COMPANION TO THE
HISTORY OF MODERN SCIENCE

COMPANION
TO THE
HISTORY OF
MODERN SCIENCE

EDITED BY
R. C. OLBY, G. N. CANTOR,
J. R. R. CHRISTIE and M. J. S. HODGE

ROUTLEDGE
LONDON AND NEW YORK

First published in 1990
by Routledge
11 New Fetter Lane, London EC4P 4EE
29 West 35th Street, New York, NY 10001

© 1990 Routledge
Chapter 18 © 1974 Princeton University Press

Set in 10/12pt Ehrhardt, Linotron 202, by Promenade Graphics, Cheltenham
Printed in Great Britain
by Richard Clay Ltd, Bungay

British Library Cataloguing in Publication Data
Companion to the history of modern science.
1. Science, history
I. Olby, Robert, 1933–
509

ISBN 0-415-01988-5

Library of Congress Cataloging-in-Publication Data
Companion to the history of modern science/edited by R. C. Olby
. . . [et al.].
o p. oo cm.
Bibliography: p.
Includes index.
ISBN 0-415-01988-5
1. Science—History. I. Olby, Robert C. (Robert Cecil)
Q125.C565 1989   89–10483
509—dc20   CIP

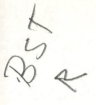

CONTENTS

Section IC: Philosophical problems

PART II: SELECTED WRITINGS IN THE HISTORY OF SCIENCE

Section IIA: Turning points

CONTENTS

PREFACE

This book concerns the momentous story of modern science as it has developed in the Western world since the Renaissance. The coverage is selective rather than comprehensive; the main goals are to show what a broad diversity of subjects comes within the history of science, and what a varied array of approaches historians of science are currently pursuing. We have explained in the Introduction how the volume is structured so as to serve these goals, and how it may answer to the interests of the general reader, as well as to the preoccupations of specialists in historical, philosophical, sociological and scientific fields.

The preparation and publication of this *Companion* traces to a proposal made by Jonathan Price of Routledge. From the beginning the intention of the publisher was to have a single volume, comprising substantial articles rather than entries in either encyclopedic or dictionary form. This intention was one that we, as editors, readily agreed was appropriate, given what was already available, given that a volume on the History of Technology was also being prepared by Routledge, and given what a wide readership would find most useful. To mark the departure from encyclopedic or dictionary forms, the title *Companion* was chosen; its usages seemed to provide precedents for several kinds of publication, including what we had in mind. The final scope and structuring of this book were then settled in discussions among the four of us and Jonathan Price as the publisher's representative. We are delighted that there is now this chance to extend our thanks to Jonathan Price for all he has done. It has been a great pleasure to join forces with him in producing this book. We give our thanks, likewise, to Mark Barragry of Routledge for his conscientious supervision of the production of the book.

We count ourselves very fortunate in having worked with two very able assistant editors. Early on Ros Thompson provided valuable aid, for which we are very grateful. The main burden has been taken up since by Laura Fransella, to whom we are greatly indebted for a most conscientious and congenial collaboration. The whole enterprise has depended decisively on her energy and expertise. Andrea Charters and Gay Lowe have our warm thanks for taking care of extensive correspondence and typing on top of their normal demanding duties.

We have a great debt of gratitude to those who have contributed articles, especially for their willingness to fulfil what were challenging assignments within stringent editorial constraints. We are particularly grateful to several who accepted invitations to write for the volume at a late stage when time was getting short. Most particularly, we thank our colleague Jerry Ravetz, now retired from the programme at Leeds to which he has given so much since its earliest days; he kindly agreed to write on the Copernican revolution when at the very last moment the article originally commissioned could not appear.

Book titles have been placed in the Index of Subjects followed by the authors' names in brackets to facilitate identification. For entries in the Index of Names the style used in *The Dictionary of Scientific Biography* vol. xvi, has been followed. Consequently the prefixes 'da', and 'de', 'Von', etc., have not been used to start names except in a few cases: thus Moivre not De Moivre, Lamarck not Monet de Lamarck, but De la Beche not Beche, and similarly Hevesy not Von Hevesy, and Naegeli not Von Naegeli, but Von Neumann not Neumann.

We alone have responsibility for the introduction, errors and all. Engaging our academic discipline in the synoptic way required by a volume such as this has been a rewarding experience. We recommend it to others, mindful that this is a very appropriate time to recognise what a large and growing audience there is for the history of science.

R. C. OLBY
G. N. CANTOR
J. R. R. CHRISTIE
M. J. S. HODGE
Leeds

INTRODUCTION

1. THE *COMPANION* AND ITS USES

The principal aim of this *Companion* is to introduce the reader to the historical development of modern Western science itself, and to the extensive scholarly literature that has been written about it. Modern science is here defined as science – excluding medicine and technology – from the sixteenth century to the present. The subject comprises, therefore, a significant portion of human endeavour over some four centuries. It has been studied, however, mainly by a small body of historians of science, most of them working during the last four decades. The results of their researches now fill many monographs and journals. A recent (1986) annual bibliography on the history of science lists over three thousand new books and articles. There are more than three dozen journals devoted entirely to the history of science and ten times that number carry occasional articles on the subject.

No individual, whether historian of science or not, could ever hope to have a detailed knowledge of all this literature; but there are many people who for various reasons may wish to have some familiarity with specific subjects within the history of science. The *Companion* has been produced in response to this widespread interest. It seeks to meet the requirements of several different audiences, including not only scientists and those specialists concerned with science from a historical, philosophical or sociological perspective, but also, indeed especially, the general reader who is curious as to how modern science has developed. For all these audiences the *Companion* aims to provide succinct but authoritative articles on major subjects within the history of science, articles written by acknowledged experts. Each article offers an overview of its subject and, where appropriate, discussion of the problems of interpretation and the current state of historical scholarship. With the non-expert in mind, the material has been made as accessible as possible with a minimum of technical knowledge required.

This volume is designed to complement other works of reference on the history of science without duplicating their form or function. There are several biographical dictionaries devoted to scientists, most notably the invaluable *Dictionary of Scientific Biography* (ed. C. C. Gillispie, Scribners, New York, 1970–8) in sixteen volumes. This provides accounts of individual scientists and their work, extensive treatment being given to major figures such as Newton and Einstein. However, with the exception of one volume that includes special articles on Indian, Mesopotamian, Egyptian, Japanese and Mayan science, the *DSB* is not arranged so as to enable the reader to pursue particular historical topics and themes. *The Dictionary of the History of Science* (eds. J. Browne, W. Bynum and R. Porter, Macmillan, London, 1981) contains short entries on numerous historical and historiographical subjects, while *Information Sources in History of Science* (eds. P. Corsi and P. Weindling, Butterworth, London, 1983) concentrates on bibliography for certain areas of the field.

The present *Companion* differs, therefore, from these extremely useful works in presenting substantial articles on its chosen subjects. In this respect the *Companion* is closer to such works as the five-volume *Dictionary of the History of Ideas* (ed. P. Wiener, Scribners, New York, 1973–4) and the eight volume *Encyclopedia of Philosophy* (ed. P. Edwards, Collier-Macmillan, New York, 1968), both of which contain some longer pieces on science while covering areas beyond science. Surprisingly few works written in recent decades have offered comprehensive coverage of the history of the sciences. The four volumes of R. Taton (ed.), *Histoire Générale des Sciences* (Presses Universitaires de France, Paris, 1957–64), published in English translation as a *General History of the Sciences* (Thomas and Hudson, London, 1963–4), proceed by region – Greece, say, or Egypt – for the early centuries, and then by discipline – for example, Chemistry, or Astronomy – for the modern era. Among books by a single author, one that was first published in 1956 is still valued for its integration of intellectual and social developments: Stephen F. Mason, *A History of the Sciences* (rev. ed. Collier Books, New York, 1962).

The organisation of the *Companion* in its sections and articles reflects the views of the editors, views shared by many working in the field of history of science. It is widely recognised that the complexity of the development of science prohibits a chronological arrangement of material. Moreover, the map of the sciences – the array of distinct sciences and their relations with one another – has changed so fundamentally over the last four centuries as to preclude structuring a historical work in accord with those disciplinary boundaries that exist today. So, with neither past chronology nor present disciplines offering organising principles, the editors have adapted this book's structure to their view that historiographical issues are often paramount in writing about the history of science, and that science often has to be understood through its connections with other social and intellectual activities. These considerations have guided the decision to make the following divisions within the *Companion*:

PART I: THE STUDY OF THE HISTORY OF SCIENCE
IA.   History of science and related disciplines
IB.   Analytical perspectives
IC.   Philosophical problems

PART II: SELECTED WRITINGS IN THE HISTORY OF SCIENCE
IIA.   Turning points
IIB.   Topics and Interpretations
IIC.   Themes

This partitioning should not be taken to impose sharp segregations but, especially in Part II, to introduce some order within a wide variety of subjects. Thus 'Turning points' comprise major changes in particular branches of science, changes that have mostly occurred in fairly short periods of time; these are accordingly arranged in rough chronological order. 'Topics and Interpretations' deal mainly with longer-term matters that are less closely related to particular branches of science. Finally, 'Themes' concern perennial subjects, often involving historical relations between science and issues outside the sciences.

While the reader will usually be able to locate an article from the Table of Contents, the Index provides a further way of finding material. The Index gives key words and the names of all persons discussed in the text. Finally, articles contain cross-references to appropriate material to be found elsewhere in the volume. If the text includes a reference (see art. 7, sect. 3) further discussion will be found in the third section of the seventh article. The articles themselves are written so as to keep notes and references to a minimum, references being confined mainly to giving sources for quotations in the text. Suggestions for further reading are listed at the end of each article so as to enable the reader to pursue further any subject of interest.

In any work of this kind, there are necessarily various limitations. One concerns the omission in the *Companion* of four major areas: non-Western science, science before the sixteenth century, technology, and medicine. These four are all now areas of such productive scholarly interest, however, that including any one of them would have entailed doubling the length of the work. Another kind of limitation arises from the treatment given to subjects within the scope assigned to the *Companion*. No selection of some six dozen articles can offer anything like complete coverage of the whole history of modern science, and readers may well find a favourite portion of the field not represented. In most cases, this is because the editors have had to be selective, and have had to decide that certain items should take precedence over others. What they have sought to do is to provide between two covers a selection of articles that reflect as fully as possible the diversity of current concerns within the history of science community. Towards this end, a selection has been made from a larger list of possibilities. While not claiming to be comprehensive, the *Companion* does aim to reflect the state of history of science as it is taught and researched in the 1980s.

2. SCIENCE AS HISTORY

The most obvious rationale for any work in the history of science is familiar enough, but still deserves to be kept constantly in mind. Put simply and abstractly, it is that for every attempt modern Western man may make to understand himself and to make himself understood to others – including what he has done to others – nothing is more essential than an understanding of science as it has developed in history.

What is perhaps less easy to appreciate at first glance is the breadth in the range of issues that such a historical study must comprehend, if it is to enlighten us fully as to the place science holds in our civilisation, our culture and our society. One way to get a feel for the range of issues involved is to consider the task historians will face a century from now if they ever set themselves to make sense of science as it exists today. That task might be construed in many ways, but at a minimum it would comprise some six distinguishable, although inseparable, components. Two of these components come readily to mind: future historians will have to treat the theories held by the experts – molecular genetics, quantum electrodynamics and so on; and they will have to consider the applications made of those theories in industry and technology, in bio-engineering, computers and the rest. But such would be only part of the story. For, to take two further issues, science has a political life and diverse institutional embodiments that must also be taken into account. The scientific profession in a modern industrial state is perceived and managed as a national economic resource, and has therefore a political economy in just the same way as do the armed forces or agriculture. This political economy of science is based both on the politics of the state itself, and on the institutionalisation of science as a profession with a characteristic reward system, recruitment, training routines and career models. This much is manifest as soon as one recalls that science today is not a pastime for a handful of wealthy amateurs, as it mostly was in Newton's day, but a livelihood for millions of people employed in government agencies, private companies, universities and so on.

Less obviously, beyond these components in the life of science in the history being made at present, our future historians would have to do justice to the pervasiveness of science as a cultural force and as an ideological resource. The novels, plays, music, films, sermons and advertisements of our time, not to mention the comics and the cults – in sum, the art, philosophy, religion, entertainment and commerce – are all suffused with and often constructed around concepts, techniques, images, anxieties and attitudes deriving from the presence, the omnipresence, of science in our society. Where would Madison Avenue be without Freud to exploit, Evangelical Christianity without Darwin to confront, Hollywood without Frankenstein to invoke – the list could go on indefinitely. Standing even further back from the daily research and teaching duties of particular scientific disciplines, our historians would have to take on the role of science itself as an element in fundamental ideological alliances and conflicts. Here, for instance, a seeming paradox would be encountered. One bloc of countries, the Socialist states, despite many divergences, agree in taking their socialism to be scientific, indeed to be the only scientific theory of society, socialist or otherwise. Yet a constant refrain among Western intellectuals is that the very spirit, let alone the letter, of that socialism is completely inconsistent with those ideals of freedom and reason that are intrinsic to science as a progressive, self-critical enterprise. Science, as a contested ideological resource, is central to the history of our time.

This parable of the future history of our time will have made its point if it has brought out that there is much more to the history of science than a chronicling of who got what right when among the scientists of the past. That there is so much more to the scope of the history of science, at any one time, implies directly that there is an equivalent scope to the study of change in science over time. The six elements cited in our parable are not constants. The whole point is that none of them is projectible back into the Renaissance or the Enlightenment, but that duties comparable in scope although contrasting in content do face historians of the science of those periods. Accordingly, any history of the changes that take science from one period to another has to comprehend transformations across as broad a range of issues as those half-dozen inconstant elements may exemplify in our century.

From what has already been said, it will be clear that the present *Companion* is premised on the assumption that the true measure of the history of science, as a subject, is not to be taken from the fact that a small, marginal, even esoteric, scholarly community has it as its special disciplinary charge. Rather, this measure should be taken from considering what scope and significance must be given to the whole array of topics and themes that have to be considered as soon as science, in its every aspect, is taken as a subject in history.

To see what taking science as a historical subject can and cannot do for us, it is worth asking how the rationales that may be given for the historical study of science compare and contrast with the rationales that may be given for other forms of historical study. Once again, the commonplaces that come most quickly to mind may not provide the most telling response to this query. For a start, it is easy enough to justify the history of science as needed alongside other enquiries directed at particular parts of the past. Given that political historians can shed light on life in Shakespeare's England, much more can be clarified if they then work together with historians of Elizabethan science. Quite generally, any enquiry into past times is aided by including enquiry into the *science* of those times.

Turning from the many pasts to the single present, another commonplace insists that the sequence of those pasts illumines the present as its latest outcome. As for politics, then, so for science: the understanding of the present, its consensuses, controversies, alignments, in theories and in practices, is indispensably enhanced by discerning the sources of what is present in what went before. The strength of the Labour party in Wales or of bacteriology in Paris are far from anomalous when traced to legacies from traditions now more than a century old. So, quite generally, an argument for the history of science, as for the history of anything else, can be drawn from the explanatory power of the past in regard to the present.

What such commonplaces overlook, however, is that there is a further rationale for turning to the past that is not even implied by what has been said so far. This further rationale derives from the truism that because the present is a short-run affair and the future is inaccessible, the past is the only long run to which we have access. So if, as is often the case, we wish to find out how something goes over big stretches of time, it is to the past we must turn as the only accessible long run. For economists the thought is second nature. To study those trends and tendencies that take decades or centuries to make themselves discernible, economic theorists join forces with economic historians. Likewise, then, for the life of science: there is every reason to think that the short run can mislead us. After all, to take just one example, the study of scientific life over the short run of the present may suggest a strong independence thesis: the conclusion, that is, that scientific communities are largely self-sufficient and self-regulative in generating and pursuing their own goals and in devising and evaluating the strategies they require for doing so. It is a conclusion, however, that it is risky to extrapolate to a longer run of centuries or even decades. Many historians reflecting on such larger periods would be inclined to reject any such conclusion, in favour of the view that communities devoted to science are conditioned in their aims and methods by events originating in all sorts of other spheres of life from the economic to the literary, the political to the religious. It is not, then, simply that all sorts of things change in the long run that appear permanent under shorter run scrutiny; it is rather that things change in more extreme ways, for more remote reasons and with more remote consequences than a student of the shorter run is ever likely to contemplate.

The insights that the longer run is able to provide can, however, only be gathered provided we are prepared to travel across the centuries without taking too much of the present with us. The industrialised suburbanite tourist who travels far up the Amazon only to concentrate his attention on deficiencies in the telephone system or in the hygiene has, in a sense, never left home; and so he can gain little insight into his own cultural location by contrasting it with what his travels might otherwise have served to bring before him. Likewise for the historian: a past that is viewed too exclusively from the perspectives of the present cannot provide the contrasts needed to contribute understanding of the present. More than that, to travel in time without leaving the present which is home is to forego the insights that the long run can supply, and that can correct the impressions arising from confinement to the short run.

For these reasons the history of science requires study and interpretation of a sort that science itself cannot supply. It is not simply that one does not accept as sufficiently critical scientists' history of science, any more than one accepts, say, politicians' history of politics. Beyond that, there is the commitment of science to its own progress which prevents science producing the history that others, beyond science, require. Modern science is indeed almost definable as science that believes in a progressiveness of scientific change that makes the past *passé*, a past only to be turned to in order to reveal how science, inevitably and cumulatively, leaves its past behind. Precisely, then, because the life of science includes this history on the terms of science itself, there is a constant need to study the past of science on terms drawn not from science but from history in all its forms. Here, as elsewhere, the self-sufficiency and self-regulation of science cannot be accepted uncritically if we are to have an understanding of science that serves purposes beyond those of science itself. For such reasons, this *Companion* seeks to exhibit the historical study of science as it can serve many purposes and so contribute in various ways to what, in an earlier abstraction, was called modern Western man's quest to understand himself and make himself understood to others. After all, at this point in history, he needs all the kinds of help he can get.

3. HISTORY OF SCIENCE AS SUBJECT AND DISCIPLINE

As practised now, the history of science is a highly diversified field of scholarship. Not only does its subject matter range from the teachings of Classical Greece and Ancient China to the latest theories and inventions of physics and biochemistry; its emphases and strategies are equally diversified. For some, a general Scientific Revolution, taken to have occurred in the seventeenth century, will always remain the essential moment from which the life of science in history ultimately derives; while for others the principal concern is with the way later developments, especially in the nineteenth and twentieth centuries, have given rise to numerous new sciences, such as biology, psychology and cybernetics, in a continually expansive process.

Recognition of modern science as a complex, expanding process has led to a striking variety in the efforts to understand that process. At one time, a quarter of a century ago now, it was customary to draw one main contrast. This was between accounts that emphasise the internal, technical history of particular sciences, and those that mobilise a wider range of factors, in an effort both to link history of science to other aspects of history, and to explain the structure and content of science not just through the problems, methods and solutions science assigns to itself, but through the economic, social and ideological imperatives of particular epochs. It was often in making up their minds about this contrast that historians of science were invited to confront further issues concerning both intellectual and social aspects of history. For much of the development of science, some maintained, there is no realistic distinction to be made between scientific, religious and philosophical thought, so that the history of science must include these forms of belief in its analyses. Again, while some historians of science contented themselves with studying the institutional basis of science, in scientific societies, universities and research institutes, others resolved to demonstrate how scientific knowledge is itself inextricably involved in the value systems and social formations within which the production of scientific knowledge occurs.

Although the diversity of current historiographical alignments is often no longer characterisable through these versions of the contrasts, it is truer than ever that the discipline of history of science possesses a relatively open cognitive structure that is marked by its ability to incorporate, if not fully to accept, novel approaches. This situation in turn arises from the condition of a field of study that does not have, and never has had, an autonomous professional structure. Historians of science are, in their backgrounds, a heterogeneous group, coming from the sciences, from philosophy, from sociology, from history, from classics, and so on, and are liable to find themselves working within or alongside these other disciplines. History of science inevitably reflects this diversity in the variety of its methods, problems and solutions; and, if it is unable to integrate this multiplicity into a unified perspective, it possesses nonetheless the advantages of a plural nature: it is lively and it is receptive. On the other hand, this condition has its drawbacks. Lacking an autonomous and unified existence, history of science can often appear vulnerable to the colonising ambitions of philosophy, say, or sociology; at times, it can also seem overly involved in debates concerning the true and proper groundings of the discipline. The best history of science attempts to balance these conflicting demands, and the *Companion* has sought to do just this by devoting initial attention to foundational historiographical issues and the relation of history of science to other disciplines, and then ensuring that the diversity of approaches expressed in the first part is exemplified in the articles in the second.

The *Companion*, with the organisational policy and judgements it embodies, is itself a product of history: the history of the history of science community and, within that, of one particular group at Leeds. Thirty years ago, when a programme of teaching and research in the history of science was first formally instituted at the University of Leeds, the disciplinary alliance with philosophy was recognised in a decision to have a Division of the History and Philosophy of Science within the Department of Philosophy. With the subsequent expansion of the programme, teaching in history of science was offered to students of all kinds, in the Arts, the Sciences, the Social Sciences and Engineering. At the same time, the research undertaken in the Division spread into areas that often lay beyond those envisaged in the original commitment to the field. A tradition emerged, therefore, of pluralistic, eclectic studies – historical, philosophical and socio-political studies – of science. Awareness grew, too, of the interest history of science held, or could come to hold, among academics in other disciplines and among the general public. Far from being exceptional, this experience has been broadly paralleled at several other universities, and, in so far as it has been, a Leeds *Companion to the History of Modern Science* may stand as a representative rather than idiosyncratic text.

4. HISTORY OF SCIENCE AND ITS AUDIENCE

When scholarly experts turn from communicating with other specialists to address a wider public, there are difficult demands to be met in adapting the presentation to the larger audience. The editors of this *Companion* have worked to meet these demands by imposing uniform standards and conventions throughout this volume and by ensuring that the articles are not written as research papers would be. To this end, the space – on average 6,000 words – for each contribution has been restricted; documentary evidence has been minimised; far larger subjects have been engaged than any single research paper would address; and contributors have been encouraged not to avoid controversy. By these means, and through the suggestions for further reading, it is hoped that the articles will serve as doors that can provide entries for readers who are coming to these subjects for the first time.

Science can appear both fascinating and daunting to anyone who is not a scientist. The possibilities for fascination are exhibited in any museum of science or science park. On occasion, perhaps only rarely, radio and television offer a compelling glimpse of the discoveries of modern science. Yet the lay person knows that science is a closed world, that he or she is excluded from the knowledge. The doors of the laboratory are not open and scientific literature is composed in an incomprehensible language. Moreover, the lay person may well feel an ambivalence towards science, since its most visible and tangible manifestations – the products of technology – have been a mixed blessing. Because science is such an important and problematic element in our culture, the general reader often wishes to know both about the content of science – the prerogative of the scientific community – and how science relates to other forces shaping our culture. The history of science – in alliance with such neighbouring disciplines as the philosophy and sociology of science – is unique in offering resources relevant to both quests.

In preparing this volume the editors have also had in mind the interest of working scientists in the history of their own fields and in the state of the art of historical researches in the field of science. In the English-speaking world it has been a commonplace that historical and scientific researches, both in terms of methods and results, are viewed as fundamentally different, if not directly opposed. According to this popular view, science is objective; it deals with replicable events and it achieves certainty thus bringing about consensus. History is only accessible through the eyes of observers and actors, by reading what they have written or by listening to their recollections. Such evidence is inherently subjective, and since it concerns past events is by definition unrepeatable. Is it any wonder, then, that certainty and consensus are only dreamt of, never achieved?

The response of historians of science to these assertions is to admit the limitations inherent in their subject, but to argue that, like the scientists, they are concerned with empirical data, and that as the body of this data has increased, due to archival and historical researches, so elements of consensus have formed. The more we have come to know about such much-researched figures as Newton and Darwin, the smaller has become the number of alternative interpretations that the historian can plausibly offer of their work. Yet whether we turn to science or to history, consensus is never final. Scientists have accepted the conclusions of philosophers that scientific laws are based on the strength of inductive reasoning rather than on the necessity of deductive argument; scientific knowledge cannot claim certainty. Nor is this the only factor which has brought about a change in the scientist's image of science. The overthrow of classical mechanics and of Newtonian space-time undermined any such confidence in the truth claims of science. Also, the revelations which the best of scholarly historical and sociological researches have provided, as to the influence of subjective elements and social factors in the construction of scientific knowledge, have had an impact. In these revelations scientists have themselves played a part: Stephen J. Gould on the 'mismeasure' of man, Robert Hare on the birth of penicillin, to name but two.

Scientists recognise that as members of professional disciplines they are influenced by the career goals of those professions. They bring to their research the expectations and claims of legitimacy that those professions seek. One trend in the historical study of science has been to place greater emphasis on these constraints as part of the context in which science is conducted, validated and disseminated. Among scientists, it was James D. Watson who brought this aspect of scientific activity most dramatically to the attention of the public in his best seller, *The Double Helix* (1968). In this *Companion*, scientists will find articles especially devoted to this topic.

Any work such as the present *Companion* may serve as a supplementary aid in the teaching of science at secondary school and at college or university level. Students of the sciences feel crushed at times by the empirical detail of the subjects as traditionally taught. Some of the articles here could be used to point out the fundamental principles underlying a science, and to delineate the context in which particular scientific theories proved acceptable and applicable, and why in a different context they have come under criticism. For the teaching of science to the arts student, on the other hand, this volume offers perspectives on science with which such students should feel able to identify.

A general work on the history of science, such as the present *Companion*, can do at least three things for philosophers. Firstly, a moment's reflection on anyone's list of leading figures, from Plato and Aristotle to Russell and Wittgenstein, is enough to show that the single preoccupation that most obviously distinguishes Western philosophy over the centuries is, indeed, science. Here, then, taking history seriously means taking science seriously. There is now, moreover, a strong movement among historians of philosophy to do just that: to take the history in the history of philosophy seriously. Instead of treating past figures quite unhistorically, as so many colleagues who happen to be dead, but whose writings can be read and appreciated regardless of their original motivation and context, a new breed of historians of philosophy are making questions of motivation and context integral to their studies. In doing so, they are often complementing the work done by historians studying the science that the philosophers were confronting and assimilating at the time. The present *Companion* will contribute, it is hoped, to this integrative venture.

Secondly, among philosophers of science, it has been a commonplace since the 1960s that a main challenge is to comprehend scientific change, and the issues it raises concerning rationality, for instance, in scientific theorising. One corollary of this commonplace is that philosophers of science no longer see themselves as mere consumers of illustrative examples of scientific achievements, as originally produced by scientists and chronicled subsequently by historians of science. Rather, philosophers of science have had to engage the study of the history of science at first hand, so as to have an immediate access to primary documentation of the processes of scientific theory construction, dissemination and criticism. This engagement is not without its difficulties. Historians of science may feel that the history of science is historically too exacting to be properly undertaken by philosophers; while philosophers of science may feel it is too instructive philosophically to be safely left to historians. The mere fact that such misgivings have been expressed in recent years shows that both parties have an obligation to learn more about each other's interests in the development of science.

Finally, philosophers, committed as they are to a life of self-examination, are beginning to express curiosity about philosophy itself; not in the sense of individuals and their philosophies, from Thales on, but in a broader sense. For in this broader sense, philosophy has an institutional and ideological history as well as a doctrinal development. For instance, in the middle of the last century, philosophy as a profession and as a branch of learning had a quite different place in university curricula, and a quite different relation to the church, in England, in Scotland and in Germany. And these differences are strongly reflected in the different institutional and ideological lives that philosophy lives today, not only in those three countries but also in the United States and Australia. Historians of science have had to learn to confront such ideological and institutional differences as fascinating historiographical challenges. By facing these challenges as they arise for philosophy, philosophers can enhance their own understanding of their collective enterprise.

Sharp contrasts have sometimes been drawn between what philosophy, on the one hand, and sociology, on the other, have brought to and taken from the history of science. On one stereotype, philosophers hold an intellectualist view of the development of science, construing it, that is, as a progressive succession of disembodied ideas; while sociologists have seen it rather as a sequence of individual and group responses made by human, social beings to changing social circumstances. One use of this *Companion* will be, however, to convince philosophers and sociologists alike that such stereotypical contrasts cannot be sustained when historical cases are considered in detail.

A decade or two ago, sociologists were often content to present some particular sociological explanation for some development in science – Darwin's theorising, say, or the rise of the mechanical philosophy in the seventeenth century – and then to insist that any expression of dissatisfaction with that particular explanation was tantamount to a prejudicial denial that any sociological perspectives had any place at all in the history of science. The present *Companion* should serve to show that the state of discussion has now moved beyond such fallacious gambits. For any historical development in science a variety of interpretations and explanations may be worth considering seriously. Some may be more sociological, others less so, but the ultimate legitimacy of sociology as a source of historiographical resources will not stand or fall with any one of them.

Equally, this *Companion* should show sociologists that no one tradition within social theory – whether Marxist or Weberian, structuralist or post-structuralist – has now a privileged standing in relation to the history of science. No general presumptions of social theory made in regard to any particular historical case study are likely to be conceded, therefore, in the present state of discussion. Conversely, however, it is manifest that those who now work at the history of science are more willing and able than at any time past to avail themselves of what sociologists and social theorists have to offer in understanding science.

Historians generally, of politics, society, economy and culture, have tended to suffer from the kinds of institutionalised separations which have worked to maintain history of science as something of an independent sub-discipline within the historical sciences. Because history of science often seems to present a forbiddingly technical aspect, demanding highly specialised kinds of understanding, general historians have on the whole inclined, in research and teaching, to leave the history of science to its specialised practitioners. This kind of separation arguably benefits neither group. There need surely to be ways in which the general discipline of history can continually and as a matter of course incorporate the work of history of science, making it available to students and scholars, and integrating it within wider frameworks of historical reference. Unless and until such practices become conventional, history overall runs the danger of treating less effectively than it might a major shaping feature of modern Western history, for the history of science reaches out in crucial ways to affect the nature and form of culture, economy and politics. The coverage of modern Western science offered by the *Companion*, dealing both with major and more specialised aspects of scientific development, offers to historians an easily usable resource for the work of recognising and integrating history of science within the overall discipline of history. As an initiatory introduction to history of science, outlining the contours of the field, indicating as succinctly as possible the substance of the field, and also as a critical reference guide offering direction for further exploration, the *Companion* hopes to make available to historians the contemporary range of resources produced by historians of science.

Historians of science can obviously find several sorts of uses for the *Companion*. In these days of specialisation, any coherently collected set of up-to-date summary treatments which incorporate much of the discipline's total range must be valuable. The *Companion* offers the chance to take in the state of the art, presented in an easily accessible and readable form, together with pointers as to how particular items of special interest may be further pursued. It may help, in addition, to revive interests abandoned for the sake of special research aims, and even to indicate future areas of possible interest and activity.

The *Companion* forms a contemporary compendium of approaches, themes and topics in the discipline, and is of potential utility in many circumstances of teaching and supervision: to introduce students to particular subjects; to give them a sense of the range of possible approaches and interpretations; to instil historiographical and critical awareness; to initiate a track of reading and research. While history of science does not lack for research outlets, for pure bibliographical guides and for textbooks, there is a range of needs not automatically fulfilled by these forms of writing, and it is this range of needs which the *Companion* can help to supply.

We have dwelled insistently on the multiple audiences and uses for the historical study of science, because it is our conviction that the time is long gone when this study needs to present itself, diffidently and apologetically, as a peripheral minority interest. Many developments within and beyond the profession of history of science have made such diffidence and apology no longer appropriate. We would like to think that this volume gives a sense of what these developments have been, and that the volume thereby makes its contribution to this same end.

THE EDITORS

PART I

THE STUDY OF THE HISTORY OF SCIENCE

SECTION IA. HISTORY OF SCIENCE IN RELATION TO NEIGHBOURING DISCIPLINES

1

THE DEVELOPMENT OF THE HISTORIOGRAPHY OF SCIENCE

JOHN R. R. CHRISTIE

1. INTRODUCTION

Historiography is the study of the writing of history, and the study of the historiography of science therefore takes as its subject the variety of ways in which science's past has been written about. As an academic discipline, history of science is a relatively recent speciality, yet it has nonetheless an ancestry stretching back several centuries. This history of the historiography of science has its own intrinsic fascination, but also possesses a wider value. By examining the sequence, growth and proliferation of historical writing on science, it is possible to achieve a sense of the lineage and formation of history of science as a field of enquiry and scholarship. In achieving this sense, it is also possible to discern the emergence of the typical kinds of understanding, communication and expression whose development has been crucial in shaping the practices which now collectively constitute the disciplinary existence of historians of science. In what follows, therefore, we will be pursuing in a preliminary fashion the story in whose course first appear many of the basic themes, topics and interpretations which form the subject-matter of this *Companion*.

2. THE HISTORICAL STARTING-POINTS

When does the historiography of science start? There is a genuine problem in assigning definitive, ascertainable origins for the historiography of science. This is because any scientist, in his actual scientific work, already has an orientation towards the past. He will have been educated into certain intellectual traditions, certain scientific practices, and his work will inevitably be involved in extending, or perhaps breaking with these traditions and practices. These efforts can often involve overt consideration of selective aspects of his science's history, so that it is no exaggeration to say that history of science is itself present, and can often appear within, works of scientific research and teaching. Two examples, from the science of chemistry in the eighteenth century, can reinforce this point. When Antoine Lavoisier (1743–94) came to publish some of his earlier studies of gases, he supplemented the account of his own research with the recent history of researches in this area.[1] Similarly, the influential Dutch physician and chemist Herman Boerhaave (1668–1738) would introduce his students to the study of chemistry in part through providing a brief history of the science, a teaching practice which was often followed by later chemists.[2]

Intellectual disciplines of all kinds tend to generate and produce their own relatively informal histories in these ways, and they offer a convenient starting-point, a locatable series of origins for the historiography of science. Yet if we merely remained with these starting-points, we would emerge with only a rather scattered and incomplete sequence of incipient histories of scientific disciplines and their research programmes. Some other perspective, of broader and deeper significance for the origins of historiography of science, can perhaps be found. This perspective should seek more than the partial and individual recognitions of history contained within the scientific teaching and research of such as Lavoisier and Boerhaave, important and revealing though such examples are. But where might more significant origins be found, and of what might they consist?

They consist firstly in the recognition that science is not just a sequence of separate disciplinary activities, each with a discrete historical existence, but is also and much more importantly an activity possessing a general significance with respect to the overall course of human history itself. This recognition of the global significance of science, its world-historical importance, is part of the spectrum of justification for science which was promoted during the Scientific Revolution of the seventeenth century, most notably at the hands of the philosopher-scientist Francis Bacon (1561–1626). According to Bacon, it is the aim of science to discover 'the knowledge of Causes, and secret motions of things; and the enlarging of the bounds of Human Empire, to the effecting of all things possible'.[3] This was a succinct, confident and ambitious statement of the nature and purpose of science, and its focus brought together the notions of scientific knowledge, power and progress. For Bacon and his followers in the seventeenth century, the implications of such an attitude were directed towards the future history of the human race, for whom science offered a progressive future based upon the power over nature which science now promised. Bacon and the other scientific revolutionaries of his period were therefore less concerned with elaborating upon science's past than with promoting an image of science which disengaged human history from its past and brought it into a new epoch. Thus, to discern the global origins of the historiography of science, we need in addition to specify that moment when this Baconian conception of science becomes itself an object of interest and enquiry for the historical consciousness of the West, as it seeks to understand and explain this distinctive feature of its historical existence.

3. DEVELOPMENTS DURING THE ENLIGHTENMENT

We can date the emergence of this specifically historical concern with the global and epochal significance of science to the middle decades of the eighteenth century. It is associated with the intellectual movement which dominated that time, known to historians as the Enlightenment.[4] The Enlightenment was essentially a programme of reform produced by philosophers and scientists dedicated to changing the intellectual, political and social terrain upon which humans had hitherto been obliged to live. They sought in particular a greater degree of individual political liberty and social equality than currently existed. A key to this attainment was intellectual liberation, and it was this presupposition of the Enlightenment which rendered science central to its aspirations, for Enlightenment thinkers erected science as the model of what the unfettered human intellect could achieve. The work of Galileo, Descartes, Bacon and Newton was mobilised as exemplary, as producing authentic knowledge of nature. This authentic knowledge not only liberated the human mind from the shackles of superstitious religion and outmoded metaphysics, but could be turned to productive material uses which would enhance prosperity, and thereby guarantee political and social progress. To make this claim, which echoed many of the original Baconian claims, Enlightenment intellectuals needed to pay a kind of detailed attention to the history of science which it had hitherto not received, for the claim was not simply a repetition of the original Baconian promise, but rather that this promise, since the time of Bacon and Galileo, had been partially fulfilled, and that this fulfilment justified the Enlightenment's progressive optimism. It was the Enlightenment, therefore, which first constructed and launched upon the world a historically-based view of science's intellectual, political and social significance for humanity. In the course of so doing, it laid down a series of assumptions concerning science and its historical existence which have been so influential that *all* Western historians of science have been formed within them. This holds equally whether historians have been persuaded of the Enlightenment's commitments, or whether they have attempted to modify or overthrow them.

4. THE SCIENTIFIC REVOLUTION

These assumptions can be seen emerging with particular clarity in the 1750s and 1760s. It was then that certain fundamental narratives, subjects and structures were developed in forms which became foundational for the historio-graphy of science. In narrative terms, the Enlightenment wrote the history of what we now call canonically the Scientific Revolution (see art. 15). This may be read, for example, in attenuated form, in Jean d'Alembert's *Preliminary Discourse to the Encyclopedia of Diderot* (1751), where d'Alembert (1717–83) rehearsed a story which led from Galileo's trial by the Inquisition, through Bacon, Des-cartes, Kepler and Huyghens to Newton and Locke, a sequence whereby 'a few great men . . . prepared from afar the light which gradually, by imperceptible degrees, would illuminate the world'.[5] It was a history of intellectual emancipa-tion from the influence of politically and spiritually repressive forces. The prota-gonists in this narrative take on heroic and exemplary status for d'Alembert and his readers: 'Such are the principal geniuses that the human mind ought to regard as its masters'.[6] Short as d'Alembert's narrative is, it nonetheless embodies features which continue to appear in Western accounts of this histori-cal phenomenon. Firstly, it sets it within a bounded historical period, the seven-teenth century. Secondly, it takes the events under view as connected and developmental, forming a coherent narrative unit. Thirdly, it presents these events as a significantly progressive contrast with what had preceded them. Fourthly, the developments have a fundamentally revolutionary nature. Fifthly, they are the mental products of individual men of genius who form the cast of characters essential to the narrative. Sixthly, they include developments in philosophy as well as science. Finally, they are intellectually authoritative.

Many of these features may now seem unremarkable as an account of the Scientific Revolution. This is precisely a measure of the success of the Enlightenment's invention of the Scientific Revolution: the elements it selected and to which it gave a coherent narrative expression now appear so natural to our understanding of the origin of modern science that we find it very difficult to imagine any account functioning without those elements. It is as well to be reminded, therefore, that d'Alembert's narrative is a humanly selected and con-structed interpretation undertaken for particular purposes, and in principle as alterable as any other such interpretation.

The *History of Astronomy* by Adam Smith (1723–90) was written at much the same time as d'Alembert's *Preliminary Discourse*, and illuminates another and rather different foundational tendency in Western historiography of science. This tendency is referred to in the full title of Smith's work: *The Principles which Lead and Direct Philosophical Enquiries; Illustrated by the History of Astronomy* (1795). Smith's work was by no means a straightforward disciplinary history of astronomy. Although it treated the development of astronomical thought from ancient times up until Isaac Newton, this development was subsidiary to his main interest, which was focused upon the universal principles by which the human mind understands and explains the natural world. Smith saw the human mind as constantly attempting to produce simple, unified and coherent representations of nature. It is provoked into this exercise by the perception of unusual, anomalous observations which do not fit with conventional expectations of how nature behaves. Faced with such observations, the mind produces a novel set of ideas, a scientific theory, which satisfactorily explains the disturbing observations. Although the detail of Smith's views bears some comparison with more modern philosophical accounts of science and scientific change, it is more significant in other ways. In Adam Smith we find a rather complex intertwining of history of science with philosophical concerns, in the course of which a view of the developmental or progressive view of the nature of science is expressed. Smith created a specific role for history of science in relation to the broader philosophical attempt to understand what general principles, if any, underlie and structure the course of scientific development.

In so doing, Smith was forging a link between the history and philosophy of science which has proved to be of enduring importance. Its continuing importance can be seen in works which have made a major impact on historiography of science in the nineteenth century, such as those of William Whewell (1794–1866), and in the twentieth century, such as those of Thomas Kuhn.[7] Historiography of science, in other words, has from its origins onwards often accompanied a more specifically philosophical quest for understanding the nature of science, and this feature has in turn often affected the historiography, lending it a philosophical vocabulary and motivation. In this too, historiography of science is a child of the Enlightenment, which sought not only to make science the pre-eminent form of intellectual activity, but sought also within the human mind and within human history to discover the principles of scientific reasoning and progressive scientific development.

5. THE CONTRIBUTION OF JOSEPH PRIESTLEY

This preliminary survey of the Enlightenment's historiography of science would not be complete without attention to the historical work of Joseph Priestley (1733–1804), England's most famous man of science in the latter half of the eighteenth century. Priestley wrote, among other historical works, a work entitled *The History and Present State of Electricity* (1767). Less polemical than d'Alembert's, less philosophical than Smith's, Priestley's historiography is nonetheless just as revealing. Although its historical focus is confined largely to the development of electrical science in the eighteenth century, it avowedly wished to illustrate the theme illustrated in their different ways by d'Alembert and Smith, namely the progress of the human mind: 'It is here that we see the human understanding to its greatest advantage, . . . increasing its own powers . . . and directing them to the accomplishment of its own views; whereby the security and happiness of mankind are daily improved'.[8] As such, historiography of science is preferable to, more instructive and delightful than histories of politics and warfare. Historiography is given here a directly educative, moralising role by Priestley, but perhaps more interesting is the way he conceives his subject matter, since it is here for the first time that historiography of science portrays science definitively as an active, highly instrumentalised, above all *experimental* activity. This contrasts notably with the versions of science portrayed by d'Alembert and Smith, where history of science is the history of mind, of intellectual ideas. Priestley, himself an instrument-maker and experimenter of note, understood science and its progress in less exalted terms. It was a history of practical discoveries made through experiment, aided by the construction of appropriate material apparatus. Discovery was innovative for Priestley, but constituted by small steps, a gradual series of improvements.

6. THE NEGATIVE ASPECT OF SCIENTIFIC HISTORIOGRAPHY

Thus far, we can see how the Enlightenment set in place basic features of the historiography of the origins of modern science and installed within it liberal notions of freedom, progress and individualist creativity. Additionally, it set forth a structural connection between historiography of science and philosophy, and it pioneered a historiographical focus on innovative experimental discovery. These are all features of major import for the development of historiography of science, but it would be wrong to leave the Enlightenment without noticing one further feature which its historical understanding of science produced. Common to all aspects of Enlightenment historiography so far has been a deeply positive evaluation of science. Yet the Enlightenment also produced negative evaluations of science's role in history. The philosopher Jean-Jacques Rousseau (1712–88), in his *Discourse on the Moral Effects of the Arts and Sciences* (1750) characterised science not as promoting freedom, but as substantially negating it.

> So long as government and law provide for the security and well-being of men in their common life, the arts, literature, and the sciences, less despotic though perhaps more powerful, fling garlands of flowers over the chains which weigh them down. They stifle in men's breasts that sense of original liberty, for which they seem to have been born; cause them to love their own slavery, and so make of them what is called a civilized people.
>
> Necessity raised up thrones; the arts and sciences have made them strong . . . [9]

Here, the civilised pursuit of knowledge and culture, with which Enlightened progress is identified, now becomes more sinister in its historical effects. It distracts men from the pursuit of true liberty, and at the same time both obscures the recognition of oppression while propping up the agents and instruments of oppression. The example of Rousseau could be added to. It makes the point that the Enlightenment's historiography of science did not finally produce a unified, single-valued representation of science's historical significance. Rather, it produced a split conception, with positive and negative aspects which seem incapable of being brought together. And in this too, our own contemporary historiography is an authentic descendant of the Enlightenment.

7. SCIENTIFIC SOCIETIES AND DISCIPLINARY HISTORIES

Between the 1780s and 1830s the principal historiographical development which occurred was arguably related to the forms of development which science itself was undergoing at this time. Hitherto science had existed institutionally in universities and in learned societies such as the Royal Academy of Sciences in Paris and the Royal Society of London. The later eighteenth and early nineteenth centuries witnessed the growth of disciplinary-based scientific societies, whose members were devoted to the pursuit of one particular scientific discipline, such as geology or astronomy, rather than to the pursuit of natural philosophy in general. Science itself was therefore undergoing a process of division of labour which produced increasingly specialised disciplinary orientations. The historiography of science itself responded to these developmental features of scientific life, producing a number of disciplinary histories. These were noteworthy not simply for their recognition of coherent disciplinary formations, and for their attempts to create discrete and unified histories of scientific disciplines, complete with founding figures, fundamental innovations and so forth. As we have already seen, there had by this time long existed a tendency for particular sciences to generate their own informal histories in particular circumstances of research and teaching. More noteworthy was the way in which the construction of a disciplinary history could itself make visible and begin to define basic problems of historical understanding which in one form or another still pertain, and still continue to preoccupy disciplinary historians. When and how does a specialised discipline come coherently together? Does the process mark a cumulative development of pre-existing elements, or else mark a definite break with what went before?

8. THE HISTORIOGRAPHY OF CHEMISTRY

Perhaps the most enduring location of such questions lay, and still lies, in the historiography of chemistry, for historians of chemistry are compelled to consider the problem of the science's historical lineage with respect to the pre-existing practice of alchemy. This represents a key problem, for alchemy can be seen as an embarrassingly 'pre-scientific' activity, a jargon-ridden, secretive practice with impossible aims. Yet alchemists were also considerable experimenters, and developed theories of chemical 'elements', both of which features mean that, in historical terms, chemistry cannot simply be cut off from its alchemical past. This historical problem, of the emergence of the authentic scientific discipline in relation to its problematic past, was tackled for example in Thomas Thomson's *History of Chemistry* (1830–1). It also recurs within historical writing on the recently emerged science of geology, where the attempts of Charles Lyell (1797–1875) to re-establish the methodological and conceptual foundations of geological science entailed a historical designation and account of its origin.[10] Such historical reflection on the 'genuine' origins often tends to accompany the emergence of particular scientific specialities. It is this process which constitutes the formulation of a discipline's identity, along with specification of subject-matter, methods, techniques and theories. While disciplinary historiography of science has, since the early nineteenth century, achieved a professional distance from such direct identity formulations, the nature and form of the problem of originary identity must always continue to haunt its efforts.

9. 'HISTORICISM'

For intellectual historians generally, the nineteenth century is often seen as the period in which historiography as a whole took on its modern form, producing many classics of historical writing. This itself can be seen as an outgrowth of the nineteenth century's devotion to what is termed 'historicism'. 'Historicism' is that view of man, nature and society which insists that all these are formed by processes of development through time, rather than by abstract, eternal static principles such as reason or justice. The two pre-eminent exemplars of nineteenth-century historicism are Gottfried Hegel (1770–1831) and Karl Marx (1818–83), both united in seeing human existence as being fundamentally produced by historical change. They adopted, however, radically different views of what constituted the dynamic core of historical development. For Hegel, development was essentially mental in nature, the growth of the human mind and human society towards full and rational self-consciousness, a position known as 'idealism'. For Marx, by contrast, the basic form of historical development was material, economic production. As men produce the essential material features of their life, they also derivatively produce their social and political relations, their consciousness, learning and culture, a position known as 'historical materialism'.

10. THE WORK OF WILLIAM WHEWELL

These two forms of historiographical approach have been profoundly influential, for historiography generally and for certain aspects of the historiography of science in particular, and these aspects will be examined in more detail below. For the time being, however, our question is the impact of historicism upon the nineteenth-century historiography of science. Did it produce a home-grown equivalent of Hegel or Marx? The most likely pretender to such a title was the Cambridge-based scientist, philosopher and historian, William Whewell. Whewell produced a massive and erudite *History of the Inductive Sciences* (1837). It incorporated two features we have designated as already foundational for historiography of science. Firstly, it was a history of *sciences*, which divided up the historical world of science into the development of discrete scientific disciplines, such as astronomy, physical science, geology and so forth. Indeed, Whewell pushed this policy of division and subdivision to hitherto unheard-of lengths, inventing neologisms such as 'geological dynamics', 'thermotics' (the science of heat) and 'atmology' (the study of vapour). This process of division and subdivision created a representation of scientific development as an endless series of continual branchings, proliferating as history advanced towards the present day. Secondly, Whewell's history was also specifically tied to an explicitly philosophical project, which indeed appeared as *The Philosophy of the Inductive Sciences* (1840). The history was to function as the essential background to and basis of an analysis of the principles of progressive scientific reasoning. As a mobilisation of history in the service of philosophy, it has never been surpassed in its thoroughness, which is itself an index of Whewell's historicist leanings.

Whewell's overall developmental picture of history of science is very much an extension of the Enlightenment's. It saw science's origins in the speculative works of Greek philosophy, defective in their lack of factual content; the Middle Ages were a 'stationary period', lacking progressive elements because weighed down by intellectual dogmatism and mystical forms of knowledge such as astrology and alchemy. Genuine scientific development was then resumed in the sixteenth and seventeenth centuries with Copernican astronomy and Newtonian physics. From that time successive scientific specialities had emerged and grown to maturity.

Whewell, however, considerably added to this basic picture, and not only with respect to the sheer amount of detail his work contained. Present in Whewell's work was a far greater methodological sophistication and narrative complexity than ever before. Methodologically, he insisted that for science to develop authentically, pre-conditions were required: in this case, the co-existent presence of both facts and theories, each being necessary for the progressive existence of the other. He also exemplified what has since become a standard technical method in studies which conjoin history with philosophy of science, the method known as 'rational reconstruction'. This method, rather than following a strictly factual chronological narrative of the emergence of a discovery or theory, attempts instead to reconstruct the process of rational developmental relations which, it is held, pertain to the discovery or theory's emergence. Whewell's pioneering use of this technique can be seen in his account of Newton's discovery of the principle of universal gravitation.[11] Whewell analysed this down into five logically and conceptually distinct constituent propositions, and his history portrayed the separate emergence of each proposition, the order and connection of emergence being disconnected from any thorough and coherent chronological analysis.

As well as these methodological innovations, Whewell also introduced higher levels of narrative complexity than any of his predecessors. He saw history of science developing in 'epochs', highly charged periods of progress identified usually with the work of one individual, such as Newton. But this individual's work was not simply the individual's sole creative mind confronting and explaining nature unaided. Rather, the individual existed in already historically-formed circumstances, created by the relevant discoveries of preceding scientists, which constituted the 'prelude' to the 'epoch'. The epochal significance of an individual such as Newton then consisted in drawing a whole series of pre-existing discoveries within one unified, generalised framework, re-arranging a diverse and perhaps disconnected series of discoveries as functions of a single scientific proposition or law. This account of fundamental scientific change represented it as non-revolutionary. Underlying apparently revolutionary changes was a cumulative sequence of changes, and their culmination smoothes out any apparent contradictions. Nothing of scientific value is lost as science moves forward. In so far as they are true, former discoveries are preserved and incorporated within the culminating, unifying development.

> Nothing which was done was useless or unessential, though it ceases to be conspicuous and primary.
> Thus the final form of each science contains the substance of each of its preceding modifications; and all that was at any antecedent period discovered and established, ministers to the ultimate development of its proper branch of knowledge. Such previous doctrines may require to be made precise and definite, to have their superfluous and arbitrary portions expunged, to be expressed in new language, to be taken into the body of science by various processes; but they do not on such an account cease to be true doctrines, or to form a portion of our knowledge.[12]

Whewell's historical exposition of this narrative principle preserves the notion of progress essential to science while discarding the idea of progress as being discontinuous or revolutionary in nature. It is a conservationist, consolatory image of change also, for nothing of significance is ever lost. But above all it is historicist in outlook, for each present moment of scientific development incorporates the truth and value of its past, and so is definitively formed and produced by its history.

11. SCIENTIFIC BIOGRAPHY

The nineteenth, historicist, century was also a great age of biographical writing, and historiography of science was also responsive to this larger tendency of nineteenth-century culture. Biography was an extremely popular form of writing, and served to communicate to a wider than scientific public aspects of the historiography of science. David Brewster (1781–1868), the Scottish physicist, wrote popular biographies of Galileo, Tycho Brahe and Kepler,[13] and also produced a monumental biography of Isaac Newton, a work only recently superseded, so considerable was its range and detail.[14] Brewster's biographies of scientists still have historiographical interest, for they often focus upon a problem which retains technical and general significance for historians of science. This problem is most clearly delineated in Brewster's treatment of Newton's alchemical interests. These constituted problematic matter for Brewster, revealing as they did Newton's involvement in the intellectually contemptible and morally reprehensible practice of alchemy. Brewster himself was finally at a loss to produce any coherent explanation for Newton's alchemy, and the problem he faced, of understanding how Newton, the paragon of scientific rationality, also took seriously the mystical practices of alchemy, has never disappeared for Newtonian scholarship. Although approaches to the problem are now more sophisticated than anything Brewster could manage, the issue of how one integrates these apparently opposing aspects of Newton's work still persists.[15]

Biography has become conventional for historians of science since the mid-nineteenth century, continuing to provide a useful focus of research and writing. Its tendency is to stress the individualist element in historiography of science, namely, to see the unique agent of scientific development as the individual mind as it grapples with scientific problems. Biography however adds also a humanising element often lacking in histories of particular theories or sciences. Because biography takes the human life as its narrative unit, and because any successful biography needs to clarify the personal meanings which the protagonist's life and career held for him, it must focus on what a scientist's work means for him personally, how it expresses the scientist's personality in psychological and social terms. While the individualist aspect of biography can lead to over-emphasis on individual genius at the expense of more thoroughly historical explanation, and while biography after Freud can sometimes give way to reductive and implausible psychoanalytic explanations, it remains the case that with appropriate and sensitive handling, a biographical focus upon a scientist's work can provide an important range of insights which other kinds of historiography cannot. This, combined with the greater popularity of biography with a more general reading public, ensures the continuing survival of scientific biography.[16]

12. HISTORIOGRAPHY OF SCIENCE IN THE TWENTIETH CENTURY

As historiography of science moved into the twentieth century, it moved into a radically new situation. Before the twentieth century, historiography of science was produced largely by scientists themselves, and philosophers. During the twentieth century, historiography of science has become an increasingly professionalised discipline, produced by people who practise history of science as a specialised academic occupation within universities and colleges. This process, it is important to realise at the outset, has not yet been total. It remains true that historians of science are not simply recruited from a straight career ladder consisting of an undergraduate degree in history of science, followed by an academic career of teaching and research. Historians of science often have a prior educational background in some other subject, a science, philosophy, sociology or history, before switching into history of science. Its practitioners often include workers in museums, and the membership of its associations includes individuals whose professional occupations are largely unrelated to the business of teaching and researching history of science. This means that history of science has a peculiarly open professional structure, which partially may account for its singularly responsive and diverse intellectual history in the twentieth century.

With these qualifications entered, history of science has nonetheless generated the kinds of academic forms, publications and networks, and professional associations, which conventionally characterise academic professions. It has learned societies, many specialised journals, and has university and college departments devoted to it, although the departments tend to be fewer in number and smaller in size than those of most other academic disciplines.

The growth of these departments, journals and associations occurred most notably after the Second World War, but it was a process already well in train during the first half of the century. The Collège de France in Paris had a short-lived professorship devoted to history of science from 1892 to 1913, and although the professorship was suppressed, Paris remained an important centre for history of science from the late nineteenth century onwards, through the work of the chemist Marcelin Berthelot (1827–1907), the historian-philosopher Paul Tannery (1843–1904), and later in the 1920s, 30s and 40s, the historians Hélène Metzger (1889–1944) and Alexandre Koyré (1892–1964), who published both scholarly monographs and articles in journals such as *Archeion* and *Scientia*.[17]

In 1912 the Belgian historian George Sarton (1884–1956) initiated and carried through plans to found *Isis*, which became and still remains the leading journal in the history of science. The importance of such journals is easy to underestimate, but they did more than simply provide a venue for the publication of scholarly work. Journals also provide a network of professional communication, helping thereby to create and solidify a bonding sense of community for scholars who might otherwise have remained isolated individuals or small cadres. They thus have a considerable significance for a nascent but still struggling academic discipline, such as history of science in the inter-war period.

Sarton's career and the vision which impelled it are revealing. History of science for Sarton was the only arena of human activity which unequivocally demonstrated the progress of mankind. Science was the religion of this progressive, secular humanist, who could declare, in his *Introduction to the History of Science* (1927–48) that 'The history of science is the history of mankind's unity, of its sublime purpose, of its gradual redemption'.[18] Despite the intensity of his commitments, and his success in maintaining *Isis* as a viable project, Sarton's career nonetheless never managed to solidify itself institutionally. Moving to Harvard after the First World War, and undertaking some undergraduate teaching there over the next three decades, he nonetheless failed to persuade Harvard to support a department for the history of science. There were signs too that the involvement of scientists under the German Reich in the 1930s and 1940s shook his earlier faith in the history of science as the record of mankind's progressive redemption. That said, Sarton's attempts to provide bibliographic resources for history of science, his commitment to laying down basic and professional methodological criteria for his subject and of course *Isis* itself, all remain enduring contributions to his chosen field.

Of more intellectual influence than Sarton was another emigré from Europe, the Russian Alexandre Koyré. Koyré was a historian of science whose work on seventeenth-century science, notably the *Etudes Galiléennes* (1939) came to provide an intellectual model for many younger historians. Whereas Sarton had pursued a broad introductory overview, Koyré's scholarship was characterised by close textual exegesis of important scientific texts, carefully tracking their conceptual structures, to clarify the fundamental intellectual ideas which underlay the advances made by a Galileo or a Newton. Koyré's historiography has therefore a strongly idealist cast. For him, science was a kind of pure thought, approximate to philosophy, and Koyré himself approached scientific texts as a philosopher whose own philosophical commitments derived from the paramount idealist thinkers in the Western philosophical tradition, Plato and Hegel.

Koyré worked in France before the Second World War, then in New York during its course. From 1945 to 1964 he divided his time between Paris and American universities such as Harvard, Yale and Princeton. It was in this American setting that his work became particularly influential. This influence attained its full significance not only because it profoundly affected the approaches of a number of scholars who were to publish significant work in the

1950s, 1960s and 1970s. It was additionally significant because this period coincided with the notable professional expansion of history of science in higher education in America and elsewhere, witnessing an increasing number of academic programmes and departments being devoted to the history of science. It was in this setting, the coming-together of an expanding profession and a distinct historiographical approach, that Koyré's work took on central importance for the discipline and enabled him to have a structural effect upon modern historiography of science. That effect can be measured out in the work of influential American researchers and teachers such as Thomas Kuhn, Charles Gillispie and Richard Westfall, a generation of scholars who have all variously acknowledged Koyré's profound intellectual impact.

If professional American historiography bears the decisive imprint of Koyré's idealism at its formative stage, this by no means completes the description of recent and contemporary historiographical development. Materialist approaches, looking back ultimately to the work of Karl Marx, have also made considerable headway in the twentieth century. Historical materialism as applied to historiography of science, sees science as being produced and determined by the social and economic relations in which science takes place. Thus, instead of seeing science as a purely intellectual activity, developing according to its own, internal conceptual dynamics, historical materialism interprets science as a form of intellectual production, tied to the economic preoccupations, class interests and ideological values of particular historical periods and cultures.

A very basic form of this kind of work may be read, for example, in the Soviet historian Boris Hessen's account of Newton's *Principia*, which systematically relates the scientific content of Newton's work to specifically economic aspects of the society in which Newton lived.[19] Since Hessen's work, materialist historiography of science has developed considerably more sophistication, and has resulted in major scholarly endeavours. Joseph Needham's huge *Science and Civilization in China* (1954–84) not only attempts to see science as something shaped by the culture which produces it, but in so doing has opened up to scholarly understanding a whole vast area with which Western scholars have been unfamiliar. Historiography of science tends very much to adopt a Eurocentric perspective, and Needham's work is a valuable corrective to the historical vision of things scientific which most Western scholars promote.

13. THE PROFESSIONALISATION OF HISTORY OF SCIENCE

From historical materialism, and from other intellectual resources such as sociology, has developed a kind of historiography known as 'social history of science', which has had increasing impact within the discipline. Aspects of social history of science, and the resources which it draws upon, may be pursued in more detail in several of the articles which immediately follow in this section of the *Companion*. Overall, social history of science incorporates several different kinds of study. It may rest content with providing a detailed history of science's institutional development at particular times and places, showing how particular communities of scientists are formed.[20] It may also relate institutional development to wider social and political features of a culture or nation. From there, it may point out ways in which particular fields of science have been formed by, or become responsive to, features of social and political change.[21] It may further point to the ways in which the content of certain scientific theories is produced by and contains ideological commitments typical of the society in which the theory is produced.[22] It may point out how science itself affects the wider social, economic and political spheres.[23] Much theoretical and practical labour has been devoted to such topics by historians, sociologists and philosophers of science over the last three decades. This work has not been uncontroversial. Although few would disagree that historical knowledge of science's social development is both useful and desirable, as is knowledge of science's impact upon society, social history of science can nonetheless question some of the cherished historical images produced originally by the Enlightenment and developed thereafter. Is science, after all, historically typified by the term 'progress'? The role of scientifically-produced technologies for military purposes and for ecologically-damaging manufacturing processes questions the suitability of terms such as 'progress' for understanding science's history. If science can be seen as responsive to social, economic, political and cultural forces and values, in what sense can it still be maintained that science produces authentic, neutral, objective knowledge? If scientists work typically in collective, institutionalised settings, should we continue to conceive of the individual scientist as the unique agent of scientific development? In short, social history of science tends overall to call in doubt the liberal certainties of progress, authenticity and individualism centralised by Enlightenment historiography and its nineteenth- and twentieth-century successors. It may be, then, that historiography of science, in recently questioning its old, foundational assumptions, has initiated a revolution in its own historical understanding.

The increasing professionalisation of history of science has also aided in the abandonment of old historiographical assumptions. Two in particular deserve mention; firstly, the view that the Middle Ages were devoid of scientific interest, and secondly the view that science, historically speaking, was an activity typified by its secular nature, which was held to contrast with the religious belief-systems which preceded the rise of modern science. The scientist-philosopher Pierre Duhem (1861–1916) was among the first to question the view that the medieval centuries lacked any significant scientific development, showing in particular how medieval physical thought was subject to historical changes in ways which anticipated the sorts of changes usually attributed to the period of Galileo. The rich and variegated nature of medieval science has since been further revealed by scholars such as Crombie and Claggett.[24] Historians have also had to come to terms with the impossibility of characterising science's history as something separate from religious belief and theological principle. Once there existed sufficient and detailed attention to the works and manuscripts of scientists such as Newton, Kepler, Boyle and many others in the seventeenth, eighteenth and nineteenth centuries, it became increasingly obvious that their scientific work could not simply be separated off from their religious beliefs and theological reasonings. Any sympathetic consideration of their science has to realise how it was integrated within the patterns of religious culture, rather than posing itself as an alternative to religion.[25]

As well as these structural alterations in historiographical interpretation of the overall historical course and nature of Western science, the professionalisation of history of science has also and quite simply meant that far more of science's history has been discovered and written about in the last forty years than in the two preceding centuries. This process is incapable of summary, so diverse is the range of work that it covers, but in general terms what it has produced are increasing degrees of specialisation. Whereas for a Whewell or a Sarton it was still possible to write general histories of science, historians of science now tend to identify themselves in much more specialised terms: as historians of biology, or of chemistry, or of the social sciences; of American science or German science; of medieval science, or of early modern science, or of twentieth-century science. Among other things, the proliferation of specialised journals marks this process. This kind of specialisation allows much closer and more detailed scrutiny of scientific development than was ever possible for pre-professional or early professional practitioners.

Is historiography of science now therefore simply comparable to other disciplines, divided into narrowly focused specialities, and losing sight of larger issues and perspectives? This is significantly not the case, and for two reasons. Firstly, specialisation applies particularly to research, rather than to teaching. Because historians of science teach in rather small departments which are often obliged to offer general, introductory courses, they are equally obliged, as lecturers and tutors, to retain a general and updated awareness of the field as a whole, and to be professionally familiar with subjects as far apart as medieval optics and the Manhattan Project which produced the atomic bomb. This feature of professional life keeps in place an attention to the larger issues of scientific development.

Secondly, because history of science is an open professional structure which involves and includes practitioners of other disciplines such as philosophy, sociology and history, it is peculiarly sensitive and responsive to the kinds of information, theoretical perspectives and practical techniques which those other disciplines produce. Philosophers persist in producing new and different unifying theories of scientific development. Sociologists originate a variegated array of social approaches to science. Historians pioneer novel techniques of historical investigation. Many of these work their way, more or less rapidly, into the developing body of knowledge, technique and interpretation which make up the historiography of science. The field is now therefore constituted in a way which both allows fruitful specialisation and encourages generalist perspectives and a process of theoretical and methodological innovation, maintaining thereby its commitment to tackling the fundamental and global meanings of science in the history of the Western world.

NOTES

1. A. Lavoisier, *Opuscules physiques et chimiques* (Paris, 1774).
2. H. Boerhaave, *New method of chemistry* (trans. P. Shaw and E. Chambers, London, 1727).
3. F. Bacon, 'New Atlantis' (1626), in J. Spelling, R. Ellis and D. Heath (eds.), *The works of Francis Bacon* (14 vols., London 1872–74), vol. III, p. 156.
4. For a general treatment of the Enlightenment and science see T. L. Hankins, *Science and the Enlightenment* (Cambridge, 1985).
5. J. d'Alembert, *Preliminary discourse to the Encyclopedia of Diderot* (1751), ed. R. Schwab (New York, 1963), p. 74.
6. Ibid., p. 85.
7. T. S. Kuhn, *The structure of scientific revolutions* (Chicago, 1962).
8. J. Priestley, *The history and present state of electricity* (London, 1767) (vol. 1), p. iv.
9. J. J. Rousseau, 'Discourse on the moral effects of the arts and sciences', in G. D. H. Cole (ed.), *The Social Contract and Discourses* (rev. ed. London, 1973), pp. 4–5.
10. See R. M. Porter, 'Charles Lyell and the principles of the history of geology', *British journal for the history of science*, 9 (1976), 91–103.
11. W. Whewell, *History* (vol. 2), pp. 160–87.
12. Ibid., (vol. 1), pp. 10–11.
13. D. Brewster, *Martyrs of science: lives of Galileo, Tycho Brahe and Kepler* (Edinburgh, 1841).
14. D. Brewster, *Memoirs of the life, writings and discoveries of Sir Isaac Newton* (2 vols., Edinburgh, 1855).
15. See, e.g. the treatment of this issue by R. S. Westfall in *Never at rest: a biography of Isaac Newton* (Cambridge, 1980).
16. For examples of good recent scientific biography, see E. Fox Keller, *A feeling for the organism: the life and work of Barbara McLintock* (New York, 1983), and P. Pauly, *Controlling life: Jacques Loeb and the engineering ideal in biology* (New York, Oxford, 1987).
17. For the Collège de France professorship, see H. W. Paul, 'Scholarship versus ideology: the Chair of the General History of Science at the Collège de France, 1892–1913', *Isis*, 62 (1976), 376–87.
18. G. Sarton, *Introduction* (vol. 1), p. 132.
19. H. Hessen, 'The social and economic roots of Newton's *Principia*', in N. I. Bukharin *et al.*, *Science at the crossroads* (1931, 2nd ed. London, 1971), pp. 147–212.
20. E.g. R. Hahn, *The anatomy of a scientific institution: the Paris Academy of Sciences, 1666–1803* (Berkeley, Los Angeles, London, 1971).
21. E.g. Hahn's work again, and J. Christie, 'The origins and development of the Scottish scientific community', *History of science*, 12 (1974), 122–41.
22. E.g. R. M. Young, 'Malthus and the evolutionists: the common context of biological and social theory', *Past and present*, 43 (1969), 109–45.
23. E.g. B. Latour, *The Pasteurization of France* (Cambridge, Mass.), in press.
24. P. Duhem, *Le système du monde: histoire des doctrines cosmologiques de Platon à Copernic,*

A. Crombie, *Robert Grosseteste and the origins of experimental science* (Oxford, 1953); M. Claggett, *The science of mechanics in the Middle Ages* (Madison, 1959).

25. See e.g. C. Webster, *The Great Instauration: science, medicine and reform in England, 1626–1660* (London, 1975) for a treatment of seventeenth-century English science which makes its religious context unavoidably clear.

FURTHER READING

J. Christie, 'Narrative and rhetoric in Hélène Metzger's historiography of eighteenth-century chemistry', *History of science*, 25 (1987), 99–109. See also the accompanying articles on Metzger by J. V. Golinski and B. Vincent-Bensaude.

——, 'Sir David Brewster as an historian of science', in A. Morrison-Low and J. Christie (eds.), *'Martyr of science': Sir David Brewster 1781–1868* (Edinburgh, 1984).

M. Finocchiaro, *The history of science as explanation* (Detroit, 1973).

H. Kragh, *An introduction to the historiography of science* (Cambridge, 1987).

A. Thackray, 'Science: has its present past a future?', in R. Stuewer (ed.), *Historical and philosophical perspectives of science* (Minneapolis, 1970), pp. 112–27.

——, and R. Merton, 'On discipline building: the paradoxes of George Sarton', *Isis*, 63 (1972), 473–95.

——, 'History of science' in P. Durbin (ed.), *A guide to the culture of science, technology and medicine* (New York, 1980), pp. 3–69.

M. Teich and R. M. Young (eds.), *Changing perspectives in the history of science* (London, 1973).

History of science (1962, 26 vols.). This journal publishes a great many articles of historiographical analysis and review.

2

THE HISTORY OF SCIENCE AND THE WORKING SCIENTIST

JOHN R. G. TURNER

The brief story about the relationship of the working scientist to the history of science is that, as far as he or she is concerned, there isn't one. A scientist who is not fascinated by the way the world is put together, and not convinced that the scientific method provides the best means towards understanding it, or that the successive efforts of scientists provide a progressive improvement in that understanding, so that their project could just possibly be better than anything that has gone before, is in the wrong job. Many working scientists regard – or affect to regard – a real interest in the history of the subject as some kind of intellectual weakness, or as an occupation suitable for ageing members of the profession who have lost their flair and are being put out to grass, a phase of life for which one scientist coined the pejorative term 'philopause'. Old theories are either right, in which case we have adopted them, or wrong, in which case they are a waste of time. A hard-centred scientist's interest in history extends no further than an understanding of the basis for the current controversies in his or her field – what is commonly understood as 'scientific review'. Science was until recently an intellectual profession which, unlike the arts and humanities, was criticised internally by its own practitioners, and had no 'parasitic' cadre of critics carping on the sidelines. Scientists when they were old enough, famous enough or bold enough, wrote their own history, to their own advantage.

This may or may not be considered to be an odd stance for scientists to take: it lays them open to charges of intellectual philistinism, and makes them prone to distorted perceptions of their own field. We have then to ask whether the practice of any craft or creative art is really improved by a cool objective under-standing of its history. Does one make better cabinets for knowing the history of carpentry? One may write better symphonies from a deep study of Mozart and

Mahler, but are the compositions necessarily improved by an understanding of their place in musical history? Historians may be said to study history, but the notion that scientists study science is a linguistically generated illusion: scientists study not science but the physical universe.

How much of the history of science the practising scientist knows and understands is perhaps itself a subject worthy of several Ph.D. theses in the sociology of science. Most of us have some perception of the historical development of our own field, and a general perception of the history of the whole of science from Bacon onwards, picked up at school, from television and from popularisers such as Koestler and Bronowski. Historical awareness is probably greater in some fields than in others: subjects which are themselves historical may encourage more of an interest in the history of the subject. Evolutionary biologists, for example, seem to have a greater penchant for scientific history than many others, perhaps enhanced by the domination of their subject by the historically and biographically fascinating figure of Charles Darwin.

In those few sciences which are themselves historical, archival history has a small but important part to play. Use of early records of comet appearances or supernovae, like the calculation of the period of Halley's comet by Halley and subsequent astronomers, and the Chinese record of the explosion which now forms the Crab nebula are much-quoted examples in astronomy. Old records of temperature have been used for estimating long-term trends in the climate, such as the important issue of whether the Earth is slowly warming up from the greenhouse effect of carbon dioxide. A more whimsical exercise is the use of Tycho's barometer readings and the ships' logs to construct the weather map of the deep autumn depression that wrecked the Spanish Armada. Historical ecology and biogeography chart the changes in the ranges of species, or their adaptation to new habitats, such as the change of the rabbit from a delicate species that had to be carefully nurtured in Britain into a hardy agricultural pest. Synthesis of landscape history with evolutionary ecology can reconstruct the history of evolving populations of snails. In effect the scientist is tapping archives or ancient data banks, and although she or he must be historically aware in order to understand the nature of the instruments used (the siting and functioning of early thermometers for example), and to a lesser degree the intellectual climate in which the readings were taken, there need be no tension between the methods of science and the methods of history.

It is when history becomes an interpretative critique that the ways of the scientist and of the historian begin to part. Scientific history as it used to be written by scientists served the tribe of scientists much as the hero-myths serve any other human tribe. Neophytes, undergraduates and research students were taught which of the ancestor-figures to venerate: naturally those among the earlier generations of scientists whose theories and interpretations could be construed as pointing in the direction of the modern 'correct' view of the subject. Even ancient Greeks came in for this method of classification into forward-looking theorists and dead-enders – there was nothing more deadening than a professor of a physical science trying to review his subject from Democritus onward. The neophyte might hope in the end to become one of the deified ancestors, by developing his or her chosen field further in the 'correct' direction, or very rarely by making the sort of discovery that significantly widens or alters the field of enquiry. The thoughtful student could of course see a problem inherent in this view: the progress of science to which he or she would, if very able, contribute, itself ensured that all scientific theories were in some sense 'wrong', and that the only thing that distinguished a good theory from a bad one was the Oscar Wilde distinction between a life-long passion and a mild flirtation – the mild flirtation, or successful theory, lasted longer. A quick examination of the literature would reveal that most of the scientists of the past were non-entities, only a very small minority 'got it right', and that there was a rather larger number of heroic failures, who were gloriously and terribly wrong. Here was a view that consigned almost all scientists to the historical scrap-heap. It has a rather sinister modern extension in the use of 'citation-ratings' (counting the number of times a paper is cited in the reference lists of other papers in the 'primary' journals) as a method of assessing the quality of scientific research.

This traditional view of scientific history then provided the young scientist with a small number of hero-myths, of which the most pervasive was that of Galileo versus Rome. As with any myth, the behavioural norms that this drama inculcated were deep, but in outline could be seen as loyalty to the scientific community in the face of organised political power (a loyalty that transcended loyalty to party, nation or creed), and respect for experiment and observation in preference to written authority. Scientists with a leaning towards agnosticism and other varieties of atheism liked to read the lesson as being the evil influence of organised religion. A similar interpretation can be put on the suppression of modern genetics by the organised authority of the Soviet state.

The scientists' view of science tended to be excessively reverential to hero-figures among the sheep on the right hand, excessively condemnatory of scientists who have been separated with the goats on the left, and to interpret disputes over fundamental theory naïvely as religious or philosophical obscurantism (Rome) versus scientific enlightenment (Galileo). (The uniformitarian-catastrophist debate in geology was very easily simplified in this way, as was the debate over Darwin.) The losing side in major disagreements tended to be caricatured as knaves or fools: the unwritten assumption was that if the correct interpretation of the world is obvious to us now, it should have been obvious then, and only prejudice could have prevented them from seeing it. What there was of history in the scientists' perception was a backward extension of scientific review – an attempt to sort out the correct from the incorrect, the winners from the losers, and one's own camp (winners, naturally) from the opposition. As it is impossible for a scientist to un-know what has occurred since, even a serious attempt at historical writing becomes fraught with the wisdom of hindsight, and that peculiar habit of interpreting the past in terms of the present, which the scientist as scientist knows to be a non-sensical reversal of causality and time's arrow.

History is harder than scientists think. Once the matter is more than a few decades old, the practising scientist finds it very difficult even to understand what an earlier scientist is saying, because of a deep inability to read the text in its contemporary context. Words in scientific discourse can shift their meaning in less than a decade in a rapidly developing field, making the reading of even slightly old texts an assault course of pitfalls for the linguistically naïve scientist, who often regards words as having the fixed meanings assigned to them by scientific authority. Consequently, even when merely reviewing earlier work for scientific and scholarly purposes the scientist tends badly to distort the meaning of the earlier texts.

Tensions and contradictions or no, this was a view of scientific history with which scientists felt comfortable. Naturally in view of the fact that it was mostly generated by scientists who had developed an interest in the archives, it conformed with the nineteenth-century view of science as progress towards an increasingly accurate view of the world. Dividing the scientists of the past into those who had and had not caused their fields to move in the 'right' direction not only reinforced this very important view of science: it allowed historical assessment to merge with the normal behaviour of scientists when in dispute with contemporary rivals – to show that the other side has got it wrong, and should be assigned to the scrap-heap. It has been common practice to cite hero-figures, rather superficially, in an attempt to show that one's own theory is in the dominant and correct camp in its field. Citing Darwin is a good way for any evolutionary biologist to validate his or her claims to serious attention, and the writings of so rich a master can be combed, much as the Bible, for quotations which will validate deeply opposed views: was Darwin a 'neutralist', was he a 'punctuationist', or was he a 'pluralist', and therefore all things to all biologists? A daring and hazardous variant of this tactic is to attempt the resurrection of one of the rejected figures of the past who can be claimed as ancestral to one's own unorthodox views. It is doubtful if even with a balanced view of historiography, a scientist writing the history of his or her own field can ever completely resist the temptation to use the matter for self-justification, or to turn the exercise into personal intellectual genealogy and extended autobiography.

History can in this way become a valuable adjunct in the political fight for recognition and funding. Much as evolutionary biology looks back to Darwin, the recognition of molecular biology as an independent discipline, with chairs, fellowships, departments and resources is validated by reference to the heroic, monographed, biographied and (literally) dramatised discovery of the Double Helix by Watson and Crick.

Scientists are often ignorant of, or even hostile to, developments in the historiography of science during the last twenty years. Science sets its own standards for the acceptance or rejection of theories, interpretations and observations, which are widely regarded by scientists as being internal, and not affected by external philosophical, political or religious criteria. Suggesting that the opposition has some kind of external axe to grind is usually regarded as a professional foul, and hence interpretations of the history of science which relate it to external intellectual and social developments are regarded with deep suspicion. To say that an ecologist may have been drawn to a theory about competition because it conformed with his Quaker views on the nature of conflict, for instance, would be seen as at worst scurrilous, and at best irrelevant to the assessment of the theory within the framework of science. Suggesting that the earlier proponents of hereditarian theories of intelligence were motivated by racial or social prejudice is harder to shrug off, and tends to be dealt with by placing these practitioners in the outgroup of 'frauds' or 'pseudoscientists'; (almost the entire corpus of the work of Sir Cyril Burtt has been eliminated from psychology in this way). At the extreme, an entirely relativistic or social theory of science, which evaluates theories and observations purely in their historical or social context, cannot be acceptable to a practising scientist: he or she knows that some constructions explain or predict the behaviour of the real world better than others, and that the theories should be used or discarded according to their ability to make these explanations and predictions. There are probably rather few thoughtful scientists who still see science as establishing the 'Truth', but even if one takes a more pragmatic view of science as the Bus-Timetable of the Universe (a person with a timetable is more likely to catch a bus than someone who is completely ignorant of the causes which generate the arrival of the buses), it has to be acknowledged that some methods of calculating the timetable predict the arrival of the buses more accurately than others. In Platonic terms, if there is only one physical reality, then the existence of two equally useful ways of describing it can only be a temporary flaw in our construction of scientific theories: ultimately a better single description will appear to replace both competitors. True pluralism in the scientific world is not possible, except perhaps for that very small minority of scientists who believe in plural realities.

The relativism which rightly or wrongly is often thought to be implicit in the Kuhnian view of science is therefore deeply distasteful to most scientists. The Galileo myth teaches that science transcends religious, political and philosophical predispositions, and that (*eppur si muove*) the physical world does not obey our prejudices. If a functionally superior description of the world sits uncomfortably with our Marxism or Christianity, then in theory it is our Marxism or

Christianity that has to make the adjustment. A totally relativistic view would dictate that Lysenkoist genetics was as valid a description of heredity as Mendelian genetics, and that we should choose between them according to our feelings about bourgeois capitalism; it would imply also that, as there is indeed a Jewish culture with its own literature, humour, religion and so on, perhaps there is also a particular kind of science embedded in that culture. The thought that this implies that Hitler could have been right to classify the theory of relativity as 'Jewish science' (leaving him subject only to moral but not intellectual condemnation) will convince most scientists that they have brought the relativist to the asses' brigg.

The relativistic view of science as reification of its external social context is nonetheless used to some extent as a stick for beating the opposition, by scientists of radical persuasion who espouse theories unpopular with their more politically conventional colleagues. A theory which states that all science is reified prejudice allows one to dismiss the more broadly accepted view as merely capitalist or racist, and to assert the superiority of the radicalised theory, not by the internal criteria of scientific verification, but on the external criterion of the moral superiority of one's socio-political leanings. Thus the claim of Marxism itself to represent a scientific and objective description of history automatically renders false in a real scientific sense all scientific theories that point in the opposite direction (the truth shall set you free). It follows immediately that the data on which the theories rest must be either falsified or misinterpreted. The recent debate over the supposed inheritance of intelligence (in which data on both sides has indeed been falsified) provides plentiful examples.

But this kind of dismissal on the strength of external criteria remains hazardous, and can be performed successfully only on scientists who can somehow be placed in the out-group designated as pseudoscientists. In this way most of the leaders of the twentieth-century eugenics movement can be safely removed from the community of scientists, and criticised on purely socio-political grounds. A historian would find it a lot harder to separate the real scientists and the pseudoscientists.

There is therefore a natural gulf between the scientist and the historian; do we agree with the scientist that history is bunk, or suggest to him or her that those who do not understand history are condemned to repeat its mistakes? A sophisticated scientist certainly learns strategies within the scientific method by studying the masterworks of the earlier generation (which is merely the equivalent of absorbing Mozart), and scientists show by their use of citations, which have become ever more important as a token of exchange within the body-scientific, that they are quite as interested in other scientists as they are in the physical world. If a scientific theory is 'correct', then its past is in a sense irrelevant. But if it is wrong, one of the ways to understand how and why is to understand the intellectual context in which it arose, and the philosophical, social and political prejudices of its originators; observations are harder to categorise in this way, but it seems generally understood by scientists now that there is no such thing as a theory-free observation. However, the cumulative nature of science dictates that *all* theories are incorrect: therefore no theory can be understood fully without reference to its external relations. I believe that, without realising it, I discovered this fact for myself in the course of twenty years spent trying to comprehend R. A. Fisher's 'fundamental theorem of natural selection', one of the knottier problems in evolutionary theory: only when I could relate it not simply to Fisher's views about biology and his admiration for Darwin, but to his eugenic idealism and his welding of Darwinism with his Christianity, did the theorem finally make sense.

This divide has naturally been crossed from time to time, probably more easily in the past when all history was Whiggish, than in the present when scientists have little access in their training or professional lives to the methods of modern historians. Viewing history as local history and biography, some scientific societies have treasured their archives, publishing obituaries, biographies and even historical memoranda. They have assembled scientific manuscripts, letters and documents relating to the history of their field (the [British] Genetical Society is currently attempting this for example), or, as in the British Association, inaugurated historical sections. Some scientists have converted to become good non-partisan historians; a very few have combined both careers. Scientists who write history in this way bring to the field a deep understanding of the actual scientific subject-matter which is hard to match. They tend of course to write in their own subject – it must be rare indeed for a working scientist to do archaeology in some corner of a foreign field – and to deal with its recent history: the eighteenth and earlier centuries are a period which requires more training in its mastery than a busy scientist is likely to achieve. It would be interesting to investigate the hypothesis that the less committed a scientist is or has been to a clearly formulated set of hypotheses in his or her field, the more objective the history will be, and that those who turn to history do not often return to the bench (the 'philopause' is, like other signs of senility, irreversible). In what may be a temporary phase in the development of science, scientists assess each other more on the size of their research grants than on their output: history is inexpensive and attracts little funding. Its pursuit is not a profitable career-strategy for most scientists.

If this is so, then we can ask to what extent history attracts those who are beginning to find less satisfaction in the physical world, to what extent the scientist sees history as a handy stick with which to thump his or her less sophisticated colleagues over the head in purely scientific debates, and to what extent the study of history gives the scientist such a Paschalian gulf at his or her side that the practice of science comes to seem futile or impossible. Again, the answers are largely unknown.

The scientist should be able to gain from the study of history a more balanced understanding of the nature of scientific controversy in general, and of disputes and choices in his or her own field in particular. Seeing that the way forward has much more often been a matter of synthesis than of the outright rejection of the views of the 'losing' camp (whatever the traditional hero-myths say) should produce a more flexible approach to current theories, an increased ability to question their assumptions and a greater willingness to re-examine older, discarded viewpoints. The training of most scientists largely lacks in anything that would inculcate self-awareness: introducing the working student or scientist to even a little history can produce a disproportionate broadening of the mind. As the modern approaches to history percolate, more scientists are becoming willing to stand back and look at science in its human context, though they will always take a different view from the professional historian. The profound interest which most scientists take in precedence (or 'I got there first!') renders them very prone to the now historically unfashionable habit of treating everyone significant as a forerunner of someone more significant. The independence of science from the social context is largely a self-delusion on the part of scientists, many of whom are intensely political animals, jockeying for position, status and resources, and repeatedly having to justify themselves to committees of their peers appointed by their political masters. As science comes increasingly under the control of large organisations, manipulated more or less directly either by the state or by industry, the scientists' wish to view science purely as self-monitored activity with practical output but no socio-political input, will come increasingly under stress. An understanding of the history of science may become a valuable resource for any scientist who wishes to continue doing science in the remaining years of the century.

As for the history of science itself, it is like any other branch of the humanities in that only the worst philistines – a category that now unfortunately includes the holders of the purse-strings for the British universities – would regard its justification as primarily its practical or economic value to the scientist at the bench or to the industry which employs him. The history of science has the same uses as other branches of history. With the dominance of science and its technologies in the modern world and the intellectual impact of the Scientific Revolution, the history of science is clearly a heavily under-developed branch of history, rating vastly fewer practitioners than economics or politics: it is quite clearly much too important to be left to the self-interested and distorted perceptions of the working scientists themselves.

NOTE

For arguments of various kinds, I am indebted to all my colleagues in the Division of the History and Philosophy of Science at the University of Leeds.

FURTHER READING

S. G. Brush, 'Should the history of science be rated X?', *Science*, vol. 183 (1974), 1164–72.

S. J. Gould, *Ontogeny and phylogeny* (Cambridge, Mass., 1977).

——, *The mismeasure of man* (New York, 1981), (reprinted Harmondsworth, 1984).

R. Gregory, *Discovery or the spirit and service of science*, first published 1916, abridged and partly re-written (Harmondsworth, 1946).

D. J. Kevles, *In the name of eugenics* (New York, 1985). (Reprinted Harmondsworth, 1986.)

H. Kragh, *An introduction to the historiography of science* (Cambridge 1987).

E. Mayr, *The growth of biological thought* (Cambridge, Mass., 1982).

Zh. A. Medvedev, *The rise and fall of T. D. Lysenko* (translated by I. M. Lerner), (New York, 1969).

S. Rose (ed.), *Towards a liberatory biology* (London, 1982).

——, *Against biological determinism* (London, 1982).

3

THE HISTORY OF SCIENCE AND THE HISTORY OF SOCIETY

ROY PORTER

In 1949, the general historian, Herbert Butterfield, staked out a dramatic claim for the part played by science over the last five centuries in shaping Western society. In Butterfield's view, the Scientific Revolution of the sixteenth and seventeenth centuries.

> outshines everything since the rise of Christianity, and reduces the Renaissance and Reformation to the rank of mere episodes, mere internal displacements, within the system of medieval Christendom.[1]

Well over a generation later, however, a glance at almost any textbook history or synoptic survey of 'the rise of the West' will show that infinitely greater space and significance are still being attached to poets and popes than to Pasteur. Historians at large are still blind to the possibility that science has made a special contribution in the unique development of Western civilisation; and this stricture applies to the best historians no less than to the mass. Fernand Braudel's massive and magisterial *Civilization and Capitalism, 15th to 18th Century* (1979–81) illuminates many aspects of the material culture of early modern Europe, but the fact that man's scientific understanding of the physical world all around was then undergoing stupendous transformation finds no place in Braudel's account. Similarly, the four volumes of the admirable *Fontana History of Europe* which cover the sixteenth and seventeenth centuries contain only seven pages which even mention science: contrast the literally hundreds of pages given over to religion, and the tens to the arts. Likewise, in his *A Social History of England* (1983) Asa Briggs assumes that on one occasion alone has science made its mark on English society: the time of the foundation of the Royal Society. (Newton, however, gets no mention.)

Certain historians and historiographical schools have of course been more sensitive to the social role of science. Not surprisingly, Marxists have been prominent amongst these. Christopher Hill rightly saw the Scientific Revolution of the seventeenth century as falling within his general designation of the *Century of Revolution* (though his attempts to demonstrate how specific scientific breakthroughs, such as Harvey's theories of the heart and of the circulation of the blood, reflect political events have not met much acceptance). For their part, economic historians have been forced to weigh up science's part in the technological transformations of the First Industrial Revolution (and subsequent ones as well), even if nowadays, looking for the causes of industrialisation, they mainly give preference to more strictly 'economic' factors, such as capital formation investment and the rise of effective consumer demand. Literary, cultural and social historians, when addressing periods with a high scientific charge (e.g. the mid-Victorian age and its intellectual revolutions), have of course confronted the impact of science, though even here, latter-day revisionist studies have played down the role of Darwinism in the Victorian crisis of faith, and even in the long march of secularisation in general.

Overall, however, no great symbiosis is taking place between general historians and historians of science. General historians still think they can, to all intents and purposes, safely ignore the impact of science upon modern society – precisely at a time when science has given governments the capacity to put an instant end to civilisation as we know it. Was Butterfield wrong to judge that science 'outshines everything'? Is there, instead, something wrong with the way the history of science is written? After all, a flourishing academic discipline of the history of science has grown up, practised – one would think, beneficially – by a mixture of the scientifically and the historically trained. Is this admittedly relatively specialist, research being cold-shouldered by the historical community at large? Perhaps historians of science are content to burrow away in isolation, believing that science has truly had a 'tunnel history' of its own, hermetically sealed off from wider social causes and effects. A glance at the chequered history of attempts to grasp the social history of science will illuminate these issues.

1. THE MARXIST MANIFESTO

From the first mobilisation of the 'New Science' of the seventeenth century, its spokesmen contended that science and society must interact synergistically for mutual benefit. After all, from Francis Bacon, through Enlightenment philosophies to nineteenth-century Positivists, it was axiomatic that the progress of science demanded a favourable environment, which meant freedom of thought and publication, state protection and adequate rewards. Science would, in turn, transform social existence. ('Experiments of fruit,' argued Bacon, would forward 'relief of man's estate'.) Following Enlightenment visions of progress it is no surprise that , in its turn, Marxism should assume the mantle of scientific socialism. Marxism envisaged a crucial role for science in man's self-emancipation from the chains of Nature.

According to Marxist thought, science would remain equivocal, at least until the advent of communist society, bourgeois science being ideological through and through. It was in that sense that Marx regarded Darwinism as the projection onto Nature of the alienating and mystifying values of the capitalist mode of production: cut-throat competition and the survival of the fittest. Yet Marxist historians and theorists also regarded science as a progressive force. These were the prospects conjured up in the formulation of a Marxist 'science policy' during the 1930s, prominent in which were the Soviet historian, Boris Hessen, and a cluster of British left-wing scientists, amongst them J. D. Bernal, whose vision found classic expression in *The Social Function of Science* (1939) and his awesome *Science in History* (1954).[2]

A generation later, *Science in History* lives on as the boldest attempt yet to interpret the whole history of Western science within its wider framework. Yet it now appears a deeply flawed enterprise because, contrary to the Marxian dialectic, Bernal rested content with merely juxtaposing the successive phases of science alongside parallel, but essentially unconnected, accounts of economic, political and social changes. Within a historical determinism in which it was the 'social being of man which determines his consciousness', and in which 'the hand mill gives you society with the feudal lord; the steam mill, society with the industrial capitalist',[3] science might have been identified as the crucial variable mediating between modes of production, instruments of production and class formations. However, the opportunity was missed. Instead, 1930s' Marxism traded heavily upon a sloganising economic reductionism. Surveying the Scientific Revolution, Hessen wrote:[4]

> The struggle of the university, and non-university science serving the needs of the rising bourgeoisie, was a reflection in the ideological realm of the class struggle between the bourgeoisie and feudalism.

Such doctrinaire 'vulgar Marxism' of this kind helps explain why the work of Hessen and Bernal proved not a new dawn but a dead end.

Comparable, but non-Marxist, attempts to establish the wider social correlations of science hardly met with greater long-term success. The most ambitious and promising of these was the attempt of the sociologist, R. K. Merton, to link Protestantism (especially in its Calvinist and Puritan manifestations) with the quickening of science in the seventeenth century. Paralleling Max Weber's attempts to demonstrate an inner coherence between the Protestant ethos and the spirit of capitalism, Merton argued that the Puritan mind, with its commitments to experience and to stern self-discipline, underwrote the experimental, co-operative, utility-orientated science which blossomed during the Scientific Revolution.

During the 1960s especially, the putatively Puritan roots of modern science were widely debated, under the stimulus of Christopher Hill's seeming conviction that all the seeds of modernity lay in Puritanism. But biographical and prosopographical research in depth have cast doubts upon Merton's correlations, particularly when the international and multi-confessional dimensions of the scientific movement are taken into account. Indeed, paradoxically, the one sphere of science enduringly illuminated by the Marxism of the 1930s lay quite beyond Europe. Bernal's colleague, the eminent biochemist Joseph Needham, grew fascinated with Chinese science. Aware of its nonpareil achievements during those medieval centuries when Western science had wallowed in the doldrums, Needham posed the riddle of why China hadn't pioneered the 'Scientific Revolution'. His answer was that China had not developed capitalism either, with its special demands and opportunities. Today, Needham's *Science and Civilization in China* is still in progress, the greatest attempt to relate science to society within the history of scholarship, even if many scholars today find Needham's initial question something of a side issue.

2. SCIENCE SHEDS ITS SOCIAL HISTORY

As part of the rejection of everything Marxist in the years of the Cold War, Anglo-American history of science was to distance itself from all such concerns with the social roots and even the social fruits of science. Instead, from the 1950s it became profoundly fascinated with the internal intellectual challenges posed by science, understood as a sequence of highly abstract, theoretical attempts to express the truth about Nature. If the essence of science lay in the methods, concepts and theories successively advanced from (say) Copernicus to Einstein, Marxist priorities seemed trivial, question-begging, or simply false. Moreover, the fact that the Marxist doctrine of the social determination of consciousness so readily translated in practice into the brutality of Stalin's brainwashings and purgings discredited it morally as well. The Free World, by contrast, stood for intellectual freedom; and in that light, interpreting the achievements of science primarily as the work of intellects 'free and unconfined' and individually fathoming the secrets of the natural world purely out of the love of truth, had great attractions. Fired by the Platonist 'white' Russian emigré, Alexandre Koyré, a body of extremely technically accomplished historians of science emerged in the post-war years. These included A. Rupert Hall, I. B. Cohen, Marshall Clagett, R. S. Westfall, A. C. Crombie, C. C. Gillispie and numerous others, pioneering what came later to be known as 'internalist' history of science. Against vulgar Baconians, they contended that science was far more than an accumulation of facts; it entailed high-level theorising. Against vulgar Marxists, they argued that such theories were not to be subject to economistic reductionism. As Koyré put it, 'science . . . is essentially *theoria*, a search for the truth . . . an inherent and autonomous . . . development'.[5] Thus it followed (in Hall's words) that 'intellectual change is one whose explanations must be sought in the history of the intellect';[6] or as Gillispie judged, 'science, which is about nature, cannot be determined in its content by the social relations of scientists'.[7]

Such pronouncements more or less ruled out of court the project of a social history of science, or the attempt to trace intimate links between science and society. Ironically, a particular social development may well have expedited this separation. For the 'internalist' school was flexing its intellectual muscles at precisely the moment when study of the history of science was securing its own separate and autonomous departmental existence in many universities. Thus, the situation of historians of science, and that of past scientists, apparently mirrored each other in their independence.

This is not the place to pay tribute to the massive contributions such scholars have made to understanding the conceptual foundations of modern science. What is relevant to note here is that in their writings they consistently ratified the autonomy of mind. (Gillispie approvingly quoted an anecdote in which Newton, asked by a bystander how he made his discoveries, answered: 'By thinking constantly unto them').[8] Scientists, Hall argued, were not 'puppets' of external forces. Hall was even sceptical about whether science, though a monumental *intellectual* achievement, was even commonly of much practical utility. The early modern period saw the creation of the science of ballistics. But ballistic theory, he argued, was of scant use to practical gunners, who worked out projectile paths themselves by trial and error. Science, in other words, was principally a thought odyssey, rising above banausic reality as a testament of the life of the mind. In the post-Hiroshima twilight when science had lost its innocence, this could be comforting news.

3. THE ORGANISATION OF SCIENCE

Certain social approaches to the history of science could, however, peacefully coexist with what became the prevailing 'internalism', above all, those focusing on the development of scientific institutions. (Within traditional positivism, questions of social organisation were not believed to impinge upon the laws of thought.) Almost from their very inception, of course, prestigious scientific societies such as the Royal Society of London and the Paris *Académie Royale des Sciences* had their own historians, and most of the provincial and metropolitan scientific bodies – many of a specialist nature – which mushroomed during the nineteenth century had their in-house centenary history. But from the early 1960s, the archives of scientific institutions have been scrutinised on a vast scale (they form ideal raw materials for the Ph.D. industry). A more critical stance than formerly has been conspicuous. Thus Morris Berman's history of the early years of the Royal Institution, to mention just one instance, was to dwell on the rapidity with which the initial idealistic aims of the Institution were abandoned under pressure from its financial backers. Such histories of formal scientific institutions have broadened out into studies of informal networks of practitioners ('invisible colleges'), into examinations of amateur as well as professional science and into analysis of wider 'audiences' for science. They have often drawn fruitfully upon the conceptual apparatus developed by sociologists of contemporary science, probing the 'social system of science' with its career structures, citation patterns, reward systems, intellectual property rights, publication networks and so forth.

Micro-studies of scientific organisation, formal and informal, have proved fruitful in other directions. For one thing, they have stimulated a few brave attempts to map out the scientist's place in society, in the contexts of social change and national cultural differences. Here the pioneering work, spelt out in an over-compressed and rather schematic book, has come from the sociologist Joseph Ben-David. In Ben-David's analysis, seventeenth-century England was able to support a precocious scientific community because of the presence of a cadre of amateur enthusiasts ('virtuosi'). This, however, proved an ambiguous legacy. The amateur tradition in this event lacked high-level vocational commitment, and so scientific leadership passed to France, whose centralised, absolutist state machine supported a corps of eminent professional scientists, concentrated around the Académie Royale des Sciences. This scientific bureaucracy, though attacked by the French Revolution as an arm of the *ancien régime*, was buttressed by Napoleon, but languished as an engine of scientific innovation during the nineteenth century through administrative ossification and over-centralisation. Instead, in the nineteenth century it was the German-speaking world which evolved the optimal social role for the scientist, as professor in the competitive *Lehr- und Lernfreiheit* atmosphere of the multiplicity of reformed universities, surrounded by faithful posses of Ph.D. students. Ben-David's scheme incorporates a distracting teleology. But, at this distance, its most frustrating feature is its explicit disavowal that the sociology of scientific organisation can generate a sociology of scientific knowledge itself. Ben-David openly endorsed the idealist denial of the social determination of the content of science. Yet the floodtide of research has steadily rendered that distinction impossible to sustain. Of crucial importance in this respect – not necessarily for what it overtly stated but for what were taken to be its implications – was Thomas S. Kuhn's *The Structure of Scientific Revolutions* (1962).

Kuhn presented a picture of science proceeding within 'paradigms'. These were structures of thought (*Gestalten*). But they were also identified with an elaborate social scenario – the innovating scientist in his fief-like laboratory, flanked by a bodyguard of colleagues and students, pioneering a distinctive repertoire of techniques, experiments and (more widely), the endorsement of such paradigms through discipleship, text-books, patronage and scientific education. Scientific paradigms, Kuhn argued, were sustained and fostered by frames of mind, group loyalties and by a tenacious conservatism. The process whereby science abandoned an exploded paradigm and embraced a new one was not at all the joyous, liberating act of falsification in the quest for naked truth, as envisaged by Karl Popper, but rather a series of agonising psychosocial upheavals, the best analogy for which was religious: loss of faith and conversion.

Because Kuhn argued that paradigms were strictly speaking incommensurable, i.e. one could not be judged better than its predecessor according to an accessible objective truth criterion, his opponents accused him of encouraging a subjectivist and relativist view of the status of science. If that were so, factors which were (in the wider sense) ultimately social would count, after all, in theory choice. Kuhn later backtracked on various of the inferences derived from his ideas, but his hyper-influential book gave impetus and respectability to many new currents from the mid-1960s. For example, a powerful genre of studies has emerged, investigating the 'cognitive styles' of particular research groups, schools and the dynamics of scientific laboratories. Similarly, scientific controversy has been explored in terms of the wider commitments of the competing parties. By challenging the distinction – so fundamental to positivism – between the social and the cognitive, such studies have embraced the 'social construction of knowledge'; the view that science is not a body of self-evident facts, just 'read off' from Nature, but is rather manufactured or shaped (no criticism is necessarily implied) through the agency of formal and informal scientific institutions. Via an elaborate anthropological case-study of an advanced laboratory, Latour and Woolgar have provided a particularly detailed demonstration of how modern research findings are essentially man-made artifacts, ratified and authorised by science's conventions rather than through direct correspondence with Nature.

Scientific apparatus may likewise be seen as creating a man-made (i.e. social) milieu for science. Shapin and Schaffer have recently argued, for example, that the development of pneumatology in the seventeenth century hinged upon the invention – and not least the highly-prized actual physical possession – of specific pieces of apparatus, above all, the air pump, as a means of generating experiences unknown in the regular course of Nature and of creating intellectual authority. The point is an important one. From the vantage-point of the late twentieth century, science's authority is adamantine (even if, because of that very stature, it is widely suspected and criticised). Three hundred years ago, the credit of natural science was far more precarious. Possibly the central dilemma, therefore, for the seventeenth-century natural philosopher was to win control of the grounds of belief, particularly when – as so often – his conclusions contradicted common sense, the expectations of the eyes and the entrenched erudition of the traditional texts. The spectacular experiment, conducted under artificial conditions controlled by the experimenter, provided an exemplary demonstration of truth, or at least of the manipulative potency of the scientist, rather as, in the late nineteenth century, possessing the most successful laboratory became, for Pasteur, the paramount symbol of scientific invincibility.

4. THE EXTERNAL HISTORY OF SCIENCE

When, from the mid-1960s, the interpretations of the 'internalists' were first challenged, that challenge did not come, initially at least, from latter-day Marxists aiming to lead scientific theories in terms of classes and class struggles. Rather it stemmed from practitioners of traditional disciplines in the broad domain of intellectual and cultural history and the history of ideas and from scholars alert to the perils of Whig history. They were aware of the anachronism of regarding the scientists of previous centuries as men whose mental topography, canons of rationality and criteria for proof were identical to our own. Careful reconstruction of scientists' thoughtworlds – particularly those of the early modern age such as Copernicus and Kepler – showed their absorption in metaphysical and philosophical systems, in the occult arts and magic and in alchemy and astrology, all of which disciplines are clearly alien to today's sciences of which they have been called the founding fathers. It thus appeared that such men of science lived in divided, compartmentalised universes – a solution certain internalists lamely favoured – or that traditional ('prescientific') disciplines had indeed contributed some sort of input into modern science. Above all, through the stimulus of Frances Yates's studies of the Hermetic Corpus, the so-called irrational roots of modern science were laid bare, setting off a whole series of violent scholarly controversies as to the rationality of science, which cannot be explored here.

Now, of course, to point out that Copernicus may have been 'influenced' by Hermeticism, or that Newton's deep involvement in alchemy may have played a part in his formulations of the physics of force, did not necessarily fling open the doors to the *social* history of science, for these were simply alternative intellectual discourses. But it did prove the consequence. For one thing, the very act of admitting alternative traditions was an acknowledgement that the making of modern science was the product of the confluence of an exotic mix of diverse currents. No longer could the Scientific Revolution be seen as a small, closed seminar of great minds lost in thought. For another, the disciplinary structure of modern science now came up for question for the first time. Individual scientific theories had clearly had their histories but so, it now seemed, had the configurations of the disciplines themselves. So how had the different sciences successively constituted and reconstituted themselves? How, when and why did 'physics', 'chemistry' and 'biology' take shape? When had the undivided empire of 'natural philosophy' become fragmented? Had 'magic' yielded to 'science'? Such fundamental repatternings of natural knowledge could not be understood without a sociology of knowledge.

If the occult arts, Hermeticism, magic, alchemy and so forth had all contributed to the melting pot of seventeenth-century speculation about Nature, by what means had modern science (the 'New Philosophy') consolidated itself, growing confident, successful and capable of holding its own over much older traditions, which were increasingly vilified as obsolete? At precisely the time (the height of the Vietnam War, the student revolt, and the counter-culture) when the politics of contemporary science were raising profound questions about science's present authority, the question of the generation of ideological authority by science in earlier centuries became a burning issue. The era from the Reformation at least to the close of the Thirty Years War involved times of appalling social struggle and upheaval, terminated by what has been seen as the re-imposition of 'stability' by an emergent ruling order, dominant in thought no less than in politics and sheltered in many nations by the carapace of emergent centralising Absolutism. What finally emerged victorious as modern science (with its mechanical philosophy, its vision of Nature as dead rather than alive and its valorisation of cosmic law and order) emerged thus only after profound definitional struggles. These were over and against a plurality of other (ultimately losing) traditions for understanding and manipulating the natural world – struggles often waged in the thick of other, wider conflicts, such as the events of the English Civil War. In those circumstances, one of the leading currents of the social history of science over recent years has been to seek out the links between science, power and politics, and to explore how to mobilise intellectual resources (above all, symbols of nature), both to assert their own dominion and to serve various social interests. Thus, for example, science could be used to advance the values of particular social groups. Examining the espousal of Newtonianism by Whig apologists for the English political establishment around the turn of the eighteenth century, M. C. Jacob showed how the science of the Boyle Lectures, through demonstrating the existence of God, of hierarchy in Nature, of the conjoint presence of spirit and matter and of cosmic order and providential superintendence, thereby ratified, by analogy, hierarchical order both in Church and state.

To take a slightly different social use of social science's authority could be to undermine the legitimacy of rival cultural traditions. By increasingly denying the reality of demonology, science was to lend its support to the ending of witch persecution – a 'progressive' and 'enlightened' cause, but one which also backed elite against popular values. In a similar way, emergent psychiatry in the eighteenth century redefined religious inspiration as deluded enthusiasm and a species of mental disorder, helping to discredit the validity of radical movements of faith such as Methodism. Over the centuries, in scores of contexts, natural science pronounced freely upon such issues as race, gender, normal sexuality, the healthy mind, and man's place in Nature. This has occurred so commonly that it is implausible to speak of such instances as mere 'abuses' of science: they have been integral to its uses. The social sciences, naturally, have pontificated more freely still. As powerful schools of scholarship over the last decades have argued, science was able to act as an ideological mouthpiece in this way precisely because the 'objectivity' and fact/value distinction on which it was built gave it the promise of being beyond ideology.

5. THE 'NEW MARXISM' AND OTHER DEMYSTIFICATIONS

It was at this point that a 'New Marxism' made its impact, by enlisting detailed research of this kind under the banner of a wider programme of ideological demystification. Traditional Marxism à la Bernal was mistaken, it was now argued, because it had been entirely uncritical towards science. Indeed, Marxism itself had traded all too readily upon the distinction between bad ideology and good science, a mistake which itself provided a wonderful example of the mystifying ideological power of the shibboleth, 'science'. The 'New Marxism' dropped economism and the naïve Utopianism about science, and instead concentrated its energies upon exposing the dazzling conjuring trick whereby science had acquired and legitimated authority precisely while claiming to be value-neutral – indeed to be a force for human liberation. In his historical and polemical writings, R. M. Young in particular has aimed to combat such idealist 'sacralisations' of science ('science *is* social relations').[9] It is, he argues, a mistake to assume that science grows progressively less ideological, less socially-determined over time: today's socio-biology is at least as contaminated as yesterday's social Darwinism. Moreover, the counter-argument mentioned above that it is only the *abuses*, and not the *uses* of science which are ideological, is a liberal smoke-screen. For moral, political and gender prejudices are water-marked right into the very fabric of science, in its language, metaphors, concealed metaphysics and methodological devices. For instance, through complex processes and at a variety of levels, not all of them conscious, Malthus's socio-politics of human overpopulation became naturalised in Darwin's evolutionism, and were seen as normative for all living beings.

This New Marxism has aimed to deprivilege science, restoring it to the same plane as other belief systems. Similar goals have been central to or implicit in other theoretical directions. Important amongst these has been Structuralism, which programmatically treats all objects for analysis with absolute parity as 'texts', inscribed within bodies of 'discourse'. Repudiating empiricism in all its manifestations, structuralism and its successor, 'deconstructionism' have both denied the validity of all reference to 'objectivity' outside texts themselves. Thus for structuralists such as the late Michel Foucault, science cannot look to an outside reality to guarantee its privileged status. Hence Foucault treats the sciences as he does other forms of discourse, such as linguistic theory – i.e. as organised and given meaning within the deeper 'epistemes' of their times, the conditions of possibility for thought in successive ages. Such thought structures are separated by yawning gulfs. There are no continuities; thus to look to scientific progress is essentially a *question mal posée*. Foucault, it should be noted, has different fish to fry from the Marxists, whose notion of human liberation he regarded as a relic of nineteenth-century anthropocentrism. Regarding man as the mouthpiece of discourse, rather than discourse as the ideology of ruling classes, Foucault stressed that knowledge is power (*savoir/pouvoir*), but saw man as the expression, rather than the agent, of such power.

Another formulation of a 'sociology of knowledge' distanced from Marxist reductionism is that adumbrated by the anthropologist Mary Douglas. This starts from a basic Durkheimian sociology which sees ideas of God and Nature as functions of society, and proceeds to argue that beliefs differ from tribe to tribe, and within particular societies, correlative to specific modes of social position – above all, the strength of group solidarity and ascribed social role. Douglas has highlighted the boundary-establishing, definitional quality of key ordering concepts in cosmologies – such basic dualities as order and disorder, higher and lower, white and black, pure and polluting and such normative devices as time and space. There has been little application to date of her ideas in detailed research by historians of science, but considerable interest in their potential had been expressed by those – for example, the proponents of the Edinburgh 'strong programme' in the sociology of science – who have contended that the scholar's task, faced with the explanation of beliefs, must be to treat all of them symmetrically, whether conventionally 'true' or 'false', scientific or ideological.

6. FUTURE OPTIONS

The proof of puddings is in the praxis. It is a simple empirical fact that the number and range of plausible and powerful currents in the micro-social history of science are rising fast. Historians now know much more about the ways in which particular groups of scientists, in the laboratory or in the field, 'negotiated' their readings of nature, and how such negotiations profoundly mediated clusters of interests. Researchers are now much more sensitive to the ways in which scientific texts, from the individual paper to the *Principia*, embody social experiences and values and carry a whole host of messages, warnings and judgements, to peers and society at large.

But such demystifications of the ideological aspects of science too frequently stop where they start, at the level of *ideas*. They highlight how scientific formulations constitute vehicles for transmitting values, as when popularisers of Newton encoded value-judgements about political order and religious piety. It is easy to leap from there to larger statements to the effect that science served the function of 'social control'. Two key difficulties, however, arise at this point. One is the problem involved in ascribing motives and purposes. Can we really be certain that in proposing a particular 'biased' reading of Nature a scientist was (unconsciously?) endorsing a particular set of values? This, however, is a problem not unique to the history of science – it is one which historians in general have to cope with all the time.

The second difficulty is more serious. It is the problem of investigating the relations between assumed aims and accomplished achievements. If we take the view that in various ways science was an instrument for regulating conduct, did it succeed? Did it prove more or less effective than other ideological vehicles – such as sermons – or than more tangible rewards and punishments? Such questions have been too often neglected. It is one thing to speak at length of the hegemonic functions of popular science in Mechanics' Institutes; it is perhaps more valuable to note that such science was not in practice welcomed by their members. It is one thing to show, in depth and detail, how during the first half of the twentieth century eugenics encoded within its supposedly neutral scientific framework a vast range of social, political and moral prejudices about the 'labouring and dangerous classes'; it is another to be reminded that English eugenics programmes were never in fact put into effect. It is important to recognise that science ('the mode of cognition of industrial society') has the power to assume the status of the normative, the natural, the real and the rational. But that must surely be the starting line of the task of the social historian of science, not its winning post.

It is with good reason that current history of science has rejected simple Whig history, has peered at the past through eyes other than those of hindsight and has paid attention to scientific 'losers' as well as 'winners'. No general historian these days celebrates the triumph of the West in the eupeptic tones of Lord Macaulay or Herbert Spencer, and it is good that historians of science have learnt that lesson too.

However, there are dangers too in the alternatives to Whig history. On the one hand looms the prospect of over-specialisation, narrowness and fragmentation. Few general historians are any longer prepared to chance their arm at writing the histories of whole societies over spans of centuries; and historians of science have caught the same disease. Even at the level of student textbooks, professional historians of science have ceased to write synoptic histories of science. Our standard histories of great transformations such as the Scientific Revolution are now twenty or thirty years old; in specialisation lies safety. But it is particularly distressing that the last hundred years or so of science leading up to the present has, until now, lacked comprehensive interpretation. Micro-studies are all very well, but without an adequate sense of scale and perspective, the real interplay of forces – intellectual, social, economic and political – cannot be grasped; history becomes impoverished, and our grasp of the present is thereby impaired by default.

Moreover, there is a further pitfall if the social history of science becomes too closely identified with the priorities of demystification, with exposing the hidden authoritarian, sexist and elitist ideologies encoded into science. It is important to de-privilege science in this way. But we may be in danger of creating a new mystification in its place, by rendering profoundly mysterious how and why science has proved such a dramatically successful and powerful enterprise in the West. The science that can put a man on the Moon or destroy our civilisation in a flash certainly carries a capacity for social control, but it is also a collective social, institutional and cognitive movement which has (to return to Butterfield) 'outshone' similar endeavours – organised religion or philosophy come to mind – which, just five centuries ago, were much more imposing activities.

Understanding how and why science gained such power and prestige raises profound questions. Some of these are relatively internal to the social practices of science itself. We may thank recent critical history and sociology of science for showing that so many of science's vaunted ethical norms (such as openness and internationalism) are belied by its actual practice. All the same, it remains true that science has become a relatively multi-national enterprise, and the scientific community has acquired immense strength, cohesion and bargaining-power because it possesses an organic life of its own beyond individual laboratory or national boundaries. Science has been remarkably successful in generating new knowledge, solving problems, expanding its frontiers and in policing its own advances (the discrediting stagnation of late medieval theology, or of many bureaucratic systems, stand in stark contrast). In other words, science has its own internal, often highly technical dynamics which require careful attention.

Of particular importance for grasping the phenomenal success of science over the last 150 years is the fact that so many of science's 'discoveries' or 'breakthroughs' have been perceived to have direct and powerful social effects. In the short term at least, few people experienced any immediate impact from the work of Copernicus or Newton, just as the investigations of medical scientists from the Renaissance to the Enlightenment made scant actual impact on the health of individuals or nations, whereas, say, the work of Pasteur wrought dramatic changes.

In part, that means that the interactions of science and production and of science and society actually became closer. At the dawn of the Industrial Revolution, James Watt did not actually need to know the theory of latent heat to hit upon the idea of making the steam engine more efficient by introducing a separate condenser; a hundred years later, by contrast, only a first-rate chemist would have been able to develop synthetic dyes. But it means something more significant too that the traditional boundaries between science and industry and science and its applications began to dissolve; the very introduction of the terms 'pure science' and 'applied science' paradoxically witnesses that process. The development of electricity during the nineteenth century offers a classic instance of this. Without top-level scientific research by men such as Faraday, the electrical industry could never have developed; yet all the electricity which the scientist investigated and utilised was entirely man-made. In the present century, the development of plastics and artificial intelligence offers further instances of how the scientist has become utterly bound up with society precisely because what he is investigating is no longer 'Nature' ('out there' as it were) but the products of previous scientific-technical ingenuity and industry.

As Latour has convincingly argued, this transformation has immeasurably enlarged the scope of scientific-technical inquiry; but it also sets new problems for the historian or historical sociologist of science, since the categories traditionally deployed for understanding the work of a Kepler or a Newton (notions for example of 'discovery') seem patently inappropriate for an adequate grasp of the modern laboratory or international research network. Latour's own work, which draws heavily upon the language of anthropology, and focuses upon the dimension of science *as an activity* is one valuable attempt to grapple with these difficulties.

In these respects, science today is immensely successful in setting work for itself and in setting and controlling its own activities. The channels and the rhetoric through which this success story are publicly communicated form a key area of investigation for the social historian of science. But it remains no less important to grasp how science achieved that degree of public favour in the first place, and how its findings gradually exercised command over public attention, particularly bearing in mind the fact that in nations such as England and the United States, science became assimilated into the outlooks of key social classes long before it was adopted by the state. It is surely a symptom of today's alienation from science, rather than a mark of any real advance in historical interpretation, that we seemingly lack the empathy to grasp how attractive scientific culture was to 'progressive' sectors of society in the past. We urgently need to give an account of the rise of science which can explain the informal and voluntaristic foundations upon which today's centrally controlled, state-funded science empire is based. Not till then will we have a rounded understanding of the ambiguities of science's social development. Something similar lay behind Gibbon's account of how the 'enthusiasm' of the early Christians was translated into the pride of the Medieval Church. It will hardly be a mark of the progress of historiography if two hundred years later that task is beyond our grasp.

NOTES

1. Herbert Butterfield, *The origins of modern science, 1300–1800* (London, 1949; new ed., 1957).
2. A good Marxist account of Bacon is Benjamin Farrington, *Francis Bacon, philosopher of industrial science* (London, 1951).
3. Karl Marx, *The poverty of philosophy* (written 1847; reprinted ed., Moscow, n.d.), p. 109.
4. Boris Hessen, 'The social and economic roots of Newton's *Principia*', in *Science at the crossroads* (reprint ed. by P. G. Werskey, London 1971; original ed., 1931), pp. 151–2.
5. A. Koyré, 'Commentary', in A. C. Crombie (ed.), *Scientific change* (London, 1961, 1963), 847–56, p. 856.
6. A. R. Hall, 'Merton revisited', *History of science*, 2 (1963), 1–16, p. 11.
7. Quoted in Roy MacLeod, 'Changing perspectives in the social history of science', in I. Spiegel-Rosing and D. Price (eds.), *Science, technology and society* (London and Beverly Hills, 1977), pp. 149–95, p. 156.
8. C. C. Gillispie, *The edge of objectivity: An essay in the history of scientific ideas* (Princeton, 1960), p. 117.
9. R. M. Young, 'Science *is* social relations', *Radical science journal*, 5 (1977), 65–129.

BIBLIOGRAPHY

J. Ben-David, *The scientist's role in society. A comparative study* (Englewood Cliffs, NJ, 1971).

M. Berman, *Social change and scientific organization: The Royal Institution, 1799–1844* (London, 1978).

J. D. Bernal, *Science in history* (London, 1957).

M. Douglas, *Purity and danger* (Harmondsworth, 1970).

M. Foucault, *The order of things* (London, 1970).

R. Hahn, *The anatomy of a scientific institution: The Paris Academy of Sciences, 1666–1803* (Berkeley, 1971).

A. R. Hall, *The Scientific Revolution 1500–1800* (London, 1954).

——, 'The scholar and the craftsman in the scientific revolution', in M. Clagett (ed.), *Critical problems in the history of science* (Madison, 1959), pp. 3–23.

M. C. Jacob, *The Newtonians and the English Revolution, 1689–1720* (Ithaca, 1976).

A. Koyré, *Etudes galiléennes*, 3 parts (Paris, Hermann, 1939, English translation, Hassocks, 1978).

T. S. Kuhn, *The structure of scientific revolutions* (Chicago, 1962; rev. ed., 1970).

B. Latour, *Science in action* (Milton Keynes, 1987).

S. F. Mason, *A history of the sciences; main currents of scientific thought* (New York, 1962).

R. K. Merton, *Technology and society in seventeenth century England, Osiris*, 4 (1938), 360–632 (reprinted with new introduction, New York, 1970).

J. Needham, *Science and civilization in China* (Cambridge, 1954–84).

G. S. Rousseau and Roy Porter (eds.), *The ferment of knowledge: Studies in the historiography of eighteenth century science* (Cambridge, 1980).

S. Shapin, 'History of science and its sociological reconstructions', *History of science*, 20 (1982), 157–211.

C. Webster, *The Great Instauration: Science, medicine and reform, 1626–1660* (London, 1975).

F. Yates, *Giordano Bruno and the Hermetic tradition* (London, 1964).

4

THE HISTORY OF SCIENCE AND THE PHILOSOPHY OF SCIENCE

LARRY LAUDAN

Both history of science and philosophy of science have long genealogies as academic specialities. Philosophers of science generally trace their roots to Aristotle's *Posterior Analytics*. That work – with its emphasis on the structure of explanation, the nature of causation and the linkage between concepts and experience – effectively paved the way for much of the subsequent development of the discipline. History of science is a comparative newcomer, usually seen as emerging from the pioneering studies of Priestley, Smith and Montucla in the late eighteenth century. Despite their quite divergent origins, each of these disciplines first came into its own during the nineteenth century. It was then, for instance, that philosophy of science began to assume an identity distinct from epistemology and when history of science came to be seen as more than an ancillary branch of the general history of learning.

During the great flowering of these disciplines in the century from the 1830s until the 1930s, the two subjects developed side-by-side, generally in very close liaison. Scholars such as William Whewell, John Herschel, Augustus De Morgan, Auguste Comte, Ernst Mach, Pierre Duhem, Abel Rey, Pierre Duhem, Emile Meyerson, E. A. Burtt, Arthur Hannequin, Kurt Lasswitz, Paul Tannery, Ernst Cassirer and Alexandre Koyré happily intermingled historical and philosophical concerns in their research. They inclined to the view that science needed to be understood in cognitive terms, and that such an understanding must encompass both what science had been (hence the historical component) and what science ought to be (the philosophical element). Despite numerous disagreements about specific points of doctrine, all believed that there were

47

important epistemological lessons to be learned from a detailed understanding of the genesis and development of scientific ideas.

Beginning sometime during the 1930s, however, each discipline began to go its own way. Philosophers of science, smitten with logical positivism's alluring promise of rigour, began to think that the method of conceptual analysis alone was sufficient to formulate an adequate understanding of the scientific enterprise; a detailed familiarity with the history of science (particularly of science before the twentieth century) was thought to have no particular bearing on questions about the conceptual and methodological foundations of the sciences. Significantly, none of the towering figures of logical empiricism (e.g. Schlick, Carnap, Reichenbach and Hempel) saw any need to follow in the footsteps of Comte, Whewell, Mach and Duhem, who had insisted on the necessity of using history to illuminate and sometimes to adjudicate between rival philosophical doctrines. Formal, logical analysis tended to replace historical research as the preferred mode of presentation.

Historians of science, for their part, began to maintain that there was something perniciously 'Whiggish' about using historical materials to address general questions, philosophical or otherwise, about the nature of science. Historians of science from Whewell to Conant had formerly argued that the great virtue of the history of science is that it serves the cultural function of teaching us how science works and how scientific knowledge is wrought; but historians of science since the 1940s and 1950s have generally been chary about using the historical record to address broad or general questions about the nature of scientific change and about the justification of science. By the late 1950s, therefore, history and philosophy of science had become as remote from one another's concerns as they had once been intimately intertwined. Historians thought it inappropriate to address epistemological questions in their research; philosophers saw no need to 'stoop' to consulting the historical record.

During the 1960s, there emerged a small but influential handful of scholars (e.g. Feyerabend, Hanson, Buchdahl, Toulmin and Kuhn) who sought to persuade philosophers to re-think their dismissal of the relevance of historical research to philosophy of science. It had become clear by then that the positivist account of science was a gross misconstrual of science. Explanation in science did not typically satisfy the formal models of the positivists. Scientists did not draw the line between theory and observation in anything like the way that positivists had supposed. Empiricist theories of empirical support and confirmation – apart from generating their own internal contradictions – had dismally failed to account for the manner in which scientists used evidence and made theory choices. For such reasons, it was suggested that the philosophy of science associated with logical positivism was ill-suited to provide any epistemic rationale for real science.

As a result of this critique, philosophical research in the last two decades has seen the return to respectability, if not yet to dominance, of the older tradition of pursuing philosophical and historical researches in tandem.[1] Shapere, Laudan, McMullin and Lakatos, along with many others, are heirs to that tradition. The return of philosophers of science to historical concerns has been prompted by many factors, but the two chief among them are: (1) a belief that processes of theory, change and temporal progress are among the central epistemic determinants of science; and (2) a realisation that the *justification* of philosophical claims about how science works rests in part on the adequacy of those claims to actual science. One might have thought that the former factor would be especially potent as a basis for renewing the ties between historians and philosophers of science, since an account of scientific change must be, *inter alia*, a general theory about the historical development of science. And so it has been for philosophers, who now recognise that 'historically-orientated philosophy of science' is one of the major genres for approaching philosophical questions.[2]

By contrast, and despite the emergence of theory change as a central problem on the philosophers' agenda, the attitudes of many historians of science towards the philosophy of science have hardened considerably, to the point where historians of science nowadays venture at their peril (and on pain of compromising their reputations) to address overt epistemological questions in their research. Prestigious journals in the history of science fail to carry articles which express explicit philosophical concerns, and many historians of science (especially in the English-speaking scholarly community) go to considerable lengths to disavow an interest in philosophical questions, and adamantly deny the mutual relevance of historical and philosophical research.

If my claims are correct about the hostility of historians to engaging the philosophical questions which have traditionally motivated the historical study of science, then the interesting case of Thomas Kuhn and the reception of his work by his fellow historians of science may be instructive. Here is a scholar who has doubtless had a greater impact on the broader intellectual community than any other historian of science in our century, perhaps even more than any general historian of his generation. Moreover, his central works – *The Structure of Scientific Revolutions* and *The Essential Tension* – are quite open about addressing themes of a general and philosophical sort about theory change. His handling of those themes has been widely cited by social and natural scientists, philosophers and literary theorists. Yet, reading the current scholarly literature of the history of science, one would scarcely be aware of the existence of Kuhn as a theorist of science.[3] I know of no other active discipline which, over the course of almost a generation, has managed so systematically to fail to address the ideas of its most influential theorist. And what goes for Kuhn is just as valid for all the other theorists of scientific change, whether card-carrying historians of science (such as Holton or Cohen) or philosophical interlopers (like Lakatos, Toulmin, Feyerabend and a host of others).

49

As a result, relations between history and philosophy of science are sorely strained. Philosophers of science, at least many in their ranks, have become convinced that the history and philosophy of science make sense only if conducted in consort. By contrast, the prevailing view among historians of science is to the effect that the philosophical suitor proposing matrimony should be summarily dismissed.

All of this raises a key question, namely, whether there is a coherent rationale for historians to resist so tenaciously a marriage which the philosophers thought had already been consummated. Interestingly, there is virtually no discussion in print, which explains why historians are resisting the proposal. One can point to no classic essay or monograph which shows definitively why the call of Kuhn, Crombie, Conant and Koyré (echoing the earlier call of Whewell, Mach and Duhem) for historians of science to engage issues in the theory of knowledge has fallen on such deaf ears. In the absence of written sources, one must depend on the oral tradition to find out why historians are unmoved by the clarion call. That means that a part of my analysis will be evidentially suspect, for, since historians have not grappled with this issue in print, I have had to rely on more devious and less reliable avenues of information.[4] When I ask many historians of science why they feel that there is little commonality between their attempts to understand science and the efforts of their philosophical counterparts, or why they so rarely engage the larger questions about processes of scientific change and knowledge formation, the answers I get are quite diverse, though there are some common threads running through them. It is in reflecting on those answers that I have come to conclude that the reservations historians of science have about tackling philosophical (or other sorts of) theoretical issues about the dynamics of scientific knowledge rest on a set of dubious premises and ill-considered arguments. These arguments (which I shall attempt to summarise below) appear to function more as slogans for excusing non-engagement than as mature and carefully thought-through positions. It is some of those discussions which have prompted the remarks that follow.

1. COGNITIVE VS. NON-COGNITIVE HISTORY

One clear cause for the relative indifference of many recent historians of science to theories of scientific change has to do with shifting interests within the larger historical community about the central problems of history. Virtually all models of scientific change, whatever their differences, are concerned with explaining the vicissitudes of scientists' *beliefs* about what the world is made of. In a phrase, scientific theories and their cognitive fortunes are the central preoccupation of virtually all the philosophical theorists of scientific change. But, for a growing number of historians of science, there is no longer a consuming interest in understanding or explaining the cognitive fluctuations of the historical record. A concern with theory, or with the arguments and evidence adduced by scientists, smacks for some, these days, of a kind of outmoded 'internalism' or, even more offensively, of the study of 'disembodied ideas'. To many who take this line, the study of scientific ideas has been rendered obsolete by the emergence of the study of the social life of science. Science, we are told nowadays, usually in the portentous tones normally reserved for the enunciation of profound truths, is a human activity – nay, a social and human activity. Somehow the older focus on scientists' ideas is thought to de-humanise science by neglecting the larger social dimension in which science arises and by which it is transformed. According to some, it is not science, but *scientists*, which form the proper subject of historical narrative. These scientists seek to build careers, they organise themselves into societies, communities and disciplines. They jockey with one another for position and prestige, they form institutions, they found laboratories and – especially if they are involved in 'big science' – they build political careers and empires: they become scientist politicians. The new and apparently influential breed of social historians of science often attends to virtually everything about such scientists *except their ideas about the natural world*![5]

It is fairly clear why those engaged in history of science have little or no use for the available models of scientific change. Those models, after all, concern themselves primarily with describing how scientists come to form their beliefs about the world. Since the social historians are evidently uninterested in understanding the cognitive processes of the fixation of scientific belief, they see little promise in those models. I have no quarrels with institutional and more broadly social history when seen in its proper perspective. But I do believe that the questions addressed in such history of science are ultimately subordinate or peripheral to the main concerns of the history of science. Because social and institutional studies show some signs of coming to be regarded as harbingers or exemplars of a new genre of history of science, I want to explain why I find their concerns subordinate and secondary.

Science matters in our culture chiefly, albeit indirectly, because of what it says about the world. The political influence of science, its prestige, its level of financial support and even its size all depend on its theories and how those theories in turn have enabled scientists to anticipate and manipulate nature. Take away those theories, and the manipulative and predictive skills they confer, and science would arguably occupy a very different place in the intellectual landscape. To tell the history of science without explaining why scientists come to hold the beliefs about the world that they do is to confuse trappings with substance, effects with their causes. In sum, if it is true that science matters (both intellectually and institutionally) because of the manipulative and predictive skills which its ideas confer on their possessors, then a concern with science as a cognitive process must be primary, for until we have understood how science works cognitively, the largest question about science will remain unanswered. The theorists of scientific change recognise the centrality of the cognitive; that is why their theories focus primarily on the dynamics of scientific belief change.

Consider a close analogy. No one would entertain for a moment the idea that the central problem in the history of music was how symphonic performers organised themselves. They would reject out of hand the idea that the central problem in the history of painting should be the question of how painters' patronage was arranged. Yet it is today seriously being proposed (especially among English-speaking historians of science) that the *central* questions about science have to do, not with the master works which science has produced, but rather with the mundane minutiae of the life of a 'normal' scientist or with the ways in which scientists garner political support for their activities.

Such institutional historians of science, by failing even to confront – let alone to answer – the question of why scientists believe what they do, have opted out of the cognitivist game altogether. Many have evidently concluded that the only alternative to the disembodied history of scientific ideas is a lobotomised history of scientific institutions.

2. THE RESISTANCE TO THEORY

Fortunately, however, many – perhaps most – historians of science are not committed to such institutional history as the sole or primary vehicle for understanding science. They seek to meet what I have just been calling the cognitivist challenge. If there is hope for constructive interaction between historians and philosophers of science, one might expect it to show up in the work of those concerned to explain the history of scientific ideas. Indeed, the cognitive historian of science is already dealing with epistemological issues, whether he cares to call them so or not. Typically, he is explaining why and how particular scientists discover, pursue, accept, modify and reject the theories of their time. What influence did Cambridge Platonism exert on Newtonian theories of space and time? How large a role did Darwin's observations on the *Beagle* play in shaping his notion of extinction? What importance, if any, did the Michelson-Morley results have for Einstein when he was developing the Special Theory of Relativity? These are precisely the sort of issues which modellers of scientific change engage. Yet the irony is that cognitively-orientated historians of science have shown little more interest than their institutionalist brethren in criticising, amending or even acknowledging the existence of the various theories of scientific change. As Kuhn once put it, 'few of the current practitioners of internal history are particularly philosophically minded'.[6] Although virtually every piece of cognitivist history has implications for the general claims of theorists of scientific change, very few of the authors of such studies bother to explore their implications. This phenomenon is as perplexing as it is ubiquitous. What we are dealing with, after all, are distinguished historians, talking about particularly interesting and potentially revealing episodes of scientific change, who are wholly indifferent to exploring what implications their own narrative accounts have for a variety of widely discussed theories about scientific change.

It is rather as if a whole community of paleontologists collected enormous amounts of evidence about the extinction and distribution of species, but conspired never to reveal what their evidence entailed for prevailing theories of extinction and biogeography. I use the term 'conspired' deliberately; there appears to be an unstated rule of research in the history of science nowadays that one must never acknowledge the existence of any general theories about how science develops (not even to refute them), let alone use one's historical skills and evidential resources to go so far as to explore in detail how well or badly those theories fit the data.

When I ask my cognitively-inclined friends in history of science about the rationale for this self-effacing and self-denying convention, they often tell me that it is in keeping with the general tendency in historical research to eschew theorising or generalising from one case to another. The historian's duty, they say, is to tell a coherent story, preferably in narrative form, about a particular sequence of events. It is no part of the task of history, they insist, to subsume disparate and unique events under some over-arching pattern or grand design. As they see it, the construction or evaluation of 'theories' about the past is beyond the pale of legitimate historical inquiry. The authority of Herbert Butterfield and his repudiation of 'Whig history' is often invoked as a rationale. This is unfortunate since, although Butterfield was a fine historian, his published essays on historiography are a *mélange* of confused *non sequiturs*. Yet it is Butterfield who seemed to sum up the anti-theoretical, anti-generalising bias of the current generation of historians of science when he wrote, in *The Whig Interpretation of History* (1931) that:

> The eliciting of general truths or of propositions claiming universal validity is the one kind of consummation which it is beyond the competence of history to achieve.

Because of Butterfield, the term 'Whiggism' has come to be used disparagingly of any general theory of scientific change, especially if that theory represents science as progressing through time.

The Butterfield analysis, and that of all the other anti-Whigs who defer to it, appears to me to rest on several dubious assumptions about history in general and history of science in particular. Not the least of them is that it ignores the fact that several highly respected and influential branches of general history – think of economic history, historical demography, labour history or much of social history – engage quite explicitly in formulating and testing generalisations (whether they be about patterns of corporate behaviour, forms of economic life, the location of cities and ports, or the vicissitudes of crime and punishment). My first observation, then, is this: if it is legitimate to engage general theories in these well-established areas of history, why is it not so in the history of science?

Equally dubious is the assumption, implicit in the policy of non-engagement, that the writing of history can be, and ought to be, an atheoretical activity. One simply goes out, collects the relevant evidence, consults all the relevant archives and then proceeds . . . how? To tell it as it really happened? Few historians would admit to being as naïve as that. But why is it any less naïve to imagine that theoretical views about the processes of scientific change can or should be cordoned off from writing the history of those changes? If the study of science itself has taught the rest of the world any lessons, it is that the most interesting research emerges from the interplay of theory and observation and that any effort sharply to separate the two is doomed. Yet, when it comes to their own craft, historians of science seem to exhibit the same suspicious resistance to engaging theoretical issues which was once associated in the natural sciences with narrow-minded Baconian inductivists. That whole approach to inquiry has been discredited, not least by the work of prominent historians of science.

Surely a degree of reflexivity is called for here. We know of few, if any, disciplines which, by limiting themselves to a narration of the 'bare facts' and by eschewing theory, manage to make significant and lasting contributions to the growth of knowledge. Whenever it has been tried, it has failed to produce significant results, for, try as one might, one cannot conduct research without bringing general presuppositions to bear. Why then does the historian of science imagine that virtue resides in writing about the history of scientific ideas as if no one had ever said anything of a general nature about how science develops? It is neither logically possible nor conceptually desirable to dissociate general and theoretical concerns from the construction of a narrative of specific events.

I have thus far argued for the logical impossibility of cleanly separating theory from practice in writing history of science. I have yet to address the desirability of intermingling the two, and that brings me to the real nub of the issue. The fact that general theories about scientific change have been developed, or even that they have achieved a fair degree of notoriety, is after all no compelling reason for the historian explicitly to engage them. (One might, however, have expected that the historian's much-admired passion for getting it right might have moved him at least to point out where these theories go astray.) I want to suggest that there is an urgent reason for taking this enterprise seriously, even if it should turn out – as I suspect it will – that most of the extant theories of scientific change will prove to be woefully inadequate. It has to do with the rationale or justification for history, and especially history of science, within the larger intellectual scheme of things.

Cast your minds back for a moment to that period in the 1950s when post-war, English-speaking intellectuals were attempting to re-think the character of higher education. It had become clear that science and technology were key components of our cultural heritage and our contemporary life; it was equally clear that those activities had not received due scrutiny in academic circles. Indeed, virtually every major institution of our culture, whether the church, the military or the body politic, had received more systematic scrutiny from historians than had science. It was argued widely and cogently (e.g. by James Conant, Vannevar Bush and C. P. Snow) that what was needed was serious scrutiny of science by scholars in the humanities and the social sciences. The point of that exercise was to make science *intelligible*, i.e. to explain something about how science operates, about the factors which impede or enhance its advance and about the relations between science and the other components of our culture. History of science and philosophy of science both profited institutionally from this thrust. Several countries set up funding panels for the humanistic study of science and universities founded departments, or more modestly, positions in history of science or philosophy of science where formerly there had been none. Degree requirements were rewritten so as to encourage students to study these disciplines in some depth. If it were not for that rewriting, most of the current practitioners of history or philosophy of science would be otherwise engaged.

The larger purpose behind these developments was not only to discover how science worked, but to communicate that understanding to scientists and the general public alike. History, quite properly, was given pride of place in this undertaking because it was thought that one could *learn* about science by scrutinising its past. That is why Conant published the *Harvard Case Studies* and that is why Kuhn wrote the *Structure*, a book which opens with the pregnant observation that:

> History, if viewed as a repository for more than anecdote or chronology, could produce a decisive transformation in the image of science by which we are now possessed.[7]

But, as Kuhn would be the first to stress, history can teach lessons, and transform cultural images, only if it explicitly addresses *general* issues. A lesson, to be a lesson, must have general applications. If the episodes that the historian discusses have no significant elements in common, or nothing in common with the scientific experiences of our own time, then every episode becomes *sui generis* and we emerge from the exercise as impoverished as we were at the outset. Kuhn once chastised general historians for their 'abdication . . . of responsibility for evaluating and portraying the role of science in the development of Western culture'.[8] That indictment, thoroughly deserved, considering what short shrift science is given in general historical studies, is coming more and more to apply to historians of science as well. The latter, confronted with a choice between the Conant-Kuhn thesis that history can teach lessons, and the

Butterfield doctrine that there are no general patterns to be gleaned from history, are moving dangerously close to refusing to evaluate the place of science in Western culture. I venture a conjecture: that virtually all historians believe that they have something to say to our time about how science works. But how are these insights to be communicated, and how are they to be authenticated, except by framing them as general theories or hypotheses?

3. PROGRESS, SUCCESS AND WHIGGERY AGAIN

The divide separating many philosophers of scientific change from historians of science is broader still than is suggested by the distinction between those who make theories about cognitive processes of change and those who prefer to 'let the facts speak for themselves'. Philosophers' concerns are not only general and theoretical; they are also normative and evaluative. Philosophers of science generally believe that science has been a very successful enterprise for producing ideas which give us manipulative and predictive control over nature. They hold, moreover, that science through time has conferred greater and greater degrees of control over nature. In sum, philosophers generally see science as a *progress*, at least along this dimension, and they believe that a central task of historical research is both to record and to explain that progress.

Historians of science used to think so too. From Whewell to Sarton, traditional historians recorded the various steps on the progressive route of science from a largely ineffectual body of quasi-mythical philosophies of nature to the impressive achievements of a Newton, a Lagrange or a Maxwell.[9] As late as the 1960s, historians of science still felt comfortable with these themes as guiding narrative threads.[10] But, along with the rush from theory, historians have also been pulling back from an acknowledgement that science has become more successful through time and have dropped altogether any concern to explain the conditions which made that progress possible. Just as with the repudiation of theory, any concern with scientific progress as an explanatory challenge has been rejected as 'Whiggism'. As before, the brief has been developed at greatest length by Herbert Butterfield. He objected to any effort to write history as a progression because, as he saw it, that led to a falsification of the past; more specifically, it led to historians ignoring all those figures who did not lie on a straight line projecting from then to now.[11] This, he thinks, is 'part and parcel of the Whig interpretation of history'.[12]

One can sympathise with Butterfield's concern that a tale of victory, told only by the victors, makes for bad history. But in denying that historians are ever justified in recognising that certain parts of science are better than others, and in asserting that it is no part of the historian's task to explain the conditions which made them more successful, Butterfield (and those historians of science who follow him) would appear to be abandoning the programme of telling the full story of the past to which they are otherwise so deeply committed. It is, to take a specific example, a fact that Newtonian celestial mechanics is more successful empirically than Cartesian cosmology. It might explain much about science in general if we could come to understand what it was about Newton's way of proceeding which enabled him to produce a theory so strikingly more successful than its immediate predecessor. Philosophers, indeed, attempt to elicit just such an understanding. But if, with Butterfield, one denies at the outset that it is ever appropriate for the historian to ask whether one event represented progress over another, then one cannot even address the question, let alone answer it.

If he once grants that certain scientific theories or approaches have proved more successful empirically than their rivals, then the historian who disavows any interest in scientific progress is confessing that there are some facts about the past which he has no interest in explaining. Given that no history can be complete, that alone would not be very distressing. But the progressiveness of science appears to everyone *except the professional historian of science* to be the single most salient fact about the diachronic development of science. That, above all else, cries out for historical analysis and explanation.

If I seem to have dealt harshly with some of my historical colleagues, it is not because I see no promise in the historical study of science. On the contrary, I think historians of science have a splendid opportunity before them. Thanks largely to a concatenation of casual circumstances, there is now a large audience of scientists, philosophers, sociologists and others, looking to the history of science to move the discussion of how science works beyond the preliminary efforts of Kuhn, Feyerabend and the other early modellers of change. There are large intellectual issues which, it is now conceded, the history of science can uniquely illuminate. But if historians continue to refuse the challenge of giving a *general* account of scientific change and if they continue to imagine that science evolves altogether without direction and improvement, then others (especially philosophers and sociologists), possibly less well-suited for the task, will step into the breach. Indeed, they are already doing so. Kuhn, for one, is on record as predicting that this process is inevitable, for he has lately questioned whether 'professional' historians of science are any longer prepared to write the history of scientific ideas with a view to addressing questions of a philosophical or theoretical sort.[13] I, for one, hope that he is wrong.

NOTES

1. For a dissenting voice, however, see Giere, 1973. (I believe that Giere is no longer the doubter he once was on this issue.)

2. As evidence of this renewed interest in history, one can cite the fact that specialist journals in philosophy of science, which twenty years ago would have been apt to dismiss historically-orientated contributions as so many shaggy-dog stories, now routinely carry essays which involve historical case studies designed to illuminate some philosophical problem or other.

3. Ironically, even Kuhn himself has so internalised the prevailing conviction that one should keep

one's philosophical musings separate from 'real' history, that he makes virtually no use of his own model of scientific change when discussing – as he does at length – the history of quantum theory.

4. There are occasions when historians of science have (usually quite rightly) faulted the historical analyses offered by one or another philosopher. Peirce Williams has even asked, not facetiously, whether philosophers of science should be allowed to do history. But the question whether philosophers of science do good or bad history is wholly distinct from the question whether historians of science should address philosophical questions in doing their research.

5. If this seems an unfair generalisation, consider three of the recent books by historians of science that have attracted much interest and critical praise: D. Kevles's *The physicists*, C. Gillispie's *Science and polity in 18th-century France*, and A. Thackray's and J. Morrell's *Gentlemen of science*. Despite their immense erudition, all three works studiously avoid telling us anything whatever of the views concerning the natural world of the scientists they study. Indeed, there is virtually no history of science (as that term was traditionally understood) in any of these works.

6. T. S. Kuhn, 'History of science', in P. Asquith and H. Kyburg (eds.), *Current research in philosophy of science* (1979), p. 126.

7. T. S. Kuhn, *The structure of scientific revolutions*, p. 1. Contrast this attitude with Butterfield's sturdy insistence that:
   behind all the fallacies of the whig historian there lies the passionate desire . . . to make history answer questions and decide issues. (Butterfield (1931), pp. 64–5)

8. T. S. Kuhn, *The essential tension*, p. 130.

9. Historians of science, of course, disagreed amongst themselves about exactly how the 'progressive' story of science should be told, and about some of its central elements. But there was near unanimity that science had become more successful through time and that the historian's task was to study the conditions which made that progression possible.

10. Recall, for instance, Charles Gillispie's *The edge of objectivity* (Princeton, 1962).

11. The young Butterfield thought that, if one succumbs to this temptation, then 'historical personages can easily and irresistibly be classed into the men who furthered progress and the men who tried to hinder it . . . ' (Butterfield (1931), p. 11). Later in his career, Butterfield changed his mind almost entirely on this issue; when he wrote on the history of science, indeed, he was Whiggish in the extreme.

12. Ibid., p. 11.

13. See especially Kuhn's *The essential tension* (Chicago, 1977), chap. 6.

BIBLIOGRAPHY AND FURTHER READING

J. Agassi, 'Towards an historiography of science', *History and theory*, Beiheft 2 (1963).

P. Asquith and H. Kyburg (eds.), *Current research in philosophy of science* (Ann Arbor, 1979).

R. Burian, 'More than a marriage of convenience', *Philosophy of science*, 44 (1977), 1–42.

H. Butterfield, *The Whig interpretation of history* (London, 1931).

I. B. Cohen, 'History and the philosopher of science', in F. Suppe (ed.), *The structure of scientific theories* (Urbana, 1977), pp. 308–49.

R. Giere, 'History and philosophy of science: intimate relationship or marriage of convenience?' *British journal for the philosophy of science*, 24 (1973), 282–97.

C. Gillispie, *The edge of objectivity* (Princeton, 1962).

T. S. Kuhn, *The structure of scientific revolutions* (Chicago, 1962).

——, *The essential tension* (Chicago, 1977).

Imre Lakatos, 'History of science and its rational reconstructions', in R. Buck and R. Cohen (eds.), *Boston studies in the philosophy of science*, vol. 8 (Dordrecht, 1971), pp. 91ff.

Larry Laudan et al., 'Scientific change: philosophical models and historical research', *Synthèse*, 69 (1986), 141–224.

J. Losee, *Philosophy of science and historical inquiry* (Oxford, 1987).

Ernan McMullin, 'The history and philosophy of science: a taxonomy', in R. Stuewer (ed.), *Minnesota studies in philosophy of science* (Minneapolis, 1970), pp. 12–67.

L. P. Williams, 'Should philosophers be allowed to write history?' *British journal for the philosophy of science*, 26 (1975), 241–53.

5

SOCIOLOGICAL THEORIES OF SCIENTIFIC KNOWLEDGE

BARRY BARNES

1. SOCIOLOGICAL CONCEPTIONS OF KNOWLEDGE[1]

All societies make a systematic distinction between knowledge on the one hand and mere belief on the other. Knowledge is that which is entitled to general acceptance and trust; belief is that which one or more individuals, rightly or wrongly, happen to cleave to. In any given society knowledge may be described as true beliefs, or justified beliefs, or beliefs both justified and true. There will also be methods of identifying such beliefs, of ascertaining what is true and/or justified and there will be agents charged with the task of recording and remembering which beliefs are indeed to be counted as knowledge. Unfortunately, in different societies different beliefs are accepted and taken for granted as knowledge, and different methods are employed to determine which beliefs deserve so to be accepted. What counts as knowledge in one society, or social context, may count as mere belief in another. To obtain a sense of this great diversity it is only necessary to cast a cursory glance towards any of the four main classes of cultural others: aliens, ancestors, deviants and experts all sustain or have sustained bodies of knowledge distinct from, and in many cases in conflict with, our own.

Sociologists and anthropologists have treated the different forms of knowledge established in different social contexts as empirical phenomena, and have tried systematically to describe their features and to compare them with each other. Here are some general features which bodies of knowledge seem typically to manifest when they are studied as empirical phenomena.

(1) At any given time and place knowledge exists, for the most part, as received knowledge or inherited knowledge. It has been handed down routinely from the ancestors, and is in the course of being handed on to the next generation. It is a

part of, or perhaps more accurately an aspect of, the cultural tradition of the society.

(2) In the first instance, it is the fact that a belief is a part of the cultural tradition which marks it out as knowledge rather that 'mere' belief, and counts as the grounds for its acceptance. The authority surrounding custom and tradition sustains certain beliefs as parts of the stock of knowledge of a given society. If a belief is generally accepted, or if it is accepted by authoritative figures, or if it is set out in a sacred text or an accepted repository of wisdom, that in itself may be enough to mark it out as knowledge. The most important although not the sole single criterion in identifying a belief as knowledge is its general acceptance as knowledge.

(3) Knowledge is generally acquired or inherited in association with specific practices or procedures, carried out in specific contexts or situations. Where its recipients make further enquiry as to its validity or its adequacy, they do so with reference to these practices and procedures and the extent of their efficacy in the actual situations of their use. Thus, for example, bodies of knowledge in tribal societies, whether one considers the detailed technical lore of hunting or agriculture, or the (formally speaking) completely general assertions of religion and cosmology, tend to have bounded domains of application and to be evaluated in relation to specific, local requirements and objectives.

(4) Where received knowledge is critically evaluated in the course of use, that evaluation is logically problematic. This is because what the knowledge implies in any given situation of use does not follow logically from the knowledge itself. The application of received knowledge is a matter of its active interpretation. It must be developed and understood in a specific way if it is to be applied in any given case, and different agents may always develop and apply it differently. The proper application of an item of received knowledge is, formally speaking, contestable. Thus, for example, we may find it not at all surprising when learned judges, all of unquestionable competence in so far as their knowledge and understanding of the law is concerned, nonetheless vote three to two in deciding a particular case with both the majority and the deviating minority offering grounds and reasons for their finding.

In a nutshell, then, what counts as knowledge in most social contexts it is tempting to call 'customarily accepted belief'. It is sustained by consensus and authority much as custom is sustained. It is developed and modified collectively, much as custom is developed and modified. This we might call the standard sociological conception of knowledge, the conception which both inspires and is confirmed by most of the empirical studies of knowledge undertaken in the social sciences. On inductive grounds one might expect this standard, widely applicable conception to make good sense of scientific knowledge and of the distinctions between knowledge and mere belief sustained and enforced by natural scientists. And so indeed it does. Scientific knowledge assimilates to the standard conception very readily, and much of profound importance can be discerned and understood when science is analysed in this way. But this is something that has only readily been acknowledged and accepted over the last two decades, and even now a sociological conception of scientific knowledge is still vigorously challenged and opposed, and, more significantly, what such a conception suggests about the nature of science is still not adequately understood.

What held back the application of the sociological conception, and staunched, for a time, the natural flow of inductive inference, was the existence of an alternative, long-established notion of the nature of evaluation in science. According to this alternative conception, evaluation had nothing to do with custom and consensus; it involved nothing more than competent observation and rational inference. Any reasonable agent could infer which beliefs deserved to count as established scientific knowledge by comparing their logical implications with the indications of observation and experiment. Consistency with experience was the key criterion which distinguished knowledge from mere belief in the context of science, and if this made scientific knowledge systematically different from putative 'knowledge' in other contexts this was merely because scientific knowledge was *genuine* knowledge, and what was supposed to be knowledge elsewhere was no such thing. The standard sociological conception might indeed apply everywhere but in the context of science, since error and ungrounded belief might indeed be posturing as genuine knowledge everywhere but in the context of science. As far as science itself was concerned, knowledge was rationally accepted belief and not customarily accepted belief: the only custom of interest in the realm of science was the custom of evaluating knowledge in the light of reason and experience. One might perhaps wish to understand why scientists chose to adhere to this custom, but that was the limit of the role of custom in scientific evaluation.

It is as the plausibility of this individualistic *rationalist* account of evaluation in science has declined that the alternative sociological conception has come to be taken seriously. As we have become more sceptical and uncertain about the privileged status of scientific knowledge, so we have become more willing to tolerate analogies between it and other varieties of knowledge and to accept that what appertains to knowledge generally might also appertain to science in particular. Why, though, has the rationalist account gone into decline? Why does it no longer command the uniform assent it once enjoyed? There are many causes. Perhaps the most important of all is the collective achievement of historians of science over the last two decades. One does not have to point to any specific discovery here, or any emergent agreed doctrine or overall vision of scientific change. The real achievement of the historians is that they have so developed their methodological sophistication and so intensified the rigour and thoroughness of their studies that they have successfully been able to convey much of the real complexity of cognitive processes in science. Simple idealised images of scientific evaluation have become harder and harder to reconcile with the detailed results of uncompromising professional historical investigations. Even though the historians have generated no agreed general conception of scientific change of their own, even though they are inclined to lament their own differences of approach and conviction and the reluctance of a complex historical reality to settle these differences for them, the overall contribution of their work to the development and refinement of our general understanding of the evaluation of scientific knowledge has been second to none. In particular, they have enriched our awareness of the *context* of scientific work, both the immediate professional context and the wider social context, and have documented the many subtle interactions of context and cognition.

Philosophical analysis has also undermined the rationalist account. Rationalist philosophers themselves have explored its problems and weaknesses with admirable penetration. Looked at from a philosophical point of view the main problem for rationalism is that scientific knowledge is theoretical knowledge. There is no independent language of observation and no set of theory-independent observation statements. All verbally formulated knowledge of science has something of a theoretical character. All of it represents an interpretation of experience rather than an unproblematic reflection of experience. Even simple observation reports may stand as knowledge only on the basis of the acceptance of a theory of the associated instrumentation, a theory of the conditions of observation and a theory of perception. Observation does, in a sense, discipline theory in science, but theory disciplines observation also: observation reports may be discarded on theoretical grounds just as theories may be discarded on observational grounds. Theory, consequently, is underdetermined by experience, in science as much as in any other context. Alternative interpretations of experience are always possible; alternative theories are always viable. Accordingly, reason and experience do not sufficiently determine the knowledge which an individual scientist should accept. Where a specific body of knowledge is recognised and accepted by a body of scientists, there would seem to be a need to regard that acceptance as a matter of contingent fact, since an alternative body of knowledge might well be equally reasonable in a purely formal sense. A recognition that knowledge is underdetermined by experience leads away from an individualistic rationalist account of evaluation towards a collective conventionalist account, even if it does not refute the one or completely justify the other.

It must be acknowledged too that the general climate of thought and opinion had long been slowly moving towards a more matter-of-fact orientation to science and scientific knowledge. Whereas once the pressing concern was to overcome residual prejudices and to obtain proper recognition of the merits and accomplishments of science, more recently the need has been to turn upon science itself as an object of study and reflection, to seek the understanding that can only arise from detailed empirical investigation and to tell it how it is. To this extent it may be said of the sociological conception that its time has come. This is no idle point. The philosophical basis for the sociological conception has long existed, for example in the work of the American pragmatists and in Duhem, but for over half a century there was no interest in making appropriate use of this material. In 1935, Ludwik Fleck published a marvellous pioneering sociological study of the evaluation of scientific knowledge, which described in detail the historical variations in what counted as scientific fact and the social processes through which what was accepted as fact at any time became consensually established. Fleck was a practising scientist who wrote on a topic close to his scientific interests: syphilis and the standard means used in its diagnosis, the Wasserman test. His work combined striking sociological and historical originality with a high level of technical scientific competence. But it is only very recently that there has been any widespread interest in appraising this work and making use of its insights.[2]

Thomas Kuhn was altogether more fortunate when *The Structure of Scientific Revolutions* appeared in 1962. Now at last there was an audience willing to consider the fundamental defects of the rationalist vision of science, even if only because it was willing to consider the fundamental defects of anything generally accepted as part of the established order. Kuhn's famous dramatisation of the insufficiency of reason and experience in scientific evaluation, his comparison of theory change with political revolution and his highlighting of the dogmatic and authoritarian aspects of scientific practice, all assured him of a ready hearing.[3] In some quarters he attained an instant of inadvertent celebrity as a radical critic of science, his attack on the rationalist version of science being misconstrued as an attempt to denigrate and devalue natural science itself. (This same misconstrual is still occasionally visited upon modern sociologists of scientific knowledge. With what increasingly comes to seem like wilful perversity, some scholars still refuse to accept that an anti-rationalist view of evaluation in science may co-exist with a high evaluation of science.)

When Kuhn first published the *Structure*, not, needless to say, as a critique, but rather as an attempt to understand what was valuable and distinctive in the natural sciences and what accounted for their extraordinary degree of success, it was his attack upon rationalist orthodoxy which commanded attention. Now that the heady days of the 1960s have passed, it is the positive claims in his alternative account of science which sustain the continuing interest in his thought. We are now able to recognise in Kuhn's work the foundation stone upon which the modern, well-developed sociological conception of scientific knowledge has been built. All the four previously listed general features of bodies of knowledge are present in Kuhn's account of science, clearly described and convincingly illustrated. The nature of scientific knowledge as inherited knowledge is explicitly recognised. The quasi-dogmatic character of its transmission, relying upon the authority of teacher and text and the artful use of various pedagogic devices, is analysed and illustrated. The intimate association of belief and practice, theory and practical accomplishment in science, is duly emphasised: indeed, there is no more profound and consequential insight in the whole of Kuhn's work than his identification of the scientific *paradigm*, the accepted example of good scientific practice, the specific scientific achievement upon which future research will be modelled, as the fundamental unit in the transmission of scientific knowledge. Kuhn makes it clear not only that the standing of scientific knowledge is determined within specific contexts of scientific activity, but that what such knowledge amounts to is determinate only in such contexts. Divorced from actual situated practice the words and symbols of scientific laws and theories become empty marks on sheets of paper, all connection with natural phenomena lost. Finally, Kuhn stresses the logically problematic nature of evaluation in science. He shows that neither an initial choice of scientific paradigm nor a choice between competing paradigms is fully intelligible in terms of logic and experience alone, and must always involve an element of consensus and agreement within the appropriate community. More profoundly, he shows how the adequacy of a paradigm in the course of routine use, in the context of *normal science*, as Kuhn would say, is itself something which cannot be ascertained by formal, unproblematic methods.[4] What follows from a paradigm, what it properly applies to and what confirms and what disconfirms it, must all be *decided* rather than formally inferred by the members of the relevant community. A paradigm must not be thought of as being or embodying a set or rules which determine research practice: scientists may ' . . . agree in their *identification* of a paradigm without agreeing on . . . a full *interpretation* or *rationalisation* of it.'; ' . . . like an accepted judicial decision in the common law, it is an object for further articulation . . .'[5]

The achievement of work in the sociology of scientific knowledge over the last two decades has been to confirm further and to develop and elaborate the conception of scientific knowledge embodied in these four points. An impressive array of empirical studies has accumulated over this period, all of which support the view that scientific knowledge is analogous to, and on a par with, other forms of knowledge. In these studies, the skill, the ingenuity and the intellectual virtuosity of gifted natural scientists shine through as strongly as in any traditional historical or philosophical study, but the epistemologically privileged status of science is not assumed, and not being assumed, it fails to make itself evident. What these studies invariably show is that a particular move in the scientific game could have been made differently without offence to reason or lack of respect for observation. The move in question may be a large one, requiring major modifications in the practice and procedure of many scientists, or it may be a minute adjustment to the conceived mode of correct operation of, or the conceived correct interpretation of readings from, a specific scientific instrument. In either case empirical studies exist which seek to show the lack of compelling reasons for the move, and the way that social interactions amongst involved parties lead to its being agreed upon as the correct move and hence consensually established. It is characteristic of these studies that they either study scientific practice in very considerable detail as it occurs in the laboratory, or that they focus upon disputed and controversial issues. The open-endedness of scientific practice is revealed in the first case by very high-resolution observation and in the second by exploiting the refined perceptions of natural scientists themselves.[6]

2. SOCIOLOGICAL EXPLANATIONS OF KNOWLEDGE

I have spoken of a general conception of knowledge which sociologists accept, and which they now largely agree to be applicable to scientific knowledge as well as to knowledge of other kinds. I could equally well have spoken of a 'descriptive theory'. Current agreement on a descriptive theory of scientific knowledge represents, for sociologists and those inclined to agree with them, a significant advance. One should guard against thoughts of 'mere description'; the importance of an adequate description and characterisation of phenomena is hard to overstate. But if there is a measure of agreement amongst sociologists about how to describe science and scientific knowledge, there is as yet no such agreement about what the consequent description suggests and implies. Indeed, opinion is systematically divided on the matter.

One school of thought in the sociology of science takes the description of science as the limits of its task, and seeks only to illustrate and justify a sociological description through the study of specific empirical and/or historical cases. Most of those of this persuasion see their work as a kind of celebration of indeterminacy. The point is to show that things might have been otherwise, that people are not compelled and constrained in how they act and what they believe, not even by reason and experience, not even in science: human action is always, in a sense, free action involving choice. Customs and conventions are seen as the creations of human agents, actively negotiated and actively sustained, under the collective control of those who initially negotiate them and subsequently sustain them. Scientific knowledge is seen as customarily accepted belief, actively sustained by specific agents in specific situations, owing its existence to their activity and its specific form to the specific form of that activity. Proponents of this approach tend to be reluctant to generalise. They may occasionally seek to document some of the techniques and procedures commonly employed in the negotiation of social convention and the accomplishment of consensus, some of the devices put to work to create a sense of the externality and objectivity of knowledge and some of the artful strategies used to win arguments and gain assent. But even here the dominating intention is to

66

assert the priority of human agency over its supposed products – systematic proofs, objective laws, replicable findings and real objects. The crucial task is to display scientific knowledge through and through as a *social construct*.[7]

A second school of thought regards the sociological description of scientific knowledge as raising profound problems of *explanation*. Suppose that a change occurs in what counts as accepted scientific knowledge. It may be a major change involving assimilation of the work of a Darwin or an Einstein, or a minor one whereby a new star is plotted on the maps or a new insect species added to the lists. Such a change is not intelligible solely and simply as a collective rational response to new experience: reason and experience are insufficient in themselves to account for it. What then are we to refer to, in addition, to produce a more satisfactory, more nearly sufficient explanatory account of the change? What extra ingredients might solve our explanatory problems? It might be said that the change is a change in custom or convention, and is sustained by consensus. True, no doubt, but what is the provenance of this consensus, and why did it come to surround this particular convention and not another? It might be said that the particular convention was socially negotiated and then collectively enforced. True, perhaps, but little if anything is added to our understanding by this statement: why should scientists, with no compelling need, trouble to negotiate and enforce a convention at all, and why should they fasten upon one particular convention rather than another? For those content to describe processes of scientific evaluation and do no more, these are illegitimate questions, or at least questions without answers: they are content merely to note that a convention was established, by social processes which could have unfolded other than as they did. But for others these are genuine questions about the causes of human behaviour, and the search for answers to such questions is a legitimate and indeed an important objective for sociological research. From this point of view what matters is not the celebration of indeterminacy but engagement in the endless task of getting rid of it.

One way of working towards an adequate explanation of evaluation in science is to adopt a sociological form of instrumentalism. Specific objectives and interests may be posited to reside in specific situated scientific communities. When beliefs are evaluated in such communities and the business of deciding what precisely is to count as knowledge is under way, there will be alternative possibilities available for consideration, all rationally defensible as compatible with experience. Where a specific collective choice is made it may be amenable to explanation as the choice most appropriate to some relevant objective or interest. The objective or interest may be considered as a *cause* of the choice. What cannot be explained in terms of reason and experience alone may perhaps be explicable if reference is made to a relevant objective or interest, operating in a specific context or situation, against a background of pre-existing accepted knowledge and technique. Thus, Dean has considered the simultaneous tence of 'morphological' and 'genetic' theories of plant species, and has related the extent and distribution of their acceptance and use to the practical objectives and interests of scientists in herbaria and museums on the one hand, and in laboratories and settings where systematic experimentation is possible on the other.[8] Pickering has suggested that elementary particle physicists accepted the 'charm' model of the properties of hadrons in the 1970s, and discarded the competing 'colour' model, because only the charm model could be readily incorporated into the practice of a significant number of subgroups of these physicists, and used to further their interests and objectives. Because the 'charm' model was used in many separate contexts within the larger community of high-energy physicists it lost its association with any one specific context, and its characteristic theoretical entities came thereby to be seen as real.[9] MacKenzie has sought to account for controversies over the appropriate procedures for the measurement of statistical association by reference to associated divergences in the general political interests and objectives of scientists.[10] Shapin, in a study of early-nineteenth-century Edinburgh anatomy, has traced disagreement over the correct pictorial representation of the structure of the human brain to the social and political uses of these representations, and hence to systematic social and political conflicts in that specific situation.[11]

As it happens, work of this kind has been predominantly historical in orientation, and historians of science should experience no difficulty in appraising the quality of its methods and techniques. It will be useful, however, to say a little more about the form of sociological explanation employed in these studies, and to make a strong distinction between what it involves and what is implied by the commonly accepted stereotypes of explanation through interests.[12]

First of all it must be emphasised that references to interests in modern sociological theories of scientific knowledge do not seek to do more than contribute to the task of explanation. Clearly, reference to interest alone is insufficient as a basis for understanding knowledge. Indeed, knowledge itself is not the focus of explanation when interests are invoked in modern studies, but rather change in knowledge: a particular body of existing knowledge is taken as *given* in the formal explanatory structure.

Secondly, and given accepted stereotypes this is perhaps the most important

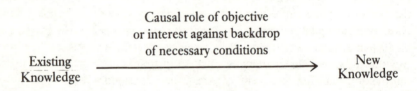

68

point of all, interests are not to be thought of as distorting or biasing forces pressing, as it were, upon the operation of reason. Rather, it is a matter of alternative prima facie reasonable evaluations being available, and the selection from these reasonable alternatives being caused by the operation of interests. It is a matter of reason and interest being fused together in symbiosis, together helping to fix what a community sensibly takes to be true or valid, not of reason and interest operating in opposition, the former leading to truth, the latter to error.

Thirdly, reference to interests or objectives does not provide an 'externalist' explanation of scientific evaluation. The suggestion is that all evaluation in science without exception is underdetermined by reason and experience, and takes on a systematic determinate pattern only because of the operation of some contingent causal factor. Dean and Pickering refer to the narrow esoteric objectives of professional scientists as causes of specific technical evaluations. MacKenzie and Shapin refer to exoteric, more broadly-based political interests and objectives for the same purpose. The work of Dean and Pickering has close affinities with 'internal' history of science, that of MacKenzie and Shapin with 'external' history, as these terms have traditionally been used. But the basic form of the explanation employed in all these four contributions is identical.

Finally, since interests and objectives act causally and contingently upon specific moves in the scientific game, they must not be thought of as indissolubly connected to specific established bodies of knowledge themselves. A body of knowledge exists as a tradition, with a history. Its state at any time must always be understood by reference to its history. During its historical development different kinds of interests and objectives may be relevant at different times, so that today's science may be descended in line from yesterday's metaphysics or yesterday's ideology. Or indeed, different kinds of interest and objective may act in concert on the development of a body of knowledge, which knowledge may hence be multifunctional: it may have, for example, at one and the same time an esoteric utility for the professionals carrying it, and a more wide-ranging political utility, and be evaluated and developed in relation to both.

Those sociologists who seek only to describe the construction of scientific knowledge, and those who look also for explanations are unlikely rapidly to resolve their differences. Against the first, it can be objected that they leave too much that appears systematically patterned, ordered and coherently organised entirely unaccounted for, apparently no more than a matter of random chance or coincidence. Nor does their refusal to speculate and explicitly theorise about the causes of belief and action offer any advantage from a methodological or epistemological point of view, since, as they themselves recognise, there is no clear demarcation to be drawn between observation statements such as they make and theory-laden statements such as they avoid, and hence no evident means of producing 'innocent' descriptions superior to those which they criticise and reject. On the other hand, to accept the additional task of explanation is to encounter additional difficulties and to create additional problems. And long, bitter experience in the history of the social sciences reveals the problems and difficulties involved in the explanation of belief and action to be inordinately complex and recalcitrant.

It is indeed, at the present time, commonplace to find social scientists pessimistic about the possibility of systematic sociological explanations of action and belief, and negative in their evaluation of attempts to do so. Completely general explanatory sociological theories continue, nevertheless, to be put forward, and each one provides a possible framework within which the specific task of explaining action and belief in science may be set. Worthy of specific mention here is the 'grid-group analysis' initiated by the anthropologist Mary Douglas, since it has actually been used by some historians of science to analyse and interpret their empirical findings.[13] Douglas makes two central claims. Firstly, she holds that a cosmology, a shared understanding of the natural order, always emerges in the course of the practical activity of a society, and is always related to the furtherance of practical interests: a cosmology is resorted to in efforts to justify or legitimate what one does, and to control or influence what others do; all the time, it is re-evaluated and re-constituted with a mind to its utility in the performance of these tasks. Secondly, she suggests that different social environments present individuals with different problems of justification and control, and encourage the emergence of different cosmologies. In particular, strongly and weakly bounded social environments, conditions of high and of low 'group', present systematically distinct practical problems of participants, and encourage systematically distinct conceptions of nature. And so, similarly, do environments with strong and weak internal differentiation, high and low 'grid'. If the 'grid-group co-ordinates' of a social environment should change, then Douglas would expect an associated change of cosmology within that environment. More equivocally, where the 'grid-group co-ordinates' of two social environments differ, she would expect, other things being equal, to observe an associated difference in the two relevant cosmologies. Thus, to offer an altogether too crude and inadequate example, Douglas would expect a significant move to lower 'group' and lower 'grid' in a given social environment to be accompanied by a move to a more impersonal secular cosmology, a weakening of anthropocentric and anthropomorphic orientations to physical phenomena, and an increased willingness to recognise and tolerate anomalies and exceptions standing out against the general pattern of the natural order.

Douglas's ideas are still actively evolving. It remains to be shown how precisely concerns to legitimate and justify social activity make their effect upon generally-held conceptions of nature. And it remains to be seen whether such concerns may be regarded simply as causes of change to an existing cosmology, or whether a more ambitious project is feasible, wherein a simple taxonomy of basic kinds of cosmology may be reliably correlated with an equally simple taxonomy of kinds of social environment. If a correlation of this last kind could indeed be made, then it could be made the basis for prediction. The general form of a cosmology, even of a scientific cosmology, could be read off from the 'grid-group co-ordinates' of the relevant social environment: secular, individualistic cosmologies would be characteristic of low 'grid' and low 'group'; witchcraft cosmologies of low 'grid', high 'group'; and so on. Needless to say, such an attempt to link cosmology and society into what amounts to a law-like regularity gives rise to misgivings, even among those who have no fundamental objection to the causal explanation of knowledge. But it deserves mention nonetheless as a bold conjecture which represents the most ambitious extant vision of the scope of the sociology of knowledge, yet which is currently being operationalised with some precision and assessed in the light of historical findings.

3. SOCIOLOGICAL THEORY AND HISTORICAL PRACTICE

Rationalist philosophers of science have been known to argue that the best available account of the nature of scientific knowledge and scientific evaluation should be sought out by historians, and explicitly presumed in the constitution of historical narrative.[14] If this were the case then historians would have to master the sociological conception of science as a prerequisite for their research. Such a course is not, however, recommended by the present author. Better by far in an ideal world might be utter ignorance on the part of historians of all general conceptions of evaluation and judgement in science: then historical work might be used yet more reliably to test alternative conceptions, and establish a preference for one over another. But to hope for ignorance here must be Utopian: no historian can search for truth without prior knowledge and the selective perception it is prone to encourage; and modern historians with their formidable learning cannot hope even to come close to this ideal state. The sociological conception of knowledge and evaluation in science is already a part of the consciousness of historians of science. Indeed, from the start historians have played an invaluable part in developing it, both at the level of theory and in the context of detailed empirical enquiry. Fine sociological studies are continually appearing in the current literature of the history of science. The best that can be hoped for, therefore, as far as the social sciences are concerned, is that even as historians make use of sociological theories and perspectives for their own specific purposes, so they will keep a weather-eye open for weaknesses and defects in these same theories, and not fail to give them prominence. On that basis, a sociologically-informed history of science such as is currently flourishing will surely make a worthwhile contribution both to sociology and to history.

NOTES

1. In this article I discuss sociological theories which claim to describe the characteristics of scientific knowledge, and theories which offer explanations of the production and acceptance of specific bodies of scientific knowledge. I do not refer to sociological theories of the origin of modern science, even though the work of Zilsel, for example, might be legitimately regarded as offering, in one sense, a sociological theory of scientific knowledge. The theories of Marxist sociologists and the writings of the critical theorists and other speculative, philosophically-orientated European scholars are omitted on other grounds: they are discussed elsewhere in this volume. Finally, I must regretfully acknowledge the lack of any discussion of the ethnomethodological studies of natural science which have recently begun to appear: it is, at least for me, still too early to attempt a fair exposition and evaluation of this work.

2. L. Fleck, *Entstehung und Entwicklung einer wissenschaftliche Tatsache* (1935); English translation by F. Bradley and T. J. Trenn, *Genesis and development of a scientific fact* (Chicago, 1979).

3. Strictly speaking, Kuhn speaks of paradigm change rather than theory change, and the difference is most important. But he was widely read at the time as speaking of theory change.

4. '... "normal science" means research firmly based upon one or more past scientific achievements, achievements that some particular scientific community acknowledges for a time as supplying the foundation for its further practice'. T. S. Kuhn, *The structure of scientific revolutions*, (2nd ed. Chicago, 1970), p. 10.

5. Ibid., p. 44 and p. 23. For a discussion of this deeply interesting point see B. Barnes, *T. S. Kuhn and social science* (London, 1982), pp. 83–90.

6. B. Latour and S. Woolgar, *Laboratory life: the social construction of scientific facts* (London, 1979); K. D. Knorr-Cetina, *The manufacture of knowledge* (Oxford, 1981); H. Collins (ed.), 'Knowledge and controversy', special issue of *Social studies of science*, 11 (1981); M. Lynch, *Art and artefact in laboratory science* (London, 1985).

7. The materials referred to in note 6 serve to illustrate this approach, although they differ amongst themselves on many points of detail.

8. J. Dean, 'Controversy over classification: a case study from the history of botany', in B. Barnes and S. Shapin (eds.), *Natural order* (London, 1979), pp. 211–30.

9. A. Pickering, 'Interests and analogies', in B. Barnes and D. O. Edge (eds.), *Science in context* (London, 1982), pp. 125–46.

10. D. MacKenzie, 'Statistical theory and social interests', *Social studies of science*, 8 (1978), 35–83.

11. S. Shapin, 'The politics of observation', in R. Wallis (ed.), *On the margins of science: the social construction of rejected knowledge*, Sociological review monograph 27 (1979), 139–78.

12. The discussion in the next few paragraphs is condensed and less than precise. For a more adequate treatment of essentially these points see B. Barnes, *T. S. Kuhn and social science* (London, 1982), pp. 101–20.

13. M. Douglas, *Natural symbols* (London, 1973); *Implicit meanings* (London, 1975); *Cultural bias* (London, 1978); M. Douglas (ed.), *Essays in the sociology of perception* (London, 1982). D. Bloor, 'Polyhedra and the abominations of Leviticus', *British journal for the history of science*, 11 (1979), 245–71. K. Caneva, 'From galvanism to electrodynamics', *Historical studies in the physical sciences*, 9 (1978), 63–159. J. L. Gross and S. Rayner, *Measuring culture* (New York, 1985).

14. See, for example, L. Laudan, *Progress and its problems* (London, 1977).

FURTHER READING

1. Sociological conceptions of knowledge

D. Bloor, *Knowledge and social imagery* (London, 1976).

A. Brannigan, *The social basis of scientific discoveries* (Cambridge, 1981).

H. Collins, *Changing order* (London, 1985).

T. S. Kuhn, *The structure of scientific revolutions* (2nd ed. Chicago, 1970).

M. Mulkay, *Science and the sociology of knowledge* (London, 1979).

2. Sociological explanations of knowledge
   B. Barnes, *Interests and the growth of knowledge* (London, 1977).
   M. Douglas, *Implicit meanings* (London, 1975).
   ——, *Cultural bias* (London, 1978).

3. Sociological theory and historical practice

Reviews
   S. Shapin, 'Social uses of science', in R. Porter (ed.), *The ferment of knowledge* (Cambridge, 1980); and 'History of science and its sociological reconstructions', *History of science*, 20 (1982), 157–211.

Specific studies
   D. MacKenzie, *Eugenics in Britain: 1865–1930* (Edinburgh, 1981).
   A. Pickering, *Constructing quarks: a sociological history of particle physics* (Edinburgh, 1984).
   S. Shapin and S. Schaffer, *Leviathan and the air-pump: Hobbes, Boyle, and the experimental life* (Princeton, 1985).

SECTION IB. ANALYTICAL PERSPECTIVES

6

MARXISM AND THE HISTORY OF SCIENCE

ROBERT M. YOUNG

The main thing to be said about Marxism and the history of science is that more, much more, has been written that is explicitly or implicitly anti-Marxist than has been written which is avowedly an attempt to see the history of science in Marxist terms. Another class of writings can be seen as watered-down Marxism, while still another is silent about Marxism but does not make much sense unless one knows that Marxism is the silent partner in a one-voice dialogue or polemic in which the other position is not named. The analogy which springs to mind is that of a planet which is not seen but is inferred because of the perturbations of the other planets due to the gravitational effect of the unseen one.

The defining feature of Marxist approaches to the history of science is that the history of scientific ideas, of research priorities, of concepts of nature and of the parameters of discoveries are all rooted in historical forces which are, in the last instance, socio-economic. There are variations in how literally this is taken and various Marxist-inspired and Marxist-related positions define the interrelations among science and other historical forces more or less loosely. There is a continuum of positions. The most orthodox provides one-to-one correlations between the socio-economic base and the intellectual superstructure. This is referred to as economism or vulgar Marxism. The classical source is a set of comments in the preface to *A Contribution to the Critique of Political Economy* (1959):

> My enquiry led me to the conclusion that neither legal relations nor political forms could be comprehended whether by themselves or on the basis of a so-called general development of the human mind, but that on the contrary they originate in the material conditions of life, the totality of which Hegel, following the example of English and French thinkers of the eighteenth century, embraces within the term 'civil society'; that the anatomy of this civil society, however, has to be sought in political economy. . . . The general conclusion at which I arrived and which, once reached, became the guiding principle of my studies can be summarised as follows. In the social production of their existence, men inevitably

enter into definite relations, which are independent of their will, namely relations of production appropriate to a given stage in the development of their material forces of production. The totality of these relations of production constitutes the economic structure of society, the real foundation, on which arise a legal and political superstructure and to which correspond definite forms of social consciousness. The mode of production of material life conditions the general process of social, political and intellectual life. It is not the consciousness of men that determines their existence, but their social existence that determines their consciousness . . . The changes in the economic foundation lead sooner or later to the transformation of the whole immense superstructure. In studying such transformations it is always necessary to distinguish between the material transformation and the economic conditions of production, which can be determined with the precision of natural science, and the legal, political, religious, artistic or philosophic – in short, ideological forms in which men become conscious of this conflict and fight it out. Just as one does not judge an individual by what he thinks about himself, so one cannot judge such a period of transformation by its consciousness, but, on the contrary, this consciousness must be explained from the contradictions of material life, from the conflict existing between the social forces of production and the relations of production. No social order is ever destroyed before all the productive forces for which it is sufficient have been developed, and new superior relations of production never replace older ones before the material conditions for their existence have matured within the framework of the old society. Mankind thus inevitably sets itself only such tasks as it is able to solve, since closer examination will always show that the problem itself arises only when the material conditions for its solution are already present or at least in the course of formation.[1]

The attentive reader will notice that science is here distinguished from ideology, but all versions of Marxist history of science generalise the position taken here about intellectual life and treat science as lying within the historical forces described by Marx in this passage, which is of fundamental importance to Marxist historiography.

Next to economism is the theory of mediation, according to which there are various degrees of relative autonomy, elasticity, lag and room for contradictions. There is ample warrant for this in the writings of Marx and Engels. For example, Engels wrote to Bloch in 1890:

According to the materialist conception of history, the *ultimately* determining element in history is the production and reproduction of real life. More than this neither Marx nor I have ever asserted. Hence if somebody twists this into saying that the economic element is the *only* determining one, he transforms that proposition into a meaningless, abstract, senseless phrase. The economic situation is the basis, but the various elements of the superstructure – political forms of the class struggle and its results, to wit: constitutions established by the victorious class after a successful battle, etc., juridical forms, and even the reflexes of all these actual struggles in the brains of the participants, political, juristic, philosophical theories, religious views and their further development into systems of dogmas – also exercise their influence upon the course of the historical struggles and in many cases preponderate in determining their *form*. There is an interaction of all these elements in which, amid all the endless host of accidents (that is, of things and events whose inner interconnection is so remote or so impossible of proof that we can regard it as non-existent, as negligible) the economic movement finally asserts itself as necessary. Otherwise the application of the theory to any period of history would be easier than the solution of a simple equation of the first degree.[2]

All of this falls within the general framework which asserts that:

The ideas of the ruling class are in every epoch the ruling ideas: i.e. the class which is the ruling *material* force of society, is at the same time its ruling *intellectual* force. The class which has the means of material production at its disposal, has control at the same time over the means of mental production, so that thereby, generally speaking, the ideas of those who lack the means of mental production are subject to it. The ruling ideas are nothing more than the ideal expressions of the dominant material relationships, the dominant material relationships grasped as ideas; hence of the relationships which make the one class the ruling one, therefore the ideas of its dominance.[3]

Marx stresses the historicity of all concepts throughout his writings, for example, in the *Grundrisse*:

This example of labour shows strikingly how even the most abstract categories, despite their validity – precisely because of their abstractness – for all epochs, are nevertheless in the specific character of this abstraction, themselves likewise a product of historic relations, and possess their full validity only for and within these relations. . . . In the succession of the economic categories, as in any other historical, social science, it must not be forgotten that their subject – here, modern bourgeois society – is always what is given, in the head as well as in reality, and that these categories therefore express the forms of being, the characteristics of existence, and often only individual sides of this specific society, this subject, and that therefore this society by no means begins only at the point where one can speak of it *as such*; this holds *for science as well*.[4]

To summarise the less rigid form of Marxist approaches to the history of science which fall within the domain of mediation theory, one should begin with the concept of labour and the labour process as the key to human history. History or historicity is, in turn, the key to everything: 'We know only a single science, the science of history'.[5] The net effect of this approach is to broaden and deepen one's perspective: to root explanations in labour and the labour process, to treat concepts historically, to investigate connections and articulations as fully as possible and constantly to bear in mind that the arrow of causality moves from being to consciousness. This means that a number of distinctions on which the false self-consciousness of science depends are seen as permeable and interactive, for example, the distinctions between fact and value, substance and context, science and society, the context of origination and the context of justification. If one connects these perspectives to recent developments in the philosophy of science, a useful simplification would be to say that all facts are theory-laden, all theories are value-laden, and all values are derived from world-views or ideologies which permeate and constitute what count as facts, theories, priorities and acceptable scientific discoveries. A further consequence is that the sharp distinction between science and technology vanishes. All is mediation – mediation of social and economic forces involved in the production and reproduction of real life. Science is inside society, inside history.

At the extreme of the position I have described as the theory of mediation lies structuralist Marxism with its concept of immanent or structural causality in which the formal features of an intellectual sphere correspond to formal features of the base, but in the most arcane writings of the structuralist Marxists, the lonely moment of the last instance never comes. My own experience of the trajectories of structuralist Marxist writers is that they eventually find themselves moving into the New Right and are therefore not a reliable guide to this point of view.

At the outermost extreme of Marxist historiography lies the point of view of totality. The entire effort of Marxist writings in this tradition is to transcend the attempt to treat science in isolation from society. Science was seen as 'incapable of grasping reality as a totality'.[6] At the extreme, the theory of totality argues that all aspects of reality are interconnected with and reflect all others. This is a point of view rather akin to Leibniz's monadology and it runs the risk of losing the directionality of causality from base to superstructure which is the bedrock or axiom of Marxist explanation. On the other hand, the point of view of totality insists on embedding ideas in society. As Lukács wrote,

> For the Marxist as an historical dialectician both *nature* and all the forms in which it is mastered in theory and practice are *social categories*; and to believe that one can detect anything supra-historical or supra-social in this context is to disqualify oneself as a Marxist.[7]

The appearance of Marxist history of science in the Anglo-American literature can be linked to a single catalytic event: the surprise appearance of a Soviet delegation at The Second International Congress of the History of Science and Technology in London in 1931. The delegation was headed by Nikolai Bukharin, Lenin's favourite, who was still years away from his own dramatic purge trial. Another contributor to the volume of their essays, *Science at the Cross Roads*, was N. I. Vavilov, an eminent plant breeder who died of persecution a decade later, while among the others, E. Colman survived and slipped into Finland decades later.

Far and away the single most important document in the Marxist historiography of science is the essay from that volume, 'The social and economic roots of Newton's "Principia" ' by Boris Hessen. This is the *locus classicus* of the base-superstructure approach to the history of science, using the greatest work of modern science's most revered hero as its case study. Hessen argued that each of Newton's main theoretical preoccupations could be rooted directly and unambiguously in technical issues in his historical setting. He began by reviewing Marx's views from the Preface to *A Contribution to the Critique of Political Economy* (quoted above). The following sentence appears in bold: 'The method of production of material existence conditions the social, political and intellectual process of the life of society'.[8] Moving on to Lenin, he claims that Marxism eliminates two main defects in previous historical writing:

> Previous historical theories considered only the intellectual motives of the historical activity of people as such. Consequently they could not reveal the true roots of those motives, and consequently history was justified by the individual intellectual impulse of human beings. Thus the road was closed to any recognition of the objective laws of the historical process. "Opinion governed the world." The course of history depended on the talents and the personal impulses of man. Personality was the creator of history . . . The second defect which Marx's theory eliminates is that the subject of history is not the mass of the population, but the personalities of genius. The most obvious representative of this view is Carlyle, for whom history was the story of great men . . . The ideas of the ruling class in every historical period are the ruling ideas, and the ruling class distinguishes its ideas from all previous ideas by putting them forward as eternal truths. It wishes to reign eternally and bases the inviolability of its rule on the eternal quality of its ideas.[9]

He then traces the economics, physics and technology of the period of the English Civil War and the Commonwealth and dwells on communications, water transport, industry (especially mining) and war (including division of labour, army and armaments, and ballistics). He then concludes:

> If we compare this basic series of themes with the physical problems which we found when analysing the technical demands of transport, means of communication, industry and war, it becomes quite clear that these problems of physics were fundamentally determined by these demands . . . We have compared the main technical and physical problems of the period with the scheme of investigations governing physics during the period we are investigating, and we come to the conclusion that the scheme of physics was mainly determined by the economic and technical tasks which the rising bourgeoisie raised to the forefront.[10]

Moving on, he says,

> We cite all these facts in opposition to the tradition which has been built up in literature, which represents Newton as an Olympian standing high above all the 'earthly' technical and economic interests of his time, and soaring only in the empyrean of abstract thought.[11]

Then, casting his net wider, he allows for a less vulgar view than is often attributed to him:

> It would, however, be too greatly simplifying and even vulgarizing our object if we began to quote *every problem* which has been studied by one physicist or another, and every economic and technical problem which he solved.[12]

He goes on to repeat that the economic factor is not the sole determining factor — only the 'creation and recreation of actual life'. He then argues that it is important to 'analyse more fully Newton's epoch, the class struggles during the English Revolution, and the political, philosophic and religious theories [that] are reflected in the minds of the contemporaries of these struggles'.[13] Hence, he discusses wider issues, including the history of concepts of energy, and the history of Luddism leading up to his own time.

I have considered this classical paper at some length, mostly because it is richer than is often supposed. Among the other writings in *Science at the Cross Roads*, Bukharin's essay seems to me the most interesting. In discussing 'Theory and Practice from the Standpoint of Dialectical Materialism', he puts forward a theory of science which roots it in practice. He argues that

> the idea of the self-sufficient character of science 'science for science's sake' is naïve: it confuses the *subjective passions* of the professional scientist, working in a system of profound division of labour, in conditions of a disjointed society, in which individual social functions are crystallised in a diversity of types, psychologies, passions (as Schiller says: 'Science is a goddess, not a milch cow'), with the objective *social role* of this kind of activity, as an activity of vast *practical* importance. The fetishizing of science, as of other phenomena of social life, and the deification of the corresponding categories is a perverted ideological reflex of a society in which the division of labour has destroyed the visible connection between social function, separating them out in the consciousness of their agents as absolute and sovereign values.[14]

He goes on to include scientific theories within the superstructure, and says that the 'mode of production' determines also the 'mode of conception'.[15] Therefore, the 'highest forms of theoretical cognition'[16] are included in historical analysis; '*scientific cognition* is the practice of material labour continued in particular forms (natural science)'.[17]

In my view, this approach lays the foundations for a labour process perspective in the history of science in which the relations between theory and practice — the connections or articulations of science — are always to the fore as constitutive rather than contextual, while science itself is seen in terms of raw materials, means of production, purposive human activity and the goals or use values which emerge from the labour process.

The effect of the appearance of the Soviet delegation has been described as electrifying — though not on the day, when hardly anyone responded. The papers were printed and made available in five days and appeared in book form ten days after they were delivered.

The historians of science whose work was most directly influenced in Britain were J. G. Crowther, a journalist and free-lance writer; Hyman Levy, a physicist; Joseph Needham, a chemical embryologist who became the historian of a massive work on *Science and Civilization in Ancient China*; and a polymath crystallographer, J. D. Bernal, who essayed broadly on the history of science, especially in his multi-volume *Science in History*. There were others, but I would say that the direct effect on historical writing (*pace* Needham) was not very great. It certainly did not influence the teaching of the history of science in the major British universities in the ensuing decades. Benjamin Farrington wrote interestingly on Francis Bacon, but the only noteworthy young historian of science in Great Britain, S. F. Mason, author of *Main Currents of Scientific Thought*, had to return to chemistry because he could not find work as a historian of science.

Instead, the history of science developed two deeply un-Marxist strands: the history of discovery and the history of ideas. Both were cut off from the study of the sorts of determinations which characterise the writings of Marx, Engels, Soviet writers and their English followers. There were a few English-speaking writers of note, especially Edgar Zilsel and Dirk Struik, but there was certainly no school or tradition. Indeed, an avowedly anti-Marxist historian of ideas, Rupert Hall, bragged in 1963 about how little Marxist writing there was[18] and reiterated his position a decade later when he was badly out of touch.[19]

Did it all drain into the sands? I would say no. Rather than look for directly Marxist historiography, it is worth noticing watered-down versions of it – linking ideas to their times but filtering out the nasty subversive and revolutionary potential of a fully Marxist analysis. I refer to the writings of Max Weber, Karl Mannheim and Robert K. Merton in sociology, the sociology of knowledge and the sociology of science. I will dwell on the last two, while noting in passing that Max Weber has been seen as the bourgeois Marx, placing ideas in history but rooting them in an irrational human nature rather than in the socio-economic base. Karl Mannheim, the father of the sociology of knowledge, has been called 'the bourgeois Lukács', since his work was deeply influenced by the Hungarian Marxist dialectician whose writings on reification and the concept of totality were of fundamental importance in challenging economism or vulgar Marxism and providing a rich conception of the interrelations between forms of thought, ideas of nature and conceptions in science. Mannheim rooted ideas, including some ideas in the foothills of science, in human interest. He began with the concept of the value-ladenness of ideas which represented the interests of particular groups and then moved on to the sociology of knowledge. He wanted to determine the parameters of situationally conditioned knowledge versus detached knowledge. Mannheim acknowledged his debts to Marx and

Lukács,[20] but his own work was distinct from theirs in that his goals were avowedly epistemological rather than political. His aim was to avoid taking sides and to find a standpoint from which to view knowledge as a social product, while the Marxist position is to assert that knowledge always takes sides and to support the relatively progressive tendency in any particular circumstance. Mannheim attempted to rise above the dangers of relativism into the observer's viewpoint of 'relationalism', while Marxists always see their work as fundamentally polemical and partisan.

Many adherents to the perspective of the sociology of knowledge have joined Mannheim in attempting to stand above the battle and have drawn on other social sciences, including anthropology, to enrich their views on scientific knowledge. The approach of the sociology of knowledge has grown dramatically in recent years as a way of rooting science in society without endangering the career or detached academic perspective of the investigator, drawing a firm line between theory and practice.

A similar path was taken by Robert K. Merton, the doyen of bourgeois sociology of science, whose original work in the 1930s was littered with footnotes and homages to Hessen. Merton focused on the origins, the class perspectives, the choice of topic, and other parameters of scientific knowledge while avoiding any commitment to seeing the resultant discoveries in ideological terms. The sociology of knowledge thereby became an elaborate study of the context of origination while carefully keeping away from the context of justification, the holy of holies which is so dear to non-Marxist philosophers of science. Within this framework of sociology of science as sociology of knowledge, quite subtle work has been done about scientific communities, patronage, honours, the culture of laboratories, scientific accountability (or the lack of it) to the rest of society, and other topics which take the existing mode of production as given.

There are traditions of Marxist history of science in Eastern Europe, but there has been very little communication between writers in the Soviet bloc and those in the West. There are also Marxist and communist writers in, for example, France, Italy and Germany, but Anglo-Saxon scholars have not been particularly powerfully influenced by them. The single exception to this judgement is the work of Michel Foucault, who wrote within the structuralist tradition and always claimed to do so in the light of Marxism. However, his voluminous and brilliant writings have always struck me as lacking historical specificity. He paints boldly and audaciously on large canvases, dipping into historical particularity at moments, but his concept of power is relatively ahistorical in that a particular claim about it could often be moved fifty years in either direction without affecting his argument. My own experience of most writing in the wake of Foucault's ideas is that the practitioners lack his brilliance, do not do their homework, and tend to drift into relatively apolitical stances, bedazzled by *belles lettres*.

84

The best defence of Foucault's writings is that, like a Marxist, he treats theoretical and practical knowledges as forms of power. His most illuminating work has been about human knowledges – psychiatry, clinical medicine, penology and sexology. Yet he is un-Marxist in cutting these off from most of their articulations and in treating them formalistically. In this sense he is also anti-Marxist, or, at least, anti-reflectionist. Yet he leaves open the question of the appropriate conceptualisation of the relationship between knowledge and society: it remains to be investigated. For a Marxist, in the elusive last instance the question is not an open one. The arrow of causality must point, however circuitous its path, from the production and reproduction of real life to knowledge, whether theoretical or applied.

Would that I could cite a significant volume of avowedly Marxist writings in the English language to counterpose against the watered-down and disappointing versions discussed above. It could, of course, be argued that the flowering of Marxist writings in the later 1960s and early 1970s only glanced at problems which the history of the mode of production is not yet ready to solve. As Albert Camus, a fellow traveller of French Marxism, once wrote, 'One must imagine Sisyphus happy'.[21]

In my own view, when future historians find themselves able to provide a richer Marxist history of science, the Marxist writer whose views they are likely to find most fruitful – along with those of Marx, Lukács and Marcuse – is Antonio Gramsci. I shall cite two passages to give a flavour of his insight – the first on objectivity and the second on science and nature:

> the idea of 'objective' in metaphysical materialism would appear to mean an objectivity that exists even apart from man; but when one affirms that a reality would exist even if man did not, one is either speaking metaphorically or one is falling into a form of mysticism. We know reality only in relation to man, and since man is historical becoming, knowledge and reality are also a becoming and so is objectivity, etc.[22]

> Matter as such therefore is not our subject but how it is socially and historically organised for production, and natural science should be seen correspondingly as essentially an historical category, a human relation . . . Might it not be said in a sense, and up to a certain point, that what nature provides the opportunity for are not discoveries and inventions of pre-existing forces – of pre-existing qualities of matter – but 'creations', which are closely linked to the interests of society and to the development and further necessities of development of the forces of production? [23]

Here, I propose, lie the germs of a richer Marxist history of science.

NOTES

1. K. Marx, *A contribution to the critique of political economy* (1859) (London, 1971), pp. 20–1.
2. ——, *Grundrisse: foundations of the critique of political economy (rough draft)* (1857–58) (London, 1973), pp. 105–6.

3. ——, and F. Engels, *Selected correspondence* (1955), 2nd ed. (Moscow, 1965), p. 417.
4. ——, and F. Engels, *The German ideology* (1845–46) (London, 1965), p. 61.
5. ——, and F. Engels, *The German ideology*, p. 28.
6. M. Jay, *Marxism and totality: the adventures of a concept from Lukács to Habermas* (Cambridge, 1984), p. 117.
7. Quoted in ibid., p. 116.
8. N. I. Bukharin *et al.*, *Science at the crossroads* (1931), 2nd ed. (London, 1971), p. 152.
9. Ibid., pp. 153–4.
10. Ibid., pp. 166–7.
11. Ibid., p. 174.
12. Ibid., p. 177.
13. Ibid.
14. Ibid., p. 20.
15. Ibid., p. 22.
16. Ibid., p. 23.
17. Ibid., p. 24.
18. A. R. Hall, 'Merton revisited, or science and society in the seventeenth century', *History of science*, 2 (1963), 1–16.
19. ——, 'Microscopic analysis and the general picture', *Times literary supplement* 26 Apr. 1974, pp. 437–8.
20. K. Mannheim, *Ideology and utopia: an introduction to the sociology of knowledge* (1936) (London, 1960), p. 279.
21. A. Camus, *The Myth of Sisyphus and other essays* (1942) (New York, 1959), p. 91.
22. A. Gramsci, *Selections from the prison notebooks of Antonio Gramsci* (1929–35) (London, 1971), p. 446.
23. Ibid., pp. 465–6.

BIBLIOGRAPHY AND FURTHER READING

J. D. Bernal, *Science in history* (1954), 2nd ed. (London, 1957).

T. M. Brown, 'Putting paradigms into history', *Marxist perspectives*, 9 (1980), 34–63.

J. G. Crowther, *The social relations of science* (1941), 2nd ed. (London, 1967).

M. Foucault, *The order of things: an archaeology of the human sciences* (London, 1970).

L. R. Graham, *Science and philosophy in the Soviet Union* (London, 1973).

D. Joravsky, *The Lysenko affair* (Cambridge, Mass., 1970).

L. Levidow (ed.), *Radical science essays* (London, 1986).

S. F. Mason, *Main currents of scientific thought* (1956); reprinted as *A history of the sciences* (New York, 1962).

R. K. Merton, *Science, technology, and society in seventeenth century England* (1938) (New York, 1970).

J. Needham *et al.*, *Science and civilization in China* (Cambridge, 1954–84).

Radical Science Collective, 'Science, technology, medicine and the socialist movement', *Radical science journal*, 11 (1981), 3–70.

D. J. Struik, *Yankee science in the making* (1948), 2nd ed. (New York, 1962).

Gary Werskey, *The visible college: a collective biography of British scientists and socialists in the 1930s* (London, 1978).

R. M. Young, 'The historiographic and ideological contexts of the nineteenth-century debate on man's place in nature', in *Darwin's metaphor* (Cambridge, 1985), pp. 164–247.

E. Zilsel, 'The genesis of the concept of scientific progress', in P. P. Wiener and A. Noland (eds.), *Roots of scientific thought* (New York, 1957), pp. 251–75.

7

THE SOCIOLOGY OF THE SCIENTIFIC COMMUNITY

TREVOR PINCH

1. INTRODUCTION

Over the last decade and a half the sociology of the scientific community has become inseparable from the sociology of the products of that community – namely scientific knowledge. For epistemological reasons it had been previously assumed that there was nothing of interest which sociologists could say about scientific knowledge. That has all changed. Undoubtedly the major development in the field of sociology of science has been the emergence of the sociology of scientific knowledge.

The strictures which Karl Mannheim placed on the sociology of knowledge, whereby certain areas of knowledge such as the sciences and mathematics could not be usefully examined because they were considered to produce immutable asocial truths, have at last been challenged. The natural sciences, including physics and mathematics, are no longer seen as possessing a special epistemological warrant which makes their sociological analysis irrelevant. Research in the sociology of scientific knowledge today places a high premium on the analysis of physics, mathematics and other so-called 'hard' sciences.

The new type of analysis attempted places less emphasis on traditional aspects of the scientific community such as scientists' career structures, the reward system and the norms of scientific behaviour – features which were the major foci of interest for the Mertonian sociology of science of the 1950s and 1960s. The new sociology of science which has emerged in Europe and in Britain in particular, breaks with this tradition in that it examines the very content of scientific knowledge. Studies carried out within the new sociology of scientific knowledge are concerned to relate aspects of the scientific community to the content of scientific ideas, methods, procedures and practices. As a consequence of needing to take into account the actual content of science many of the leading practitioners of this approach are themselves ex-natural scientists.

2. THE EMERGENCE OF THE SOCIOLOGY OF SCIENTIFIC KNOWLEDGE

Several developments have contributed towards the recent emergence of the sociology of scientific knowledge. Of prime importance has been the breakdown of the 'standard' empiricist view of scientific knowledge in the philosophy of science. Undoubtedly a major influence here has been the work of Thomas Kuhn and the subsequent debate generated amongst philosophers such as Popper, Lakatos and Feyerabend. Although it is doubtful whether logical empiricism ever achieved total dominance in the philosophy of science, many philosophers, and indeed many scientists in the early 1970s, would probably have subscribed to key elements of the standard empiricist view. However, there are now a variety of versions giving different weights to the role of experiment and theory and different accounts of the type of empirical evidence which scientists should seek (see art. 5).

The crux of the matter is that in the standard view, scientists are seen to be in dialogue with a fixed natural world. They are assumed to be able to discover the truth about it, or at least to increase the verisimilitude of their theories, through experiments and observations embedded in a web of theory. According to the particular version being put forward, the process is attended to with varying degrees of difficulty. In the most sophisticated versions, the difficulty is great and the process is time-consuming and uncertain. The key feature, however, even in these sophisticated versions, is that given the appropriate circumstances, the data can speak, if only to add another nail to the coffin of a degenerating research programme.

Well-known difficulties with the standard view, such as the problem of theory-laden observation and the failure of correspondence theories of truth, have led to a re-examination by philosophers of the grounding of scientific knowledge. Detailed sociological and historical studies of specific episodes of scientific development have shown that science does not conform to the activity portrayed in the standard philosophical view. Such studies have brought added emphasis to the search for a more satisfactory account of scientific development.

Although the reappraisal is still underway, the approaches of philosophers and sociologists are no longer always antithetical. For instance, philosophers such as Hesse, Nickles and Hacking have in recent works drawn attention to the sociological input in their theories of science.[1] It is not my intention here to go over these philosophical developments in any detail. It is sufficient to point out the current fragmented state of philosophy of science. Conventionalist, relativist, realist, falsificationist and even anarchist accounts of science proliferate. It is clear that there are no agreed universal canons of scientific rationality which would make the task of a thorough-going sociology of scientific knowledge redundant.

Also of significance in the development of the sociology of scientific knowledge has been the influence of the phenomenological, ethnomethodological and ordinary-language philosophy tradition, associated with, for example, the writings of Schutz, Garfinkel, Wittgenstein and Winch.[2] This tradition has been particularly prevalent in Britain where North American functionalist sociology has always held less sway. Indeed this influence has led to Kuhn being interpreted in a much more radical way in Britain (by writers such as Barnes) than in North America. The phenomenological tradition showed how all human activity could be understood in terms of the generation of cultural meanings in the context of localised social interaction. It was a short step to include scientific activity within this analysis. Again, scientific knowledge is treated as if it possesses no special epistemological warrant.

Finally, no account of the emergence of sociologists' interest in scientific knowledge as an object of study is complete without reference to the Mertonian tradition in the sociology of science.[3] It would seem that Merton shared Mannheim's reservations concerning the possibility of a sociology of scientific knowledge. The standard empiricist philosophical view of science seems to have underpinned Merton's normative framework. Scientists' commitment to norms, such as that of universalism, ensured that the publicly-warranted objective knowledge demanded by the empiricist view was maintained. The collapse of the standard empiricist view has thus taken away much of the momentum from the Mertonian approach. Norms are now usually treated as interpretative resources or accounts of action rather than constraints upon action.

The new focus upon the study of knowledge and, in particular, the location where knowledge is produced (such as specific episodes at the research frontiers of science or the scientific laboratory) has meant that the Mertonian research tools, generated in the context of an analysis of the institutional features of the scientific community, have become less salient. Mertonian and non-Mertonian large-scale studies of the scientific community using mass-aggregate techniques continue. Research instruments stemming from such approaches, such as the Science Citation Index, are important for addressing many issues of science policy. However, the constitutive questions of the sociology of science are now mostly generated by the sociology of scientific knowledge. Consequently there has been a switch in the national research traditions which dominate the field. Although the new sociology of scientific knowledge has taken root in North America, the heartland of the field is now to be found in Europe and, in particular, in Britain.

3. THE NEED FOR SYMMETRICAL EXPLANATIONS

The analytical assumptions of the new sociology of scientific knowledge have been presented in a number of different forms. One influential statement has come from Bloor, who has outlined a 'strong programme' in the sociology of scientific knowledge.[4] The most important principle of his programme is a commitment to a *symmetrical* sociological analysis of knowledge claims. By 'symmetry' Bloor means that sociologists should offer the same type of explanation for beliefs that are perceived to be 'true' as is offered for beliefs that are perceived to be 'false'. This requires the sociologist to exercise charity in the interpretation of belief systems – 'true' beliefs can no longer be regarded as unproblematic because they simply are true. Furthermore, the easy option of explaining adherence to 'false' beliefs in terms of 'social epidemiology' (in other words, by the imputation of some sort of social characteristic shared by the adherents of deviant beliefs) or 'false consciousness' is not encouraged within this approach. Sociologists of scientific knowledge must be impartial as to the 'truth' or 'falsity' of the beliefs that they attempt to explain. Just as a sociologist of religion would not wish to explain the domination of the Hindu faith over the Muslim faith in India in terms of Hinduism being better able to represent God, so too should the sociologist of science resist easy explanations for the triumph of particular scientific ideas in terms of those ideas being better able to represent the natural world.

Such a position, of course, entails a form of relativism. There has been much debate over relativism – and many ways around the so-called paradoxes of relativism have been offered. The easy rejection of sociology of scientific knowledge on the grounds that it is relativist will today no longer suffice. Few sociologists of scientific knowledge today would want to claim any special epistemological warrant for their own findings. Like all knowledge, that produced by the sociology of science can be understood as a social construct. Relativism for most researchers functions as a methodological heuristic. It is difficult to see how anything other than a 'relativistic attitude' can be taken when studying areas of contemporary science, where what is to count as the 'truth' has not even emerged.

4. RESEARCH SITES FOR THE STUDY OF THE SCIENTIFIC COMMUNITY

The emphasis upon knowledge-creation processes in the scientific community has meant that new research sites have had to be found which exemplify such processes and which allow them to be studied. Concepts for identifying groups in science, such as 'invisible colleges', 'schools', 'disciplines', 'co-citation networks' or even Kuhn's term 'paradigm' have proved difficult to operationalise. Because such means of identifying groups tend to be based upon an artificial separation of scientists' social relationships and cognitive relationships, they are unsuitable for capturing the new view of scientific knowledge – a view which sees the cognitive and social as being irretrievably linked. Several new research sites and means of identifying the salient groups have arisen in tandem with the new sociological studies of science.

4.1. Core-set studies

The 'core-set' is the term coined by Collins to designate a group of scientists engaged in a scientific controversy over some particular scientific fact or theory.[5] They are the group who contest and produce new knowledge of the natural world. The scientists in the core-set may be drawn from a variety of disciplines and areas of expertise and they will typically be located in a variety of geographical and institutional settings. They may include both theoreticians and experimentalists. A typical core-set for, say, a controversy in modern physics over a particular experimental observation, comprises anywhere between ten to 30 scientists. Because scientific controversies are public and polarising phenomena – the debate between protagonists often being fought out in the literature and at conferences – the relevant scientists can easily be identified. In a contemporaneous core-set study, it is usually possible to interview all the main protagonists plus less central figures who may play a significant part in the debate.

The core-set is surrounded by the scientific 'on-lookers', who follow the debate and wait for the core-set scientists to pronounce on the controversial issue. Ludwik Fleck in his prescient study of the genesis and development of a scientific fact can also be seen to have drawn a distinction between the core-set and the rest of the scientific community. Fleck refers to the scientific community as being divided between 'a small esoteric circle and a larger exoteric circle. . . . Any individual may belong to several exoteric circles but probably only a few, if any, esoteric circles'.[6] A similar point is made by Collins who argues that most scientists spend only a comparatively small part of their activities engaged within a core-set. Indeed, many scientists may never be engaged in controversy at all throughout their careers.

Recently Rudwick, in his study of the Great Devonian Controversy, has used the almost complete record of the correspondence between the protagonists to provide the most detail yet of how a core-set forms and changes during the course of a controversy.[7] The core-set for the Devonian controversy was made up of scientists with a variety of competences. It included, for instance, geologists, palaeontologists and amateur fossil collectors. Rudwick's study is particularly useful not only for showing how knowledge is constructed within the confines of the core-set, but also for mapping out how scientists at the periphery can, at various points in the controversy, be transported to 'centre stage'.

The rationale for studying the scientific community in this way, by defining a key group of knowledge producers engaged in debate at the research frontiers of science, is provided by Collins in a three-stage 'empirical programme of relativism' (EPOR). In the first stage of the programme the priority is placed upon the demonstration of the interpretative flexibility of scientific knowledge. In other words, it is shown how different interpretations of the natural world are available to different scientific actors. Scientific controversies provide a particularly suitable location for achieving this aim. Typically the rival scientific viewpoints on offer provide the basis for showing how Nature alone cannot settle the dispute. Interviews with protagonists and an analysis of scientific papers produced in the course of the dispute (or, for historical cases, correspondence and notebooks) usually reveal how the water-tight experiments and unquestionable theory of one side can be questioned by the other side. This stage of the programme is consistent with Bloor's Strong Programme tenet whereby the truth and falsity of scientific knowledge are held to be irrelevant to sociological analysis. In a scientific controversy both sides claim that scientific truth is with them – it is truth which is at issue.

In the second stage of the programme the explanatory work shifts to the identification of 'closure mechanisms'. These are processes whereby the potentially endless interpretative flexibility of scientific knowledge is limited or closed down. In other words, explanations are sought for why scientists reach agreements about the 'truth' and 'falsity' of particular claims. These 'closure mechanisms', such as the role of rhetoric or funding, are usually to be found within the confines of the scientific community and are one of the main ways in which scientific knowledge is socially shaped. Several studies have identified specific closure mechanisms.

The final stage of the empirical programme of relativism – a stage which has yet to be reached in most studies – aims to show the effect of the wider social cultural milieu upon the processes whereby consensus is reached within the scientific community. If this programme was carried out in full for a piece of knowledge belonging to a modern mainstream science with substantial institutional autonomy then, as Collins writes:

> The impact of society on knowledge 'produced' at the laboratory bench would . . . have been followed through in the hardest possible case.[8]

4.2. Lab studies

Another important research site to emerge from recent sociological work on the scientific community has been the individual scientific laboratory. Researchers following anthropological methods have studied how scientists produce new knowledge 'at the lab bench'. It has been shown, using detailed field notes, audio recordings and even video recordings of laboratory activity, how scientific facts are constructed and deconstructed in the course of routine laboratory work. Again the standard empiricist view of scientific knowledge whereby the truth or falsity of particular scientific facts are to be found in Nature, is rejected in favour of a more symmetrical analysis. As Latour and Woolgar write:

> . . . we do not conceive of scientists using various strategies as pulling back the curtain on pregiven, but hitherto concealed truths. Rather objects (in this case substances) are constituted through the artful creativity of scientists.[9]

Symmetry forms only the starting point for the analysis and lab studies offer a variety of other theoretical and explanatory themes. For example, Latour and Woolgar outline a model of 'credibility cycles' whereby scientific careers can be understood in terms of cycles of investment in equipment, resources and information. A related approach has been developed by Law and Callon, who advocate a network model of science where interdependencies or links between different scientists and different laboratories constrain the knowledge produced. Knorr-Cetina has analysed how scientific facts are produced in the context of 'trans-scientific fields' defined in terms of resource relationships. The relationships of laboratory administrators and funding officials with scientists are all seen to play a part in the formation of scientific knowledge.

Lab studies, with their focus upon the microcosm of day-to-day scientific activity, provide much fine structure of the work of a cross-section of members of the scientific community (many different sorts of scientists, including technicians and administrators, are to be found in laboratories). The strengths of lab studies are their heterogeneity and their ability to concentrate in great detail upon the everyday social construction of scientific knowledge. Within their strengths, however, also lie their weaknesses. In their concern with identifying contingencies significant in the local setting, they choose to place less emphasis on the processes across space, time and community which may play a part in settling the eventual outcome – particularly in cases where knowledge is disputed. Some scientific facts are constructed and deconstructed over a period of time, and by many different scientific actors, located at a variety of different laboratories. For example, a study of Blondlot's laboratory in 1903 may miss the crucial social processes whereby Blondlot's findings were deconstructed. However, in an interesting twist to this argument Latour, in his work on Pasteur (1983), has argued that it is possible to study how the wider society is actually transformed within the laboratory. This draws attention to the important point that not only is science socially shaped in laboratories, but also that society too can be shaped in the laboratory.

Core-set studies, although they do address phenomena across space, time and community, conversely suffer from the weakness that their analysis may be less detailed in regard to day-to-day scientific activities. Also, by focusing upon core-sets such studies may miss processes going on in the wider community which settle the controversy. Finally, it is worth noting that since most science is not controversial, paying too much attention to processes associated with controversy may provide a misleading picture of social aspects of the scientific community.

4.3. The social shaping of scientific knowledge

As indicated already, a variety of approaches towards the relationship between scientific knowledge and the community of knowledge-producers is evident in recent sociology of science. One approach which has been especially influential has become known as the 'interest model'. Studies of interests and how they shape scientific knowledge tend to be based upon traditional historical methods. That is to say, a number of different aspects of scientific activity are examined across space, time and a range of communities. There are no particular research sites where it is recommended that the interest model is especially likely to be of relevance. Indeed, it is a general model derived from broad considerations in the sociology of knowledge. It is an approach which is fully commensurate with Bloor's strong programme stipulation of symmetrical explanation. Both successful and failed knowledge claims are to be explained in terms of putative social and cognitive interests.[10] The key interests may arise from inside or outside the context of the scientific community. The approach has now been developed and extended to include the analysis of contemporaneous scientific disputes. The notion of interests has also been shown in Pickering's work to relate to the practices, research techniques and exemplars shared by particular scientific specialities.

A recent historical study by Shapin and Schaffer of Robert Boyle's famous air-pump experiments falls broadly within this tradition of analysis and is unrivalled in its treatment of the detailed processes of the social shaping of scientific knowledge.[11] The study takes to task the standard account of Boyle's experiments which are often regarded as the classic success story of the new experimental method. By a detailed analysis of the neglected controversy between Boyle and Hobbes, Shapin and Schaffer illustrate the micro-politics of the negotiation of what counts as experimental knowledge. They further show how at this crucial institutional juncture, the conception of experimental method by Boyle and the Royal Society was shaped by political events in the wider arena of seventeenth-century Britain. What is striking about this study is that many of the features of contemporaneous experimental controversies are evident in the seventeenth century. This encourages the view that the recent work on the social aspects of scientific communities, and how knowledge is socially shaped within such communities, has a wide applicability.

4.4. Ethnomethodology and discourse analysis

Finally, to round off this very brief account of the major foci of recent work on social aspects of scientific communities, reference must be made to ethnomethodology and discourse analysis. Writers within these traditions have shifted the emphasis from the traditional goals of sociological explanation in terms of the motives, interests and actions of scientists towards concerns over *accounts* of scientific activities. For example, in one of the earliest studies of this type, Woolgar looked at how discovery-accounts (of pulsars) were organised so as to produce a particular reading. The theme of scientific discovery has also been explored by Brannigan who has shown in a number of cases how scientific discoveries are attributed and made accountable. The focus of such work is often on the discourse whereby discoveries and other scientific activities are made available. Thus the 'talk' and literary discourse of science take on a special significance. However, the literary products of scientists are not used here in the traditional way as evidence for the imputation of actions. Rather they are used to show how particular readings, accounts, or interpretations are constructed. This even applies to the use made of interviews with scientists conducted by sociologists.

Despite the radical claims of ethnomethodologists such as Lynch, Livingston and Garfinkel, who profess that they have no interest in traditional sociological issues, many of their concerns parallel those to be found within more standard sociology of scientific knowledge. The object of the analysis becomes the determination of the processes whereby different types of account are systematically produced in different local contexts. Also the transformation of accounts between different contexts (e.g. the laboratory notebook, the published article, the press statement and the interview) overlaps with the concerns of the laboratory and core-set studies where also, on occasions, the processes by which particular texts are constructed and transformed are examined in detail.

Despite the different analytical intentions of the ethnomethodological and discourse-analytical inspired work, it can also be said to share the Strong Programme assumptions concerning symmetry and impartiality. In other words, it does not make any difference to the analysis whether the discourse studied or the ethnomethodological account offered is of a 'true' or 'false' discovery. The common focus upon how 'reading', 'accounting' and 'talk' are achieved leaves no specially reserved place for the natural world as an arbiter in such matters. Science is treated straightforwardly as part and parcel of culture. Garfinkel, Lynch and Livingston, in their analysis of a tape recording of the discovery of the optical pulsar by Cocke and Disney, write:

> Cocke and Disney's discovery is this: from the local historicity of the embodied night's work they extract a cultural object, the Independent Galilean Pulsar. The IGP retains the material contents of astronomical *things* in their entirety. Nevertheless, the IGP, the potter's object, is a *cultural* object, *not* a 'physical' or a 'material' object.[12]

Perhaps the *differences* between all the different strands of modern sociology of scientific knowledge lie in where they locate the constraining features of the social world as arising. For the ethnomethodologist the constraints are to be found in the accounting features themselves. For the interest theorist they reside in the wider society.

5. UNITY, DIVERSITY AND DISPUTE

The diversity of approaches to be found within recent work on the scientific community is clear, but it would be wrong to present the above research sites and strands of analysis as being mutually exclusive. Often similar topics have been illuminated by a range of different perspectives. For example, the problems of pseudoscience and the problem of drawing boundaries between science and pseudoscience has formed an important analytical focus for many studies within the recent sociology of science from a variety of perspectives.[13]

It can be seen that there is much agreement in the sociology of scientific knowledge over the underlying assumption that scientific knowledge can be treated as a social construct and that science is not special in any important epistemological sense. However, the consequences of this assumption for the study of the scientific community, as we have seen, have not been uniform. Different types of sociological explanation have been advanced and there has been no agreement as to the most appropriate research site as where best to pursue the analysis. These differences have recently become more overt (in one or two cases) and have had the unfortunate effect of transforming the unity of the 1970s into the present (as of 1986) rather more fragmented state of the field.

For example, the 'interest' explanation has met with criticism from some ethnomethodologists and discourse analysts. One criticism levelled by Woolgar and Yearley is that the imputation of interests is less straightforward than commonly assumed.[14] This is because (it is claimed) such explanations ignore actors' own 'interest work'. That is to say, scientists will themselves impute social interests to the work of others in order to try and discredit it. For this reason it is difficult to impute the 'real' social interests at stake. A similar criticism has been made by Gilbert and Mulkay of all work in the sociology of scientific knowledge which relies on interviews with scientists as evidence for social action. The argument is that interview data cannot be used to impute motives or actions to scientists – at the most such data merely reflect scientists' repertoires of discourse. In short, these critics draw attention to the problems of interpreting interview data and historical data for the purposes of imputing actions and interests.

Several answers to these types of criticism have been offered. Perhaps the most pertinent response has been to point out that we can never have access to a realm of 'pure' uninterpreted data, and that therefore every analyst is faced with this type of dilemma. Even the data presented by ethnomethodologists and discourse analysts are interpreted and it is not clear how, for example, putative social interests can be excluded such as to provide a realm of 'pure' data.

The 'reflexive attitude', which has recently been advocated as a response to the unavoidable difficulties of interpretation, can be seen as an alternative to or as an extension of the 'relativistic attitude'. The 'reflexive attitude' means that analysts should always attempt to draw their readers' attention to the constructed nature of the sociologist's account. This leads to the exploration of the sociologist's own form of discourse and alternative forms of discourse, such as unconventional texts and 'New Literary Forms'.[15]

Although not everyone would like to go as far as this (and some would not like to go very far along this path at all!) such work does indicate the special place which texts and discourse possess in science. Scientists spend much time arguing and writing about their ideas and discussing them. Even scientific instruments can be seen as devices for producing written inscriptions. If we include diagrams, graphs and other forms of visual representation within the analysis, then we are clearly talking about central features of scientists' activities. The recent attention given to texts and discourse, or to what has been referred to as the 'linguistic turn' in the sociology of science, does not seem to be misplaced. However, it is to be hoped that in the long term such detailed textual analysis can be related to more traditional sociological concern in the development of the scientific community.

6. CONCLUSION

As in most reviews of this type, this one has been both partial and selective. Other work in the sociology of science has continued in other national contexts and individuals in Britain have also worked within a variety of different perspectives from those discussed here. For instance, Whitley has produced a comparative taxonomy which attempts to link the social and cognitive dimensions of a whole variety of scientific disciplines. Also, in North America Gieryn's recent work has many resonances with the 'strong programme' and a 'weak programme' in the sociology of science has been advocated by Chubin and Restivo which attempts to bring together the concerns of sociology of science with those of science policy within a framework for political action. Finally it is worth noting that the contention that scientific knowledge is socially shaped has parallels with the political analysis of science offered by the Radical Science Group.[16]

The sociology of scientific knowledge as it has developed during the 1970s and early 1980s is now widely recognised as having made a significant impact upon how we understand scientific knowledge and its relationship with the wider society. Such work has had, and is continuing to have, an impact on how we understand technology, science education, public-science disputes (e.g. scientific disputes that endender public interest) and the public's understanding of science.[17] This has been an exciting period of development for one of the liveliest areas of science studies.

NOTES

1. See Mary Hesse, *Revolutions and reconstructions in the philosophy of science* (Bloomington, 1980); and Ian Hacking, *Representing and intervening* (Cambridge, 1984); and T. Nickles, 'Twixt method and madness', in N. Nersessian (ed.), *The process of science* (The Hague, 1987).

2. A. Schutz, *The phenomenology of the social world* (London, 1980); H. Garfinkel, *Studies in ethno-methodology* (Englewood Cliffs, NJ, 1967); Ludwig Wittgenstein, *Philosophical investigations* (Oxford, 1974); and Peter Winch, *The idea of a social science* (London, 1958).

3. See B. Barber, *Science and social order* (New York, 1952); W. O. Hagstrom, *The scientific community* (New York, 1965); J. Gaston (ed.), *The sociology of science: problems, approaches and research* (London, 1973).

4. D. Bloor, *Knowledge and social imagery* (London, 1976).

5. H. M. Collins, 'The place of the "core-set" in modern science: social contingency with methodological propriety in science', *History of science*, 19 (1981a), 6–19.

6. L. Fleck, *Genesis and development of a scientific fact* (English edition, Chicago, 1979).

7. M. J. S. Rudwick, *The great devonian controversy: the shaping of scientific knowledge among gentlemanly specialists* (Chicago, 1985).

8. See H. M. Collins, 'Stages in the empirical programme of relativism' *Social studies of science*, 11 (1981b), 3–10, p. 7.

9. B. Latour and S. Woolgar, *Laboratory life* (Beverly Hills, 1979), p. 129.

10. See B. Barnes, and D. MacKenzie, 'On the role of interests in scientific change', in R. Wallis (ed.), *On the margins of science: the social construction of rejected knowledge*, Sociological review monograph 27 (1979). B. Barnes and S. Shapin (eds.), *Natural order: historical studies of scientific culture* (Beverly Hills and London, 1979). D. MacKenzie, *Statistics in Britain, 1865–1930, the social construction of scientific knowledge* (Edinburgh, 1981) and A. Pickering, *Constructing the quark* (Chicago, 1984).

11. S. Shapin and S. Schaffer, *Leviathan and the air-pump: Hobbes, Boyle and the experimental life* (Princeton, 1985).

12. H. Garfinkel, M. Lynch and E. Livingston, 'The work of discovering science construed with materials from the optically discovered pulsar', *Philosophy of the social sciences*, 11 (1981), 131–58, 141. See also M. Lynch, *Art and artefact in laboratory science: a study of shop work and shop talk in a research laboratory* (London, 1985).

13. See, for instance, R. Westrum, 'Social intelligence about anomalies: the case of UFOs', *Social studies of science*, 7 (1977), 271–302; S. Shapin, 'The politics of observation: cerebral anatomy and social interests in the Edinburgh phrenology disputes', in Wallis (1979), pp. 139–78; H. M. Collins and T. J. Pinch, *Frames of meaning: the social construction of extra-ordinary science* (London, 1982); T. Gieryn, 'Boundary-work and the demarcation of science from non-science: strains and interests in professional ideologies of scientists', *American sociological review*, 48 (1983), 781–95.

14. S. Woolgar, 'Interests and explanation in the social study of science', *Social studies of science*, 11 (1981), 365–94, and S. Yearley, 'The relationship between epistemological and sociological cognitive interests: some ambiguities underlying the use of interest theory in the study of scientific knowledge', *Studies in the history and philosophy of science*, 13 (1982), 353–88. For replies to Woolgar's and Yearley's arguments and continuation of the debate, see Barry Barnes, 'On the "hows" and "whys" of cultural change', *Social studies of science*, 11 (1981), 481–98, D. MacKenzie, 'Interests, positivism, and history', ibid., 498–504; S. Woolgar, 'Critique and criticism: two readings of ethnomethodology', ibid., 505–14; and D. MacKenzie, 'Reply to Steven Yearley', *Studies in the history and philosophy of science*, 15 (1984), 251–9.

15. See M. Mulkay, *The Word and the world* (London, 1985).

16. B. Young, 'Science is social relations', *Radical science journal*, No. 5 (1977), 65–131.

17. For its extension to technology see, for example, T. Pinch and W. Bijker, 'The social construction of facts and artefacts: Or how the sociology of science and the sociology of technology might benefit each other', *Social studies of science*, 14 (1984), 399–442. For the relevance of such work to science education see H. M. Collins and S. Shapin, 'Experiment, science teaching, and the new history and sociology of science', presented to the International Conference on using history of physics in innovatory physics education, Pavia, Italy (September 1983); for the case of public science disputes, see B. Wynne, *Rationality and ritual* (Chalfont St Giles, Bucks.: BSHS

Monographs, 1982); and for the public understanding of science see T. Shinn and R. Whitley (eds.), *Expository science: forms and functions of popularisation* (Dordrecht, 1985).

BIBLIOGRAPHY

B. Barnes, *T. S. Kuhn and social science* (London, 1982).

A. Brannigan, *The social basis of scientific discoveries* (Cambridge, 1981).

M. Callon and J. Law, 'on interests and their transformation: enrolment and counter-enrolment', *Social studies of science*, 12 (1982), 615–62.

D. E. Chubin and Sal Restivo, 'The "mooting" of science studies: research programmes and science policy', in Knorr-Cetina and Mulkay (1983), pp. 53–84.

H. M. Collins, *Changing order* (Beverly Hills and London, 1985).

G. N. Gilbert and M. Mulkay, *Opening Pandora's box: a sociological analysis of scientists' discourse* (Cambridge, 1984).

K. Knorr-Cetina, *The manufacture of knowledge* (Oxford, 1981).

—— and M. J. Mulkay (eds.), *Science observed: perspectives on the social study of science* (London and Beverly Hills, 1983).

T. S. Kuhn, *The structure of scientific revolutions* (Chicago, 1970).

B. Latour, 'Give me a laboratory and I will raise the world', in Knorr-Cetina and Mulkay (1983), pp. 141–70.

R. K. Merton, *The sociology of science: theoretical and empirical investigations* (Chicago, 1973).

T. Pinch, *Confronting nature: the sociology of solar-neutrino detection* (Dordrecht, 1986).

R. Whitley, *The intellectual and social organization of the sciences* (Oxford, 1984).

S. Woolgar, 'Discovery: logic and sequence in a scientific text', in K. Knorr, R. Krohn and R. D. Whitley (eds.), *The social process of scientific investigation, Sociology of the sciences yearbook* 4 (1980), pp. 239–68.

8

FEMINISM AND THE HISTORY OF SCIENCE

J. R. R. CHRISTIE

1. WHAT FEMINISM SEEKS TO DO

In recent decades, feminism has resurfaced as a considerable and widespread
political movement throughout the world, devoted to obtaining equal rights and
status for women in the economic and political spheres. Put more generally,
feminism seeks a world where the biological, *sexual difference* between female
and male does not entail an economic, social and political inequality between
the lives of the two *genders*, feminine and masculine. In theoretical, scholarly
terms, the focus of feminism is upon the term *gender*, the socially and culturally-
produced difference of identities attributed to biologically female and male persons. Around these different gender identities is organised the phenomenon
known as *patriarchy*, the system which embodies and assures the inequitable
distribution of power between women and men, to the continuing advantage of
men. Patriarchy, then, is the structure of social relations which ensures that
men tend to have better access to career, salary, status and power in any given
set of economic, social and political circumstances. It further ensures that in
situations usually thought of as 'private' or 'personal', men also tend to occupy
the most powerful position. The point of concentrating upon gender is therefore to discover, understand, criticise and overthrow the means by which feminine and masculine identities are made; are socially-constructed artefacts
which support and produce a fundamental, systematic and arguably universal
condition of inequality which holds across boundaries of class, culture and race.

Feminism fights on many fronts, from the conventionally political to the personal, and does so less as a centrally-organised political party or unit than as a
series of linked but diverse groups whose activities are free to be geared to the
needs and demands of women as they occur in a great variety of conditions
across the world. Academic feminism forms one portion of this spectrum of
activities, and contains its own diversity within it. Its main presence is within

arts or humanities subject-areas such as literary and art criticism and history, but it has also made its presence felt within history generally, and more recently within history of science. There are a number of reasons why science and its history should have come to preoccupy feminism, and to these we can now turn.

2. FEMINISM AND SCIENCE

Feminist interest in science has often derived from the broader political issues and struggles with which it is engaged. Two in particular place science on feminism's agenda: the women's health movement and the anti-nuclear peace campaigns. Both of these involve confronting extremely powerful groupings of predominantly male scientific expertise, to wrest from them the rights of women to control their own bodies and what is done to them in the name of medicine, and the right to a future unshadowed by the threat of planetary destruction. In these forms, science can be seen as an obvious and often particularly dangerous location of patriarchal actions and attitudes. This in turn raises the wider, theoretical and historical question of the nature of science itself. To what extent might modern science, in its historical formation and contemporary development, be seen as a significant aspect of patriarchy?

Once this question is asked in these terms, a potentially large field of enquiry is opened up. Firstly, why does science appear historically as such a male-dominated project? Is it the case that female scientific activity has been as small and as negligible as much as conventional history of science makes out, and if so, how did this come about? Or is it the case that female presence in the history of science has tended to be ignored or marginalised, in line with the treatment meted out to women in history generally, as written by males in a male-dominated historiography? In answering these questions, feminist history of science tends to affirm that science in history has indeed often been a predominantly male-run enterprise, whose values of objectivity, instrumental rationality and manipulative, exploitative power over nature tend towards the exclusion of female practitioners from the world of science, as do the educational structures which support that world. Even so, and despite the efficacy of these values and structures, there has also been an active female presence throughout science's history which is both valuable and significantly recoverable.

3. FEMINISM IN HISTORY

A historically wide-ranging attempt to recover the significant presence of women within science's history can be found in Margaret Alic's *Hypatia's Heritage: A History of Women in Science from Antiquity through the Nineteenth Century*. Alic's introductory remarks can stand as an apt description for the feminist project of recovery generally within history of science:

... (We) think of the history of science as a history of men. More than that, we think of the history of science as the story of a very few men – Aristotle, Copernicus, Newton, Einstein – men who drastically altered our view of the universe. But the history of science is much more than that. It is the story of thousands of people who contributed to the knowledge and theories that constituted the science of their eras, and made 'great leaps' possible. Many of the people were women. Yet their story remains virtually unknown.[1]

Alic's work is able to demonstrate consistent female involvement in Western science since its earliest beginnings. It draws renewed attention to women scientists such as Hildegard of Bingen (1098–1179), who wrote on natural history, medicine, cosmology and cosmogony; Lady Anne Conway (1631–79), who produced a vitalistic cosmology; and Margaret Cavendish, Duchess of Newcastle (1623–73), who wrote on theoretical and experimental natural philosophy. Additionally, it points to the way in which women with scientific interests clustered significantly in subjects such as natural history and botany throughout the seventeenth, eighteenth and nineteenth centuries.

Alic makes, therefore, a relatively straightforward case for recognising frequently ignored 'women's contributions' to scientific development. In this perspective, women's scientific work is seen as additional to men's. Historical understanding can be improved and corrected by adding female achievement to the existing record. This is a perspective and method of work which, however, tends to leave certain kinds of questions unasked and unanswered. It does not address, though it sometimes documents, the kinds of social and educational pressures and prejudices which tended systematically for much of Western history to militate against the entry of women into the world of learning in general and science in particular. It also seems to accept, relatively unquestioningly, a subaltern and supplementary role for women scientists in history. 'Great leaps forward' remain the province of male heroes, while women labour in more humdrum and humble roles, with only occasional exceptional or aristocratic women able to move beyond this station.

4. FEMINIST HISTORIOGRAPHY

Many feminists would therefore see the project of straightforward recovery of the history of women in science as being somewhat limited, however valuable, and would wish to move beyond it. Margaret Rossiter, for example, in her study of women scientists in America, does not simply recover a significant female presence in American science.[2] She is able to relate this presence to more general trends in higher education. Most tellingly, she delineates the kinds of work and career to which women, in contrast with men, were assigned, and documents the specific kinds of resistances to women and side-trackings and marginalisations of their work that were produced by men able to define and control the nature of women's scientific labour and careers. Rossiter thereby clarifies not only the sources and forms of an expanded female presence in American science from 1880, but explains further the ways in which that expanded presence was not permitted to affect the overall structure of male domination in American science. That women took up subaltern roles, as assistants in laboratories and observatories, as junior professors, or confined to 'feminine' scientific fields such as cosmetic chemistry, is no longer seen as a straightforward historical fact, but as a distinctive and problematic phenomenon to be analysed and explained. Given such notably consistent data, the category of gender has an obvious and direct explanatory relevance. Women scientists achieving careers in the Progressive Era had the kind of career they had because they were women moving into the traditionally male world of knowledge, expertise and power, and thereby constituted a potential threat to this male monopoly as it moved into an important developmental phase of more thorough professionalisation and bureaucratisation. Rossiter's work effectively demonstrates how the simple historiographical project of recovery can be widened and deepened by adopting a persistently questioning attitude towards what is factually recovered, seeking beyond the subaltern existence of women scientists for reasons which explain that subalternity. These reasons, once uncovered, tend to reveal American science as a patriarchal institution of limited adaptability, which, like the culture at large, operated gender identities to the disadvantage of women.

In this more advanced historiography there is a significantly critical dimension at work, and it is precisely this critical perspective which gives feminist historiography its own particular and distinctive purchase within history of science. The gains it can make are not necessarily confined to subject-matter which includes women scientists. Donna Haraway's challenging analysis of the genesis and production of the African Hall in the American Museum of Natural History in New York foregrounds the analytical terminology of gender and patriarchy to provide an in-depth historical account of the meanings embodied in this major cultural and scientific institution between 1903 and 1936.[3] Haraway is able to show that the Museum's public activities were moulded by the perceived 'threat' of 'decadence' to American culture at this time. The activity of exhibition was to 'produce permanence, to arrest decay'; of eugenics, 'to preserve hereditary stock, to assure racial purity'; of conservation, 'to preserve resources . . . for moral formation, the achievement of manhood'.[4] Haraway does not confine her analysis to New York, but pursues it into the kinds of labour, organisation, technology and skill which produced the African Hall, and the values which motivated and became embodied in that production. Behind the African Hall lies a fascinating narrative of African safari: hunting, killing, photography and taxidermy, all expressing an overweeningly male ethos of sportsmanship, the trial of confronting nature, of conquest over nature by killing and of the attainment of manhood through these processes. This brought back to New York, in the form of dead gorillas and elephants, an ennobled nature, to be preserved and displayed as the sphere of possibility for the moral attainment of unadulterated manhood. The African Hall, ostensibly about the fading zoological African present, is also and equally about being a man in a threatened post-Roosevelt America.

By viewing the African Hall, realising the stories behind its activities and clarifying the ideological tenor of its complex history, Haraway reveals a relay of patriarchal meanings and a closed circuit of masculine messages. By that token, a critical feminist historiography of science obviously need not confine itself to the overt subject of women in science, but needs to pursue all the dimensions of patriarchy in science as and when they occur, whether or not this includes women.

What other such dimensions can feminist historiography reveal? A critical issue in feminism is the subject of essentialism, of whether women can be said to have an essential nature which therefore fits them for a certain sort of life. Contemporary feminist theory tends to retreat from essentialism, which ties feminine gender identity to female reproductive biology, her biological nature, rather than seeing gender identity as a changing social and cultural construct. The perils of biological essentialism for feminism are fairly obvious. If woman's nature is defined essentially by her reproductive capacities and functions, then this all too easily becomes the basis of stereotypical conceptions and images of women which have often functioned to the benefit of patriarchy: woman as wife, child-bearer, home-maker and so on. Essentialism therefore becomes a topic close to the top of feminism's critical concerns, and this in turn finds expression in feminist historiography of science.

Whereas Alic and Rossiter tackle the issue of women as subjects in science, that is, as active agents within sets of institutions and practices, the issue of essentialism raises the issue of women as objectified by science, as objects of scientific study. Here, much of the territory of the history of the life sciences and of medicine becomes immediately relevant, because, historically speaking, it is these discourses and institutionalised practices which have exercised theoretical and practical power over women, defining and treating women in authoritative ways. The objectified images of woman which science has historically produced have many variations, but contain nonetheless some dominant aspects. Woman tends to be identified with materiality, with the body, and comes to be seen, in crucial aspects of woman's life, as a creature of the material body. Aristotle, for example, identified the female reproductive role with the provision of 'matter', which was given 'form' only by male seed. In the eighteenth and then the nineteenth century, medical works increasingly portray woman as at the mercy of her own reproductive physiology and the ungovernable, literally hysterical passions which derived from it. Women thereby becomes identified with 'nature', with animality, with the affective, the emotional, lacking the male attributes of objectivity, rationality and self-control. The life and medical sciences have therefore often produced understandings of woman which consistently characterise her by her biological nature. This biological nature in turn fits woman for wifely, motherly, domestic roles in life, while specifically unfitting her for the male activities of learning, directing and governing. In these ways too, feminist historiography can therefore see male-produced science as providing a series of authoritative sanctions for conceptions of women which serve patriarchal interests.[5]

Nor is it only in these ways which science displays deeply gendered biases at the core of its presuppositions, methods and operations. These gender biases are discernible in different forms in recent scientific specialities such as primatology, as Haraway's work has demonstrated;[6] and are equally discernible when feminist historians examine the seventeenth century, the period of the genesis of modern Western science. This latter is important territory for feminist historiography of science. If it can be shown that modern Western science generated and deployed gender identity distinctions as part of its foundational manœuvrings, if the origins of modern science were predicated in part upon a politics of gender, then feminism is enabled to make a strategic and structurally critical point about the connection of science and patriarchy in Western history.

5. FEMINISM AND THE SCIENTIFIC REVOLUTION

Feminist historians and philosophers have endeavoured with some success to produce new understandings of the Scientific Revolution which examine the ways in which modern science in its historical origins was a highly gendered construction. Carolyn Merchant argues that the conception of nature which eventually emerged as dominant in the seventeenth century, a mechanistic materialistic conception, was a distinctively masculinised conception which replaced an older feminised view of nature.[7] The new, male version of nature saw it as disenchanted matter working according to mechanical principles. This replaced a feminised nature seen as vital, organic and productive. In this scenario, traced out by Merchant in many words and images from the sixteenth and seventeenth centuries, the old, beneficent Mother Nature is increasingly deprived of her vital and productive aspects as she is subjected to the measured and measuring canons of reductive mechanistic materialism. In brief, to emerge fully, modern science has to subdue and kill off female nature, for the two cannot occupy the same conceptual and practical space. This is a process which Merchant, a feminist historian with strong ecological sympathies, sees continuing apace into present times.

The process delineated by Merchant indicated one possible and often plausible set of interpretations of the Scientific Revolution's gender politics. Other feminist historians have added to and complexified the picture she presents. Evelyn Fox Keller's study of Francis Bacon, while recognising the consistent drive to male mastery and power over a female nature explicit in much of his writing, argues for the possibility of a more subtly gendered dialectic in Bacon than might first appear.[8] While Bacon often emphasises that nature is a woman to be conquered, subdued and penetrated by the aggressive, scientific male mind, man is also characterised as the servant and interpreter of a nature which can only be commanded by being obeyed. The male mind is thereby also required to possess a receptive and responsive, that is, more female mode, of understanding nature. For Keller, the Baconian mind therefore actually takes on a dialectic and hermaphroditic quality, incorporating and appropriating the feminine while appearing to deny and subdue it. This kind of dialectical reading, which attempts to track all the levels and kinds of gender images and concepts in their interaction, indicates that the Scientific Revolution's politics of gender may be less straightforward than the direct confrontational politics of male conquest and female death envisaged by Merchant.

Keller's analysis of gender ideology in relation to seventeenth-century science gains further depth in an examination of the debates subsequent to the founding of the Royal Society of London over the nature of true science and the methods proper to it.[9] Once again, although full play is given to elements demanding science as a 'Masculine Philosophy', capable of resisting 'The Woman in us . . . an *Eve*, as fatal as the *Mother* of our miseries', Keller also tracks the persistence, albeit declining, of hermetic and alchemical views which emphasised creative, feminine principles, and affective modes of understanding. The recognition of the persistence and influence of such elements is not particular to feminist historiography. What is particular is the view that these elements form part of a debate which cannot be simply understood in terms of new mechanistic science versus old magic, nor even in more complexly socialised and politicised terms of class-fractional or occupational clashes of interest over what constitutes legitimate knowledge. Particular to feminist historiography is the realisation and depiction of such debates as possessing an ineliminable and important gender dimension, which cannot be ignored if any reasonably coherent and full understanding of the Scientific Revolution is to be achieved. As Keller summarises:

> It is through the analysis of such debates that we can begin to understand the selection pressures exerted by ideology in general – and gender ideology in particular – on the competition between different visions of science. These pressures are part of the process that transforms a complex pluralistic tradition into a monolithic rhetoric, overlaying, obscuring, and often distorting a wide diversity of practice.[10]

A certain sympathetic identification with the Puritan scientific reformers of seventeenth-century England is also present in Sandra Harding's analysis of the origins of modern science.[11] This analysis comes towards the end of an extended philosophical investigation of the relations between science and feminism, and incorporates and extends many of its findings. Harding first redesignates the nature of the issues involved: it is less a question of 'women in science', more a question of science in feminism. The aims, strategies and values of feminism are hereby placed in the foreground of the analysis, whose aim is to provide a philosophical, historiographical critique of science from a feminist standpoint, and indicate a possible feminist science to succeed the patriarchal science which has hitherto held sway. In the course of this analysis, Harding overturns many of the commonplace assumptions purveyed by masculine history and philosophy of science. It takes physics as the paradigmatic, exemplary science, but why should we continue to hold with this convention? Placed alongside the array of life sciences and social sciences, the practices, methods and historical developments of the physical sciences are less than typical. And why should women accept unreflective, progressivisit characterisations of science's development and impact upon the world? The relevant question is surely, 'progressive for whom?'; if it has not been progressive for women, why should we persist with this characterisation of science as a progressive endeavour? Harding comes to view Western science, produced by and tied to the needs of expanding capitalist economies and imperial polities, as deeply regressive in its nature and its effect upon the world.

One large part of this regressiveness is the patriarchal nature of Western science, the ways in which masculine gender identity and the dominant ideologies of science are bound together by deep mutual implications which act continually to reinforce one another, while consigning other kinds of work and values to the sphere of the feminine. Instead of recognising and analysing these processes, historiography of science has tended to rehearse the origins of modern science as a mythic tale, enshrining heroic male creativity which constitutes its own principle of development, producing an abstractly intellectualised activity, objective, value-free, and disconnected from any context of social and political relations.

Harding proceeds to spell out the ways in which this and other accounts of the emergence of modern science suffer from obvious contradictions and defects. Narratives which focus on scientific development as a purely rational process owing nothing to anything outside of itself erect a paradox. Science is portrayed as the true pattern of enquiry into the natural causes of things, but science itself is simultaneously exempted from an enquiry which would reveal its own causal origins as a social phenomenon. While this historiography fails to take account of social, economic and political influences on the formation of modern science, attempts which contrastingly do emphasise such features suffer from a different problem. If science develops in response to the workings of social causation, in what coherent senses can the objectivity, rationality and progressiveness of science be maintained? We are left only with the variable standards and patterns of belief of different times and cultures against which to assess scientific development, and these do not constitute a stable ground.

Harding's critical historiography does not, therefore, wish simply to abandon criteria of rationality and objectivity with respect to science. Instead, it removes such criteria from their traditional residence in science and philosophy of science, and relocates them in political and moral discourse. By so doing, it reconnects the standards of objectivity and rationality with the sphere of values, the designation of what is good, just, non-exploitative and genuinely progressive. It is this reconnection of science and value which leads Harding to make a sympathetic identification of a new, feminist science with the science of the Puritan reformers in mid-seventeenth-century England. Feminist and Puritan science hold common assumptions: they are anti-authoritarian, have a radical belief in progress, are participatory, seek educational reform, are humanitarian, and wish for a combination of scientific with moral and political understanding. It is this conception of science which Harding sees as being replaced in the latter half of the seventeenth century by a process which included a newly institutionalised and hierarchised division of scientific labour, an atomistic cosmology, a norm-based, highly methodised version of scientific enquiry and a view of science as value-free. In taking on these attitudes and practices, science was locking itself into a patriarchal mode which erased the progressive possibilities inherent in the period of Puritan reform. It is these possibilities which the project of a feminist science seeks to revive. Harding's feminist historiography, overtly evaluative in both negative and positive ways, offers an interesting combination of radicalism and traditionalism. Its feminist radicalism insists upon foregrounding feminist values as the basis of analysis and judgement; its traditionalism consists in its refusal to abandon scientific objectivity and its willingness to learn from history.

6. CONCLUSION

The strands of feminist historiography of science surveyed here constitute an innovative and potentially powerful set of approaches to the history of science. They have much in common with Marxist-orientated, social history of science (see art. 6) and also draw upon the methods of language analysis increasingly present in the field (see art. 9). To these they add a set of concepts and questions which are more than a simple supplement to existing approaches and methods. By centralising the subjects of gender and patriarchy and beginning to trace out their relevance for history of science, feminism currently foreshadows a qualitatively altered view of science and its history. Although the contours of this view are as yet only emerging, they are becoming clear enough to suggest that some old certainties, induced by a historiography blind to the subject of gender, will have to be radically altered or discarded. The recovery of women's place and women's work in the history of science, the reasons for women's assignment to largely subaltern positions in science, the embodiment and construction of patriarchal interests and values by science, the degrading objectification of women by science and the masculine-gendered construction of modern science in its formative phase, all demonstrate a re-mapping of the historical world of science which gives new and different meanings from those found in more conventional and unreflective historiography. As ever, new and different meanings tend to generate resistance and controversy as well as interest and support, but as feminism and feminist scholarship grow, and as it increasingly recognises the crucial position occupied by science in modern and contemporary history, further feminist attention to this subject should consolidate and further extend the insights it has so far produced.

NOTES

1. M. Alic, *Hypatia's heritage* (Boston, 1986), p. 1.
2. M. Rossiter, *Women scientists in America: struggles and strategies to 1940* (Baltimore, 1982).
3. D. Haraway, 'Teddy bear patriarchy: taxidermy in the Garden of Eden, New York City, 1908–1936', *Social text*, 11 (1984–5), 20–64.
4. Ibid., p. 57.
5. For work dealing with aspects of these issues, see the journal *Representations*, 14 (1986).
6. D. Haraway, 'Animal sociology and a natural economy of the body politic, parts I and II', *Signs*, 4 (1978), 21–36, 37–60.
7. Carolyn Merchant, *The death of nature: women, ecology and the scientific revolution* (San Francisco, 1979).
8. E. Fox Keller, 'Baconian science: the arts of mastery and obedience', in her *Reflections on gender and science* (Yale, 1985), pp. 33–42.
9. E. Fox Keller, 'Spirit and reason at the birth of modern science', ibid., pp. 43–65.
10. Ibid., p. 65.
11. S. Harding, *The science question in feminism* (Ithaca, NY and Milton Keynes, UK, 1986), chaps. 8–9.

FURTHER READING

In addition to works cited under Notes, the following are also important and useful.

B. Easlea, *Witch-hunting, magic and the new philosophy: an introduction to the debates of the Scientific Revolution, 1450–1750* (Brighton, 1980).

D. Haraway, 'Sex, mind and profit: from human engineering to sociobiology', *Radical history review*, 20 (1979), 206–37.

——, 'The contest for primate nature: daughters of man the hunter in the field, 1960–1980', in M. Kann (ed.), *The future of American democracy* (Philadelphia, 1983), pp. 175–208.

L. J. Jordanova, 'Natural facts: a historical perspective on science and sexuality', in C. MacCormack and M. Strathern (eds.), *Nature, culture and gender* (Cambridge, 1980), pp. 42–69.

E. Fox Keller, *A feeling for the organism: the life and work of Barbara McClintock* (New York, 1983).

M. McNeil (ed.), 'Gender and expertise', *Radical science series* 19 (London, 1987).

9

LANGUAGE, DISCOURSE AND SCIENCE

J. V. GOLINSKI

1. INTRODUCTION

Language has emerged as a central concern of many areas of the humanities and social sciences in recent decades. The increasing pervasiveness of the highly ambiguous term 'discourse' in much contemporary debate is a result of this concern, which has so far extended over the disciplines of philosophy, anthropology, sociology, and literary criticism, and is beginning to have an effect in history itself. To date most historians of science have proved reluctant to execute a 'linguistic turn', and to join their colleagues in other fields in giving serious attention to problems of language. Their reluctance is regrettable, since it passes up the opportunities that linguistically-orientated studies would offer of forging new connections between the history of science and other contemporary disciplines; but it is also perhaps understandable in view of the disagreements and confusions which exist in the current understanding of language. For, despite widespread agreement that language is the central problem of modern human studies, there is no unanimity as to what this implies methodologically. As Martin Jay has put it, 'Linguistic turns . . . may take many different directions.'[1]

Beneath the apparent coherence of the modern attack on the problem of language lie widely disparate philosophical views on its nature and human significance. Thus, while most analytical philosophers would regard language as an entity which mediates between the human subject and objects in the external world, others such as structuralists and post-structuralists see it as an autonomous system governing the construction of meaning independently of human intention or reference to the objective world. To some, language is a defining feature of human existence, to others (such as semioticians, structuralists and hermeneuticists) it provides a model for the understanding of all human action. In view of this diversity of available philosophical perspectives on language, the urgent need is for some clarification of the theoretical issues at stake, and discussion of the ways in which they have been and might be applied to research in the history of science. Brief as it must be, this essay will attempt to address these needs.

That the turn towards the study of language is deeply rooted in the fundamental assumptions of many areas of contemporary human studies can hardly be denied, though it has never been satisfactorily explained. Michel Foucault has however suggested elements of an explanation in his brilliant but much-contested 'archaeology' of the human sciences, *The Order of Things* (1970). Foucault argues that language did not exist as a problematic entity in the eighteenth century, in the sense that it was regarded simply as a means of representation, albeit one which was not always properly used. With the rise of historical studies of grammar in the early nineteenth century, language lost its transparency, and acquired a historical 'density'. It became an attribute of the newly-constructed entity, 'man'; it was both an object of knowledge and also an irreducible limitation on what could be known. This development had two consequences, in Foucault's view. Firstly it stimulated consistent attempts to construct a formal, logical representation of thought, which would be free from the ambiguities and loosenesses of human language. Secondly, there developed a critical focus on the various ways in which language functioned as an *a priori* determinant of what human beings could think. Marx, Freud and Nietzsche are portrayed by Foucault as contributors to this latter enterprise, which has revealed how much we are all 'governed and paralysed by language.'[2]

In this way, Foucault suggests that two apparently opposite aims, the reduction of human thought to its logical form, and the interpretative understanding of the way in which language constrains thought, are both in fact symptoms of an underlying awareness of the density of language, an awareness which is characteristic of the modern view of man. Similarly, Ian Hacking has noted how several apparently distinct philosophical traditions of our time share what he calls 'immense consciousness of language'. Foucault's point is also paralleled by that of Richard Rorty, in a review of the evolution of recent British and American linguistic philosophy. Rorty claims that both those philosophers who sought to solve philosophical problems by a logical formalisation of language, and those who looked for solutions through a closer understanding of the common usage of language, shared the basic belief that a philosphical problem was 'a product of the unconscious adoption of assumptions built into the vocabulary in which the problem was stated'.[3]

The identification of this basic assumption of much recent philosophy, and of many other areas of the human sciences, provides one reason for historians of science also to take language more seriously. To take the 'linguistic turn' in this sense is to relinquish the view that the language of science (any more than that of philosophy) is simply a means of representation, separable from and irrelevant to the 'content' of science. Such a move carries with it the implication that historians should no longer seek to penetrate *through* the linguistic practices of scientists, to isolate ideas and conceptual structures in their minds, and should instead start to investigate those verbal and textual practices themselves.

Historians who take this step are undertaking to look sensitively at the ways in which scientists use language – in writing texts, giving lectures, preparing research reports, holding conversations, and so on. I shall adopt that embarrassingly overloaded term 'discourse' to cover all of these practices.[4] But to adopt the term is not to specify how it should be used; and to take the 'linguistic turn' is not to commit oneself to any particular mode of analysis of scientific language. There remain in fact a number of options available. In the discussion that follows, some examples of recent historical research on scientific language will be mentioned, and related in each case to the philosophical view of language that appears to underlie the investigation. The purpose of such a discussion is to clarify the theoretical issues in the field, not to suggest that historians are (or should be) guided by the views of particular philosophers. For the sake of simplicity, I shall distinguish just three kinds of approaches, characterised by three distinct attitudes to language: the 'symbolic', the 'hermeneutic or semantic' and the 'rhetorical'. Broadly, the first approach studies language in relation to the objects to which it refers, the second interprets it as a system of meanings, and the third analyses the way in which it serves the interests of its producer. These categories are intended to aid analysis, rather than to restrict it; it is not suggested that all relevant work will fit neatly within any one of them.

2. 'SYMBOLIC' APPROACHES

The 'symbolic' approach takes as its object of study the ways in which language exercises its function as a system of symbols. It starts from the assumption that language is a means of symbolic communication, that it attaches verbal signs to things, and uses them to convey meaning. Rather than seeking to grasp the meanings that the signs are given, this approach concentrates on understanding the way in which the connection between sign and thing is made. The connection is studied in the light of views on the nature of language articulated by those whose linguistic usage is under investigation, or by others in their cultural milieu.

The rationale of this approach has been described by Ernst Cassirer. In his work, *The Philosophy of Symbolic Forms* (1955), Cassirer portrays language as the primary attribute of human culture. But he makes it clear that he wishes to grasp the function of language symbolically, rather than semantically. Philosophy, he claims, cannot penetrate behind language; it can only discern the way in which language works, namely by attaching labels to sense-data, so that objects are brought within the range of the understanding. Linguistic symbols denote objects, and thereby appropriate them within the structure of the mind through which the world is apprehended.

On this view of language, the interesting questions about linguistic usage concern the way in which symbols are attached to the objects they name or denote. Two overlapping pairs of alternatives must be considered. Firstly whether the denotation is made unambiguously, i.e. whether there is a one-to-one correspondence of word with thing; and secondly, whether the naming is taken to be entirely conventional, dependent solely on human choice, or is thought to rely on some essential (natural or divinely-revealed) connection between an object and its name. Several historians have investigated shifts between these alternative methods of denotation, particularly in the crucial period of the seventeenth-century Scientific Revolution, and have related them to concurrent changes in scientific and philosophical ideas.

On the issue of ambiguity, the options are distributed between two extremes: at one pole, unambiguous word-for-object denotation; at the other, complete freedom in attaching any name to any thing. Although in fact neither extreme is possible, all language occurring at some point between the two, there is pressure in some contexts for denotation to be more precise and ambiguity to be restricted. For example, historians of the seventeenth century have portrayed the 'plain style' espoused by some natural philosophers of the time as an attempt to push usage towards the pole of unambiguous naming.[5] Thomas Sprat, a prominent apologist for the new science as practised by the Royal Society of London, denounced 'this vicious abundance of *Phrase*, this trick of *Metaphors*, this volubility of *Tongue*, which makes so great a noise in the World', and called for 'a close, naked, natural way of speaking'.[6] John Locke's critique of linguistic inaccuracies, his identification of six types of 'abuses of words', and his castigation of rhetoric as 'that powerful instrument of error and deceit', developed and formalised themes which Sprat and other seventeenth-century natural philosophers had already explored.[7]

Schemes for artificially constructed 'universal' or 'philosophical' languages, which were also commonplace in the seventeenth century, appear to have taken this desire for unequivocal denotation to its practical conclusion. In these schemes, precisely one name was to be given to each thing, and compounded objects were to be given names synthesised from the names of their parts, so that the processes of analytic and synthetic reasoning could be exactly reproduced linguistically. Historians such as James Knowlson, Vivian Salmon, Hans Aarsleff and Mary Slaughter have studied these proposals, found in the writings of J. A. Comenius, George Dalgarno, Francis Lodowyck and John Wilkins, among others. They have pointed out various connections with scientific developments of the period, but have not reached any consensus as to what the original motivation for the schemes was.

In Aarsleff's account, the issue of conventionality is crucial in this connection. In his view, the schemes for 'universal languages' indicate the survival of the 'Adamic' view of language, which holds that words and things were originally connected by God's command at the Creation. Although the proposed languages were to be explicitly artificial constructions, their espousal demonstrates to Aarsleff that it was still thought possible to recover the original divine link between language and the world. The 'Adamic' view of language had its roots in pietistic mysticism, feeding through from Protestant Germany to the English Puritan reformers of the mid-seventeenth century. It was displaced towards the end of the century by the view, expounded forcefully by Locke, of the inescapably conventional nature of language as an entirely human construction.

To Slaughter, on the other hand, the universal language schemes bespeak the continued predominance, until the late seventeenth century, of what she describes as a 'taxonomic episteme', based on Aristotle's philosophy of essentialism. They mark the final stages of a basically scholastic enterprise of exhaustive classification of natural objects, with the aim of knowing them in their essences. In this way Slaughter differs from Aarsleff on the real motivations for the universal language schemes, though she agrees on the chronology of their rise and decline, and on the importance of Locke in sealing their eventual fate. On balance, it seems likely that both Aristotelian essentialism and the Adamic language doctrine were influential upon those who proposed linguistic reforms in the seventeenth century, though neither seems established as a completely comprehensive explanation of the popularity of such schemes.

While the historians remain divided over significant details in this area of scholarship, the basic orientation of their studies seems clear. Their work falls under the heading of what I have called the 'symbolic' approach, because they assume that the symbolic function of language, the way in which names are attached to objects, is the relevant issue. They thus devote attention to the practices of naming, whether ambiguous or precise, conventional or natural. The assumption made is that the choice of particular methods of denotation on behalf on language-users is a voluntary one. Hence, expressed views about the nature of language can be used as evidence of usage, and connections between, for example, scientific use of language and philosophical views *about* language in the relevant milieu, can be expected to be uncovered. Geoffrey Cantor's research on connections between theories of language and theories of light in the eighteenth century illustrates how this approach can be extended into the history of science in the period since the Scientific Revolution.[8]

3. 'HERMENEUTIC OR SEMANTIC' APPROACHES

The second category of approaches to scientific language is the one I have called 'hermeneutic or semantic'. I am applying this label to studies which give serious attention to the problems of interpretation of the meaning of scientific language, in other words, which do not follow Cassirer in restricting their attention to the mechanisms of denotation. In a sense, of course, historians have always been concerned with meaning; some measure of interpretation in inseparably part of their enterprise. But when they take the linguistic turn, they are forced to confront afresh the problems of interpretation of past scientific theories. Meaning is now seen, in science as in other linguistic activities, as emerging from an interaction between the human subject, the world, and the formal structures of the language in which it is expressed. In future, history of science which aims at the interpretation of meaning will have to take account of the wide range of linguistic codes in which the substance of science has been communicated.[9]

Recent historical research has used this kind of approach to illuminate two particular types of problems. Firstly, the problem of the meanings given to scientific theories in certain cultural contexts. Studies in this area offer new perspectives on the popularisation of science. Secondly, the question of metaphor in scientific language is also illuminated by this kind of study. Whereas in the 'symbolic' approach, metaphorical language was seen simply as an imprecise method of denotation, a 'hermeneutic' approach permits metaphors to be read as devices for the transfer of meaning between different disciplines, or between science and general culture.

A brilliantly-sustained recent analysis of the first kind of problem is Roger Cooter's study of nineteenth-century phrenology, *The Cultural Meaning of Popular Science*. Cooter cuts across simplistic accounts of the popularity of phrenology at this time with a detailed analysis of the meanings ascribed to phrenological discourse in various cultural contexts. This involves him in discussion of the ways in which written texts were interpreted, the iconography of illustrations, and the messages conveyed by popular phrenological lectures. In each case, the historian is interested in processes of interpretation and the construction of meaning, and at the same time his own procedure is explicitly interpretative, in seeking to capture the meanings of past discourse. Thus Cooter seeks to grasp the appeal of phrenology to its audiences 'by decoding the science's signs and symbols'; he exhibits those symbols as 'personal, intimate, common, flexible, and "real" (because of their external palpably empirical nature)', and describes in great detail the variety of personal meanings which their flexibility might make them able to carry. Phrenology emerges as 'a multifaceted symbolic resource'; a mode of discourse whose success stemmed from its extraordinary adaptability as a way of making sense of a wide range of human social relations.[10]

This brief summary does no justice to the complexity of Cooter's analysis and it neglects altogether his argument for the importance of the symbolic functions of phrenology in relation to the stability of Victorian society at large. My point is to show the potential productivity of an approach which attempts to interpret the meanings of scientific discourse in specific cultural contexts. Such a perspective allows historians to dispense with the idea that science is always straightforwardly and inevitably 'popularised', and encourages us to grapple with the problems of understanding the actual meanings which scientific discourse had to those who comprised its audience.

This perspective is also capable of yielding new insight into the importance of metaphorical language in science. Semantically, metaphor can be understood as a transfer of a term between different contexts of meaning. Metaphors thus emerge, in the 'hermeneutic' approach, as crucial for understanding conceptual transfer between scientific disciplines, or between science and other areas of culture.

A stimulating discussion of this has been provided in a paper by Karl Figlio on the metaphor of organisation in the early-nineteenth-century bio-medical sciences. Figlio describes metaphorical language in science as a link between the formal elements of scientific theories and the ideological role of science in general culture. His discussion touches on the example of notions of irritability in eighteenth-century physiology, notions which while 'precisely specified in a technical sense, . . . were obviously infused with all the shades of meaning attached to ideas of life'.[11] The wide metaphorical implications of the terms employed allowed for the investment of crucial social interests in debates in this area. Questions of materialism, determinism, and others, were hotly contested; and Figlio holds that this was because a range of important personal interests were involved in commitments to one side or another. He concludes that an understanding of the metaphorical meanings of scientific terms provides a method by which these social investments in science may be exposed:

> It remains the task of the history of science to elucidate these interests – philosophical, theological, social, national, or political (i.e. ideological) – but it is an unapproachable problem until the concealed level at which these interests impinge upon each other is uncovered; i.e. until the meanings conveyed in the scientific language in which they are expressed are unveiled at the level at which ideas metaphorically flow between apparently separate domains.[12]

Thus the interpretation of the role of metaphor in scientific language appears to be essential, if historians are to understand the way human interests are invested in science. A study which parallels Figlio's in this respect is Robert M. Young's discussion of Darwin's metaphor of selection.[13] Young shows that the term 'selection', as used by Darwin, functioned technically in a description of the mechanism of evolution, but that it also had wider connotations which included an evocation of divine design. The term therefore served to weld together a diverse group of adherents to Darwin's theory, covering a wide range of different views as to the extent of God's intervention in the world.

The 'hermeneutic or semantic' approach which I have attempted to identify thus offers promising new perspectives on the relations between science and general culture. By undertaking the interpretation of the language of science, it offers the prospects of grasping the meanings of scientific terms within and outside technical disciplines. It is nevertheless largely unperceived as a distinctive approach in the history of science; and this is a pity, because the price of non-recognition is that the methodological problems of interpretation are not confronted explicitly, and the possible links with other disciplines are not explored.

Other groups of historians have been bolder in advancing this kind of method. For example, both Keith Michael Baker and William J. Bouwsma have made the call for intellectual history to be transmuted into 'the history of meaning', a history which would embrace all aspects of culture and all forms of symbolic expression of human experience.[14] Although the history of science would presumably wish to secure the boundaries of its own territory within such an all-embracing 'history of meaning', an expanded awareness of the range of human symbolic activity, and of the methods of its interpretation, would surely offer new views of a wide range of issues concerning the relations between science and human culture at large.

4. 'RHETORICAL' APPROACHES

The third category of methods for studying scientific language, the 'rhetorical' approach, concerns itself not with the meaning of language, but with its other functions. In its widest sense, the discipline of rhetoric studies the ways in which language is used in argument, the means by which persuasion is effected by a certain form of words deployed in a specific relationship between speaker and audience (or, by extension, between writer and readership). In other words, rhetoric deals with the uses of language, as opposed to its meaning; or with its ritualised production in certain situations, as opposed to its conceptual content.

Unfortunately, philosophical discussions of rhetorical theory have been few and far between. The ancient antagonism between philosophy and rhetoric, dating from Socrates' arguments with the Sophists, has inclined philosophers to believe that rhetoric is unworthy of their attention, except in so far as it requires denunciation in the terms which Locke pioneered. On the other hand, some recent theorists of language, including hermeneuticists and semioticians, have been keen to link their approaches to that of the ancient discipline. And historians of science have also been given increasing attention to rhetoric in recent years.

One aspect of this has been the recovery of the historical importance of the discipline, particularly in relation to the Scientific Revolution; another has been the attempt to discern rhetoric in action within scientific discourse of various forms and periods. The second of these fields will be our main concern here, although it is worth noting that significant work has also been done in the former area. From the research of Paul Oskar Kristeller since the 1940s, it has been recognised that the revival of classical rhetoric was an important part of the learned culture of the European Renaissance. Historians such as Walter Ong and Lisa Jardine have mapped changing attitudes in the Humanist disciplines of rhetoric and dialectic, and have suggested how such changes might have had a lasting influence on the progress of the Scientific Revolution. More recently, scholars such as Steven Shapin and Peter Dear have been showing how scientists of the seventeenth century faced problems concerning the literary representation of their experiments, and the mobilisation of linguistic resources to persuade their readers; problems which were implicitly rhetorical. Barbara Shapiro has further argued that the methods and standards of demonstration which were found appropriate for deployment in the new science were those of traditional rhetorical fields, such as the law. From this work, an outline picture is emerging of the long-term importance of the renaissance revival of rhetoric, as a contributory factor in the seventeenth-century Scientific Revolution.

Quite independently of the results of this historical enquiry into the influence of rhetoric as a discipline, it can be argued on theoretical grounds that rhetorical properties always inhere in scientific language. Any use of language to persuade or move an audience can be analysed rhetorically, and this applies to science as to all fields in which language is used. The distinctive features of such a rhetorical analysis are twofold. Firstly, it does not distinguish between the 'content' of science (its theoretical ideas) and the 'style' in which they are presented. Rhetoric has always treated content and style as inextricable; its analysis is focused on the ritual regularities of expression which make a particular piece of language representative of a certain oratorical or textual genre. It is this feature of rhetorical analysis which gives it appeal to modern linguistic theorists anxious to deny 'metaphysical' distinctions between content and style in discourse. Secondly, rhetorical analysis concerns itself with the relationship between speaker or writer and audience, and in this way opens out to wider historical study of the contexts of scientific communication and the functions of scientific texts.

Understood in this sense, an analysis of scientific language as rhetoric can find encouragement in the writings of authors as widely influential, but as divergent in their general outlook, as Thomas Kuhn and Michel Foucault. One of the implications of Kuhn's crucial concept of a 'paradigm', introduced in his major work *The Structure of Scientific Revolutions* (1962), is that some kind of rhetorical analysis of science is called for. Kuhn describes a paradigm as a model problem-solution, concretised in the form of a textbook and perpetuated by a system of instruction, from which it cannot be entirely abstracted. As David Hollinger has indicated, Kuhn's importance for historians lies primarily in his having related scientific practice to the continuing authority of tradition; a tradition which is understood not as comprising certain abstract principles or concepts, but as embodied in the textual forms of concrete exemplars enforced as conventions of practice. To adopt M. D. King's phrase, Kuhn has made science out to be, not a world view or a set of methodological prescriptions, but 'a system of traditional authority'.[15]

If he is interpreted in this way, Kuhn's analysis has points of contact with that of Foucault in his 1971 address, 'L'Ordre du discours'. Foucault commends a study of discourse which would concentrate particularly on the institutions of pedagogy, such as academic disciplines, which 'constitute a system of control in the production of discourse'. He therefore urges that we are 'not to burrow to the hidden core of discourse, to the heart of the thought or meaning manifested in it; instead, taking the discourse itself, its appearance and its regularity, . . . we should look for its external conditions of existence'.[16]

Given the recommendations of Kuhn and Foucault, it is perhaps unsurprising that one of the main problems recently illuminated by a rhetorical perspective on scientific language is that of the maintenance of disciplines. Wilda Anderson, for example, has suggestively discussed the contribution of certain rhetorical forms to sustaining the identity of the discipline of chemistry during the Enlightenment. Focusing on the *Dictionnaire de Chymie* (1766) of Pierre-Joseph Macquer, she shows how its structure manifested the possible interconnections of the different parts of chemistry, but avoided imposing a dogmatic system upon it. Macquer's introductory review of the history of the subject also consolidated its unity by providing a historical legitimacy for its practitioners, and justified its claims to be a 'philosophical' discipline with authority to oversee a variety of practical arts.

Other historians have applied a rhetorical approach to understanding the functions of public addresses and orations. These have been shown to utilise traditional linguistic forms to appeal to certain audiences, thereby securing the legitimacy of disciplines and the positions of particular practitioners therein. Herman Boerhaave's orations at the University of Leyden in the early eighteenth century, the eulogies of Vicq d'Azyr in the Société Royale de Médecine in the 1770s and 1780s, and the *éloges* of Georges Cuvier in the Institut de France in the 1800s, have all been subjected to rhetorical analysis of this kind.[17]

Aside from serving to sustain the unity of disciplines, rhetoric in scientific language can have other functions. For example, the means by which scientific writings attempt to convey a representation of the 'facts' of experiments can also be seen as inherently rhetorical. A number of writers have advanced the argument that scientific language can never be simply and purely descriptive, that it inevitably deploys linguistic artifice and formal devices to persuade the reader of the 'factual' status of what is described. This point of view has been developed, and applied to examples of modern scientific research papers, by Joseph Gusfield, Steve Woolgar, Nigel Gilbert and Michael Mulkay, among others.

Some of these writers have argued that, because scientific 'facts' are rhetorically constructed, analysts should abandon any attempt to read through scientific texts to the social or experimental context in which they were produced. Gilbert and Mulkay, for example, argue that any sociological account of scientists' practices of operating upon nature would be an arbitrary imposition of a single meaning upon the many varieties of scientific rhetoric. The sociologist's is just one account among many, and 'almost every single account is rendered doubtful by its apparent inconsistency with other, equally plausible, versions of events'.[18]

To this kind of argument, historians are likely to respond that the variation among possible accounts of science does not by itself indicate that choice between them is entirely arbitrary; it simply raises the question of the methods which are appropriate to elucidate a valid historical description. Arguing along these lines in their recent book, *Leviathan and the Air-pump* (1985), Steven Shapin and Simon Schaffer have used techniques of the rhetorical analysis of scientific discourse, but have not shirked the historian's duty to place that discourse in its historical context.[19]

Shapin and Schaffer have investigated the pioneering construction of a language of experimental description by Robert Boyle in the mid-seventeenth century. They describe how every feature of what they call Boyle's 'literary technology' was tailored to the purposes of conveying a persuasive account of the experiments he described. The prolixity of Boyle's prose, his relentless description of circumstantial details, even of failed experiments, and the meticulous diagrams of apparatus he provided, were all means towards a basically rhetorical end: the persuasion of the reader of the factual status of his accounts. 'Appropriate moral postures' also enhanced the persuasiveness of Boyle's descriptions; these included candidness about failures, modesty in advancing opinions and a reluctance to engage in disputes. And in addition, the factual credentials of the accounts depended upon their being correctly witnessed by reliable men, preferably of gentle birth, and on the names and rank of those witnesses being recorded. According to these authors, many of the features of the rhetorical construction of scientific research papers, which sociologists of science have identified in modern examples of the genre, had their origins in the verbose writings of Robert Boyle.

Shapin and Schaffer push their analysis further, beyond the level of the rhetorical devices in Boyle's texts. By exploring the differences between Boyle and Thomas Hobbes, they show how disagreements about the interpretation of experiments disclose fundamental epistemological differences over the way in which knowledge was to be constructed, and these in their turn are connected with alternative political visions. The social order or 'polity' which was constructed among experimentalists, or between them and their audiences, was integrated within the social and political order of society at large. In this way,

Shapin and Schaffer link the experimental and discursive practices of Robert Boyle and his allies in the early Royal Society with the consolidation of social and political stability in Restoration England in the 1660s.

This well-received recent book shows how the rhetorical dimension of scientific discourse is beginning to be recognised among historians. It also indicates that the discussion of scientific language as rhetoric opens out naturally into the elucidation of the context of science, because to portray language as rhetorical is to indicate its uses in the situation in which it is deployed. The rhetorical approach then, no less than that which I have called 'hermeneutic or semantic', is well adapted to the needs of historians who seek to grasp the development of science in its historical context. The 'symbolic' approach, as we have seen, is likewise capable of connecting the language of science with its context; in this case via an account of the attitudes to language which are found to be characteristic of the cultural milieu.

All three approaches seem compatible with the historian's usual aim of understanding the development of science in its cultural and social context; they thus promise to reward further development and application in historical research. There remain of course theoretical problems, which I have not been able to broach in an essay of this length. In particular, the question arises of the compatibility of the three methods, given the very different philosophies of language which underlie them. Historians have a tendency to be eclectic in their choice of conceptual tools, but the genuine philosophical difficulties in the way of reconciling these perspectives should not be brushed aside. What is needed of course is further conceptual analysis of methods in conjunction with more empirical investigations of areas of the history of science where they might profitably be applied. This review is intended to point the way to such further investigations, by suggesting a pattern for understanding what has already been done.

ACKNOWLEDGEMENTS

I am grateful to Greg Myers and John Christie, for their helpful comments on an earlier draft of this paper.

NOTES

1. Martin Jay, 'Should intellectual history take a linguistic turn? Reflections on the Habermas-Gadamer debate', in Dominick LaCapra and Steven L. Kaplan (eds.), *Modern European intellectual history: reappraisals and new perspectives* (Ithaca and London, 1982), p. 106.
2. Michel Foucault, *The order of things: an archaeology of the human sciences* (London, 1970), p. 298.
3. Ian Hacking, *Why does language matter to philosophy?* (Cambridge, 1975), p. 10; Richard Rorty, *Philosophy and the mirror of nature* (Princeton, 1979), p. xiii.
4. The phrase is from Mark Cousins and Athar Hussain, *Michel Foucault* (Basingstoke, 1984), pp. 77–8, who give four meanings of the term 'discourse' in contemporary theory.

5. Richard F. Jones, 'Science and English prose style in the third quarter of the seventeenth century', *Publications of the modern language association of America*, 45 (1930), 977–1009.
6. Thomas Sprat, *The history of the Royal Society of London* (London, 1667), pp. 112, 113.
7. John Locke, *An essay concerning human understanding* (Oxford, 1975), pp. 490–508, quotation on p. 508.
8. Geoffrey Cantor, 'Light and Enlightenment: an exploration of mid-eighteenth-century modes of discourse', pp. 67–106, in David C. Lindberg and Geoffrey Cantor, *The discourse of light from the Middle Ages to the Enlightenment* (Los Angeles, 1985).
9. For discussion of the historical background, and general philosophy of hermeneutics (though neither offers much help with methods), see: Hans-Georg Gadamer, *Philosophical hermeneutics* (tr. D. E. Linge, Berkeley, 1976); Paul Ricoeur, *Hermeneutics and the human sciences* (tr. John B. Thompson, Cambridge, 1981).
10. Roger Cooter, *The cultural meaning of popular science: phrenology and the organisation of consent in nineteenth-century Britain* (Cambridge, 1984), quotations on pp. 110, 119, 190.
11. Karl M. Figlio, 'The metaphor of organisation: an historiographical perspective on the biomedical sciences of the early nineteenth century', *History of science*, 14 (1976), 17–53, quotation on p. 26.
12. Ibid., p. 26.
13. Robert M. Young, 'Darwin's metaphor: does nature select?' pp. 79–125, in Young, *Darwin's metaphor: nature's place in Victorian culture* (Cambridge, 1985).
14. Keith Michael Baker, 'On the problem of the ideological origins of the French Revolution', pp. 197–219 in LaCapra and Kaplan (eds.), *Modern European intellectual history*; William J. Bouwsma, 'From history of ideas to history of meaning', *Journal of interdisciplinary history*, 12 (1981), 279–92.
15. M. D. King, 'Reason, tradition, and the progressiveness of science', pp. 97–116, in Gary Gutting (ed.), *Paradigms and revolutions* (Notre Dame, Indiana, 1980), esp. pp. 103, 108–9.
16. Michel Foucault, *L'Ordre du discours*, tr. as 'The discourse on language', pp. 215–37 in Foucault, *The archaeology of knowledge and the discourse on language* (Tr. A. M. Sheridan Smith, New York, 1976), p. 229.
17. *Boerhaave's orations* (tr. E. Kegel-Brinkgreve and A. M. Luyendijk-Elshout, Leiden, 1983); Daniel Roche, 'Talent, reason and sacrifice: the physician during the Enlightenment', pp. 66–88, in Robert Forster and Orest Ranum (eds.), *Medicine and society in France* (Baltimore and London, 1980); Dorinda Outram, 'The language of natural power: the *éloges* of Georges Cuvier and the public language of nineteenth-century science', *History of science*, 16 (1978), 153–78.
18. G. Nigel Gilbert and Michael Mulkay, *Opening Pandora's box: a sociological analysis of scientists' discourse* (Cambridge, 1984), p. 11.
19. For theoretical comments, and for an introduction to the literature covering these arguments, see Steven Shapin, 'Talking history: reflections on discourse analysis', *Isis*, 75 (1984), 125–30.

FURTHER READING

Hans Aarsleff, *From Locke to Saussure: essays on the study of language and intellectual history* (London, 1982).

Wilda C. Anderson, *Between the library and the laboratory: the language of chemistry in eighteenth-century France* (Baltimore and London, 1984).

Andrew Benjamin, Geoffrey Cantor and John Christie (eds.), *The figural and the literal* (Manchester, 1986).

William J. Bouwsma, 'From history of ideas to history of meaning', *Journal of interdisciplinary history*, 12 (1981), 279–92.

Ernst Cassirer, *The philosophy of symbolic forms* (3 vols., New Haven, 1955).

Roger Cooter, *The cultural meaning of popular science: phrenology and the organisation of consent in nineteenth-century Britain* (Cambridge, 1984).

Peter Dear, '*Totius in verba*: rhetoric and authority in the early Royal Society', *Isis*, 76 (1985), 145–61.

Hubert L. Dreyfus and Paul Rabinow, *Michel Foucault: beyond structuralism and hermeneutics* (Brighton, 1982).

Michael Ermath, 'Mindful matters: the empire's new codes and the plight of modern European intellectual history', *Journal of modern history*, 57 (1985), 506–27.

Michel Foucault, *The order of things: an archaeology of the human sciences* (London, 1970).

G. Nigel Gilbert and Michael Mulkay, *Opening Pandora's box: a sociological analysis of scientists' discourse* (Cambridge, 1984).

Joseph Gusfield, 'The literary rhetoric of science: comedy and pathos in drinking driver research', *American sociological review*, 41 (1976), 16–34.

David Hollinger, 'T. S. Kuhn's theory of science and its implications for history', pp. 195–222 in Gary Gutting (ed.), *Paradigms and revolutions* (Notre Dame, Ind., 1980).

Lisa Jardine, *Francis Bacon: discovery and the art of discourse* (Cambridge, 1974).

Ludmilla Jordanova (ed.), *Languages of nature: critical essays on science and literature* (London, 1986).

James Knowlson, *Universal language schemes in England and France 1600–1800* (Toronto and Buffalo, 1975).

Paul Oskar Kristeller, *Renaissance thought and its sources* (New York, 1979).

Thomas S. Kuhn, *The structure of scientific revolutions* (Chicago, 1962).

Dominick LaCapra and Steven L. Kaplan (eds.), *Modern European intellectual history: reappraisals and new perspectives* (Ithaca and London, 1982).

J. G. Merquior, *Foucault* (Fontana Modern Masters, London, 1985).

Walter J. Ong, *Ramus: method and the decay of dialogue* (Cambridge, Mass., 1958).

Richard Rorty (ed.), *The linguistic turn: recent essays in philosophical method* (Chicago, 1967), 'Introduction', pp. 1–39.

Vivian Salmon (ed.), *The works of Francis Lodwick* (London, 1972).

Simon Schaffer, 'Making certain', *Social studies of science*, 14 (1984), 137–52.

Steven Shapin, 'Talking history: reflections on discourse analysis', *Isis*, 75 (1984), 125–30.

Steven Shapin, 'Pump and circumstance: Robert Boyle's literary technology', *Social studies of science*, 14 (1984), 481–520.

Steven Shapin and Simon Schaffer, *Leviathan and the air-pump: Hobbes, Boyle and the experimental life* (Princeton, 1985).

Barbara Shapiro, *Probability and certainty in seventeenth-century England* (Princeton, 1983).

Mary M. Slaughter, *Universal languages and scientific taxonomy in the seventeenth century* (Cambridge, 1982),

Steve Woolgar, 'Discovery: logic and sequence in a scientific text', pp. 239–68, in Karin D. Knorr, Roger Krohn and Richard Whitley (eds.), *The social process of scientific investigation* (Dordrecht, 1981).

SECTION IC: PHILOSOPHICAL PROBLEMS

10

CONTINENTAL PHILOSOPHY AND THE HISTORY OF SCIENCE

GARY GUTTING

Although twentieth-century philosophy of science in the dominant Anglo-American tradition has shown unparalleled sophistication in its analyses of the content and methods of science, it has offered little in the way of a reflective assessment of the overall significance of science as a way of knowing. The positivists simply assumed that science is the only source of knowledge about the world. Even their discussions of the verifiability principle, which concerned demarcating science from non-science, presupposed that only science yields synthetic knowledge. More recent analytic philosophers of science have rejected many of the fundamental positivist theses, especially those concerning the relation of scientific theories to observations. However, even though post-positivist thinking about science has been a decisive advance in several respects, it has, for the most part, left untouched positivism's legacy of an uncritical attitude towards the ultimate significance of scientific knowledge.

One of the most distinctive and valuable features of recent Continental history and philosophy of science (which we may take to mean work in this area done in Germany and France for roughly the last 60 years) has been its explicit focus on the *critique* of science. This is not to say that Continental historians and philosophers have been uniformly negative in their assessment of the cognitive status of science; as we shall see, there have been sharp divisions on this issue. But almost all Continental work, in contrast to its Anglo-American counterpart, pays a great deal of attention to the cognitive value of science in comparison to other ways of knowing.

The following survey focuses on three major areas of Continental work in the history and philosophy of science:

(1) philosophers (particularly, Husserl, Merleau-Ponty and Heidegger), associated with the phenomenological and existentialist traditions;

(2) Marxist historians and philosophers associated with the Frankfurt School, particularly Jürgen Habermas;

(3) historians and philosophers associated with a major French network of thinkers that includes Gaston Bachelard, Georges Canguilhem and Michel Foucault.

The survey is selective and makes no pretence to comprehensiveness. For example, it deliberately ignores a significant body of recent European work (by, e.g. Stegmüller and by the German Popperians) that is closely and explicitly tied to standard Anglo-American history and philosophy of science. Also, there is no treatment of important French work, especially by Cavaillès and Ladrière, on the philosophy of mathematics. Further, particular emphasis has been given to the work of Bachelard and Canguilhem, firstly because it is not well known in the English-speaking world and secondly because it has a particularly strong historical emphasis.

1. PHENOMENOLOGICAL AND EXISTENTIALIST APPROACHES

Phenomenology and existentialism dominated Continental philosophy from the end of the Second World War until the 1960s. Although the most important Continental thinkers today are definitely outside these traditions (Paul Ricoeur is a major exception), they remain a powerful historical influence. Phenomenological and existentialist attitudes towards science varied considerably. Some writers – Sartre, for example – paid science scant attention, apparently regarding it as irrelevant to the central concerns of philosophy. Others, however, made it a fundamental theme of their reflection. Husserl, in particular, gave a great deal of attention to the philosophy of logic and of mathematics and to the philosophy of the natural sciences. Especially important is his discussion in *Die Krisis der europäischen Wissenschaften und die transcendentale Phänomenologie* of scientific idealisation, a discussion strongly influenced by the historical work of Alexandre Koyré on Galileo. Husserl's one-time student, Martin Heidegger, was also centrally concerned with science and, especially, the significance of technology in human existence. Another student of Husserl, Alfred Schutz, developed a very important phenomenological approach to the social sciences. In France, Maurice Merleau-Ponty's phenomenological analyses were deeply informed by (and critical of) work in behavioural and Gestalt psychology.

All these thinkers had, of course, their own distinctive emphases and positions. But they all also shared a general view of science that can be fairly characterised as the 'phenomenological view.' This can be summarised in three fundamental propositions. The first is an epistemological thesis, asserting that scientific concepts are abstractions from the concrete givens of immediate ('lived') experience. The second is the metaphysical claim that scientific descriptions of the world express just one abstract dimension of the world's reality. The third is the ethical judgement that profound moral evils such as dehumanisation and alienation ensue if we ignore the truth of the first two theses and regard scientific truth as the only or ultimate truth about the world.

The key to understanding the first thesis is Husserl's concept of the *Lebenswelt* (life-world). The life-world is, roughly, the pre-scientific world of our immediate everyday experiences; experiences that, in Husserl's view, form the ultimate ground for even the most highly theoretical of our scientific concepts. The life-world is marked by two key features. Firstly, it is *complete* in the sense that it contains in a fully concrete way every reality there is. Secondly, it is *fundamental* in the sense that it is the ultimate source and ground of all meaning and truth. Science, by contrast, is *incomplete* and *derivative* in relation to the life-world. This is because it selects just some features of the life-world (for example, those susceptible to mathematical analysis) and develops its own realm of meaning and truth by abstracting and idealising the features selected. Because of this, a proper assessment of science requires a twofold movement of understanding. On the one hand, we need to explicate the various methods of abstraction and idealisation whereby science constructs its concepts from the experiential givens of the life-world. On the other hand, we must attain an understanding (via phenomenological analysis) of the concrete life-world structures that have provided the starting-point of science. In this way we can appreciate the significance of a scientific result by putting it in its proper place as derivative from the life-world.

The second thesis moves from this view of science as epistemologically subordinated to the life-world to a corresponding view of science as metaphysically subordinated to the life-world. This does not mean that phenomenologists deny the objective reality of the scientific world. On the contrary, they insist that science reveals a realm of objective facts. But they claim that it is precisely its objectivity that makes the scientific description of reality abstract and derivative. This conclusion follows from the phenomenological view of the nature and origin of objectivity. On the concrete level of the life-world, reality is not split into the duality of experiencing subject and experienced object. Rather, the fundamental reality is a unity of subject and object ('man-in-the-world'). What is ultimately real are the concrete relations of presence, encounter and dialogue; the notions of separate subjects and objects (e.g. Descartes's thinking and material substances) are abstractions from lived reality. It is, however, both possible and useful to work with such abstractions and, particularly, to focus on the isolated material object. The advantage of such a move lies in the possibilities it opens up for precise, quantitative description and technological control. The move is made by considering a thing entirely in its own right, ignoring all dimensions tied to its encounter with an experiencing subject (e.g. secondary qualities and emotional connotations). In the – admittedly ideal – limit, when all relations to subjects have been eliminated, we reach pure objective reality, the ultimate object of science. So, while there is no doubt that science reveals objective reality, this reality is in fact just one abstract dimension of the full concreteness of the world.

The third thesis concerns the unfortunate but natural tendency of science to ignore its origins and present the world it has abstracted from lived experience as an autonomous, concrete and – at least potentially – complete reality. According to Husserl, this self-misunderstanding arises because each new generation is typically able to take for granted as pre-given and unproblematic the achievements of its predecessors. Thus, the world-view of Newtonian mechanics, which originally appeared as a highly counter-intuitive theory, was regarded by the beginning of the twentieth century (by Bohr, for example) as no more than a formulation of common sense. The difficulty is that scientists lose sight of the elaborate abstractions and idealisations by which the results they take for granted were achieved. Inverse to the continual progress of science is a continual forgetting of its origins and a resulting loss in our understanding of the ultimate meaning of scientific concepts.

This inevitable loss of scientific meaning leads to crises, such as occurred in physics in the early twentieth century, that require the scientist to return to the roots of his concepts and rethink them in terms of their life-world origin. But much more significant than these internal scientific crises are the effects of the loss of scientific meaning on society and civilisation as a whole. If human beings accept as the ultimate reality a world from which everything connected to their individual and communal subjectivity is excluded, they will end by renouncing the aesthetic, cultural and moral values that are essential to their humanity. In particular, our current moral and cultural crises result from a failure to situate science properly in the human life-world. Husserl and also Heidegger (in his reflections on technology) have developed this line of thought with great acuteness and sensitivity.

2. MARXIST APPROACHES

At just about the same time that Husserl's *Krisis* initiated the major strand of phenomenological reflection on science, the German philosopher Max Horkheimer was developing what became a highly influential neo-Marxist approach to science. Horkheimer agreed with Husserl's central claim that the objectifying methods of science do not represent the only legitimate sort of knowledge and that the delusion that they do is a major threat to human values and culture. But Horkheimer thought Husserl's phenomenological approach was no remedy for the crisis posed by our misunderstanding of modern science. In his view, the root of the crisis was the 'traditional' concept of scientific theory as an entirely disinterested, value-neutral account of the world, a conception that denies from the beginning any intrinsic connection between scientific knowledge and the practical interests of human life. Like all major Western thinkers from Plato to Hegel, Husserl accepted this traditional conception of theory and so, for all his sensitivity to the crisis of Western science, still acquiesced in the split between knowledge and action that sustained the crisis. According to Horkheimer, the solution was to reject the traditional notion of theory in favour of a new concept of *critical theory*; i.e. of theory as deriving from the fundamental practical interests of human life and hence essentially and intrinsically directed towards the improvement of human existence.

The work of Jürgen Habermas represents a systematic and sustained effort to develop and ground this conception of critical theory. Habermas's fundamental project is to provide a contemporary counterpart to the classical ideal of building human society on the basis of a body of *practical knowledge* (i.e. a knowledge of basic human values). Before the modern era, Western societies generally thought they had an adequate grasp of the ultimate values that should guide human lives; but they lacked the technical resources to realise these values. Today we have greater technical resources than our ancestors ever dreamed of; but, ironically, the very advances in scientific rationality that have brought this about have also apparently undermined the rational standing of values. It seems that our ultimate values must be regarded simply as non-cognitive givens (e.g. pure expressions of will or feeling). The relation of reason to values seems entirely instrumental; it can tell us how to attain goals most effectively but can say nothing about what goals should be pursued.

Habermas rejects this typically modern view and undertakes to show that reason itself is essentially value-oriented. Specifically, he argues that: (1) all human knowledge is value-oriented in the sense that its very status as knowledge derives from its essential connection with certain basic human interests (which he calls 'cognitive interests'); and (2) these cognitive interests are themselves not just contingent givens but rather correspond to necessary orientations of reason itself.

In supporting these theses, Habermas takes a fundamentally Kantian epistemological stance; that is, he treats knowledge as the result of the constituting activity of a transcendental subject. However, he accepts, first, Hegel's correction of Kant according to which the transcendental subject must be regarded as a temporal entity subject to historical evolution; and, second, Marx's correction of Hegel, according to which the history of consciousness must not be understood idealistically as the life of a pure spirit but rather materialistically as the life of the human community rooted in the realities of our biological nature. Habermas develops his epistemology in a way that frequently comes very close to the viewpoint of the American pragmatists.

Because his approach is broadly Kantian, Habermas sees it as fundamentally opposed to positivism, which he takes to be in essence a rejection of any conception of transcendental subjectivity. Specifically, he develops his epistemology by a sustained critical reflection on the nineteenth-century origins of contemporary positivism, with particular emphasis on positivist methodology of science. His central criticism of positivist methodology is very similar to that urged by many Anglo-American critics of positivism: that the positivist account distorts science by regarding it solely as a system of propositions and hence ignoring the human activities that create this system. If, Habermas maintains, we rigorously follow out the conception of science as a human activity, the resulting methodology of science will inevitably lead us to the standpoint of transcendental epistemology.

The key to this return to Kant is the notion, mentioned above, of a cognitive interest. This Habermas defines as follows: 'I term *interests* the basic orientations rooted in specific fundamental conditions of the possible reproduction and self-constitution of the human species'.[1] As such, an interest corresponds to a general need that must be satisfied if humans are to survive and develop as specifically human. According to Habermas, there are three basic cognitive interests: the empirical-analytic interest, the communicative interest and the emancipative interest. The empirical-analytic interest is concerned with technical control of the natural world, the communicative interest with the mutual understanding presupposed by the functioning of society and the emancipative interest with the liberation of persons from psychological and political forces of oppression. For each of these interests, Habermas maintains not only that it is necessary for the survival or the fully human development of our species but also that it corresponds to a distinctive and irreducible form of theoretical knowledge. Thus, human knowledge takes the form not only of the predictive-explanatory theories of the natural sciences but also of the understanding (*Verstehen*) of hermeneutic social sciences and of the liberating knowledge of what Habermas calls critical social science.

The core of Habermas's work has been the elaboration and implementation of his idea of a critical social science. He finds a model for such a science in psychoanalysis, which is designed to free individuals from the tyranny of neurotic symptoms by uncovering the true meaning of thoughts and actions, meanings distorted by the process of repression. Roughly, what psychoanalysis does for individuals, critical social theory will do for society. In both psychoanalysis and critical social theory, the notion of communication is central. Just as psychological liberation is attained by removing distortions in the communication of unconscious meanings, so social liberation requires the elimination of the power mechanisms that prevent free communication among the members of society. Consequently, much of Habermas's effort to ground a critical social theory has focused on the development of a 'theory of communicative competence' designed to determine the conditions of possibility for ideally free communication. Given this as a foundation, Habermas proposes to construct a critical theory of social evolution through a reconstruction of Marxist historical materialism. All this has added up to a major interdisciplinary enterprise, drawing on and contributing to work in philosophy, linguistics, psychology and sociology.

3. THE FRENCH NETWORK: BACHELARD, CANGUILHEM AND FOUCAULT

The phenomenological and Marxist approaches to science discussed so far have operated on a rather high level of philosophical generalisation and have paid little attention to specific episodes in the history of science. There is, however, a major twentieth-century French approach to the philosophy of science that is deeply and firmly rooted in the history of science. This approach is closely tied to a long French tradition in the history and philosophy of science that began with Comte and was continued in the work of Duhem, Poincaré, Meyerson and Koyré. The central figures of this approach are Gaston Bachelard, who developed his views on science in a series of books published from the 1920s through to the 1950s, and Georges Canguilhem, Bachelard's successor as director of the Institut d'Histoire des Sciences et des Techniques at the University of Paris. Both these thinkers have exerted a strong influence on such major contemporary philosophers and historians as Michel Foucault, Louis Althusser and Michel Serres. Although not so well known outside France, Bachelard and Canguilhem have provided a major alternative to both the phenomenological and the Marxist approaches to science.

Bachelard's thought can be fruitfully viewed as a sustained attempt to understand the nature of reason and rationality by reflecting on the history of science. History of science is relevant because, according to Bachelard, reason is best known by an understanding of science, and science is best known by an understanding of its history. The first thesis derives from Bachelard's conviction that the structures of reason are apparent not in abstract principles but in the concrete employments of reason. Norms of rationality are constituted in the very process of applying our thoughts to particular problems, and science has been the primary locus of success in such applications. The proof of the second thesis – that science is best known through its history – lies in the repeated refutation of *a priori* philosophical ideals of rationality (e.g. those of Descartes and Kant) by historical scientific developments. There are, then, no viable accounts of rationality except those derived from the historical developments of scientific reason. To understand reason, philosophy must 'go to the school of science'.

The rationality that philosophy tries to discover in the history of science is no more fixed and monolithic than that history itself. As we shall see shortly,

Bachelard finds sharp breaks in the history of science and corresponding changes in the conception of reason. Moreover, Bachelard reminds us that there is, strictly speaking, no such thing as the history of science, only various histories of different regions of scientific work. Correspondingly, philosophy cannot hope to uncover a single, unified conception of rationality from its reflection on the history of science; it will find only various 'regions' of rationality.

Because of his demand that the philosopher of science work from the historical development of the sciences, the centre of Bachelard's philosophy of science is his model of scientific change. This model is build around three key epistemological categories: epistemological breaks, epistemological obstacles and epistemological acts.

Bachelard employs the concept of an epistemological break (*rupture*) in two contexts. First, he uses it to characterise the way in which scientific knowledge splits off from and even contradicts common-sense experiences and beliefs. This sense of 'break' is fundamental for Bachelard, since he sees it as constituting science as a distinctive cognitive realm. One very simple example of such a break is modern chemistry's claim that glass is very similar to wurtzite (zinc sulphite). The comparison is one that would never occur to common sense, since it is not based on any overt resemblance of the two substances but on the fact that they have analogous crystalline structures. Thus, science breaks with ordinary experience by placing the objects of experience under new categories that reveal properties and relations not available to ordinary sense perception.

The second sort of epistemological break is that which occurs between two scientific conceptualisations. For Bachelard, the most striking and important of such breaks came with relativity and quantum theory, which he saw as initiating a 'new scientific spirit'. This 'new spirit' involved not only radically new conceptions of nature but also new conceptions of scientific method (e.g. new criteria of explanatory adequacy). Bachelard's detailed treatments of this topic preceded by two or three decades similar discussions by Anglo-American historians of science such as Kuhn and Feyerabend.

The language of epistemological 'breaks' suggests that there is something to be broken, a barrier that must be shattered. Bachelard follows out this suggestion with his notion of an *epistemological obstacle*. An epistemological obstacle is any concept or method that prevents an epistemological break. Obstacles are residues from previous ways of thinking that, whatever value they may have had in the past, have begun to block the path of inquiry. Common sense is, of course, a major source of epistemological obstacles. Thus, the animism of primititive common sense, which inclined people to explain the world by analogy with vital processes (sex, digestion, etc.) was an obstacle to the development of a mechanistic physics. Likewise, the still strong common-sense idea that phenomena must be the attributes of an underlying substance blocked the rejection of the ether as the locus of electromagnetic waves. More generally, Bachelard regards the common-sense mind's reliance on images as a breeding ground for epistemological obstacles. However, epistemological obstacles may also arise from successful scientific work that has outlived its value. The most striking of such cases occur when the concepts and principles of an established theory lead us to regard new proposals as obviously absurd; e.g. the counter-intuitive feel of the rejection of classical determinism in quantum physics. But previously successful scientific methods can also become epistemological obstacles. For example, the emphasis on direct observation that led in the seventeenth century to major breaks with Aristotelian science became an obstacle to eighteenth-century developments of atomic theories. Finally, traditional philosophy, with its tendency to canonise as necessary truths the contingent features of one historical period of thought, is another major source of epistemological obstacles.

The views and attitudes that constitute epistemological obstacles are often not explicitly formulated by those they constrain but rather operate at the level of implicit assumptions or cognitive and perceptual habits. Consequently, Bachelard proposed to develop a set of techniques designed to bring them to our full reflective awareness. He spoke of these techniques as effecting a 'psychoanalysis' of reason. Bachelard's use of this term signals his aim of unearthing unconscious or semi-conscious structures of thought, but it does not express a commitment to the details of Freudian theory.

The concept of an *epistemological act* counterbalances that of an epistemological obstacle. Whereas epistemological obstacles impede scientific progress through the inertia of old ideas, 'the notion of epistemological acts corresponds to the leaps of scientific genius that introduce unexpected impulses into the course of scientific development'.[2] An epistemological act is not, however, just a change; it has a positive value that represents an improvement in our scientific accounts. There are, accordingly, different values that must be accorded to different episodes in the history of science. Consequently, Bachelard holds that writing history of science is different from writing political or social history. In the latter case, 'the ideal is, rightly, an *objective* narration of the facts. This ideal requires that the historian *not judge*; and, if the historian imparts the values of his own time in order to assess the values of a past time, then we are right to accuse him of accepting "the myth of progress" '.[3] But in the case of the history of the natural sciences, progress is no myth. Present science represents an unquestionable advance over its past, and it is entirely appropriate for the historian of science to use the standards and values of the present to judge the past. Application of these standards results in a sharp division of the scientific past into '*l'histoire périmée*' (the history of 'outdated' science) and '*l'histoire sanctionée*' (the history of science judged valid by current standards).

This Bachelardian writing of the history of the past on the basis of the present is not equivalent to the now generally disdained 'Whiggish' approach to the history of science. For one thing, Bachelardian history does not try to understand past science in terms of present concepts. It realises the need to explicate the past in its own terms. For another, there is no assumption of the immutable adequacy of present science. Precisely because they are scientific, the present achievements by which we evaluate the past may themselves be surpassed or corrected by future scientific development.

However, even though all scientific results are open to revision and some have been definitively rejected, others must be accepted as permanently valid achievements. Thus, Bachelard says that phlogiston theory is 'outdated because it rests on a fundamental error'. Historians who deal with it are working 'in the paleontology of a vanished scientific spirit'.[4] By contrast, Black's work on caloric, even though most of it has long been jettisoned, did yield the permanent achievement of the concept of specific heat.

How is this idea of unalterable progress consistent with Bachelard's insistence that all scientific results are open to revision? How can an achievement be 'permanent' and at the same time open to correction in the wake of an epistemological break? Bachelard's response is that an epistemological break is not merely the rejection of past science but also a preservation, via reformulation, of old ideas in a new and broader context of thought. Specifically, past results are replaced by generalisations that reject them as unconditionally correct but preserve them as correct under certain restricted conditions. Bachelard finds a model here in the development of non-Euclidean geometry. This development refutes the claim that the Euclidean postulates express the sole truth about geometry but at the same time presents these postulates as defining one exemplification of a more general class of geometries (i.e. Euclidean geometry is the structure geometry possessed by a space of zero curvature). In just the same way, Bachelard sees Newton's astronomy as a special case of Einstein's 'pan-astronomy'. This is so not merely because, to a certain approximation, Newtonian calculations yield the same numbers as Einsteinian calculations but because key Newtonian concepts such as mass and velocity can be shown to be special simple cases of the corresponding Einsteinian concepts. Bachelard characterises this process of replacement by generalisation as 'dialectical', not in the Hegelian sense of a synthesis of opposites but in the sense of a process of conceptual expansion whereby what previously appeared to be contraries (e.g. Euclidean and Lobachevskian geometries) are seen as complementary possibilities. Earlier concepts are not mysteriously 'sublated' into a higher unity but are *rectified* (corrected) on the basis of superior successor concepts that allow us to explain precisely the extent to which they are applicable.

This account of scientific change allows Bachelard to reject the *continuity* of science and still accept its *progress*. Science develops by a series of epistemological breaks that make it impossible to regard its history as a linear accumulation of truths within a single conceptual framework. The conceptual framework of science at one stage will be rejected as erroneous at later stages. Nonetheless, some of its results may be permanent scientific achievements in the sense that they will be preserved as special cases within all subsequent scientific frameworks. Each successive framework will represent progress over its predecessors in the sense that it has a more general perspective from which the range of validity of previous perspectives can be assessed.

The work of Georges Canguilhem complements that of Bachelard, in two ways. Firstly, whereas Bachelard was a philosopher who employed a historical method of analysis, Canguilhem is a historian with an acute (and essentially Bachelardian) philosophical sensitivity. Secondly, while Bachelard's reflection on science was primarily directed towards the physical sciences, Canguilhem's focus is on biology and the medical sciences. These differences give Canguilhem's thought its own distinctive cast and even on occasion lead him to significant disagreements with Bachelard (e.g. on the nature and significance of epistemological breaks). But on the whole, Canguilhem's work represents an extension and deepening of certain aspects of Bachelard's. Of particular interest for our purposes is Canguilhem's detailed formulation of a Bachelardian conception of the history of science.

For Canguilhem, the history of science is primarily the history of concepts; not, to cite some major alternatives, the history of terms, the history of phenomena, or even the history of theories. A history of terms reflects the naïve and all too common idea that there is some historical significance in finding people who, for example, spoke of mass before Newton, of atoms before Dalton, or of evolution before Darwin. Such history is misled by superficial similarities in language and ignores the really important question of whether two scientists had the same understanding of a given aspect of nature. A history centred on phenomena is concerned with who first observed or accurately described a given natural process or structure, without taking into account that the crucial factor is not what was observed but the interpretation involved in the observation. Thus, Priestley may have discovered oxygen in the sense of being the first to produce it in a laboratory and describe its phenomenal features accurately. But such a 'discovery' is of little significance for Canguilhem's history of science, since Priestley failed in the decisive matter of providing an adequate scientific understanding of oxygen, which he incorrectly interpreted as dephlogisticated air. The decisive achievement was Lavoisier's understanding of oxygen as a chemical element.

It might seem that Canguilhem's rejection of history of science as the history of the discovery of phenomena corresponds simply to a rejection of the positivists' sharp distinction of theory and observation. He is, we may think, drawing the obvious consequence of recognising that there are no scientifically interesting observed facts apart from their theoretical interpretations. This would suggest that Canguilhem's is, in fact, a history of theories. Why then does he insist that his primary concern is with concepts and not with theories?

To understand Canguilhem's view here, we need to distinguish – in a way that Anglo-American philosophers of science typically do not – between interpretation and theory. Most recent work in analytic philosophy of science has emphasised that scientific observation does not present us with pure, uninterpreted data; all scientific data are given as already interpreted. Canguilhem would agree with this point, which was, after all, emphasised by Bachelard long before Hanson, Kuhn, *et al.* But the typical Anglo-American discussion of this topic also assumes that the interpretation of data is a matter of reading them in terms of a theory; that is, in terms of a set of scientific generalisations put forward to explain the phenomena under investigation. Interpretation is seen as deriving from theoretical commitments. Aristotelians saw the motion of a heavy body swinging from a chain as a constrained fall because of their theory that falling bodies were seeking their natural place. Galileo saw it as the nearly periodic movement of a pendulum because of his theoretical principle of inert. On this view, the concepts whereby data are interpreted derive from the theories whereby they are explained. It is not surprising that some philosophers holding this view (Feyerabend, for example) took the further step of maintaining that the entire meaning of a concept or term is given by the role it plays in the statements of theory. This led to the puzzling conclusion that any revisions in theory entailed changes in the meaning of scientific concepts.

For Canguilhem, however, it is essential to separate the concepts that interpret data from the theories that explain them. A concept provides us with the initial understanding of a phenomenon that allows us to formulate in a scientifically useful way the question of how to explain it. Theories provide a variety of (often competing) ways of answering the explanatory question. Thus, Galileo introduced a new way of conceiving the motion of falling bodies. But in order to explain the motion so conceived, he, Descartes, and finally Newton introduced a series of different theories. Accordingly, Canguilhem can make sense of the same concept playing a role in very different theories – of, as he says, concepts that are 'theoretically polyvalent'. This in turn allows him to write historical accounts of the formation and transformation of concepts that operate at a different – and more fundamental – level than accounts of the succession of explanatory theories.

Canguilhem places great emphasis on the point that his history of scientific concepts does not itself pretend to have scientific status. This is in contrast with a number of other influential alternative conceptions of the history of science. There is, for example, the essentially positivist conception, articulated by Dijksterhuis (and earlier by Comte's disciple, Pierre Lafitte), of history of science as the 'laboratory' of epistemology. Here the idea is that the events and results of science's past are simply given to the historian as already constituted objects. The historian's function is to scrutinise these data – Lafitte spoke of the historian's 'mental microscope' – and use them to evaluate epistemological accounts of science.

Two other examples of history of science modelled on science itself are the 'externalist' and 'internalist' approaches so much discussed by Anglo-American historians of science. The externalist uses the techniques of psychology or the social sciences to relate scientific developments to economic, social, political or religious conditions. The internalist ignores such conditions in favour of the internal logic of a science's development; but he is still interested in employing the facts about this development to evaluate, in a broadly scientific way, generalisations about the nature of science. This, we might add, is particularly true of internalist history – e.g. that of Kuhn, Lakatos and Laudan – that is designed to illumine the philosophy of science. Here the historian views himself as an experimenter in Dijksterhuis's laboratory, using the data of history to test methodological principles and models of scientific development.

According to Canguilhem, what is common to all these scientific approaches to the history of science is their failure to see history itself as passing normative judgements about the science it studies. Consequently, to the model of history of science as a laboratory, he opposes the model of history of science as a law court in which 'judgements are made regarding the past of knowledge, or the knowledge of the past'.[5] On such a model, history of science is not a scientific discipline precisely because its explicitly normative intent excludes the value-free orientation characteristic of a scientific analysis.

But in just what sense does Canguilhem see history of science as evaluating (judging) the past of science? Here he invokes Bachelard's distinction of *l'histoire périmée* and *l'histoire sanctionée*, according to which past science is evaluated as outdated or validated on the basis of its relation to the results of current science. Thus, the historian's judgements are based on norms derived from an epistemological analysis informed (*à la* Bachelard) by current science.

Canguilhem also expresses the non-scientific nature of history of science in terms of the difference between its object and the object of a science. Whereas the object of history of science has, of course, a historical character, the objects of science have, as such, no history. In this context, an object's 'having a history' is not a matter of its merely having existed and changed over time. Rather, an object is historical (has a history) when it is regarded as essentially part of a process of historical development that is not finished. As historical, the object is essentially incomplete and hence not given in its full reality. The objects of sciences (even of 'historical' sciences such as geology or evolutionary biology) are not historical in this sense because science treats them – along with any history they may have – as givens completely available for analysis. The objects of the history of science are rather treated as only partially given, not fully determined. Specifically, this means that the normative judgements of the historian are not absolute assessments of the intrinsic scientific merit of a scientific development but are rather relative to the present state of science. The value and even the meaning of science's past may alter with its future progress. In this regard, the work of the historian of science is very similar to that of critics of art and literature.

Canguilhem regards his conception of the history of science as eliminating one major concern of many historians of science: the search for precursors of major scientific discoveries. A precursor, according to his wry definition, is 'someone of whom we know only after that he came before'.[6] In speaking of precursors, Canguilhem has particularly in mind the claim, frequently made by historians, that major scientific innovations by, for example, Copernicus and Darwin, were essentially anticipated by much earlier thinkers (e.g. Aristarchus and Diderot). Sometimes, in fact, it seems that the historian's goal is to find ever earlier precursors for any important scientific work. As Canguilhem points out, if this search for precursors is taken to the limit, then science ceases to have a history; all scientific achievements occurred in some initial golden age. In any case, he argues that the 'discovery' of a precursor is usually based on a failure to recognise fundamental conceptual differences that underlie superficially similar formulations. Those, for example, who think that Réaumur or Maupertuis were precursors of Mendel's work on heredity do not understand the distinctive nature of Mendel's concept of an independent hereditary character. Only under the most stringent conditions does Canguilhem allow any talk of scientists from different historical periods having pursued the same line of research or having made the same discovery.

But, although Canguilhem is firmly opposed to what, following J. T. Clark, he calls 'the virus of the precursor', this does not mean that he denies the need to understand the influence of earlier scientific work on later. Because science is a part of human culture, its discoveries are conditioned by the (explicit and implicit) education of those who make them. Here Canguilhem speaks very positively of understanding scientists' work in terms of what they have learned from their 'predecessors' and argues that failing to do this leads to the sort of empiricist or positivist history of science that denies the genuine historicity of science. Accordingly, we should not misunderstand Canguilhem's rejection of the search for a scientist's precursors in different historical periods as a refusal to consider the undeniably important influence of his predecessors in his own historico-cultural context. An adequate history of scientific concepts will have to pay detailed attention to such influences, as indeed Canguilhem himself does on many pages of his history of the concept of the reflex.

We turn finally to the work of Michel Foucault. Foucault made major contributions as a philosopher, a social historian, a literary analyst and a social and political critic. But his intellectual *métier*, as is apparent from the topics of his major books, was the history of thought; and, particularly, the history of scientific (or would-be scientific) thought. Foucault's approach to the history of scientific thought has strong connections to that of Bachelard, who taught at the Sorbonne during Foucault's student days, as well as to that of Canguilhem, who was Foucault's thesis advisor for his *doctorat d'état* in the history of science. (This thesis was published in 1961 as *Folie et déraison: l'histoire de la folie à l'âge classique*.) Foucault's earliest work (e.g. *Maladie mentale et personnalité*, published in 1954) was strongly influenced by phenomenology and existentialism. But he soon became disillusioned with what he later called their 'transcedental narcissism' and developed a historical method, the 'archaeology of knowledge', designed to analyse bodies of knowledge in terms of linguistic and social structures that operate at a level more fundamental than that of any constituting consciousness. This archaeology of knowledge can be regarded as a radicalisation of Bachelard's project of a psychoanalysis of knowledge. It is also in important respects an extension and transformation of Canguilhem's history of concepts.

Whereas Bachelard and Canguilhem focused on the physical and the biological sciences, respectively, Foucault was primarily concerned with the more 'dubious' human sciences (e.g. psychology and the social sciences). Contrary to some of his critics (and supporters), Foucault does not attempt to undermine the rationality and objectivity of science in general or even of the human sciences taken as a whole. He is, however, concerned to raise critical questions about key aspects of the contemporary self-understanding of the human sciences. For example, psychology and psychiatry regard themselves as nothing more than scientifically objective disciplines that have discovered the true nature of madness as 'mental illness'. They further see themselves as employing their knowledge of mental illnesses for the purely humanitarian purpose of curing those who suffer from them. In his first major book, *Folie et déraison*, Foucault traces the historical origins of psychology and psychiatry with a view to showing, first, that 'mental illness' is more an artefact of contingent features of modern thought than it is an objective, scientific category. Second, he tries to show that the mad are regarded as threats to the moral order of modern society and that their medical treatment has been more a matter of social control than of compassionate relief. Here he is particularly concerned to debunk the myth of Pinel and Tuke – the founders of the modern asylum – as the enlightened liberators of the mad.

In Foucault's next book, *The Birth of the Clinic*, he moves from mental to physical illness. Like psychiatry, modern medicine sees itself as based on a body of objective, scientific knowledge (e.g. that of pathological anatomy). Foucault does not deny this, but he does question modern medicine's positivist assumption that this knowledge was achieved simply by, for the first time, looking at the human body and its diseases with a clear and unbiased empirical eye. Foucault maintains that modern medical knowledge is no more a matter of pure observation than was that of the seventeenth and eighteenth centuries. In both cases, medicine was based not on a pure experience, free of interpretation, but on a very specific way of perceiving bodies and diseases, structured by a grid of *a priori* conceptions. Foucault presents the new, modern mode of medical perception as intimately tied to the new system of public clinics and teaching hospitals that emerged after the French Revolution. He also emphasises the importance of Bichat's work on pathological anatomy and Broussais's on fevers as key stages in developing the modern view of disease as an organic disorder of the individual body.

In 1966 Foucault published his most ambitious work, *Les mots et les choses* (translated as *The Order of Things*). Here his ultimate goal is to understand the cognitive status of the modern 'human sciences' or 'sciences of man' (*Geisteswissenschaften*). To do this, he proposes to place these disciplines in the overall epistemological field of modern knowledge. But this project in turn leads him to an effort to situate modern knowledge in the broader context of Western culture and science since the Renaissance. As a result, *The Order of Things* becomes an analysis of key aspects of Western thought over the last three hundred years. Foucault's approach to this history is based on several fundamental propositions. The first is that what knowledge means has varied from one historical period to another; specifically, the Renaissance (roughly the sixteenth century), the Classical Age (from the mid-seventeenth century to the end of the eighteenth century) and the Modern Age (from the beginning of the nineteenth century to at least the middle of the twentieth) have all had very different conceptions of knowledge. Second, a given epoch's conception of knowledge is ultimately rooted in its 'experience of order'; i.e. the fundamental way in which it sees things connected to one another. For example, in the Renaissance, order was a matter of resemblance between things, whereas in the Classical Age it was understood in terms of relations of strict identity and difference. Third, since knowledge is always a matter of somehow formulating truths about things, its nature in a given period will depend on the period's construal of the nature of the signs – especially linguistic signs – used to formulate truths. A given period's conceptions of order, signs and language, along with the conception of knowledge they entail, constitute what Foucault calls the *episteme* of the period. The goal of *The Order of Things* is to understand the place of the human sciences in the modern *episteme* on the basis of a historical analysis of the relation of this *episteme* to those of the Renaissance and the Classical Age.

The central thesis of *The Order of Things* is that the entire body of modern positive knowledge of human beings is based on a particular conception of human beings, a conception Foucault labels *man*. The defining feature of man, in this sense, is that he is both an object in the world and the knowing subject through which there exists a world of objects. Although modern thinkers have taken this conception as definitive of human reality as such, Foucault maintains that it is just one historical construal of that reality – and one that is presently passing away. Overall, *The Order of Things* can be regarded as a critique of the concept of man carried out in three stages. Firstly, Foucault shows that the concept had no role at all in the Classical Age that preceded our modern period. Secondly, he analyses modern philosophical efforts to develop a coherent understanding of man and exhibits their failure. Finally, he analyses the more successful efforts of the human sciences to attain knowledge of man and shows that they are based on disciplines ('counter-sciences') such as Lacan's psychoanalysis and Lévi-Strauss's anthropology that undermine the concept of man. Foucault concludes that the age of thought dominated by this particular way of conceiving human reality is nearing its end.

In the course of developing this thesis, Foucault makes a variety of more specific historical points. He argues, for example, that the empirical sciences of biology, economics and philology are peculiar to modern thought and cannot be properly regarded as continuous with Classical disciplines (natural history, analysis of wealth and general grammar) that seem to deal with the same phenomena. In particular, he maintains that there is no genuine conception of evolution in the seventeenth and eighteenth centuries. Diderot, Maupertuis and even Lamarck never thought of species as essentially produced by temporal processes. Here, his position recalls Bachelard's and Canguilhem's emphasis on sharp breaks in the history of science and the folly of searches for precursors. On the other hand, Foucault in other contexts rejects conventional views about the importance of famous divisions in the history of thought. He holds, for example, that the distinctions between Ricardo's pessimism and Marx's optimism and between Cuvier's fixism and Darwin's transformism are merely superficial differences between thinkers operating within the same *episteme*.

As he pursued his historical case-studies, Foucault became increasingly sensitive to questions about the methods of analysis he was using. In his next book, *The Archaeology of Knowledge*, he offered an extended reflection on the archaeological method developed in his preceding works. Foucault presents archaeology, like any historical inquiry, as beginning with *documents*, collections of statements that we have received from our ancestors. Ordinary history – and especially the history of ideas – sees documents as clues to the intentional acts (beliefs, thoughts, desires, feelings) of those who produced them. It uses the objective linguistic data of statements to reconstruct the inner life of subjects. Foucault, by contrast, proposes to take statements as objects of study in their own right, making no effort to use them as means to revive the thoughts of the dead. This is why he calls his enterprise an 'archaeology' – an objective analysis of linguistic 'artefacts'. We are, of course, already familiar with two (non-historical) areas of inquiry that treat statements in their own right: grammar, which defines the conditions under which a statement is meaningful and logic, which specifies what can and cannot be consistently added to a given set of statements. But it is obvious that the set of statements actually made in a given domain and epoch is a very small sub-set of those permitted by grammar and logic. Ordinarily, we explain the vast number of grammatically and logically possible statements that are *not* made on the basis of the experiences, beliefs and intentions of subjects. We do not speak of Jupiter hurling thunderbolts because we do not believe in him; the ancient Greeks did not speak of space travel because they had no experience of it; the Victorians suppressed certain aspects of sexuality out of shame. Foucault suggests that in many fundamental cases the explanation for such linguistic gaps is rather that statements are subject to a further set of rules (neither grammatical nor logical) to which speakers unwittingly conform. A set of statements governed by such a set of rules constitutes what he calls a *discursive formation*.

Foucault's account of the relation of discursive formations to sciences is based on the special sense he gives to the distinction between *connaissance* and *savoir*. By *connaissance* he means (in accord with ordinary French usage) any particular body of knowledge such as nuclear physics, evolutionary biology, or Freudian psychoanalysis; thus, *connaissance* is what is found in scientific (or would-be scientific) disciplines. *Savoir*, on the other hand, refers to the discursive conditions that are necessary for the development of *connaissance*; it refers, in Foucault's words, to 'the conditions that are necessary in a particular period for this or that type of object to be given to *connaissance* and for this or that enunciation to be formulated'.[7] In Foucault's view, a particular science is the locus of *connaissance* whereas a discursive formation is the locus of *savoir*. As such, the *savoir* of a discursive formation provides the objects, standards of cognitive authority, concepts and theoretical strategies that are necessary for a body of scientific *connaissance*. Or, we might say, a discursive formation provides the pre-knowledge (*savoir*) necessary for the knowledge (*connaissance*) achieved by a science. *Connaissance* is an achievement of an individual or a group consciousness and so is naturally the focus of a subject-centred enterprise such as traditional history of science. *Savoir*, by contrast, is the concern of Foucault's archaeology.

From an archaeological view, a science is just one, localised formation in the 'epistemological site' that is a discursive formation. Science neither supersedes nor exhausts the discursive formation that is its background. Hence, an archaeological approach to science differs essentially from Bachelardian history of science. It does not proceed on the basis of the assessment of the significance and validity of the past provided by the norms of current scientific practice. Rather, it seeks the origin of epistemic and scientific norms in the relevant discursive formations, seeing such norms not as unquestionable givens for historical reflection but as themselves the outcomes of historical processes. Here we find a key difference that sets Foucault's work off from that of Bachelard and Canguilhem. He proposes a method of writing the history of scientific reason without presupposing present norms of scientific rationality. Because of this, Foucault thinks his archaeological history can provide the basis for a historical critique of scientific rationality, something that is beyond the capacity of Bachelardian history of science.

The Archaeology of Knowledge clearly marks the end of one major stage of Foucault's work. After its publication in 1969, he remained relatively silent for six years. *Discipline and Punish*, published in 1975, resumes his critique of the human sciences but now in a mode that places far more explicit emphasis on social and institutional mechanisms of power. Here Foucault's primary concern is to show how bodies of knowledge – particularly the modern social sciences – are inextricably interwoven with the techniques of social control. They are not, he maintains, autonomous intellectual achievements applied, *à la* Bacon, as instruments of social power. Rather, their very constitution as knowledge depends essentially (although it is not reducible to) mechanisms of power. In *Discipline and Punish*, for example, Foucault details the essential dependence of criminology on the development of prisons in the nineteenth century; and he suggests similar ties between other social sciences and such controlling social structures as schools, military camps and factories. Similarly, in the first volume of his *History of Sexuality*, he argues that the 'sciences of sexuality' developed in the nineteenth and twentieth centuries are integral parts of another aspect of modern society's control of its members. Roughly, the disciplinary techniques associated with criminology, pedagogy, etc. control by making men objects, while the sciences of sexuality make them self-monitoring subjects.

The theme of the essential connection of knowledge with power develops fully and explicitly what was suggested at numerous points in Foucault's earlier work. What is distinctive in *Discipline and Punish* and *History of Sexuality* is Foucault's new conception of the nature of power. He rejects the standard view that power is a purely negative, repressive social force that is challenged and overcome by the liberating light of truth. According to Foucault, power, although frequently destructive and always dangerous, is also a creative source of positive values (including those of truth and knowledge). He further rejects the common picture of social and political power as flowing from a single dominant centre (e.g. the ruling class, the monarch). Instead, he sees a society as shot through with a multiplicity of power relations, interacting but mutually irreducible.

In order to analyse the development of bodies of knowledge out of systems of power, Foucault employs a new historical method that he calls 'genealogy'. Genealogy does not replace archaeology, which is still needed to uncover the discursive rules that constitute bodies of knowledge. But genealogy does go beyond archaeology to explain changes in the history of discourse (which are merely described by archaeology) by connecting them to changes in the non-discursive practices of a society's power structure. Like other historians, Foucault sees the latter changes as deriving from a wide variety of economic, social, political and ideological causes. But, contrary to many standard accounts, he maintains that these causes cannot be fitted into any simple, unified, teleological scheme (e.g. the rise of the bourgeoisie, the ambition of Napoleon). Rather, he holds that non-disursive practices change because of a vast number of small, often unrelated facts (e.g. *ad hoc* adjustments of existing procedures, a chance discovery of a new implement or technology), the sorts of 'petty causes' Nietzsche made the concern of *his* genealogy. Thus, for Foucault, changes in the non-discursive practices that constitute a society's power structure must be understood as due to an immensely complex and diffuse variety of micro-factors.

As Foucault researched and wrote the later volumes of his history of sexuality, his conception of the project broadened considerably. Rather than just looking at the emergence of the modern notion of the self as subject, he proposed to trace the Western concept of the self from the ancient Greeks on. Moreover, he began to combine this historical project with the ethical one of constructing alternatives to modern moral codes. Two volumes on Greek and Roman views of sexual ethics (*The Use of Pleasure* and *The Care of the Self*) appeared in 1984 just before his death. Another volume (*Les Aveux de la Chair*), centring on the Christian practice of confession, may appear posthumously.

Conclusion

This selective survey has emphasised aspects of recent Continental history and philosophy of science that might challenge or inspire parallel Anglo-American work. There is no suggestion that these approaches, separated by much more than bodies of water, should, or profitably could, merge. It is, indeed, likely that the vigour of each approach depends on features that separate it from the other. But short of misleading or enervating syntheses, there is surely ample room for a rich range of constructive encounters between Continental and Anglo-American efforts to understand science.

NOTES

1. Jurgen Habermas, *Knowledge and human interests*, trans. J. Shapiro (Boston, 1971), p. 196.
2. Gaston Bachelard, *L'activité rationaliste de la physique contemporaine* (Paris, 1951), p. 25.
3. Ibid., p. 24.
4. Ibid., p. 25.
5. Georges Canguilhem, *Etudes d'histoire et de philosophie des sciences* (Paris, 1970), p. 13.
6. Ibid., p. 22.
7. Michel Foucault, *The archaeology of knowledge*, trans. A. Sheridan (New York, 1972), p. 15, translator's note 2.

FURTHER READING

Richard Bernstein, *The restructuring of social and political theory* (New York, 1976).
——, *Beyond objectivism and relativism: science, hermeneutics, and praxis* (Philadelphia, 1983).
Georges Canguilhem, 'Gaston Bachelard' (set of three essays), in *Etudes d'histoire et de philosophie des sciences* (second edition, Paris, 1970).

Hubert L. Dreyfus and Paul Rabinow, *Michel Foucault: beyond structuralism and hermeneutics* (second edition, Chicago, 1983).

Charles Guignon, *Heidegger and the problem of knowledge* (Indianapolis, 1983).

Gary Gutting, 'Continental philosophy of science', in Peter Asquith and Henry Kyburg (eds.), *Current issues in philosophy of science* (East Lansing, Michigan, 1979), pp. 94–117.

——, *Foucault's Archaeology: science and the history of reason* (Cambridge, Mass., 1989).

Ian Hacking, 'Michel Foucault's immature science', *Nous*, 13 (1979), 39–51.

Martin Jay, *The dialectical imagination: a history of the Frankfurt School and the Institute of Social Research*, 1923–1950 (Boston, 1973).

Joseph Kockelmans and Theodore Kisiel (eds.), *Phenomenology and the natural sciences* (Evanston, 1970).

Thomas McCarthy, *The critical theory of Jurgen Habermas* (Cambridge, Mass., 1978).

Edo Pivcevic, *Husserl and phenomenology* (London, 1970).

Alan Sheridan, *Michel Foucault: the will to truth* (London, 1980).

Roch Smith, *Gaston Bachelard* (Boston, 1982).

Mary Tiles, *Bachelard: science and objectivity* (Cambridge, 1984).

11

DISCOVERY

THOMAS NICKLES

1. DISCOVERY AS A PROBLEM FOR HISTORY

How to treat scientific creativity is perhaps the chief problem facing historians of science. Genuine historical accounts are not mere chronologies or collections of anecdotes; they provide coherent descriptions and illuminating, intelligible explanations of the activities and beliefs of individual scientists and of scientific communities. Not surprisingly, then, the successful treatment of innovative research coincides with the maturation of history of science as a scholarly discipline.

Some writers (especially philosophers) have identified the problem of historically explaining discoveries with that of the existence of a *logic* of discovery. For them, genuine discovery explanations must exhibit a (or *the*) logic of discovery. A contemporary example is illustrated by those artificial intelligence (AI) experts who demand that adequate discovery explanations be fully constructive – a set of heuristic and logical procedures capable of actually producing the desired solution from the available information. For them the historical and logical enterprises are strongly coupled: an exact method of discovery is necessary and sufficient for historical explanation.

A weaker view is that discovery explanations must be deductive arguments from scientific law statements and factual claims to a conclusion describing the discovery. This is Carl Hempel's famous 'covering law' theory of explanation. Still weaker is the view that discovery explanations are merely plausible arguments leading to the discovery as a conclusion. On this view the possibility of historical explanation presupposes the *rationality* of the discovery process but no *logic* of discovery. Some critics of the Hempel model have denied that explanations necessarily have the form of arguments from premises to a conclusion. Do intelligible discovery explanations imply or presuppose a methodology of discovery? Must an adequate philosophical account of discovery provide a model for historical explanation?

Given the overwhelming complexity of historical developments of any sort, global understanding of history and even neat, local explanations are difficult to achieve. Any ordering scheme or intellectual grid imposed to structure historical accounts threatens their accuracy and historicity and possesses all the dangers of general history. General history tends to be 'Whig' history – misguided attempts to understand the past in terms of present (or non-historical) categories of thought. For example, early historians of science embraced logic of discovery as a boon to historical writing, because writing about particular applications of the method provided a standard (internalist) technique for explaining discoveries. In so far as the discovery method was a general logic, uncluttered by the technical details of particular subjects, historians could provide discovery accounts intelligible to a wide, unspecialised audience. A unified logic of research also conveniently served to demarcate science from other pursuits, helping to explain why science was uniquely progressive.

Thus we see the attraction of *inductivist* history of science. In so far as scientific discoveries are inductions from bodies of data, it is clear how they are to be explained. Inductivist methodologies of science became especially popular in the seventeenth century, in conjunction with the strong empiricist view that the facts can be unproblematically read off nature. Later the scientific revolution as a whole was explained as an inductive-empiricist turning away from pure reason to nature. It is understandable why most history of science was inductivist history, of one sort or another, until well into the twentieth century.

The primary historical competitor to inductivism as a general methodology of science has been hypothetico-deductivism (H-D) or hypotheticalism. On this view, scientific discoveries are not derived from phenomena or generated from previously established results. Rather, discoveries result from proposing hypotheses and then successfully testing their predictions. Hypotheticalists of the twentieth century such as Karl Popper and several of the logical positivists have denied that there can be any logic of discovery. They have tended to reduce the discovery process to a momentary flash of insight. Such an extreme hypotheticalism is clearly disastrous for history, since it leaves the historian little to say about theory construction except to relate anecdotes about the strange conditions under which ideas popped into the heads of great scientists and to describe the ensuing empirical tests. Limited to a choice between global inductivism and global hypotheticalism, the early historians therefore found inductivism the more attractive option, at least until they began to portray scientists romantically as heroic individual geniuses (see below).

Those who believe in the possibility of genuine history of discovery appear to face a dilemma. If there is no method or rationale of discovery whatever, as extreme hypotheticalists hold, then there can be no genuine history of discovery. But if scientific work is driven by a strong logic of discovery (as inductivists, *inter alia*, hold), then genuine history is again impossible. History reduces to applied logic – filling an ahistorical formal schema with historical content.

This is a false dilemma, however. We are not forced to choose either of these extremes. Modern, internalist history of science provides a compromise, which partly explains its attraction to both historians and methodologists. Internalist history since mid-century has certainly not been a slave to logic, inductive or deductive; but neither has it sacrificed rational intelligibility for amusing anecdote. Thanks to detailed, largely internalist examinations of the creative work (both successful and unsuccessful) of Newton, Lavoisier, Fourier, Darwin, Faraday, Maxwell, Planck, Einstein and a host of others, it has become clear how impoverished are standard H-D accounts of the research process. Historical studies of scientists' notebooks and other sources have revealed the rich texture of reasoning typically involved in creative research. This and the fact that this reasoning did not fit neatly under either of the traditional methodological rubrics – 'inductive' and 'H-D' – have served to open methodological thinking to fresh ideas. Doctrinaire inductivism and hypotheticalism grossly oversimplify scientific practice and are absent from the better histories.

Apart from notable exceptions, it is only within the past few decades that historians have learned how to do history of science well. The recent mass of historical work has decisively refuted older claims that scientists in all fields employ a single, *general* method of discovery. This work demonstrates that historians somehow have managed to wean themselves from simple and universal developmental formulas such as inductivism and, accordingly, that detailed historical explanations are inevitably technically demanding. (The other side of this coin is the problem of decreasingly small audiences for technical historical writing.) Correspondingly, philosophers can no longer take for granted that there is an interesting, content-free logic of science of any sort, let alone a general logic of discovery. Historical work seriously challenges older claims for the methodological unity of the sciences, even claims for the methodological unity of a single science as it develops over time.

For all its attractions, rational, internal history of discovery faces certain difficulties. Hempelians and (even more strongly) constructivist AI experts criticise typical discovery explanations for being logically imprecise, too fuzzy and intuitive to be genuinely explanatory. But while high standards are admirable, these particular standards would seem to be out of place; for such constructive means were plainly available to the historical discoverers (Kepler, Black, Ohm, *et al.*) discussed by AI. And, given their failure to fit most historical cases, it is too much to expect even deductive explanations of discoveries from scientific laws, in accordance with Hempel's model.

Secondly, 'externalist' historians and sociologists criticise internalist explanations from another quarter entirely. In substituting rational explanation for logical derivation, internal histories remain too 'idealist', too idea-driven, when in fact our ideas and their reception are, at least in part, products of our social existence. In *The Social Basis of Scientific Discoveries* (Cambridge, 1981), Augustine Brannigan challenges the appropriateness of the 'discovery' label itself and treats discovery as a matter of social attribution rather than as a successful interpretation of nature. To regard discovery attributions as simple reports about the successful mastery of objective nature is to beg all of the interesting questions. It is to take as given precisely what needs historical and social explanation. This is also a central theme of Andrew Pickering's *Constructing Quarks* (Chicago, 1984). Further, discovery attributions are often retrospective reconstructions. Hence, historical and philosophical accounts which take those attributions at face value will be Whiggish. If we suppose that discoveries are localisable as to place, time and agent, then it is doubtful whether there can be a genuine history of discovery, critics say, since historians have found it surprisingly difficult to make such identifications. Thus we have a sort of 'uncertainty principle' for discoveries. They are wave-like smears in time rather than precisely locatable historical particles.

Internalists reply that it is the externalist who is being unhistorical. The breakup of a major discovery into a historical series of smaller innovations makes discovery more rather than less tractable to historical explanatory treatment. As Noretta Koertge points out (see Further Reading), such a breakup also naturally occurs for logico-analytical reasons when we specify what is to be explained in terms of full propositions instead of nouns or noun phrases. We do not simply explain 'the discovery of oxygen' but why and how Priestley succeeded in discovering that heating mercury calx produces a gas supporting respiration and combustion, how Lavoisier showed *that* such-and-such and Scheele *that* so-and-so. There need be no conflict among these explanations, and we need label none of this work simply 'the discovery of oxygen' in our sense of 'oxygen'.

Another difficulty for 'rational', internalist explanations of discoveries in terms of the unfolding logic or rationality of ideas is in seeing how creative departures can be guided by (or even logically consistent with) extant knowledge. Are not the great revolutions inconsistent with the past and hence irrational by previous standards? The internalist may reply, firstly, that even a logical proof, which cannot of course be logically ampliative, may nonetheless be epistemically ampliative. This is especially obvious in much mathematical discovery, but also recalls Newton's theory of light (see below). Secondly, a piece of new information, combined with a generalisation (abstracted logical consequence) of previous results can have revolutionary implications. For example, a mathematical generalisation of the Galilean transformation plus the fact of the constancy of the velocity of light entails the Lorentz transformation, which, under a natural interpretation, is incompatible with its predecessor. In 1911 Ehrenfest showed that Planck's empirical radiation law, in conjunction with unproblematic principles of classical statistical mechanics, entails the existence of energy quanta!

Externalist accounts of discovery face their own difficulties. The primary objection is that they do not, and cannot, genuinely explain the specific intellectual *content* of discoveries. It is one thing to explain the precise mathematical and physical content of, say, Newton's law of universal gravitation, and quite another to discuss the socio-political and psychological context in which Newton's ideas developed and were received. Non-rational, externalist explanations of innovation in terms of social conditions make the sources of discovery exogenous to research; hence, innovation is not something that arises naturally out of research itself. This is, at any rate, what the internalists claim. In the past decade scholars have explored ways of transcending this internalist-externalist dichotomy.

One other problem for the historian may be mentioned at the outset. There is a troublesome ambiguity in the term 'discovery' and in the idea of accounting for discovery. On the one hand 'discovery' is an achievement term: the word signifies a final result, a finished, successful *product*. On the other hand, 'discovery' suggests an elusive *process* by which, in the more striking cases, new world pictures and new languages of scientific description emerge. Must history of science remain content to describe and explain the processes that historical investigators have employed, without judging the adequacy of these efforts and the correctness of their products? Or, on the contrary, must fully adequate history explain the success of science by showing that scientific conclusions are in some sense justified – if not as truths about the universe then at least as reliable results and techniques? In recent years most historians, in reaction to the Whig histories of earlier generations, have taken the moderate course of examining in detail the problem-solving and justification procedures employed by the scientific communities studied and have only occasionally made explicit judgements about the validity of these procedures. Nonetheless, the correctness or incorrectness of particular results and procedures is frequently presupposed in historical writing.

To summarise: In the wake of positivist and Popperian attacks on the whole idea of a method of discovery, and simultaneous attacks on the possibility of serious intellectual history of discovery, the appearance of interesting internalist histories of discovery encouraged some philosophers to treat the existence of these histories as evidence for the existence of a logic of discovery. But the availability of rational histories falls far short of entailing the existence of a discovery logic. Eventually, given the difficulty – or impossibility – of finding a strict, general logic of discovery, and noting that rationality is distinct from logicality, many so-called 'friends of discovery' retreated from *logic* of discovery to the *rationality* of discovery. History remains coupled to methodology of discovery but at a different level; and now the history drives the methodology rather than vice versa. For these friends, the availability of internal explanations of discovery is sufficient to establish the methodological interest of discovery. Of course, in the absence of precise logical articulation, both internalist history and rationality of discovery appear 'fuzzy' to methodologists accustomed to crisp logical precision. On the other side, historians of an 'externalist' bent question the adequacy of internalist history and the very notion of a discovery.

2. THE HISTORICAL BACKGROUND

In the seventeenth century, at the dawn of modern science, men such as Bacon, Descartes and Newton called for a method of discovery, a way of ordering investigation such that discoveries could be produced in abundance and not merely occasionally, by fortunate accident. The topic of discovery has always been tied to debates about method, and there were substantial differences among the methods they proposed. Some writers equated method of discovery with 'the method of analysis' as they construed it – the method of discovery reportedly employed by the ancient Greek mathematicians but concealed by them. According to Pappus of Alexandria, 'analysis' is somehow convertible into 'synthesis', a method of demonstration. What these ancient methods were and how the seventeenth-century discovery programmes related to them, are still topics of scholarly debate.

It is widely held (especially by philosophers) that seventeenth-century methodologists proposed *algorithmic* methods of discovery, which they intended to function simultaneously as logics of justification. These savants supposedly equated logic of discovery with logic of justification: use of the right discovery method simultaneously and infallibly justifies the discovery, indeed, justifies it more securely than the testing of hypotheses ever could. Hence method of discovery, as such, carries special epistemic weight.

This view is anachronistic for several reasons. Firstly, the distinction between algorithms and heuristic procedures was not fully articulated until the twentieth century. If we do apply contemporary concepts to early methodology, seventeenth-century discovery methods are probably better considered as strong heuristics rather than as algorithms. Secondly, the modern idea of logical proof was not, of course, available. Descartes, for example, still conceived of logical proof as an intuitive grasping of the argument as a whole rather than merely as a discursive, step-by-step procedure conforming to logical rules. Not until a few decades later did Leibniz anticipate the modern view. Some early investigators still fancied that deductive reasoning could be logically ampliative. But also, thirdly, terms like 'deduce' and 'deduction' were used more loosely than today. For those men, as for Sherlock Holmes, 'deduction' (a leading or 'drawing from') could mean any argument (including an inductive argument) from numerous premises or involving a long chain of reasoning. Fourthly, although epistemically confident, few seventeenth-century men of science were strict infallibilists. Newton, for example, sometimes acknowledged that future revisions would be necessary if contrary cases should come to light.

Fifthly, no seventeenth-century thinker possessed our conceptions of history and of deep historical change. Hence the 'radical novelty' view of discovery, as something which breaks out from all previous conceptual frameworks was not part of their perspective. The idea of a conceptual framework and of alternative frameworks seems to date from Kant and his successors. Bacon and even Descartes held that scientific laws and theories could be formulated in terms of the conceptual language already available, or a straightforward extension of the same. Nor does such a view necessarily reduce method to simple, inductive 'stamp collecting', as Descartes's own research demonstrates. Newton held that his theories of gravitation and of light were 'deductions from the phenomena', yet these theories posit the existence of novel entities and process.

Finally, Newton did not restrict his derivations from the phenomena to low-level, 'data' statements anymore than Descartes confined his premises to *a priori*, philosophical truths. Among his premises Newton included phenomenal claims and also principles accepted by the leading investigators of his day. The precise nature of Newton's reasoning is currently the subject of lively debate, but no one would characterise him as a naïve inductivist! Nor was Descartes the naïve deductivist as he has often been portrayed.

The most serious misunderstanding of seventeenth-century methodologists of discovery is that they simply equated logic of discovery with logic of justification, where 'discovery' now means the original, historical occurrence to someone of an idea or theory, and 'justification' means 'final, conclusive justification'. Not even Bacon considered his inductive method a 'single-pass' affair in which, at one stroke, a new and fully justified 'form' (or 'law' as we should call it) is derived from the completed tables of discovery. Rather, Bacon directed that the tables themselves were to be improved as candidate generalisations were examined against the evidence, the result of these multiple passes being both conceptual refinement of the language of science and doctrinal refinement of the scientific claims made. The first appearance of a law candidate did not justify it as an established law. Bacon's idea seems to have been that, in successful cases, the tables and the law candidates they generate eventually provide enough, refined information to generate all possible law candidates relevant to the problem and to refute all of them but one. After the generation step, this 'eliminative induction' proceeds deductively. Bacon realised that employing his full, inductive method could be uneconomical; accordingly, he provided several short-cuts of a heuristic nature in the 'prerogative instances' of the *Novum Organum* (1620). It is even doubtful whether Bacon held his method of discovery to be a purely logical organon, independent of the content of previous results. The final line of the *Novum Organum*, Part I, reads: 'the art of discovery may advance as discoveries advance'.

In modern terminology, Bacon's generation phase is 'constrained generation'. It yields only candidates which are relevant to the problem at hand (with respect to the variables employed and their relationships). Once the refuting instances are built into the process as additional constraints, the process *as a whole* generates true, justified laws. Knowing all of this in advance could, in principle, have led an investigator directly to the correct law, in which case discovery and justification would have coincided. But, as Bacon recognised, this information is not normally known in advance and must be obtained through the hard work of applying the method. We are wiser after the event. The method represents a process of inquiry and not merely a final logic of justification.

Thus it may be more accurate to say that Bacon equated justification not with original discovery but rather with discoverability, generatability, or derivability from what is already known. Justification is not identical with the original, historical generation of the idea. Instead, it amounts to knowing enough to see how the claim could be uniquely generated from what we know about the world *now*, at the end of our investigation. Justification is *idealised* or reconstructed discovery.

This point is clearer in Newton's scientific practice, once misinterpretations of his famous remark, *hypotheses non fingo*, are set aside. Newton's work was, of course, infinitely more sophisticated, more 'modern' than Bacon's, which still carried a medieval stamp. In the famous 1672 paper in which he announced his theory of light and colour, the young Newton wrote as if, in a single afternoon, he had performed the series of prism experiments which led him to his striking conclusion that white sunlight actually consists of a mixture of rays of different refrangibility. However, historians have discovered that Newton had actually been considering and testing numerous hypotheses about light for years previously, as indicated by his *Optical Lectures* at Cambridge.

Does this historical disclosure that Newton's 1672 report was disingenuous debunk his claim to have derived his conclusions from the phenomena? Not at all. Although sometimes disguised as such, a scientific paper is not normally an accurate historical report of the original discovery path. Newton's central claim was that his conclusions about the nature of light are derivable from the phenomena exhibited by his carefully arranged series of experiments – that his theory of light was derivable from what has already known about the world. The derivation here is a logical argument, not a historical discovery process – although it *could* have produced the original discovery had the relevant information been available to Newton at the beginning of his inquiries. Newton's chief interest lay in showing that his was a justified theory and not merely a well-tested hypothesis, much less one conjectural hypothesis among others. It is beside the present point that Newton's reasoning actually contained a subtle mistake.

There is now convincing historical evidence that Newton tolerated the use of hypotheses and hypothesis testing but insisted that genuine theories must be justified by showing how to generate them from what we eventually know about the world. Newton employed H-D methodology as a heuristic for finding and gathering information concerning theory candidates; however, a hypothesis did not become a theory until its derivability from the phenomena was established. Thus for Newton scientific justification was ultimately generative. It is arguable that many other prominent natural philosophers held similar views about discovery and justification during the seventeenth, eighteenth, and even nineteenth centuries. Nor, contrary to later commentators, does generative reasoning reduce to simple, inductive inference. In principle it may be purely deductive. In practice, because of the complexity of the subject matter, such derivations typically include a subtle inter-weaving of deductive and inductive steps. On the generative view of justification, there is no need to ascribe to the original discovery process any special epistemic weight. The epistemic justification derives from the generative argument, regardless of how somebody in fact originally acquired the new idea.

According to Larry Laudan and other historians of methodology, there was a major change in methodological temper in the decades around the turn of the nineteenth century. Hypotheticalism replaced inductivism as the dominant methodology of science, with the result that logic of discovery rapidly lost importance.

There is much truth in this picture. Several investigators rejected the doctrinaire Newtonianism of the day. During the eighteenth century, Newton's followers had adopted a rigid, narrow empiricist conception of scientific methodology which forbade the use of hypotheses, even empirically testable hypotheses employed heuristically. According to the 'Newtonian' *vera causa* principle, only causes whose actual existence could be observed in nature were admissible. Scottish philosophers such as Dugald Stewart and several men of science throughout Europe rebelled against this methodological strait-jacket and emphasised the heuristic value of hypotheses and analogies.

It was during the first half of the nineteenth century that several of the so-called 'Baconian' sciences (electricity, magnetism, physical optics, heat theory, geology, biology, matter theory, etc.) began to attain theoretical maturity, with a corresponding loss of applicability for inductive methods. It is also true that, reflecting upon these scientific changes, John Herschel, in the *Preliminary Discourse on the Study of Natural Philosophy* (1830), and William Whewell, in *Philosophy of the Inductive Sciences, Founded upon their History* (London, 1840), spoke favourably of hypothetical methods and stressed the importance of novel predictions over the original mode of discovery. Traditional inductivism would not do. However, it is a mistake to interpret these writers as simply abandoning a generative conception of methodology (discovery and justification) for an H-D, consequentialist theory of justification. For one thing, actual scientific practice during this period was masked by changes in the style of discovery attribution adopted by historians and by the scientists themselves. Previously, the discoverer was one who employed the correct method, but henceforth, the discoverer was romantically portrayed as an individual genius. (The precise relationship of these changes to the literary and social movements of the time awaits definitive treatment.) This new, heroic style of discovery attribution made scientific work appear more H-D and less constructive than it really was.

For another thing, recent commentators have taken methodological statements out of context. Only in isolation do some of Herschel's remarks (for instance) remind one of Popper's full-blown hypotheticalism. Indeed, in the context of Popper's views on discovery, it sounds strange to speak of a strongly heuristic role for the method of hypothesis. But against the background of rigid, 'Newtonian' inductivism, hypothetical methods offered a heuristic means to open up new fields of investigation, gain new information and develop new ideas. The probable falsity of the initial hypotheses did not matter for this purpose. They were only tools for acquiring information that could eventually be employed in a generative mode. The larger context reveals that Herschel's methodology was generative and similar to Newton's actual methodology, sketched above. In favourable cases, thorough testing yields enough information, in conjunction with previous results, to derive the hypothesis from these premises. The hypothesis thus acquires a new logical status as a fully-fledged *theory*.

Whewell's relationship to traditional methodology was still more complex. His *History of the Inductive Sciences* (London, 1837) provided a new model for writing the history of discovery. Whewell claimed to derive his philosophy of science, including his philosophy of discovery, from his historical work.

It is only with William Stanley Jevons's *Principles of Science* (1874) that a purely hypotheticalist theory of justification appears. Jevons's statement that 'agreement with fact is the sole and sufficient test of a true hypothesis' jettisons traditional, generative theory of justification for a thoroughgoing consequentialist theory. (However, Jevons remained more interested in heuristic aids and economy of research than most consequentialists today.) A purely consequential theory asserts that testing the logical consequences (predictions) of a hypothesis is the source of all empirical justification, whereas a purely generative theory insists that the derivability of the theory itself from the phenomena and/or previous results is justification enough. Until Jevons, most methodologists combined generative and consequential elements in their methodologies, although strong inductivists were pure generativists. For them, only information used to construct a theory counts in its support; whereas for pure consequentialists only successful test predictions count, and derivations from the phenomena (for example) count for nothing. Accordingly, the fundamental change from strong generativism to strong consequentialism represents a complete logical inversion. How are we to explain this nineteenth-century inversion in the logic of science, this abandonment of classical methodology of discovery? Does it reflect a basic change in scientific practice or primarily a change within philosophy of science? If the latter, then its explanation is a problem for history of methodology rather than for history of science proper. So far, these important questions have received little attention.

Around the turn of the twentieth century, Ernest Mach in Vienna and the American pragmatists, notably Charles Peirce and John Dewey, adopted a viewpoint which, in another incarnation, would eventually transform the study of discovery. These philosophers held that scientific discovery is problem-solving. Mach's interest in discovery as a topic for theory of inquiry is perhaps surprising, given that he was an intellectual father of the later, logical positivists. At any rate, the rise of the logical postivist movement in the 1920s and 1930s soon eclipsed the pragmatic epistemologies of Mach and the Americans.

The history of logical positivism on the discovery issue is also complex, however. The official, logical positivist position on discovery is usually attributed to Hans Reichenbach (1891–1953), who, in *Experience and Prediction* (Chicago, 1938), distinguished 'context of discovery' from 'context of justification' and supposedly ruled context of discovery out of bounds to epistemology. A careful reading of that work reveals that Reichenbach's distinction had a different purpose. Indeed, Reichenbach himself believed in the existence of a sort of inductive-probabilistic logic of discovery, or rather, a logic of discoverability. It was primarily in Reichenbach's and other positivists' later writings that the 'two context' distinction became an invidious one. Ironically, at the very time these writers banished discovery as a legitimate methodological topic, some of them were contributing to the development of statistical inference and data reduction methods, such as factor analysis, which amounted to logics of discovery.

The later positivists came to focus more and more on the logical structure of the final products of research – theories, laws, explanations and empirical testing. Having stripped the process of research of all interesting cognitive-epistemic features, they assigned this topic to psychologists and historians!

Karl Popper (b. 1902), who differs from the positivists on several points, rejected discovery as an epistemological topic in his *Logik der Forschung* (Vienna, 1934), later expanded and translated as *The Logic of Scientific Discovery* (London, 1959). Popper treated creative work in science in a grand, romantic fashion, as a kind of poetic inspiration which could not be studied epistemologically or even as serious intellectual history. Although Popper did emphasise the importance of problems as the starting point of research, by contrast with the logical positivists, and tracing the sources of major scientific problems to metaphysical disagreements, only in his later work did he have anything to say about what problems actually are. No epistemic account of creative work in science grew out of Popper's problem-oriented approach to inquiry, as he persisted in his opposition to methodology of discovery. Popper's methodology consists almost entirely of a theory of criticism of candidate problem solutions already 'on the table'. It is a 'critical-eliminative' rather than a 'constructive' theory of inquiry.

Popper's views on problems did encourage his student and colleague, Imre Lakatos, to develop a constructive theory of inquiry. Lakatos's 'methodology of scientific research programmes' (MSRP) was an attempt to reconcile Popper's purely consequentialist epistemology with the constructive methodological tradition which flowered in the seventeenth century. It was also an attempt to reconcile Popper's philosophy of science with Thomas Kuhn's theory of science (see below). Lakatos attempted to make heuristics philosophically respectable as a body of discovery guides and constraints falling between algorithms and logical proofs, on the one hand, and unreasoned inspiration and luck on the other. According to MSRP, scientists do not construct theories in isolation but as part of a series produced by a 'research programme'. A research programme is defined by a 'hard core' of unrevisable principles plus a 'protective belt' of claims subject to revision. Both components provide substantial heuristic guidance to theory construction. The negative heuristic warns, 'Do not violate the hard core'; and the positive heuristic urges, 'Do develop the programme, stage by stage, by producing more sophisticated, protective-belt theories'.

Kuhn has a threefold relevance to our topic. Firstly, he is perhaps the most visible representative of mature, internalist history of science, which has transformed all science studies topics, including methodology of discovery (yet his work has also inspired social accounts of science). Secondly, in an early paper Kuhn pointed out the radical-conservative 'essential tension' of innovative work. For a puzzle or problem to be well defined, it must be rooted in previously established results and principles; yet innovative solutions must somehow break out of the reigning conceptual framework, hence transforming the original problem, including, in the more revolutionary cases, the criteria of appraisal. This appreciation for the 'historicity' of scientific work makes it all the more difficult to provide a uniform, rule-based account of discovery, and forces us to distinguish ordinary puzzle-solving from extraordinary problem-solving and further to distinguish routine solutions (e.g. standard applications of mathematical techniques) from the non-routine solutions that even ordinary research puzzles may demand. While critics of discovery logics underestimate the number and power of routine, problem-solving methods, the 'friends of discovery' tend to underestimate the difficulties posed by novel problem-solving. Major, historical, scientific change resists capture in terms of a uniform system of constructive rules, a general logic of discovery.

Thus, the influx of reliable historical information has both encouraged and discouraged efforts to deal with discovery and innovation. The work of N. R. Hanson exemplifies this tension. One of the first philosophers of science to take seriously the new history of science, Hanson, in *Patterns of Discovery*

(Cambridge, 1958), revived some of Peirce's ideas on discovery, viz. Peirce's 'logic of abduction'. Yet Hanson was also one of the first philosophers to emphasise the magnitude of historical, conceptual change.

In *The Structure of Scientific Revolutions* (Chicago, 1962; 2nd ed., 1969), Kuhn himself proposed a rule-like, 'stage' theory of scientific development in which his 'essential tension' of innovation and tradition was reified into alternating periods of conservative (normal) and radical (revolutionary) science. The major contribution of Kuhn's theory to the discovery debate was his thesis that the unit of scientific achievement is the solved problem (or research puzzle) rather than the discovered truth. Scientific research consists mainly in solving problems rather than in directly establishing truths. Moreover, problem-definition, problem-ranking and the adequacy of a solution are, in part, matters of social decision by the relevant community.

In *Progress and its Problems* (Berkeley, 1977) Larry Laudan went a step further and defined scientific rationality in terms of problem-solving success, rather than vice versa. Laudan advanced a detailed, problem-solving model of scientific change and called attention to the importance of heuristic appraisal in science. He interposed a 'heuristic pursuit' stage of research between the two traditional stages of discovery and justification.

By the late 1970s, the Popperian and positivist injunctions against dealing with discovery had lost their force, and pragmatic ideas were regaining academic respectability. The work of Herbert Simon and Nicholas Rescher is noteworthy here. Philosophers began to recognise Simon – economist, cognitive psychologist and AI expert – as a major pragmatic philosopher. In his classic, *Administrative Behavior* (New York, 1945; 3rd ed., 1976) and later works, Simon revived the discussion (prominent in Mach and Peirce) of economy of research, and investigated the resulting constraints on institutional organisation. Economy is required for research to proceed efficiently. Economy, in turn, requires that scientists be 'satisficers', content with a solution that works well enough, rather than 'maximisers' or 'optimisers', seeking the best possible solution. Applied to discovery, economy demands that scientists normally employ heuristics rather than algorithms. Algorithms are rarely available, and even when they are, heuristics are usually more efficient despite their carrying no guarantee of success. Again, like Mach and Peirce, Simon equated discovery with problem-solving behaviour, a move which immediately related the previously arcane topic of discovery to research already well underway in cognitive psychology, AI, engineering, history and philosophy. The resulting problem-solving models make discovery something internal to ordinary scientific work rather than exogenous or purely serendipitous. A close look at actual scientific research, whether historical or contemporary, reveals the presence of problems to be solved in all phases of inquiry, including justification procedures. The AI expert Douglas Lenat soon explicitly drew the consequence that discovery is ubiquitous in research. Clearly, treatment of discovery, so construed, is central to any adequate theory of inquiry.

As methodologists became more interested in the process of inquiry, methodology itself became more closely identified with theory of inquiry and somewhat less with the study of logical structures. The message of Rescher's *Methodological Pragmatism* (Oxford, 1977) was that pragmatism must undergo a (further) methodological turn if theoretical claims are to be warranted by what works in practice. Roughly, it is methods which succeed or fail in practice, and theories are in turn warranted by their being the products of good methods. In Pierce's *Philosophy of Science* (Notre Dame, 1978), Rescher employed his study of Pierce as a vehicle for reviving interest in the economy of research. Economy, Rescher argued, demands the heuristic coupling of original discovery with 'final' justification. It remains a matter of dispute what sort of coupling, if any, is required by economy of research.

During the 1970s, a new sort of 'constructive' sociology of science, which emphasised the technical content of scientific ideas, emerged in Britain and spread to the Continent. The resulting spate of historical and contemporary case studies, together with the steady increase in standard historical studies, provided new information of ever-increasing detail about scientific inquiry and called for a more sociologically informed treatment of innovative research.

By the late 1970s and early 1980s, several developments converged to make discovery and innovation a lively topic of discussion in science studies. Even philosophers acknowledged the need to understand better how science actually works before engaging in normative methodology. Understanding how science works means studying the research *process*. 'Theory of inquiry' is, in effect, the successor subject to methodology of discovery, just as the latter largely superseded the 1960s preoccupation with the problem of deep conceptual change. The discovery movement was, in part, an attempt to study the sources of conceptual change, a task which formal logical theories of justification had not attempted. The 'theory of inquiry' movement presupposes that problem-solving and opportunity for innovation pervade scientific work and its reception.

3. SCIENTIFIC DISCOVERY TODAY

Developments over the past decade have broadened the discussion of discovery in several ways. Formerly, discovery studies were concerned exclusively with how laws and theories and, to some extent, facts are discovered. Moreover, discovery was considered to be a single temporal and/or logical stage of research, namely the first stage, preceding both preliminary evaluation or 'pursuit' and final justification. Treatments of discovery focused on a few, glamorous discoveries and neglected nearly everything else, including failed theories and the challenging but fairly well-defined work that constitutes the great bulk of research. Today the 'discovery' label covers problem-solving generally. Discovery topics include search and generation (or construction) tasks of all kinds in science – the search for, or generation of, problem solutions of any sort and not just the construction of elaborate, new theories. Since interesting problems occur in all phases of research, from problem-finding to 'final' justification, the topic of discovery is virtually co-extensive with study of the entire research process.

Ironically, under the new conception of discovery, discovery tasks pervade what used to be considered 'context of justification' as opposed to discovery. For instance, in a critical-eliminative, H-D methodology such as Popper's, two kinds of search tasks which are absolutely crucial are error searches and searches for novel predictions. These non-trivial search tasks are epistemically interesting, but Popperians and everyone else have neglected them. Thus discovery is an important topic even for purely consequentialist accounts of the justification process. Discovery issues are still more important to generative methodologies, which insist upon derivability (discoverability) or partial derivability as a component of full justification. A few Bayesian-probabilistic theorists of science join some friends of discovery in demanding such an account.

One sort of justification problem which crucially arises at many points of research is that of *heuristic appraisal*. Which of the available research problems would it be most fruitful to choose? Which line of research is likely to solve a given problem or to solve it more efficiently? Which of two competing theories or research programmes will be more productive of new results? Which will better overcome standing difficulties? Such appraisal is necessarily future-oriented and therefore different from the evaluation of past empirical performance, which has virtually exhausted philosophers' discussions of justification. Heuristic appraisal is largely a (highly fallible) evaluation of the heuristic potential of a problem or line of solution, e.g. the power of an approach to direct research in promising ways. Discovery issues are obviously relevant to such evaluations of heuristic fertility.

Whereas an older generation of methodologists considered discovery issues pertinent only to the efficient generation of new theories at the initial stage of research, today discovery is widely recognised to be relevant to all manner of justification processes. In the contemporary view, the treatment of discovery does not merely fill a lacuna in older methodologies of science. By appreciating how early, faltering, problem formulations and solutions are progressively refined by later stages of research, the entire conception of research, including the process and logical structure of scientific justification, is transformed. Taking scientific reconstruction seriously may help to bridge the gap, mentioned at the outset, between logical and historical treatments of discovery and innovative research.

Today, methodologists and science studies experts are exploring the variety of problems and solution techniques that appear among the various sciences and speciality areas. One implication of this body of work is nominalistic and 'centrifugal' in tendency: scientific problems are many and diverse. There is no one sort of problem or solution strategy which characterises all research at all times or even much research at any time. Older conceptions of both the methodological unity and the doctrinal unity of science are yielding to an appreciation of the integrity of diverse modes of investigation and to the domain- and content-specificity of the more powerful problem-solving methods which characterise mature research. In this light the old debate between inductivists and hypotheticalists looks naïve indeed as simple, general, inductive and H-D methods are only two of the many problem-solving strategies. Moreover, *both* are among the weakest problem-solving strategies, precisely because of their content-neutrality and near-universal applicability. Scientists resort to them only when more powerful methods are unavailable. Recently, AI theorists have explicitly articulated what nineteenth-century scientific investigators implicitly discovered in a host of scientific disciplines then reaching theoretical maturity: problem-solving power and generality of application are inversely related (roughly speaking). One cannot understand the 'logic' of scientific inquiry without attending to the specific content of the particular discipline concerned. This holds even for highly general mathematical methods, as Kuhn reminds us. In this sense the existence of an interesting, general logic of discovery distinct from, but analogous to, deductive logic, is extremely doubtful.

On the one hand, those who conceive a logic of discovery as a magic formula, a distinctive logical technique which taps the well-springs of creativity, will find this conclusion disappointing. On the other, simply to retreat from a precise logic to a fuzzy rationality of discovery is to give up too quickly, for there do exist powerful, local, problem-solving methods in every fairly mature science. The solution of several interesting theoretical and experimental problem-types has been reduced to routine and even mechanised. The power of these local 'logics' of discovery (and of the laboratory devices which implement them) resides in their ready access to well organised, discipline- and problem-specific knowledge. Since these logics are unremarkable in a purely logical sense, the knowledge and its mode of organisation must be considered part of the very method of inquiry. As AI research has shown, judicious use of available information can cut down vast search spaces more effectively than powerful heuristics or faster processing speeds. The price is locality. What works powerfully for one range of problems in one domain of knowledge will not work at all for quite different problems in that and other domains. For example, experimental and theoretical problem-solving within the same field are often quite different. Recently, Ian Hacking (in *Representing and Intervening*, Cambridge, 1983) and others have argued that experimental inquiry is less dependent on theoretical investigations and controversies than philosophers and historians have imagined. Thus positivists and Popperians tended to view experimental contexts in the same way that they regarded discovery contexts – as too poor in intellectual resources to raise sophisticated research problems or to support complex reasoning of epistemically interesting varieties. Do not experimentalists simply construct their apparatus and then just *observe* what happens? Experimental *discovery* was doubly condemned by such accounts. Yet Ludwik Fleck, in his long-neglected work, *Genesis and Development of a Scientific Fact* (Basel, 1935; Chicago, 1979), had already shown what an epistemically and socially complex process it can be to construct and establish a scientific fact. It can be difficult to pinpoint factual discoveries as to author, place, time and objective relation to nature.

Although Kuhn highlighted this point, he, too, may have underestimated the extent to which scientific research reconstructs its own previous results with a resulting need for radical breaks in the development of science. Work at the frontier is constructed largely by modelling it on previous problems and solutions, as Kuhn pointed out, but in the process those resources are themselves conceptually reconstructed and not merely further articulated. A scientific revolution is often a retrospective reconstruction of accumulated transformations which were themselves fairly 'normal'. The point for discovery is that much or most of the innovation may occur after the original result is published, justified and 'accepted'. Again, the good news for historians is the breakdown of momentous revolutionary breakthroughs into more manageable pieces. The new wave of micro-studies (e.g. work on Faraday's research and its transformation by Maxwell and his generation) supports this constructive-reconstructive viewpoint. Further support might be expected from studies of the writing of technical survey articles, *Handbücher*, and even textbooks. Surprisingly little attention has been given to these topics.

The major task facing methodologists of discovery is to integrate the now-dominant, problem-solving theory of inquiry with a thoroughly social account of inquiry, to integrate logic and individual psychology with history and sociology. Especially in philosophy and the cognitive sciences, problem-solving models have presupposed idealised, individual investigators, working in isolation. In this respect, these models of discovery and innovation are still 'Cartesian'.

Whether and to what extent such integration can be achieved are open questions. Further attention to scientists' own reconstructions of previous work may be one key. In successful cases the problems become sufficiently well defined and the solution methods sufficiently routinised that even AI work is applicable. On the other hand, some socio-historical critics of discovery programmes insist that integration is impossible, that the sociality and historicity of research leave nothing for logic of discovery to capture. Social critics have narrowed the discovery topic to vanishing point by insisting that, in the traditional sense, discoveries simply do not occur in research – while at the very same time, the friends of discovery have broadened discovery to encompass all of research!

FURTHER READING

H. Collins (ed.), *Social studies of science*, 11 (February, 1981). Special issue on the determination and replication of scientific facts.

J. Dorling, 'Demonstrative induction: its significant role in the history of physics', *Philosophy of science*, 40 (1973), 360–72.

M. Finocchiaro, 'Aspects of the logic of history-of-science explanation', *Synthèse*, 62, 429–54.

C. Glymour, R. Scheines, P. Spirtes and K. Kelly, *Discovering causal structure: artificial intelligence, philosophy of science, and statistical modeling* (Orlando, 1987).

D. Gooding and F. James (eds.), *Faraday rediscovered* (London, 1985).

M. D. Grmek, R. S. Cohen and G. Cimino (eds.), *On scientific discovery* (Dordrecht: 1981).

J. Hintikka (ed.), *Synthèse*, 47 (April 1981). Special issue on problem-solving methodologies of science.

J. Holland, K. Holyoak, R. Nisbett and P. Thagard, *Induction: processes of inference, learning, and discovery* (Cambridge, Mass., 1986).

C. Howson (ed.), *Method and appraisal in the physical sciences* (Cambridge, 1976). (Historical applications of Lakatos's MSRP.)

N. Koertge, 'Explaining scientific discovery', *PSA 1982*, Vol. 1, 14–28.

T. S. Kuhn, *The essential tension* (Chicago, 1977).

I. Lakatos and A. Musgrave (eds.), *Criticism and the growth of knowledge* (Cambridge, 1970).

P. Langley, H. A. Simon and G. Bradshaw, *Scientific discovery: computational explorations of the creative processes* (Cambridge, Mass., 1986).

L. Laudan, *Science and hypothesis* (Dordrecht, 1981), Chap. 11.

T. Nickles (ed.), *Scientific discovery, logic, and rationality* and *Scientific discovery: case studies* (Dordrecht, 1980).

——, 'Lakatosian heuristics and epistemic support', *British journal for the philosophy of science*, 38 (1987), 181–205.

H. Post, 'Correspondence, invariance, and heuristics', *Studies in history and philosophy of science*, 2 (1971), 213–55.

S. Schaffer, 'Scientific discoveries and the end of natural philosophy', *Social studies of science*, 16 (1986), 387–420.

H. A. Simon, *Models of discovery* (Dordrecht, 1977).

J. Strong, *Studies in the logic of theory assessment in early victorian Britain, 1830–1860*, Ph.D. dissertation, University of Pittsburgh, 1978; available from University Microfilms International, Ann Arbor, Michigan.

E. Zahar, 'Logic of discovery or psychology of invention?', *British journal for the philosophy of science*, 34 (1983), 243–61.

12

RATIONALITY, SCIENCE AND HISTORY

LARRY BRISKMAN

Man, declared Aristotle, is a rational animal. Not only is man capable of rationality; this is his defining or essential characteristic – that which sets him apart from other animals. Yet despite Aristotle's assertion, men look as capable of acting and thinking irrationally as of acting and thinking rationally; as easily moved by passion and prejudice as by evidence and calculation. If men are by nature rational, they often seem successful in keeping their rational natures under pretty effective control.

Traditionally, however, there is one area of human life where, it is thought, rationality reigns supreme – natural science. Many consider the empirical sciences (and mathematics) to be paradigms of rationality, and their rules of procedure or method the encapsulation of its fundamental rules. Yet despite the widespread appeal of this view, all is not plain sailing: there exists a striking diversity of *theories* as to how rationality in general, and the rationality of science in particular, are to be characterised and understood. Even worse, it is unclear how these disagreements may be settled rationally – for each theory of rationality will, quite rationally, imply a different answer to the question of how these disagreements may be rationally settled! Theories of rationality thus appear to have the peculiar property of being reflexive: when in the dock they seem to be required to act as judge and jury as well.

The problem of how rival theories of rationality can themselves be rationally evaluated will be broached again later. First, however, it will be useful to survey some of the most influential conceptions of rationality, and to indicate some of the main difficulties they face. I will then consider some possible interactions between theories of rationality and the History of Science; in particular, whether the History of Science can make an important contribution to our understanding of rationality. Finally, the idea of rationality as a universalistic ethic will be highlighted.

1. RATIONALITY: WEAK AND STRONG

Let us begin with a common-sense variety of rationality – that of rational action. An action is rational if it is goal-directed and if the person pursuing the goal believes that the action is required in order to achieve it. If an agent wishes to reap crops, and if he believes that for crops to be reaped seeds must be sown, then his sowing of seeds is a rational action. Equally, if an agent wishes to reap crops, and if he believes that the seeds will not grow properly without rain, and if he also believes that there will be no rain unless the gods are cajoled by the performance of a rain dance, then his rain dance is also a rational action. We may call this idea of rationality (following Jarvie and Agassi) 'rationality in the weak sense'.[1]

Weak rationality (in the guise of the Rationality Principle, or of the rule of maximising expected utility) is an almost universal assumption of the social sciences. Economists, anthropologists, sociologists and social psychologists take it for granted that men are, in the main, weakly rational, and this assumption provides a paradigm for the social scientific explanation of individual action. Even when confronted by seemingly 'irrational' actions, such as rain dances or magic, anthropologists will seek to understand them as weakly rational. Closer to home, Freud sought to understand neuroses, and R. D. Laing, in *The Divided Self* (1960), to understand even schizophrenic behaviour, as weakly rational – as an attempt to make the best of an impossible situation. Rationality in the weak sense is thus a fairly basic and neutral notion – almost everyone is, or can be considered to be, weakly rational. Thus the idea of weak rationality does not discriminate between the rationality of the modern farmer's use of chemical fertilisers and the 'primitive' farmer's performing of rain dances.

It is precisely when we attempt such discriminations that philosophical theories of rationality proper come into their own. For such theories can be taken, roughly, as concerned to explain not so much the rationality of actions as the rationality of the beliefs on which weakly rational actions are based. Philosophical theories of rationality thus aim to tell us how to discriminate between theories, statements or claims about the world that deserve to be taken seriously (may be rationally accepted) and those that do not (are not rationally acceptable; ought to be rejected). Thus philosophical theories of rationality are part of methodology; their purpose is to inform us as to how we can become more than merely weakly rational.

2. CLASSICAL JUSTIFICATIONISM: RATIONALITY AS PROOF

The historically dominant solution to the philosophical problem of rationality is *justificationism*: the rationally acceptable theories, statements or claims about the world are those that have been proven, or demonstrated, or established as true by sound arguments. Any claim so proven is worthy of rational acceptance; any claim not so proven is unworthy of such acceptance. This latter class divides into two: those claims whose negations have been proven and are thus to be rationally rejected; and those claims that are not decided either way, for which the rational course is to suspend judgement. The traditional justificationist view of how we can be more than merely weakly rational is, then, this: if we act on the basis of claims about the world that have been proven, demonstrated or established as true by sound arguments, then we are being more than merely weakly rational; we are being, one might say, 'strongly' rational. The modern farmer is more rational than the 'primitive' farmer because the claim that chemical fertiliser improves crop yields has been established by arguments (i.e. rationally established); while the claim that rain dances improve these yields has not (it has either been rationally disproved or it is unproven).

Echoes of this traditional view of rationality sound in the writings of the ancient Greek philosophers (and of most modern and contemporary philosophers too). Yet already in antiquity, sceptics had pointed out that the unbridled demand for argumentative proofs, or demonstrations, threatens an infinite regress, for since all such proofs must start from assumptions (premises) it is impossible, by argument, to prove or demonstrate all assumptions. It follows that the procedure of argumentative proof must start from assumptions that have not been argumentatively proven and are thus, given justificationism, unworthy of rational acceptance. The traditional view of rationality thus threatens to collapse the very distinction between strong and weak rationality it was designed to secure – for if argumentative proof or demonstration must start from assumptions that are not worthy of rational acceptance, the 'strongly rational' modern farmer is just like his 'weakly rational' predecessors, whose actions are also predicated upon rationally unacceptable assumptions.

The traditional view of rationality as argumentative proof thus faces a dilemma: either rationality depends upon irrationality, for example, some form of dogmatic or fideistic commitment to certain 'ultimate assumptions', and is thus a particular species of irrationality; or there can be something like non-argumentative, or non-logical, proof. That is to say, there can be proof that does not proceed from further premises but from some different kind of basis altogether.

3. INTELLECTUALISM AND EMPIRICISM: DESCARTES AND BACON

Historically, two main philosophical schools arose in the attempt to save the classical view of rationality from unwanted, and irrational, dogmatic or fideistic consequences – *intellectualism* (usually called rationalism) and *empiricism*. Both sought to identify an unproblematic basis from which argumentative proof could proceed. According to intellectualism, the sceptical regress is stemmed by premisses ('axioms') that are seen clearly and distinctly to be true by an infallible faculty of Reason, or intellectual intuition. Such axioms are self-evident to any rational being – provided, that is, that his faculty of Reason (which Descartes called the *Lumen Naturale*, or Natural Light) is unimpaired. Rationality, in the sense of proof by logical argument, is then possible because the axioms of proof are themselves 'proved' by Reason; they are known immediately to be true since their truth is self-evident to the intellect.

Empiricism, in contrast, sought to stem the regress in an infallible faculty of Sense, or in experience. Some premisses (empirical or observational 'basic statements') are known to be true on the basis of sense experience; they are, so to speak, proven by experience, not by logical argument. But given such 'proven' premisses, we can then reason argumentatively, by logical induction, to the truth of other claims about the world. Rationality, in the sense of proof by logical arguments, is then possible because the basic premisses of proof are themselves 'proved' by experience.

In classical Greek philosophy, proponents of both views can be found. Parmenides (c. 510–c. 450 BC) more or less invented rationalism, and Plato (429–347 BC) expounded a version of it. The Greek atomists, on the other hand, and Aristotle (384–322 BC) (in some moods) held identifiably empiricist views. In modern (post-Reformation) philosophy, rationalism was re-invented by René Descartes (1596–1650) and empiricism by Francis Bacon (1561–1626). Both saw their philosophies as antidotes to the reigning, Church-sanctioned, Aristotelian dogmas. They hoped that, by setting human inquiry upon a new and secure road, the deep and powerful knowledge of nature that had so far eluded us could be won. Thus, both Descartes and Bacon saw their task as that of displaying the methodological basis, the rules of rationality, by which a genuine science of nature could be achieved.

In standard accounts of the history of modern philosophy, Descartes's rationalism and Bacon's empiricism (usually identified with Locke's) are taken to be arch rivals. Yet despite their undoubted differences, the bonds that unite them run deep.[2] Firstly, both views are *optimistic* in maintaining that truth will manifest itself (either to Reason or to Sense), and thus that rational knowledge is possible. (Compare this to the sceptical pessimism about the power of rationality of, say, Montaigne (1533–92) or Erasmus (1466–1536).)[3] Secondly, both views are *individualistic* in holding that every individual possesses all the necessary equipment (of Reason or Sense) to obtain rational knowledge, and thus to contribute to the growth of science. Thirdly, and more strikingly, both views are *egalitarian* in holding that all individuals possess this equipment in equal measure.[4] Fourthly, both views are *radicalist* or *anti-traditionalist*: both hold that the proper use of man's rational equipment requires that we first discard all traditional learning (which, for Bacon, is a source of prejudice) and start all over again, so as to build a secure rational structure of knowledge upon proper foundations.[5] Finally, both views hold that although knowledge is our birthright, it is our fault that we have not yet attained it. Thus they teach the historically influential (religious) doctrine that *error is sinful*, and that the well-functioning, and unprejudiced, rational mind reaches the truth by avoiding all error.

Descartes's rationalism and Bacon's empiricism are grand philosophical structures. They are responsible, in part, for the birth of modern science, and for the Enlightenment ideal of the rational unity of mankind. Unfortunately they are false. Cartesian intellectualism has been in disarray since the time of Newton: the triumph of Newtonian over Cartesian physics, coupled with Descartes's claim to have based his physics only upon clear and distinct ideas, guaranteed true by intellectual intuition, undercut confidence in the Cartesian 'Natural Light'. In addition, the Kantian antinomies showed that arguments of equal intuitive cogency could be given for contradictory cosmological propositions. The conclusion seemed inescapable: pure Reason is not a reliable guide to truth. Add to this the nineteenth-century discovery that Euclid's 'self-evident' postulates are not true in all possible worlds, and Russell's discovery of paradoxes in intuitive set theory, and the destruction of Cartesianism is more or less complete – the Natural Light cannot be trusted even in mathematics.

Bacon's empiricism historically fared much better, largely as a result of Newton's insistence that his discovery of the laws of motion and of gravitation was based upon experience and induction. Yet Hume (1711–76) showed, in his *Treatise of Human Nature* (1739), that justificationist empiricism is inconsistent with induction – in that the latter requires the acceptance of a principle whose own proof, or justification, cannot rest upon experience. But this implies that empiricism cannot provide a rational justification for universal laws, and hence that it fails to exhibit natural science as a rational enterprise. More importantly, Hume's result collapses the empiricist's distinction between strong and weak rationality: for action almost always relies on universal laws (rain dances produce rain; the application of potash improves crop yields). So if the justificationist empiricist can provide no rational justification for the acceptance of universal laws then the 'strongly rational' modern farmer is just like his 'weakly rational' predecessors, whose actions also rely on universal laws that cannot be rationally justified.

Just as Hume's sceptical criticism (in his *Dialogues Concerning Natural Religion*) of the theological argument from design lay dormant until Darwin (1809–82) gave an alternative, non-theological, account of (apparent) design, so his sceptical criticism of the justifiability of induction lay dormant (except for Kant (1724–1802)) until Einstein (1879–1955). With the triumph of Einstein's physics, the Baconian (and Newtonian) idea that Newton's laws were demonstrated by induction from experience became untenable.

4. RATIONALITY AS INCONCLUSIVE PROOF: PROBABILISM

Despite the overthrow of Newtonian physics, and thus of its claim to have been rationally established, many empiricists felt that something could be saved from Bacon's programme. Observation and experience might be too weak to enable rational proof that universal laws, or theories, are true; but, they insisted, this does not show that laws or theories cannot be supported by empirical evidence, that evidence cannot raise (or lower) the probability that they are true. Bacon was thus right to think that the rational man reasons from experience; his mistake was to think that such reasoning can amount to strict proof.

The probabilist view of rationality has some attractive features. It need not be embarrassed by the overthrow of Newtonian physics. Newton's theory may have been highly probable given the evidence available before, say, 1905; but Einstein's was even more probable given the (increased) evidence in, say, 1919. Now the probabilist's rule for rational acceptance is this: accept the theory with the highest probability given the available evidence. In 1905, rationality demanded the acceptance of Newton's theory; by 1919 it demanded the acceptance of Einstein's. The overthrow of Newton's theory is thus rationally explicable on the probabilist's model. Moreover, this model provides a new means to discriminate strong from weak rationality: strongly rational actions are those that rely on the best-supported, and so most probable, laws or theories; less rational are those actions relying on less probable ones; while irrational (but still weakly rational) are those relying on highly improbable ones.

All variants of probabilism are forms of fallibilism – scientific laws or theories cannot be proved true from empirical evidence; there is no certainty in science except, perhaps, at the level of empirical evidence itself. Here, already, is a problem for probabilism: for it is widely held that if evidence is uncertain, it cannot 'probabilify' laws or theories. Yet every attempt to secure the certainty of empirical evidence, such that it remains useful for science, has utterly failed. More worrying is the fact that if laws or theories have absolute probability equal to zero, then their probability given any empirical evidence remains zero. But as Popper (b. 1902) and Carnap (1891–1970) have shown, the absolute probability of universal laws is zero.[6] So the probabilist demarcation between weak and strong rationality collapses: *all* actions rely on highly improbable laws or theories.

This difficulty for probabilism has led to a wide diversity of responses. Yet whatever their fate, a paramount difficulty remains: no one has explained the value of high probability relative to evidence. Even if we could reason from 'h is highly probable given e', and e, to 'h is highly probable' (no such rule of detachment is valid), it is unclear what 'h is highly probable' tells us. For, as shown by the lottery paradox, some highly probable hypotheses must be false; and some highly improbable ones must be true.[7] However, in action, we desire to act effectively or successfully (that is, we wish to maximise *actual*, not merely *expected*, utility), and so what we desire is that our actions be underwritten by *true* laws. Since high probability bears no connection to truth, it is obscure why anyone should want to be rational in the probabilist's sense.

5. RATIONALITY, REASONS AND CHOICE

Behind the idea of rationality as proof, and behind most forms of probabilism, lies the demand that rationality be a decision-procedure, or choice-determinant or consensus-forming operator. Accordingly, an adequate theory of rationality should specify an objective procedure for determining, among a set of competing claims about the world, which is the rational one to adopt (the provably true one; the most probable one). Only one choice can be the rational choice; if several are equal from the rational point of view, there cannot be a rational choice between them since any choice must then be rationally arbitrary.

This idea of rationality as a choice-determinant is connected to the popular view that rationality involves more than just reasoning, or employing logic. Rather, it involves the use of reasoning in order to give reasons, in particular, good reasons. The madman who claims he is Napoleon may reason in a perfectly logical way from that claim; but he is irrational because he has no good reasons for making the claim, for believing it true (or nearly true). It follows that if reason is indifferent between two alternative claims, there are no good reasons for preferring one to the other; hence, no choice between them can be rational. The common-sense idea of rationality as the giving of good reasons thus implies that rationality be a choice-determinant. It was because of this that the Romantics viewed rationality as the enemy of individuality; a rational choice is no longer *my* choice, rather it is Reason's choice.

The requirement that rationality be a choice-determinant is, I think, a disastrous one; for before good reasons can determine our choices we must first choose to be rational! That is, we must first decide to allow them to do so (assuming, of course, they exist). The decision or choice to be rational cannot then be a rational decision or choice – it cannot have been determined by good reasons unless it was already made. But then the decision to be rational must be an irrational decision, and so rationality requires irrationality. The distinction between rational and irrational choice thus collapses: *all* choice is irrational, since none can be determined by good reasons.

This result is pertinent to current discussion of the problem of scientific rationality, for almost everyone takes this problem to be that of explaining how rational choices between competing theories in science can be made. Moreover, it is almost universally assumed that a rational choice must be determined by good reasons. Thus, Kuhn and Feyerabend argue that since rational considerations can never determine a scientist's choice; whether of theory, paradigm or research project, science is not rational, for choice is determined by socio-psychological factors (Kuhn) or by opportunistic propaganda (Feyerabend). But as we have seen, the demand that rational choice be determined by (good) reasons makes *all* choice irrational, and so of course makes all choice in science irrational. The problem however lies, I suggest, not with the rationality of science but with the demand that rationality be a choice-determinant, and that rational choices be determined by good reasons.[8]

6. RATIONALITY AS CRITICISM: POPPER

In opposition to the view that rationality is the giving of good reasons, Karl Popper sees rationality as fundamentally a *learning procedure* (not a decision-procedure). The sole aim of rationality is to help us learn whether claims about the world are true or false. For Popper, the search for good reasons is pointless – for there are none to be found; not, that is, if we are interested in truth. However good the reasons for accepting a theory as true, it may nevertheless be false. Thus anyone interested in truth has no good reason to be interested in good reasons.

Popper's view of science is fallibilist – there is no certainty in science, not even at the level of empirical or observational 'basic statements'. But unlike probabilism, Popper's fallibilism is critical, not justificational. That is, probabilists hold that science *aims* to prove or justify its hypotheses; but that such proof or justification can never be perfect; so that certainty in science can never be reached. Popper's fallibilism is quite different: he rejects not only the possibility of attaining certainty (as do all fallibilists), but also the *quest* for it. His fallibilism rests not on the impossibility of perfect proof but on the constant necessity for detecting errors, and on the conscious adoption of methodological policies designed to help us detect them.

According to Popper, the method of science is that of trial and error; of conjecture or hypothesis, and of the detection and elimination of those that are in error. The conjectures themselves are not rational; rationality resides solely in the (socially institutionalised) method of error-detection and elimination. For this, logical argument is crucial; by logical reasoning from the conjectures we attempt to discover the errors they contain; and by logical reasoning from such discovery to the falsity of the conjecture, we eliminate it as a candidate for the truth. The madman who reasons logically from his claim to be Napoleon is, as common sense suggests, irrational; but this is because he will not allow that such reasoning can lead to the detection of error in his claim. For Popper, then, rationality is critical; and strongly rational actions are those based on proposals for action that survive criticism – criticism that freely employs laws or theories that have themselves survived our best critical efforts to detect error in them.

173

Popper's critical rationalism is a version of empiricism, for observation and experiment are among the main tools science employs to detect error in its hypotheses. Indeed, only those hypotheses whose errors are capable of detection by such means should be allowed to enter empirical science (this is Popper's famous demarcation criterion). Among those that enter there may be competitors in which, despite our best rational efforts to date, no error has been detected. One or the other may then be rationally accepted. Thus critical rationalism supplies no decision-procedure: rational methods are a constraint system imposed with the aim of helping us learn. In fact, empirical testing does not even negatively decide the fate of theories – *we* must decide their fate, by deciding in the light of experiment to accept as true a statement reporting its result. Such a statement is, in effect, a further conjecture; to be subjected, if challenged, to rational procedures in the attempt to detect error in it. Rational procedures are thus like life: they involve risk. Venture nothing, gain nothing.

Popper's view of rationality has been widely criticised (and, in my view, widely misunderstood).[9] It is often argued that empirical evidence cannot falsify theories unless it is certain; and that if observation does not make the acceptance of evidence-statements rationally obligatory, empirical criticism is mere arbitrary whim. It is often argued that Popper cannot solve the problem of (strongly) rational action, and that no reasons can be given for thinking falsificationist methods conducive to the pursuit of truth. It is often argued that rational procedures extend beyond ones for eliminating trials, to ones for generating and/or supporting them. Whatever the fate of these criticisms, however, Popper's theory offers a novel, and challenging, alternative to the more traditional approaches.

7. RATIONALITY AS HISTORY: HEGEL

The ideas of rationality canvassed so far are all methodological. But there is a rather different tradition, stemming from Parmenides and Plato, that views rationality as *ontological*. Its slogan is that 'The Real is Rational and the Rational is Real'. Accordingly, Reason is a reliable source of knowledge of Reality. Though this ontological view thus leads to a form of intellectualism, it must be distinguished from Cartesian intellectualism.

As we have seen, Kant showed (in his *Critique* of 1781) that Pure Reason leads to antinomies, or contradictions. He concluded that it is not a source of knowledge of Reality and that it must be confined within the bounds of sense experience if it is to lead to consistent results. Hegel (1770–1831), whose philosophy is the culmination of post-Kantian German idealism, responded to Kant's criticism of rationalist metaphysics with the astounding reply that since Reason contradicts itself, and since the Real is rational, Reality must contain contradictions! These 'real contradictions' are, Hegel thinks, the motor by which Reality changes and develops; they thus underlie, and explain, History.

Hegel's philosophy is dialectical: reality evolves by a process of 'thesis' being confronted by contradictory 'antithesis', whose struggle is resolved by the emergence of a 'synthesis' at a 'higher' level. This synthesis is then a new thesis to be confronted by a new antithesis; and so on. Thus in Hegel's philosophy we have the following equation: The Rational = The Real = The Contradictory = The Dialectical = History. History is thus seen as the 'March of Reason'; and it displays what Hegel calls The Cunning of Reason – the great historical actors are the agents of Reason. But where Reason is heading, and thus Reason itself, can only be seen at the *end* of History – 'The owl of Minerva flies at dusk'.

Hegel's philosophy is obscurantist. It denies that consistency is a requirement of rational thought, and inconsistency a touchstone of falsity. It thus renders criticism impossible: for criticism involves the unearthing of contradictions. Secondly, it entails that history, and thus the history of science, is rational willy-nilly, whatever the facts of its development. Finally, it leads both to an uncritical 'progressivism', and to a historical relativism: for if History is the march of Reason, then the rational standard of 'betterness' is 'laterness'. Newton's theory is thus better than Descartes's, and Einstein's better than Newton's, simply because of their historical positions. Even worse, if Reality itself is the historical development of Reason (which is Hegel's idealist view), then in the fourteenth century Ptolemaic astronomy was *true* (since it was then the highest expression of Reason), whereas now it is false. Thus truth changes with theory-change; and all theories are true (in their own time).[10]

8. RATIONALITY AND THE HISTORY OF SCIENCE

As is clear from the example of Hegel, theories of rationality can greatly affect our view of the history of science. Indeed, a number of philosophers have argued that no serious history of science can be written in the absence of a philosophy of science, or of a theory of scientific rationality. As Lakatos put it (parodying Kant), ' . . . History of Science without Philosophy of Science is blind'.[11] In this section I want to explore some interactions between the theory of rationality and the history of science.

The first point to emphasise is that theories of rationality have not been developed with an eye to the historian of science, with the aim of providing him with a historiographical theory. Rather, they have been developed with an eye to *science itself*; they aim to display the rules of rational inquiry by which scientific knowledge can be achieved (and thus the means by which we can improve on mere weak rationality). Indeed, in the case of radicalist theories such as Bacon's and Descartes's, it could hardly be otherwise, for such theories hold that the pursuit of genuine science requires the rejection of all traditional learning. In other words, both entail that there was, at the time of their proposal, no genuine science to speak of, and thus no science of which to write history.

Does it follow that the historian of science can safely ignore theories of rationality? Not at all, for given that such theories aim to found or influence the practice of science they are, in so far as they have succeeded in this regard, important elements of the History of Science. They are part of the 'situational logic' of scientists themselves; in order to understand their actions and decisions (as weakly rational) we often need to know the theory of *strong* rationality that they held. For example, one can hardly understand the rejection of wave theories of light by many early-nineteenth-century British physicists without realising that such theories required an unobservable 'ether', and thus did not satisfy the justificational empiricist demand that rational science be 'provable from experience'. Equally, the response of most modern physicists to Weyl's unified field theory is hardly explicable without reference to the fact that it is not independently testable (relative to its intended *explananda*), and thus fails to satisfy an accepted requirement of empirical science. The historian of science thus needs to be conversant with philosophical theories of rationality, for they have deeply influenced the historical development of science itself.

But more can be said, for such theories have also deeply influenced the historical development of the History of Science as an intellectual discipline. The explanation of this influence is that most historians adopt the widespread view that natural science is a strongly rational enterprise. They thus view its history from the standpoint of whatever theory of strong rationality *they* accept. For example, historians of science who accept Bacon's theory try to write the history of science as the history of the discovery of hard empirical facts and the inductive 'ascent' from such facts to empirically-justified theories.[12]

These two roles that philosophical theories of rationality play in the writing of the history of science must be sharply distinguished. In their first role, as part of the 'situational logic' of scientists themselves, historians of science need not pass judgement on them. Just as the anthropologist need not judge Azande theories of witchcraft correct to use them in the weakly rational explanation of Zande magical practices; so the historian of science need not judge justificational empiricism correct to use it in the weakly rational explanation of the rejection of wave theories of light. But in their second role, as positive theories of scientific rationality held by the historian himself, and used by him as a historiographical tool, he must be directly concerned with their correctness. For if his theory of strong rationality is inadequate, this is likely to lead to inadequacies in his historical writings about science.

This last point brings us back to the problem, raised earlier, of how disagreements between competing theories of strong rationality may be rationally settled, for each theory will demand that it be employed in the settlement procedure. A number of recent philosophers of science (e.g. Lakatos) have suggested, in response to this problem, that since inadequate theories of rationality will, if used historiographically, lead to inadequate history of science, History of

Science (as an intellectual discipline) plays a special role in the attempt to understand strong (scientific) rationality. Inquiry into the history of science can, it is argued, be used to test a proposed model of strong rationality: the more of the actual history of science that can be reconstructed as rational in its light, the better the model.[13]

This suggestion will, no doubt, warm the hearts of historians of science: instead of being an arcane, esoteric study, History of Science strikes at the core of man's rational essence. But before joy be unconfined, it is well to realise the difficulties of this suggestion. To begin with, the proposal to test theories of strong rationality against the history of science assumes that that history has, by and large, been strongly rational. Yet it would be surprising if this were the case. Science is, after all, a human endeavour, and so as likely to be full of pig-headed prejudice as of sweet, strong, rationality. More importantly, given that competing theories of strong rationality have themselves influenced the historical development of science, it is hard to see how that history can provide a 'neutral' testing ground for competing theories of strong rationality. Even worse, the suggested test implies Hegel's doctrine of the 'Cunning of Reason'; for it requires us to assume that Newton (for example), despite his proclaimed Baconianism, unwittingly acted in accord with the best theory of strong rationality – and this even if he did not hold that theory, and even if that theory is unknown to anyone, Newton or ourselves! Finally, the suggested test is such that the best theory of strong rationality is Feyerabend's 'non-theory', whose sole rule is 'Anything goes', for clearly the entire history of science will, in its light, be reconstructable as 'strongly rational'.

This last point hits the nub. However 'congruent' with the history of science Feyerabend's 'anarchistic' theory may be, this matters little, for the theory utterly fails to solve the philosophical problem at hand. Theories of strong (scientific) rationality are not proposed as naturalistic empirical theories; they are proposed as normative methodologies – as attempts to answer the question of how we can improve on the (weak) rationality of acting to achieve our goals in accordance with our beliefs, by acting to improve our 'beliefs' themselves. Philosophical theories of rationality aim to solve this normative problem; they can no more be criticised by appeal to the facts of history than can the moral injunction against murder be criticised by appeal to the fact that murders are committed.

Once this is seen, however, our old problem of rationally evaluating competing theories of rationality re-emerges: for how can we improve our 'beliefs' as to the best methods for improving our 'beliefs' except by employing what we believe to be the best methods for improving our beliefs? This problem is, I suggest, not as serious as it might appear. Firstly, theories of strong rationality need not be self-serving; if tested by their own standards they are not guaranteed to emerge unscathed. In fact, the history of the discussion of such theories shows that, rather than being self-serving, they are often self-defeating. For example, the theory that rationality is logical proof provably leads to irrationality (since proof must start from unproven, and so rationally impermissible, assumptions). Secondly, and more importantly, we always have available the test of the problem itself; if the distinction between weak and strong rationality proffered by a theory of rationality can be shown to collapse, then that theory can hardly be acceptable as a solution to the problem of how we can improve on mere weak rationality. Competing theories of strong rationality can thus be criticised by logical and philosophical argument; there is no need to turn to the History of Science (as an intellectual discipline) in order rationally to debate them.

Does this mean that the student of rationality has nothing to learn from the history of science? No – for although theories of strong rationality should not be tested *against* the history of science, they have been tested *in* the history of science. Indeed, a striking feature of the history of science has been the frequency with which supposed 'requirements of rationality' (such as the demand that physical theories have mechanical models, or that science abjures speculative hypotheses) have had to be re-evaluated. Just as theories of strong rationality have been part of both the history of science and the History of Science (as an intellectual discipline) – and are thus ignored by the historian at his peril; so the history of science has included debate over theories of strong rationality – and is thus ignored by the philosopher at his peril.

9. CONCLUSION: RATIONALITY AS AN ETHICAL IDEAL

It is then a mistake to divorce the (scientific) debate of competing theories of the world from the (philosophical) debate as to competing theories of how we can rationally undertake the task of improving our (scientific) knowledge of the world. The one debate is part and parcel of the other. This explains why science is more than a mere repository of positive knowledge; why at the same time it embodies our best normative ideals as to the methods by which we can become more than merely weakly rational.

This fact partially accounts, I suggest, for the cultural importance of science; for science represents an ethical ideal – that of the rational unity of mankind – whose central tenet is that we can all learn about the correctness of our own views, even from those whose views may be incorrect. The example of Priestley (1733–1804) is apposite here. He clung to an incorrect phlogistonism in the face of Lavoisier's antiphlogistonism; yet in the process, he pointed out difficulties in Lavoisier's theory which led, in Davy's work, to the discovery that oxymuriatic acid contains no oxygen – and thus to the refutation of Lavoisier's theory that oxygen is the principle of all combustion, calcination and acidulation. Thus, we can all learn from each other, even from those who are mistaken. It is for this reason that science cannot tolerate the relativist view that 'two wrongs can make two rights' – for then no one has need to learn at all, and so no need to learn from others. Science is, therefore, an ethical enterprise, whose core is the universalistic (and anti-relativistic) ideal that mankind is united by its capacity to learn through rational argument.

ACKNOWLEDGEMENTS

I should like to thank David Miller for criticism of an earlier version of this paper, and for saving me from a number of mistakes. I also wish to thank the John Dewey Foundation (Carbondale, Illinois) for financial support in the form of a Senior Research Fellowship.

NOTES

1. I. C. Jarvie and J. Agassi, 'The problem of the rationality of magic' in B. Wilson (ed.), *Rationality* (Oxford, 1970), pp. 172–93. Also in I. C. Jarvie and J. Agassi (eds.), *Rationality: the critical view*, Nijhoff International Phil. Series, vol. 23 (Dordrecht, 1987), pp. 363–83.

2. See K. R. Popper, 'On the sources of knowledge and of ignorance' in *Conjectures and refutations* (London, 1963), pp. 3–30.

3. For the sceptical background to Cartesian and Baconian optimism, see R. H. Popkin, *The history of scepticism from Erasmus to Spinoza* (Berkeley, 1979).

4. See, for example, the beginning of Descartes's *Discourse on method*, in E. S. Haldane and G. R. T. Ross (eds.), *The philosophical works of Descartes*, vol. 1 (Cambridge, 1968), pp. 81–2.

5. See, e.g. Descartes's use of the method of hyperbolic doubt in the first Meditation – Haldane and Ross (eds.), *The philosophical works*, vol. 1, pp. 144–9. See also Aphorisms XLIV and LVI of Bacon's *Novum organum* (1620).

6. R. Carnap, *Logical foundations of probability* (Chicago, 1950), pp. 570ff.; K. R. Popper, *The logic of scientific discovery* (London, 1959), pp. 257ff. For criticism of the development of Carnap's probabilism, see I. Lakatos, 'Changes in the problem of inductive logic' in J. Worrall and G. Currie (eds.), *Philosophical papers of Imre Lakatos*, vol. 2 (Cambridge, 1978), pp. 128–200.

7. For the lottery paradox, see H. E. Kyburg, Jr., 'Probability, rationality, and a rule of detachment' in Y. Bar-Hillel (ed.), *Logic, methodology and philosophy of science*, Proceedings of the 1964 International Congress (North-Holland, Amsterdam, 1965), pp. 301–10. See also R. Hilpinen, *Rules of acceptance and inductive logic* (Amsterdam, 1968).

8. For criticism of the idea of rationality as the giving of good reasons, see D. Miller, 'A critique of good reasons' in Jarvie and Agassi (eds.), *Rationality: the critical view* (1987), pp. 343–58. The idea that rationality should be seen as guiding, but not determining, choice is stressed by W. Berkson in 'Skeptical rationalism', *Inquiry*, vol. 22 (1979), 281–320; reprinted (in part) in Jarvie and Agassi (eds.), (1987), pp. 21–43.

9. See, for example, A. O'Hear, *Karl Popper*, The Arguments of the Philosophers Series (London, 1980) – but see also my review in *The philosophical quarterly*, vol. 32 (1982), 285–7; W. Newton-Smith, *The rationality of science* (London, 1981), esp. chap. 3; and W. Salmon, 'Rational prediction', *British journal for the philosophy of science*, 32 (1981), 115–25.

10. For an introduction to Hegel, see I. Soll, *An introduction to Hegel's metaphysics* (Chicago, 1969). For criticism of Hegel, see K. R. Popper, 'What is dialectic?' in *Conjectures*, pp. 312–35. For an attempt to avoid Hegelian 'historicism' while acknowledging its main insight that all of our knowledge develops historically, see my 'Historicist relativism and bootstrap rationality', *The Monist*, vol. 60 (1977), 509–39; reprinted (in part) in Jarvie and Agassi (eds.), (1987), pp. 317–38.

11. I. Lakatos, 'History of science and its rational reconstructions' in R. C. Buck and R. S. Cohen (eds.), *P.S.A., 1970*, Boston studies in the philosophy of science, vol. VIII (Dordrecht, 1971), p. 91.

12. For details of the effects that the adoption of certain philosophical theories of rationality have

had on the writing of history of science, see Joseph Agassi's path-breaking monograph *Towards an historiography of science* (Middletown, 1963).

13. See I. Lakatos, 'History of science' in Buck and Cohen (eds.), *P.S.A. 1970*, pp. 117–18. A similar idea has been advanced, in a slightly different form, by L. Laudan, and others, in 'Scientific change: philosophical models and historical research', *Synthèse*, vol. 69 (1986), pp. 141–223.

FURTHER READING

W. W. Bartley, *The retreat to commitment* (2nd ed., LaSalle, 1984).

J. R. Brown (ed.), *Scientific rationality: the sociological turn* (Dordrecht, 1984).

P. K. Feyerabend, *Against method* (London, 1975).

T. F. Geraets (ed.), *Rationality today* (Ottawa, 1979).

I. C. Jarvie and J. Agassi (eds.), *Rationality: the critical view* (Dordrecht, 1987).

T. S. Kuhn, *The essential tension* (Chicago, 1977).

I. Lakatos and A. Musgrave (eds.), *Criticism and the growth of knowledge* (Cambridge, 1970).

L. Laudan, *Science and values* (Berkeley, 1984).

W. Newton-Smith, *The rationality of science* (London, 1981).

G. Radnitzky and G. Andersson (eds.), *Progress and rationality in science*, Boston Studies in the Phil. of Sci., vol. LVIII (Dordrecht, 1978).

W. Salmon, *The foundations of scientific inference* (Pittsburgh, 1967).

P. A. Schilpp (ed.), *The philosophy of Karl Popper*, 2 vols. (LaSalle, 1974).

B. Wilson (ed.), *Rationality* (Oxford, 1970).

13

REALISM

W. H. NEWTON-SMITH

1. VARIETIES OF REALISM

Realism construes theories in the natural sciences as being about the physical world, a world taken to exist independently of the theoretician. For the realist, that world includes non-observable items: forces, fields, electrons and quarks, for example. These non-observable items are introduced in order to explain observed phenomena. It is held that in order to explain a theory it must be true. Consequently, realists typically characterise the aim of science as the discovery of explanatory theoretical truths about the world. Realists vary in the extent to which they think that this aim has been realised in the development of modern science. However, realism in the philosophy of science, unlike realism in some other areas of philosophy, standardly involves an epistemological claim that it is possible to ascertain whether theories are achieving the aim, and a historical claim that the natural sciences have been in fact been accumulating truth in some sense at the theoretical level.

Realism is a theory about the nature of science; in particular, a theory about its aim and achievements. If a historian of science is to offer rational explanations in partial explanation of scientific change, he needs a theory of science. To explain, for example, the transition from classical mechanics to relativistic mechanics on a rational basis one would seek to show that given the evidence available at the time, relativistic mechanics was a better theory; that the scientific community perceived this; and that that perception motivated them to change their allegiance. In so far as such explanations in terms of internal factors (factors relating to the theories and the evidence) have any role to play in providing histories of science, one needs an account of the aim of science if one is to have a framework within which to talk of one theory being better than another. Realism is one of the available theories. Moreover it is a theory which makes quite specific claims about the history of science; namely, it has produced progress of a particular kind. As will be seen below these claims have proved to be controversial.

Realism as characterised can seem rather commonplace and uncontroversial. The contested matters at stake can best be displayed by contrasting realism with the most significant opposing theory of science. Historically speaking, this has been instrumentalism. The instrumentalist treats theories as being mere tools or calculating devices designed to provide correct observational predictions. It is assumed that there is a defensible distinction between the domains of the observable and the non-observable. Observational claims are true or false as the case may be and it is in principle possible to ascertain which. With regard to sentences involving non-observational or theoretical terms, questions as to truth or falsity are not to be pursued. For some instrumentalists these questions cannot even be properly considered, for the theoretical sentences are like uninterpreted formulae of a logical calculus which as such do not make any assertions that could be true or false. This has been called the semantical form of instrumentalism. The form which is currently more fashionable, epistemological instrumentalism, holds that the theoretical sentences are in fact either true or false. However, as it is impossible to ascertain which, there is no point in being concerned in science with questions of truth or falsity at the theoretical level. That the theoretical sentences are either true or false is seen as a mere matter of logic that has no role to play in accounting for the aims or methods of science. The semantical and the epistemological instrumentalists are agreed that theories are to be evaluated in terms of their utility in generating true observational predictions.

In both everyday life and in scientific contexts we appear to evaluate explanations in the categories of truth and falsity. To the extent that the laws or theories cited in an explanation are shown to be false, we regard the explanation as unsatisfactory. Given this connection between truth and explanation any instrumentalist would seem to be debarred from representing science as concerned with explanation. This is because in theoretical matters the instrumentalist takes it that either truth is not at stake or that truth, while at stake, is not to be had. This might seem to count decisively against instrumentalism in favour of realism. However, the most influential instrumentalist, Duhem, simply denied that scientists were in the business of providing explanations. And other instrumentalists, such as van Fraassen, have sought to develop pragmatic theories of explanation according to which truth is not a requirement of a good explanation. The fact that both these instrumentalistic moves run contrary to our untutored inclinations has given rise to the claim considered further below that realism is the common-sense theory of science.

In our characterisation of realism, primacy has been given to the notion of the truth of scientific theories; the realist being the one who aims to discover explanatory truth at the theoretical level. Not infrequently, realism has been characterised directly as the doctrine that theoretical entities really exist; that is, the theoretical terms of a theory (i.e. 'electron') stand for or denote unobservable entities (i.e. electrons). This latter doctrine has been called 'entity-realism' and the former might well be called 'truth-realism'. The truth-realist certainly believes in the real existence of theoretical entities. For he believes in the real existence of whatever has to exist to make his theoretical beliefs true. Thus, for example, believing it to be true as part of his theory that electrons impinging on fluorescent screens cause scintillations, he posits the existence of electrons. For that claim could not be true unless they did exist. This conclusion could only be avoided if some sort of reductionism were feasible. A reductionism of the required sort would treat all discourse about electrons as translatable into purely observational discourse. Reductionism, although once forcefully advocated by Russell, among others, now has virtually no support, as it has not proved possible to carry out this reduction. And furthermore it would treat discourse at the theoretical level as a mere redescription of discourse at the observational level rather than as providing a theoretical explanation of the observable. Truth-realism in fact thus leads to entity-realism in the absence of any successful reduction of the theoretical to the observable.

Recently, however, there have been entity-realists who are not truth-realists. These realists (notably Cartwright and Hacking) hold that we are justified in believing in the existence of theoretical entities only when we are in a position to use these entities to produce effects. For example, electrons exists for we can use them to produce scintillations. Unless we could use quarks to do things, discourse about them would not be construed realistically by the entity-realist. On this account, we introduce terms like 'quark' into our theories without thereby necessarily taking on any commitment to the existence of quarks. The commitment to existence comes only when we talk of the items in question as things which can be used to produce certain effects. The entity-realist differs from the truth-realist in holding that we do not have and may not be able to have any theories which are true about, for example, electrons even though we have good reasons to believe in their existence. Some of the difficulties in truth-realism that have prompted this move to entity-realism are noted below. The truth-realist, while acknowledging these difficulties, maintains, contrary to the entity-realist, that if we are to know that we are using electrons to produce a certain effect, we must know some significant things about them; that is, that our theories about electrons must be true to some extent. In this case, to be an entity-realist one has to be a truth-realist. On this admittedly contentious assumption, entity-realism and truth-realism differ only in emphasis and this is how we treat them for the remainder of this essay.

2. ARGUMENTS FOR REALISM

Realists have used what might be described as local and global strategies in defence of their position, both of which involve an appeal to the notion of explanatory power. An example of the former is found in Galileo's hypothesising the existence of mountains on the moon in order to explain the variation in patterns observed on the surface of the moon, patterns which we now know more directly to be shadows cast by the mountains. At the time of Galileo the mountains had not been observed, but if the hypothesis were true it would give a fine explanation of the observed phenomena. That it was the best available explanation was taken as a grounds for conjecturing it to be true, a conjecture which the subsequent direct observation of the mountains has confirmed. Realists have laid great stress on the fact that items not observable at the time that they were introduced for explanatory purposes have frequently been observed later. However, some items introduced for explanatory purposes are not amenable to subsequent direct observation by humans. For example, J. J. Thomson posited the existence of small negatively-charged particles, electrons, in order to explain the scintillations observed when an electric charge was applied to the cathode in a glass tube with a phosphorescent surface at the opposite end. The realist sees the explanatory power of that hypothesis as providing good grounds for taking it to be true even though electrons are not capable of observation by the sensory apparatus of humans. And the fact that the items – such as quarks – introduced for explanatory purposes in contemporary sciences are typically incapable, even in principle, of direct observation does not seem to the realist an epistemologically significant reason for refusing to posit their existence.

The style of reasoning employed by the realist has been called 'inference to the best explanation'. It is held to be a form of inference which we standardly employ in everyday life. For instance, I may never see a mouse in my house. But I may infer the existence of the mouse on the grounds that if there were a mouse that would provide the best explanation I can think of for the disappearance of bits of food in the night, the occurrence of scrabbling noises and the appearance of droppings. In the scientific context, a theory, such as Thompson's theory of the electron, is argued to be more likely to be true than any available rival theory on the grounds that it provides the best available explanation. As will be seen below, this style has been also used in a more large-scale fashion by the realist in defence of his position.

The realist finds it implausible to suppose that a theoretical term as useful as, say, 'electron' could function merely as a device in the making of correct observational predictions without corresponding to something in the world. In addition, the realist is impressed by the fact that an idea introduced to solve a particular problem often has application to the solution of other quite different problems. For example, Planck's quantum of action which was posited to account for black body radiation proved in addition to solve the problem of the specific heat of solids. If the quantum of action corresponded to an important underlying constituent of physical reality, one would expect it to be manifested in a range of observable features of matter. The realist does not see how the instrumentalist can explain this transfer of theoretical ideas from one domain to another. If those ideas did not correspond to anything in the world but were mere devices to facilitate predictions, the realist thinks that the transference could not be expected.

It is sometimes said, albeit controversially, that realism is the practising scientist's philosophy of science. For, if one has a theory that talks about, say, detecting electrons and about the effect of electrons, and if that theory is relatively successful, it is natural to think that there are electrons and that the theory has articulated some important if partial or approximate truths about them. The naturalness of this presumption no doubt arises in part from the fact that it is in effect a projection into the scientific domain of a common-sense attitude. In the realm of common sense we are realists, taking it that objects such as the moon exist even when they are not actually being perceived. If the moon does exist unperceived that would explain the continuities in our perceptions. The realist admits that there is a difference between the moon and an electron in that while the moon is not always perceived it is always perceivable. Electrons while unperceived are also unperceivable by humans in any direct fashion. But there are many reasons why something may be unperceivable by us. These would include the fact that some things may be too small or that others may produce electromagnetic radiation of the wrong frequency.

If our faculties had been different, in ways that they might well have been different, what we now count as unperceivable might have been perceived. The realist does not think that this accident should count against the existence of items the postulation of which does explain features of our experience. If it were conceded that the existence of items not perceivable by us with our faculties might be posited for explanatory purposes, the realist does not see why we might not further postulate the existence of items even though we cannot tell a story of how alterations in our powers could enable us to perceive them. In a nut-shell, the realist position is that it would be *ad hoc* to be a realist about the moon without being a realist about electrons. And to deny the reality of the moon by, say, advocating, as some instrumentalists have done, the doctrine of phenomenalism which restricts existence to the perceptual experiences is, according to the realist, utterly implausible.

Furthermore, the realist argues that in everyday life we do posit the existence of states which are not directly observable. For we ascribe to other persons psychological states which we do not directly observe and which it is not clear could in any sense be observed. For example, in the face of the appropriate behaviour we say that someone is courageous or loving. We do not see the courage or the loving. However, the postulation of these states explains what we do observe of the behaviour of others. The thought that someone's courage or loving could in some sense be observed is as dubious as thinking that quarks could in some sense be observed. The realist is consequently inclined to see the instrumentalist as basing his position on an objectionably narrow empiricist epistemology which would limit what can be said to exist to what can be directly perceived as existing, and which tends to lead to the behaviourist identification of being courageous or being loving with behaving in a courageous or loving manner. This sort of limited epistemology, deriving from a strong form of verificationism which denies cognitive meaning to sentences which cannot be tested in some fairly direct fashion, would license instrumentalism as a theory of science but at the cost of committing us to behaviourism and phenomenalism.

3. ARGUMENTS AGAINST REALISM

Realism has been opposed not only by instrumentalism but also, particularly in recent years, by those sceptical of the entire notion of scientific progress. It is to be noted that instrumentalists are not sceptical about science and scientific progress. For them, progress consists in the increase in the predictive power of scientific theories. Relativistic mechanics is better than classical mechanics in that the former provides more accurate predictions over a wider range of phenomena. The realist on the other hand relates scientific progress to the discovery of theories that are more approximately true at the theoretical level. For him the improvement in predictive power does not in itself constitute progress. It is rather a fallible indicator of progress which is constituted by an increase in truth. The instrumentalist is here joined by those of relativistic tendencies with regard to scientific progress. The relativist draws attention to the fact that past scientific theories have been discovered in due course to be false. And he argues that there is no reason to assume a privileged position for our current theories: these will be discovered to be false. That being so, he questions the appropriateness of taking truth as the aim of science.

If that is the aim of the activity it is not particularly rational, for we have good reason for thinking that it will never be achieved. Realists have tended to respond by characterising the aim as the production of theories that are more approximately true or have more truth and less falsity in them. In this way the realist can maintain that the aim of science relates to truth while acknowledging the fact to which the sceptic draws attention; namely, that theories turn out to be false, strictly speaking. That could be so while the theories were nonetheless improving in the amount of truth which they contained. Even if this move by the realist answers this particular negative argument of the sceptic, the onus is on the realist to produce some positive reason for thinking that the history of a mature science such as physics does indeed include a sequence of theories which are, by and large, better approximations to the truth. But even before that argument can be advanced, a more radical negative argument of a relativistic character must be answered.

Relativists deny the legitimacy of any objective notion of scientific progress. Notions of truth and reasonableness must be relativised to particular points of view. Furthermore, there is no legitimate way of comparing differing points of view. Consequently any transition in the history of science from one theory to another can only be explained by reference to external factors. Not infrequently, relativists base their case on the phenomena of scientific revolutions. These revolutions are seen as producing such dramatic shifts in the concepts deployed in the theories that there is no common language in which the successive theories can be expressed. That being so, it is argued that the theories simply pass each other by with no possibility of comparing the contents.

In addition it is argued that these revolutions produce changes in the very standards used for selecting theories or hypotheses and so there is no independent basis for arguing that one is better than the other. The realist's response is to reiterate as a brute fact the claim supported by the instrumentalist, that in the natural sciences successive theories have been providing more predictive and manipulative power. The relativist is asked to reflect on the impressive technological spin-off of modern scientific theories. If theories were simply incomparable as to content or if there were no grounds for preferring one theory to another, it would be quite mysterious that the sequence of theories should be generating this increase in our power over the physical world.

Realism is thus opposed to both instrumentalism and relativism. However, in an important sense the realist has much more in common with the instrumentalist than the relativist. For both the realist and the instrumentalist believe that there has been real progress in the history of the natural sciences. And they are likely to be largely in agreement as to what factors scientists should properly take into account in choosing between theories. They differ in the interpretation to be given of the notion of scientific progress. The relativist in contrast rejects the very idea of scientific progress. This means that the only account a relativist historian of science could offer would be a purely externalist one. Instrumentalism and realism represent options among others which could be adopted by a historian who wished to use internal factors in explaining, in part at least, historical change on a rational model.

4. THE REALIST EXPLANATION OF SCIENTIFIC SUCCESS

Assuming agreement that there has been an impressive increase in predictive and manipulative power, the realist deploys what has been called his global strategy. Applying inference to the best explanation, he argues for his central contention that there has been an increase in the accumulation of approximate truth at the theoretical level. In a global move he asks why is it that, say, Einstein's relativistic mechanics gives better predictions than Newtonian mechanics or why contemporary theories of the structure of the atom are empirically more successful than Bohr's theory of the atom. That is, he asks what it is about the more successful theory that makes it more successful. If the empirically successful theories did involve uncovering some significant truth about the underlying theoretical structure of the world, one would expect those theories to provide more predictive power. They do provide that power and the realist argues that the best explanation of this brute fact is that they do indeed represent the discovery of better approximations to the truth at the theoretical level. It would, the realist argues, be utterly mysterious that contemporary theories should have the success that they do if it were not for the fact that they are progressing at the theoretical level.

There has been considerable discussion as to whether there is any phenomenon needing explanation. It has been claimed that the reason for the increase in the observational success of physical theories is simply that we select theories for their observational success. The realist does not deny that we typically select theories on the basis of our conjectures about their likely observational success. He insists, however, that it makes perfectly good sense to inquire what it is about observationally successful theories that makes them observationally successful. The answer for the realist is that those theories have been capturing more truth about the world at the theoretical level. Whether the realist has offered a good explanation in response to a genuine question remains a matter of considerable controversy.

In particular, it has been argued that a detailed examination of the history of science shows that the central concepts of many successful theories have turned out not to apply to anything: phlogiston, caloric, circular inertia and spontaneous generation, for example. If historical studies were to show, as Laudan has argued they do (see Laudan 1984), that this is typically the case, the realist theory is threatened. For it would lead to the expectation that our own theories will be replaced by theories with quite different central concepts, in which case there will be difficulties in explicating a sense in which successful theories are more approximately true, given that there is a radical change in what is taken to exist. As noted below, Laudan's response to this is to seek to explicate a notion of progress that does not involve truth. Whatever the results of the historical investigations and whatever the fate of their interpretation, realism is a theory of science for which historical investigations are of particular relevance.

In defences of realism reference is made to explanatory power, manipulative power and predictive power. Of these notions the third is the more basic. Manipulative power refers to the ability a theory gives us to affect the world. While it can provide dramatic evidence of the predictive power of a theory, it is not always applicable to some theories such as cosmological ones which may be used to make successful predictions about features of the world that we are in no place to manipulate. Explanatory power refers to the ability a theory gives us to explain features of the world. While the relation between the explanatory power and predictive power of a theory is a matter of controversy, on most theories of explanation the greater the predictive power of a theory, the greater its explanatory power.

In deploying this global argument, the realist is not committing himself to the view that the accumulation of truth is a steady and irreversible process. While some realists have thought this, most realists allow that the rate of this accumulation may be variable and that much of what we took to be approximately true may be jettisoned or modified during scientific revolutions. This more sophisticated realist assumes only that, by and large, the chances are that current theories in natural science have more truth in them than their predecessors.

It is common to describe this realism as empirical realism. For the argument is based on claims about how best an observed phenomenon can be explained; namely, the observed fact that current theories tend to provide more successful predictive power than their predecessors. Some realists might seek to defend on purely *a priori* philosophical grounds their assumption that the theoretical sentences of scientific theories are true or false, but the claim that science is actually making progress towards the aim of truth requires an empirical argument. For it could turn out that such progress is no longer made. Realists regard this claim that there has been progress as an essential tenet of their position as there would be no point in caring about truth in science if it were not something which we have been having some success in achieving. This global strategy has proved contentious. In addition to difficulties with the notion of truth noted below, the notion of inference to the best explanation in this context has been found to be dubitable. Those who deny any connection between explanation and truth do not think that the fact that the realist conclusion provides the best explanation is any reason to think that it is true. Others, who accept that there is a connection, deny that inference to the best explanation is a legitimate epistemological strategy. It is said that to show an explanation to be the best, one must show that it is the one most likely to be true and hence it is useless as a tool of inference. It is clear therefore that the realist is committed to developing and defending a particular conception of explanation and of inference to the best explanation.

Realists have sought to support their position further in an explanatory way by considering various features of scientific practice, arguing that realism makes the most sense of actual scientific practice. One feature which the realist cites in this context is the drive for the unification of theories. It is not uncommon to find two theories, each relatively successful in their own domains but in conflict if interpreted in realist terms. This is said, for instance, of quantum mechanics and general relativity. In such circumstances considerable efforts are made by the scientific community to produce a single unified theory. The realist claims that this drive is entirely appropriate on the realist assumption that the aim is truth. If the aim were merely predictive, there would be no reason, according to the realist, not to rest content with simply using the different theories in different domains. The instrumentalist replies that unless there is a unification the theories are likely to give incorrect predictions for phenomena in the intersection of the domains of the theories; that is, for phenomena partly covered by each theory. The fact that the unification of theories has led in the past to an increase in empirical adequacy is also cited as a justification for pursuing that end. Little by way of definite results decisively favouring one side over the other has been reached from reflections on actual scientific practice and it may be that, in so far as accounting for that practice is concerned, the choice between realism and instrumentalism is an open question.

5. THE PROBLEM OF VERISIMILITUDE

The realist's conclusion is frequently expressed in terms of a notion of verisimilitude, a notion given prominence by Popper. To say that one theory has greater verisimilitude than another is to say that the one theory contains more truths than the other or, more modestly, that more theoretical claims of the one theory are more approximately true than more of the other theory. Embarrassingly for the realist, attempts to give a precise definition of this notion of verisimilitude have been quite unsuccessful. It turned out on Popper's own definition that no two false theories would differ in their degree of verisimilitude. And as verisimilitude was to be used to compare theories which were false, strictly speaking, this renders Popper's notion of verisimilitude useless.

Attempts by others to provide alternative explications of this notion which would be applicable to the complex theories of modern science have been no more successful. The failure of these attempts is cited by some critics of realism as a reason for thinking that the very notion of verisimilitude is illegitimate. This failure has accordingly prompted renewed interest in instrumentalism and other theories of science which do not explicate the aim of science in terms of a truth-related notion. Laudan, for example, advocates his theory that scientific progress consists in problem-solving capacity in part on these grounds. Realists on the other hand take it that the definition of verisimilitude is desirable but not essential. Attention is drawn to the fact that many terms occur in successful scientific theories (such as 'field' or 'spacetime') for which we do not have a satisfactory definition. Opponents of realism also draw attention to the fact that not only can we not say what we mean by 'verisimilitude'; we have no way of actually ascertaining whether one theory has more verisimilitude than another. But the realist argues that we can have good but indirect reasons for thinking in some cases that one theory has more verisimilitude than another; namely, that this assumption explains the greater empirical success of the one theory.

Popper, who describes himself as a realist, cannot consistently deploy any such argument for thinking that an increase in empirical success is a sign of an increase in verisimilitude. For Popper denies the legitimacy of any form of inductive inference and inference to the best explanation is a particular form of induction. This means that while a Popperian may believe that science has been discovering more truth at the theoretical level, that belief is entirely a matter of faith. No reason whatsoever can be given for thinking that progress has been made. Popper's realism is thus seen to differ significantly from more standard versions as it cannot involve any epistemological claims about the possibility of finding out whether theoretical hypotheses are true or have a degree of truth in them. Popperian realism is simply the claim that such hypotheses are true or false and that the aim of science is to discover the truth. There is no prospect of having any reason to think that any truth has been discovered. And consequently, in Popper's sense of the term 'realist', one could be a realist even if no truth were ever discovered.

It is often taken that the problem with verisimilitude is a largely technical one, to be solved by explicating some measure of the relative number of truths and falsehoods in a theory. However, it may be that there are more intractable issues at stake. For instance, aiming merely to increase the truth-content of a theory while decreasing the falsity-content does not seem appropriate. For we are interested not just in truth but in interesting truth. And it is not clear how to give a sufficiently objective explication of what it is that makes a truth interesting. It has also been claimed that the core of many successful scientific theories consists of a metaphor or metaphors. As such, these call for evaluation in terms of the categories of fruitfulness or appropriateness rather than truth and falsity. Whatever is made of these points it remains more or less agreed on all sides that any viable form of realism ultimately requires the articulation of a satisfactory notion of approximate truth.

6. UNDERDETERMINATION OF THEORY BY DATA

Historically, the most important theoretical argument against realism derives from the idea of the underdetermination of theory by data. This is the idea that for any subject-matter there will be more than one, perhaps indefinitely many, incompatible rival scientific theories each of which fits all actual and possible data. Historically this idea has been very influential. It appeared, for example, that both the Ptolemaic and the Copernican theories could be made to fit the astronomical data. That situation created a dilemma for the realist, for if he inferred the truth of one of the theories on the basis of its success in accounting for the data, he would be obliged equally to infer the truth of the other theory. In this case he would be committed to the absurd view that each of two incompatible theories was true. Prima facie, the realist is forced to embrace some form of instrumentalism with regard to the underdetermined theories. One possibility is to move in the direction of semantical instrumentalism, holding that the theories in question are mere calculating devices which are not intended to make truth-claims about the world. The other possibility is to insist that the theories are true or false but to concede that there are facts about the world which science is powerless to ascertain. In either case this is a major departure from the realist hope of having knowledge of truths about the world at the theoretical level.

Osiander's advice to Copernicus was to claim only that his theory worked and not that it was true. And Cardinal Bellarmine attempted similarly to persuade Galileo to view the Copernican theory in an instrumentalistic light. In Bellarmine's case this was prompted perhaps more by the desire to avoid a conflict with the Scriptures as the Church interpreted them than by purely philosophical considerations. If it was only claimed that the theory gave the correct predictions and not that it was true, there would be no conflict. Galileo, realist that he was, argued the theory to be true and suggested to Bellarmine that as the Scriptures were likewise true, the Church should find an interpretation which rendered them consistent with the theory.

Galileo's presumption that the Copernican theory was true rather than the Ptolemaic theory, in the face of the apparent ability of both theories to 'save the phenomena', was grounded in part on the fact that he held the Copernican theory to be the simpler. And this illustrates a ploy that realists have sought to use when faced with two theories which apparently fit the data equally well. This is to find some other factor defeasibly indicative of truth in regard to which a pair of underdetermined theories differ. This strategy has generated considerable controversy. For these factors either tend to be uncontroversial (such as internal logical consistency) and not particularly useful, or more useful but controversial. Simplicity provides an example of the latter since many have doubted whether simplicity can be shown to be indicative of truth. Simplicity might be an attractive feature of a theory without being a sign that the theory has more truth in it than more complex rival theories.

It is important to note that the underdetermination which would provide a threat to realism is underdetermination by all actual and possible data. In the case of underdetermination by the actually available data, the realist can simply take an agnostic stance, deferring any decision as to which theory is the one more likely to be true until further evidence is available. In the case of underdetermination by all actual and possible data, no data could be obtained which would count in favour of one theory over the other. The claim that there are any such cases is very controversial. And most realists would feel that there is no threat from this quarter. However, contemporary instrumentalists such as van Fraassen have tended to follow the lead of Duhem in arguing that every theory does in fact suffer from underdetermination, even though we do not have to hand underdetermined alternatives to our current theories. The alleged fact that such theories could be articulated if we were clever and willing enough would undermine the grounds the realist has for claiming any degree of truth for our current theories.

Realists generally hold that neither Duhem nor van Fraassen who take underdetermination to be a general phenomenon have provided any good reason for assuming this to be so. Some realists think that underdetermination can be shown *a priori* to be impossible. On this view, if theory A and theory B both fit all actual and possible data and fare equally well on any epistemically viable principles of theory choice (i.e. simplicity), then A and B are not really distinct theories. A and B are merely notational variants of one another which appear incompatible. And in so far as there is any genuine underdetermination, it may be a limited phenomenon affecting only limited parts of theories. Just as the instrumentalist has failed to convince the realist that all theories are underdetermined in a massive way, so the realist has failed to convince the instrumentalist that underdetermination cannot arise.

The realist holds that the most serious threat to his position rests on a purely speculative assumption which finds no support from the history of science nor any convincing *a priori* demonstration. In addition the realist feels that his position, unlike that of the instrumentalist, does not assume the legitimacy of a dichotomous distinction between theory and observation. The instrumentalist would seem committed to some such distinction even if he concedes that its determination in practical terms is difficult or impossible. For the instrumentalist takes a different stance with regard to observational and theoretical matters. In the case of the former one can know their truth or falsity. In the case of the latter, either they are not candidates for evaluation in these categories (semantical instrumentalism) or such evaluation is of no interest as it cannot be performed (epistemological instrumentalism). It is not enough to make some sort of distinction or other between the observational and the theoretical. The distinction has to be drawn in terms which would rationalise, taking a quite different stance towards the theoretical and the observational. In view of the difficulties in drawing any sort of distinction between the observational and the theoretical, let alone a distinction that would license the required difference in treatment, the realist will argue that his theory, which provides a uniform treatment of all scientific discourse, is superior.

Even if there is no reason to assume that underdetermination is in fact of significant extent, it can be used as a thought experiment in explicating a realist's underlying commitments. This can be seen by considering theories A and B which are underdetermined by all actual and possible data. In this case there will be some sentence h entailed by A where the negation of h is entailed by B (A and B are incompatible ex hypothesi). Given the characterisation of realism, h is true or false and it is in principle possible to ascertain which. But given underdetermination, these two assumptions cannot be satisfied simultaneously. Retaining the assumption that h is either true or false forces the realist to admit the existence of utterly inaccessible facts, facts which transcend our capacity to discover them. The alternative is to drop the assumption that truth is at stake in regard to h. In this case no inaccessible facts are embraced but theoretical sentences such as *h* are construed as a semantical instrumentalist would construe all theoretical sentences; that is, as not capable of being true or false. Many realists take it that the essence of their position is the claim that theoretical sentences are either true or false. They would regard one who withdrew the assumption that truth was at stake in the case of underdetermination as a closet instrumentalist. In any event, realists are likely to regard the existence of such undecidable sentences as being at best a marginal phenomenon.

7. THE NATURE OF TRUTH

Certain familiar philosophical difficulties arise at the very core of realism. For the realist aims at having true, explanatory theories that are about the world independently of ourselves. And this commits him to articulating an appropriate theory of truth. Generally, a version of the correspondence theory of truth is offered; that is, a hypothesis is said to be true if it corresponds to the facts. But such a theory is fraught with difficulties. It has been doubted whether one can give an explication of the notion of a fact without resource to the notion of truth, thereby generating a vicious circle. And the notion of correspondence is a metaphor which has seemed to many philosophers to have defied any attempts to unpack it. Furthermore, the idea of a correspondence theory of truth has been held to embody an objectionable metaphysical picture since it suggests that there is some vantage point from which the world of facts can be compared to our theories, a vantage point which we as things in the world could never attain. In the face of these and other difficulties in the correspondence theory of truth, scientific realists have arguably been too cavalier in appealing to that theory.

In an attempt to circumvent these difficulties, there has recently been a revival of interest in theories of scientific truth inspired by pragmatism. Instead of focusing on an illusive notion of correspondence it is suggested that we should look to the deliverances of the scientific method. Truth should be taken to be by definition what would result in the long run from the ideal employment of the scientific method in ideal circumstances. The pragmatist envisages a kind of convergence of belief in certain theories as more and more evidence is more and more carefully processed. Truth is what would be converged upon in ideal circumstances. The realist finds the notions of 'ideal employment', 'ideal circumstances' and 'the long run' as opaque as the pragmatist finds the notion of truth as correspondence. It will argued by the realist that what we mean by a true theory is not one which is licensed by the scientific method even in some ideal sense but one which describes the world as it is. And it will be objected that the pragmatist has no explanation of scientific success.

It remains the case, however, that the viability of realism depends on the articulation of a satisfactory theory of truth. This is a genuine and difficult problem. But it is not a problem that arises specifically in the context of our understanding of scientific theories. It is already there at the level of our com-mon-sense beliefs about, say, tables and chairs. In so far as we are realists at that level, we need such a theory of truth which, if forthcoming, can be deployed by the scientific realist in the context of scientific theories. And our inclination (shared with the instrumentalists) to be realists at the level of beliefs about ordinary objects may, in the end, provide the most persuasive starting-point for the scientific realist as it amounts to the extension of that orientation into the scientific domain. According to the realist, no convincing reason has been given for thinking that the extension is illegitimate. And making that extension provides the best available explanatory account of the nature and suc-cess of the scientific enterprise.

FURTHER READING

N. Cartwright, *How the laws of physics lie* (Oxford, 1983).

P. M. Churchland and C. A. Hooker (eds.), *Images of science* (Chicago, 1985).

P. Duhem, *The aim and structure of physical theory* (New York, 1981).

I. Hacking, *Representing and intervening* (Cambridge, 1983).

R. Harré, *Varieties of realism* (Oxford, 1986).

N. Jardine, *The fortunes of inquiry* (Oxford, 1986).

L. Laudan, *Progress and its problems* (Berkeley, 1977).

——, *Science and values* (Berkeley, 1984).

J. Leplin (ed.), *Realism* (Berkeley, 1984).

W. H. Newton-Smith, *The rationality of science* (London, 1981).

K. Popper, *Objective knowledge* (Oxford, 1972).

B. C. van Fraassen, *The scientific image* (Oxford, 1980).

PART II

SELECTED WRITINGS IN THE HISTORY OF SCIENCE

SECTION IIA: TURNING POINTS

14

THE COPERNICAN REVOLUTION

J. R. RAVETZ

1. INTRODUCTION

This title refers to one of the most momentous events in the history of modern European natural science. More than any other, it exemplifies the rise of the world-view of modern European culture. The Copernican revolution was prolonged and complex. Its inception can be dated to within a few years of the opening of the sixteenth century, just as 'Renaissance' was on the point of giving way to 'Reformation', and the European wars of exploration and conquest were underway. The scientific aspect of its completion can be precisely dated to 1687, a year before the Glorious Revolution secured the Protestant ascendancy in Britain and hence fixed the political, social and cultural framework of Europe. The inception was the discovery, or perhaps the better realisation, by the young Polish astronomer Nicholas Copernicus (1473–1543), that the earth is not stationary and at the centre of the cosmos, but rather rotates on its axis and also orbits the sun. The completion is the publication of Isaac Newton's *Philosophiae Naturalis Principia Mathematica* (1687), which incorporated Copernican principles in the construction of a uniquely powerful dynamical astronomy.

The revolution was also complex. Its history can be traced in three inter-related aspects: astronomy, physics and natural philosophy. For astronomy, it not only reflected the change in the conception of the relative positions of earth and sun; it also produced an astronomy where calculations were based on the applications of a universal physical law rather than on the compounding of simple circular motions. In physics, it stimulated the theoretical effort that led to the replacement of the Aristotelian physics of qualities, with one based on quantities. In that old system, in some ways closer to common sense, every thing had its natural place, depending on its degree of gravity or levity; and every motion had its natural sort, those on earth normally involving qualitative change and those in the heavens being circular and perfect. Its successor, our modern orthodoxy, deals nearly exclusively with the quantitative attributes of matter, called the 'primary qualities' in the seventeenth century. In natural philosophy, it replaced an earth-centred cosmos which had been reconciled with Christian teaching, by an infinite, uniform, nearly empty universe; and it also established a conception of knowledge based on experiential facts rather than on ecclesiastical authority.

We should not infer that the astronomical work simply *caused* this transformation of scientific culture. The vast process of 'the disenchantment of the cosmos', which defines the unique consciousness of modern Europe, and the demise of the Medieval world-picture, seems to have depended rather less on Copernican astronomy than some enthusiastic scholars have tended to claim. But the Copernican revolution was the central scientific programme around which all the other changes were organised and debated, from the scientific task of the creation of a new mechanics appropriate for an earth moving through homogeneous space, to the political struggle over authority when the results of science were apparently in conflict with the teaching of the Church.

The revolution required men of great genius and also courage for its making. Copernicus was a man of many parts, devoting most of his life to public administration and the defence of the Polish realm against the Teutonic Knights; among his minor works is a pioneering treatise on money. At the midpoint of the revolution came two men who transformed its nature, and who were colleagues and to some extent friends; but whose personal circumstances and scientific styles were nearly as different as they could be. Such were Galileo (1564–1642) and Kepler (1571–1630). Finally came Newton (1642–1727), a man whose public lustre as a scientist successfully concealed his private face as a speculative natural philosopher, until the present generation of historians of science finally unravelled his secret.

After its effective completion in its scientific aspect, the Copernican revolution continued in the cultural and political realms. The scandal of the trial of Galileo was a severe embarrassment to the Catholic Church, and (since Galileo chose to recant) not an unmixed propaganda victory for its enemies. Copernicus's own book of 1543 remained on the Catholic Index of Prohibited Books until the early nineteenth century. A direct observational demonstration of the orbital motion of the earth, in stellar parallax, waited until the 1830s for its genuine achievement by F. W. Bessel (false claims go back nearly to the time of Copernicus). A similar demonstration for the earth's rotation came even later, with the Foucault pendulum of the 1840s.

Because of its length, complexity and involvement with issues of religion and authority, the Copernican revolution has raised important questions for the philosophy of science and also for the writing of its history. These latter naturally tend to focus on the case of Galileo: was he a martyr to scientific truth and intellectual freedom; or was he a proud man lacking in a sense of social responsibility when he insisted on broadcasting his unproven and dangerous ideas? (This is not merely a Catholic apologists' view; the atheist writer Arthur Koestler (1905–83) argued for it in *The Sleepwalkers* (1959).) In the philosophy of science, Copernicus caused a second, delayed revolution when it was realised that the combination of the astronomy of Ptolemy with the physics of Aristotle was a genuinely scientific system. Since Copernicus (with his successors) undoubtedly showed this to be false, then in this crucial case science did *not* progress by the accumulation of facts and the refinement of theories. A young scholar at Harvard University in the late 1940s found this deeply unsettling to all the ideas he had imbibed about science; out of Thomas Kuhn's questioning came the modern classic entitled *The Copernican Revolution* (1957), and also the seminal philosophy of *The Structure of Scientific Revolutions* (1962). (See art. 54, sect. 3.)

2. THE INCEPTION OF THE COPERNICAN REVOLUTION

Nicholas Copernicus was born in Torun, in north-western Poland, in 1473. His family were of good social standing; an uncle was a leading bishop of the church. He attended university at Cracow, then an outpost of humanistic studies, and afterwards went to Italy for his professional education. He stayed there as long as he could, working with a leading astronomer. He returned to Poland in 1512 to take up a career as canon of Frauenburg Cathedral. His service to the Catholic Church and thus to the Polish nation occupied all his working life; for his astronomical work, he was known only by reputation and some short papers. One of these was the *Commentariolus*, a sketch of an early, simple version of his theory; and the other, a *Letter Against Werner*, dealing with the problems of the reference-frames for astronomy. Copernicus also wrote a short treatise on money, a pioneering work on a modern interpretation, motivated by the disturbed conditions in the area for which he was a responsible administrator. Near the end of his life he was visited by a young Lutheran scholar from Wittenberg, George Joachim Rheticus (1514–74). He overcame Copernicus's long resistance to the publication of his great work, and secured a text to take back to publish. On his return he also published a popular account of the system, the *Narratio Prima* (1540). Copernicus received the printed text of the *De revolutionibus orbium coelestium* (*On the revolutions of the celestial spheres*) on his deathbed in 1543, and the theory was launched on the world posthumously.

The world did not rush to accept Copernicus's theory, for it was introduced in competition with a system of the heavens which, in spite of some anomalies and paradoxes, integrated astronomy, physics, theology and educated common sense. The basic model came from the classical Greek natural philosophers, as interpreted by Aristotle. The cosmos had the spherical earth at the centre, and above it the spheres of the seven planets, starting with the moon. Beyond them all was the sphere of the fixed stars, rotating daily. All qualitative change took place on earth; the heavens were perfect and immutable, experiencing only circular motion. On the earth, everything had its natural place, depending on the degree to which it possessed gravity or levity. At the centre was the element earth, then water, then air, then fire; all levity, which extended to the sphere of the moon. This Aristotelian scheme harmonised with Christianity, with Hell down at the centre and Heaven up in the sky, beyond the fixed stars. It also fitted nearly perfectly to an astronomical system of mathematical models based on compounded uniform circular motions for the description of the planets' motions. This was achieved by Claudius Ptolemy of Alexandria in the second century, in his book known by its Arabic title of *Almagest*. Later astronomers embellished it, and also introduced mechanisms for explaining some peculiar slow motions of the planetary orbits; but as a coherent system of frameworks, observations and models, it survived intact until the time of Copernicus.

To see how the Copernican revolution was launched, we consider the structure of Copernicus's theory as it came before his public. It involved three different motions of the earth. Only the first two are remembered now; but as the three elements went their somewhat separate ways through the rest of the sixteenth century, their varying receptions provide us with many clues as to how Copernicus was understood in his time.

The first motion is the diurnal rotation of the earth about its axis, replacing the supposed rotation of the 'eighth sphere' of the stars about its axis through the North and South celestial poles. This motion involved the greatest strain on common sense and indeed on physics; it was hard to explain why there would not be continuous high winds, why people would not be thrown off by centrifugal force, and how birds manage to return to their nests. Yet without this rotational motion as the foundation, there could be no theory of the orbiting motion of the earth through the heavens.

Copernicus's second motion involves making the earth one of the moving heavenly bodies, while the sun is stationary near the centre. By this means the mathematical theories of the planets' motions could be unified, and perhaps also simplified. The 'retrograde' motion of the planets (which had motivated astronomical theory for the previous two millenia) could be explained as a mere appearance, as the result of the relative motion of the planets with respect to the earth; they were simply moving more slowly than the earth against the background of the fixed stars. Also, the whole system would then have determinate dimensions, with the radius of the earth's orbit around the sun being the unit. However, these advantages, largely aesthetic and philosophical, were considered by most authorities in the later sixteenth century to be outweighed by the numerous anomalies and paradoxes afflicting such a theory. On the astronomical side, the orbital motion of the earth should make it closer to different sets of fixed stars at different times of the year; and so there should be an annual apparent change in their patterns. Evidence of this was being claimed from the six-teenth century onwards, but it was rightly rejected until the very small effect was finally established by F. W. Bessel in the 1830s. As a physical system of earth and heavens, that of Copernicus contradicted all the accepted teaching of Aristotle, with its plausible and coherent structure of a heavy, central earth and light, fiery heavens. Furthermore, the new theory contradicted one of the very few theological propositions on which there had been no debate through all of Christendom: that when Joshua commanded the sun to stand still at Jericho (Joshua 10: 12–13) he meant just what he said and so caused a miracle.

It is not surprising that reception of the theory was slow, and in its way opportunistic. Copernicus's followers would tend to pick and choose among the parts of his theory, taking and adapting those they found useful or acceptable, and rejecting the rest. What astronomers mainly wanted were mathematical methods for improving the tables of planetary positions, so that astrological science could be provided with a more secure base. Ptolemy, who had created the great synthesis of mathematical astronomy in the second century AD, had been an astrologer of renown; and Copernicus's own teachers at Cracow had lectureships in the school of medicine, teaching what in sixteenth-century England was known as 'Mathematicall Physick' (astrological medicine). Copernicus himself did not cast horoscopes, and after him Galileo rejected astrology; otherwise the two subjects were closely united until the mid-seventeenth century. (See art. 37, sect. 2.) The Lutheran scholars who showed such interest in Copernicus had a strong astrological commitment, notably Rheticus and the great teacher Melanthon. Astronomers were also concerned with the improvement of navigation, through solving the 'problem of longitudes'; and with the reform of the solar-lunar calendar for the Christian year based on Easter. Copernicus's theory offered little for the former task, but promised much for the latter.

For the calendar, the fundamental problems, including the variety of definitions of the year, seemed to be resolved by the *third* motion posited by Copernicus. This was rendered obsolete before the end of the century, and soon afterwards forgotten. It is a slow motion of the earth's axis, mainly in a conical path, to produce the 'precession of the equinoxes'. This explains the apparent slow rotation 'in consequence' (backwards) of the stellar sphere, which produces a steady change in the position of the constellations (and hence also of the astrological houses of the zodiac) with relation to the sun's apparent orbit. Copernicus explained this regular motion, and then added little variations to it, and also to the orbits of the planets and even to the sun as it lay near the centre of the earth's circular orbit. In this way he hoped to solve the long-standing crisis in the definition of Easter, a lunar-solar event, and also lay the foundations for a truly perpetual calendar. On rather dubious grounds Copernicus was later given credit for the basis of the Gregorian calendar, still in use today. This restoration of harmony and coherence to a collection of motions that had, over the centuries, gone seriously awry, was the starting-point for Copernicus's analysis in the early *Commentariolus*; there he diverged significantly from Ptolemy's scheme for basic measurements. This aspect of his work was also one of the main bases for Copernicus's reputation among competent astronomers as one of their greatest and gave some protection to his paradoxical theory of the earth and planets, until such time as a new common sense rendered it less implausible.

3. FIRST RESPONSES TO THE COPERNICAN THEORY

It was a long time before the Copernican theory became an issue for violent contention in religion and philosophy; that occurred with Galileo, with premonition in the case of Giordano Bruno. But from the beginning it was felt to be very sensitive in those respects, and its early career was muddled on that account.

The *De revolutionibus* was a collection of very different materials. Its bulk was mathematical astronomy, where Copernicus first re-cast the reference frames for observation and then produced his revised models for the moving bodies. Before that came Book I, an argument for the reality of the earth's motions, relying on various heuristic considerations. At the beginning was Copernicus's own preface, telling of problems he solved and warning that astronomy is a matter for experts. Before the preface came an unsigned note addressed to the reader, consisting of an apology for the strange theory and a disclaimer that it represented reality. As a result, those who liked the mathematics but not the physics could use this note as evidence that Copernicus himself did not take his models literally. This confusion was deliberate; the friend of Rheticus who saw the book through the press, Andreas Osiander (1498–1552), wrote the note in order to avoid possible trouble from the theologians! The matter was finally cleared up by Kepler, by whose time the whole debate had been transformed away from Copernicus's own views to much broader issues concerning his theory.

This first phase of the Copernican revolution covers the period when the learned arts were undergoing their great renaissance in Europe. Around the end of the fifteenth century the classic texts from antiquity first became widely available in well-edited printed versions. Before then, in almost all scientific fields Europe was still a pupil, and a not very competent one, of Islamic culture. Thus the first high-level commentary on *Almagest* appeared in Italy just as Copernicus arrived there for his studies. During the career of Copernicus, the scientific heritage of classical antiquity was fully recovered. By the later sixteenth century, European technique and science began to surpass its sources in many areas; and the first great original achievements of European science, for example, those by Vesalius, and then Tycho Brahe and William Gilbert, date from that period. Studies of the surviving copies of the *De revolutionibus* have shown that it was read and annotated by scores of men all over Europe, who were interested primarily in its mathematical contents. For astronomers and learned men of that period, Copernicus stood out as the great restorer of astronomy, who gave hope that the science would regain its mathematical coherence and observational accuracy. His cosmological theories, to a great extent separable from his mathematical techniques, were a matter for each scholar to cope with in his own way.

An important example of this respect is provided by the astronomers and scholars at the University of Wittenberg. Even though Luther himself dismissed Copernicus with a joke in his 'table talk', his most loyal and influential scholars took Copernicus very seriously indeed; it was they who saw to the publication of the *De revolutionibus*; and they established a link that extended through to Kepler. Moreover, they made early popularisations of the system as they interpreted it, for example, Reinhold in his *Prutenic Tables* (1551).

Another important early supporter was Thomas Digges (*c.*1546–95), an English mathematical practitioner and textbook writer. In a translation of Book I of the *De revolutionibus*, called 'A Perfit Description of the Celestial Orbes' (1576), he faced the problem of absence of stellar parallax in 'the most ancient doctrine of the Pythagoreans'. He solved it by letting the stars extend indefinitely far into space, in a region described on the illustration as 'This orbe of stars fixed infinitely up extendeth hit self in altitude spherically, and therefore immovable. The palace of foelicity garnished with perpetuall shining glorious lights innumerable, farr excelling our sonne both in quantitiye and qualitye, the very court of coelestiall angelles devoid of greefe and replenished with perfite endlesse joye, the habitacle for the elect.'[1] For him there was no theological problem of the displacement of the earth; heaven was still 'up'.

The most significant dialogue with Copernicus was conducted by Tycho Brahe (1546–1601), who flourished towards the end of the sixteenth century. Himself an astrologer and alchemist of renown, he determined to use his fame and Royal patronage to establish observational astronomy on a firm footing. For this he built huge observational instruments on his island near Copenhagen, and operated them with unprecedented concern for rigour and accuracy. He took the Copernican theory seriously, produced arguments which eventually convinced him it was wrong, and finally published a 'compromise' system of the world which may not have been entirely his own original thought. On the issue of the earth's rotation, he imagined an experiment, with cannons shooting to the East and to the West. If the earth were really in motion, then it would catch up with the eastwards cannonball, causing an apparent decrease in its range. He also analysed the stellar parallax problem, calculating a lower bound to the distance of the fixed stars if the effect was too small to be seen on his uniquely accurate instruments. Combining this with the visual diameter of the fixed stars (accepted on the basis of naked-eye observations) he calculated a minimum size for them that was fantastically large, indeed larger than the supposed orbit of the earth around the sun. Thus the first motion of the earth was refuted by a plausible thought-experiment, and the second by a physically implausible conclusion on the size of the fixed stars. Together, these two arguments might be considered reasonable refutations in the sense used by Karl Popper, or part of the 'ocean of anomalies' in which every new theory drowns, in the sense of Imre Lakatos. (See art. 54, sect. 2.) Tycho also satisfied himself that the slight, slow irregular motions in the orbits of the earth and planets, which Copernicus incorporated in his third motion of the earth, were non-existent, being merely the result of observational errors occurred over the centuries. Thenceforth the third motion of the Copernican theory was forgotten.

Tycho's compromise system adapted a device that had been known to Islamic astronomers, some of whom had imagined that Venus and Mercury orbit the sun. That provides a neat explanation of why these two planets remain close to the sun in the heavens, unlike Mars and the other planets. Tycho extended this to all the planets, so that he kept the earth stationary in the centre, with the sun moving around it, and all the other planets moving around the sun. This may seem cumbersome, but it fitted nearly all the phenomena as satisfactorily as Copernicus's model, whilst avoiding the cosmological paradoxes with which that model was afflicted. It did involve an anomaly of its own, in that the spheres of the planets' orbits intersected; but Tycho had already claimed that this occurred in the case of comets, and so for him it was no great problem. The system was thereby inconsistent with Aristotelian natural philosophy; and for convinced Copernicans (starting with Galileo) it had nothing significant in its favour. But it had a surprisingly long life, as it was later adopted by Jesuit astronomers as *their* compromise against Galileo, and lasted until well into the next century.

By the end of the sixteenth century, Copernicus's theory had attracted much respectful attention, because of his eminence as an astronomer. But on balance, it could not overcome all the anomalies in common sense, physics, natural philosophy and theology with which it was afflicted. Although various practitioners had proclaimed their support for it, as a full system of planetary astronomy it had won no converts among eminent astronomers.

The last of the significant sixteenth-century figures in the Copernican revolution was not an astronomer at all, but a wild, heretical Dominican monk, Giordano Bruno. Sharing the religious enthusiasm that was more prominent on the Protestant side, he attempted a comprehensive critique of the corrupted churches of his time. This included rejection of the Aristotelian philosophy in favour of a neo-Platonic one; and in this, exalting spirit over matter, there was no privilege given to heavy, dense things. So Bruno imagined not only our sun-centred system, but an infinity of them, and each with its own human and religious drama. From this point, roughly the 1580s, the Copernican system was irrevocably linked to religious conflict. Bruno spent the last ten years of his life with the Inquisition, recanting nothing, and was burned at the stake in 1600. Scarcely ten years later Galileo announced his telescopic discoveries including what could be interpreted as life-support systems on the moon. The name of Bruno was never mentioned by Galileo or his opponents; that would have been breaking the rules of a game which, however harsh it eventually became, never lost its etiquette.

4. THE TURNING-POINT: GALILEO AND KEPLER

There is no lack of strong or interesting characters in the making of the Copernican revolution; but with Galileo and Kepler we have men who would have been great fictional creations had they not existed already. They were colleagues, and even friends of a sort; but their circumstances, lives and styles were as contrasting as opposite sides of an artistic pattern. We have Galileo the Italian, or better the Florentine, proud, argumentative, the friend of the great and noble, and even in his days of old age and disgrace the object of admiration on all sides. In contrast, Kepler, the Central-European provincial, was forced to a career of drudgery. Although humble and loving, he was dogged by bad luck, death and danger, and finally died in poverty on a journey to plead for his wages. The contrast extends to their paradoxical achievements. Kepler was a speculator and a visionary, but his lasting contribution was achieved in the most technical of studies in mathematical astronomy, on the orbit of the planet Mars. Galileo was the prototype hard-headed scientist; but while he discovered many new phenomena in the heavens that *suggested* the inadequacy of the old systems, all his attempted *proofs* of the new system ended in failure.

Kepler was first on the scene, with his discovery in 1596 of a great 'cosmographic mystery', in structural harmonies of the Copernican system of the planets, related to the five regular solids of Plato. He knew of Galileo as an astronomer and a Copernican, and sent a copy of his book to him; Galileo's reply was a masterpiece of tact and caution. For Galileo was then biding his time, while he slowly built a career through university prestige and ducal patronage, and also awaited something that would provide convincing proof of the Copernican theory. Kepler kept working, and in 1605 began a study of Mars, using data left by his former master Tycho. For four years he struggled with the orbit, testing various hypotheses which always produced just too much error in relation to the accuracy of Tycho's observations. Finally he produced the two laws which define the modern theory of planetary motion: elliptical orbits, with the sun at one focus; and the radius vector of the planet sweeping out equal areas in equal times. At once, the uniform circular motions, the mainstay of astronomy since classical times, were obsolete. New problems, not least of calculation, but also of physical explanation, were created. In the absence of the compounded uniform circular motions, with their natural physical basis in rotating spheres, there would be a need for a *dynamical* explanation of planets' motions. This made Kepler's work more revolutionary for technical astronomy than had been the cosmological innovation of Copernicus.

By way of distraction, Kepler had to protect his mother from accusations of witchcraft; and during this period he wrote a little 'Dream' of a voyage to the moon, picking up on ancient speculations about 'selenites' that had recently become identified as anti-Catholic propaganda. If there were men on the moon, how could they have heard of Christ, or, even more to the point, of St Peter? This, more than the displacement of Man from the centre of the Cosmos, seems to have been the practical point of ideological sensitivity in the new astronomy.

Meanwhile, Galileo heard of a 'spyglass' that makes distant objects seem closer; re-inventing it for himself, he quickly realised the crucial technical feature, that a useful telescope would need better lenses than any in existence. With his skill in instrumentation, and also with his location in a city renowned for fine glassware, he was able to design a process and produce lenses of unique excellence. These served for prestige, patronage and also income. First securing an increase in status and pay from the University of Padua with a presentation spyglass, he then turned it to the heavens, and there discovered phenomena promising a proof of Copernicus, together with fame, glory and secure patronage back in Florence.

His first discoveries are retailed in the *Sidereus nuncius* (*Starry messenger*, 1610) perhaps the greatest classic ever of popular science, and also a masterpiece of subtle propaganda for the Copernican system. We start with the moon, and are guided away from the 'ancient' spots to those made visible to us through Galileo's telescope or at least his drawings based on it. The dividing line between dark and light portions of the moon is wavy and rough; the light and dark spots on either side are observed, described, interpreted and suddenly transformed into peaks and valleys. The analogy with earth is driven home repeatedly, even to the point of a mathematical demonstration of the heights, in terrestrial miles, of those lunar mountains whose very existence had been unsuspected until that moment. Then Galileo argues that the large dark spots are seas; and he later argues for an atmosphere around the moon, so that (by implication) it is complete with a life-support system ready for Kepler's space-travellers, though of course Galileo would never say as much.

Following on the moon-mountains, other discoveries tumbled out of the telescope, so dramatically that Galileo may well have been sure that he would soon effectively see the earth in motion. A myriad of fixed stars appeared, together with a Milky Way revealed as stars and not as a smear; and then the crowning achievement of that phase of observation: the moons of Jupiter. With typical Galilean logic, he interpreted them as evidence *for* Copernicus, since they weakened one of the standard arguments *against* him, the uniqueness of the earth-moon system. And with typical Galilean opportunism, he named them after the house of Medici, thereby securing his return to Florence under proper auspices.

All this was reported in January of 1610; within a few years Galileo could also report the phases of Venus (proving that she orbits the sun, contrary to Ptolemy but not to Tycho), spots on the sun that show it to be rotating and also to have growth and decay (against the Aristotelian insistence that these occur only on earth and not in the heavens), and the 'ears' of Saturn. He was now famous, and rather notorious, and he continued his campaign of indirectly arguing for Copernicus on all fronts. In the inevitable reaction, his enemies created a scandal, and the books of Copernicus and of others less prudent than Galileo were examined by theologians.

Galileo was provided, through a friend, with informal written admonitions from the two greatest statesmen of the Church (Cardinals Barberini and Bellarmine), speaking from their great respect and admiration for him; one mentioned the men on the moon, and the other Joshua. The message was clear: take care not to be seen to be challenging the Holy Mother Church, and all problems can be resolved. They may have been too late, for the *De revolutionibus* was soon put on the Index of Prohibited Books, 'pending correction' but actually remained there for some three centuries. Galileo's name was officially kept clean, but everyone knew that he had lost that round in his campaign.

Galileo seemed to have another great chance in 1623, when his friend Maffeo Barberini was elected Pope. He quickly identified himself with Galileo in a bruising dispute over the comets of 1618, to the discredit of the Jesuit astronomers who had formerly been Galileo's strong, if covert, supporters. Galileo then wanted to write his great book, with a physical proof of Copernicus: a theory of the tides as caused by the compound motions of the earth, caused rather like water swishing round a bowl. It would also disprove the ridiculous theory of the astrologers (including Kepler) that the tides are influenced by the moon. The Pope demurred, and required Galileo to write a book in which the inconclusiveness of all the physical arguments would be demonstrated. Thus, through the seventh decade of his life Galileo worked on a book that would somehow convey the Copernican message whilst seeming not to do so. When it appeared, the *Dialogo* (*Dialogue Concerning the Two Chief World Systems*, 1632) (ostentatiously ignoring Tycho's compromise) was a masterpiece as literature and a disaster as scientific argument and political persuasion. The theory of the tides was incomprehensible in its argument, and also patently incorrect in predicting a single tide each day. And the Pope himself was outraged by Galileo's choice of 'Simplicio' as the character to utter his, the Pope's, profundities in scientific method. Galileo's task was one of supreme difficulty: to get a subversive message past the censor when the censor is the Holy Father himself. In these terms we may get a clue to the blunder in which he so antagonised his friend and protector.

With the Pope now an implacable enemy, Galileo was hauled before the Inquisition, his remaining well-placed friends powerless to protect him. Some manœuvring was required to frame an appropriate charge for a confession; but in the end he confessed to believing a proposition that was false in virtue of its being condemned as such by the Church. The idea that the Church can decide on the truths of science was thus expressed with brutal, and ultimately damaging, clarity; but then Galileo was less than perfect in his role as martyr for science, since he confessed to something he did not believe. The trial and condemnation were a disaster in many ways; not least in fostering an atmosphere of fear and repression that accelerated the intellectual decline of Counter-Reformation Catholic Europe. Galileo retired to his house-arrest, producing his great work on mechanics, the *Discorsi* (*Discourses . . . Concerning Two New Sciences*, 1638), which (as Brecht suggested in his play) was a nearly acceptable reason for avoiding martyrdom.

While Galileo was engaged in his publicist's battles for Copernicus, Kepler continued his work of reconciling celestial visions with astronomical observations. The 'music of the spheres', a theme of mystical writers since classical antiquity, was now analysed from the real motions of the (Copernican) planets; Kepler produced musical scores for describing the various ratios of their motions. In the course of this study, he found the third of his immortal laws, relating the times of revolution of the planets in their orbits to the radii of the orbits. It is (*T*imes)-*S*quared proportional to (*R*adii)-*C*ubed, easily remembered as T-S-R-C. he also produced his *Epitome* of Copernican astronomy (1621) in which he argued for the system mainly on aesthetic grounds, and a set of astronomical tables (the 'Rudolfine') in which the Copernican system (in his version) was presupposed and thus corroborated.

If we look at the strictly scientific aspect of the Copernican revolution, Kepler's contribution was much greater than Galileo's. Working astronomers had no choice but to use his ellipses; this model incidentally resolved some classic problems of planetary astronomy (as that of planetary 'latitudes'); and through Kepler's work the Copernican system became the working hypothesis for astronomy. But Galileo, with all his blunders and failures, quite demolished the old Aristotelian-Ptolemaic system of an integrated physical astronomy. Whatever took its place would be designed around the wreckage of those plausible, neat distinctions between earth and heavens that had set the rules for scientific astronomy from its origins in classical antiquity.

5. THE COMPLETION

The Copernican revolution, being so extended and complex, provides us with a good example of a classic problem in the philosophy of science: at what point, or by what criteria, does it become 'scientific' to believe in the truth of a previously rejected theory? In the present case, Kuhn has given an illuminating answer in *The Copernican Revolution*. It was not so much any single piece of evidence that was conclusive; but rather that by the time of Galileo and Kepler, all the evidence was running one way; if not directly for Copernicus, then at least directly against Aristotle-Ptolemy. It was possible for competent astronomers to hold the line for Tycho; thus the Jesuit Giambattista Riccioli (1598–1671), in the frontispiece of his *Novum Almagestum* (1659), argued that the Tychonic system was more weighty in the scales of evidence that the Copernican. But by then such an opinion was becoming eccentric.

By the middle of the seventeenth century, the tide was flowing, not merely in technical problems, but also in the common sense of plausibility concerning scientific questions. Students at universities were beginning to read textbooks of natural philosophy written by Descartes and Gassendi and their followers. Among them, the Copernican system was either demonstrated or presupposed. It was all part of the loss of plausibility of a structured cosmos, where everything had occupied its place in the hierarchy, and where all things and actions had been imbued with meaning. Astrology was in rapid decline by this time, in spite of there being no demonstration of its falsity. The exciting, creative medley of natural philosophies of the turn of the century, including all sorts of traditions descended from Plato and from Aristotle, was now dwindling; with the rapid progress of the 'disenchantment of the cosmos', all philosophical paths were leading towards a universe where sentience and meaning were ever more restricted. In such a context of plausibility, the old Aristotelian objections to Copernicus lost their force, and the old neo-Platonic enthusiasm for him was an irrelevance.

Among natural philosophers, the central physical problems being studied were closely related to those raised by the defence of Copernicus. Chief among these was mechanics. There were many debates about the composition of motions, with experiments, both hypothetical and real, of balls dropped from masts of ships and high places; these would resolve the paradoxes of motion on a rotating earth. But mechanics was also the paradigm science of this new philosophy, which abolished all meaningful structures and substituted matter and motion for its reality. Progress was not immediate; and laws of impact described by Descartes were, with the exception of the trivial case of complete symmetry, wrong. But the paradigm was established, and in this *latter* phase of the Copernican revolution, the 'scientific revolution' was intimately related, and crucial in its support. (See art. 15, sect. 3.3.)

By the time that the young Isaac Newton was studying at Cambridge, all the fundamental problems of natural philosophy were cast within this framework of 'experimental corpuscular-mechanism' (to use John Schuster's term; see art. 15, sect. 3.3) with a Copernican world-system presupposed at its base. Astronomy had proceeded onwards from Kepler to produce ever more refined mathematical analyses of elliptical motions, more effective computational techniques and more plausible explanations of the dynamics of such orbits. Kepler's magnetic solar force was enriched by G. A. Borelli (1608–79) to the assumption of a straight-line inertial motion of the planet, which was modified both by a centripetal solar magnet and by a centrifugal *anima motrix*. Robert Hooke (1635–1702) took a simple pendulum as a model, and produced an elliptical motion by an impulse force perpendicular to the plane of vibration. In this he implicitly assumed the identity of terrestrial with celestial mechanics; and in that respect another phase of the Copernican Revolution in physics was accomplished.

Thus the elements of Newton's problems were well defined in advance. He was able to move directly on to the problems of the dynamics of the heavens, and to imagine 'gravity' extending to the 'sphere' of the moon (we note the archaic language preserved in his epochal discovery). This force of gravitation accounted for a spectacular range of phenomena: the fall of bodies near the earth, the orbits of the earth and other planets, the moon and the moons of Jupiter and even comets and tidal motions. In his work, Copernicus is presupposed as automatically as Euclid, and Kepler's laws are empirical truths which furnish excellent test-beds for his mathematical theories. Of course, even then, Newton's task was stupendous, particularly since he had to break with the programme laid down by his philosophical mentors, and assume the existence of a force for which he could give no mechanical explanation. Also, there was the problem of the false value for the moon's distance, which put him off the scent for a number of years; and of course Newton had his own special style of interaction in scientific debate. But all that is part of another great historical narrative; for us it suffices that with the publication of the *Principia*, the scientific aspect of the Copernican revolution was complete. (See art. 16.)

There still remained popularisation, and also the resolution of the Church's opposition to Copernicus. The former task was simpler and more pleasant. By the late seventeenth century, the plurality of inhabited worlds had lost its ideological sting; and (charmingly written by Fontenelle) it formed the theme of the first of a series of successful books on science for ladies. The return of Halley's comet in the eighteenth century seemed to prove that Newton's theory of universal gravitation was as true as Euclid's geometry. There were always those who managed to doubt the new doctrine; such were the 'Hutchinsonians' in England; but however reasonable they were in their Biblical arguments, they were limited in their influence.

For the Roman Catholic Church, the issue of the truth of the Copernican theory had, in the Galileo case, been overwhelmed by that of obedience and authority; and in retrospect the dominant question was that of which side was responsible for the tragedy. By the later eighteenth century, Newtonian dynamical astronomy was being taught in Jesuit schools, while Copernicus remained on the Index and Galileo was vilified. Eventually common sense prevailed on the scientific issue, and by stages the *De revolutionibus* was released, long after it ceased to have any scientific interest. As far as Galileo is concerned, the issue is still alive; the Church has not quite said that he was right in his actions.

In the popular mind, the completion of the Copernican revolution may be said to have occurred only at the moon-landings, with the sight of the living earth rising over the horizon of the dead lunar landscape, and then floating in the heavens. This vision, a product of high-technology and high-publicity science, seen live on television all over the world, may be said to have shown humanity at last that the earth is truly *not* at the centre of creation. But, perhaps paradoxically, it helped greatly to inaugurate the next revolution in the scientific imagination, that of 'only one earth', where we must all live, or die, with our ecosystem.

6. AN HISTORIOGRAPHICAL POSTSCRIPT

The term 'Copernican revolution' seems to have been first used by the philosopher Kant (1724–1804) as an analogue for his own; this was just before the change in meaning of 'revolution' from a cyclic action to one which destroys. The story offers obvious temptations both for hagiography and for Whiggery in the history of science. These were compounded with nationalism, for nineteenth-century German historians wanted to give empirical support to the *a priori* truth that no Pole could have been so intelligent as to discover the true system of the world. Hence they invented a 'deutsche Kopernicus', based on the mixture of spoken languages in the area of Copernicus's birth. This effort had one good effect, which was to stimulate Polish scholars to equally thorough research; the culmination of this came with the celebration of the quincentenary of the birth of Copernicus in 1972, marked by critical editions of all his works, and by many special studies on his background, work and influence. Although centred on Poland and promoted there, this has been a great example of co-operative international scholarly research.

In the Anglo-American sphere, studies of the Copernican revolution flourished as part of the history of ideas in the 'scientific revolution' period. Thomas Kuhn's pioneering work, written as a general introduction, combined the 'history of ideas' approach of Alexandre Koyré with a keen insight and great popularising skill on scientific matters. He had been criticised for failing to anticipate later currents of historiography more concerned with the social context of science; from my point of view the book is insufficiently sensitive to the science as it was practised at the time. Thus Kuhn accepts (implicitly in his history and explicitly in his philosophy) the legend that there was a crisis in astronomy over a multiplicity of epicycles, which Copernicus attempted, with mixed success, to solve. My reading is that in the early sixteenth century, astronomy was not a matured academic science, in the sense of having a community of competent practitioners concerned with such esoteric problems, without which one cannot speak of crises. The problems that motivated Copernicus and his successors derived only in part from the practice of 'normal science'; what was generically called 'philosophy' was influential throughout. However, Kuhn's *The Copernican Revolution* has, like its successor *The Structure of Scientific Revolutions*, never been superseded.

A complementary popular treatment was provided by I. B. Cohen's *The Birth of a New Physics*, concentrating more on Galileo and the physical sciences. A jarring note was introduced by the writer Arthur Koestler in *The Sleepwalkers*, in which Kepler is the gentle hero, Galileo an arrogant and unscrupulous operator who deserved everything he got and Copernicus a 'timid canon' who wrote a book so boring that no-one would read it! The worthwhile part of the book, on Kepler, was republished as *The Watershed*, in 1960.

With the decline of the 'history of ideas' approach studies of the Copernican revolution have languished somewhat. One new style of historiography, high-lighting social and institutional factors, has analysed the social roles of the astronomers who popularised and developed the Copernican system; but without significantly changing our picture of the whole event. The Copernican revolution is still waiting for a successor to Kuhn, to put the conceptual history into a context that includes the contemporary scientific, social, institutional and ideological factors as well. For that we might well need a very new conception of the history of science, and hence of science itself.

BIBLIOGRAPHY

I. B. Cohen, *The birth of a new physics* (New York and London, 1985).

A. Koestler, *The sleepwalkers* (New York and London, 1959).

——, *The watershed* (New York, 1960).

T. S. Kuhn, *The Copernican revolution* (Cambridge, Mass., 1957).

——, *The structure of scientific revolutions* (Chicago, 1971).

J. R. Ravetz, 'Copernicus', *Journal of the British astronomical association*, 84 (1974), 257–71.

R. Westman (ed.), *The Copernican achievement* (Berkeley, 1975).

15

THE SCIENTIFIC REVOLUTION

JOHN A. SCHUSTER

1. EXPLAINING THE SCIENTIFIC REVOLUTION: HISTORIOGRAPHICAL ISSUES AND PROBLEMS

The Scientific Revolution is commonly taken to denote the period between 1500 and 1700, during which time the conceptual and institutional foundations of modern science were erected upon the discredited ruins of the Medieval world-view, itself a Christianised elaboration of the scientific and natural philosophical heritage of classical antiquity. The central element in the Scientific Revolution is universally agreed to be the overthrow of Aristotelian natural philosophy, entrenched in the universities, along with its attendant earth-centred Ptolemaic system of astronomy. These were replaced by the Copernican system of astronomy (see art. 14) and the new mechanistic philosophy of nature (see art. 38), championed by René Descartes, Pierre Gassendi, Thomas Hobbes and Robert Boyle. Historians of science agree that by the turn of the eighteenth century, Isaac Newton's scientific and natural philosophical work had subsumed and solidified Copernican astronomy, unified the terrestrial and celestial mechanics deriving respectively from Galileo Galilei and Johannes Kepler, and transformed the mechanical philosophy by adding to it an ontology of immaterial forces and 'ethers' acting on ordinary matter according to mathematically expressed laws. It is also agreed that conceptual breakthroughs in related areas complemented these major transformations: Galileo and Newton laid the foundations for classical mathematical physics; William Harvey established the circulation of the blood, based on the achievements of the sixteenth-century anatomical tradition; and Descartes, Pierre Fermat, Newton and Gottfried Wilhelm Leibniz created the first modern fields of mathematics, co-ordinate geometry and differential and integral calculus.

The Scientific Revolution is also usually seen as having produced unprecedented changes in the social orgnisation and social role of natural philosophy and the sciences. The Royal Society of London and the Parisian Académie des Sciences, founded in the 1660s, were the first successful institutions devoted solely to the promotion of the new science of the seventeenth century, and they provided the models for such institutions which proliferated in the eighteenth century. Their organisation and publications did much to shape the scientific community and to create a continuing, stable domain of scientific debate and communication, although this by no means amounted to the sort of professionalisation of science that was to occur in the nineteenth century. (See art. 64.) They also embodied and propagated a triumphant new public rhetoric which praised the usefulness of science, its putative contributions to social and material progress and its objective detachment from the value-laden realms of politics and religion. Although the contributions of science to technological and economic development remained small until the nineteenth century, this public rhetoric, largely derived from the writings of Francis Bacon, did play a role in motivating and legitimating subsequent scientific work. Similarly, despite the fact that the rhetoric of value-neutrality and objectivity was itself an ideology, occluding the values and aims which the new science embodied, this public rhetoric had a significant role in shaping the eighteenth-century Enlightenment, and in promoting liberal and revolutionary social and political causes during the next two centuries.

Although there is general agreement that such major changes occurred in science and natural philosophy during this period, historians of science have been unable to achieve consensus about any of the historiographical issues central to understanding the Scientific Revolution. They cannot agree on what is to be explained. Was there, for example, a truly revolutionary transformation of the sciences and natural philosophy, and if so, where precisely in the period was this break located – in the work of Newton, or perhaps earlier in the generation of Kepler, Bacon and Harvey? Alternatively, does the period display a slower process of continuous change with developments starting in the Middle Ages and only gradually evolving toward the synthesis of Newton? On a deeper level, no consensus has emerged about what would constitute an adequate explanation of either revolutionary or more continuous change. Much of the discussion of this problem has been bogged down in the debate between internalist and externalist approaches to the history of science. (See art. 3, sects. 2–4.)

To all intents and purposes the canonical statements of the internalist and externalist positions derive from the writings of Alexandre Koyré (1892–1964) and Boris Hessen (1893–1938).[1] Whilst only a few externalists would share Hessen's commitment to a rather crude Marxist economic determinism, his work, contrasted with that of Koyré, defines the boundary between externalism and internalism. This boundary divides those concerned with the intellectual contents of science, with concepts, theories and ideas, on the one hand, and those concerned with the non-cognitive, social, economic and institutional conditions, causes, constraints and (possibly) determinants of scientific theory and practice, on the other hand.

Koyré held that the development of modern science depended upon a revolution in ideas, a shift in intellectual perspective, involving the establishment, within or above scientific thought, of a new metaphysics or set of deep conceptual presuppositions, which in turn shaped thinking, experience and action in the emerging fields of modern science, especially classical mechanics and Copernican astronomy. Galileo's constitution of classical mechanics within the framework of a loosely 'Platonic' metaphysics was Koyré's exemplary case of the emergence of modern science. According to Koyré, the strategies and practices of scientific research always follow from within one's particular categorical framework, or metaphysics, hence Galileo had no need of the abstract and vague dictates of some presumed correct 'scientific method', which might have provided post-facto legitimatory rhetoric. Galileo succeeded in founding the first version of classical mechanics because he worked, perceived and argued within the correct sort of metaphysical framework, a kind of non-mystical Platonism; a conviction that the basic furniture of the world consists in mathematical objects, moved according to simple and symmetrical mathematical laws. If Galileo had experimented (which Koyré doubted) and if he exploited new 'facts', the experiments and the facts were shaped by cognition and action themselves constrained by this metaphysics. For Koyré such a Platonic metaphysics was the only viable framework for scientific advance, at least in the physical sciences. Other frameworks might have their virtues, but not scientific virtues. For example, Aristotelian natural philosophy and cosmology, themselves coherent as a categorical framework, could never structure experience and reasoning so as to produce modern mathematical physics, since they were too closely enmeshed with the categories of natural language and everyday life.

Hessen's main subject was Newton, and his explanation of the Scientific Revolution depended on showing that Newtonian physics was a response to practical, economically relevant questions raised during the previous century and a half by the development of the fledgling commercial capitalist economy. From the early sixteenth century, capitalist development and the centralisation of states had focused a number of technical problems in areas such as mining, shipbuilding, gunnery, navigation and cartography. In retrospect one sees that in essence these problems pertain to fundamental areas of physics and it is not therefore surprising that at the time they invited solution by the development of Newtonian physics. For Hessen, the content of the new science reduced to (1) provision and use of the correct scientific method, leading to (2) the development of classical physics having clear economic and technological applications.

Hessen granted no essential role to the sort of intellectual factors studied by Koyré, or to merely local social factors, those which could be considered to be contingent in relation to the overriding dynamics of the secular rise of capitalism and the capitalist class. Hessen's detailed argument made this clear. On the one hand he correctly read Newton's *Philosophiae Naturalis Principia Mathematica* (*Mathematical Principles of Natural Philosophy*, 1687) as a philosophy of nature, rather than as a compendium of piecemeal results in applied physics, because he recognised the theological, philosophical and political resonances of Newton's scientific work. On the other hand, however, he had to view these elements as not essential to Newton's science, but rather as the inevitable but superficial reflections of the immediate historical and social conditions of men of Newton's class; reflections, for example, of the particular political form the 'class war' took at that time, and of the particular legal, religious and political 'superstructures' through which the underlying historical process was reflected in the minds of Newton and his contemporaries. For Koyré such resonances were essential, for they are symptomatic of the metaphysics which shapes more narrow theorising and problem-solving in the sciences. However, Koyré was only interested in these resonances as systems of ideas and not as signs of underlying socio-economic causes of scientific work.

The contrast between the views of Koyré and Hessen begins to suggest the range of disagreement amongst historians of science concerning what needs to be explained in the Scientific Revolution and how it should be explained. Koyré and Hessen focus on different 'sites' of the Scientific Revolution, Galileo versus Newton;[2] they concentrate on different objects of explanation, Galileo's mechanics versus Newton's physics and natural philosophy; and, as noted, they offer widely different sorts of explanations: the triumph of the correct metaphysics versus the technical needs of rising capitalism. Beyond these differences lies a fundamental difference of epistemology and philosophy of science; for Hessen, science is the essentially correct method applied to practical ends, while for Koyré science is essentially correct metaphysics, method being irrelevant, and intellectual comprehension is the main end.

Nevertheless, for all their differences Koyré and Hessen do concur on a critical point – there *was* a revolution in science, a temporally delimited radical transformation of the concepts, aims, techniques and social organisation of science. Hence they fail to provide a measure of the distance separating such (otherwise opposed) advocates of revolution from those who seek the explanation of the origin of modern science in the gradual and continuous evolution of elements originating in the Middle Ages. For example, advocates of continuity such as Alistair C. Crombie and John Herman Randall see the development and application of scientific method as the central feature of the Scientific Revolution. They trace the slow and continuous development of method from Medieval and Renaissance articulations of Aristotle's methodogical doctrines, down to the heroic methodologists (and founders of modern science) of the seventeenth century, such as Bacon, Descartes, Galileo and Newton, who added to previous ideas about method a better managed dose of experiment, and, above all, more mathematics.[3] Other forms of the continuity thesis stress the debts of Galileo's physics to discussions of difficulties in Aristotle's physics, emanating originally from fourteenth-century Oxford and Paris, or they concentrate on the continuity of Medieval scholastic doctrines of natural law and voluntarist theology (stressing the will and absolute power of God) with those current in the mechanical philosophy of the mid-seventeenth century. Interestingly, for each advocate of continuity pointing to method or natural law as the essence of modern science, there can be found an advocate of revolutionary change concerned with the sudden and dramatic appearance of method or the concept of natural law.[4]

As these examples indicate, the cross-cutting debate amongst internalists and externalists, advocates of continuity and advocates of revolution depends on the assumption that some essence or defining property of modern science, be it method, natural law or Platonic metaphysics can be identified and then used to explain the slow or sudden appearance of that essence. For any given defining property it is possible to find contrasting internalist and externalist explanations of its origin and causes, as well as contrasting revolutionary or continuist interpretations of its historical career. This suggests that the fundamental difficulty with the existing literature is not the unresolved debate between internalists and externalists, and 'revolutionaries' and continuists. Rather, the difficulty and the reason for the continuing lack of resolution of these debates, resides in the universal assumption that modern science has some simply graspable defining feature which, turned into an historical category, invites explanation of the Scientific Revolution through the search for general causes of the appearance, sudden or otherwise, of that feature.

In the last two decades three developments have tended to reduce the plausibility of attempts to grasp the essence of science. In the first place, recent research has highlighted the historical contours and interpretative difficulties of the later periods, making it much more difficult to believe that grasping the putative essence of the Scientific Revolution provides the key to the nature and course of modern science. Secondly, there has been an accelerating accumulation of meticulous but piecemeal studies of seventeenth-century topics, of individual figures and of institutions, schools and traditions. The detail and nuance of much of this literature further weakens the credibility of the traditional search for simple defining features and their equally simplistic causes. Finally, the work of T. S. Kuhn, Paul Feyerabend and Gaston Bachelard has cast doubt on the conviction that science is based on a unique, efficacious and transferable method. Almost all historians of science now question whether the origin and development of modern science can be explained by means of the emergence, refinement and application of 'the scientific method'. Ironically, however, these developments, by dampening enthusiasm for new grand synthetic explanations of the Scientific Revolution, have in effect left in place the older internalist/externalist and revolution/continuity theses. (See art. 1, sect. 10.)

They have been challenged and are increasingly seen as irrelevant, but the lack of credible alternatives means that they still influence discussions of the origins of modern science in a subtle way.

In sum, it is no exaggeration to say that the historiography of the Scientific Revolution is in a parlous state. Scholarly debate has been dominated by the clash of simplistic interpretations running along the two axes of internalism-externalism and revolution-continuity. For lack of anything better, such orientations linger, despite rising scepticism about their worth. The major issues in the field, the chief problems of interpretation and the categories available for addressing them have been ossified by the clash, and non-engagement, of contending forms of explanation which now lack credibility. The way out of this impasse lies in adopting perspectives embodied in recent work in the sociology of scientific knowledge and the so-called contextualist historiography of science, both of which have tended to concentrate on nineteenth- and twentieth-century science.

The newer sociology of scientific knowledge (see arts. 5 and 7) has elucidated how scientists within a given field or scientific speciality manufacture knowledge claims, negotiate their status and reinterpret and redeploy them in further cycles of knowledge production. They have observed that this 'social construction' of knowledge is set within the grids of power and cognition characteristic of the community at a given moment, the grids themselves being subject to modification as claims are variously established, extended, reinterpreted or dismantled, and credit is allocated for these accomplishments. Thus social and cognitive issues cannot be separated at the sites where a scientific community manufactures knowledge; instead, scientific knowledge is made in and through social processes that are in turn altered by the changing fabric of knowledge. Contextualist historians of science have reached analogous conclusions; but they have attended more closely to the problem of relating scientific sub-cultures to their larger social, political and economic environments or contexts. They see that although such sub-cultures have their own internal social dynamics and are, to various degrees, insulated from larger social forces, they nevertheless depend for their existence on the configuration of larger forces, which, additionally, can at any time intervene more directly in a sub-culture.

These considerations allow us to see that much of the self-defeating debate between internalists and externalists was due to their exclusive concentration on, respectively, cognitive and social issues. Internalists were inclined to believe that scientific ideas have a special and autonomous cognitive status, and hence that the history of science unfolds through the internal logic and dynamics of ideas alone. They failed to grasp that scientific sub-cultures are relatively autonomous just because they have well-developed social and political micro-structures through which knowledge is produced, and that the micro-structures are variously exposed to, and depend on, the larger factors studied by the externalists. A similar point was missed by the externalists from the other direction. Concentrating on large-scale social and economic factors, they were loath to grant autonomy, and an inner dynamic, to intellectual traditions and sub-cultures. Therefore they, like the internalists, failed to appreciate that intellectual sub-cultures are not merely systems of ideas, but also have 'internal' social structures and political dynamics, partially buffered from the direct impact of larger factors, through which knowledge is manufactured.

The debate between advocates of revolution and continuity can also be defused by adopting this perspective. The sociology of scientific knowledge and contextualist history of science show how, within a given field, scientists struggle to impose significant revisions of the existing conceptual fabric on their peers. This involves bids to reinterpret parts of the existing fabric and often necessitates the importation of conceptual resources from other realms of discourse. Any such process of revision, reinterpretation, negotiation and consensus formation can be variously glossed as involving 'revolutionary' or merely 'continuous' alterations of the conceptual fabric, and this glossing can be done by the scientists who are involved in the struggle, as well as by observing historians and sociologists. In other words, no revisions are inherently and essentially revolutionary or continuous in nature; rather, these are terms deployed by interested parties, historical actors or historians, seeking to explain the process. On the one hand, historians who advocate continuity are simply over-stressing the existence of conceptual borrowing and reinterpretation. They therefore tend to hypostatise a history of *ideas* and their inner, gradually unfolding logic of development. On the other hand, historians who advocate revolutionary displacement of conceptual fabrics are simply overplaying the fact that no revised conceptual framework is exactly like any previous one. A case for 'revolution' can almost always be made out by selectively stressing certain aspects of change at the expense of others.

For an adequate historiography of the Scientific Revolution historians of science must avoid the above pitfalls and instead recognise that natural philosophy and the various sciences constituted sub-cultures: hence the challenge is to describe and explain the processes of change (not necessarily 'progressive') which characterised the systematic natural philosophies and the existing and nascent sciences in the early modern period. This involves forming empirically-based and historically-sensitive conceptions of these sub-cultures as social and cognitive enterprises. It also involves the notion that natural philosophy and the sciences, so conceived, conditioned each other at the same time that they were variously open to, and affected by, the larger social, political and economic contexts in which they were practised or promoted. Finally, this also involves having some working model of the key moments in the process by which these sub-cultures interacted and changed, both amongst themselves and in relation to working models of their (equally historically changeable) contexts. Whether the term 'Scientific Revolution' is retained to denote the period is less important than forming these adequate historical categories and a working description of the processes of change they experienced.

2. APPROPRIATE CATEGORIES: NATURAL PHILOSOPHY, THE SCIENCES AND THE PRACTICAL ARTS

The Scientific Revolution consisted of a process of change and displacement among and within competing *systems of natural philosophy*. The process involved the erosion and downfall of the dominant Aristotelian philosophy of nature and its replacement during the middle third of the seventeenth century by variants of the newly constructed mechanistic natural philosophy, which, after a period of consolidation and institutionalisation, were modified and partially displaced by the post-mechanist natural philosophies of Leibniz, and especially Newton, setting the stage for the eighteenth century. The erosion of Aristotelianism in the sixteenth and early seventeenth centuries was connected with the proliferation of alternative natural philosophies of magical, alchemical and Hermetical colorations, and the mechanical philosophy was as much a response to the social, political and theological threats seemingly posed by these competitors as it was a response to Aristotelianism. Consequently, the crucial moment in this process resides in the first two generations of the seventeenth century, an age of heightened conflict amongst Aristotelianism, its magical/alchemical challengers and nascent mechanism. This in turn suggests that Newtonianism was hardly the teleological goal of the process, but rather a complexly conditioned, contingent (and surprising) modification of the classical mechanism of the mid-seventeenth century.

Viewed in this way, the Scientific Revolution takes on an interesting rhythm as a process of change and transformation of an appropriate 'object' – systematic natural philosophy. There is a preliminary sixteenth-century stage, which will be termed the Scientific Renaissance, characterised by the erosion of Aristotelianism in some quarters, its deepening entrenchment in others and by a ferment of revived alternatives. There follows a 'critical' period (*c.*1590–1650) of natural philosophical conflict marked by the initial construction of mechanistic philosophies, and then a brief period of relative consensus about, and institutionalisation of, a range of variants of the mechanical philosophy (*c.*1650–90), punctuated and complicated by the advent of Newtonianism.

In the period of the Scientific Revolution, every system of natural philosophy, whether of a generally Aristotelian, mechanistic or Neo-Platonic magical/alchemical type, purported to describe and explain the entire universe and the relation of that universe to God, however conceived. The enterprise also involved, explicitly, a concern with the place of human beings and society in that universe. Each system of natural philosophy rested on four structural elements whose respective contents and systematic relations went a considerable way towards defining the content of that system: (1) a theory of substance (material and immaterial), concerning what the cosmos consists of and what kinds of bodies or entities it contains; (2) a cosmology, an account of the macroscopic organisation of those bodies; (3) a theory of causation, an account of how and why change and motion occur; (4) an epistemology and doctrine of method which purports to show how the discourses under (1), (2) and (3) were arrived at and/or how they can be justified, and how they constitute a 'system'.

At the basis of any system of natural philosophy resided one or more privileged images, metaphors or models, the articulation of which underlay one or more of the elements and/or their modes of systematic interrelation. Such images and metaphors could be drawn from a variety of discursive resources: from common discourse about some phenomenon or craft; from already systematised discourse about politics, society or theology; or from the presumed guiding concepts of some especially valued field of scientific research. Because natural philosophers were selective in their choice of constitutive metaphors and models, the resulting systems embodied and expressed certain values and interests at the expense of others. However, a natural philosophy was not a simple metaphor, but a complex system, the parts of which and their interrelations could be given differential emphases and interpretations. Hence, the values and goals 'belonging' to a given natural philosophy were necessarily open to some variation and reinterpretation, and no system had an unequivocal, single meaning impressed upon it by its inventors or by its audience, hostile or receptive. This explains how natural philosophies could be integrated with political, social or religious systems of thought, and could be used to illustrate and support varied viewpoints about mankind, politics, society and God. They were sensitive to historical changes in their social contexts and helped contribute to them, for they could be focal points in shifts of attitude and interest amongst the educated elite.

It follows that natural philosophies cannot be reduced and explained away as 'reflections' of the social structure of early modern Europe. The construction, modification and purveying of natural philosophies was a rich, *sui generis* social enterprise, to which individuals devoted themselves with seriousness and hard-won skills, just because of the social, intellectual and religious value placed on having the 'correct' view of nature. Natural philosophies were, in short, context-sensitive and context-affecting; but they are not reducible to some simplistic reading of the social context.

Beyond having a workable conception of natural philosophy, the historian of science must also consider those narrow scientific disciplines, or traditions of highly specialised and technical research which either existed or first developed during the Scientific Revolution. Sixteenth-century Europe possessed two sets of mature scientific disciplines. T. S. Kuhn termed the first set the 'classical physical sciences', including geometrical astronomy and optics, statics and mechanics (study of the simple machines), harmonics and geometry itself. To this group of sciences, which were first constituted in classical antiquity, Kuhn added the mathematical treatment of natural change, as it had developed in the Aristotelian schools of the Latin West from the fourteenth century and been enriched in the Renaissance by connection with the statics and hydrostatics of Archimedes, the pseudo-Aristotelian *Mechanical Questions*, and the medieval 'science of weights', thus forming an additional domain of physical inquiry concerned with the quantitative treatment of local motion. These fields shared an essential reliance on mathematical articulation, and they were sufficiently developed in conceptual and technical terms to be able, in principle, to support cumulative traditions of posing and resolving problems about their respective objects of inquiry. Each of them commanded a body of esoteric conceptual material embedded in classical 'textbook' expositions and linked to exemplary sorts of problem situations and solutions.[5]

Similar, though not identical conditions held in the second set of mature sciences, those linked to medical practitioners and medical institutions: human anatomy, physiology and medical theory, the classical medical sciences. These too embodied esoteric, textbook-grounded bodies of material; but they lacked, of course, the mathematical articulation and hence the same degree of specification of problems and modes of solution. However, they did contain outcroppings of a serious and disciplined concern with observation and even in some cases experiment, which played only a minor role in the geometrically-based sciences.

Some enterprises not included in Kuhn's schema may well be added. Astrology was widely considered to be a science because it had a mathematical articulation, a textbook tradition going back to Claudius Ptolemy's *Tetrabiblos* and a long traditional linkage with medicine and with the practitioners of the other mathematically-based sciences. Alchemy should also be included, although its lineage was not so tightly bound to the existing cluster of sciences, and its moral-psychological aspirations and its search for redemption through esoteric knowledge and successful practice, tended to set its adherents apart from other practitioners.

The sciences existed in relation to the enterprise of natural philosophy. Indeed, each science was variously considered to be part of, or conditioned by, one or another system of natural philosophy. In Kuhnian or Koyréan terms the 'metaphysics' of a science was often supplied or enforced by one or another system of natural philosophy. For example, although the elaborate geometrical tools of Ptolemaic astronomy fell outside any plausible realistic interpretation, and hence outside any natural philosophical gloss, the main lines of Ptolemy's astronomy, its 'metaphysics', was clearly shaped by Aristotelian and Platonic natural philosophy: the finite earth-centred cosmos, the distinction between the celestial and terrestrial realms and the primacy of uniform circular motion. When, in the later sixteenth and early seventeenth centuries, Copernican astronomy became a critical issue, it was not as a set of new calculational fictions, but rather as a system with realistic claims implying the need for a framework of non-Aristotelian natural philosophy adequate to justifying its existence and explaining its physical mechanisms.

The shape of a science, its direction of development, and indeed its very legitimacy often depended upon the character of its natural philosophically-enforced metaphysics, which itself might have been the outcome of conflict and debate. So, for example, the mechanical philosophy supplied its spokesmen with metaphysical machinery which could be used either to marginalise scientific enterprises which were subsumed by antagonistic natural philosophies; or to co-opt acceptable portions of otherwise dubious scientific enterprises by reinterpreting them in terms of a mechanistic metaphysics, as was done with portions of the work of such non-mechanists as Harvey, Kepler, William Gilbert and Francis Bacon. Conversely, rapid change in a science and/or a shift in its social evaluation could lead to the constitution, alteration or abandonment of a natural philosophy through the borrowing or rejection of privileged images or models. Paracelsus's 'alchemisation' of natural philosophy comes to mind here, as does the rise of the mechanical philosophy, which was grounded in the concerns of practical mathematicians and devotees of 'mechanics'.

All of this suggests that the Scientific Revolution involved more than a process of change and displacement of natural philosophies. One also needs to attend to the sciences in the period: to their individual patterns of change (which largely conform to the three-stage model); to their relations with the existing natural philosophies; and to the shifting hierarchical patterns imposed on them by the contending systems of nature.

Finally, before the stages in the Scientific Revolution are discussed, one additional category has to be introduced, that of the practical arts, amongst which were numbered at the time navigation, cartography, architecture and fortification, surgery, mining, metallurgy and other chemical arts. In the period of the Scientific Revolution important questions surrounded the social role of the practical arts and the status of their methods, tools and results as 'knowledge'. These questions and the answers they received on the plane of natural philosophical discourse shaped the aims and contents of competing systems of nature and some developments in the individual sciences. The deeper social and economic structures of the age prompted these questions and therefore they affected natural philosophy and the sciences by this mediated pathway.

3. STAGES IN THE PROCESS OF THE SCIENTIFIC REVOLUTION

We can now return to the working periodisation of the process of the Scientific Revolution, articulating it in the light of the discussion of generic natural philosophy, the classical sciences and the practical arts. By concentrating on the so-called critical period as a function of the larger process, we can, on the one hand, prevent misunderstanding such characteristic 'Scientific Renaissance' figures as Nicholas Copernicus and Andreas Vesalius, and, on the other hand, we can avoid conceiving of the Scientific Revolution as a series of events destined to culminate in Newton.

3.1. The Scientific Renaissance: c.1500–1600

The Scientific Renaissance owes its name to the fact that it displays in the realm of the classical sciences as well as that of natural philosophy many of the scholarly aims and practices which already characterised the treatment of classical literature, history and languages in earlier stages of the Renaissance. In the sixteenth century the established humanist practices of textual recovery, editing, translation and commentary were increasingly focused upon the scientific, mathematical and natural philosophical heritage of classical antiquity. This late maturation of the scientific phase of the Renaissance was due to several interacting factors. Firstly, there was the increasing penetration of university curricula by humanist studies which partly shifted the foci of intellectual interest and increased the pool of able individuals interested in directing humanist concerns into the sciences, mathematics and natural philosophy. Moreover, increasing numbers of university-educated men, tinged by humanism and possessing practical experience in law, administration, the military and even commerce, came to consider Scholastic Aristotelianism to some degree irrelevant. Such individuals were the instigators of, and audience for, increased attention to non-Aristotelian natural philosophies. Printing also appears to have been a critical factor determining the timing and shaping the outcome. The lure of authorship, authority, prestige, patronage and business made possible by print helped to focus attention on pursuits such as algebra, anatomy, surgery, mechanics and fortification, and natural magic. Ferment in these areas was crucial to some developments in natural philosophy and the sciences. A final factor is the re-evaluation of the status of the practical arts, their products and practitioners, which first began to gain momentum in the sixteenth century, and which catalysed developments in natural philosophy and the sciences.

The sixteenth century was marked by historically high levels of population increase and price inflation, and by an expanding commercial capitalist economy, set against the background of a significant development in the power, and to some degree the size, of state administrations. Overseas trade, and more importantly, internal trade within Europe increased, and the Dutch, followed by the English and hesitantly by the French, began their challenges to the established Spanish and Portuguese overseas empires. The earlier efflorescence of German mining, manufacture and trade continued until it was crippled in the Thirty Years War, and throughout the century the centre of internal European trade began to shift from the Mediterranean basin to the North Sea and Baltic region.

All of this had important consequences for the role and status of the practical arts. The number and diversity of potential patrons and clients for their output increased. At the same time expanded literacy, partly spurred by the Protestant Reformation and partly by access to print on the part of some master practitioners, their cultural allies and patrons, created a domain in which practitioners could compete for recognition and honour, whilst simultaneously contributing to a disparate chorus of claims that the practical arts and artisans deserved higher status, and that their skills and craft knowledge warranted the cultural status of 'science'.

Various groups were touched by this ideological and attitudinal development. There were, for example, leading literate craftsmen and engineers for whom School natural philosophy was irrelevant. Their attitudes could range from bald assertions that facts were better than words and practical action better than verbal disputation, to more sophisticated calls for the reorganisation of education with greater emphasis on the practical arts. The latter demands were sometimes reinforced by educated gentlemen or scholars, including anti-Aristotelian humanists seeking a revised curriculum of 'useful' subjects, ranging from improved rhetoric and dialectic, useful for the diplomat and administrator, to mathematics, useful for the gentleman officer.

Such developments spurred the outcroppings of anti-Aristotelianism which mark the sixteenth century, expressed as piecemeal challenges to traditional pedagogy, as well as adherence to non-Aristotelian natural philosophies. This in turn helps to explain the currency of Platonic themes in the alternative natural philosophies of the sixteenth century. If a practical mathematician, interested gentleman or scholarly humanist had some natural philosophical training and interest, a re-evaluation of the practical arts could support or motivate the advocacy of some philosophical alternative to Aristotle. Here Platonic modes of thought had considerable appeal, because of the great stress which was placed upon mathematics. This also allowed the mathematical arts to be placed in a better light, as, for example, in the work of a figure such as John Dee (1527–1608), for whom magical, neo-Platonic and mystical elements combined with a strong interest in the advocacy of the mathematical arts.

By attending to the sixteenth-century re-evaluation of the practical arts, one can clarify the long-standing question of the status of the classical Marxist explanations of the Scientific Revolution of Hessen, J. D. Bernal and Edgar Zilsel. It becomes clear that the crux of the matter is not how science responded to the technical problems created by nascent commercial capitalism. Rather, the issue becomes one of understanding how this larger development conditioned the re-evaluation of the arts, and how that re-evaluation in turn affected the aspirations, thought and behaviour of natural philosophers and practitioners of the sciences.

Sixteenth-century natural philosophy, which has proved notoriously difficult to analyse, receives some orientation from the notion of a Scientific Renaissance. The recovery, assimilation and publication of natural philosophical systems made available a wide and confusing array of non-Aristotelian approaches. These ranged from neo-Stoicism and Lucretian atomism, through varieties of neo-Platonism, some more or less flavoured with Hermetic influences and variously amalgamated with alchemy, natural and demonic magic and cabala; to more eclectic and idiosyncratic alternatives, derived from figures such as Bernardino Telesio, Paracelsus, or even Pietro Pompanazzi, an Aristotelian whose natural philosophy was theologically suspect and shared some of the imperatives of natural magic. Nevertheless, it is also crucial to appreciate that throughout the sixteenth century, and frequently well into the seventeenth century as well, Scholastic Aristotelianism was officially entrenched and constituted the central element in the education of virtually all of the men who had any serious concern with natural philosophy. Indeed, the late sixteenth and early seventeenth centuries represented an 'Indian Summer' of Scholastic Aristotelianism, which, having survived the theological fissions of the Reformation, and the onslaughts of humanists and Platonists, found new life in the rapidly rigidifying academic curricula of the Protestant churches and their militant post-Tridentine Catholic opponents. Nor was Aristotelianism yet moribund as a metaphysics for scientific work. It was still a guide to the cosmological foundations of astronomy, while in physiology and anatomy Aristotelian concepts continued to flourish, as in the work of William Harvey.

Aristotelianism was, however, under fire from many directions. The central scientific challenge came from a Copernicanism construed in some very limited quarters as cosmologically true; but this challenge was largely latent until the last generation of the sixteenth century, and only gathered momentum in connection with the career of Galileo after 1609. (See art. 14, sect. 4.) On a more subtle level Aristotelianism was dismissed as irrelevant by elements of the avant-garde literati and by some scientific specialists, as well as by exponents of the practical arts. In seeking to establish the scientific credentials of their fields and their claims to higher status, men as diverse as Giovanni Battista Benedetti and Galileo in mechanics, and Paracelsus in medicine and alchemy had to engage in polemics with the teachings of the Schools. Anti-Aristotelian rhetoric was repeatedly heard outside the universities, in princely courts, print houses and workshops of master artisans; indeed anywhere the practice of a science or art fell outside the scope of Aristotelianism. Such rhetoric, often accompanied by articulation of alternative systems of natural philosophy, indicates that Aristotelianism was losing credibility and relevance within certain social groupings. However, the range of alternatives against Aristotle (and within Aristotelianism) was wide, eclectic and confused. Natural philosophical initiatives subserved a wide variety of social, educational and religious interests and no clear pattern is discernible. Rather than prematurely subsuming these alternatives under simple classifications such as 'the Hermetic tradition' or 'the Chemical philosophy', as some historians do, we should accept this confusion as a complex product of the larger structures of the age.

Turning to the existing classical sciences, one finds a marked increase in their recovery, reconstruction and extension in the Scientific Renaissance. The timing and the pace of recovery, revision and extension differed from field to field. In mathematical astronomy, the Renaissance phase is discernible from the late fifteenth century, whilst in mathematics and geometrical optics the pace of the Renaissance phase only accelerated a century later. Anatomy and medical theory followed more closely upon astronomy, the programme of editing and publishing the body of Galen's works culminating in the 1520s and 30s. In each case there was an initial stage of recovery, improvement and, if necessary, translation of texts. This could lead to positive extension in some cases, even if the advance was imagined to consist in a purification of sources or a return to lost ancient wisdom. The entire process took place amid the catalysing influence of the pedagogical and philosophical assault on Scholastic philosophy; the reassertion of Platonising modes of thought which helped revalue mathematics as the key to knowledge; and the more general trend towards recasting the ideal of knowledge in the image of the ideals of practice, use and progress, rather than contemplation, commentary and conservation.

By the mid- or later-sixteenth century, European scholars were offered a much enriched opportunity for work in each of the classical sciences. In astronomy Copernicus could enter into the highly technical tradition of planetary astronomy, basing himself on the prior labours of Regiomontanus (Johann Müller) and Georg Puerbach, the late-fifteenth-century renovators of the field, who themselves had tried to appropriate and perfect the tradition as it had emerged from the later Middle Ages. In geometry the process of assimilation and purification is even easier to discern, for the century saw not only improved texts and commentaries on Euclid's *Elements*, but the recovery, translation and edition of the texts of higher Greek mathematics.

The work of such Scientific Renaissance figures as Copernicus (1473–1543) and Andreas Vesalius (1514–64) needs to be seen in context and not merely as the first steps towards the 'inevitable' triumphs of Kepler, Harvey and Newton. For example, the work of Vesalius and its standing in the anatomical tradition of the sixteenth century is highly typical of the dynamic of the Scientific Renaissance. Vesalius, like Copernicus, stood roughly in the second generation of the Renaissance of his field. He was heir to, and contributed towards the establishment of, the corpus of Galenic writings. Like Copernicus, he was trying to grapple with newly available or improved classical texts, and in so doing made certain initiatives, all the while claiming that he was clarifying, purifying or recapturing the classical intent and achievement of the field. He stood near the beginning of a critical and cumulative tradition, grounded in the availability of the printed word and the high quality woodcut, and prompted by the rhetoric of the re-evaluation of practice (doing the surgeon's work oneself). Yet Vesalius and later figures in the tradition remained largely Galenic in physiological theory, and they should not be read as providing steps towards Harvey, nor Whiggishly criticised for failing to reach his results. (See art. 36.)

3.2. The critical period: *c.*1590–1650

The critical period is characterised by a conjuncture between an unprecedented burst of conceptual transformation in the classical sciences, and a heightened, often desperate, competition amongst systematic natural philosophies (some tried to Utopian and eirenic programmes of religious and social reform) which issued in the construction and initially successful dissemination of the mechanical philosophy. The Renaissance themes of the re-evaluation of practical knowledge and desire for command over nature continued to be sounded, and all of this occurred within a context of apparently heightening political, religious and intellectual turmoil.

The two generations after 1590 saw dramatic developments in mathematical astronomy and the emergence with new urgency of the question of the cosmological status of the Copernican system. The last working years of Tycho Brahe (1546–1601) open the critical period. His attempt to fashion a mathematical and cosmological compromise between Ptolemy and Copernicus raised the issue of cosmology more clearly than had Copernicus, and largely unintentionally did much to undermine the more rigidly Scholastic versions of the Aristotelian basis of the accepted cosmology. Kepler (1571–1630) was certainly the key figure, his active career virtually spanning the period in question. His laws of planetary motion, although not widely recognised during the period, marked the decisive technical break with the tradition of mathematical astronomy and posed the mathematical and physical problem of the motion of the planets in a new light. As he himself recognised, this work marked the birth of a new physico-mathematical field, celestial mechanics, although a sustained tradition of practice did not emerge from it, and Newton's later celestial mechanics was not entirely continuous with it in conceptual terms. More generally, Kepler contributed to the ripening of a cosmological crisis in the minds of early-seventeenth-

century thinkers by vigorously asserting, in the light of his overriding philosophy of nature, that empirically determinable simple mathematical harmonies
expressed and governed the motions and structure of the heavens and that their
existence established the truth of his brand of Copernicanism. The crisis was
brought to a head by the telescopic discoveries of Galileo and his polemical agitation starting with his writings of the 1610s.

The critical significance of the period needs little comment in the domain of
mechanics and the mathematical study of local motion. With Simon Stevin
(1548–1620) and Galileo, the two main trends of sixteenth-century studies of
mechanics reached a climax and pointed towards qualitatively different concerns. Through a subtle mixture of practical, theoretical and pedagogical interests, Stevin enriched mechanics with novel insights, for example, a generalised
notion of the parallelogram of forces, and a conception of hydrostatic pressure.
But his insistence upon strict adherence to Archimedean methods, tied to conditions of equilibrium, led him to deny the possibility of a mathematical science
of motion. Galileo's early work also brought him to the point of transcending
the sixteenth-century tradition, albeit from a more dynamically-orientated perspective, at least at first, and throughout his career he sought in various ways to
exploit geometrical-mechanical exemplars in the formulation of a new mathematical science of local motion. The mathematical account of falling bodies
and projectile motion in his *Discorsi* (*Discourses . . . Concerning Two New Sciences*,
1638) capped the sixteenth-century agitation for a mathematical and anti-
Aristotelian science of motion somehow grounded in 'mechanics'. It constituted
a radical innovation, the first version of a classical mechanics, which is best seen
not as an approximation to or forerunner of Newtonian mechanics, but rather as
an initial and *sui generis* species of a new genus.[6]

It can be argued that mathematics revealed the most profound conceptual
shifts in the period. With the recovery of the texts of higher Greek mathematics,
interest was aroused in the precise manner in which the ancient mathematicians
had produced their results. The synthetic and axiomatic style of the extant texts
masked the procedures by which the results had first been discovered, although
Pappus and other classical writers had hinted at the existence of general
methods of discovery for solving problems and finding proofs of theorems. The
search for the secret of Greek geometrical analysis became associated with and
drew rhetorical force from the broader and very fluid contemporary interest in
'method' as a tool of discovery, proof and teaching, on the part of humanists
and Aristotelians alike. In this intellectual environment it was easy for some to
construe the hints in Pappus as implying that the Greeks had possessed a
method of analysis. The humanist pedagogue and methodologist Petrus Ramus
(1515–72) suggested that the traces of this unified analytical method might
be found in the problem-solving techniques of the contemporary practical
mathematical art of algebra, which itself was profiting from the prevailing

re-evaluation of practical pursuits. François Viète (1540–1603) realised this insight, although in fact he drew more inspiration from the revised logistical art of Diophantus than from the procedures of contemporary 'cossic' algebra.

Viète envisioned the extension of his symbolic algebra or 'logistic of species' through the reconstruction of the texts of Greek geometrical analysis and their translation into his improved algebraic syntax. In the early seventeenth century Alexander Anderson, Willebrord Snel and Marino Ghetaldi, as well as the giants Descartes and Fermat, worked within this tradition, drawing into it more of the resources of algebra, which they simultaneously developed further. With the appearance of Descartes' *Géométrie* (1637) and the mature work of Fermat, the analytical enterprise emerged as a self-conscious new approach to mathematics in which an improved algebra and emergent analytical theory of equations assimilated the field of analysis as previously conceived. New vistas emerged which led, amongst other things, to the invention of calculus later in the century. Greek geometry – synthetic, essentialist and tied to spatial intuition – began to be replaced by an abstract, relational, symbolic and analytical view of mathematics. This was the deepest conceptual transformation of the age, grounded in the attempt to recover and master the classical heritage in an environment coloured by changing views of the aims and bases of mathematical work, as embodied in the up-grading of algebra.

These changes in the classical sciences, included those in optics and physiology which have not been discussed, come closest to looking individually like scientific revolutions and jointly as *the* Scientific Revolution. Yet, even here it is not really fruitful to speak in this manner. One might, for example, try to explicate the expression 'revolution' by invoking a philosophical theory of scientific revolutions, for example Karl Popper's or T. S. Kuhn's. It is far from clear, however, that these would adequately explain the processes of change in each of the domains involved, and it is certainly clear that they would provide no serious rationale for a sense of revolution transcending and embracing all the individual cases. Moreover, one cannot neglect the processes of change in natural philosophy and the relations of those processes to these developments in the classical sciences. It is equally clear that the accelerating transformations of the classical sciences in the period 1590 to 1650 require for their historical comprehension a grasp of the nature of the Scientific Renaissance which they punctuated. This task outstrips the resources of any abstract theory of revolution applicable discipline by discipline. Therefore, these changes have been termed 'radical transformations' or 'significant conceptual shifts' in order to avoid the suggestion that some model of revolution can grasp them in the context of the larger and longer process. That process of the Scientific Revolution is not the sum of these smaller transformations and these transformations require delicate case-by-case treatment in relation to the stages in the larger process, including specific attention to the domain of natural philosophy.

In natural philosophy, the late sixteenth and early seventeenth centuries witnessed a proliferation of and climactic struggle amongst, competing systems.
The period is critical, because out of the conflict and confusion of the natural
philosophies of the Baroque age, there emerged the mechanical philosophy,
which was self-consciously designed and constructed by a handful of innovators, notably Descartes and Pierre Gassendi, who were encouraged by Marin
Mersenne, partly inspired by Isaac Beeckman, and followed shortly thereafter
by Thomas Hobbes and other early English assimilators of this initially Continental invention, such as Kenelm Digby and Walter Charleton.

In the critical period, the most obvious threat to Aristotelian natural philosophy came from a variety of often Hermetically-tinged, neo-Platonically-based
natural philosophies orientated towards alchemy and natural (or even demonic)
magic. (See art. 37, sect. 2.) The seventeenth century had opened with the
burning in Rome of Giordano Bruno (1548–1600), whose teaching combined
appeals to a *prisca theologia* pre-dating Moses, astrology, cabala and magic of the
natural and demonic sort. These elements yielded a magical gnosis of distinctly
non-Christian temper and misplaced eirenic ambitions. Bruno had not been
condemned for his natural philosophy *per se*, of course; nevertheless, his
thought marks one extreme point of development of Hermetically- and
magically-orientated alternative natural philosophies, and it haunted advanced
but orthodox thinkers of the next generation, such as Mersenne and Descartes,
who were to forge mechanism. Quite apart from the religious issues raised by
the teaching and career of Bruno, cognitively *avant garde* but religiously orthodox thinkers had to contend with the ideological pall which Bruno's work cast
upon novelties in natural philosophy, especially those linked to atomism or
Copernicanism, or which embodied a high evaluation of mathematics as a key
to practical, operative knowledge of nature.

Bruno, however, was only one of a number of challenging alternative figures
in natural philosophy who surfaced in the early seventeenth century. Tommaso
Campanella advocated a similar brand of general reform mediated by magical
and astrological Hermeticism. The Rosicrucian fraternity, in its first incarnation amongst German Lutherans in the 1610s, seemed to be proposing a
policy of Protestant reunion, linked to the promise of personal redemption to be
achieved through a magical-alchemical science offering medical and spiritual
benefits. Although the original wave of agitation was swallowed up in the opening stages of the Thirty Years War, the reputation and aspirations embodied in
the Rosicrucian manifestos lived on in the very real persons of Robert Fludd
and Michael Maier.

In the early seventeenth century Hermetically-orientated natural philosophies posed a particular challenge to those who stayed abreast of the latest
scientific and philosophical currents, and whose commitment to Aristotle was
weak or non-existent. Natural philosophies tinctured with Hermeticism were

vehicles, but not the exclusive vehicles, of those sixteenth-century currents of opinion which had placed a premium on operative knowledge, on the search for command over the powers of nature. Such systems could marshal powerful sentiments in favour of the combined practical and spiritual value of mathematics. To the extent, which was considerable, that the founders of mechanism resonated similar sentiments, they had to design the mechanical philosophy so that the values were maintained, but the perceived moral, theological and political dangers and associations were held at bay.

The founders of classical mechanism hoped to resolve the conflict of natural philosophies in a way which was cognitively progressive, but religiously and politically conservative; that is, by exploiting and co-opting the achievements of the classical sciences, including the Copernican initiative in astronomy, by amplifying the premium placed upon mathematics and operative knowledge by sections of Renaissance opinion, whilst avoiding the perceived religious, political and moral pitfalls of the alchemical, magical, Hermetic and eclectic atomistic systems then bidding to displace Scholastic Aristotelianism. The mechanical philosophy was constructed so as to embody an arguably orthodox 'voluntarist' vision of God's relation to nature and to mankind, without threatening to collapse the divine into nature and/or to elevate man, as seeker of operative knowledge as well as wisdom, to the level of a 'magus', a status morally and cognitively unacceptable to mainline Catholic and Protestant thought alike. Accordingly, the selection and moulding of conceptual resources to form the mechanistic systems was a nice and dangerous task, firstly because it involved endorsing some values and aims characteristic of magical-alchemical systems, whilst explicitly opposing them as such, and, secondly, because the resulting product was itself intended to displace Aristotelianism in the institutional centres of natural philosophy, a task delayed in the event by one or two generations in virtually all instances.

The rise of mechanism paralleled the final triumph of Copernicanism; indeed an 'elective affinity' existed between the two. Not all realist Copernicans were mechanists; but all mechanists were realist Copernicans. Cause and effect cannot easily be disentangled here. The infinite universe of the mechanists, and the search for a mathematical-mechanical account of order and change, could prompt or reinforce anti-Aristotelianism; or could be selected in order to express such a pre-existing sentiment. On balance it seems that the acceptance of mechanism – for its many perceived cognitive, ethical, political and religious virtues – played a larger role in the widespread acceptance of Copernicanism by the educated public than vice versa.

Several other questions surround the interpretation of the rise of mechanism. Firstly, mechanism was constructed partly with the purpose of co-opting or defeating a certain erudite scepticism current in the early seventeenth century and destructive of dogmatic knowledge claims. But whether one can join some historians in speaking of a 'sceptical crisis' of the time to which the new philo-sophy proved to be an antidote, is a matter of debate.[7] Similarly, on a still broader contextual plane, the vogue of scepticism and the outbreak of Utopian and eirenic natural philosophies both relate to the religious and political turmoil of the period, notably the tensions within and amongst states leading up to the outbreak of the Thirty Years War in 1618. England can be understood as undergoing a delayed, idiosyncratic version of the process in the generation leading to the outbreak of the Civil Wars of the 1640s. For natural philoso-phers, systems of nature had valued and significant relations to religious, politi-cal and social discourses, and so problems and tensions were viewed through the filter of natural philosophising. This tended to suggest that the problems of the age had some of their basis in the very confusion of competing systems, a view which raised the stakes in finding and enforcing the true philosophy of nature and so fostered the proliferation of competing systems. But, again, whether the disturbed religious, political and social context deserves the title 'crisis' in the sense of a supposed 'general crisis of the seventeenth century' is questionable, as is the role of mechanism as one of the sources of 'resolution' of that crisis.[8]

In order to understand the critical period, it is not sufficient to pay attention only to the victors, the founders of mechanism. For example, Francis Bacon (1561–1626) and Johannes Baptista van Helmont (1579–1644) were major figures filtering and re-ordering the natural philosophical alternatives cast up in the sixteenth century, in order to devise programmes expressive of and respon-sive to the shifting value-orientations towards operative knowledge and the reform of pedagogy and communication in natural philosophy. Their careers display a driven but idiosyncratic commitment to constructing a novel natural philosophy in a situation viewed as void of credible alternatives.

Van Helmont stood for a transformed and sanitised alchemical natural philosophy, toning down the potential excesses – religious, psychological and political – of Paracelsianism, without sacrificing its stress on 'experience'. He, like certain other reformers of the Paracelsian tradition who exploited Ramus's pedagogical tenets, emphasised a new dispensation of a 'chemical philosophy' under the aegis of sober pedagogy and methodology. One could imagine that had the contextual conditions ultimately favouring mechanism not been pres-ent, van Helmont, Fludd and Maier might have been contending for natural philosophical hegemony, rather than Descartes, Gassendi and Hobbes.

Bacon can be seen as a brilliant *bricoleur* of disparate sixteenth-century value re-orientations and natural philosophical attitudes, whose discourse defeats attempts to conjure away his enterprise under the simple rubrics of Aristotelian, alchemical, Puritan or Ramist 'influence'. He was a filter and refiner of the dis-parate polemics and attitudinal shifts characteristic of the sixteenth century, addressing on the level of natural philosophical culture the debates over the status of practical knowledge, the aims and method of 'useful' education of gentlemen, and the Protestant stress on cultivating socially useful, secular vocations. Bacon did not construct a system of natural philosophy; rather, he emphasised institutional programmatics, the ethical/valuational position of the natural philosopher, and, of course, method, a crucial but not exhaustive dimension of natural philosophy. An unsystematised and often implicit ontology was present in his work, however, and, like the more systematic and explicit elements of his thought, it was open to selective adoption and reinterpretation by mechanists and a rump of Hermeticists in the succeeding generation.

In sum, all of the major innovators in natural philosophy, whether mechanists or not, were shaped by and responded to the context of the critical stage of the Scientific Revolution. They all aimed to fill a perceived void of natural philosophical authority; they all overtly rejected Scholastic Aristotelianism whilst remaining to varying degrees dependent upon its vocabulary and conceptual resources; they all resonated on the plane of natural philosophical discourse with some positive interpretation of the sixteenth-century revaluation of the practical arts; and they all drew models and exemplars from the accrued catalogue of achievements in the practical arts and classical sciences of that century, although the choice and weighting of privileged items did vary greatly. In addition, most of the innovators stressed proper method and pedagogy as the salient feature of a new natural philosophy. Their strivings grew in all cases from sensitivity to the apparently irreconcilable divisions within religion and natural philosophy. Beyond all this there was the suspicion that natural philosophical dissension was a conditioning cause of the larger political and religious conflicts, which, accordingly, could be wholly or partially cured by the installation of a true philosophy.

3.3. The stage of consensus and consolidation: *c.*1650–1690

The third stage in the process of the Scientific Revolution is characterised by the dissemination and widespread acceptance of varieties of the mechanical philosophy, and by the progressive melding of mechanism with a doctrine of method, loosely attributable to Bacon, emphasising experimental grounding, tentative theorising, exploitation of instruments and possible technological benefits. A consensus formed around an experimentally-orientated corpuscular-mechanical natural philosophy [hereafter ECM]. It was a loose consensus, to be sure, but none the less real, especially when compared with the conflict of natural philosophies characteristic of the two earlier stages. A further consequence and symptom of the existence of this consensus was the founding of the new permanent scientific societies and the establishment of the newly proclaimed social role and public rhetoric of science (see section 1). The Scientific Revolution, conceived as a process emerging from the previous two stages and centred on the career of natural philosophy and the transformation and reordering of the sciences, ends at this stage.

The dominant natural philosophy of the third stage of the Scientific Revolution was not one definitive system, derived, for example, from Gassendi, Descartes, Hobbes, or, in the period itself, from Robert Boyle or Christiaan Huygens. Rather, ECM was a loose template from which were derived specific variants. There was, however, broad agreement about the methodological component of ECM, and it was not at all like the simplistic inductivism sometimes credited to Bacon and later forcefully proclaimed by Newton. In the hands of Boyle, Huygens or Jacques Rohault the methodological discourse of ECM asserted that the fundamental commitment to the metaphysics of corpuscular-mechanism was not, in fact, a metaphysical dogma at all, but rather a modest, albeit highly likely hypothesis. The method further dictated that any particular class of phenomena was to be explained by first devising a specific corpuscular-mechanical model, consistent with, but not deducible from, the deep ontology of 'matter in motion' and the fundamental laws of collision and motion, and then deducing from the model the phenomena in question. Considerations of the range of phenomena explained, the accuracy of the explanations and the absence of any obvious counter-instances, all served as criteria of the heightened probability of the model and explanation. Beyond this, the method stressed, in the manner of Bacon, 'experience' as the outcome of experimentation grounded in the use of instruments, a robust approach to nature promising deeper and more accurate indications of what there was and how it worked, a form of knowledge convertible to power over nature as its test and fruit.

This doctrine of method hardly sufficed to guide the development of ECM or the sciences subordinate to it. Yet, like any such otherwise ineffective and vague method doctrine, it did help to shape the way knowledge claims were assembled, negotiated and entrenched or rejected. It also functioned at the institutional level in providing some of the rhetorical resources for solidifying and delimiting legitimate practitioners and practices, as in the apologetics and programmatic rhetoric of the Royal Society. Under its loose label as 'Baconianism' this method doctrine also helped to solidify the new public rhetoric of science (see section 1).

Experimental corpuscular-mechanism drew great strength from the policy, adopted by the earliest of the mechanists, of co-opting and reinterpreting the scientific triumphs of the critical period, so that they appeared to support or to be derived from the mechanical philosophy and its proclaimed method. Kepler's work was winnowed of its unacceptable neo-Platonism; Harvey was made out to have been a mechanist; and Galileo was, erroneously, turned into a full-blooded systematic mechanical philosopher. Bacon's eclectic ontology and implicit natural philosophy were repressed, and his method, or rather strategic chunks of it, were grafted onto mechanism. Large parts of alchemy, astrology and natural magic were pushed to the periphery of orthodox natural philosophy and culture; yet, in a sanitised form, 'rationalised' by ECM, surprisingly substantial slices of them remained to be pursued.

The impact of ECM upon the existing sciences was correspondingly complex. It would be a mistake simply to assume that the sciences all thoroughly succumbed to the metaphysical determination of ECM; or, in cases where that did happen, to assume that it was necessarily a good thing. Medicine and physiology came rather fully under the sway of ECM, a view which persisted well into the eighteenth century. The body was seen as a machine, both in gross macroscopic terms and on the level of mircro-structure and function. Much was learned in a fairly trivial way about the mechanics of the body; but the really basic problems of biology – those centring on the functional interrelation of the organs and systems and the self-regulation of the body – were systematically occluded by the mechanical model. In celestial mechanics, the domain opened by Kepler's work, the picture was more equivocal. Descartes had attempted a completely mechanistic, if qualitative and verbal, account of the causes of the heavenly motions in the Copernican system. Newton, who, for the time being, solved the main problems of celestial mechanics, had to break with strict mechanism and reintroduce into natural philosophy immaterial forces and agencies of neo-Platonic, Keplerian, or, some argue, Hermetic derivation. And even in the period leading up to the work of Newton, non-mechanical forces had entered the celestial mechanical speculations of Giovanni Alfonso Borelli and Robert Hooke. (See art. 16, sect. 5.)

It is possible, however, to misunderstand the rhythm of the development of modern science by focusing too intently upon Newtonian celestial mechanics. It is arguable that experimental corpuscular-mechanism and its attendant sciences, in their conceptual, institutional and rhetorical garb of the third stage, might have proceeded qualitatively rather undeterred for some considerable time had not something odd and unexpected happened in the form of Isaac Newton (1642–1727). Newton, it is true, redefined the consensus of the third stage whilst building upon it, with his post-mechanical philosophy of nature, reintroducing immaterial forces and powers, and with his dazzling re-working of the existing mathematical sciences – optics, mathematics and celestial and terrestial mechanics – which he unified. But the fact of Newton does not in itself prove that he was the teleological goal of the Scientific Revolution. To see things that way truncates our view of the process leading to the third stage, that of consensus and consolidation. Moreover, historians of science increasingly acknowledge that the eighteenth century was not simply the age of Newton, in natural philosophy, rational mechanics or the emerging fields of experimental science, such as electricity and magnetism, and heat. One can now see, for example, that much of eighteenth-century mechanics and mathematics followed from Continental developments deriving from the work of Huygens,

Leibniz, Jakob and Johann Bernoulli, Nicolas Malebranche and others; that early and mid-eighteenth-century natural philosophers often espoused a fairly strict mechanistic ontology, rather than believe in Newtonian forces or ethers; and that the emergent experimental fields of the eighteenth century are not usefully viewed as the straightforward products of some inevitably fruitful Newtonian metaphysics. It is also generally agreed that Newtonianism was institutionalised and popularised in Britain and later on the Continent through institutional, social and political manœuvrings which in turn point up the con-tingency rather than inevitability of the Newtonian dispensation. (See art. 39.)

Our periodisation of the history of modern European science should take all this into account, starting by seeing the Scientific Revolution in terms of its three stages or moments, punctuated – contingently – by Newton.[9] His work, superimposed upon and partially redefining the third stage of the Scientific Revolution, should then be seen as setting, to a considerable degree, the boun-daries of possibility in natural philosophy and the sciences in the eighteenth century, which in turn led to that period of accelerated development of the sciences and their institutional and professional structures between about 1770 and 1830, termed in some quarters 'the second scientific revolution'. (See art. 18, sect. 4.)

NOTES

1. A. Koyré, *Etudes galiléennes* (Paris, 1939); English trans. by J. Mepham, *Galileo studies* (Has-socks, 1978); B. Hessen, 'The social and economic roots of Newton's *Principia*', in *Science at the crossroads*, N. I. Bukharin *et al.* (eds.) (2nd ed., London, 1971), pp. 150–212.
2. This point is only reinforced by the fact that Koyré's other works locate the revolution else-where; e.g. *Newtonian studies* (Chicago, 1965) [Newton, as well as Descartes]; *La révolution astronomique. Copernic, Kepler, Borelli* (Paris, 1961) [Copernicus and especially Kepler].
3. A. C. Crombie, *Robert Grosseteste and the origins of experimental science: 1100–1700* (Oxford, 1953); J. H. Randall, *The school of Padua and the emergence of modern science* (Padua, 1961).
4. For example, on natural law cf. M. B. Foster, 'The Christian doctrine of creation and the rise of modern natural science', *Mind*, 43 (1934), 446–68; F. Oakley, 'Christian theology and the Newtonian science', *Church history*, 30 (1961), 433–70 and E. Zilsel, 'The genesis of the con-cept of physical law', *Philosophical review*, 51 (1942), 245–79. On method cf. Crombie and Ran-dall [note 3] with E. Zilsel, 'The origins of William Gilbert's scientific method', *Journal of the history of ideas*, 2 (1941), 1–32 and any 'internalist' account of the genesis of method in the seventeenth century.
5. T. S. Kuhn, 'Mathematical versus experimental traditions in the development of physical science', in T. S. Kuhn, *The essential tension. Selected studies in scientific tradition and change* (Chicago, 1977), pp. 31–65.
6. The fundamental character of Galileo's mechanics is best grasped through an elaboration of Gaston Bachelard's notion of how mathematico-experimental disciplines function, as for example in the work of Maurice Clavelin, *The natural philosophy of Galileo*, trans. A. J. Pomerans (Cambridge, Mass., 1974).
7. R. H. Popkin, *The history of scepticism from Erasmus to Spinoza* (Berkeley, 1979).
8. T. K. Rabb, *The struggle for stability in early modern Europe* (Oxford, 1975).
9. Such a periodisation and conceptualisation of the historical categories in play can provide the basis for a critique of the existing major interpretations of the period as they appear in the works by Koyré, Kuhn, Merton, Yates and Hessen in the Bibliography, and in the works of the crisis theorists [notes 7 and 8].

FURTHER READING

E. A. Burtt, *The metaphysical foundations of modern science* (rev. ed., London, 1932).

M. Clavelin, *The natural philosophy of Galileo*, trans. A. J. Pomerans (Cambridge, Mass., 1974).

B. Easlea, *Witch-hunting, magic and the new philosophy. An introduction to debates of the scientific revolution: 1450–1750* (Brighton, 1980).

O. Hannaway, *The chemists and the word. The didactic origins of chemistry* (London, 1975).

B. Hessen, 'The social and economic roots of Newton's *Principia*', in *Science at the cross-roads*, N. I. Bukharin *et al.* (eds.) (2nd ed., London, 1971), pp. 150–212.

M. Hunter, *Science and society in Restoration England* (Cambridge, 1981).

A. Koyré, *Galileo studies*, trans. J. Mepham (Hassocks, 1978).

T. S. Kuhn, 'Mathematical versus experimental traditions in the development of physical science', in T. S. Kuhn, *The essential tension. Selected studies in scientific tradition and change* (Chicago, 1977), pp. 31–65.

R. Lenoble, *Mersenne ou la naissance du mécanisme* (2nd ed., Paris, 1971).

P. Rossi, *Francis Bacon: from magic to science*, trans. S. Rabinovitch (Chicago, 1968).

——, *Philosophy, technology and the arts in the early modern era* (New York, 1970).

S. Shapin and S. Schaffer, *Leviathan and the air-pump: Hobbes, Boyle and the experimental life* (Princeton, 1985).

C. Webster, *From Paracelsus to Newton: magic and the making of modern science* (Cambridge, 1982).

——, *The Great Instauration: science, medicine and reform, 1626–1660* (London, 1975).

F. Yates, *Giordano Bruno and the Hermetic tradition* (New York, 1964).

E. Zilsel, 'The sociological roots of science', *American journal of sociology*, 47 (1941–2), 544–62.

16

NEWTON AND NATURAL PHILOSOPHY

ALAN GABBEY

1. INTRODUCTION

The work of Isaac Newton (1643–1727) has always attracted scholarly attention, yet only within the past thirty or forty years has it begun to benefit from
properly historical treatment. On the mathematical, astronomical and optical
writings, and signally on the *Philosophiae Naturalis Principia Mathematica* (*Mathematical Principles of Natural Philosophy*, 1687), there is now a wealth of literature
illuminating origins and antecedents, conceptual and methodological innovations, and influences within the relevant sciences. There is a variorum edition
of the *Principia*, a magnificently annotated edition of the mathematical writings,
and the optical work is currently in scholarly editorial hands. Editorial initiatives
are turning towards Newton's extensive writings on alchemy, theology, prophecy and chronology, which at last begin to enjoy serious attention from historians. There is now an excellent modern biography by R. S. Westfall.

These researches have brought with them a sharper appreciation of the need
to explore Newton's life, beliefs, attitudes and achievements as functions of
their properly constituted respective historical contexts. Hagiography and positivist historiography of Newton's science are no longer common coin in Newtonian studies. A cognate issue that merits attention is the relation of the
content, structure and style of Newton's scientific discourse, both experimental
and theoretical, to its author's intentions *vis-à-vis* the presumed expectations of
his audience.

His unpublished writings raise other issues. Modern Newtonian scholarship
depends heavily on the extant manuscripts, and will continue to do so. The
published work provides only partial and often misleading reports of his
researches and intellectual interests, so the relation between manuscript and
corresponding printed text (where there is such a text) is rarely unproblematic.
Even in the case of the *Principia* there are manuscripts whose obvious bearing

on the printed text has not yet been fully examined. The problem takes on new dimensions in the case of the alchemical and theological writings, of which only a tiny number of related texts have ever appeared in print. Yet these manuscripts will prove crucial for an adequate account of what Newton was trying to achieve as a natural philosopher. The manuscripts also bring into focus the intriguing issue of how Newton's undoubted belief in the doctrine of the *prisca theologia* squares with his active immersion in the scientific advances of his own time.

The alchemy is an issue in itself. No consensus has yet emerged on the meaning of Newton's enormous investment of time and energy in pursuit of the Great Work. One reason for this lack of agreement is that not all of the immense fund of manuscript material has been thoroughly studied, or fully understood. A more interesting reason is that historians' readings of this material are often guided by evaluative presuppositions concerning Newton's involvement with alchemy. For some it was a misguided attempt to do for chemistry what he had done so successfully for the mathematical and physical sciences. For others it was an unenigmatic involvement in an integral component of seventeenth-century culture, and was in no way incompatible with the rest of his scientific investigations. For others, the entanglement with alchemy was simply a mystifying aberration best relegated to the bottom drawer of Newtonian studies.

In this article the alchemy is presented (with qualifications) as a part of natural philosophy, a step that constitutes no doubt another issue. It derives from the belief that Newton's conception of the business of natural philosophy, the appropriate disciplinary framework for interpreting much of his work, was richer and much wider than one might think on reading only the mathematics and the significantly-titled *Mathematical Principles of Natural Philosophy*.

2. SOURCES AND INTELLECTUAL BACKGROUND

In his second year as an arts undergraduate at Trinity College, Cambridge (which he had entered in June 1661), Newton began the formal study of 'natural philosophy', the discipline that in the philosophy textbooks of the day bore variously the broadly equivalent names *physica, physiologia*, or *philosophia naturalis*. Among the more popular of these textbooks was Johannes Magirus's *Physiologiae Peripateticae libri sex cum commentariis* (*Six Books of Peripatetic Physiology, with commentaries*, 1597), which was the introduction to natural philosophy prescribed for Newton by his college tutor. Magirus's textbook is a typical example of Peripatetic natural philosophy, the traditional teaching of the schools that took as its basis the physics of Aristotle, and thus exemplifies a major component of the intellectual matrix within which Newton's explorations in natural philosophy began.

According to the *Physiologia Peripatetica*, natural philosophy is the science of natural bodies, that is, of the causes of real change and rest in the natural world. These causes or principles (*principia*) constitute 'nature', and those that constitute and are intrinsic in bodies are either active or passive, active principles being the forms from which all actions and change derive, passive principles being the matter that is the seat of natural capacities to retain conferred change. In other words, natural philosophy deals with the capacities of natural bodies to act and be acted on, and with their associated actions and properties. This synoptic description of natural philosophy is culled not from Magirus himself, but from Newton's own student notes crammed from his reading of *Physiologia Peripatetica*.[1]

This sense of the aims of natural philosophy did not change significantly during Newton's lifetime. Thus scientific dictionaries of the early eighteenth century likewise defined the discipline as the science of natural bodies, of their powers, natures, operations and interactions. As in the seventeenth century, a scientific knowledge of the powers and operations of nature required a knowledge of the causes of natural change. There should be nothing surprising in finding this continuity. Natural bodies exhibit powers and properties, they act on each other producing changes whose origins we explain through conceptual categories that encompass the causes or *principia* of change and the capacities of bodies to undergo change and retain newly-acquired states or properties. This is so whether we are Peripatetics or Newtonians. We may choose (for example) to equate inferred active and passive principles in nature with the forms and matter of Peripatetic physics, or to follow Newton and use precisely the same terms 'passive' and 'active principles' as labels for (respectively) inertial forces in bodies, and the hazily understood ontological grounds of gravity, chemical and geological phenomena, the heat of the sun, the heat and activity of animal bodies, the power of the will.

Again, the range of topics understood to fall within the domain of natural philosophy underwent no substantial change. The *Physiologia Peripatetica* deals with the principles of natural things, place, vacuum, motion, time, the infinite; planets, the fixed stars, solar and lunar eclipses; the elements, primary, secondary and occult qualities, mixed bodies; meteors and comets, tides, winds, the motion of the earth; metals, minerals, plants, spirits, animals, man, embryology, zoophytes; the soul, the senses, dreams, the intellect, the will. A comparable agenda was assumed by most compilers of general treatises on natural philosophy during Newton's maturity and last years. And Newton too wrote and meditated on most of these topics, though with significantly differing degrees of commitment, and of achievement.

These considerations indicate that it is simplistic to assume, as is often done in the secondary literature, that Newton abandoned Magirus and Peripatetic notions once his university courses were completed, or that his intellectual development as a natural philosopher began only after he had put aside the traditional curriculum and espoused the mechanical philosophy. It is true that when he died in 1727, he left a body of achievement that had effected irrevocable transformations, both directly and indirectly, in the major natural philosophies of his day, including that of the Peripatetics, the arch-exemplar of this new kind of physics being the *Principia*. However, quite apart from vestiges of Peripatetic physics in Newton's mature thought, it must be remembered that Peripateticism in one form or another was the earliest contact the protagonists of the Scientific Revolution had individually with serious scientific or philosophical concerns. (See art. 15, sect. 3.) In the young Newton's Cambridge, Peripatetic philosophy may have been on the decline, but it did offer a sophisticated, rigorously organised system of thought, and as far as natural philosophy was concerned, Peripateticism afforded a unified and coherent systematisation of the manifold diversities of nature. The coherent picture of the world elaborated within the Peripatetic tradition caught the young Newton's attention, in that it showed that an intelligible and comprehensive system of nature was a *prima facie* possibility, and the search for just such a system was Newton's lifelong central concern. Once he began to discern its limitations, Peripateticism stood as a challenge to Newton, as it did to others in his century, to create something better.

There already existed something better, or at any rate something promisingly different, in the writings of several authors – not in the Cambridge Arts curriculum – whom Newton began to study on his own about 1663. There he discovered new kinds of natural philosophy, new methods and new issues arising out of the innovations of those who had already found the physics of the Schools to be ineffectual. He studied the Greek atomists, and probably Pierre Gassendi, the reviver in France of Epicurean atomism; he read closely Walter Charleton, the English Gassendi and author of the informatively-titled *Physiologia Epicuro-Gassendo-Charltoniana* (1654). He familiarised himself with Thomas Hobbes's *De corpore (On Body,* 1655); he took extensive notes from Robert Boyle's experimental works of the 1660s, and read Robert Hooke's *Micrographia* (1665). The works of his future friend Henry More, the Cambridge Platonist, also captured his interest, as did to a lesser extent the natural philosophy of Kenelm Digby and the epistemological scepticism of Joseph Glanvill. He also read Galileo's *Dialogo (Dialogue on the Two Great World Systems,* 1632).

Above all, Newton discovered René Descartes, the principal champion of the new 'mechanical philosophy'. (See art. 38.) He studied closely and with a critical eye the 1656 edition of the *Opera philosophica*, which contained the Latin text of the *Principles of Philosophy* (1644), the most effective of all the texts of the moderns in exciting Newton to the creation of his own principles of natural philosophy. In addition, the *Dioptrics, Meteorology* and parts of the *Discourse on Method* provided him with arresting specimens of Descartes' achievements in particular sciences. He also made serious studies of Descartes' ontology and epistemology.

In mathematics too Descartes was the supreme influence. In the *Geometry* Newton found his greatest inspiration for his mathematical development as a whole, including the creation of the fluxional calculus. He studied William Oughtred's influential *Clavis mathematica* (*Mathematical Key*, 1652), the works of François Viète, and the *Arithmetica infinitorum* (*Arithmetic of Infinites*, 1656) of John Wallis, which set him on the path towards the binomial theorem and infinite series in general. He learned the basics of astronomical theory and practice from several treatises, and in Thomas Streete's *Astronomia Carolina* (*Caroline Astronomy*, 1661) he first encountered Kepler's First and Third Laws of planetary motion, which were to figure importantly twenty years later in the *Principia*. He read the 1653 edition of Gassendi's *Institutio astronomica* (*Introduction to Astronomy*), in which volume he would have seen also Galileo's *Sidereus Nuncius* (*Starry Messenger*, 1610) and Kepler's *Dioptrice* (*Dioptrics*, 1611).

3. NEWTON'S INNOVATIONS

This singular programme of extra-curricular study accompanied, and in large measure occasioned, one of the most extraordinary bouts of creativity in the life of any scientist, past or present: Newton's *anni mirabiles* of 1664–1666.

In mathematics, there were researches on cubic curves and on the classification of cubic equations. There was the binomial theorem, discovered by applying the algebraically free variable (of Cartesian inspiration) to John Wallis's method of indivisibles for finding quadratures. In developing Descartes' construction for sub-normals, Newton discovered a general method of differentiation to find slopes of tangents and radii and centres of curvature. He saw that finding tangents (differentiation) and quadratures (integration) are inverse operations, and began to use his 'fluxions', that is, rates of change of a variable with respect to an independent time dimension; he evolved kinematic solutions of curvature and tangent problems by employing the resolution and composition of motions. Later, in 1671, he reformulated his calculus techniques using the notion of 'first and last ratios', a formulation that was to be employed in the *Principia*.

In mechanics, the model and at the same time the target was Descartes' laws of motion and rules of collision in the *Principia Philosophiae* (*Principles of Philosophy*). Newton reformulated Descartes' version of 'the principle of inertia', and developed the idea that a force impressed on a body is to be measured by the *change* in the quantity of the body's motion; he argued that in a collision action and reaction are equal and opposite. (These findings were later formalised in the *Principia* as the First, Second and Third Laws of Motion.) Accordingly,

Newton was able to replace Descartes' rules of collision with empirically adequate analyses of elastic and non-elastic collisions, including oblique collisions, which were beyond the resources of Cartesian mechanics.

Newton was also able to treat quantitatively the forces associated with circular motion. Both Descartes and Newton explained the phenomena (e.g. the tension in the cord of a sling) by invoking the innate tangential tendency of a body constrained to move in a circle. However, unlike Descartes, Newton found significant measures for the centrifugal force of a ball revolving round the inside of a circular shell, by conceiving of the shell as the limit of a series of circumscribed polygons of an increasing number of sides. Later (*c.* 1669) he derived the full formula for centrifugal force (mv^2/r) in another way by considering the infinitely small displacement away from the centre of motion of a body momentarily allowed to escape along the tangent before being, so to speak, pulled back to its circular path. In the *Principia* this procedure became a key element in his treatment of orbital motion about a central force. Applying his findings on centrifugal force to the conical pendulum, Newton also determined experimentally a value for g, the acceleration due to gravity.

More strikingly, he applied this analysis of centrifugal force to the motions of the moon and planets. In 1666 (or possibly a year or two later), he combined the above formula with Kepler's Third Law to show that for the moon and planets, assuming circular orbits, the centrifugal force varies inversely as the square of the orbital radius, so there must be an agent or agents of some sort exerting an equal and opposite force constraining each body to move in its orbit. Furthermore, according to Newton's own recollections in 1718, he 'thereby compared the force requisite to keep the Moon in her orb with the force of gravity at the surface of the earth, and found them answer pretty nearly', the whole episode being mysteriously occasioned, according to the testimonies of two contemporaries, by the fall of the famous apple.[2]

Whatever the role (or relevance) of the apple, and whether or not the 'moon test' actually took place in the mid-1660s (as opposed to the more likely mid-1680s), it is certain that 1666 or thereabouts did *not* see the discovery of the inverse square law of universal gravitation. At that time Newton thought that the power keeping the moon in its orbit (and causing apples to fall) was twofold: an unexplained, possibly non-mechanical 'gravity', and the action of the vortices of swirling subtle matter that Descartes had offered as a qualitative, purely mechanical (i.e. action-by-contact) explanation of celestial orbital motions and of gravity itself. Indeed it seems that Newton attributed the 'pretty near' but not wholly satisfactory mathematical comparison between the restraining force at the lunar orbit and that at the earth's surface, to the unknown relative effects of 'gravity' and the Cartesian vortex. It was not until 1684 that Newton began to employ in his celestial mechanics the notion of a *centripetal* attractive force, now without benefit of vortices.

In optics, the wonderful years 1664 to 1666 saw the beginning of Newton's researches on 'the celebrated phaenomena of colours'.[3] Using a wide variety of observations, some taken from Boyle, Descartes, Charleton and Hooke, some the results of his own investigations, Newton criticised traditional accounts of the origin of colours, arguing that they do not arise from reflections or from modifications of light and darkness; nor could Hooke be right in claiming that light consists in pulses and that colours originate in a confusion of pulses and their impressions. Instead, argued Newton, it is white light that is a confusion of colours, which are to be interpreted not as pulses, but as corpuscles moving at speeds hypothetically corresponding to different colours and their differing degrees of refrangibility. In the 'Questions' (see below) Newton noted that 'slowly moved rays are refracted more than swift ones', that is, that blue and purple rays move more slowly than red and yellow ones.[4] As yet there was no suggestion that a given colour is associated with some inherent *inalienable* property of the corresponding ray. This important insight came in the essay 'Of Colours' (probably 1666), in which more sophisticated and more systematic prism experiments convinced Newton of the heterogeneity of white light and of its decomposition into constituent immutable colours. This essay also contained the first observations of 'Newton's Rings'.

In addition to this catalogue of 'positive' achievements, the *anni mirabiles* are also notable for broader and often more speculative explorations in natural philosophy. The important 'Questiones quaedam philosophicae' ('Certain Philosophical Questions'), compiled during the period early 1664 to late 1665, follow in approximate order roughly the same sequence and range of topics that one finds in Magirus and other typical Peripatetic manuals. The comprehensiveness of Newton's involvement in the study of all things natural is clear from the variety of topics, which include: atoms ('first matter'), divisibility, the vacuum, cohesion, place and time, natural and violent motion, celestial bodies, the tides, the qualities of bodies, rarity and density, generation and corruption, the four elements, magnetic and electric phenomena, perpetual motion devices, vegetables and minerals, light and colours (prism experiments, chemical reactions), sensation, the physiology of vision, memory, imagination, sympathies and antipathies, hydrostatics, method, God's designs in nature, the soul, sleep and dreams, the final conflagration.

Out of such heterogeneity emerge several general points about Newton the burgeoning natural philosopher. First, it is clear from the 'Questions' that Epicurean cosmology provided the framework for his thinking about the natural world. He argues for the actual infinity of space (not the mere limitlessness of Cartesian extension), and maintains the doctrine of atoms moving through this infinite void, both of which positions he held throughout his life. In the 'Questiones' Newton entertains initially the Epicurean doctrine of indivisible magnitudes (atoms of matter, time, distance and motion), for which he later substituted the twin doctrines of indivisible minima of the physical existent matter and infinite space, and of Wallis-inspired infinitesimals for use in mathematical contexts. Despite the implications of this ontological dichotomy, Newton never relinquished the ideal of a mathematical realism in which mathematical entities and operations map onto structures and changes in the physical world, thereby promising the mathematisation of nature, once its laws could be established. The *Principia* is an eloquent witness to that ideal.

Second, in keeping with his atomism was Newton's inclination always to search out mechanical explanations of natural phenomena. He was not a whole hearted disciple of any of the mechanists of the day, nor did he ever view as unproblematic the presumed explanatory sufficiency of Cartesian action-by-contact, or assume or imply that atomism equals materialism. Yet explanations in terms of mechanical models (the most developed example at this time being the optical researches) invariably suggested themselves to him as the natural mode of inquiry in physics, allied to experimentation and 'the mathematical way'. And failure to discover such models in particular cases did not mean abandoning the search for mathematical laws applicable in those cases. The supreme proof of this point is the law of universal gravitation in the *Principia*. Other than showing that gravity could not be explained by vortical mechanisms, Newton was never able to devise a mechanical explanation of the gravitational phenomena that he succeeded in bringing under mathematical rule.

Third, the 'Questiones' show that Newton's interest in optics arose in large measure out of a desire to understand the physiology (modern sense) of perception, especially colour perception, his accounts of the latter deriving from the physicalist treatment that he found in Hobbes's *De corpore* and again, though fulfilling anti-Hobbesian purposes, in More's *Immortality of the Soul* (1659). Hobbes had argued that only matter exists in the world, so thought, sense and perception are ultimately nothing but bodies in motion. For More, Hobbes's denial of spiritual substance was an impious absurdity, but he did accept that *if* it were supposed that nothing exists but matter, then a Hobbesian account of sense and perception would obtain. Newton shared More's views, including his rejection of Hobbes's materialism, but his interest lay principally in determining empirically how perceptions relate to their corporeal causes. Accordingly, the 'Questiones' contain reports of observations and experiments involving the seeing eye, including Newton's proddings at his own eyeball (using in one instance, gruesomely, a bodkin to get between eyeball and bone), his aim being to see how colour images and their alterations correspond to motions impressed on the eye. The methodology underlying these and the other optical researches is intriguingly summarised in the following passage:

> The nature of things is more securely and naturally deduced from their operations one upon another than upon our senses. And when by the former experiments we

have found the nature of bodies, by the latter we may more clearly find the nature of our senses. But so long as we are ignorant of the nature of both soul and body we cannot clearly distinguish how far an act of sensation proceeds from the soul and how far from the body.[5]

Here the operations of bodies on each other include those of the human body and other objects, and the distinction between the natures of bodies and of 'our senses' reflects the dualism between those bodily operations and the soul's perceptions of representations in the *sensorium*, the seat of sensation in the brain.

Fourth, the vast range of topics investigated in the 'Questiones', taken in conjunction with the lessons of Magirus's manual, conveys a correct picture of what Newton took 'natural philosophy' to be. Without that understanding, we cannot adequately evaluate Newton's achievements in the context of his time, or appreciate their significance within the context of his own view of his intentions and hopes in the discipline.

We have seen that in assessing Newton's development as a natural philosopher we should not undervalue the formative and indeed lasting influences of the other writers he studied: Epicurus, Charleton, Hobbes, More, Boyle and Descartes. In the case of Descartes, this point is strongly reinforced by the role of his doctrines in the manuscript 'De gravitatione', written probably in the early 1680s, just before the *Principia*. 'De gravitatione' marks a decisive stage in the evolution of the principles of Newton's physics. It begins (and finishes) as though its sole concern is 'the science of gravity and of the equilibrium of fluid and solid bodies in fluids',[6] but most of the 20-folio text consists in a long critical digression on the doctrines of place, motion, body and extension that had appeared in Descartes' *Principia Philosophiae*. One of Descartes' concerns in that work had been to establish intelligible and unambiguous definitions of place, rest and motion, while maintaining the Aristotelian denial of the vacuum. Descartes defined place as the innermost surface of the surrounding medium touching the surface of the placed body, and so for him motion, i.e. change of place, is properly defined as the mutual separation of these two surfaces.

For Newton, on the other hand, a body's place is that part of *space* the body fills evenly, and motion is simply the change of that place. Defining place and motion the Cartesian way leads to anomalies, contradictions and absurdities, and in 'De gravitatione' Newton deploys to great effect numerous arguments to make his case. For example, Descartes had used his definition of motion to claim that, properly speaking, the earth is at rest, because it is embedded in the vortex that carries it round the sun, so there is no mutual separation of the relevant surfaces. If that is so, counters Newton, whence the tendency to recede from the sun (at the centre of the vortex) that Descartes attributes to the earth, and which is counter-balanced by the inward vortical pressure? Again, notes Newton, the Cartesian philosopher cannot say where Jupiter was a year ago, because Jupiter's Cartesian place in the vortex has itself changed in the meantime. In general, the Cartesian philosopher cannot say where a body was at any given time in the past, so he cannot know what path it has been following, nor can he know therefore the body's previous speed. In other words, the Cartesian definition of motion yields the conclusion that a body cannot have any determinate motion, speed or direction.

As for extension, Descartes had argued that it alone constitutes the nature of body, and that therefore the material universe is an indefinitely extended plenum, its indefiniteness standing in distinction from God's transcendent infinity. Both theses are rejected in 'De gravitatione'. Newton admits he does not know what the real nature of bodies is, except that God has willed that they, occupying space, be endowed with powers to produce in us all that we experience in them, including the most basic property, impenetrability, which we come to know of through touch. Extension is therefore distinct from body; and space, whether bodies occupy it or not, is eternal, infinite, uncreated and uniform. The parts of space are incapable of motion, and the motions of bodies can now be unambiguously specified with reference to that immutable space. The immutability, infinity and eternity of space derive from its being an emanative effect of God's existing as the immutable and infinite being, and in general 'space is a disposition of being *qua* being'.[7]

To a degree these conceptions of body and space were reaffirmations of Newton's (here Lucretian) atomistic cosmology, but they took shape more directly under the recent influence of Henry More's Neoplatonist ideas on space and body and their relations to God and mind. Newton introduces into his arguments the spatial ubiquity of God and the extendedness of mind, both typical Cambridge Platonist doctrines. Since 'De gravitatione' directly challenged Cartesian teaching with doctrines of space, time, motion, body, God and mind, which were the bases on which Newtonian natural philosophy was to develop, the document testifies to the looming presence of Descartes in Newton's intellectual life. It is an equally telling testimony to Newton's skill in forging new principles of natural philosophy. On quite a different topic 'De gravitatione' is also of importance, since despite the long critical digression on Descartes, Newton still manages after all to squeeze in some propositions on hydrostatics which form instructive complements to the corresponding treatment in the *Principia*.

4. THE ROLE OF ALCHEMY

If we think of the variety of investigations so far discussed (the mathematics excepted) as so many candidates for inclusion in a developing programme of natural philosophy, then it should not be unexpected that (al)chemical investigations also found their way into that programme. The natural philosophy of the Peripatetic tradition catered for every power and operation of bodies, and that included the bewildering multiplicity of phenomena that flowed from crucible and furnace. (Al)chymia was not allocated a separate chapter or section in the natural philosophy manuals, but that was because qua rational inquiry it was subsumed in those chapters that explicitly treated speculatively the elements, metals, minerals and stones. Viewed in this light, alchemy was part of natural philosophy; and transmutation, the central material concern of most alchemists, was compatible with and in fact implied by Peripatetic doctrines of qualitative change. On the other hand, within a disciplinary perspective alchymia was primarily an ars, not a scientia speculativa, so Peripatetic authors accorded it separate treatment in their general encyclopaedias. At the same time, this status as a practical enterprise fitted it for inclusion on the roster of the experimental sciences of Newton's day.

The suggestion that alchemy be counted part of natural philosophy, allied to experimentation, must however be qualified by recalling that it often addressed more than the task of transmutation (with or without medical applications) and the study of certain substances and their properties. For many, the Great Work that would achieve the transmutation of base metals into gold was a 'projection' of the individual's quest for spiritual purification, or (in Jungian terms) of a quest for individuation, for the integration of psychic opposites within the self. During the first half of the seventeenth century varieties of spiritual or mystical alchemy found a vigorous role among Hermeticists, Rosicrucians and other petitioners for social, educational and religious reform throughout Protestant Europe. Yet by mid-century mystical alchemy was broadly distinguishable from alchemy qua part of natural philosophy. (See art. 37, sect. 1.) In England this distinction became increasingly accentuated within a group of alchemists and natural philosophers associated with the educational and religious reformer Samuel Hartlib, which included notably Digby, Boyle and George Starkey (probably 'Eirenaeus Philalethes', one of Newton's preferred alchemical authors).

This group re-interpreted the alchemist's art in terms of some version of the mechanical philosophy, which (as Boyle showed) could account for transmutation just as easily as, and indeed better than, the Peripatetic doctrine of forms and qualities. Also, this new (al)chemical philosophy would now become the true key to unwinding the mysteries of God's Creation. By mid-century, alchemy in England was becoming so to speak 'chemicalised', though it would be claiming too much to say that it had transmuted itself into 'chemistry', or that it had disentangled itself from the arcane styles and procedures of the mystical alchemist.

This was the milieu into which entered the young Newton with his unbounded obsession to know the workings of nature. Accordingly, on the heels of the anni mirabiles came anni mirandi, thirty years of alchemical toil and meditation which began about 1668 and lasted well into the 1690s. The evidence for these exertions is the two thousand-odd pages of extant alchemical manuscripts, consisting in notes of Newton's laboratory experiments, his (al)chemical theorising, extensive extracts in his own hand from the manuscript and published writings of other alchemists, and classified lists of alchemists and their work. Newton did not content himself with just the works of his contemporaries, but also read every alchemical text he could lay his hand on, from whatever period. The enticing fact is that few men of the seventeenth century knew as much about alchemy and its (by then) voluminous literature as the author of the *Principia*.

Nor can there have been many who explored that literature as thoroughly and with such large purposes in mind, or who coupled their explorations with such a methodical commitment to the proving power of sedulous experimentation. Newton would locate and read those texts, however arcane, that promised clues to the secrets he was after; he would pore over and often transcribe the symbolic and the esoteric, the ostensibly unintelligible. Then he would interpret his material, usually in the light of his knowledge of cognate passages from other authors, to disengage alchemical meanings that conveyed something to him, and above all to elicit ideas and hypotheses that could be tested. The testing would take place in his laboratory (in the garden on the North side of the Great Gate of Trinity College), where day and night Newton performed countless alchemical experiments, not all of them recorded, and no doubt few of them crowned with success. According to his assistant and amanuensis, in his experiments he was 'most accurate, strict, exact', and 'scrupulously nice . . . in weighing his materials', a testimony corroborated by the quantitative aspects of Newton's own laboratory notes.[8]

Newton's overall alchemical purpose in the laboratory was to achieve transmutation, a project that had beckoned him on his reading of Boyle's *Origine of Formes and Qualities* (1666), though he would have known about the notion itself through his parallel or earlier reading of squarely alchemical texts. Boyle's mechanist and corpuscularian ideas had worked their influence on Newton before he began his alchemical experiments, thereby enriching the Epicurean-Lucretian atomism of the 'Questiones', and accounting in large measure for Newton's unswerving adherence, from the *anni mirabiles* onwards, to corpuscularism as the over-arching theoretical framework of his natural philosophy. (See art. 38.) Transmutation, the alchemists' dream, fitted smoothly within the domain of theoretical possibilities mapped out by the mechanical philosophy, of whatever variety. In his *Origine of Formes and Qualities* Boyle wrote:

> . . . supposing all Metals, as well as other Bodies, to be made of one Catholick Matter common to them all, and to differ but in the shape, size, motion or rest, and texture of the small parts they consist of, from which Affections of Matter, the Qualities, that difference particular Bodies, result, I could not see any impossibility in the Nature of the Thing, that one kind of Metal should be transmuted into

another; that being in effect no more, than that one Parcel of the Universal Matter, wherein all Bodies agree, may have a Texture produced in it, like the Texture of some other Parcel of the Matter common to them both.

Twenty years later, in an unpublished 'Conclusio' intended for the *Principia*, Newton was making essentially the same point, and with greater assurance:

... For the matter of all things is one and the same, which is transmuted into countless forms by the operations of nature, and rarer and more subtle bodies are by fermentation and vegetation commonly made thicker and more condensed . . .[9]

However, theoretical possibility and speculative ingenuity do not bring with them their own directions for empirical corroboration or for application in practice. Whatever mechanical hypothesis for transmutation Newton might have entertained or shared with Boyle, when he began his alchemical experiments about April 1669, their purpose, bench procedures and terminology were wholly along lines prescribed by traditional alchemy. Likewise Boyle's experimental discussions, on which Newton's initial laboratory work seems to have been modelled, also reflect the presuppositions of the alchemical tradition.

Assuming the mercury-sulphur theory of the composition of metals, Newton's first aim was to extract 'the mercury of the metals'. This he did by adding lead filings to a solution of mercury in *aqua fortis*, thereby allowing 'the sulphur of lead' to precipitate 'the mercury of lead'; then he repeated the process with tin and, less convincingly in his view, copper. Following Boyle, who had described how to 'open' metals to extract their mercury, Newton heated first a mixture of mercury sublimate (mercuric chloride) and the additive sal ammoniac (ammonium chloride), and then this mixture (successively) with iron, tin, copper and silver, concluding: ' . . . ye salts will act upon ye metalls & you shall have their mercury running at the bottom'.[10]

These mercuries of the metals did not satisfy Newton, whose higher aim was the far nobler and more esoteric 'philosophical mercury' or 'mercury of the philosophers', which would dissolve all metals, including gold, and which was approximate material to the Stone itself. So delving further into the exclusively alchemical literature, he turned his experimental dexterity to 'the star regulus of antimony', the crystalline star formation that appears when antimony is prepared from antimony ore (stibnite) using a non-metallic reducing agent under carefully controlled conditions. The star regulus of antimony was of quite singular importance for Newton, as for other alchemists. Antimony ore was 'The Wolf of the Metals', because it was used to purify gold of contaminating metals. This could explain the name 'regulus': 'little king', the cleansing companion of gold, the alchemical King. But also, in the constellation Leo the star Regulus was known as 'the heart of the lion', and Newton believed there was a correspondence between the antimony regulus and the celestial star, with the Lion of the alchemists symbolising antimony ore.

More significantly, Newton believed that there is at work in the star regulus of antimony an invisible spirit that can 'magnetically' draw the philosophical mercury out of the metals. This notion he had gathered by early 1669 from a close study of the alchemical works of Basil Valentine, Michael Sendivogius, Jean d'Espagnet and Eirenaeus Philalethes, who shared and developed the Neoplatonic doctrine of a Universal Spirit, the source of vivifying principles (the fermental virtue, the vegetable spirit, the spirituous air, the spiritual semen) drawn down 'magnetically' by terrestrial 'matrices' to effect the embodiment of specific forms. Newton therefore got down to preparing good samples of the star regulus of antimony, using both metallic and non-metallic reducing agents, and conducted into the late 1670s and early 1680s a sequence of still imperfectly understood experiments that took him deeper into the *arcana* of the Art in quest of the mercury of the philosophers and of the other 'sophic' materials essential to the Great Work.

Whether or not he thought he succeeded in preparing philosophical mercury depends partly on the authorship of a curious manuscript entitled 'Clavis' ('The Key'). The text, in Newton's hand and dating from the late 1670s, describes how the triumphant experimenter used the star regulus of antimony to coax philosophical from common mercury via a fermental sulphur activated by spiritual semen (drawn from the Universal Spirit, one supposes), the necessary mediation between the mutually familial mercury and antimony being provided by the Doves of Diana (i.e. silver). The most recent scholarly opinion is that the manuscript is Newton's copy of a work by Philalethes, rather than a personal record of one of Newton's major successes as an alchemist. [11] Nevertheless, the ideas and procedures in the 'Clavis' correspond to those to which we know from other writings that Newton subscribed at that time.

It was noted above that Newton's alchemical papers of the 1660s were not expressed or conceived in mechanist terms. His first attempts to interrelate his alchemical thinking and his mechanist doctrines date from 1672–75. In 'An Hypothesis explaining the Properties of Light discoursed of in my several Papers' (read to the Royal Society in 1675), Newton sought to explain these properties in terms of 'an aethereall Medium much of the same constitution with air, but far rarer, subtiler & more strongly Elastic'. This ether is denser outside bodies than within their pores, and its pressure deflects light corpuscles in varying directions. But Newton prescribed for his ether the task of explaining a universal range of phenomena, such as surface tension, the cohesion of solids, animal motion, the phenomena of static electricity and magnetism, and 'the gravitating principle', both on earth and in the rest of the solar system. In keeping with such a variety of phenomena (especially those of electricity, magnetism and gravitation), the ether is non-homogeneous, being 'compounded partly of the maine flegmatic body of aether partly of other various aethereall Spirits'.

Newton's ether hypothesis was of Neoplatonic origin, and is evidently a reworking of the doctrine of the Universal Spirit from which embodied specific forms are born. 'Perhaps the whole frame of Nature may be nothing but aether condensed by a fermental principle', wrote Newton in the initial version of his 1675 paper. For his Royal Society audience he expanded this idea in language rather less reminiscent of the alchemical origins of the ether hypothesis: 'Perhaps the whole frame of Nature may be nothing but various Contextures of some certain aethereall Spirits or vapours condens'd as it were by praecipitation . . . and after condensation wrought into various formes, at first by the immediate hand of the Creator, and ever since by the power of Nature . . . ' In that case, consequently, there will be unending cycles of changes from form to form, 'for nature is a perpetual circulatory worker, generating fluids out of solids, and solids out of fluids, fixed things out of volatile, & volatile out of fixed, subtile out of gross, & gross out of subtile . . . '[12]

The transformability of matter was one of Newton's abiding beliefs, as was the corresponding doctrine of the unity of matter, which is implied by the notion of nature as a 'perpetual circulatory worker'. Both doctrines were also part of mechanist teaching, so to that extent they form a bond between Newton's alchemy and his participation in the development of the mechanical philosophy. Furthermore, despite its Neoplatonic origins, Newton's ether (here and in his later writings) is material, so when set to work to explain natural phenomena, its role was virtually indistinguishable from that of analogous material media in other contemporary mechanical philosophies.

Yet precisely because of the materiality of his ether, Newton was confronted with a key problem. Do the actions of the ether themselves have material causes, or do they derive from some non-material active source? Are the ultimate sources of activity in alchemical and mechanical change material or non-material? In the unpublished 'Of Nature's obvious laws & processes in vegetation' (c. 1674), Newton claims that each natural action is either vegetable or purely mechanical, and that we must distinguish between 'vulgar' and 'vegetable' chemistry. The former deals with sensible and mechanical interactions and coalitions between larger particles, the latter revealing 'a more subtile secret & noble way of working in all vegetation which makes its products distinct from all others . . . ' This division into two kinds of chemistry, which is the basis of Newton's theory of hierarchical composition (below), promises a straightforward matter-spirit bifurcation, but Newton goes on to say that the source of the more secret way of working is 'an exceeding subtile & unimaginably small portion of *matter* diffused throughout the masse which if it were seperated, there would remain but a dead & inactive earth'. Here the principles of (al)chemical activity are material. On the other hand, in 'An Hypothesis' Newton invokes non-material 'secret principles of (un)sociableness' that account for (im)miscibility between certain fluids.[13] The vitalising magnetic principles in the star regulus of antimony, called 'magnesia' by Newton, is also non-material.

The fact is that neither we nor Newton can ever quite say if the natural changes he analyses are the effects of purely material causation or of vital causation acting via the matter undergoing change.

Such tensions and ambivalences were by no means peculiar to Newton's natural philosophy. In varying forms they were endemic in all mechanical philosophies of the period, and were sources of ineradicable difficulties for any attempt to mechanise the world picture. Yet Newton's confrontation with the problem is of revolutionary importance because he worked out a solution which, though not free of philosophical blemish, did promise a unification of mechanism and at least 'chemicalised' alchemy at the particulate level, and more importantly, provided at the same time a successful method of mathematising new domains within natural philosophy.

5. FORCES AND ACTIVE PRINCIPLES

In the decade following 'An Hypothesis' and 'Of Nature's obvious laws' Newton became temporarily disenchanted with ether hypotheses. In addition to the difficulties mentioned above, Newton surmised that an ether ought to retard the motions of the planets about the sun, but no retardation had ever been observed. So the general concept of *forces* seemed to offer a way of explaining natural phenomena, and coupled with this idea was a developed account of chemical and physical composition. All Newton's ethers, from whatever stage in his thinking, were particulate, so it was a relatively comfortable transformation from the concept of an ethereal medium to that of conglomerations of particles under the influence of inter-particulate forces, both attractive and repulsive, acting across the pores or other spaces separating the particles. The best-known example of this idea in application is Newton's account of bodies in terms of hierarchies of increasingly complex aggregations of particles held together by short-range attractive forces. In his *De natura acidorum* (*On the nature of acids*, 1692, published in 1710), aggregations of the smallest particles were labelled 'particles of the first composition', and aggregates of the latter, 'particles of the second composition', and so on; and acidity consisted in a strong attractive force between particles.[14] The culmination of Newton's work as an alchemist, the 'Praxis' (1693), contains a recipe for 'multiplication', effectively the discovery of the Stone and of how to achieve the multiplication of gold through 'projection' onto metals. The assumed particulate base underlying these mysterious happenings is the activation of particles of the first composition by 'the first agent', the force that originates all life and activity, and which is the beginning of the Great Work.[15] The idea of hierarchical composition appears in Query 31 of the second English edition (1717) of the *Opticks*, where in addition longer-range repulsive forces (still at the micro-level) explain the emission, reflection and refraction of light, and where too the ether stages a comeback (as it did in the 'General Scholium' in the *Principia*) in the tentative hope that it might after all account for gravity and optical phenomena.

Six years before the 'Praxis' Newton had published his *Principia*, his scientific masterpiece, in which one might say force concepts reached their mathematical apotheosis. In stark contrast to the forces accorded qualitative explanatory roles in the (al)chemical and optical speculations, the forces employed throughout the propositions in the *Principia* were sharply focused through being explicitly defined and then quantified in functional terms. In the carefully worded 'Definitions' at the beginning of the *Principia* appear *vis insita* (the innate force of a body endeavouring to maintain it in its state of motion or rest), *vis inertiae* (the force of inertia, another name for *vis insita*), *vis impressa* (the impressed force that changes a body's state of motion or rest) and the centripetal force that maintains a body in an orbit about a centre of motion. The second and third of the three Laws of Motion prescribe measures (a) for the *vis impressa* (proportional to change of quantity of motion); and in conjunction with the above definitions, (b) for the *vis inertiae* when maintaining a body in 'inertial' motion (proportional to the quantity of motion) or when reacting against an impressed force (equal to the latter). The precise ontological status of these forces is still an issue among Newtonian scholars, but there is little disagreement over their role in the *Principia*. They enabled Newton to apply his laws of motion in the solution of a vast range of problems in mechanics and physics, from collision theory and pendular motion to the motion of bodies in resisting media, wave motion, the speed of sound, and the disproof of Cartesian vortex theory.

Also of unsettled ontological status, yet (like the above mechanical forces) of incomparable mathematical efficacy, was the force of universal gravitation, which acts between any two particles in joint proportion to the product of their masses and to the reciprocal of the squared distance between them. Conventionally taken to be among the most original features of the *Principia* (though Hooke also merits attention in this context), the inverse square law, coupled with the above mechanical principles, allowed Newton to bring to fruition the work on celestial mechanics that began during the *anni mirabiles*. He showed that for a point-mass moving under a central force, the line joining the mass to the centre sweeps out equal areas in equal times (and conversely); that if the orbit is an ellipse, then the central force varies inversely as the square of the distance of the point-mass from one of the foci (and conversely); and that the square of the orbital period varies as the cube of the mean distance from that focus. Then on showing that the gravitational attraction of a solid sphere acts as though all its mass were concentrated at its centre, Newton was able to apply these results for point-masses to the planets, thereby achieving successful mathematico-mechanical demonstrations of Kepler's Laws of planetary motion. (See art. 14, sect. 5.) He also attempted, with mixed success, a mechanical explanation of the precession of the equinoxes, initiated modern lunar and cometary theory and tackled the (insoluble) 'three-body problem' of the perturbations caused by the three-way attractions between earth, moon and sun.

There is considerable debate on the special nature of the 'Newtonian style' of mathematical physics, that is, on the relationships and mutual influences between the mathematical apparatus of the *Principia* and the physical reality that is the subject of those mathematical procedures.[16] Whatever the outcome of that complex debate, we should take note of a significant phrase in the first sentence of Newton's preface to the first edition:

> Since the ancients (as we are told by Pappus) esteemed the science of mechanics of greatest importance in the investigation of natural things, and the moderns, rejecting substantial forms and occult qualities, have endeavoured to subject the phenomena of nature to the laws of mathematics, I have in this treatise cultivated mathematics as far as it relates to [natural] philosophy.

He did not write something like 'I have cultivated natural philosophy as far as it lends itself to mathematical treatment'. The *Principia* is primarily a work of mathematics, and its conceptual origins lie as much in the mathematical innovations of the *anni mirabiles* and later as in any of the researches in natural philosophy. In that respect the *Principia Mathematica* contrasts significantly with (say) Descartes' *Principia Philosophiae*, in which there is scarcely any mathematics worth talking about. In effect it marked a major step in the emerging partnership between two traditionally disparate disciplines: mathematics (pure and mixed) on the one hand, and natural philosophy on the other.

So Newton did not regard his *Principia* as the only possible guidebook of investigation into nature (or indeed his *Opticks* as the only domain in which assiduous experimentation would yield results). When we turn our attention to the natural philosophy of which the *Principia* is so to speak the mathematically expressible part, we are taken back to the broad domain of natural philosophy as Newton practised it. The second and third editions (1713, 1726) of the *Principia*, the Queries to the *Opticks*, the manuscript drafts relating to each of these texts, and the (al)chemical writings of the 1680s and 1690s, together with letters and other documents, reveal the mature Newton in search of knowledge and understanding of the hidden constituents of matter and of its perpetual transmutations, of the larger regenerative cycles in God's Creation (in which Newton believed comets play a role), of the sources in antiquity of truths about the natural world (including even the inverse square law), of the sources of natural activity, and of the variety of forces that activate the (al)chemical and physical worlds. As the extant manuscripts show, Newton contemplated enlarging the *Principia* to include these wider researches, at least those that could be corroborated by empirical and historical evidence. But the unending complexity of the natural world made that an impossible task. We recall for example the wistful lines from the preface to the first edition of the *Principia*:

> I wish we could derive the rest of the phenomena of Nature [other than the motions of celestial bodies and the sea] by the same kind of reasoning from mechanical principles, for I am induced by many reasons to suspect that they may all depend upon certain forces by which the particles of bodies, by some causes hitherto unknown, are either mutually impelled towards one another, and cohere in regular figures, or are repelled and recede from one another. These forces being unknown, philosophers have hitherto attempted the search of Nature in vain; but I hope the principles here laid down will afford some light either to this or some truer method of philosophy.[17]

The forces in the *Principia* functioned effectively because they were sent out to work in mathematical dress, and their mathematical roles implied no commitment to any specific doctrine of their ontological ground. This point was not appreciated by Newton's critics, who charged him with resurrecting long-dead occult qualities with his concept of gravitational attraction across interparticulate *vacua*. Newton rejected the charge, insisting that 'attraction' (whether gravitational, electric or magnetic) was only the name he used to signify the real force, whatever the nature of its cause, with which the bodies tend to move towards each other.

The mature Newton did take a view on the ultimate causes of corporeal activity, a position that seemed to him to resolve the difficulties in deciding whether these causes are material or non-material, or more accurately, seemed to reveal the ultimate ground of every cause, of whatever immediately apparent kind. In Query 31 of the *Opticks* (1717–18) we read:

> . . . The *Vis inertiae* is a passive Principle by which Bodies persist in their Motion and Rest, receive Motion in proportion to the Force impressing it, and resist as much as they are resisted. By this Principle alone there never could have been any Motion in the World. Some other Principle was necessary for putting Bodies into Motion; and now they are in Motion, some other Principle is necessary for conserving the Motion. For from the various Composition of two motions, 'tis very certain that there is not always the same quantity of Motion in the World. . . . Seeing therefore the variety of Motion which we find in the World is always decreasing, there is a necessity of conserving and recruiting it by active Principles, such as are the cause of Gravity . . . and the cause of Fermentation, by which the Heart and Blood of Animals are kept in perpetual Motion and Heat; the inward Parts of the Earth are constantly warm'd, and in some places grow very hot; Bodies burn and shine, Mountains take fire, the Caverns of the Earth are blown up, and the Sun continues violently hot and lucid, and warms all things by his Light. For we meet with very little Motion in the World, besides what is owing to these active Principles. And if it were not for these Principles, the Bodies of the Earth, Planets, Comets, Sun, and all things in them, would grow cold and freeze, and become inactive Masses; and all Putrefaction, Generation, Vegetation and Life would cease, and the Planets and Comets would not remain in their Orbs.[18]

For Newton these active (and passive) principles were God's intermediaries in his governance of his Creation. They were not intrinsic to matter, but participated in the spiritual realm of Christ's vice-regency in the world, and thereby constituted for Newton a sign of God's existence and a proof of His management of the world of the natural philosopher. All of which was in keeping with Newton's view of the scope of natural philosophy: 'And thus much concerning God; to discourse of whom from the appearances of things, does certainly belong to Natural Philosophy'.[19]

NOTES

1. University Library, Cambridge, Add. Ms. 3996 (Newton's Trinity Notebook), ff. 16r–26v. Newton's earliest informal introduction to natural philosophy was John Bate's *The mysteries of nature and art* (London, 1634), which he read while still at Grantham School.
2. Draft of I. Newton to P. Desmaizeaux, 1718, University Library, Cambridge Add. Ms. 3968.41, f. 85r. The two sources for the apple story are John Conduitt (Newton's nephew) and William Stukeley.
3. I. Newton, 'New theory about light and colors' (1672), reprinted in I. B. Cohen, (ed.), *Isaac Newton's papers and letters on natural philosophy* (Cambridge, 1958), pp. 47–59. Quotation on p. 47.
4. J. E. McGuire and M. Tamny, (eds.), *Certain philosophical questions: Newton's Trinity notebook* (Cambridge, 1983), pp. 432–3.
5. Ibid., pp. 376–7.
6. I. Newton, 'De Gravitatione', in A. R. Hall and M. B. Hall, (eds.), *Unpublished scientific papers of Isaac Newton* (Cambridge, 1962), pp. 90, 121.
7. Hall and Hall, *Unpublished scientific papers*, pp. 103, 136.
8. B. J. T. Dobbs, *The foundations of Newton's alchemy, or 'the hunting of the greene lyon'* (Cambridge, 1975), pp. 7–8. See further the important essay review of Dobbs's book by K. Figala, *History of science*, 15 (1977), pp. 102–37.
9. Dobbs, *Foundations*, p. 200 (Boyle) and p. 202 (Newton).
10. Ibid., p. 143.
11. For a full discussion see ibid., pp. 175–93.
12. I. Newton, 'An hypothesis explaining the properties of light' (1675) in Cohen, *Papers and letters*, pp. 178–235. Quotations on pp. 179–81. See also Dobbs, *Foundations*, pp. 175–93, 205–6.
13. R. S. Westfall, *Never at rest: a biography of Isaac Newton* (Cambridge, 1980), p. 307. It should be noted that in these documents Newton is using 'vegetation' in the wide seventeenth-century sense of growth and maturation not only of plants but also of metals and minerals.
14. I. Newton, 'De natura acidorum' (1692) in Cohen, *Papers and letters*, pp. 256–8.
15. Westfall, *Never at rest*, pp. 529–30.
16. See I. B Cohen, *The Newtonian revolution, with illustrations of the transformation of scientific ideas* (Cambridge, 1980) and Z. Bechler, (ed.), *Contemporary Newtonian Research* (Dordrecht, 1982).
17. I. Newton, *Mathematical principles of natural philosophy* (Berkeley, 1934), pp. xvii and xviii.
18. —— *Opticks* (New York, 1952), p. 397 and pp. 399–400.
19. Newton, *Mathematical Principles*, p. 546.

FURTHER READING

Zev Bechler (ed.), *Contemporary Newtonian research* (Dordrecht, 1982).
Paolo Casini, 'Newton: the classical scholia', *History of science*, 22 (1984), pp. 1–58.
I. Bernard Cohen, *The Newtonian revolution, with illustrations of the transformation of scientific ideas* (Cambridge, 1980).

Betty Jo Teeter Dobbs, *The foundations of Newton's alchemy, or 'the hunting of the greene lyon'* (Cambridge, 1975).

John Herivel, *The background to Newton's principia: a study of Newton's dynamical researches in the years 1664–84* (Oxford, 1965).

David Kubrin, 'Newton and the cyclical cosmos: providence and the mechanical philosophy', *Journal of the history of ideas*, 28 (1967), 325–46.

J. E. McGuire and P. M. Rattansi, 'Newton and the "Pipes of Pan" ', *Notes and records of the Royal Society of London*, 21 (1966), 108–43.

J. E. McGuire, 'Body and void in Newton's De Mundi Systemate: some new sources', *Archive for history of exact sciences*, 3 (1966), 206–48.

—— 'Force, active principles, and Newton's invisible realm', *Ambix*, 15 (1968), 154–208.

—— 'Neoplatonism and active principles: Newton and the *corpus hermeticum*', in *Hermeticism and the scientific revolution*, ed. R. S. Westman and J. E. McGuire (Los Angeles, 1977), pp. 93–142.

Ernan McMullin, *Newton on matter and activity* (Notre Dame, 1978).

Robert Palter (ed.), *The annus mirabilis of Sir Isaac Newton 1666–1966* (Cambridge, Mass., 1970).

Alan E. Shapiro, 'Light, pressure, and rectilinear propagation: Descartes' celestial optics and Newton's hydrostatics', *Studies in history and philosophy of science*, 5 (1974), 239–96.

Richard S. Westfall, *Never at rest: a biography of Isaac Newton* (Cambridge, 1980).

—— 'Newton and alchemy', in *Occult and scientific mentalities in the Renaissance*, Brian Vickers (ed.) (Cambridge, 1984), pp. 315–35.

D. T. Whiteside, 'Before the *Principia*: the maturing of Newton's thoughts on dynamical astronomy, 1664–1684', *Journal for the history of astronomy*, 1 (1970), 5–19.

17

THE CHEMICAL REVOLUTION

CARLETON E. PERRIN

During the late eighteenth century, chemistry underwent a dramatic and profound transformation that tradition has labelled 'the chemical revolution'. Its drama lay in a conflict that split the chemical community into opposing factions but its significance is more complex. According to the most popular interpretation, the chemical revolution consisted in the overthrow of the phlogiston theory and its replacement by the oxygen theory of combustion. On a grander scale, the episode has been hailed as the founding era of modern chemistry and Antoine Laurent Lavoisier (1743–94), creator of the oxygen theory, as its 'father'. In recent decades, the conventional view has been challenged.[1] In the first place, combustion was not an overwhelming concern of eighteenth-century chemists, so it is not clear why a new combustion theory should provoke such strong reaction, nor be equated with the ascendance of modern chemistry. Historians now ask what the chemical revolution was really about. Secondly, Lavoisier's contributions have often been studied out of context, with the result that continuity of chemical inquiry has been overshadowed and the epistemic break with tradition possibly exaggerated. Current investigations aim to relate Lavoisier's achievements to the work of his predecessors and contemporaries. Because the chemical revolution is a major episode in the history of science, often cited by historians, philosophers and sociologists to illustrate their conceptions of scientific change, these problems have implications that transcend the episode itself.

Chemistry in 1800 was certainly different from what it had been a century earlier. Proponents of Lavoisian chemistry shared a strong conviction that its adoption represented a rupture with the past, as the words of a young Swiss convert, Marc-Auguste Pictet (1752–1825) illustrate.

Chemistry, banished until now to a small circle of adepts whose language and ideas were equally obscure, has become the inseparable aide and companion of

264

Physics: these sciences, united and guided by experiment alone, have proceeded at a rapid pace; Chemistry itself has undergone a great revolution, a frightful scaffolding has given way to a simple and illuminating theory, based upon the immediate consequences of experiment . . . Logic, without which experiments are mere isolated facts, has become more severe in its conduct and more certain in its results: in short, everything indicates that we are on the right path, and that it will lead daily to discoveries in the natural sciences.[2]

Pictet's view was from the vantage point of a triumphant campaign for the new theory. Chemistry, in the eyes of its promoters, had been created anew with a methodological soundness and a theoretical rigour which was lacking before. But to what extent were its advances due to the Lavoisian innovations rather than a century of evolutionary development?

For an appraisal of the status of chemistry prior to the upheaval, we may turn to Gabriel Venel's article 'Chymie', written at mid-century for Diderot's *Encyclopédie*. Venel (1723–75) found that chemistry in France suffered from a twofold sense of inferiority. On the one hand, it was not perceived by French intellectuals as a science on a par with mathematical physics. Its image was still tarnished by association with alchemical 'puffers'; it seemed to lack a powerful organising theory. Secondly, French chemistry had not enjoyed the encouragement accorded to its German counterpart. Although critical of the current state of chemistry, Venel was sanguine about its potential. To make chemistry respectable required a breakthrough to an overview which would give coherence to chemical doctrine. Venel called for a 'new Paracelsus' with the insight and the dramatic flair necessary to bring about a 'revolution' in the science.[3]

Developments in the first half of the century gave Venel grounds for optimism, for there had been notable advances in chemical practice and theory. Practical chemistry contributed improvements in mineral analysis and metallurgical techniques, as well as isolation of new materials, including phosphorus. Nor did chemistry lack for theory; several frameworks were available, including the venerable theory of the four elements, the doctrine of essential chemical principles and the notion of chemical affinities. Problems arose in the compatibility of diverse theories, or, more pressingly, in the relation of theory to laboratory practice. Venel's discontent with the chemical literature was twofold. On the one hand he found a plethora of petty chemical treatises competently treating matters of detail but supplying little interpretation. At the other extreme were speculative treatises, written by philosophers with little chemical knowledge and contributing little to advance the science. Venel espoused a 'philosophical chemistry' that would follow an intermediate path, guided by an intuitive method grounded in laboratory experience rather than extrinsic philosophical doctrine.

Most French chemists at mid-century accepted that natural bodies were composed ultimately of earth, water, air and fire. The conviction had been reinforced by Stephen Hales's discovery in the 1720s that air could be extracted from animal, vegetable or mineral substances and trapped (by displacement of water) in a 'pneumatic apparatus'. In principle any substance could be analysed into its elements, in practice the theory was of limited utility. When chemists decomposed a substance, the typical result was several products, none of which was a pure element; moreover, the products often varied depending upon the method of analysis. Chemists required a theoretical framework more directly related to reagents found on laboratory shelves. One such scheme was provided in the table of chemical affinities systematised by the French chemist Étienne-François Geoffroy (1672–1731) around 1718. The principle was a simple one: affinity tables were divided into several columns, each headed by a common reagent – a mineral acid, an alkali or a metal. Below each reagent were listed the principal substances that would react with it, in order of decreasing affinity. The tables encapsulated information about chemical reactions and facilitated prediction by analogy, but even more importantly, their use encouraged chemists to distinguish substances by systematic reaction with a series of reagents, rather than mere observation of their individual properties.

The brightest prospects for chemistry, in Venel's eyes, lay in the teachings of Johann Becher (1635–82) and Georg Stahl (c. 1660–1734), founders of the doctrine of essential chemical principles. In the eighteenth century, substances were classified into generic groups defined by a shared property, that is, according to whether they were earthy, metallic, combustible, acidic, caustic, and so forth. In essence the doctrine of Becher and Stahl embodied the defining properties in a set of hypothetical, quality-bearing material 'principles'. The notion had long roots reaching back to the Paracelsan *tria prima* and beyond to Aristotelian essences, but Stahl had cast the doctrine into a viable form by his dramatic success with the inflammable principle. He did not invent the concept, though he gave it a new name-*phlogiston*. Stahl's celebrated achievement was his taming of the elusive principle. Phlogiston could not be isolated or displayed, but Stahl showed that it was identical in the three realms of nature and could be passed from one combination to another at the chemist's whim. Phlogiston from charcoal could restore the principle that a metal lost upon calcination or could regenerate sulphur from its combustion product, sulphuric acid. It was the chemist's ability to manipulate phlogiston that made its existence plausible.

Lavoisier entered chemistry during the 1760s at a time when the efforts of the encyclopedists promoted a growing appreciation of its utility and philosophical interest. He did not arrive by the traditional routes of medicine, pharmacy or metallurgy. Instead he received a broad exposure to mathematics and the natural sciences through formal education at the Collège des Quatre Nations and the family connections that introduced him to leading Parisian men of science. The deepest influence upon the young Lavoisier was probably that of Jean-Étienne Guettard (1715–86), who engaged him as an assistant on excursions to chart the mineralogical resources of France. It was a desire to extend this preparation for geological work that led Lavoisier to follow Guillaume Rouelle's popular chemistry lectures in the early 1760s. After his study with Rouelle, Lavoisier continued his education by reading extensively in mineralogy and chemistry throughout the middle years of the decade. There is a common impression that he was disenchanted from the start with current chemical concepts. Surviving documents do not support that contention: he defended the theory of the four elements and used the concepts of phlogiston and chemical affinity in the same routine way as his contemporaries. However, his approach to the chemical literature was exceptional, for he read with an unusually critical eye, alert to discrepancies among different authors or to 'singular' phenomena, that did not follow simply from accepted doctrine. Such loose ends appealed both to Lavoisier's intellect and to his ambition as opportunities for 'a beautiful course of experiments'.[4] What further set him apart from typical students of chemistry was the taste he had developed for the rigour of mathematical logic and the precision afforded by instruments in physical experiments. He found such rigour and precision were often lacking in chemical investigations, but they became the hallmark of his own work. Lavoisier's experiments did not yield new substances, such as the gases and organic acids isolated by his distinguished contemporaries Joseph Priestley (1733–1804) and Carl Wilhelm Scheele (1742–86). Throughout his career Lavoisier's efforts were focused upon *problems* and his discoveries were solutions to those problems.

One of the most consequential of the problems that captured Lavoisier's imagination during that youthful period was inspired by reading an essay on the elements by the German chemist, Johann Theodor Eller (1689–1760). Eller had revived van Helmont's attempt to reduce the number of *bona fide* elements, by claiming that water was transmutable into both earth and air. Lavoisier was intrigued by Eller's argument that air was 'factitious', that is, composed of water combined with fire which made it expansive. However, he rejected Eller's conclusion that air was the same thing as water vapour, suspecting instead that it might consist of an *unknown* substance rendered into vapour form by union with the matter of fire. This notion, conceived in 1766, was the seed that Lavoisier gradually articulated into his theory of the vapour state.[5]

At that time Hales's discovery that air could be elicited from many substances had spawned quite different traditions in Britain and France. In Britain it inspired pneumatic chemistry: the isolation and study of different kinds of air. Joseph Black (1728–99) was the first to characterise a species of air differing from atmospheric air; it would not support combustion but had the property of precipitating limewater. Because it entered concrete substances like chalk or magnesia alba, he called it 'fixed air' (carbon dioxide). In 1766, Henry Cavendish (1731–1810) similarly described a species of air that was inflammable. But Joseph Priestley, in the early 1770s, emerged as the most creative discoverer and leading authority in pneumatic chemistry, by his isolation of a series of airs and his tests to distinguish them. Meanwhile, in France, Lavoisier remained unaware of the post-Halesian work until the end of 1772. Disseminated in Rouelle's lectures, Hales's results gave rise not to a tradition of pneumatic researches but to a theoretical dispute. Was the air obtained from bodies truly combined in them, or was it merely physically trapped in their pores? Then again, might the air be factitious, that is, not actually present in the bodies at all, but formed during their decomposition by the union of some other substances? Lavoisier's hunch of 1766 offered a simple resolution to the fixation of air. Removal of the combined fire that made air expansible would reduce it back to a concrete substance capable of entering chemical combination in the ordinary way. This promising notion did not immediately lead to an experimental investigation, perhaps because of competing demands on Lavoisier's time, but perhaps also because a line of attack had not yet crystallised in his mind.

Only in the summer of 1772 did Lavoisier undertake a sustained programme of research to elucidate the chemical role of air. The origin of his pivotal experiments on combustion and calcination, executed in the autumn of that year, has been the subject of controversy. H. Guerlac placed those experiments in a new light by showing that during the previous summer Lavoisier drafted a theoretical paper on the chemical role of air and fire; moreover he specifically intended to extract air from a variety of minerals by means of a large burning lens. It remains a moot point how Lavoisier proceeded from those plans to his crucial discovery (deposited at the Academy of Sciences in a sealed note on 1 November 1772) that combustibles or metals, when burned, gain weight by absorption of air. One view (favoured by Guerlac) is that the mysterious weight gain of calcined metals aroused Lavoisier's curiosity; alternatively, it has been proposed that an interest in combustion or in the formation of acids actually provided his starting point. Although none of these topics was foreign to Lavoisier as a possible area of study, the evidence does not support an explicit intent on his part to investigate any one of them. A more likely scenario is that continuing themes of his research were channelled in new directions by a series of contingencies, leading to an unforeseen discovery.[6]

In the spring of 1772 Lavoisier's name had been put forward to a committee set up by the Academy to investigate the puzzling disappearance of diamond when heated in a potter's kiln. Members of the committee requested that a large burning lens belonging to the Academy be brought out of storage in order to extend the study of the diamond and other gems to higher temperatures. Lavoisier seized the opportunity as a new means to pursue an old interest in minerals. Hales's results on a few minerals convinced him that many contained air – which he hoped to disengage with the burning lens and capture in a pneumatic device. He suspected, too, that metals (known to effervesce with acids) might also yield 'fixed air'. These were the most original of the experiments he proposed to try with the burning lens; but because of the difficulty of finding vessels to withstand its intense heat, they were never completed.

Lavoisier's participation in the burning lens investigations brought him into frequent contact with Pierre Mitouard, a Parisian pharmacist who had recently obtained a good sample of white phosphorous from Germany. Several authors had noted that phosphoric acid obtained by spontaneous combustion was heavier than the original phosphorus; some attributed the gain to absorption of air by the acid, others to attraction of atmospheric moisture. Mitouard probably mentioned these opinions, which were not, however, a focus of his own research. Lavoisier, at the time preoccupied with the chemical role of air, purchased an ounce of phosphorus from Mitouard to try his hand at resolving the question. Initially, the solution evaded Lavoisier, for he had to expose his phosphorus to the atmosphere in order to burn it; the resulting acid absorbed moisture by deliquescence as it formed, gradually dissolving itself. It remained unclear how much of the increased weight was due to moisture and how much, if any, might be due to air. Never one to waste his efforts, Lavoisier saw that repeated combustions could yield a concentrated sample of the acid from which he could derive its little-known salts. Over the following weeks he laboriously collected his sample and began a paper on the formation of the acid and its salts. But as he proceeded, a resolution to his original problem dawned upon him. He placed his acid solution in a flask, marked its level and weighed it; he then filled the flask to the mark with distilled water and weighed it again. The difference in weight gave the amount of phosphoric acid in solution, which turned out to be markedly greater than the weight of phosphorus consumed – an increase, Lavoisier concluded, that could only be due to absorbed air.

The discovery so excited Lavoisier that he dropped his study of phosphoric acid salts and deposited his unfinished paper at the Academy (on 20 October 1772) to retain priority. Having demonstrated the absorption of air by burning phosphorus, he wanted to see if the same might occur with sulphur. A positive result with sulphur then led him to speculate whether what was true of phosphorus and sulphur might apply to *any* combustible that gained weight by burning. In particular, he suspected that the weight acquired by metals during calcination (in Stahl's theory merely a slow combustion) might involve absorption of air. Within a week he confirmed his conjecture by the reverse process of reducing litharge (a calx of lead), from which he obtained a volume of air nearly a thousand times that of the calx.

The result with litharge completed a striking reversal of Lavoisier's expectations of the previous August. At that time he had hoped to extract air from metals by intense calcination; he now saw that on the contrary, under such circumstances they *absorb* air. His understanding of the relation of metal to calx (or sulphur to its acid) was inverted! Success in monitoring the entry of air into combination, and his resulting insights into the composition of familiar materials, inspired Lavoisier to predict a 'revolution' in chemistry. It is often assumed from hindsight that he meant the overthrow of phlogiston. However, the evidence does not support that claim, because he believed initially that air entered a combustible *as phlogiston left*. Subsequently, his doubts about the role of phlogiston grew until, in the early months of 1773, he came to the verge of total rejection of the concept. Therefore, the dismissal of phlogiston was a consequence rather than a cause of his revolutionary programme (and did not become final for several years).

The scope of Lavoisier's programme is more fully set out in a research memorandum he drafted on 20 February 1773. In the interval he had read other discoveries relating to 'fixed' air (including the British work) which he now saw as isolated links of a great chain – one he personally hoped to join together. The key to his anticipated synthesis was to concentrate upon the processes which absorbed air; in that way he hoped to learn about the *origin* of air in substances and to follow its progress from one combination to another. As promising starting-points, he singled out the processes of vegetation, animal respiration, combustion, calcination and certain chemical combinations. From the start Lavoisier had a larger goal than a new combustion theory. His vision embraced a new system of chemistry in which atmospheric air, or some component of the air, entered by traceable chemical paths into operations of the animal, vegetable and mineral kingdoms.

From one perspective, the remainder of Lavoisier's career can be viewed as the fulfillment of that programme. His early publications aimed at demonstrating the role of air in calcination; his emphasis shifted in the mid-1770s to combustion and the constitution of acids, then in the 1780s to fermentation, vegetation and respiration. This interpretation stresses the continuity and momentum inherent in his programme. From another point of view, however, Lavoisier's early conceptions were far from the system that he eventually published in 1789 as his *Traité Elémentaire de Chimie*. To that point his departure from convention consisted in (1) an emphasis upon air and an embryonic theory of its fixation, (2) an inversion of familiar assumptions about composition, and (3) a recognition of the incompleteness of Stahl's combustion theory. On the other hand, he had not yet distinguished 'fixed' air from ordinary air, still regarded air and water as elements, had not definitively rejected phlogiston and he still comfortably worked within the framework of chemical principles. Indeed, Lavoisier's programme of 1772–3 might be characterised as an attempt to establish air as a chemical principle, much as Stahl had established phlogiston. The further transformation of his views resulted partly from articulation of his programme and partly from its collision with discoveries and ideas advanced by his contemporaries.

Response to Lavoisier's innovations occurred in three phases. The first public disclosure of his work came in a paper on calcination read at the Academy's

Easter public meeting in 1773. There he hinted at differences with Stahl and ventured that deeper study of fixed air would lead to a period of 'almost complete revolution'. That brash forecast drew an admonition from his academic colleague, Antoine Baumé (1728–1804), who complained in print of certain physicists who wished to substitute fixed air for phlogiston. It may have been reproof from his colleagues, as much as the conceptual difficulty arising from the elimination of phlogiston, that led Lavoisier to avoid confrontation over Stahlian theory when he published an account of his research, *Opuscules Physiques et Chymiques* early in 1774.

Outside Paris, Lavoisier's early publications attracted attention primarily where his conclusions about calcination and combustion clashed with other views. The most prominent of the early encounters was with Joseph Priestley, whose concurrent investigations led to ideas on the role of air in combustion diametrically opposed to Lavoiser's. Like Lavoisier, Priestley was indebted to Hales for many of his experiments – which were conducted, however, from a distinctive point of view. Priestley set out not to reform chemical notions, but to explore the role of air in larger economies of nature. His experiments aimed at elucidating the constitution of atmospheric air, the nature of other kinds of air and their effects upon such processes as the respiration of mice and the growth of plants. Aware that certain processes, including combustion and respiration, 'spoilt' the air, he sought ways to restore its 'goodness', measuring the 'goodness' by diminution of a sample when mixed with a predetermined amount of nitrous air (nitric oxide). Priestley's work found enthusiastic emulators on the continent; Lavoisier himself first showed an interest in respiration after reading Priestley's early paper on gases and learned to distinguish gases qualitatively by repeating Priestley's experiments.

In his *Opuscules*, Lavoisier criticised Priestley's view that ordinary air was diminished during combustion by phlogistication and implied that the British philosopher had failed to note the *absorption* of a portion of air by the burning substance. Priestley was quick to deny any suggestion that phlogiston diminished the elasticity of air, pointing out that it had the effect of precipitating 'fixed' air from the atmosphere – hence the shrinkage. Differences between Priestley and Lavoisier were exacerbated in 1775 when Lavoisier published his famous paper showing that the red calx of mercury (upon reduction without charcoal) yielded not Black's 'fixed' air, but an air capable of supporting combustion. Priestley himself had obtained such an air from the red calx in August 1774 and had mentioned it in Lavoisier's presence during a Paris visit in October. In the second volume of his *Experiments and Observations on Different Kinds of Air* Priestley not only chided Lavoisier for failing to observe that the air was a species much better than ordinary air (Priestley proposed to call it dephlogisticated air), but also implied that Lavoisier ought to have acknowledged his own priority. Theoretical differences between Priestley and Lavoisier were therefore compounded by an apparent breach of 'philosophical' etiquette – plus perhaps, a rivalry for authority in the popular new field of pneumatic chemistry.

In its early manifestations, Lavoisier's programme was not perceived as a threat to the foundations of chemistry because its revolutionary implications were concealed and the validity of its limited claims disputed. A second phase in its reception was launched with his reading of a paper 'On Combustion in General' in the autumn of 1777. On that occasion Lavoisier made clear his intention to account for combustion without employing the concept of phlogiston; accompanying thermal effects were instead attributed to the matter of fire released as air relinquished the vapour state. For several years, Lavoisier refrained from direct confrontation with colleagues over the existence of phlogiston, electing instead to develop the positive implications of his theory. He proceeded with analyses of acids (showing that they contained dephlogisticated air, which he renamed *oxygen*, the acid-former), and elaborated his theory of heat in collaboration with Laplace. Around 1781–2 he sketched an outline of a systematic presentation of his views, in which for the first time he articulated his new understanding of the elements, defined pragmatically as simple substances that were the end result of chemical analysis. His list included the metals, sulphur and phosphorus as well as the more traditional earths and water. Despite the growing power and coherence of his system, he was confronted by rival theories and disconcerting counter-evidence. His colleague, Pierre Macquer, had advanced a compromise theory that granted the absorption of air in combustion (and hence could explain weight relations precisely as Lavoisier did), but retained phlogiston as the pure matter of sunlight (allowing him to account for reduction without charcoal). The theory attracted a following in France as a way of incorporating Lavoisier's compelling results within a conventional theoretical framework. Another serious competitor was the theory-favoured by Jean-Claude de Lamétherie (1743–1817) in France and R. Kirwan (*c.* 1733–1812) in England – that inflammable air was pure phlogiston. Metals were known to release inflammable air when they dissolved in acid; even more compelling was Priestley's observation in 1782 that a calx of lead was successfully reduced by heating it in inflammable air (which was consumed as the metal formed). How could such phenomena be explained without the assumption of an inflammable principle in the metal? The second phase closed with a startling discovery that turned these phenomena to Lavoisier's advantage. Repetition of Cavendish's ignition of a mixture of inflammable and dephlogisticated airs, yielding water as a product, led Lavoisier to recognise that water was not an element but a compound of the two gases. So inflammable air evolved 'from metals' could be attributed instead to decomposition of water. This insight was supported by an analysis of water, by passing steam over heated iron filings. The water was decomposed, its oxygen combined with the iron and its inflammable air (which

Lavoisier now renamed *hydrogen*, the generator of water) was set free in considerable quantity.

A third phase in the reception of Lavoisier's views began with public response to the alleged composition of water and to his provocative 'Reflections on Phlogiston' read to the Academy in the summer of 1785. In it he argued that Stahl's theory was based upon circular reasoning, that variations of phlogiston theory were incompatible with Stahl's and with one another, and that the principal phenomena of chemistry could be simply explained without phlogiston – a strong indication of its non-existence. Although Stahl's theory might have benefited chemistry initially, its retention had become an obstacle to further progress. The 'Reflections' produced an uproar of protest, at first within the Academy then later more widely with the paper's publication in 1786. The tacit truce on fundamental issues was abandoned. The existence of phlogiston was perceived as the central issue and the analysis of water as a crucial experiment. Stahl's followers objected that the formation of water from the two gases indicated that it was a constituent of the gases, rather than the other way around; in the alleged analysis of water, the abundant inflammable air came, they said, from the iron filings, not the water. The experiments were difficult to repeat and both the results and the interpretation remained contentious for several years.

As the deeper implications of Lavoisier's programme spread and especially as a few prominent members of the French community declared their support, its threat could no longer be ignored. A schism began to develop within the French community. A couple of the Academy's younger chemists, Claude Louis Berthollet (1748–1822) and Antoine François de Fourcroy (1755–1809) – and many of its mathematicians and physicists – rallied to Lavoisier's side; from Montpellier Jean Antoine Chaptal (1756–1832) declared his support. Promotion of the new chemistry increasingly took on the aspect of a collaborative campaign; its advocates were dubbed 'antiphlogistians' and their activities were described in political metaphor. Active opposition to the new chemistry grew in proportion, finding its voice in the *Journal de physique*, under de Lamétherie's editorship. Criticism was initially reasonable, stressing counter-evidence and theoretical objections, but as the strength of the antiphlogistic party grew, it sometimes turned acrimonious and personal.

Early in 1787, Louis Bernard Guyton de Morveau (1737–1816) travelled to Paris to consult leading chemists on the reform of chemical nomenclature that he had been urging for several years. Long a respected defender of phlogiston, Guyton had gradually modified his position, in the light of new evidence, until little separated it from Lavoisier's. In Paris he was finally won over. In collaboration with the antiphlogistians, he then drew up a new method of chemical nomenclature grounded on Lavoisian principles. The language reflected the new view of chemical composition. It was founded upon a set of operationally-defined 'simple' substances', each given a simple name. Compounds received binomial names revealing their elemental constitution and assigning them a genus and species. So a lead calx, for example, was allotted to the genus oxide, species lead. It is the familiar naming system for simple inorganic substances such as sulfides, nitrites, nitrates and so forth, still in use today. Promoters of the new nomenclature saw it as a significant advance. Not only would chemistry become easier for beginners to learn, but the systematic and analytical nature of the language would also improve reasoning in chemistry. To opponents, on the other hand, the new terms had a barbarous ring. The system was objectionable because, from a practical point of view, experienced chemists would not understand the foreign terms; philosophically, the whole system was founded upon hypotheses which might collapse; politically, it was seen as a blatant attempt to impose the new theory by forcing beginners to learn the new language.

Despite vocal opposition, the trickle of converts to the new chemistry turned into a stream during the late 1780s. Its early promoters included several of France's most successful chemistry teachers: each year hundreds of students assimilated the new view through the able lectures of Fourcroy in Paris, de Morveau in Dijon and Chaptal in Montpellier. However, the transition was not simply a matter of an older generation dying off to be replaced by a younger and more flexible one. The community as a whole shifted to the new system, though not all at once, nor with uniform enthusiasm. Conversion proved more difficult for older chemists, who were possessed of deeper attachment to the old theory and acute awareness of the limitations of the new. Yet many of them managed partial adoption of the antiphlogistic system as its experimental claims were confirmed and its theory clarified. The campaign was significantly advanced by publication of several antiphlogistic treatises – especially Lavoisier's *Traité* – providing a coherent overview of the new system to combat the fragmentary and often distorted perceptions of it in circulation.

The struggle for the new chemistry in France was effectively accomplished by 1789–90, although some prominent figures persisted in their opposition. During the early 1790s many sceptics quietly began to employ the new concepts. By the middle of the decade, even that inveterate opponent, de Lamétherie, found himself obliged to use the new nomenclature in order to be understood by readers of the *Journal de physique*. Elsewhere, dissemination of the new theory proceeded at different rates, according to the commitments of local communities and the quality of their communications with France. In Britain, where mutual interests and excellent lines of communication facilitated awareness, the course of debate closely paralleled that in France; antiphlogistic publications were rapidly translated into English. By the early 1790s the new chemistry was well established in Edinburgh and Glasgow where it was endorsed by Black and his students. Prominent English philosophers were reluctant to concede the superiority of the Lavoisian system: Cavendish appears to have abandoned the defence of phlogiston (without championing oxygen) by about 1787; James Watt adopted the new ideas with reservations, while Richard Kirwan capitulated to the antiphlogistians in 1791 but never became a whole-hearted supporter. Of course, Priestley and his friend James Keir remained against it to the very end. The stubborn German opposition to the antiphlogistic chemistry is well known. Ironically, it owed much to the self-sufficiency of the German chemical community (reinforced by emergent cultural nationalism), which did not encourage chemists to pay attention to foreign developments. More generally, the implications of the Lavoisian system tended to be ignored until they were championed locally by a few individuals. Typically, those individuals were young; many had travelled and come into contact with antiphlogistians. Once the issue had been raised, arguments followed similar patterns to those in France and Britain, but with local variations; the existence of phlogiston always remained at the heart of the debate. By the close of the century the new chemistry had penetrated even the remote corners of Europe and America. Paris emerged as the leading European centre for chemical instruction; students flocked there to hear lecturers by Lavoisier's supporters who, since the political revolution, had dominated all of the Parisian scientific institutions.

The new chemistry was established amidst dissension; today its interpretation continues in controversy. There is consensus that the overthrow of phlogiston is too narrow a focus, but no suitable synthesis has taken its place. Novel (and sometimes incompatible) interpretations have been proposed. The Lavoisian achievement has been portrayed as the reaffirmation of material principles over British attempts at mechanisation, or alternatively, as the subordination of chemistry to physics.[7] Several authors shift the emphasis away from phlogiston or combustion to the nature of the vapour state, or the theory of acidity, or the new view of composition. But insistence upon any one of these aspects would be just as restrictive.

A more promising approach would be to treat the transformation as a complex process with several layers of meaning – perceived differently according to time and place. Lavoisier first spoke of 'revolution' when he saw a way to elucidate the nature of air; ultimately he succeeded in his goal of establishing air (or rather oxygen) as a key chemical entity. His path led through detailed studies of calcination, combustion, acids, fermentation, organic analysis and respiration; it was his specific claims about these processes that constituted the manifest implications of his work. But his programme had deeper consequences (some unforeseen in the autumn of 1772), notably the elimination of phlogiston and the overturning of the traditional hierarchy of composition. Close colleagues had an early glimmer of these implications, but the community as a whole remained unconcerned until the direct attacks upon phlogiston and the publication of the nomenclature. On a disciplinary level, Lavoisier employed physical methods, received support from physicists and brought chemistry much closer

275

to its sister science – an intrusion that was resisted. Even more imperceptibly, Lavoisier's synthesis undermined the entire doctrine of chemical principles, substituting a combinatorial view in which the properties of simple substances bore no necessary relation to those of their compounds. These changes were considerable. Nineteenth-century historians, comparing the concepts, language and methods of Lavoisier's chemistry with its predecessors, saw in them the beginnings of modern chemistry.

The Chemical Revolution is a classic instance of conceptual change in science – one of the first to be foretold. Venel had called for a breakthrough that would exploit the distinctive methods and concepts of chemistry to establish it as the independent peer of physics. Ironically, Lavoisier found that breakthrough in the chemical role of air, but pursued it by the methods of experimental physics. His innovations transformed the structure and language of chemistry, generating a crisis that split the community. Chemistry emerged from the conflict as a more mature discipline with the public recognition Venel had desired. A new historiographic synthesis is called for, one that neither imposes another straitjacket nor trivialises the episode, but incorporates the full richness of the transformation.

NOTES

1. The conventional view is clearly articulated in H. Butterfield, *The origins of modern science, 1300–1800* (rev. ed., New York, 1965), chap. 11; for recent reviews see M. Crosland, 'Chemistry and the chemical revolution', in *The ferment of knowledge*, (eds.), G. S. Rousseau and R. Porter (Cambridge, 1980), pp. 389–416; J. R. R. Christie and J. V. Golinski, 'The spreading of the word: new directions in the historiography of chemistry 1600–1800', *History of science*, 20 (1982), 235–66.
2. M. A. Pictet, 'Lettre de M. le professeur Pictet aux rédacteurs du Journal', *Journal de Genève*, 28 November 1789.
3. G. F. Venel, 'Chymie', *Encyclopédie, ou dictionnaire raisonné des sciences, des arts et des métiers*, vol. 3 (Paris, 1753), pp. 409–10.
4. Lavoisier's reading notes from the period have been preserved, Archives de l'Académie des Sciences, Lavoisier Papers, Dossier 251.
5. The significance of the notes on Eller was first brought out by J. Gough, 'Lavoisier's early career in science: an examination of some new evidence', *British journal for the history of science*, 4 (1968), 52–7.
6. The reconstruction given here relies upon a recently discovered manuscript; see C. E. Perrin, 'Lavoisier's thoughts on calcination and combustion, 1772–1773', *Isis* (forthcoming).
7. R. Schofield, 'The counter-reformation in eighteenth-century science – last phase', in *Perspectives in the history of science and technology*, ed. D. H. D. Roller (Norman, 1971), pp. 39–54; E. M. Melhado, 'Chemistry, physics, and the chemical revolution', *Isis*, 76 (1985), 195–211.

FURTHER READING

M. P. Crosland, *Historical studies in the language of chemistry* (London, 1962).

M. Daumas, *Lavoisier-théoricien et expérimentateur* (Paris, 1955).

C. C. Gillispie, 'The rationalization of matter', in *The edge of objectivity* (Princeton, 1967), pp. 202–59.

H. Guerlac, *Antoine-Laurent Lavoisier, chemist and revolutionary* (New York, 1975).

—— 'Chemistry as a branch of physics: Laplace's collaboration with Lavoisier', *Historical studies in the physical science*, 7 (1976), 193–276.

F. L. Holmes, *Lavoisier and the chemistry of life – an exploration of scientific creativity* (Madison, 1985).

K. Hufbauer, *The formation of the German chemical community (1720–1795)* (Berkeley, 1983).

J. R. Partington, *A history of chemistry* (4 vols., London, 1961–70), vol. 3, esp. chaps. 7 and 9.

18

LAPLACIAN PHYSICS

ROBERT FOX

1. INTRODUCTION

The period from Napoleon Bonaparte's assumption of power as First Consul in 1799 until his final overthrow in 1815 is generally recognised to have been one of the most glorious in the history of French science. It was a period when France led her European rivals in the quantity and in the quality of her scientific contributions, especially in the physical sciences. Great names, such as those of Laplace, Berthollet, Biot, Poisson, Gay-Lussac, Thenard and Malus abounded, and there were some remarkable successes, of which the most celebrated is perhaps the discovery and study of the polarisation of light. It is not surprising, therefore, that both the 'declinists' of Britain in 1830, such as Charles Babbage (1792–1871) and David Brewster (1781–1868), and those who complained no less bitterly about the state of French science in the 1860s and 1870s, notably Louis Pasteur (1822–95) and Charles Adolphe Wurtz (1817–84), looked back to the years of Napoleon's rule as a truly golden age for science.

It is not difficult to identify at least some of the conditions that allowed French science under Napoleon to become a byword for excellence. The supply of able graduates from the Ecole Polytechnique, public recognition and the encouragement given even by Napoleon himself, the attractive career possibilities that were available to young men trained in science and the select research school centred on Berthollet's country house at Arcueil, just outside Paris, all played their part. On the other hand, we also know something of the weaknesses of French science in the Consulate and First Empire. For example, although weaknesses were rarely acknowledged at the time, at least in public, there existed grave deficiencies in education, especially at the elementary level. It is also clear that the First Class of the Institute (the revolutionary successor of the Académie des Sciences) became increasingly a manifestation of Napoleon's vision of science and culture as means of enhancing the reputation of his regime.

It is the main contention of this article that the course and content of much of French physics and physical chemistry under Napoleon were strongly influenced by the zeal of the mathematician and physicist Pierre-Simon Laplace (1749–1827) and the chemist Claude Louis Berthollet (1748–1822) for a programme of research which they jointly sought to pursue. In the years of its greatest success, from 1805 to 1815, the programme both raised problems and laid down the general principles for solutions; and, in so doing, it gave French physical science a most uncommon unity of style and purpose. It also stimulated much good work yet it owed its dominant position not simply to its merits, considerable though these appeared to be at the time, but equally to the effectiveness with which Laplace and Berthollet were able to control the scientific establishment of France in teaching as well as research. Once this control was lost (a process which will be discussed in Section 3), the programme became vulnerable, and, beset by the challenges of new discoveries and theories in heat, optics, electricity, magnetism and chemistry, as well as by a new generation of younger scientists who felt no allegiance to Laplace and Berthollet, it was abandoned, quite suddenly, between 1815 and 1825.

2. LAPLACIAN PHYSICS

Laplacian physics was a style of physics that depended on and was embraced by what J. T. Merz, with an acknowledgement to Maxwell, first called the astronomical view of nature.[1] It was a physics that sought to account for all phenomena on the terrestrial and, more particularly, the molecular scale, as well as on the celestial scale, in terms of central forces between particles which, although treated by analogy with Newtonian forces of gravitation, could be either attractive or repulsive. The forces were conceived as being exerted by and upon imponderable as well as ordinary ponderable matter; in fact, an essential and highly characteristic element in Laplacian physics was the system of imponderable fluids of heat, light, electricity, and magnetism. In accordance with beliefs that had come to be widely accepted by the end of the eighteenth century, each fluid was thought to consist of particles which were mutually repulsive but which in all cases were attracted by ponderable matter. In the hands of the Laplacians, models of such fluids, founded on the assumption that the forces between imponderable and ponderable matter were effective only over 'insensibly small' distances, were capable of being translated into systems of differential equations whose approximate solutions could 'save' the phenomena already known and even predict new ones. The suggestiveness of the models is beyond question. Indeed, it was in the attempt to refine and quantify a theory of imponderables which had hitherto been vague and qualitative that Laplacian physics found its main problems and had its most notable achievements.

The imponderable fluids, like the rest of Laplacian physics, did not originate with Laplace himself. As far as the basic model for their structure is concerned, they have their roots in Newton's speculations on the subtle electrical spirit in the second edition of the *Principia* (1713), in his speculations on the ether which appeared in the second (1717) and subsequent editions of the *Opticks*, and even more clearly perhaps in what was generally recognised through the eighteenth century as the Newtonian view of gas structure – the view that the particles of gases were stationary and that repulsive forces between these particles accounted for gas pressure and the other characteristic gaseous properties.[2] This Newtonian model had been applied with increasing frequency in discussions of the properties of imponderable fluids since the 1740s, when Franklin used it in his widely-read speculations on the nature of the electric fluid. By 1780 the theory of the imponderables was recognised to be imperfect to the extent that it was still almost entirely qualitative, but it was coherent, simple and, above all, it had the merit of possessing what appeared to be a thoroughly Newtonian pedigree. (See art. 39.)

So for a Frenchman such as Laplace, whose interest in the experimental aspects of physical science, especially the study of heat, grew rapidly in about 1780, it was to be expected that the imponderable fluids would provide an entirely acceptable explanation of the phenomena of physics. Moreover, it was just at this time that the writings of Laplace's friend Lavoisier were beginning to attract favourable attention to the fluid or caloric theory of heat and to give it the form it was to have for the next seventy years; and it was only shortly afterwards that Coulomb produced some of his most important work in electricity and magnetism, work which did much to win support for the two-fluid theories that Coulomb himself favoured. But Laplace, of course, did more than merely accept the legacy of Newtonian physics as this was normally understood towards the end of the eighteenth century. It was his great achievement to build on the Newtonian tradition, to restate many of its principles in a mathematical form, to take up its outstanding problems, especially with regard to the short-range forces that were thought to operate on the molecular scale and thereby to create a physics which, although Newtonian in origin, was unmistakably and characteristically Laplacian.

Signs of what was later to emerge as the true Laplacian programme can be detected as early as 1796 in the first edition of the *Exposition du système du monde*, where Laplace stated that not only optical refraction and capillary action but also the cohesion of solids, their crystalline properties, and even chemical reactions were the result of an attractive force exerted by the ultimate particles, (*molecules*) of matter. Already Laplace looked forward to the day when the law governing the force would be understood and when, as he put it, 'we shall be able to raise the physics of terrestrial bodies to the state of perfection to which celestial physics has been brought by the discovery of universal gravitation'.[3] In Laplace's view, there was good reason to believe that the molecular forces might themselves be gravitational in nature, even though they did not obey the simple inverse-square law, a complication that resulted from the effect, on the molecular scale, of the shape of the individual molecules.

But in all this he was saying no more than what so many eighteenth-century Newtonians, with an eye on Newton's *Queries*, had already accepted as standard doctrine. Throughout the eighteenth century, molecular forces, usually assumed to be negligible except over a very short range, had been invoked as a standard element of Newtonian physics in treatments of optical refraction, capillary action, surface tension and crystal structure, and they had been invoked also in a continuing tradition of work on chemical affinities. (See art. 17.) Although molecular forces had been equally acceptable to British and to French Newtonians, it was probably the French, in particular Alexis-Claude Clairaut (1713–65) and Georges-Louis Leclerc de Buffon (1707–88), who (next to Newton himself) exerted the greatest influence on Laplace.

Despite the evidence of continuity with at least one kind of eighteenth-century Newtonianism which had a strong following in France, Laplace's statement of the range of phenomena that could be treated in terms of molecular forces, as given in 1796, was far more comprehensive than any made previously. Laplace also made a new departure by placing unprecedented emphasis on the goal of a unification of terrestrial and celestial physics. Although the unification was advanced, in the *Exposition du système du monde*, as the goal of the systematic programme of research which Laplace wished to launch, it was not until the publication of the fourth volume of the *Traité de mécanique céleste* in 1805 that his brief and rather formal statement was transformed into the basis for a truly Laplacian style of science. It is crucial to our understanding of this transformation that by 1805 Laplace had gained a close and highly influential ally in Berthollet, his intimate friend since the early 1780s, his next-door neighbour at the village of Arcueil from 1806 and a man who saw chemistry in precisely those Newtonian terms that Laplace sought to apply more particularly in physics. In the *Recherches sur les lois de l'affinité* of 1801 and more fully in the *Essai de statique chimique* of 1803, Berthollet had expounded his view that chemical affinity was the result of attractive forces between the particles of matter. Indeed, he had gone so far as to begin the *Statique chimique* by declaring:

> The forces that bring about chemical phenomena all derive from the mutual attraction between the molecules of bodies. The name affinity has been given to this attraction so as to distinguish it from astronomical attraction . . . It is probable that both are one and the same property.[4]

The similarity between Berthollet's notions of affinity and Laplace's conception of molecular forces is unmistakable. It meant that when, between 1805 and 1807, Laplace published his theoretical studies on the refraction of light and capillary action in the fourth volume of the *Mécanique céleste* and when he based these studies on the assumption that there were short-range attractive forces both between the particles of ponderable matter and those of light, he was using an approach which had the sanction not only of a strong eighteenth-century Newtonian tradition but also of the most eminent French chemist of the day.

There can be no doubt, then, that by 1805 Laplace had a clear conception of his programme for physics and for physical science as a whole. It is true that he had not even now set down his programme formally, as he was to do rather sketchily some three years later; but on this point, the 1805 volume of the *Mécanique céleste* and its two supplements, published in 1806 and 1807, are clear. They show unmistakably that Laplace had formulated the basic idea of the reduction of all physical phenomena to a system of densely distributed particles exerting attractive and repulsive forces on one another at a distance (albeit at a very short distance) and that he had identified areas in which the idea could be put to the test. In this earliest work on his programme, Laplace gave lengthy mathematical treatments of optical refraction and capillary action, basing both treatments on the supposed existence of short-range attractive forces of the type that had first been postulated by Newton and discussed so often through the eighteenth century. By contrast with earlier attempts to solve these problems, Laplace's treatments of both refraction and capillarity were lengthy and, to all appearances, comprehensive. Not surprisingly, the problem of discovering the law relating molecular force and distance, which had remained in much the same state for some six decades, was one that the *Mécanique céleste* and its supplements did not solve. Nevertheless, Laplace's demonstration that the form of the law was unimportant at least made the situation appear less scandalous, and to that extent it was a minor triumph. In his mind, however, there was obviously far more to be achieved by a study of short-range forces than the mere tying up of loose ends, and between 1805 and 1807 he appears to have immersed himself totally in the problems of molecular physics.

In these years, Laplace brought his writings on capillary action to the notice of the Institute on no fewer than four occasions and engaged others in experiments designed to confirm and enlarge on his theoretical work. For example, René-Just Haüy (1743–1822), the Parisian engineer Jean-Louis Trémery, and Joseph-Louis Gay-Lussac (1778–1850), then a young protégé of Berthollet, were all asked to undertake experiments on capillary action, while Jean-Baptiste Biot (1774–1862), perhaps the closest Laplacian disciple at this time, was chosen to undertake the experimental investigation of refraction in gases which was proposed to the Institute by Laplace himself.

The collaborative nature of this activity reflects the importance of the influence that Laplace was able to wield in the scientific community. He did not hesitate to use his position to promote his beliefs, and the direct patronage which he and Berthollet dispensed to promising young graduates of the Ecole

Polytechnique – Biot, Arago, Gay-Lussac and Siméon-Denis Poisson among them – was only one of his methods. Laplace also wielded to extraordinarily good effect the system of prize competitions organised by the First Class of the Institute. Hence it is not surprising to find him serving on, and presumably dominating, the five-man committee which in December 1807 proposed a mathematical study of double refraction as the subject for the prize for mathematics to be awarded some two years later.

Clearly the intention in setting the subject was that the treatment of refraction, given in the fourth book of the *Mécanique céleste*, should be extended to embrace double refraction as well. The prospect of success in the enterprise was all the more attractive from the Laplacian point of view because the explanation of double refraction had presented notorious problems since the discovery of the phenomenon in crystals of Iceland spar in 1669. Now, moreover, the problems seemed likely to become increasingly troublesome, since, for some years, Haüy had been using double refraction as a valuable exploratory tool for the investigation of crystal structures, and his work was still proceeding. Predictably, it was a confirmed supporter of the corpuscular theory of light and one of the most brilliant of Laplace's disciples at Arcueil, Étienne Malus (1775–1812), who was awarded the prize of 3000 francs on 1 January 1810. It is very probable, in fact, that the subject for the competition was conceived by Laplace not simply in the hope of a glorious victory for the corpuscular theory but with Malus specifically in mind. Not surprisingly, Malus duly produced the vindication of the Laplacian position that was expected of him.

As a patron, Laplace had been well served. Specific problems had been answered for him, and the position of his programme had been strengthened. And Malus had more than just his prize-winning paper to contribute to the Laplacian programme. For example, after his discovery of the polarisation of light in the autumn of 1808 he had given his now considerable authority to the view that the new phenomenon could not be explained by Huygens' wave theory, and instead had given an explanation in terms of the various forces which he supposed, in the best Laplacian fashion, to act on the particles of light. (See art. 40, sect. 4.) Indeed, Malus did so much for Laplacian physics in general and for the furtherance of the Laplacian programme in particular that his premature death from consumption in February 1812, after some five years of intensive research, must have come as a grievous blow to Laplace.

By this stage, however, there was no question of abandoning the programme, if only because a number of outstanding issues were waiting to be settled. Foremost among these were the problems concerned with the behaviour of elastic surfaces. Laplace had already stated that the theory of such surfaces might be established in terms of short-range intermolecular forces of repulsion, and in 1809 a competition on the subject had been set by the First Class of the Institute. Although the competition was said to have been suggested by Napoleon, we may be sure that Laplace, whose zeal for his programme was then at its height, had a hand in the matter. In the event, by the closing date on 1 October 1811, no entry of sufficient merit had been received, and the competition had to be set twice more before the prize was eventually awarded to Sophie Germain (1776–1831) in January 1816. This award represented something of a defeat for Laplacian interests, since Germain's approach was fundamentally different from that of Poisson, whose paper on elastic surfaces, read to the First Class of the Institute on 1 August 1814, used short-range forces in the orthodox Laplacian manner. Moreover, the very fact that it was a defeat gives it significance as a mark of Laplace's declining influence and reputation after the downfall of Napoleon (which will be discussed later).

Another outstanding problem that was tackled in the last years of Napoleon's rule, though this time with rather more success from the Laplacian point of view, concerned the theory of heat. Again, the issue was raised in a prize competition of the Institute, set in January 1811. As the committee that proposed the subject made clear, it was hoped above all that the competition, which asked for a detailed experimental study of the specific heats of gases, would lead to a decision on an important point in the caloric theory. Since the point was one that had to be resolved before even the simplest mathematical treatment of the theory could be undertaken, it was of obvious interest to Laplace, and he duly sat on the committee that set the competition. The aim was to decide whether it was possible for some caloric to exist in a body in a latent, or combined state (i.e. without being detected by a thermometer) or whether all of the caloric was present in its 'sensible' form and therefore as a contribution to the body's temperature. Predictably enough, victory went, in January 1813, to two young men, François Delaroche and Jacques-Etienne Berard, who had performed their experiments at Arcueil and who, by upholding the distinction between latent and sensible caloric, vindicated the position long favoured by Laplace. One cannot help feeling that the only other competitors, Nicolas Clément and Charles-Bernard Desormes, who deviated from the Laplacian view, simply had no chance and were fortunate to receive even the 'honourable mention' that was accorded them.

Despite some slackening of corporate research activity from 1812, Laplacian physics was still, to all appearances, in a strong position in France towards the end of the Napoleonic period. Certainly the fact that regular meetings of the Society of Arcueil stopped in 1813 did not augur well for the future. But Laplacian influence was still just as great in French scientific education as it had long been in research and, because of strong administrative centralisation, it was just as easily exercised. An examination of syllabuses, textbooks and sets of lecture notes of the period shows clearly that pure Laplacian physics was being taught as standard doctrine both in science courses in the *lycées* and, what is even more important, in the courses that mattered most for the future of French physical science, those at the Ecole Polytechnique. In Aléxis Thérèse Petit's lectures at the Ecole Polytechnique in 1814–1815, for example, the existence of the imponderable fluids – caloric, light, electricity, and magnetism – went virtually unquestioned, and other aspects of Laplacian physics, notably the treatment of capillary action, were given great prominence. Even as late as 1823 Laplace could state his programme in its most definitive form in the fifth and final volume of his *Traité de mécanique céleste*. He wrote:

> By means of these assumptions, the phenomena of expansion, heat and vibrational motion in gases are explained in terms of attractive and repulsive forces which act only over insensible distances. In my theory of capillary action I related the effects of capillarity to such forces. All terrestrial phenomena depend on forces of this kind, just as celestial phenomena depend on universal gravitation. It seems to me that the study of these forces should now be the chief goal of mathematical philosophy. I even believe that it would be useful to introduce such a study in proofs in mechanics, laying aside abstract considerations of flexible or inflexible lines without mass and of perfectly hard bodies. A number of trials have shown me that by coming closer to nature in this way one could make these proofs no less simple and far more lucid than by the methods used hitherto.[5]

It must be stressed that the uniformity to which the programme aspired was by no means complete. In the first place, there were those, outside the Arcueil circle and usually outside the Parisian 'establishment' of science, who opposed Laplace. Two 'outsiders', Clément and Desormes, have already been mentioned and in the next section it will be argued that Fourier's mathematical treatment of the distribution of heat in solids appeared as a major challenge as early as 1807. Moreover, by the time of the Bourbon Restoration, Augustin Jean Fresnel (1788–1827) was already working, in almost total isolation, towards his critique of the corpuscular theory of light. And there were many more whose research was not opposed to Laplacian principles but independent of them. For example, the work of Gay-Lussac and Thenard on the alkali metals and electrochemistry, Gay-Lussac's experiments on the combining volumes of gases and J. P. Dessaignes' study of phosphorescence simply did not bear on the Laplacian programme or, in any direct way, on the theories on which the programme was based. But, despite these deviations and independent traditions of work and despite Laplace's own occasional vacillation, the uniformity in the physical science of Napoleonic France is striking. Even if in chemistry there was little progress, the programme in physics was pursued for a decade with vigour and, to all appearances, success. Certainly in France at the beginning of 1815 there seemed no reason why the dominant orthodoxy that had emanated from Arcueil since the early years of the century should, at least in the foreseeable future, be abandoned.

3. THE REJECTION OF LAPLACIAN PHYSICS

Yet within about ten years, by the mid-1820s, the intricate structure of Laplacian physical science had collapsed, leaving just a few increasingly isolated diehards to pursue the chimera that the programme and its attendant beliefs were then generally recognised to be. In these ten years of revolt against Laplacian orthodoxy, the tradition that had gone almost unchallenged in the physical sciences in the Napoleonic period was abandoned. To the men who led the revolt it undoubtedly seemed that a new and more glorious era was dawning. Indeed, it may lead us to see Napoleonic science in a somewhat less favourable light if we accept that these men shared much of the feeling of exhilaration and liberation of the intellect that was felt by many literary and political figures associated with the Bourbon Restoration. The men of science may not have gone so far as to see the Empire as an intellectual 'desert', as Edgar Quinet did,[6] but, contrary to general belief, most of them participated fully in the new optimism which so many Frenchmen experienced in those early Restoration years. Sadly, this enthusiasm and spirit of optimism, which was to be so fruitful in literature and the arts, in science came to nothing. For what eventually emerged from the ruins of Laplacian orthodoxy was not the new, revivified physical science that the early years of the Restoration had seemed to promise, but only a burst of creativity whose duration was no less brief, and whose decline was even more drastic, than that of Napoleonic physical science.

The men chiefly responsible for the revolt of the decade 1815–25 were Joseph Fourier, Pierre-Louis Dulong, François Arago, Augustin Jean Fresnel, and Alexis Thérèse Petit. Of these only Fourier, born in 1768, was over thirty in 1815, so that, with this one exception, they had learnt their science and performed their earliest work in the period when Laplacian principles had enjoyed their greatest success in France. Dulong, Arago, Fresnel and Petit had all been thoroughly indoctrinated with these principles as students at the Ecole Polytechnique; and Dulong and Arago had even been members of the Arcueil circle (though, significantly perhaps, only since about 1810), and both had benefited in their careers from the patronage that was offered at Arcueil. Petit, by contrast, was not a member of the circle, but his brilliant doctoral thesis of 1811 on capillary action and his first lectures as professor of physics at the Ecole Polytechnique in the winter of 1814–15 were wholly Laplacian in their general tone.

It is probably no coincidence that the challenge to the prevailing orthodoxy was first raised by the two members of the anti-Laplacian group, Fourier and Fresnel, who had spent the greater part of the Napoleonic period in relative obscurity, far from Paris and hence far from the centre of Laplacian control. Fourier had shown his colours be preparing a conspicuously non-Laplacian treatise on the distribution of heat in solid bodies, which he read to the First Class of the Institute in December 1807, but the paper was published only in the form of an abstract, drawn up by a less than enthusiastic Poisson. In 1811 Fourier took his work further when he submitted a revised version of the 1807 paper for a prize competition set by the First Class of the French Institute, and in January 1812 he was awarded the prize. But even this paper was criticised by the judges, and its impact was reduced by a delay in publication which meant that it did not appear in print until more than a decade later, when Fourier himself was one of the permanent secretaries of the Académie des Sciences.

Fresnel began to make his mark in October 1815, when he deposited his first paper on the diffraction of light at the Institute.[8] In the paper he gave powerful support to the wave theory of light and in doing so exposed serious shortcomings in the rival corpuscular theory. Immediately he won over Arago and Petit, hitherto good Laplacians, and by December 1815 these two new converts had even performed some experiments on refraction in gases which they interpreted in such a way as to support Fresnel. Ampère, whose rather idiosyncratic commitment to the anti-Laplacian cause became really apparent only in the early 1820s, had been privately won over by May 1816, and even Berthollet's former protégé Gay-Lussac, now beginning to take on the mantle of his master as France's leading chemist, was sympathetic. Interest in the challenge to the Laplacian position was enormous, and it bore important fruit in January 1817 in the decision of a committee of the Académie des Sciences, to offer the prize in physics for a study of diffraction. It seems likely that in this way the still-powerful Laplacian party hoped to settle the issue finally in its own favour by bringing this important phenomenon of physical optics into line with polarisation and double refraction, which had been explained so successfully in terms of the corpuscular theory. But the ruse – if such it was – backfired. For, despite the fact that among the five judges were Laplace himself and the two arch-Laplacians, Biot and Poisson, Fresnel won the prize in March 1819 with a paper of unquestionable brilliance.[9]

The successful attack on the corpuscular theory of light helped to create an atmosphere in which it was natural that other cognate beliefs should be subjected to a new scrutiny. Once action at a distance was discredited in one branch of the Laplacian programme, it became far easier to attack it in other branches; and the programme in its strict and complete sense naturally collapsed rapidly as new weaknesses in the Laplacian approach were identified. One such weakness was exposed by Sophie Germain, whose victory in the Académie's prize competition in 1816 was both a blow to Laplacian interests, as represented above all by Poisson, and a sign of diminishing Laplacian control. Like the criticism of the corpuscular theory of light, Germain's treatment of elastic surfaces stimulated a prolonged controversy, which lasted far into the 1820s, engaging an increasingly isolated Poisson in a bitter but vain debate with a group of critics inspired by Fourier.

In view of this mounting criticism, it seems plausible to interpret the attack on the caloric theory which accompanied Petit and Dulong's announcement of their famous law of atomic heats in 1819 as a natural product of the questioning mood that had come to prevail in French science since 1815. A similar illustration of the changing atmosphere may be found in chemistry, where, at precisely the same time as the first attacks on Laplacian physics were being launched, there was a turning away from related chemical principles that had gone virtually unchallenged in the Napoleonic period. In this challenge the break with the past was manifested not so much by an explicit, open confrontation with Berthollet's chemistry as by the gradual acceptance of Dalton's atomic theory, which directed attention away from molecular forces to combining weights. Again it is the year 1815, when France renewed close contact with Britain, which seems to have been the turning-point, for until then the atomic theory, opposed by Berthollet, had made little headway in France.

Discoveries and experimental evidence also contributed to the weakening of the Laplacian position. The point is best illustrated by electromagnetism. (See art. 22.) Following Oersted's observation of the magnetic effect of a wire carrying an electric current in 1820, French physicists zealously engaged in the investigation of the new phenomenon, and Biot and André-Marie Ampère (1775–1836) were soon among the most prominent of them. The problems that were raised for the Laplacians were plain enough. For example, electromagnetism introduced a rotational force which had no obvious connection with the central forces of Laplacian physics; moreover, Coulomb, whose views on the electrical and magnetic fluids had become part of the Laplacian orthodoxy, had denied the possibility of an interaction between electricity and magnetism. But Biot, then at his most belligerent, was undaunted and more than ready for the conflict that ensued between him and Ampère.

Ampère's theory of electromagnetic interaction contained much that Biot found objectionable. In particular, Biot protested at Ampère's attempt to reduce not only electromagnetic phenomena but even the forces between magnets to interactions between current-carrying conductors; magnetic forces, in his view, had been explained perfectly well in terms of Coulomb's two fluids of magnetism. The fact that Ampère retained fluids of electricity was no consolation, for his fluids were thoroughly unLaplacian and apparently had more in common with Fresnel's ether than with the fluids of Coulomb. In response, Biot put forward his alternative explanation, while pursuing a policy of faint praise, misrepresentation and open criticism towards the work of Ampère. By 1824 he had developed fully a theory in which the forces of electromagnetism were explained in terms of magnetic interactions between tiny magnets which he supposed to be arranged in a circular fashion around the current-carrying wire. For Biot, convinced of the correctness of Coulomb's explanation, the cause of magnetic interactions was, of course, not in doubt, so that his electromagnetic theory was presented as having utterly sound foundations. But the model did not withstand the scrutiny of Ampére, who demonstrated its weaknesses and defended himself against the charges that his own theory was unNewtonian. So discredited, Biot's theory was soon forgotten. His attempt to treat the exciting new phenomena in accordance with Laplacian principles had failed.

By the mid-1820s, then, the position of the Laplacian orthodoxy had been gravely weakened. Most tellingly, there had emerged in France certain anti-Laplacian principles, not only in physics but also in chemistry and mechanics, to which all critics of Laplacian science could subscribe. Of these, scepticism towards the traditional imponderable fluids, sympathy for Dalton's atomic theory, the new rational mechanics of Fourier and his followers and Ampère's electrodynamics were the most obvious. That those who sought to break with Laplace and his school had so many shared beliefs and operated on such a broad intellectual front is striking. For instance, Petit, as well as evidently sharing Dulong's doubts about caloric and his enthusiasm for the atomic theory, was among the earliest supporters of Fresnel's wave theory, as were Dulong and Ampère. Fresnel, for his part, was a critic of the traditional caloric theory and influenced Ampère in his work on electromagnetism, and Arago not only championed Fresnel in his difficult early years after 1815 but also took a keen and highly favourable interest in the work of Petit and Dulong on heat. This degree of unanimity is, in fact, hardly surprising, for the members of the anti-Laplacian group were in close, almost daily contact in the scientific circles of Paris, where they all lived and worked. Between some of them the relationship was especially close. Petit and Dulong were intimate friends (until Petit's untimely death in 1820), and the same may be said of Ampère and Fresnel and of Arago and Fresnel. Arago, moreover, became Petit's brother-in-law when Petit married in November 1814.

Throughout the Restoration period the reaction of the Laplacian party to the growing criticism was complex. The vigour of response to Fresnel's wave theory would suggest that the party felt the attacks keenly. But in their publications, at least, they generally preferred to give the impression that little had changed.

The case of the ever-loyal Poisson is particularly striking. As late as 1835, he published a lengthy work, the *Théorie mathématique de la chaleur*, in which the existence of caloric and its traditional properties were taken as entirely axiomatic. But by 1835 Poisson's book, although its author does not seem to have recognised the fact, was a relic of a bygone age, an anachronism in terms both of its physics and of its laborious and inelegant mathematics. And, to judge by the almost complete silence in which it was received, it was seen as such by his contemporaries. By the 1830s Poisson was a lone, almost pathetic figure, clinging vainly to an ideal of a 'physical mechanics', based on Laplacian principles, which was unrealisable.

Naturally enough, purely intellectualist factors were not alone in bringing about the move from Laplacian science. This was not simply a case of new principles being measured against old ones and being found superior, although there was something of this in the situation, especially with regard to the debate over the nature of light. Other relevant factors include the weakening of the authority of the Arcueil circle after regular meetings ceased in 1813. And it may well be that the personal unpopularity incurred by Laplace in the early years of the Bourbon Restoration played its part too. In this unpopularity political considerations loomed large. It is relevant to observe, for example, that Laplace's name became a byword for illiberalism in certain quarters in the early years of the Restoration, and that it remained so until long after his death. Indeed, in the freer atmosphere of the Orleans monarchy, which did little to encourage restraint, criticisms of Laplace's 'pliability' in political and personal matters and of his failure to defend the freedom of the press became common, further tarnishing his already flawed reputation.

As Laplacian influence faltered and then waned, so the leading members of the new anti-Laplacian generation were able, if only by virtue of age and seniority, to gain control of the still-centralised scientific community of Paris. It was important, for example, that when the need for a wholesale reorganisation of the *Annales de chimie* was felt in December 1815, it was Arago (rather than, say, Biot) who became one of the two new editors. The publication of the work of Fourier and Fresnel, which followed with remarkable (and significant) rapidity, soon gave a clear intimation of the changing allegiance of the *Annales* and, because of the established authority of the journal, did much to accelerate the abandonment of Laplacian principles. Almost as important as this new domination of the most prominent French journal of physical science was the way in which critics of Laplace were able to exert influence at the Ecole Polytechnique after 1815. Petit, for instance, had been made professor of physics there in 1814 and he occupied the post until his death in 1820. Petit was followed in his turn by Dulong, who remained as professor until 1830, when he became Director of Studies for the Ecole Polytechnique as a whole.

Changes that told against Laplacian interests also took place in the Académie des Sciences. Here, the really decisive event occurred in November 1822, when the anti-Laplacian cause gained its most glorious victory through the defeat of Biot by Fourier in the election for the post of permanent secretary for the mathematical sciences. The vote, thirty-eight to ten, was not overwhelming, but from that point Laplacian science was doomed, and the election of Arago to replace Fourier as permanent secretary in 1830 only sealed its fate, ushering in a period that the remaining sympathisers of Laplace resented bitterly.

By the mid-1820s, therefore, the style of science that had appeared so right and unassailable in the Napoleonic period had been irreversibly abandoned by the leading figures in a new generation; and the peculiar organisational structure centred on Arcueil, which had provided essential support for the old science, had collapsed, leaving power in new hands.

4. THE LEGACY OF LAPLACIAN PHYSICS

Despite its eventual collapse as a coherent programme of research, Laplacian physics left an indelible mark within and outside France. Historians are generally agreed that the age of Laplace witnessed the definitive establishment of the discipline of mathematical physics, with the techniques of mathematics being used to unprecedented effect in the elaboration of theories that could then be subjected to the control of experiment. Despite this consensus, however, analyses of the period have taken many different forms. Maurice Crosland, Robert Fox, Eugene Frankel and Ivor Grattan-Guinness are among those who have set the scientific influence of Laplace and his circle in an institutional as well as an intellectual context.[10] They have stressed the importance of the Arcueil circle and the French Institute as settings for the performance and diffusion of research and of the Ecole Polytechnique both as a source of mathematically-gifted recruits and as a vehicle for perpetuating doctrinal orthodoxy. Enrico Bellone, by contrast, has taken a more determinedly 'intellectualist' approach.[11] For him, Laplacian physics has to be seen as part of a 'second scientific revolution' in which the characteristically seventeenth-century quest for explanation in terms of qualitative mechanical models gave way to an approach that eschewed the simple determinism of the mechanical philosophy in favour of a far greater emphasis on mathematics and empirically-controlled theory. In Bellone's analysis, the 'revolution' to which Laplacian physics contributed was a more protracted one than many historians would allow; it had roots in the last years of the eighteenth century, its main fruits in the mathematical theories of thermodynamics and electrodynamics, and repercussions extending even into the twentieth century. The approach is an intriguing one, not least because it makes the emergence not only of Laplacian physics but also of the non-determinist physics of our own day as parts of a continuing process of change.

Of course, it would be extravagant to claim that the Laplacians alone were responsible for the new union of mathematics and the tradition of 'physique expérimentale' that had come about by the 1820s. Clearly they built on an incipient adjustment of disciplinary boundaries whose effects had already been patchily visible since the mid-eighteenth century, notably in the work of Coulomb. But the Laplacians' demonstration of the power of the new techniques was conclusive. It is a mark of the conviction which they carried at the methodological level that their approach was quickly adopted abroad. This diffusion did not necessarily imply an acceptance of specific Laplacian doctrines. Indeed, in Britain, it was the work of Fresnel and Fourier that most conspicuously influenced mathematical physics in the second quarter of the nineteenth century. George Biddell Airy and George Gabriel Stokes were just two members of the Cambridge 'school' who continued work on the properties of Fresnel's ether. And it was their influence, along with that of John Herschel, which helped to establish the mathematical theory of optics as an essential topic for undergraduates reading for the Cambridge Mathematical Tripos. Here in Cambridge, it seems, the curriculum of the Tripos provided a particularly favourable context for the assimilation of mathematical physics, though variants on the 'Cambridge style' flourished simultaneously elsewhere, notably at Glasgow under William Meikleham and at Edinburgh under James David Forbes.

Within France, the legacy of Laplacian physics had a somewhat different character. Partially in reaction against the bold hypotheses of Laplace and his closest associates, many French physicists moved towards a more cautious, even positivistic approach. For some of these physicists, Fourier's *Théorie analytique de la chaleur* (1822) served as a procedural model. Gabriel Georges Lamé and Jean-Marie-Constant Duhamel, for example, followed Fourier's principle of reducing speculations on the causes of phenomena to a minimum, and produced mathematical analyses of heat transfer that were very much in the Fourier tradition. Ampère, too, showed certain positivistic tendencies in his *Théorie mathématique des phénomènes électro-dynamiques* in 1826. And the spirit of caution was given formal and very visible expression in Auguste Comte's *Cours de philosophie positive* (1830–42). In the event, Comte's philosophical prescriptions seem to have exerted little influence: in physics, at least, declared positivists were few. Nevertheless, the reluctance to go beyond the bounds of the strictly observable made its mark about the mid-century in some masterpieces of precise experimental physics and in a distinguished tradition of metrology that eventually made France the natural home of the Bureau International des Poids et Mesures. In these years, the painstaking measurements of Hippolyte Fizeau, Léon Foucault, Victor Regnault, and Eleuthère Mascart came to symbolise French physics and, unwittingly, to set it on a track that detached it increasingly from the more theoretical trends that by then were flourishing in other countries.

What occurred in France about the mid-century, in fact, was a reopening of the gap between experiment and mathematical techniques which the Laplacian physicists had done so much to bridge. The consequences were serious and enduring. Despite the early contributions of Sadi Carnot and Ampère, the elaboration of thermodynamics and electromagnetic theory took place largely in Germany and Britain, and in the twentieth century French physicists still tended to play a secondary role in the emergence of the theory of relativity and quantum mechanics. Clearly, theoretical physics had not died completely in France. But the distinction of a small pantheon of major contributors – Henri Poincaré, Marcel Brillouin and Louis de Broglie among them – could not conceal an underlying weakness. It is no coincidence that discussions of the supposed decline of science in nineteenth-century France, have tended to draw their evidence from the contrast between the golden age of mathematical physics in the age of Laplace and the period from the mid-nineteenth century in which French contributions ceased to lead the field.

NOTES

An earlier version of this article was first published in R. McCormmach (ed.), *Historical studies in the physical sciences* (Princeton, 1974) vol. 4, and is copyright © 1974 by Princeton University Press. Excerpt pp. 89–136 reprinted with permission of Princeton University Press.

1. J. T. Merz, *A history of European thought in the nineteenth century* (4 vols., Edinburgh and London, 1896–1914), vol. 1, pp. 341–8.
2. I. Newton, *Philosophia naturalis principia mathematica*, 2nd ed. (Cambridge, 1713), p. 484; Newton, *Opticks*, 2nd ed. (London, 1717), pp. 322–8.
3. P. S. Laplace, *Exposition du système du monde* (2 vols., Paris, an VII (1796)), vol. 2, p. 198.
4. C. L. Berthollet, *Essai de statique chimique* (2 vols., Paris, an XI (1803)), vol.1, p. 1.
5. P. S. Laplace, *Traité de mécanique céleste* (5 vols., Paris, 1799–1825), vol. 5, p. 99.
6. E. Quinet, *Histoire de mes idées. Autobiographie*, 7th ed. (Paris, 1895), p. 241.
7. *Procès-verbaux des séances de l'Académie tenues depuis la fondation de l'Institut jusqu'au mois d'août 1835* (10 vols., Hendaye, 1910–22), vol. 3, p. 632; J. B. J. Fourier, 'Mémoire sur la propagation de la chaleur dans les corps solides', *Nouveau bulletin des sciences par la Société Philomathique de Paris*. vol. 1 (1807–1809), pp. 112–16; Fourier, 'Théorie de mouvement de la chaleur dans les corps solides', *Mémoires de l'Académie Royale des Sciences de l'Institut de France*, vol. 4 (1819–1820), pp. 185–555 and vol. 5 (1821–1822), pp. 153–246.
8. A. J. Fresnel, 'Mémoire sur la diffraction de la lumière . . . ', *Annales de chimie et de physique*, vol. 1 (1816), pp. 234–81.
9. ———, 'Mémoire sur la diffraction de la lumière', *Mémoires de l'Académie des Sciences*, vol. 5 (1821–1822), pp. 339–445.
10. Full references to the work of these authors are provided below.
11. See the work of Bellone cited in Further Reading.
12. For one such discussion, see the paper by John Herivel cited in Further Reading.

FURTHER READING

Enrico Bellone, *The world on paper. Studies on the second scientific revolution*, trans. by Mirella and Riccardo Giacconi (Cambridge, Mass, 1980).

Maurice Crosland, *The Society of Arcueil. A view of French science at the time of Napoleon I* (London, 1967).

—— and Crosbie Smith, 'The transmission of physics from France to Britain: 1800–1840', *Historical studies in the physical sciences*, 9 (1978), 1–61.

Robert Fox, 'The rise and fall of Laplacian physics', *Historical studies in the physical sciences*, 4 (1974), 89–136.

Eugene Frankel, 'The search for a corpuscular theory of double refraction: Malus, Laplace, and the prize competition of 1808', *Centaurus*, 18 (1974), 223–45.

—— 'J. B. Biot and the mathematization of experimental physics in Napoleonic France', *Historical studies in the physical sciences*, 8 (1977), 33–72.

Charles Coulston Gillispie *et al.*, 'Pierre-Simon, Marquis de Laplace', in C. C. Gillispie (ed.), *Dictionary of scientific biography* (16 vols., New York, 1970–80), vol. 15, pp. 273–403 (especially sections 22–4 and 27).

Ivor Grattan-Guinness, 'Mathematical physics in France, 1800–1840: knowledge, activity, and historiography', in *Mathematical perspectives. Essays on mathematics and its historical development*, (ed.) Joseph W. Dauben (New York, 1981), pp. 95–138.

John W. Herivel, 'Aspects of French theoretical physics in the nineteenth ccentury', *British journal for the history of science*, 3 (1966–7), 109–32.

Robert H. Silliman, 'Fresnel and the emergence of physics as a discipline', *Historical studies in the physical sciences*, 4 (1974), 137–62.

David B. Wilson, 'Experimentalists among the mathematicians: physics in the Cambridge Natural Sciences Tripos, 1851–1900', *Historical studies in the physical sciences*, 12 (1982), 325–71.

—— 'The educational matrix: physics education at early-Victorian Cambridge, Edinburgh and Glasgow Universities', in *Wranglers and physicists. Studies in Cambridge mathematical physics in the nineteenth century*, (ed.) Peter M. Harman (Manchester, 1985) pp. 12–48.

19

NATURAL HISTORY, 1670–1802

PHILLIP R. SLOAN

I. THE ORIGINS OF THE SCIENCE OF NATURAL HISTORY

The roots of a science of natural history, originally meaning an inquiry into the facts of nature (*res naturae*), have a long history beginning in antiquity. Originally the concept designated very little beyond a collection of observations or reports on geological, meteorological, biological and astronomical phenomena. The writings on zoology by Aristotle, especially his *History of Animals*, and the *De plantis* of his pupil Theophrastus (*c.* 381–276 BC) on botany can be seen as early expressions of this collection of observations in the Western tradition.

It is the *Natural History* of Pliny the Elder (AD, 23–79), consciously modelled on the chronological history of Livy and embodying the ideal of the 'encyclopaedic' learning of the Roman Humanists, which established the archetype for later Western expressions of the idea. The Plinian ideal of natural history intended it to be a collection of reports on all topics, particularly those of detail about natural objects which had been otherwise ignored in the Roman humanistic-literary ideal of culture.

Pliny's long-winded summary in thirty-seven books of the writings of various authorities on cosmology, astronomy, geography, anthropology, obstetrics, zoology, botany, pharmacology and mineralogy provided the prime source for information on the ancient opinions on these matters, and established the model upon which the 'encyclopaedic' tradition of the Renaissance humanists could be subsequently modelled. It also established as part of this tradition a concern to make practical application of this information. The continued availability of Pliny's text to the Latin West during the Middle Ages made this a primary source of information and misinformation which later commentators were to utilise.

Natural history, conceived in these terms, has less the character of organised scientific inquiry than that of an empirical data base for such inquiry. The theory and method of science, pursued primarily in antiquity by Aristotle and Galen, which sought a causal understanding through philosophical principles, was not properly a concern of the early natural histories. This underlies the sharp distinction made later between natural philosophy and natural history.

2. WORK IN THE RENAISSANCE

The Renaissance natural histories of Konrad Gesner (1516–1665), Ulisses Aldrovandi (1522–1605), Guillaume Rondelet (1507–56), Pierre Belon (1517–64) and the herbals of Leonhard Fuchs (1501–66) and Kasper Bauhin (1550–1624), retain a clearly Plinian, or in botany, a Dioscoridean character, in spite of the new material, illustrations and attention to anatomical detail contained in them. In their attempt to identify the plants, animals and minerals mentioned in the ancient texts, and in their critical concern to correct the errors of the Ancients in the light of renewed empirical inquiry, the natural historians of the Renaissance stood in a similar relation to the ancient tradition as Vesalius did to that in anatomy – revising, correcting and even criticising the ancient tradition in the light of new information, but remaining within a similar perception of the value and nature of the inquiry.

New issues, insufficient in themselves to generate a conceptual revolution, but nevertheless capable of creating new questions, were raised by the discovery of the New World. In addition to its demonstration of the errors of the ancient geographers, this discovery also confronted the European tradition with new questions concerning the classification of animals and plants. Joseph Acosta's reports (1589) of the numerous new forms in the New World raised issues of classification and also of theology as Europeans sought to explain the origins of these new forms. Many of the new exotic forms could not be placed in the general categories of the ancient authors, nor matched with their descriptions. The alphabetical arrangements of objects utilised by many of the Renaissance Encyclopaedists could locate these new forms in many instances only by giving them a name, without supplying a higher-order rationale for their ordering.

Francis Bacon's methodological reform of learning was of deep importance for development of this understanding of natural history in its early modern sense. Bacon's concern, developed in his *Advancement of Learning* (1605), was to systematise the various branches of knowledge in a natural arrangement of learning, relating each form of learning to the primary human faculties of Memory, Imagination and Reason. In this classification Bacon gave natural history a place in the hierarchy of learning, while codifying its distinction from natural philosophy proper. Bacon's ordering separated natural history, along with sacred, ecclesiastical and civil history, as subjects of Memory, from natural philosophy, a topic of Reason, and implied that it was an enterprise concerned solely with a collection of information. In Bacon's words, it was devoted to inquiry into 'the history of creatures, history of marvels, and history of arts'.[1]

This Baconian natural history, best exemplified by his posthumous *Silva Sylvarum*, primarily differed from the Plinian approach in its critical spirit of inquiry, treating with scepticism the reports and fabulous dimensions of prior natural histories. It also emphasised a more systematic inductive collection of empirical observations (experiments) as a means of supplying a basis for the work of natural philosophy in its search for causal explanation. This understanding of natural history, institutionalised in the inductive inquiries of the early Royal Society of London in their natural histories of heat, wind, colour and more arcane phenomena, developed this Baconian approach in the seventeenth-century. As the term was defined by John Harris in his influential lexicon of scientific terms and concepts at the opening of the eighteenth-century, natural history was 'a Description of any of the Natural Products of the Earth, Water or Air, such as Beasts, Birds, Fishes, Metals, Minerals, Fossils, together with such *Phaenomena* as at any time appear in the material world; such as Meteors &c'.[2]

To this point, one well-defined tradition of natural history had developed through the early modern period in an isomorphic relation with that of antiquity. With Bacon it had received a clearer location in a more general systematisation of knowledge, and the strong development of British natural theology in the seventeenth century, with its emphasis on the argument from design, supplied a theological rationale for this collecting and classifying of natural objects in the search for the 'natural system'. The 'historical' character of this inquiry did not imply a deep concern with temporality or temporal process, but was directed at synchronic collection and systematisation, even if it utilised reports of earlier authors. To this extent Michel Foucault's claim about the 'non-historical' character of early modern natural history is warranted.

3. THE SEVENTEENTH-CENTURY TRADITION

This meaning of natural history formed the strong, even dominant tradition in natural history of the seventeenth-century, and in this form led directly into the eighteenth-century and the systematic natural history of Linnaeus.

At the same time, however, the roots of a very different conception of 'natural history' were also being developed in the seventeenth century. For this second tradition, natural history was a science in the classical meaning of the term, rather than a propaedeutic to science. Furthermore, in this tradition its historical character was to be more profoundly developed.

This second, and ultimately more important, wing of natural history, sought a causal understanding of natural objects in terms of historical genesis, and in its modern form began with the writings of the Hermetic philosophers of the

Renaissance, who were concerned to formulate a Christian philosophy on chemical premises distinct from those of Greek science and its traditions. Paracelsus's *Philosophia ad Atheniensis* (1564), and the various attempts subsequently to develop a 'Mosaical' philosophy by Robert Fludd (1638), Athanasius Kircher (1644) and Johannes Baptista van Helmont (1648), produced rational theories to explain such matters as the presence of fossils, earthquakes, volcanoes, mountains and floods by historical processes involving chemical mechanisms. These attempts to combine scientific categories with the chronological ordering of events provided by Scripture, developed the suggestions of some of the Church fathers, particularly St Augustine, whose *De genesi ad litteram* provided a model for the scientific readings of Genesis. Such accounts, like other aspects of the Hermetic developments of the Renaissance, lacked the systematic power needed to render these compelling to more than a minority of individuals. As with many other aspects of the Renaissance science, Cartesianism provided the key to future developments of these speculations.

4. DESCARTES

Descartes occupies a central position in the natural history tradition through his presentation in his *Principles of Philosophy* (1644) of a secular history of the solar system and the earth, in which the present formation of the earth is conceived as produced by natural mechanisms in accordance with the operation of natural laws. The Cartesian 'theory of the earth', as these speculations were commonly termed, posited the formation of the earth from the gradual accumulation of matter in the centre of a celestial vortex, initially forming a star which then gradually cooled to form solid earth. Continued cooling results in the cracking and faulting of the surface, releasing subterranean waters and forming the continents and mountains. Minerals are formed by similar natural processes.

In this comprehensive speculative account, organic life was, surprisingly, omitted, primarily because Descartes had not been able to solve the problem of the organisation of the embryo by the laws of motion. The Cartesian account therefore skips from the formation of the inorganic world to the level of pre-existing life and consciousness. (See art. 24.)

Many of the details of Descartes's accounts can be shown to be derivative of a preceding Renaissance tradition. More important, however, Descartes made these speculations part of a larger epistemological and metaphysical reform of all philosophy, in which the categories of the Classical tradition were replaced by those involving an ontology of matter and mind, combined with a novel understanding of the concepts of natural law, the principle of inertia and the exclusively mechanical action of material bodies. Furthermore, Descartes provided an epistemological rationale for understanding nature in this way and no other. On Cartesian principles, rational certitude was only preserved by the

Cartesian method, which moved from a claimed foundation in the unassailable certitude of the *cogito ergo sum* (I think therefore I am) to the *a priori* proofs of God's existence as a non-deceiving being, terminating with the principles of physics and natural philosophy. This suggested to at least many of his contemporaries that only through this Cartesian understanding of phenomena, in terms of secondary causation and universal mechanism, could nature be understood at all. Because God's existence was proven *a priori* in the Cartesian philosophy, it was not necessary to rely on the argument from design, and by this development, Cartesianism could proceed to develop a fully secularised account of geology and cosmology. (See art. 53.)

However, this ambitious philosophical programme was modified throughout by a pervasive hypotheticalism which made the historical character of Descartes' speculations uncertain to his readers. As he wrote in the *Principles of Philosophy* (1644):

> I do not doubt that the world was created in the beginning with all the perfection which it now possesses: so that the Sun, the Earth, the Moon, and the Stars existed in it, and so that the Earth did not only contain the seeds of plants but was covered by actual plants: and that Adam and Eve were not born as children but created as adults. The Christian faith teaches us this, and natural reason convinces us that this is true; because, taking into account the omnipotence of God, we must believe that everything He created was perfect in every way. But, nevertheless, just as for an understanding of the nature of plants or men it is better by far to consider how they can gradually grow from seeds than how they were created by God in the very beginning of the world; so, if we can devise some principles which are very simple and easy to know and by which we can demonstrate that the stars and the Earth, and indeed everything which we perceive in this visible world, could have sprung forth as if from certain seeds (even though we know that things did not happen that way); we shall in that way explain their nature much better than if we were merely to describe them as they are now. . . . [3]

Although Descartes did not himself utilise the designation 'natural history' to denote these speculations, this new conception of a science which presented a historical and genetic account of the means by which the present order of things came into being under the action of natural laws, gave a new meaning to the term in the seventeenth century. The most creative Cartesian investigators, e.g. the Dane Nicholas Steno (1638–86), took these speculations as fertile hypotheses pointing to a true description of nature, and proceeded to develop Descartes' explanations in more empirically rigorous ways, utilising Descartes' general theory of the earth to develop a careful genetic account of the means by which organic bodies had arisen and their remains naturally fossilised and enclosed within the earth by hydrogeological processes.

In other directions, the secular character of Descartes' theories was modified in the 1680s by the British divine, Thomas Burnet (c.1635–1715), who attempted to synthesise the Cartesian and Mosaical philosophies by harmonising

Descartes' historical account with the Book of Genesis. By the late seventeenth century, the use of the terms 'natural history' to cover these speculations about the history of the earth can be found in the writings of John Woodward and Thomas Robinson.[4] For this tradition the issues were no longer concerned with the collection and arrangements of observations, but were those involved with the formulation of historical theories of nature in which creation, including that of organic beings, takes place in time by secondary causation.

By their close association with Cartesianism, these early attempts at a 'history of nature' were also subject to the Newtonian critique of Cartesian physics and cosmology. Newton's attack on the Cartesian vortex theory and on other aspects of Cartesian physics carried with it a parallel critique of Cartesian 'world-building', Newton's term for these speculative theories of the earth. Such efforts were a prime example of hypothesis-making, and in Newton's name much of this speculation came to a historical cessation in the early eighteenth century. As the thirty-first query to Newton's *Opticks* was to put this:

> it's unphilosophical to seek for any other Origin of the World [except divine creation], or to pretend that it might arise out of a Chaos by the mere Laws of nature; though being once form'd, it may continue by those Laws for many Ages.[5]

Consequently, although Newton formulated a physics based on the objective existence of infinite time and space, he also placed emphasis on the presentist analysis of the motions of bodies and the celestial motions in terms of contemporaneous laws, while expressing scepticism about the possibility of a scientific understanding of the means by which the present order of things had come to be in time. Although there were efforts to develop Newtonian cosmological, if not geological, theories on Cartesian models, the main thrust of Newtonianism was opposed to these. Movement beyond these powerful strictures required substantial developments in eighteenth-century philosophy and science.

5. EARLY ENLIGHTENMENT DEVELOPMENTS

The post-Newtonian developments in the concept of natural history in the Enlightenment can be outlined as proceeding along the following lines. The older, classificatory tradition had never waned in the seventeenth-century, with a strong tradition running from the important work of Cesalpino (1519–1603) through that of John Ray (1627–1708) and Francis Willughby (1635–72) in zoology, and through the work of Ray, Rivinus (1652–1723) and Tournefort (1656–1708) in botany. This tradition was assisted by the development of Baconian science and its ideal of induction. These activities fed into the strong programme of Linnaean natural history in the middle of the century, with its primary emphasis on specimen collection and classification of the three kingdoms of nature. Through the work of Carl Linnaeus (1707–78) and his pupils this led to the rational systematisation of the main groups of organisms into subordinating groups with the establishment of the binomial system of nomenclature and the Linnaean hierarchy of seven main groups (Kingdom, Class, Order, Genus, Species, Variety). Linnaeus codified the prior usages by Cesalpino, Ray and Tournefort of the reproductive structures for the classification of plants, and extended the earlier utilisation by Wotton, Willughby and Ray of parts of locomotion and function for the definition and classification of main groups of animals. Such 'artificial' systems provided the groundwork for the mature attempts of Linnaeus and his pupils to develop more natural plant groupings. Linnaeus' disciples, such as Petrus Osbeck and Peter Forsskl, produced foundational works in special group zoology.

Linnaean natural history provided the impetus for numerous natural history societies and was behind the sponsorship of natural history collection by the scientific academies. Linnaean students, for example Anders Sparrmann, Daniel Solander and Carl Thunberg, accomplished collecting expeditions in the Far East and South Africa. Collection by government sponsorship was also undertaken on a large scale by the French government, which had institutionalised its work in natural history with the establishment of the *Jardin du Roi* in 1635 and its attendant *Cabinet d'histoire naturelle*. This was to grow into a major centre of French botanical and zoological collection during the eighteenth century, developed to its greatest extent under the long supervision (1739–88) of Georges-Louis Le Clerc Comte de Buffon (1708–88).

The Linnaean tradition, while primarily concerned with collection, systematisation and development of the natural system of classification, also made limited attempts at a more historical approach. Linnaeus began this with his own attempt at a Mosaical 'history' of the earth in his treatise *Oratio de telluris habitabilis incremento* (1744). This was an attempt to develop a theory of the origin of animals and plants by hybridisation, developing these from a primeval stock placed on an Edenic island created by God. Other Linnaean treatises developed the ideas of the harmony and balance of nature through the interaction of species in a larger economy of nature.[6]

Although these activities indicate that the Linnaean programme was much more complex than simple collection and identification of specimens, this vision of natural history remained conceptually confined by a limitation on the focus of what constituted the domain of this science, restricting itself in Linnaeus's own formulations to a kind of school scholasticism in combination with hermetic and religious principles.

The second Enlightenment development of natural history involved the revival of Cartesian-style secular histories of the earth and cosmos after their period of decline following the critique of speculative cosmology by Newton. The revival of this tradition in parallel with, and also in self-conscious opposition to, the Linnaean tradition, implies that the eighteenth-century was never dominated by an ahistorical concept of 'natural history' to be contrasted with the historical 'biology' of the nineteenth-century. We are rather presented with competing research programmes which involved incompatible assumptions and agendas, both designating their inquiries as 'natural history'.

This renewal of historical natural history required substantial theoretical development along three different lines. The first involved the revival of the Renaissance concept of Nature as a substantive agency intermediate between God and individual creatures. This Renaissance view of Nature as an active, intermediary power had been undercut in some respects by the mechanical philosophy of Descartes himself, who had explicitly denied that nature was anything more than a created order of matter.

The Renaissance-Stoic conception of nature was, however, revived by the Cambridge Platonists Ralph Cudworth and Henry More, and was further developed, as an alternative means to explain creation, by authors such as John Toland who were concerned to formulate a Deistic theology. This restoration of a creative agency to Nature provided a means of avoiding the consequences of Cartesian mechanism, particularly in biology, and also supplied an explanatory framework in which organisms could be integrated into a naturalistic theory of the earth. Organisms could, in this case, arise by the creative powers of nature itself, rather than by simple mechanical laws of motion. Such a notion was also a means of avoiding theological problems associated with such issues as the production of embryological monsters. Newton also gave impetus to this development, in spite of his opposition to historical developmentalism, by his theory of the pervasiveness of active ether throughout nature, and by his suggestion that attractive and repulsive forces, analogous to the attractive forces in the planetary realm, were operative in the material activities of bodies. This new status of Nature as a creative and dynamic agency, an 'immense living power which animates the universe', as Buffon was to term it in 1765, gave an object of reference for a science concerned with a 'history' of Nature.

We see the deeper development of the consequences of this view of Nature in the philosophy of Gottfried Leibniz (1646–1716) and his disciple and interpreter Christian Wolff (1679–1754). As the Leibnizians viewed the mechanical philosophy of Descartes, nature had been deprived of a concept of 'live force' (vis viva), a concept demanded by the phenomena of mechanics. The mechanical philosophy also implied, for the Leibnizians, a nature devoid of teleological purpose. In opposition to this the Leibnizian conception of matter, based on centre of force rather than on material extension or mass, gave reality a dynamic character which was applied to nature as a whole. It also restored the Aristotelian concept of an immanent teleological agency in nature itself. Leibnizian nature was not an inert system acting by contact action. Instead, it followed out an internal, telos-laden career, governed by in-dwelling law, directed to rational ends. God's intervention was unnecessary in this system precisely because it carried out by its own power its divine mandate. In this respect, Leibnizian nature was at least practically autonomous, and able to fulfil and even create by its own internal dynamism without divine intervention. For eighteenth-century thinkers able to draw upon these developments, the ideal of a science of Nature distinct from rational mechanics or experimental physics, presented new possibilities.

The second development was an indirect implication of Leibniz's critique of Newton's concepts of absolute time and space as these were related to the phenomenal world. The notions of absolute and infinite time and space, most clearly expressed by Newton in the Scholium to Definition Eight of the second edition of the *Principia* (1713), had divorced the infinite space-time container of the world from an essential connection to its historical process. For this reason there was no inherent difficulty for Newtonians to conceive of a world with an effective age of approximately 6,000 years located within infinite time and space.

The Leibnizian critique of the foundations of Newtonianism, developed most explicitly for the eighteenth century in the Leibniz-Clarke correspondence (1717), rejected this hiatus, and made time and space immanent in phenomena. For Leibniz, time and space do not exist apart from things, but are realised through them. Leibniz's complex metaphysical system of the monads prevented this concept from having an immediate empirical application, although it is significant that he was willing to renew a Cartesian-style 'theory of the earth' in his posthumous *Protagea* (1749). More direct application of Leibnizian principles in ways which could be applied to natural history was reserved for his interpreter and synthesiser Christian Wolff. Wolff's tendency to give more concrete and empirically-meaningful interpretations of Leibnizian concepts is evident in his discussion of the notions of time and space. Time does not exist apart from objects, but is grounded in their successional existence. Similarly, in opposition to Newton, space exists only in the relationship of bodies, and not as a container in which they are located. At least on a philosophical level, these developments opened up the possibility that only through the material history and successional relations of objects was time even realised.

The third development flowed directly from this Leibnizian-Wolffian analysis. By the middle of the eighteenth-century, a distinction appeared in the literature, directly indebted to Leibniz and Wolff, between two orders of scientific inquiry. The first, an 'abstract' order, was that dealt with by mathematical science. In a surprising reversal of seventeenth-century conclusions, the abstract character of mathematical science meant that it was also divorced from the reality of concrete things. This was then contrasted to a second order, that which became the domain of inquiry into historical process, natural history and ecological and genetic relationships of organisms. In this 'concrete' or 'physical' order, one dealt with the temporal and spatial relationships of actually existent particulars. Surprisingly, this meant that for some inquirers, the most certain science, with the strongest claim to truth, was not physics, but rather natural history and geology.

6. THE WORK OF BUFFON

The importance of these three metaphysical revisions of the philosophical foundations of seventeenth-century science is to be most clearly followed in the writings of Buffon (1707–88). Following out the implications of each of these developments, Buffon opened his monumental *Histoire naturelle générale et particulière* (1749–89 with supplements) with an essay intended to function almost as a *Discourse on Method* for this new conception of natural history. In this he placed himself in direct opposition both to the natural history of Linnaeus, and also to certain key assumptions of mathematical physics. The value of hierarchical classification and the development of 'abstract' systems of nature by Linnaeus, Tournefort and the other classifiers was openly attacked. In its place Buffon proposed to substitute a science based on a 'physical' understanding of relationships and processes of nature which alone could give certainty. By this he explicitly meant a science which sought its conceptual grounding in concrete successional and temporal process. Distinguishing 'physical' truths, grounded on succession and repetition of events, from the 'abstract' truths of mathematical physics, he wrote in 1749, in his 'Initial Discourse':

> Physical truths, on the other hand, are in no way arbitrary, and in no way depend on us. Instead of being founded on suppositions which we have made, they depend only on facts. A sequence of similar facts or, if you prefer, a frequent repetition and an uninterrupted succession of the same occurrences constitute the essence of this sort of truth. . . . One goes from definition to definition in the abstract sciences, but one proceeds from observation to observation in the real sciences. In the first case one arrives at evidence, while in the latter the result is certitude.[7]

The implications of this novel development were most directly expressed in Buffon's analyses of historical cosmology, geology and biology. In cosmology, Buffon revived the speculative theories of the historical genesis of the solar system, combining aspects of Descartes' theory with Newtonian revisions suggested by William Whiston's cometary theory. His theory of succession and causation received their most clear application in geology, where Buffon proposed in 1749 that sudden, catastrophic events should not be utilised as causes in developing a theory of the earth, but effects which are daily repeated, motions which succeed each other without interruption, and operations that are constant, ought alone to be the ground of our reasoning.[8]

Buffon's geological theory, for this reason, is based on uniform, temporally sequential causes, particularly the recurrent action of the tides and sea in the formation of the topography.

Even more revolutionary is the significance of this development for Buffon's understanding of biological species. For the classificatory tradition, most immediately represented for Buffon's generation by Linnaeus, a 'species' was a logical category, one of the five Porphyrian predicables, designating the lowest class of entities above that of the individual and the local variety. On this conception of species, there was no difference between a 'species' in mineralogy, or other inanimate objects, and one in botany or zoology.

Buffon's successional and historical understanding of physical relationships implied for him a radically different understanding of a species in biology. Rather than being an 'abstract' class of individuals, it was exclusively to be understood as a 'physical' historical lineage, a concept only applicable to the temporal and spatial relationships manifested by organisms. As he writes in his most influential discussion of this question in 1753:

> It is neither the number nor the collection of similar individuals which forms the species. It is the constant succession and uninterrupted renewal of these individuals which comprises it. . . . The species is thus an abstract and general term, for which the thing exists only in considering Nature in the succession of time, and in the constant destruction and renewal of creatures. . . .
>
> Since the species is nothing else than a constant succession of similar individuals which reproduce themselves, it is clear that this designation must be extended only to animals and plants.[9]

Buffon's grounding of such concepts on the temporal recurrence and material connectedness of natural events implied an emphasis on material relationship and natural causation as components of his conception of natural history. Whereas the Linnaean programme concerned itself with the classification of nature and the search for the 'natural system', Buffon's programme emphasised historical process, the study of the distribution, migration of forms, geological change, and even study of the degenerative change of species in time. Developing these concepts in a series of articles in the 1760s, Buffon expanded his concept of physical species to include degenerative change in historical lineages of forms as they underwent geographical migration. Finally, by the synthesis of all these biological and geological speculations in the great *Epoques de la nature* of 1778, Buffon presented a full system of historical geology and biology with enormous impact on the succeeding discussions. The age of the earth was extended to more than 37,000 years, with forms arising and diversifying as the earth underwent geological change. (See art. 24.)

This contrast of the Linnaean and Buffonian programs, both given institutional support in different social structures in Europe and England, provided a fertile set of options upon which the late eighteenth century could easily draw.

The Linnaean approach, followed by numerous natural history societies on the Continent and in England, continued the cataloguing, collecting and classifying of the works of created nature, with numerous naturalists working out the main lines of contemporary groupings of plants and animals under its banner. The Linnaean Society of London, founded in 1788, was created to preserve Linnaean manuscripts and collections, and to promote the study of Linnaean natural history in England.

Buffon's approach, on the other hand, achieved its institutional locus at the Paris *Jardin du Roi* during his long superintendence from 1739–88. This institution provided a location where more novel researchers in comparative anatomy, distribution and geology could be carried out alongside the continuation of Linnaean systematic botany practised by the long succession of the Jussieu family. Through its complicated history during the Revolutionary period, when the autocratic *Jardin* was transformed into the democratic *Muséum National d'histoire naturelle*, French natural history continued to explore new issues and raise new questions. In comparative anatomy, the inquiries initiated by Buffon's collaborator Louis-Jean-Marie Daubenton, were continued by Etienne Geoffroy Saint-Hilaire and Georges Cuvier. Possibilities of species transformation, raised by Buffon, were continued by Lamarck, Bernard de Lacépède and Geoffroy Saint-Hilaire; new lines of inquiry into invertebrate form and function were pursued by Lamarck; while the foundations for modern ichthyology were laid by Bernard de Lacépède and Georges Cuvier. Modern paleontology was begun by the researches into the significance of fossils by Cuvier and Brongniart. The charter for a 'science' of natural history, provided by Buffon, had clearly destroyed the invidious distinction between 'natural history' and genuine 'natural philosophy'.

7. KANTIAN NATURAL HISTORY

For most of the late eighteenth and early nineteenth century, the Linnaean and Buffonian approaches to natural history did not stand clearly distinct, and the inherent tensions and even incompatibilities between these two programmes offered no obstacles to their synthesis. Georges Cuvier, for example, advocated moving repeatedly from one to the other for inspiration. Buffon and Linnaeus served more as two conceptual fonts, used often eclectically, to provide a dual focus of inquiry into nature.

In the German tradition there was, however, a more conscious attempt to systematise the distinction of these two different conceptualisations of natural history. Immanuel Kant's philosophical reform of the 1770s carried with it direct implications for this clarification of issues. Kant had personally been involved with issues in theoretically natural history through his teaching of physical and geographical anthropology, and by thus was aware of the differences between the Linnaean and Buffonian approaches to natural history. His recognition of the distinction is first shown in his *Allgemeine Naturgeschichte des Himmels* of 1755. In this speculative attempt to construct a historical cosmology, Kant's meaning of *Naturgeschichte* was clearly in the sense of Buffon, Woodward and Robinson, not that of Bacon and Linnaeus. This point was made explicit in the opening lecture to Kant's course on physical geography (*c.* 1775), where he distinguished sharply between a *Naturbeschreibung*, meaning a Linnaean account of the taxonomic relations of nature, and a historical understanding, a *Naturgeschichte* proper:

> The history of nature [*Naturgeschichte*] contains the multiplicity of geographical objects, as it has been in different times, but not how it is now at the same time. Because in this case it would be a description of nature [*Naturbeschreibung*]. But if the events of collected nature, as they have been constituted through all times, are brought forth, we are supplied for the first time with a natural history properly so called.[10]

In 1775 Kant made practical application of this distinction in a discussion of the races of man. Linnaean analyses of the varieties of humankind had classified human beings into several taxonomic varieties, and in later editions of the *Systema naturae* (1771) had gone so far as to admit four species in genus *Homo*, with several distinct varieties. This was in direct contrast to Buffon's conclusion that humankind formed a single reproductively-compatible 'biological' species capable of undergoing geographical and historical diversification.

In dealing with this issue in the 1770s and 80s, Kant made an important distinction between the concepts belonging properly to the 'description' of nature, and those proper to its 'history'. The designations of 'race' or 'variety' used in these discussions of humankind, were thereby separated by Kant, with 'variety' confined to descriptive and classificatory natural history, and 'race' confined to its historical conception. This broadly defined for Kant two distinct approaches in studying the relationship of organisms. As he was to write in his 1775 paper:

> The logical division [of nature] proceeds by classes according to similarities; the natural division considers them according to the stem, and divides animals according to genealogy, and with reference to reproduction. One produces an arbitrary system for the memory, the other a natural system for the understanding. The first has only the intention of bringing creation under titles; the second intends to bring it under laws.[11]

Kant's distinction became critical for the subsequent discussions of this problem in German contexts. As debates on polygenesis progressed into the

1780s and 90s, Kant argued that in the Buffonian, historical sense of natural history, humankind formed only one species with distinct historical races united in a common stem.

Kant's splitting of Linnaean and Buffonian natural history along lines rendering one essentially a science of space, and the other a science of time, are further codified by his introduction into the literature in 1788 of the terms *Physiographie* and *Physiogonie* as synonyms of his terms *Naturbeschreibung* and *Naturgeschichte*. For his German successors, if not clearly for those in other national traditions, 'natural history' from this date had two meanings and two approaches, one confining itself to data available contemporaneously to sense, and the other involving itself in historical speculations about historical origins and developmental process. Whereas some naturalists, such as Johann Blumenbach, would primarily explore under the label of 'natural history' taxonomic relationships, comparative anatomy, and physiology, others would seek to develop the historical and genetic approach under the guise of a 'History' or 'Physiogony' of nature. The latter programme, especially explored by those influenced by the *Naturphilosophie* of Schelling, removed many of the epistemological strictures that Kant himself placed on the status of speculative knowledge, and its advocates were willing to give realist interpretations to theories of the historical genesis of organisms, the origins of species and the derivations of kinds. Through Samuel Taylor Coleridge, these views were introduced into England in the 1820s, and received public expression in the lectures at the College of Surgeons in the late 1820s by Coleridge's disciple Joseph Henry Green.[12]

However, in the wake of Kant's distinctions, others advocated the confinement of natural history and related inquiries into geology and minerology to non-historical analyses. Kant's own restriction of scientific knowledge to the categorised knowledge of the Understanding (*Verstand*) could be taken to mean that only the Linnaean approach was a true science. 'History' of nature was confined to the domain of speculative Reason (*Vernunft*), having no more than a regulative function. Depending on how one read Kant's intentions, his distinctions could be interpreted either as warranting the development of historical speculations of nature, along lines suggested by his discussions in such works as the *Kritik der Urteilskraft* of 1790, or as implying the confinement of all scientific inquiry to the domain of description and analysis of contemporaneously available process. As these Kantian distinctions were disseminated in the early nineteenth century, the consequence was a methodological debate. This debate was strongest in the Germanies (Humboldt, Johannes Müller, Schelling, Carus, Tiedemann and Blumenbach), but gradually extended into France (Cuvier and Etienne Geoffroy Saint-Hilaire) and England (Grierson, Lyell, Green and Owen), which pitted positivistic attempts to restrict natural history to its contemporaneous and descriptive functions against the more speculative attempts to construct valid histories of nature. Tension between these approaches was to last into the Darwinian period.

8. HISTORIOGRAPHIC CONSIDERATIONS

The foregoing analysis has supplied an 'intellectual history' of the concept of natural history without attending to substantial historiographic issues raised by the recent history and sociology of scientific knowledge.

Traditionally, the historiography of this material in Anglo-American literature has taken two forms. The first is that of positivist histories, representing the development of scientific rationality in progressive stages leading up to Darwin and beyond, with the conclusive scientising of the natural history tradition. In this analysis of the history of the science, static 'creationist' natural history is superseded by evolutionary biology; essentialist taxonomy is rendered genealogical and populational; while branching evolution is formulated in a form which avoids the pitfalls of the linear evolution of Lamarck and Geoffroy Saint-Hilaire. The unity of biology, embryology, biogeography and geology is achieved and the primary mechanism of change – natural selection theory – is accepted. Twentieth-century natural history, represented by the 'New Synthesis' of evolutionary biology, populational genetics and critical systematics, constitutes the extension of this into the present.[13]

Such histories, serving a normative rather than a descriptive function, have a different purpose from that of the 'History of Ideas' approach as practised by A. O. Lovejoy, Alexandre Koyré and Jacques Roger. This approach seeks to isolate primary ideas, such as 'nature', 'evolution' and 'natural system', and to discuss these as elements undergoing historical development within specific historical contexts. It seeks a full contextual understanding of the ideas without attempts at making them into stages of a historical progress. In recent years, this approach to the history of science has felt strongly the impact of the new historicism introduced into the history of science by Thomas Kuhn. (See art. 54.)

Kuhn's model of scientific development begins with the formulation of monolithic 'paradigms', able to define a normal scientific tradition. Associated with this are the concepts of 'crisis', 'revolution' and new paradigm formulation. This model of analysis has deeply affected the writing of Anglo-American history of science since the 1960s. However, although the Kuhnian model has been successfully applied to several case histories in the physical sciences, it has met with only limited success in the life sciences. Most problematic in the application of this model to the natural history tradition is the discernment of the necessary body of shared assumptions, processed 'ways of seeing' and clear paradigmatic texts and principles which are capable of generating the incommensurabilities necessary for the application of Kuhn's revolutionary model.

The difficulties in applying this historiography to natural history have been described with reference to the Darwinian revolution.[14]

Developing in response to both Thomas Kuhn and also to the positivist historiography of the philosopher Karl Popper has been the historiographic analysis of the late Imre Lakatos, and to some extent that of the philosopher Larry Laudan.[15]

Lakatos's model is, in the present author's view, the most historiographically useful for the mundane analyses of questions presented by the subject-matter of the natural history tradition. This seeks to analyse scientific development in terms of dynamic research traditions, research programmes or similar combinations of intellectual content and socio-historical embodiment. Typical of such programmes is that they are in competition with one another. This allows for the important interactions of institutional structures and cognitive considerations and personalities, while at the same time allowing greater flexibility in the conceptual structure than is permitted by Kuhn's notion of paradigms. This also avoids search for single defining conceptual structures in a given period, a particular difficulty in applying the paradigm concept to natural history.

In recent decades, the most radical revisions in historiography have been through the activities of two intellectual schools, one Continental and the other located originally at the University of Edinburgh. Both present claims which are now strongly contested among Anglo-American historians and philosophers of science.

Most explicitly with reference to the concept of natural history generally, the writings of the late French philosopher Michel Foucault, and the German historian Wolf Lepenies have sought to relate the conceptual changes in this domain to factors outside the internal history of scientific ideas.[16] Linguistic structures, the embedding of thought and language in larger social context and the possibility of more radical 'epistemic' revolutions have been seen to underlie the change from 'natural history' to the 'history of nature' or more generally to 'biology'. (See arts. 9 and 10.)

Foucault's arguments have been particularly influential in the analysis of the history and theory of classification. The analysis of the various classification systems of organisms since the Renaissance in terms of their manifestation of deeper social and political interests has proved useful, and has given a means for analysing the observed changes from linear to network, and finally to branching models of arrangements in natural history.

Foucault's intent has been to develop an 'archaeological' approach to the writing of history which incorporates many of the themes of modern Deconstructionism, generally associated with the name of Jacques Derrida. Furthermore, Foucault has explicitly applied these concepts to the analysis of the themes in the natural history tradition and to the history of biology and medicine, drawing heavily on the work of the French historian of biology Georges

Canguilhem. (See art. 10, sect. 3.) Because of this explicitly biological reference point, Foucault's work has affected these domains more deeply than is evident in the historiogaphy of the physical sciences. Traditional approaches to texts and archival sources employed normally by historians are rejected in this analysis, and the stock assumption of historians concerning the transmission and transparency of ideas through texts and documents is itself questioned. In its place is presented an archaeology of thought which seeks to discern the underlying patterns of thought, institutional relationships and even the relations of domination and power encoded in the texts from the textual relationships and the units of discourse employed. Consequently, the apparent autonomy of conceptual developments and theoretical structures in scientific discourse is at some point interpreted, if not reduced, within an analysis of economic structures, institutions, class-struggles, technological changes, relations of power and domination, or other socio-economic factors. Foucault's explicit intent is to 'derationalise' and 'de-anthropomorphise' historical thinking by relating thought to underlying structural changes in the material ground-work of thought, at the same time abolishing any sense of teleological development of historical consciousness.

The general acceptability of these Continental approaches to historical writing is strongly contested among contemporary English-speaking historians, and these positions are more favourably received by historians of science than by historians generally. Some have characterised this movement critically as a 'neo-Ramism', linking it with the attacks on traditional logic by the Renaissance thinker Petrus Ramus. The Foucauldian analysis, applied to natural history, derives much of its force from the interesting conjunctions of scientific and socio-political events in the period from 1790–1810, a particularly fertile period in the development of modern natural history. Under debate are the claims that this synchrony of definable scientific changes and the French and Industrial Revolutions is causal, and not simply the association of a 'loose montage' of ideas with no more than superficial connections with one another. The theoretical character of the Foucauldian analysis, denying the autonomy of the transcendental historical observer, renders such a position difficult to criticise by appeal to historical data itself. On the level of ordinary historical analysis and dicourse, where Foucault's analysis seems most commonly employed among historians of science, his claims depend on a high degree of selectivity of texts and authors.[17]

Sharing some features in common with Foucault's radical critique, but significantly less ambitious in its vision, is the 'reflexive' sociology of knowledge, introduced into the analysis of the history of science particularly by the Edinburgh school, but with debts to the sociology of Emil Durkheim, Marx and to the philosopher Ludwig Wittgenstein. As with Foucault, the issue of classification has also been a particular object of attention, in this case with the claim being made that the world radically underdetermines classifications, with social structures and interests implicit in their produced forms.[18] (See arts. 5 and 7.)

This historiography generally seeks to relate the content of scientific theory to underlying sociological structures, reducing science to one naturalised expression of culture among many, without special claims to theoretical autonomy determined by the structure of reality. The Edinburgh 'strong programme' differs from the more traditional sociology of knowledge deriving from Max Weber, and represented for the history of science by the studies of Robert K. Merton and Joseph Ben-David. The Weberian tradition has sought to analyse the sociological setting of scientific ideas, but retains the distinction between external context and rationally independent internal content. It is this separation which is denied by the Edinburgh school, and the studies done in this mode have attempted to relate even the hard content of scientific theories in biology, mathematics and physics to underlying social structures. Critics of the Edinburgh approach have often emphasised the problems presented by self-reference in their attempts to reduce rationality to sociology, and have made a more limited critique by arguing that the case histories presented do not warrant the conclusions drawn. A recent defence of a realist interpretation of classification against the relativism of the sociological analysis has been presented by Scott Atran.[19] The incompatible assumptions represented by these alternatives suggest that historiographic debate among historians of the life sciences will be an important issue for some time to come.

NOTES

1. Francis Bacon, *Advancement of learning*, in: *The works of Lord Bacon* (London, 1871), vol. I, p. 28.
2. J. Harris, *Lexicon technicum* (London, 1710), vol, II, no pg. no.
3. Descartes, *Principles of philosophy*, trans. V. R. Miller and R. P. Miller (Dordrecht, 1983), p. 105–6.
4. T. Burnet, *The Sacred theory of the earth* (London, 1684); John Woodward, *Essay toward a natural history of the earth* (London, 1695); Thomas Robinson, *New observations on the natural history of this world of matter and this world of life* (London, 1694).
5. Isaac Newton, *Opticks* (3rd ed., ed. F. Cajori, Berkeley, 1952), p. 402.
6. Carl Linné, *Oratio de telluris habitabilis incremento* (Leyden, 1744), I. J. Biberg, *Specimen academicum de oeconomia naturae* (Uppsala, 1749).
7. Buffon, 'Initial Discourse on the Manner of Studying Natural History', in: J. Lyon and P.R. Sloan (eds.), *From natural history to the history of nature. Readings from Buffon and his critics* (Notre Dame and London, 1981) pp. 123–24.
8. 'Second discourse', *ibid.*, p. 149.
9. Buffon 'L'Asne' *Histoire naturelle*, vol. IV (1753) in *Oeuvres philosophiques de Buffon*, ed. J. Piveteau (Paris, 1954) p. 356.
10. Kant, *Physische Geographie*, ed. F. T. Rink (1802) in: Immanuel Kant, *Sämmtliche Werke* ed. K. Vorländer 7 vols. (Leipzig, 1905), Vol. 6, p. 14.
11. Kant, 'Von der verschiedenen Racen der Menschen', in *Kants gesammelte Schriften Werke* (29 vols., Berlin, 1912), vol. 2, p. 429.
12. Phillip R. Sloan, 'Darwin, vital matter and the transformism of species', *Journal of the history of biology*, 19 (1986), 369–445.
13. See Ernst Mayr, *The growth of biological thought* (Cambridge, Mass., 1984).

14. J. Greene, 'The Kuhnian paradigm and the Darwinian revolution in natural history', in: D. H. and D. D. Roller (eds.), *Perspectives in the history of science and technology* (Norman, 1971), pp. 3–25, and comments by W. Coleman.
15. Imre Lakatos, 'Falsifiability and the methodology of scientific research programmes', in: I. Lakatos and A. Musgrave (eds.), *Criticism and the growth of knowledge* (Cambridge, 1970), pp. 91–195, and 'History of science and its rational reconstructions', in: C. Howson (ed.), *Method and appraisal in the physical sciences* (Cambridge, 1976), pp. 1–39. L. Laudan, *Progress and its problems* (Berkeley, 1977).
16. M. Foucault, *The order of things*, (New York, 1970), chapter 5. W. Lepenies, *Das Ende der Naturgeschichte* (Munich, 1976), and 'De l'histoire naturelle à l'histoire de la nature', *Dix-huit siècle*, 11 (1979), 175–84.
17. A. Megill, 'The reception of Foucault by historians', *Journal of the history of ideas*, 48 (1987), 117–41. Donald R. Kelley, 'Horizons of Intellectual History', *Journal of the history of ideas*, 48 (1987), 143–69. See G. Huppert, '*Divinatio et Eruditio*: thoughts on Foucault', *History and theory*, 13 (1974), 191–207.
18. B. Barnes, *Scientific knowledge and sociological theory* (London, 1974). Concrete applications of some of these principles to specific case histories in science are to be found in B. Barnes and S. Shapin (eds.) *Natural order* (Beverly Hills, 1979). A useful programmatic article on this general approach is S. Shapin, 'History of science and its sociological reconstructions', *History of science*, 20 (1982), 157–211. See also D. Bloor, 'Durkheim and Mauss revisited: classification and the sociology of knowledge', *Studies in history and philosophy of science*, 13 (1982), 267–92 and commentary on this which follows.
19. S. Atran, *Fondements de l'histoire naturelle* (Paris: Editions complexe, 1986).

FURTHER READING

Scott Atran, *Fondements de l'histoire naturelle: pour une anthropologie de la science.* (Paris, 1986).

Michel Foucault, *The order of things* (New York, 1970).

Wolf Lepenies, *Das Ende der Naturgeschichte.* (Munich, 1976).

John Lyon, and Phillip R. Sloan (eds.), *From natural history to the history of nature: readings from Buffon and his critics* (Notre Dame, 1981).

Jacques Roger, *Les sciences de la vie dans la pensée française du xviii siècle.* (2nd ed., Paris, 1971).

Paolo Rossi, *The dark abyss of time*, translated by L. G. Cochrane. (Chicago, 1984).

Martin Rudwick, *The meaning of fossils.* (London, 1972).

Phillip R. Sloan, 'Buffon, German biology, and the historical interpretation of biological species', *British journal for the history of science*, 12 (1979), 109–53.

—— 'John Locke, John Ray, and the problem of the natural system', *Journal of the history of biology*, 5 (1972), 1–53.

Frans A. Stafleu, *Linnaeus and the Linneans: the spreading of their ideas in systematic botany 1735–1789.* (Utrecht, 1971).

20

THE HISTORY OF GEOLOGY, 1780–1840

RACHEL LAUDAN

1. INTRODUCTION

The period between 1780 and 1840 has long been regarded as a crucial one in the development of geology. In 1780, relatively little was known about the structures and processes of the earth in spite of the efforts of individual mining engineers and bureaucrats, mineralogists, fossil collectors and cosmogonists. By 1840, the sequence of the European rocks was well on the way to being sorted out. This laid the groundwork for the reconstruction of the history of the earth and also of life on the earth. Sophisticated theories of geological causes, consistent with contemporary physics, were in hand. The appropriate methodologies for both historical and causal investigation had been much debated, and a coherent and self-conscious body of men devoted themselves almost exclusively to geology.

Thus without exception, historians of geology have fastened on this period as the formative one in the history of the discipline (though as a cautionary note, it should be pointed out that the concentration on this period has meant that we know almost nothing of earlier or later developments so that it is possible that the identification of the period 1780–1840 as crucial may have to be revised). Nonetheless, the historiography of geology has been transformed in the past two decades and scholars have modified almost every aspect of the older 'received view' of the subject's history.

I shall first briefly review the standard account of the history of geology, then I shall indicate how the history of these particular eight decades is now understood and finally I shall look at three themes that have had particular importance, namely the methodology of geology, the relation between geology and religion and the social history of geology.

2. THE RECEIVED VIEW OF THE HISTORY OF GEOLOGY

The traditional historiography of the 'heroic' period of geology (as the period from 1780–1840 used to be called) derives from that very period. Its outlines were laid down, sometimes explicitly, sometimes by default, in the four historical chapters with which Charles Lyell (1797–1875) prefaced the first volume of his *Principles of Geology* (1830) and in the responses to that volume of the Victorian polymath, William Whewell (1794–1866). It was reinforced by the eminently readable work by Sir Archibald Geikie, *The Founders of Geology* (1905), still in print and still the introduction to the subject for many readers. The received account remains standard in many geology texts, in secondary works on the history of science, and in popular works such as John McPhee's best-selling books.

In essence, the received view comprises five interrelated theses. The first is that geology took a 'historical' turn at the point at which it became a 'science' in the early nineteenth century. The second is that the historical turn was accompanied by (and probably caused by) a new empiricism and an enthusiasm for facts, particularly those gathered in the field, rather than for theory. The third is that both these developments were made possible by separating the earth sciences from religion, by distinguishing geology from Genesis and by freeing geology from a restrictive time span. The fourth is that they were accompanied by the creation of institutions for the collection, publication and transmission of geological knowledge and finally, that the making of modern geology was a British accomplishment.

According to the received view, the emergence of geology as a science took place in three distinct stages. From about 1790 to 1810, debates between the Neptunists and the Plutonists dominated the field. Abraham Gottlob Werner (1750–1817), the leading Neptunist and professor at the famous mining academy of Freiberg, is presented as an armchair geologist with an *a priori* cosmogony that, it is hinted, owed more to Genesis than to field work. He and his followers are supposed to have argued that all the rocks of the earth's surface had been deposited from and consolidated in a formerly universal ocean. James Hutton (1726–1797), the Edinburgh natural philosopher, and his followers (the Plutonists) 'believed' by contrast that the rocks had been eroded from older land surfaces, deposited at the bottom of the ocean and there consolidated by heat. According to the Wernerians, the present land surface was revealed when the waters that had deposited the rocks gradually receded; but according to the Huttonians, the present land surface was revealed when the rocks consolidated under the ocean were elevated.

Power was on the side of the Wernerians, it is said, for Werner attracted pupils from all over Europe. But right was on the side of the Huttonians, for Hutton subscribed to the uniformity of geological causes, to the necessity for field observations and to the immensity of geological time. As he said, 'We see no vestige of a beginning, no prospect of an end'. The result was a period of 'sterile wrangling' as many contemporaries called it.

The second stage in the development of geology, again according to the received view, came when the Geological Society of London was founded in 1807. Explicitly committed to a programme of Baconian co-operative fact-gathering, the members of the Geological Society set theories to one side for the time being. The members – and certain others like the mineral surveyor, William Smith (1769–1839) who were excluded from membership by lower social status – concentrated instead on amassing a solid database for geology, particularly in surveying and mapping the strata.

The third and final stage, purportedly, was marked by the resurgence of debate, in this case the debates between the uniformitarians and the catastrophists, followed by the eventual triumph of the uniformitarians. These debates are seen as a replay of the earlier ones. The catastrophists, represented most prominently by Georges Cuvier (1769–1832) in France and William Buckland (1784–1856) in England, are said to have believed that the earth's history was punctuated by periodic revolutions or 'catastrophes'. The interpretation of the last of these catastrophes as a Flood and conventional Christian dogma are thought to have been mutually reinforcing. Catastrophists supposedly accepted a short time-scale, the possiblity of miraculous intervention, and the priority of theory over field work.

Charles Lyell's doctrine of uniformitarianism, so it is said, effectively exposed the catastrophists' errors. Lyell argued that nature's laws had been uniform, that the geologist had no need to resort to miracles and that, given a sufficiently long time-scale, presently observable geological causes were capable of producing all known geological phenomena. Like Hutton, Lyell believed that the present was the key to the past and that detailed observation of current geological processes was the way to advance the science. With the uniformitarian programme established, geology was set on a sound footing. Geologists set about establishing the details of the history of the earth and of life on earth. The heroic tale of the 'discovery of time' and of the earth's past was underway. Such, in outline, is the old version of the history of this science.

3. THE NEW ACCOUNT

A cautionary note about the new history of geology is in order. With few exceptions, the new work has been confined to British geology within the 'heroic' period. In spite of the considerable need to look at geology on the continent and in the periods before and after 1780–1840, we are still in a state of great ignorance about continental geology at any period and about British geology following 1840. Only when that is corrected will we be able to set the well-documented parts of the story in some perspective.

In the new history of geology, James Hutton and the Plutonists fade in importance. As a result of extensive scholarly investigations, the picture of Hutton as one who constructed his system purely by observation has been replaced. In its stead, Hutton is recognised as the heir of two eighteenth-century traditions, both of which played a role in shaping his system. The first tradition is that of deism. Hutton, like many of his friends in Scotland, rejected traditional Christianity with its reliance on truth by revelation, and instead argued that the nature of the deity could best be understood by the use of reason and the examination of his works. Surely, he surmised, no deity would have created a world that contained the seeds of its own destruction. Rather, he would have created one that could maintain itself indefinitely. Thus at the very least these beliefs predisposed Hutton to assert the uniformity of geological causes and the immensity of geological time.

The second tradition to which Hutton was indebted stemmed from Newton. One interpretation of Newton common amongst eighteenth-century natural philosophers suggested that 'ethers' or 'subtle fluids' were the causes of a whole range of physical phenomena ranging from gravitation and heat to electricity and magnetism. Hutton fell squarely within this tradition. His theory of the earth, and of consolidation and elevation in particular, although too complicated to be traced in detail here, was in fact a theory of the circulation of the subtle fluid of heat. Emanating in the first instance from the sun, heat fluid was transformed in the earth into 'latent heat' (a concept introduced by his friend, the chemist Joseph Black) which caused the fluidity that preceded consolidation, and then subsequently into specific heat which caused expansion and hence elevation.

Thus Hutton's theory was one more in a long line of cosmological systems, albeit a rather unusual one. His field work was done in order to check hypotheses arrived at by theoretical considerations. Hutton's system is a fascinating one to unravel. But its impact on the geology of the succeeding thirty years, at least until Lyell resurrected a much-transformed version of it in the *Principles*, was rather slight.

By contrast, the Wernerians (or the school of Freiberg as they were often called) dominated geology from 1790 to the late 1820s. They actively extended the framework for thinking about both the historical and causal geology that Werner had proposed and many were early members of the Geological Society of London. In his *Short Classification and Description of the Rocks* (1787) and in his very influential lectures at the Mining Academy of Freiberg, Werner argued that geologists should divide up the rocks of the earth's surface into 'formations' – groups of rocks formed at particular times – rather than into mineralogical units. This seemingly innocuous change brought about very important consequences. Beforehand, the study of the earth had either taken the form of mineralogy – the study of the mineral substances comprising the earth – or of cosmogony, the postulation of a sequence of events by which the supposedly original spherical, fluid, chaotic globe had reached its present state. These two activities had meshed nicely, for minerals were basically distinguished by their reactions to heat and water, the two causes assumed to be most important in shaping the earth's surface. In the Wernerian tradition both mineralogy and cosmogony declined in relative importance, particularly the latter. The history of the earth was not to be a matter of speculation about possible causes, but a painstaking reconstruction of the order of formations.

Werner and his followers thus initiated what might be called the 'historical' turn in geology. The reconstruction of the earth's past by examining natural monuments (that is, strictly historical geology), although not without precursors, was the invention of the early nineteenth century. It largely displaced cosmogony and, because of its success, mineralogy was relegated to secondary importance. Once the methods for reconstructing the order of the rocks had been articulated, enthusiasm for historical geology according to the 'school of Freiberg' swept beyond Germany to France, to England and to other parts of the world including America.

What did historical geology involve in more detail? It involved, first and foremost, arranging the rocks in chronological order. In the long run, geologists hoped that this would serve as a basis for constructing past environments, but the primary order of the day was to sort out the order of the rocks. Put in the technical, taxonomic language of the day (which geologists and mineralogists used), the aim was to arrange rocks according to their age. That is to say, the *essential* character of rocks was to be age of deposition, which overrode mineralogy, structure, geographical location and so on. In short, time was of the essence. The problem, of course, was that time was unobservable. Thus the methodology of historical geology boiled down to the trick of finding other characters that corresponded to age. Everybody's favourite was order of superposition. At least for those rocks deposited in water (the vast majority, according to the early Wernerians) and at least for those that had not subsequently been overturned, the order of superposition gave the relative age of the rocks. It was quickly realised that the second of these assumptions was too simple; only in rare instances was the structure of the rocks a simple sequence of horizontal beds. In practice, then, the geologist devoted much of his attention to unravelling structure, for order of superposition could only be determined once this was done. Having determined the succession in one location, the geologist tried to correlate with successions in other locations until a complete sequence was obtained. If simple in theory, correlation was difficult in practice because rocks often differed in height above sea level, and in mineralogy from one place to another and in addition had frequently been distorted in various ways.

Soon afterwards, fossils – which had been just one among many identifying characters of rocks for Werner – began to play a larger role in correlation. At the beginning of the nineteenth century two scientists who had close ties with the Wernerians, J. F. Blumenbach (1752–1840), the prominent anatomist and natural historian at Göttingen University and E. F. Schlotheim (1764–1832), his pupil, argued that certain forms of life had become extinct in the past. From this it followed that certain time-periods were characterised by certain forms of life. Blumenbach's and Schlotheim's example was soon followed; Cuvier in particular publicised the use of fossils by his work on the Paris Basin and Alexandre Brongniart (1770–1847), his collaborator, used them extensively. Debates proliferated as to exactly how fossils should be employed. Did the variation of fossil forms with prior environments vitiate the attempt to use them for dating (as the Scot, John Fleming pessimistically asserted), or were they essentially reliable (as everyone else optimistically hoped)? Could one characteristic fossil identify a formation or did a whole fauna and flora have to be used? Did whole fossil faunas and floras change abruptly and simultaneously (as Cuvier believed) or slowly and gradually (as Lyell maintained)? But these were debates within a framework of acceptance for, from the 1820s onwards, fossils were firmly in place as essential to the historical geologist.

Historical geologists found the problem of the 'independence of rocks' (as it was called) particularly vexing. Were there real breaks between rocks of different ages (i.e. were the formations really different entities) or were the breaks arbitrary (i.e. were the formations simply a matter of convention)? Neither theory nor data gave a clear answer to this. Initially, Werner had postulated that rocks were continuously deposited from an ocean of gradually changing composition. Perhaps as a result of his famous survey of the Paris Basin, Cuvier suggested in 1812 in the *Preliminary Discourse* to the *Researches on the fossil bones of quadrupeds* (translated into English in 1813 as the *Essay on the Theory of the Earth*) that the breaks between formations were not conventional but the result of dramatic upheavals in the order of nature. Then in 1829, in his classic *Recherches sur quelques-unes des révolutions de la globe*, Léonce Elie de Beaumont (1798–1874), professor at the Ecoles des Mines in Paris, suggested a physical mechanism for this, to be discussed shortly.

The formulation of the programme of historical geology led to a period of intense activity in the surveying, mapping, correlating and establishing of the geological succession from the 1820s to the 1840s. Geologists devoted most of their effort to describing the sequence of formations. Omalius d'Halloy, Brochant de Villiers, Alexandre Brongniart, Alexander von Humboldt and Leopold von Buch on the Continent and Adam Sedgwick, Henry de la Beche and Roderick Murchison in England were only some of the more prominent people who contributed to the effort. For all these historical geologists, reconstructing the conditions that had prevailed at different periods, or understanding the history of life on earth for its own sake, took decidedly second place. Consequently, questions about the conceptual foundations of historical geology faded, particularly in Britain, and historical geology came to be regarded as a largely atheoretical activity, in which the virtues of hard work in the fresh air paid off. Historians of geology have recently undertaken detailed studies of particular episodes in the development of British stratigraphy, studies designed to throw light on scientific practice in general, as well as on the history of geology.

The Wernerians pursued causal geology as well as historical geology, though largely independently. Werner's causal theory grew out of a long tradition of 'chemical cosmogonies'. These went back to the *Physica subterranea* (1669) of the chemist J. J. Becher (1635–82). All postulated that the rocks had been sequentially deposited from an ocean, the composition of which consequently changed gradually and predictably. In the 1810s and 1820s, the Wernerians widened their interest to include causes (presumed to be related) for elevation of land and for volcanoes and earthquakes. They retained a fondness for chemical causes and for mineralogy. The reasons for this shift are complex. The recognition of rocks of the same chemical composition at all levels of the geological column, the recognition that igneous rocks were found more widely than Werner had originally believed, the recognition that many rocks had been deformed and the recognition that rocks of the same age occurred at very different heights above sea level probably all played a role.

Leopold von Buch (1774–1853), one of Werner's most distinguished pupils, put forward the two most important theories, namely the theory of elevation craters and the theory of dolomitisation. The theory of elevation craters explained the uplift of areas larger than those round volcanic craters (eruption craters). Drawing on Mexican observations of another of Werner's pupils, Alexander von Humboldt, (1769–1859) and on his own experience in Tenerife, Buch postulated that wide areas of land could be heaved up by the intrusion of the volcanic rock, basalt, and by the creation of steam when this occurred below the surface of the ocean. The theory was extremely successful, and despite opposition by Lyell and a few others, was strongly supported until the 1860s.

However, this still did not account for mountain chains and in the mid-1820s, after travelling in the Dolomites and the Alps, von Buch proposed the theory of dolomitisation. According to this, the intrusion of another kind of igneous rock, porphyry, caused the elevation of mountain chains and the conversion of ordinary limestone to dolomite. This proposal did not fare so well, in part because it was quickly replaced in the early 1830s by Elie de Beaumont's theory of elevation.

Elie de Beaumont broke with the tradition of explaining elevation in terms of chemistry and mineralogy and instead drew on recent work by J. B. Fourier (1768–1830) and L. Cordier (1777–1861) in theoretical physics and in geophysics. Their work on cooling had confirmed the belief, common since at least the seventeenth century, that the earth was cooling from an originally molten body. Elie de Beaumont suggested that as the earth cooled it contracted. When the stresses on the crust passed a certain threshold, a paroxysmic shrinking and wrinkling of the crust occurred. Mountain chains with a characteristic direction were thrown up, in line with the evidence that Wernerian research had collected which suggested a correlation between the ages of the rocks making up different mountain chains and their directions. Waters rushing down the slopes of the mountains caused erosion and the extinction of life forms. In this way, Elie de Beaumont synthesised historical and causal geology, which had developed largely independently for the previous generation. His theory, published almost simultaneously with Lyell's *Principles*, received immediate acclaim and stimulated the construction of broad causal theories of mountain elevation.

In sum, the term 'catastrophist', retrospectively applied to this causal tradition by William Whewell, did not carry the pejorative overtones of unscientific behaviour that it has subsequently acquired. Nor did Lyellian uniformitarianism carry the day in geology as has been so frequently suggested. We now need to turn to recent work on the interpretation of uniformitarianism.

4. THE METHODOLOGY OF GEOLOGY

Discussions of geological method have concentrated almost exclusively on 'uniformitarianism', a doctrine usually presumed to have been pre-shadowed by Hutton and fully articulated by Lyell in the *Principles of Geology*. But since Lyell never gave a succinct formulation of 'uniformitarianism', by the mid-twentieth century it had come to mean things as various as that geological processes took place slowly, that the present was key to the past, or that miracles had no place in geology.

In the last two decades, historians have succeeded in giving a clear exegesis of Lyell's doctrine. Lyell's uniformitarianism comprises a bundle of three distinct theses, which can be characterised as law, kind and degree uniformitarianism. Law uniformitarianism asserts that the laws of nature have not changed, kind uniformitarianism that the kinds of causes operating on the earth have not changed and degree uniformitarianism that the intensity of the causes acting on the earth has never changed.

Nineteenth-century geologists were of one mind that law uniformitarianism was a reasonable stance (with the possible exception of the problem of the creation of new species, but there even Lyell abandoned his uniformitarianism). They were much more dubious about kind uniformitarianism. If the earth had cooled, for example, as most geologists believed, then presumably there had been a time when ice was not a geological agent. And almost all geologists were aghast at degree uniformitarianism, for the suggestion that the intensity of causes had never varied seemed both arbitrary and improbable. This explains why geologists almost to a man rejected uniformitarianism and signed up with Whewell in the catastrophist camp.

Why did Lyell espouse a position as improbable as degree uniformitarianism? The most likely explanation is that he was adapting one of the most commonly-held methodologies of the day to geology. Natural philosophers and scientists espoused a range of views about the correct relation between theories and evidence. At the one extreme, some scientists – including G. B. Greenough (1788–1855), founding President of the Geological Society – thought that strict enumerative induction was the only reliable methodology. According to this view, theory, in geology as in any other science, would only emerge as the result of the collection of massive amounts of data. At the opposite extreme, some scientists – Lyell accused seventeenth-century cosmogonists of this, though he seems not to have realised that Hutton was equally suspect – believed in the method of hypothesis. According to this, any hypothesis was deemed acceptable as long as it was consistent with the data. Lyell rejected both these extremes, the first because the hope of any reasonable theory faded into the indefinite future, and the other because there was too little empirical control. Instead he opted for the so-called *vera causa* method (method of true causes), first advocated by Newton in the 'Rules of Reasoning' in the *Principia* and given canonical form in the late eighteenth century by the Scottish philosopher, Thomas Reid. The *vera causa* method was popular at the time, advocated by the highly-regarded scientist, John Herschel. According to this, any postulated cause must satisfy two conditions: it must be known to exist and it must be known to be adequate to produce the effect.

Lyell ingeniously modified the *vera causa* principle to the particular problems of geological science. Compared to, say, physical causes and effects, geological causes and effects were hard to observe in conjunction, acting as they did over long periods of time, or in the centre of the earth. How could the geologist be sure that the cause he was postulating was *known* to exist? By observing it, of course, which meant that only observable (and hence largely present-day) causes could be invoked. How could the geologist be sure that the cause he was postulating was *adequate* to produce the effect? By observing it causing the effect, which meant that only causes of intensity that had been observed could be invoked. But the introduction of it into geology was (rightly) regarded by most geologists as hopelessly restrictive. Lyell had introduced a methodology for causal geology that was at odds with most of the successful causal theories in the discipline.

5. GEOLOGY, RELIGION AND THE DISCOVERY OF TIME

Here again, scholars have cleared away a lot of old myths about the relation (or more accurately, the antagonism) between geology and religion. Once it was thought that early-nineteenth-century geologists were engaged in a battle to free geology from a literal interpretation of the Bible. Geological evidence, after all, suggested that the earth had existed much longer than the 6000-odd years that seventeenth-century theologians had allowed and that the Biblical account of events like the Flood early in the earth's history was seriously flawed. But this battle has been shown to be largely illusory and a more complex story put in its place.

In parenthesis, here again we need to remember that we know practically nothing about the relation between religion and geology on the Continent. What little we do know suggests that Continental geologists did not bother themselves much about religion. Why the British should have been so much more vexed over the question is not clear. One possible answer is that critical historical scholarship had already convinced the Germans, at any rate, that the Bible was not to be taken literally so that the potential for conflict with geology was defused.

In Britain, geologists were concerned about the relation between religion and geology but not quite in the simple way the myth suggests. What was at stake was a debate between liberal Christians and deists. There were fundamentalist Christians, who asserted the literal truth of the Bible, but they had little to do with the geological community, and little clout within the British establishment. Most geologists were Anglicans and they believed that there was an overall consistency between the geological record and a liberal reading of the Bible. The occurrence of loose, unsorted surface deposits and the existence of 'erratic' boulders seemed to point to some recent widespread Flood. Not until after the period we are discussing were these attributed to the Ice Age. The general trend of increasing sophistication and complexity in the fossil record seemed to support a liberal reading of Genesis. The apparently very recent origin of man confirmed his special place in the universe. Devoutly Christian men like Sedgwick, Buckland and Whewell could interpret geology as being part of the evidence for Christianity.

The challenge came from Hutton and Lyell, both of whom were Deists, not Christians; that is to say, they believed in the existence of a deity, but not in the revelations of the Old and New Testaments. These texts they thought to be the work of ignorant and superstitious people. The nature of the Deity had to be inferred from reason and from the evidences of nature, not from the Bible. Thus they saw no reason to assume that the earth had a directional history. Indeed, quite the reverse, for reason suggested that the deity would not make a world that contained the seeds of its own destruction. Consequently it is not surprising that Hutton and Lyell, with similar theological commitments, erected similar geological systems in which the igneous and aqueous causes could maintain the world forever in habitable condition.

6. THE SOCIAL HISTORY OF GEOLOGY

The major question in the social history of geology has concerned the interpretation of the fact that geology appeared to come of age at just the time that Europe became industrialised. Particularly for those who accepted the received view – that geology was an English creation – the coincidence was striking. There *must* have been a connection, it seemed.

Yet a detailed examination of the evidence suggests that the Industrial Revolution and the development of English geology were largely independent. Most English geologists were gentlemen amateurs who neither contributed know-how to the industrialising north nor relied on new data from, say, the opening-up of new industrial mineral resources. They took scant interest in matters practical. The few who did were the large landowners, like Sir Joseph Banks, but their attempt to create a useful, mineralogical society was thwarted. The *laissez-faire* structure of British capitalism discouraged mineowners from sharing their knowledge. The few geologists who were not gentlemen – primarily the mineral surveyors – were excluded from national scientific life, at least until William Smith was retrospectively elevated to prominence by the gentleman geologists of the Geological Society of London. And while one can admire the mineral surveyors' intelligence and their determination to make sense of the data they dealt with in their lives as practical men, they contributed little to the science of geology. So far as one can see, then, there was no significant interaction between geology and industrial development in England.

This was not the case on the Continent. There the development of industry, particularly the mining and porcelain industries, went hand in hand with the development of geology from the mid-eighteenth century on. Unlike English industrial concerns, many of the continental ones were state owned. Rulers accepted the mercantilist theory that the wealth of the state should be enhanced and regarded support for these industries as one means to that end. In order to supply trained personnel to manage state industries, institutions were founded from the 1750s on in Sweden (the *Bergskollegium*), in Schemnitz, in Berlin, in Freiberg (the *Bergakademie*), and in Paris (the *Ecole des Mines*). Almost all the prominent European geologists were trained in one or another of these institutions. Even those, like Alexander von Humboldt and Leopold von Buch, who were wealthy enough to pursue their science independently, studied at such schools. And in turn the schools provided limited but stable employment for a number of those who did not have private money.

Whether or not these institutions in fact enhanced the development of industry is not clear. But that they contributed to the growth of European geology is unquestionable. Unlike their English counterparts, continental geologists had the benefit of sustained systematic training in all branches of geology and mineralogy. Consequently they brought a much clearer understanding of the intellectual traditions within geology, as well as a much more rigorous background in its technical aspects to their geological work.

After a long period in which the history of geology was one of the most stagnant areas of the history of science, the past few years have seen a flurry of new interest. New questions have been asked about the nature of geological controversy, about the social setting of geology, about the relative importance of theory, experiment and field work in the discipline and about its relations with other sciences.

FURTHER READING

Gordon Davies, *The earth in decay: a history of British geomorphology* (New York, 1969). A useful discussion of one theme in causal geology, albeit from an exclusively British perspective.

Charles Gillispie, *Genesis and geology: a study in the relations of scientific thought, natural theology, and social opinion in Great Britain, 1790–1850* (New York, 1959). Now dated, especially by insufficient attention to deistic positions, but still the classic source on religion and geology in Britain.

Mott Greene, *Geology in the nineteenth century: changing views of a changing world* (Ithaca, NY, 1982). Not as broad as the title indicates, but a fascinating account of theories of mountain building not only in Britain but also on the Continent and in America.

Rachel Laudan, *From mineralogy to geology: the foundations of the earth sciences, 1660–1830* (Chicago, 1987). An intellectual history of the origins of historical and causal geology.

Roy Porter, *The making of geology: earth science in Britain 1660–1815* (Cambridge, 1977). A detailed account of the social origins of British geology, with some discussion of theoretical issues, particularly Hutton's geology.

——*The earth sciences: an annotated bibliography* (New York, 1983). A useful introduction to the available secondary literature.

Martin Rudwick, *The meaning of fossils: episodes in the history of palaeontology* (New York, 1976, reprinted Chicago, 1985). An excellent introduction to the history of paleontology, particularly strong on Cuvier's and Lyell's contributions to the subject in the period 1790–1840.

——*The great Devonian controversy: the shaping of scientific knowledge among gentlemanly specialists* (Chicago, 1985). A detailed study of one particular dispute within historical geology and its implications for wider theories of science.

Nicholas Rupke, *The great chain of history: William Buckland and the English school of geology (1814–1849)* (Oxford, 1983). A sympathetic account of Buckland's geology, with remarks on the nature of historical geology that go well beyond Buckland's particular contribution,.

James Secord, *Controversy in Victorian geology: the Cambrian-Silurian dispute* (Princeton, NJ., 1986). Another detailed study of a particular debate within historical geology that makes a nice companion volume to Rudwick 1985.

21

ENERGY

CROSBIE SMITH

Between Isaac Newton and Albert Einstein no development in physics is more significant than the replacement of the concept of force by the concept of work. Historians usually argue that the *energy* revolution occurred around 1850, but that interpretation fails to recognise that the concept of work remained the essential measure of energy until energy acquired a status independent of mechanics late in the nineteenth century.

As early as 1854, William Thomson (later Lord Kelvin, 1824–1907) told the British Association for the Advancement of Science that James Prescott Joule's discovery of the conversion of work into heat by fluid friction in 1843 had 'led to the greatest reform that physical science has experienced since the days of Newton'. And in 1908, Sir Joseph Larmor, Lucasian Professor of Mathematics at Cambridge, regarded energy as the most far-reaching achievement of nineteenth-century physical science: 'This doctrine has not only furnished a standard of industrial values which has enabled mechanical power . . . to be measured with scientific precision as a commercial asset; it has also, in its other aspect of the continual dissipation of available energy, created the doctrine of inorganic evolution and changed our conceptions of the material universe'.[1] Such remarks are symptomatic of a fundamental reformulation of physical science which took place after 1840 and which redefined physics itself in the second half of the century as the study of energy and its transformations.

1. 'FORCE' VERSUS 'WORK'

The concept of force has a long history. In his *Philosophiae Naturalis Principia Mathematica* (*Mathematical Principles of Natural Philosophy*, 1687), Newton (1642–1727) expressed the wish that we could 'derive the rest of the phaenomena of Nature by the same kind of reasoning from mechanical principles [as in the case of gravitation], for I am induced by many reasons to suspect that they may all depend upon certain forces by which the particles of bodies . . . are either mutually impelled towards one another . . . or are repelled and recede from one another'.[2] Many subsequent writers followed Newton's prescription and attempted to account for diverse phenomena by combinations of attractive and repulsive forces between particles or point atoms. While most attempts were qualitative and speculative, some, notably Coulomb's formulation of an inverse square law of electrical attraction, were numerically-based.

In the early nineteenth century, Pierre-Simon Laplace's (1749–1827) programme for the reduction of all physical phenomena to the action of inverse square forces between point atoms marked the high tide of force physics. (See art. 18.) Unlike Newton's infinitely hard atoms, Laplace's atoms could never collide, not only because they were mere points but also because they repelled one another with forces that increased as the distance diminished. Hence, while Newton's inelastic atoms lost motion at every collision, Laplace's atoms could never lose *vis viva* which he defined as mass times the square of the velocity. Laplace's universe had no need of Newton's God who acted continually to replenish motion in a world which would otherwise run down.

Laplace's reductionist programme was comprehensive. He announced that:

> . . . the phenomena of expansion, heat, and vibrational motion in gases are explained in terms of attractive and repulsive forces which act only over insensible distances . . . All terrestrial phenomena depend on forces of this kind, just as celestial phenomena depend on universal gravitation. It seems to me that the study of these forces should now be the chief goal of mathematical philosophy.[3]

With his French followers, he carried this programme into most branches of physics. Siméon-Denis Poisson (1781–1840), in particular, developed the mathematical theories of heat and electricity (electrostatics). A proper derivation of the equations of heat conduction, for example, began with an explicit model of the relation between ponderable molecules and caloric fluid in a solid. From a complex and speculative picture, Poisson extracted by rigorous but laborious mathematical methods the general equation for the motion of heat. Again, his theory of electricity was a theory of action at a distance between point masses of electrical fluid, an approach at once rigorous and complex, leading to equations insoluble for all but the simplest cases.

By contrast, the approach of Joseph Fourier (1768–1830) marked a decisive shift away from the force physics of the Laplacians. He continued the Laplacian priority on mathematical analysis, but at a practical rather than at a hypothetical level. Fourier therefore treated heat conduction as though it were a phenomenon of continuous flow, without regard to its true physical nature. His technique brought the power of mathematical analysis to bear directly on empirical laws without any appeal to microscopic models of the Laplacian kind. His theory of heat was essentially macroscopic, geometrical and practical. Thus against Poisson's view from *inside* the machine, so to speak, Fourier set the engineer's view from *outside* the machine.

The development of a strong tradition of theoretical engineering in France, especially following the Revolution, greatly strengthened the trend away from centrally-directed forces, as exemplified in the Laplacian programme. In particular, Lazare Carnot and Gaspard Monge, key figures behind the new Ecole Polytechnique, maintained close contact with engineering needs and emphasised the mechanics of machines and geometrical analysis in their textbooks and teaching. As early as 1782, Carnot's *Essai sur les machines en général* had begun to give the concept of 'work' (force times distance) priority over force in dynamics. Under various names such as 'mechanical power' (John Smeaton) or simple 'effect' (James Watt), work was the basic measure of engine achievement (weight times height) and derived from those practical engineers of early industrialisation who required a useful comparison of the relative performances of water, wind, animal and steam sources of power. Work did not, in general, appear as an independent concept in the abstract dynamical literature where the principle of conservation of *vis viva* occupied an important position.

The generation after Carnot and Monge transformed engineering mechanics into a new science of work. In the period 1819–1839 work terms such as *quantité de travail* (Coriolis) or *travail mécanique* (Poncelet) were introduced, *vis viva* redefined as $\frac{1}{2}mv^2$ such that work achieved and retained priority over the old mv^2, and the equation between work and half *vis viva* explicitly formulated. Largely as a result of the pressing needs of French industry to match Britain after 1815, this new generation did not concern itself with trial-and-error methods but with improving industry through a better understanding of the principles of machines. These practically-orientated theories of machines came much closer to Fourier's mathematical physics than to the abstract force physics of Laplace.

Sadi Carnot's *Reflexions sur la puissance motrice du feu* (1824) belongs to this generation of French theoretical engineers. Impressed by the fuel economy of Woolf's 'high pressure' compound steam engine compared to 'low pressure' Watt engines, Carnot (1796–1832) aimed to explain this relative economy and to consider whether further improvements were possible. His answer was that the motive power produced by heat engines depended only on the temperature difference between boiler and condenser and not on the working substance (steam, air, etc.) employed. In other words, the larger the temperature difference, the greater the work produced by a given quantity of heat. He reasoned that no engine could be more efficient than a perfectly reversible one in which the motive power produced by a quantity of heat falling between two temperatures could be employed to raise the same quantity of heat to its original temperature. Violation of this principle would yield work for nothing. He therefore set a theoretical limit to the possible improvements to heat engines operating between fixed temperatures.

Though Carnot's reasoning later formed one of the twin pillars of energy physics and thermodynamics, his text was almost wholly ignored by his French contemporaries. Nevertheless, one engineer, Emile Clapeyron, published an exposition of Carnot's views, in analytical form, in the *Journal de l'Ecole Polytechnique* (1834). Significantly, this paper was translated for a British publication in 1837 and for a German scientific journal in 1843. In this way, Carnot's ideas were introduced to most of the principal characters in the formulation of energy physics: Joule, Thomson, W. J. M. Rankine, Hermann von Helmholtz and Rudolf Clausius.

To understand the reception of Carnot in Britain, and the concomitant development of energy or 'work' physics, we must consider briefly the industrial context. Especially from the 1830s, the expansion of railways and steamships accentuated the need for improved economy in the production of motive power. At the centre of the new industrial universe stood the rapidly-growing cities of Manchester and Glasgow. In Manchester, William Fairbairn's giant steam engine, boiler and locomotive building works provided tangible proof of the city's industrial progress, wealth and power through steam and iron. In Glasgow a similar trend towards heavy engineering was evident in the activities of the marine engine-builder Robert Napier who had laid the foundations for the spectacular growth from 1840 of iron and steam ship-building on the River Clyde. For these and other industrialists at the forefront of engineering progress, questions of economy could only be solved by an understanding of engineering and physical principles and not by the trial-and-error methods which permeated most of the older industries. This quest for economy thus involved feeding back the advances made by French textbook writers and their British successors into industrial practice.

Symptomatic of the trend was the rapid professionalisation of British academic engineering from 1840. In that year, the appointment of Lewis Gordon (1815–75) to the University of Glasgow marked the creation of the first British engineering chair. Gordon and his successor, Rankine, developed close links with scientifically-minded industrial chemists, engineers and reforming academics via the Glasgow Philosophical Society. In 1840–41 at Cambridge, William Whewell (1794–1866) and Robert Willis published their complementary engineering textbooks on *The Mechanics of Engineering* and *The Principles of Mechanism*. The appearance of these very practical texts for the use of both university students and students in colleges of engineering is all the more striking when set against the traditional academic concerns of the University of Cambridge.

Whewell's textbook explicitly adopted the term 'labouring force' from the French 'travail' employed by writers on industrial machines. Apart from being the first major British text to employ 'work' as central to mechanics, Whewell's use of the term 'labouring force' expressed his parallel interest in the science of political economy and its labour theory of value. 'Labouring force is the labour that we pay for', Whewell explained, and went on to develop the economic theme by distinguishing work done by machines (equivalent to the wages of labour) from work accumulated in storehouses such as reservoirs of water or flywheels (equivalent to capital).[4]

Gordon was particularly concerned with the correct measure of work. Listing a variety of British and French synonyms, he chose 'mechanical effect', from the German 'mechanische Wirkung', which virtually coincided with Watt's practical employment of 'effect', and which was the term most often used by Thomson and his circle until their more frequent usage of 'energy' from the early 1850s. With practical engineers very much in mind, Gordon emphasised that mechanical effect was correctly measured as 'the produce of the *effort* and the *distance through which it is exerted* which should be obtained directly from a dynamometer'.[5]

2. WILLIAM THOMSON AND THE NEW PHYSICS OF 'WORK'

William Thomson's education in Glasgow and Cambridge brought him into close contact with these engineering trends. But above all, the passionate engineering enthusiasms of his elder brother, James (1822–92), led him to place mechanical effect at the very centre of his physics. First as a pupil of Gordon's and later as an apprentice at Fairbairn's Thames shipbuilding and marine engineering subsidiary, James's concern with designs for more economical marine steam engines and water wheels was all-pervasive. As early as 1844 he initiated discussion with William of the Carnot-Clapeyron theory of the motive power of heat. Throughout these discussions, the production of mechanical effect and its efficient use formed the central theme. For example, they were concerned with the problems of losses of mechanical effect in water spilling into canal locks and in steam engines. These issues would be vital to William's reception of Joule's claims presented at the 1847 meeting of the British Association.

Meanwhile, William had begun to reformulate mathematical physics. The attempt marked a major step in the transition from force physics to energy-field physics. In his earliest papers, he had frequently drawn a mathematical analogy between electricity and heat. In 1841, for instance, he had compared Poisson's theory of electricity (based on action at a distance force) with Fourier's theory of heat conduction (based on continuous and hence conserved fluid flow) and shown that the distribution of lines of electrical force in space obeyed the same equation as the distribution of heat flux in a homogeneous conductor. Electricity, like heat, he treated not as a fluid substance, but as a state of intensity of a body. Thus the high temperature of a steam boiler corresponded to a state of intensity of heat, and the low temperature of the condenser to a state of diffusion of heat.

Not until 1845, however, did Thomson begin to compare a charged electrostatic system with a steam engine.[6] His approach developed fully while he worked during the spring of 1845 in Victor Regnault's physical laboratory. Regnault was then carrying out for the French government precise quantitative experiments on high pressure steam aimed at improving the economy of steam engines. Thomson wanted an expression for the total force (ponderomotive force) between two electrified conducting spheres which would allow easy comparison with experimental measurements. He could have conceived the calculation as a sum of forces acting at a distance between point particles of electrical fluid on both spheres. Such a calculation required, however, a complicated double integral over the two spheres and presupposed knowledge of the mutually influencing electrical distributions. Instead, he recognised that this problem was of the same kind as the problem of work derived from a steam engine.

In a letter of 1844 James had been concerned with the capacity for work of a steam engine, a capacity which derived from the *tendency* of the system towards its lowest level of mechanical effect (the sea, for example). William considered the meaning of Carl Freidrich Gauss's (1777–1855) minimised function for a proof of existence and uniqueness of electrical distributions on conducting surfaces. He realised that the function could be interpreted as the mechanical effect contained in the system, and that therefore the electrical distribution would be such as to reach the lowest level of total mechanical effect, as with water and other mechanical systems. For the two spheres problem, then, the ponderomotive force between them was the tendency of the system to reach its lowest state of mechanical effect.

Thomson's new view, centred on the concept of mechanical effect, expressed the work expended or absorbed by an electrical system in exactly the same way as a waterfall or steam engine, with electrical potential analogous to the height of a waterfall or temperature difference between boiler and condenser, and quantity of electricity analogous to mass of water or quantity of heat. Total force became total work contained in the system, with attention focused not on summing over elementary forces among the parts but on the work entering or leaving the system. Total mechanical effect thus became a potential (soon to be potential energy) for the gross forces exerted by the system.

Thomson's deployment of these analogies began a process which changed mathematical physics. Work became the central concept of physical theory. Statics became a special case of dynamics. Within two years, he was employing the new conception over a wide range of phenomena. For example, he derived the total force on a piece of soft iron placed in a magnetic field as the tendency for the mechanical effect in the entire field to attain its lowest level. Mechanical effect was now located *in the field* rather than in the forces exerted on magnetic matter. Here he advanced the mathematical basis of field theory. (See art. 22, sect. 2.)

Equally important was his new conception of measuring quantities or agents such as electricity and heat by their mechanical effect, independently of materials, arrangements and other variables; the work done by an electrical or heat engine gave an absolute measure of physical quantities. Thomson now began to develop a theory of absolute measurements in terms of the behaviour of physical systems as engines, the best-known example being his absolute scale of temperature developed in 1847–48. His concern with absolute electrical measurements also provided the foundation for the British Association's work, from 1861, on electrical units. Such concerns were vital to the development of nascent electrical industries of telegraphy and power.

Thomson's new perspective, then, originated within the context of the Carnot-Clapeyron theory of heat engines in which the passage of heat from a hot to a cold body produced mechancial power (work or *vis viva*). In 1847, however, he met Joule (1818–89) for the first time and discovered that three years earlier Joule had mounted a strong attack on the Carnot-Clapeyron theory. Joule objected to the implication that by an improper disposition of the engine (leading to waste by conduction or collision, for example), the *vis viva* would be destroyed: 'Believing that the power to destroy belongs to the Creator alone, I entirely coincide with Roget and Faraday in the opinion that any theory which, when carried out, demands the annihilation of force, is necessarily erroneous'.[7] Joule's own theory substituted for the temperature difference a straightforward conversion of the heat (contained in the steam expanding in the cylinder of a steam engine) into an equivalent quantity of mechanical power.

The Thomsons were very sceptical of Joule's claim for the *mutual* conversion of heat and work. Their careful study of his papers seemed to show that Joule's experimental researches had only demonstrated the conversion of mechanical effect into heat. His measurements offered a resolution to the problem of 'loss' or 'waste' which had troubled the brothers for some years, but his major claim to displace the Carnot theory with the conversion of heat into work remained unacceptable to them.

Apart from this disagreement over the recoverability of mechanical effect 'lost' as heat, however, much about Joule's perspective appealed to the Thomsons. They shared his engineering interests, his quest for economy and his enthusiasm for accurate quantitiative measurement. They certainly shared his theology of nature whereby an omnipotent God created and held in being a universe whose basic building blocks (matter and other agencies such as 'force' or 'energy' discovered by experiment) could not be increased, annihilated, or otherwise altered by any human or natural agency. Such a metaphysical belief was one to which all Christians, irrespective of denomination or status, had to give allegiance. It made possible the wide acceptance of the new conservation of energy doctrine on account of its perceived non-sectarian, non-speculative and non-hypothetical character. Thus William entirely admitted Joule's specific objection to the Carnot-Clapeyron theory. The consensus illustrates the importance of a shared metaphysics in rendering a doctrine acceptable. For Thomson, as for Joule, energy (measured as mechanical effect) had to be conserved: 'Nothing can be lost in the operations of nature – no energy can be destroyed'. In this 1849 footnote to his exposition of Carnot's theory, Thomson introduced the term 'energy' into mathematical physics.[8]

Committed to Carnot's theory and to a concomitant view of heat as a state of intensity (rather than to material caloric as was often assumed), Thomson was, however, still not prepared to accept Joule's preference for a mechanical (soon called dynamical) theory of heat. Joule's hypotheses on the nature of matter and its properties were avowedly mechanical. In 1843, for example, he made clear that if 'we consider heat not as a *substance*, but as a state of vibration, there appears to be no reason why it should not be induced by an action of a simply mechanical character'. Here he did not attempt to establish a dynamical theory of heat from the experimental results; rather, he used the general theory (heat as a state of vibration) to render these results plausible or intelligible. In 1844, however, he reversed his argument. The near constancy of the mechancial equivalent of heat afford 'a new and, to my mind, powerful argument in favour of the dynamical theory of heat'. He proceeded to construct a tentative model involving atmospheres of electricity revolving very rapidly (and hence possessing *vis viva*) around atoms.[9]

When in 1848 Thomson acquired from Lewis Gordon a copy of the very rare Carnot text, he was uniquely placed to offer an up-to-date exposition of Carnot's theory in the light of the problems raised by Joule. As Thomson presented Carnot's theory in his 1849 'Account', the logic had four stages:

1. The heat in a body is a state function (i.e. in any cyclic process the change in heat content is zero).
2. Any work obtained from a cyclic change of state thus derives from the only change that can occur in such a cycle: namely, transfer of heat (without loss) from high to low temperature.
3. Application of (2) to a reversible process, together with denial of perpetual motion, yields Carnot's criterion for a perfect engine: no engine is more efficient than a reversible one.
4. From (3) it follows that the maximum efficiency obtainable from any engine operating between heat reservoirs at different temperatures is a function of those temperatures (Carnot's function).[10]

Familiar with Clapeyron's memoir, with Joule's results, and now with Thomson's latest analysis, the German theoretical physicist Rudolf Clausius (1822–88) produced in 1850 the first reconciliation of Joule and Carnot. Accepting a general mechanical theory of heat (that heat was *vis viva*) and hence Joule's view of the convertibility of heat and work, Clausius retained that part of

Carnot's theory which demanded a transfer of heat from high to low temperature when work is produced. Under the new view, then, a portion of the original heat was converted into work according to the mechanical equivalent of heat, the remainder descending to the lower temperature. Having abandoned (1) and part of (2) above, Clausius attempted to demonstrate (3) by reasoning that if it were false, then 'it would be possible, without any expenditure of force or any other change, to transfer as much heat as we please from a cold to a hot body, and this is not in accord with the other relations of heat, since it always shows a tendency to equalise temperature differences and therefore to pass from hotter to colder bodies'.[11]

Thomson had also moved towards a resolution. In 1851 he laid down two fundamental propositions, the first a statement of Joule's proposition of the mutual equivalence of work and heat, and the second a statement of Carnot's criterion for a perfect engine (3). His final acceptance of Joule's proposition rested primarily neither on experiment nor on Joule's arguments but on resolving the problem of the irrecoverability of mechanical effect lost as heat. He now believed that work 'is *lost to man* irrecoverably though *not lost in the material world*'. Thus although 'no destruction of energy can take place in the material world without an act of power possessed only by the supreme ruler, yet transformations take place which remove irrecoverably from the control of man sources of power which . . . might have been rendered available'.[12] In other words, God alone could create or destroy energy (i.e. energy was conserved) but men could make use of transformations of energy, for example in water wheels or steam engines.

Thomson, then, accepted as a fundamental principle what he soon termed the universal dissipation of mechanical energy. Work dissipated as heat would be irrecoverable to man; to deny this principle would imply that we could produce mechanical effect by cooling the material world with no limit except the total loss of heat from the world. This reasoning provided the basis for Kelvin's 'second law of thermodynamics': 'it is impossible, by means of inanimate material agency, to derive mechanical effect from any portion of matter by cooling it below the temperature of the coldest of the surrounding objects',[13] a statement which Thomson used to demonstrate (3) above. Having resolved the recoverability issue, he quickly adopted the dynamical theory of heat, making it the foundation of Joule's proposition of mutual equivalence which replaced (1) above.

With Thomson's paper 'On a universal tendency in nature to the dissipation of mechanical energy' (1852), the energy synthesis reached a wide audience. There Thomson made explicit the dual principles of conservation and dissipation of energy: 'as it is most certain that Creative Power alone can either call into existence or annihilate mechanical energy, the 'waste' referred to cannot be annihilation, but must be some transformation of energy'.[14] In this short paper published in the *Philosophical Magazine*, the new term 'energy' achieved prominence for the first time. It was no longer a mere footnote; instead the shared theology of nature emphasised the primary status of energy. Here the dynamical theory of heat, and with it a whole programme of dynamical (matter-in-motion) explanation, went unquestioned. And here too, the universal, cosmological primacy of the energy laws opened up new questions about the origins, progress and destiny of the solar system and its inhabitants.

Thomson and others, such as Hermann von Helmholtz (1821–94) and Julius Robert Mayer (1814–78), soon considered the consequences of the energy laws for traditional accounts of the sun's heat, the great source for most of the mechanical effect on earth. In the 1850s, Thomson argued that the sun's energy, too great to be supplied by chemical means or by a mere molten mass cooling, was probably provided by vast quantities of meteors orbiting around the sun but inside the earth's orbit. Retarded in their orbits by an etherial medium, the meteors would progressively descend or spiral towards the sun's surface in a cosmic vortex analogous to James Thomson's vortex turbines (horizontal waterwheels). The meteors would generate immense quantities of heat energy as they vaporised by friction. In the 1860s, however, he adopted instead Helmholtz's version of the sun's heat whereby contraction of the body of the sun released immense quantities of heat over long periods. Either way, the sun's heat was held to be finite and calculable, making possible order-of-magnitude estimates of the limited past and future age of the sun. Thomson made similar estimates for the earth's age based on Fourier's conduction law applied to a cooling mass. The limited time-scale of about 100 million years (later reduced) posed problems for the much longer time demanded by Charles Darwin's new theory of evolution by natural selection (1859). But the new cosmology was itself evolutionary, making claims to trace the history of the solar system from origins to endings via the energy laws. (See art. 20.)

While Thomson, Rankine, Helmholtz, Clausius and many others developed specific experimental and theoretical consequences of the energy laws in most areas of cosmology, physics and engineering, the nineteenth-century programme of energy physics received its most celebrated embodiment in Thomson and Peter Guthrie Tait's *Treatise on Natural Philosophy* (1867). Originally intended to treat all branches of physics, the *Treatise* was limited to mechanics. Its approach was nevertheless radical. Taking statics to be derivative from dynamics, it aimed to interpret Newton's third law (action-reaction) as conservation of energy, with 'action' viewed as rate of working. Fundamental to this work-based physics was the move to make extremum conditions, rather than point forces, the theoretical foundation of dynamics. The tendency of an entire system to move from one place to another in the most economical way would determine the forces and motions of the various parts of the system. Variational principles (least action, for example) thus played a central role in the new dynamics.

3. RIVAL CONNCEPTUALISATIONS OF ENERGY: MECHANICAL VERSUS NON-MECHANICAL THEORIES

In 1959 T. S. Kuhn named twelve European men of science and engineering 'who, within a short period of time, grasped for themselves essential parts of the concept of energy and its conservation'.[15] Recognition of this phenomenon of simultaneous discovery had already led to several bitter priority disputes (often in terms of national rivalries between Britain and Germany) in the second half of the nineteenth century. Yet a closer historical analysis of four of these 'pioneers' (Joule, Faraday, Mayer and Helmholtz) shows the very divergent nature of their conceptualisation, theories shaped by widely differing cultural perspectives ranging from Manchester engineering to German metaphysics. Only after the energy synthesis of Thomson, therefore, did the issue of simultaneous discovery arise.

Just as James Thomson devoted much time to researching and designing vortex turbines as an alternative to steam power, Joule's researches in Manchester began with attempts to design economical electro-magnetic engines. 'I can hardly doubt that electro-magnetism will ultimately be substituted for steam to propel machinery', Joule wrote in 1839.[16] Like James, Joule's major concern was with measuring and improving the economy of engines, although (unlike James) he never patented and marketed them. His published investigations from 1838 were based on work-related measurements. Lifting power (weight times unit height per unit time) yielded the criterion by which to judge the performance of an electro-magnet.

At a public lecture in 1841, Joule admitted disappointment with the performance of electro-magnetic engines: 'Now the duty of the best Cornish steam-engine is about 1,500,000 lb. raised to the height of 1 foot by the combustion of a lb. of coal, which is nearly five times the extreme duty that I was able to obtain from my electro-magnetic engine by the consumption of zinc'. The comparison was so unfavourable that he confessed: 'I almost despair of the success of electro-magnetic attractions as an economical source of power: for although my machine is by no means perfect, I do not see how the arrangement of its parts could be improved so far as to make the duty per lb. of zinc superior to the duty per lb. of coal'. In addition, the cost of the zinc and the battery fluids, compared to the price of coal, prevented 'the ordinary electro-magnetic engine from being useful for any but very peculiar purposes'.[17]

While some historians of science have seen Joule's subsequent research as a shift away from engineering and towards 'purer' science, others have interpreted Joule's researches in terms of a British matter theory tradition (especially the conversion and unity of natural powers) or in the context of the contemporary British chemical community. Support for each of these diverse perspectives can be found in Joule's texts. For example, Joule's evident familarity with Fara-

336

day's recent electro-chemical and electro-magnetic investigations has been used to argue for Joule's and Faraday's common goals in terms of the conversion and unity of natural powers, electrochemistry, or experimental conversion processes.[18] However, a fundamental difference between Faraday and Joule explains why it was Joule, and not Faraday, who enunciated the mechanical equivalent of heat.

Foremost an experimental philosopher, whose lack of mathematical techniques has tended to obscure the often quantitative nature of his researches, Michael Faraday (1791–1867) nonetheless never attempted to measure exact conversion equivalents. As early as 1833 he stated that 'for a constant quantity of electricity, whatever the decomposing conductor may be . . . the amount of electro-chemical action is also a constant quantity, i.e. would always be equivalent to a standard chemical effect founded upon ordinary chemical affinity'.[19] Soon after, he discussed the use of a voltameter as a 'comparative standard, or even as a measurer' of electricity, while recognising also the importance of the voltameter as an 'absolute measurer' in terms of spatial units (the volume of gases evolved). Faraday's researches here and elsewhere show his use of comparative or relative quantitative measures; but his apparent unwillingness to make absolute ('mechanical') measures clearly differentiates his approach from Joule's. At a fundamental level, Faraday's concept of force was not a mechanical one and as such could not be quantified. Above all, he did not adopt the crucial concept of work which in the hands of Joule and Thomson provided the common measure and link for the numerous experimental conversion processes. In short, Faraday, who worked at the Royal Institution in London, lacked the engineering interests so entirely characteristic of Joule in Manchester and Thomson in Glasgow.

A vital clue to interpreting Joule throughout his researches, and not merely up to 1841, in terms of his engineering concerns, lies in the all-pervasive theme of heat, culminating in his 1843 phrase 'on the mechanical value of heat'. If the meaning of 'value' is again taken not merely in the quantitative but also in the economic sense, then Joule, after the 'almost despair' with his engine, did not turn to pure research, electrochemical in nature, and then from that research suddenly produce a series of papers on the mechanical equivalent of heat. Rather, his investigations throughout must be seen to involve a fundamental search for an understanding of the failure of his engine to match the economy of heat engines. That quest led him directly to the mechanical value of heat, that is, to the amount of work obtainable from a given quantity of heat. Significantly, Joule's primary interest lay with the mechanical value of heat, and not with the thermal value of mechanical work, the latter being Thomson's subsequent perception of the real achievement of Joule's experiments.

Joule's mechanical conceptions, which in general admitted only 'the existence and elementary properties of matter',[20] not only emphasise his distance from Faraday, but serve also to distance him from Mayer. Although Mayer's 'discovery' of the mechanical equivalent of heat has usually placed him among the 'pioneers' of energy, he did not accept a mechanical theory. In his view, the mere fact of interconversion did not justify taking any particular form of 'force' as fundamental. His refusal to accept a mechanical theory of heat may be understood in terms of his lingering adherence to (despite a professed rejection of) certain assumptions of the German metaphysical creed known as *Naturphilosophie*. For Mayer, force held a middle position between inert matter and *Geist* (which implied both mind and soul). All three categories (matter, force and soul) were by their nature indestructible, i.e. conserved. Forces expressed the rationality or causality of nature, especially in terms of relationship. Forces were not simply located in isolated matter (as for the Laplacians, for example), but arose only in the interrelations of matter. Although Mayer rejected the assumption of *Naturphilosophie* that we could construct the true system of nature by thought, he nevertheless seemed to employ empirical results primarily as confirmation of *a priori* conservation. This approach, together with his maintenance of force as some kind of substance, independent from matter but with equal status, rendered his arguments largely unacceptable to contemporary German physicists who had gone much further in their rejection of *Naturphilosophie*. For many empirically and practically-minded British physicists, Mayer's work remained largely within metaphysics, although Faraday's successor at the Royal Institution, John Tyndall, became a staunch defender of Mayer's claims to the discovery of energy conservation.

Helmholtz's famous 1847 memoir *Über die Erhaltung der Kraft* also illustrates the way in which different cultural perspectives shaped the central physical doctrines. His memoir brought together a German methaphysical perspective (from Kant) and French physics (from Laplace). Thus his philosophical introduction explained that 'the science whose object it is to comprehend nature must proceed from the assumption that it is comprehensible . . . Finally, therefore, we discover the problem of physical natural science to be, to refer natural phenomena back to unchangeable attractive and repulsive forces, whose intensity depends solely upon distance. The solvability of this problem is the condition of the complete comprehensibility of nature'.[21] This assumption of the rationality of nature (Kant) via the physics of point atoms and attractive and repulsive forces (Laplace) guaranteed conservation of *vis viva*. Furthermore, the assumption of the impossibility of perpetual motion, based on empirical considerations (Clapeyron and others), also supported conservation of *vis viva*.

Fundamental to Helmholtz's memoir was a relational view of force. Independently of Helmholtz, Mayer had neatly summed up this German perspective of *Verwandschaft* (relationship) in 1842: 'spatial separation of ponderable objects is a force'.[22] Helmholtz reasoned more specifically that if force did not always return to the same value for the same spatial relation, *vis viva* might be continuously produced from nothing, which would violate both the equality of cause and effect (the principle of sufficient reason) and the impossibility of perpetual motion. His arguments depended for their articulation on the Kantian distinction between quantity and intensity. For Helmholtz, in the realm of forces between point atoms, Newtonian moving force became the measure of the intensity of force, while the conserved quantity of force was measured by *vis viva* or potential or work. Thus the relation between two atoms at any instant possessed intensity (producing changes in spatial relation) and quantity (connecting the past history of the relation to its future).

Helmholtz's 1847 memoir, with its Kantian-Laplacian synthesis, was vastly different from Thomson's work-centred field physics developing in Britain at the same time. Helmholtz's assumptions related to German philosophy, French theoretical physics and German physiology (concerned especially with the elimination of all traces of *Geist*). Thomson's assumptions related to French engineering physics (Fourier and Carnot) and to British engineering (James Thomson and Joule). Nevertheless, the generally low profile of Helmholtz's metaphysics (relative to Mayer), and his mechanical reasoning – especially work as a measure of quantity of force – soon rendered his memoir acceptable to both German and British physicists.

Mechanical conceptualisations of energy, with work as its essential measure, dominated British and German physics in the second half of the nineteenth century. Towards the end of the century, however, a different perspective, which emphasised the independence of energy from mechanics, emerged in Germany. In the 1880s, Ernst Mach condemned the assumption that mechanics comprised the basis of all physical phenomena and argued instead for a phenomenological view in which sensations would constitute the real object of physical research. The principle of energy conservation served as an ideal: though mechanical theories had aided the formulation of the principle, once established it described only a wide range of facts concisely, directly and economically with no need for mechanical hypotheses.

The so-called 'Energeticist' school of physics also explicitly aimed to replace mechanics as the fundamental science. In 1890, Georg Helm attempted to derive the equations of motion from the conservation of energy and thus to subsume mechanics and its extensions under energetic foundations of physics. His ally Wilhelm Ostwald similarly wished to replace atomism in chemistry by energetics, and proposed a corresponding change from an absolute mechanical system of measurement to an energetic system in terms of energy, length and time. Overall, energetics aimed not to construct mechanical pictures but to connect measurable quantities with each other, a goal shared by Mach and later by the French physicist and philosopher Pierre Duhem whose critique of nineteenth-century British physics for its factory mentality is well known. But the energeticist school had formidable critics. Ludwig Boltzmann, for example, labelled energetics as mere classification, while Max Planck pointed out that it failed to distinguish between reversible and irreversible processes in nature. Of much more far-reaching consequences for the foundations of mathematical physics at the dawn of the new century were the questions posed by electromagnetism (see art. 22) in which energy considerations had, through the role of Thomson, Maxwell and their successors, come to play a major role.

NOTES

I am much indebted to Norton Wise for several of the interpretations included here, especially his insights into the central role of work in nineteenth-century British physics. This chapter draws extensively on material developed at length in our biographical study of Lord Kelvin.

1. W. Thomson, 'On the mechanical antecedents of motion, heat, and light', *Mathematical and physical papers* (6 vols., Cambridge, 1882–1911), vol. 2, p. 34; J. Larmor, 'William Thomson, Baron Kelvin of Largs. 1824–1907', *Proceedings of the Royal Society*, 81(1908), i–lxxvi, on p. xxix.
2. I. Newton, *Mathematical principles of natural philosophy*, trans. A. Motte, rev. F. Cajori (2 vols., Berkeley and Los Angeles, London, 1971), vol. 1, p. xviii.
3. P. S. Laplace, *Traité de mécanique céleste* (5 vols., Paris, 1799–1825), vol. 5, p. 99.
4. W. Whewell, *The mechanics of engineering* (Cambridge, 1841), pp. 146–57. Developed in M. N. Wise with the collaboration of C. Smith, 'Work and waste: political economy and natural philosophy in nineteenth-century Britain; *History of science* (forthcoming).
5. L. D. B. Gordon, 'On dynamometrical appartus; or, the measurement of the mechanical effect of moving powers', *Proceedings of the Philosophical Society of Glasgow*, 1(1841), 41–2; *A synopsis of lectures to be delivered. Session 1847–8* (Glasgow, 1847), p. 5.
6. This issue and related analogies are discussed more fully in M. N. Wise and C. Smith, 'Measurement, work and industry in Lord Kelvin's Britain', *Historical studies in the physical and biological sciences*, 17(1986), 147–73.
7. J. P. Joule, *The scientific papers of James Prescott Joule* (2 vols., London, 1887), vol. 1, pp. 188–9.
8. W. Thomson, 'On the mechancial antecedents . . .', *Mathematical and physical papers*, vol. 1, p. 118n.
9. Joule, *Scientific papers*, vol. 1, pp. 123; 187–8; 204–5.
10. W. Thomson, 'An account of Carnot's theory of the motive power of heat, with numerical results deduced from Regnault's experiments on steam', *Mathematical and physical papers*, vol. 1, pp. 113–55. I am grateful to Norton Wise for this concise formulation.
11. R. Clausius, 'On the motive power of heat, and on the laws which can be deduced from it for the theory of heat', in E. Mendoza (ed.), *Reflections on the motive power of fire by Sadi Carnot* (New York, 1960), pp. 109–52.
12. W. Thomson, *Preliminary draft for the 'Dynamical theory of heat'*, PA 128, Kelvin papers, Cambridge University Library.
13. W. Thomson. 'On the dynamical theory of heat; with numerical results deduced from Mr. Joule's "equivalent of a thermal unit" and M. Regnault's "observations on steam" ', *Mathematical and physical papers*, vol. 1, p. 179.
14. W. Thomson, 'On a universal tendency in nature to the dissipation of mechanical energy', ibid., vol. 1, p. 511.
15. T. S. Kuhn, 'Energy conservation as an example of simultaneous discovery', in M. Clagett (ed.), *Critical problems in the history of science* (Madison, 1959), pp. 321–56.
16. Joule, *Scientific papers*, vol. 1, p. 14.
17. Ibid., vol. 1, p. 48.
18. See respectively P. M. Heimann, 'Conversion of forces and the conservation of energy', *Centaurus*, 18(1974), 147–61; J. Forrester, 'Chemistry and the conservation of energy', *Studies in history and philosophy of science*, 6(1975), 273–313; T. S. Kuhn in Clagett, *Critical problems*, pp. 325–27. H. J. Steffens, *James Prescott Joule and the concept of energy* (New York, 1979), pp. 1–60 emphasises Joule's shift towards purer science.

19. M. Faraday, *Experimental researches in electricity* (3 vols., London, 1839–55), vol. 1, para. 505.
20. Joule, *Scientific papers*, vol. 1, p. 52.
21. Hermann Helmholtz, 'On the conservation of force; a physical memoir', in J. Tyndall and W. Francis (eds.), *Scientific memoirs. Natural philosophy* (London, 1853), pp. 114–62, on pp. 115–17.
22. Translated in M. N. Wise, 'German concepts of force, energy, and the electromagnetic ether: 1845–1880', in G. N. Cantor and M. J. S. Hodge (eds.), *Conceptions of ether: studies in the history of ether theories, 1740–1900* (Cambridge, 1981), p. 273.

FURTHER READING

J. D. Burchfield, *Lord Kelvin and the age of the earth* (London, 1975).

D. S. L. Cardwell, *From Watt to Clausius. The rise of thermodynamics in the early industrial age* (London, 1971).

J. Forrester, 'Chemistry and the conservation of energy', *Studies in history and philosophy of science*, 6(1975), 273–313.

D. Gooding, 'Metaphysics versus measurement: the conversion and conservation of force in Faraday's physics', *Annals of science*, 37(1980), 1–29.

P. M. Harman [Heimann] 'Conversion of forces and the conversation of energy', *Centaurus*, 18(1974), 147–61.

——*Energy, force and matter. The conceptual development of nineteenth-century physics* (Cambridge, 1982).

C. Jungnickel, and R. McCormmach, *The intellectual mastery of nature. Theoretical physics from Ohm to Einstein* (2 vols., Chicago, 1986).

T. S. Kuhn, 'Energy conservation as an example of simultaneous discovery', in M. Clagett (ed.), *Critical problems in the history of science* (Madison, 1959), pp. 321–56.

C. Smith, 'Natural philosophy and thermodynamics: William Thomson and "The dynamical theory of heat" ', *British journal for the history of science*, 9(1976), 293–319.

——'William Thomson and the creation of thermodynamics: 1840–1855', *Archive for the history of exact sciences*, 16(1976), 231–88.

——'A new chart for British natural philosophy: the development of energy physics in the nineteenth century', *History of science*, 16(1978), 231–79.

C. Smith and M. N. Wise, *Energy and empire. A biographical study of Lord Kelvin* (Cambridge, 1989).

M. N. Wise, 'William Thomson's mathematical route to energy conservation: a case study of the role of mathematics in concept formation', *Historical studies in the physical sciences*, 10(1979), 49–83.

——'German concepts of force, energy, and the electromagnetic ether: 1845–1880', in G. N. Cantor and M. J. S. Hodge (eds.), *Conceptions of ether: studies in the history of ether theories, 1740–1900* (Cambridge, 1981), pp. 269–307.

——'The flow analogy to electricity and magnetism, part I: William Thomson's reformulation of action at a distance', *Archive for history of exact sciences*, 25(1981), 19–70.

——With the collaboration of C. Smith, 'Work and waste: political economy and natural philosophy in nineteenth-century Britain', *History of science*, (forthcoming).

22

ELECTROMAGNETIC THEORY IN THE NINETEENTH CENTURY

M. NORTON WISE

Electromagnetism presents issues of quite general historiographical interest. In purely intellectual terms, it offers one of the major transformations of theory in the history of physics, that from action at a distance to field theory. This transformation involves two others, of even wider import: the birth of energy physics, with energy transformations as the most basic object of research (see art. 21), and the rise of theories that were essentially mathematical, without definite reference to physical models. Broadening our traditional preoccupation with theory, however, we find around mid-century experimental work of a new order, involving a precision of measurements and sophistication of instrumentation unimaginable even thirty years earlier. Concomitantly, the first research laboratories for physics were founded between 1850 and 1870.

To pursue electromagnetism into the new activities and institutions of physics would immediately raise issues of paramount concern to social and economic historians, issues of science-based industry and the so-called second industrial revolution, based on electric telegraphy and electric power, as well as on the chemical industry. From another perspective, cultural historians will want to explore the differences in national style evident in electromagnetism, especially differences between German and British physics. These broader historiographical issues await thorough investigation. Intellectual developments, therefore, dominate the following discussion.

By the mid-nineteenth century, the subject of electromagnetism involved attempts to unify three phenomena: 'electrostatic' forces between electrified bodies; 'electromagnetic' forces between an electric current and a magnet or between two electric currents and 'electromagnetic induction' of currents by moving magnets and by moving or changing currents. Two approaches to the problem of unity are readily identifiable. In the manner of Isaac Newton and Pierre-Simon Laplace, one could seek a single force acting between atoms of electrical matter which would subsume the different phenomena. Wilhelm Weber (1804–91), who achieved great success in 1846, epitomises this tradition. Alternatively, one could seek a specific quantity, common to the three phenomena, which would serve to measure their capacities or energies, and in terms of which they could be interrelated. James Clerk Maxwell (1831–79), in his first paper on 'fields' of electric and magnetic energy in 1855, followed by the electromagnetic theory of light in 1863, established this programme as a search for energies in the ether. Relatively separate tracks of Weberian force physics and Maxwellian energy physics continued in electromagnetism until the end of the century, but an intermediate development ultimately dominated. Hermann von Helmholtz (1821–94) combined a reductionist view of atoms and forces with his fundamental emphasis on conservation of energy to produce a powerful and disturbing mixture of ideas in 1871. From the mixture came the electron theory of Hendrik Antoon Lorentz (1853–1928) in the 1890s.

We have then to distinguish between the roots of force physics and of energy physics. In the older literature the distinction of two traditions has usually been drawn between action at a distance and contiguous action, or between forces and fields. More recent scholarship, however, suggests that the force-energy distinction is more appropriate. It places Helmholtz, for example, who held both force and energy as fundamental physical entities, in his historical role as mediator, even though he pursued action at a distance rather than field explanations. Furthermore, in analysing early-nineteenth-century developments, we are able to distinguish the essentially mathematical tradition of force physics from the essentially experimental tradition that produced the major discoveries of electromagnetism and simultaneously motivated their energy interpretation.

I. FORCES AND POTENTIALS

The programme for reducing all physical phenomena to the mathematics of forces acting at a distance between point atoms was established in France by Laplace and his followers during the first decade of the nineteenth century. (See art. 18.) Its defining feature mathematically was an abstract function V, later labelled a 'potential' function, from which the components of force at any point could be derived by simple differentiation with respect to three coordinate axes: e.g. $R_x = -\partial V/\partial x$, or in vector notation,

$$\vec{R} = -\text{gradient } V,$$

where $\vec{R}$ is force per unit mass ($\vec{R} = \vec{F}/m$, if $\vec{F}$ is the total force which would act on a mass m placed at the point). For a system of inverse square forces produced by point masses m_i, the function V was defined at any point in space by the equation,

$$V = \Sigma m_i/r_i,$$

or,

$$V = \iiint \varrho \, d\tau/r,$$

where r_i is the distance from the point to the mass m_i or to the density ϱ in the volume element $d\tau$. For points not occupied by a mass, furthermore, the function V satisfied 'Laplace's equation',

$$\partial^2 V/\partial x^2 + \partial^2 V/\partial y^2 + \partial^2 V/\partial z^2 = 0,$$

so that the problem of finding the force at any point in space reduced to the problem of solving this differential equation for a given case. The mathematical theory of forces was devoted during much of the nineteenth century to general methods of solution for Laplace's equation and its generalisation. Closely related problems and solutions derived from the wave equation, associated with Fresnel's development of the wave theory of light, and the diffusion equation, associated with Fourier's theory of heat conduction. The new techniques of 'continental analysis' demanded mathematical sophistication. With them, mathematical physics in a modern sense began; they still provide the classical tools of the subject.

With respect to electrostatics, the Laplacian programme found its leading expositor in Siméon-Denis Poisson (1781–1840). He applied it in papers of 1812–13 to the empirical inverse square law of Coulomb, which Poisson regarded as a force acting between atoms of two electrical fluids, positive and negative. 'Poisson's equation' for the function V is valid both within and without an electrical distribution ϱ,

$$\partial^2 V/\partial x^2 + \partial^2 V/\partial y^2 + \partial^2 V/\partial z^2 = -4\pi\varrho.$$

The major problem Poisson sought to solve concerned the attraction between two electrified conducting spheres. His methods did not yield a general solution despite their sophistication. Nevertheless, he founded the mathematical theory of electricity.

Poisson developed a similar analysis for magnetism in 1822–24, again basing his mathematical theory on Coulomb's measurements and on an interpretation of Coulomb's inverse square law for magnetism as a force acting between atoms of two magnetic fluids, northern and southern. Using a microscopic model of 'magnetic elements' inside a magnetised substance, and suitable averages over them, Poisson obtained quite general results for permanent and induced magnets. He also applied those results to correcting the errors of navigational compasses in ships containing iron, a problem of increasing economic and military significance.

Such practical problems, which immediately bring issues of wealth and power to bear on the development of mathematical physics, have not usually appeared in the history of potential theory; but many of the major figures in its development, including Gauss and William Thomson, considered them carefully. Present historiography asks what difference that made, and suggests some answers.[1]

The analysis of V for electrostatics and magnetostatics was pursued with great elegance and power by Green (1828) and Gauss (1839–41), who independently labelled it the potential function. Green, however, whose work remained unknown until William Thomson resurrected it in 1845, eliminated Poisson's microscopic models and based his analysis on macroscopically-defined electrical densities and magnetisations (magnetic moment per unit volume). In this, Green joined an emerging British tradition, which made macroscopic energy densities the fundamental physical referent and which attributed to potential the connotations of potential energy. Gauss continued to insist on the Laplacian approach, in which the potential function provided a formalism for describing forces. Aside from this emergent split in methodology and in physical reference, however, Green and Gauss established many of the same mathematical relations.

Following Oersted's discovery of electromagnetism in 1820, Ampère had shown that a force existed between current-carrying wires, just as between magnets, and had obtained a new law describing the electromagnetic force. He also had speculated that all magnetism was produced by electric currents and had proposed a model of 'electrodynamic molecules' in magnetic substances, involving currents of electrical fluid circulating around the molecules. Ampère's force is remarkably unlike Laplacian forces. It acts, not between atoms, but between elements of current, sections of infinitesimal length imagined to make up a line of current. Furthermore, although it is an inverse square force, acting along the line between elements, the orientations of the elements also enter.[2]

Although Ampère had not supplied a potential function for his force law, Gauss, following Ampère's ideas, obtained a potential for magnetic forces produced by closed currents. Preoccupied, however, with finding the optimal data for mapping the earth's magnetic field over its entire surface, Gauss did not pursue more general forms of electromagnetic potentials.

The first such potential function was discovered by Franz Neumann, founder of the Königsberg seminar in mathematical physics. Neumann's potential, described in papers of 1845 and 1848, supplied a mathematical form for Faraday's 'electromagnetic induction', the induction of electric currents in conducting circuits subjected to changing magnetic forces, whether produced by magnets or currents. The induced electromotive force at a point could be expressed as the time derivative of a function whose spatial derivatives gave the magnetic force at the point, but in a complex way. This function, labelled a 'vector potential' by Maxwell, gives the magnetic force at any point as the circulation of the vector potential around the point. Here were the beginnings of unity in the mathematical tradition of forces and potentials, for the forces of both electromagnetism and electromagnetic induction could be derived from a single 'potential function', in its newly extended meaning.

In 1846, Gauss's collaborator at Göttingen, Wilhelm Weber, approached the ultimate goal; he found a law of force that encompassed all three of the major phenomena of electricity and magnetism. Having been dismissed from his Göttingen professorship for political dissent, Weber then occupied the chair of physics at Leipzig, recently vacated by Gustav Theodor Fechner. Fechner had proposed a model of currents in a wire as consisting of oppositely-charged electric particles travelling in opposite directions with equal velocity. He suggested that both Ampère's and Faraday's results could be regarded as net effects obtained from summing four pairs of forces between like and unlike charged particles in two currents. Within this model, Weber discovered, the law of force between any two particles would involve not only their relative separation, but also their relative velocity and relative acceleration, yielding a three term relation.[3] The three terms give electrostatic force between particles at relative rest, electromagnetic force between particles with a relative velocity and induced electromotive force between particles with relative acceleration a. With good reason, then, Weber considered his law the *Grundgesetz* of electrodynamics, for it subsumed all known electrical phenomena and promised even to explain the electrical constitution of matter. He hoped ultimately to include gravitation.

Weber showed by 1848 that his force could be derived in the simple Laplacian manner as the gradient of a potential function, albeit a velocity-dependent one. His analysis thus continued the tradition of reducing all physical phenomena to the mathematics of point atoms and forces, analysed through the theory of potentials. Within that tradition, the appearance of a velocity dependence – an implicit time dependence – in the function V was not necessarily disturbing, for that abstract function served primarily a mathematical role. Even the physical quantity, force, expressed only a relation between two atoms, and a relation in space and time seemed, especially in the context of the German idealist tradition, no less valid than one in space alone. Indeed, for Weber, the law of force expressed the essential interrelation of space, time and matter, which he expected to reduce to a single measure in his absolute system of units.

Potential theorists after the mid-century incorporated the new conservation of energy doctrine, but for them potential energy did not take on the status of a substantial reality, analogous to matter. It acquired two alternative meanings, however, depending on two different interpretations of potential: electrokinetic potentials and retarded potentials. The former introduce 'kinetic' terms, like Weber's v^2/c^2, into the notion of 'potential', making the distinction of potential and kinetic somewhat arbitrary. In addition to Weber himself, Rudolf Clausius contributed most to this line. Clausius did not use the notion of potential energy at all, but only of a function which completed the conservation law for kinetic energy. The alternative theories of retarded potentials supposed the velocity dependence to derive from a delay in the action of a force at a distance, as though it propagated at the speed of light. Carl Neumann, son of Franz Neumann, represented this interpretation. He regarded the potential as a true potential energy, but only in the sense of a space-time relation, a transcendental concept not subject to explanation. Energy theorists like Helmholtz raised a variety of objections to both of these alternatives during the 1870s, and a considerable debate ensued. This debate and later developments in the theory of action at a distance potentials by Lienhardt, Wieckert and Schwartzschild have been largely ignored in historical literature.

2. FIELDS OF ENERGY

The mathematical tradition of forces and potentials depended for its vitality on alliance with an experimental programme new at the beginning of the nineteenth century. The modern experimenters, exemplified by Coulomb and Ampère, but more especially at mid-century by Weber and William Thomson, emphasised precision measurements and instruments. Interestingly, however, neither the mathematisers nor the measurers seem to have inspired the most dramatic new theoretical programme of the century; in which physical research was based on the idea of a conserved physical quantity converted from one form to another in the operations of nature. That idea, once mathematised at mid-century by being joined to the older metaphysics of conservation of *vis viva*, became the doctrine of energy conservation. (See art. 21.) But its inspiration in the nineteenth century derived largely from qualitative discoveries aimed at revealing directly the unity of nature: the voltaic pile by Volta (1800), electromagnetism by Oersted (1820) and electromagnetic induction by Faraday (1831). These phenomena seemed to display interconversions from one form of power to another: chemical to electrical, electrical to magnetic and magnetic back to electrical. Hans Christian Oersted (1777–1851) and Michael Faraday (1791–1867), in particular, pursued their researches on interconversion with conscious commitment to the unity of all natural powers, to the belief that all physical forces are but manifestations of a fundamental conserved 'force'.

Although variously based, such doctrines found particularly consistent expression in German *Naturphilosophie* and related idealist schemes, in which the powers of nature were seen as realisations of the powers of mind and ultimately of God's power, or of Idea in general. (See art. 56, sect. 2.) The tradition of atoms and forces had made atoms real and force the relation of them, so that force did not exist in space, but only where it acted on matter. By contrast, the *Naturphilosophie* of the later Kant, and of Schelling and Hegel, made force – as natural power – the essential reality and matter a phenomenal manifestation of it. To advocates of point atoms, space was empty; to *Naturphilosophen*, it was a plenum of force, in which a point atom could possess only geometrical significance, as the centre of a distribution of force. Thus, to Oersted, the power of an electric current did not exist in the wire which served as its axis but in the space surrounding the wire. Faraday, in a similar fashion, regarded molecules as force distributions, although his debt to *Naturphilosophie* appears tenuous.

Forces, in the sense of interconvertible powers, had two noteworthy characteristics: polarity, which gave them their dynamic character, and a quantity-intensity duality, which gave them their descriptive adequacy. With his famous language of 'lines of force', Faraday transformed these characteristics into a powerful new theory of 'fields'. An electric line of force represented a polar axis, with its opposite ends constituting plus and minus electricity. No electrical particles or fluids existed, but still Faraday could speak of one electricity 'inducing' the other by 'contiguous action' along the lines of induction. Magnetic lines represented a similar state of polarisation, although they formed closed loops with no terminations, so that northern and southern fluids had no corollary.

Lines of force did not exist separately in Faraday's picture, but as systems of lines. He characterised the systems by *intensity* of force measured longitudinally, giving the tension of the polarisation along a line, and by *quantity* of force measured laterally, or by the number of lines, giving the quantity of electricity represented at the terminations. All properties of electric and magnetic systems, Faraday believed, could be described in this language, with suitable extensions. Thus, since the lines represented propagation of force through space, he expected that any change in the quality of that space would affect its capacity to transmit the lines, and therefore would change the relations of quantity and intensity. Searching for such effects in electrostatics he discovered the 'inductive capacity' of 'dielectrics' in 1837, which reduces the intensity between two charged conductors for a given quantity. A long search for effects of contiguous action on light yielded in 1845 magneto-optic rotation, or the rotation of the plane of polarisation of light when propagating through a special glass along lines of magnetic force.

The glass itself, and many other media, exhibited a strange new magnetic behaviour, opposite to that of known magnetic substances. It was repelled from the poles of a magnet, or as Faraday put it in his own theoretical terms, it tended to move from *places* of stronger to *places* of weaker force. He soon showed that this 'diamagnetic' behaviour could be explained in terms of a lower conducting power for lines of force, as compared with mere space, while normal 'paramagnetic' substances like soft iron possessed a higher conducting power. This description marks the beginning of field theory, where 'field' is Faraday's term for the places of stronger and weaker force. Objects in the field are not so much acted on by the field as they participate in it, and the action they experience expresses the effect they have on the distribution of force in the field, which obeys an overall principle of economy. Diamagnetics, being poor conductors, are squeezed out of a region of strong fields while paramagnetics are drawn in. The principle means, in fact, that the direction of the lines of force in a field does not in general give the direction of the moving force on an object at all. This ponderomotive force may even be perpendicular to the lines of force.

Faraday's ideas did not translate easily into the conceptual structure of existing mathematical theory. They required not only propagating forces and a distinction of forces in a field from ponderomotive forces, but also a measure of the amount of natural power contained in a field or converted from one field to another. Mathematicians showed little interest. But in the mid-forties, William Thomson (1824–1907), a precocious Cambridge graduate from Glasgow, stepped in with the requisite mathematics already at hand, and with a pre-established interpretation. The ponderomotive force, Thomson showed, could be described as the tendency of the field to minimise the quantity of work it contained, where 'work' meant literally the mechanical work one would have to do to establish the field, whether by assembling its sources from bits of magnetised matter at infinity or by generating electric currents. Equivalently, the magnetic system could restore this mechanical work, if treated as an engine for lifting weights, for example.

Thomson made three preliminary steps, largely in 1845, before arriving at this notion. Firstly, drawing on the work of Fourier, he developed a mathematical analogy between electrostatic induction and heat conduction, which showed that the action at a distance theory could be translated into Faraday's theory of contiguous action (minus the quantity-intensity distinction), with specific inductive capacity playing the role of conductivity. The force at a point, given by potential gradient, then behaved exactly like a temperature gradient. Secondly, he reinterpreted a mathematical result of Gauss in potential theory, to show that electricity distributed itself at equilibrium so as to minimise the work contained in any given electrical system. This interpretation, which Thomson obtained by analogy with steam engines, brought the theory of potentials into association with standard principles of mechanics, such as those of virtual velocities and conservation of *vis viva*. Gauss had minimised the function,

$$\Phi = \Sigma m_i dV_i,$$

which Thomson recognised as $\Sigma m_i R_i dr_i = \Sigma F_i dr_i$, a function which is minimum at equilibrium according to the principle of virtual velocities, and which measures changes in *vis viva* for conservative systems. He also recognised it as the measure of work used by engineers: force times distance moved. Thus the work Φ contained in the system was minimum at equilibrium. Reinterpreting the potential function V, it became the work required to bring a unit of matter from infinity to any given point.

Finally, Thomson reinterpreted a theorem of both Gauss and Green as showing that the work in the system could be regarded either as localised in the sources of density ϱ at their respective potentials V, or as spread throughout a 'field' in space, with a density varying as the square of the field strength R,

$$\Phi = \iiint \varrho V d\tau = \iiint R^2 d\tau.$$

Generalising this form in 1847, Thomson obtained Faraday's view of ponderomotive forces $\vec{T}$ on magnetic material of 'conductivity' k,

$$\Phi = \iiint k R^2 d\tau$$
$$\vec{T} = -\text{gradient } \Phi.$$

That is, the work contained in the entire field behaves like a total potential for the system, which is minimum at equilibrium and yields the ponderomotive forces within it as gradients. (Compare the earlier definition of V.) Diamagnetics therefore move to places of weaker force and paramagnetics to stronger.

Unlike Faraday, however, Thomson understood the reality of the field to consist not in 'powers' distributed in space, but in states of a material substance, the luminiferous ether. As a definite, if unknown, mechanical structure, the ether would contain work in the same way as other materials: e.g. in elastic deformation or in *vis viva*. Concomitantly, he interpreted Faraday's magnetic rotation of light as due to rotations of the ether around the direction of propagation, thus around the magnetic lines. He concluded that the magnetic lines actually consisted in these rotations, a view that motivated his recurrent quest for a vortex theory of ether and matter.

In 1847, when Thomson achieved these results, he also met Joule, who insisted that mechanical work was interconvertible with heat, as well as with the conservative force fields of electricity and magnetism, and that he had measured their equivalents. His measurements epitomise a new attitude to the older qualitative doctrine of conservation, an attitude soon apparent on a broad front both in Britain and on the continent. (See art. 21.) The general axiom of conservation of energy that arose from the reformulated alliance of quantitative measurements and mathematical theory, greatly enhanced the significance of

Thomson's interpretation of Faraday's fields, as fields of potential and/or kinetic energy.

So far only electrostatic and magnetostatic fields have appeared in the energy scheme. Impetus for a correlative theory of electromagnetism came from Faraday's attempt in 1851 to carry his quantity-intensity description into a unified dynamical picture of lines of electric current and magnetic lines. The two sorts of lines, he argued, were related like linked rings, or as James Clerk Maxwell soon put it, in a 'mutual embrace'.[4] Each system obeyed its own longitudinal and lateral dynamics, but the longitudinal property of the one (e.g. contraction in the magnetic line) produced the same effect as the lateral property of the other (attraction between current lines). The reciprocal equivalence exhibited what Faraday called the 'oneness of condition' of the two forms of power.   In a magnificent synthesis of Faraday's qualitative reciprocity with Thomson's mathematics, Maxwell, another young Scot just graduated from Cambridge, produced his first field theory in 1855. The mutual embrace, however, encompassed only constant lines of current and constant magnetic lines, or simply Ampère's force of electromagnetism. Electromagnetic induction required an additional relation. Eight years later Maxwell reformulated the embrace for fields varying in time, based on the belief that a variation in either field would produce the other. This mutual induction of fields, he showed, if it occurred at all, would produce electromagnetic waves propagating through space at the velocity of light. In one grand speculation, the electromagnetic theory of light was born. (See art. 40, sect. 6.)

Maxwell's speculation took very seriously Faraday's view that electricity was nothing other than the termination of lines of electrostatic induction, as well as his related quantity-intensity distinction. This implied that as the intensity of the lines increased, the associated increase of quantity would behave like a conduction current, carrying electricity to the opposite ends of the lines. Conceiving this quantity as a displacement in the ether, Maxwell called the supposed current a 'displacement current', given by the rate of change of displacement. Adopting modern symbols, we may interpret Maxwell's equations for the fields in source-free ether as stating that the lines of electric quantity $\vec{D}$ and magnetic quantity $\vec{B}$ form closed curves (quantity conserved). Moreover, the total electric intensity $\vec{E}$ (or magnetic $\vec{H}$) summed around any closed curve measures the time rate of change of total magnetic quantity $\vec{B}$ (electric $\vec{D}$) passing through the area enclosed by the curve.[5] The latter reciprocal relations of electric (magnetic) intensity to *changing* magnetic (electric) quantity give the mutual embrace as mutual induction propagating at the speed of light.

These relations capture only the mathematical superstructure of Maxwell's 1863 theory. Beneath it lay a most imaginative model representing the dynamical relations that a mechanical ether would have to exhibit. Prominent features were vortex cells to represent magnetic lines and idler wheels to transmit the rotation between cells and to represent electricity, both in conduction and displacement. In later treatments Maxwell avoided such detailed pictures.

Not until after Lorentz's development of electron theory in the 1890s did 'Maxwell's equations' acquire their present meaning, with ϱ representing a density of charged particles, $\vec{E}$ and $\vec{B}$ as the fundamental fields and $\vec{D}$ and $\vec{H}$ as convenient macroscopic fields in the presence of matter. Nevertheless, with Maxwell's theory a new form of unification of electromagnetism, alternative to Weber's *Grundgesetz*, had to be taken seriously, especially because it encompassed the wave theory of light. Its physical realities were not atoms and forces, but ether and energy.

Thomson, Maxwell and a number of their British compatriots sought to ground not only electricity and magnetism, but matter itself, in the mechanics of ether. Lacking any adequate theory of how matter might be related to ether, however, they proposed a formulation of mechanical theory that avoided, in the first instance, specific models of the underlying reality, especially forces acting at a distance. In their respective *Treatises*, on *Natural philosophy* (1867) and *Electricity and magnetism* (1873), Thomson and Maxwell grounded dynamics on energy and extremum conditions, adopting the variational principle of William Rowan Hamilton. Hamilton's principle allowed them to generalise Thomson's earlier approach, subordinating forces between parts of a system to an extremum condition on the whole, so that forces could be regarded as manifestations of the existing distribution of energy. The problem of mechanical theory was reduced to finding appropriate forms for potential and kinetic energies in a given system.

From this point, Thomson and Maxwell differed on how one ought to proceed. Thomson insisted on direct empirical reference for all theoretical entities (thus excluding displacement current) and on the pursuit of an adequate mechanical model for ether. Concomitantly, he founded his electromagnetic conceptions and his vortex ether on the material and economic reality of mechanical systems: engines, pumps and telegraph lines. Maxwell sought more general mathematical structures, whose validity did not depend on a mechanical representation of them, even though mechanical explanation remained his goal. Most British theorists followed Maxwell in this methodological direction, as George Francis Fitzgerald, Oliver Heaviside, J. J. Thomson, John Henry Poynting and Joseph Larmor. The 'Maxwellians' have even been defined as those who pursued electromagnetic theory exclusively in terms of macroscopically-defined energy densities in ether and matter. This definition underestimates the role of mechanical models among the Maxwellians, who often followed Thomson in the attempt to find a vortex structure for the ether. Concomitantly, it eliminates the great importance of engineering and industry for the pursuits of at least Fitzgerald, Heaviside and Lodge. Nevertheless, in Maxwellian mathematical theories, matter merely modified ether, so that all properties of matter were to be explained by appropriate modifications of the energies for ether and by applying the procedures of generalised dynamics.

Maxwellian theory achieved some phenomenal successes in the Hall effect (1879) and in Poynting's theorem (1885). It ultimately foundered, however, on its inability to give coherent accounts of such fundamental phenomena as conduction in wires, the interaction of two magnets and the reflection of light from a metal surface. Through intense interaction with Lodge and Fitzgerald, Larmor began in the early 1890s to develop an analytic scheme that, in effect, added discrete particles of electricity to the Maxwellian notion of matter as a modification of ether. The ether, furthermore, increasingly took on the role of a mere symbol for the electromagnetic field, rather than a mechanical structure. After his reading of Lorentz in 1895, Larmor's scheme became an explicit electron theory of matter, drawing a firm distinction between the mechanics of electrons and the electrodynamics of ether.

3. MEDIATORS: HELMHOLTZ, HERTZ, AND LORENTZ

In a major paper of 1870, Helmholtz, the giant of German physiology and physics, placed himself squarely between Weber and Maxwell. Like Thomson, he had, in 1847, in his classic memoir *Über die Erhaltung der Kraft* (*On the conservation of force*), brought potential theory into association with the capacity of a system to do work, and thus with potential energy. His deep commitments to the idea of energy entailed an unwillingness to accept Weber's *Grundgesetz*, with its velocity dependent potential, even though Helmholtz himself believed that the ultimate reality of nature lay in atoms and forces. Already in 1847 he argued that no velocity-dependent force could satisfy the principle of conservation of *vis viva*, which seemed to require forces dependent only on position, so that a return of a system to its initial spatial arrangement would yield its initial velocities. Even after Weber showed in 1848 that his potential would satisfy this condition, Helmholtz refused to accept it. Apparently he saw in velocity-dependent potentials an opening for the mystifying vital forces in physiology that he believed he had expunged through the doctrine of conservation of energy. A related factor was his belief in potential energy as a real physical quantity, for velocity dependence obscured its unique interpretation.

Helmholtz's 1870 theory depended on a generalised form of Franz Neumann's potential, that is, on a potential for current elements, and not on an underlying model of what a current would be in terms of atoms and forces. With different choices for a parameter, it gave the potentials for currents of Weber and Carl Neumann, as well as Franz Neumann, and showed that they would have different experimental consequences for open circuits (where Maxwell's displacement also had its consequences). The experiments, however, did not yet exist. Helmholtz's theory also included an electrostatic potential and electric and magnetic polarisations of ether and matter. Although all the forces acted instantaneously at a distance, Helmholtz showed that with a certain limiting assumption, the theory predicted waves of polarisation spreading through the ether at the speed of light, much as in Maxwell's theory.

Largely ignored in Britain, Helmholtz's conceptions provided the starting point for the main line of development on the continent. Lorentz's attempts from 1875 to the early 1890s to derive optical consequences from the electromagnetic theory of light, all began from Helmholtz's theory. Hertz's extensive researches of the 1880s, which ultimately established the existence of electromagnetic waves, began similarly as an attempt to confirm Helmholtz's version of Maxwell's theory, which, like the original, required electromagnetically-induced polarisation of dielectrics and also electromagnetic forces produced by changing polarisation.

By the early 1890s, however, Helmholtz, Hertz and Lorentz had all adopted the contiguous action view. It has often been supposed that Hertz's experiments alone account for this shift away from potential theory; but more is needed, for retarded potentials could explain all that Maxwell's theory could, as Hertz was aware. In seeking a broader explanation, we must look to the central role that energy had come to play in physical theory. It had acquired the status of a substance, much like matter itself. Concomitantly, research into the transformations of energy required that energy be located and traced from place to place. Theories of action at a distance, even delayed action at a distance, did not treat energy in this concrete way. If an electrified body, for example, produced motion in another body at a distance, one could not say that the energy was propagated across the space with the retarded potential, for the potential did not represent a physical entity existing in space, but an abstract function. This was Max Planck's view in 1887. Similarly, Hertz regarded his 1888 experiments on electromagnetic waves in wires as most appropriately understood through Poynting's theorem, whereby the energy entered the wire from the immediately surrounding field. And Lorentz in 1891 objected to the electrokinetic potentials of Weber and Clausius because they mixed the kinetic energy of moving masses with potential energy. The views of Helmholtz, Planck, Hertz and Lorentz, not to mention the more sweeping philosophical commitments of positivists and energeticists such as Ernst Mach and Wilhelm Ostwald, are highly suggestive of the dominant role energy had come to play.

With the adoption of contiguous action among a substantial group of continental theorists by the early 1890s, the character of electromagnetic theory rapidly changed. Although the story is complex, several markers stand out. Firstly, Hertz reformulated Maxwellian equations for free ether, providing what seemed a clean and comprehensible picture of a pure electromagnetic field, independent of mechanical considerations. Secondly, extending Hertz's conceptions in 1893, Helmholtz developed a theory of the interaction of light with matter that sharply distinguished the electromagnetic field from discrete charged particles, or ions, scattered within matter. It was through this formulation that German physicists developed sophisticated theories of optical phenomena, especially magneto-optical phenomena, and first learned to treat fields and ions as two separate realities. Already in 1875 Helmholtz had produced a two-substance theory, explaining dispersion in terms of an elastic-solid ether with oscillating particles embedded in it. But whereas both substances in that theory consisted of normal inertial materials interacting mechanically, the new theory distinguished substances of two kinds, electromagnetic and mechanical, whose motions, though linked, did not obey the action-reaction law.

Thirdly, Helmholtz's new scheme contained nothing that Lorentz had not already produced in 1892. But Lorentz's classic works, which are now regarded as having established the distinction of fields and matter, were almost unknown in Germany until the late 1890s. Lorentz, in fact, also starting from Hertz's field equations, offered a much more general electron theory than Helmholtz and his followers. It treated matter as consisting of nothing other than charged particles, required statistical averaging procedures to obtain the detailed interactions of light and matter and attempted to solve the famous problems of matter in motion through the ether which led to relativity theory. (See art. 28.) After 1895 his microphysical approach to magneto-optics and his field transformations for moving bodies began to attract widespread attention, so much so that by 1900 Lorentz's electron theory provided the primary conceptual structure for electromagnetism.

NOTES

1. E.g. Bruce Hunt, ' "Practice vs. theory": The British electrical debate, 1888–1901', *Isis*, 74 (1983), 341–55; M. N. Wise and Crosbie Smith, 'Measurement, work, and industry in Lord Kelvin's Britain', *Historical studies in the physical sciences*, 17 (1987), 147–73.
2. Ampère's force between two elements dl_1 and dl_2 carrying currents i_1 and i_2 is,

$$F = -i_1 i_2 dl_1 dl_2 (2 \cos \alpha - 3 \cos \beta_1 \cos \beta_2)/2r^2,$$

where α is the angle between the elements, and β_1 and β_2 are the angles they make with the line between them, of length r.
3. Weber's *electrodynamische Grundgesetz* for the force between particles with charges e_1 and e_2 separated by r is,

$$F = (e_1 e_2/r^2) [1 - (1/c^2)v^2 + (2r/c^2)a],$$

where c is a constant giving the ratio between electrostatic and electromagnetic units, later shown to differ from the velocity of light by a factor $\sqrt{2}$.
4. M. N. Wise, 'The mutual embrace of electricity and magnetism', *Science*, 203 (1979), 1310–18.
5. In this special case, Maxwell's equations take the following symmetric form:

divergence $\vec{D} = 0$
divergence $\vec{B} = 0$ } closed electric and magnetic lines

$$\left.\begin{array}{l} \text{curl } \vec{E} = -(1/c)\partial\vec{B}/\partial t \\ \text{curl } \vec{H} = +(1/c)\partial\vec{D}/\partial t \end{array}\right\} \text{ mutual embrace as mutual induction}$$

The presence of electric charge and current requires: divergence $\vec{D} = \varrho$; curl $\vec{H} = (1/c)(\vec{i} - \partial\vec{D}/\partial t)$. In addition, Maxwell included quantity-intensity relations for each field and relations for electrostatic and vector potentials, which he considered integral to the theory.

FURTHER READING

Fabio Bevilacqua, 'H. Hertz's experiments and the shift towards contiguous propagation in the early nineties', *Rivista di storia della scienza*, 1 (1984), 239–56.

J. Z. Buchwald, *From Maxwell to microphysics: Aspects of electromagnetic theory in the last quarter of the nineteenth century* (Chicago, 1985).

Salvo D'Agostino, 'Hertz's researches on electromagnetic waves', *Historical studies in the physical sciences*, 6 (1975), 261–323.

C. W. F. Everitt, 'Maxwell, James Clerk', in *Dictionary of scientific biography* (New York, 1974).

David Gooding, 'Final steps to the field theory: Faraday's investigation of magnetic phenomena: 1845–1850', *Historical studies in the physical sciences*, 11 (1981), 231–75.

Tetu Hirosige, 'Origins of Lorentz' theory of electrons and the concept of the electromagnetic field', *Historical studies in the physical sciences*, 1 (1969), 151–209.

Walter Kaiser, 'Einleitung', to Ludwig Boltzmann, *Vorlesungen über Maxwell's Theorie des Lichtes* (Graz, 1982), 5–32.

Ole Knudsen, 'Mathematics and physical reality in William Thomson's electromagnetic theory', in *Wranglers and physicists: Studies on Cambridge mathematical physics in the nineteenth century*, (ed.) Peter Harman (Manchester, 1985), 149–79.

Nancy Nersessian, *Faraday to Einstein: Constructing meaning in scientific theory* (Dordrecht, 1984).

Daniel Siegel, 'The origin of the displacement current', *Historical studies in the physical sciences*, 17 (1986), 99–146.

Crosbie Smith and M. N. Wise, *Energy and empire: A biographical study of Lord Kelvin* (Cambridge, 1989).

M. N. Wise, 'German concepts of force, energy, and the electromagnetic ether: 1845–1880', in *Conceptions of ether: Studies in the history of ether theories, 1740–1900*, (eds.) G. N. Cantor and M. J. S. Hodge (Cambridge, 1981), 269–307.

23

CELL THEORY AND DEVELOPMENT

JANE MAIENSCHEIN

Cell theory has passed through various stages of understanding during the three centuries since researchers first noticed the existence of cells. Likewise, the role of cells in development has also gone through different interpretations. Theories have included an elementary conception of basic microscopic units in the mid-seventeenth century, a more fully articulated cell theory in the early nineteenth century which held that cells are the basic building blocks of living organisms, a later nineteenth-century conviction that the actions of cellular material actually bring about organic development and differentiation, and the idea that cells hold a key to evolutionary development as well. Controversies and disagreements about detail have occurred, but some version of cell theory and the fundamental role of cells in development has persisted.

This essay will examine the intersection of studies of cells and studies of development, which necessarily leaves out much of both cytology and embryology. Yet the study of cells and their role in individual development has raised important questions and has shaped both the direction of cytology and the study of embryology. It is worth focusing on the intersection and on those few but valuable historical examinations of both cell theory and development.

1. CYTOLOGY AND CELLULAR STUFF

In 1665, Robert Hooke's *Micrographia* (1665) first brought cells to public attention.[1] Intended as a popularly accessible book rather than a specialised report, the *Micrographia* illustrated and described cells which Hooke had studied with his microscope. Taking a thin slice of cork, for example, he observed what looked like a honeycomb of pores, which he called cells since they were essentially spaces surrounded by walls and not unlike the monastic cells of the time. Then he observed similar textures in a number of other plant forms as well. Though convinced that these cells must have a proper purpose, this English observer was not quite certain what that purpose might be. He concluded that they might serve as channels to carry fluids through the plant material in just the way that arteries and veins move fluids through the animal body. Hooke thus established that structural units called cells exist in some organisms, but was not confident about further conclusions.

A few years later, other observers turned their microscopes to organic material as well. In particular, the Englishman Nehemiah Grew and the Italian Marcello Malpighi both began to observe more clearly the detailed structure of plant cells with their work which they called vegetable anatomy. Because the cellular structure of plant material is more obvious than that of most animals, they each clearly observed cells. Malpighi's *Anatomes plantarum* (London, 1675, and 1679) referred to the 'utricles' (or cells) and to the 'basic utrical structure' of the plants. At the same time, in work also communicated to the Royal Society of London, Nehemiah Grew addressed the question raised by Hooke as to whether plants have circulatory systems like animals. He did not find any valves or perfectly analogous vessels to answer that question, but he did provide more detailed and definitive descriptions of the cells in his work which culminated in *The Anatomy of Plants* (London, 1682). The contemporaneous work by Malpighi and Grew set the standard for discussion of cells as structural units for some time. It also demonstrates the close connection between microscopic exploration and cell study in the early years.

Since microscopic aid is valuable for seeing most cells, the increasing interest in microscopy in the seventeenth and eighteenth centuries brought with it an enthusiasm for describing the structure of materials, including the apparent cellular structure of living materials. Thus, some historians have cited the crucial directive role of technical advances, while others have argued that ideas preceded technical innovation. Whatever the technical contribution, questions arose among the microscopists. While Hooke, Grew and Malpighi located cells in plants, others questioned what those cells were: whether the basic units of life or parts of an interconnected fabric; whether accidental and occasional or ubiquitous structures; or whether perhaps only unimportant microscopic artifacts. Others asked whether cells exist in animals as well. The late eighteenth century brought discussion of 'globules', for example, as alternative fundamental material structures. Others saw 'fibrilles' as the more proper units of organic material, and some invested the latter with vital properties such as 'irritability'.

This proliferation of ideas creates problems for the historian who wants to examine cell theory, because it remains unclear what to count as cells. Do we include only those discussions that actually label their entities as 'cells', or do we also include references to 'globules' or 'fibrilles'? When examining cell theory *and* development, such work as Caspar Friedrich Wolff's seems important since he regarded embryos as made up from globules, which produced a sort of 'cellular tissue' analogous to plant cells. And yet the globules do not really correspond to visible cells or to basic organic structural units, as Shirley

Roe has clarified in *Matter, Life, and Generation* (Cambridge, 1981). It is reasonable, therefore, to exclude Wolff as belonging to a different tradition, with different concerns and commitments, and to remain with the microscopic-based study of what cells are and what their role is in development.

In order to begin addressing those developmental questions and to turn those structural spaces surrounded by walls into something more functional, it was useful, firstly, to fill them with something and, secondly, to determine how they arise. Felix Dujardin began to answer the first question in 1835. His 'sarcode' was the material which fills living cells: 'a glutinous, diaphanous substance, insoluble in water, contracting into spherical masses, sticking to the dissecting needles and letting itself be drawn out like slime, and, finally, being found in all the lower animals interposed between the other structural elements'.[2] Dujardin's work on infusoria, designed to examine the internal structure of that organic group, also raised the question of whether similar substances exist in other organisms. In 1839, the Bohemian researcher Jan Purkinje confirmed this and identified the fluid stuff inside the cell walls as 'protoplasm', a concept which Hugo von Mohl extended and developed into its modern form (Purkinje, *Übersicht über die arbeiten und Veränderung der schlesichen Gesellschaft für vaterländische Kultur im Jahre 1839* (Breslau, 1840); von Mohl, 'Über die Saftbewegung im Innern der Zellen', *Botanische Zeitung* 4 (1846), pp. 73–8 and pp. 89–94.)

Both Dujardin and Purkinje suggested that the internal fluid protoplasm might be the basic material of life, but it remained for the German cytologist Max Schultze to carry that suggestion into a fully developed theory – the protoplasm theory. In a paper of 1861 directed at clarifying the nature of a cell, Schultze acknowledged that a cell had been defined as a structure with 'membrane, nucleus, and contents', but that in fact only the nucleus and protoplasm appeared as universally basic. Thus 'A cell is a lump of protoplasm inside of which lies a nucleus'.[3] The membrane or cell wall separates the cell contents from the external environment but is not, in fact, really necessary since the unique protoplasmic substance is kept distinct from the surrounding material simply by the fact that it does not mix with water. He pointed out, in particular, that cells which are undergoing division have no membranes. For Schultze, the crucial internal contents do not consist of a simple watery fluid but rather of a thick viscous mucous substance, comparable to soft wax. This protoplasmic material is basic to life, while the nucleus plays an as yet unknown role. Though he worked with a variety of animals himself, Schultze also cited work on plants to demonstrate the uniform protoplasmic basis of all living material in protoplasm.

By 1861, the cell had acquired a very different consistency and role ascribed to it from the one Hooke had suggested nearly two centuries earlier. Thomas Henry Huxley's popular essay of 1868 suggesting that protoplasm was the 'physical basis of life' brought the protoplasmic view to wide attention ('On the

Physical Basis of Life', *The Fortnightly Review* 5, (1869), pp. 129–45) and stimulated further discussion. What was the relative importance of nucleus and protoplasm, and in what sense were the cells the *units* of life if protoplasm was the *stuff* of life? The different lines of research, with respective emphases on plants or animals, or on adult or dividing embryonic cells, for example, gave rise to different views of the cells and their importance. Generally, those stressing the central importance of protoplasm de-emphasised the significance of cellular units and of what has historically been called 'the cell theory' which an alternative tradition stressed. It is the latter tradition which provided the strongest basis for progress in interpreting the cellular role in development and which must remain central for historians concerned with both cells and development.

2. CELL THEORY AND CELLULAR DEVELOPMENT

At the same time as the theory of cell substance was evolving, in the mid-nineteenth century, a very different theory of how cells come into existence was also emerging. The German botanist Jakob Mathias Schleiden and the zoologist Theodor Schwann collaborated to present what has come to be labelled as *the* cell theory. Their theory depended very directly on their definition of how cells come into existence as part of their life cycle and it differed from the protoplasm theory in emphasising the essential role of the cell wall for defining this basic unit of life.

Schleiden was one of those young biologists of the early nineteenth century who could not accept the then traditional preformationist interpretation of the origin of organic form.[4] Preformationists of the previous century had answered the age-old question: 'how does an individual come to have his particular differentiated form?' with the answer: 'from pre-existing form'. An individual organism inherits its form from its parent. Logically, therefore, an individual cell would also inherit its form from earlier cells. But Schleiden and others, such as the German embryologist Karl Ernst von Baer, had begun to reject such a preformationist interpretation and to turn instead to epigenesis. (See art. 33.) An epigenetic position holds that form emerges anew, shaped by the interaction of living internal material and its external environment. As an epigenesist, then, Schleiden wanted cells to emerge anew in each generation. He maintained that those newly-arising material cells serve as the fundamental units of both organic structure and organic function for all of organic nature.[5] Cells are the basic units of life. Schleiden and his collaborator Schwann further insisted that all cells in both plants and animals originate according to the same general set of procedures; all cells must therefore be fundamentally the same sorts of things. Unity of nature reigned, as it did for most early-nineteenth-century German naturalists.

Schleiden's theory of free cell formation held that the following process occurs for plants: inside the contents of a cell a granular substance arises; by accumulating surrounding material, this gives rise to a nucleus; as the nucleus grows a cell forms and a surrounding membrane appears to set it off as a new cell. Schleiden maintained that this process occurs as an 'altogether absolute law'. The resulting cell consists almost incidentally of those internal contents labelled by others as protoplasm, but also necessarily includes a nucleus and cell wall.

Stimulated by his discussions in Berlin with Schleiden, Schwann further developed the 'Schleiden-Schwann cell theory' with his animal investigations.[6] He suggested that, beginning with a structureless substance or 'cytoblastema', a dark granule arises, which in turn gives rise to a nucleus. Then layers of substance accumulate around this core to produce a full cell. For Schwann, this process takes place in material surrounding, rather than inside, the old cells, so that in this respect, he differed from Schleiden. For both, nonetheless, the new cells are really new and not simply inherited or pre-existent in any sense. They both maintained that cell formation strictly follows the inorganic and hence materialistic process of crystallisation. Then once formed, the cells serve as structural and functional units for living organisms.

Published together and translated in 1847, the claims of Schleiden and Schwann became the basis for a 'cell theory', which held cells to be the fundamental organic units common to all living beings and as developed by 'free formation' out of formless cytoblastemic substance in the same basic way. Some challenged the exact definition of the cell – whether it requires an enclosing membrane or wall to define it, for example. Others questioned the mode of cell origin – whether always *de novo* rather than from pre-existing cellular material in particular. Work on plants and animals also diverged as researchers questioned the respective natures of plant and animal tissues. Yet most researchers had nonetheless begun to accept some version of cell theory by the mid-nineteenth century. The problem remained of sorting out the details and of elaborating the extent to which cells function as *the* fundamental units of life and living processes. In particular, Jacob Henle and Albert von Kölliker adapted the theory into classic full discussion within anatomy and histology, but cell theory as a basis for development took longer to elaborate. Maintaining a focus on cells, the German zoologist Robert Remak and the pathologist Rudolf Virchow moved towards a different and eventually more widely acceptable interpretation of cell theory, which proved more useful for embryology.

In 1855 Remak published the results of his extended study of freshly laid frogs' eggs and concluded that the cells in his embryos developed in a different manner from the one that Schleiden had described for adult plant cells. In citing the substantiating support of other researchers' results as well as his own earlier work, Remak endorsed an endogenous theory of cell formation, whereby cells form only from material internal to other cells. Indeed, all cellular development begins with the fertilisation of the egg cell, while subsequent cell cleavages result from a series of divisions directed by the nucleus (*Untersuchungen über die Entwicklung der Wirbelthiere* (1850–55)).

Also in an essay of 1855 and with much more detail in his classic work *Die Cellularpathologie* (1858), Virchow agreed with Remak and other cytologists who had begun to question free formation, asserting that all cells arise only from other cells: 'Omnis cellula a cellula'. Cells do not crystallise in any intercellular cytoblastema, and since cells require both a nucleus and membrane, they must begin as more than tiny material nucleus-producing granules. Life is continuous as one cell gives rise to another, one generation to another. The complex and responsive cellular material is not only the basic *structural* unit of living material, it can also be the basic unit of *life*.

Virchow and others had come to the conclusion that cells somehow divide. Rather than new cells crystallising in a strictly materialistic manner around a granular core, Virchow saw the existing cellular material accumulate new material and grow larger, eventually reaching a point at which it divides. According to this vitalistic interpretation, living material does not emerge from non-living material. In fact, the history of the cell theory in the nineteenth century became closely tied with arguments about materialism vs. vitalism. According to Ackerknecht's (1953) interpretation, Virchow's particular interpretation of cell theory reflected his political vision of the role of individuals within the state.

Not everyone who accepted the doctrine that cells arise only from other cells also agreed with Virchow's politics or his form of vitalism. But continuity of cellular, living material made the epigenesist's task easier. If cells provide continuity from one generation to the next, then the epigenesist need not explain the production of form from completely homogeneous matter. Instead, he may assume the existence from the beginning of something which is already living, inherited from the past. As John Farley has pointed out, 'the re-emergence of sex' and sexual reproduction as a driving biological problem in the 1870s, accompanied by improvements in microscopic and cytological techniques and hardware, served to refocus attention on the cells – notably on the egg and sperm or ovule and pollen cells – and their roles in development.

What resulted, as researchers embraced Virchow's view of cell formation and substantiated it with observations resulting from improved microscopic techniques, was a move towards emphasis on cell division. As it stood at mid-century, the cell theory depended on an interpretation of how cells develop, but did not provide significant clarification of how individual organisms develop and become differentiated. If each cell grows by accretion of material, then the question remains of how cells mutate, and in such a way that a whole organism is created. What guides development?

Pursuing epigenetic interpretations of development, researchers began to accept that cell division may be the key to development of individual organisms and hence the key to what differentiates life from non-life, namely, the ability to reproduce successive generations of individuals. By the 1870s, enthusiasm for the materialistic Schleiden/Schwann interpretation of cellular development and for protoplasm ideas had faded. Research had begun to enter a new stage, exploring the importance of cell division for development. This change in problems and approaches, with attendant shifts in meanings of words and in emphases, creates pitfalls for unwary historians who cast backwards for the roots of today's ideas. Unfortunately, biologists who have written casually about the history of cell theory have also fallen into that trap and have made the picture seem rather clearer than it was. It is important to recall that 'cells' do not even refer to the same thing as we move from the seventeenth to the nineteenth century, for example.

Out of the proliferation of studies in the 1870s, two very different lines of research emerged which need to be examined as separate traditions. One, growing out of the cytological tradition, carefully examined the structure of the cell. Using histological techniques for fixing, staining, preserving and cutting cells, the cytologists began to be able to look more deeply and to discern fine differences between cells. The nucleus attracted the first and most concentrated attention, but gradually other cellular parts also attracted interest. And with their discovery, researchers began to ask also what the cellular parts were for.

A second line of research took a wider look. Instead of focusing down into smaller and smaller parts, this group asked how the cells fit within the whole organism. Of particular interest for our purposes, embryologists began to see that distinctions between different cells might begin to explain established facts of heredity and evolution, since an individual organism begins as a single egg cell which is the product of an evolutionary past and of inheritance from its parent. That individual egg cell is also the beginning of a new individual and hence must contain whatever is needed to pattern that individual. This second group of researchers began to examine more closely what happens in the course of cell division: what, in fact, happens as the one original egg cell divides? Different groups focused respectively on the nucleus or on the whole cell.

3. CELL THEORY AND DEVELOPMENT: INTO THE NUCLEUS

The cell nucleus seems first to have attracted the serious attention of British botanist Robert Brown. In 1831 he determined that the nucleus is, in fact, an important part of at least living cells and not just an artifact of microscopic observation ('Observations on the Organs and Mode of Fecundation in Orchideae and Asclepiadaea', *Transactions of the Linnaean Society* 16 (1833), pp. 685–742). Brown was the first to label this body the nucleus and to observe systematically that it occurs in a range of types of organisms. Yet he did not develop his observations into a more general theory, nor did he speculate about the significance of that nucleus. In time, others did, as they also extended his sketchy suggestions concerning fertilisation as a result of kinetic interaction of ovule and pollen in plants.

In fact, work on fertilisation highlighted the first line of research into cell theory and development.[7] Advances in microscopic techniques such as improved sectioning, fixing, and staining as well as the advent of the oil immersion lens, allowed a closer look at cell contents. Observers could now distinguish more than just a general nucleus, protoplasm and membrane. Thus, the 1870s and 1880s brought a flurry of new studies, of which those by the Belgian Edouard van Beneden, the Germans Walther Flemming and Oscar Hertwig, the Polish/German Eduard Strasburger and the Frenchman Hermann Fol were particularly important. Their technical disagreements, aggravated by imperfect microscopic evidence, make it more difficult – and also particularly valuable – for historians to clarify the threads of thought during this time.

Each of these men declared that the egg and sperm cell – for by then fertilisation was generally agreed to involve the union of those two cells – contain a distinct nucleus. Therefore, the nucleus does not come into being simply for the purposes of cell division and then disappear, as some believed, but maintains its individuality across generations. And yet, Fol, at least, denied that the structure of the nucleus has any purity or continuity and that the nucleus could play any significant role in heredity. However, as he continued work through the 1880s, Fol began to see the centrosomes as permanent structures, with each parent cell contributing two centrosomes or one which divided soon after fertilisation. Centrosomes might play a role in heredity. Hertwig disagreed, maintaining that the nucleus itself and its components have continuity but that centrosomes do not. Furthermore, for both Hertwig and Strasburger, the nucleus served as the bearer of heredity while for Fol it did not. When Hertwig, Strasburger and others actually saw the nucleus divide during cell division, that evidence considerably strengthened their case for a nuclear role in heredity and subsequent development.[8]

If the cell, and particularly the nuclear part of the cell, really exists as an identifiable and continuous entity, and if fertilisation actually involves the joining of a nucleus from each of two parents, then the nuclei must play a basic role in heredity. But how? And how does the stability between generations, assumed to be brought by heredity then translate itself into the differentiation of individual development? For this group of researchers, inquiry began to focus on details of the process of nuclear division.

The occurrence of mitotic nuclear division (or mitosis) had been recognised as early as 1873. Many researchers immediately attacked the subject and determined that nuclear division is basic to cell division. Strasburger insisted that nuclear division occurs transversely, that is, across the chromosome, dividing it into two separate pieces of different materials. In contrast, van Beneden and Flemming insisted on longitudinal division. Van Beneden observed the movement of chromosomes as they moved during cell division. Then Flemming provided a striking set of studies demonstrating the stages of mitotic division, which he presented in three papers published from 1879 to 1881. He believed that this indirect division of what he called chromatin (the stainable nuclear material, which Wilhelm Waldeyer labelled as chromosomes in 1888) provided the basis for the process of cell division in all forms of cells. By the 1880s a group of researchers had decided that the nucleus plays a role, if not *the* critical role, in cell division generally and thus in the development of individuals. Flemming's *Zellsubstanz, Kern und Zelltheilung* (1882) provides an excellent review of work prior to that time.

Furthermore, by the late 1880s it began to seem as though the nucleus also plays a – or the – critical role in moving from one generation to the next. Van Beneden and Theodor Boveri from 1887–8 and Hertwig in 1890 had each clearly observed that something unique happens during the production of germ cells.[9] During this process of maturation division when one cell gives rise to the ripe germ cells, each chromosone divides once while each cell divides twice. Thus, each ripe germ has only half the original full complement of chromosomes. The chromosomes must play some important role in heredity to result in this complex process, but what? Earlier, equally careful cytologists such as Strasburger had insisted on transverse division of chromosomes and did not see an important difference between germ cell and adult cell production (or mitosis and what was later called meiosis). Only gradually during the 1880s and 1890s did researchers work out details of the structural and chemical constitution of the chromosomes and of the nucleus. And only after 1900 did theories begin to emerge, explaining the chromosomal role in heredity. (See art. 33, sect. 6.) The work of the British researchers John Bretland Farmer and John E. S. Moore first explicitly stated what happens in reduction division and the workings of the 'maiotic phase'. Their classic paper 'On the Maiotic Phase (Reduction Division) in Animals and Plants' (*Quarterly Journal of Microscopical Science* 48 (1904), pp. 487–569) also provides a useful survey of material to date.

Yet such detailed researches into the nucleus and nuclear division focused more and more narrowly on the fine structure and parts of the cell. This concentration drew attention away from development, partly because no one saw how nuclear change translated into epigenetic developmental change. By the 1890s, it was the second line of research, looking at whole cells, that still concentrated on cell theory and on development.

4. CELLS AND DEVELOPMENT:
THE CELL'S ROLE IN DEVELOPMENT

Cell theory, as American cytologist Edmund Beecher Wilson wrote in his classic *The Cell in Development and Inheritance* (New York, 1896), was the second great generalisation of biology in addition to evolution theory. He realised that only recently had the two ideas begun to converge in a way that promised major progress for biology. In addition to those researchers concentrating on applying new microscopic techniques to observe more clearly the fine structure of intracellular material, others such as Wilson focused on the cell as a whole or on the organism as a whole. A tradition emerged, directed at showing how the different cells resulting from division of the egg give rise to different parts of the body. The researchers participating in this tradition were concerned with embryology (and evolution) rather than with the earlier stage of fertilisation or with nuclear change. They included especially a group of Germans and a group of Americans.

In the 1870s, embryologists had concentrated on the collections of cells making up germ layers rather than on particular cells. For one thing, it was simply too hard to see individual cells and what they did during development. Furthermore, evolutionary theory and Ernst Haeckel's particular interpretations of what happens suggested that the broader-reaching germ layers rather than individual localised cells held significance for understanding evolution and genealogical relationships. How could the peculiarities of one individual cell be the product of evolution, selectionists would have wondered?

Stimulated by improved research techniques, embryologists began to ask what happens to individual cells. Given that the egg and sperm and their union are all cells, perhaps careful detailing of what happens to cells in development could be worthwhile. A group of German physiologists and zoologists began to study *Entwickelungsmechanik* or *Entwickelungsphysiologie*. Alongside the work of researchers including Wilhelm His, Eduard Pflüger, Gustav Born and Hans Driesch, Wilhelm Roux devised an elaborate theory of the action of blastomeres, cleavage and then of cells and cellular parts and their roles in development.

Roux and other developmental researchers studied the factors which cause the egg cell to divide and how this division occurs. They investigated the effects on development of conditions such as experimentally-altered gravitational field, artificial light source, altered nutrients and chemical manipulations. With manipulative experimental studies, the researchers could begin to establish that not only does the individual organism respond to external conditions but it also exhibits a great deal of internal control over its development and differentiation. Eventually, Roux constructed a theory of mosaic development, according to which each cell division separates off cellular material which then, because of its constituent material, develops in a unique and appropriate way.

In particular, Roux performed a famous experiment in which he used a hot needle to kill one of the two cells resulting from the first cell division of a frog's egg, as discussed in his summary work *Die Entwickelungsmechanik der Organismen* (1890). He left the dead material but it did not grow, so he considered that the cell had been functionally eliminated. The other cell developed into precisely the half embryo that it would have done under perfectly normal conditions. Therefore, Roux concluded, it must have been something inside the cell itself, part of its own material which directed it, in this case, to develop as a half embryo. He presumed that the same constituent would also direct a normal cell product to develop in its appropriate manner. Thus, cells are parts of organisms but develop largely independently, according to their own internal instructions. Those instructions, he decided, came from the nucleus and specifically from the chromosomes.

For Roux, the chromosome is a complex mixture of different chromatin granules, which represent different qualities. These align themselves in preparation for cell division and then divide. Division may occur quantitatively, so that the original granules reproduce and then separate, with all qualities represented in each of the two daughter cells. Division may also occur qualitatively, so that the two daughter cells end up with sub-sets of the original materials and are thereby differentiated. The latter process occurs during embryonic development. By this process, each nucleus receives its own unique set of chromatin, and the course of development involves a successive separating-out of original pieces into the various cells. Because it contains its own chromatin qualities, each cell is capable of self-differentiation and experiences some autonomy even while it is part of the whole, complex organism.

In *Das Keimplasm* (1892), August Weismann developed a similar theory, carrying much further the idea that separate bits of chromatin represent different qualities. He constructed an elaborate hierarchy of cellular parts with biophores as the basic units. These are then aggregated progressively into determinants, ids, and idants, the latter of which finally represent the visible chromosomes. The complex chromosome structure is inherited from one generation to the next because the cells of the germ plasm retain the full complement of sub-units, while body cells receive only part and become differentiated accordingly. Mitosis serves to distribute the smallest differentiated bits of chromatin to the different cells and thus becomes the mechanism for effecting individual development as well as intergenerational heredity. Eventually, each cell will have only one kind of determinant in it, which will give it its specific character.

For both Roux and Weismann, whose ideas came to be labelled the Roux-Weismann theory in the mid-1890s, the cell remained basic. Chromatin carries the material of heredity, but it is the division into separate cells that brings development. Cell theory was once again a basic assumption for these biologists, but with a very different emphasis. Roux and Weismann had explained a mechanism by which individual cells become differentiated and hence by which complex organisms grow, but many others did not find this explanation satisfactory. The resulting discussions provide valuable material for historians examining cells and development.

Hertwig and others in Germany rejected the Roux-Weismann interpretation of development, saying that it really explained nothing. For Hertwig, Weismannism represented a hopeless sort of preformationism which throws everything back on to the nucleus and chromatin rather than on to preformed little beings, but which is preformationism nonetheless (*The Biological Problem of Today* (1894)). Questions of cells and development therefore became tangled with traditional debates about whether epigenesis or preformation better explains development. A further question arose as to whether perhaps cell theory itself had been overtaken. Perhaps the cell is not the smallest basic unit of life after all. Roux and Weismann expanded discussion about the role of cells in development and about their status as the smallest basic functional, structural and even developmental units of life, but others disagreed.

Reactions became particularly lively among American biologists around the turn of this century, especially among researchers who gathered at the Marine Biological Laboratory (MBL) in Woods Hole, Massachusetts, each summer. The first MBL director, Charles Otis Whitman, directly questioned the dominance of the 'cell standpoint' in his paper 'The Inadequacy of the Cell Theory of Development', (*Biological Lectures* 1893 (1894), pp. 105–24). In particular, he regarded the cell theory of development as inadequate. The whole individual organism directs development, he insisted, for the individual has an organisation that the study of cells alone cannot explain. Whitman endorsed Huxley's view that cells are like seashells. They are left behind by the tide and map the tide's effects, but the seashells themselves do not represent or record the tidal process of change, which is ultimately the interesting phenomenon. Organisation of an individual, then, does not result simply from cell division but instead precedes and directs cell division. Whitman rejected the full implications of the Roux-Weismann theory of independent development of individual cells.

And yet he certainly did not claim that cells have no importance. In fact, Whitman inaugurated a series of cell lineage studies during the 1890s by his students and colleagues at the MBL and at the University of Chicago. These studies were designed precisely to illustrate the patterns of cellular development and the way in which the original egg takes on differentiation. Cell lineage studies consisted of using exacting histological and microscopic techniques to trace what happens to the cell and its nuclear and cytoplasmic parts as the cell divides. What happens inside, and what is the result as the cell products each begin to assume their own individualities as well? Researchers including Whitman, Wilson, Edwin Grant Conklin and a host of others carried out these detailed studies on a variety of organisms in order to assess similarities and differences which might reveal ancestral evolutionary relationships.[10] They also sought to evaluate the extent to which the original egg cell is already differentiated by determining how regular or 'determinate' the cleavage process and products are from one individual to another. If every organism of the same type divides in the same way, and if each cell product gives rise to the same differentiated adult parts as that same cell product in other organisms, then individual development must somehow be strongly determined by the structure or content of the egg cell. If, however, there is considerable variation and flexibility, then the egg is not strictly determined, and environmental factors must direct development. Cell lineage study, in fact, focuses on cells and cell fates and reveals a complex interaction of external and internal directive factors operating on development.

Whitman insisted that it was the whole functioning organism which ultimately directs differentiation. Cell boundaries simply do not follow predetermined and invisible lines in the egg. Nor does cell division respond blindly to internal nuclear directions. Instead, cells respond, following the laws of a sort of organic physics and chemistry, to the needs of the whole, which in turn result from the long-term action of evolutionary selection. Conklin agreed, priding himself on his being 'a friend of the egg' as a whole. While some emphasised the role of either nucleus or cytoplasm in development, Conklin and others joined Whitman in stressing the significant role of both and of the integrated organism. For example, Charles Manning Child stressed that 'It is the organism – the individual, which is the unit and not the cell'.[11]

Yet other American researchers, including E. B. Wilson who also worked closely with Whitman at the MBL, did regard the cell as basic. One could study the cell and its role in directing development and inheritance to productive effect because each cell does have significant individuality, even if co-ordinated with other cells within a more complex organism. As Wilson interpreted the revised cell theory of 1896, it held that higher life forms, whether animal or plant, consist of structural units known as cells. Out of these cells arise tissues and the other body parts. Cells are not hollow, as Hooke's choice of words would suggest, but are filled with protoplasm. The cell and its protoplasm serve as the 'physical basis of life'. Cells are all the basic, elementary units of both organic structure and function, even though they appear very diverse. In higher organisms, according to Wilson, as cells become more specialised, they enter a 'physiological division of labor'. Study of the cells and their actions must provide a basis for all study of life, Wilson felt, for:

Each bodily function, and even the life of the organism as a whole, may thus in one sense be regarded as a resultant arising through the integration of a vast number of cell-activities; and it cannot be adequately investigated without the study of the individual cell-activities that lie at its root.[12]

The result of the co-existence of these alternative interpretations and emphases on the cell's importance even at the same summer laboratory resulted in heated discussion. This discussion, as it found expression in published lectures and papers, stimulated further attention to the cell.

By 1900, the cell was generally accepted as a legitimate subject of study in its own right. And yet at least for this group of researchers, understanding of cell theory had changed. The cell could still be the most common, fundamental unit of life, but researchers did not have to take the cell as the proper unit for *all* analysis. Cells are not completely independent and do not either develop or live alone – at least most cells from multicellular organisms do not. Cell theory and its role in interpreting development had gained considerable complexity by 1900, but this complexity complemented and refined rather than undercut the value of older cell theory. It is the historian's task to sort out the different traditions, and to assess the influence of new techniques and questions in modifying early observations, in order to explain the move from early observations of cellular structures to the cell theory and on into the developmental examinations of the late nineteenth century. So far, only parts of the story have been told, and too often from a retrospective perspective, unquestioningly seeking past equivalents of modern cells and missing such important questions as how cell theory influenced theories of development.

5. CELL THEORY IN THE TWENTIETH CENTURY

In this century, researchers have recognised that the most serious weakness of the cell theory is its inability in itself to explain cell-to-cell interaction or that organisation of many cells which became Whitman's stumbling-block. By mid-century, Hans Spemann and others did, however, begin to attack such interactions in various ways. Considerable recent work, especially since the Second World War, has been directed at dealing with this weakness. Studies of exchanges at cell junctions and across cell membranes have begun to show the ways in which cells join together into functional multi-cellular units. Advances in biochemistry and molecular biology, as well as the advent of observation techniques and equipment such as electron microscopes which allow ever more detailed resolution, have led the way in this work.[13]

Since the Swiss physiological chemist Johann Friedrich Miescher theorised in 1869 that nuclei of cells may all consist of a characteristic substance (which he went on to identify as 'nuclein', later called nucleoprotein), biochemists have provided increasingly detailed information about the cell. While the researchers discussed above concentrated on the structural elements: on the nucleus or the cytoplasm or the whole cell and its relation to other cells, a few other researchers analysed what substance is *in* the cell. In the twentieth century, it has gradually become clear that cells of different types exhibit remarkable consistency in their cell substances. (See art. 32, sect. 5.) DNA material is remarkably uniform throughout all living cells, and so is much of the rest of the cellular material. This discovery has reinforced the view of the cell as the basis of all life. It has also returned biologists to the sorts of questions about evolution and the relationships among cells that earlier cell lineage researchers were asking.

If all cells contain much the same substance, as well as exhibiting similar structural elements, then perhaps the cell is the ancestral unit of life. Perhaps a simple cell actually came first, rather than a complex multicellular and even multilayered ancestral organism such as Ernst Haeckel and most other nineteenth-century naturalists had envisioned. Such a hypothesis certainly satisfies the often-repeated call for simplicity in science.

Unicellular organisms presumably preceded multicellular organisms, perhaps (as it seems recently) with the boundary having been crossed several times. Studying cells and their similarities and subtle differences among different types of cells or between eukaryotes and prokaryotes, can provide a key to evolutionary or phylogenetic development, as Margulis's recent investigation into *The Origin of Eukaryotic Cells* has shown (1970). The twentieth century has thus added a new layer of significance to the original cell theory. Evolutionary study has not replaced embryology or the study of cell division or the biochemistry of cells certainly, but has complemented it. The cell theory – as the statement that all life consists of basic cellular units, which arise only from other cells – has gained new dimensions and new confirmation.

NOTES

1. Selections of this and a number of the other works mentioned in this article are translated in Thomas S. Hall (ed.), *A source book in animal biology* (Cambridge, 1951).
2. Felix Dujardin, 'Sur les prétendus estomacs des animalcules infusoires et sur une substance appelée Sarcode', *Annales des sciences naturelles; zoologie*, 4 (1835), 343–77; quotation from Hall, p. 438.
3. Max Schultze, 'Über Muskelkörperchen und das, was man eine Zelle zu nennen habe', *Müller's Archiv für Anatomie, Physiologie und wissenschaftliche Medecin* (1861), 1–27; Hall excerpts, pp. 449–55, quotation Hall, p. 451.
4. Ernst Mayr, *The growth of biological thought* (Cambridge, Mass., 1982), p. 655. On Schleiden, see Marcel Florkin, *Naissance et déviation de la théorie cellulaire dans l'œuvre de Theodore Schwann* (Paris, 1960).
5. Matthias Jakob Schleiden, 'Beiträge zur Phytogenesis', *Müller's Archiv* (1838), 137–76; translated as 'Contributions to Phytogenesis', with Theodor Schwann's *Microscopical researches into the accordance in the structure and growth of animals and plants* by Henry Smith (London, 1847), pp. 231–68; Schleiden, *Grundzüge der wissenschaftliche Botanik* (Leipzig, 1842, 1843), translated

by Edwin Lankester as *Principles of scientific botany* (London, 1849), and reissued with introduction by Jacob Lorch (New York, 1969), pp. ix–xxxiv.

6. Theodore Schwann, *Mikroscopische Untersuchungen über die Übereinstimmung in der Struktur und dem Wachstum der Tiere und Pflanzen* (Berlin, 1839), translated by Henry Smith. As Frederick Churchill has pointed out, 'Rudolf Virchow and the pathologist's criteria for the inheritance of acquired characteristics', *Journal of the history of medicine and allied sciences*, 31 (1976), 117–48, p. 124, Schwann's ideas about cells first appeared in a series of letters.

7. For an early summary discussion of such work see John Gray McKendrick, 'On the modern cell theory and the phenomena of fecundation', *Proceedings of the Royal Philosophical Society of Glasgow*, 19 (1887–8), 71–125.

8. Hermann Fol, 'Le Quadrille des Centres. Un épisode nouveau dans l'histoire de la fécondation', *Archives des sciences physiques et naturelles*, 25 (1891), 393–420; Oscar Hertwig, *Altere und neuere Entwicklungs-theorieen* (Berlin, 1892); Eduard Strasburger, *Zellbildung und Zellteilung* (Jena: 1875, 3rd edition, 1880); Strasburger, 'Die Controversen der indirekten Zelltheilung', *Archiv für mikroscopische Anatomie*, 23 (1884), 246–304. The details of chromosomal and related division were explored by many researchers in the late nineteenth century, as discussed by Gloria Robinson, *A Prelude to genetics: theories of a material substance of heredity* (Lawrence, Kansas, 1979).

9. Eduard van Beneden, 'Recherches sur la maturation de l'œuf et la fécondation', *Archives de biologie*, 4 (1883), 265–640; Hall excerpts, pp. 456–58; van Beneden, 'Nouvelles recherches sur la fécondation et la division mitosique chez l'Ascaride mégélocéphale', *Bulletin de l'Academie Royale des Sciences, des Letters et des Beaux-Arts de Belgique*, 14 (1887), 215–95; Theodor Boveri, *Zellenstudien* (Jena, vol. 1 1887, vol. 2 1888, vol. 3 1890, vol. 4 1900); Oscar Hertwig, 'Experimentelle Studien am tierischen Ei vor, während und nach der Befruchtung', *Jenaische Zeitschrift*, 24 (1890), 268–313. Other related studies proliferated as well, including especially important contributions to the study of cell division and heredity by Richard Hertwig and Theodor Boveri and work on reduction division by August Weismann.

10. Reports of the cell lineage work appeared in a numbr of articles in the *Journal of morphology* which Whitman edited and in the MBL's *Biological lectures* through the 1890s. Jane Maienschein, 'Cell lineage, ancestral reminiscence, and the biogenetic law', *Journal of the history of biology*, 11 (1978), 129–58 discusses the work.

11. Charles Manning Child, 'The significance of the spiral type of cleavage and its relation to the process of differentiation', MBL's *Biological lectures* 1899 (1900), 231–66, quotation p. 265.

12. Wilson, *The cell*, pp. 4–6, quotation p. 6.

13. For introductions to some of this work: C. H. Waddington, *Biological organisation. Cellular and sub-cellular* (New York, 1959) presents results of a working discussion-oriented symposium of 1957. Jean Brachet and Alfred E. Mirsky's *The cell* (New York, 1959) presents six impressive volumes of papers summarising the conclusions about methods and problems (vol. I), cell components (vol. II), meiosis and mitosis (vol. III), specialised cells (vol. IV and V), and a supplement (vol. VI). Since then there has been an explosion of books, journals, textbooks and even popular books devoted to study of the cell and cell theory.

FURTHER READING

Erwin Ackerknecht, *Rudolf Virchow. Doctor, statesman, anthropologist* (Madison, 1953).

John R. Baker, 'The cell-theory: A restatement, history, and critique', *Quarterly review of microscopical science*, 89 (1948), 103–25; 90 (1949), 87–108; 93 (1952), 157–90; 94 (1953), 407–40; 96 (1955), 449–81.

Jean Brachet and Alfred E. Mirsky (eds.), *The cell* (New York, 1959), 6 vols.

William Coleman, *Biology in the nineteenth century* (Cambridge, 1977), chaps. 2 and 3.

—— 'Cell, nucleus, and inheritance: an historical study', *Proceedings of the American philosophical society*, 109 (1965), 124–58.

John Farley, *Gametes and spores* (Baltimore, 1982), especially Chap. 6.

Gerald L. Geison, 'The protoplasmic theory of life and the vitalist-mechanist debate', *Isis*, 60 (1969), 273–92.

Thomas S. Hall, *Ideas of life and matter* (Chicago, 1969), vol. II, pp. 121–304 on 'Tissue, cell and molecule, 1800–1860'.

Arthur Hughes, *A history of cytology* (London, 1959).

Julius Sachs, *History of botany* (Oxford, 1890).

Edmund Beecher Wilson, *The cell in development and inheritance* (New York, 1896, 2nd ed. 1900).

24

ORIGINS AND SPECIES BEFORE AND AFTER DARWIN

M. J. S. HODGE

1. AN ALTERNATIVE TO THE DOMINANT HISTORIOGRAPHIC TRADITION

Most languages distinguish different kinds of things and most peoples have theories about the origins of things, including the origins of animal and plant kinds, their diverse designs for living and diverse degrees of life, from the highest to the lowest. Diversity in designs and degrees has been an explicit preoccupation throughout the long run of Western thought. This preoccupation has always concerned the nature and fate of our own species, and so the understanding of the soul, morality and polity. The Jewish account of the Creation includes the forming and the falling of the first humans, a narrative later elaborated into the Christian doctrine of original sin. Among the Greek philosophers, Aristotle taught that any species is distinguished by the purposes embodied in its natural actions; and this teleology of specific natures provided foundations for his politics, his views on man as a political animal, no less than for his interpretation of plant reproduction.

Today, as for over a century now, such issues are always likely to be subsumed under two catchwords: evolution and Darwin. For even people who find neither congenial are conditioned in their belief and attitudes by both. Whenever a culture engages modern Western science, there to be confronted is evolution: the proposal that extant species, including man, have arisen by the modification of earlier ones, in an extremely long process that began with a few simple forms of life – a proposal first made scientifically respectable, and also more generally notorious, by Charles Darwin (1809–82) in his book *On the Origin of Species* (1859).

Ever since the great debates of the 1860s, and initially in efforts to win them

374

for Darwin, people have been rewriting the history of Western thought as the history of *evolution*: the rise of *evolution*, as an idea or world-view or whatever, and its eventual triumph, with Darwin, over its natural contrary, *creation* or *stasis* or some combination of both, *static creationism*, say. Surprisingly, that historiographic tradition continues to dominate even current specialist writing. The present article will be more easily understood if it is explained straightaway how it seeks to show that at least one alternative to that tradition is possible.

The trouble with all *evolution* historiographies is that they project back into earlier centuries the issues and distinctions, the conflicts and the alliances, that were decisive for the great debates of the 1860s. One way to avoid this fault is to adopt an *origins* and *species* historiography instead. This has at least three advantages. Firstly, we are working with words and therefore issues that the people saw themselves as working with at the time, any time at least since the middle of the last millenium BC. Secondly, we can operate not with a binary scheme of contrary options, but with as many differences as we find reason to recognise among the positions that have been held on questions about origins and species. Thirdly, we can interpret any steps taken away from earlier positions as they were taken, that is as deliberate departures from what was previously held, rather than as so many unknowing steps towards the options, evolutionary or otherwise, that will later be contested in the wake of Darwin's work.

These three points are to be kept especially in mind as we turn to Medieval Christian attempts to integrate Greek and Hebrew intellectual legacies concerning questions of origins and species. Consideration of such attempts is indispensable for any understanding of how Western scientific thought on these questions has developed in the four centuries since the Renaissance.

Plato's theory of Forms or Ideas was a theory both of origins, *archai*, and of species, *eide, gene*. Moreover, it provided for objective moral and political values, as well as for the foundations for the mythic cosmogony of his dialogue, *Timaeus*. For not only does the Form Justice constitute a standard for judging acts in so far as they are just, the Forms of natural kinds – Fire, Horse, Man and so on – were the recipes and standards looked to by the Craftsman when he made an orderly cosmos by imposing on a chaos the order eternally available in the Forms. Plato's pupil Aristotle also took forms to be *archai*. But he rejected Plato's view that forms can exist separately from formed individuals; Horse and Man as forms are not, he held, separable from individual horses or men; and he denies that the cosmos ever had a beginning in time. The form of an individual has an origin in the generation of the individual from its parents, but man or horse as species are perpetuated, not originated thereby. There is then, for Aristotle, a cyclic perpetuation of forms, in species life cycles, among animals and plants, matching the endless, everlasting cycling of the divine, unchanging heavenly bodies, the planets and stars. Forms, as species, are *archai* of formed individuals, and are origins so original as to have, themselves, no origins.

By contrast, for the Greek atomists, as represented most fully in the Roman Lucretius's long poem *De Rerum Natura*, species are in no sense *archai*. For the atomists divided and distributed Being not into so many distinct Forms, as did Plato, but into myriad uncuttable chips of matter, the atoms. For that is all there is: material atoms moving mindlessly in the beingless void of space. Species must then be referred to atoms, as the *archai* for everything. Lucretius finds in the motions and shapes of atoms his explanation for why there are the species of animals and plants there are. When the earth was young and hotter than now, all sorts of permutations of animal and plant parts were formed on the earth's surface. Only some, however, could survive and reproduce to continue their lives in stable species, and it is those that have lived ever since.

Any Medieval Christian found many themes affirmed in the Biblical account of God's making and populating the heavens and the earth, the account set forth in the first thirty-five verses of the book of Genesis. God is supreme and worked without assistance; the world is a good work; plants and animals have been fitted to life on land and in the seas, and following their first appearance have perpetuated their species under God's command to increase and multiply; man is unique in being made in God's image; the Sabbath is a special day of rest; the work of making the heavens, earth, plants, animals and men was completed then and God has done no comparable work since.

As a representative writer on creation in the thirteenth century, Thomas Aquinas (1225–74) is typical in continuing the preference for the Platonic over the atomist tradition, but he is an innovator in being the first to give a sustained explication of the work of the six days as the creation of an Aristotelian cosmos. Confronting the issue of why a single, simple God could and would create many differing creatures, Aquinas upholds the Platonic tradition in arguing that God can do so, because the singularity and simplicity of his essence is imitable in creatures in many diverse ways existing as so many distinct Ideas in the divine mind; and in arguing that God would do so, because he creates so that his goodness shall be communicated to creatures and represented in them, and because that goodness can only be represented by a multitude of creatures distributed in the scale of perfections, from the lowliest of the corporeal to the highest of the angelic species. The distinction of creatures according to their species must be God's work and not left to any delegated agency, because, Aquinas insists, a craftsman who intends to produce an ordered whole intends all the elements of its order; and the ordered elements that together constitute the order of the universe are the specific natures forming the scale of natures.

For Aquinas, therefore, the doctrine of God as the *arche* without *arche, principium* of all else, is integrated with Plato's view of forms as exemplars of the cosmic Craftsman's ordering work and with Aristotle's view of forms as sempiternally embodied natures. The work of the six days is thus constitutional work for species. In introducing forms into matter, in working initially to instantiate these exemplars, the Divine Ideas, God is giving species their constitutions. Then, once complete with the creation of man, God's working has been administration, sustaining and governing species in accord with their constitutions given them during the six days. No introduction of new forms into matter can come within the administrative course of nature, because such introductions are completed in the constitutional work. Here, therefore, species, as the *naturae* of the *scala naturae*, are the ultimate constituents of the very order of the cosmos. Aquinas, as an Aristotelian, believes that for God to form a cosmos is for Him to distinguish in matter a central, terrestrial realm from a surrounding celestial realm replete with heavenly bodies and angelic souls, and for Him to complete the cosmos by adorning the earth with species of all the animal and plant natures in the full *scala*. Thus, the forming of the earth and its first stocking with life is constitutional work.

Christian writers in the Middle Ages made various selective uses of Greek traditions concerning origins and species, both in making sense of the general teaching in Genesis that God was the ultimate origin of everything and therefore of specific diversity, its degrees and designs; and in making sense of the difference between what was involved in the originating work of the six days and the way the world has run in the four or five thousand years since. Only by keeping these uses of these traditions in mind can we understand the implications, for Western thought about origins and species, of the fundamental shifts in cosmology and natural philosophy that took place in the seventeenth century.

2. ORIGINS AND SPECIES IN THE AGE OF ENLIGHTENMENT

To understand the implications of these shifts in thought, we should start with René Descartes (1596–1650). For, according to Descartes, the earth is not stationary and central in a finite spherical cosmos, but is a planet circling the sun in a boundless material universe whose workings are ultimately the mechanical transactions of a universal matter of a single common essence, transactions conforming to a few universal laws of motion. Descartes's cosmogony can therefore differ fundamentally from Aquinas's, for it can treat the earth's origin within a general theory of planet formation. Any planet has arisen from a swirling vortex of material particles. The individual case of the earth's formation, including the acquisition of its shape, atmosphere, mountains, soil and inhabitants, can be given, then, in a separate narrative. Because Descartes is a mechanical philosopher, the earth's formation need not belong to the original imposing of lawful motion on matter, but can come much later in the subsequent governing of matter in conformity with those laws. The Cartesian geogony was, explicitly, only a hypothetical narration, only a demonstration, as Descartes puts it prudently, of how God, had He so chosen, could have produced the earth and its inhabitants gradually by means of natural, secondary causes; rather than working, as Descartes assures us He really did, a miraculous creation in the Biblical six days.

Thomas Burnet (1635–1715) was the first deliberately to reject this contrast between hypothetical Cartesian narration and sacred Biblical history. The new astronomy, he says, allows answerable questions about terrestrial history to be separated from unanswerable mysteries about the earlier origin of the whole universe. Genesis concerns only this, our earthly world. By referring the events it records to lawful Cartesian matter in motion, a hypothesis can be had as to how a chaos became this habitable world. An early earth, enjoying a perpetual spring thanks to rotation at right angles to its orbit, would provide the warmth and nutrition of a womb. The sun could naturally initiate generations of the first animals and plants in this soil. New species never arise today, but they did once and all at once. Nature's laws are constant, but the conditions natural agencies operated in made them more productive then than nowadays.

Newton's protégé William Whiston (1667–1752) upheld the Newtonian rather than the Cartesian account of matter and motion. But, like Burnet, he assumes that Moses treats only of our planet and its origin from its own chaos. Moses does not say, Whiston notes, what the earth owes to nature and what to miracle. Among the items that Whiston decides are beyond nature's ability, and so due to God's direct, miraculous action, are Adam and Eve, their bodies and souls, and the production of all the animals and planets that were ever to live on the earth. Whiston holds that these were formed minutely encapsulated in the first members of each species, in accord with the new boxes-within-boxes emboîtement theory of pre-existent germs.

Whiston's official Newtonian replacement for Burnet's theory of the earth shows that the eighteenth century inherited from the seventeenth a host of new issues, at once historical and causal, concerning two cosmogonies: the macrocosmogony of the origin of the solar system in general and of the earth in particular, and the microcosmogony of any individual animal or plant as it appears to move from seminal chaos to adult organisation. Many ambitions motivated Georges Buffon (1707–88) to write what he did in the many volumes of the Histoire Naturelle, which began appearing in 1749 and was incomplete still at his death. But one ambition throughout was to uphold Newton's account of matter and motion – and force – while developing natural Newtonian macrocosmogonical and microcosmogonical alternatives to all Divine miracles, or Biblical chronologies, such as Whiston had included in his integration of Moses and emboîtement.

Buffon's alternative to pre-existent boxed germs was his theory of organic

molecules and organic moulds. The molecules are miniscule, universal components of living bodies. The diversity of living species is grounded, therefore, in
the diversity of the ordinary, brute matter with which the organic molecules are
associated. The distinctive combination of organic molecules and brute matter
that forms the body of an organism acts as an internal mould. By internal
mould, Buffon means a constellation of active, penetrating forces, analogous to
gravitational force. Such an internal mould goes to work on incoming nutrients,
which will include more organic molecules, and moulds are stable in that they
make more of themselves.

Organic molecules can differ in their activity and their numerousness. The
organisation of the highest animals is due to many active molecules and their
moulds are the most stable. Within lower grades of life there is less stability,
and so one finds families of species that have diversified from a common stock.
The numerousness and activity of the organic molecules depend in turn upon
heat. Gravity, which is attractive, and heat, which is repulsive in its action, are
the ultimate agents in nature for Buffon. The history of nature's productions
has then to be reconstructed as the history of the diverse effects of gravity and
heat; and, since gravity is constant and never wanes, the changes in the living
world must be referrable to changes in heat. Buffon is resolute in his thermal
determinism. The same degrees of heat, he says, would, other conditions
being the same, always produce the same grades and types of organisation.
Eventually, after conducting experiments on cooling spheres, Buffon is ready
to provide a chronology for the habitability of the earth, and indeed of other
planets. His chronology – which has the earth first cool enough to sustain life
tens, perhaps hundreds, of thousands of years ago – is a direct alternative to all
Scriptural chronologies which it challenges throughout.

The early heat of the nascent earth formed the first organic molecules from
unorganised matter, and these molecules organised themselves into the first
species. Nature was then in her first force and elaborated organic matter with a
greater heat; hence the early, giant, extinct quadrupeds and molluscs that we
find today only as fossil remnants. As Buffon's treatise on the *Epoques de la
Nature* (1779) proceeds, it explains how the first and hottest land was formed in
the northern regions. In the Old World the highly organised products of that
first land were able to migrate into the younger land formed to the South; hence
the grandeur of African fauna. By contrast the mountains of Central America
blocked migration in the New World. The South American fauna is less grand,
because it was formed from organic molecules produced there, when nature
was older and cooler. The llama differs from the giraffe because it is due to a
sparser and more feeble stock of organic molecules. Thus did Buffon find, in
the history of Newtonian heat and gravity, sources for the diversity of the
species that have originated at different times and places on our planet.

The great innovators of the seventeenth century, most obviously Descartes and Newton, to whom Buffon was heir, had seen themselves as replacing once and for all the Aristotelian cosmology. Moreover, in the theory of matter, Newton, especially, had drawn knowingly although not exclusively, on Greek atomism as transmitted by writers such as Gassendi. But it would be a mistake to think that we have with Buffon a simple substitution of the Lucretian heritage for the Aristotelian. The *Epoques de la Nature* is not a rewriting of *De Rerum Natura*. Enlightenment cosmogonists were not reduced to making new choices among old, classical options. There is, however, this element of accord between Buffon and Lucretius: for both, as contrasted with Aristotle, species are not origins in a way that precludes them having origins within the workings of nature.

Just as we can not identify Buffon simply as Lucretius updated, nor can we characterise his celebrated contemporary Carl Linné (Linnaeus in Latin: 1707–78) as a recycled Aristotle. Certainly, Linnaeus's main aim and role was to reform and consolidate a tradition in natural history that he knew went back to Andrea Cesalpino (1519–1603), a man who had, in turn, appointed himself to bring Aristotle's logic of classification to bear on the classifying of plants, on the understanding that, as Cesalpino saw it, in doing this one was displaying the constitution of an Aristotelian cosmos. Certainly, too, Linnaeus had no time for the theories of the earth in the cosmogonical sense of Burnet, Whiston and Buffon. But his cosmogonical reticence and his commitment to the Aristotelian taxonomy inaugurated by Cesalpino, did not mean that Linnaeus always took the species living today, and demanding classification into genera, families and so on, as merely given; as perpetuated by nature now, having been initiated by God as so many distinct kinds tracing to the first, Mosaic week of creation. By the end of his life, Linnaeus was proposing that there are many more species now than God made in that first week, because within each of the broad groupings – families and orders – later species have arisen from the hybrid crossings of earlier ones. Sexual generation, newly found to be as ubiquitous among plants as among animals, is a means not only for species to perpetuate themselves but also to join in making others. (See art. 19.)

Buffon and Linnaeus set very contrasting precedents, both for systematic taxonomy and for the understanding of origins and species. Jean Lamarck (1744–1829) had debts to both men in his early work, but in 1800 he began taking a position that is best understood as a new Newtonian alternative to Buffon's Newtonian account of life's place in nature.

For Lamarck's most general claim, eventually made quite explicit, is that, yes, nature – which is to say the collaboration of attractive and repulsive forces of heat and gravity – has indeed produced all bodies, living and lifeless, organised and otherwise, the animals and planets no less than the minerals. However, among living bodies, nature can only make the simplest directly, in direct spontaneous generations from lifeless matter; the more complex have therefore been produced indirectly through the gradual complexification of these over vast eons of time. Where Buffon has nature making organic molecules from brute matter and then these molecules suddenly making animals and plants, simple and complex, Lamarck has the simplest organisms formed as intermediaries and the rest formed gradually from them. Buffon although correctly Newtonian about the nature's agencies, is incorrect about their powers and their history, according to Lamarck. The earth's heat is constantly revived by the circulation of fire to and from an unfading sun; so nature now can do no more, and no less, than at any time in our planet's apparently unlimited past. Always obliged to begin the production of living bodies with the simplest, she has always to produce the higher forms of life by modifying the simplest in a progressive, successive production of the classes forming the two or more series of animal and of plant organisation. This successive production of the several class series involves a successive production of species that are unlimitedly mutable.

This unlimited mutability serves two complementary ends for Lamarck. Firstly, fossil remains of animals that match no known living species need not be interpreted, as they were by Buffon, as relics of species that have failed to survive changing circumstances and ended in extinction; but as relics of species that have survived by being changed by those circumstantial changes. Secondly, the serial rankings of the main classes of animals and plants can be interpreted as giving the order of their production over long periods of time, an order that is not determined by circumstantial change but by a tendency of the movements within the living bodies that constitute life itself, a tendency to produce increases in organisational complexity that are conserved and so accumulated in reproduction. Species have the successive origins they have in Lamarck, because the indirect production of all living bodies except the simplest has necessarily been successive.

Lamarck was exceptional in his generation in being a professional zoologist who responded to the full range of natural philosophy and natural history integrated in Buffon's macrocosmogonical and microcosmogonical hypotheses. The norm among those in the early nineteenth century who saw themselves contributing to zoology or botany or geology as branches of knowledge, as sciences, appropriate to professorial profession, was to pursue such sciences in ways that postponed or circumvented direct sustained engagement with the problems those hypotheses purported to solve.

Georges Cuvier (1769–1832), Lamarck's Parisian colleague, developed the Linnaean quest for a natural taxonomic system in bringing to it the comparative anatomy of internal organisational structures and functions. He extended the results to cover the fossil animals, insisting that they were indeed often remains of extinct species that had lived and died at different periods in the earth's long past. He was prepared to imply that the oldest extinct species had been replaced by newer, younger species; but he declined to say how such replacements took place, insisting that the origin of life and organisation lay beyond science, even inclining to the pre-existence of germs with its corollary that the origin of individual organisation lay there too. Alexander von Humboldt (1769–1859) likewise insisted that the science of the geographical distribution of plants and animals is concerned with where species have originated, but leaves as a mystery beyond science the causes for their originating when and where they have.

Lamarck did have allies, if not followers. Another Parisian colleague, Etienne Geoffroy Saint-Hilaire (1772–1844), accepted the indefinite modifiability of species and supported that thesis from his work on embryology. However, the precedent set by Buffon's integration of the theory of the earth and theory of generation was not an invitation most professional naturalists and natural philosophers were inclined to accept. Even those, many of whom were in Germany, who were pursuing new interests in comparative embryology on the assumption that pre-existent germs were discredited once and for all, did not move willingly and comprehensively from their theorising about generation to the theory of the earth. Developments in geology were, however, opening up new contexts of inquiry where integrative efforts might find a place. It was in such contexts that Darwin was to pursue his work on origins and species.

3. THE EMERGENCE OF DARWIN'S ZOONOMICAL PROGRAMME

Darwin has often been portrayed as an amateur, gentleman beetle collector who had learned little from his formal education, and who was innocent of intellectual ambition or ideological orientation. But such portrayals are now known to be highly misleading. A better sense of the man's early years can be had by noting the obvious biographical landmarks. His school years were followed by, successively, five student years (1825–31) at Edinburgh and then at Cambridge, five voyage years (1831–36) and then five London years (1837–42). It was during the London years that he arrived at almost all the main theoretical conclusions that were to dominate the rest of his life, especially the theory of natural selection – his theory of the origin of species – and, very probably too, pangenesis – his theory of reproduction, including heredity and variation. Even before going to Edinburgh, he had developed serious scientific interests, especially under the influence of his older brother Erasmus who went with him to study at the Scottish university. Once there, he engaged, through reading, lectures and field trips, a range of scientific issues, especially in general zoological theory. Likewise, at Cambridge the botanical lectures he attended provided far more than an introduction to taxonomy and field work. Again, the voyage years were as much years of reading (there were some four hundred volumes on the boat) and writing and reflecting as they were of observing and collecting. It is, then, simply a mistake to think that Darwin's biological theorising is confined to later London years that followed an earlier phase of observation by a naïve voyaging naturalist.

It is also a mistake to make Darwin the young theoriser nothing but a precursor of the mature author. We should not reduce our study of his earlier years to a hunt for the germs of those ideas that are familiar from his later books. To do this would be to overlook much that mattered to him when he first began working on issues of general theoretical import.

We can confirm these biographical and historiographical themes by beginning our narrative with Darwin in mid-1834, when he was halfway through his voyage and about to leave eastern South America for the western coast. His main writing throughout the voyage was in two scientific diaries (still unpublished today): one on zoology, one on geology. A good way to grasp Darwin's permanent preoccupations as a biological theorist is to see what issues of theory were dominant in these two diaries in 1834.

One cluster of issues traces directly to what can be called his Grantian generational preoccupations. For at Edinburgh he had learned from Robert Grant (1793–1874) to compare and contrast various modes of generation or reproduction, sexual and otherwise, in invertebrate animals, and to reflect on the way a colony of more or less independent individuals often grows and acts in a co-ordinated way as if pervaded by a single principle of life or vital force. Thanks to this Grantian heritage, Darwin in mid-1834 was investigating whether the matter making up the central living mass of a polyp colony was growing continuously so as to connect the component individual polyps; and he was concluding that the gemmules, minute buds, whereby many invertebrate animals reproduced, often arise from a distinctive granular matter in the parent.[1]

As for geology, by mid-1834 Darwin was embracing the controversial theoretical teachings of Charles Lyell (1797–1875) as set out in his *Principles of Geology* (1830–33). All the causes of change are presumed, in Lyell's system, to persist undiminished into the present, the human period, and on into the future. Now, as at all times, habitable dry land is being destroyed by subsidence and erosion in some regions, while it is being produced by sediment consolidation, lava eruption and elevationary earthquake action in others. Equally, Lyell has the long succession of faunas and floras brought about by a continual, one-at-a-time extinction of species and their replacement by new ones. In defending this last thesis about species replacement, Lyell had explicitly countered the views of Humboldt and others that the origins of species were mysteries beyond all science. The geologist, Lyell insisted, has to consider whether species are now coming into being and what is determining the timing and placing of these species' origins. He had considered at length Lamarck's system and rejected it in favour of a separate creation of fixed species. How these creations occurred Lyell left unspecified, but he did lay down that adaptational constraints alone determine when and where species originate and so determine which genera and families of species originate in which areas of the world.

In mid-1834, Darwin had no disagreement with these Lyellian doctrines. By mid-1837 he had shifted far away, and knowingly so, from Lyell's account of the organic world, while remaining committed to Lyell's views on the inorganic, physical world. To understand Darwin's moves away from Lyell's views on the world of life, we have to see that they were being made by the same Darwin who was preoccupied with the issues deriving from his Grantian generational heritage. Nothing conditioned Darwin's entire life as a scientific theorist more than his lifelong habit of integrating and adjudicating between these two (Scottish) intellectual legacies: the Lyellian-geological (including biogeography and ecology) and the Grantian-generational.

A first break from Lyell came in 1835, when Darwin rejected Lyell's view that species become extinct when physical changes in an area lead to competitive imbalances and so competitive defeats, wherein some invasions of alien species succeed and some retreats of other species do not. Darwin favoured instead a generational theory of extinctions, whereby the succession of individuals in a species is propagating a limited, original duration of life, and so dies out eventually of old age just as a single animal does or a grafted succession of plant shoots had often appeared to.

A second break came, it seems, in mid-1836 shortly before the voyage ended. For it was then, there is reason to believe, that Darwin first inclined toward the view that new species arise by the modification of earlier ones. The rationale for this inclination was most likely a conviction that there were resemblances between very similar but distinct congeneric species that could not be explained, à la Lyell, as due to adaptation to similar conditions; for these species had evidently originated in areas with very different conditions, desert, rain forest and so on. If new species can arise in the modification, the transmutation, of earlier ones, then such resemblances can be explained as due to heredity rather than adaptation.[2]

The third and final break with Lyell came in the spring of 1837, a few months after Darwin's return to England. New judgements by London naturalists, especially on the birds and fossil mammals he had collected, seem to have convinced Darwin that his 1836 rationale for favouring transmutation was dramatically vindicated by several groups of biogeographical and paleontological facts. Accordingly, he decided to go all the way with transmutation and to construct a system of laws of life, a zoonomical system, as comprehensive as that system of Lamarck's which Lyell had rejected.

Darwin's zoonomical system, which is articulated in the first two dozen pages of his *Notebook B*, opened in July 1837, is a generational system in its two most general claims. Firstly, change in species and so adaptation, is credited ultimately to the distinctive powers of sexual generation, as contrasted with all asexual modes of generation. Secondly, all organisation, high and low, is traced to organisational progress beginning with the simplest organisms of all – monads, so called – whose eventual issue over eons of time is a branching propagation of species, analogous to the branching propagation of buds whereby a tree grows. Thanks to sex, a tree of life can arise from a monad.

From the start, Darwin was explicitly including in his system man and his mental life. Within a year he was also explicit in taking a materialist view of human mental, including moral, faculties. His metaphysics, at this time, was theistic as well as materialistic, however. The lawful causation whereby species are adapted and diversified is taken to be benevolently instituted originally by a Divine Creator.

His notebook programme set itself two tasks. The first was to understand how sexual generation in changing conditions allowed species to change into new species adapted to the new conditions. The second was to show how far otherwise inexplicable facts in biogeography, paleontology and morphology can be explained on the theory that many new species could have arisen in the branching and rebranching descent from a single ancestral stock. Here Darwin extended quite generally the form of argument first encountered in his use of transmutation in resolving biogeographical problems. Resemblances – for instance, in the forelimbs of bats, moles and monkeys – are often not explicable as adaptations to a common way of life, for those lives differ; they are explicable as a shared heritage from a common ancestor. Differences – among those fore-limbs, say – can be referred to adaptive divergences in distinct lines of descent from a common ancestral species.

The branching tree of descent arises from the reiteration of adaptive species formation. The most general quest is, therefore, for causes that are adequate for the formation of species and their unlimited, arboriform, adaptive diversification into distinct genera, families and so on.

4. THE CONSTRUCTION, PRESENTATION AND RECEPTION OF THE DARWINIAN THEORY

Darwin's initial presumption, in 1837, was that sexual generation would ensure the adaptiveness of change, because in changing conditions adaptive inno-vations of character would be impressed on the maturing organisation of the offspring from sexual generation, and only adaptive acquisitions would be transmitted to future generations.

The movements Darwin made away from this view in the next year, 1838 – movements which eventually brought him to his theory of natural selec-tion – are much more complex than even many specialist writers on Darwin seem willing to recognise. Misled, still, by Darwin's later brief recollections, they often imply that Darwin read one book, Thomas Malthus's *Essay on the*

Principle of Population (the fifth edition, 1826), and on one day, September 28th, 1838, in a few notebook sentences, reached the theory then and there in all its essentials. The truth is, however, that Darwin's theory of natural selection was not arrived at until late November or early December that year, and that it was not, indeed could not have been, reached in the way that various versions of the myth of a single moment of Malthusian insight all imply.[3]

Certainly, the reflections on reading Malthus were decisive. Up to then, Darwin inclined to think that a whole species is able to adapt to changes in the conditions throughout its area, because local adaptations to local changes are eliminated, as are occasional congenital peculiarities, by crossing with unaffected individuals in the same species. Malthus impressed him that were it not for limited food, populations – in animals as well as man – would increase at very great rates. So, in the struggle to survive and reproduce, many lose out in each generation. Here, then, is a force making for adaptation, through the elimination in a few generations of maladaptive variations and the retention of adaptive variations.

This conclusion left in place, however, Darwin's confidence that the impressionable maturations and blending crossings, distinctive of sexual as contrasted with asexual generation, are what ultimately makes adaptive change possible. The Malthusian crush of population supplements this causation, but its inclusion in Darwin's theorising calls for no rethinking of the necessity and efficacy of sex. Such a rethinking happens two months later, when Darwin comes for the first time to think that species in the wild owe their adaptive formation to a process analogous to the selective breeding of hereditary variants practised by animal breeders, in producing distinctively adapted races of domesticated species: greyhounds and bulldogs, race horses and draught horses, for instance. With this selection analogy, Darwin sets aside the assumption that adaptation is ensured by the maturation and crossings distinctive of sex; for, rather, adaptation – whether to the needs of a wild species or to man's ends – now depends on the selection to which any variation is subject, even variation that may be arising by chance, and not as an adaptive response to changed conditions. Species are now, for Darwin, like the races of dogs and horses, in being adapted products of selected breeding; but they are more slowly and therefore more permanently adapted; and they are more discriminatingly, consistently and comprehensively selected and therefore more perfectly adapted.

It is this argument concerning chance variation, adaptation and selection that remains for Darwin, ever thereafter, as constituting his theory of the origin of species. Over the next twenty years, he refines it, extends it and supports it in many new and significant ways, while never quite getting around to publishing it.

He was prompted finally to prepare his book, *On the Origin of Species*, for publication in 1859, when, quite unexpectedly the year before, he received a sketch of a theory of natural selection very like his own theory, sent by a younger English naturalist Alfred Russel Wallace (1823–1913), who was then working at natural history in the East Indies. Wallace's sketch and some manuscript pieces by Darwin were read as a joint paper at the Linnean Society and appeared in print in 1858. Wallace was like Darwin in following the line of historical, biogeographical enquiries opened up by Lyell, and he was like Darwin in taking a materialist view of man and mind. There was, however, nothing in Wallace corresponding to the generational preoccupations that can be traced in Darwin back to Edinburgh and medicine. Wallace was content to be a junior partner in the whole business, rather than claiming equal entitlement; and, although members of the scientific community were aware that the theory had been converged on independently by two men, they and the wider public associated it principally with Darwin.

The argument of the *Origin* makes three successive cases for natural selection: that it exists, that it is sufficient to produce, adapt and diversify species, and that it has probably been the main agent responsible for producing the species extant today and those extinct ones found as fossils. The existence of selection in nature is argued for on the grounds that it follows from the existence of hereditary variation, together with the struggle to survive and reproduce that is entailed by the powers of reproductive multiplication and limited resources, especially food. The adequacy of natural selection to produce species is defended by arguing that man, as a selective breeder, had produced distinctive races adapted to different uses within domesticated species; and by arguing that because natural selection is far more prolonged, precise and comprehensive as a selective breeding process, it is able to produce not only distinct races, but distinct species, starting from a single common ancestral species. The races produced by natural selection will meet the criteria for counting as species: inability or disinclination to interbreed; distinction by character gaps with no intermediate varieties; and true breeding, that is, perpetuation of characters over successive generations.

The third and final section of Darwin's argument presents a revised version of the view he had taken back in 1837. The theory that species have arisen in branching divergences due mainly to natural selection is more probable than the theory of separate creations of fixed species, because the branching divergence theory allows for more facts of various kinds – biogeographical, morphological and so on – to be explained by being referred to general laws rather than to particular Divine willings.

The reception of Darwin's proposals was also a much more complicated affair than is sometimes appreciated. Too often, a single, unrepresentative moment is taken to indicate the overall trend. That moment is the meeting at Oxford of the British Association for the Advancement of Science, where Darwin's supporter T. H. Huxley clashed with the Bishop of Oxford, Samuel

Wilberforce and, according to legend, won the day for Darwin against the Bishop's reactionary religious prejudices and flippant debating ploys. One way to move towards a less misleading account of that occasion in particular, and of the issues generally in play at that time, is to see that Darwin's argumentation was often raising questions of authority, especially the authority of physics on the one hand and of the churches on the other.

The authority of what was taken to be the best science of the day, namely the Newtonian celestial mechanics of the solar system, was such that reviewers of Darwin's book and appraisers of his theorising were expected to ask how fully Darwin was satisfying the standards set by this, the best science. They often concluded that his science was defective by those standards. A main difficulty was in supporting the theory by comparing its consequences with relevant, ascertainable facts. With Newton's theory of gravitation, it seemed possible to deduce precisely the consequences of the forces acting under specifiable conditions; to establish when those conditions have been met in the world, and to confirm the theory by showing that its consequences are matched by what has occurred under those conditions. By contrast, what the consequences of natural selection would be under any specifiable conditions was not easily decided from the theory itself. What is more, comparing those consequences with the changes species have undergone was not at all easy, for the obvious reason that there was no direct access (via a moving picture record of life's changes in the past) to those changes. A theory, it was implied by the critics, that was subject to these difficulties was not sufficiently like Newton's physics to count as good science. This criticism raised, therefore, the question of whether a scientist working on the problems Darwin had addressed should be expected to submit to the authority of physics.

The authority issue as it concerned the churches took a different form. It had long been agreed between some men of science, at least, and some men of the church that some possible conflicts of authority should be avoided by a suitable distinction of responsibilities. For instance, geologists had concerned themselves with the history of the earth and its animal and plant inhabitants before the arrival of man; leaving churchmen, including those scientists who were churchmen, responsible for the subject of man's life on earth under the moral government of God, a government that had no place in the pre–human epochs. The Darwinian camp's willingness, signalled already in the *Origin*, to subsume our species under the general theory of descent obviously indicated a deliberate unwillingness to negotiate any comparable divisions of responsibility in constructing and presenting that theory. Darwin's general account of species, independently of the case of man, made trouble for various versions of the argument from design: the argument that only an intelligent designer, identifiable with God, could have fitted structure to function as we find it fitted in a bird's wing or rabbit's eye. Even if one insisted that natural selection was God's chosen means of bringing species naturally into being, there remained the difficulty that it seemed a very unreliable, wasteful and cruel way for the Divine intentions to be carried out. Darwin did, then, seem to take the goodness out of nature and to deprive Adam and Eve of literal life. A God who would choose natural selection was not a God who would send his Son as saviour; an earth that had never been trodden by the first Adam was not an earth that needs that saviour as the second Adam.

Historians of science have been moving away in recent decades from the familiar thesis, now a century old, that science and religion have been forever destined to conflict by virtue of their permanent and opposed natures. In place of this conflict thesis they have often proposed another that it is surely time to insist is equally indefensible, namely that Western science was a legitimate child of Christianity and so normally and properly, if not invariably, has lived in natural accord with Christianity to the benefit of both parent and offspring. One trouble with both the conflict thesis and this revisionist alternative to it is that they appeal equally to assumptions of a natural relationship between two abstract entities, a relationship whose naturalness traces to the characters of the entities that are presumed invariant. Whatever else we can learn from considering the long run of theories about origins and species, including the issues arising in the wake of Darwin's work, we must see that any such assumptions are highly problematic. (See art. 50.)

5. WIDER MOVEMENTS AND DEEPER SIGNIFICANCE

Ever since the 1860s people writing about Darwinian science have sought the ultimate implications of what Darwin was doing, and in seeking these they have sought to place his science in some larger context of major trends in history, including social and economic as well as intellectual history. The scope and variety of these proposals illustrates once again that there is much more to the history of science than might at first appear.

Writers of philosophical bent have often wished to fit Darwinian science into some comprehensive generalisations about the way fundamental conceptions of the universe have altered through the ages. For example, it has been suggested that for the Greeks the universe was a permanently adult organism, while for the seventeenth-century metaphysicians it was a lifeless machine; and that, thanks to Darwin and others, there was a shift in the nineteenth century to a universe conceived of as a growing organism.

There are always two sorts of difficulties with any such proposals. First, even when put in more qualified and sophisticated forms, they often seem open to the obvious objection that, at any one time, there is serious disagreement over what the science of the day presupposes or implies as to the ultimate nature of the universe. Second, there is uncertainty as to how we are to understand such a proposal in relation to particular individuals. True, Newton did take a stand on the question of whether nature was ultimately mechanical – although it was, contrary to legend, a stand against that view; but Darwin nowhere commits himself concerning the universe as a whole, and among those who have taken his science most seriously there is little consensus.

However, even if we find these two difficulties insuperable, we can still consider what insights can be had concerning Darwinian science, by seeing what range of different metaphysical positions it has been enlisted to support. For example, several writers, notably John Dewey early in this century, and Ernst Mayr more recently, have argued that Darwinism is fatal to any version of Platonic essentialism, any version, that is, of the view that the contents of the world fall into so many types – like types of figures in geometry: triangle, square and the rest – distinguished by essential differences specifiable in appropriate definitions. For, argue anti-essentialists, any theory of gradual change brought about by selective accumulation of variation within species cannot accept that species are delimitable and definable types, with the differences within species understood as defects due to imperfections in the individual embodiments of the type. So, they also argue, the typological conception of species that supports racialist doctrines, of more and less perfectly human races within mankind, is discredited by Darwinian theory. Whatever we make of this line of argument, we can certainly benefit, as historians, from being prompted by it to consider how far the emergence of Darwinian science involved departures from the metaphysics and ideology of the original sources of Platonism, Plato himself and his many followers.

The search for a social history of Darwinian science has been much developed in recent years. One point of departure for such quests has been the Marxist tradition of relating the emergence of Darwinian science to the changes historians identify as the Industrial Revolution. On the face of it the existence of some such relation would seem an obvious conclusion. The timing seems right: England in the 1830s had just become the world's first industrial nation. Darwin's theory has ideas of progress and competition integral to it. The conclusion would seem to be, therefore, that the theory represents one of the ways whereby the new economic order of industrial capitalism was expressed intellectually. (See arts. 6 and 66.)

Sometimes proposals of this kind are met with general arguments to the effect that this is not how history happens, because scientific change cannot be conditioned by economic life as the proposal requires. The conduct of this general debate about science and society is obviously relevant to any particular case such as the Darwinian one. But, equally, there are considerations peculiar to this case that need clarifying if that general relevance is not to be misunderstood. One consideration is that we have to be more critical that many writers on Darwinism have been concerning the economic history that may be involved.

It is all too easy, for instance, especially in thinking of England, to identify capitalism principally with industry in the sense of manufacturing. However, in looking at Darwin's biogeographical theorising, his Malthusian notions and his selective breeding analogies, it is plain that the relevant economic context is often not the new world of urban factories and mills, with Manchester as its exemplar; rather it is the earlier developments that gave England its new agricultural capitalism and its empire. Malthus after all is principally concerned, as Adam Smith so often was, with food and land, including land as ground won or lost in invasions that lead to struggles between aliens and natives. The animal and plant breeders, after all, were themselves often captains of a new scientific, agricultural industry.

Reflecting on the relevance of the economic history of these developments in agriculture and empire should suggest that Darwin's science drew its cultural resources less from the nineteenth and more from the eighteenth century than is often thought. If so, then the mediation between economic change and scientific theory may be less direct than is sometimes implied. Instead of seeing Darwin as directly reflecting on any innovations in urban and manufacturing life going on up the road from where he sat in his study, so to speak, we should see him drawing on intellectual traditions that had arisen in response to earlier changes in the agricultural and imperial life of his country.

A further way to raise larger questions about Darwin and his science is to ask whether there was, in any reasonably precise sense, a Darwinian revolution in biology, comparable, say, to the Copernican revolution in astronomy, the revolution in the Renaissance whereby the earth ceased to be central and stationary and became a rotating planet in orbit around the sun. The main challenge in maintaining that there was a Darwinian revolution is in showing that there was a shift from one consensus before Darwin to another after him, and that he was the main agent in bringing that shift about. One thing we can say, perhaps, is that in the decades before 1859, many leading biologists took species to be independently initiated in their origins and fixed in their characters, while within a few years of Darwin publishing, very few professionals were defending that position at length as Lyell and Agassiz had, for instance, in their very different ways in the 1850s. What is more, there is plenty of testimony from the time that this change in opinion did occur and that Darwin is responsible.

However, this generalisation hardly shows that there was a Darwinian revolution. On the one hand, there was, before Darwin, a great variety of approaches to questions of form and function, creation and design, progress and development, and life and matter; what is more, Darwin's implicit and explicit teachings on these questions were wholeheartedly embraced by very few biologists even well into this century, let alone in the last. Biologists who have agreed with Darwin that species are not separately originated and fixed perpetuated have often agreed with him on that issue alone, and have disagreed with him on others so fundamental as to make that agreement look almost superficial. To take just one example, there were biologists in the last century who agreed with Darwin that new species do arise from the modification of earlier ones, but who interpreted evolution as a developmental process subject, as individual embryonic developments are, to developmental laws that ensure the progressive realisation of a pre-existing Divine plan for the earth, life and man. In general, then, we have to be very careful not to over-estimate how fully Darwin's proposals were accepted in the last century by professional biologists, let alone people outside that scientific community. Certainly, many considered Darwin's views carefully and some welcomed much of what he said; but only a few, very few, had no serious disagreements with his position as a whole.

6. TWENTIETH-CENTURY EPILOGUE

There is a familiar stereotype as to what happened to evolutionary biology in this century, but it is now discredited by recent historical research. The stereotype says that in 1900 there was agreement that evolution had occurred but no consensus concerning what had caused it, especially, no consensus that natural selection was the cause. However, the stereotype continues, in that year there were rediscovered Mendel's laws of heredity, laws that allowed natural selection to be vindicated against all the objections then current. After two decades or so of misunderstandings, this vindication of Darwin by Mendel began to be appreciated, and a new theory, the new so-called synthesis, or neo-Darwinian synthesis, began to emerge with the integration of Mendel on heredity and Darwin on selection as its principal doctrine. By the 1950s this synthesis had been extended successfully to the reinterpretation of botany, paleontology and so on. Since then the synthesis has been modified but not replaced as a consensus.

There are at least two fatal difficulties with the stereotype. The first is that the characterisation of the state of discussion around 1900 is quite inadequate. The issues dividing the different schools of thought cannot be reduced to the single one of what the causes of evolution was. For a host of prior matters were in dispute too: whether evolution is to be understood as a regular development conforming to laws of development, or whether it is irregular and contingent in its branching and rebranching precisely because it conforms to no such laws; whether evolution is directed mainly by inner forces or, rather, mainly by external conditions and circumstances; whether it is smooth and gradual in its course or jerky and advanced by jumps.[4] These were all obviously complex questions and the bearing of Mendelism on all of them taken together was by no means straightforward.

A second difficulty is that when we see how the new synthesis emerged in the 1930s, it is plain that the integration of the new genetics with the old problems about species and their origins involved far more than demonstrating that Mendelism can rescue selectionism, by resolving difficulties about the hereditary variation selection needs to accumulate if it is to be effective in causing evolution. A glance at one book can show how much more was involved, and that is the book that did more than any other to convince biologists that new developments in genetics meant that a new synthesis of causal theory in evolution was at hand: Theodosius Dobzhansky's *Genetics and the Origin of Species* (1937). For Dobzhansky's book is a synthesis not merely of Mendel's and Darwin's legacies, but of a Western tradition in theoretical population genetics and a Russian tradition in experimental genetics of populations; of genetics and systematics and of cytology and biogeography. So, even if we confine our attention to how one decisive text came to be written, we can see that the stereotype misleads us thoroughly.[5]

The last two decades have seen various challenges to the new synthesis as it was celebrated, with little dissent, at least in the English-speaking biological world, in 1959, the centennial of the *Origin*. Some writers have even declared that evolutionary biology is now in such a state of uncertainty and disagreement that talk of crisis is appropriate. Others, however, are not at all persuaded that such talk is called for. If there is a crisis, it is not one that is ever likely to be resolved to the satisfaction of all those dissatisfied with the orthodox consensus, for they seem to have little in common beyond that dissatisfaction. Thus some dissenters question the genetical doctrines accepted by the orthodox, but other dissenters do not; again some dissenters want evolutionary and embryological biology unified by a common foundation in developmental laws of form, while others think evolution is even more stochastic or random than the orthodox do.

What has been subject to a more univocal critique is not the new synthesis as such, but a distinctive programme in evolutionary biology, called sociobiology; it is a programme constructed by extending that synthesis to include social behaviour in animals and man so as to subsume topics – such as incest, kinship and altruism – traditionally treated by anthropologists and moral philosophers. Critics, many of them professional biologists on the political left, have found the programme making erroneous and unwholesome assumptions about nature and nurture, competition and adaptation; assumptions that involve, in turn, fallacious presumptions in favour of the *status quo* in class, race and gender politics.

From evangelical Christians, on the other hand – who, in the United States, especially, often tend to right-wing politics – has come a renewed attack on evolution itself, particularly as a dogma imposed by distant, liberal, secular scientists on children whose schools should properly, it is argued, be under local, electoral control in this matter as in any other of moral import.

These various politicisations of evolutionary biology may seem malfunctioning lapses from the proper norms of scientific discourse, but historically considered, as part of the long run of thinking about origins and species, they are far from exceptional; indeed they are what one expects. It is likewise, with the recurrent concern among philosophical analysts of evolutionary biology to compare and contrast the theory of natural selection with one or another branches of physics; at least since Newton and certainly since Darwin, there has been sustained discussion of the precedents set by successes in physics for any efforts to understand the history and diversity of life on earth. That discussion has been continued in this century by a new professional community of philosophers of science, who have taken up the questions raised in asking how far the concepts of evolutionary biology resemble the paradigm examples of scientific concepts taken by philosophers from physics. One issue that is at stake in this discussion is the unity of science itself. If evolutionary biology is really very unlike physics, then one can hardly talk of the structure of scientific theories, or indeed of the nature of science itself, without begging contentious questions.

Many evolutionary biologists may sometimes wish that the ideological critiques and philosophical explications of their theories could be suspended so that they can get on with their work undistracted. But not all feel this way, as is apparent from the way several leading general textbooks on evolution have been written recently.[6] In continuing the tradition of seeing questions about origins and species as involving perennial issues of politics, philosophy and religion, such texts would seem to have history very much on their side.

NOTES

1. See P. R. Sloan, 'Darwin's invertebrate programme', in D. Kohn (ed.), *The Darwinian heritage* (Princeton, 1985) pp. 71–120; M. J. S. Hodge, 'Darwin as a lifelong generation theorist', ibid., pp. 207–44.
2. For differing accounts of how Darwin may have first inclined to transmutation, see F. J. Sulloway, 'Darwin's conversion: the *Beagle* voyage and its aftermath', *Journal of the history of biology*, 15 (1982), 325–96, and M. J. S. Hodge, 'Darwin, species and the theory of natural selection' in S. Atran *et al.*, *Histoire du concept d' éspèce dans les sciences de la vie* (Paris, 1986), pp. 227–52.
3. For a much fuller account, see M. J. S. Hodge and D. Kohn, 'The immediate origins of natural selection', in D. Kohn (ed.), *The Darwinian heritage* (Princeton, 1985).
4. P. J. Bowler, *The eclipse of Darwinism: anti-Darwinian evolution theories in the decades around 1900* (Baltimore, 1983).
5. On the emergence of the new synthesis, see E. Mayr and W. B. Provine (eds.), *The evolutionary synthesis: perspectives on the unification of biology* (Cambridge, Mass., 1980).
6. See, for example, T. Dobzhansky, F. Ayala, G. L. Stebbins and J. W. Valentine, *Evolution* (San Francisco, 1977) and D. J. Futuyma, *Evolutionary biology* (Sunderland, Mass., 1979).

FURTHER READING

P. J. Bowler, *Evolution: the history of an idea* (Berkeley, 1984).
—— *The non-Darwinian evolution: reinterpreting a historical myth* (Baltimore, 1988).
T. F. Glick (ed.), *The comparative reception of darwinism* (Austin, 1974).
J. C. Greene, *The death of Adam. Evolution and its impact on Western thought* (Ames, 1959).
D. L. Hull (ed.), *Darwin and his critics. The reception of Darwin's theory of evolution by the scientific community* (Cambridge, Mass., 1973).

D. Kohn (ed.), *The Darwinian heritage* (Princeton, 1985).

E. Mayr, *The growth of biological thought. Diversity, evolution and inheritance* (Cambridge, Mass., 1982).

D. Oldroyd, *Darwinian impacts: an introduction to the Darwinian revolution* (Milton Keynes, 1980).

R. J. Richards, *Darwin and the emergence of evolutionary theories of mind and behaviour* (Chicago, 1987).

M. Ruse, *The Darwinian revolution: science red in tooth and claw* (Chicago, 1979).

E. Sober (ed.), *Conceptual issues in evolutionary theory. An anthology* (Cambridge, Mass., 1984).

R. M. Young, *Darwin's metaphor. Nature's place in Victorian culture* (Cambridge, 1985).

25

WILHELM WUNDT AND THE EMERGENCE OF EXPERIMENTAL PSYCHOLOGY

K. DANZIGER

The name of Wilhelm Wundt (1832–1920) remains indissolubly linked to the origins of experimental psychology. This is so even though he cannot be credited with a single significant scientific discovery, any genuine methodological innovation or any influential theoretical generalisation. Recognition on such grounds is far more readily granted to other German experimentalists of the second half of the nineteenth century for their contributions to the emerging field of experimental psychology. Among these it is appropriate to mention Gustav Theodor Fechner (1801–87), the inventor of the field of psychophysics with its 'psychophysical methods', Hermann von Helmholtz (1821–94), remembered for his monumental work on vision and hearing; and Hermann Ebbinghaus (1850–1909), who pioneered the experimental study of memory.

Nevertheless, there has always been a pervasive intuitive appreciation among experimental psychologists that it was Wundt rather than these others who played the crucial role in constituting the field. In other words, his role is felt to be intimately tied up with the emergence of the field as such, rather than with the emergence of specific issues within the field.

At the most accessible level, Wundt's achievements are clearly reflected in certain historical landmarks. From 1875 onwards, he occupied a chair in philosophy at the University of Leipzig, one of the largest and best-funded academic institutions in Germany. As such, it attracted a large number of foreign students who flocked to Germany during this period to complete their academic training. Wundt's tenure happened to coincide with the period of Germany's undisputed ascendancy in the field of higher learning, especially in the sciences. Over a period of about four decades Wundt supervised nearly two hundred

Ph.D. theses, many of them by non-Germans. Thousands more attended his lectures and witnessed his demonstrations. His international reputation was assured, particularly in countries with inadequate but expanding systems of higher education. American research students were the most numerous, with the Russians forming another major group.

Of course, Wundt would not have done so exceptionally well in attracting students if they had not felt that he had something special to offer them. What he offered was both a systematic and a practical link between two sets of promises, one represented by the term 'psychology', the other by the idea of 'science'. Both fascinated many young intellectuals in the latter part of the nineteenth century – their combination proved wellnigh irresistible.

Faith in the almost limitless promise of scientific methods was not limited to Wundt's American students. His own appointment to a chair in philosophy was a direct result of the prevalence of such sentiments among German academics during the third quarter of the nineteenth century. Wundt had no formal qualifications in philosophy when he was appointed to represent that subject at Leipzig. He was a graduate in medicine from the University of Heidelberg, where he had subsequently spent many years as a lecturer and sometime assistant to Helmholtz. He had written a textbook on human physiology and a series of research monographs published as *Contributions to a Theory of Sensory Perception* (1862). The closest he had moved to some of the traditional concerns of philosophy was in his *Lectures on Human and Animal Psychology* (1863). But the University of Leipzig had decided that at least one of its three philosophy chairs must be occupied by someone with a background in natural science rather than in traditional philosophy. The period when systematic philosophy was regarded as the crown of learning had ended by the middle of the nineteenth century. Now, the answers were expected from science rather than from grand metaphysical systems. This attitude was not to last, but it was very helpful to Wundt at the crucial point in his career.

1. PSYCHOLOGY BEFORE WUNDT

By the time that Wundt made his contribution to it, the topic of psychology had had a complex, though relatively short, history. It was short because, prior to the eighteenth century, nothing approaching what we mean by psychology had constituted a coherent domain of discourse, reasonably distinct from other topics. The very term, 'psychology' was unknown in most languages, including English. It is in the first half of the eighteenth century that we must locate the emergence of reflective psychological discourse in a recognisably modern form. This does not means that psychological topics were not addressed previously, but that systematic reflection within a psychological framework is a rather modern phenomenon.

Even when it did emerge, psychological discourse remained very closely tied to non-psychological problems. In the main, eighteenth-century writers did not discuss psychological issues because that was their primary interest, but because they were fundamentally interested in certain kinds of answers to non-psychological questions. These non-psychological questions were quite varied, and this variation produced a wide spectrum of psychological concepts, each tailored to the role it played in discussions propelled by non-psychological concerns. There were four major distinguishable intellectual contexts within which the construction of modern psychological categories took place, and we will briefly consider each in turn.

The first such context was undoubtedly philosophical. A rationalist philosopher, Christan Wolff (1679–1754), published the first systematic treatises whose titles announced their subject as being 'Psychologia', and whose content did not deal with the different kinds of spirits, as earlier works on this topic had done. But historically more important was the emergence of the subject of 'mental philosophy' within the context of British philosophical empiricism. The British empiricists were interested in explaining knowledge and morality in terms of the natural constitution of the individual human mind. To further this aim, they developed theories about mental functioning that emphasised the role of experience and eventually led to the constitution of such psychological categories as *sensation* and *association*. The psychological ideas of this school were systematised by James Mill in 1829. Just before this, Johann Friedrich Herbart (1776–1841) had developed a 'mental mechanics' which owed something to empiricism but at least as much to rationalism. Herbart tried to demonstrate that mental processes and their interaction could be represented mathematically. Where the empiricists talked of the association of elements, Herbart described the *assimilation* of elements by previously existing structures.

A second major context within which the categories of modern psychology developed was provided by discourse about the foundations of human society. In its attempts to show that social order was possible on the basis of the natural constitution of the independent human individual, eighteenth-century empiricist moral philosophy constructed the modern psychological category of *motivation*, among others. But somewhat later a more organicist kind of social thought developed the category of *culture*, beginning with the writings of Johann Gottfried Herder (1744–1803), and promoted an interest in the way in which psychological processes depend on a social medium, for example, language.

Thirdly, we have to note the profound role played by medical-physiological discourse in tracing the origins of modern psychological thought and practice. Certain psychological topics had, of course, appeared in medical writings since ancient times. But, with the differentiation of a specifically physiological literature in the eighteenth century, it became customary to discuss psychological issues within a framework provided by the physiology of the organism. This was a natural consequence of the vitalistic perspectives that dominated early physiology. The use of the term *stimulus* in its modern sense dates from this period, as does the systematic raising of psychological questions in a functional, biological context. It was only the new mechanistic physiology of the middle of the nineteenth century that led to the expulsion of psychological questions from strictly physiological discourse.

Finally, it is necessary to mention the regular appearance of fundamental psychological discussions in a fourth context, best designated as natural philosophy. In both Britain and Germany there existed a tradition of speculation about the Grand Design incorporated in living nature in particular. This tradition began as natural theology but gradually took on secularised forms. It was not uncommon for psychological topics to occupy a prominent place in this literature. Outstanding examples are provided by David Hartley (1705–57) who presented a speculative psychophysiology embedded in a theological framework, Erasmus Darwin (1731–1802), who developed a comprehensive system of biopsychological explanation in the context of a secularised natural philosophy and Herbert Spencer (1820–1903), who wrote a well-known treatise on psychology inspired by a speculative evolutionary biology.

In the course of the nineteenth century, there were important developments on the level of psychological theory within each of these four contexts of discourse. However, in the light of subsequent events, it seems that the developments which were most fraught with consequences occurred not on the level of theory, but on the level of practice, including discourse about practice. Earlier discussions of psychological issues had usually drawn on common experience or anecdotes for illustrative material, with experimental or more systematic observational evidence being involved only very occasionally. But in the nineteenth century, the use of systematic techniques for gathering evidence gradually became more common and also more self-conscious. We can distinguish several of these techniques, usually associated with one or other of the major contexts of discourse.

Within an empiricist philosophical context, *introspection* gradually began to be thought of as a method. This happened much later than has sometimes been assumed and partly in response to attacks like those of Immanuel Kant (1724–1804) and Auguste Comte (1798–1857), who adduced reasons why evidence produced by employing the so-called 'inner sense' could have no scientific value. In its classical period, empiricist philosophy had not really distinguished between subjective awareness and systematic observation of that awareness. The English term, 'introspection', borrowed from theological writings, came into use towards the middle of the nineteenth century to refer to a method for gathering empirical knowledge about the human mind. This method generally aroused scepticism among rationalists and those who stressed the limitations of individual consciousness because they regarded it as essentially a reflection of physiological or social processes.

At about the same time, the *experiment*, was moving into prominence as the method of choice in a physiological context. Initially promoted by men such as François Magendie (1783–1855) in France, it began to flourish in Germany where a considerable experimental literature grew up on the physiology of the senses and of muscular movement. Wundt's earliest contributions were part of this literature.

Reflection on social processes also took a much more empirical and methodological turn in the second and third quarters of the nineteenth century, with the increasing availability and use of statistical data on the one hand and of comparative philological methods on the other. Two major lines of social research with psychological implications emerged, one that relied essentially on census type aggregate data, leading for example to crime and suicide statistics, and another that employed systematic analyses of cultural products such as languages. Out of the latter a fledgling discipline called *Völkerpsychologie* emerged around 1860, which sought to use this approach to draw conclusions about the nature of human mental processes. As we will see, Wundt became a major figure in this field.

2. WUNDT'S ACHIEVEMENTS

When the young physiologist Wundt began to be interested in psychological questions, he would have been faced by a diffuse set of issues scattered over widely varying domains. At first he tended to react to this like everyone else by restricting himself to a rather narrow band of issues and methods. On the whole, his early work on sense perception has this character. But even here one can see the beginnings of what were to become the hallmarks of the Wundtian style, firstly, a remarkably broad synthetic sweep, and secondly, a strong emphasis on methodological questions. While many shared Wundt's interest in psychological questions, none equalled the breadth of his perspective on these questions or his understanding of the role of methodology in bringing some order to this diffuse collection of topics. These strengths were the source of his exceptional personal appeal, given the rising tide of interest in matters psychological.

Wundt's influence rested on achievements in the areas of codification and institutionalisation rather than on specific thematic contributions. The first of these achievements was a text book entitled *Grundzüge der physiologischen Psychologie* (1873–74), first published just before his appointment at Leipzig. It had a much wider scope than the term 'physiological psychology' would suggest to the modern reader. However, it was unique at the time in that it clearly used the existence of experimental evidence as a primary criterion for establishing a distinct domain of psychological studies. Unlike earlier psychological texts, its construction was not subordinated to the exposition of a speculative system but attempted, as far as possible, to ground the discussion of theoretical issues in a presentation of experimental evidence. This feature had great appeal and Wundt's text came to define a new sub-division of science for a whole generation. The book went through six successful editions, growing in size from one to three volumes and presenting a more clearly worked out theoretical synthesis with each subsequent edition.

Four years after he had taken up his duties at Leipzig, Wundt began to assign experimental psychological research topics to his students which they would then discuss in their doctoral dissertations. He set aside some space for this work, and by 1883 had obtained official recognition for his 'Institute of Experimental Psychology'. In the same year the first number of what was essentially Wundt's house organ, the *Philosophische Studien*, appeared. This provided a vehicle for the dissemination of the experimental psychological studies that were emanating from his laboratory in ever-increasing numbers. Not that this was simply a journal of experimental psychology – it contained a characteristically Wundtian mixture of philosophical and experimental studies – but the latter did form a significant proportion of the material published. Wundt's journal inspired the appearance of new psychological journals elsewhere, such as *The American Journal of Psychology*, which was initiated by G. Stanley Hall (1844–1924) who had been an early visitor at the Leipzig laboratory. However, from 1890 onwards, the style of psychological journals began to change as philosophical articles disappeared from their pages. By the turn of the century, Wundt's journal was already something of an anomaly.

However, during the last two decades of the nineteenth century, Wundt was generally seen as the European 'pope' of what was often referred to as the 'New Psychology'. (In the United States he soon had to share that position with William James (1842–1910).) Wundt had assembled a unique organisational framework for the systematic and continuous production of experimental psychological knowledge. This framework was not limited to external props such as texts, journals and laboratory space, but extended to the internal organisation of psychological research itself. The work of Wundt's laboratory depended on the use of certain pieces of apparatus for the controlled presentation of stimuli and the measuring and recording of particular aspects of human behaviour. This apparatus quickly came to define what a proper psychological laboratory looked like, and, as new laboratories were founded, the inventory of Wundt's laboratory provided a standard to aim for. Inevitably, the existence of relatively rare and expensive hardware tended to channel experimental research in certain specific directions.

But it was not only on the level of hardware that Wundt's laboratory acted as a model. Previous psychological experiments in a physiological context had usually been conducted somewhat informally by independent investigators interested in rather specific questions, which were often not even regarded as psychological questions. At the Leipzig laboratory, however, there was a very different pattern. Here there was a definite community of investigators who worked on a range of related topics within an overall conceptual framework provided by Wundt. They assisted each other in various practical ways and, because of the collective nature of their enterprise, developed certain rules and conventions which regulated their joint work. These partly implicit rules and conventions governed such matters as the division of labour among the participants in a psychological experiment, the constraints on the actions of each participant and on their interaction and the definition and recognition of the phenomena that were of interest. For instance, the division of functions among two kinds of participants, now called 'experimenters' and 'subjects', became a matter of accepted routine in the wake of a pattern developed at Leipzig. Before that, the more usual procedure had been that of experimenting on oneself. Wundt's many students left his laboratory with a definite idea of what constituted a psychological experiment and often proceeded to implement this idea in other parts of the world.

Wundt also passed on to his students a distinct corpus of problems that defined the domain of experimental psychology. Many of these problems fell within the area of sensory experience, while others were based on the measurement of response times under various conditions (so-called mental chronometry), and still others involved the recording of responses dependent on the autonomic nervous system. There was little attempt at investigating central processes, the big exception being attention, a phenomenon to which Wundt attached great importance on theoretical grounds.

3. THE PLACE OF EXPERIMENTAL PSYCHOLOGY

When we turn from the level of research practice to the level of theory, we find that Wundt occupies a much less exalted place in the history of psychology. This is certainly not because he was essentially a technician who lacked an interest in the more fundamental theoretical issues. That is something which might have been true of another early experimentalist, Georg Elias Muller (1850–1934), at the University of Göttingen, but it was not true of Wundt. In fact, his theoretical output was of staggering proportions. The foundation of his laboratory coincided with the publication of a major work, entitled *Logik*, of which the first volume (1880) was devoted to 'the principles of knowledge' and the second (1883) to 'the methods of scientific research'. This work, which was never translated into English, makes it clear that Wundt's role in codifying psychological research practice was not just a matter of *ad hoc* arrangements, but involved a great deal of reflection on the then current conceptions in the philosophy of science.

These reflections led Wundt to a very distinctive definition of the place of psychology among the sciences and of the place of experimentation within psychology. He started from the common division between the natural sciences (*Naturwissenschaften*) and the moral sciences (*Geisteswissenschaften*) and assigned to psychology a mediating role between the two. This meant that psychology was always obliged to have one foot in each camp. That was true both for its content and for its methods. Experimental psychology represented the natural science part of the subject but it was far from being the whole of psychology. The experimental method was extremely valuable where it could be properly applied, but there were important areas of psychology which were beyond its reach. In general, those psychological processes which could be most directly linked to the physical manipulations of laboratory experimentation were the ones which yielded most readily to experimental investigation. This meant that complex cognitive and affective functions, thinking, problem solving, motivation and complex feelings were beyond the reach of laboratory methods. Moreover, it was precisely these kinds of processes which depended most strongly on the individual's embeddedness in a cultural matrix. Laboratory experimentation, however, created an artificial isolation of experimental subjects from their cultural background, removing the most important determinants of their experience and behaviour from view.

Wundt therefore proposed that a different kind of psychology would have to provide a complement to experimental psychology. This was the *Völkerpsychologie* which was already in existence at the time. The term is really untranslatable ('folk psychology' is a bizarre mistake), but it refers to a kind of social psychology which emphasises the analysis of culture rather than social behaviour. In its methods, *Völkerpsychologie* would rely on the comparative, often historical study of cultural products, especially language, myth and custom. Wundt believed that this would lead to an understanding of psychological processes such as thinking, fantasy and volition. As soon as his laboratory had been established, Wundt increasingly turned his attention to this side of psychology. His *Ethics* of 1886 already contained a great deal of material from this context, but the first volume of his *Völkerpsychologie* did not appear till 1900, to be joined by up to nine additional volumes over the following two decades. Towards the end of his life Wundt intimated that this was a far more important part of psychology than the experimental part, which he had done so much to establish.

Virtually no one shared this view; rather, they dismissed it as the opinion of an old man who had apparently outlived his time. The emerging social sciences did not like *Völkerpsychologie* because of its psychologising of language and culture. The new generation of psychologists who had succeeded Wundt had neither sympathy nor understanding for a position that seemed to put in doubt psychology's claim to be counted among the natural sciences. What Wundt had tried to hold together now drifted apart: experimental psychology in one direction, the social sciences in another. Had he managed to codify and institutionalise a distinct body of investigative practices that was not limited to experimental psychology, the fate of his later work might have been different. As it was, it amounted to no more than one man's encyclopaedic vision.

4. THE REPUDIATION OF WUNDT

The repudiation of Wundt by a new generation of scientific psychologists, many of whom had been his students, affected far more than his *Völkerpsychologie*. He left no disciples and founded no school. His lasting achievements had been entirely on the level of research practice. On the level of psychological theory, he began to be regarded as excessively 'metaphysical' even before the turn of the century. (Indeed, his incredibly prolific pen had produced a *System of Philosophy* in 1889.) He had always shown a marked tendency to interpret experimental findings in terms of broader issues, and he favoured theoretical concepts with connotations that went far beyond the limited scope of particular experiments. He called his psychological system 'voluntarism' to give expression to his belief in the primacy of goal-directed affective processes in human psychology. The cognitive aspect of these processes became manifest in the process of *apperception*, which unified the components of sensory experience into wholes by a process of *creative synthesis*. In his autobiography, which he completed shortly before his death in 1920, he summed up his theoretical goal as follows: 'Whereas physiology believed it had to restrict itself to the strictly delimited area of sensation, it became my aim, on the contrary, to show, wherever possible, how the elementary processes of consciousness, sensations and associations, everywhere already reflected the mental life in its totality'.[1]

He might just as well have applied this contrast to his immediate successors as to his predecessors. For various reasons, many of the students who learned the practice of psychological experimentation in Wundt's laboratory did not share his broader theoretical interests or his perspective on psychology as a whole. Many of his foreign students, particularly the Americans, had come primarily to learn certain techniques and were not about to adopt a philosophical framework which they experienced as culturally alien to them. Some of the most effective voices among his students, like the young Oswald Külpe (1862–1915) and Edward Bradford Titchener (1867–1927), were impressed by the anti-theoretical positivism of Ernst Mach (1838–1916) (see art. 53), and preferred reductionistic explanations to the theoretical scaffolding erected by Wundt. Above all, many of the serious experimentalists among his students did not take kindly to the restrictions he placed on the scope of experimental psychology and his assignment of a peculiarly hybrid status to the subject as a whole. They were convinced that the future of psychology lay in its affiliation with the natural sciences and in its ability to demonstrate the applicability of the experimental method to all psychological problems.

Accordingly, they attempted to bring under experimental scrutiny many of those 'higher' mental processes which, according to Wundt, could only be investigated indirectly by a comparative analysis of cultural products. The most determined efforts in this direction were those on the psychology of thinking by Kulpe's 'Würzburg School' and by Titchener in the United States. Because these investigators did not question the tradition that defined the proper objects of psychological investigation as mental objects, their attempts at widening the scope of psychological experimentation inevitably led to a tremendous intensification of introspective analysis. They referred to their approach as 'systematic experimental introspection', and their experimental publications soon began to look very different from those of Wundt's laboratory, where introspection had only been employed within narrowly defined limits. This led to difficulties all round. Wundt criticised these new introspective studies as 'pseudo-experiments'; Titchener disagreed with most of the other systematic introspectionists about the phenomena to be discovered by these means, and many psychologists began to feel that the whole enterprise was quite irrelevant to their real scientific and professional interests.

In America there had emerged a variant of empirical psychology which owed nothing whatever to Wundt's influence and which was not experimental in nature. Its methods were those of the census rather than of the laboratory. It circulated questionnaires about psychological matters and collected the products of mental activity from large groups of individuals in order to tabulate the results, and to show the distribution of psychological characteristics among various sections of the population. Through the mediation of men like James McKeen Cattell (1860–1944), the statistical and anthropometric ideas of Sir Francis Galton (1822–1911) gained a following among American psychologists. In due course, these elements fused in the mental test movement which provided a major alternative focus to the laboratory of Wundtian vintage for psychological practice. These developments were greatly strengthened by a growing determination among psychologists to demonstrate the practical usefulness of their discipline.

Such developments were anathema to Wundt. Not only did he disapprove of what he regarded as a superficial methodology, incapable of throwing any light on the legitimate problems of psychology, but he objected in general to any move in the direction of severing the ties between psychology and philosophy. Such a development, he felt, threatened to turn psychology from a serious intellectual discipline into a mere craft dominated by considerations of practical applicability. It was highly characteristic of his approach that psychology's turn to experimental and other empirical methods was not regarded as entailing the institutional independence of psychology as a discipline. He was, of course, much more directly concerned with the German situation, where, by the beginning of the twentieth century, the main pressure for the divorce of psychology from philosophy had come from philosophers rather than from psychologists. In Germany the transformation of psychology into a separate profession with essentially technical tasks was not, in fact, completed until the Nazi period.

The emergence of modern psychology thus appears to have occurred in two major steps. Wundt was the key figure only in the first of these steps and did what he could to prevent the second. This ambiguous role has led to numerous problems of historical interpretation.

5. HISTORIOGRAPHIC PROBLEMS

For convenience of exposition, the historiographic problems which have developed around the present topic may be divided into extrinsic and intrinsic problems. Such a division is based on a distinction between problems whose main source must be looked for among Wundt's commentators, and problems whose main source lies within the material itself. Needless to say, these two kinds of problems interact with one another.

The major sources of extrinsic difficulties are linked to two sets of circumstances: firstly, the fact that the historiography of this topic has been left to professional psychologists and secondly, the predominance of specifically American perspectives in this area. Accounts of the origins of experimental psychology by psychologists have been subject to a number of influences that must be taken into account in assessing the significance of these contributions: (1) The accounts are those of amateur historians who tend to decontextualise their topic and who are predisposed by their background to personalise and 'psychologise' historical issues. (However, recent years have seen considerable improvement in this respect among a new generation of psychologist historians.) (2) Historical accounts tend to be presented in the context of disciplinary self-examination or for the purpose of socialising prospective members of the discipline. Therefore, they often show a justificationist bias, deteriorating at times into the realms of 'origin myths'. (3) Because of the existence of deep divisions within the discipline, extending to fundamental issues, there is a tendency to interpret history in the light of current controversies.

These problems are compounded by the fact that most of the English-language literature in this area is American literature which is burdened by the legacy of a troubled relationship between the ethos of American psychology and the European roots of the subject. From the time of William James and G. Stanley Hall, American psychologists had a vision of their subject which was very different from that of Wundt, and there was no reason for them to take him seriously, except in the narrow area of laboratory methodology. In this situation the British expatriate, Titchener, took on the role of a kind of American surrogate for Wundt. However, although Titchener was unusual in America for the seriousness with which he treated many of Wundt's ideas, he had his own idiosyncratic notions about the nature and scope of experimental psychology. He invented the distinction between his own 'structuralism' and the 'functionalism' of many of his American colleagues. That was a distinction which made sense in a specific local and historical context, but when the label of structuralism was retroactively applied to Wundt, it only led to confusion. This confusion was compounded after the rise of behaviourism, when the most diverse pre-behaviourist experimentalists tended to be lumped together as 'introspectionists'. After Titchener's death in 1927, his historical perspectives were largely preserved in the work of his student, E.G. Boring, whose writings dominated the historiography of experimental psychology for half a century. Eventually, the centenary of the founding of Wundt's laboratory provided the occasion for a re-examination of the historical origins of modern psychology by a new generation of scholars.

Quite apart from these complications, which are really extrinsic to Wundt's own work, there are intrinsic difficulties which cannot be separated from his contribution. First of all, there was a distinct change in Wundt's priorities over the years, and this was accompanied by changes in his formulations and emphases.[2] Broadly speaking, the young Wundt was more sanguine about the prospects of psychology as a natural science than the mature Wundt of the middle period (1880–1900), while the old Wundt had gone even further in abandoning the enthusiasms of his early years. This means that it is relatively easy to construct different versions of his position by selectively emphasising the work of different periods. However, if one is interested in understanding his contribution in its historical context, rather than in image making, certain considerations become appropriate. Firstly, one must try to understand the long-term shifts in his priorities in relation to the response of his academic generation in Germany to the changes that were taking place around it. Secondly, one must understand the very real continuities that characterised his outlook over the years in terms of the intellectual tradition to which he was heir. Finally, one has to keep in mind that the historically effective figure was the Wundt of the middle period, so that it is the formulations of this period which merit the greatest emphasis in the context of a history of experimental psychology.

The enormous range of Wundt's work has also been a source of difficulties. It meant that he often discussed the same topic in different contexts and for different types of audience. This produced differences of emphasis which made it difficult to pin him down. But beyond such surface problems there is the deeper problem of a contradiction between an intellectual style nurtured on speculative and synthesising traditions and a subject matter that was rapidly breaking up into separate technical specialisms. Wundt embodied a transitional phase which was clinging to the past even as it was breaking with it. Such a period has to be grasped on its own ambiguous terms if historiographic blunders are to be avoided.

The internal tension that runs through Wundt's work emerges particularly clearly in connection with his most significant contribution, the systematic linking of an experimental methodology in psychological theory. In reality, the techniques he had inherited from physiology were completely inadequate for the ambitious theoretical goals he had in mind, namely the investigation of human volition, psychic causality and so on. Broadly speaking, he reacted to this by holding fast to his theoretical vision and trying either to have it both ways or to adapt his methodology. His successors and some of his contemporaries, on the other hand, were much more inclined to trim their theoretical sails to the methodological wind. Unless this difference is recognised, his role in the history of modern psychology is likely to be misunderstood. Like many of his age, Wundt was caught in the paradox between his technological and his metaphysical commitments. But was not this paradox essential for the emergence of modern psychology?

NOTES

1. W. Wundt, *Erlebtes und Erkanntes* (Stuttgart, 1920), p. 195 (translated from the German original).
2. For an account of some of these changes see especially W. van Hoorn and T. Verhave, 'Wundt's changing conceptions of a general and theoretical psychology', in W. G. Bringmann and R. D. Tweney, *Wundt studies* (Toronto, 1980).

FURTHER READING

M. G. Ash, 'Academic politics in the history of science: experimental psychology in Germany, 1879–1941', *Central European history*, 13 (1981), 255–86.
—— 'The self-presentation of a discipline: History of psychology in the United States between pedagogy and scholarship,' in L. Graham, W. Lepenies and P. Weingart (eds.), *Functions and uses of disciplinary histories* (Sociology of the Sciences, vol. 7), (Dordrecht, 1983).
A. L. Blumenthal, 'Wilhelm Wundt: Psychology as the propadeutic science', in C. E. Buxton, *Points of view in the modern history of psychology* (London, 1985).
W. G. Bringmann and R. D. Tweney (eds.), *Wundt studies: a centennial collection* (Toronto, 1980).
K. Danziger, 'The positivist repudiation of Wundt', *Journal of the history of the behavioral sciences*, 15 (1979), 205–30.
—— 'Wundt's psychological experiment in the light of his philosophy of science', *Psychological research*, 42 (1980), 109–22.
U. Geuter, 'The uses of history for the shaping of a field: observations on German psychology', in L. Graham, W. Lepenies and P. Weingart (eds.), *Functions and uses of disciplinary histories* (Sociology of the Sciences, vol. 7), (Dordrecht, 1983).
R. A. Littman, 'Social and intellectual origins of experimental psychology', in E. Hearst (ed.), *The first century of experimental psychology* (Hillsdale, N.J., 1979).
R. W. Rieber (ed.), *Wilhelm Wundt and the making of a scientific psychology* (New York and London, 1980).

R. S. Turner, 'Helmholtz, sensory physiology, and the disciplinary development of German psychology', in W. R. Woodward and M. G. Ash (eds.), *The problematic science: Psychology in nineteenth-century thought* (New York, 1982).

W. B. Weimer, 'The history of psychology and its retrieval from historiography: I. The problematic nature of history', *Science studies*, 4 (1974), 235–58.

W. R. Woodward, 'Wundt's program for the New Psychology: Vicissitudes of experiment, theory and system', in W. R. Woodward and M. G. Ash (eds.), *The problematic science: psychology in nineteenth-century thought* (New York, 1982).

26

BEHAVIOURISM

ROGER SMITH

'Behaviourism' has become a complex and exciting topic in the history of the human sciences. There are perhaps three kinds of debate about historiographic as well as empirical issues. Firstly, there is an attempt to determine the relation between 'scientific', 'experimental' and 'behaviouristic' psychology from *c.* 1910 to *c.* 1970, and, correlatively, whether and in what sense behaviourism was the heartland of psychology in that period. Secondly, it is at issue whether the historian should be looking primarily to a body of scientific knowledge, to an attempt to reduce science to a set of methodological prescriptions, or to a social movement for human technology with psychologists providing the expertise to manage modern urban and industrial society. Thirdly, there is a philosophical debate – greatly enriched by the historical dimension – about the place of behaviourism in psychology and the human sciences. It is therefore foolish to offer a narrow definition of what behaviourism was (or is): its history must deal with a range of major themes in the development of twentieth-century psychology. An awareness that these themes are still very much alive is important to understanding the range of relevant literature.

1. BEHAVIOURISM AS A SCIENTIFIC PRACTICE

For many observers, the dominant activity in the academic specialism of psychology, from about 1910 to the 1960s, was studying animal learning in highly controlled laboratory settings. Many psychologists viewed this activity as a model for scientific psychology: it elaborated objective, experimental techniques for studying physical variables; it advanced knowledge of a cluster of related, core phenomena; and it provided training and a sense of coherent endeavour for a legitimately distinct scientific specialism. This model originated in, and continued to be dominated by, psychology in the United States. More specifically, it was agreed that the programme began with J. B. Watson's polemic, 'Psychology as the behaviorist views it' (1913),[1] following many 'anticipations' (by Max Meyer and James McKeen Cattell, among others). Similarly, it was agreed that the movement declined in the 1950s when subjected to 'internal' criticism (that it both failed to explain learning and that its terms were imprecise) and from without (that it could not, logically, explain human action). In the 1960s, this decline, and an associated loss of direction in psychological research, fostered a sense of crisis. Many psychologists feel that the replacement of behaviourism by cognitive psychology resolved this crisis. This general picture sometimes encourages the use of T. S. Kuhn's language of 'paradigms'.[2] Such a description, however, does not fit. Critics have shown that behaviourism never dominated psychology in a clear-cut way, even in the United States, while elsewhere there always have been major alternatives (such as phenomenological psychology or differential psychology). In itself, moreover, it was not a united endeavour, but consisted rather of competing research schools, and further, there never was a core of paradigmatic knowledge, but attempts instead to constitute science by commitment to methodological principles. It has therefore become a temptation to treat behaviourism only as a set of prescriptions for accrediting would-be researchers as scientists. This, however, is over-simplification of another kind. Recent work makes it possible to flesh-out these generalisations with some historical detail, but, as more research is done, particularly for the period after 1920, considerable reinterpretation may become necessary.

1.1. Origins

The setting is the establishment of academic departments of psychology in North America from the 1880s to the First World War. These departments turned a German ideal of *Wissenschaft* and a home-grown tradition of 'moral science' into an autonomous psychology discipline legitimated by its social utility. By 1903, over 40 laboratories had been established. The academics responsible for this, such as William James, Stanley Hall, Cattell and James Baldwin, claimed to be institutionalising *scientific* psychology, and this concern with psychology as 'science' was fundamental to the subsequent career of behaviourism. Their ideal was motivated in various ways: it distanced psychology from the liberal arts curriculum characteristic earlier in the century (and still influential later); it implied continuity with the high-status German universities (whether or not this 'continuity' involved much actual transfer of practice and values); and it sought to capitalise on enthusiasm for the progress of physical science. In practice, the ideal translated into a concern with method and technique – the means of achieving objective description and measurement of mental content and capacities. Much less adequately, the ideal translated into theory – the means by which knowledge of mind integrated with natural scientific knowledge. Integration appeared to be possible by following one of two broad programmes:

analysing mind's dependence on the brain and nervous system, or developing evolutionary theory to include mind as a biological function.

It was clear by 1900 that 'scientific' psychology, though possessing a partially unified institutional framework (e.g. the American Psychological Association, founded in 1892), consisted of very different approaches, more varied than the conventional separation of structuralist and functionalist schools would suggest. Certainly, at Cornell E. B. Titchener imposed a precise conception of scientific psychology as the description of conscious contents, using techniques of controlled introspection. By contrast, James at Harvard and J. R. Angell and John Dewey at Chicago conceptualised a Darwinian view of mind as functional – as part of the organism's adaptation to the surrounding world (or a human being's to society). But there were many other activities, such as Baldwin's work on the stages of child development, or E. L. Thorndike's studies of animal learning. Thorndike showed that the long-standing 'pleasure-pain principle' of motivation could be studied experimentally in animals by correlating behaviour with its consequences ('the law of effect').[3] Sometimes known as 'connectionism', Thorndike's approach to learning theory established a pattern that much influenced behaviourism, though he himself continued to refer to the animal's mind.

While psychology existed in the early years of the century, in the eyes of practitioners and outsiders alike, as 'the science of mind', its objects of study were exceedingly diverse: the brain, the rat, the child in school and the habitual criminal. Very importantly, outside pressures on psychologists to produce useful knowledge about what people do and how that can be altered, coincided with inside pressures to maximise the objectivity of experimental technique by recording physical variables. The desire for practical facts coincided with the desire to legitimate psychology with fact-finding methods. The result was a progressive concentration on descriptions of physical behaviour and the conditions under which it occurred as well as the results it yielded. Though it remained common to refer behaviour also to conditions of mind, these mental conditions were in practice specified by observations of the experimental conditions modified to vary behaviour. It thus began to occur to various psychologists that causal explanations which invoked such mental states were not only in danger of being subjective but also otiose.

Varied statements that the future of psychology as a science lies with the analysis of behaviour, not consciousness, existed in the opening decade of the century. To talk therefore, about a founder of behaviourism is unhelpful. What can be said about Watson is that he was especially subject to some of the pressures already described.[4] As a graduate student and young teacher, Watson had to balance his personal enthusiasm for experimental and field studies of animals against claims from different teachers for physiological or functionalist prescriptions for objective psychology. In moving towards restricting himself to descriptions of physical conditions and behaviour, Watson achieved a liberation of animal psychology from its position as an appendage of human psychology, and he side-stepped the insoluble logical problem of drawing on analogy to deduce the content of the animal mind. By the time of his (now) famous paper of 1913, he had an established institutional position at Johns Hopkins University from which to claim that the basis for a practical science of humans lay in observing animals. The 1913 paper did not cause a revolution; indeed F. Samelson has shown that it did not attract much immediate attention.[5] It is in retrospect that the paper has become a classic. It threw down the challenge that only behaviourists among psychologists could qualify as strictly objective natural scientists. Watson supported this claim with telling attacks on pursuing 'the animal mind' or descriptive agreement about mental contents. In addition, in retrospect, he isolated an autonomous subject matter for human science, behaviour, thus lessening the very real danger of psychology losing itself intellectually and institutionally in philosophy (studying mind) or in physiology (studying the material basis of mind). (See art. 46.) In this sense, Watson brought into focus the general orientation of functionalism – a 'biological' way between the Scylla of philosophical idealism and the Charybdis of physiological reductionism. (In practice, Watson soon made it clear that he was the crudest of materialists; the conceptual development of functionalism produced pragmatism and the 'social behaviourism' of G. H. Mead.)

1.2. Development

Watson certainly did not reorganise the discipline around his programme, nor did his 1913 paper create a crisis. Psychologists continued using the techniques and language with which they were already familiar, but of course these included many behaviouristic elements. During the years of the First World War, psychologists were much more excited by applying psychological testing in the army than pursuing a purist behaviourism. Watson himself amplified his programme in *Behavior: an Introduction to Comparative Psychology* (1914) and in *Psychology from the Standpoint of a Behaviourist* (1919). His research and publications at this time show just how loose and *ad hoc* his programme really was. He was more interested in 'practical' observation of animals and humans outside the laboratory than in refining theoretical or experimental detail. Thus, when he proposed a behaviouristic analogue for the higher mental process of thinking, as sub-vocalised speech movements in the laryngeal muscles, he first tried to observe it directly; only secondarily did he introduce Pavlovian conditioning as a technique for the objective study of such processes. (This set a pattern in North America for treating Pavlov's work as merely a valuable addition to the technique of studying learning.)

Watson's behaviourism was initially methodological, in the sense that he argued for it in order to satisfy an objectivity criterion. In his interpretation of this requirement, psychology tended towards atomism (i.e. its subject matter can be broken down into elementary units having physical character), peripheralism (i.e. its subject matter concerns stimulus and response rather than central processes), and environmentalism (i.e. that behaviour is acquired and fluid rather than innate and fixed). These characteristics are actually very variable in behaviourism's subsequent development (Watson himself accepted love, rage and fear as instincts), but the core topic remained the S–R (Stimulus–Response) relation. Watson also pushed eagerly towards a 'metaphysical' behaviourism, denying the existence of mental processes altogether, which was highly controversial. When this was refined it was by philosophers rather than psychologists, such as E. B. Holt and by the later 'philosophical' behaviourists, notably Gilbert Ryle in *The Concept of Mind* (1949). The only clear metaphysical materialist psychologist in 1919 was probably A. P. Weiss; but his reductionist programme, eliminating distinct behavioural as well as psychological categories, was an alternative to behaviourism. Nevertheless, contemporaries (as well as later commentators) did not always clearly distinguish between physiological reductionism and psychological behaviourism, and critics discerned a common materialism.

By the early 1920s, many psychologists were using the label 'behaviourism', but in an extraordinary variety of ways. The situation is still not really clear (though greatly illuminated by the works of Samelson). Watson himself was forced out of academic life by his divorce in 1920, moving on to a successful career in the J. Walter Thompson advertising agency and as a populariser of psychology (particularly with his new wife, Rosalie Rayner, on 'scientific' child rearing). The 1920s was a period of competing 'schools' in psychology, with a great expansion of psychological activity but no overall sense of direction and certainly no agreed theory. Even less, those sympathetic to a behaviourist orientation accepted that not everything could be simplified to S–R functions. In particular, psychologists conceptualised the central or S–R linkage in terms of either brain processes (e.g. Karl Lashley) or hypothetical variables (e.g. E. C. Tolman). While resistance of a philosophical character to behaviourism was widespread (e.g. William McDougall's 'battle of behaviourism'), most psychologists were preoccupied with narrow experimental programmes, often behaviourist in orientation, which they did not try to justify in theoretical terms. A reaction to this beginning in the late 1920s led to what is often termed neo-behaviourism.

The neo-behaviourists introduced a new concern for systematic theoretical structure. This began autonomously in the North-American setting with dissatisfaction at the diversity and triviality of experimental work. It was influenced during the 1930s, however, by developments in the philosophy of science, which arose in response to the overthrow of classical physics (see art. 54). For a time, psychology was quite exceptional as a science because it attempted to build knowledge on explicit methodological prescriptions derived from the philosophy of science. Part of the explanation must be the congruence of a behaviourist preoccupation with collating observable variables with the philosophy of positivism. Two broadly 'positivist' arguments influenced psychology in the 1930s: firstly, that operational definition gave meaning to scientific terms (following the American physicist, Percy Bridgman); secondly, that science should be unified under a logically consistent scheme of meaningful observation statements. The emigrant German-speaking logical positivists perhaps indeed achieved their greatest influence on a science in neo-behaviourism. (See art. 54, sect. 2.)

It was characteristic of neo-behaviourist psychology that it consisted of different schools, each led by a researcher combining particular experimental techniques with a comprehensive vision of the field, each developing highly technical studies of the constitution of the S–R connection. But no unification was forthcoming and each programme developed by refining its position in response to the other schools. As a simplification, the four most important schools were those of Tolman (1886–1959) (followed by I. Krechevsky), E. R. Guthrie, Clark Hull (1884–1952) (followed by Kenneth Spence), and B. F. Skinner (b.1904). Hull was the most influenced by logical positivism, creating a dauntingly formal system remote in the extreme from Watson's earlier loose ideas. Hull and the other neo-behaviourists accepted a variety of central variables (Tolman even advocated a 'purposive' or 'molar' behaviourism) as long as they were studied in a methodologically rigorous way.

The work of B. F. Skinner should be distinguished, not least because he belonged to a younger generation and managed to sustain his programme, though increasingly isolated, into the 1970s. Skinner, in *The Behaviour of Organisms* (1938) introduced the technique of operant conditioning and the claim that learning occurred by reinforcement – by a tendency to repetition or aversion as a result of behaviour. He soon abandoned an interest in assimilating this empirical claim to an operationalist philosophy of science and subsequently eschewed 'theory' altogether. He argued that scientific psychology was (or should be) nothing but a set of statements about the observed order or pattern of behaviour. Reactions to Skinner's work have encapsulated both the enthusiasm for, and antagonism towards, behaviourism in general.

Though studies of the history of psychology in Europe in the twentieth century are few and incomplete, it appears fair to restrict the development of behaviourism to North America until 1945. After 1945, many aspects of behaviourism, though especially its experimental techniques and traditions of training students, were important to the academic take-off of psychology (and the social sciences generally) in Britain, Scandinavia and West Germany. In the West German case, behaviourism perhaps offered what appeared as a rigorously objective psychology, quite independent of German traditions, and thus provided the discipline with a new start. Scientists in Europe certainly turned to American work for a model of highly professional scientific practice. The climate of opinion supported research that appeared to equip society with a knowledge of its own foundations free from the possibility of ideology.

1.3. Decline

There are no histories of the decline of behaviourism; rather, it is in the collective memory of active psychologists. Though the dominance by neo-behaviourism has clearly gone, deep-lying elements of behaviourism as a way of thought and interest in behaviourist techniques of objective description remain. It appears wrong to regard psychology as going through a distinct 'revolution'; instead, alternative traditions which had always been present, if excluded from certain North-American institutions, slowly attracted attention. Questions came from both inside and outside the psychological community in Europe and North America.

Behaviourism, of course, never monopolised psychological activity even in the United States, let alone anywhere else. Studies in perception and physiological psychology sustained major alternative experimental traditions. By the early 1950s, there was serious disquiet at the inability of the schools to agree a common body of knowledge and techniques even for learning theory – the heartland of neo-behaviourism. The sheer imprecision and variation of meaning in key terms, such as stimulus, response and behaviour, was an embarrassment. Hull's programme appeared to demonstrate the practical impossibility of achieving a consistent and full positivist reduction. Non-Skinnerians did not agree that learning was solely a product of reinforcement in animals, let alone in humans. The entrenched institutional position of behaviourist practices, supported by an image of their scientific character, ensured their survival for many years, but they became what Imre Lakatos described as 'degenerating' research programmes. At the same time there were large shifts of interest, often associated with the desire to place human beings centre stage. Thus developmental psychology, personality theory, social psychology and neo-Freudianism all flourished. Even in animal studies, a new ethology suggested that observations did not have to be laboratory-based to be rigorous.

Behaviourists had a somewhat ambivalent attitude towards central processes. While agreeing on the need for psychology to avoid reference to unobservables (including mental processes), they differed in the way they translated central processes into observables and viewed the relationship between brain science and behavioural science. Tolman and Hull devoted considerable effort to theorising central processes, though without specifying a causal relation to the brain. Skinner considered that psychology could develop by describing 'schedules of reinforcement' without reference to central variables. But in the 1950s, and overwhelmingly in the 1960s, psychologists turned to theorising central processes, whether in neurobiological or psychological terms. It no longer seemed a pressing concern for psychologists to eliminate a mentalist language as a precondition of objective research.

Several outside developments probably helped legitimise these changes. Firstly, there were marked advances in knowledge and technique in the neurosciences which revived hope in a programme to elucidate the physical causes of behaviour. Secondly, new technologies – cybernetics, systems analysis and computing – prompted major new ways of conceptualising and modelling central processes and behaviour. The impact of these ideas is such that many modern psychologists no longer think in terms of there being a problem about linking behaviour and 'mind'. Thirdly, philosophers of science rejected logical positivism, since its meaning criteria could not be sustained, particularly once it became clear that all observation statements were theory-laden. Lastly, a considerable body of work, developing within analytic philosophy, argued that human action required explanation in terms of reasons or intentions. From this point of view, to explain in terms of mental purposes is part of what we mean by human action (and does not presuppose 'unobservables'). The behaviourist explanation is *different* and cannot, in principle, replace it. By contrast, a cognitive psychology that built mental processes into psychological explanation appeared compatible with principles of the philosophy of mind. In perhaps the single most famous attack on behaviourism, Noam Chomsky brought some of these points to bear in opposing his own idea of a universal, innate grammar to Skinner's account of verbal behaviour.[6]

These developments, as well as broad political changes, fostered a climate of crisis in the late 1960s. It became a common fictional device to refer back to an age when psychology had had a unified programme, behaviourism, in order to try to understand where present changes were leading. But in this period there was also the first serious investment in the history of psychology. This new history both traced the roots of present troubles and achieved a wider sense of the place of both psychology and behaviourism in western culture.

2. BEHAVIOURISM AS A SOCIAL TECHNOLOGY

Two kinds of historical and critical work have extended an understanding of behaviourism in significant directions, and these are introduced in this and the following section. Firstly, historians have begun to explain 'the origins' of behaviourism in social conditions, establishing ideas which are being extended in due course to interpret the academic response and outside receptivity to behaviourism into the 1950s. The social conditions which have been implicated are of two interrelated kinds: the process by which psychology became a distinct academic discipline and professional occupation; and the conditions of large-scale social change which generated outside support for this process. Much of this work occurs in a series of papers by John Burnham and in a book by John O'Donnell.[7] They have tied the growth of American psychology to a general commitment to the social sciences, this in turn embodying a new conception of academic research and the value of its contribution to social reform. Reform was pivotal for the Progressive Era's response to post Civil War industrialisation and the dramatic shift of population and political influence to the cities. The huge scale of immigration up to the First World War, particularly involving southern and eastern Europeans, greatly encouraged a search for new forms of social organisation. Under these circumstances, academic claims for funding and leadership based on cultural status changed to claims based on expertise. The curricula and purposes of the older American colleges were widely reformed, influenced by German models and the innovative graduate school at Johns Hopkins. There were also new social science organisations. But the shift to an emphasis on practical expertise was most evident in new universities, whether state-funded (under the Land-grant Act) or dependent on local business communities (as with the University of Chicago). The universities were in the business of rapid growth, but this meant financial dependency on student numbers and on satisfying boards answerable to businessmen or state politicians.

Many ambitious students were attracted by a scientific conception of psychology in the late nineteenth century. This, and of course the desire for a career, led a certain number to study in Germany. In North America, however, personal interest, academic interest and social pressure coincided to foster a pragmatic conception of science as propaedeutic to technology. In the 1890s this fostered close relations between psychology and education, and career shifts from 'pure' to 'applied' work were common. The existence and boundaries of an autonomous psychology were quite problematic. What did identify psychology most clearly was a series of expert techniques: for describing conscious contents, measuring capacities and for predicting and controlling learning, memory or conduct. A claim for expertise in technique therefore became central to the argument in support of psychology's independent value to society.

The shift towards defining psychology as the study of behaviour happened when it became evident that this was a psychology which might reconcile objective methods, expert technique and applicable results. Elementary schools, courts of law, or personnel boards required knowledge of what people do in specified circumstances. The early behaviourist orientation claimed special aptitude for setting out 'the facts' to satisfy this need. It also defined an area of practice uniquely occupied by the psychologist and enhanced psychology's argument for institutional autonomy as a scientific discipline. Many of these points applied equally to functionalism, but if, as Watson claimed, behaviourism was the only logically consistent functionalism, then behaviourism added a greater sense of scientific rigour. It should be noted that this is not an argument that applied psychology, and hence behaviourism, was uniquely American. The value attributed to applying knowledge was a central feature of psychology's growth everywhere. But the correspondence between psychology's claim to offer 'facts' and the cultural valuation of 'facts' was particularly forceful in America.

Thus Thorndike followed his early experimental work on learning in animals by becoming a professor of experimental pedagogy, when he declared that 'there can be no moral warrant for studying man's nature unless the study will enable us to control his acts'.[8] Watson followed his call for objective psychology in 1913 with a series of studies, in which he freely and loosely referred to instincts, habits, feelings and capacities, for a practically-oriented human psychology. Far from imposing restrictive methodological constraints, Watson engaged in open-ended observation of babies and in studying the effect of anti-VD propaganda films on the military. In 1918, in association with the Johns Hopkins psychiatrist Adolf Meyer, he revived his interest in mental illness. He began to elaborate entirely speculative behaviourist explanations for disorders and initiated some of the ideas that later entered into behavioural therapy.

When Watson left academic psychology in 1920, it involved little change in motivation for him to become an advertising executive and populariser of psychology; after all, the point of science was its application. One may perhaps see in Watsonian behaviourism the anti-intellectualism associated with American political culture. It never considered philosophical and ethical problems inherent in behavioural engineering. Watson himself was pragmatic and unsubtle, whether dealing with babies, sex, advertising or deviancy. The origins of these attitudes in small-town rural America, the loss of community in the movement to the cities and the appeal of a technological panacea, are brought out in a bold psycho-historical study by David Bakan.[9] It is striking that Skinner shares a similar background, similar conception of psychology as human technology and similar indifference to philosophical analysis and ethical discourse.

O'Donnell has suggested that both early behaviourism and the popular behaviourism of Watson in the 1920s were continuous with a long-standing tradition of popular and practical psychology. Citing phrenology as the most important variant, he points to the avid consumption of guides to psychology applicable to everyday affairs. Behaviourism scientifically legitimated commonplace correlations between the observable world and conduct. In its emphasis on the environment, its de-mystification of mind and its marketing of tools, it was the embodiment of a democratic technology. This said, it should also be remembered that, by the 1920s, academic psychology had become an institutionalised scientific discipline and hence did not have to answer constantly to lay audiences. The generation of psychologists before 1914 was harassed by the need to claim funds or to fend off fears of scientific materialism. Later generations took the institutional base of psychology for granted and pursued careers in esoteric knowledge and technique such as neo-behaviourism. Nevertheless, the many substantial areas of applied psychology, now often institutionally separate, sustained the earlier traditions. Skinner reintegrated the esoteric and the applied when, in his Utopian novel *Waldon Two* (1948), and in *Science and Human Behavior* (1953) and *Beyond Freedom and Dignity* (1971), he sought a general audience for his most ambitious of all visions, that of an engineered answer to world problems.

A related conception of the potential of social science expertise underlay the currency of the term 'behavioural science' from the early 1950s. The entry of the Ford Foundation in 1952 into social-science funding created behavioural science almost overnight – 'an administrative arrangement that became intellectually institutionalised'.[10] According to the Ford Foundation's usage, behavioural science included the study of 'subjective behaviour' (i.e. attitudes, beliefs and motivation) as well as overt behaviour. In other usages, it meant the search for a general theory of behaviour. But it is clear that the term 'behaviour' had come to mean almost anything of relevance in human relations.

3. BEHAVIOURISM AS A NATURAL SCIENCE

The history of behaviourism inevitably focuses on the North-American setting. As a way of thought, and viewed in the light of modern science generally, however, behaviourism has a deeper structural dimension. It can be argued that behaviourism is logically implicit in the form of scientific explanation dominant since the seventeenth century. This leads on to the question of whether behaviourism was an 'aberration' in the development of scientific psychology or whether its underlying forms of explanation remain intact in much of the human sciences. It may be that consideration of behaviourism's strengths and weaknesses cannot be undertaken independently of fundamental questions about explanation in the human sciences generally. It is certainly impossible to divorce behaviourism's successes from the role of mechanistic explanation and empiricism in natural science.

Behaviourist explanation is deterministic, linking one set of physical changes ('the stimulus') with a second set ('the response'). The possibility of describing organisms in these terms developed historically with the concept of the reflex, already associated after Descartes with the elimination of mind from animals. The reflex described how mechanism produced an appearance of purposiveness and hence of mind. The reduction of the human mind to reflex events became increasingly conceivable with the development of physical metaphors for mental processes; for example, the empiricist account by Locke and Hume of the origin of ideas in atomic sensations, David Hartley's theory of the 'associ-

ation' or causal linking of ideas, and the analysis of motivation into consequences of the pleasurable or painful qualities of ideas. The association psychology and utilitarianism of Bentham and James Stuart Mill, and later of
Alexander Bain, Herbert Spencer and Charles Darwin (however modified by
evolutionary theory), conceptualised psychological explanation in which the
work was done by causal relations rather than by mental faculties (such as
reason). Then the great refinement of theoretical and experimental studies of
the reflex concept in the mid-nineteenth century encouraged hopes that psychology could become literally (as opposed to metaphorically) physiological.
Physiological psychologists of the period suggested that mind was either epiphenomenal or a causally impotent parallel to physical causal relations, and in
either case, was an embarrassment if brought into the scientific endeavour.

Whether because of the sheer complexity and difficulty of brain research or
because of philosophical naïvety, these very real failures in the physiological
approach to psychology significantly influenced the direction of research. One
response, associated with Wundt, adapted experimental technique for the study
of mental content and sought to make psychology competent to address philosophical questions. (See art. 25.) A second response became behaviourism. It
was argued that scientific psychology did not depend on knowledge of the
physical mechanisms underlying mind. Instead, the psychologist should correlate the physical input to the organism with the physical output, leaving the
causal nature of the linkage to future research. It was plausible to claim a
unique rigour for this approach since it searched directly for regularities
between observables. In his enthusiasm for behaviourism and impatience with
neurophysiology, Watson sometimes talked as if environment and behaviour
constituted the whole of human (or animal) life. But there was no problem, in
principle, in introducing central physical variables into the explanation, if and
when these variables became observable. And of course this was done, by Watson in a loose way and by the neo-behaviourists with more precision. S–R
(Stimulus–Response) theories were therefore a development from reflex theory
and associationism, with the physiological mechanism or association of ideas
being replaced by environmental mechanism and behaviour, in the interests of
facility of observation and control.

The behaviourists identified closely with the progress of the physical
sciences. Their claim to dominance among psychologists rested on their being
the true heirs of the mechanistic explanation and empiricist methodology that,
they believed, made the physcial sciences triumphant. Watson was explicit: it
was only behaviourism which enabled psychologists to observe their subject-
matter in the way that natural scientists observed theirs. The ideal behind this,
that psychology is continuous with the other branches of natural science, was a
potent force with Watson's generation. And it has remained so with psychologists, supporting the continuing use of many aspects of behaviourist technique

as 'obviously' scientific. As Brian Mackenzie has argued, this ideal led the neo-behaviourists to 'the most sustained attempt ever made to construct a science of psychology through the use of detailed and explicit rules of procedure'.[11] He suggests, further, that the ideal showed behaviourism to be a set of methodological prescriptions rather than a body of knowledge and that this starkly exposes the limits of a preoccupation with method in the advancement of science. He concludes that the attempt to formalise method has in fact restricted the human sciences.

Descartes's conception of the reflex and of the mechanistic form of purposive movements was influenced by contemporary mechanical toys. Later mechanistic psychologies, whether Bentham's or Watson's, were similarly part of a wider technological culture. Watson, in a famous phrase, defined the aim of psychology as 'the prediction and control of behaviour', apparently taking it for granted that all scientific explanation was not only equivalent to prediction but also of value because of the controlling power which it provided.[12] Quite simply, Watson and many other psychologists did not discriminate between knowledge and power. Skinner later achieved notoriety by identifying 'the good' with what has reinforced behaviour in the past, and by identifying knowledge of conditioning with a political programme for ensuring human survival. Thus, in making human beings a proper subject for natural science, behaviourism also made human beings a proper object for technology.

It has been relatively easy for critics of behaviourism to show that behaviourist knowledge is not adequate for the controlling purposes required of it, and that the ends for which such control is intended do not circumscribe human desires. Behavioural modification techniques do have a continuing application for specific and limited ends (as in giving mentally-handicapped children a particular skill), but even here it is accepted that they are more complex than the theories on which they were originally based. Not surprisingly, an association between behaviourism and political constraint on human liberation, widely perceived in the 1960s, helped its demise. Nevertheless, 'the excesses' of behaviourism prompt deeper questions for the human sciences. Such questions belong to debates which have continued since the late nineteenth century and which are still very much unsettled.

Behaviourism rode on the back of a 'commonsense' view that treats scientific epistemology as essentially unproblematic and the activity of science as 'self-evidently' rational. The behaviourists, among many other twentieth-century social scientists, assumed that it was in principle only prejudice which prevented science's comprehension of human beings. The behaviourist technologists went further, believing that science itself clarified the ends for which knowledge was to be deployed. Whatever has happened to behaviourism in a narrow sense, the underlying structure of behaviourist beliefs and values continues to have a central place in the world-view of esoteric and popular scientific psychology alike. In the debate comparing artificial and human intelligence, for example, the question of whether computational processes can duplicate conscious mental operations repeats earlier arguments over behaviourism. (See art. 34, sect. 4.) Such continuity of philosophical argument suggests that it is right to locate behaviourism as an exemplification of natural-science explanation. But if so, its limitations may in reality indicate the abstraction, simplification and mechanisation that natural science must practice on human reality. The question then returns of whether such science should possess the unique status that it does (and of whether the scientist has the unique position as expert) in the organisation of human affairs. The work of Watson and Skinner may now look crude but it only simplified a fundamental intellectual and political challenge.

NOTES

1. J. B. Watson, 'Psychology as the behaviorist views it', *Psychological review*, 20 (1913), 158–77; often reprinted, e.g. in W. Dennis (ed.), *Readings in the history of psychology* (New York, 1948), pp. 457–71.
2. For an introductory discussion: T. H. Leahey, *A history of psychology: main currents in psychological thought* (Englewood Cliffs, NJ, 1980), pp. 326–77. See also discussion by D. S. Palermo, N. Warren and W. Weimer in *Science studies*, (1971), 135–55, 407–13; 3 (1973) 211–44; 4 (1974), 195–200, 235–58.
3. *Animal intelligence* (New York), 1911); L. Postman, 'The history and present status of the law of effect', *Psychological bulletin*, 44 (1947), 489–563.
4. For a biography, see D. Cohen, *J. B. Watson: the founder of behaviourism. A biography* (London, 1979). This account should be corrected by the work of O'Donnell and Samelson.
5. F. Samelson, 'Struggle for scientific authority: the reception of Watson's behaviourism 1913–1920', *Journal of the history of the behavioural sciences*, 17 (1981), 399–425.
6. N. Chomsky, 'Review of Skinner's verbal behavior', in L. A. Jakobovits and M. S. Miron (eds.), *Readings in the psychology of language* (Englewood Cliffs, NJ 1967), pp. 142–71; originally published 1959.
7. J. C. Burnham 'Psychiatry, psychology and the Progressive Movement', *American quarterly*, 12 (1960), 457–65; Burnham, 'The new psychology: from narcissism to social control', in J. C. Braeman, R. H. Bremner and D. Brody (eds.), *Change and continuity in twentieth-century America: the 1920s* (Columbus, 1968), pp. 352–98.
   J. M. O'Donnell, *The origins of behaviorism: American psychology, 1870–1920* (New York, 1986).
8. Quoted in Leahey, p. 294.
9. D. Bakan, 'Behaviorism and American urbanization', *Journal of the history of the behavioral sciences*, 2 (1966), 5–28.
10. 'Behavioral sciences' in D. L. Sills (ed.), *International encyclopaedia of the social sciences* (New York, 1968), vol. 2, pp. 41–5.
11. B. D. Mackenzie, *Behaviourism and the limits of scientific method* (London, 1977).
12. Watson 1913, in Dennis (1948), p. 457.

FURTHER READING

H. Cravens and J. C. Burnham, 'Psychology and evolutionary naturalism in American thought, 1890–1940', *American quarterly*, 23 (1971), 635–657.

W. K. Estes, S. Koch, K. MacCorquodale, P. E. Meehl, C. G. Mueller, Jr., W. N. Schoenfeld and W. S. Verplanck, *Modern learning theory: a critical analysis of five examples* (New York, 1954).

F. Samelson, 'Organising for the kingdom of behavior: academic battles and organizational policies in the twenties', *Journal of the history of the behavioral sciences*, 21 (1985), 33–47.

C. Taylor, *The explanation of behavior* (London, 1964).

T. W. Wann (ed.), *Behaviorism and phenomenology: contrasting bases for modern psychology* (Chicago, 1964).

P. P. Wiener (ed.), *Dictionary of the history of ideas* (5 vols., New York, 1973–4), articles on 'Behaviorism', 'Man-machine from the Greeks to the computer' and 'Psychological theories in American thought'.

R. M. Young, 'Animal soul', in P. Edwards (ed.), *Encyclopaedia of philosophy* (New York, 1967), vol. 1, pp. 122–27.

27

FREUD AND PSYCHOANALYSIS

RAYMOND E. FANCHER

The term 'psychoanalysis' denotes both the specific system of psychotherapy and the general psychological theory developed by the Viennese physician Sigmund Freud (1856–1939). Accordingly, students of the field commonly distinguish between Freud's *clinical theory*, which mainly addresses psychopathology, repression and the experiences of analytic therapy sessions, from his *metapsychology*, which attempts to explain the mechanics of mental functioning in a general model of the mind.

Freud's ideas constantly developed and changed over the course of his long lifetime, and are best understood in their proper chronological and situational contexts. Thus the first part of this essay introduces Freud's major works in the order in which they were written, and within the framework of his life history. The second part describes major historical and philosophical studies of Freud which have been conducted after his death.

1. FREUD'S LIFE AND WORK

1.1. Background and training

Sigmund Freud was born on 6 May 1856 in the Moravian town of Freiberg (now Prîbor, Czechoslovakia), but moved to Vienna in 1860 where he remained until the Nazi menace forced him to flee to London in 1938, for the final year of his life. The son of a Jewish wool merchant of modest means, young Sigmund always excelled academically, and developed early interests in history and literature. A chance encounter with Goethe's essay *On Nature* during Freud's final year at *Gymnasium* inspired him about science, and led to his impulsive enrolment at the University of Vienna's medical school in 1873.

For the first three years of medical school, Freud's primary attention was captured by a non-medical teacher, the philosopher and 'act psychologist',

Franz Brentano (1838–1917), who taught that classical associationistic psychology had to be modified by consideration of motivational and 'dynamic' factors such as intentions, desires, and judgements. Then Freud's interests turned strongly towards the mechanistic 'new physiology' promoted by his teacher Ernst Brücke (1819–1892), according to which all animate processes, of whatever degree of complexity, must ultimately be explained in terms of ordinary physico-chemical processes. Freud enthusiastically conducted and published neurophysiological research from Brücke's laboratory for six years, passing his final medical examinations almost off-handedly (and belatedly) in 1881. In 1882, he reluctantly concluded that a physiological research career was not feasible for an impecunious Jew living in anti-Semitic Vienna, and decided to obtain the clinical training required for medical practice at Vienna's General Hospital.

At the hospital, Freud's neurophysiological background led him to gravitate towards the psychiatry clinic directed by the brain anatomist Theodor Meynert (1833–1893). Meynert, a fervent proponent of the new movement to localise cortical functions, taught that ideas or memories are contained in specific brain cells and interconnected in a system called the 'ego', whose physical disruption can produce phenomena such as dreams and psychopathological symptoms. Under Meynert, Freud became proficient in diagnosing organic brain disorders, and developed ambitions of making his living as a specialist in neuropathology.

During this training period Freud also experimented with the then little-known drug, cocaine, and published a series of controversial papers recommending it for a variety of medical problems. Falsely believing it was non-addictive, he prescribed it to a friend as a substitute for morphine, with disastrous eventual results which led Freud to rue his early and incautious endorsements. Understandably, this episode was not a phase of his early career that he later chose to emphasise.

A more positive set of interests began to develop late in 1885, when Freud won a six-month travelling fellowship to study in Paris with the eminent neurologist, Jean Charcot (1825–93). Charcot was then deep into the study of hysteria, a condition whose symptoms often mimicked the disabilities caused by localised injuries to the brain and nervous system, but which occurred in the absence of such injuries. Most physicians of the time regarded hysteria as malingering, but Charcot observed that similar effects could be produced by hypnosis, and hypothesised that both hysteria and hypnosis were caused by hereditary and generalised (as opposed to localised) degeneracy of the nervous system. Charcot's neurological theory was soon proven incorrect, but his dramatic clinical demonstrations of hysteria and hypnosis kindled Freud's interest in these medically unfashionable subjects.

On returning to Vienna, Freud married Martha Bernays (1861–1951), his fiancée of five years, and tried to establish a practice in neuropathology.

Between 1888 and 1893 he published well-received studies of aphasia and infantile cerebral palsy, but despite a growing reputation, could not make a living treating just these kinds of cases. He had also kept up with the literature on hysteria, however, translating into German not only Charcot's work but also that of Hippolyte Bernheim (1840–1919), Charcot's principal theoretical opponent and leader of the so called 'Nancy School'. Bernheim denied Charcot's neurological degeneracy theory, and used direct hypnotic suggestion as a *treatment* for hysteria, with some success. Freud now began accepting patients with hysteria to fill out his practice, and confirmed that the Nancy technique was considerably better than orthodox medicine, though still imperfect. His search for improved therapy for hysteria marked the real beginnings of psychoanalysis.

1.2. Studies on hysteria

Important first clues in the search came from Freud's friend, Josef Breuer (1842–1925), who years earlier had treated a single remarkable case of hysteria with an experimental *cathartic method*. His patient, a young woman called 'Anna O.' in published accounts of the case had been repeatedly hypnotised and asked to try and recall the first time she had ever experienced a sensation similar to that of a particular symptom. Invariably, she recalled emotion-laden but previously 'forgotten' memories; e.g. of suppressing tears and squinting her eyes in order to tell the time for her terminally-ill father, about whom she was greatly upset. Afterwards she forgot the incident, but the squint persisted as a hysterical symptom. Upon recalling the scene under hypnosis, and now 'abreacting' the distressed emotion she had previously suppressed, she was relieved of the symptom. Most of her numerous symptoms were removed in this way, but Breuer became highly uncomfortable about Anna's growing emotional attachment to him as the treatment proceeded, and could never be persuaded to repeat the method on another hysterical patient.

Freud recalled this case as he worked with his own hysterical patients in the early 1890s, tried the technique and found it more effective than direct hypnotic suggestion. With some difficulty, Freud persuaded Breuer to collaborate in writing *Studies on Hysteria* in 1895, a book which included five case studies (including Anna O.) and a new theory of hysteria. According to this theory, symptoms originate in emotion-laden memories which somehow lose access to conscious recollection, thus becoming *pathogenic ideas*. Stimuli which should normally bring the pathogenic ideas to consciousness fail to do so, but arouse the *strangulated affect* or suppressed emotional energy associated with the ideas. Denied its normal route to expression, this energy literally 'discharges' into the musculature to create physical symptoms which Freud labelled *conversions* (representing the 'conversion' of emotional into physical energy). Pathogenic ideas could apparently be restored to consciousness through hypnosis, their strangulated affect belatedly expressed or *abreacted* and the symptoms made to disappear.

Two important problems remained; the first a theoretical question as to *why* pathogenic ideas became unconscious in the first place, and the second, the practical issue of discovering a memory-enhancing technique that could be used on non-hypnotisable patients. Freud's invention of *free association* as his substitute for hypnosis led indirectly to his answer for the theoretical problem, as well as to a monumental broadening of his theory.

To free associate, a normally conscious patient (but still reclining on the hypnotic subject's couch) was simply asked to recall and relate everything that came to mind in association with a symptom, without editing or censoring the account. Simple in concept, this was difficult in practice because patients inevitably experienced *resistance* – blocking, editing, censoring their accounts, or sometimes openly refusing to continue because of anxiety or embarrassment. Nevertheless, the technique often led to the recollection of *repressed* and emotion-laden pathogenic ideas, whose abreaction produced relief of symptoms.

Moreover, Freud learned more about the structure of hysteria and the nature of pathogenic ideas. He regularly found several pathogenic ideas behind an individual symptom, leading him to describe that symptom as 'overdetermined'. He also found that the pathogenic ideas uncovered with greatest difficulty but also with greatest therapeutic effect regularly involved sexual misadventures in childhood. This led to Freud's notorious *seduction theory*, published in 1896, which held that sexual mistreatment in childhood caused hysteria in adults. Freud believed that the memories of these events became sexualised 'after the fact' with the onset of puberty, and then had to be repressed from normal consciousness to escape from their disturbing affect.

The seduction theory was poorly received, and Freud himself soon concluded it was mistaken. Though patients remained convinced of the accuracy of their sexual 'memories', other evidence too often disconfirmed them. Freud's eventual resolution of this contradiction arose from his self-analysis, which prominently entailed his first serious consideration of dreams.

1.3. Dreams and self-analysis

In 1895, Freud began his decade of greatest creativity. At the same time as *Studies on Hysteria* was being published, he began an ambitious theoretical attempt to integrate his neurological knowledge with his new insights about hysteria and unconscious psychological processes in a 'psychology for neurologists'. He summarised his ideas in a draft manuscript which he never published, but sent to his Berlin friend and confidant, Wilhelm Fliess (1858–1928). Fortunately, Fliess saved the manuscript, along with much other correspondence from Freud which has been published since Freud's death. Originally untitled, the manuscript was called *Project for a Scientific Psychology* in the English translation of 1954.

Here Freud tried to explain hysteria as well as normal mental functioning in the mechanistic, neurological terms prescribed by Brücke's teaching. Also borrowing from Meynert, he proposed that individual ideas or memories are localised in individual cortical neurons, each one capable of being aroused or 'cathected' by some undefined process of electrochemical excitation. Still following Meynert, Freud saw these neurons as being interconnected in a system called the 'ego'. Freud's ego concept went beyond Meynert's however, in that it allowed for the influence of motivational or dynamic factors on the flow of thought (as had been emphasised by Brentano), as well as for the unconscious nature of much psychic activity. Freud accounted mechanistically for the unconscious production of 'primary process' phenomena such as over determined hysterical conversion symptoms. Perhaps most momentous of all, he also considered dreams and showed how his neurological theory predicted that dreams should resemble hysterical symptoms in many ways. In addition, however, the theory also suggested that dreams should represent the fantasied gratification of endogenously arising needs – that is, dreams should represent the fulfilment of wishes.

As he was formulating this theory, Freud also began to study dreams empirically by subjecting them to free association. A frequent recaller of his own dreams, he became his own best subject. Moreover, his father died in late 1896, precipitating a personal crisis which Freud sought to resolve largely through interpreting his dreams – his famous self-analysis. Following his rule of allowing associations to go where they would without censoring, Freud discovered in himself the elements of the *Oedipus complex*: evidence that he had wished as a child for the 'sexual' possession of his mother as the source of sensual gratification, and for the 'death' (removal) of his father as a rival for his mother's attention. Many of Freud's followers have seen this self-anlaysis, conducted in the absence of any supportive therapist except for his distant correspondent Fliess, as Freud's most courageous and significant personal accomplishment.

The self-analysis and new theory of dreams pointed to a solution to Freud's seduction-theory riddle. He now saw dreams and hysterical symptoms as structurally similar, both being overdetermined symbolic representations of ideas too dangerously emotion-laden to be accepted in consciousness directly. In dreams, however, the originating unconscious ideas (called the dream's 'latent content', as opposed to the 'manifest content' of the conscious dream experience) were unacceptable *wishes*, often reflecting sexual urges dating from childhood. In hysteria, the pathogenic ideas had seemed to be false *memories* of sexual experience in childhood. Taking the cue from dreams, Freud began to reinterpret pathogenic ideas as thinly-disguised reflections of childish sexual wishes like those which initiated his dreams.

Sensing that unconscious primary processes were surprisingly widespread, Freud began analysing everyday mistakes by free association. Here too he found evidence of unconscious motivation – the now-famous, 'Freudian slips'. Unconscious psychic processes which had first seemed pathological, in the context of hysteria, were now seen as pervading much of 'normal' experience as well. Freud explored these ideas in his book, *The Interpretation of Dreams* (1900) (regarded by many, including Freud himself, as his greatest work), and in the more popular *The Psychopathology of Everyday Life*, published a year later.

1.4. Sexuality

Freud's theories of hysteria and dreams had highlighted the importance of sexuality, and he developed this theme in his book, *Three Essays on the Theory of Sexuality* (1905). Here Freud argued that the sexual instinct was *not* the traditionally accepted heterosexual and genitally-oriented urge which appears only after puberty, but was instead a highly general drive for sensual gratification of many kinds, present from infancy onwards. At first, rhythmic stimulation of *any* body part satisfies the drive; hence an infant is 'polymorphously perverse'. With development, however, a sequence of specific *erogenous zones* come to be singled out as focal locations for this broadened form of sexual pleasure: first the mouth or *oral zone*; then, during the period of toilet training the *anal zone*; and only at the age of five or so does the genital or *phallic zone* become dominant. Such, at least, was Freud's conception of the 'normal' sequence of development.

Throughout these changing phases of childhood development, the person most closely associated with sensual pleasure – the chief object of the sexual instinct, in Freud's language – is usually the mother. The father usually becomes the chief rival, thus establishing the Oedipus complex. The child's Oedipal thoughts become increasingly anxiety-arousing, however, and at age five or six are repressed to establish a relatively tranquil *latency period*. At puberty, physiological maturation markedly increases the pressure or impetus of the sexual instinct, and threatens the Oedipal repressions. For psychic tranquillity, a new object must be found to replace the mother – ideally a socially acceptable member of the opposite sex. Only now, after extensive development and channelling, does the sexual instinct take on its traditionally-assumed configuration.

Freud went on to argue that the 'normal' sequence described above is not pre-ordained, but may be interrupted by *fixations* or *arrests* at particular stages, resulting in adult propensities for non-standard sexual practices. In this context, 'perversions' are interpreted as remnants of childhood sexuality. Neurotic symptoms, as in hysteria, are relatively extreme and maladaptive *'defences'* against the conscious recollection of childhood sexuality. And even when the normal sequence is followed, the infantile forms of sexuality are never completely abandoned, but only repressed into unconsciousness where they lie in wait to express themselves in a multitude of indirect ways: in dreams, slips, jokes, or the proclivity towards everyday activities of an 'oral' or 'anal' nature (e.g. eating, drinking or smoking for the former; extreme cleanliness, tidiness or perfectionism for the latter).

Freud now saw the sexual drive as ubiquitous, expressing itself in a multitude of indirect and unconsciously determined ways, some maladaptive and some 'normal'. The maladaptive expressions were potentially treatable through free association and the informed interpretations of a psychoanalyst, for once the underlying ideas and impulses became conscious, the psychic energy previously necessary for repression could theoretically be released for more open and creative use.

1.5. The psychoanalytic movement

By 1905, Freud had developed and published his basic psychoanalytic ideas, and though his open treatment of sexuality was highly controversial he had begun to attract a number of followers. A small group of Viennese, including Alfred Adler (1870–1937), Otto Rank (1884–1939) and Wilhelm Stekel (1868–1940) formed the Psychological Wednesday Society for weekly discussions at Freud's house. The band grew and renamed itself the Vienna-Psycho-Analytical Society in 1908, moving to larger quarters in 1910. Foreigners such as Karl Abraham (1877–1925) from Berlin, Sandor Ferenczi (1873–1933) from Budapest, Ernest Jones (1879–1958) from London and Carl Jung (1875–1961) from Zurich visited Freud and the Society, and formed the nucleus of the International Psycho-Analytical Association, established in 1910. In 1909 Freud and Jung were invited to lecture at Clark University in Worcester, Massachusetts, marking the first official American recognition of psychoanalysis. (Freud's Clark lectures, published in 1910 as *Five Lectures on Psycho-Analysis*, remain an excellent introduction to his theory.)

Perhaps inevitably, internal turmoil quickly beset the young psychoanalytic movement. Some members accepted Freud's general emphasis on unconscious psychic factors but resisted his stress on sexuality. Personality clashes occurred too, and several prominent figures including Stekel, Adler and Jung formally defected from Freud in the early 1910s.

Those who remained in the movement helped build on the basic theoretical foundations already laid by Freud, and became the primary audience for much of his subsequent work. Addressed to a specialist rather than a general readership, much of his writing inevitably became increasingly technical. (Two important exceptions were the *Introductory Lectures on Psycho-Analysis* (1916–17), and the posthumously published *An Outline of Psycho-Analysis* (1940), both of which were directed at a general audience.)

In the early 1910s Freud became preoccupied with 'narcissistic' conditions, where concerns for the self posed an apparent challenge to his theory of sexuality. Major works here included *Leonardo da Vinci and a Memory of his Childhood* (1910) (sometimes regarded as the first published attempt at 'psychobiography'), and the 1914 paper, 'On Narcissism: An Introduction'. In mid-decade, a series of 'Papers on Metapsychology' explored the fine details of repression and the unconscious, and a series of clinical articles described new cases and suggested refinements in therapeutic procedure. The horrors of the First World War sensitised Freud to the destructive elements in human nature, leading him to postulate a death instinct ('Thanatos') as a rival to the sexual instinct ('Eros') in his book, *Beyond the Pleasure Principle* (1920).

In 1923, concern over ambiguities in psychoanalytic language (e.g. the use of 'unconscious' as both a noun and an adjective) led Freud in *The Ego and the Id* to suggest his famous division of the psyche into *id* (the reservoir of unconscious instincts and impulses), *ego* (the psychic agency responsible for creating adaptive compromise solutions to psychic conflict) and *superego* (the acquired inner repository of moral demands). Two years later, one of Freud's most notoriously controversial papers ('Some Psychical Consequences of the Anatomical Distinction between the Sexes') tentatively suggested that a woman's propensity towards 'penis envy' typically leads to a less demanding superego than is found in most men.

In the meantime, mouth cancer had been detected in Freud, necessitating a long series of painful and disfiguring operations that darkened the last sixteen years of his life. During this final period his writings became increasingly philosophical and sombre. In *The Future of an Illusion* (1927) he interpreted orthodox religious beliefs as illusions deriving from infantile wishes; in *Civilization and Its Discontents* (1930) he speculated that the destructive aspects of Thanatos were likely to triumph in the end over the more creative aspects of Eros: and in 1937 ('Analysis Terminable and Interminable') he concluded that a complete therapeutic psychoanalysis was impossible. His final provocative work, *Moses and Monotheism* (1939), enraged many of his fellow Jews with its hypothesis that the historical Moses had actually been an Egyptian.

Thus Freud remained controversial to the end of his life. Nevertheless his basic message – that human beings are creatures in conflict with themselves, beset by irreconcilable and usually unconscious demands from the inner as well as the outer worlds – struck a responsive chord. His ideas concerning repression, the importance of early experience and sexuality, and the inaccessibility of much of human nature to ordinary conscious introspection have become part of our common intellectual currency. As W.H. Auden put it in his poem, 'In memory of Sigmund Freud', Freud became not just a historical person, 'but a whole climate of opinion/ Under whom we conduct our differing lives'.

2. HISTORICAL AND PHILOSPHICAL STUDIES

2.1. The Standard Edition

The extensive Freudian corpus has many complexly interrelated parts, and pit-falls await those who comment on isolated parts of it in ignorance of the whole. Accordingly, English-speaking students of Freud are fortunate to have available to them the 24 volumes of *The Standard Edition of the Complete Psychological Works of Sigmund Freud* (1953–74) (commonly referred to as the *Standard Edition* or just the *S.E.*), translated from the German under the general editorship of James Strachey, in collaboration with Freud's daughter, Anna. This uniform edition presents all of Freud's major psychological writings, omitting only a few of his early neurophysiological and neurological studies, the papers on cocaine and his posthumously-published collaborative study (with William Bullitt) of Woodrow Wilson. Volume 24 contains complete indexes and bibliographies for the entire edition, as well as useful lists of cases, dreams, symbols, analogies, personal names and works of art referred to in the texts. Each individual work throughout the collection is preceded by a summary of its previous German and English publication history, as well as an Editor's Introduction by James Strachey. Varying in length from a few lines for minor works to many pages for the major ones, these invaluable introductions describe the circumstances under which the pieces were written, and refer the reader to other works in the edition where Freud dealt with the same or similar topics.

Since a single person edited all the works in the *S.E.* and personally translated much of it as well, terminology and usage are consistent throughout. As translators must, Strachey sometimes imposed his own biases onto Freud's work, and his efforts have recently been criticised in Bruno Bettelheim's well publicised *Freud and Man's Soul* (1983). Bettelheim, who grew up with Freud's works in their original German, argues that the English translations distort their 'essential humanism', rendering Freud's prose as inappropriately abstract, theoretical, mechanistic and 'scientific'. Bettelheim cites several instances where Strachey replaced Freud's original everyday language with highly technical terms or even neologisms: e.g. *Ich* and *Es* (literally, 'I' and 'it') became 'ego' and 'id'; *besetzen* ('to occupy, invest or fill up') became the neologism 'to cathect'; and *Fehlleistung* (Freud's terms for a slip, meaning literally 'faulty achievement') became 'parapraxis'. Among other complaints, Bettelheim objects to Strachey's rendering of *Seele* as 'mind' (instead of 'soul'); *Deutung* as 'interpretation' (instead of 'attempt to grasp the deeper meaning'); and *Abwehr* as 'defence' (instead of 'parrying' or 'fending off'). Bettelheim believes that the net effect of these kinds of inappropriate translations is to put an unfortunate and unnecessary distance between Freud and his readers.

In Strachey's defence, it should be noted that some of the translations Bettelheim dislikes were conventional, and in common use before Strachey undertook Freud: e.g. 'ego' for *Ich*;'interpretation' for *Deutung*; and 'mind' for *Seele* if the German term is used in an explicitly mentalistic context. Bettelheim's complaint about the translations' mechanistic and 'scientific' connotations overlooks the fact that much psychoanalytic theory and language actually originated in Freud's explicitly mechanistic and scientific model-building of the 1890s. And most importantly of all, Strachey straightforwardly explains most of his problematic translations in notes, giving the original German terms as well as their literal translations, and openly acknowledging the disadvantages of his final choices. For example, he candidly admits that Freud himself objected to the neologism 'cathect' for *besetzen*, and explicitly says that the English 'defence' is more passive in meaning than the German *Abwehr*. In matters of translation as well as in general scholarship, Strachey's attention to detail is superior to that of Bettelheim, who provides neither index nor even original page references for the 'translation errors' quoted in his book. Indeed, in many respects the *S.E.* is more complete, and benefits from more extensive editorial scholarship than the *Gesammelte Werke*, its 18-volume German counterpart. Bettelheim's caveats should be kept in mind by the reader of the *S.E.*, and of course a working knowledge of German is highly desirable for any serious student of Freud's works. But still, the edition remains an enormously helpful tool.

2.2. Correspondence and private papers

A very large quantity of Freud's private papers, correspondence and unpublished work has survived, much of it collected by the Sigmund Freud Archives of New York, and deposited in the Library of Congress in Washington. Much of this material is still closed to scholars, however, as some of its donors specified release dates that extend well into the next century. Until recently, the management of the Archives added restrictions of its own to the viewing of papers, leading to considerable controversy and charges of favouritism. Now, however, most documents are supposed to be open to scholars on the basis of equal access, and the Archives have announced their intention of releasing currently unavailable material from restriction as soon as possible. Interested scholars may apply directly to the Library of Congress for permission to view the open parts of the collection.

Among the most important of the items to be published so far are the letters and draft manuscripts Freud sent to his intimate friend Wilhelm Fliess between the years 1887 and 1904. The most scientifically relevant portions of this correspondence, including the *Project for a Scientific Psychology* (1895), appear in Volume 1 of the *S.E.*; a larger though still incomplete selection from the correspondence was published in 1954 as *The Origins of Psychoanalysis: Letters to Wilhelm Fliess, Drafts and Notes: 1887–1902*, edited by Marie Bonaparte, Anna Freud and Ernst Kris, with an informative introduction by Kris. Even though incomplete, these candid letters and tentative draft manuscripts never intended for publication provide an extraordinarily close and intimate look at the development of Freud's thought during the most creative phase of his career.

After years of speculation about the remaining letters, the full correspondence (except for the *Project*) appeared in 1985 as *The Complete Letters of Sigmund Freud to Wilhelm Fliess 1887–1904*, translated and edited by Jeffrey M. Masson. This edition revealed many previously unknown details about Freud's deteriorating friendship with Breuer, his intensely emotional and dependent relationship with Fliess during this critical period and the case of Emma Eckstein, one of his most important early patients.

In 1974, the executors of the Freud and Jung literary estates co-operated in order to publish the most extensive correspondence in print so far between Freud and one of his early disciples: *The Freud/Jung Letters: The correspondence between Sigmund Freud and C.G. Jung*, edited by William McGuire. Here the flowering and then the deterioration of one of Freud's most important professional relationships is vividly documented, as the personalities of both men come through clearly and honestly, if not always entirely positively. The reader gets an excellent first-hand picture of the internal politics of the young psychoanalytic movement.

Letters of Sigmund Freud 1873–1939 (1970), edited by his son Ernst, presents a general selection of Freud's personal letters to nearly a hundred different correspondents, including many to Martha Bernays during their long engagement. Several briefer sets of correspondence have also been published – with his followers Karl Abraham and Oscar Pfister, for example, and the writer Stefan Zweig – and more are being prepared for publication, including the Ernest Jones letters. With the new policies of the Sigmund Freud Archives, it seems certain that other important archival date-sources will continue to emerge over the next few years.

2.3. Biographical and theoretical studies

Following Freud's death, his family authorized Ernest Jones to write his biography, with full access to private family records and papers; the three volumes of Jones's *The Life and Work of Sigmund Freud* appeared in 1953, 1955 and 1957. Though marked by some of the problems to be expected in an authorised biography by an admiring disciple who was also an interested party to many of the events he describes, this large work remains the standard account of Freud's life and career. Some important supplementary material, particularly about Freud's medical history and his relationship with Fliess, was added by Freud's personal physician Max Schur in *Freud: Living and Dying* (1972). Ronald Clark's *Freud: The Man and the cause* (1980) and Peter Gay's *Freud: A Life for our Time* (1988) lack the first-hand intimacy of the Jones and Schur biographies, but benefit from an abundance of recent historical scholarship on Freud. Gay appends an outstanding bibliographical essay to his volume that will guide the interested reader to much of this scholarship.

An enormous number of more specialised studies of Freud's life and background have appeared, and can be sampled only very incompletely here. The works cited below are themselves extensively referenced, however, and should adequately introduce the reader to the larger literature.

William J. McGrath's study, *Freud's Discovery of Psychoanalysis: The Politics of Hysteria* (1986) offers a good summary of the literature on Freud's religious, educational and philosphical background, including the influences of Brentano, Charcot and the general atmosphere of *fin de siècle* Vienna. McGrath also provides an original and useful account of Freud's interest and involvement in politics. Peter Amacher's short monograph, *Freud's Neurological Education and its Influence on Psychoanalytic Theory* (1965), explicates the neurophysiological theories of Brücke, Meynert and some of Freud's other Vienna teachers. An outstanding and full account of the more general biological teachings to which Freud was exposed as a young man, and of the idiosyncratic theories developed by Wilhelm Fliess during his period of great intimacy with Freud, is Frank Sulloway's *Freud: Biologist of the Mind* (1979). Sulloway argues that Freud's early synthesis of these biological ideas formed the real core of psychoanalysis, which Freud later disguised in non-biological terminology.

While Sulloway argues for an essential continuity among the phases of Freud's work, other scholars have seen marked disjunctions – particularly between his subjectively oriented *clinical theory*, expressed in terms of wishes, feelings, insights etc.; and his more objective and deterministic *metapsychology*, which treats the mind as a mechanism. George Klein, in his book *Psychoanalytic Theory* (1976), argues that the two approaches are based on totally different data sources, and are logically separate; moreover, Klein argues that the metapsychology was based on a sterile and outdated neurological reductionism, and predicts that it will soon become little more than a historical curiosity to practising psychoanalysts, who will continue to find great wisdom in the clinical theory. Karl Pribram and Merton Gill approach the issue somewhat differently in *Freud's 'Project' reassessed* (1976). After documenting the central importance of the ideas expressed in the *Project* to all of Freud's later metapsychology, they debate the actual scientific value of the work. Gill basically agrees with Klein that the *Project* and all metapsychology based on it were a dead end; Pribram, however, sees in the *Project* a highly promising model for a modern theory of cognitive functioning.

Always controversial, and with the personal details of his life so fully documented, Freud has been the target of many attacks on his personal character as well as on his work. Some of these have asserted sensational theses (that Freud was a lifelong cocaine addict, for example, or impregnated his sister-in-law) which received more attention from the popular press than from serious students of Freud. But one recent accusation of intellectual cowardice against Freud aroused scholars as well as the public, because it came from someone who was, at least temporarily, very much an insider in the psychoanalytic establishment. Jeffrey Masson, as Projects Director of the Sigmund Freud Archives and editor of the complete Freud-Fliess correspondence, had privileged access to material from which he concluded that Freud did not abandon his seduction theory because of contrary evidence, as the standard account of his life asserts, but because he lacked the courage to hold to a theory which was unacceptable to the Viennese medical authorities. After expressing this view publicly, Masson was summarily fired from his positions with the Freud Archives. A lively account of these events – though one that Masson has disputed in a libel suit – is given in Janet Malcolm's *In the Freud Archives* (1983).

Masson presented his case most fully in the provocatively-entitled book, *The Assault on Truth: Freud's Suppression of the Seduction Theory* (1984). A major part of Masson's argument derived from the case of Emma Eckstein, Freud's hysterical patient of the early years, who figured prominently in previously unpublished parts of the Fliess correspondence. (Eckstein was a family friend and for a time a psychoanalytic colleague of Freud's; Masson does not say so, but it seems likely that considerations of confidentiality and professional courtesy led earlier editors of the correspondence to leave details of her case unpublished.) Masson's reading of Freud's comments on this case, along with some other circumstantial evidence from Freud's library, led him to conclude that Freud still privately accepted the veridicality of his patients' 'seduction memories' after he had publicly abandoned the seduction theory.

Most informed reaction to Masson's book has been negative. Critics have noted that the passages of correspondence which Masson emphasises are ambiguous, and that the rest of the newly available full correspondence is still consistent with the standard view. Moreover, there is strong evidence in favour of the standard view which Masson overlooks, such as Freud's discovery of the importance of sexual fantasy (as opposed to reality) in his self-analysis, which was ongoing at the time he renounced the seduction theory. Throughout his career, Freud bore considerable abuse because of the ideas he did publish, and hardly behaved like one who had compromised his principles to please the medical establishment. In sum, Masson's research into the Fliess episode has resulted in the publication of considerable and interesting new material about Freud's early career, but it seems unlikely that his inflammatory interpretation of that material will be widely accepted by future scholars.

2.4. The social history of psychoanalysis

Besides his published work, Freud also left a well-developed psychoanalytic establishment with innumerable practitioners and followers, which continues as

a major social institution today. Thus the history of the psychoanalytic movement has attracted interest, with the focus not so much on Freud himself as on
the other individuals who were associated with him, and the organisations they
created. Paul Roazen's *Freud and his Followers* (1976) provides one comprehensive survey of these developments, including details about the dissensions of
Adler, Stekel and Jung; the politics and policies of the group who remained
loyal to Freud and created the international psychoanalytic movement; and
accounts of the most important female psychoanalysts (including Freud's
daughter, Anna) who came to occupy prominent places in the mature psychoanalytic movement. Separate full biographies of several of these figures (e.g.
Adler, Jung, Jones, Marie Bonaparte and Helene Deutsch) have also been published and help fill out Roazen's picture.

The reception of psychoanalysis by the larger scientific, medical and cultural
establishments in Germany and America has been usefully investigated by
Hannah S. Decker in *Freud in Germany* (1977), and by Nathan G. Hale in *Freud
and the Americans* (1971). The phenomenal popular success of psychoanalytic
ideas in pervading modern culture has been examined by Ernest Gellner in *The
Psychoanalytic Movement* (1985). Gellner attributes this success not so much to
the scientific validity of the theories, as to the fact that they filled a void in the
general religious and philosophical atmosphere of our times. Unfortunately,
Gellner's entirely plausible case for the importance of extra-scientific and cultural factors may be dismissed by some because it is paired with an arch and
sometimes misleading description of psychoanalytic theory proper, based
almost entirely on secondary sources rather than on Freud himself.

2.5. Psychobiography and psychohistory

Besides being the subject of considerable historical investigation, psychoanalytic theory has sometimes been employed by biographers and historians as a tool
to help understand their subjects. (See art. 1, sect. 11.) Unquestionably the
person studied most extensively in this way, and perhaps to best effect, is Freud
himself. Freud left behind many accounts of his own dreams, fantasies and
childhood memories – the basis of his self-analysis – which were put to use by
Jones, Schur and Gay in their biographical studies, and by many other psychoanalysts in shorter or more specialised studies of their founding father.
Examples of this kind of work, by a group of analysts associated with the Chicago Institute for Psychoanalysis, may be found in *Freud: The Fusion of Science
and Humanism: The Intellectual History of Psychoanalysis* (1976), edited by John
Gedo and George Pollock. A rather different but still illuminating example of the
use of depth-psychological (though obviously 'non-Freudian') material is Carl
Jung's appropriately entitled autobiography, *Memories, Dreams, Reflections* (1963).
Needless to say, most historical figures have not left behind the kind of

material that Freud and Jung did, and moreover cannot be placed 'on the couch' to obtain the kinds of associations that would be of most interest and use to a psychoanalytically-inclined biographer. Accordingly, most psychobiographical investigations – and there have been many of them in spite of the difficulties involved – have had to make do with sparse information, and to indulge in some rather speculative reconstruction. Freud's own pioneering study of Leonardo da Vinci's childhood turned out to be based on a mistranslated word, and his highly unflattering portrait of Woodrow Wilson (with William Bullitt) has been severely criticised for its totally unverifiable assertions that childhood traumas and repressed Oedipal feelings produced undesirable adult characteristics in the American President. Some other works by Freud's followers have suffered from deficiencies as bad or worse.

Given these problems, some historians such as Jaques Barzun and David Stannard have argued that the entire enterprise of 'psychohistory' (i.e. the use of depth-psychological and generally Freudian hypotheses to solve historical problems) is intellectually disreputable, and ought not to be practiced at all. Three charges are seriously considered but also rebutted by the psychoanalytically-trained historian Peter Gay, in *Freud for Historians* (1985). Gay grants that serious abuses have occurred, but argues that there are still genuine ways in which the prudent application of psychoanalytic insight can be (and has been) useful to historians – particularly in offering a more sophisticated alternative to the relatively superficial 'common-sense psychology' so often assumed by them. Gay cites some specific psychoanalytically-informed biographies and other historical studies that he believes have succeeded – though it must be conceded that his list is short, and does not include a major work in the history of science.

2.6. Psychoanalysis and the philosophy of science

Freud's psychoanalytic theories have long been debated with respect to their status as 'science'. Karl Popper's assertion that psychoanalytic propositions are inherently unscientific because they are largely unfalsifiable – i.e. data which at first appear to disconfirm them are too easily explained away with alternative hypotheses – is probably the best known criticism (see art. 54). On another level, Jurgen Habermas and Paul Ricoeur have each charged Freud with being overly 'scientistic' in his metapsychological theorising, agreeing with Klein and Gill that the most solid part of psychoanalysis is its clinical thoeory, grounded in real subjective experience. Philosopher Adolf Grünbaum has critically examined these positions in his new and widely reviewed book, *The Foundations of Psychoanalysis* (1986), and concluded that while Freud was mistaken in many of his most important conclusions, he was nonetheless vastly superior to his critics in the sophistication of his philosophy of science. The June 1986 issue of the journal *Behavioral and Brain Sciences* contains a précis of the book by Grünbaum, followed by thirty-nine invited commentaries on his argument and a concluding author's response.

These and related controversies about the scientific value and legitimacy of psychoanalysis will undoubtedly continue into the indefinite future. Probably for a variety of emotional as well as intellectual reasons, Freud's theory has succeeded in capturing the attention of philosophers, historians and scholars from many other disciplines, as well as the educated general public. Since the theory is so multifaceted, and involves so many different problematic and controversial but nonetheless important aspects of human experience, a wide variety of different evaluations will undoubtedly continue to be both supported and supportable.

FURTHER READING

P. Amacher, *Freud's neurological education and its influence on psychoanalytic theory* (New York, 1965).

B. Bettelheim, *Freud and man's soul* (New York, 1983).

R. W. Clark, *Freud: The man and the cause* (New York, 1980).

H. S. Decker, *Freud in Germany: Revolution and reaction in science, 1893–1907* (New York, 1977).

R. E. Fancher, *Psychoanalytic psychology: The development of Freud's thought* (New York, 1973).

S. Freud, *The standard edition of the complete psychological works of Sigmund Freud*, 24 vols., ed. and trans. by J. Strachey in collaboration with A. Freud (London, 1953–1974).

S. Freud, *The origins of psycho-analysis: letters to Wilhelm Fliess, drafts and notes: 1887–1902*, ed. by M. Bonaparte, A. Freud, and E. Kris (New York, 1954; London, 1954).

S. Freud, *Letters of Sigmund Freud 1873–1939*, ed. by E. L. Freud, trans. by T. and J. Stern (London, 1970).

S. Freud, *The complete letters of Sigmund Freud to Wilhelm Fliess 1887–1904*, ed. and trans. by J. M. Masson (Cambridge, Mass., 1985).

S. Freud, and W. Bullitt, *Thomas Woodrow Wilson: a psychological study* (Boston, 1966).

S. Freud and C. G. Jung, *The Freud/Jung letters: the correspondence between Sigmund Freud and C. G. Jung*, ed. by W. McGurie, trans. by R. Mannheim and R. F. C. Hull (Princeton, N J, 1974).

P. Gay, *Freud for historians* (New York and Oxford, 1985).

—— Freud, *A Life for Our Time* (New York and London, 1988).

J. E. Gedo and G. H. Pollock (eds.), *Freud: The fusion of science and humanism: The intellectual history of psychoanalysis* (New York, 1976).

E. Gellner, *The psychoanalytic movement* (London, 1985).

A. Grünbaum, *The foundations of psychoanalysis: a philosophical critique* (Berkeley and Los Angeles, 1984).

A. Grünbaum, 'Précis of *The foundations of psychoanalysis: A philosophical critique*', with commentary and author's response, *Behavioral and brain sciences*, 9 (1986), 217–84.

N. G. Hale, *Freud and the Americans: the beginnings of psychoanalysis in the United States, 1876–1917* (New York, Oxford, 1971).

E. Jones, *The life and work of Sigmund Freud*, 3 vols. (New York, 1953–57; London, 1953–57).

C. G. Jung, *Memories, dreams, reflections* (New York, 1963).

G. Klein, *Psychoanalytic theory* (New York, 1976).

J. Malcolm, *In the Freud archives* (New York, 1983).

J. M. Masson, *The assault on truth: Freud's suppression of the seduction theory* (New York, 1984).

W. J. McGrath, *Freud's discovery of psychoanalysis: the politics of hysteria* (Ithaca, NY and London, 1986).

K. H. Pribram and M. M. Gill, *Freud's 'Project' re-assessed* (New York, 1976; London, 1976).

P. Roazen, *Freud and his followers* (New York, 1975; London, 1976).

M. Schur, *Freud: living and dying* (New York, 1972; London, 1972).

F. Sulloway, *Freud: biologist of the mind* (New York, 1979).

28

THE THEORY OF RELATIVITY

JOHN STACHEL

'The theory of relativity' is an umbrella term for two distinct theories, the special theory and the general theory. Both might not bear this common appellation if they were not so closely associated with the name of Albert Einstein (1879–1955), who developed the second in an attempt to generalise his original theory of relativity, now called the special theory.

Einstein often compared the principles of special relativity to those of thermodynamics. Each theory starts with a few principles, which incorporate a wealth of empirical data into generalisations at a high level of abstraction. For thermodynamics, these principles generalise the failure of attempts to construct perpetual motion devices. For special relativity, they generalise the failure of attempts to distinguish a state of absolute rest from states of uniform translational motion.

These principles are used to derive criteria that must be satisfied by constructive theories at a lower level of abstraction. For special relativity, these criteria are kinematical: the laws of physics are the same in any inertial frame of reference, i.e. they are invariant in form under a group of spatial and temporal transformations, called the Lorentz group.

The general theory of relativity is a theory of gravitation. In contrast to the other forces of nature, gravitational effects are a result of the structure of space and time; modifications of which can be brought about by the distribution of matter and energy, which act as sources of the gravitational field. Hence, space, time, matter, energy and gravitation are inextricably intertwined. Whether the resulting theory is a theory of 'relativity', in some sense of the word analogous to its use to describe the special theory, is still actively debated by physicists and philosophers of science.

Einstein regarded the theory of the free gravitational field (i.e. in the absence of matter and other non-gravitational fields) as his major accomplishment.

However, he was not satisfied with the treatment of the sources of the gravitational field in general relativity. These sources must be specified by additional field or particle variables, which are independently and arbitrarily introduced into the theory. Einstein hoped to find some mathematical structure to serve as the basis of a 'unified theory' of the gravitational and electromagnetic fields, without the introduction of any additional entities.

The history of the theory of relativity thus naturally subdivides into: the development of the special theory of relativity; the development of the general theory of relativity; the search for a unified theory of gravitation, electromagnetism and, more recently, of the weak and strong forces.

1. THE SPECIAL THEORY OF RELATIVITY

The special theory of relativity arose from attempts to reconcile Newton's mechanics with Maxwell's electrodynamics. If Newton's laws of motion are valid initially with respect to some frame of reference (Newton's absolute space), they hold equally well in any frame of reference in uniform translational motion with respect to the first. The term 'inertial frame' was introduced late in the nineteenth century to denote any such reference frame.

Newton's description of motion is based on the concept of absolute time, assumed to be independent of all physical processes and the same for all inertial frames. Newton distinguished between absolute and relative space, time and motion. (See art. 16.) The relative quantities are the ones that are directly accessible to observation. Newton's famous rotating bucket experiment provides a simple method for distinguishing absolute from relative rotations.[1] But he was unable to provide a method for distinguishing absolute from relative uniform translations since the laws of Newtonian mechanics take the same form in every inertial frame; all inertial frames of reference are mechanically equivalent. We shall refer to this equivalence as the Newtonian principle of relativity. In going from a description of some motion with respect to one inertial frame to its description with respect to another, one must use a set of transformations connecting the spatial coordinates of the two inertial frames that are now called the Galilean transformations. Since the Newtonian time is the same for all inertial frames, there is a trivial, identity transformation for the time.

As long as the laws of mechanics were assumed to form a foundation for the explanation fo all physical phenomena (the mechanistic world-view), the Newtonian principle of relativity seemed to be valid for all phenomena. However, a particular inertial frame might still be singled out under certain circumstances. For example, the laws of sound propagation assume a much simpler form in the frame of reference in which the medium is at rest, through which the sound waves propagate.

In the latter half of the nineteenth century, the wave theory of light appeared to require such a privileged frame. Light propagates through the almost perfect vacuum of interstellar space with no difficulty. So it was assumed that all of space is permeated by a subtle medium, called the ether, in which light propagates as a wave. Maxwell's theory makes the ether the bearer of all electromagnetic fields, which included light waves. Attempts were made to construct mechanical models of the ether, but gradually the electromagnetic ether came to be accepted as a non-mechanical physical system, the behaviour of which was completely characterised by Maxwell's equations. Attempts were even made to derive the laws of mechanics from those of electrodynamics (the electromagnetic world-view).

By the end of the nineteenth century, the views of Hendrik Antoon Lorentz (1853–1928) on electrodynamics were widely accepted because of their success in explaining most electrical and optical phenomena. Lorentz assumed that:

(1) All of space, including the interior of ordinary matter, is permeated by a completely immobile ether, the seat of all electric and magnetic fields. Maxwell's equations hold in the inertial frame in which the ether is at rest.

(2) Ordinary matter contains charged particles, the motions of which are affected by the electric and magnetic forces exerted on them by the fields.

(3) The motions of these charged particles generate the electric and magnetic fields in the ether.

Lorentz's viewpoint singles out one inertial frame, the ether rest frame. It is the only frame of reference in which the velocity of light is constant in all directions. Hence, motion with respect to the ether should be detectable by means of optical experiments performed in a moving frame, such as the earth. However, numerous attempts to detect the motion of the earth through the ether by optical or other electrodynamical experiments ended in failure. In 1874, Eleuthère Mascart (1837–1908) suggested, on the basis of the negative result of a series of 'first order' experiments (i.e. experiments sensitive to terms of order v/c, where v is the speed of the earth and c is the speed of light with respect to the ether), that it might be impossible to detect a privileged inertial frame by optical means. Albert Abraham Michelson (1852–1931) used refined interferometric techniques to carry out a 'second order' experiment (i.e. sensitive to terms of order $(v/c)^2$) in 1881, repeated with greater accuracy by Michelson and Edward Morley (1838–1923) in 1887, with a similarly negative result.

The situation at the end of the nineteenth century may be summarised as follows: Maxwell's theory, as interpreted by Lorentz, postulated an immobile ether frame of reference. Motion with respect to this ether frame should be detectable. But all experiments indicated that the Newtonian principle of relativity holds for electromagnetic phenomena as well as for mechanical ones, without any need to consider uniform translatory motion relative to the ether.

The people who contributed most to the resolution of this problem were Lorentz, Henri Poincaré (1854–1912) and Einstein. Lorentz's method of resolving the discrepancy was to show that Maxwell's equations, although they really hold only in the ether frame of reference, appear to remain valid in a moving inertial frame. To do this, the equations have to be transformed to the moving frame, using the Galilean transformations supplemented by certain additional transformations, which 'compensate' for motion through the ether. In 1892, he succeeded in explaining the failure of 'first order' experiments to detect motion through the ether by introducing a transformation from Newtonian time to 'local time', as he called it. In order to explain away 'second order' effects, Lorentz introduced in 1895 a contraction in that dimension of a body in the direction of its motion through the ether.

In 1904, Lorentz achieved exact compensation for motion through the ether with a set of transformations for both the space and time variables, which Poincaré soon named the Lorentz transformations. Lorentz regarded the spatial transformations as reflecting a contraction of bodies, produced by their motion through the ether. He explained this contraction electrodynamically, on the assumption that the forces holding matter together either were electrodynamical in origin, or behaved similarly. Lorentz regarded the time transformation, a new version of the transformation to the 'local time', as a technical device. He did not discuss the relation between the 'local time' and the readings of clocks at rest in the moving frame. For Lorentz, then, the ether was not only real, but physically efficacious. It is true that the relativity principle appears to hold for ordinary matter alone, without any need to take into account its motion with respect to the ether. But this is the result of compensating effects that arise from the motion of matter through the ether.

Poincaré's approach to electrodynamics was based on Lorentz's work. Around 1900 he called attention to the conventional element in the definition of the simultaneity of distant events, and interpreted Lorentz's 'local time' as giving the readings of clocks at rest in a moving inertial frame that are synchronised by means of light signals. In 1904, he listed the relativity principle among those principles, such as the conservation of energy, the scope of which extended beyond mechanics. In 1905, he recognised that the Lorentz transformations form a group, analysed its mathematical structure and showed that Maxwell's equations remain invariant in form under the transformations of this group. He accepted the ether, while occasionally suggesting that it is no more than a convenient hypothesis that might some day be discarded. In spite of these important contributions Poincaré never organised his many insights into a theory that transcends its electrodynamic origins, or that resolutely discards the concepts of ether and absolute time and establishes a new kinematical foundation for all of physics.

Einstein was the first person to create such a theory. Although he was working on the electrodynamics of moving bodies by 1899, only a few references in his letters shed any light on the development of his ideas between then and

1905. Given the dearth of contemporary data and the plethora of possibilities, it is not surprising that scholars disagree in their reconstructions of how Einstein arrived at the formulation of the special theory that he published in 1905.[2]

Einstein opened this paper by rejecting the ether concept and adopting two principles: the relativity principle and the light principle. Einstein's version of the relativity principle requires that not only the laws of mechanics, but *all* the laws of physics must take the same form in any inertial frame. The light principle asserts that there exists an inertial frame in which the speed of light is independent of the motion of its source. The two principles are drawn from previous theory and experiment: the relativity principle from the Newtonian relativity principle and the failure of all optical and electrodynamical attempts to detect the supposed translational motion of the earth through the ether and the light principle from the vast amount of evidence supporting a wave theory of light. But these principles were elevated by Einstein to the status of postulates, in need of no further justification within the theory.

Einstein noted that the two principles appear to be irreconcilable: if the speed of light is constant in one inertial frame, and there is no ether to single out that frame from all others, then the relativity principle requires that the speed of light be the same constant in *all* inertial frames. This conclusion is inconsistent with the familiar, Galilean law of addition of velocities. If the two principles are both to be upheld, Newtonian kinematical ideas must be modified.

By means of a careful analysis of the concepts of spatial length and temporal interval, Einstein demonstrated that the two principles do indeed imply a new kinematics. He used light signals to define the synchronism of clocks at rest in an inertial frame of reference. It follows from this definition of simultaneity, together with the two principles of the theory, that time can no longer be considered to be absolute but is relative to an inertial frame of reference: events which are simultaneous with respect to one such frame are not simultaneous with respect to another. He derived the transformations between the spatial and temporal coordinates of an event in two different inertial frames. Although these transformations are mathematically equivalent to the Lorentz transformations, they have a quite different physical interpretation in Einstein's theory.

Einstein derived a formula for the composition of relative velocities that removes the apparent contradiction between the two principles: the velocity of light, compounded relativistically with any lesser velocity, remains unchanged in magnitude. Einstein also derived relativistic formulae for various optical effects, such as aberration and the Doppler effect. He showed that Maxwell's equations do not change their form under his transformations, and derived relativistic dynamical equations, replacing Newton's for the motion of a charged particle. Later in 1905, he concluded that inertial mass and energy are equivalent ($E = mc^2$).

During the next few years, Einstein worked on applications of the principles of the special theory to various branches of physics, and wrote several review articles on the subject. In 1907, while other physicists were just beginning to engage the special theory, he sought a generalisation of the theory that would include gravitation (see below).

A very important mathematical reformulation of the special theory was given in 1907–8 by Hermann Minkowski (1864–1909). He realised that the Lorentz transformations could best be pictured by uniting space and time in one mathematical structure, a four-dimensional space-time now often called 'Minkowski space', in which all physical processes can be represented. This formulation makes explicit the space-time symmetries implicit in Einstein's formulation of the special theory. A four-dimensional vector and tensor analysis for Minkowski space developed by Arnold Sommerfeld (1868–1951) in 1910 was soon widely adopted.

Numerous tests of kinematical, dynamical, optical and electromagnetic consequences of the special theory have been carried out since 1905, and the theory has survived them all. It has become an everyday working tool of both experimental and theoretical physicists. It would be impossible, for example, to design modern particle accelerators, electron microscopes, high-voltage television tubes or klystrons, in all of which sub-atomic particles move at speeds comparable to the speed of light, without taking into account the relativistic variation of mass with velocity. It would be just as impossible to classify theoretically the many particles discovered with the aid of high-energy particle accelerators without taking into account the criteria that special relativity imposes on theories of such elementary particles. (See art. 43.) The uses of nuclear reactions, for both constructive and destructive purposes, provide striking examples of current technological applications of the mass-energy equivalence relation, examples that have made $E = mc^2$ the most widely known equation of our age.

However drastically certain classical concepts and laws are modified by the special theory, in many respects it represents a culmination of the classical tradition in physics, and an extension of its scope. Yet novel features of the theory, such as the new concepts of time and space, led to many difficulties and misunderstandings in the course of its assimilation by the physics community. A number of German physicists accepted various aspects of the special theory fairly rapidly, although often showing considerable misunderstanding of its essential features. For example, it was often referred to as the Lorentz-Einstein theory, thereby emphasising the identity of many of the formulae given by Lorentz and by Einstein, and obscuring the crucial differences in the conceptual basis of the two theories, and in the interpretation of these formulae. Max Planck (1858–1947) played a major role in promoting early discussions of the special theory. He worked on the theory himself, as did several of his students, notably Max Laue (1879–1960) who, in 1911, wrote the first monograph on special relativity. By this time, the theory was generally accepted by physicists in German-speaking countries, with some notable exceptions. Hostility to the theory developed in some quarters and became manifest on a large scale in post-First World War Germany, especially after the Nazi seizure of power.

In other countries, acceptance of the theory was much slower. There was practically no discussion of special relativity among French physicists until the 1920s, after the general theory started to receive widespread popular attention. British physicists continued to approach the problems of electrodynamics in the spirit of Joseph Larmor (1857–1942) and Oliver Lodge (1851–1940): like Lorentz, they continued to refine models of the ether and of the electron. Special relativity was accepted only to the extent that it could be fitted into this programme. It was not until much later that a change in attitude occurred. The few American physicists who mentioned the special theory before the First World War were generally hostile to the new concepts of space and time, which they considered contrary to common sense.

2. THE GENERAL THEORY OF RELATIVITY

Einstein started to look for a relativistic theory of gravitation in 1907. While not alone in this quest, he was the only physicist who felt the need to generalise the special theory of relativity in order to solve this problem. The story of the origins of the general theory is thus the story of Einstein's search.

In 1907, Einstein started to look for a theory of the gravitational field that would generalise Newton's gravitational theory by making it satisfy the criteria required by special relativity. He easily found such a theory, but it lacked a fundamental property of gravitation: any body, regardless of its composition, has equal gravitational and inertial masses. As a consequence of this equality, all bodies fall with the same acceleration with respect to an inertial frame of reference in which there is a uniform gravitational field. Einstein noted that the motion of such a body is indistinguishable from the motion of a body not subject to a gravitational field, but moving with respect to a frame of reference accelerated upward (relative to an inertial frame) with an acceleration numerically equal to the acceleration produced by the gravitational field. He generalised this result by assuming that *all* physical phenomena taking place in an inertial frame *with* a constant gravitational field are physically equivalent to similar phenomena taking place in an accelerated frame of reference *without* any gravitational field. Einstein took this principle of equivalence, as he later called it, as the key to understanding gravitation. This means that taking gravitation into account requires an extension of the principle of relativity from inertial frames of reference to accelerated frames of reference; and thus a generalisation of his original relativity theory.

While still far from possessing a complete theory of gravitation, Einstein found that the equivalence principle implied several novel effects of gravitation on other physical processes. He predicted that a light ray would bend, and that a clock would run slower, in a gravitational field. Since the frequencies of the spectral lines produced by an atom provide natural clocks, such lines originating in the sun or other stars should be shifted to measurably lower frequencies compared to terrestrial lines. Attempts soon began to separate this predicted gravitational red shift of spectral lines from other astrophysical effects on the positions of such lines. Over the years, a number of observers claimed that the gravitational red shift had been quantitatively verified, while others gave equally strong refutations of these claims. Only with a successful terrestrial test of the gravitational red shift in 1960 by Robert Pound and Glen Rebka was this controversy finally settled, in favour of Einstein's theory.

In 1911 Einstein noted that starlight reaching the earth after passing near the edge of the sun should be deflected sufficiently by the sun's gravitational field to produce a measurable displacement of the star's observed position. Measurements of the positions of stellar images near the sun, on photographic plates taken during an eclipse, made it possible to test the predicted solar light deflection when compared with their positions on plates taken on an ordinary night. Attempts to observe this effect were made during eclipses in 1912 and 1914, but failed due to poor observational conditions. By the time such observations were first reported, after the 1919 solar eclipse, Einstein had developed a full theory of gravitation, which predicted twice the deflection of light that he had derived from use of the equivalence principle alone.

Starting in 1912, Einstein worked intensively for three years on the problem of finding a generalised theory of relativity that includes gravitation. With the help of Minkowski's four-dimensional space-time approach he developed a totally new outlook on gravitation. Instead of being a force like electricity or magnetism, gravitation is a warping of space-time. According to the law of inertia, which holds in both Newtonian and special-relativistic mechanics, a particle not acted upon by any force moves in a straight line with uniform velocity. In space-time, this motion is represented by a four-dimensional straight line, which may be called an inertial path. When they are acted upon by forces, particles are deflected from inertial paths in space-time. Gravitation was considered to be one such force, which causes a particle to follow a non-inertial path in a flat space-time. Einstein now saw that, thanks to the equivalence principle, gravitation could be understood as a 'warping' or curvature of space-time: a particle under the influence of gravitation *still* follows an inertial path, but the path lies in a *non-flat* space-time. (See art. 42, sect. 2.)

By late 1912, Einstein had found the correct mathematical representation for his concept of the gravitational field: the metric tensor, which is used to describe the geometry of a non-flat space-time. A space whose geometry is fully characterised by such a metric tensor is called a Riemannian space. Given any two points in such a space, there is a curve in the space called a geodesic, which is the straightest of all the curves joining these two points. For Einstein, the inertial paths of particles in a gravitational field are geodesics of some Riemannian space-time. (See art. 42, sect. 4.) Collaborating with the mathematician Marcel Grossmann (1878–1936), formerly a fellow student and now his colleague, Einstein learned to use the mathematical tools needed for this new way of looking at the gravitational field: Riemannian geometry and tensor analysis.

Einstein had now solved the problem of the effect of gravitation on other physical processes; what remained unsolved was the problem of the effect of all other processes on gravitation, that is, the problem of the equations governing the gravitational field. In 1912, Einstein came close to solving this problem in the way that he finally adopted three years later. As we saw, he interpreted the equivalence principle as indicating the need to generalise the relativity principle from inertial frames to at least some accelerated frames of reference. For Einstein, a change in the frame of reference corresponds to a change of coordinate system in space-time. This implies that the gravitational field equations must be invariant under a wider group of space-time transformations than the Lorentz group of special relativity. Einstein felt that the most natural generalisation of the relativity principle would be to demand invariance under *all possible* space-time transformations. This requirement is called the requirement of general covariance. Generally covariant field equations for the metric tensor exist; that is, there is a set of field equations which do not change their form under any possible space-time transformation. Indeed, the field equations are almost uniquely determined by this requirement. But, until late in 1915, Einstein rejected these equations.

Einstein found an argument that seemed to prove that generally covariant field equations must allow more than one solution corresponding to a given source of the gravitational field. That such a source uniquely determines a unique gravitational field is a physically compelling requirement for a theory of gravitation. So Einstein abandoned general covariance. The flaw in this argument involves a unique feature of general-relativistic field theories. In such a theory, the points of space-time are not physically individuated before a solution to the field equations is specified. Once this is recognised, it is seen that all the apparently distinct mathematical solutions corresponding to a given source really represent the same gravitational field. But this did not become clear to Einstein for several years.

Convinced that the field equations could not be generally covariant, Einstein formulated non-covariant field equations for the gravitational field. By mid-1915, various problems with these non-covariant equations led him to re-examine the whole problem. By the end of the year, he discovered the flaw in his argument against general covariance, and adopted a set of generally covariant field equations which differ only slightly from the ones he had rejected three years earlier.

One of the most noteworthy features of the resulting theory is its 'dynamising' of the geometry of space and the chronometry of time. In all previous physical theories, space and time constitute a kinematical framework, within which the dynamical laws that operate govern the behaviour of various particles and fields. The special theory unites the three-dimensional geometry of space and the one-dimensional chronometry of time into the four-dimensional chronogeometry of space-time; but this chronogeometry is still fixed *a priori*; it influences all physical processes, but is not influenced by them. In the general theory, the chronogeometry of space-time is described by the metric tensor, which is also responsible for all gravitational phenomena. Hence, this chronogeometry is no longer fixed *a priori*, but is subject to gravitational field equations that link it with all other physical processes.

By solving his non-linear field equations in a linear approximation, Einstein showed that a test particle in the gravitational field of a spherically symmetrical mass would not simply describe an elliptical orbit, as in the Newtonian theory of gravitation, but that the orbit would precess. Einstein thus succeeded in explaining the well-known anomalous precession of Mercury's orbit, known since Le Verrier's work in the 1840s and 1850s. Shortly afterwards, in 1916, Karl Schwarzschild (1873–1916) found the exact spherically-symmetric solution to Einstein's equations. This most famous of all exact solutions to these equations is now known as the Schwarzschild solution.

Using this solution, Einstein re-evaluated the angular gravitational deflection of a light ray just grazing the sun's edge. He obtained about 1.7″, twice his previous prediction for the deflection. Roughly speaking, half the amount is due to the equivalence principle, and half to the curvature of space produced by the sun's gravitational field. A first, inconclusive attempt to test this revised prediction was made during the partial solar eclipse of 1918. But the British solar eclipse expeditions of 1919, headed by Frank Dyson (1868–1939) and Arthur Stanley Eddington (1882–1944), first reported reasonably close agreement between their observations and Einstein's prediction. This announcement received banner headlines in the British and American press, which heralded the overthrow of Newton's gravitational theory. Thus Einstein achieved fame among the general public. The reasons for his celebrity, for its persistence and for the development of the many myths about Einstein, have been the subject of considerable speculation, but only recently have such questions begun to be seriously studied.

As noted above, in the general theory of relativity, the chronogeometry of space-time is not fixed. This implies another unique feature of the theory: the topological structure of space and time in general also not given *a priori*. It must be determined for each particular solution to the field equations, with the help of some physical and mathematical criteria for an acceptable global solution. (See art. 41, sect. 1.) Starting in 1917 with the Einstein static universe, various cosmological solutions have been proposed. Some of these are spatially closed, e.g. they may have spatial cross-sections with the topology of a three-sphere. Other cosmological solutions are spatially open, i.e. they have spatial cross-sections which have the topology of three-planes. But even non-cosmological solutions to the field equations, i.e. solutions representing the gravitational fields of localised sources, can have remarkably complicated topological structures. For example, in 1935 Einstein and Nathan Rosen proposed the 'bridge' interpretation of the Schwarzschild solution, and more recently, Martin Kruskal proposed another topologically non-trivial interpretation of the same solution.

In 1916, Einstein showed that, in the linear approximation, his field equations have solutions representing gravitational waves. Exact solutions representing plane and cylindrical gravitational waves were later found. In the early 1960s, Hermann Bondi started the study of a large class of asymptotic solutions, representing the gravitational radiation field far from a source. No exact solution representing the radiation field from a finite source has yet been constructed, but in 1918 Einstein showed that, in linear approximation, variation with time of the quadrupole moment of a source's mass is responsible for gravitational radiation. Because of the smallness of the constant that determines the coupling of the energy of such a source to the gravitational field, gravitational radiation from sources in the solar system is minuscule. (The sun radiates about as much energy in gravitational waves as a small light bulb does in electromagnetic waves.) Only very large-scale astrophysical or cosmological events can produce enough radiation to be observable with current gravitational wave detectors. One observer has claimed the detection of such radiation over the last twenty years, but his observations have not been confirmed by other observers. However, secular changes observed in the orbit of one component (a pulsar) in a binary star system have been interpreted as an effect of the gravitational waves radiated by the system.

By about 1920, Arthur Stanley Eddington and Hermann Weyl, among others, realised that the equations of motion of the sources of the gravitational field are not independent of the gravitational field equations themselves; in certain cases, in fact, these equations of motion are completely determined by the field equations. Einstein also worked on this problem later in the 1920s. In 1937, he collaborated with Leopold Infeld and Banesh Hoffmann to develop an approximation method for finding general-relativistic corrections to the Newtonian equations of motion of a system of slowly-moving bodies with comparable masses, interacting through gravitation. In the last twenty years, a method has been developed for taking into account the effect of gravitational radiation by such a system on its motion.

Observations of the binary pulsar mentioned above are consistent with the quantitative predictions of the theory.

For many years, attempts to verify the general theory were confined to the three classic tests proposed by Einstein: the gravitational red shift, the advance of the perihelion of Mercury and the solar light deflection. Within the solar system, other general relativistic effects involve only minute corrections to Newtonian gravitational effects, which are still generally beyond the limits of observation. This paucity of possibilities for experimental work in the field combined with the interest among mathematicians in the technical elaboration of the theory has resulted in physicists turning away from research on the general theory for several decades. This was especially true after the development of quantum mechanics, which provided them with so many problems of immediate interest and potentially rapid applicability. In contrast to special relativity, which every physicist was expected to master, general relativity existed in splendid isolation. It was recognised by most physicists as the best theory of gravitation, but was not regarded as part of the mainstream of physics. In recent years, this isolation has been considerably mitigated.

Starting in the 1960s, the development of new technologies, such as radar ranging and long base line interferometry, led to a revival of interest in repeating the classic tests with much greater accuracy. Irwin Shapiro also proposed a fourth test: due to the sun's gravitational field, radar signals reflected from Mercury or Venus should take measurably longer to return to earth when these planets are near the sun than when they are far away. Recent data from all four tests have confirmed the predictions of Einstein's theory with a high degree of accuracy. A series of discoveries starting in the 1960s revived interest in general relativity among astrophysicists. A number of objects were observed, such as quasars, pulsars and phenomena in galactic centres, the theoretical explanation of which seems to involve significant general-relativistic corrections to Newtonian theory. Relativistic astrophysics is now a recognised and growing subdiscipline.

After the new quantum mechanical formalism began to be applied to the quantisation of the electromagnetic field equations in the late 1920s, the question naturally arose of whether the gravitational field should also be quantised. In 1932 Leon Rosenfeld made the first attempt to quantise the field equations of general relativity, in linear approximation. Since then, many attempts have been made to apply various methods of field quantisation to the Einstein field equations. However, the features which make general relativity unique as a physical theory create formidable technical and conceptual difficulties for each of these attempts, none of which has been completely successful. Some physicists doubt whether such attempts at formal quantisation of the theory are the correct way to proceed. Einstein himself did not believe that quantum mechanics provides a complete description of physical reality, and continued to search for a quite different explanation of quantum phenomena, but with even less success. The existence of two such apparently incommensurable modes of approach to the theoretical comprehension of the physical world as quantum field theory and general relativity, each so successful within its own domain, remains an outstanding challenge to theoretical physicists.

3. UNIFIED FIELD THEORIES

The search for theories which unify apparently distinct realms of physical phenomena has a long history. The mechanistic world-view assumed that a mechanical explanation could be found for all phenomena, and the 'central force' programme attempted to realise that goal by explaining all phenomena on the model of Newton's gravitational theory. Maxwell's theory explained light in terms of interacting electric and magnetic fields, which in turn were unified into a single electromagnetic field by the special theory of relativity.

The electromagnetic world-view, espoused by Wilhelm Wien, Max Abraham and others around the turn of this century, attempted to explain the electron and its mechanical properties on the basis of Maxwell's theory of the electromagnetic field, or some suitable modification of that theory. (See art. 22, sect. 3.) Einstein himself made such an attempt around 1909, and Gustav Mie worked on a non-linear electrodynamical model of the electron for many years. There were also attempts to include gravitation in such a unified theory. In 1915, Gunnar Nordström proposed a five-dimensional theory that united his relativistic scalar gravitational theory with Maxwell's electromagnetic theory.

In 1918, Hermann Weyl proposed a unified theory, that includes electromagnetism by generalising the geometry used as the basis of Einstein's theory of gravitation. Weyl's theory was soon rejected by Einstein and others as physically unsatisfactory; but its historical significance is great. It is the first example of a theory which introduces a field in order to satisfy the criterion of invariance under a local gauge group, a technique which is of great importance in current gauge theories of elementary particles.

Weyl's mathematically elegant theory utilises a special class of affine connections. The affine connection is the closest four-dimensional mathematical analogue of the Newtonian gravitational force. A connection defines a family of preferred curves in space-time, which may be interpreted physically as the paths of test particles under the influence of gravitation (inertial paths). In 1921, Eddington utilised a more general affine connection as the basis of a unified theory of gravitation and electromagnetism. After some initial scepticism, Einstein became intrigued with the idea and started to work on it himself. Two years later Elie Cartan utilised affine spaces with torsion to generalise Einstein's theory of gravitation. Earlier, Theodor Kaluza suggested, in 1919, the possibility of unifying Einstein's gravitation theory and electromagnetism on the basis of a five-dimensional theory, a programme which Einstein encouraged. The unified field theories of gravitation and electromagnetism that grew out of attempts to generalise general relativity fall into one or more of the following categories:

(1) Theories that utilise spaces of more than four dimensions;
(2) Theories that utilise a metric tensor, symmetric or asymmetric;
(3) Theories that utilise an affine connection, with or without torsion.

These categories are not mutually exclusive; for example, there are metric-affine theories, pentadimensional metric theories, etc.

From the outset of his work on unified theories, Einstein aimed for more than the unification of gravitation and electromagnetism; he also hoped that non-singular solutions to the proper set of unified field equations would yield an explanation of the discreteness associated with so many quantities in physics, such as electric charge, energy and the atomic structure of matter. He regarded a constructive explanation of such quantum phenomena as the major goal of physics. He felt that quantum mechanics had not provided such an explanation but merely postulated what had to be explained. Therefore, he persisted in the search for a unified field theory, even after the development of quantum mechanics in the 1920s convinced most physicists that his search was quixotic. At the present time, there is no strong indication that any such programme can succeed in providing an alternative explanation of quantum phenomena.

For many years, the unified field theory programme was so closely associated with Einstein's goal of superseding quantum mechanics that attempts at unification fell out of fashion as quantum mechanics and quantum field theory proved ever more successful. However, in recent years, a special-relativistic, locally gauge-invariant field theory has successfully unified the electromagnetic and weak interactions into a single, so-called electroweak interaction. An extension of this approach shows promise of including the strong forces, as well, in a so-called grand unified theory. As a result, there has been a rebirth of interest in unified field programmes, with the ultimate aim of also including gravitation. Current proposals differ from Einstein's in both scope and motivation; however, they aim to unify the electroweak and the strong interactions with gravitation, and they take for granted that classical unified field theories, rather than being substitutes for quantum mechanics, are only preliminaries to their quantised versions of such theories.

4. INFLUENCE OF THE THEORY OUTSIDE PHYSICS

As from about 1910, philosophers attempted to assimilate the theory of relativity. Einstein's theory modified traditional views of basic philosophical concepts such as space, time and matter, presenting a challenge to philosophers claiming to have developed a comprehensive world-view. Such outstanding philosophers as Henri Bergson, Ernst Cassirer, Emil Myerson, Bertrand Russell, Hans Reichenbach, Moritz Schlick and Alfred North Whitehead devoted books to the theory of relativity in the 1910s and 1920s. Some of these philosophers attempted to show that the theory was quite compatible with their previous views, which required little or no modification. Others attempted to create a 'scientific philosophy', which would take account of the novel features of recent scientific theories, such as the theory of relativity. Perhaps the most influential such attempt was that of the so-called Vienna Circle of logical positivists. (See art. 54, sect. 2.) After the development of quantum mechanics in the late 1920s, interest shifted to that theory, which presents even greater challenges to classical philosophical doctrines than does the theory of relativity. In the last few decades, the growth of philosophy of science as a separate sub-discipline, with more modest aims, has led to renewed critical studies of the foundations of space-time theories, starting with the work of Adolf Grünbaum.

Although the theory of relativity is a highly mathematical branch of physics, its history has been surrounded by extra-scientific controversies. Some physicists attacked Einstein for subverting common sense and sound physical intuition. After he became world famous in 1919, attacks were levelled at Einstein, and at relativity, from other quarters since it was well known that he was a Jew, a pacifist and a man of the left. In Weimar Germany, such attacks were often politically motivated, even if they were covered with a scientific or philosophical veneer. During the Nazi era, the anti-Semitic animus behind some of these attacks emerged into the open, and the teaching of the theory was considered a subversive act. Some philosophers and physicists in the Soviet Union maintained a continuous attack on the theory as incompatible with the official doctrine of dialectical materialism, and at certain times during the Stalinist era the theory was semi-officially condemned.

After Einstein became well known in 1919, a number of books and articles appeared attempting to explain the theory of relativity to a wider public. Einstein himself had written such a book in 1917, which was eventually translated into most major languages and is still in print in several of them. A host of scientists, philosophers, educators, journalists and laymen joined in the attempt to meet the continuing popular demand for accessible explanations. The theory of relativity has consequently become widely known, but it would be rash to say that it has been widely understood. It has been subject to a number of misinterpretations. For example, it has often been invoked in support of various 'relativisms'; assertions that all things of some type, such as ethical judgements, are relative to the points of view of different individuals or social groups. Whatever the merits of such doctrines, they must be sharply distinguished from the theory of relativity. Einstein did not assert that 'everything is relative'; indeed, it is more correct to understand his theory as a theory concerning invariants – the invariance of the laws of physics and of such quantities as the velocity of light.

NOTES

1. I. Newton, *Mathematical principles of natural philosophy*, trans. A. Mottle, rev. F. Cajori (2 vols., Berkeley and Los Angeles, 1934), vol. 1, pp. 10–11.
2. A. Einstein, 'Zur Elektrodynamik bewegter Körper', *Annalen der Physik*, 17 (1905), 891–921.

FURTHER READING

Albert Einstein, *Autobiographical notes* (LaSalle, 1979). First published in Paul Arthur Schilpp (ed.), *Albert Einstein: Philosopher-Scientist* (LaSalle, 1949), pp. 2–94.

Thomas Glick, *The comparative reception of relativity* (Dordrecht, 1987).

Stanley Goldberg, *Understanding relativity: origin and impact of a scientific revolution* (Boston, 1984).

Tetu Hirosige, 'The ether problem, the mechanistic worldview, and the origins of the theory of relativity', *Historical studies in the physical sciences*, 7 (1976), 3–82.

Gerald Holton, *Thematic origins of scientific thought from Kepler to Einstein* (Cambridge, 1973).

Arthur I. Miller, *Albert Einstein's special theory of relativity (1905) and early interpretation (1905–1911)* (London, 1981).

John Norton, 'How Einstein found his field equations: 1912–1915', *Historical studies in the physical sciences*, 14 (1984) 253–316.

Abraham Pais, *'Subtle is the Lord . . .' the science and the life of Albert Einstein* (Oxford, 1982).

José Manuel Sánchez Ron, *Relatividad especial, relatividad general (1905–1923): Orígenes, desarollo y recepción por la comunidad científica* (Barcelona, 1981).

Marie-Antoinette Tonnelat, *Histoire du principe de relativité* (Paris, 1971).

Roberto Torretti, *Relativity and geometry* (Oxford, 1983).

Vladimir P. Vizgin, *Relyativistskaya teoriya tyagoteniya (istori i formirovanie, 1900–1915)* (Moscow, 1981).

—— *Yedinye teorii polia v pervoi treti XX veka* (Moscow, 1985).

29

QUANTUM THEORY

MICHAEL REDHEAD

The history of the quantum theory has received rather uneven treatment from professional historians of science. There has been a great deal of emphasis on the early period from 1900 to 1926, during which time the classic formulations of the so-called old and new quantum theories were laid down. But there have been many important subsequent improvements in the underlying theory, its applications and interpretation. The present article attempts a more balanced perspective on the whole theory from the initial inception to its ongoing development. The subject is necessarily a technical and mathematical one, and no account, worthy of any pretensions to accuracy, can avoid reference to some technical matters. An attempt has been made to keep these to a minimum, but it is not entirely possible to eliminate them. This probably helps to explain why the more recent history has largely been dealt with by practising physicists, rather than by historians.

An important controversy in the historiography of quantum theory has concerned the relevance of the background of wider cultural influences, where some authors have sought to identify the source of the new scientific ideas.[1] These writers have probably overstated their case. The quantum theorists were driven by great intellectual ingenuity in confronting what most of them, arguably correctly, regarded as objective problem situations arising from the interplay of theory and experiment in atomic physics. In this article we shall concentrate on the many complexities in the history, from a predominantly internalist point of view. (See art. 3, sects. 2–4.)

The quantum theory involves two basic ideas: (1) The possible values to be accorded to some observable properties of physical systems on the atomic scale are restricted to a discrete 'quantised' set, as compared with the continuous 'unquantised' set of possible values envisaged in classical physics; and (2) A maximally specific description of the state of the atomic system does not allow the prediction of the outcome of all subsequent measurements on the system, but only the probability that an outcome permitted by quantisation will occur.

I. THE RISE OF THE 'OLD QUANTUM THEORY'

The history of quantum theory begins in 1900 with the work of Max Planck (1858–1947) on the distribution of energy in the spectrum of black-body radiation. The background to this problem is as follows. Classical thermodynamics and electromagnetic theory predicted that, for a perfectly absorbing cavity, the energy density u per unit frequency range at frequency v and absolute temperature T satisfied the equation

$$u(v, T) = v^3 f\left(\frac{v}{T}\right)$$

where f is a universal function, quite independent of the particular physical nature of the cavity. During the closing years of the nineteenth century much effort was expended on determining the form of this function. Wilhelm Wien proposed in 1896 the form $e^{-const(v/T)}$, which agreed well with experiment at high frequencies (short wavelengths). But in 1900 Otto Lummer and Ernst Pringsheim demonstrated deviations from Wien's law for lower frequencies and, more decisively, Heinrich Rubens and Ferdinand Kurlbaum showed that u was proportional to T at sufficiently low frequencies. Planck tackled the problem in three stages. Firstly he showed that u could be related to the mean energy U of harmonic oscillators in the walls of the cavity by the relation

$$u(v, T) = \frac{8\pi}{c^3} U(v, T)$$

where c is the velocity of light in *vacuo*.

Planck realised that the Wien formula could be derived from this result by investigating the entropy S of the oscillators and was in fact equivalent to the statement

$$\frac{\partial^2 S}{\partial U^2} = \frac{const}{U}. \tag{1}$$

For the low-frequency behaviour Planck recognised that (1) had to be replaced by

$$\frac{\partial^2 S}{\partial U^2} = \frac{const}{U^2}. \tag{2}$$

In 1900 Planck suggested an 'empirical' interpolation between (1) and (2), viz.

459

$$\frac{\partial^2 S}{\partial U^2} = \frac{a}{U(U + b)} \tag{3}$$

where a and b are constants, which leads via the thermodynamic identity

$$\frac{I}{T} = \frac{\partial S}{\partial U}$$

and the requirement of reducing to the Wien formula in the high-frequency limit, to the empirically very well supported distribution

$$U(v, T) = \frac{Av^3}{e^{Bv/T} - I} \tag{4}$$

where A and B are new constants. Planck now set himself the task of justifying equation (3). In a short communication published in 1900 he utilised the Ludwig Boltzmann relation

$$S = k \ln W$$

relating the entropy S to the thermodynamic probability W. To compute W he used the mathematical artifice of dividing the total energy NU of N oscillators (of a given frequency) into Z 'units' of value ε, so NU=Zε, and then computing W as the number of ways of distributing Z indistinguishable energy elements among the N oscillators according to the formula

$$W = \frac{(N + Z - I)!}{(N - I)! \, Z!}.$$

For large N and Z he could recover (3) and by choosing ε=hv, with h a universal constant, he finally obtained (cp. equation (4))

$$U(v, T) = \frac{8\pi v^2}{c^3} \frac{hv}{e^{hv/kT} - I}. \tag{5}$$

The two vital steps in arriving at equation (5) are (1) keeping ε finite, and (2) choosing ε=hv. These steps seem to have been motivated by the requirement of recovering equations (3) and (4) respectively from the new approach.

At that time Planck does not seem to have appreciated the revolutionary nature of restricting the total energy NU to an integral multiple of hv. The now familiar gloss, that the energy of *each* oscillator is restricted to a discrete set of multiples of hv, a genuine concept of quantisation as applied to oscillator energy, was first stated explicitly by Albert Einstein (1879–1955) in 1906. Indeed it is arguable that Einstein, not Planck, was the real discoverer of the quantum theory and its revolutionary conceptual implications. This is further supported by considering Einstein's famous 1905 paper[2] in which he computed the volume dependence of the entropy of the radiation field in a 'black-body' cavity in the Wien regime and found that the result was the same as if the radiation were composed of a finite number of localised energy quanta hv. This corpuscular theory of light (the 'particles' of light were designated photons by Gilbert Lewis in 1926) led Einstein to his explanation of the laws governing the photo-electric effect, in particular, that the maximum energy of the ejected electrons depended not on the intensity but only on the frequency of the incident light. Further clarification was provided by Einstein in 1909 when he computed the mean square energy fluctuations in a cavity of radiation subject to Planck's distribution law, and found a result which was the sum of two terms, one of which was expected on a wave theory of light and the other on a particle theory. Already the idea of wave-particle duality, the necessary fusion of two apparently incompatible points of view, began to appear.

Einstein's other early contribution to the development of the quantum theory, was his application of the idea of energy quantisation to the theory of the specific heats of solids, and his explanation of their decrease in value at low temperatures, in violation of the classical prediction of a temperature-independent specific heat. Einstein used the Planck formula for the mean energy of an oscillator to compute directly the specific heat, $C = \partial U / \partial T$.

It was clear from Einstein's work that quantum conceptions could be applied both to material systems, such as molecular oscillations in a crystal, and also to immaterial systems such as fields of radiation. Indeed in 1910 Peter Debye, developing ideas of Paul Ehrenfest, gave a new derivation of Planck's distribution law by quantising the field oscillations directly instead of Planck's method of quantising the energy of the oscillators responsible for *producing* the radiation.

The next major development in the quantum theory was due to Niels Bohr (1885–1962) who proposed in 1913 a theory of the hydrogen atom which explained the well-known regularities in the frequencies of line-spectra emitted by the gas. These regularities were summarised in empirical formulae that stemmed from the work of Johann Balmer (1885) and culminated in the combination principle (1908) of Walter Ritz which exhibited the frequency of every spectral line as the difference between two terms, each of which involved an integer.

Bohr moved from Cambridge to join Ernest Rutherford in Manchester in 1912. His own theory was based on Rutherford's nuclear model of the atom (1911) and consisted in identifying the energy and hence the frequency of the radiated energy quantum with the difference in energy of two 'stationary' states in the atom. While moving in a 'stationary' orbit the electron was supposed not to radiate, in defiance of the classical laws of electromagnetic radiation, radiation only occurring when the electron 'jumped' from one stationary state to another. Bohr showed parenthetically that the stationary states could be characterised, for the simple case of an electron moving in a circular orbit, by the 'quantisation condition' that the angular momentum was an integral multiple of

$h/2\pi$. Apart from explaining the already-known Balmer and Paschen series in the hydrogen spectrum, the theory also predicted a further series of lines in the ultraviolet spectrum, which were confirmed by Theodore Lyman in 1914. An apparent difficulty posed by lines observed by Edward Pickering (1896) in the spectrum of the star ζ Puppis was turned into a major triumph by Bohr who attributed them to ionised helium, and obtained remarkable numerical agreement with the observations, when proper account was taken of the finite mass of the nucleus.

The idea of stationary states for electrons in atoms was apparently suggested to Bohr by the experiments of Richard Whiddington (1911) on the discontinuous changes in the X-rays emitted when cathode rays (electrons) of increasing energy bombarded the anticathode. Similar observations in the visible spectrum by James Franck and Gustav Hertz (1914) directly confirmed Bohr's frequency condition.

During the next decade a great deal of effort was expended in developing Bohr's simple model into what later came to be known as the 'old quantum theory' of atomic structure and associated line spectra. A very significant development was the generalisation of Bohr's angular momentum quantisation condition for circular orbits in hydrogen-like atoms to the general case of multiple periodic motions analysed in celestial mechanics by the familiar angle and action variables appropriate to the problem. Thus, in 1915, Arnold Sommerfeld (1868–1951) postulated further quantum conditions for the action variables and applied them to the general problem of the relativistic motion of the electron in the hydrogen atom, obtaining results which explained in quantitative detail the fine structure of hydrogen-like spectra, in particular the precision measurements on the spectrum of ionised helium by Louis Friedrich Paschen (1916). Similar quantum conditions were proposed independently by William Wilson and Jun Ishiwara. A further remarkable success was the explanation of the effect of an electric field (the Stark effect) on the Balmer lines of the hydrogen spectrum by Karl Schwarzschild and by Paul Epstein (1916), while further experimental support for the Sommerfeld conditions came from the demonstration by Otto Stern and Walther Gerlach (1922) of space quantisation, the discrete angular alignments of atomic magnetic moments in a magnetic field.

Ehrenfest (1916) provided important theoretical support for the Sommerfeld conditions by noticing that an action variable is adiabatically invariant, i.e. remains constant in value when the mechanical system is subject to adiabatic (infinitely slow) variation in the parameters defining the motion. The Adiabatic Principle in the old quantum theory claimed that those mechanical quantities subjected to quantisation, and which, therefore, could not vary in a continuous manner, must be adiabatic invariants.

A second overriding principle, much exploited in the old quantum theory, was what came to be called the Correspondence Principle, first explicitly formulated by Bohr in 1918 (although he did not use the term 'correspondence' until two years later). According to this principle, for large quantum numbers the quantum theory of spectral lines must tend smoothly to the classical results predicted for the motion in the stationary states themselves (without transitions). This was employed by Bohr and his student Hendrik Kramers to extend the old quantum theory to cover the intensities and polarisations of spectral lines, in addition to their frequencies.

From its inception Bohr envisaged that the quantum theory of atoms should be applied to the much more difficult problem of the structure of complex atoms. He proposed a 'building-up' principle in virtue of which various permitted states for the motion of a single electron could be successively filled by all the electrons in an atom in a way which would reflect the periodicities in chemical behaviour of successive elements in the Periodic Table, the chemical properties being controlled by the outermost ring or 'shell' of electrons. In particular, Bohr predicted in 1921 that element 72, hitherto undiscovered, should not belong, as had been thought, among the rare earths. This was confirmed very soon afterwards by the discovery of hafnium by Dirk Coster and Georg von Hevesy.

In addition, much effort was expended in trying to explain the multiplet structure of complex atomic spectra and the closely associated problem of the Zeeman splitting of spectral lines in a magnetic field. Indeed, in the early 1920s Sommerfeld and Alfred Landé formulated the so-called magnetic core hypothesis according to which the magnetic moment associated with the nucleus and the inner (non-optical) electrons acted on the optical electrons with an 'internal' Zeeman effect. Considerable clarification was introduced in 1925 by Sommerfeld's student Wolfgang Pauli (1900–58), with his Exclusion Principle – no two electrons can share identical quantum numbers – and by Samuel Goudsmit and George Uhlenbeck with their concept of electron spin as a physical interpretation of Pauli's fourth quantum number. These two contributions mark the high point in the achievements of the old quantum theory. Moreover, 1925 marked the opening of a new era with the discovery by another of Sommerfeld's erstwhile students, Werner Heisenberg (1901–76), of what came to be known as matrix mechanics.

2. THE NEW QUANTUM THEORY

Heisenberg had worked with Kramers earlier on the theory of optical dispersion, the effect of atomic structure on the propagation of a light wave through a medium constituted by atoms. For this purpose the atom was conceived as a collection of 'virtual' oscillators each associated with a frequency allowed by a transition between two energy levels in the atom characterised by quantum numbers n and m. These frequencies $\nu_{n,m}$ constituted a two-dimensional array as contrasted with the one-dimensional array $n\nu$ of harmonic frequencies associated with classical oscillators of frequency ν. The two sorts of frequency were connected via the Correspondence Principle by the relation $\nu_{n,n-r} \rightarrow r\nu_n$, where ν_n is the frequency of classical motion in the nth state, for large quantum numbers n.

Heisenberg then developed a new non-commutative algebra for arrays of the general form $X_{n,m}$, which was recognised by Max Born (1882–1970) as equivalent to the rules for multiplying matrices. The formal development of Heisenberg's approach proceeded very rapidly. Collaborating with the young mathematician Pascual Jordan, Born published in 1925 a fundamental paper entitled 'Zur Quantenmechanik',[3] and then in 1926 appeared what came to be known as the 'three-man paper' co-authored by Born, Heisenberg and Jordan.[4] In these two papers matrix mechanics was developed in much the same way as it is taught today. The problem of finding the quantised energy levels was reduced to choosing matrix representations for the co-ordinates and momenta which satisfied the basic commutation relation

$$qp - pq = \frac{ih}{2\pi} I$$

and in terms of which the classically computed Hamiltonian reduced to a diagonal matrix whose elements gave directly the energy levels in question. In 1926 Pauli used matrix mechanics to derive anew Bohr's familiar formula for the Balmer series in hydrogen but in the same paper he already showed the superiority of the new methods by investigating the perturbation of the Balmer series by crossed electric and magnetic fields.

Matrix mechanics was formidably abstract in its approach, and really only accessible to mathematicians. By contrast, a very different version of quantum mechanics, the so-called wave mechanics of Erwin Schrödinger (1887–1961), used the much more familiar mathematics of partial differential equations, and, while shown by Schrödinger himself to be actually equivalent in empirical content to Heisenberg's matrix mechanics, led in practice to a host of new applications. To understand the background to Schrödinger's work we must return to Einstein's contribution to the development of quantum theory. Einstein's proposal of the light quantum met with very little favour from other physicists, and in particular was not accepted by Bohr. Nevertheless Einstein continued to pursue the problems of radiation theory. In 1916–17 he obtained a new derivation of Planck's distribution law by considering the dynamic equilibrium between the absorption and emission of radiation by atoms. He found it necessary to introduce besides emission stimulated by the external field, a new process of spontaneous emission occurring quite independently of any external cause and governed only by probabilistic considerations. Furthermore he attributed directed momentum $h\nu/c$ as well as energy $h\nu$ to the light quanta. The idea of the light quantum as a 'particle' of light was finally turned from a fanciful conception to a generally accepted hypothesis by the explanation of the Compton effect, the change in wavelength of X-rays scattered off free electrons, in terms of a classically described collision between the light quantum and the electron (Arthur Holly Compton (1923)). In 1924 Bohr, Kramers and John Slater proposed that conservation of energy was only satisfied in an average sense during the interaction of matter and radiation, but this proposal was soon disproved by experiments which confirmed Compton's analysis for individual events (Walther Bothe and Hans Geiger (1924) and Compton and Franz Simon (1925)). The light-particle conception was used furthermore by Satyendra Nath Bose (1924) in yet another derivation of the Planck radiation law, in which radiation was considered as a 'gas' of identical and indeed non-individual particles, subject to a novel statistical treatment. This work was seized on by Einstein, who suggested applying the same statistical treatment (Bose-Einstein statistics) to a gas of material molecules. Einstein showed that for such a gas there was a kind of statistical attraction between the molecules, which would lead to condensation at sufficiently low temperatures. Furthermore he calculated the mean square energy fluctuations in the gas, and found, just as for photons, a sum of two terms, one characteristic of an assembly of particles and the other characteristic of an assembly of waves. Thus Einstein recognised that wave-particle duality might have to be extended from light to matter.

It is this wave aspect of matter which forms the subject of wave mechanics. The idea of matter waves was introduced into physics quite independently by Louis de Broglie (1892–1987) in 1923. De Broglie's starting point was the optical-mechanical analogy of William Rowan Hamilton who demonstrated in 1833 that the motion of a system of particles could be understood in terms of rays associated, as in geometrical optics, with a moving wave surface. The analogy was not regarded as of any physical significance, since the velocity of the particle did not in general correspond to the velocity of the ray. De Broglie considered how the light-quantum hypothesis of Einstein could be reconciled with phenomena of interference and diffraction. In some way the particle must be accompanied by a wave, and if this were true of light particles, should it not also be true of material particles? With a particle of rest mass m_0, moving with a velocity βc, where c is the velocity of light, de Broglie associated an internal frequency $v_0 = m_0 c^2/h$, which to a stationary observer would appear as $v_0 \sqrt{1-\beta^2}$, by Einstein's time dilatation formula. But the stationary observer should see a frequency $v_0/\sqrt{1-\beta^2}$ if the variation of mass with velocity is taken into account. The discrepancy between these two frequencies led de Broglie to the conception of a wave of frequency $v_0/\sqrt{1-\beta^2}$ and velocity c/β associated with the particle which he easily showed would always keep in phase with the 'internal' frequency $v_0 \sqrt{1-\beta^2}$ as viewed from the stationary frame. The wavelength associated with the wave is h/p, where p is the momentum of the particle, while the group velocity of the wave turns out to be just βc, the velocity of the particle. He considered that these phase waves 'guided' the displacement of energy associated with the particles and that their existence for light particles explained how diffraction and interference phenomena could occur, which should also be demonstrated when electrons were scattered by crystals. The experimental confirmation of this prediction came in 1927 with the work of Clinton Davisson and Lester Germer and of George Thomson. Moreover, de Broglie could understand the Bohr quantisation condition as expressing the condition that the phase wave in a circular orbit would keep in phase with itself, in the sense that the perimeter of the orbit contained an integral number of wavelengths.

De Broglie's work was reported by Paul Langevin to Einstein, who remarked on its relevance to his own work on energy fluctuations in a quantum gas. What was needed was a wave equation that would govern the propagation of the new matter waves. This was produced in 1926 by Schrödinger in a very important four-part paper.[5] Schrödinger's attention had been drawn to de Broglie's ideas by reading Einstein's second paper on the degenerate quantum gas. Initially he followed de Broglie in trying to derive a relativistically invariant equation. No manuscript of this work survives, but apparently he had obtained what later became known as the Klein-Gordon equation. He rejected this as it did not reproduce the well-verified Sommerfeld result for the fine structure of the hydrogen spectrum. A few months later he returned to the problem in non-relativistic approximation and obtained what is now known as the time-independent Schrödinger wave equation, whose eigenvalue spectrum for a Coulomb potential reproduced exactly the Bohr energy levels. In the published work Schrödinger applied this equation also to the linear harmonic oscillator and the rigid rotator, obtaining in the former case the same result as Heisenberg had found with his matrix mechanics, namely a spectrum of the form $(n+\frac{1}{2})h\nu$, $\eta=0$, 1, 2, ... Schrödinger developed a perturbation theory by extending the classic work of Lord Rayleigh on acoustic vibrations, and also obtained the more general time-dependent form of his own wave equation. Although Schrödinger's whole approach appeared very different from Heisenberg's, he showed that a formal identity could be established between the two methods, as noted above.

A third approach to the new quantum mechanics was developed by Paul Adrien Maurice Dirac (1902–84) in Cambridge. This was even more austerely abstract than Heisenberg's approach, but in its fulfilment embraced the methods of Heisenberg and Schrödinger on a uniform basis. Shortly after being shown the proofs of Heisenberg's 1925 paper, Dirac developed what he called a quantum algebra for the abstract quantities represented by the two-dimensional matrix arrays of complex numbers in the work of Heisenberg, Born and Jordan. He demonstrated a thorough-going correspondence between the commutator bracket of two quantum variables and the classical Poisson bracket for the corresponding dynamical variables. In a second paper published in 1926 he introduced the terminology of q-numbers and c-numbers to distinguish quantum (non-commuting) and classical (commuting) variables, and applied his abstract algebraic approach to obtain a very neat solution of the hydrogen spectrum problem. Later the same year, Dirac developed the general transformation theory for representations of his q-numbers (the transformation theory was also arrived at independently by Jordan), and showed how Heisenberg's matrix mechanics and Schrödinger's wave mechanics were simply related by a canonical (unitary) transformation. In the course of this work Dirac introduced states of infinite norm and had recourse to his famous δ-function which was zero everywhere except at the origin where it displayed an infinite singularity. The properties attributed by Dirac to the δ-function were mathematical nonsense, and it was this lack of rigour in Dirac's work which led John von Neumann (1903–57) to develop a mathematically rigorous formulation of abstract quantum mechanics in the period 1927–9. He had come to Göttingen in 1926, together with another assistant, Lothar Nordheim, to work with David Hilbert on the mathematical foundations of quantum mechanics. Von Neumann's work on quantum mechanics was collected together in 1932 in his magisterial work *Mathematische Grundlagen der Quantenmechanik* (*Mathematical foundations of quantum mechanics*). The arena for quantum mechanics was not the space of discrete or continuous variables, but rather *Hilbert space*, an abstraction from the isomorphic realisations provided by the space of square-summable sequences and square-integrable functions (in the Lebesgue sense). The dynamical variables or observables (Dirac's q-numbers) were appropriately chosen (hypermaximal) self-adjoint linear operators on this abstract space. Von Neumann assumed that every hypermaximal operator corresponded to an observable. This condition was only relaxed in 1952 when Gian Carlo Wick, Eugene Wigner and Arthur Wightman introduced the idea of superselection rules which reduced the Hilbert space to a direct sum of incoherent subspaces. The only other significant development of von Neumann's mathematical treatment of Hilbert space was the proof provided in 1957 by Andrew Gleason that the von Neumann density operators exhausted all possible constructions of probability measures over the projection lattice of the space, provided the space had a dimension greater than two. Von Neumann's book was matched in elegance, if not in rigour, by Dirac's monograph *The Principles of Quantum Mechanics* (1930). With these two books the first phase of technical innovation in quantum mechanics came to fruition.

3. THE INTERPRETATION OF QUANTUM THEORY

In the meantime, there had been a great deal of discussion about the interpretation of the new formalism. Heisenberg in his original 1925 paper adopted an avowedly Machian or positivistic approach, insisting that the theory should be couched in terms of quantities directly related to what could actually be observed, in particular, the frequencies and intensities of spectral lines. Heisenberg believed himself to be following here the methodology of Einstein in rejecting the notion of an unobservable ether frame of reference to provide a standard of absolute rest. Einstein himself pointed out to Heisenberg that what can be observed is actually decided by the theory and cannot be known independently. Like many of the early quantum physicists, Heisenberg's philosophical approach was very much conditioned by the prevalent ascendency of logical empiricism. Schrödinger had a totally different attitude. He wanted to interpret wave mechanics as a classical wave theory. For an electron of charge e he interpreted $e|\psi|^2$, where ψ is the wave function governed by his equation, as the spatial density of electrical charge. The corpuscular aspect of electrons he believed consisted in the possibility of constructing localised wave packets that would represent the moving particles. Several difficulties emerged. Firstly, the wave function was a complex-valued function of position and time, and so could not be given a direct physical interpretation. Secondly, the wave packets would suffer dispersion, so particles could not maintain their localisation except in exceptional circumstances. Thirdly, and most decisively, the wave function for a many-particle problem was a function in the configuration of space of all the particles, rather than the three-dimensional physical space.

In 1926 Born introduced what came to be known as the Born interpretation or probabilistic interpretation of the wave function. He did this originally in connection with the application of wave mechanics to the problem of the collision of a free particle with an atom. Rejecting Schrödinger's interpretation, Born regarded $|\psi|^2$ as measuring the probability density for finding a particle in a small element surrounding the positional argument of the wave function. This interpretation was adopted and given a much more general setting by Dirac and Jordan in their transformation theory. The modulus squared of the elements of the transformation matrix measured the probability that a particle prepared in an eigenstate of one observable would be observed on measurement to reveal the eigenvalue of another observable.

In 1927 Heisenberg wrote a famous paper in which he identified the physical content of the quantum theory with the impossibility of simultaneously measuring canonically conjugate quantities, when due account was taken of the physical conditions under which such measurements could be performed.[6] He adopted an operationalist stance: meaning could only be attached to concepts like the position and momentum of an electron if an experiment could be specified which would actually measure these quantities. Introducing his famous *gedanken* experiment of the γ-ray microscope, Heisenberg explained how increasing the accuracy of position measurement by increasing the microscope's resolving power using radiation such as γ-rays of very short wavelength would necessarily disturb to a higher degree, and in an uncontrollable manner, the momentum of the electron due to Compton scattering of the radiation photons. A qualitative analysis showed that the product of uncertainties in the position and momentum of the electron was of the order of Planck's constant. This was an example of Heisenberg's celebrated Uncertainty Principle, that the more accurately one tried to know one variable, the less accurately one could at the same time know the canonically conjugate variable. This epistemological principle, Heisenberg believed, was the physical reason behind Born's probabilistic interpretation. Heisenberg viewed the uncertainty relations as the conceptual starting point for the whole theory. Dynamical quantities lacked definition in so far as they could not be measured precisely.

A much more profound analysis of the philosophical implications and preconceptions of quantum mechanics was initiated by Bohr. He rejected Heisenberg's starting point. It was not a case of quantities not being defined because they could not be measured, rather, they could not be measured because they were not defined. Bohr introduced his so-called complementarity interpretation of quantum mechanics in a lecture given at Como in 1927. Classical concepts could and indeed must still be used in the atomic domain, but their use was restricted to 'complementary' experimental contexts. Space-time description, for example, was complementary to the 'claims of causality', identified with conservation laws of momentum and energy. The 'quantum postulate' necessitated an uncontrollable disturbance of atomic systems by the very act of observation, thus preventing simultaneous measurement of conjugate quantities in the way described by Heisenberg. Paradoxically it was Einstein, who had done so much to develop the idea of wave-particle duality, who opposed Bohr's interpretation. Bohr considered that with complementarity he had arrived at a major epistemological discovery that indeed had wider implications in the fields of psychology and the social sciences, but Einstein rejected the claim of ultimate limitations on human knowledge of what he regarded as an objective, independently existing, physical reality, and sought by many ingenious thought experiments to show how the Heisenberg uncertainty relations could be circumvented. The discussions were carried on between Bohr and Einstein, particularly at the Fifth and Sixth Solvay Conferences in 1927 and 1930 respectively. On the latter occasion Bohr refuted Einstein's objection to the time-energy uncertainty relation by an appeal to Einstein's own relativistic conception of the effect of a gravitational field on the rate of a clock.

The Bohr-Einstein dialogue culminated in the paper published by Einstein, Boris Podolsky and Nathan Rosen in 1935, in which they claimed to establish the incompleteness of the orthodox quantum-mechanical description by showing that elements of reality simultaneously existed corresponding to the noncommuting dynamical variables associated with the position and momentum of a particle. The example considered by Einstein and his co-authors involved two particles spatially separated in a specially chosen quantum-mechanical state, which would allow the prediction of either the momentum or the position of one particle by measuring the corresponding momentum or position of the other particle. Assuming a locality principle, that measurements on the second particle could not create elements of reality associated with the first particle, they claimed to establish their incompleteness result. Einstein was proposing a dilemma, either that the quantum-mechanical formalism is incomplete or that instantaneous non-local action must be admitted. Einstein rejected the second horn of the dilemma on relativistic grounds and enthusiastically embraced the first horn. But Bohr simply rejected the whole argumentation essentially on the grounds that concepts of position and momentum for the first particle were only sharply defined when an experiment had actually been performed of one sort or the other on the second particle, and both the relevant experiments could not of course be performed simultaneously on the second particle. In fact the 1935 discussion led Bohr to a more sophisticated understanding of complementarity, in which he no longer talked of disturbance of microsystems by observation, but emphasised rather the wholeness and the essential individuality of a quantum 'phenomenon', specified by a description in classical terms of the whole experimental arrangement.

The majority of physicists sided with Bohr in this debate and for the next thirty years Copenhagen orthodoxy in the interpretation of quantum mechanics reigned supreme. Additional support for this view came from an argument by von Neumann in his 1932 monograph purporting to show the logical inconsistency with certain plausible general principles, of supplementing the quantum-mechanical state description with a more complete specification afforded by additional 'hidden variables'.

It came as some surprise, then, when David Bohm published just such a hidden-variable interpretation of quantum mechanics in 1952. The Bohm interpretation, however, involved wildly non-local actions, and attracted much less attention by physicists than, with hindsight, it deserved. The whole question of the possibility of hidden-variable theories and their connection with non-locality was greatly clarified by John Bell in the 1960s.[7] In a paper published in 1964 Bell showed that any hidden-variable reconstruction of the quantum mechanics of two spin-1/2 particles that did not exhibit non-locality must satisfy an inequality (which came to known as the Bell inequality) involving certain correlation functions between the spin projections of the two particles along different directions. But inserting the correlation functions which could readily be calculated from the quantum-mechanical formalism showed that under appropriate conditions the inequality would be violated. The significance of this result was that the Einstein dilemma referred to above could not escape non-locality by embracing the incompleteness horn as Einstein had supposed. A 'completed' quantum mechanics would itself exhibit non-locality. There was a great deal of interest in the question of whether the violation of the Bell inequality predicted by the quantum-mechanical formalism would be confirmed by experiment or whether, perhaps, the formalism itself would at last be shown, in this type of prediction, to be deficient. A series of experiments were conducted from 1972 onwards, which, after some initial indecisiveness, came down firmly in favour of the inequality being violated. These experiments culminated in 1982 with the publication of the results of work carried out by Alain Aspect and his collaborators in Paris showing that the non-local action was propagated instantaneously (outside the light-cone in relativistic terms). However, further analysis had demonstrated that the non-locality involved could not be used to transmit signals at superluminal speeds, and was of a more delicate and subtle kind than anything contemplated in classical physics.

In the meantime Bell had also clarified, in a paper published in 1966, the question of von Neumann's no-hidden-variable theorem, and had identified an overly restrictive assumption involved in the proof. A further noteworthy attempt to establish the impossibility of hidden variables in quantum mechanics was made by Simon Kochen and Ernst Specker in 1967. But again 'hidden' assumptions in their proof were challenged by Bell, Bas van Fraassen and others, so that the question of the viability of hidden-variable theories such as Bohm's became much more open in the 1980s and allowed picturable classical-style accounts to be given of the standard 'paradoxical' thought-experiments of quantum mechanics, although always at the expense of allowing a mysterious, and to many physicists still an unacceptable, action-at-a-distance to operate.

Another vexed question was the problem of measurement. If a microsystem was initially in a pure quantum-mechanical state, then interaction with a piece of apparatus would leave the joint system still in a pure state, i.e. in general the apparatus could not properly be said to be in a state corresponding to the measurement result, but was, in a sense, entangled in a superposition of states corresponding to definite measurement results. This was clearly appreciated by von Neumann, who devoted the last two chapters of his 1932 book to the topic. To put the matter bluntly, application of the formalism of quantum mechanics to the measuring apparatus as well as to the system being measured did not permit measurement to issue in any definite result at all. To deal with this serious difficulty, von Neumann introduced what came to be known as the Projection Postulate, namely, that in a measurement time-evolution of the state of the microsystem an apparatus would ultimately 'project' this composite state into one or other component of the offending superposition. Since this projection could not consistently be supposed to occur at any physical stage of the process, however long a chain of successive measurement interactions was envisaged, von Neumann presumed it must occur when the conscious mind of the observer became aware of the result of the measurement. In this way an essential subjectivity, the self-awareness of the observer, was introduced into the theory. This approach was denied by Bohr, who regarded the classical description of the apparatus, with definite pointer readings, as arising from the epistemological considerations embodied in his complementarity philosophy. However, von Neumann's point of view was vigorously expounded and defended by Fritz London and Edmond Bauer in 1939, and has continued to find support, most famously by Wigner, and more recently by John Archibald Wheeler, up to the present day.

Other approaches to the measurement problem have been developed, in addition to the classic positions of Bohr and von Neumann. In particular, attempts have been made to explain the disappearance of the mysterious interference effects involving pieces of macroscopic apparatus apparently predicted by the formalism, by invoking the irreversible character of the completed measurement process. A bizarre proposal that has continued to have some currency was made by Hugh Everett, one of Wheeler's students, in 1957. In a measurement all the possible outcomes are simultaneously realised in parallel universes, and the result we observe corresponds to what is actually the case in the universe we happen to inhabit. Suffice it to say no generally agreed and entirely satisfactory resolution of the problem of measurement has been arrived at.

4. QUANTUM FIELD THEORY

We want now to return to developments in quantum mechanics associated with systems of identical particles and the closely related subject of quantum field theory. We have already described how Bose and Einstein developed a new statistical mechanics for assemblies of identical (more accurately, indistinguishable) particles, which were 'non-individuals', so that permuting the particles among themselves produced no change in the overall physical state of the assembly. In 1926 Enrico Fermi showed how the Bose-Einstein statistics had to be modified if the particles were subject to the Pauli Exclusion Principle, so that no more than one particle could occupy any given quantum state. Later in the same year Heisenberg and Dirac showed independently how these new statistics could be accommodated in the formalism of the new quantum mechanics. For identical particles the quantum-mechanical state of the assembly had to be the unique linear combinations of permuted states which were either symmetric (Bose statistics) or antisymmetric (Fermi statistics) under exchange of any pair of particles. Then, in 1927, Dirac showed how the quantum mechanics of an assembly of bosons could be reformulated mathematically as equivalent to regarding the Schrödinger wave equation of a single particle as a 'mechanical' field, subject to canonical quantisation in terms of commutator brackets for canonically conjugate quantities, but involving, as distinct from the quantum mechanics of particles, an infinite number of degrees of freedom. In this way the N-particle Schrödinger equation in a configuration space of 3N dimensions could be reduced to a 'second quantised' one-particle Schrödinger wave equation in physical three-dimensional space. Applying these ideas to the light quantum or photon, Dirac showed how, starting with the particles, he could arrive at a description in terms of a second-quantised wave, but equally he recognised that the concept of the light quantum could be extracted from a first quantisation of the classical electromagnetic field governed by Maxwell's equations. This was the seminal source of quantum field theory and the thoroughgoing correspondence between a quantised field and an assemblage of 'particles' or more properly field quanta, although the idea of quantising the electromagnetic field was not, of course, original to Dirac, and goes back, as we have seen, to Ehrenfest and Debye. The question now arose, how could these methods be adapted to deal with assemblies of fermions rather than bosons? The solution to this problem was finally achieved in 1928 by Jordan and Wigner, who showed how the 'second quantisation' for fermions, subject to antisymmetric wave functions, must proceed by formally replacing commutator brackets by anticommutator brackets in the canonical quantisation of the one-particle wave equation. The new second-quantisation approach to systems of identical particles was more than just an equivalent reformulation of the old N-particle theory. It allowed that theory to be extended in an obvious and natural way to variable N, i.e. to describe processes of the creation and annihilation of particles. This idea was resisted, by Dirac for example, even in the case of the light quantum, in which case he considered the emission or radiation of such a particle to be, not a genuine creation process, but a transition from some unobservable 'reservoir' state. We shall return to this view of Dirac in a moment, when discussing his so-called hole theory of the positive electron. For the moment we remark that Fermi, in his theory of β-decay (1933) was the first to contemplate genuine particle creation and corresponding annihilation in fundamental physics. This led to the wholesale application of quantum field theory to the various unstable particles discovered originally in cosmic ray phenomena, during the 1930s and 1940s. Most famously, Hideki Yukawa in 1935 discussed the properties of what was later identified as a 'mesotron' field, which would mediate the strong nuclear force, in the same way that photons mediated electromagnetic interactions.

Only in 1928 did Dirac arrive at a satisfactory relativistic quantum theory of the electron. The relativistic wave equation written down by Schrödinger, Oskar Klein and Walter Gordon, which we have already referred to, was, unlike the non-relativistic time-dependent Schrödinger equation, of second order in the partial time derivative. Dirac sought to 'linearise' the Klein-Gordon equation by introducing an algebra of 4 x 4 matrices, which constitute an example of what mathematicians know as a Clifford algebra. Dirac showed how the extra internal degrees of freedom introduced in the new equation gave the electron a spin and an associated magnetic moment exhibited in an external magnetic field, exactly corresponding to the Goudsmit and Uhlenbeck spin discussed above. In addition he showed that the new equation, when applied to the energy levels of the electron in the hydrogen atom, exactly reproduced the experimentally well-confirmed fine structure predicted by Sommerfeld using the old quantum theory. There was, however, a major difficulty with the new Dirac equation – it permitted the electron to exist in states of negative energy. In order to deal with this problem Dirac introduced his hole theory in a paper published in 1930. Dirac supposed that all the negative energy states were occupied individually, as permitted by the Exclusion Principle, by an infinite sea of unobservable electrons. If one of these negative energy electrons made a transition to a state of positive energy, the resulting 'hole' in the negative energy sea would behave as a particle of opposite, i.e. positive, charge. Dirac tried to interpret these holes as protons. However Hermann Weyl showed that these holes must have the same mass as the electrons. These positive electrons or positrons were subsequently discovered experimentally by Carl Anderson in 1932. The Dirac equation described particles with spin quantum number $1/2$. During the 1930s relativistic wave equations were investigated for particles of arbitrary spin and in a famous paper published in 1940, Pauli showed that when the spin quantum number was half integral, quantisation according to the Exclusion Principle was required, while for integral spin it was necessary to postulate Bose statistics.

Meanwhile, in the period 1929 to 1930, Heisenberg and Pauli developed a fully-fledged relativistic quantum electrodynamics, describing the interaction between electrons and the electromagnetic field, based on a second quantisation of the Dirac equation. But the theory immediately encountered difficulties when Ehrenfest pointed out that divergencies (infinite results) would arise if it was used to calculate radiative reaction effects in which virtual photons were reabsorbed by the same particle as emitted them. Detailed calculations by Ivar Waller and by Julius Robert Oppenheimer, published in 1930, confirmed Ehrenfest's expectation. The problem of divergencies plagued quantum electrodynamics throughout the 1930s. Many empirically successful calculations were carried out to the first non-vanishing order of perturbation in the coupling between the electron-positron field and the electromagnetic field, but any attempt to improve on these results by calculating higher-order terms in the perturbation series yielded absurd infinite results. This difficulty was finally resolved in the period 1947 to 1949 by exploiting the idea of so-called renormalisation of the mass and charge of the electron, that had been particularly advocated by Kramers. Divergent terms were absorbed into contributions to the mass and charge of the electron and these renormalised parameters were identified with the experimentally-observed values. The renormalisation technique was shown to eliminate divergencies in all orders of perturbation theory by Freeman Dyson in 1949, and the new renormalised quantum electrodynamics gave rise to extremely accurate predictions for anomalies in the hydrogen spectrum (the Lamb shift) and in the gyromagnetic ratio of the electron. Diagrammatic methods for calculating these effects were introduced by Richard Feynman in 1949 which made the very complicated calculation of these and other radiative reaction effects mathematically tractable. The further development of renormalisable relativistic quantum field theories takes us beyond the confines of general quantum theory into the more specialised topic of elementary particle physics. (See art. 43.)

5. APPLICATIONS AND AXIOMATICS

So far, we have discussed the successes of quantum theory in dealing with simple fundamental problems like explaining the regularities in the hydrogen spectrum. But directly after the inception of the new quantum mechanics, particularly in its accessible wave-mechanical version, the theory was applied with astonishing success to a host of more complex problems. As we have seen, Schrödinger in his original papers developed a perturbation theory for problems that could not be solved exactly. Supplemented by powerful variational techniques, quantum mechanics was brought to bear on the structure and spectra of complex atoms. Remarkable numerical accuracy was achieved by Egil Hylleraas in 1929 for the helium ground state and the associated ionisation potential. For atoms of higher atomic number, Douglas Hartree (1928) introduced his method of the self-consistent field, which allowed for inter-electron interaction by making the best estimate of an appropriately modified central field. This was improved by Vladimir Fock in 1930 to allow for antisymmetrising the electron wave functions. Meanwhile group-theoretic methods had been introduced by Wigner, Weyl and von Neumann to exploit the symmetry properties of atomic states in the problem of their classification. These methods were unfamiliar to the majority of physicists at the time, who were delighted when Slater showed them how to avoid, in the theory of atomic spectra, what had come to be known as the 'group-pest', by using his method of determinant wave functions, incorporating spin from the outset of the calculation. However, it has been a feature of the subsequent history of quantum mechanics that a more profound understanding of many of its applications has depended on symmetry considerations. A major triumph of the early application of quantum mechanics was the explanation given by Walter Heitler and Fritz London in 1927 of the homopolar (covalent) chemical bond in terms of so-called exchange forces arising from superposition of the single atomic wave functions. This introduced the field of quantum chemistry, which was rapidly developed by Linus Pauling, Slater, Robert Mulliken and others. Another important application of the theory was to the solid state and in particular to metals. In 1927 Sommerfeld and Pauli applied Fermi-Dirac statistics to a simple model of a 'gas' of free electrons within a metal, and succeeded in resolving problems associated with specific heats and the magnetic properties of metals. The theory was much improved by Felix Bloch in 1928 who investigated the perturbation of the electron states by the periodic potential provided by the crystal lattice of the metal. The resulting band structure in allowable states enabled the distinction between insulators and metals to be drawn in terms of whether the top band of states to be occupied was, or was not, completely filled. Bloch was able, moreover, to give the first really adequate account of electrical resistance in terms of the scattering of electrons by the lattice vibrations from one Bloch state to another. For many years the phenomenon of superconductivity posed a major problem for quantum-mechanical explanation. But in 1957 John Bardeen, Leon Cooper and John Schrieffer showed how to do this in terms of a quantum state corresponding to a coherent superposition of paired electron states. This state was produced at sufficiently low temperatures by interaction with the very lattice vibrations which, at higher temperatures, are responsible for the electrical resistance of the pure metal.

The first successful application of quantum mechanics to nuclear physics, as distinct from atomic physics, was the explanation of α-decay in terms of the characteristic tunnelling of quantum waves through a potential barrier given independently by Edward Condon and Ronald Gurney and by George Gamow in 1928. Many further applications arose later in the theory of nuclear structure, nuclear collision processes and, more generally, in the field of elementary particle physics. Deserving special mention is the beautiful demonstration of superposition and interference effects in the states of the neutral kaon by Abraham Pais and Oreste Piccioni in 1955.

Despite these impressive successes, much of the detailed quantitive application of quantum mechanics to complex problems depended on very questionable mathematical approximations which were often validated only by agreement with experiment and not by strict mathematical analysis. The assumption that quantum mechanics could, in principle, explain everything became an article of faith, rather than a proven fact.

Although, by 1927, the formalism of quantum mechanics had become firmly established, there have been a number of significant attempts to base quantum mechanics on an alternative axiomatic basis. Jordan, von Neumann and Wigner in 1934, following earlier ideas of Jordan, laid the foundations of the 'algebraic approach' to quantum mechanics, which abstracted a non-associative algebraic structure from the properties of self-adjoint operators on a Hilbert space, and then investigated this structure axiomatically, independently of its model in terms of Hilbert space. This approach was developed by Irving Segal (1947) and led in 1964 to the C*-algebra formulation of quantum field theory by Rudolph Haag and Daniel Kastler. In the meantime, an alternative approach stemmed from a paper published in 1936 by Garrett Birkhoff and von Neumann which abstracted from Hilbert space the lattice structure of its projection operators. This lattice was non-Boolean (non-distributive) and Birkhoff and von Neumann suggested that quantum mechanics really involved a modification in logic, replacing the Boolean lattice of classical propositions by the new non-Boolean lattice of quantum propositions. This approach was developed enthusiastically on the mathematical side by George Mackey at Harvard and by Josef Jauch, Constantin Piron and other collaborators in Geneva during the 1960s. The relevance of this logico-algebraic approach to resolving the paradoxes of quantum mechanics in terms of a revision of logic, that would parallel the revision of geometry necessitated by general relativity, has been canvassed by Hilary Putnam and others since the late 1960s. This was essentially an alternative development to the three valued quantum logic published by Hans Reichenbach in 1944, with a similar aim of resolving the conceptual paradoxes associated with the theory, but in the 1970s the whole idea of quantum logic came under attack from the philosophers, although many interesting technical improvements in the logic-algebraic approach continued to be made.

Meanwhile, in the 1940s, Feynman, in introducing his diagrammatic methods in quantum field theory, developed a new 'path-integral' approach to quantum mechanics (the basic idea goes back to Dirac). In this approach transition amplitudes were exhibited as a sum or integral over all possible classical paths or trajectories linking the initial and final states. Finally, in 1943, Heisenberg introduced a novel programme which instituted the scattering or S-matrix, in place of the quantum field, as the basic object of study. This was greatly developed in the 1960s, with mathematical properties of analyticity used as axioms in specifying the properties of the S-matrix, and for a time this programme virtually eclipsed quantum field theory as a basis for the theory of the elementary particles, but it ran into intractable mathematical problems and, in the early 1970s, quantum field theory returned to the centre of the stage with the proof by Gerardus 't Hooft of the renormalisability of the Weinberg-Salam electro-weak unified gauge theory and the extension of gauge field theories to the attempted unification of all the fundamental interactions, including even gravitation.

The quantum theory has proved a wonderfully versatile and adaptable framework in which to accommodate the properties of atomic and subatomic systems. In spite of continued debates about the paradoxes of interpretation, it remains the most successful attempt at a foundational theory for the whole of physics.

NOTES

1. P. Forman, 'Weimar culture, causality, and quantum theory, 1918–1927: adaptation by German physicists and mathematicians to a hostile intellectual environment', *Historical studies in the physical sciences*, 3 (1971), 1–115; J. Hendry, 'Weimar culture and quantum causality', *History of science*, 18 (1980), 115–80; P. Kraft and P. Kroes, 'Adaptation of scientific knowledge to an intellectual environment. Paul Forman's "Weimar culture . . . ": Analysis and criticism', *Centaurus*, 27 (1984), 76–99.

2. A. Einstein, 'Über einen die Erzeugung und Verwandlung des Lichtes betreffenden heuristischen Gesichtspunkt', *Annalen der Physik*, 17 (1905), 132–48.
3. M. Born and P. Jordan, 'Zur Quantenmechanik', *Zeitschrift für Physik*, 34 (1925), 858–88.
4. M. Born, W. Heisenberg and P. Jordan, 'Zur Quantenmechanik. II', *Zeitschrift für Physik*, 35 (1926), 557–615.
5. E. Schrödinger, 'Quantisierung als Eigenwertproblem', *Annalen der Physik*, 79 (1926), 361–76, 489–527 & 734–56; 80 (1926), 437–90.
6. W. Heisenberg, 'Über den auschaulichen Inhalt der quantentheoretischen Kinematic und Mechanik', *Zeitschrift fur Physik*, 43 (1927), 172–98.
7. J. S. Bell, 'On the Einstein Podolsky Rosen paradox', *Physics*, 1 (1964), 195–200.

FURTHER READING

The Bohr-Einstein letters (New York, 1971).

J. Hendry, *The creation of quantum mechanics and the Bohr-Pauli dialogue* (Dordrecht, 1984).

A Hermann, *The genesis of quantum theory (1899–1913)* (English translation of *Frühgeschichte der Quantentheorie (1899–1913)* (Cambridge, Mass., 1971).

F. Hund, *The history of quantum theory* (English translation of *Geschichte der Quantentheorie*) (London, 1974).

M. Jammer, *The conceptual development of quantum mechanics* (New York, 1966).

—— *The philosophy of quantum mechanics: the interpretations of quantum mechanics in historical perspective* (New York, 1974).

H. Kangro, *History of Planck's radiation law* (English translation of *Vorgeschichte des Planckschen Strahlunggesetzes*) (London, 1976).

T. S. Kuhn, *Black-body theory and the quantum discontinuity, 1894–1912* (Oxford, 1978).

E. MacKinnon, *Scientific explanation and atomic physics* (Chicago, 1982).

J. Mehra and H. Rechenberg, *The historical development of quantum theory* (4 vols., New York, 1982).

A. Pais, *'Subtle is the Lord ....': The science and the life of Albert Einstein* (Oxford, 1982).

—— *Inward bound: of matter and forces in the physical world* (Oxford, 1986).

D. ter Haar, *The old quantum theory* (Oxford, 1967).

B. L. Van der Waerden, *Sources of quantum mechanics* (Amsterdam, 1967).

B. Wheaton, *The tiger and the shark: empirical roots of wave-particle dualism* (Cambridge, 1983).

30

CLASSICAL ECONOMICS AND THE KEYNESIAN REVOLUTION

BILL GERRARD

The publication of Adam Smith's book *An Inquiry into the Nature and Causes of the Wealth of Nations* in 1776 marked the beginning of modern economic thought. *The Wealth of Nations* was the first attempt to produce a systematic account of the workings of a capitalist economy. Smith (1723–90) saw the economic sphere as an arena of order; he sought to explain the principles of economic order just as Newton had done for the physical world through the law of gravity. For Smith the equivalent principle of economic order is the price mechanism. Smith argued that individuals pursuing their own private interest would be led by the price mechanism to maximise the general welfare. This is the famous invisible hand doctrine. The price mechanism acts as an invisible hand, ensuring a harmony of interests between individuals; there is no need for a Leviathan or Social Contract within the economic sphere other than to ensure that no individual or group of individuals ever becomes a powerful-enough monopoly to control and subvert the operation of the price mechanism.

Smith's vision dominated mainstream economics in the nineteenth and early twentieth centuries. Initially the theoretical details of Smith's vision were developed by the classical school of economists, particularly David Ricardo. However, following the so-called marginalist revolution of the 1870s, Smith's vision was given a very different theoretical form by the neo-classical school. But the message remained the same: the price mechanism would ensure the achievement of the best of all possible worlds.

This orthodoxy held sway within mainstream economics until the publication of John Maynard Keynes's book *The General Theory of Employment, Interest and Money* in 1936. Writing against the background of the Great Depression in which the invisible hand quite clearly had failed to prevent mass unemployment, Keynes attempted to show that not all economic activity is regulated by the price mechanism. In particular Keynes argued that the level of employment is determined by forces quite different in kind to those of the invisible hand. Orthodox economics had failed to recognise the limitations to its own one-dimensional approach.

This essay charts the rise and fall of the invisible hand doctrine within economic theory from Adam Smith to John Maynard Keynes. Section 1 covers Smith's own theory of price and its subsequent development by Ricardo. This is followed in Section 2 by an account of the later neo-classical formulation of the invisible hand doctrine and its application to the problem of unemployment. Finally, Section 3 deals with Keynes's critique of the invisible hand doctrine.

1. ADAM SMITH AND THE CLASSICAL THEORY OF PRICE

Smith's theory of price began with the distinction between the natural price of a commodity and its market price. The natural price of a commodity is a centre of gravitation, the price which the dominant and persistent forces at work in the economy will continually tend to bring about. The market price, on the other hand, is the price which actually holds at any point in time. The market price will tend to diverge from the natural price because of the existence of various transitory influences which continually impede the actual achievement of the natural price. Thus Smith's theory of price involved two separate elements: (i) a theory of the dominant forces determining the natural price; and (ii) a theory of the transitory forces which cause the market price to diverge from the natural price at any point in time.

In his theory of natural prices, Smith set himself two questions: (i) how should the natural price be measured? and (ii) what determines the natural price? In answer to the first, Smith advocated a labour-commanded measure; price should be measured in terms of how many units of labour could be purchased for the same amount. The price of a unit of labour, that is, the wage-rate, became the numeraire of Smith's system, the standard against which all other prices would be measured. In adopting a labour-commanded measure, Smith showed himself to be well aware of the need to differentiate between real and nominal prices. This distinction was important for Smith in his subsequent discussions of growth and capital accumulation where the concern is with changes in physical quantities rather than nominal values.

Turning to the question of the determination of natural price, it must be noted immediately that Smith made little progress. Smith began with the simple case in which labour is the only input in the production of commodities. In this case Smith argued that the labour theory of value would hold, that is, commodities would exchange against each other in proportion to the amount of labour required to produce each commodity. For example, if commodity X required 10 hours of labour and commodity Y required only 5 hours of labour, the natural price of commodity X would be twice the natural price of commodity Y.

However, as Smith pointed out, the simple labour theory of value does not hold if labour is not the sole factor of production. Thus Smith rejected the labour theory of value as the theory of natural prices appropriate to a capitalist economy, since such an economy is, by definition, characterised by labour being combined in the production process with capital in the form of plant and machinery. Smith made no attempt to develop a more complex labour theory of value to deal with the situation of multiple factors of production. Rather, Smith merely stated that the natural price of a commodity would equal the total value of the factors of production used in the production process, each factor itself being valued at its own natural price. Each type of labour used would have its own natural wage level while the natural price of all types of capital would be some uniform rate of profits. This is not a theory; it is a definition. All Smith has done is to move the question of what determines the natural price of a commodity back one step to the question of what determines the natural prices of the various inputs used in the production of the commodity.

While Smith may not have advanced very far in constructing a theory of natural price, he did make substantial progress in analysing the transitory forces which cause market prices to diverge from natural prices. In particular, Smith considered what happens if the quantity of a commodity to be sold differs from that needed to ensure that the market price equals the natural price. This equality holds if the quantity of a commodity supplied is equal to what Smith termed the effectual demand. If the quantity supplied is less than the effectual demand, the market price will tend to rise above the natural price as buyers compete against each other to purchase the relatively limited quantity of the commodity available. If, on the other hand, the quantity supplied exceeds the effectual demand, the market price will tend to fall below the natural price. This is known as the law of supply and demand.

If the market price diverges from the natural price because the quantity supplied differs from the effectual demand, Smith showed that there would be a tendency for the quantity supplied to adjust towards the effectual demand. If, for example, the quantity supplied is less than the effectual demand, the market price will exceed the natural price. This means that the rate of profit earned by the producers of this particular commodity will be above the natural (or uniform) rate of profits earned elsewhere in the economy. This will attract new entry into this industry as other capitalists also seek to earn these supra-normal profit rates. The already existing producers may also expand their production levels to increase their share of these supra-normal profits. Overall, the effect will be to increase the level of production until it coincides with the effectual demand, at which point no further expansion of production will occur since the market price will equal the natural price, implying that the natural rate of profits is now being earned in this industry. Similarly, in an industry in which supply exceeds the effectual demand so that the market price is below the natural price, there will be a tendency for the level of production to contract since the level of profits will be below the natural rate.

Thus Smith showed how individual capitalists, acting in their own self-interest, would move their capital from low-profit industries to high-profit industries and, in so doing, would create, quite unintentionally, a tendency for the market prices of commodities to be equal to their natural prices with a uniform rate of profits being earned across all industries. It is this process of competition whereby individuals moved their resources to where they could obtain the most favourable terms of exchange which, according to Smith, is the central principle of economic order.

In the field of price theory, then, Smith gave a detailed account of how the interaction of demand and supply could lead market prices to diverge from natural prices but he failed to provide a theory of the determination of natural prices. Smith, however, did at least clear the way for subsequent writers by showing the inadequacies of the simple labour theory of value as a theory of natural price, unable as it is to deal with the existence of factor inputs other than labour. It was David Ricardo who made most headway in developing a labour theory of value which could cope with the existence of capital. Ricardo achieved this by recognising that the capital used in the production process is itself produced using labour. Ricardo argued that capital should be treated as the embodiment of past labour inputs. A commodity could, therefore, be seen as consisting of a direct (or current) labour input as well as an indirect (or past) labour input in the form of plant and machinery. In this way, Ricardo revived the labour theory of value as a theory of natural price. Commodities would exchange in proportion to the labour input, both direct and indirect, used in their production.

Despite making substantial progress, however, Ricardo failed to produce an adequate theory of natural price, as he himself realised. The labour theory of value as formulated by Ricardo only holds in the special case where: (i) all capital has a uniform durability; and (ii) all industries use capital and labour in the same proportion. If either of these two conditions does not hold, the relationship between the natural prices of commodities will diverge from that in line with the labour theory of value.

Other classical economists, especially John Stuart Mill, took Ricardo's analysis as the definitive work on the subject of price. Natural prices, Mill held, would mainly depend on the labour input but not strictly so, for the reasons that Ricardo had indicated. The labour theory of value was quietly laid to rest. One notable exception to this was Karl Marx. For Marx the labour theory of value was much more than a theory of price. It also laid bare the social relations within the capitalist mode of production. Using the labour theory of value, Marx showed that labour did not receive a wage equal to the full value of its productive output. Rather, capitalists used their ownership of the means of production to exploit labour by retaining what Marx termed the surplus value, the difference between the value of labour's productive output and the wage that labour actually received. But when it came to using the labour theory of value as a theory of price Marx ran into the same problems as Ricardo before him and although he made some progress he never solved what become known as the 'transformation problem'.

In summary, classical theory distinguished between the natural price and the market price of a commodity. The natural price was seen as depending on the costs of production, these costs being mainly conceived of in terms of labour inputs. The market price, on the other hand, depends on the interaction of demand and supply. There would be a tendency for the market price to converge on the natural price as supply adjusts towards the effectual demand, the level of demand consistent with the natural price. This convergence results from the reaction of producers to the differential profit rates across industries that occur if there are any deviations from the natural price. Thus the price mechanism was seen to act like an invisible hand, ensuring the co-ordination of decisions made by individuals.

2. NEO-CLASSICAL THEORY

In the 1870s, in what became known as the marginalist revolution, economic theory was changed quite markedly at the hands of economists such as Jevons, Menger and Walras. These neo-classical economists shared Smith's vision of the economic system as an arena of order, but they formulated a very different theoretical model to that held by Smith and the other classical economists. In so doing they greatly extended the power of the invisible hand doctrine. Whereas price theory had been only one element within classical theory, in neo-classical theory it became the central issue. In classical theory, questions such as the distribution of income, employment levels and growth and capital accumulation were considered quite separately from the question of price determination. In neo-classical theory all of these other questions now became just applications of price theory.

Neo-classical theory adopted a market-theoretic approach to the understanding of the economic system, in which the economy is viewed as a series of interdependent markets. The operation of each market is explained by the demand-and-supply theory of price determination. The equilibrium price in any market is that price which equates the quantity demanded by buyers with the quantity supplied by sellers. If price is above its equilibrium level, supply will exceed demand so that sellers will be forced to reduce both price and their level of supply in order to prevent themselves from being left with unsold stocks. The fall in price will tend to stimulate demand since the commodity is now cheaper to buy. Eventually, price will reach its equilibrium market-clearing level. Similarly, if price is below its equilibrium so that demand exceeds supply, there will be a tendency for price to rise towards the equilibrium level as sellers try to take advantage of the excess demand for the commodity. This convergence towards the equilibrium market-clearing price occurs provided the market is perfectly competitive in the sense of no agent or group of agents possessing any monopoly power with which to affect the market price.

Thus, in neo-classical theory there is no distinction between natural price and market price. The equilibrium price is the market-clearing price determined by the interaction of both demand and supply. In classical theory, on the other hand, the equilibrium (or natural) price depends solely on the costs of production, that is, the conditions of supply, and is completely independent of market forces.

Neo-classical theory is a theory of the allocation of resources by means of the price mechanism. Economic behaviour, in all its many forms, is reduced to a market exchange in which the price and the quantity transacted are determined simultaneously by the forces of demand and supply. Neo-classical theory has developed by applying this demand-and-supply theory to all types of economic activity. One of the main areas of development in neo-classical theory in the early part of this century was in understanding the macro-economic issues of how the economy functions as a whole. In particular, attention focused on what determines the total levels of employment and unemployment in an economy.

In neo-classical theory, the macro economy consists of three aggregate markets: the labour market, the loanable funds market and the money market. The most fundamental of these is the labour market which explains the supply-side of the economy, the driving force of the system. The equilibrium level of aggregate supply is determined in the labour market by the interaction of the demand for labour by producers and the supply of labour by households. Both the demand and the supply of labour are seen to depend on the 'price' of labour, namely, the real wage, i.e. the money wage measured relative to the general price level. Market forces, if allowed to operate freely, would move the real wage towards that level at which the demand for labour equals the supply of labour. Full employment is the equilibrium market-clearing outcome; there will be sufficient jobs on offer to employ all those seeking employment. Thus the price mechanism ensures that, on the supply-side, there is a continual tendency towards the full employment level of output.

For the economy as a whole to be in equilibrium, there must be sufficient aggregate demand such that the whole of the aggregate supply of output is purchased. Initially the sufficiency of aggregate demand was a matter of assertion, an article of faith. The early classical theorists, Mill and Marx excepted, held to

Say's Law that supply creates its own demand. Say's Law implies that all income generated by the act of supplying output is fully spent on the purchase of that output, so that there is always enough demand. Such a proposition is true of necessity in circumstances in which there is no alternative but to use current income to purchase currently-produced output. However once a monetary economy with savings is considered, Say's Law is no longer obviously true. Savings represent a leakage from demand in the sense of being a part of current income that is not used to purchase currently-produced output. For Say's Law to hold when savings exist requires that savings be exactly equal to investment. Investment is an injection into demand caused by firms borrowing to purchase currently-produced capital goods such as plant and machinery to use in the production process. Say's Law now becomes a matter for analysis since there is a need to explain how investment and savings decisions, made as they are by two separate groups of individual agents, are rendered equal in aggregate. The loanable funds market provided the neo-classical economists with the theoretical support for their adherence to Say's Law. Investment is treated as a demand for loanable funds while savings is a supply of loanable funds. The rate of interest acts as the price mechanism ensuring market-clearing within the loanable funds market, and thereby generating sufficient aggregate demand to purchase the aggregate supply of output.

The final element in the macro theory of neo-classical economics is the money market. The neo-classical theory of the money market is a development of the age-old notion that the general price level depends on the amount of money in circulation. This quantity theory of money was recast in terms of demand-and-supply theory. Money is demanded as the medium of exchange. The quantity of money demanded would depend on the total value of the transactions to be undertaken which, in turn, would depend on the general price level. As the general price level rose, the demand for money would rise. Thus if the money supply changed, movements in the general price level would be the mechanism by which equilibrium in the money market would be restored.

It follows from this analysis that, in equilibrium, money is neutral in the sense that it determines only the general price level; the quantity of money does not affect real variables such as output, employment, the real wage and the rate of interest. This creates what is known as the classical dichotomy, in which money acts simply as a veil behind which the real sector operates, entirely unaffected in equilibrium by the presence of money.

In neo-classical theory, the economic system tends to gravitate towards a position of full employment, provided that all markets are perfectly competitive. Real wage adjustments ensure that a full employment level of output emanates from the supply-side while interest rate adjustments ensure that sufficient aggregate demand is generated. This position of full employment is associated with a level of unemployment now known as the natural rate of unemployment.

This natural rate of unemployment consists of two elements: (i) frictional unemployment and (ii) voluntary unemployment. Frictional unemployment arises from the difficulties in translating equilibrium in the labour market at the aggregate level into a realised consistency at the level of individual workers and firms. Frictional unemployment includes seasonal unemployment due to seasonal fluctuations in the demand for labour as well as structural unemployment due to changes in the location and relative size of individual industries. Voluntary unemployment, on the other hand, arises from the decisions by some households not to seek employment given existing wages and conditions.

If the level of employment should fall below full employment this implies that unemployment will be above the natural rate. In neo-classical theory such a situation is caused by the failure of a market or markets to clear owing to the existence of imperfections that impede the adjustment process. Neo-classical theory recognised two main sources of imperfection causing this type of unemployment. Firstly, rigidities on the supply-side may prevent the establishment of the market-clearing real wage. For example, trade union activity may lead to the money wage being inflexible downwards. This possibility was recognised by both Marshall and Pigou. Secondly, rigidities on the demand-side may prevent sufficient aggregate demand being generated. The focus fell on the interest rate and the effects of the banking and credit system on the determination of the interest rate. Again, this line of reasoning is to be found in the work of Marshall. It was particularly developed by Wicksell who argued that if the banking system set the rate of interest too high, this would tend to deflate the economy, since saving would exceed investment. However, this deflation would be only a temporary phenomenon since the banking system could not sustain such a position indefinitely. The build-up of idle reserves would lower the profitability of the banking system, putting downward pressure on the rate of interest as banks sought to stimulate the demand for loanable funds and reduce the interest payments on deposits.

Thus, to summarise, in neo-classical theory the economy tends towards a position of full employment if the price mechanism is free to operate unhampered within a perfectly competitive system of markets. In particular, real wage and interest rate adjustments play a crucial role in the achievement of full equilibrium. If unemployment exceeds the natural rate, this is a disequilibrium phenomenon created by imperfections on the supply-side and/or on the demand-side leading to real wage and interest rate maladjustment, respectively. Such maladjustment occurs because of structural imperfections that allow certain agents the power to control market price. Specifically, trade unions represent a monopolistic element on the supply-side that can influence wage levels while the banking system is a monopolistic element on the demand-side that can influence the rate of interest. Thorough-going competition, as Pigou pointed out, is a sufficient condition for full employment. The presence of monopoly power represents a structural imperfection which limits the extent of competition in a market economy and thereby prevents the attainment of full employment.

It follows from neo-classical theory that, as regards reducing the level of unemployment in general, policies should be directed towards the supply-side. Ultimately the supply-side is where the problems mainly lie since the price mechanism is believed to be reasonably effective in generating sufficient aggregate demand. If there is a problem of interest rate maladjustment, there could be a role for a degree of monetary expansion to help increase the downward pressure on the market rate of interest and thus speed up the adjustment process, overcoming any inertia created by the financial institutions. On the whole, however, unemployment was not viewed as being caused by deficient demand beyond that resulting from the rate of interest being too high. Government attempts to stimulate aggregate demand through a fiscal expansion financed by higher borrowing were considered to be self-defeating since they would push up the rate of interest thereby inducing an off-setting reduction in private investment. This is known as the crowding-out effect.

On the supply-side the advocated policies were of two general types: (i) measures to reduce the natural rate of unemployment and (ii) structural adjustments to remove rigidities that block the free functioning of the market mechanism. The natural rate of unemployment could be reduced by lowering frictional unemployment through a variety of measures designed to promote the dynamic efficiency of markets. Provision of information on vacancies to aid job search and retraining schemes and relocation allowances to improve labour mobility are examples of this type of policy. Policies to reduce the level of voluntary unemployment were also advocated, the focus being primarily on the disincentive effects of unemployment benefits. An alternative type of supply-side policy is direct intervention to restructure markets in order to reduce the degree of monopoly power, thus improving the allocative efficiency of markets. In particular, the labour market could be made more competitive by restricting the extent of trade union power, making wage levels more responsive to the forces of supply and demand.

Overall, neo-classical theory represents the pinnacle in the development of the invisible hand doctrine. If only the price mechanism is allowed to operate freely throughout the economy, the outcome will be one of general equilibrium with the full employment of labour. The free operation of the price mechanism would maximise the general welfare. This implies that, in the economic sphere, governments should adopt a policy of *laissez-faire*, allowing individuals complete freedom to pursue their private gain under conditions of perfect competition. The only role of government in the economic sphere is as the protector of the invisible hand, intervening only when imperfections impede the operation of the price mechanism.

3. KEYNES'S *GENERAL THEORY*

The experience of prolonged mass unemployment throughout the Western world in the 1920s and 1930s was at odds with the teachings of neo-classical economics. It was clear that the invisible hand was not operating. Neo-classical theorists answered by arguing that there must be imperfections within the economic system which were blocking the operation of the price mechanism. In particular, attention focused on the power of trade unions to enforce wage settlements above the level consistent with market-clearing in the labour market. It followed that the remedy for mass unemployment was for individuals to price themselves back into jobs by accepting reductions in their wage levels. Thus the problem of unemployment was seen to be a matter for individual, not government, action.

It was just this type of analysis and policy prescription which Keynes sought to refute in *The General Theory of Employment, Interest and Money* published in 1936. Keynes believed that neo-classical theory had over-extended itself by attempting to use its market-theoretic approach to explain all aspects of economic activity. There was no recognition of any limitations to the application of demand-and-supply theory. Keynes aimed to produce a general theory within which the demand-and-supply theory of neo-classical economics would be treated as a special case with well-defined limits to its relevance. The notion that there are limits to the validity of the market-theoretic approach is the revolutionary essence of Keynes's *General Theory*.

Keynes accepted that neo-classical theory could explain how the price mechanism leads to the allocation between competing uses of resources that are fully employed. But for Keynes, neo-classical theory could not explain the determination of the level of employment. Neo-classical theory had provided theories to show how the price mechanism could ensure full employment but in so doing, Keynes believed that neo-classical theory had gone beyond the limits of its relevance. The way in which the economic system actually operates is such that the price mechanism is not the means by which the level of employment is determined.

According to Keynes, neo-classical theory could explain only two types of unemployment: frictional unemployment and voluntary unemployment. Both these types of unemployment are consistent with a position of full employment. Neo-classical theory explained any prolonged period of below full employment as the result of wage rigidities. But Keynes argued that this type of unemployment should also be considered as voluntary since it is unemployment resulting from the actions of workers themselves. What Keynes sought to provide was a theory of involuntary unemployment, a type of unemployment which could not be conceived of within the market-theoretic approach. Involuntary unemployment, as its name suggests, occurs for reasons outside the control of individual workers or groups of workers. Wage cuts would not solve the problem of involuntary unemployment; indeed, Keynes showed that they could make matters worse. Involuntary unemployment is a type of unemployment with which the price mechanism could not deal. Hence it followed from Keynes's analysis that there is a need for collective action to reduce involuntary unemployment.

The starting point for Keynes's theory of involuntary unemployment is his rejection of the notion of a labour market in which wage and employment levels are determined simultaneously by the interaction of demand and supply. According to Keynes, the industrial sector of the economy just did not behave in this way. Wages and employment levels are determined quite independently by different sets of forces. The money wage is determined in the wage bargain between employers and employees, with employees being mainly concerned with maintaining their relative wage level in the light of the wage bargains of other groups of workers. The influence of relative wages would, Keynes believed, dominate the wage bargain rather than market forces. Furthermore the wage bargain only determines the money wage, not the real wage as neo-classical theory postulated. In Keynes's theory the real wage emerges as a residual outcome once the general price level is determined by the aggregate effect of the pricing decisions of individual firms. The real wage has no behavioural significance whatsoever. In particular, Keynes rejected the neo-classical notion that the demand for labour by firms depends on the level of the real wage.

Instead of depending on the real wage, Keynes argued that the employment decision of firms depends on the level of demand for their product. Firms estimate the level of demand for their product and then set their level of output accordingly. Given their production techniques, the required level of employment is now determined. In other words, the industrial sector behaves according to what could be termed Keynes's Law that demand creates its own supply; given the level of demand which exists for their product, firms set their output and employment levels accordingly. Keynes's Law represents a complete inversion of Say's Law that supply creates its own demand. By recognising the actual nature of the employment decision Keynes at a single stroke transformed the nature of macro-economic theory. Neo-classical theory had been a supply-side economics in which the labour market is the driving force and the price mechanism ensures the existence of sufficient demand. Keynes's theory, on the other hand, gave primacy to the demand-side with employment and output levels being determined as a consequence, not vice versa.

For Keynes the total level of employment in an economy depends on the total level of effective demand, that is, the demand for commodities backed by the means of payment. Keynes sought to show that the level of effective demand in an economy could be in equilibrium at a level below that required to support full employment. This lack of effective demand is the cause of involuntary unemployment.

Keynes explained the determination of the level of effective demand through what he termed the principle of effective demand: the proposition that savings and investment are brought into equality by changes in the level of income. Neo-classical economists had recognised that equilibrium on the demand-side requires that the level of savings equals the level of investment. The loanable funds market theory provided an explanation of how this equality would be achieved by movements in the rate of interest while the level of income would remain constant at the full employment level. Keynes rejected the notion of a market for loanable funds. Savings and investment are brought into equality not by changes in the rate of interest but rather by changes in the level of income. This follows from Keynes's empirical generalisation that the levels of consumption expenditure and savings by households depend primarily on the level of income. Using this consumption function Keynes showed that given some level of investment, the level of savings would adjust towards that same level through induced changes in the level of income. Suppose, for example, that initially investment and savings are equal and then for some reason the level of investment rises. This means that there is now a higher level of demand in the economy. This will induce firms to increase their output and employment levels, generating a higher level of income which, in turn, will generate higher levels of consumption and savings. The higher level of consumption will lead to further rises in income and employment. Eventually this multiplier process will establish a new equilibrium with savings once again equal to investment, but at a higher level of income and employment than before. The multiplier process will also operate in a downward direction leading to a reduction in income and employment levels if for any reason there is a fall in the level of investment.

From Keynes's analysis it follows that the level of effective demand and hence the level of employment, depend ultimately on the level of investment. Keynes believed that the level of investment depends on two main factors: (i) the marginal efficiency of capital and (ii) the state of long-term expectations. The marginal efficiency of capital is the old neo-classical notion that, as the rate of interest falls, more and more capital projects would become profitable, and hence the level of investment would increase. However, although Keynes accepted that the level of investment would depend on the rate of interest, unlike neo-classical theorists, he did not believe that the level of investment would determine the rate of interest. Specifically, there is no tendency for the rate of interest to move to that level which would bring about enough investment to generate full employment. The rate of interest is determined by a very different set of factors from that postulated by neo-classical theory. Anyway, Keynes believed that the rate of interest is of secondary importance in determining the level of investment. By far the most important determinant is the state of long-term expectations. The expected returns from investment depend on the judgements which businessmen make about the unknowable future. Such judgements are not based solely on mathematical calculations, as neo-classical theory implied. Rather, they ultimately depend on psychological factors, how businessmen feel about the current state of the world and the likely future changes. If businessmen lack sufficient confidence in the future, no amount of prodding by an invisible hand will overcome this obstacle to full employment.

Having replaced the loanable funds market theory by the principle of effective demand, Keynes needed to develop an alternative theory for the determination of the rate of interest. Keynes achieved this through his theory of liquidity preference in which the rate of interest replaces the general price level as the mechanism which ensures equilibrium in the money market. The key to this development was Keynes's recognition that households demand money balances not only for transactions purposes but also for store-of-value purposes. Money is one form in which the accumulated stock of financial wealth may be held. As an asset, money offers the advantages of liquidity in the sense of being capable of immediate usage for transactions purposes without any risk of loss in nominal value. However against this must be set the disadvantage that money, unlike other assets, does not earn a rate of interest. Keynes believed that as the rate of interest rises, the speculative demand for money as an asset would fall since the lack of interest payments would exceed the value that households attached to money's perfect liquidity. Overall it followed from Keynes's analysis that, since the transactions demand for money depends on the level of income which is determined outside the money market, it falls upon the rate of interest, through its regulation of the speculative demand for money, to act as the mechanism to ensure equality between the supply of money and the total demand for money.

Keynes's theory of liquidity preference rendered invalid the neo-classical notion that money is neutral. It is possible, under Keynes's analysis, for changes in the supply of money to affect output and employment levels permanently. This occurs through the operation of the so-called Keynes effect in which changes in the supply of money alter the equilibrium rate of interest in the money market, leading, in turn, to changes in the level of investment and, eventually, to changes in output and employment levels. Thus in Keynes's *General Theory* there is no classical dichotomy; the real and monetary sectors of an economy are inextricably linked.

Taken as a whole, Keynes's *General Theory* represents the rejection of the unitary view of the economy adopted by neo-classical theory. Keynes showed that the market-theoretic approach is not applicable throughout the economy. Instead Keynes proposed a dualist conception of the economy which recognises that the industrial and financial sectors display very different modes of activity. The financial sector operates in accordance with the principles of demand-and-supply analysis as formulated in liquidity preference theory. The rate of interest operates to ensure that within the money market there is sufficient demand for money to allocate fully the available supply. Say's Law holds in the financial sector; the price mechanism ensures that supply creates its own demand. But in the industrial sector there is a very different pattern of behaviour. Unlike the financial sector, the industrial sector must determine the level of employment of its resources. Through the principle of effective demand Keynes showed that it is changes in the level of the flow of income via the multiplier process which regulate the level of employment. The level of employment is not under the control of the price mechanism. In the industrial sector it is Keynes's Law which holds; demand creates its own supply. If there is not enough demand (and there is no reason why there should be), involuntary unemployment will occur with no automatic self-correcting mechanism to return the economy to full employment.

Keynes's analysis of involuntary unemployment pointed towards very different policy prescriptions from those proposed by neo-classical economists. The defining characteristic of involuntary unemployment is that it occurs for reasons beyond the control of individuals or groups of individuals. Involuntary unemployment is due to a lack of demand in the economy as a whole which can only be remedied by collective action. Keynes proposed the socialisation of investment but never defined what he meant by this. His analysis implied that to ensure full employment it is necessary to have some collective control of the aggregate level of investment, the key to the whole problem. Keynes did not detail what this collective control should involve. The followers of Keynes interpreted the socialisation of investment to mean that governments should use their fiscal and monetary policies to maintain the level of demand in the economy at a sufficiently high level to ensure full employment. This is the basis of Keynesian demand-management which dominated the economic policies of Western governments after the Second World War.

Keynes had shown the belief in the invisible hand doctrine to be a case of misplaced optimism. In the face of mass unemployment it is wrong for governments to adopt a *laissez-faire* attitude, advocating the need for the price mechanism to be allowed to operate freely. The revolutionary message of Keynes for policy-makers is, quite simply, that there is no price mechanism which regulates the level of employment. If society wants full employment, it must itself intervene in the economic process to bring about that result.

4. CONCLUSION

This essay has surveyed the development of Adam Smith's invisible hand doctrine in its early classical and later neo-classical forms and the subsequent rejection of this doctrine by Keynes. It has been shown that neo-classical theory and Keynes's *General Theory* offer two very different views of the significance of the price mechanism. Neo-classical theory portrays the price mechanism as the sole means of regulation within the economic system. Keynes, on the other hand, saw the price mechanism as limited to the regulation of the financial sector only. He believed that output and employment levels in the industrial sector are determined in a very different manner.

Despite Keynes's rejection of neo-classical economics, most subsequent developments in economic theory have remained wholly within the market-theoretic approach. Indeed, within a decade of its publication, Keynes's *General Theory* had been incorporated into neo-classical theory to produce the Neo-classical Synthesis which interpreted Keynes as dealing with the consequences of money-wage rigidities in the labour market. The wheel came full circle in the 1970s and 1980s when, in the face of another period of prolonged mass unemployment, most Western governments repudiated Keynesian demand-management policies in favour of a return to a *laissez-faire* approach. Keynes may have marshalled logic and experience to reject the invisible hand doctrine but he failed to convert the vast majority of economists who still believe that the invisible hand doctrine is the fundamental and universal principle of economic order.

FURTHER READING

A highly readable account of the development of economic theory from Smith to Keynes is to be found in William J. Barber's *A history of economic thought* (Harmondsworth, 1967). A much more detailed study with excellent guidance for further reading is Mark Blaug's *Economic theory in retrospect* (4th edition, Cambridge, 1985).

Adam Smith's *The wealth of nations* edited by Andrew Skinner (Harmondsworth, 1970) has a very useful 'Introduction' by the editor. John Eatwell's essay entitled 'Competition' in *Classical and Marxian political economy* edited by I. Bradley and M. Howard (London, 1982) explains the differences between the early classical and later neo-classical theories of price and the competitive process while Mark Casson's book *Economics of unemployment: an historical perspective* (Martin Robertson, 1983) gives a detailed account of pre-Keynesian theories of unemployment.

Keynes's *General theory* appears as Volume VII of *The collected writings of John Maynard Keynes* edited by E. Johnson and D. Moggridge (London, 1973). Alvin Hansen's *A guide to Keynes* (London, 1953) is probably the most useful step-by-step guide to the *General theory*. An assessment of the relationship between Keynes's theory and preceding classical and neo-classical theories is to be found in Will Hutton's recent book *The revolution that never was* (London, 1986).

For a survey of the different strands of thought among the followers of Keynes, see Alan Coddington's article 'Keynesian economics: the search for first principles' (*Journal of Economic Literature*, 1976). I have dealt with the incorporation of Keynes's ideas into neo-classical theory in the essay 'Keynesian economics: the road to nowhere?' in *J. M. Keynes: in retrospect* edited by John Hillard (Newent, Gloucestershire, 1988).

31

FROM PHYSIOLOGY TO BIOCHEMISTRY

NEIL MORGAN

I. INTRODUCTION

Any account of the history of biochemistry must begin with a definition and must set the historical boundaries to its enquiry. Historians have chosen, by and large, to use broad definitions, for example, that of a 'timeless, extended family of biochemistries' (Kohler)[1], or perhaps the even wider 'interplay of chemistry and biology' (Fruton)[2]. The reason for this is that the history of biochemistry is a complicated one, both conceptually and institutionally, and broad definitions allow a sense of continuity without which the enterprise would fail. Its study involves the historian not only in the study of physiology, but also in medical chemistry, physical chemistry, microbiology and a wide spectrum of associated sciences, as well as sociological questions of institutional growth and discipline identity.

Writing in 1851, Henry Bence Jones looked back to the experiments of A.L. Lavoisier on pneumatic chemistry some seventy years previously as evidence of a first *rapprochement* between physiology and chemistry proper. Such knowledge was legitimately the province of physicians, so that medical chemistry looms large in the early history of biochemistry. While progressive nineteenth-century physicians recognised the need to reduce empiricism in medicine, chemistry was far from being accorded a central role in that undertaking. Early-nineteenth-century medicine attempted to promote scientific medicine primarily through morbid anatomy, attempts being directed to link disease symptoms with lesions found in the organs and tissues *post-mortem*.

By the end of the 1830s such studies had reached a high degree of sophistication. Medical interest in morbid anatomy had its roots in a *structural* rather than a *chemical* model of life and disease, so that it dealt with a different conceptual framework from that to which we have become accustomed. Its subject was specifically *the structure of vitality*, rather than the *chemistry of life*. Nevertheless, it remained true that some attention was paid to chemical physiology through-out the first half of the nineteenth century. Medical diagnosis, for example, had traditionally used the body fluids as an indicator of disease. Early-nineteenth-century physicians interested in chemistry wanted to expand on the diagnostic value of the senses and reached towards rigorous chemical criteria.

Another feature of medical chemistry before the mid-nineteenth century was its interest in urinary calculi, 'the stone' being a far more common complaint in the last century than this. (The best-remembered sufferer, perhaps, was the seventeenth-century diarist Samuel Pepys. Cut for the stone, he used to hold annual parties in thanksgiving, displaying the stone – the size of a tennis ball – in a specially-designed glass cabinet). With the hope that chemical analysis might, in the long run, offer patients an alternative to cruel lithotomy, it was via the 'stone' that chemistry entered medicine. Outside the 'chemical' diseases – the stone, gout, diseases of the urine and diabetes – medical chemistry remained peripheral. Against this background, Justus von Liebig's *Animal Chemistry or Organic Chemistry in its application to Physiology and Patho-logy*, published in English in 1842, presented a more comprehensive and systematic chemical perspective in which to understand health and pathology.

During the 1840s clinical chemistry became well developed on the continent. A laboratory of clinical chemistry was set up at the Charité Hospital (1840) and J.F. Heller supervised a similar institute at the Allgemeines Krankenhaus in Vienna (from 1844). Simon published a journal on physiological and pathologi-cal chemistry in relation to medicine from Berlin, which competed with Heller's *Archiv für Physiologische und Pathologische Chemie*. Significantly, as Büttner and others have shown, medical chemistry failed to develop further conceptually or institutionally.[3] Eugen von Gorup Besanez at Erlangen described his discipline as one that fell into disconsolate and *ad nauseam* statements of the composition of body fluids. The degeneracy of medical chemistry, coupled with the concep-tual growth of organic chemistry and the chemical industry on the continent gradually bled attention from biological chemistry after 1850.

2. CHEMICAL PHYSIOLOGY

From 1860, with the expansion of physiology as a discipline inside scientific medicine, first in Germany and France, and somewhat later in Britain, the chemistry of life was reconceptualised as chemical physiology. (See art. 48, sect. 4.) The fact that chemical physiology developed as part of physiology, and at one remove from medicine, had important consequences. To assert their independence and importance, physiologists developed an expansionist pro-gramme of which chemical pysiology was only one part. At Carl Ludwig's insti-tute in Leipzig, for example, a tripartite division was developed with separate sections given over to chemical physiology and histology as well as the more important physical physiology section. Although in a few cases chemical physiologists occupied chairs of physiology (for example Willy Kühne at Heidelberg and Albrecht Kossel at Marburg), in the main it was physical physiology that held centre stage. Emil du Bois-Reymond and Edward Pflüger stressed the notion of a *gesamte Physiologie* – a discipline which formed a comprehensive and unified whole, in order to give a coherent picture of the animal machine.

In Britain, almost none of the leading figures in physiology were orientated to strictly chemical questions. Michael Foster at Cambridge and John Burdon Sanderson at University College London were interested in cardiovascular physiology, and classic problems of muscle and nerve physiology.[4] Although at Kings College London William Halliburton developed a research programme in chemical physiology in the period 1880 to 1890, the research was always designed to illuminate distinctly physiological and pathological issues. Hence, much of the research at Kings College centred on the chemistry of muscle and nerve tissue, influenced by nearby research on neuro-anatomy and neuropathology. Halliburton wrote that 'chemical physiology cannot be studied apart from other branches of physiology, so closely are both root and branches intertwined'.[5]

Here, in an English context, was a description of a conceptual and institutional relationship between subject areas that was also felt in Europe. In 1877 when Hoppe-Seyler canvassed in the first volume of his new journal *Zeitschrift für Physiologische Chemie* for an independent biochemistry, Pflüger insisted that 'the division of physiology into physiological physics and chemistry is philosophically inadmissable and impossible in practice'.[6] Hoppe-Seyler's annexation of different aspects of various fields could preserve neither a coherent and defined nucleus of leading research problems, nor could it define an independent institutional base.

3. BIOCHEMISTRY AS AN INDEPENDENT DISCIPLINE

Between 1880 and 1900, there were several developments in science that together supplied the conditions for biochemistry to become more narrowly focused, and to develop as a separate discipline. One of these changes was the rapid expansion of the fields of microbiology and bacteriology, creating an atmosphere in which chemistry was able to offer a potential breakthrough in the understanding, and even cure, of infectious disease. While much early bacteriology was morphological in character, it became clear that a primary need was to develop an understanding of the *chemistry* behind specific infections. This can be seen for example in the work of Brieger, Selmi and others on the ptomaine theory of infection around this period.[7]

The identification and culturing of pure strains of bacteria, using the techniques of Koch and Hansen, together with the discovery of the protein exotoxins of diphtheria and anthrax gave scientists the confidence to employ chemical techniques much more stubbornly than they had done before. Renewed optimism and confidence led to chairs and departments of chemical pathology being set up within universities, together with the building of new research institutes. The Pasteur Institute opened its doors in 1888, and the Robert Koch Institute in 1889. The Lister Institute of Preventive Medicine was established in London in 1891, and was at the forefront of institutional support for scientific medicine. Arthur Harden, for example, did his classic work on carbohydrate metabolism there. The first chair of chemical pathology in Britain was Vaughan Harley's appointment at University College London in 1896, where it was a direct forerunner of the Department of Biochemistry.

While chemical pathology continued to expand, the concurrent study of fermentation created another model for the further development of biochemistry. Indeed, in the work of Pasteur, Hansen and others the close relationship between brewing science and bacteriology in general should be emphasised. At Burton-on-Trent in England, Cornelius O'Sullivan and Horace and Adrian Brown contributed significantly to enzymology and kinetics. At the Carlsberg laboratories in Copenhagen, established by the brewer J.F. Jacobsen in 1875, key contributions to biochemistry were quickly made.

As Kohler has pointed out, the context of contemporary medical bacteriology critically influenced the discovery of cell-free fermentation by Eduard Buchner in 1897. Taken along with the work on exotoxins, the work on zymase altered the model of chemical physiology and gave it a new unity. The living cell was now to be viewed not in terms of an integrated protoplasm but as a membrane-bound bag containing a whole series of defined protein catalysts. Biochemistry began to emerge as a science concentrating on *dynamic* metabolism and intracellular chemical conversions. At the same time in physiology the concept of hormones was put on a firm foundation by Bayliss and Starling's study of the mechanism of pancreatic secretion. In 1905 Starling, in his Croonian lecture 'The Chemical Control of the Functions of the Body' suggested that the products of the ductless glands could be classified, like secretin, as chemical messengers.

F. Hofmeister in 1901 chose to depict the living cell as an enzyme-based machine-shop. Similar programmatic statements were made by Marceli Nencki (1902) and in Britain by Frederick Gowland Hopkins. Hopkins's address on 'The Dynamic Side of Biochemistry', given before the British Association for the Advancement of Science in 1913, has often been taken as the classic statement formulating biochemistry as a unitary science based on the study of dynamic metabolism mediated through enzymes. It should be remembered, however, that this was a retrospective statement of biochemistry's new identity. The first decade of the century had already promoted the formation within the international scientific community of a new communications network of journals, texts and societies, although the fine details of metabolic pathways were not traced until later.

The first use of the term 'biochemistry' in a journal was in 1902 in F. Hofmeister's *Beiträge zur Chemische Physiologie und Pathologie*, subtitled significantly *Zeitschrift für die gesamte Biochemie*. Similarly the abstracting journal *Biochemische Centralblatt*, founded in 1903, overtook the *Jahresbericht über die Fortschritte der Tierchemie*. From 1900 to 1910 biochemical journals and scientific societies proliferated internationally. In the United States, J.J. Abel and C.A. Herter founded the *Journal of Biological Chemistry* in 1905, while in Britain the *Biochemical Journal* was founded in 1906. In the same year the *Biochemische Zeitschrift* began to be published in Germany. Benjamin Moore had been appointed to the first chair of biochemistry in Britain at Liverpool in 1902, and by 1913 the British Biochemical Society could boast a membership of 150. In France the Société de Chimie Biologique began publishing its *Bulletin* in 1914. By 1920 biochemistry's self-identity was assured, buttressed with all the aspects of a discipline in its own right. Expansion continued outside Europe, for example in Japan (*Journal of Biochemistry* 1922) and in the Soviet Union (Biochemical Institute of the Ukraine 1925).

From 1923, the Dunn bequest to Gowland Hopkins's department in Cambridge helped free it from a service role to physiology, and the Cambridge school rapidly expanded. In America, as a result of the United States Medical Reform movement, biochemistry was given a key place in pre-clinical medical teaching, and expanded accordingly. Also significant in the early decades of the century were the Agricultural Experiment Stations, for example in T.B. Osborne and Vickery's analysis of vegetable proteins in Connecticut, and E.V. McCollum's work on vitamins at the Wisconsin College of Agriculture in Madison. From 1901 the Rockefeller Institute of Medical Research provided the institutional background for a wide range of biochemical researches at the hands of scientists of the calibre of Donald van Slyke, Oswald Avery, Karl Landsteiner, Leonor Michaelis and John Northrop.

4. THE PARADIGM OF DYNAMIC BIOCHEMISTRY

From 1932, both Britain and the United States were enriched by German emigrés. Amongst these were biochemists who had been working at the Kaiser Wilhelm Institutes in Berlin-Dahlem. Hans Krebs moved to England, and Otto Meyerhof, Max Bergmann and others to the United States. Otto Warburg, who influenced both Krebs and Meyerhof, remained in Germany. In the late 1920s, Meyerhof and his associates had been able to reconstruct *in vitro* the main steps of the glycolytic pathway, using active muscle extracts. This extended the work of the biochemist Gustav Embden, and that of Arthur Harden on carbohydrate metabolism in yeast. In 1929 Karl Lohmann, working in Meyerhof's laboratory discovered Adenosine Triphosphate (ATP); and in the period after 1930, Meyerhof and his colleagues played a leading part in laying the foundations for an understanding of the part played by this and other 'energy-rich' phosphorus-related compounds in biochemical energy transfer.

Otto Warburg, who influenced Meyerhof considerably, was another of the true architects of the conceptual edifice of the biochemistry erected at this time, both via his fundamental work on the oxidative processes going on in the cell, and significantly, through his contribution to instrumentation (manometry, spectrophotometry) and enzyme purification. Early in his career he made important contributions to the study of the intracellular iron-porphyrin pigment that he named the *Atmungsferment*, and which was later designated cytochrome a3. In 1931, the Rockefeller Foundation endowed a special institute at Berlin-Dahlem, the Kaiser Wilhelm Institute for Cell Biology, where Warburg identified the flavines and nicotinamide as hydrogen carriers in the complicated processes of biological oxidation. Warburg's use of the absorption of light at a specific wavelength (340nm) by reduced NAD enzyme became the basis for a large number of spectrophotometric probes for redox and coupled biochemical reactions.

Hans Krebs, an associate of Warburg, cemented another of the important cornerstones of intermediary metabolism through his discovery of metabolic cycles. In 1932 he described the ornithine cycle for the production of urea but, shortly after Hitler's rise to power in 1933, was forced to leave Germany. It was in England at the University of Sheffield that he performed the research that led him to elucidate the structure of the citric acid cycle in 1937. This basic discovery built on earlier work, including that of Albert Szent-Györgyi, which had demonstrated the catalytic acceleration of the carbohydrate metabolism of pigeon-breast muscle suspension by certain dicarboxylic acids. The mapping of this cycle, which acts as a cross-roads for major metabolic pathways, and its linkage on the one side to the Embden-Meyerhof pathway and on the other to the electron-transport chain terminating in cytochrome oxidase, was a landmark in the history of biochemistry, and a fruition of the biochemical programme of earlier decades, as set out by Gowland Hopkins.

5. ORGANISATION IN THE CELL

Alongside the purely dynamic, metabolic biochemistry of this programme there ran a supplementary concern for biological structure at the ultramicroscopic level, and the way in which such biochemical structure governed the function and regulation of cellular activity. To develop the metabolic programme properly, biochemists who championed the enzymological model had to skirt around such issues, ignoring them or at least laying them to one side. Between 1915 and 1940, however, new physical probes of ultramicroscopic structure began to be used in biological research, creating a distinct tension between biophysics and biochemistry and making a potential disciplinary interface.

In the period 1910–1930, some biologists turned to cross-disciplinary studies in colloid science, using new techniques to probe biochemical materials, beginning with the ultramicroscope of Zsigmondy, and protein electrophoresis. In Britain, this movement was centred around the Cambridge biologist William Bate Hardy. While in Germany the *Kolloidzeitschrift* had been publishing since 1906, it was not until 1930, at Hardy's instigation, that an active Colloid Committee, drawing members from the Biochemical, Chemical and Physical Societies was drawn up in Britain. The expansion of this area, especially as newer physical probes were introduced, caused enzymological biochemists some concern over the unity of their discipline. Hopkins, in his Linacre lecture of 1938, for example, showed renewed interest in just those features of cell chemistry which had previously been excluded from the paradigmatic programme of classical dynamic biochemistry. Cell organisation, and importantly, the question of the anatomy of large molecules, were invited back into the biochemical fold.

Ever since Emil Fischer's precocious work on the amino-acid sequence of polypeptides at the turn of the century, some biochemists had suggested that the functional diversity of proteins might be based upon the structural arrangement of the amino-acids in the molecule. Such speculations were given added point by the injection of new and expensive machines such as the ulracentrifuge and X-ray diffraction apparatus into biochemical institutes, often backed by Rockefeller cash. Svedberg, in the late 1920s, found that haemoglobin was monodisperse, that is, its ultracenrifugation gave a distinct band in the ultracentrifuge cell. This was suggestive of uniform particle size, and did not fit at all the popular colloidal model for protein, in which the particle was visualised as made up of a large but variable number of relatively small molecules, loosely bound together by electrostatic forces. Rather, Svedberg's findings were soon interpreted as indirect corroborative evidence for the *macromolecular* concept put forward by Hermann Staudinger, a German polymer chemist, in 1922. Staudinger argued that proteins are very large molecular weight molecules in which all the atoms are linked together by normal covalencies.

Faraday Society meetings in England in the period 1930–5 mark the transition from colloid science to macromolecular chemistry. Especially important was the development of X-ray diffraction as a powerful tool to attack the structure/function relationship in biochemically-important molecules. In the early 1930s, William Astbury in Leeds used the technique to probe the structures of the k-m-e-f group of fibrous proteins. Independently, Linus Pauling in America and Wu in China suggested that in protein molecules the polypeptide chains were folded in precise ways, such that macromolecular structure and function were intimately connected. (See art. 32, sect. 1.)

Some two decades separate the peak accomplishments of metabolic bio-chemistry from similar achievements in structural studies. Examples of these are the elucidation of the three-dimensional shape of globular proteins at increasingly higher resolution, in the late 1950s and early 1960s, with the work of J.C. Kendrew on myoglobin and that of M.F. Perutz on haemoglobin, both in Cambridge. Taken together with the complete amino-acid sequence of proteins (first achieved for beef insulin by Frederick Sanger in 1955), these analyses led to a far more detailed understanding of the biochemistry of respiratory pig-ments and enzymes.

6. SUMMARY

This account has aimed to be more than a chronology of biochemistry's expan-sion. It is hoped that in its reference to the recent work of other historians, it reflects the diversity of approaches to the subject now being used and explored. But a word of warning! Biochemistry is a complicated subject, and it is doubtful if its history can be fully grasped from one perspective alone. I believe this to be especially true of the sociological approach. Recent emphasis, for example, on the relationship between biochemistry and its institutional base has been a use-ful corrective to narrowly intellectual history, and it has enriched, but not replaced, the work of historians who rightly catalogue the importance of – for example – new instrumental techniques and conceptual advance. The current diversity of historiography is welcome just so long as it makes no claim to com-pleteness. Neither a text based on the purely political squabbling of different scientific groups for public funds, *nor* an aseptic and bleached account of facts and techniques is likely to reflect the reality of the subject's development. The history of biochemistry, emerging from physiology, demonstrates that for this discipline, the relationship is a complex one.

NOTES

1. R. E. Kohler, *From medical chemistry to biochemistry. The making of a biomedical discipline* (Cam-bridge, 1982), p. 9.
2. J. S. Fruton, *Molecules and life. Historical essays on the interplay of chemistry and biology* (New York, 1973), p. 2.
3. J. Büttner (ed.), *History of clinical chemistry* (Berlin and New York, 1983), *passim*.
4. Gerald Geison, *Michael Foster and the Cambridge school of physiology: the scientific enterprise in late Victorian society* (Princeton, 1978).
5. W. D. Halliburton, *Biochemistry of muscle and nerve* (London, 1904), p. 2.
6. E. Pflüger, 'Die Physiologie und ihre Zukunft', *Pflüger's Archiv*, 15, 363; note the significance of the full title of this journal, *Archiv für die gesamte Physiologie des Menschen und der Tiere*.
7. N. Morgan, 'Pure science and applied medicine. The relationship between bacteriology and biochemistry in England after 1880', *Bulletin of the society for the social history of medicine*, 37 (1985), 46–9.

FURTHER READING

J. Büttner (ed.), *History of clinical chemistry* (Berlin and New York, 1983).

Noel G. Coley *From animal chemistry to biochemistry* (Amersham, 1979).

C. Debru, *L'Esprit de biochemie. Histoire et philosophie biochemiques* (Paris, 1983).

M. Florkin, *A history of biochemistry*, 3 vols., *Comprehensive biochemistry* 30–33 (1972–9).

J. S. Fruton, *Molecules and life. Historical essays on the interplay of chemistry and biology* (New York, 1973).

E. Glas, *Chemistry and physiology in their historical and philosophical relations* (Delft, 1979).

V. M. D. Hall, 'Biochemistry', in C.A. Russell (ed.), *Recent developments in the history of chemistry* (London, 1983).

H. Hølte and K. M. Møller, *The Carlsberg laboratory, 1876–1976* (Copenhagen, 1976).

R. E. Kohler, 'The background to Eduard Buchner's discovery of cell-free fermentation', *Journal of the history of biology*, 4 (1971), 35–61.

—— 'The reception of Eduard Buchner's discovery of cell-free fermentation', *Journal of the history of biology*, 5 (1972), 327–55.

—— 'The history of biochemistry: a survey', *Journal of the history of biology*, 8 (1975), 275–319.

—— *From medical chemistry to biochemistry. The making of a biomedical discipline* (Cambridge, 1982).

N. Morgan, 'William Dobinson Halliburton, F.R.S. (1860–1931) pioneer of British biochemistry?', *Notes and records of the Royal Society*, 38 (1983), 129–45.

J. Needham and E. Baldwin (eds.) *Hopkins and biochemistry, 1861–1947, a commemorative volume prepared on the occasion of the first international congress of biochemistry* (Cambridge, 1949).

P. R. Srinivasan, J. S. Fruton and J. T. Edsall (eds.), 'The origins of modern biochemistry – a retrospect on proteins', *Annals of New York Academy of Science*, 325 (1979).

S. Strobanova, 'Biochemical journals and their profile in 1840–1930', *Acta historiae rerum naturalium nec non technicarum*, 16 (1981), 149–95.

—— 'Formation of interdisciplinary sciences. The case of biochemistry', *Acta historiae rerum naturalium nec non technicarum*, 19 (1985), 193–245.

M. Teich, 'From "enzyme" to "cytoskeleton" – the development of ideas on the chemical organization of living matter', M. Teich and R. Young (eds.), *Changing perspectives on the history of science* (London, 1973), pp. 439–71.

32

THE MOLECULAR REVOLUTION IN BIOLOGY

ROBERT OLBY

'It is no exaggeration', declared a group of British experts in 1968, 'to suggest that biology today is in a phase as dynamic and productive as was physics during the first 25 years of the century'. This spectacular progress, they claimed, centred on the kind of research 'which has for its object the description of the structure, organisation and function of living cells in chemical and physical terms, a branch of biology, part of which has become known as 'molecular biology'. Molecular biology, they explained, was based largely on the concepts of physics, chemistry and mathematics – they did not mention biology – and it had given to fundamental biological research not only sophisticated new physical tools, but also an 'immensely powerful intellectual stimulus'.[1]

Whilst they admitted the breadth of the 'molecular approach' in biology these experts associated molecular biology with specific achievements – the elucidation of the structure of DNA by J. D. Watson and F. H. C. Crick in 1953 and of the proteins myoglobin and haemoglobin in 1958 and 1959. Molecular biology concerned not merely powerful techniques, not just analysis at the molecular level, but also the relation between the proteins and the nucleic acids in terms of the encoding, copying, transmission and translation of 'information'. This relationship was seen as the key to understanding how genetic 'information' is encoded in the chemical substance (DNA) of which genes are made and how that information is expressed in the process of gene action. The structure of carbohydrates and fats, the steps in intermediary metabolism, the mechanism of energy transfer – subjects which deeply interested the biochemists – were not prominent in this picture.

It is this association between structural investigation and genetic mechanisms that gave to the molecular biology of the 1950s its alleged novelty, and justified the claim that here was a new discipline formed out of the fusion of specialisms, and quite unlike anything that had preceded it. This *narrow* conception is in contrast to the *broad* conception of the subject held by those responsible for introducing the term 'molecular biology' in the 1930s and 1940s. There exist, it appears, two conceptions of molecular biology and historically there have been three phases, the first broadly conceived, the second more narrowly delimited and crude, the third more sophisticated and possessing considerable explanatory power. Although elements of discontinuity can be located between these three phases, there are also important features common to them all. Any attempt to force the history into the framework of a single 'molecular revolution' will therefore appear somewhat contrived and crude. Thus from the 1930s onwards the research programme of molecular biology was always considered to be reductionist in character, i.e. biological function was to be accounted for in terms of structure going right down to the molecular level. By the 1950s it was becoming increasingly apparent that the ultimate determinant of structure was residue sequence. When we come to the 1980s a new and more complex view has emerged as to the ways in which the expression of these fundamental sequences is controlled. This view of the expression of genetic information in the cell is one of a series of levels at which the process may be influenced. This hierarchical – one might say organismic – view is at the same time molecular, and most of its supporters would say still fundamentally reductionist.

Prior to the emergence of molecular biology in the 1930s there existed a *biophysical* tradition which appealed to the laws governing molecular aggregates, rather than to those governing molecules, in its reductionist programme of explaining the nature of protoplasm, and the properties of compounds of biologically important compounds. These laws were those of colloid chemistry. (See art. 31, sect. 5.) Although this biophysical tradition drew attention to the importance of electric charge, to membranes and to dynamic aspects of cell organisation, it was transformed and virtually supplanted by the molecular tradition of the 1930s. But it is noteworthy that this transformation was only achieved by using the powerful techniques which biophysicists had themselves developed.

1. THE TERM 'MOLECULAR BIOLOGY'

The first person to use the term 'molecular biology' with the intention of specifying a broad research programme was Warren Weaver. In 1938, as Director of the Natural Sciences Section of the Rockefeller Foundation, he waxed eloquent over a 'new branch of science . . . which may prove as revolutionary . . . as the discovery of the living cell . . . A new biology – molecular biology – has begun as a small salient in biological research'. Modern tools, he wrote, were reaching deeper and deeper into the living organism; they were revealing new facts about the structure and behaviour of the 'minute cellular substances'. Because these techniques were delicate it had now become possible to 'investigate ever more minute details of certain life processes'.[2] Weaver's conception was thus instrument-dominated, interdisciplinary, and the most promising level of its analysis was ultra-structural.

This *broad* programme of molecular biology was most explicitly implemented in the 1930s by W. T. Astbury (1898–1951) at the University of Leeds. Starting with keratin, the protein of wool, horn and nail, he put forward molecular structures for a whole family of proteins the k-m-e-f group. Turning to the nucleoproteins of viruses and chromosomes, his laboratory produced the first X-ray photographs of nucleic acids which he interpreted in terms of long-chain molecules, the separation between the units of which approximated closely to that separating the units in a protein chain. This fact caused him to speculate that the key to an understanding of the mechanism by which viruses and genes are duplicated lay in this dimensional 'fit' between the two classes of master molecules.

Looking back on his work in the 1930s, Astbury remarked that it was unlikely that he had invented the term 'molecular biology', but he had 'long tried to propagate it'. He went on,

> It implies not so much a technique as an approach from the viewpoint of the so-called basic sciences with the leading idea of searching below the large-scale manifestations of classical biology for the corresponding molecular plan. It is concerned particularly with the forms of biological molecules and with the evolution, exploitation and ramification of these forms in the ascent to higher levels of organization.[3]

In turning from the X-ray crystallography of small molecules to that of large molecules, Astbury realised he was entering a largely uncharted field. Only the studies of cotton, silk and rubber fibres by German staff of the Kaiser Wilhelm Institut für Faserstoffchemie offered any guidance. Nevertheless, Astbury achieved the first molecular structures of keratin which accounted not only for their chemical properties but also for their functional properties of elasticity, tensile strength and shrinkability. In so doing he demonstrated the potential fruitfulness of structural analysis for the classification of biologically important large molecules and for revealing the molecular basis for their biological functions.

Because of the great importance of the proteins for biology many workers contributed to the study of their structure in the 1940s. In the United States Maurice Huggins and Hugh Taylor introduced the concept of helical chains for proteins in opposition to Astbury's 'ribbon' chains. The proteins had also attracted the interest of Linus Pauling (b.1901) when he discussed the molecular mechanism of their denaturation and renaturation in 1936. The biological activity of the molecule depended upon the specific folding of the long polypeptide chain. Denaturation caused the chain to unfold and lose its biological activity, while renaturation caused it to fold once more into its functional shape.

This conception of molecular form could be applied to the problem of biological specificity also. The power of the immunological system to 'recognise' the slight differences between closely related pathogens, and to synthesise an appropriate anti-body to a novel antigen could be accounted for in molecular terms. Using the 'instructional theory' according to which the antigen of the invading pathogen 'instructs' the synthesis of an anti-body by the host, Pauling and co-workers envisaged the process of folding of the long polypeptide chain as being under the influence of the antigen, so that the resulting shape of the anti-body *complements* that of the antigen.

But it was in the study of viruses that the molecular approach was most actively pursued in the 1930s and 1940s. This was because the viruses could be prepared in crystalline or para-crystalline form and subjected to chemical and physical analysis. They represented the smallest particles with the power of replication aided only by the environment of the host cell. At first it was the plant viruses that dominated the field following the success of W. M Stanley (1904–71) in extracting a crystalline preparation of the Tobacco Mosaic Virus (TMV). Owing to difficulties with this system, attention turned to the bacterial viruses, bacteriophages (phages). Beginning in 1938 Max Delbrück (1906–81) joined by Salvador Luria (b.1912) in 1942 concentrated their attention upon the problem of viral replication, and the Phage Group which formed around them explored the roles of viral protein and nucleic acid in this fundamental life process.

The approach of the phage biologists was strongly influenced by genetics, and the result of their successes in identifying hereditary transmission of viral characters with DNA played a decisive part in launching the second phase of molecular biology which, as we have noted, was more circumscribed than its forebear. In 1953 a member of the Phage Group, J. D. Watson (b.1928), and F. H. C. Crick (b.1917) a member of the MRC Laboratory of Molecular Biology at Cambridge, put forward their structure for Desoxyribonucleic acid (DNA). This was a double helix, the structure of which suggested how its function of gene duplication might be conceived at the molecular level. The modern and more narrowly defined field of molecular biology has been built very much around the researches emanating from the pursuit of the implications of their model.

2. MOLECULAR BIOLOGY AS A DISCIPLINE

When a subject possesses disciplinary identity it can be identified not only in terms of its conceptual and methodological features, but also in terms of institutional and sociological features. Molecular biology has fewer features of this kind than disciplines like biochemistry and genetics. Thus there are no societies for molecular biology, no international congresses and most of the University departments which bear its name do so more to mark a conscious effort to integrate existing disciplines and departments than to create new entities. It is true that the *Journal of Molecular Biology* did come into existence in 1959 but this was due neither to the initiative of the molecular biologists, nor to their determination to overcome resistance to their subject by existing journals. On the contrary, the idea of this journal originated from the founder-manager of Academic Press, Kurt Jacoby, who persuaded the scientists that his idea was worth supporting. It is also true that research institutes and laboratories bearing the name of molecular biology have been formed, for instance those at Cambridge, Brussels, Paris and Rome, but molecular biology is too close to existing disciplines like biochemistry to have achieved broad institutional identity at the undergraduate level.

At the same time it would be a poor sociologist who looked no further than these public evidences of disciplinarity. If, behind the scenes, those calling themselves molecular biologists have had influential positions as advisors to governments, and if they have been able to influence the funding of biology to such an extent as to direct money away from traditional areas into molecular approaches, then they have at least the status of an influential network. An attempt at such action is seen in the Kendrew Report. As a result of the brain drain of molecular biologists from the UK to the United States, Sir John Kendrew (b.1917) persuaded the Advisory Council on Scientific Policy to appoint a Working Group on Molecular Biology. The Report it produced in 1968 called for modernisation of biology teaching in the UK to ensure the wider dissemination of the new knowledge of molecular biology, and the allocation of more funds to that subject. Specifically it called for the creation of centres of excellence in which molecular biology could be carried on under conditions of support as favourable as those available in the United States.

The publication of the Kendrew Report exposed the rift which was developing between biochemists and molecular biologists. Certain members of the Biochemical Society were outraged. They asked the Biochemical Society to respond. The result was a sub-committee chaired by Sir Hans Krebs (1900–1981). Its report took a conciliatory tone. It welcomed the request for modernisation of teaching and provision of more funds, but it made quite clear its view that molecular biology, or 'biology at the molecular level', the term adopted in the Kendrew Report, was very much a part of biochemistry. The approaches of molecular biology, it considered, concerned applying to large molecules the techniques and methodology traditionally employed by biochemists to smaller molecules.

It is true that biochemists had been involved in collaborating with geneticists in the work on the genetics of anthocyanin pigments in the 1930s, and in the study of the genetics of *Neurospora* metabolism in the 1940s. They were also involved in the study of the biological function of the protein and nucleic acid portions of the phage particle. As a profession, however, biochemists took little interest in the problem of gene structure and function. The question of the chemical basis of biological specificity did concern them, as it was one aspect of the great subject of protein synthesis. However, biochemists were most prominent as supporters of the 'multi-enzyme' theory of synthesis, in preference to the 'template' theory.

Since disciplines are the product of a process of negotiation as well as the custodians of particular methodologies and theoretical systems, it was natural that biochemists should absorb the contributions of molecular biologists, to whom one biochemist referred as 'biochemists practising without a licence'. Others argued that a satisfactory definition of molecular biology could not be found. This did not concern Crick who explained that he was forced to call himself a molecular biologist 'because when inquiring clergymen asked me what I did, I got tired of explaining that I was a mixture of crystallographer, biophysicist, biochemist, and geneticist . . . '[4]

Whilst some authors and editors of multi-volume works explicitly appropriated the new subject by adding 'molecular biology' to their titles, others warned against the adverse effect of over-concentration upon the molecular approach. Ernst Mayr (b.1904) urged that the study of organisms at each level – from the molecular to the species aggregate – is equally legitimate. Pointedly, he added:

> It is fortunate both for physics and for biology that systems at higher levels can be studied with profit long before the elementary units at the lower levels are fully understood. The past history of biology has shown that progress is equally inhibited by an anti-analytical holism and a purely atomistic reductionism. A healthy future for biology can be guaranteed only by a joint analytic and synthetic approach.[5]

Whether or not molecular biology has the status of a discipline, there can be no question but that those who have played a leading part in developing the subject have won considerable public acclaim and influence within the political economy of science. Although direct practical applications of molecular biology seemed far away in the 1960s, the potential for therapeutic and industrial applications has been transformed by the discoveries of the 1970s, which opened up the possibility for genetic manipulation. Equally, developments in our understanding of the molecular biology of viruses have supported the long-held suspicion that many forms of cancer are caused by viruses. The molecular biologist is, as a result, a known species both in the stock marker and in the cancer ward.

3. THE CONCEPTS OF MOLECULAR BIOLOGY

Some of the founders of the new molecular biology, unlike their predecessors, have expressed themselves vehemently on the importance of the molecular approach and the unimportance of analysis at higher levels. J. D. Watson is reported to have remarked that there is sociology and everything else is molecular. F. H. C. Crick stated that the ultimate aim of the modern movement in biology was to explain '*all* biology in terms of physics and chemistry'. He added: 'Thus eventually one may hope to have the whole of biology "explained" in terms of the level below it, and so on right down to the atomic level'.[6] Whether this aggressively confident, even strident, reductionist approach has been belied by the actual practice of molecular biologists we shall discuss later. Suffice it to say that the concepts of molecular biology are embedded in the language of chemistry, physics and biology.

Consider the 'classical' concept of biological specificity, i.e. the property of an organism to 'recognise' and to distinguish its own tissues and fluids from those of another organism, the property of an enzyme to act on a specific substrate and the many subtle differences between organisms determined by heredity and so on. Molecular biologists speak of 'information', taking the term from information theory, in which information is treated in very general terms and the mathematical treatment is modelled on thermodynamics. The specific differences between organisms are then bits of information each of which is encoded in the genetic constitution. Gene expression involves the processes of *transcription* and *translation* of the encoded information of the gene into a specific sequence of amino acids which make up the protein gene product. Immunological differences are due to differences in the protein gene product, and these in turn are determined by differences in the encoded information of the gene.

When they advanced their model for DNA, Watson and Crick suggested that the genetic information was contained in the sequence of the four bases, one of which is attached to each link in the long DNA chain. The possibility thus arose of discovering the nature of the chemical code in which the genetic information is written. Perhaps the most dramatic achievement of the molecular biologists and biochemists was the unravelling of the genetic code, a task completed in 1970. The success depended on advances made in the understanding of the machinery of protein synthesis. Crick codified the emerging theoretical picture in a classic lecture entitled simply, 'On Protein Synthesis', delivered to the Society of Experimental Biologists in 1957. Here he spelt out two hypotheses and one 'dogma'. The Sequence Hypothesis states that 'the specificity of a piece of nucleic acid is expressed solely by the sequence of its bases, and that this sequence is responsible for that of a particular protein'; the Colinearity Hypothesis states that to a specific sequence of the bases of DNA there corresponds a specific sequence of amino acids in the polypeptide chain of the protein determined by that DNA; the Central Dogma states that 'once "information" has passed into protein it cannot get out again'.[7]

The strictly reductionist character of the view expressed in Crick's lecture is seen in the assertion that the biological specificity of proteins is due to their chemical constitution and three-dimensional shape, and that the latter is in turn due to amino acid sequence. The claim that the machinery for the transmission of this chemical specificity from DNA to proteins only allows it to operate in the one direction constituted the molecular basis for the rejection of the possibility of any form of Lamarckian heredity.

Molecular biology has also been applied successfully to the subject of the control of gene expression, an area virtually untouched by geneticists hitherto. At the Pasteur Institute, François Jacob (b.1920) and Jacques Monod (1910–1976) introduced the hypothesis of 'regulator' and 'operator' genes which controlled the expression of the 'structural' genes responsible for the synthesis of a specific enzyme – β galactosidase. More recently a segment of DNA found in many organisms, and called the 'homeobox', has been identified which controls the expression of whole batteries of genes.

It is also now clear that another mechanism exists for the control of gene expression which acts not upon the DNA of the gene, but upon the chemical message ('messenger RNA') produced by the gene. Enzymes which cut and join stretches of messenger RNA are employed by the cell to produce different gene products in different parts of the organism, thus causing differentiation. These examples show that the modern phase of molecular biology, though conceived more narrowly than its forbear, has been able to do much more than merely describe genetics in molecular terms. It has enabled a fresh approach to be adopted to traditional problems in many areas. It has placed protein-nucleic acid relations at the heart of biology, integrating major features of genetics, biochemistry, embryology, cytology and virology. Moreover, evolutionary relations which hitherto had been pursued through study of the fossil record, and by hybridisation and cytogenetics, could now be attacked at the molecular level by the comparative study of DNA and protein sequences. Comparative studies of the amino acid sequences of the respiratory proteins have provided strong ammunition for those evolutionists – the 'neutralists' – who claim that *some* characteristics of organisms owe their presence to increases in the frequencies of the genes which determine them. Such increases are held to be due to cumulative sampling errors or so-called 'random drift' and not to selection.

4. REDUCTIONISM AND THE EMERGENCE OF MOLECULAR BIOLOGY

Attempts to reconstruct the history of molecular biology have brought to the fore the question as to whether or not molecular biologists were pursuing a reductionist programme. Whilst Kenneth Schaffner has argued that reductionism was peripheral to molecular biology, John Fuerst has urged that it was of central concern. When Schaffner looked at the history of the operon theory he did not find that the research was directed exclusively from the molecular level, but rather that biological entities were studied, and biological concepts and theories utilised, alongside chemical and molecular ones. Fuerst argued that the logical positivist conception of reduction used by Schaffner was not appropriate to the study of scientific practice. It sufficed that the early molecular biologists *believed* in the long-term possibility of explaining biology in terms of physics and chemistry. Whether they were using the techniques of physics and chemistry without being committed to a belief in the possibility of reducing biology to those sciences – 'methodological reductionism' – or whether they did also believe in such reduction – 'ontological reductionism' – could only be decided by appealing to their programmatic statements. These he showed to favour ontological reduction in the long term.

This reductionist view has had the effect of stressing the importance of the intellectual migration of physicists into biology. Stimulated by Schrödinger's little book, *What is Life?* (1944), they turned to biology as a promising area for research. Crick's justification for his outspoken advocacy of reductionism was that physics and chemistry offered a sound foundation of knowledge which would guide the discovery of new knowledge. The effect of these reductionist claims has been to create an asymmetry in the assumed influence of biological and physical sciences upon molecular biology, to the effect that 'backward' biology was revolutionised and modernised by 'progressive' physics. But as empirical research has shown, biological theories, concepts and techniques have been just as important as physical techniques, witness the theories and experimental methods of genetics, the dilution technique and plaque count of virology, and the parasexual processes of gene transfer developed in bacteriology and virology.

Nor is it true that the majority of the founders of molecular biology were trained as physicists. Whilst Crick, Delbrück and Wilkins were trained as physicists, Astbury, Rosalind Franklin (1920–55) and Linus Pauling were trained in physics and chemistry, Max Perutz (b.1914) in chemistry, Salvador Luria in medicine (his attempt to train as a physicist failed), and Jacob, Monod and Watson in biology. Of physicists, only those who immersed themselves in biology can be said to have had a major influence on the shaping of molecular biology.

Biochemists have expressed their concern at the way their contributions to molecular biology have been minimised, or ignored. Yet it was they who supplied the invaluable techniques of enzymology, chromatography, sequence analysis and tracer techniques. In truth the chief feature of molecular biology has been its interdisciplinarity. The most important contribution from physics came from a hybrid of physics and crystallography – X-ray crystallography – but the 'language' of molecular biology owes more to chemistry and biology than to physics.

In contrast to those who have argued for the importance of conventional physics in molecular biology, Stent has claimed that an important motivation behind the move of physicists into biology was the romantic view that biology was not reducible to orthodox physics. Rather, by studying biology, physicists could hope to discover fresh paradoxes, like those which had caused an earlier generation of physicists to formulate quantum mechanics. With the emergence of these new paradoxes, new physical principles would be formulated adequate to explain biology. The inspiration for this hope was the famous 1933 lecture of Nils Bohr (1885–1962) on 'Light and Life'. Yet the only molecular biologists who were motivated by this hope appear to have been Delbrück and Stent. In *What is Life?* Schrödinger had urged that there was no alternative to the molecular account of the gene.[8]

Whilst it is true that there has been a mutual influence of physics, chemistry and biology in the evolution of molecular biology, it would be a perverse historian or philosopher who refused to accept that the description of concepts like gene, mutation, specificity and development in molecular terms represents a form of reduction. Of course these descriptions all presuppose the organised structure of the cell. A string of nucleic acid bases on a polynucleotide chain has no significance for the biologist without the machinery of the cell in which its 'information' can be expressed. As Polanyi remarked: ' . . . the analysis of the hierarchy of living things shows that to reduce this hierarchy to ultimate particles is to wipe out our very sight of it. Such analysis proves this ideal to be false and destructive'.[9]

Recently the discovery that the same genetic code can be 'read-off' or transcribed starting at different points giving rise to different gene products has caused concern that, after all, the gene cannot be defined unambiguously in terms of its molecular sequence. Must we return to the definition of the gene in terms of its product? The presence of these 'jumping genes' has complicated the picture, but has not caused the abandonment of the molecular account. Nor has the earlier discovery of 'nonsense DNA', but the simple picture of the chromosome as a collection of 'structural' genes represented by a continuous DNA chain has given place to a much more sophisticated view.

The emphasis placed on the migration of physicists into biology has given rise to a radically different interpretation of the reductionist claims of molecular biology by Abir-Am. She sees the relations between the sciences involved as one of imperialism. Physicists as members of a high-status field saw themselves as invading and conquering the low-status field of biology. They exercised their power by the battery of instruments which they, as physicists, were qualified to operate. The success of molecular biology, she claimed, came from the pursuit of biological thinking rather than from mere instrumentation. Clearly there is a sociological dimension to reductionism such as Abir-Am has claimed, but that does not make the intellectual dimensions of reductionism redundant. Nor is her claim at all convincing that this instrument-led conquest lacked biological modes of thought.[10]

5. MOLECULAR BIOLOGY AND SCIENTIFIC REVOLUTIONS

It is tempting to depict modern molecular biology as an example of a Kuhnian phase of revolutionary science leading to the establishment of a new paradigm. Twentieth-century science can then be neatly packaged into two major revolutionary phases – first quantum physics, then molecular biology.

No-one would deny that since 1953 there has been a burst of activity in the area of protein-nucleic acid relations, the structure of the gene, its coding, expression and mutation, protein synthesis, etc. Crick's theoretical scheme of 1957 pointed the way to a consensus in the field, but there were many surprises ahead. Thus, the discovery, in 1970, of an enzyme which copied DNA from RNA – the reverse transcriptase – met with widespread incredulity on account of the popular conception of the Central Dogma, although this partial reversal of the machinery of gene expression was not excluded in Crick's scheme.

If we compare the treatment of these subjects in the 1950s with the treatment of them in the 1930s and 40s the contrast is striking. The most obvious difference is that protein, not DNA, was considered as the material of the genes, that gene expression therefore involved no translation from one class of compounds into another for gene and gene product were both proteins. A genetic code in terms of an amino acid sequence was envisaged, but since there was no call for a translation process, the questions of the size of the codon and the degree of redundancy in the codon were not raised.

Even when it became clear that nucleic acids were essential to gene duplication in the nucleus and protein synthesis in the cytoplasm, their role continued to be considered a minor one. Since gene duplication was treated as a special case of protein synthesis, these processes going on in the nucleus and cytoplasm appeared to be fundamentally the same, and the nucleic acids fulfilled the role of 'midwife' molecules in both. Those who adopted the 'template hypothesis' pictured the nucleic acid chain as a framework upon which the polypeptide chain of the gene was stretched out, in order to serve as a template upon which a new polypeptide chain could be laid. This view was only directly challenged after the publication of the Watson-Crick model for DNA.

Meanwhile the assumptions hitherto made about the limited variety of nucleic acids, based on their tetranucleotide structure, were revised following the demonstration by O. T. Avery (1877–1955), Colin Macleod (1909–72) and Maclyn McCarty (b.1911) in 1944, that the Transforming Principle was DNA. This Principle is said to 'transform' because it causes the recipient bacteria to acquire a heritable character from the dead bacteria from which the Transforming Principle has been taken. Although a great variety of interpretations of this curious phenomenon was entertained, for instance that the transforming principle merely caused genetic mutation to occur in a given direction, it functioned as a serious 'anomaly' which stimulated Erwin Chargaff to pioneer the application of chromatography to the nucleic acids in order to put the tetranucleotide hypothesis to the test. As a result he succeeded in demonstrating the chemical basis to the biological specificity which Avery had claimed for DNA.

According to the Tetranucleotide Hypothesis all nucleic acids contain equal quantities of their four constituent nucleotide 'bases' arranged in a repetitive manner. The number of possible sequences was therefore very small – 16. If, on the other hand, the arrangement was not repetitive, although the sum total of the four bases conformed to that of a tetranucleotide, then much greater variety was possible. This was called a 'statistical tetranucleotide' by J. M. Gulland (1898–1947) in 1945. But it was only with the aid of chromatography that Chargaff was able in 1949 to announce the destruction of the tetranucleotide hypothesis when he showed how far his base analyses for the DNA of four very different organisms departed from expectation.

At the same time, biochemists reasoned that if the genetic material is composed of DNA then the DNA content of haploid and diploid cells should differ by a factor of 2. In other words, the presence of two sets of chromosomes in diploid cells as opposed to one set in haploid (germ) cells should mean twice as many genes in the former and twice as much DNA. This prediction was confirmed in 1948, and by 1950 cell chemists had followed up several other parallels between DNA and genes, all of which supported the identification of the genes as DNA rather than protein.

This conclusion gave a new meaning to the knowledge already attained of the chemical geography of the cell. T. Caspersson (b.1910) and J. Brachet (b.1909) had shown that DNA is confined to the nucleus, and protein synthesis occurs chiefly in the cytoplasm associated with the presence of ribonucleic acids (RNA). They had interpreted their results in terms of protein genes, but on the basis of DNA genes this chemical geography was more intelligible. Somehow the specificity of the DNA was transmitted in the RNA to the cytoplasm where it served as a template for synthesis of the protein product of the gene.

Because the phages studied by the Phage Group possessed a lot of DNA which did not have a genetic function, the results of following the DNA from parent to progeny phage particles by the tracer technique were inconclusive. However, by 1952 it was clear that the DNA packed in the head of the phage particle is injected into the host cell whereas the protein coat is discarded. This 'visual' demonstration by electron microscopy alongside the biochemical demonstration by tracer technique brought conviction where tracer studies alone had failed.

A full-scale Kuhnian analysis would seek to demonstrate the existence of an articulated paradigm in the pre-1950s incommensurable with the paradigm of modern molecular biology. There is little support in the literature for the existence of such incommensurable views. Thus the pre-1950s did not differ from the modern period in terms of the fundamental explanatory approach adopted. Save for the paradox-hunters inspired by Bohr, the founders of modern molecular biology were at one with their forebears in seeking straightforward chemical and physical explanations of biological phenomena. The notion of copying a sequence of 'residues' on a template was introduced in the 1930s, 'like-with-like' and 'complementary' schemes of replication were discussed in the 1940s, while hydrogen ' bridges' (bonds) and salt-linkages were invoked as the mechanisms for holding polypeptide chains in particular conformations in both the 30s and 40s. Finally, the specificity of large molecules was attributed to their three-dimensional shape and the presence in them of 'active groups'.

Given these points of agreement, the two phases of molecular biology differed on two major points:

(1) The repository of genetic specificity lay in the proteins according to the first phase of molecular biology, but in the second phase it lay in the nucleic acids. Anomalies which emerged in the 1930s and 40s were interpreted in accordance with the assumption of protein genes. The fact that alterations to the protein of viruses did not yield altered offspring, and the observation that ultra-violet light, specifically affecting DNA, caused inactivation or mutation of a variety of organisms called for the construction of supplementary hypotheses to preserve the proteins as the repository of inheritance. As two radiation biologists remarked:

> It is probably somewhat dangerous to overemphasize the importance of nucleic acid in the study of radiation effects on living cells. It is very well possible that in radiation-produced mutations, the nucleic acid is only the 'absorbent' agent, then transfers the absorbed energy to the protein closely associated with it.[11]

Not until 1958 when the protein and nucleic acid portions of the virus particle were separated in sufficiently native state to preserve activity was it possible to demonstrate the genetic role of the nucleic acids in these plant viruses.

(2) The second major difference concerns the determination of biological specificity. In the early period two features of the chemistry of proteins were advanced as determining specificity – composition (i.e. what amino acids it contains) and constitution (i.e. the arrangement of the amino acids). Those who discussed this second aspect thought in terms of *repeating* sequences. In view of the large number of different amino-acids in proteins this assumption of repetition did not seem unduly restrictive. The much-studied proteins of silk, collagen and fish protamine gave analyses suggestive

for repeating sequences (which modern work has confirmed). Moreover, the results of ultra-centrifugal study of proteins suggested to T. Svedberg (1884–1971) the existence of standard sub-units in all proteins. Such sub-units could be built from standard repeating sequences. Astbury tried to show that features on the X-ray diffraction pattern of proteins which related to long distances of separation along the polypeptide chains were produced by long-distance *chemical* repeats (for, given a repeating sequence, the rarest amino acid would occur at only widely-spaced and constant intervals).

Modern molecular biology considers repeating sequences as the exception rather than the rule. Moreover, biological specificity under a given environment is believed to be determined *only* by the nature and sequence of the amino acids, i.e. linear sequence determines three-dimensional conformation. The notion that an antigen can affect the folding of the polypeptide chain (as stated in the instructional theory of anti-body formation) is therefore rejected.

Clearly the views advanced in the first phase of molecular biology were less precise than those put forward in the second phase, but they were sufficiently detailed to stimulate experimental researches. The early molecular biologists recognised some of the limitations within which they worked. They knew, until the advent of chromatography, that their separation methods were inadequate, they were all too aware of the paucity of data on their X-ray diffraction patterns of the fibrous proteins. But they were confident that the proteins lay at the very centre of life and that their biological functions could be understood in terms of their structures and environments. Modern molecular biology has brought the nucleic acids into that centre and has transformed our conception of their relation to the proteins. This transformation has taken less than two decades to effect. Within a generation the teaching of molecular aspects of biology and biochemistry has been profoundly altered. A historian of the twenty-first century looking back on this episode would surely conclude that something like a revolution had occurred in a very short space of time, even if it did not exemplify many of the important features claimed by Kuhn for revolutionary science.

The conception of molecular biology as an example of a revolution has been criticised by H. Judson. He argues that revolutions may be found by the historian in physics, but they are not to be found in biology. In contrast to physics, where there have been 'towering, overarching' theories, in biology 'no large-scale, closely interlocking, fully worked out, ruling set of ideas has ever been overthrown'. Instead of the 'set-piece battles' and 'overturnings' of physics, biology has proceeded by 'openings up'.[12] As for a philosophical model of scientific change which fits biology Judson appealed to the 'Correspondence Principle' according to which new theories have to account for the success of their predecessors by degenerating into them under the conditions in which they were confirmed. Thus at low velocities, Einsteinian mechanics collapses into Newtonian mechanics. This preserves the logical relationship of successive theories and stresses the scientists' commitment to an attitude of conservatism.

This model of scientific change succeeds on the assumption that those parts of the old theory worthy of preservation and therefore to be explained by the new theory can be clearly identified at the time. This is indeed a convenient way of disposing of the problem presented to any rational theory of scientific change by rejected knowledge. To argue that the rejected knowledge was not really knowledge and hence that nothing has been overturned is a highly arbitrary way of handling the historical data! The facts of the matter are that the Lamarckian theory of enzyme adaption, of bacterial resistance to phage and antibiotics and the protein and nucleoprotein theories of the gene, have all been rejected.

The reason why examples of rejected knowledge are not more evident is that Whiggish success-stories simply excise the rejected knowledge. Thus the history of protein synthesis has been recounted in terms of a series of attempts to arrive at a genetic code and translation process which successively approach our modern view. As D. Bartels has shown, however, there were two rival research programmes in existence out of which our modern conception has emerged, The first, the 'multi-enzyme programme', conceived protein synthesis in terms of the reversal of protein breakdown, and envisaged a battery of enzymes which played the dual role of peptide bond formation and specification of the appropriate amino acid at each link. This programme made important contributions to our understanding of phosphorylation and the involvement of enzymes in protein synthesis, but the multi-enzyme theory was rejected in favour of the rival 'template theory'. This course of events exemplifies a general feature of scientific change, namely, that new theories rarely result from the mere triumph of one rival theory over another, or of one research programme over its rival. Rather, out of the controversy between rival programmes a new theory emerges. In 1953 Watson and Crick had questioned whether enzymes were needed for DNA synthesis. No biochemist would even have entertained such a preposterous idea, and nor would we today. On the other hand no molecular biochemist would today suggest that enzymes might play a part in the determination of sequence in protein synthesis. In 1953 the biochemists Peter Campbell and T. S. Work described the multi-enzyme and template theories, and explained their reasons for rejecting the latter theory, among which is their opinion that the gene, which supposedly acts as a template, is 'essentially an abstract idea and it may be a mistake to try to clothe this idea in a coat of nucleic acid or protein'.[13] But this does not make their attitude to the template theory 'incommensurable'. Moreover, those who supported the multi-enzyme theory were not thereby prevented from contributing to and adopting the template theory. Indeed, three of those who are closely associated with the establishment of the modern theory of protein synthesis: Heinz Fränkel-Conrat (b.1910), M. B. Hoagland (b.1921) and Paul Zamecnik (b.1912) were initially adherents of the multi-enzyme research programme.

6. INTERPRETING THE HISTORY OF MOLECULAR BIOLOGY

Much energy has been expended in identifying the several strands which together have produced molecular biology. When Stent claimed that the chief root of the subject lay in the work of the Phage Group, Kendrew replied that there were two roots – the American Phage Group whose interest centred on 'information' and the British 'structural' school, who were commited to the unravelling of the three-dimensional structure of biologically important molecules. The Watson-Crick model for DNA can then be seen as representing the synthesis of both informational and structural viewpoints, for the structure of DNA was suggestive of its biological function, that of carrying herditary information. The model also represented the result of collaboration between a member of the Phage Group (Watson) and a member of the structural group (Crick). Furthermore, since both groups were led by physicists (Delbrück and W. L. Bragg), this picture of the history underlines the importance to be attributed to the roles played by physicists. Those who have advanced this picture recognise the need to include the discovery of the chemical nature of the transforming principle in 1944. This is done by claiming the important impact of that discovery on the thinking and research of the Phage Group.

Whilst this picture is simple and neat, it does less than justice to the rich variety of the specialisms which were influenced by the 1944 discovery. It gives attention to the Phage Group at the expense of other research programmes, for instance those working on the plant viruses, and the histochemical and biochemical aspects of nuclear division. The biochemists of the New York Academy of Arts and Sciences organised a meeting in 1978 at which a broader and more balanced view was presented by focusing attention on the history of protein research.

From a historiographical point of view it can be argued that such attempts to trace 'paths', 'roots' and 'origins' must necessarily involve a Whiggish approach – starting with modern molecular biology and tracing its elements back to identify its roots. Thus Edward Yoxen has suggested that the identification of Schrödinger's book, *What is Life?* as the seminal work drawing many phycisists into biology, resulted from a retrospective reinterpretation of this text, which in fact was taken at the time to be addressed chiefly to the question of whether or not life obeys the second law of thermodynamics. Schrödinger's mention of the 'hereditary codescript' which has been stressed in several accounts, Yoxen noted, was really quite brief. It has been magnified by our present knowledge of the importance of this concept. In fact, concern over the

Second Law and over the basis of the fidelity of the genetic system were not mutually exclusive, for as Schrödinger emphasised, the most striking case of the Second Law apparently being disobeyed was seen in the remarkable constancy of the gene.

In contrast to the 'path-finding' approach it may be more fruitful to explore the methodologies of what in their day were recognised as acknowledged achievements, in order to grasp the manner in which modern molecular biology has evolved. First, we note that there already existed in the 1930s a broad conception of a molecular approach via the exploration of the three-dimensional structure of macromolecules. The achievements which were recognised at this time were the structures of natural and synthetic fibres which had been formulated on the basis of a variety of physical and chemical data. Second, the concept of long-chain macromolecules embodied in these structures were also applied to the nucleic acids, and the relation between these compounds and the proteins was discussed in terms of biological function resulting from chemical structure. Third, the importance of physics for biology was seen most strikingly in the study of X-ray mutagenesis. Recognising the difficulties standing in the way of a direct analysis of the chemical structure of the gene, attempts were made to discover its secrets indirectly by damaging it and observing the results. This approach was taken by H. J. Muller (1890–1967), and by Timoféeff-Ressovsky (b.1900), K. G. Zimmer (b.1911) and Delbrück, in their classic 1935 study 'On the Nature of Gene Mutation and Gene Structure'.[14] It was this study which informed the analysis in Schrödinger's *What is Life?* Fourth, plant viruses were crystallised and shown to consist only of nucleoproteins. Fifth, through the researches of bacteriologists and biochemists, carbohydrates and nucleic acids, as well as proteins, were shown to possess biological specificity, and this was attributed to their chemical constitution. Finally, biological specificity was described in the language of information theory, the deployment of which, some have argued, marks a fundamental departure from the old conception of specificity.

Rather than searching for the immediate antecedents of modern molecular biology, let us explore the broad conception of a 'molecular' biology from which has emerged and evolved the molecular biology we know today. The manner in which this modern molecular biology has been rendered more complex and in some of its aspects transformed, is a chapter which awaits the historian. No one should be dissuaded from such a task by the prediction of Gunther Stent that in 1968 the decline of molecular biology was approaching, and that the *avant-garde* of biological research will be formed by students of the nervous system, not geneticists.[15]

NOTES

1. Council for Scientific Policy, 'Report of the working party on molecular biology', *Parliamentary papers* (1967–8), vol. 31 Cmnd 3675, p. l.

2. W. Weaver, 'Molecular biology: origin of the term', *Science*, 170 (1970), 581–2.
3. W. T. Astbury, 'Adventures in molecular biology', *Harvey lectures*, Series 46 (1950–1), p. 3.
4. F. H. C. Crick, 'Recent research in molecular biology: introduction', *British medical bulletin*, 21 (1965), 184. Cited in: G. S. Stent, 'That was the molecular biology that was', *Science*, 160 (1968), 390.
5. E. Mayr, 'From molecules to organic diversity', *Federation proceedings*, 23 (1964), 1235. Reprinted and revised in: E. Mayr, *Evolution and the diversity of life. Selected essays* (Cambridge, Mass., 1976), p. 72
6. F. H. C. Crick, *Of molecules and men* (Seattle and London, 1966), p. 14.
7. F. H. C. Crick, 'On protein synthesis', *Symposium of the Society for Experimental Biology*, 12 (1958), 153.
8. E. Schrödinger, *What is life?* (Cambridge, 1944), p. 57.
9. M. Polanyi, 'Life's irreducible structure', *Science*, 160 (1968), 1312.
10. P. Abir-Am, 'The discourse of physical power and biological knowledge in the 1930s: a reappraisal of the Rockefeller Foundation's "Policy" in molecular biology', *Social studies of science*, 12 (1982), 341–82. See also: 'Responses and replies', 14 (1984), 225–63.
11. A. Hollender and C. W. Emmons, 'Wavelength dependence of mutation production in the ultraviolet with special emphasis on fungi', *Cold Spring Harbor symposia on quantitative biology*, 9 (1941), 185.
12. H. F. Judson, *The eighth day of creation. The makers of the revolution in biology* (London, 1979), p. 612.
13. P. N. Campbell and T. S. Work, 'Biosynthesis of proteins', *Nature*, 171 (1953), 1000. See also: R. C. Olby, 'Biochemical origins of molecular biology: a discussion', *Trends in biochemical sciences*, 11 (1986), 303–5.
14. N. W. Timoféeff-Ressovsky, K. G. Zimmer and M. Delbrück, 'Uber die Natur der Genmutation und der Genstruktur', *Nachrichten von der Gesellschaft der Wissenschaften zu Göttingen. Math. phys. Kl., Fachgruppe VI*, 1 (1935), 189–245.
15. G. S. Stent, 'That was the molecular biology that was', *Science*, 160 (1968), p. 395.

FURTHER READING

D. Bartels, 'The multienzyme program', *History and philosophy of the life sciences*, 5 (1983).

F. H. C. Crick, *What mad pursuit. A personal view of scientific discovery* (New York, 1988).

C. Debru, *L'Esprit des protéines* (Paris, 1983).

P. Fischer, *Licht und Leben. Ein Bericht über Max Delbrück, den Wegbereiter der Molekularbiologie* (Konstanz, 1985), English translation entitled: *Thinking about science. Max Delbrück and the origins of molecular biology* (New York and London, 1988).

H. F. Judson, *The eighth day of creation. Makers of the revolution in biology* (New York, 1979).

M. McCarty, *The transforming principle: discovering that genes are made of DNA* (New York, 1986).

J. Monod, *Pour une éthique de la connaissance. Textes choisis et présentés par Bernardino Fantini* (Paris, 1988).

R. C. Olby, *The path to the double helix* (London, 1974).

P. R. Srinivasan, J. S. Fruton and J. T. Edsall (eds.), 'The origins of modern biochemistry', *Annals of the New York Academy of Sciences*, 325 (1979), 1–373.

J. D. Watson, *The double helix* (New York, 1968).

E. J. Yoxen, 'Where does Schrödinger's "What is Life" belong in the history of molecular biology', *History of science*, 17 (1979), 17–52.

33

THE EMERGENCE OF GENETICS

ROBERT OLBY

A nineteenth-century biologist would have been perplexed if he were asked to explain what a 'geneticist' studies. A 'genetic' study implied a developmental one, tracing the history of, for example, the growth of intelligence from birth to maturity. Those who studied hereditary transmission were regarded as students of the broad field of 'inheritance', which was concerned as much with questions of development and evolution as with transmission. The narrower conception of inheritance, in which attention was focused on hereditary transmission, was referred to as 'heredity' in the latter part of the nineteenth century, and it was this conception of the field which was understood by the term 'genetics'. Yet, like psychology, which has a long history rooted in the philosophy of mind, genetics has a long history located in theories of 'generation'. A problem for the historian is, then, to settle on a strategy for relating the genetics of the twentieth century with the study of inheritance and of hybridism in previous centuries.

If we turn to definitions of inheritance in the earlier period we find that they rely on the analogy with the inheritance of estate, thus emphasising the transmission of the possessions of one individual, some of which he may have acquired in his own lifetime. The use of the term 'inheritance' was thus metaphorical, and to an extent misleading. As J. Arthur Thomson (1861–1933) pointed out, the use of phrases borrowed from the inheritance of property is 'apt to cause obscurity and fallacy when applied to the inheritance of characters which literally constitute the organism and are inseparable from it'.[1] In the biological literature, inheritance was not really a subject in its own right, rather it was a feature of a fundamental property of living things, namely generation. Discussions of inheritance tended, as a result, to be closely concerned also with theories of fertilisation and development. From the Greeks came the material theory of Hippocrates, several versions of which were offered in the eighteenth century. Charles Darwin resurrected the theory in the nineteenth century and called it 'Pangenesis'. The 'seed' or representatives of the various parts of the body of both male and female was accumulated in the gonads. Such a process allowed for the inheritance of acquired characters since acquired structures, just like congenital structures, could supply their representatives. Many other features of generation could also be explained by the theory, for example, regeneration and development. From Aristotle came the form and matter theory. The female contributed the matter and nourishment of the embryo, the male the form. This theory rested in turn upon his conception of substance, according to which the existence of an organism depended upon the intimate union of matter and form. Such a conception allowed the development of the organism to be envisaged as a progressive transformation starting with the apparently formless matter of the egg. This 'epigenetic' theory contrasted with the 'preformationist' theory according to which a miniature of the adult was formed which was not transformed but simply enlarged in development, and with the theory of 'pre-existence' which claimed that all individuals were present at Creation in miniature form, packed one within the other like Russian dolls.[2]

The eighteenth century witnessed several attempts to subject such theories to experimental test by hybridising species and varieties. Although to our eyes the results constitute a refutation of pre-existence, whether on the male (spermist) or female (ovist) side, such data were not interpreted in this way. Thus Charles Bonnet (1720–93) and Albrecht von Haller (1708–77) both selected those data which, taken in isolation, supported their own preformationist views. By the nineteenth century, however, preformation no longer held sway, so that the results of hybridisation could be evaluated in the light of epigenetic development. Now clearly, if the specific form of the offspring was not already present in the 'germ' before fertilisation, it should be possible by hybridisation to change this form, a change which might affect not only the immediate offspring, but subsequent generations also. This possibility opened up the debate on the transmutation of species, for it would then appear that hybridisation could lead to species multiplication, or if not multiplication, at least the transmutation of one existing species into another. Much of the experimental study of hybridisation in the eighteenth and the nineteenth centuries was conducted to test this point.

1. THE HEREDITARIANS

Between the eighteenth and nineteenth centuries, the medical literature shows a development from preoccupation with discussions of the evidence for the inheritance of acquired characters and the effects of the imagination of the mother upon the foetus, to concerns about the effects of consanguinity (inbreeding) and the urbanisation of society leading, it was widely believed, to hereditary 'degeneration'. It was within the debate on the possibilities or the limits to progress of man, his 'perfectibility', that a new school of thought arose, which we may describe as 'hereditarian'. The hereditarians were opposed to the claims of the 'perfectibilists' because they rejected the assumption of the perfectibilists that the effects of civilisation and amelioration of society were in the course of generations acquired by heredity. Into this debate entered the historian, Henry Thomas Buckle (1821–62), arguing both against those who claimed the inheritance of acquired characters and those who denied it. He perceived that selective citation of pedigrees could be used to support almost any claim. Consequently, in order to account for the development of modern civilisation in Europe he turned to the *social structure* of European nations, rather than to their biology or climate. As the most prominent hereditarian, Francis Galton (1822–1911) opposed this nihilism by reconceptualising inheritance as a statistical relation between populations of successive generations. This definition took the subject out of its old context of generation, extricating it from its association with embryology, and establishing a clearly-defined research programme concerned only with the data of hereditary transmission. As Ruth Cowan has pointed out, Galton's new conception of the subject was signalled by his replacement of the old metaphor 'inheritance' by the term 'heredity', after the French term '*hérédité*'.[3]

Galton's work was debated chiefly within the context of inheritance in man, and had virtually no impact upon the work of the hybridists and animal and plant breeders until the 1890s. Gregor Mendel (1822–84) appears to have remained completely ignorant of Galton's work, and it was only when Mendel's papers were discovered in 1900 that attempts were made to relate the work of these two pioneers. Many biologists sought to link the new field of cytology with the data of hybridism and heredity. Darwin's hypothesis of Pangenesis of 1868 was really a pre-cytological hypothesis based on the analogy between a higher organism and the colony of polyps in a coral, but his admirer, Hugo de Vries (1838–1945) transformed it into the hypothesis of Intracellular Pangenesis, in which the hereditary determinants, or 'Pangenes' were stored in the nucleus from which they migrated into the cytoplasm in order to form the characters for which they were severally responsible. Such migration, however, did not extend beyond the cell wall.[4] Continuity between cellular and individual generations was therefore traced to the source of pangenes, the nucleus. August Weismann (1834–1914) and Oscar Hertwig (1849–1922) also used the results of cytology in formulating theories of heredity, but it would be a mistake to assume that the development of the understanding of cell division, the formation of germ cells and their fertilisation, led inevitably towards a Mendelian type of hereditary theory. On the contrary, the same cytological assumptions served to support quite distinct theories of inheritance.

With the discovery of Mendel's papers in 1900 we enter a new period, during which the principles of the animal and plant breeders were as far as possible reinterpreted in Mendelian terms. Mendel's papers served as a significant achievement which was emulated in experiments with an increasing range of species. A number of these did not appear to follow the Mendelian scheme without introducing ancillary hypotheses such as linkage and the compound character, and it was only gradually that Mendelian heredity became established as a *general* theory of heredity. In the first phase of the subject in the present century it was widely believed that there were at least two forms of heredity – Galtonian and Mendelian – indeed many biologists, particularly those in Germany, held that Mendelian heredity concerned only unimportant characters, and that characters of evolutionary significance to the species were subject to a different form of hereditary transmission in which acquired characters could be inherited. These characters were 'carried' not by the nucleus but by the cytoplasm.

Although the claims made for Mendelism by the Mendelians were enthusiastic, they were nevertheless tentative. Confidence was tempered by the recognition that examples of the presence of Mendelian heredity were as yet limited and scattered. The subject which the Mendelians studied they therefore called 'Mendelism' rather than 'heredity'. Their subject was launched more confidently and effectively when Bateson coined the term *'genetics'* in 1906. Three years later the Danish biologist, Wilhelm Johannson (1857–1927), introduced the term *'gene'* in his widely read textbook, *Elemente der exakten Erblichkeitslehre* (1909), and made the fundamental distinction between 'genotype' and 'phenotype' thus adding considerable precision to what Galton had called the effects of 'nature' and 'nurture'. Meanwhile, the successful welding together of Mendelian heredity and the cytology of chromosomes had to await the work of the Columbia school under T. H. Morgan (1866–1945) in the years 1911 to 1913, by which time it could be said that genetics was established. This essay, therefore, does not go beyond the year 1913.

2. THE BREEDERS AND THE HYBRIDISTS

Charles Darwin greatly prized the knowledge of the practical breeders of his time and was convinced of the power of inheritance by the willingness with which sheep breeders paid out large sums of money for the privilege of using the rams owned by Robert Bakewell (1725–95). Little did he know that these breeders were being 'milked' by Bakewell who at the time was facing bankruptcy and needed all the money he could get! Nor were the successes of the animal breeders a guarantee that the theoretical assumptions behind their practices were well founded. Thus Nicholas Russell has pointed out the practice of horse breeders in the seventeenth century of importing fresh Arab stallions rather than relying on indigenous stallions of Arab blood[5]. This expensive procedure was due to their belief that the transmission of Arab qualities depended upon the stallion having been reared in the oriental climate. Equally, their lack of concern about the qualities of the mare stemmed from their assumption of the predominant influence of the male in hereditary transmission.

The fear that changed conditions of life would destroy breed characters was based on the then-current theory of adaptation according to which the distinctive characters of the breed represented adaptations to the locality in which that variety lived. Under changed conditions the breed would acclimatise, but in the process it would 'degenerate' losing the breed's special characteristics. By the end of the eighteenth century breeders had found definite evidence that degeneration did not occur. Arab horses and Merino sheep bred in England retained their breed characteristics. This discovery led animal breeders to attach much more importance to hereditary constitution and much less to the effects of the environment.

Although by the nineteenth century the animal breeders achieved a clearer understanding of their art, they pictured heredity in terms of characters of different 'strengths' in the 'blood', the longer the character had been in the breed, the greater its strength. Thus older breeds were held to be 'prepotent' over more recent breeds. Sometimes a character that had not been seen in a breed for generations would suddenly reappear producing what was called a 'reversion' to a long-lost breed – as in Darwin's hybrid pigeons. Here the plumage of the wild rock dove was produced in domestic brown and white breeds. The breeders were clear that crossing yields variability, and that selfing of hybrid offspring was essential to achieve constancy of type. However, they had no theoretical grounds for being able to predict how long such a process would take and no expectation that it could be achieved rapidly as in Mendel's pea experiments.

Among the hybridists, those experimenting with plants contributed the most useful results. Carl Linnaeus introduced a controversy in the 1760s when his prize essay on plant sexuality was published.[6] Here he claimed that hybridisation occurs in nature and leads to the production of new species. This assertion was tentatively supported by the Swabian botanist, J. G. Gmelin (1709–55) who called for experiments to decide the question. There followed a long line of responses, first J. G. Koelreuter (1733–1806) followed by Carl Friedrich von Gaertner (1772–1850), Charles Naudin (1815–99), D. A. Godron (1807–80) and William Herbert (1778–1847). They all admitted that new varieties could thus be formed, but only Herbert in his work on the Amaryllidaceae claimed that new species also are yielded by hybridisation.[7] The others were too impressed by the strength of reversion which brought hybrid progeny back to one or other of the originating species to accept Linnaeus's claim. As for those hybrids which did not revert, Gaertner was convinced that they suffered a general weakening such that they were unlikely to form the starting point of new species. Mendel, as we shall see, appears not to have taken so pessimistic a position.

The result of the plant hybridists' studies was the clear demonstration of the very different behaviour of the immediate offspring of hybrids (known as F1) and the behaviour of their progeny (F2). The former were uniform, the latter variable. Many individuals of the latter generation tended to revert to the originating partners in the cross. Naudin found examples of complete reversion in the F2 generation, and he speculated that it had been achieved by the separation of the specific essences in the formation of the pollen grains and the germinal vesicles. Unions in fertilisation between the specific essences thus separated would produce the reversions observed. This theory of germinal segregation was like the Mendelian theory, but differed in that Naudin treated the specific essence as a whole rather than considering the character differences themselves as independent units in heredity. Nor was complete reversion the only result of hybrid reproduction, for some of Naudin's experiments gave what he called *variation désordonnée*. Gaertner, too, concluded that the species acts as a whole although he found evidence of apparently independent transmission of characters.

Ernst Mayr has argued that the distinction between typological and populational thinking in biology marks an important feature of the differing approaches to biology throughout its history.[8] Naudin and Gaertner treated species as 'types' following the 'essentialism' of the old systematists, whereas Mendel and plant breeders like Henry Louis de Vilmorin (1843–99) and Henri Lecoq (1802–71) saw no fundamental difference between species and varieties and looked to the individual characters for the stable units. As for the basis of heredity, they did not look to particles but to fluids and forces. Naudin spoke of heredity 'ploughing the furrow more deeply, generation after generation' so that new varieties gained strength with the passage of time. Variation was treated as a force opposing heredity, not as a feature of heredity itself.

3. MENDEL'S EXPERIMENTS

The inspiration of the famous experiments of the Moravian priest, Gregor Mendel (1822–84), has been a subject of much debate among historians, as has been the meaning and significance of the papers he wrote. Sir Gavin de Beer (1899–1972) claimed that the science of genetics could be traced directly to Mendel and that its birth took place in 1865, the year in which he described his experiments with the edible pea (*Pisum sativum*). Vitszlav Orel has urged the importance of the attention devoted in Moravia to practical animal and plant breeding in providing Mendel with an informed and enthusiastic environment in which to pursue questions concerning the nature of hereditary transmission. L. A. Callender and Robert Olby, on the other hand, have argued that however important this environment may have been for making the techniques of breeding accessible to Mendel, his work was addressed to an unresolved question concerning hybridisation, namely whether or not hybridisation leads to the production of new species, as Linnaeus had claimed.[9] This question was of major concern to botanists, as is seen in the number of prizes which were offered by scientific academies for answers to it. Among the prizewinners were Naudin and Gaertner.

This question focused Mendel's attention upon hybrid descendants (F_2 and beyond) rather than upon the immediate hybrids (F_1). When he surveyed the literature he failed to find any reports which classified hybrid offspring accurately with respect to each of the differentiating characters in the cross, yet he saw that without such information it was impossible to draw any firm conclusions as to the power of hybrids to give rise to new species. Having guessed that the characters which show constancy of type behave independently, Mendel planned a brilliant set of experiments in which he grew statistically significant numbers of each generation, not a small sample merely to exemplify the variety of forms in a generation, as was the custom among breeders and hybridists hitherto. The result was his discovery of the approximation of the frequencies of the contrasted characters in the F_2 generation to the integral ratio of $3:1$. From his study of the next (F_3) generation he was able to show that the fundamental ratio in F_2 was $1:2:1$, which the phenomenon of dominance obscured. As a student of mathematics and physics he was thrilled to find that this ratio represented, on the one hand, the terms in a binomial expansion $(A + a) = A^2 + 2Aa + a^2$, and on the other, the terms in the expansion of 'hybrid' series, or the 'development' of the hybrid in its offspring – $A + 2Aa + a$. When he considered two pairs of contrasted characters, the different classes of offspring and their proportions reflected the terms produced by combining two binomials. This fact, he considered, clinched the case for the independence of the characters he dealt with.

The manner in which the parental characters were recovered in unadulterated form in the hybrid offspring convinced Mendel, as it had convinced Naudin, that there is a process of segregation between the elements brought together in the hybrid, but it was clear to Mendel that the species or variety did not act as a whole. His atomistic conception of the independence of the characters fitted with his belief in the material basis of heredity located in the constituents of the germ cells and the fertilised egg resulting from their fusion. Yet it is not obvious from any of his writings that he intended his fundamental concept – the character pair – to be translated into a pair of elements, factors, or *Anlagen*, as in the theory of the gene. J. Heimans and J. H. Bennett were the first to point out this distinction between Mendel's theory of heredity and the gene theory to which it gave rise. Nor is it credible to claim that Mendel's 1865 paper was simply a contribution to the laws of heredity. As the opening and the closing sections show, the paper was addressed to the question of species multiplication by hybridisation. The results with *Pisum* suggested that a limited number of constant forms carrying new combinations of existing characters could be produced, but that the character of the immediate hybrid (F1) was not preserved.

Mendel seems to have been convinced that other hybrids exist which do not follow the law found for *Pisum*. These allegedly showed no reversion, they were 'constant hybrids'. Despite the scepticism of the chief authority, Carl von Gaertner, on this point, Mendel was hopeful that such hybrids did exist in nature and could be produced by experiment. Before he communicated with the eminent authority on the hawkweeds (*Hieracium*), Carl von Naegeli (1817–91), Mendel had decided to explore the behaviour of this genus, aware though he was of the exceeding difficulty of hybridising its species. In 1865 he had argued that just as the contrasting character pairs separate in germ cell formation in the hybrids of *Pisum*, so in other genera this separation might not take place, but instead the contrasted characters remain attached in a lasting union. In such cases 'constant hybrids' would be produced at once which, by virtue of their constancy, would constitute new varieties or species. His experimental test of other so-called constant hybrids proved negative, but the hawkweeds mystified him. Not all members of the first generation of hybrids were the same. This, as Callender has pointed out, was not what he expected. Some of them gave rise to constant forms – a vindication of his hope to discover such forms, and thus to account for the great polymorphism of this genus, the feature about the hawkweeds which had attracted him to them in the first place.

4. THE DISCOVERY OF MENDEL'S WORK

The neglect and 'rediscovery' of Mendel's work has been a subject of much debate. Compared with his fellow-countryman, Christian Doppler (1803–53) who, like Mendel, started his professional life as a teacher, Mendel made very little effort to publicise his work. Those who knew it found it supportive of the belief that hybrid offspring revert to their originating species. His paper on hawkweeds, though better known than his work on the pea, was too brief and inconclusive to have much impact. Within the context of middle-European botany in Mendel's day it is hardly surprising that the remarkable significance of his work was unappreciated.

In 1900 three botanists, Hugo De Vries (1848–1935), Carl Correns (1864–1933) and Erich Tschermak von Seysenegg (1871–1962), claimed to have rediscovered Mendelian ratios and the Mendelian explanation of germinal segregation, and to have gone on to discover Mendel's paper of 1865. Mendelian heredity has thereafter become the most famous example of 'rediscovery' and 'multiple' discovery in science. Attempts to establish these claims on the basis of a thorough reading of the documents have only been made recently.

The results throw doubt on most of the claims made by the three 'rediscoverers'.

First we must ask what constitutes the discovery of Mendelian ratios. Darwin and other nineteenth-century biologists reported data which we can identify with the advantage of hindsight as exemplifying Mendelian ratios. However, when Mendel reported a Mendelian ratio, he perceived that the numbers he gave represented an *approximation* to a specific ratio such as 3:1, and that such a result indicated the operation of a statistical law of some kind. When De Vries reported the numbers 3167 and 1082 for yellow and white maize seeds in 1899 he merely remarked that these maize hybrids were capable 'of reproducing the types of their two parents'.[10] In truth the concept of a Mendelian ratio is not a simple and unadulterated fact, but a theory-laden fact. It is the theoretical component that identifies certain data among a host of results as peculiarly significant.

From the documents available we can be fairly confident that both Correns and Tschermak were aware that the numerical results they recorded had some special significance. Therefore they knew that they had made some sort of discovery. This prompted them to undertake a literature search, the result of which was that they independently discovered Mendel's 1865 paper. Then they realised that they had really rediscovered what Mendel had already found. Very likely Correns had understood how germinal segregation could yield these ratios. The same cannot be said for Tschermak. In the first place he did not have the data showing how the 3:1 ratio was composed of a 1:2:1 ratio until the summer of 1900. In the second place, he treated the numerical predominance (3:1) like the total predominance observed in all F1 individuals and called 'dominance' by Mendel. For Tschermak these were *both* manifestations of the combining power or 'valency' of the two contrasted characters. He appears not to have accepted Mendel's view that F1 dominance and F2 reversion are due to different causes, the latter to the operation of a stochastic process. One would expect that De Vries, being the first to announce the discovery of ratios in 1900 and to offer the explanation in terms of segregation, could claim independence from Mendel. But as Onno Meijer has conclusively shown, there is no evidence to support such a claim other than De Vries's own recollections. Rather, it appears that it was not until he received a reprint of Mendel's paper early in 1900 that he was able for the first time to organise his results on a rational plan based on Mendel's theory.

Augustin Brannigan has argued that scientific discovery is a process of 'social attribution' rather than an intellectual or psychological process.[11] Clearly the public recognition of Mendel's work as a discovery of importance to science was the work of the scientific community, and hence a social process in which the 'rediscovery' in 1900 was the first step. It involved attributing the discovery to Mendel, which was clearly a social act. At the same time Mendel, Correns and

Tschermak seem to have realised by themselves that they had made a discovery of some importance. This was surely a psychological process. Equally the attribution of the status of discovery to Mendel's work on *Pisum* involved experimental work to corroborate it, and intellectual activity to integrate the new results with the old. The recognition of the fundamental importance of Mendel's work was not therefore simply a process of social attribution.

5. HEREDITY IN MAN

It was above all social and political questions which exposed the need for sound knowledge of the nature of hereditary transmission in man. Among those who were concerned about the state of modern urban society were Prosper Lucas (1833–85), Augustin Morel (1809–73) and Francis Galton. Although all three advocated some policy to guide human reproduction, it was Galton who introduced the name *eugenics* in 1883 to refer to the study of the means by which the race of man might be improved.

His starting point was the long-term stability of racial characters. Despite the fact that not all offspring are like their parents, the characteristics of a race are preserved constant over many generations. This must mean that the physiological basis of racial constancy is not what common sense would have us believe. The link connecting parent and offspring is not through their *bodies* but through the elements from which they are formed. He drew the analogy with a necklace, the chain being like the germinal material, the pendants on the chain like the bodies of individuals of successive generations. Equally, we do not inherit all the characters of one parent or grandparent, but some characters from one parent and some from another. Heredity must be due to many independent bearers or particles. To discover the laws of heredity it was necessary to investigate large numbers of related individuals, not just the members of a few families. Whatever these laws might be, they must express the statistical relations between generations.

It is well known that Galton discovered the tendency of offspring on average to be pulled back towards the mean of the population. Exceptional parents had on average less exceptional offspring, yet average parents were here and there throwing out more exceptional offspring and the two effects were balanced thus yielding racial stability. If a population was to evolve, he concluded, it would have to suffer a sudden change which would introduce a new racial mean to which future generations would cling. Galton was thus an advocate of the quantitative study of populations (biometry) and of a saltatory (mutationist) theory of evolution.

Methodologically and conceptually Galton had stepped well beyond the position reached by such authorities as Lucas and Morel, who were the best-known writers on human heredity before him. Unlike them he demanded sufficient data for statistical treatment, and in opposition to them he viewed variation, reversion and inheritance as belonging to the same phenomenon – heredity. Variation did not oppose heredity, as Lucas claimed, but was a feature of it. Degeneration was not, as Morel claimed, due to the effects of environmental pollutants, but to the reproductive pattern of urban societies. For the law of heredity Galton turned to the widely accepted hypothesis of *fractional* heredity, according to which the contribution of each ancestor to the offspring is halved in each generation. Thus the parents contribute between them one half the heritage, the grandparents one quarter, etc. He claimed that the statistical relations which he had found between the generations – the regression coefficients – were in harmony with this fractional or *Ancestral Law* as he called it. Although the first data he used to establish the law concerned a *continuously* varying character (stature), he went on to attempt to establish the same law also for 'alternative' or non-blending characters (eye colour in man and the coat colour of basset hounds). The law, he explained, was expressed in a different way in the two cases. In blending characters the law related to the blend of the differing ancestral expressions of the character in each individual although it still had to do with averages of many individuals. In the case of non-blending characters, it was expressed in the number of individuals which showed exclusively the character of a particular ancestor. This meant that the Ancestral Law was *the* law of heredity.

Galton was thrilled to learn that the cell divisions leading to the formation of the egg involve throwing out half of the germinal material, thus offering a possible material basis to the fractions in his Ancestral Law. Equally the discovery of the ova of the child in the foetal stage reassured him that he had been right to claim that the physiological link between generations was through the reproductive cells and not through the body cells. Galton's success in developing the statistical tools with which to investigate the data of human heredity and his vigorous promotion of eugenics, which included furnishing liberal funds in support of research, resulted in his becoming known as the founder of eugenics, although, as Victor Hilts has described there was a previous tradition of eugenic thought to which the phrenologists, among others, belonged.[12] Galton's notion of hereditary filiation through the 'stirp' was not known outside Britain, and August Weismann's development of the 'continuity of the germ-plasm' in 1889 was independent of him. Unlike Galton, Weismann was deeply immersed in biology, and as a true Darwinian he believed that the evolution of species had been due entirely to natural and what he called 'germinal selection' acting on the abundant variations which were shuffled and distributed by the mixing process of bisexual reproduction.

In Continental Europe the debate over the role of selection and the possibility of the inheritance of acquired characters were major subjects of controversy up until the Second World War. In Britain the selectionists were a small band, but there grew up around Galton a vigorous group of 'hereditarians' which set about demonstrating selection in action. This was the 'biometric' school led by Karl Pearson (1857–1936) and by the hard-working experimental zoologist Raphael Weldon (1860–1906). The climate of opinion concerning the role of selection at this time was also sceptical in Britain, and has been described by Peter Bowler in his book *The Eclipse of Darwinism* (1986). Dissatisfaction with the speculative, descriptive embryology which relied upon the theory of recapitulation was allied to the growing demand for experimental approaches to the questions of evolution. Foremost among such experimentalists was William Bateson (1861–1926). He sought to demonstrate the truth of Samuel Butler's aphorism: 'The origin of species is the origin of varieties', by an investigation of clearly-marked 'discontinuous' variations. He saw in hybridisation an experimental technique for exposing the behaviour of these variations. By 1900 he was convinced that they were the source of new varieties because they persisted when outbred and, having originated in one step, were not dependent upon natural selection to accumulate their divergence from the existing population gradually over many generations. When he read De Vries's French paper on hybrids (which did not mention Mendel), Bateson thought the numerical ratios might represent a modification of Galton's Ancestral Law for non-blending heredity. Only after he had read Mendel's own paper did he realise that here was a new theory which he could deploy very effectively in his fight for experimentalism and in his attack on the biometric school.

The controversy which took place between the biometricians and the Mendelians has been the subject of much discussion. Mackenzie and Barnes claim that empirical, scientific data did not determine the attitudes of the contestants, but rather that socio-political factors were decisive. William Provine emphasised personal animosities, and Bernard Norton, while recognising that the broad cultural milieu throws some light on the debate, concluded that there did not exist clear differences between the social groups to which the contestants belonged, and that differences in fundamental views concerning philosophy and methodology of science were of far greater significance.

It would, in any case, be misleading to assume that the biometric-Mendelian controversy marked the only significant difference of opinion over the nature of heredity in the first decade of this century. Other disagreements were not charged with personal animosity, and were less dependent upon the presence of a few major figures. When Weldon died prematurely in 1906 the controversy over heredity in animals and plants died down, but it continued in the field of human heredity, the disputants being Pearson and C. C. Hurst (1870–1948). Yet opinion was divided over the relative merits of Mendelian, Galtonian and Weismannian heredity. We are apt to assume that because Weismann believed in the presence of reduction division, which was both quantitative and qualitative and because Mendel assumed a process of germinal segregation, that the two theories were complementary. Indeed, this was how Correns viewed them. Others saw the situation differently.

First, it is clear that Weismann assumed the presence of many determinants of one character trait, not just a single pair in each cell. The representation of such determinants in the organism depended upon a process of 'germinal selection' which did not lead to the sort of clear predictions which follow from Mendel's scheme. In his *Lectures on Evolution* (1906), Weismann was not particularly enthusiastic about Mendelian heredity.[13] Authors like J. Arthur Thomson followed Weldon, who had offered a rival explanation of dominance and segregation in terms of the expression or latency of determinants. He argued that just as the recessive character is hidden in F_1, so in F_2 the recessive character is hidden in all the dominant segregates, but expressed in all the recessive segregates, and there has been no segregation of determinants. The reappearance of ancestral characters long lost from the breed could be attributed to the stimulating effect of cross-breeding causing the expression of the latent determinants.

6. GENETICS AS A DISCIPLINE

It was in the course of Bateson's struggle to fund his Mendelian research that he hit upon the term 'genetics'. First in a letter to Adam Sedgwick in 1905, and the following year at the Third Conference on Hybridisation and Plant Breeding in London, he publicised the word, defining it as: 'The elucidation of the phenomena of heredity and variation: in other words, to the physiology of Descent, with implied bearing on the theoretical problems of the evolutionist and systematist, and application to the practical problems of the breeders, whether of animals or plants'.[14] When the conference proceedings were published; genetics was adopted as the alternative title. The subsequent growth of genetics was brought about by a combination of factors. Firstly, there was the undoubted success of the Mendelian theory and method as the basis for a research programme. Then there was the interest of academic agriculturalists who were striving to make their subject genuinely scientific and who found in Mendelian experimentation a fruitful avenue to pursue. Last, but not least, there was a strong interest in the possible social applications of genetics. This eugenic concern was an important stimulus to the support of the subject in its early days, witness the Eugenics Laboratory at University College London (1906), the Balfour Chair of Genetics at Cambridge (1912) and the Eugenics Record Office at Cold Spring Harbor (1906).

In Germany, the subject of heredity remained broad in conception, embryological and physiological aspects being included. Heredity was not to be confined to transmission genetics other aspects being ignored. Clearly *Erblichkeitslehre* was not the same as *genetics*. Whilst the American geneticists, led by

T. H. Morgan, attributed all heredity to the chromosomes in the nucleus, the Germans argued for the importance of determinants in the cytoplasm. They rejected his 'nuclear monopoly', and argued not just for the cytoplasmic determination of the plastids, which are responsible for the colour of foliage, and could be considered a special case, but also for the determination of important specific and generic characters by a structure in the cytoplasm which they called the 'Plasome'. Although Correns became the director of the Kaiser Wilhelm Institut für Biologie in 1913, he did not convert it into a Morgan-style laboratory, for he was himself more interested in non-Mendelian than in Mendelian heredity.

It has been argued persuasively by Jan Sapp and Jonathan Harwood that the historiography of genetics has been constructed in a misleading manner owing to the concentration of studies upon Anglo-American genetics.[15] A broader approach embracing the work of German-speaking scientists reveals a rather different picture. Nor is it true that British genetics was as completely devoted to Mendelian genetics and nuclear transmission as some accounts would suggest. Bateson urged his followers to treasure their exceptions. He devoted much time himself to the study of graft hybrids and to plastid inheritance. Indeed, he does not seem to have been convinced that segregation is a unique event identified with germ cell formation.[16]

It is clear at the same time that British geneticists did not all follow closely the Morgan model. Thus J. S. Huxley was successful in demonstrating the action of 'rate genes' in his study of eye colour in the fresh water shrimp (*Gammarus*) and R. Scott-Moncrieff, continuing earlier studies of the genetics of flower colour by the Bateson school, was able to display the close parallel between genetically distinct strains of snapdragon (*Antirrhinum*) and the chemically distinct organic pigments in their flowers. The mode of gene action in terms of the catalysis of specific biochemical reactions was clear in these early studies.[17]

The literature on the early history of genetics has been adversely affected by the Whiggish tendency to read into the texts the concepts of modern genetics. Thus Mendel's theory was allegedly about the transmission of factors or genes and Mendelian segregation was the segregation of genes. Equally, Mendel was making a contribution to the Darwinian theory of evolution by showing that new characteristics are not diluted and lost in bisexual reproduction. In fact there is now strong evidence that Mendel was not talking about what later became known as genes, and he was not sympathetic to Darwin's views on variation and heredity. Mendel's remarks on transformism, though guarded, would seem to align him with the theological tradition of evolution by species multiplication from a limited set of created stocks as held by Linnaeus and by William Herbert, Dean of Manchester. On the other hand, there is no doubt that Mendel's conception of heredity was revolutionary. Weismann and Galton had sought to distance themselves from *personal* notions of inheritance as discernable in the body of the individual, but they did not abandon the assumption that the germinal matter contains determinants representative of each individual. Admittedly these determinants were subject to repeated fractionation until in subsequent generations they became mere traces. Even then it was possible for long-forgotten ancestral traits to reappear. Hence the establishment of purity of type ought to be a long and difficult task, rather than an often rapid process as the Mendelian theory predicted. The establishment of genetics on the basis of Mendelian heredity therefore marks a clear discontinuity in the history of hereditary theory and practice.

Another tendency which has produced misleading accounts of the establishment of genetics is that of placing so much emphasis on the Biometric-Mendelian debate. Quite apart from this controversy, Mendelian heredity was not at once seen as the model for all hereditary phenomena, even by its supporters. Nor was Bateson alone in his scepticism towards chromosomes. As Scott Gilbert has shown, it was research and debate over the determination of sex which led to the resolution of uncertainties about the relation between chromosomes and genes, and which set ground rules in the United States for the demarcation of genetics from embryology.[17]

NOTES

1. J. Arthur Thomson, *Heredity* (London, 1908), p. 5; see also: W. Johannsen, 'The genotype conception of heredity', *American naturalist*, 45 (1911), 129–59.
2. S. A. Roe, *Matter, life and generation: eighteenth century embryology and the Haller-Wolff debate* (Cambridge, 1981).
3. R. S. Cowan, 'Nature and nurture in the work of Francis Galton', *Studies in history of biology*, 1 (1977), 133–208.
4. Hugo De Vries, *Intracellular pangenesis*, translated by Stuart Gager (Chicago, 1910), pp. 63–6.
5. N. Russell, *Like engend'ring like, heredity and animal breeding in early modern England* (Cambridge, 1986).
6. C. Linnaeus, 'Disquisitio de sexu plantarum, . . .' *Amoenitates Academicae*, 10 (1790), pp. 127–8.
7. W. Herbert, *Amaryllidaceae; . . . followed by a treatise on cross-bred vegetables* (London, 1837), pp. 17–18, 335–80.
8. E. Mayr, 'Darwin and the evolutionary theory in biology' in: *Evolution and anthropology: a centennial appraisal* (New York, 1959) pp. 409–12, reprinted in: E. Mayr, *Evolution and the diversity of life, selected essays* (Cambridge, Mass., 1976), pp. 26–9.
9. L. A. Callender, 'Gregor Mendel – an opponent of descent with modification', *History of science*, 26 (1988), 41–75, and R. Olby, *Origins of Mendelism*, 2nd. ed. (Chicago, 1985), pp. 259–99.
10. Hugo De Vries, 'Sur la fécondation hybride de l'albumen', *Comptes rendus hebdomadaire de l'Académie des sciences*, 129 (1899), 973.
11. A. Brannigan, *The social basis of scientific discovery* (Cambridge, 1981) chap. vi.
12. V. L. Hilts, 'Obeying the laws of hereditary descent: phrenological views on inheritance and eugenics', *Journal of the history of the behavioral sciences*, 18 (1982), 62–77.
13. A. Weismann, *Lectures on evolution*, translated by J. A. and M. R. Thomson (2 vols., London, 1906), vol. i, pp. 56–8.
14. W. Bateson, 'Inaugural Address', *Proceedings of the third conference on hybridization and plant breeding* (London, 1906), p. 91.
15. J. Sapp, *Beyond the gene: cytoplasmic inheritance and the struggle for authority in genetics* (New York, 1987). J. Harwood, 'The reception of Morgan's chromosome theory in Germany: inter-war debates over cytoplasmic inheritance', *Medizinhistorisches Journal*, 19 (1984), 189–232.

16. See L. Doncaster, *An introduction to the study of cytology* (Cambridge, 1920), p. 219.
17. R. Scott-Moncrieff, 'The classical period in chemical genetics', *Notes and records of the Royal Society*, 36 (1981), 125–54.
18. Scott F. Gilbert, 'The embryological origins of the gene theory', *Journal of the history of biology*, 11 (1978), 307–51.

FURTHER READING

A. Baxter and J. Farley, 'Mendel and meiosis', *Journal of the history of biology*, 12 (1979), 137–73.

F. Churchill, 'Hertwig, Weismann and the meaning of reduction division circa 1890', *Isis*, 61 (1970), 429–57.

A. G. Cock, 'William Bateson's rejection and eventual acceptance of chromosome theory', *Annals of science*, 40 (1983), 19–59.

W. Coleman, 'Bateson and chromosomes: conservative thought in science', *Centaurus*, 15 (1970), 228–314.

A. W. F. Edwards, 'Are Mendel's results really too close?', *Biological review*, 61 (1986), 295–312.

A. E. Gaissinovitch, 'The origins of Soviet genetics and the struggle with Lamarckism, 1922–1929', *Journal of the history of biology*, 13 (1980), 1–51.

D. Kevles, 'Genetics in the United States and Great Britain 1890–1930: a review with speculations', *Isis*, 71 (1980), 441–55.

B. A. Kimmelman, 'The American Breeders' Association: genetics and eugenics in an agricultural context, 1903–13', *Social studies of science*, 13 (1983), 163–204.

R. de Marrais, 'The double-edged effect of Sir Francis Galton: a search for the motives in the biometrician-Mendelian debate', *Journal of the history of biology*, 7 (1974), 141–74.

O. G. Meijer, 'De Vries no Mendelian', *Annals of science*, 42 (1985), 189–232.

R. Olby, 'William Bateson's introduction of Mendelism to England: a reassessment', *British journal of the history of science*, 20 (1987), 399–420.

V. Orel, *Mendel* (Past Masters) (London, 1984).

D. B. Paul and B. A. Kimmelman, 'Mendel in America: theory and practice, 1900–1919', in R. Rainger, K. R. Benson and J. Maienschein (eds.), *The American development of biology* (Philadelphia, 1988), pp. 281–310.

W. W. Piegorsch, 'The Gregor Mendel controversy. Early issues of goodness of fit and recent issues of genetics', *History of science*, 24 (1986), 173–82.

G. Robinson, *A prelude to genetics* (Lawrence, Kansas, 1979).

C. Rosenberg, 'The special environment of scientific innovation: factors in the development of genetics in the United States', in C. Rosenberg, *No other gods: on science and American social thought* (Baltimore, 1976), pp. 196–209.

F. Weiling, 'Die wissenschaftliche Tätigkeit J. G. Mendels und ihr Milieu sowei der Niederschlag seiner wissenschaftlichen Intentionen und Arbeit in Bonner Bibliotheken', *Decheniana*, 126 (1974), 1–68.

34

CYBERNETICS AND INFORMATION TECHNOLOGY

MICHAEL S. MAHONEY

Since the Second World War, 'information' has emerged as a fundamental scientific and technological concept applied to phenomena ranging from black holes to DNA, from the organisation of cells to the processes of human thought and from the management of corporations to the allocation of global resources. In addition to reshaping established disciplines, it has stimulated the formation of a panoply of new subjects and areas of inquiry concerned with its structure and its role in nature and society. Embodied in the computer, theories based on the concept of 'information' have so permeated modern culture that it is now widely taken to characterise our times. We live in an 'information society', an 'age of information'.

Current awareness of the fundamental nature of information and of its determinative role in modern life makes it difficult to unravel the threads of its history, especially when following them back to a time when 'information' had only common meaning. One may speak today of the printing press, typewriter, telegraph or telephone as 'information machines', but that is not how they were originally conceived, and including them in the history of information risks losing sight of the time and place at which the concept itself emerged and of the process by which it came to shape modern thought and even self-consciousness.

Information in the modern technical sense emerged from a complex of activities which, underway just before the Second World War, gained impetus from wartime research and culminated in 1948 with the appearance of Norbert Wiener's *Cybernetics: or Control and Communication in the Animal and the Machine* (1948) and Claude E. Shannon's *The Mathematical Theory of Communication* (1948). Although neither work encompassed the full variety of current research related to it, both provided initial points of reference for organising and directing subsequent investigation. In addition, Wiener's cybernetics and Shannon's 'information theory' (as it was commonly called, despite his disapproval) attracted the attention of scholars in other fields, who sought to apply or adapt these new concepts and methods to their own concerns.

1. CYBERNETICS AND INFORMATION THEORY

Wiener used the term 'cybernetics' to characterise the common elements of his work with Vannevar Bush on computing machines, with Yuk Wing Lee on electrical networks, with Julian Bigelow on the prediction of flight paths and with Arturo M. Rosenblueth and Walter Pitts on neuromuscular behaviour and neuro-physiology.[1] Fundamentally, Wiener concluded that control in both mechanical and biological systems depends on feedback, which in turn requires communication of information within the system. Secondly, 'the ultra-rapid computing machine, depending as it does on consecutive switching devices, must represent an ideal model of the problems arising in the nervous system' and conversely 'was in principle an ideal central nervous system to an apparatus for automatic control'.[2]

The intimate link between control and communications shifted attention from the specifics of electrical engineering to the more general notion of the message, however transmitted. Viewed as time series, messages become predictable through statistical analysis and prediction can be optimised by means of the calculus of variations. Messages transmitted over physical channels are subject to distortion by background noise and hence raise the problem of their accurate reconstruction. Consideration of that problem led Wiener to the question of the measure of information and through it to the relation of information and entropy, by which he arrived again at the living organism.

The nature of information linked Wiener's work to Shannon's, whose paper had the more narrowly defined goal of defining the capacity of a communications channel, of determining 'the effect of statistical knowledge about the source in reducing the required capacity of the channel, by the use of proper encoding of the information' and of setting the limits of possibility of correctly construing a message transmitted in the presence of noise.[3] Starting from the principle that information resolves uncertainty, Shannon measured information with reference to the number of possible messages that could be sent in a given time using a given set of symbols. The precise form of measure being arbitrary, Shannon chose as the unit of information for discrete channels the single binary digit or 'bit' (coined by John Tukey of Bell Labs.) A set of n symbols s_i, each with a corresponding probability p_i, has the informational content of $H = -\Sigma p_i \log_2(p_i)$ bits; if the symbols are equiprobable, the measure reduces to $H = \log_2 n$, which is the maximum. More usual are messages in which the different p_i depend on previous sequences (Markov processes) and in which the distributions in randomly chosen messages of sufficient length are representative of distributions over all messages (ergodic processes).

Viewed as a measure of uncertainty or surprise, information can be construed as a form of entropy and Shannon chose his function with Boltzmann's H theorem in mind. By increasing the uncertainty about the source of signals and hence about the message being transmitted, noise adds to the entropy of a channel, detracting from its useful capacity. However, as Shannon showed, given sufficient capacity, the entropy of noise can be overcome to an arbitrary degree by a suitable encoding of the message, which in essence lowers the entropy of the source through redundancy. That one pays for certainty at the cost of information places a premium on efficiency of coding, a subject which, already under investigation at the time, gained new impetus from Shannon's results.[4]

Tied to systems of communications and thus to the problem of selecting the correct message from a range of possible ones, Shannon's measure of information did not meet the needs of others seeking to quantify 'constructive' information, for example Donald McKay and Dennis Gabor.[5] Nonetheless, it soon became a touchstone for work in a range of fields. Léon Brillouin's analysis in depth of the relation of entropy and information led in the mid-1950s to the formulation of statistical thermodynamics as a branch of information theory. Joining Shannon's theory with John von Neumann's research on automata and the construction of reliable organisms from unreliable components, Samuel Winograd and Jack D. Cowan established the principles of reliable computation in the presence of noise (1963). Other applications were less successful. Enthusiasm among biologists in the 1950s for applying Shannon's results to genetic information waned in the 1960s, largely owing to equivocal use of the term 'information' itself. Similar overextensions of the theory led to a certain disenchantment with it by the late 1960s. Nonetheless, Shannon's work remained fundamental to the theory of coding and hence made its continuing presence felt not only in communications research but also in computer science.

Cybernetics followed a similar pattern of enthusiastic reception followed by overextension and disenchantment. By the late 1960s the term itself gradually disappeared from use in the United States and Western Europe, although it is still common in the Eastern bloc. Yet, the themes and approaches it encompassed have continued to develop since then, pursued separately in the disciplines Wiener sought to bring together and in new disciplines spawned from them.[6] Both the fate of cybernetics and its effect on other subjects are perhaps best understood by examining more closely the technological context in which it arose.

As Wiener himself emphasised, in both conception and implementation, cybernetics was intimately tied to the new forms of automatic computation developing rapidly during the decade from the late 1930s to the late 1940s. In addition to providing a tool for solving the problems in applied mathematics that Wiener's methods entailed, it served as his model of the nervous system. The design of computers in turn posed problems of a cybernetic nature and hence constituted a field of application for his methods, as it did for Shannon's. Yet, the computer had its own intellectual and technical roots, which determined its development independently of its role in cybernetics and which thereby conditioned that role. Especially for those who viewed cybernetics in the wider sense of systems theory, the computer ultimately offered resources that far exceeded Wiener's vision or even contradicted it.

In particular, the computer both accommodated and encouraged a broader view of 'information', and of how it can be transformed and communicated over time and space, than that which underlay the new theory. It thereby transformed traditional methods of accounting and record-keeping into a new industry of data processing, posing both unprecedented possibilities and unanticipated dangers. Since the 1950s the computer, both as processor of information and as vehicle of communication over both space and time, has come to form the core of modern information technology. What the English-speaking world refers to as computer science is known to the rest of Western Europe as *informatique* (or *Informatik* or *informática*). Much of the concern over information as a commodity and as a natural resource derives from the computer and from computer-based communications technology.[7] Hence, the history of the computer and of computing is central to that of information science and technology, providing a thread by which to maintain bearing while exploring the ever-growing maze of disciplines and subdisciplines that claim information as their subject.

2. COMPUTERS AND COMPUTING

The computer itself is the product of two lines of historical development corresponding roughly to the distinction between the physical machine, or *hardware*, and the programs or *software*, that guide its operation. As a physical device, the first all-electronic calculator, ENIAC, crowned longstanding efforts to automate large-scale computation and tabulation. As logic machines, the first stored-program computers, EDSAC and EDVAC, emerged as by-products of theoretical inquiry into the nature and limits of logical thought, in particular as a foundation for mathematics.

2.1. The electronic calculator

The mechanisation of computation began in the late Middle Ages with the invention of such analog devices as mechanical clocks, planetaria and related automata. The first digital mechanisms appeared in the seventeenth century. The machines of Wilhelm Schickard (1623) and Blaise Pascal (the 'Pascaline', 1654) used geared wheels to perform addition and substraction automatically upon entering the terms. While Schickard retained logarithmically scaled rods ('Napier's Bones') for multiplication and division, Gottfried Wilhelm Leibniz devised a shifting mechanism for translating those operations into repeated addition and subtraction (1672). Legend would have it that these machines responded to computational needs; one hears, for example, of Pascal seeking to ease his father's job as tax collector. Yet, in practice, none operated at the speed of a skilled human reckoner. Rather, they were viewed as objects of wonder in their capacities as automata to emulate not physical actions, but the highest form of rational thought.

Only in the early nineteenth century did the computational needs of science, especially the new fields of thermodynamics and electricity and magnetism, together with their applications to industry, begin to stimulate a steady development of practical devices of increasing power. The hand-driven mechanical calculator reached its final configuration, while new designs appeared in the form of the 'difference engine', the planimeter and the harmonic analyser. The first of these, invented in 1823 by Charles Babbage to automate the calculation of mathematical and astronomical tables and subsequently improved by Georg Scheutz and others, reflected the recent development of the calculus of finite differences and approached the limits of digital computation by mechanical linkage, thus encouraging a turn to analog devices. Various planimeters (J. H. Hermann (1814), Jacob Amsler (1854), Clerk Maxwell (1855), J. Thompson (1876)) translated the integration of curves into continuous compound mechanical action, while the harmonic analyser (Kelvin (1873), Michelson and Stratton (1898)) linked the integrators to model the solution of differential equations via Fourier series.

By the middle of the nineteenth century, new commercial and industrial organisations, especially those that conveyed the increasing output of new forms of production to an ever-widening consumerate, enhanced the demand for improved accounting machines while adding to it the need for new means of mechanical record-keeping and tabulation of data. Governments, too, added to the demand as industrialisation placed new responsibilities on them in the realms of finance, regulation, public health and social services and thus multiplied both the volume and the importance of social statistics. In the United States, where apportionment of congressional representation rests on a decennial census, it was clear by the late 1880s that without automatic tabulation the count for 1890 could not be completed before the year 1900. Herman Hollerith's electrically activated punched-card tabulating machine (1894) responded directly to that need and became the basis for a new industry.

While responding to immediate needs, some inventors looked beyond them to longer-range possibilities, thus focusing attention on the nature of computation itself. Foremost among them was Charles Babbage. Before completing the construction of his Difference Engine, he became absorbed in overcoming its limitation to executing only a single compound calculation at a time, the form of which is built into the machine, and in 1834 conceived an 'Analytical Engine' which would automatically carry out a variety of operations in response to a sequence of commands. His design, modelled in part after Jacquard's loom and in part after the maze of gears and shafts that was the early English factory, was a microcosm of the Industrial Revolution: values placed in 'storage' moved in and out of an arithmetical 'mill' performing operations recorded on punched cards. Since its mechanical form dictated that power varied with size, Babbage looked beyond hand-driven models to the driving force of steam. Except for a few sub-units, the engine never went beyond the stage of intricate drawings and was soon all but forgotten. Its structure probably exceeded the capabilities of machine technology and would in any case have been too slow to be useful. It did, however, provoke the first effort to specify the nature of the operations involved in instructing a machine and thereby earned Ada, Countess Lovelace the reputation of the world's first programmer.

The distribution of electrical power and telephone service in the early twentieth century posed new computational problems, while providing new models for their solution. The design of electric power grids entailed the solution of large systems of simultaneous equations, both finite and differential. Here analog devices taking increased advantage of electrical technology continued to lead the field. A 'product integraph' developed at MIT under the guidance of Vannevar Bush (1927) integrated expressions of the form $f_1(x)f_2(x)dx$ by mechanical analog multiplication followed by integration via electric meter and mechanical rotation. Bush's differential analyser (1931) reversed that action, adding the output of electronic torque amplifiers to multiply via integration, i.e. $uv = \int u\,dv + \int v\,du$.

Telephone switching systems involved increasingly complex configurations of electrical relays opening and closing circuits in response to input from users, a process which was soon recognised as itself a form of computation. The logical analysis of such systems (in particular by Shannon at MIT in the late 1930s) suggested the linking of relays to model binary arithmetic. A simple adder circuit designed by George Stibitz at Bell Telephone Laboratories in 1937 soon led to a relay device capable of handling complex numbers (Model I, 1939); reached in New York via telegraph lines from Hanover, New Hampshire, it also provided the first demonstration of remote computation in 1940. During the same period, Howard Aiken at Harvard, with the support of IBM, began the construction of a general-purpose electromechanical computer, the Mark I (1943).

While electrical relays made binary computation practical, the remaining mechanical components placed a physical limit on the speed of computation.

Even as the relay machines were being designed, they stimulated experiments with circuits using electronic tubes instead of relays. J. V. Atanasoff constructed a small device at the University of Iowa (1939–40). Under circumstances still not entirely clarified, Atanasoff's work came to the attention of John Mauchly soon before he moved from Ursinus College to the Moore School of Engineering at the University of Pennsylvania to take charge of a Bush differential analyser then being pressed into national service for the computation of firing tables for the United States Army's Ballistic Research Laboratory. With the support of Herman Goldstine, the Army's technical liaison to the project, Mauchly and his colleague J. Presper Eckert gained approval in 1943 for the development of the first all-electronic computer, the Electronic Numerical Integrator and Automatic Calculator (ENIAC), which came on line in 1946.[8]

Using some 18,000 vacuum tubes in a circuit design that seemed to defy the inherent probability of failure, ENIAC retained in its design some of its origins in mechanical calculation. It did arithmetic decimally, using ring counters and storing intermediate results in accumulators consisting of banks of such counters. Fixed data (constants) were held in function tables set manually by switches and, in a manner similar to computation using electrical accounting machinery, the computer followed a fixed program set up manually by setting switches and connecting wires. Nonetheless, operating at a speed of some 5000 ten-digit additions a second, it marked the advent of modern high-speed computing and served as prototype for all hardware to follow.

2.2. The stored-program computer

As progress on ENIAC demonstrated the feasibility of large-scale electronic calculation, thought turned to internalising its programs by enabling it to modify its instructions in response to the results it was generating. Again, the precise details have not been resolved, but it seems clear that John von Neumann played a major role in laying out the logical structure of the stored-program computer. In addition to his own ideas on automata, he brought to the task an understanding of the work of Alan Turing, whose article, 'On Computable Numbers, with an Application to the *Entscheidungsproblem*', defined the abstract structure of machines capable of logical calculation and who was himself at work designing one of England's earliest computers, the Pilot ACE.[9]

Turing's theoretical work belonged to a quite different line of scientific development from that of mechanical calculators, yet one that also stemmed from the early nineteenth century, with roots reaching back initially to the seventeenth. In addition to designing the earliest four-operation calculator, Leibniz also explored binary arithmetic and discussed the idea of a symbolic logical calculus.[10] But these ideas remained separate in his mind and undeveloped in his works. Not until the nineteenth century did they again emerge as sustained themes of mathematical inquiry, first in the efforts of George Boole to develop an algebra of logic that might serve as a vehicle for the 'laws of thought'. His study of the theory of operators led him to the notion of classes as operators on sets of objects and then to an algebra of those classes. For example, if C is a deck of cards, one may take x as an operator selecting the hearts from the deck, y as one selecting the diamonds and z as one selecting face cards. Then $xC + yC = (x + y)C$ selects all red cards and $z(x + y)C$, all red face cards. Clearly, $x^2(C) = x(x(C)) = x(C)$. Moreover, if $C-xC = (1-x)C$ designates all non-hearts, then $x+(1-x) = 1$, and $x(1-x) = x-x^2 = x - x = 0$ and so on. Since the criterion of selection in each case is binary, Boole's classes correspond to logical functions and their relations to an algebra of logic.

Given the cultural presence of machinery in the nineteenth century, it is not surprising that efforts to mathematise or quantify the rules of logic should issue in the design of logic machines such as those of James Jevons in England and Allan Marquand in the United States. Marquand's friend Charles S. Peirce even suggested replacing the rods and strings of the machine with electrical circuits. But the devices served no practical purposes and remained at best aids to understanding the structure of logical reasoning.

In the late nineteenth century attention shifted from the mathematics of logic to the logical foundations of mathematics, as new fields like non-Euclidean geometry, vector algebra and abstract finite algebras undermined reliance on intuition and spurred a drive toward rigorous formalisation. In that context, Gottlob Frege attempted a reduction of arithmetic to logic (*Grundlagen der Arithmetik*, 1884) and produced instead the first of the antinomies (Russell's paradox) that soon cast the consistency of logic itself in doubt; an equally troubling paradox issued from the work of Georg Cantor and Cesare Burali-Forti on transfinite numbers (1895–7). David Hilbert's famous Program of 1900 included in its agenda for mathematics a formalisation of the subject capable of resolving what he later (*Grundzüge der theoretischen Logik*, 1928, with W. Ackerman) termed the *Entscheidungsproblem*: is there a general procedure for deciding whether a statement of a given axiom system has a proof in that system? Bertrand Russell's and Alfred North Whitehead's *Principia mathematica* (1910) unintentionally emphasised the centrality of the problem when Kurt Gödel ('On formally undecidable propositions in *Principia mathematica*', 1931) showed that any logic powerful enough to generate arithmetic had to be either incomplete – that is, include formally undecidable propositions – or inconsistent.

Gödel's proof employed the technique of assigning numbers to the statements of a system and then couching the proof of a proposition from the axioms in terms of an effective procedure for computing the proposition's number from those of the axioms. Decidability came down to computability. Turing's paper of 1936 gave a precise definition to the notion of an effective computational procedure by expressing it as an abstract finite-state machine consisting of a potentially infinite tape divided into cells and passing under a device capable of reading from a cell, or writing to it, one of a finite set of symbols and of moving right or left to the neighbouring cell. The machine carried out an effective procedure by passing through a finite set of states in a finite number of steps from an initial configuration of symbols on the tape to a desired final configuration. Each state could be characterised as a vector containing the symbol in the current cell, the action to be taken and the state to follow; a vector of the state vectors then characterised the procedure and thus the machine itself.

On the basis of this definition, Turing showed that there exist numbers which are definable but not computable. Moreover, since by a suitable convention the last vector could be translated into a configuration of symbols on the tape, Turing machines themselves were subject to computation by Turing machines. On that basis, Turing proved that 'there can be no general process for determining whether a given formula [A] of the [restricted Hilbert] functional calculus K is provable, *i.e.* that there can be no machine which, supplied with any one [A] of these formulae, will eventually say whether [A] is provable'.[11]

Turing set out as the most general form of his machine a universal procedure for reading the description of any Turing machine at the beginning of a tape and then instantiating it for the configuration on the remainder of the tape. That universal machine contained the germ of the stored-program computer, for it meant that the same tape could contain both instructions and data, interpreted as one or the other in accordance with the state of the scanning head. In essence, the computer replaced the tape by an addressable memory holding sequences of binary digits and the read-write head by separate arithmetical and control units, the former of which operates on those sequences and the latter of which interprets them as instructions. Treated as data, instructions can be modified in the course of computation; more importantly a set of instructions can be self-modifying in response to the results it is generating.

The original ENIAC group had taken some steps toward the internal storage of its instructions when von Neumann joined their efforts, but the fundamental logical structure of a stored-program device emphasised in his 'First draft of a report on the EDVAC' (1945) appears to have stemmed from him. With that report and the 'Preliminary Discussion of the Logical Design of an Electronic Computing Instrument' composed together with Arthur Burks and Herman Goldstine in 1946, the electronic digital computer assumed its basic form. Cambridge University's EDSAC, under the direction of Maurice Wilkes, first realised that form in a working machine in 1949. Eckert and Mauchly's BINAC soon followed in the United States.

3. THE COMPUTER INDUSTRY

Viewed before the war as an esoteric device of unproved value, the electronic computer was born of extensive government funding in response to specific military needs. In the immediate post-war years also, even after ENIAC had demonstrated the feasibility of the computer and its importance to scientific research, further development still depended on government funding, either by direct subvention or through contracts for the development of specific machines. Although Ferranti Ltd joined with the University of Manchester in 1949 to develop a commercial version of its prototype Mark I, it was not until 1950, as the first stored-program computers went into operation, that major corporations in the United States began to take an interest in them as potential products. Remington Rand acquired Engineering Research Associates and the Eckert and Mauchly Company, then building the famous Univac, and was in turn acquired by Sperry. IBM, which in 1948 had built the (partially electro-mechanical) Selective Sequence Electronic Computer as a single showpiece for its world headquarters, entered the market only in response to Univac's threat to its line of electrical accounting machinery. Its first commercial machines, the 701 and 704 appeared in 1953, followed a year later by the popular 650 with its magnetic drum storage.

The first trickle of commercial machines soon became a flood. By 1965, customers in the United States could choose among more than 100 models offered by over twenty manufacturers; an additional 100 models were available from over 25 companies world-wide. The advent of the minicomputer around 1970, and of the microcomputer a decade later, brought similar spurts of growth to the industry. Side by side with the manufacture of the devices themselves emerged a new data-processing industry, which by 1970 accounted for some 2 per cent of the gross national product of the United States.

The commercialisation of the computer shaped its development both as a scientific and technical device and as the focus of an emerging professional discipline with its attendant institutions. Conceived for scientific purposes and born of military needs, the device initially responded to no immediate demand from the world outside science and engineering. Few, if any, of IBM's customers clamoured for electronic versions of their electrical and electromechanical accounting equipment. Rather, that demand had to be created by devising applications for the computer in the realms of finance, management and communications. Those applications and the machines needed to implement them meant keeping pace with scientific and technological development, which in turn meant closer and more open ties between industrial research institutions and the rapidly expanding scientific community in the universities and at now-permanent government installations. Dependent in turn on the computer industry for funding and for technical support, academic computer science took

546

shape partly in response to corporately defined research needs. From the outset, the careers of computer people show a characteristic pattern of regular and easy movement between campus, industry and government facilities.

3.1. Computer science

From about 1950 onwards, computing gradually assumed a shape and place of its own among the disciplines of science and engineering. In 1954, the seven-year-old Association for Computing Machinery (ACM) announced in the first number of its *Journal* that it would henceforth leave questions of hardware to the American Institute of Electrical Engineering and the Institute of Radio Engineers and direct its efforts instead to 'the other phases of computing systems, such as numerical analysis, logical design, application and use and, last but not least, to programming'. Far from last or least, programming soon emerged as a body of concepts and techniques distinct from the architectures of particular machines, as its practitioners identified the algorithms, data structures, search and sort routines on which programs rest. *Preparation of Programs for an Electronic Digital Computer* (1951) by Maurice Wilkes, D. J. Wheeler and Stanley Gill marks perhaps the beginning of that line of development, while Donald E. Knuth's *The Art of Computer Programming* (1969) represents a major stage of consolidation.

In the early 1960s the ACM followed the National Academy of Sciences and the Mathematical Association of America in recognising 'computer science' as a distinct field of study 'embracing such topics as numerical analysis, theory of programming, theory of automata, switching theory, etc.' and undertook, with considerable discussion, to define a suitable curriculum at graduate and undergraduate levels. Soon after, in 1967, recurrent difficulties encountered by large-scale programming projects prompted the NATO Science Committee to set up a study group on computer science, which in turn urged the establishment of a discipline of 'software engineering', which would base the manufacture of software 'on the types of theoretical foundations and practical disciplines that are traditional in the established branches of engineering'. With professionalisation and ramification into sub-disciplines came a panoply of new organisations and publications. By 1970 some 400 journals strove to meet the informational needs of several hundred thousand computer scientists and data-processing professionals.

The intellectual origins of the computer combined neatly with the exigencies of its commercialisation in directing much of the research agenda during the next decades. Making the computer accessible to users from a wide range of backgrounds was essential both to exploring its theoretical potential and to marketing it. Computer scientists and business users had a common stake in the development of programming languages, of operating systems and of applications to non-numerical data.

3.1.1. Programming languages

Essential both to Turing's theory of computing machines and to von Neumann's theory of self-reproducing automata was the notion of the self-programming computer. The stored program realised that notion to the extent of enabling the computer to modify its instructions and thus control the flow of computation in response to the results being generated. But those instructions initially had to be specified in excruciating detail using the machine's own language of sequences of binary digits, or 'bits'. 'Automatic programming' aimed at bringing the language of specification closer to human usage and at automating such standard tasks as allocation of memory, calling sequences for subroutines, assembly of subroutines from libraries, input/output protocols and loading formats.

The first 'assemblers' in the early 1950s gave rise to a 'Tower of Babel' of programming languages by the late 1960s and then to a measure of standardisation in the 1970s. The major achievements include FORTRAN (Backus, 1956), LISP (McCarthy, 1958), COBOL (Hopper, 1959), APL (Iverson, 1962), BASIC (Kemeny and Kurtz, 1965) and the succession of ALGOLs (international committees, 1958, 1960, 1968) capped by PASCAL (Wirth, 1971). The first report on ALGOL in 1959 set the standard for specifying the syntax of languages with John Backus's Normal Form (BNF), later modified by Peter Naur (whence 'Backus Naur Form'). That technique and others drawn from ongoing research in automata theory and mathematical linguistics, especially the work of Noam Chomsky, placed the design of languages and, to some extent, their compilers on theoretical foundations independent of any particular machine and hence made the languages themselves portable between different machines.

At the same time most of these languages remained tied through their primitive terms (integers, real numbers, characters and arrays) to the basic architecture of the computer. During the 1970s emphasis began to shift to languages which included a wider and more flexible range of data structures and objects – including programs – and which focused on the objects of computation and relations between them rather than on procedures. That development, in particular FORTH (Moore, 1969), C (Ritchie, 1972), Small Talk (Kay, 1972–80), ADA (Ichbiah, 1978) and MIT's LISP machine, aimed at embedding languages in a programming environment and reflected both the concomitant development of operating systems and the recent advent of powerful small computers.

3.1.2. Operating systems

Suitably programmed, the computer also had the capacity to oversee its own efficient operation. The high cost of computers spurred efforts to minimise the time during which the processor stood idle, either between jobs or during transfers of data (I/O for 'input/output') to and from much slower peripheral devices. Operating systems began in the early 1950s with simple monitor programs to schedule and set up jobs handled sequentially. Between 1955 and 1964, more elaborate multiprogramming systems supervised several programs at once, switching them in and out of the main processor as they waited for I/O; new multiprocessing systems allocated the work of programs over several processors. Beginning in 1962 'timesharing' systems adapted the notion of multiplexing to enable several users to share the resources of a single computer and to use the device interactively. In the United States these systems derived in part from the earlier development of the SAGE air defence system (1951–8) and SABRE airline reservation system (1963), both of which monitored transactions from many users working simultaneously, and served as prototypes for later real-time process control systems.[12]

Operating systems entered a new phase of development in 1964 with IBM's OS/360, designed to provide users with a common interface over a range of different machines and hence with generically defined systems services. Subsequent versions embodied the notion of the 'virtual machine', which presented each of many users with the image of an independent machine with its own operating system and permitted different users to use different systems. UNIX, introduced by Bell Labs in 1976, offered a highly interactive, multi-user environment linked by single file system. Operating systems perhaps reached the peak of their size and complexity in the late 1970s, as subsequent development, sparked by the advent of minicomputers and microcomputers, focused attention on the sharing of information and services between computers distributed over a network.

3.1.3. Software and its problems

Operating systems constituted only one sort of sophisticated, large-scale programming project undertaken in the 1960s. Others included, in addition to SAGE and SABRE, air-traffic control systems, large databases for government and industry, electronic switching systems for communications networks and control and communications systems for the United States's space programme. While many remarkable achievements issued from such projects, they also encountered difficulties that caused growing concern among practitioners about the industry's capacity to produce reliable software on time and at reasonable cost. By 1969, leaders in the field were speaking of a 'software crisis' and urging that software be placed on a more scientific footing. One response was the concept of 'structured programming'. Introduced by Edsger Dijkstra in 1969 and developed further by C.A.R. Hoare in England and Niklaus Wirth in Switzerland and the United States, it aimed at a discipline of programming supported by appropriate languages and under-pinned by methods of theoretical verification (as opposed to empirical debugging). However, the movement encountered resistance among data processing workers. Despite the growing effort of software engineering during the 1970s software continued to resist efforts to automate its production and to establish standards of productivity and reliability.

3.2. Miniaturisation

The problems of software loomed even larger by contrast to the rapid development of hardware over the same period. During the 1950s the limitations of hardware both shaped and hindered the design of software. Assemblers and compilers require large memories to hold the intermediate tables and files they create in translating source code. So too do operating systems, which must remain resident (at least in part) while monitoring programs and responding to requests for system support. The more sophisticated the compiler or operating system, the greater the demand for memory and processor speed. Hence many of the developments in software depended on a series of revolutionary developments in electronics that produced order-of-magnitude increases in the speed and internal capacity of computers while reducing their cost and external dimensions to the same degree. As computer designers in the late 1940s looked to mercury delay lines, cathode ray tubes and diodes to reduce the number of vacuum tubes, researchers at Bell Laboratories assembled the first transistor (Brattain, Bardeen and Schockley, 1947–9). By the late 1950s, as transistor based computers were coming on the market, offering more computing power in less space for less money, experiments got underway with the first integrated circuits (Kilby, 1958; Noyce, 1959) which in turn made their commercial appearance in IBM's System 360 in 1964. Thereafter, the combination of miniaturisation and large-scale integration, spurred and supported by military research and the space program, produced a succession of ever more powerful chips, which by the late 1970s were capable of holding an entire central processing unit, thereby giving rise not only to supercomputers capable of carrying out 80–250 million operations per second but to the microcomputer and to the creation in the 1980s of a consumer market for computers and a return to the single-user system.

4. FROM CYBERNETICS TO COMPUTATION: ARTIFICIAL INTELLIGENCE

The increasing power and accessibility of computers ironically reinforced the autonomous tendencies of fields Wiener had envisioned united by cybernetics. By making feasible techniques like linear programming using George Dantzig's simplex method (1947), computers directed such fields as operations research and management science away from traditional applied mathematics and toward new methods of modelling and simulation using discrete mathematics, thus triggering new developments in that area while appropriating a major segment of Wiener's agenda. Interactively adapting to the computer, each discipline designed applications that best suited its own needs and in turn shaped its research to take advantage of what the device could do.

That turned out to be particulary true for the agenda perhaps closest to Wiener's heart: the computer as a model of the human nervous system and hence of human thought. Here, cybernetics' initially suggestive concepts of negative feedback, pattern recognition and stochastic learning proved unfruitful, as did efforts to emulate human perception by modelling neural structures.[13] Yet, by suggesting and supporting a representational approach to the meaning of 'control and communication' in the realm of human thought, that is as a tool for modelling rather than as a model itself, the computer became the foundation of the new field of artificial intelligence. (See art. 11.)

From the beginning, Turing viewed the computer as a manipulator of symbols and hence as capable of emulating any behaviour representable symbolically, in particular, game playing and similar manifestations of human intelligence. Turing machines, no less than Boole's algebra of logic, were meant to embody the laws of thought and hence to express human thinking. His design of the ACE reflected that intent, as did his early efforts to write a chess program and his espousal of machine intelligence. By contrast, von Neumann originally thought of the computer as a tool for the large-scale, high-speed calculations necessary for solving non-linear systems of equations and the basic architecture that bears his name likewise reflected this view, as did most programming languages with their focus on functions and procedures, even in the realm of data processing.

While scientific calculation and business data processing dominated the field of computing during its first decades, Turing's vision had its American adherents. In the early 1950s Shannon, impressed by chess-playing programs, took up the question of logical automata capable of self-directed behaviour. His colleagues at MIT included Marvin Minsky, then engaged in modelling neural networks on the computer in an effort to emulate perception and John McCarthy, working on a formal logic of human thought. Elsewhere, attracted to the computer as a tool of rational decision-analysis in management, Herbert

Simon teamed in the early 1950s with Allen Newell and J.C. Shaw to explore the heuristic capabilities of information processing. A 'Logical Theorist' program capable of finding and proving mathematical theorems led to the design of a 'General Problem Solver'. These first efforts came together in 1956 at a conference at Dartmouth College on 'artificial intelligence' (AI).

Despite the common designation, artificial intelligence encompassed from the outset a range of methods and agendas of research, diverse views concerning its short-range and long-term goals and changing relations with other disciplines such as psychology, neurophysiology and linguistics. Its (yet unwritten) history is correspondingly tangled and unclear, but one abiding feature has been the common emphasis on working programs as the embodiment of theory.[14] Main lines of investigation in the United States, Europe and Japan have included goal-directed planning, learning, understanding of natural language both syntactically and semantically, analysis and understanding of visual images, the organisation of knowledge about the world, the production of knowledge, and the emulation of expert problem-solving based on detailed knowledge in specific domains.[15] This last area, which emerged in the mid-1970s with programs capable of analysing molecular structure, diagnosing diseases and designing computer circuits, represented a new orientation of the field towards empirically-based systems aimed at assisting humans in solving problems of immediate practical significance. With expert systems, artifical intelligence moved into the market-place.

Although largely independent of mainstream computer science until the 1980s, AI spun off several major contributions to computing in general, for example time-sharing, techniques of graphical simulation, interactive debugging and computer design of VSLI circuits. In turn, its development by the end of the 1970s made it clear to many that application of such data-intensive strategies to more general realms of human thought lay beyond the limits of von Neumann architecture, as did significant progress on the earlier goals reached. Computers that can understand spoken and written speech, that can translate common language into programs and that can learn from their own experience, it was argued, require a 'Fifth Generation' of computer hardware and software. In the early 1980s Japan made the development of such computers a national goal, while several private ventures got underway in the United States. The outcome remains at present undecided.

NOTES

1. From the Greek *kybernetes* for 'steersman' (= Latin *gubernator*); often credited to Wiener, the neologism stemmed from Ampère's *Philosophie des sciences* (Paris, 1838), where it denoted a subdiscipline of the study of government.
2. Wiener, *Cybernetics* (2nd ed., Cambridge, Mass., 1961), p. 14, p. 26.
3. Shannon, in Claude E. Shannon and Warren Weaver, *The mathematical theory of communication*,

(Urbana, IL., 1949), p. 39; Shannon's paper originally appeared in the *Bell system technical journal*, 27 (1948), 379–423; 623–56.

4. Cf. Richard W. Hamming, 'Error detecting and error correcting codes', *Bell system technical journal*, 29 (1950), 147–60.

5. Cf. Donald M. MacKay, 'The wider scope of information theory', in Machlup and Mansfeld, *The study of information* (New York, 1984) pp. 485–92; esp. pp. 486–7.

6. Cf. Peter Elias, 'Cybernetics: past and present, east and west', in Machlup and Mansfield, *The study of information*, pp. 441–4; see especially p. 442.

7. As in Simon Nora and Alain Minc's *L'Informatisation de la société* (Paris, 1978), translated into English under the title *The computerisation of society* (Cambridge, Mass., 1981). To characterise the unprecedented capabilities of computers linked to telecommunications, Nora and Minc coined the term *télématique*.

8. Meanwhile in Germany between 1934 and 1945 Konrad Zuse independently and single-handedly recapitulated the development from mechanical calculator through relay machine to electronic, stored-program device in his computers Z1–Z4. The last of these formed the basis for the early computing program at Zurich's ETH.

9. *Proc. Lond. Math. Soc.*, series 2, 42 (1936), 230–65.

10. Cf. Wiener, *Cybernetics* (1961), p. 12: 'If I were to choose a patron saint for cybernetics out of the history of science, I should have to choose Leibniz. The philosophy of Leibniz centers about two closely related concepts – that of a universal symbolism and that of a calculus of reasoning.'

11. Turing, 'On computable numbers', p. 259.

12. SAGE = Semi-Automatic Ground Environment. The computer was an outgrowth of the massive Whirlwind computer built by Jay Forrester at MIT in the late 1940s.

13. Marvin L. Minsky, 'Computer science and the representation of knowledge', in Michael L. Dertouzos and Joel Moses (eds.), *The computer age: a twenty-year view* (Cambridge, Mass., 1979), pp. 392–421; esp. pp. 401–2. Recent developments in parallel distributed processing (PDP) have revived research in neural networks, overriding some of Minsky's conclusions.

14. Allen Newell has made a stimulating attempt to sort out the main lines in 'Intellectual issues in the history of artifical intelligence', in Machlup and Mansfeld, *The study of information*, pp. 187–227.

15. While the agendas of AI in the United States and elsewhere have looked much the same, the research communities differ on the question of language. *Lingua franca* for Americans is John McCarthy's LISP (for LISt Processing), an outgrowth of his work on the mathematical foundations of thought which was better suited than procedural languages to expressing the patterns of inference and search that researchers were investigating. During the 1970s European and Japanese investigators turned increasingly to PROLOG (Colmerauer and Roussel, 1972), aimed at facilitating the development of programs based on logical relations.

FURTHER READING

S. J. Heims, *John von Neumann and Norbert Wiener* (Cambridge, Mass., 1980).

Andrew Hodges, *Alan Turing: the enigma of intelligence* (London, 1983).

Vernon Pratt, *Thinking machines. The evolution of artificial intelligence* (Oxford, 1987)

SECTION II B: TOPICS AND INTERPRETATIONS

35

ARISTOTELIAN SCIENCE

A. GEORGE MOLLAND

In January 1663 Samuel Pepys's younger brother John took his BA at Cambridge. Later in the year we find the following entries in Samuel's diary:

> *August 5th*: At home, my brother and I fell upon Des Cartes, and I perceive he hath studied him well and I cannot find but he hath minded his book and doth love it.
> *August 7th*: I find [John] not so thorough a philosopher, at least in Aristotle, as I took him for, he not being able to tell me the definicion of fire nor which of the four Qualitys belonged to each of the four elements.
> *August 8th*: I [asked] many things in physiques of my brother John, to which he gives me so bad or no answer at all; as, in the Regions of the ayre he told me that he knew of no such thing, for he never read Aristotle's philosophy, and Des Cartes owns no such thing; which vexed me to hear him say. But I shall call him to task and see what it is that he hath studied since his going to the university.[1]

Two years after John Pepys, Isaac Newton received his BA from Trinity College, Cambridge. Newton was a more conscientious student, and made inroads into Aristotle, but his inclinations also were towards a more mechanical kind of philosophy. However, until about this time Aristotelianism had provided the conventional wisdom in natural philosophy for most of Europe, and it is historically distorting to regard the now more familiar avant-garde thinkers, such as Kepler, Galileo and Descartes, as representing the norm; nor can we properly assess their achievements without a study of the background against which they worked.

1. THE DEVELOPMENT OF ARISTOTELIAN SCIENCE

To someone trained in modern science, especially physical science, an exposition of Aristotelian science presents the particularly frustrating problem of where to begin. In a certain way this difficulty parallels Aristotle's own procedures. Aristotle was a firm believer in beginning from where he was, and not from some hypothetical superior starting-point. This could sometimes give him the appearance of a down-to-earth empirical scientist in quite a modern guise. For instance, he spoke of how art or science was gained ultimately from sensations being fed into memory.

> From memory experience is produced in men; for the several memories of the same thing produce finally the capacity for a single experience. And experience seems pretty much like science and art, but really science and art come to men *through* experience . . . Now art arises when from many notions gained by experience one universal judgment about a class of objects is produced. For to have a judgment that when Callias was ill of this disease this did him good, and similarly in the case of Socrates and in many individual cases, is a matter of experience; but to judge that it has done good to all persons of a certain constitution, marked off in one class, when they were ill of this disease, e.g. to phlegmatic or bilious people when burning with fever, – this is a matter of art.[2]

Aristotle also emphasised that 'men of experience know that the thing is so, but do not know why, while the others [men of art] know the "why" and the cause'.[3] The 'modern' character is again apparent in the *Posterior Analytics*, where Aristotle held that the proper form of a science is to be axiomatic and deductive. All the pertinent conclusions should be derivable by deductive argument from a small number of premisses, reached inductively or otherwise. The model is geometrical, and this form is found to a greater or lesser degree in other Greek sciences, but ironically is not really exemplified by Aristotle's own science. His biological works are descriptive and classificatory, and his physical works are also far from conforming to the rigorous deductive model. (See art. 53.)

2. THE TOPICS

In order to understand this we should look at the beginning of Aristotle's *Topics*, which casts a different complexion on the idea of starting from where one is. The treatise concerns dialectical reasoning, that which 'reasons from opinions that are generally accepted',[4] and 'those opinions are "generally accepted" which are accepted by every one or by the majority or by the philosophers – i.e. by all, or by the majority, or by the most notable and illustrious of them'.[5] This form of reasoning has various uses, among them one

> in relation to the ultimate bases of the several sciences. For it is impossible to discuss them at all from the principles proper to the particular science in hand, seeing that the principles are the *prius* of everything else: it is through the opinions generally held on the particular points that these have to be discussed, and this task belongs properly, or most appropriately, to dialectic: for dialectic is a process of criticism wherein lies the path to the principles of all inquiries.[6]

In this way opinions join sensations as sources of scientific knowledge, and it is this path Aristotle followed for the most part in the physical treatises. It is also the path that predominated in the Aristotelian tradition, especially in the medieval and early modern universities, where dissection of opinions was a far more popular pusuit than dissection of animals.

Moreover, it is this feature that makes Aristotelianism so difficult to expound systematically. Aristotle did not start from a *tabula rasa*, as he might have done if he had been working deductively from first principles, or even if, in the manner of Plato's *Timaeus*, he had been presenting a creation myth. Instead he began from the basis of what could be seen, heard and read in the Greece of the fourth century BC, and proceeded to mould this material into shape. The result was that the parts of his system became strongly interdependent rather than following a linear order of development. This means that just about anything that one says about Aristotle will to an extent anticipate something that is to come later. But we have to start somewhere, and so let us first look very crudely at the general structure of the Artistotelian universe. It was finite and spherical, and beyond it there was nothing, not even space and time. As Aristotle had recognised, the absence of space outside the heavens is not easy to imagine, but it was standard within the tradition to blame the imagination itself for this, and appeal instead to the higher cognitive faculty. Some thinkers, it is true, did allow the existence of an infinite space outside the heavens, but this shows how easy it was to modify Aristotelianism without coming near to destroying it.

3. THE ARISTOTELIAN UNIVERSE

Between the centre of the Aristotelian universe (where lay the earth) and its extremities a radical break occurred at the moon. From the moon outwards the world consisted of a number (perhaps 55) of sperical shells which moved continually with uniform circular motions and some of which carried planets or stars. The heavenly regions were composed of a special or fifth element, whose nature it was to be moved with such motion. The motion was not completely self-caused, for ultimately the spheres were moved by desire for Aristotle's First Cause or God, and sometimes Aristotle also posited the existence of intelligences as movers of the individual spheres.

Below the sphere of the moon we are in the realms of generation and corruption, and all bodies are composed of the four elements earth, water, air and fire. None of these are found in a pure state, and all bodies are a mixture of all four, but naturally earth is the dominant element in solids and water in liquids. The elements are determined by two sets of defining properties. The first set comprises four qualities which are regarded as more fundamental than the elements – hot, cold, wet and dry. Earth is cold and dry, water cold and wet, air hot and wet and fire hot and dry. The elements are not immutable, but by changes in their qualitative structure may convert into one another. The other set of defining properties comprised heaviness and lightness. Earth is absolutely heavy and fire absolutely light, whereas water is relatively heavy and air relatively light. Associated with this is the doctrine of natural places and motions. The natural place of earthy bodies is at the centre of the world, whereas that of fiery bodies is at the periphery of the elementary regions. If a body is not in its natural place, then, if unimpeded, it will move towards it.

This idea of bodies fulfilling their own natures, and the general tendency to speak of things moving from potentiality to actuality, are characteristic of Aristotle's science, and can be associated with his predilection for biology. Aristotle may be said to be at his most 'scientific' in his biological works, which contain a wealth of meticulous observations (including evidence from dissections), along with some rather unreliable travellers' tales. By comparison with the physical works theses treatises were not widely studied in medieval and early modern Europe, but it can still be plausibly argued that biological modes of thought permeate the physical treatises also. Unlike Timaeus in Plato's dialogue of that name, Aristotle does not explicitly say that the universe is a huge (and spherical) living creature, but it does have many of the appropriate characteristics. This is particularly evident in Aristotle's concern with teleology, as in the example above when a body fulfils its nature by moving to a natural place, just as an acorn fulfils its nature by growing into an oak tree.

Obviously not all motions were natural, for when a stone is being raised it is being moved violently, that is, against its own nature. There were also voluntary motions in which animate bodies moved themselves. This threefold (natural, violent and voluntary) labelling could produce problems. For instance, the voluntary motion of an animal, in itself natural, can also be unnatural, as when it jumps. Here Aristotle appealed somewhat unclearly to a distinction between whole and parts. 'The animal as a whole moves itself naturally: but the body of the animal may be in motion unnaturally as well as naturally.'[7] 'It would seem that in animals, just as in ships and things not naturally organised, that which causes motion is separate from that which suffers motion, and that it is only in this sense that the animal as a whole causes its own motion.'[8] Examples such as this show how much the Aristotelian texts (which for the most part come to us as notes rather than as polished treatises) were in need of explication and discussion. An even bigger difficulty concerned the unnatural motions of inanimate objects, notably projectiles. If a stone is thrown upwards, it continues to move upwards after it has left the hand. But what then can be moving it since, being an inanimate object, it certainly needs a mover? Aristotle grasped the nettle firmly: the only thing in contact with it is the air, and so the air must be the mover. While moving the stone upwards, the hand also transmitted to the air the power of continuing this motion and of transmitting this power from one part of the air to the next.

4. REACTIONS TO ARISTOTLE

This explanation did not find universal favour, and many commentators, Greek, Arabic and Latin, produced thought experiments to demonstrate its implausibility. The usual alternative was to posit that some force was communicated directly to the projectile, which then continued the motion. In the fourteenth century, Jean Buridan spoke of an 'impetus', and in the late sixteenth century, the young Galileo suggested an impressed force (*virtus impressa*). It is instructive to compare their attitudes. Buridan is apologetic about diverging from Aristotle: 'In my judgement this question is very difficult, because, as it seems to me, Aristotle has not settled (*determinavit*) it.'[9] Galileo on the other hand is delightedly anti-Aristotelian: 'Aristotle, as in practically everything that he wrote about locomotion, wrote the opposite of the truth on this question too'.[10] Discussions of this problem did not occupy a big place in the Aristotelian tradition, but later scholars have seen them as an important step towards the principle of inertia of classical mechanics. There is some truth in this, but it is important to note that even Galileo at this stage was asking Aristotelian questions, even though he gave non-Aristotelian answers. It was only when he tried to stop asking such questions, and when Descartes and others conceived of motion as something that was naturally conserved, that we can really sense the transition to classical mechanics. We must, however, remember that even Newton had an innate force (*vis insita*) to account for a body's continuance in a state of rest or uniform rectilinear motion, but this was clearly contrasted with the more active impressed forces, and was in fact a force of inactivity (*vis inertiae*).

5. THE DOCTRINE OF CAUSALITY

In explaining natural and violent motion the emphasis was on two different sorts of causes: in the first case the end towards which the motion was directed, and in the second that which propelled the object. It is now time to look more closely at Aristotle's doctrine of causality, which was central to his physical thought. 'Knowledge is the object of our inquiry, and men do not think they know a thing till they have grasped the "why" of it (which is to grasp its primary cause).'[11] Again Aristotle starts from where he is, from what 'men think', and proceeds to analyse the different ways in which we may speak of causes. His principle division is into four kinds, usually referred to as material, formal, efficient and final. The material cause is that from which something is made, or from which it comes to be, as bronze may be the material cause of a statue, and letters are the cause of syllables. The formal cause is a little harder to define: it is the essence of the thing, the way the matter is organised; in a sense the definition of the thing. It is important to note that matter and form are correlative terms, and that matter can be conceived at different levels of organisation. Bronze may be matter for the statute, but itself is form with respect to the matter provided by the four elements. A final act of abstraction brings us to prime matter, matter with no qualities at all, but this never exists independently. The efficient cause is the agent that brings about a thing or event; for instance the builder is the efficient cause of a house. The final cause is that for the sake of which something is done, as reaching its natural place is the final cause of the natural motion of an object. It is this cause in particular that later thought regarded as inappropriate to natural science. The causes figure prominently in Aristotle's theory of sexual reproduction. Here the matter is the mother's menstrual blood, which is worked on and given form by the semen of the father (efficient cause), just as wood is formed by the tools of a carpenter, which, however, are not parts of the finished product. The final cause is the full-grown animal. As Aristotle noted, there is here a tendency for formal, efficient and final causes to merge together. 'The last three often coincide; for the "what" and "that for the sake of which" are one, while the primary source of motion is the same in species as these (for man generates man).'[12]

The Aristotelian insistence on both formal and material causes is of considerable significance because it gave form a degree of independence from matter not found in more mechanical views of nature, where the tendency was to explain everything in terms of the arrangement of material particles. Aristotelian science was far less reductionist, and for that reason could be accused of appealing to occult virtues, properties of bodies that had to be accepted as brute facts, not explicable in terms of something supposedly more intelligible. There was awareness of this point in the Peripatetic tradition. In the thirteenth century Albertus Magnus discussed various views on the causation of the powers that were attributed to various stones, in the course of which he reports on the reductionist position of Alexander of Aphrodisias, an early Greek Aristotelian commentator.

'He attributes all things whatsoever, whether living or not, to the elements. He even says that the intellect is the consequence of certain combinations of elements. For the elements themselves when combined, he says, are wonderfully and highly effective. And the power which in a mixed [body] rules and directs the elemental qualities is, according to him, merely the consequence of their being combined; and this, he asserts, is wonderful.'[13] Albertus himself thought this view refutable, and held instead 'that the power of stones is caused by the specific substantial form of the stone'.[14] This was almost certainly the majority view, although there were other attempts in the Aristotelian tradition to make occult virtues and suchlike more explicable.

6. ARISTOTLE AND MATHEMATICS

The holistic orientation of Aristotle's thought also caused him to have ambivalent attitudes towards the use of mathematics in science. As noted above, geometry was his paradigm for a demonstrative science, and geometrical examples abound in the corpus. Moreover, in a famous passage, he implied that in many cases in natural science, the mathematician has a distinctly superior role to the observationalist:

> The reason why differs from the fact in another fashion, when each is considered by means of a different science. And such are those which are related to each other in such a way that the one is under the other, e.g. optics to geometry, and mechanics to solid geometry, and harmonics to arithmetic, and star-gazing to astronomy . . . For here it is for the empirical [scientists] to know the fact and for the mathematical [to know] the reason why; for the latter have the demonstrations of the explanations, and often they do not know the fact, just as those who consider the universal often do not know some of the particulars through lack of observation.[15]

However, other passages reveal that Aristotle had considerable difficulty in incorporating what he called the 'more physical of the branches of mathematics',[16] such as optics, harmonics and astronomy, into his scheme of knowledge, and, with the possible exception of a problematic discussion of the rainbow, he himself did little to extend the penetration of mathematics into physics.

The ambivalence towards mathematics continued in the Aristotelian tradition. Some thinkers, such as Averroes and Albertus Magnus, saw mathematics very much as skimming over the surface of things and accordingly giving us only superficial knowledge, whereas others, such as Roger Bacon and Nicole Oresme, strove to increase its domain in the natural world. In general, however, they cannot be held to have had a significant effect on the Scientific Revolution except by expressing a general desire to mathematise. A possible exception lies in considerations of motion, and this subject also provides useful case studies for the relationship of holism and mathematics.

7. ARISTOTLE AND ASTRONOMY

For Aristotle astronomy gave a mathematical account of the heavenly motions, but there was no corresponding mathematical science to deal with sub-lunary motions. Aristotle himself started with a very generalised idea of motion and proceeded to divide it into motions in the categories of quality (e.g. from hot to cold), quantity (change of size) and place. None of these is completely reducible to any of the others, but for simplicity we shall restrict our concern to local motion, which was the most fundamental. Aristotle gave no systematic quantification, but it is clear that our initial concentration should be on a motion as a whole, the motion of the whole body through the whole time from the beginning of the motion to its end. In the development of this notion by medieval thinkers, and particularly by Nicole Oresme, it became clear that we are in effect dealing with a five-dimensional object, with three spatial dimensions (the extension of the moved body), one temporal and one of intensity of speed, which could then, so to speak, be quantified in a number of different directions. The general procedure is to work from the outside inwards, whereas Galileo and other seventeenth-century thinkers tended to work from the inside out by concentrating initially on the motions of individual points of the body across the points of space. If there was a significant medieval influence on Galileo's science of motion (and the matter is still under dispute), it is probably confined to the habit of treating instantaneous speed as a continuous quantity that can be represented by a straight line.

Aristotelian holism also entered the very heartland of mathematics. To most seventeenth-century mathematicians it was quite natural to think of lines as being composed of an infinite number of points, and to this end later mathematicians would distinguish different orders of infinity. But all this would have been anathema to an orthodox Aristotelian. For Aristotle, a line like other continua was infinitely divisible, but only potentially so; the division could go on indefinitely, but at no stage did one meet a set of ultimate elements that composed the line. Once again wholes were prior to parts, and, while wholes had a well defined existence, parts were more shadowy, and sets of parts were rarely unique, for a line could be divided into other lines in an infinity of different ways. This apparently recondite topic, to which Aristotle may seem to devote a disproportionate amount of attention, here emerges as a potent symbol of the difference between his biologically inclined world-view and the mechanical one of later thought.

8. ARISTOTELIAN NATURAL PHILOSOPHY

Aristotelian natural philsophy first became influential in the Latin west in the thirteenth century, but not unproblematically. Aristotle, even more obviously than Plato, had not been a Christian, and it was more difficult to assimilate him to the Christian tradition. It is therefore not surprising that there were repeated attempts to ban his natural philosphical works from the universities, or at least to censor them; nor, given the thirst for knowledge at the time, is it surprising that these attempts failed. There were several points of tension. Aristotle denied the Creation of the world from nothing, and claimed instead that it had always existed. He allowed at most only a shadowy form of individual survival after death. His God was not at all providential, but was engaged solely in contemplation of what was best in the universe, namely himself, and this left the way open for a thorough-going naturalism in philosophy. Aristotle often claimed that the world was a certain way because it had to be that way: to most Christians this put intolerable restrictions on God's freedom to have created the world in whatever way he chose. The tensions did not end in the thirteenth century, and it is instructive to remember that Galileo's friend and sparring partner, the rigid Aristotelian Cesare Cremonini, was continually having his own troubles with the Inquisition.

Nevertheless the intellectual Christian tradition became deeply imbued with Aristotelian concepts. In particular, these allowed an explication of the Eucharist in terms of transubstantiation: while the accidents of bread and wine remained, their substances were transformed into those of the body and blood of Jesus Christ. Mechanical philosophies, on the other hand, had notorious difficulties in coping with this. Moreover, Aristotelianism was the official philosophy of the Jesuits, an order that has often had a bad press from historians because of its members being on the 'wrong side' in certain famous disputes. But in fact the Jesuits were among the most scientifically advanced men of the age. Their colleges provided a rigorous education with greater than usual emphasis on mathematics, and figures such as Clavius, Scheiner, Cabeo, Kircher, Schott, Fabri and Pardies made no mean original contributions, even if their names are now over-shadowed by greater secular ones. However, it can be argued that this was despite rather than because of their Aristotelianism, and that, if they had been liberated from this yoke (to use Leibniz's term), they would have soared even higher. And certainly some of the greater ones were very flexible in their Aristotelianism, and prepared to make significant modifications.

9. ARISTOTLE AND THE SCIENTIFIC REVOLUTION

Positive Aristotelian influence has also been argued for in the cases of the undisputed leaders of the Scientific Revolution, notably Galileo and Harvey, both of whom significantly were associated with Padua, arguably the foremost Aristotelian centre of the time. It is now well established that many of Galileo's very early writings are drawn almost verbatim from works by Jesuits of the Collegio Romano, and it has been argued that a strong Aristotelian methodological influence remained in Galileo's mature writings. For my part I find it difficult to see much that was specifically Aristotelian in the later works, although we should remember that Galileo in his old age claimed that Aristotle would have regarded him as an Aristotelian. The case of Harvey is less problematic. He was steeped in Aristotelian thought, claimed to follow Aristotle as a leader, valued his methodology and appealed to Aristotelian analogies for the idea of circulation. In his case the dispute has been about how relevant was his Aristotelianism to his discovery of the circulation of blood.

For around 450 years Aristotelian science had been dominant in Europe. It had encouraged a rational approach to the natural world, and may in various particular ways have helped trigger off new developments in the seventeenth century. But Aristotelian science was more than a collection of theories about the world. It involved a whole attitude of mind and style of approaching natural philosophy. Like T.S. Kuhn's paradigms it determined the admissible questions about the world in a more fundamental way than that in which provided the answers. To abandon it involved far more intellectual struggle than a simple rejection of error for truth, and I see no reason to revise the traditional view that sees as one of the most significant intellectual events of the seventeenth century what a recent scholar has called the 'escape from the Aristotelian predicament'.[17] Samuel Pepys may have been shocked at his brother's ignorance of Aristotle, but some twenty-three years later he himself symbolised the coming of a new era by affixing his imprimatur to the first edition of Newton's *Principia*.

NOTES

1. *The diary of Samuel Pepys*, ed. R. Latham and W. Matthews (London, 1970–83), vol. 4, pp. 263, 267–8.
2. *Metaphysics* A.1, 980b27–981a13. I cite passages from Aristotle in the standard form, by work, book, chapter, and 'Bekker' page and line numbers. Except where otherwise stated, the translations are taken from the Oxford edition of Aristotle's works cited in the Further Reading list.
3. *Metaphysics* A.1, 980b28–30.
4. *Topics* I.1, 100a31.
5. *Topics* I.1, 100b21–4.
6. *Topics* I.2, 101a37–b4.
7. *Physics* VIII.4, 254b18–19.
8. *Physics* VIII.4, 254b30–3.
9. Johannes Buridanus, *Quaestiones super octo phisicorum libros Aristotelis*, ed. J. Dullaert (Paris, 1509; repr. Frankfurt, 1964), f.120r.
10. Galileo Galilei, *On motion and on mechanics*, tr. I. E. Drabkin and S. Drake (Madison, 1960), p. 76.
11. *Physics* II.3, 194b18–20.
12. *Physics* II.7, 198a25–7.
13. Albertus Magnus, *Book of minerals*, tr. D. Wyckoff (Oxford, 1967), p. 59.
14. Ibid., p. 65.
15. *Posterior analytics* I.13, 78b35–79a6. Translation from *Aristotle's posterior analytics*, tr. J. Barnes (Oxford, 1975).
16. *Physics* II.2, 194a7–8.
17. C. B. Schmitt, *A critical survey and bibliography of studies on renaissance Aristotelianism 1958–1969* (Padua, 1971), p. 130.

FURTHER READING

Aristotle, *The works of Aristotle translated into English*, ed. W. D. Ross (12 vols., Oxford, various dates).

M. Clagett, *The science of mechanics in the middle ages* (Madison, 1959).

E. Grant, *Studies in medieval philosophy and science* (London, 1981).

J. L. Heilbron, *Elements of early modern physics* (Berkeley, 1982).

G. E. R. Lloyd, *Aristotle: the growth and structure of his thought* (Cambridge, 1968).

A. G. Molland, 'The atomisation of motion: a facet of the scientific revolution', *Studies in history and philosophy of science*, 13 (1982), 31–54.

G. E. L. Owen, 'Tithenai ta Phainomena', *Aristote et les problèmes de la méthode* (Louvain, 1961), pp. 83–103, reprinted in *Aristotle*, ed. J. M. E. Moravcsik (London, 1968), pp. 167–90, and in *Articles on Aristotle: 1. Science*, ed. J. Barnes *et al.* (London, 1975), pp. 113–26.

W. D. Ross, *Aristotle* (London, 1923, and several subsequent editions).

C. B. Schmitt, *Aristotle and the renaissance* (Cambridge, Mass., 1983).

—— *The Aristotelian tradition and renaissance universities* (London, 1984).

F. van Steenberghen, *Aristotle in the west: the origins of Latin Aristotelianism* (Louvain, 1955).

36

THE HEART AND BLOOD FROM VESALIUS TO HARVEY

ANDREW WEAR

The heart and blood have often appeared central to an understanding of the human body. As such they have been crucial to theories of physiology. Harvey's discovery of the circulation of the blood has been taken to be one of the glories of the new science of the seventeenth century, but it was also a direct development of the work of ancient and renaissance anatomists. So, although the investigations of the heart and the blood form an important part of the history of science, it is more debatable how far they can be seen as part of the seventeenth-century movement that shaped the modern view of science. (See art. 15.)

The history of discoveries and ideas concerning the cardiovascular system is both simple and complex. Put simply (and naïvely), in 1543 Andreas Vesalius (1514–64) systematically criticised ancient anatomy. The anatomical school that followed him, based at his university, Padua, subsequently discovered more information about the body, some of which was to help William Harvey (1578–1657) in his discovery of the circulation of the blood in 1628. The discovery itself owed a good deal to the emphasis by the Paduan anatomists on personal observation and to Harvey's development of experimentation and quantification, methods which were to form part of the new science of the seventeenth century. There is a definite element of truth in this simple view but it misses a good deal, especially the philosophical and conceptual ideas of the anatomists which often had little to do with the sense of revolutionary change associated with the work of figures such as Galileo, Descartes or Newton.

Unlike the 'Newton industry', not a great deal has been written on Vesalius and Harvey. The latter, especially, has remained an enigma. Many of Harvey's papers were lost in 1642 when Parliamentary troops ransacked his London lodgings, which has meant that there is a lack of materials from which to con-

struct Harvey's intellectual biography and this has led to a good deal of speculation, inference and disagreement amongst historians. But before discussing the
question of how to interpret the work of Harvey and other anatomists, I shall
turn to Greek views of the cardiovascular system. A strong case can be made for
seeing renaissance anatomy as an elaboration and refinement of the work of the
Greeks, and in any case, renaissance ideas and observations on the heart and
blood did not start off from a clean sheet but were prompted by the existence of
a sophisticated body of anatomical and physiological knowledge.

1. THE GREEK BACKGROUND

Renaissance anatomists were concerned with retrieving and then with criticising classical views on the cardiovascular system. In the early sixteenth century,
the humanistic enterprise of going back to the Greeks (if only in Latin translation) became popular amongst medical writers and in the process, the anatomical and physiological works of Galen (*c.* 129–*c.* 200 AD), 'The Prince of
Physicians after Hippocrates', became available. In the *Use of Parts, Anatomical
Procedures* and *On the Natural Faculties* Galen had set out a two-fold system of
the heart and blood. Let us plunge into its details. He placed veins on the right
and arteries on the left side of the body (in this he followed the Alexandrian
anatomists Herophilus and Erasistratus). Galen wrote that the veins originated
in the liver and that venous blood was like food providing nourishment to the
parts of the body. The arteries had their origin in the heart, and supplied vital,
life-giving blood to the body.

Galen argued that venous blood was a product of the food we eat. In the
stomach, food was changed to chyle (milky fluid) which was then transported to
the liver. Galen believed that each part of the body had the power of attracting
nutriment to itself and changing it to its own substance. The liver, which looked
like congealed blood, was therefore able to alter the chyle to its own blood-like
substance. Arterial blood was a mixture of pneuma (spirituous elaborated air)
and blood. The air was partly changed in the lungs to pneuma, which then travelled, together, perhaps, with a little blood, via the pulmonary vein to the left
ventricle of the heart. There the incomplete pneuma, together with venous
blood that had come from the right ventricle, were concocted by the heat of the
left ventricle into thinner, brighter vital blood in contrast to the dull, dark red
venous blood while the by-products of this process, sooty vapours, travelled
back along the pulmonary vein to the lungs.

How did the blood move, and how did venous blood reach the left ventricle
of the heart? Galen wrote that the different parts of the body attracted venous
blood to themselves as and when they needed nourishment. There was no regular movement of blood, whether in a circular or backwards and forwards
motion. The idea of the same blood being regularly moved around the body was

conceptually impossible, for the purpose of the transport of venous blood was to bring it to the parts of the body where it would be used up. The movement of arterial blood did not really involve the movement of the heart. For Galen the active phase of the heart was diastole, which was when it sucked in blood rather like a bladder filling up. The heart, therefore, did not act in systole as Harvey later believed; that is, it did not, in Galen's eyes, contract and forcibly expel blood out into the aorta. Rather, Galen thought that the arteries had their own pulsative power which moved on the blood.

Galen's solution to the problem of how venous blood got from the right to the left side of the heart involved a rejection of observation in favour of theoretical preconception. He argued that the pores in the wall dividing the right and left ventricles (the intraventricular septum) did not come to a dead end as eyesight observation indicated, but continued invisibly, and that it was through these insensible pores that blood seeped from the right to the left ventricle. Galen rejected the alternative route of the pulmonary transit of the blood. He believed that only enough blood left the right side of the heart to nourish the lungs and that consequently there would be no regular movement of blood through the lungs from the right to the left ventricle. Galen was seeing the issue in terms of blood moving from the centre to the periphery (in this case the lungs) and being used up. There was also the associated issue of what the pulmonary artery and vein did. It is probable that the long held view that veins were on the right and arteries on the left made it difficult for Galen to accept that the pulmonary artery was an artery not only in structure but also in function (he called it the artery-like vein, and the pulmonary vein, the vein-like artery).

Seen from hindsight the weaknesses of Galen's system were of an observational nature: the origin of the veins in the liver, the action of the heart in diastole, the pores in the intraventricular septum, the rejection of the pulmonary transit of the blood and the conception of a two-way flow of blood and sooty vapours in the pulmonary vein.[1] These were the details which were to be contradicted by renaissance anatomists. As a system, however, it explained a lot: nutrition, growth, vitality and also reasoning and sensation (Galen had argued that a small part of the arterial blood was changed into 'animal spirits' which flowed through the nerves and the brain conveying sensation and motion). It was used by Greeks, Arabs and West Europeans in the Middle Ages and Renaissance. The long duration of the system reflects not only its intrinsic coherence but also the qualitiative, non-technical and non-quantitative world that these societies had in common and of which Galen's ideas were a product.

The only other system to rival Galen's was Aristotle's. It was inferior in anatomical detail; for instance, Aristotle did not distinguish between veins and arteries, and the physicians tended to favour Galen whilst the philosophers took the side of Aristotle in the academic disputes of the Middle Ages and Renaissance. One of the points at issue was whether the heart or the brain was the central organ of the body (Plato and Galen believed it was the brain, Aristotle the heart). There was also debate on Aristotle's opinion that all the blood vessels originated in the heart.

Sixteenth-century anatomists and Harvey did use Aristotelian ideas to support their criticisms of Galen. Moreover, interest in Aristotelian doctrines and in Aristotelian methods of embryology and comparative anatomy motivated a great deal of the work of Harvey and of his teacher Fabricius ab Aquapendente (c. 1533–1619).

2. THE RENAISSANCE ANATOMISTS

Andreas Vesalius (1514–1564) seems to tower over his fellow anatomists. Even when we discount the penchant of earlier historians for hero worship and Whig history, Vesalius still remains a point of departure for renaissance anatomy. His immediate predecessors, Berengario da Carpi (1470–1530) and Niccolo Massa (1485–1569) had criticised a few parts of Galen's anatomical knowledge and Massa had stressed the need for *anatomia sensata* based on personal observation rather than authority, but Vesalius was the first anatomist to place in doubt Galen's anatomical findings in general. He realised that Galen's description of human anatomy had been based largely on animal material, mainly simian; (unlike the Alexandrian anatomists, Galen was not able to use cadavers though he did have access to human bones). Vesalius, therefore, systematically compared his findings from human material with those of Galen and he dissected animals to show Galen's reliance on non-human material.

On the whole, Vesalius's innovations were anatomical rather than physiological and this applies to the cardiovascular system. He wrote that the vena cava did not originate in the liver but in the heart. On the crucial question of the pores in the intraventricular septum, Vesalius was at first ambivalent. In the first edition of the monumental *De Humani Corporis Fabrica* (1543) he wondered (probably without irony) at 'the skill of the Creator in allowing blood to sweat through invisible passages from the right ventricle into the left'.[2] Although he could not see the pores continuing through the septum Vesalius still believed that blood somehow went through it. In the second edition of the *Fabrica* (1555), there was a clear and explicit statement that the septum was impermeable, but Vesalius had to write that he did not know how the blood moved from the right to the left side of the heart. As Vesalius still believed in another part of Galen's cardiovascular system – that the pulmonary vein was filled with air from the lungs and sooty vapours from the heart – he could not conceive of the alternative of the pulmonary transit of the blood.

The significance of Vesalius for the history of the heart and blood centres more on his influence on the development of anatomy than on specific discoveries or theories. He helped to raise the status of anatomy. Before Vesalius, anatomy had often been seen as a craft practice closely related to surgery, but as Jerome Bylebyl has argued, by appointing a humanist scholar to the post of lecturer in anatomy and surgery, the Paduan authorities helped to integrate anatomy with medicine (medicine in Europe then had higher status than surgery, being based on books and the universities rather than on manual work and apprenticeship – though in Italy the difference was not so great and surgery did have a place in the universities). Anatomy became extremely popular in the Italian medical schools, so much so that the Paduan lectureship in anatomy had been made into a chair by the end of the century, and Paduan students declared that 'anatomy [was] the foundation of all medicine'.[3] The attack on the study of anatomy by Cesare Cremonini (1552–1631), the Aristotelian professor of philosophy at Padua, at the beginning of the seventeenth century, was a sign that the subject had risen in epistemological status and threatened to supplant philosophy as the basis of medical knowledge. Of course, neither the career of individuals like Vesalius nor the institutional history of the Paduan school of anatomy alone can account for the popularity of anatomy in the Renaissance. Other factors have to be considered, such as the humanist revival of Galen and the retrieval of his anatomical work, the popularity of anatomy with artists and their influence on anatomical illustrations and the beginnings of a sceptical approach to classical authorities. However, for whatever reasons, there is no doubt that by the end of the sixteenth century, anatomy had become a highly sophisticated discipline. It was independent of the ancients in matters of observation, learned and scholarly in theoretical issues, and its practitioners had the opinions of the ancients at their fingertips (the traditions of medieval commentary and disputation and renaissance humanist scholarship continued in anatomy well into the seventeenth century). It was this high level of sophistication, and the practice of renaissance anatomists of building upon and criticising each others' work that allowed new discoveries and ideas about the cardiovascular system to emerge.

3. THE PULMONARY TRANSIT OF THE BLOOD AND THE ACTION OF THE HEART

Although Vesalius did not discuss an alternative path for the movement of blood from the left to the right side of the heart, Realdus Columbus, his bitter rival at Padua, did. Columbus (c. 1515–59) has generally been credited with the discovery of the pulmonary transit of the blood and with elucidating the action of the heart. His views were published posthumously in the *De Re Anatomica* (1559). However, other European anatomists also wrote of the pulmonary transit around the same time. Juan Valverde da Hamusco (fl. 1552) described it in his *De la Composición del Cuerpo Humano* (1556) and attributed its discovery to his teacher Columbus. Michael Servetus (b. 1511), burnt at the stake in Calvin's

Geneva in 1553, had published in that year the heretical work *Christianismi Restitutio*. In it he wondered how the divine spirit entered man, and, drawing upon his anatomical training in Paris with Guinther von Andermacht, the teacher of Vesalius, he was able to give an answer based on the pulmonary transit of the blood. From the Bible ('But flesh with the life [soul] thereof which is the blood thereof, shall ye not eat,' Genesis 9:4) Servetus knew that the blood was the seat of the soul and that the soul was breathed into man by God.[4] Therefore, there had to be a point of contact between air and blood. This, Servetus argued, was the lungs, as they provided a larger area than the left ventricle of the heart for air and blood to mingle. He stated that blood did not go through the intraventricular septum (though a little might 'sweat' through it), but instead across the lungs where it mixed with air ('soul') and became arterial blood. In support of his view he pointed to the large size of the pulmonary artery which, he wrote, was too large merely to transmit blood for the lungs alone. One can dismiss Servetus's ideas: they were produced with religious rather than anatomical aims in mind, and, like those of the Arabic writer Ibn al Nafis, who in the thirteenth century had also described the pulmonary transit, they had no influence on contemporary anatomists or on Harvey later. (Most copies of the *Restitutio* were burned with Servetus, and it was only in 1694 that William Wootton, the English antiquary, publicised Servetus's discovery.) However, seen in a wider context, Servetus's mingling of religion and anatomy is an indication that at this time there was no sharp demarcation between the naturalistic and the religious study and signification of the body. As I discuss later, anatomists often justified their subject on religious grounds (though clearly Servetus was going well beyond the generalities found in anatomists' prefaces).

It was Realdus Columbus, teacher of anatomy in Padua and in Rome, who influenced William Harvey's views on the cardiovascular system. Harvey used Columbus's views on the pulmonary transit of the blood and on the action of the heart in the *Anatomical Lectures* (1616) and in the *De Motu Cordis* (1628) and they were stepping-stones to his discovery of the general circulation. But Columbus himself had no inkling of the systemic circulation. His belief in the origin of the veins in the liver, and his Galenic conception of venous blood being continually sent to, and used up by, the parts of the body as nourishment meant that he could not conceive of the same blood being moved round the lungs, the so-called 'lesser circulation', let alone round the body. (The lesser circulation implies that the same blood crosses the lungs and returns to them, the pulmonary transit that blood crosses the lungs but is then used up, and it is new blood that comes to the lungs – this would be the position of Columbus.)

Columbus argued for a pulmonary transit of the blood by pointing to the impermeability of the intraventricular septum, and to the size of the pulmonary artery, which was too large merely to carry blood to the lungs. Columbus made an additional and powerful series of points: the pulmonary vein, connecting the lungs to the heart, was always full of blood whether in the cadaver or in the living animal (he did a vivisection experiment to demonstrate this); the mitral valve only allowed a one-way flow of blood so smoky vapours could not travel back along the pulmonary vein and the heart was not like an oven burning green wood. He concluded that venous blood and air were mixed in the lungs rather than in the heart to produce 'shining, thin and beautiful' arterial blood.

Columbus also tackled the difficult question of the movement of the heart. This, as Harvey was to point out, was very hard to observe, since the different movements occurred so quickly. But from vivisections Columbus was able to conclude that in systole the heart is raised up and constricted, and that in diastole it moves down and relaxes. Systole could now be seen as the active phase of the heart's action, when it ejects blood outwards (an essential element for the circulation of the blood). Unfortunately, in Columbus's book the word systole was used for diastole and this confused later anatomists.[5]

The influence of Columbus on Harvey is clearly seen in the first half of *De Motu Cordis* which drew upon his ideas on the pulmonary transit and the action of the heart and the book also followed his example of using vivisection to observe the action of a part of the body. Although Columbus was, like Vesalius, concerned with the anatomical details of the body, his interest in vivisection points to a future development – the observation of the function or action of the motions of the body.

A great deal occurred in the history of anatomy between Columbus and Harvey. Specialised treatises on particular parts of the body were written, other animals apart from man were studied, and comparative anatomy and other Aristotelian approaches became popular. For the history of the cardiovascular system, the matter of real signicance was the discovery of the valves in the veins by, amongst others, Fabricius ab Aquapendente (1533–1619) in 1574 (he published the discovery in *De Venarium Ostiolis* (1603) but lectured on it much earlier). Additionally, Andreas Cesalpinus (1519–1603) may possibly have influenced Harvey by his Aristotelian emphasis on the heart as the origin of all the blood vessels, by his idea of a flow of venous blood towards the centre and by the concept of a chemical 'circulation' of the blood (i.e. a process of evaporation, cooling and condensation as in distillation). However, Cesalpinus is best seen as an Aristotelian attacking the Galenists and in the process coming up with some interesting but inchoate ideas.

4. WILLIAM HARVEY

Before discussing the vexed topic of how to interpret Harvey's work, I will give a brief account of his work on the heart and blood.

Harvey was educated in Cambridge between 1593 and 1599 and then in Padua from 1600 to 1602, where he was taught by Fabricius who was carrying out an anatomical research programme along Aristotelian lines. Like many anatomists, Harvey was a practising physician. In 1609 he was appointed physician to St Bartholomew's Hospital in London, and from 1618 he held a series of appointments as physician to James I and Charles I. Like Vesalius, who had been physican to the Emperor Charles V, Harvey was no cloistered scientist-anatomist living only for his research.

In 1615 Harvey was appointed Lumleian lecturer by the Royal College of Physicians with the duty of lecturing on anatomy and on aspects of surgery; he held the post until 1656. His notes for the lectures of 1616 on the whole of anatomy have survived together with the additions of later years. In the notes, Harvey showed himself to be a product of the Paduan school of anatomy. His main source was the *Theatrum Anatomicum* (1605) of Caspar Bauhin (1560–1624) who was also a Paduan product. Although he employed Bauhin and other authorities, Harvey introduced his own observations and used his eyes to check upon previous anatomical findings, thus following the key injunction of Paduan anatomy. In the lecture-notes, Harvey took some of the preliminary steps towards the discovery of the circulation of the blood by confirming Columbus's views on the pulmonary transit of the blood and by showing clearly that the heart acted as a muscle with the ventricles contracting and forcibly ejecting blood outwards in systole rather than attracting it in diastole. The notes contain a brief statement of the circulation:

> WH [i.e. Harvey's own opinion] it is certain from the structure of the heart that the blood is perpetually carried across through the lungs into the aorta as by two clacks of a water bellows to raise water. It is certain from the experiment of the ligature that there is a passage of the blood from the arteries to the veins. And for this reason Δ it is certain that the perpetual movement of the blood in a circle is caused by the heart beat.[6]

This was a late addition to the manuscript, inserted, in Gweneth Whitteridge's opinion, around 1627. From Harvey's own recollection of events in *De Motu Cordis*, it seems that he came to the idea of the circulation around 1619.

In 1628, Harvey published the *Exercitatio Anatomica de Motu Cordis et Sanguinis in Animalibus* and announced to the world his discovery of the circulation of the blood. The work is brief and to the point. Unlike much anatomical writing of the time, the views of previous writers did not take up a lot of space. Perhaps following the example of Fabricius, Harvey was concerned with circumscribed topics – the action of the heart and the action of the blood circulating through the body.

The book naturally splits into two parts, and it has been suggested by Jerome Bylebyl that Harvy wrote two separate treatises which he put together to form *De Motu Cordis* (the first and earlier Book on the action of the heart constituting the Proem, chapters 1 to 7 and 17; the second and later Book on the circulation constituting the Letter to Dr Argent, chapters 8 to 16).[7] The evidence for this is not conclusive and has been disputed, but it makes chronological sense and reflects Harvey's later practice in the construction of *De Generatione*, parts of which, Charles Webster has claimed, were written long before its publication.[8]

In the first half of *De Motu Cordis*, after showing the inconsistencies of Galen's views of the movement of air and blood to the heart and sooty vapours away from it, Harvey described the action of the auricles and ventricles of the heart and the pulmonary transit of the blood. Up to this point Harvey had not written anything that had not been discussed already by Columbus, though his treatment of the topics was more coherent, detailed and exhaustive.

It was in chapter 8 of *De Motu Cordis* that Harvey came to the novelty of the circulation of the blood. He wrote that it was the large quantity of blood leaving the heart, as well as consideration of anatomical structures such as the vessels and valves of the heart and the size of the arteries connected to the heart, which led him to consider whether the blood moved in a circle. Harvey then proceeded to show in chapters 9–14 that there was a circulation of the blood. He made quantitative experiments which indicated that far too much blood left the heart at a given time for it to have been used up by the body and replaced by blood manufactured in the liver from the chyle produced from ingested food. The quantitative argument indicated that blood must move in a circle, but Harvey had to show the pathways involved. He could not see the connections between the arteries and the veins (he was using a magnifying glass and not the newly-discovered microscope). However, by means of a simple experiment with ligatures, he showed that a connection must exist. Harvey ligated an arm very tightly so that no arterial blood could flow below the ligature down into the arm. He then loosened the ligature so that arterial blood flowed into the arm but the ligature remained tight enough to prevent venous blood from moving up beyond the ligature. The veins in the arm below the ligature became swollen and this indicated that blood had flowed down the arteries and then up the arm inside the veins. The last part of Harvey's anatomical demonstration of the circulation was to show that the valves in the veins always directed blood back towards the heart, and did not act, as Fabricius had believed, to prevent the extremities of the body from flooding with blood. After he had demonstrated that there was a circulation, Harvey was then able, in chapter 16, to point to previously puzzling phenomena, like the rapid spread of poisons through the body, and to explain them by the circulation; at the same time the existence of such phenomena gave further support to the circulation. In the last chapter (17) Harvey gave anatomical evidence, such as the greater thickness of the arteries close to the heart, constructed by nature to withstand the greater force exerted nearer the heart by the movement of the blood, which supported his findings on the action of the heart earlier in *De Motu Cordis*.

5. THE INTERPRETATION OF HARVEY'S WORK

Two contrasting views have dominated recent work on William Harvey. Gweneth Whitteridge has presented Harvey as one of the first modern scientists, a biologist who refuted the ancients and used the modern methods of observation, experimentation and quantification. Walter Pagel, on the other hand, although he has taken Harvey's methods into account, has emphasised that Harvey was a life long Aristotelian, a product of the late Renaissance – living at a time when the distinctions between philosophy, religion, mysticism and science were blurred and from when it could be said that science was to emerge out of the first three. There is no doubt that Whitteridge's view is simpler and easier to grasp, has a greater appeal for the student attuned to the Whig view of history as progress and makes far fewer intellectual demands on the reader. The merit of Pagel's work is that, although sometimes difficult, he gives a much fuller context to Harvey's ideas, whilst the limitations of Whitteridge's picture of Harvey are serious.[9]

Most crucially, Whitteridge cannot, because of her historiographical bias, make sense of two crucial chapters of *De Motu Cordis*. In chapters 8 and 15 Harvey set out the reasons that impelled him to concentrate on the heart and to think of the circulation. He also gave possible reasons for *why* there was a circulation. His language and ideas were vitalistic and heavily impregnated with Aristotelian concepts. The purpose of the circulation, wrote Harvey, was to transport life-giving blood to the periphery and then to bring it back to the heart where it could be enlivened again (almost like a chemical process of circulation and distillation, or Aristotle's cyclical process of evaporation, condensation and evaporation which Harvey quotes).

> So in all likelihood it comes to pass in the body, that all the parts are nourished, cherished, and quickned with blood, which is warm perfect, vaporous, full of spirit, and that I may so say, alimentative: in the parts the blood is refrigerated, coagulated, and made as it were barren, from thence it returns to the heart, as to the fountain or dwelling-house of the body, to recover its perfection, and there again by naturall heat, powerfull, and vehement, it is melted, and is dispens'd again through the body from thence, being fraught with spirits, as with balsam, and that all the things do depend upon the motional pulsation of the heart:
>
> So the heart is the beginning of life, the Sun of the Microcosm, as proportionably the Sun deserves to be call'd the heart of the world, by whose vertue, and pulsation, the blood is mov'd, perfected, made vegetable, and is defended from corruption, and mattering; and this familiar houshold-god doth his duty to the whole body, by nourishing, cherishing, and vegetating, being the foundation of life, and author of all.[10]

In chapter 15 where 'The circulation of the blood is confirm'd by probable reasons' Harvey emphasised again that:

> there must needs be a place and beginning of heat, (as it were a Fire, and dwelling

577

house) by which the nursery of Nature, and the first beginning of inbred fire may be contain'd and present'd: from whence heat and life may flow, as from their beginnings into all parts . . . And that this place is the heart, from whence is the beginning of life, I would have no body to doubt.[11]

The emphasis on the heart as the central organ of the body was, of course, Aristotelian. Harvey also shared Aristotle's (and Galen's) teleological perceptions of the body and the idea that its functions were to be viewed as the powers or faculties of the soul. This is why for Harvey the action of the heart depended on a pulsative faculty, in contrast with Descartes' innovative view that the heart acted mechanically, rather like a combustion engine.

It is very difficult to place Harvey within the 'new science' of the seventeenth century. He did not think much of Francis Bacon's philosophy (which was to serve as the programmatic base for many English scientists). John Aubrey reports Harvey as saying:

(he) would not allow him to be a great philosopher. Said he to me: He writes philosophy like a Ld Chancellor, speaking in derision.[12]

Moreover, Harvey's belief in teleology and in Aristotelian ideas would be enough to exclude him from being a full member of the 'new science', as the rejection of both were key elements in its programme.

The mislabelling of Harvey is understandable. *De Motu Cordis* was soon seen as an emblem of the success of the 'new science', even though Harvey had explicitly disagreed with its underlying mechanical-corpuscular philosophy. In *De Generatione* he emphasised the intellectual superiority of teleology over materialism:

Nor are they lesse deceived, who make all things out of Atoms, as Democritus; or out of the elements, as Empedocles. As if (forsooth) Generation were nothing in the world, but a meer Separation, or Collection, or Order of things. I do not indeed deny, but that to the Production of one thing out of another, these fore-mentioned things are requisite: But Generation her self is a thing quite distinct from them all. (I finde Aristotle in this opinion) and I myself intend to clear it anon . . .

Besides, they that argue thus, assigning only a Material cause, deducing the causes of Natural things, from a voluntary or casual concurrence of the Elements, or from the several dispositions or contriving of Atoms: they do not reach that which is chiefly concerned in the Operations of Nature, and in the Generation, and Nutrition of Animals: namely, the Divine Agent, and God of Nature, whose operations are guided with the highest artifice, providence, and wisdom, and do all tend to some certain end, and are all produced, for some certain Good.) But these men derogate from the honour of the Divine Architect, who hath made the shell of the Egg with as much skill, for the eggs defence, as any other particle; disposing the whole out of the same matter, and by one and the same formative faculty.[13]

What Harvey's successors also overlooked, was that Harvey belonged to the tradition of Paduan anatomy. He was concerned primarily in giving an anatomical 'ocular' demonstration of the heart and of the circulation, that is, in showing his procedures and results to witnesses and then describing them in print so that others could repeat them and see what he had seen. As he wrote in the *Second letter to Riolan* his concern in writing about the circulation was not so much with its causes as with its existence:

> ... this is that I did endeavour to relate and lay open by my observations and experiments and not to demonstrate by causes and approvable principles but to render it confirmed by sense and experience, as by the greater authority, according to the way of the Anatomists.[14]

Harvey's emphasis on observing for oneself, from 'the fabric of nature' was echoed by others who were also concerned with opposing authority – both Paracelsus and Galileo wrote of knowledge coming from the book of nature. The problem is that a common epistemological standpoint (knowledge can come from observation) does not entail a shared philosophical basis – as the comparison of Paracelsus and Galileo shows. Harvey's empiricism fitted the epistemology of his English successors, but it was an empiricism belonging to a tradition alien to the 'new science'. When Harvey argued for observation over reason he used the authority of Aristotle, the philosopher whose teachings were being overthrown in the seventeenth century.

The anatomists did indeed stress observation, and as the subject developed in the sixteenth century, they gained knowledge through their eyes of the actions of the body (seen through vivisection) as well as its structure. But, although discussion of action (or function, the two terms were used interchangeably) might dominate, as in Harvey's case, because it was his purpose in *De Motu Cordis* to demonstrate observationally the action of the heart and of the circulation, final causes were still important, and they underlay his thinking even though they were played down. In *De Generatione*, published in 1651 but according to Webster mainly written in the 1630s, they were given prominence. *De Generatione* is a long, very Aristotelian and traditional work, yet it was written by the same man who wrote *De Motu Cordis* and at around the same time. There were not two Harveys, the ancient and the modern, yet the contrast between *De Motu Cordis* and *De Generatione* and between chapters 8 and 15 and the other chapters of *De Motu Cordis* may at first lead to that conclusion. However, if one bears in mind the fact that the Paduan tradition of autopsy, seeing for oneself, determined the way in which *De Motu Cordis* was written and that it partly hid but did not deny the importance of final causes then the contradictions are cleared up.

6. FURTHER RESEARCH

There still remain 'Harveian problems'. Some are conceptual. For instance, John White has recently tried to show that the apparent conflict between Harvey's belief in *De Motu Cordis* that the heart was the first organ of the body and his belief in the primacy of the blood in *De Generatione* can be resolved and that Harvey was a life-long believer in the primacy of the blood.[15] However, White has not really integrated into his argument Harvey's insistence in *De Motu Cordis* that the heart gives life to the blood and it is possible that more can be written on the subject. The provenance of Harvey's methods and ideas needs further research despite Pagel's very full treatment of the issue. Here an understanding of the research methodology of Fabricius, possibly the greatest contemporary influence on Harvey, may be crucial. Andrew Cunningham's work on Fabricius shows how Fabricius developed a specifically Aristotelian programme, using comparative anatomy and concentrating on specific organs, that would lead to a universal anatomy.[16] The connections between this programme and Harvey's work need to be spelled out. But we should be asking larger questions. Why was anatomy important for the Renaissance and what can account for its popularity? Anatomy was, after all, a dirty and squalid business. As Volcher Coiter admitted in 1572, some asserted that anatomy was 'unworthy of a free man' and 'they despise it and hold it in contempt, as though useless. Those who do so, assert that it is disgraceful to touch the parts of a dead body polluted with blood and dirt'.[17]

The anatomists tried to elevate their subject by a variety of devices; they stressed the high status of its practitioners amongst whom were kings and emperors, the long tradition of the subject, the nobility of its object, the body – that 'miracle of miracles' – and they emphasised how knowledge of the body gave knowledge of God's workmanship. The rhetoric of the prefaces was augmented by a deep belief that anatomy was central to medicine and by a move to a new epistemological position which, although not doing away with knowledge derived from causes, asserted that knowledge could be gained from the hand and the eye.

All this adds up to a typical example of how a discipline becomes upwardly mobile in the learned world. But the answer to the question why, rather than how, did anatomy succeed, is less easy to give, but may provide a key to some of the problems of interpretation noted earlier. Students and the general public crowded into anatomy theatres, no doubt attracted by the prospect of the macabre, edified by the corpse as a *momento mori*, reminded by its presence 'to know thyself'[18] and also intent on seeking after knowledge. But what knowledge? Anatomy, in the writings of Vesalius and his successors, was precise, detached and yet able to enter into that favourite area of renaissance inquiry, the hidden nature of things. As such, it could be scientific in the modern sense and yet keep its sense of the mysterious. Anatomical chapters on particular organs were divided into 'structure', 'action' and 'use', and 'use', when expressed in teleological language, allowed the 'non-scientific' in our terms to remain. Whether, in fact, we have here two types of discourse, the observational-rational and the teleological-vitalistic, which were discerned *at the time* to be separate, as Brian Vickers holds, is a matter of controversy. But it is clear that, unlike the physical sciences, anatomy's traditional explanatory concepts did not become changed into 'scientific' ones (that is up to and including Harvey; later anatomists borrowed new ideas from the physical sciences). Harvey, after all, was to out-Aristotle Aristotle when he argued for a non-materialistic process of generation 'beyond the power of the elements', and that:

> likewise in the Blood, there is a spirit or virtue, doth act above the power of Elements (most conspicuous in the nutrition or preservation of each particular part) and also a nature, nay a soul in that spirit and blood answerable in proportion to the elements of the Stars.[19]

ACKNOWLEDGEMENT

I am grateful to Dr Vivian Nutton for his comments on an earlier draft of this chapter.

NOTES

1. Galen argued that the mitral valve did not close completely and allowed sooty vapours to exit through the pulmonary artery: A. J. Brock (trans. and ed.), *Galen on the natural faculties* (Harward, 1963), p. 315 (Bk. 3, 13), Furley and Wilkie, *Galen on respiration and the arteries*, (Princeton, 1984), p. 109, M. May, *Galen on the usefulness of the parts of the body* (2 vols., Ithaca, 1968) vol. 1, p. 318 (Bk. 6, 15). On the general issue of 'observational weakness' apart from the unhistorical nature of such judgement, one should take into account the 'theory-ladenness' of observations – what we see is shaped by our expectations or theories. The interesting point is that renaissance anatomists often corrected Galen's observations whilst keeping to his theories.
2. Andreas Vesalius, *De humani corporis fabrica* (Basle, 1543) pp. 275–6; 589; see also C. D. O'Malley, *Andreas Vesalius of Brussels 1514–1564* (Berkeley and Los Angeles, 1965), p. 167. There is a good discussion of the issue by Walter Pagel, *William Harvey's biological ideas* (Basle, 1967), pp. 156–69.
3. Jerome J. Bylebyl, 'The school of Padua; humanistic medicine in the sixteenth century', in Charles Webster (ed.), *Health, medicine and mortality in the sixteenth century* (Cambridge, 1979), pp. 334–70; p. 364.
4. On Servetus see Pagel, *William Harvey's bioglogical ideas*, pp. 136–55; C. D. O'Malley, *Michael Servetus. A translation of his geographical, medical and astrological writings* (Philadelphia, 1953); J. Friedman, *Michael Servetus: a case study in total heresy* (Geneva, 1978).
5. Realdus Columbus, *De re anatomica libri XV* (Venice, 1559), p. 257. Gweneth Whitteridge gives a good account of Columbus in *William Harvey and the circulation of the blood* (London and New York, 1971), pp. 49–55, 71–2.
6. Gweneth Whitteridge, *The anatomical lectures of William Harvey* (Edinburgh and London, 1964), pp. 272–3.
7. Jerome J. Bylebyl, 'The growth of Harvey's *De motu cordis*', *Bulletin of the history of medicine*, 47 (1973), 427–70; Gweneth Whitteridge disagreed: '*De motu cordis*: written in two stages?', *Bulletin of the history of medicine*, 51 (1977), 130–9; and Bylebyl's response continues on 140–50.

8. Charles Webster 'Harvey's *De Generatione*: its origins and relevance to the theory of the circulation', *British journal of the history of science*, 3 (1967), 262–74.
9. Walter Pagel, *William Harvey's biological ideas* (Basle, 1967); Gweneth Whitteridge, *William Harvey and the circulation of the blood* (London, New York, 1971).
10. The best translation of Harvey is still the first. William Harvey, *The anatomical exercises of Dr. William Harvey* (London, 1653), pp. 46–7.
11. Ibid., pp. 81–2.
12. Quoted by Pagel, *Wiliam Harvey's biological ideas*, p. 21.
13. William Harvey, *Anatomical exercitations concerning the generation of living creatures* (London, 1653), pp. 51–2.
14. William Harvey, *Two anatomical exercitations concerning the circulation of the blood* (London 1653), p. 74.
15. John S. White, 'William Harvey and the primacy of the blood', *Annals of science*, 43 (1986), 239–55.
16. Andrew Cunningham, 'Fabricius and the "Aristotle project" in anatomical teaching and research at Padua', in Wear, French, Lonie (eds.), *The medical renaissance of the sixteenth century*, pp. 195–222.
17. 'Volcher Coiter', *Opuscula selecta Neerlandicorum de arte medica*, XVIII (Amsterdam, 1955), p. 17. The quotation comes from Coiter, *Externarum et internarum principalium humani corporis partium tabulae* (Nuremberg, 1572), 'Introductio in anatomia', chap. 3.
18. On the significance of visual representations in anatomy theatres see William Schupbach, *The paradox of Rembrandt's 'Anatomy of Dr. Tulp'*, Medical History Supplement, 2 (London, Wellcome Institute for the History of Medicine 1982) especially plate 8 of the 1609 scene at the Leiden anatomy theatre and p. 95 on 'know thyself'.
19. Harvey, *Anatomical exercitations concerning the generation of living creatures*, pp. 452–3.

FURTHER READING

Margaret May (trans. and ed.), *Galen on the usefulness of the parts of the body* (2 vols., Ithaca, 1968).

A. J. Brock (trans. and ed.), *Galen on the natural faculties* (London, Cambridge, 1963).

L. R. Lind, *Studies in pre-Vesalian anatomy* (Philadelphia, 1975).

C. D. O'Malley, *Andreas Vesalius of Brussels 1514–1564* (Berkeley, 1965).

Walter Pagel, *William Harvey's biological ideas* (Basle, 1967).

—— *New light on William Harvey* (Basle, 1976).

Gweneth Whitteridge, *William Harvey and the circulation of the blood* (London and New York, 1971).

Geoffrey Keynes, *The life of William Harvey* (Oxford, 1978).

Robert G. Frank Jr., *Harvey and the Oxford physiologists* (Berkeley, 1980).

37

MAGIC AND SCIENCE IN THE SIXTEENTH AND SEVENTEENTH CENTURIES

JOHN HENRY

The claim that various magical beliefs and procedures played a crucial, even formative, role in the history of early modern science is currently being debated. In spite of the significant body of scholarship dedicated to establishing the thesis that magic has influenced science, there remain dissenters. However, this opposition does not support its contention that magic did not influence science with evidence; instead it either ignores the suggestion or simply denies it as a prima-facie impossibility. The latter argumentative strategy seems to derive from the assumption that magic was an unscientific delusion which could not have influenced so supremely rational an enterprise as modern science. Clearly, this position is utterly subjective and must therefore be regarded as a questionable basis for any historical account. The aim of this survey, therefore, is to recapitulate the major elements of the 'magic and science' thesis, with only the occasional aside to consider the opposing view. First of all, however, we must be clear about the nature of sixteenth and seventeenth century magic.

1. THE NATURE OF MAGIC

1.1. The initial premisses

Magic was (and continues to be) a system of beliefs underpinning a body of technical or craft knowledge and practice, which sought to capture and control the powers and processes of nature for man's (or perhaps merely the individual adept's) advantage. Such magical traditions appeared in the earliest civilisations and manifested themselves in a number of different but related arts and sciences. There are major divisions, such as those between Spritual, Demonic and Natural Magic, or astrology and alchemy, and innumerable smaller divisions between different sorts of divination – palmistry, scrying, sortilege, hariolation and many more. These different forms of magic had their own techniques and procedures and their own specific justifications but they were all founded upon a particular view of the world. Broadly speaking, the magical world-view of the Latin West was that nature was created by God in a hierarchy of creatures so ordered as to form the 'Great Chain of Being'. (See art. 24, sect. 1.) Each level in the hierarchy was connected directly to the beings immediately above and below but, in addition, there were a number of 'correspondences' between different parts of the Chain. Thus, there might be a correspondence between the seven planets and the seven metals; between the noblest men, kings, and the noblest metal, gold; between the inconstant moon and womankind. These putative connections and correspondences promoted magical beliefs about the secret influence of one thing on another and, therefore, the belief that knowledge about, or control of, one thing could be gleaned by study and manipulation of other things even though they might be as remote as a flower and a star. This is what John Donne meant in his *Anatomie of the World* (1611) when he asked despairingly,

> What Artist now dares boast that he can bring
> Heaven hither, or constellate any thing,
> So as the influence of those starres may be
> Imprison'd in an Hearbe, or Charme, or Tree,
> And doe by touch, all which those stars could do?[1]

The difficulty inherent in all efforts to master the magical art derived from the assumption that the way in which one entity might influence another was entirely 'hidden' or *occult*. Success as an adept depended not on a theoretical grasp of supposed causal mechanisms but on a working knowledge of the many and varied occult qualities and powers. Some magical traditions advocated the use of short cuts to the discovery of correspondences and occult virtues. The assumption of demonic magic, for example, was that even if the magician himself did not know how to bring about a desired natural effect, he could summon a demon with much greater knowledge of God's creation to bring about the result he wanted. It is important to note here that not even the Devil was believed to be capable of producing a genuinely supernatural effect – like the magician he had to rely on harnessing the powers inherent in nature:

> Though the divel indeed, as a Spirit, may do, and doth many things above and
> beyond the course of some particular natures: yet doth hee not, nor is able to rule
> or commaund over generall Nature, or infringe or alter her inviolable decrees . . .
> For Nature is nothing els but the ordinary power of God in althings created,

among which the Divell being a creature, is contained, and therefore subject to that universall power.[2]

Alternatively, the aspiring adept might prefer to rely on an interpretation of the 'signatures' of things. The doctrine of signatures held that God had provided 'signs' by which the correspondence between one thing and another could be discovered. The shape or colour or even the common name of one creature could suggest its sympathetic influence upon another. The moonstone, the sunflower and the walnut, for example, bore the signatures of their correspondence with the moon, the sun and the human brain respectively. However, both of these means of taking short cuts to magical knowledge were widely condemned, often by magicians themselves. The invocation of demons was heretical and downright dangerous, while reliance on the symbolic significance of various appearances was frequently regarded as subjective and prone to error. For many magicians, therefore, the only reliable methods for discovering the influence of one thing on another were, as we shall see, empirical investigation and mathematical analysis.

It should already be clear that magic was characteristically utilitarian in its aims. The knowledge of natural influences which the magician tried to amass was not usually regarded as an end in itself; it was merely the first stage in a pragmatic exercise which depended equally on a set of practical procedures, ranging from the astronomical mathematics of the astrologer to the technical craft of the alchemist.

Magic flourished throughout the Middle Ages and the Renaissance, receiving a series of major fillips with the recovery of various ancient magical texts. The most important of these were the writings attributed to the supposed founders of the magical arts, Hermes (or Mercurius) Trismegistus and Zoroaster. The *Corpus Hermeticum* and the *Oracula Chaldaica* were magical writings of the second and third centuries AD which combined Neoplatonic, Neopythagorean, Stoic, Persian and Gnostic Christian ideas. However, Renaissance scholars assumed that they were the geniune productions of these two ancient sages who were widely believed to have been contemporaries of Moses. Many leading scholars, such as Marsilio Ficino, Giovanni Pico della Mirandola and Francesco Patrizi, believed that the Hermetic and Chaldean writings represented an ancient wisdom derived, like Moses's writings, directly from God. Furthermore, this revival of interest in magic led to an increased appreciation of those medieval thinkers who were reputedly the best magicians; notably Roger Bacon, but also Arab thinkers like Alkindi and Avicenna.

These magical writings enjoyed a tremendous vogue throughout the sixteenth century and well into the seventeenth. Indeed, so pervasive were these ideas that Frances Yates has pointed to the 'Hermetic Tradition', as she called it, as a 'necessary preliminary to the rise of science'. Scholarly opinion now rejects her suggestion that the core of these Renaissance movements was 'Hermetic' and prefers the admittedly looser terms of Neoplatonism and magic. Yates herself wrote only in a programmatic way and much of the evidence she cited in favour of the thesis that magic was a major influence on science is circumstantial and tenuous. Lacking any detailed knowledge of the history of science, Yates all too often summed up her argument by vaguely pronouncing that 'there was indeed a vast change in the conception of man's relation to the cosmos'.[3] Nevertheless, in the hands of other scholars, Yates's ideas have proved highly suggestive.

1.2. Magic and rationality

Magic is not a monolithic subject and it is important to stress that major aspects of the history of magic seem to play no role in the rise of modern science; for example, Demonic Magic, chiromancy and the cabala. The crucial aspects of the magical tradition for the historian of science were those encompassed by the term *Natural* Magic which embraced all those arts which relied upon natural lore; for example, astrology and alchemy. However, even the general ethos of magic could provide a useful and fruitful stimulus to scientific thought. The magical and scientific world-views were not incompatible and the question of magical influence on science should not be dismissed out of hand, as some historians have tried to do, on the grounds that magic is *irrational*.[4] At the beginning of the seventeenth century, there was nothing irrational in the belief in 'correspondences' between entities and institutions. Indeed, to deny these correspondences or to act as though they had no validity was to descend into irrationality and madness, as Shakespeare demonstrated so marvellously in *King Lear*. Moreover, at a time when the world was believed to be populated by angels and demons there was nothing irrational about trying to summon them; at a time when the Church insisted that 'In the beginning was the Word' (*John*, I.1) and that the uttering of words could affect (or create) the world, there was nothing irrational about trying to discover the spells to bring about a desired result.

We cannot agree, therefore, with A. R. Hall's claim that 'the writings of some recent English historians of the more esoteric currents in Renaissance thought do tend directly to diminish the historical significance of rational discourse'. Hall also asks: 'If Copernicus wrote *De revolutionibus* because he was a Pythagorean metaphysician, what is the value of technical research into Copernicus' or Kepler's astronomical mathematics, or even into their explicit arguments for maintaining one opinion in preference to another?'[5] However, a closer analysis of Copernicus shows the importance of these 'esoteric currents' for historical explanation. (See art. 14, sects. 2 and 4; art. 15, sects. 3.1 and 3.2.)

It would clearly be wrong to suggest that *De revolutionibus* owed its origins solely to the fact that Copernicus was a 'Pythagorean metaphysician'. The claim of the historians which Hall challenges is, rather, that the influence of newly revived Neopythagorean attitudes (closely associated with, if not identical to, magical beliefs) was one of the factors which made Copernicus's *De revolutionibus* as revolutionary as it was. One of the most significant aspects of Copernicus's work was his insistence (pusillanimously disguised by Andreas Osiander in an anonymous preface) that his mathematical theory presented a *true* account of how the universe was constructed. No amount of 'technical research into Corpernicus' . . . astronomical mathematics' will explain why he believed this. Within the tradition of technical astronomy it had long been assumed that astronomical mathematics was merely hypothetical, merely a series of techniques and manipulations for predicting planetary movements, with no relevance to the physical reality of the heavens. The fact that Copernicus rejected this instrumentalist position and insisted that the mathematical system must be compatible with, and even demonstrative of, the actual physical system of the world owed much to the revival of Pythagorean and Platonic beliefs. His willingness to countenance so counter-intuitive and (by the canons of the day) so scientifically absurd a notion as the motion of the Earth merely because it provided a more 'harmonious' mathematical system and a closer fit between mathematical analysis and a putative physical reality is clear testimony to the strength of Neoplatonic influence on his thinking.

Current opinion about the mystical and anti-rational nature of magic should not blind us to the fact that many leading intellectuals in the past regarded it as a perfectly rational and legitimate source of truth about the nature of the world. Indeed, the historical evidence suggests that our present, derogatory view of magic has resulted from the fact that the most naturalistic and rational aspects of the magical belief system were absorbed into the new philosophy of the seventeenth century and only those parts of the system which were rejected continued to be called magic. Frequently associated with charlatanry and heterodoxy, magic had a bad public image, and many practitioners or other interested parties had to apologise for or simply deny their magical leanings. John Wilkins (1612–72), for example, published a book entitled *Mathematical Magick* (1648) but intimated in the preface that it was so called merely to accommodate the vulgar conceptions of these matters. The rhetorical import of Wilkins's statement is that the kind of mechanical devices whose operations are explained were not really magical but that the common people thought they were. However, it will not do for the historian to take such rhetoric at face value and believe that Wilkins was right while the common people were wrong. The fact that some aspects of what had long been part of the magical tradition were appropriated by natural philosophers in the sixteenth and seventeenth centuries cannot be used to argue that magic was irrelevant to the development of science.

It is admittedly very difficult for us, in our technological age, to see what is 'magical' about Roger Bacon's famous claim that 'chariots can be made to move without an animal with inestimable force . . . Also there can be made instruments of flying with a man sitting in the middle of the instrument and revolving a contrivance by means of which artificially composed wings beat the air like a flying bird'.[6] Nevertheless, we must accept that such 'mechanical marvels', because of the occult and secret nature of their mechanisms, were then regarded as products of the magical art. Aristotelian physics drew a distinction between natural motions (to and from the centre of the Earth in the case of heavy and light bodies; around the centre, circularly, in the case of heavenly bodies) and unnatural or forced motions. The scholastic natural philosophy of the universities concerned itself with natural motions and did not consider the unnatural operations of mechanical devices. (See art. 35.)

It is unhelpful to regard the attempts of seventeenth-century philosophers to explain the workings of such devices merely as an unexplained expansion of the scope of natural philosophy. It should rather be seen as a recognition by natural philosophers of the importance, both practical and theoretical, of certain aspects of the magical arts. The new philosophers, like the medieval philosopher Roger Bacon, believed that the study of nature could benefit from the study of artificial devices since, ultimately, their operations depended on natural laws. As Henry Power put it: 'Art being the imitation of Nature . . . the works of the one must prove the most reasonable discoveries of the other'; while for Ralph Cudworth nature was:

> another kind of art, which, insinuating itself immediately into things themselves, and there acting more commandingly upon the matter as an inward principle, does its work easily, cleverly, and silently. Nature is art as it were incorporated and embodied in matter.[7]

2. NATURAL MAGIC AND THE ORIGINS OF MODERN SCIENCE

2.1. Magic and the experimental philosophy

We can readily see that a number of characteristic features of the magical tradition, which had no significant place in medieval natural philosophy, were rapidly incorporated into the 'new philosophy' during the Scientific Revolution. (See art. 15.) For example, the emphasis on the experimental method, which is regarded as one of the most fruitful aspects of the new philosophy, derives from the magical tradition which assumed that the influences of one thing upon another could only reliably be discovered by observation and by other empirical methods. This is apparent in Cornelius Agrippa's defence of magic in *De incertitudine et vanitate scientiarum* (*The uncertainty and vanity of science*, 1531):

Therefore, natural magic is that which having contemplated the virtues of all natural and celestial things and carefully studied their order proceeds to make known the hidden and secret powers of nature in such a way that inferior and superior things are joined by an interchanging application of each to each; thus incredible miracles are often accomplished not so much by art as by nature, to whom this art is a servant when working at these things. For this reason magicians are careful explorers of nature only directing what nature has formerly prepared, uniting actives to passives and often succeeding in anticipating results so that these things are popularly held to be miracles when they are really no more than anticipations of natural operations; . . . therefore those who believe the operations of magic to be above or against nature are mistaken because they are only derived from nature and in harmony with it.[8]

The mixing of 'actives' and 'passives' to see how they interacted was a fundamental part of the natural magician's work. Only thus could he learn how to produce the effects he sought. For Giambattista Della Porta, one of the most prominent of natural magicians, only an empirical knowledge of 'the whole course of Nature' could teach us 'by the agreement and disagreement of things, either so to sunder them, or else to lay them so together by the mutual and fit applying of one thing to another, as thereby we do strange works'. Similarly, Pietro Pomponazzi pointed out that if the correspondences between things are real,

It follows also . . . that there are herbs, stones, or other means of this sort which repel hail, rain, winds, and that one is able to find others which have naturally the property of attracting them. Assuming that men are able to know them naturally, it follows that they are able, in applying the active to the passive, to induce hail and rain and to drive them away; as for me, I do not see any impossibility.[9]

Pomponazzi may have been mistaken about the existence of such herbs or stones but his assumption that there was nothing impossible about the suggestion and that it should be tested empirically is indistinguishable from what might be called the 'scientific mentality'. After all, the thinkers who refused to look through Galileo's telescope, on the grounds that what it revealed was *impossible*, were not magicians but natural philosophers; natural philosophers, moreover, who regarded any combination of lenses (or mirrors) as a magician's prop!

The natural magician's world-view was a powerful stimulus towards, and justification for, empirical investigation of nature as even Francis Bacon recognised:

Man being the servant and interpreter of Nature can do and understand so much and so much only as he has observed in fact or in thought of the course of Nature: beyond this he neither knows anything nor can do anything.

> Towards the effecting of works, all that man can do is put together or part
> asunder natural bodies. The rest is done by Nature working within.

Francis Bacon's conviction that the empirical method of the magicians was
the most effective way of understanding nature was not merely academic. Like
the magicians themselves, Bacon believed that the knowledge of nature should
be used to enlarge 'the bounds of Human Empire, to the effecting of all things
possible'.[10] This kind of utilitarianism was entirely characteristic of the natural
magician and served to distinguish him further from the academic natural
philosopher. For, while the natural philosopher was concerned to understand
the first principles involved in natural processes, the natural magician might be
satisfied merely with the ability to produce consistently, or to demonstrate, a
particular effect even though the cause remained hidden or occult. However,
paradoxical as it may seem, this did not mean that magic proved less fruitful as a
means of studying nature than the prevailing natural philosophy. On the contrary, the adoption of the magical approach by the new philosophy contributed
significantly to the overthrow of scholastic natural philosophy. (See art. 15,
sects. 3.1 and 3.2.)

The traditional role of the academic natural philosopher was to explain the
workings of nature in terms of causes. The artisan might know how to bring
about certain effects in his workshop, laboratory or forge, but only the natural
philosopher could explain how these came about. Such explanations were
almost exclusively couched in terms of the four Aristotelian causes (material,
efficient, formal and final) which ultimately depended on the substances and
the appropriate qualities of the interacting ingredients. The fact that many
natural effects had to be attributed to occult qualities, faculties and powers was
something of an embarrassment to scholastic natural philosophy. The natural
magician, however, was unconcerned. By the same token, while the natural philosopher tried to live up to the rigours of Aristotelian syllogistic logic, in which the
conclusion was explained by the combination of major and minor premisses, the
natural magician was perfectly content with inductive logic. We can see why if
we consider a standard example of an inductive argument taken from a leading
text-book of logic of the sixteenth century, Thomas Wilson's *The Rule of Reason*
(1551):

> Renyshe wine heateth,
> Malvesey heateth,
> Frenchwine heateth,
> neither is there any wyne that doth the contrary:
> Ergo all wine heateth.[11]

There has been no attempt here to explain why or how wine heats the body of the drinker; it is regarded as sufficient merely to show that it does do so, and to imply that this can be tested by administering wine to someone.

It was this concern with what natural objects do rather than with the niceties of how they do it, with effects rather than causes, which led Francis Bacon to extol the virtues of inductive logic – the very logic which was implicit in the natural magic tradition. Bacon's adoption of inductive logic, his 'theory-free' empiricist method of gathering 'facts' and his conviction that natural philosophy should have a utilitarian dimension were directly inspired by the methods of natural magic. Furthermore, his endorsement of these notions made it comparatively easy, particularly in England, for the new breed of natural philosophers to appropriate these aspects of the magical tradition. The experimental method could be presented, by its advocates in the Royal Society for example, as the only certain and reliable method of discovering truth because, unlike other methods, it was concerned not with preconceived, and thus inherently biased, theories or hypotheses but with clearly demonstrable matters of fact.

It followed from this methodology that occult powers and qualities could be held to be just as real as the 'mechanical qualities' of size, shape and motion. (See art. 38.) Thus, Robert Hooke allowed the introduction of 'unheard of Powers, Operations, Effects or Motions' into natural philosophy provided the experimenter could 'daily try, see, and find the regular working' of them. Robert Boyle, similarly, defended certain speculative qualities which he attributed to matter as 'not meerly fictitious Qualities: but such, whose Existence I can manifest, . . . by real Experiments and Physical Phaenomena'. The experimental philosopher need not assign the true cause to either gravity, the spring of the air, or any other occult quality; he need only show by experiment that bodies possess such a quality. The culmination of this magically-inspired trend can be seen in Newton's defence of his treatment of gravity and other putative 'active principles' as unexplained or occult qualities of matter (see art. 16, sect. 5):

> In this philosophy particular propositions are inferred from the phenomena and afterward rendered general by induction . . . to us it is enough that gravity does really exist . . . [12]

Until fairly recently, historians of science believed that the new philosophy explained natural phenomena in terms of contact actions between particles of matter in motion, and deliberately eschewed all occult qualities. However, it is now realised that the ability of the new philosophy to deal with occult qualities in an internally consistent and fruitful way was taken by its proponents as a clear sign of its superiority over scholastic natural philosophy. (See art. 38.) The new philosophers, who were virtually unanimous in their belief that physical phenomena could best be explained in terms of the behaviour of insensible corpuscles of matter, were concerned to argue that such insensible particles were not unintelligible. By showing that their philosophy could easily accom-modate occult qualities they were able to claim that their philosophy of invisible and insensible corpuscles was, paradoxically, more intelligible than the Aristo-telian philosophy, which could not adequately account for those same occult qualities.

It may be concluded that the natural magical belief in the usefulness of an inductive knowledge of the occult qualities of bodies and the necessarily exper-iential and observational discovery of the precise effects of such occult virtues were all absorbed into the new natural philosophy of the seventeenth century.

2.2. Magic and the mathematisation of natural philosophy

A similar case could be made for the role of magic in suggesting to Renaissance thinkers that mathematics could be a useful and valid means of understanding the physical world. At a time when the almost exclusively qualitative natural philosophy paid scant attention to the mathematical sciences, Cornelius Agrippa could insist that

> The mathematical disciplines are so necessary and cognate to magic that, if anyone should profess the latter without the former, he would wander totally from the path and attain the least desired result. For whatever things are or are effected in the inferior natural virtues are all effected and governed by number, harmony, motion and light, and have their root and foundation in these.[13]

Certainly there was a great deal of latitude in the interpretation of such a pro-nouncement. For some thinkers the belief that 'number' could express some-thing of the nature of the world led numbers to be viewed merely as symbols for other kinds of entity. Johannes Kepler (1571–1630), to take a prominent example, rejected this kind of numerology, but he believed nonetheless that the answer to the numerological question of why there are only six planets deserved serious attention. He repudiated numerology when the signification alloted to numbers was merely contingent upon a numerologist's whim because he believed that the answer to numerological questions had to derive from the for-mal structure of mathematics itself. Believing that mathematics was 'co-eternal with the mind of God' and that 'geometry provided God with a model for the Creation', Kepler felt that there must be a geometrical archetype which limited God's creation of planets, by internal geometrical rules, to only six. Otherwise, he insisted, 'we shall be driven to admit that God acted arbitrarily in the universe . . . And this is a conclusion I will not accept on anyone's authority'. Kepler guessed and subsequently established to his own satisfaction that God had placed the planets in space so that the five regular or Platonic solids could be nested between their orbits:

That is why, if I am asked why there are only six planetary orbits, my reply will be as follows: there ought not to be more than six inter-relationships, for that is the total number of the regular mathematical bodies, and six terms will fully provide that number of relationships.[14]

Idiosyncratic as this may seem, it was exactly the same belief in the mathematical structure of the world which enabled Kepler to make his discovery that planetary orbits are elliptical rather than circular. Kepler continued to struggle with Tycho Brahe's Mars data for eight years because of his paramount commitment to the Neoplatonic and magical belief that mathematics was not merely a convenient tool for 'saving the phenomena' but actually revealed the way things are. Here, then, is a clear case of a magical belief leading to a scientific discovery. (See art. 14, sect. 4.)

Kepler may be regarded as a godsend for the magic and science thesis but there is much evidence indicating the magical antecedents to the mathematisation of early modern science. Unfortunately, though, 'mathematical magic' has not yet received sufficient scholarly analysis and its role is, consequently, difficult to assess with confidence. However, there is a clear tradition within magic of regarding mathematical analysis as a means of guaranteeing the veracity of magical theories.

This can be seen not only in writers such as Cornelius Agrippa and John Dee but also in a mathematical engineer like Simon Stevin who claimed that the certainty of magical knowledge resulted from mathematics. This argument cuts both ways. Although the supreme exemplar of the new mathematical science, Isaac Newton's *Philosophiae Naturalis Principia Mathematica* (*Mathematical Principles of Natural Philosophy*, 1687), shows no sign of magical preoccupations, a number of draft Scholia intended for a second edition drew explicitly upon Pythagorean ideas concerning the harmony of the spheres in order to justify and confirm the concept of universal gravitation. Moreover, Newton carried his belief in the magical notion of the harmony of the spheres into his studies of light for the *Opticks* (1704). The British tradition of the seven-coloured rainbow stems directly from Newton's conviction that 'the Spaces which the several Colours . . . take up' were 'divided after the manner of a Musical Chord'.[15] Such views of mathematics and its applicability to an understanding of the natural world can be traced back at least as far as Roger Bacon. It would seem, therefore, that the mathematical analysis of nature was not so much an innovation in natural philosophy as an appropriation from natural magic.

3. CONCLUSION

The magic and science debate has frequently been taken beyond such general considerations of methodology and ethos. There is no shortage of detailed historical studies in which magical ideas such as sympathy and antipathy, astrological or alchemical beliefs, have been shown to constitute or effect the actual scientific theories of various natural philosophers. Among the most important of these are the works of Walter Pagel on Paracelsus, J. B. van Helmont, William Harvey, and several of their respective followers, but the *cause célèbre* in this historiographical endeavour is the claim that Newton's concept of force owed much to his meticulous and seemingly obsessive studies in alchemy. Studies of alchemical and other magical texts known to Newton and also of his own extensive alchemical manuscripts, suggest that alchemy provided him with a body of evidence and a set of concepts and arguments which he used to infer the existence of attractive and repulsive forces between particles of matter. (See art. 16, sects. 4–5.) In arguing for interparticulate forces capable of acting at a distance Newton was flouting the canons of both Aristotelian physics and Cartesian mechanics, but he was actually advocating ideas that had been commonplace in natural magic and which had recently been absorbed, at least in England, into the new natural philosophy. This did not mean that Newton accepted all the tenets of alchemy; as R.S. Westfall has said, 'with his quantified concept of force' Newton 'had extracted the essence of the art'.[16]

Newton's interest in alchemy, his development of Neoplatonic concepts of spirit (as a possible cause of gravitational and electrical phenomena), his defence of occult qualities in natural philosophy and his belief in mathematical 'harmonies' (as a means of discovering the precise nature of God's Creation) have all been recognised as indicative of the profound influence of magical traditions on his creative scientific work. For earlier historians this meant that Newton must be seen as a 'Great Amphibium' who spanned 'two worlds'. 'With one foot in the Middle Ages and one foot treading a path for modern science', he was 'not the first of the age of reason' but 'the last of the magicians'.[17] However, we no longer have to assume the existence of such tensions and contradictions in Newton's thought. It is now recognised that the transformation of natural philosophy from an academic study of one branch of 'scientia' in the medieval university to a mathematical and empirical pursuit with utilitarian ends increasingly conducted outside the cloisters of universities, was brought about by the appropriation of natural magic into natural philosophy. Accordingly, it now seems correct to say that Newton's greatness as a scientist was achieved not in spite of but because of his easy acceptance of the traditions of natural magic.

NOTES

1. John Donne, *An anatomie of the world. The first anniversary* [many editions], lines 391–95.
2. John Cotta, *The triall of witch-craft* (London, 1616), p. 34.
3. Frances A. Yates, 'The hermetic tradition in renaissance science', in Charles S. Singleton (ed.), *Art, science, and history in the renaissance* (Baltimore, 1968), pp. 255–74, 255, 257. For qualifications of Yates's views see R. S. Westman and J. E. McGuire, *Hermeticism and the Scien-*

tific Revolution (Los Angeles, 1977); Charles B. Schmitt, 'Reappraisals in renaissance science', *History of science*, 16 (1978), 200–14.

4. A. Rupert Hall, 'Magic, metaphysics and mysticism in the Scientific Revolution', in M. L. Righini Bonelli and William R. Shea (eds.), *Reason, experiment and mysticism in the Scientific Revolution* (London, 1975), pp. 275–82; Mary Hesse, 'Reasons and evaluation in the history of science', in M. Teich and Robert Young (eds.), *Changing perspectives in the history of science: essays in honour of Joseph Needham* (London, 1973), pp. 127–47; and Brian Vickers, 'Introduction', in Brian Vickers (ed.), *Occult and scientific mentalities in the renaissance* (Cambridge, 1984), pp. 1–55.

5. Hall, 'Magic, metaphysics and mysticism in the Scientific Revolution', p. 276.

6. Roger Bacon, *Opera quaedam hactenus inedita*, ed. J. S. Brewer (London, 1859), p. 553.

7. Henry Power, *Experimental philosophy, in three books: containing new experiments, microscopical, mercurial, magnetical . . .* (London, 1664), p. 192; Ralph Cudworth, *The true intellectual system of the universe* (London, 1678), Chap. III, Sect. xxxvii, Para. 9.

8. Henry Cornelius Agrippa von Nettesheim, *De incertitudine et vanitate omnium scientiarum et artium* (n.p., 1531), Chap. 42 [unpaginated].

9. John Baptista Porta, *Natural magick* (London, 1658), pp. 1–2. Pietro Pomponazzi, *Les causes des merveilles de la nature ou les enchantements* (Basle, 1556), reprinted ed. by Henri Busson (Paris, 1930), p. 124.

10. Francis Bacon, *Novum organum*, Aphorisms I and IV; in R. L. Ellis, J. Spedding and D. D. Heath (eds.), *The works of Francis Bacon* (7 vols., London, 1887–92), vol. 4, p. 47; Bacon, *New Atlantis, Works*, vol. 3, p. 156.

11. Thomas Wilson, *The rule of reason* (London, 1551), sig. H5v.

12. Robert Hooke, *De potentia restitutiva*, reprinted in R. T. Gunther (ed.), *Early science in Oxford* (14 vols., Oxford, 1921–45), vol. 8, p. 179. Robert Boyle, *Cosmicall qualities*, in *The works*, edited by Thomas Birch (6 vols., London, 1772), vol. 3, p. 307. Isaac Newton, *Mathematical principles of natural philosophy*, trans. by A. Motte, revised by F. Cajori (Berkeley, 1960), pp. 546–7.

13. Henry Cornelius Agrippa von Nettesheim, *De occulta philosophia* (n.p., 1533), II.1.

14. Johannes Kepler, *Harmonice mundi*, IV.1, in *Gesammelte Werke*, ed. by W. von Dyck, M. Caspar, F. Hammer, *et al.* (Munich, 1938–), vol. 6, p. 233. *Mysterium cosmographicum*, Preface; *Werke*, vol. 1, p. 11.

15. John Dee, 'Mathematical Preface' to *The elements of geometrie of the most auncient philosopher Euclide of Megara*, trans. by Sir Henry Billingsley (London, 1570), sig, *jr-v. Simon Stevin, *The principal works*, ed. by E. J. Dijksterhuis, D. J. Struik, A. Pannekoek *et al.* (5 vols., Amsterdam, 1955–66), vol. 3, p. 607. Isaac Newton, *Opticks: or, a treatise of the reflections, refractions, inflections and colours of light*, based on the Fourth Edition London, 1730 (New York, 1952), p. 126, 128.

16. R. S. Westfall, 'Newton and alchemy', in Brian Vickers (ed.), *Occult and scientific mentalities in the renaissance* (Cambridge, 1984) pp. 315–35.

17. Hugh Kearney, *Science and change 1500–1700* (London, 1971), p. 196; John Maynard, Lord Keynes, 'Newton, the man', in the Royal Society, *Newton tercentenary celebrations* (Cambridge, 1947), pp. 27–34.

FURTHER READING

B. J. T. Dobbs, *The foundations of Newton's alchemy, or 'the hunting of the greene lyon'* (Cambridge, 1975).

John Henry, 'Occult qualities and the experimental philosophy: active principles in pre-Newtonian matter theory', *History of science*, 24 (1986), 335–81.

Keith Hutchison, 'What happened to occult qualities in the Scientific Revolution?', *Isis*, 73 (1982), 233–53.

J. E. McGuire and P. M. Rattansi, 'Newton and the "pipes of pan" ', *Notes and records of the Royal Society of London*, 21 (1966), pp. 108–43.

Walter Pagel, *Paracelsus: an introduction to philosophical medicine in the era of the renaissance* (Basle, 1958).

—— *William Harvey's biological ideas: selected aspects and historical background* (Basle, 1967).

——*Joan Baptista Van Helmont: reformer of science and medicine* (Cambridge, 1982).

Paolo Rossi, *Francis Bacon: from magic to science,* translated by Sacha Rabinovitch (London, 1968).

Lynn Thorndike, *A history of magic and experimental science* (8 vols., New York, 1923–58).

Brian Vickers (ed.), *Occult and scientific mentalities in the renaissance* (Cambridge, 1984).

D. P. Walker, *Spiritual and demonic magic from Ficino to Campanella* (London, 1958).

Charles Webster, *From Paracelsus to Newton: magic and the making of modern science* (Cambridge, 1982).

Frances A. Yates, *Giordano Bruno and the hermetic tradition* (London, 1964).

38

ATOMISM AND THE MECHANICAL PHILOSOPHY

MARTIN TAMNY

1. THE MECHANICAL PHILOSOPHY

The Scientific Revolution of the sixteenth and seventeenth centuries was associated with the emergence of a new philosophy of nature called the 'mechanical philosophy'. Although, in part, the mechanical philosophy was a resurrection of the atomism of Democritus, Lucretius and Epicurus, it offered an exciting alternative to the dominant Aristotelian world view of the sixteenth century. Pierre Gassendi (1592–1655), René Descartes (1596–1650), Thomas Hobbes (1588–1679), Galileo Galilei (1564–1642), Robert Boyle (1627–91), Isaac Newton (1642–1727) and John Locke (1632–1704) were all, to some degree, adherents of the mechanical philosophy. The term 'mechanical philosophy' was generally used by these new scientists and philosophers to designate their methodology and their view concerning which properties, relations and entities were real (their *ontology*). This mechanical philosophy constituted a revolt against the Christian Aristotelianism which had emerged principally from the works of Thomas Aquinas, rather than an attack on the much earlier classical forms. More specifically, it was a repudiation of the doctrine of substantial forms (essences realised in matter) as causes – a doctrine that was thought to have produced empty explanations of phenomena and consequently ignorance regarding the physical world. (See art. 35.)

The form of explanation adopted by the mechanical philosophy was reductive in character. That is, it attempted to reduce the indefinitely large number of qualities manifested by bodies to just a few real properties adhering in the constituent smaller parts of the objects we see about us. Thus, most qualities were to be explained by these few properties, which were not further reducible and were thus themselves inexplicable (or, put more favourably, required no

597

explanation). These properties were regarded by the mechanical philosophers as passive, as opposed to the active properties that characterised minds or spirits. Bodies were deemed incapable of initiating any actions themselves; instead, they underwent changes. Furthermore, with the exception of those motions directly initiated by minds, all such changes were products of the inter-actions of one body with another. Such interactions were limited to exchanges of motion through contact, such as collisions, pushes or pulls. The associated methodology of the mechanical philosophy consisted, roughly, in the formation of hypotheses regarding the real properties of bodies, and these hypotheses were to be tested through rigorous experiment.

The ontology of the mechanical philosophy was 'corpuscularian', i.e. objects were considered to consist of parts that were so small as to be unobservable. Those corpuscularians who believed that there were minimum parts which could not be further divided were termed 'atomists', while those who believed that the parts were divisible without limit simply went by the name 'corpuscularian', without further qualification. This possibility of division rested in all cases on the notion of a vacuum. Those who believed in the physical reality of the vacuum were atomists, while those rejecting it were non-atomist corpuscularians.

The mechanical philosophy prospered in the hands of practitioners such as Galileo, Boyle and Newton. Never before had it been possible to describe, explain and predict such an extensive range of phenomena. Galileo had succeeded in mathematically describing the behaviour of falling bodies and pendula, while Boyle had done the same for the relationship between the pressure, temperature and volume of a gas. The great success of Newton's mechanics with its enormous predictive powers ensured the near-universal adoption of the mechanical philosophy in a relatively short time.

A consideration of two major, though common, misconceptions concerning the nature of the Scientific Revolution of the seventeenth century will help make clearer the nature of the mechanical philosophy and its connection with a corpuscular or atomistic ontology. (See art. 15.) The first misconception is the notion that the Aristotelian view of knowledge did not allow a role for observation and experience, which were central to the New Philosophy that characterised the Revolution. The second is that the New Philosophy repudiated the use of occult causes (see art. 37) – i.e. causes not directly available to sensory experience – in explaining phenomena, whereas Aristotelianism had utilised them uncritically.

2. MANIFEST EXPERIENCE

Aristotelianism has usually been characterised as dogmatic and insular to experience. This view does, however, admit that Aristotle used sense experience as the foundation of his scientific methodology in that it begins with sense experience and moves 'upward' to the increasingly general statements that characterise a particular science. However, when historians of philosophy wish to draw the lines of demarcation between Aristotle's own thought, on the one hand, and Aristotelianism, on the other, they usually do so on the issue of the relevance of sense experience to knowledge.[1] The Aristotelians, we are told, believed that Aristotle had discovered the most general truths, and no longer bothered to test the tenets of their thought against experience. This approach to Aristotelianism does capture some aspects of its character in the sixteenth and seventeenth centuries but ignores a feature of Aristotelian thought that was important for the philosophers and scientists who made the Scientific Revolution. The dominant Christian Aristotelianism of the time made direct reference to the importance, indeed centrality, of what was called 'manifest experience' and 'ocular demonstration' in the acquisition of knowledge. The fact that the Aristotelian picture of the world was remarkably consistent with ordinary experience could not be overlooked by the new scientists. One might even say that the Aristotelian picture of the world appealed to common sense, whereas Newtonian mechanics, that was to replace it, did not. It was precisely this aspect of Atristotelianism that made it so pervasive for so long. We, of course, find it difficult to recover that feeling of plausibility, since we have been taught both that it is wrong and why, but contemporary experiments on what are called intuitive physical notions have shown that the untutored mind regards the world in a way closely akin to the Aristotelian view.

Thus, although the Aristotelians may have been convinced that their basic doctrines had the force of necessity, and did not require observational evidence for their establishment, they nevertheless supported them, when under attack, by referring to their common-sense consistency with experience. These references were to what the Aristotelians regarded as manifest experience, and they believed that by these references they had offered an 'ocular demonstration' of some of the truths of Aristotelianism as against those doctrines of the new science that so clearly flew in the face of what we observe.

Galileo was very much aware of the employment of the notions of manifest experience and ocular demonstration by the Aristotelians of his day. Simplicio, the Aristotelian in Galileo's writings, is presented as making such appeals to manifest experience, while Salviati, the Copernican and 'mouthpiece' for Galileo, argues that there is no such thing as manifest experience – a position which on its surface appears inconsistent with the role of experience in the new science.

From early in the first day of the *Dialogo . . . sopra i due massimi sistemi del Mondo* (*Dialogue Concerning the Two Chief World Systems*, 1632), Simplicio continually opposes Salviati's Copernicanism with references to experience. For example, at one point he argues that Aristotle held that experiments were more valuable than arguments and that those who contradicted the evidence of their senses deserved to be punished by losing those senses.[2] Thus the commonly-held view that the Scientific Revolution introduced sense experience as the arbiter of the acceptability of scientific claims is at least an oversimplification. The Aristotelians of the sixteenth and seventeenth century were viewed by Copernicans as using sense experience to support their false claims. What Galileo shows us is that experience alone cannot serve as the arbiter of truth but only experience properly interpreted. It is not the appeal to sense experience as such that is attacked, but rather the notion that such experience is ever manifest or obvious.

Galileo attacks the notion of manifest experience by having Simplicio support an Aristotelian doctrine by reference to manifest experience and then undermining that support *not* by contesting the sense experience itself, but by showing that the same experience is consistent with the denial of the Aristotelian doctrine in question. An example will illustrate this kind of attack. On the second day, Salviati and Simplicio construct the following argument for the non-rotation of the earth. If a stone is dropped from the ceiling within a high tower and is observed not to hit the walls but to fall parallel to them, then the earth does not rotate. For, if the earth rotated, the stone could not fall perpendicularly. The argument can be reformulated as follows:

Premiss 1.   If the earth rotates, the body cannot fall perpendicularly.
Premiss 2.   But the body does fall perpendicularly.
              Conclusion. The earth does not rotate.[3]

After Simplicio accepts this argument Salviati argues that it is fallacious. The minor premiss (1) presupposes the conclusion in the sense that what we see (the stone not hitting the walls of the tower) is an indication that the stone falls perpendicularly only if we assume that the tower (and thus the earth) is not moving. We do not 'see' the stone fall perpendicularly to the earth. All we see is that the stone fails to hit the walls of the tower.

Not content to show that Simplicio can misinterpret experience without his realising that he is interpreting anything at all, Galileo goes on to show that even quick-witted Sagredo (the intelligent, uncommitted layman, who listens to both views and is moved only by the truth) can make the same mistake, albeit in a more sophisticated way. In the ensuing dialogue, Sagredo claims to see motion perpendicular to the earth (while Simplicio does not), but thought he did not (while Simplicio thought he did). But this apparent paradox is removed by recalling that Simplicio began by assuming that the earth did not move while Sagredo assumed that it did. In short, the difference in Salviati's (Galileo's) description of their respective experiences depends upon their different presuppositions and interpretations. Galileo has not only shown that our experience of the falling stone is consistent with the Copernican view, but also that there is neither manifest experience nor ocular demonstration. Some have taken the foregoing argument as evidence that Galileo was a Platonist who believed that experience is irrelevant to the acquisition of knowledge. Without examining the complexities of that problem, it can be seen that Galileo is arguing that at least some real motions are 'invisible', as when the observer shares the motion, but he is also arguing that, although such motions are invisible, they can still properly play a part in our understanding of the world. Galileo's major point, however, is that in this case we do not need *more* experience, but a way of 'looking' at past experiences. Neither manifest experiences nor ocular demonstrations are possible. Nor are they needed, so long as the New Science provides methods of correct interpretation.

Francis Bacon (1561–1626) characterised the makers of the Scientific Revolution as toilers in the 'Great Instauration' – the restoration of man to his place before the Fall. In the Garden of Eden, according to this view, Adam had no need for spectacles. All the physical universe lay before him, clear and manifest. The language with which he spoke to God was a natural language, one in which the words were not linked by mere convention to the things they named, but rather were appropriate to those things in such a way that knowing the name constituted knowing the thing named. Through the acuity of his senses and his knowledge of natural language, Adam knew and controlled the world God had given him, his dominion being exemplified in his act of naming the animals. (See art. 9, sect. 2.) But all was lost at the Fall.

In 1661, Joseph Glanvill (1638–80) attempted to show in *The Vanity of Dogmatizing* that the Aristotelianism of the previous age was not fit for the business of the great instauration. Indeed, he appears to argue that if there ever was a time that the methodology of manifest experience and ocular demonstration provided knowledge of the world, it was before the Fall. Glanvill wrote,

> *Adam* needed no Spectacles. The acuteness of his natural Opticks (if conjecture may have credit) shew'd him much of the Coelestial magnificence . . . without a *Galileo's* tube: and 'tis most probable that his naked eyes could reach near as much of the upper World, as we with all the advantages of art. . . . and 'tis not unlikely that he had as clear a perception of the earth's motion, as we think we have of its quiescence.
>
> Thus the accuracy of his knowledge of natural effects, might probably arise from his sensible perception of their causes . . . . And whereas we patch up a piece of Philosophy from a few industriously gather'd, and yet scarce well observ'd or digested experiments, his knowledge was completely built upon the certain, extemporary notice of his comprehensive, unerring faculties. His sight could inform him whether the Loadstone doth attract by Atomical *Effluviums* . . . [4]

Glanvill's Adam had no need of the mechanical philosophy of the Scientific Revolution, since for him all was known by manifest experience and ocular demonstration. Adam before the Fall is thus presented, within the context of the Aristotelian model of knowledge acquisition, as an ideal observer whose acuity of sense perception allows him to know all there is to know about the physical world. What happened at the Fall was a diminution in Adam's sensory ability and much that he knew before could no longer be known by his descendents.

This characterisation in fact fits the doctrine of Christian Aristotelianism which holds that what we cannot see (that which is not within the realm of the sensible) we cannot know; that perceivability is a necessary condition for knowledge and intelligibility. The mechanism for knowledge acquisition requires that a phantasm (image) of the object of knowledge be transmitted to the mind where its substantial form may be realised and apprehended by the active intellect. The term 'quality' was used to refer both to the properties or attributes of bodies as well as to the substantial forms (*qualitates*) that are the causes of those attributes and that are to be used to explain them. Those qualities that cannot be perceived are termed occult causes and lie outside the realm of possible knowledge. Those qualities that can be perceived and apprehended by the mind are termed *manifest* qualities and their perception, *manifest experience*.

Primary examples of occult causes were gravitational and magnetic attractions. Their effects could be known through manifest experience, but not the causes themselves. Due to Adam's folly, we cannot see these causes, but we can, through the new methodology of a non-Aristotelian mechanical philosophy, 'patch up a piece of philosophy' that argues for their nature.

3. ANTI-ARISTOTELIANISM

There is another sense in which the mechanical philosophy involves the rejection of manifest experience. The role of experience in the acquisition of knowledge about the physical world is simple observation in the case of Aristotelianism, whereas it is through experimentation in the mechanical philosophy. Experimentation is viewed as a way of wresting the truth from the world, as if there are secrets that nature does not readily give up. Thus Robert Boyle refers to the 'rack of experiment.'[5]

Mechanical philosophers not only rejected the dogmatic character of later Aristotelian thought, but also emphasised the empirical richness of the 'hands on' knowledge of the craftsman and artisan; of knowledge obtained by the direct manipulation of nature. Thus Andreas Vesalius attacked the practice of anatomical teaching that separated the professor from the physical act of dissection and the doctor from the actual treatment of his patients. Such practices led to a loss of knowledge and to students who 'are confusedly taught less than what a butcher, from his meat-block, could teach the doctor'.[6]

The very name by which the new science came to be known, the 'mechanical philosophy', was a recognition of the importance of the manipulation of nature as against the notion of simply observing manifest experience. In 1593, Gabriel Harvey was also admiring 'expert artisans, or any sensible industrious practitioners, howsoever unlectured in schools or unlettered in books'. These artisans, craftsmen and industrious practitioners went by the general name of *mechanics*, as we are told by Thomas Sydenham writing in 1669: 'The most acute and ingenious part of men being by custom and education engaged in empty speculations, the improvement of useful arts was left to the meaner sort of people, who had weaker parts and less opportunity to do it, and were therefore branded with the disgraceful name of mechanics'. In mid-seventeenth century England the term mechanic was used of anyone who placed the 'practical' knowledge garnered from manipulative experience before the claims of authority and dogma. (See art. 15, sect. 2.) Thus while the craftsman was labelled a mechanic so too, for instance, was John Bunyan, who was called a 'mechanick preacher'. *Mechanick preachers* were 'those doctrinally heretical and socially subversive laymen of the lower classes who took advantage of religious toleration to air their own disturbing views. Such men appealed to their own experience . . . to confute authority, just as the scientist appealed to experiment'.[7]

Although all the mechanical philosophers of the Scientific Revolution shared the notion that the relevance of experience to the acquisition of knowledge required interpretation and method, but *not* manifest experience, there existed no uniformity of view among them as to what that method and mode of interpretation should be. They warned against hasty inductions, unexamined presuppositions, the use of hypotheses, etc. They gave examples but not *a priori* arguments as to why to proceed one way rather than another. As the mechanical philosophy developed, some admonitions disappeared and others took their place. No single method emerged as *the* way to work until the enormous success of Isaac Newton led many to emulate a methodology that was barely spelled out. But we shall return to these issues after considering the ontology of the mechanical philosophy.

4. OCCULT QUALITIES

Another misconception is the view that the mechanical philosophy repudiated occult causes as the explanations of phenomena while Aristotelianism utilised them uncritically. This will require us to examine the way in which the Aristotelian ontology of real forms gave way to the mechanical philosophy's ontology of corpuscularianism or atomism.

A major tradition that influenced the mechanical philosophy was that of corpuscularianism and/or atomism as exemplified in the works of Galileo and Descartes, both of whom offered a new way of explaining the world in terms of motion and impacts among small bodies that had very few real properties. They attacked the facile and empty explanations of Aristotelianism that claimed to explain nearly everything and in reality explained almost nothing. Aristotelians sought to explain the behaviour of bodies in terms of their qualities (substantial forms). This led to invoking as many different qualities as there were different phenomena to be explained. These 'explanations' were considered by the mechanical philosophers to be, at best, *ad hoc*, and, at worst, meaningless. If a body was hot this was explained by its having the property of heat, if cold by its having the property of coldness. Yet this offers no adequate explanation. Galileo puts it well in the *Dialogo* when he makes Sagredo assert that gravity is but a name and not an explanation of why bodies fall. Everyone knows that the cause is called gravity, 'But we do not really understand what principle or what force it is that moves stones downward'.[8]

The Aristotelians regarded the cause of gravitation as occult and, as we have seen, unknowable, since objects are knowable only through their sensible images. These sense images transfer the manifest qualities of the object to the imagination where they then reside to be sifted later for universal and essential forms by the active intellect. Clearly, any object outside the realm of sense experience is thus outside the realm of knowledge. For Thomas Aquinas (1226–74), 'Man is not competent to judge of interior actions that are hidden but only of exterior motions that are manifest'.[9] Aquinas is typical of the Christian Aristotelians who not only did not *use* occult causes but denied that such causes were knowable. They did, however, refer to these unknown causes by name, in this way making it appear as if they were invoking them as known. Thus Aristotle referred to attraction as the occult cause of falling bodies. The standardised character of Aristotelian explanation, as we have seen, readily lends itself to this way of speaking; however, it is doubtful if many Aristotelians, when pressed, would have considered naming as an explanation. The principle point being made by Galileo and the other new philosophers is that Aristotelian explanations offer us nothing better in those cases where the Aristotelians do not regard the cause as occult.

Despite the fact that their objections applied as much to manifest qualities as to those that were occult, gravity exemplified the failure of Aristotelian explanation. The mechanical philosophy thus had at its heart an attempt to find an alternative form of explanation. This form of explanation would not only avoid the problems of substantial forms as causes, it would also allow for the explanation of those phenomena attributed to occult causes by the Aristotelians. Unlike the Aristotelians, the mechanical philosophers believed that we could achieve knowledge of those things that could not be observed. Indeed, they took the radical view that all causes are occult in the sense that they are not given in experience, but are still knowable. The mechanical philosophers' treatment of causes as occult in this sense is a direct consequence of their views regarding manifest experience, for, in rejecting any experience as simply given, they were clearly rejecting the notion that causes are given in experience. The ultimate ontology of the mechanical philosophy consists of entities that are not themselves sensible. The atoms and/or corpuscles, of which all grosser bodies are constituted, are not in the realm of the sensible, yet they and their properties are the ultimate causes and explanations of all the phenomena of nature *and* they are knowable. How is this possible?

5. REAL PROPERTIES

The form of explanation adopted was, as we have seen, reductive in character. That is, it attempted to reduce the indefinitely large number of qualities manifested by bodies to just a few real properties adhering in the constituent smaller parts of the objects we see about us. Thus, most qualities were to be explained by these few properties. The real properties of bodies were not further reducible to any others and were therefore themselves inexplicable. Mechanical philosophers thus sought to determine which properties were real. But perhaps even more important was the question of how to *justify* claims as to which properties were real since such claims went beyond experience. At the same time no mechanical philosopher wished to be, or even appear to be, guilty of the same charges made against the Aristotelians. Since any attempt at explaining the real properties would amount to no more than invoking a name, it became very important for mechanical philosophers not to claim that gravity, for instance, was a real property of the constituent bodies.

Galileo made the distinction between the real properties of bodies and those properties that are reducible to them in *Il Saggiatore* (*The Assayer*), in 1623. He calls tastes, odours, colours, etc., mere names, and places them in the consciousness rather than in external objects. On the other hand, he claims that whenever he thinks of a material object, he conceives it as bounded, having shape, relative size, a place in space and time, a state of motion or rest, contact (or not) with other bodies and as being one or more in number. These he regarded as the real properties of bodies.

Tastes, colours, odours and sensations such as heat were to be explained, according to Galileo, through the interaction of our bodies with the constitutent parts of material objects. The cause of heat is the multitude of minute particles, having certain shapes and velocities, which penetrate our bodies by means of their extreme subtlety and by their touch produce the sensation we call 'heat'.

A similar set of distinctions was made by Descartes in his *Principia Philosophiae* (*Principles of Philosophy*) of 1644. He stated that properties such as size and figure are known in a very different manner from colours, pains, etc. He asserted that they are in fact known more clearly, and 'That the nature of body does not consist in weight, hardness, colour, or other similar properties; but in extension alone'.[10] Further, Descartes believed that all the variation in matter, or all the diversity of its forms, depended on, and could be explained by, the motion of its parts. Hence, he claimed that heat consists solely in the movement of the particles of bodies.

Both Descartes and Galileo appear then to agree that the world is constituted of collections of smaller bodies ('corpuscles', 'atoms', 'particles', etc.) such that the large number of properties (or apparent properties) of the collections are reducible to the few real properties of the smaller bodies that make up the collections. The way in which the reduction was carried out varied from one mechanical philosopher to another as the example of heat in the works of Descartes and Galileo suggests.

The diversity of explanation achieved by the mechanical philosophy was made possible by the introduction of quantitative difference where Aristotelianism made use of qualitative difference. The reductive character of explanations was accomplished by accounting for the wide variety of apparent qualities by allowing a wide quantitative range that the few real properties permitted. Thus both Boyle and Descartes, among others, accounted for hotness by a single real property, motion, and attributed their difference not to a difference in kind but to a difference in degree: the more motion the hotter, the less motion the colder. Quantitative diversity thus replaced qualitative diversity and reduced the number of real properties required to explain the world.

Although the mechanical philosophy limited the number of real properties to but a few, there was no universal agreement as to which, precisely, these should be. Descartes utilised purely geometrical properties – extension, motion and shape – whereas Galileo listed being bounded, having shape, having a relative size, being spatio-temporal, having motion or being at rest, being in contact or not being in contact with other bodies and number. Newton, on the other hand, listed extension, hardness, impenetrability, mobility and inertia. While Locke's list contained solidity, extension, figure, motion or rest and number, Boyle's consisted of local motion, rest, bulk, figure, situation and texture. In the light of this diversity we must ask: how were these lists determined? Does the mechanical philosophy provide criteria for determining the real properties of corpuscles?

The first issue we must confront is whether the real properties were necessary properties. It is clear that Descartes regarded extension as *the* defining property of matter. The only properties that a material object can have are thus extensional or geometrical properties. He argued that if a piece of wax is placed near a fire, all its sensory properties change, yet we know it to be the same piece of wax. Thus what we know of the wax are not its sensory properties but those properties that remain unchanged through the wax's alteration, namely its extension, flexibility and movability. What is more, this knowledge goes beyond the senses and the powers of the imagination, since it involves infinite possibilities of shape and position. We arrive at this understanding about the wax by systematically abstracting those apparent 'properties' that can alter while it remains the same piece of wax. The properties which remain are those which are real.

Locke's criteria to determine real properties clearly reflect the atomistic ontology of the mechanical philosophy. The properties that are real are those that belong to the atoms themselves. Atoms are unobservable but they are the constituent parts of observable bodies. Those properties of observable bodies that are not lost through any change or alteration of those bodies, and most particularly those that persist through their division will also belong to the parts of those bodies, no matter how far divided. Locke regards as real those properties that are 'utterly inseparable from the body, in what state soever it be; and such as in all the alterations and changes it suffers . . . it constantly keeps; and such as sense constantly finds in every particle of matter which has bulk enough to be perceived; and the mind finds inseparable from every particle of matter, though less than to make itself singly be perceived by our sense'.[11]

Locke's criteria constitute a variety of appeals to the necessary and the contingent. In contrast to Descartes and Galileo, Locke emphasised experiential criteria in his references to the observed changes which bodies undergo and to the fact that certain properties are universally observed. On the other hand, he makes reference to those qualities that 'the mind finds inseparable from every particle of matter'.

Newton's criteria were almost certainly influenced by his reading of Locke's *Essay Concerning Human Understanding* in the early 1690s. Newton did not consider this question of criteria in the first edition of the *Principia* in 1687, but the issue does appear in Rule III of the 'Rules of Reasoning in Philosophy' of the second edition (1713). There he writes,

> The qualities of bodies, which admit neither intensification nor remission of degrees, and which are found to belong to all bodies within the reach of our experiments, are to be esteemed the universal qualities of all bodies whatsoever.[12]

Here, as in Locke, the persistence of qualities through change and particularly through division is central, but Newton has dropped any reference to whether the absence of any particular quality is imaginable. The issue of which qualities are real is to be decided by experiment, not by the imagination and its limitations. Newton proceeded to elaborate his Rule as follows:

> For since the qualities of bodies are only known to us by experiments, we are to hold for universal all such as universally agree with experiments; and such as are not liable to diminution can never be quite taken away. We are certainly not to relinquish the evidence of experiments for the sake of dreams and vain fictions of our own devising; nor are we to recede from the analogy of Nature, which is wont to be simple, and always consonant to itself.[13]

Newton's claim is that division, or any other kind of change, does not destroy extension, mobility or the object's persistence in its state of rest or rectilinear motion. Clearly, quantity can be altered by some kinds of change but if the quality remains unchanged, for example, an extended object remains just as much an extended object, then the quality is real.

Boyle's criteria for accepting or rejecting mechanical explanations and, more specifically, for determining which qualities are real, make reference only to matters of experience. He argued that, since he is not claiming that the mechanical principles are the only way to explain the qualities of bodies, all he need show is that they are sufficient for their explication. What matters is the success of our explanations in the light of future experience. Even the mechanical philosophy itself is but a reasonable hypothesis consistent with experience and superior conceptually to the Aristotelian world view.

6. CONCLUSION

It has been argued here that the mechanical philosophy does not consist of a simple appeal to experience, but attacks Aristotelianism for its views regarding manifest experience and ocular demonstration. It replaces the naïve notion of manifest experience with the notions of interpretation of experience and the conduct of experiment wherein the truths of nature are 'forced' from her. Further, far from attacking the use of explanations that refer to entities and properties that are not directly perceivable, mechanical philosophers universally adopted such explanations and attacked the Aristotelians for their reluctance to seek knowledge about that which lies beyond manifest experience.

In addition, the mechanical philosophy was not a single uniform set of beliefs. All mechanical philosophers were corpuscularians, although some were not atomists. Some properties were regarded as real or fundamental by all of them, such as extension, but no two of them had identical lists of properties. Finally, while some mechanical philosophers regarded their views as necessary truths, others regarded them as no more than a set of hypotheses consistent with experience.

Before long, the remarkable predictive success of the mechanical philosophy pushed these differences far into the background. The issue of which properties to regard as real gave way to a rough and ready set of pragmatic considerations which allowed even gravity that status, although understood as action-at-a-distance and still only a name. At the same time, these same considerations resulted in the general acceptance of the view that the world was to be explained in terms of a set of entities and properties lying outside the range of our senses yet rendered knowable through the very success of those explanations, a view that will probably outlast the Aristotelianism it replaced.

NOTES

1. See Arthur Kenyon Rogers, *A student's history of philosophy* (New York, 1925), pp. 215–16; William Turner, *History of philosophy* (Boston, 1957), pp. 433–4; and John Wick's article on Aristotelianism in *The encyclopedia of philosophy*, ed. Paul Edwards (New York, 1972), vol. I, pp. 148–51.
2. Galileo Galilei, *Dialogue concerning the two chief world systems*, 2nd edition, ed. and trans. Stillman Drake (Berkeley, 1967), p. 32.
3. Santillana reformulates the argument in essentially the same way in Galileo Galilei, *Dialogue on the great world systems*, introduction and revisions by Giorgio de Santillana (Chicago, 1953), p. 154.
4. Joseph Glanvill, *The vanity of dogmatizing: the three versions*, ed. Stephen Medcalf (Hassocks, 1970), pp. 5–6.
5. Robert Boyle, *The works of the Honourable Robert Boyle*, ed. Thomas Birch, vol. 2: *New experiments and observations touching cold or an experimental history of cold begun* (London, 1772), p. 660.
6. A. Vesalius, *De humani corporis fabrica* (Basileae, 1543), preface. See B. Farrington, 'Vesalius and the ruin of ancient medicine', *Modern quarterly* (1938), 23ff.
7. Quoted in Christopher Hill, 'Newton and his society', *Texas quarterly* (Autumn, 1967), 32.
8. Galileo, *Dialogue*, p. 234.
9. Thomas Aquinas, *Summa theologiae* 1a.2ae.91.4. Quoted in Keith Hutchison, 'What happened to occult qualities in the Scientific Revolution?' *Isis*, 73 (1982), 238.
10. René Descartes, *Principles of philosophy*, trans. V. R. Miller and R. P. Miller (Dordrecht, 1983), p. 40.
11. John Locke, *An essay concerning human understanding*, ed. A. C. Fraser (New York, 1959), vol. I, pp. 169–70.
12. Isaac Newton, *Mathematical principles of natural philosophy*, trans. A. Motte, rev. F. Cajori, *Mathematical principles*, (Berkeley, 1960), p. 398.
13. Newton, pp. 398–9.

FURTHER READING

Marie Boas, *Robert Boyle and seventeenth-century chemistry* (Cambridge, 1958).

E. J. Dijksterhuis, *Mechanization of the world picture* (Oxford, 1961).

Marie Boas Hall, *Robert Boyle on natural philosophy* (Bloomington, 1965).

Keith Hutchison, 'What happened to occult qualities in the Scientific Revolution?', *Isis*, 73 (1982), 233–53.

R. H. Kargon, *Atomism in England from Hariot to Newton* (Oxford, 1966).

Ernan McMullin, *The concept of matter in modern philosophy* (Notre Dame, 1978).

—— *Newton on matter and activity* (Notre Dame, 1978).

Stephen Toulmin and June Goodfield, *The architecture of matter* (New York, 1962).

39

NEWTONIANISM

SIMON SCHAFFER

Historical understanding of the power and influence of Isaac Newton (1642–1727) has been troubled precisely because of Newton's mastery. It is seductively easy to treat Newton's work as the culmination of the Scientific Revolution (see art. 15) and the inauguration of recognisably modern physical science. Newton seemed to have licensed a way of speaking about the world. While immensely flexible as doctrine, Newton's language suggested boundaries and conditions for the discourse of the sciences.

In retrospect, many have seen this discourse in terms of a single, simple model. Natural systems were conceived as sets of particles moving in void space under the influence of mathematically describable forces acting between the particles' centres. This model was held to depend upon the laws of motion Newton laid down in the *Philosophiae Naturalis Principia Mathematica* (*Mathematical Principles of Natural Philosophy*, 1687). These laws summarised the principle of inertia, the relationship of moving force to the change of motion of the body and the equality of action and reaction. Such laws were supposed to be true in an absolute reference frame, in which each body could be associated with an unambiguous position, mass and velocity. Such systems moved deterministically – all future states could in principle be derived from the current positions, motions and forces. These techniques could be applied outside mechanics to fields such as optics, electrostatics and the science of heat.

Every scientific discipline carries with it a history which makes sense of its origins and ends. This simple model of Newtonianism relies on just such a history. Two periods of great importance for the development of the picture of a system of particles moving under absolute mechanical laws were the late eighteenth century in France and the late nineteenth century in Germany and Austria. In late eighteenth-century France, under the authority of the astronomer and mathematician Pierre-Simon Laplace (1749-1827), Paris academicians began to pursue a research programme based on a rational and celestial mechanics attributed to Newton. In his *Exposition du système du monde* (1796), Laplace argued that the successes which this mechanical and deterministic natural philosophy had achieved in astronomy and in rational mechanics should now be extended to research into the phenomena of light, the cohesion of bodies, magnetism, galvanism and chemistry. A 'Laplacian' programme (see art. 18) emerged under the aegis of French physics, and its appeal to Newton's authority helped disseminate the view that Newton's original purposes were adequately summarised in the tenets of this mathematical and mechanical enterprise.

This reading of Newtonianism was highly influential in nineteenth-century physics. It became possible to see Newtonianism as the common sense of the physical sciences. Physics should model mechanical systems of moving mass points through an analysis of the forces operating at a distance between these points and using Newton's axiomatic laws of motion and force. This was the programmatic account of dynamical physics which the great German physicist Hermann von Helmholtz gave at Berlin University in the early 1890s. At the same period, physicists concerned to examine the philosophical foundations of their science assumed that an analysis of Newton's principles would reveal the basic assumptions of classical physics. Both Heinrich Hertz, Helmholtz's most eminent student, and the Prague physicist Ernst Mach (1838–1916) assumed that their contemporaries subscribed to this picture of Newtonian mechanics and then sought to challenge this commitment. Mach brilliantly used this picture to develop a critical history of mechanics in his *Science of Mechanics* (1883). He argued that only an historical treatment would reveal those concepts in mechanics which lacked a genuine history and were thus metaphysical. He treated the development of mechanics as nothing but a record of commentaries on the terms deployed in Newton's laws, and used these commentaries to make his own system. By juxtaposing Newton's utterances about method to be found in the *Principia* with the classical statements of terms such as mass and force, Mach suggested major revisions in what he took to be the obscure foundations of mechanical science. Mass was to be defined through the relative acceleration which a body experienced, while forces were to be referred to the arrangement of bodies in space.

The work of Mach and his contemporaries helped make it seem that Newtonianism and classical physics were synonymous. Criticism of Newtonian principles could look like criticisms of received tenets of the physical sciences. But this was only one version of the basis of physical enquiry, and only one version of what Newtonianism might mean. For example, although Laplacian physics had been responsible for the propagation of this mechanistic and deterministic reading of Newton, Laplace's colleague at the Paris Académie des Sciences, Joseph-Louis Lagrange (1736–1813), used a very different set of mechanical principles, treating dynamics as derivative from statics and banning all talk of hypothetical microscopic forces. Lagrangian mechanics posed a very severe challenge to Laplacian principles. Furthermore, the development of new sciences in the nineteenth century, such as thermodynamics and electromagnetism, using explicitly Lagrangian techniques in their dynamical analysis of heat, light and the electromagnetic field, showed that the Laplacian division of disciplines and the alleged Newtonian foundations of physics were deeply troubled.

Finally, dramatic changes in physics in the early twentieth century involved renewed claims that Newtonianism provided the conceptual and philosophical underpinnings for all of classical physical science. Albert Einstein appealed to arguments of Mach and his colleagues when mounting his critical examination of the allegedly Newtonian assumptions of classical mechanics, and his contemporaries explored Newtonianism in order to understand the fate of that mechanics. Some protagonists of these disputes assumed that such a Newtonianism was the only possible alternative to the radical theories of relativity and quantum mechanics. Thus in the 1930s the astronomer E.A. Milne argued for what he called a 'Newtonian' cosmology, based on the premises of universal gravitation, absolute space and the law of action and reaction, against its principal, Einsteinian, competitor. This sense of 'Newtonianism' now gained very widespread assent: as it vanished from modern physics it acquired a new, powerful, historical role.

The close relationship between the mechanistic reading of Newtonianism and the fate of classical physics suggests why this reading has commanded such widespread assent. At the same period as the transformations in the physical sciences during this century, historians and philosophers of science examining the Scientific Revolution and its classical aftermath began to chart Newton's work as metaphysician and methodologist. In a celebrated 1948 lecture, Alexandre Koyré described the 'Newtonian synthesis' as an accomplishment of immense philosophical significance. For Koyré, this synthesis amounted to a combination of the tools of mathematical reason and experimental enquiry. The price paid for this triumph was a loss of human value in the sciences. Thus Koyré spoke nostalgically of the passing of such values, a change he dated to the seventeenth century, and the end of the 'Newtonian synthesis' in turn, which he associated with changes in physics of the early twentieth century.[1]

This has been an enormously influential reading, yet it has posed a major problem for subsequent historians. Even though Koyré claimed that Newton achieved the union of mathematical and experimental sciences, it was all too easy to treat Newton's published legacy as split between an exact mathematical treatment of rational and celestial mechanics and an experimental enquiry into the properties of light and matter. Interpretations of early modern science due to T.S. Kuhn have contrasted these sciences of mathematical analysis and those of 'Baconian' experiment.[2] As a result, it has been common to treat the history of Newtonianism as a chronicle of the ways in which natural philosophers separated or combined these approaches. However, this commonplace can easily obscure the variant versions of Newtonianism which developed and the process by which these mutations commanded agreement from separate groups of natural philosophers, divines, physicists and philosophers in the eighteenth and nineteenth centuries. Since Newton's approval was a prize worth winning, widely differing doctrines have been associated with his name. In order to understand these loyalties and the purposes they served, it is necessary to examine the canon of Newtonian texts established during the eighteenth century, and to see how these texts were used.

1. MAKING SENSE OF NEWTONIANISM: THE INTERESTS OF INTERPRETERS

Newtonianism possesses its literary classics, the *Principia* and the *Opticks* (1704). The former is a mathematical treatise on mechanics and astronomy. Its central techniques involve ways of representing change of quantity by geometrical and dynamical models. Instantaneous changes in variable quantities become incremental variations in line lengths. The effects of continuous forces are made equivalent to sums of instantaneous impulses deflecting moving bodies from a rectilinear path. The time a body takes when moving round some point from which a single force is exerted on it is computed by the area swept out by the line linking the body to the point.

Each technique possessed its own history. In the *Principia* the work of Newton's predecessors such as Christiaan Huygens and Johann Kepler was transformed. Kepler's laws of planetary motion were generalised as motions in a central-force field. New phrases appeared; in analogy with Huygens's 'centrifugal force', 'centripetal force' referred to actions tending towards the force-centre. With these tools, the treatise presented an analysis of the motions of planets and moons, tides and comets. Newton's work in mathematics later appeared in texts on analysis, first published in 1711, and on general mathematics, edited in 1707 by William Whiston, Newton's successor at Cambridge.[3] Newton's achievement was swiftly seen as a compelling account of natural motion and its quantitative description.

Newton's book on light and colour, the *Opticks*, was assembled during the 1690s from earlier material. The treatise wore an experimental dress: it contained detailed protocols for trials with prisms, mirrors and lenses, and, as a coda, a set of queries on fire and light, matter theory and experimental philosophy, which grew in length in the successive editions from 1704 to 1717. One way of speaking about this achievement was to make the *Principia* into a programme for mechanics and astronomy and to read the *Opticks* and its associated texts as a charter for a new experimental philosophy. Both works contain some passages which present strictures on method, including a passage on experimental method first published at the end of the *Opticks* in 1706; a 'General scholium' added to the *Principia* in 1713; and some 'Rules of reasoning', as they came to be known, prefaced to the *Principia*'s third book. Newton's epigones published extracts from some other texts, including significant letters to Robert Boyle, the Anglican priest Richard Bentley and others of Newton's contemporaries, principally concerned with optics, matter theory and natural theology. The Newtonian corpus was formed out of this rather uneven mixture of documents.[4]

To chart the uses to which this legacy was put, it is necessary to consider the local interests served by its application. These interests help clarify why some writers won Newton's blessing while others attacked his system. Examples from optics and chemistry show how this worked. Many eighteenth-century natural philosophers held that Newtonianism included loyalty to a model of light as minute, rapid particles of matter affected by strong short-range forces between these particles and common matter. This was a doctrine which they claimed to find in Newton's *Opticks* and in some of his earlier papers on light and colour, composed in the 1670s and reprinted in the 1780s. Yet the doctrine of the corpuscular character of light was rejected by several natural philosophers. There was no period when Newton's writ ran throughout Europe. The greatest of mid-century academicians, Leonhard Euler espoused a wave theory of light and denied that all matter gravitated equally. Others behaved differently. While Thomas Young also developed an alternative model of light, based on vibrations in a space-filling ether, he claimed a good Newtonian warrant for his own views. (See art. 40, sect. 5.) Such examples illustrate the more general thesis that interpretation of the Newtonian enterprise has been consequent upon the interests of interpreters. We must try to understand these purposes in order to explain why a particular version of Newton's meaning was given, and to examine who it was who shared this interpretation.

Present-day historians and philosophers have their interests too. They have discussed Newtonianism in a variety of ways. Newton is treated as the legislator of modern sciences and Newtonianism as a *language*, a vocabulary and a grammar which most scientists began to use to speak about their world. His texts are combed for his views on method and his celebrated discussions of the significance of mathematics, the use of experiment, the suspicion of hypothesis and the relation between force and matter. Newtonianism becomes synonymous with 'classical' physics. A second form uses Newton to classify the variations in eighteenth-century natural philosophies. It attends to the obvious authority of Newton in the Century of Enlightenment. In this version of history, selected researchers are identified as 'Newtonian' if their views conform to those which the historian attributes to Newton. If they do not, then the natural philosophers in question can be seen as 'anti-Newtonian' or even as victims of 'misreadings' of the master's dogma. Neither approach accounts for the interpretative practices of Newton's audiences.

It is a notable feature of the development of western sciences since the Renaissance that they have formed well-defined groups of collaborating enquirers. The outward and visible forms of the scientific enterprise, such as the performance of experiments and their repetition by other credited colleagues, shared stories about the origin and progress of scientific specialities and disciplines, heroes and villains, provision of training through textbooks, laboratories and academies, networks of publication and informal communication, are all accompaniments of such groups. Much discussion has been devoted to ways in which such groups can be defined. What gives them coherence? What function do they play in research, and how do they come into being and pass away?

Each historiography answers differently. The first suggests that the local ecology of groups of co-workers is a less significant feature of scientific life than the intellectual assumptions upon which all such collaboration depends. 'Newton' becomes the name of an heroic mind which promulgated these assumptions and gave them decisive authority. Yet a wide variety of social settings can be invoked to see how Newton's authority emerged and became powerful. The period following Newton's death witnessed the emergence of scientific societies across Europe, modelled on the Paris Académie des Sciences. Members of these academies strenuously developed and debated the implications of the mathematics, mechanics and astronomy which Newton constructed. At the same period, promoters of lecture demonstrations and public shows expanded their appeal and the range of instruments and experiments. Significant commercial activity in London and elsewhere was accompanied by deliberate efforts to base the claims of speculative entrepreneurs upon Newton's natural philosophy. 'Newtonian' natural philosophy began to appear, in textbooks by writers such as Willem 'sGravesande (1688–1742) and John Theophilus Desaguliers (1683–1744), and in more popular volumes such as Voltaire's *Éléments de la philosophie de Newton* (1738) and *Il Newtonianismo per le dame* (1737) composed by Francesco Algarotti. This implies that the classification of eighteenth-century sciences into those of a 'mathematical' and those of an 'experimental' emphasis, and the division of Newton's legacy into traditions of commentary upon the *Principia* and upon the *Opticks*, can provide a preliminary model for an exploration of Newtonianism. Furthermore, as the disciplinary map of natural philosophy changed during this century, so did the various senses of Newtonianism.

2. NEWTONIAN POWERS: EIGHTEENTH-CENTURY EXPERIMENTAL PHILOSOPHIES

Between 1690 and 1727 Newton and his colleagues worked hard to establish agreement about the sense to be given to the terms of his natural philosophy and its implication for contemporary culture, religious and political. Several platforms were available for participants in these debates. At the Royal Society in London, where Newton became President in 1703, experimenters such as Francis Hauksbee (*c.* 1666–1713) and his successor Desaguliers were employed in staging shows to illustrate Newtonian principles. Command over this institution was important. Hauksbee's work on electricity, light and pneumatics, initially conceived as a development of the research programme initiated by Robert Boyle, was very rapidly absorbed by Newton into his account of the relationship between force and matter. Trials performed by Hauksbee from 1705 were reported in subsequent editions of Newton's *Opticks*.[5]

Desaguliers' role was equally decisive. From 1710 he continued the lectures on experimental philosophy delivered at Oxford by John Keill. As demonstrator at the Royal Society from 1714, Desaguliers' shows played a key role in the responses Newton organised to challenges from Continental critics. Visitors were able to witness expert and authoritative replications of Newton's optical trials. It was Desaguliers, for example, who in 1714 revived the label of 'crucial experiment' for one such trial using two prisms. The Newtonian group held that this demonstrated that light could be analysed into truly 'primitive rays' which could not then be made to change colour upon further refraction. The experiment appeared in idealised form at the front of the 1722 Paris edition of the *Opticks*. Such texts, including the translation of 'sGravesande's textbook on Newtonian philosophy which Desaguliers produced in 1721, accompanied and reported the celebrated experimental work. Experimental techniques shown at the Society and elsewhere in London were transmitted to France, Holland and Italy. Popular texts such as those of Voltaire and Algarotti appeared as a result of these contacts and the consequent emergence of audiences for this form of experimental philosophy. Desaguliers and Newton provided their performances with a commentary which stipulated the right way of interpreting the public trials. In the process, a Newtonian vocabulary was formed, involving passive particles, short-range attractive forces and active principles such as the causes of electricity, light and chemical fermentation. Newton's queries to the *Opticks* became a charter for a mature research programme.

The establishment of Newton's authority within the universities was also a significant aspect of this process. Networks of patronage and influence were decisive. At Newton's Cambridge, powerful figures such as Richard Bentley aided the careers of men who played significant roles in Newtonian debates, such as Whiston, Samuel Clarke and Roger Cotes. Political and religious controversy accompanied this process. Newton was treated by some of his allies as an exemplary member of the Whig establishment, while others saw his programme as threatening and divisive. Several of those Cambridge men who supported Newton were accused of heresy and became deeply suspect to Tories and High Churchmen, who perceived that Newton's natural philosophy seemed to attribute force to matter. The critics charged that Newtonians revelled in conceptual obscurity and offered a path to rationalist deism and free thought. In 1710 Whiston was expelled from the University. Clarke was accused of denying Anglican orthodoxy. Newton's closest colleagues found themselves enrolled in the defence of Newton's mathematics, cosmology and theology against critics such as the philosopher and divine George Berkeley, whose *Analyst* (1734) contained a brilliant assault on the foundations of Newtonian mathematics. Responses to Berkeley from mathematicians such as James Jurin and Colin Maclaurin provided opportunities for the development of Newton's programme, as did the contemporary war waged between the British natural philosophers and the allies of G.W. Leibniz, a contest which touched on issues of metaphysics, natural philosophy and religion.

Presented in polemical replies to major domestic and foreign critics, Newtonianism was a system born in conflict and a language produced for specific pugnacious purposes. The debate on the cause of gravity illustrates this formation. In the *Principia*, Newton seemed to eschew all causal talk about forces; having given their mathematical measure, he offered few indications of his account of the principles which allowed them to arise from and affect matter. The question was discussed with the Cambridge men: in the 1690s, Bentley gave sermons which enlisted Newtonianism in the defence of religion, Roger Cotes replaced Bentley as editor of the *Principia*'s second edition (1713), and Clarke translated the *Opticks* into Latin in 1706, fought Leibniz on Newton's behalf in 1715–1716, and transformed a celebrated treatise on Cartesianism, Jacques Rohault's *Traité de physique*, into a Newtonian textbook for Cambridge students (1697).

It seemed important to provide an answer to the question of the cause of forces such as gravity, since Newton faced charges from critics such as Huygens and Leibniz that an uncaused force which acted through empty space on the centres of bodies was no better than a 'miracle' or an 'occult' quality. If these accusations could be sustained, then the moral propriety of Newtonian natural philosophy would be undermined. But Newton's statements on the cause of gravity needed careful management to make them into an adequate response. Newton and his allies asked whether a force like gravity had a material cause. In passages in the *Principia* and in conversations during the 1690s Newton answered in the negative, since all matter gravitated, and any matter in space would disturb motion. Cotes told Newton in 1712 that this must mean that gravity was essential to matter, and published this view in his preface to the *Principia*'s second edition (1713). Newton and Clarke disagreed. Newton informed Bentley in 1693 that gravity could not be essential to matter, and reiterated this view in a query added to the *Opticks* in 1717. Samuel Clarke preached in 1706 that gravity must be infused into matter by God. He told Leibniz in 1715 that this did not mean that force was a 'miracle'. Arguments between Newton and his readers, whether friendly or hostile, spawned several different answers to the Newtonian question of force.

Contemporary with the contest with Leibniz, for example, Newton published statements which indicated that some fluid medium might indeed provide the cause of forces. This principle might be electrical. Newton helped himself to Hauksbee's experiments to sustain this view. Furthermore, Newton carefully changed passages in the 1713 *Principia* and the 1717 *Opticks* to allow some ethereal fluid which might be present in space and inside bodies and which could produce these forces. As presented in Britain in the first decades of the eighteenth century, Newtonianism banned certain phrases from natural philosophical discourse. No fluid made of common matter filling all space could be mentioned. It must not be said that gravity, or any force, was inherent in and essential to matter. It was allowable to remain silent on the cause of gravity. It was also permissible to tell stories about some rare fluid, itself susceptible to short-range forces, and to use electrical, chemical and optical experiments to provide support for such a substance.

This discourse provided natural philosophers with some important resources: a range of fluids evinced in demonstration experiments with electrical machines, air pumps and other devices, mathematical techniques for estimating forces and their effects, a theological claim about the first cause of all natural change and the sense that mathematical sciences might not need to state the real causes of the forces which they described. None of these resources were unique to Newton's allies. Others found them useful too. Newton's resources were applied to problems of medicine, moral philosophy and political economy. Major changes in disciplinary boundaries were implied by the use of these resources. The status achieved by mechanics and astronomy under Newton's aegis was valuable for many practitioners. The Oxford astronomy professor David Gregory and the physicians Archibald Pitcairne and John Freind construed Newton's mechanics of short-range central forces as the suitable basis for future procedures in medicine and in chemistry. These Jacobites saw Newton as a valuable ally in their restoration of proper morality and science. The great Dutch professor Hermann Boerhaave developed his own stories about the significance of an elementary fire in chemical change, and then connected this substance with statements on the ether and on force which he found in Newton. Boerhaave's views implied a new account of Newtonian disciplines. Pirated versions of Boerhaave's lectures, published as *A New Method of Chemistry* (1724) contained instructions to readers inserted by their editor, the Scarborough physician Peter Shaw. Shaw now ingeniously recast Newtonianism as pure chemistry.

This re-reading became incorporated into an experimental philosophy of active fluids. From the 1740s electrical machines and pneumatic jars seemed to give proofs of the ether Newton described. But this philosophy did not command universal assent. In histories of electricity, optics and chemistry, the radical Joseph Priestley developed a materialist cosmology in which matter and force were identified with each other. He also challenged Newton's 'divine' authority over the natural philosophical establishment. Radical attacks made it hard to preserve orthodoxy. For example, the Viennese therapist Franz Anton Mesmer claimed that his 'animal magnetism' was derived from orthodox Newtonian principles. Although it was derided by Parisian academicians, the appeal of Mesmerism showed how many other popular practitioners, including so-called 'quacks', might claim Newtonian warrant. However, French texts also implied a very significant narrowing in the scope of the discipline of physics. Natural history and chemistry were excluded and in this process a classical physical science began to appear, with characteristic institutions of teaching and research. Such institutions allowed their members to explore fundamental questions in the mathematical sciences and in new fields of enquiry. They also allowed the reconstruction of the meaning of Newtonianism so as to provide a warrant for extensive research in physics.

3. IN SEARCH OF NEWTONIAN PHYSICS

The image of Newton which was celebrated in the Enlightenment owed its power principally to the physics and astronomy pursued at the scientific academies in Paris, Berlin, St Petersburg and elsewhere. However, once again this image was a deliberate accomplishment rather than a self-evident consequence of the academies' work. An overwhelmingly Francophone scientific culture treated questions suggested by Newton's work as but one part of its agenda. Protagonists such as Euler, Alexis-Claude Clairaut or Jean d'Alembert pursued a well-defined enterprise on problems concerning vibrations, motions of rigid bodies and paths described by bodies moving under constraint. Their key techniques were not solely or dominantly due to Newton. In the Berlin Academy, Euler and Maupertuis became involved in sharp controversies over the relative merits of Newtonian and Leibnizian programmes. During the dispute these two academicians based mechanics on concepts such as 'action', the sum of products of momentum and distance for a particle system. Such systems obeyed limit principles susceptible to rational analysis: under the influence of a central force, for example, systems moved so that the total action was at either a maximum or minimum value. These techniques implied a model of an efficient natural economy dominated by conservation laws utterly alien to the cosmology of divine activity which Newton constructed. Likewise, Lagrange's mechanics of the 1780s represented an abandonment of the familiar Newtonian principles, which had been interpreted as dealing with the causes of such motions. This highly abstract approach also allowed Lagrange to construct a mathematical model of gravity which gave every point near a given massive body the value of the force which would act on an infinitesimal mass at that point. Such tactics were of immense significance for the other traditional area of Newtonian concern, celestial mechanics.

In celestial mechanics, Newton's work was sometimes challenged or ignored. His theology argued for God's role in the restoration and preservation of activity in the universe. Comets were interpreted as bearers of such activity, and many English philosophers reproduced and furthered these cosmological and moral interests in their work on spectacular celestial events and the structure of the world. While some academicians, such as the Comte de Buffon or Jérôme Lalande, did develop speculative cosmologies and claimed Newtonian licence for doing so, others were sceptical and hostile. There was criticism, too, of the premisses of Newton's gravitational theory. Euler maintained that an ether in space could affect the motion of planets and moons. In 1748 Clairaut contemplated abandoning the exact inverse square law of gravity in order to save the phenomena of lunar motion, prompting an angry dispute with Buffon, who argued that celestial mechanics must be committed to the original force law. By the 1750s Clairaut was able to show how these phenomena could fit the exact law.

Clairaut's experience was characteristic of the way in which Newtonianism was made into an ideology for enlightened savants. Essay prize competitions, official journals and the blessing of state patronage allowed academics to pose as wardens of rational philosophy and progress. Anglophile propagandists found Newton an indispensable icon for this cult. Pilgrimages to London were common: Voltaire's celebrated journey prompted his highly influential public presentation of Newtonian philosophy, while other travellers included the witnesses of Desaguliers' crucial optical experiments in 1715, followed by Delisle in 1724 and Maupertuis in 1728. Skilful campaigning by these men enabled them to make bold claims about the novel authority of Newtonian physics and mathematics.

From 1716, Delisle argued for systematic comparisons of astronomical observations with consequences deduced from Newton's gravitational theory. In 1724 he obtained copies of the astronomical tables of Edmond Halley, a monument of Newtonian science. This kind of work indicated targets at which the academicians should direct their attack. Maupertuis vigorously undermined the authority of the existing French state astronomical programme conducted from the Paris Observatory and engineered a 'crucial' test of Newton's power. He claimed that Newtonian and Cartesian theories implied different estimates of the Earth's shape. Expeditions were despatched to Lapland and Peru, equipped with good new English instruments. Clairaut was enrolled in the enterprise. Thanks to Maupertuis' publicity and Clairaut's analytic skill, it was possible to present the expeditions' results as decisive victories for the Newtonian camp.

A similar process accompanied the celebrated return of Halley's Comet between 1758 and 1759. Clairaut, working closely with Delisle's student and successor Jérôme Lalande, derived a pleasingly accurate value for the time of the comet's perihelion. These accomplishments were deliberately presented as successes for Newton's theory, even though it was widely acknowledged that Halley's cometography was imprecise and the results of the Lapland expedition ambiguous. It became possible for the academicians to present their successes in Newtonian terms. From the 1770s, Laplace and Lagrange worked to show the secular stability of the entire solar system, including both planets and moons. By demonstrating that all apparent long-term changes in the system were oscillations about mean values, and the dependence of this upon the exact inverse square law, the mathematicians held that they had completed Newton's mission for astronomy.

The coherence of this Newtonianism therefore relied upon agreements within the academies about the right methods and goals for the exact sciences. It was reinforced in Enlightenment culture through popular texts and iconography. In 1785, and again in 1800, the French Académie d'Architecture devoted its prize competition to the design of a monumental cenotaph for Newton. In 1802 the Utopian socialist Henri Saint-Simon proposed a visionary social system based on the 'Newtonian' principles of reason, order and universal law. This imagery relied on earlier programmatic statements such as those of d'Alembert in the *Encyclopédie* (1751), who invoked Newton to legitimate the supremacy of mathematical analysis in exact sciences and in experimental philosophy, while others glossed Newton's pronouncements as an argument for relentless empiricism. Branches of experimental philosophy, such as electricity, magnetism, heat and pneumatics, were systematically brought within the scope of quantitative analysis. The application of the inverse square law of forces to electrostatics by Charles Augustin Coulomb allowed Laplacians of the 1790s to envisage a general physics embracing the traditional fields of natural philosophy. Control over the scientific institutions of the French state after the Revolution enabled them to propagate this enterprise and its account of Newton's aims. For three generations the association of triumphalist mathematical physics, the French materialism and determinism of the revolutionary period and cautions about the moral and theological implications of this programme, dominated debates on the meaning of Newtonian science.

Future interpretations of Newtonianism were developed as critiques or reconstructions of Laplacian physics. The story posed as many troubles in theology and metaphysics as in the conduct of physics. In France, André-Marie Ampère attacked the foundations of Laplace's mechanism and Coulomb's electrical and magnetic theories by denying that a range of different actions at a distance could serve the purposes of the new science of electrodynamics. In what he advertised as a 'Newtonian' essay on the magnetic effects of electricity,

Ampère combined his readings in Kantian metaphysics with an enquiry into the single fundamental force which governed interactions between current-carrying circuits. He claimed to have avoided all 'hypothetical' assumptions about microscopical interparticle forces. Ampère's work aided that of others such as Joseph Fourier and Augustin Fresnel, whose dynamical investigations of heat and light used Lagrangian mathematical techniques to undermine Laplacian physics. But, as Ampère's comments suggest, Newtonianism remained a useful methodological label with considerable moral force. (See art. 18, sect. 3.)

Moral issues were also of importance in Britain, where a significant revision of Newtonianism was accomplished by the work of the Edinburgh professor John Robison (1739–1805). His most influential texts, a supplement to the *Encyclopaedia Britannica* (1801) and his posthumous *System of Mechanical Philosophy* (1822), edited by his most distinguished student, David Brewster, outlined a version of Newtonian science which he held was safe from the dangers of Laplacian atheism. This was a real concern for Robison and his colleagues: in the 1790s Robison had warned of the threat to political and religious order posed by the wrong use of Newton's authority whose deadly effects were visible in the outrages of the French radicals. The Cambridge professor Samuel Vince argued in the same way in an 1806 essay: to prevent Laplacian materialism it was necessary to 'return' to Newton and to interpret gravity as the result of direct divine action. Robison's prescription for the disease of philosophical irreligion was a combination of physics based on particles and central forces and an epistemology debated with Scottish philosophers such as Thomas Reid, deeply hostile to hypothetical models and the use of subtle fluids, such as the ether, and sceptical about the possibility of a knowledge of underlying physical causes. It was argued that Newtonians should limit themselves as far as possible to the observable motions of systems of particles. The attempted seizure of Newton's mantle by Robison and his followers was of central importance for the future form of Newtonianism. Brewster emerged as a chief spokesman in the nineteenth century, strenuously defending what he took as Newtonian truths, such as the corpuscular theory of light, and publishing a monumental biography of Newton in 1855.

Brewster constructed an exemplary picture of Newton and his legacy, and defended his hero against criticism, particularly from France. Brewster's subject was a figure fit to preside over the votaries of the religion of science. A different defence of Newtonian morality was presented from Cambridge by William Whewell in 1833. Whewell argued for a distinction between Newton, who used 'induction' to establish the true system of mechanics and astronomy on clear fundamental principles, and those such as the Laplacians, who had deduced the system's consequences. The former, Newtonian, way tended to morality, the latter to atheism.[6] The work of Brewster and Whewell illustrates the role Newtonianism had acquired in the mid-nineteenth century as a set of regulative principles for the sciences. These principles depended on rival histories of Newtonian philosophy, rival versions of a 'return to Newton'.

The dramatic transformations in scientific organisation and training prompted revisions of the stories told about Newton's methods. Debates raged about Newton's personal morality – a saint of science should live a saintly life, whatever the evidence to the contrary. Similarly, rival philosophies told different stories about Newton's path to discovery. Where Enlightenment ideologues such as Priestley had often emphasised the role of steady empirical investigation and devalued the role of sudden inspiration in Newton's style, commentators such as Brewster stressed the transcendent genius and inimitable heroism of the master scientist. Such a story could help legitimate an image of stratification in the sciences between discoverers and more pedestrian cultivators of enquiry. One of the most influential analyses of method, Whewell's *History of the Inductive Sciences* (1837), used the Newtonian achievement and its aftermath as a paradigm for scientific development in general. On Whewell's showing, Newton had brilliantly combined the clearest and deepest grasp of a set of fundamental ideas, such as causality and force, and then matched these ideas to the facts of experience. Whewell cleverly designed a model of Newtonianism which emphasised Newton's utter uniqueness and yet preserved the worth of his programme as exemplary and instructive for future scientists.

In Cambridge and in the Scottish universities, the *Principia* remained a significant part of the nineteenth-century science curriculum, suitably accompanied by student commentaries and handbooks. However, Newton's legacy might be interpreted as part of a programme in mixed mathematics, with rational mechanics as a key resource for the new work on physical optics. It might, alternatively, as at Edinburgh University, continue to be seen as the charter for experimental philosophy. These contrasting interpretations hinged on the accounts which Victorians gave of the proper path for the new disciplines in the physical sciences. The most obvious feature of Victorian physics was the development of a dynamics, a methodology for physical science in which motions and positions of particles could be derived from a general function such as 'energy' or 'work' which described the system's state and the forces acting within it. (See art. 21.) In the early 1850s, the Glasgow natural philosopher William Thomson (1824–1907) and his colleague the engineer William Rankine developed an 'energetics' based on the law of the conservation of energy. With this law, Rankine argued, a mechanical concept of energy could link together mechanics and other branches of natural philosophy – notably electromagnetism and thermodynamics.

Both Brewster and Whewell were sceptical of bold claims for the fundamental character of energetics. In 1865, the astronomer and natural philosopher John Herschel attacked the validity of energetics, arguing instead for the primacy of what he interpreted as the orthodox Newtonian view that forces were the fundamental entities in natural philosophy. Herschel drew from the resources of Newtonian natural theology to argue that observable and unobservable actions were necessarily connected, and claimed that the recognition of real forces as true causes was a key element of this programme. For these critics, mechanics in the form of extremal dynamical principles was basic, while energy laws could only be approximations to observable regularities dependent on underlying causal forces. This approach was in contrast to that developed by Thomson and his Scottish colleagues. In his powerful analysis of the invisible motions of molecular systems, for example, James Clerk Maxwell argued that his dynamical techniques were due to a great tradition fathered by Newton and continued by Lagrange and the Irish mathematician William Rowan Hamilton. In the celebrated *Treatise on Natural Philosophy* (1867) which Thomson co-authored with Peter Guthrie Tait, mechanics was grounded on principles of energy conservation and exchange, while the authors alleged that such a foundation represented a principled resurrection of true Newtonianism. (See art. 21, sect. 2.)

These fierce debates on the foundations of physics, characteristic of the late nineteenth century, reflect concern with disciplinary boundaries and the relative standing of mechanics with respect to energetics and electromagnetism. Newtonianism become a label which participants in these disputes used to claim an ancestry for their respective positions on the mechanical reduction of theoretical physics. 'Newtonianism' could become a synonym for the primacy of the mechanical world-view, or a label for theories based on central forces acting at a distance, or even an antipathy to all hypotheses about unobservable entities such as a space-filling ether or a conservative measure of energy. Ludwig Boltzmann gave a pithy example of this strategy in his inaugural lecture on the principles of mechanics at Leipzig in 1900. Drawing on the accomplishments in thermodynamics and electromagnetism of Maxwell, Thomson and Helmholtz, Boltzmann (1844–1906) argued that Newtonian mechanics now provided the foundation of the whole of theoretical physics. His imagery was political: he argued that scientific disciplines behaved like great nations, that under Newtonian leadership mechanics had successfully colonised all branches of physics and that with Darwin even biology showed signs of coming under Newtonian sway. Boltzmann conceded that even though this mechanics provided an unparalleled clarity for physical models, nevertheless some of its colonies were in revolt, notably energetics and the life sciences.[7]

The events of the next decade showed the strength of the challenge to the mechanist regime. Between 1900 and 1903 British theoreticians, such as Joseph Larmor, and German physicists such as Wilhelm Ostwald and Max Planck, publicly debated the fate of what they interpreted as Newton's mechanics and his laws of motion. The propagation of electromagnetic action and the interaction of electricity and matter seemed to violate these laws: these troubles were routinely debated in terms of rival histories of physics and thus rival accounts of the way physics might now develop. From 1905, researchers involved in the reconstruction of mechanics and electromagnetism worked successfully to portray their endeavour as the displacement by novel cosmologies of those of the 'Newtonians'.

The debate over Einsteinian relativity was the most important occasion for this work. (See art. 28, sect. 2.) From 1905, it was clear to Einstein that relativity theory needed to match what he took to be the cosmology of Newtonian gravitation, while his colleagues such as Max Planck and Hermann Minkowski worked to show that 'Newtonian' mechanics could be considered as a limiting case of relativistic motion. All this made 'Newtonianism' look like the sole alternative to Einstein's programme. In 1911 Einstein published an estimate of the amount he argued light would be deflected by a nearby massive body. Five years later he reconsidered the problem, doubling the size of this predicted deflection. Then, in 1918, the Cambridge astronomer Arthur Eddington wrote a report in which he cunningly claimed that the former value was that to be expected from 'Newtonian' assumptions, the latter from those of Einstein's general theory of relativity. As secretary of the Royal Astronomical Society, Eddington was able to stage observations of a solar eclipse during 1919 which he could present as a crucial test of the general theory's truth. He had engineered a situation in which only the so-called Einsteinian or Newtonian predictions would be considered. Despite major difficulties in the eclipse observations, Eddington's ploy worked. His triumph was widely perceived as marking the decisive victory of an Einsteinian over a generalised Newtonian world-view.[8]

It has been characteristic of most subsequent commentary on these events that Newtonian assumptions have been seen as archetypical of classical physical science and are therefore to be contrasted with those of modern physics. This has bred an awkward interpretation of the meaning of Newtonianism, in which the experimental philosophies and rational mechanics of the eighteenth century, and the debates about dynamics and energetics in the nineteenth, have been seen as little more than family squabbles among fellow Newtonians. Yet Newton himself worked very hard to stipulate the most useful sense to be given to his utterances in different settings. Shrewd observers such as Whewell or Boltzmann recognised that Newtonianism could serve many causes. This parable still has valuable lessons for contemporary historians of science.

NOTES

1. Alexandre Koyré, 'The significance of the Newtonian synthesis', in *Newtonian studies* (Chicago, 1965), pp. 3–24.
2. T. S. Kuhn, 'Mathematical versus experimental traditions in the development of physical science', *Journal of interdisciplinary history*, 7 (1976), 1–31; Henry Guerlac, 'Newton's changing reputation in the eighteenth century', in R. O. Rockwood (ed.), *Carl Becker's heavenly city revisited* (Ithaca, 1958), pp. 3–26.

3. Florian Cajori (ed.), *Sir Isaac Newton's mathematical principles of natural philosophy* (Los Angeles, 1934), pp. 2–4, 406–10; D. T. Whiteside (ed.), *The mathematical works of Isaac Newton* (2 vols., New York, 1964 and 1967).
4. I. B. Cohen, (ed.), *Newton's papers and letters on natural philosophy* (Cambridge, 1958); Newton, *Mathematical principles of natural philosophy*, trans. A. Motte, rev. F. Cajori (2 vols., Berkeley, 1934), pp. 398–400, 543–7.
5. Isaac Newton, *Opticks* (4th ed., 1730, repr. New York, 1952), pp. 393–4.
6. William Whewell, *Astronomy and general physics considered with reference to natural theology* (London, 1833), pp. 303–42.
7. Ludwig Boltzmann, 'On the principles of mechanics, I', in *Theoretical physics and philosophical problems: selected writings*, ed. Brian McGuinness (Dordrecht and Boston, 1974), pp. 129–46.
8. John Earman and Clark Glymour, 'Relativity and eclipses: the British eclipse expeditions of 1919 and their predecessors', *Historical studies in physical science*, 11 (1980), 49–85.

FURTHER READING

Peter Beer (ed.), *Newton and the Enlightenment* (Oxford and New York, 1978) (*Vistas in astronomy*, vol. 22, part 4).

R. E. Butts and J. W. Davis (eds.), *The methodological heritage of Newton* (New York and Oxford, 1970).

G. N. Cantor, *Optics after Newton: theories of light in Britain and Ireland, 1704–1840* (Manchester, 1983).

I. Bernard Cohen, *Franklin and Newton: an inquiry into speculative Newtonian experimental science and Franklin's work in electricity as an example thereof* (Philadelphia, 1956).

John Gascoigne, 'Politics, patronage and Newtonianism: the Cambridge example', *Historical journal*, 27 (1984), 1–24.

Henry Guerlac, *Newton on the Continent* (Ithaca, 1981).

J. L. Heilbron, *Physics at the Royal Society under Newton's presidency* (Los Angeles, 1983).

P. M. Heimann and J. E. McGuire, 'Newtonian forces and Lockean powers: concepts of matter in eighteenth-century thought', *Historical studies in physical science*, 3 (1971), 233–306.

M. C. Jacob, *The Newtonians and the English Revolution, 1689–1720* (Hassocks, 1976).

Christa Jungnickel and Russell McCormmach, *Intellectual mastery of nature: theoretical physics from Ohm to Einstein* (2 vols., Chicago, 1985–1986).

Robert E. Schofield, *Mechanism and materialism: British natural philosophy in an age of reason* (Princeton, 1970).

Crosbie Smith, ' "Mechanical philosophy" and the emergence of physics in Britain, 1800–1850', *Annals of science*, 33 (1976), 3–29.

Arnold Thackray, *Atoms and powers: an essay on Newtonian matter theory and the development of chemistry* (Cambridge, Mass., 1970).

Clifford Truesdell, *Essays in the history of mechanics* (New York, 1968).

David B. Wilson, 'Herschel and Whewell's version of Newtonianism', *Journal of the history of ideas*, 35 (1974), 79–97

40

PHYSICAL OPTICS

G. N. CANTOR

1. INTRODUCTION

Aristotle understood 'optics' to mean the theory of the laws of sight, and for some two millenia the word was generally considered to refer to the study of how we see. Thus, until comparatively recently, lectures and textbooks addressing this subject have been concerned with the problems of visual perception; for example, how distant objects affect our eyes and (thus) our mind, the relationship between the size and situation of an object and its retinal image, the design of optical instruments and the nature of light. The subject matter of optics is thus ill-defined, spilling into areas which we would now call physiology, psychology, engineering, mathematics and physics. Moreover, throughout most of its history, optics cannot be called a discipline since, until the early nineteenth century, there were few textbooks on the subject, no journals and a small and very diverse group of practitioners. At that time, if not somewhat earlier, a more limited definition of the subject emerged, in which optics lost its association with the sense of sight and was instead taken as referring only to the study of the nature and properties of light. It is this definition which present-day physicists will recognise as a branch of their subject.[1]

It is tempting to read the history of physical optics 'backwards'; indeed, many historians have started with the limited physicists' definition and then constructed a history linking the views of earlier writers concerning the nature of light. While there has certainly been some continuity within this mode of discourse, there has also been much discontinuity. For example, Descartes' views about the nature of light cannot simply be understood as a contribution to early physics since his optical theory was framed in response to the wider problem of explaining vision. Moreover, his theory was but part of his reform of natural philosophy, from the foundations upwards. In short, his *La dioptrique* was but one part of his projected *Le monde*.

The example of Descrates' optical writings illustrates a general point about

627

the history of optics (in its more limited sense): theories about the nature of light need to be read in relation to a scientist's other commitments, both in other branches of science and in philosophy and theology. Indeed, throughout much of their history, theories of light have been parasitic. Thus during the seventeenth century, mechanical philosophers (see art. 38) sought to account for light in terms of the motions of matter particles, while Newton's epigones explained optical phenomena by postulating small, projected particles of matter acted on by short-range attractive or repulsive forces.

Both of the above examples also illustrate another recurrent feature of optical theorising, particularly in the period since the beginning of the seventeenth century. Repeated attempts have been made to reduce physical optics to the science of mechanics; therefore contemporary views about matter, motion and force have greatly influenced theorising about the nature of light. Against this mechanisation of optics must be set the minority of writers who pursued other reductive programmes and those instrumentalists who have sought to found optics on empirically-based laws (most pointedly, Ernst Mach in his *Principles of Physical Optics* (1913)). Yet while all these approaches presuppose a clearly-defined domain for the study of optics, there has been an opposing tension which has sought to open the discourse of light to its broader, non-physical significance. The psychological, cultural and religious connotations of light have also deeply affected the way in which people, including many scientists, have conceived the nature of light. Such issues, as well as the search for laws and physical causes, constitute the history of this subject.

2. ANCIENT AND MEDIEVAL OPTICS

Light fulfils such a manifest and crucial role both in our lives and in the economy of nature that all cultures abound with myths dealing with light. In the Judaeo-Christian tradition, for example, God speaks forth light in Genesis 1:3. One issue frequently raised in exegeses of this chapter of the Bible is that light was created immediately after the heaven and the earth, but that the sun was only made on the fourth day; thus light has precedence over the sun and is independent of it. Moreover, before the advent of light 'the earth was without form, and void; and darkness was upon the face of the deep' (Genesis 1:2). Positive qualities are thus attributed to light for its role in changing this condition and, in verse 4, 'God saw the light that it was good'.

If the mythology and symbolism of light have ancient roots so too have attempts to understand how we see. The problem of explaining how a luminous body placed at some distance can affect us and provide us with an *image* of itself is an example of the more general problem of accounting for action at a distance. The Greeks offered a number of different solutions. The early atomists tried to circumvent the problem of action at a distance by explaining vision as a species of touch; they postulated an image – a skin-like material effluence – emitted from visible bodies and travelling through the intervening space before 'touching' the eye. By contrast, Plato, among others, associated light with fire and explained vision by the coalescence of sunlight with the fire emitted from the observer's eye. Aristotle, taking issue with earlier philosophers, conceived that light is the actualisation of the transparent state of a medium owing to the presence of a luminous body. Some Greeks opted for extramission (some influence travelling *from* the eye) and others for intromission (the influence travelling *to* the eye). While there was little consensus among these Greek philosophers on the question of vision, the foundations of a complementary approach to optics were firmly laid by Euclid, Hero of Alexandria and Claudius Ptolemy. In describing the paths of light rays in mathematical terms these writers provided the basis for geometrical optics.

As David Lindberg has ably demonstrated, Islamic writers extended the theories of the Greeks. Several of these writers were physicians whose interests were physiological and physical, rather than mathematical. They contributed significantly to understanding the structure and function of the eye and, drawing on Greek sources, they continued to dispute whether light proceeds from or to the eye. The decisive turn to this controversy was provided by Alhazen (c. 965–c. 1039) who devised a novel form of extramission theory in which each point on a luminous body emits light and colour to the eye. He proceeded to establish the important principle that there is a one-to-one correspondence between points on the object and the points comprising the retinal image. In his optical investigations, Alhazen effectively combined the physiological, mathematical and physical traditions, an example of the latter being his use of a mechanical model to account for refraction. Islamic theorists, especially Alhazen, provided an important source for optical writers in the West, such as Roger Bacon, John Pecham, Witelo and, in the seventeenth century, Johannes Kepler (1571–1630) and René Descartes (1596–1650).

In late medieval and Renaissance works on optics, three separable – but not separate – traditions can be identified. Firstly, a scholastic tradition which emphasised ontological and essentially psychological questions about light. Secondly, a theological tradition which drew on the Bible and on Platonism and directed attention to the cosmological role for light and to questions of cognition. Finally, a mathematical tradition drawing on Alhazen and his early followers in the West. It is this last tradition that Lindberg conceives as gaining maturity in works by Renaissance artists and anatomists who developed theories of perspective. Moreover, this tradition culminated with the highly-developed theory of image formation, including retinal images, articulated by Kepler in 1604. Lindberg argues that Kepler critically extended the medieval tradition in perspective by showing how the lens of the eye focused a cone of rays from a punctiform object on to a retinal point. This account is, however, challenged by Stephen Straker who claims that Kepler is important precisely because he broke with the medieval tradition in optics and its concern with visual perception. Unlike his predecessors (who were academics) Kepler aligned himself with artists and engineers; hence he restricted his investigations to the formation of retinal images using mechanistic and geometrical techniques. Yet Straker is not simply concerned to show that Kepler's optical work constitutes part of the new science, he also argues that Kepler played a crucial role in destroying the holistic conception of man and nature. On this account Kepler 'externalised' the subject of optics and dissociated the question of light propagation from the ancient concern with how we see and thus from consciousness.[2]

3. EARLY MODERN OPTICS

The seventeenth century saw numerous attempts to explain secondary qualities in terms of the essential qualities of matter, and optics provided some of the principal and most challenging phenomena for these mechanical philosophies to explain. (See art. 38.) Descartes, for example, offered at least three mechanistic theories; on some occasions considering light to be a pressure or tendency to motion in the particles of his second element – the subtle fluid that filled interplanetary space. He also accounted for colour by the rate of rotation of particles (which also experienced translational motion) comprising a light beam, and on yet other occasions he drew the analogy between light and the trajectory of a projected body, such as a tennis ball. Despite this diversity, Descartes' intention is clear – to explain optical phenomena solely by the motion of particles of matter. His most impressive success using a mechanical model expressed in mathematical terms was his derivation of the sine law of refraction, independently discovered by Willebrord Snell. In this derivation Descartes analysed the motion of a particle crossing the boundary between two media. Assuming that the velocity component parallel to the interface remains constant and that there is a constant ratio (n) between the velocities in the two media, he showed that $n = \sin i / \sin r$. This analysis did, however, require that light moves faster in a denser medium; faster, that is, in water than in air.

Like other seventeenth-century optical writers, Descartes paid increasing attention to colours and carried out experiments using prisms which led him to offer an account of the formation of both the primary and secondary bows of the rainbow. Nor was he alone in being dissatisfied with the Aristotelian doctrine that colour resides on the surface of visible bodies and possesses the power to actualise transparency in media. Instead Descartes considered that colour is a secondary quality, to be accounted for by matter and motion; perhaps by the rate of rotation of his second-element particles. If a beam of white light falls obliquely on a prism, different parts of that beam become *modified* into the different spectral colours. Light is thus homogeneous, red light being merely a modification of white (or blue, etc.) light.

Although mechanical philosophers offered many different theories of light, seventeenth-century theorists also had to confront an increasing number of problematic phenomena. In 1665 Grimaldi reported several experiments that seemed to show that light did not travel in straight lines. When, for example, he intercepted a narrow beam of sunlight with a small opaque object, he found coloured bands both internal and external to the geometrical shadow. Grimaldi explained these diffraction effects by a fluid theory of light and a modification theory of colours. In the same year Robert Hooke published his discovery of the colours in thin transparent laminae. He found that the colours only appeared if the thickness of the lamina fell between two limits and that the colours bore some relation to the thickness. In explaining this phenomenon, he conceived the incident light beam being partially reflected at the first and at the second surfaces, the resulting colour being determined by the relationship between the two semi-reflected pulses comprising the resultant beam travelling towards the eye. A further important class of phenomena confronting theorists was double refraction, first reported by Erasmus Bartholinus in 1669.

Probably the most startling discovery of the seventeenth century was that light – white light – was not homogeneous but a mixture of different types of light. In a series of experiments dating primarily from the mid- and late 1660s Isaac Newton (1642–1727) showed that when white light passes obliquely through a prism, the component rays suffer different 'degrees of refrangibility' – i.e. are refracted by different angles. Moreover, there was a correlation between refrangibility and colour, blue rays being refracted most and red rays least. While refrangibility could be expressed in mathematical terms, colour could not. However, as he argued in 1672, his experiments contradicted the modification theory supported by Descartes and others and instead they showed that colours are '*Original* and *connate properties*, which in divers Rays are divers'.[3]

Newton also researched the production of colours in situations other than refraction. He pursued diffraction (or what he called inflection) experiments and produced series of coloured rings with a plano-convex lens placed on an optical flat and viewed in bright light either from above or below. As in the case of refraction these two further classes of coloured phenomena appeared to be subject to simple laws. Moreover, the phenomena of diffraction and 'Newton's rings' indicated not only that each kind of ray, and thus each colour, possesses its own characteristics, but also that each kind of ray has its intrinsic periodicity. In respect to the ring patterns, Newton argued that each ray has a disposition to be reflected if the thickness of the air gap between the lens and the optical flat is equal to a constant (depending on the colour) multiplied by 1, 3, 5, . . . ; and the disposition to be transmitted by the second surface if the air gap is equal to the foregoing constant multiplied by 0, 2, 4, 6, . . . The distribution of colours within the ring patterns followed from these simple relationships.

Both Newton's early optical papers (1671–6) and his *Opticks* (1704; etc.) were major sites for controversy. One area of controversy arose from his barely-concealed preference for a corpuscular theory of light and from his stern opposition to any wave, pressure or pulse theory.[4] His position on these matters was outlined in his *Philosophiae naturalis principia mathematica* (*Mathematical principles of natural philosophy*, 1687) and in the queries added to the 1706 Latin edition of his *Opticks*. (See art. 16.) In these works Newton suggested that light consists of small particles of matter in motion, and all deviations from rectilinear propagation are explained by the action of short-range forces emanating from the reflecting, refracting or diffracting body. Thus Newton brought light within the domain of his highly successful theory of mechanics. In this unification, however, light was merely an effect of matter and it was therefore further distanced from its traditional non-material connotations.

4. THE EIGHTEENTH CENTURY

Newton's views on the nature of light and on other optical subjects proved very influential in the eighteenth and early nineteenth centuries. Writing in 1837, the English polymath William Whewell claimed that for well over a century Newton's theory was held by nearly all optical writers, and also that the dominance of corpuscular optics was responsible for the lack of progress in the eighteenth century since it 'kept down the sounder theory [i.e. the wave theory] for above a century'. Finally, he portrayed the history of optics as involving a two-cornered fight between the proponents of the corpuscular and wave theories.[5] These theses have become enshrined in the conventional historiography of optics.

A closer examination of the period shows that all of these theses are inadequate. There was certainly progress within the corpuscular theory and, particularly towards the end of the century, a number of scientists extended the theory and improved its fit with empirical data. In the opening decades of the nineteenth century, Etienne Louis Malus, David Brewster and Jean-Baptiste Biot made further significant contributions, especially in the areas of polarisation and double refraction. However, the theory's history cannot be confined solely to the field of research; since an important development occurred early in the eighteenth century, the theory was transformed into a teachable system and, together with Newton's account of the spectrum, introduced to the wider public through lectures, textbooks and other publications. The theory had become public property.

Yet the theory neither went unchallenged, nor did it stand alone. Instead, there was considerable diversity of opinion. Particularly in France, latter-day

Cartesians continued to advocate the view that light is a pressure or tendency to motion in the universal ether. Versions of the wave theory were also frequently advocated, especially by Dutch and German writers. Thus in his *Traité de la Lumière* (1690) Christiaan Huygens argued that every point on a luminous body experiences agitated motion and thus becomes a centre for a disturbance in the ubiquitous ether. If the progress of a disturbance is considered some time after it has departed its source, each point on its surface becomes the centre of a secondary wavefront. The envelope created by these secondary wavefronts thus defines the progress, including the direction, of the optical disturbance. Using this construction (Huygens' principle) he explained reflection and refraction and also extended the latter to include the double refraction of Iceland spar (calcite) by positing that the crystal contains two optical axes, so as to create a spheroidal rather than a spherical wavefront, However, it is not clear whether Huygens should be classed as a wave theorist since he claimed that 'it must not be supposed that the waves themselves follow one another at equal distances'.[6]

In his *Nova theoria lucis et colorum* (*New theory of light and colour*, 1746) Leonhard Euler proposed a paradigmatic wave theory in which each particle of a luminous body oscillates like a stretched string setting the neighbouring ether particles into oscillation, so that a sinusoidal, longitudinal wave spreads from the source. Like other early wave theorists, Euler drew a close analogy between sound and light, arguing that since the pitch of a note depends on the frequency of the vibrating air, the colour of light depends on the frequency of the wave. Although Euler incorporated Newton's wave mechanics in his account of wave propagation, he encountered considerable difficulty in explaining the colours produced by refraction.

While there were a number of wave, pulse or pression theories, Newton's corpuscular theory was also challenged by those who conceived light to be a fluid flowing from the sun. The particles comprising this fluid were not usually conceived as obeying Newton's laws of motion but were conserved and therefore circulated through the solar system. This luminous fluid was often considered as a modification of the fluids of heat and electricity, and therefore proponents of this theory paid particular attention to the role of light in chemical, thermal and electrical phenomena. Many of them also considered the fluid theory of light to be commensurate with, if not directly derived from, the Bible and therefore more fitting to Christian piety than Newton's theory.

This last point raises a more general issue. One method of studying the connection between optics and other areas is to examine the language of optics and the mutual interpenetration of terms through analogy and metaphor. This approach indicates that there has been a close conceptual relationship between optics and theology. For example, George Cheyne, who is often considered to be one of Newton's disciples, wrote in 1715:

Here, in the *Analogy of Things*, as the *Light* of the *Sun* (that Noble and Glorious *Representation*, *Image*, and *Viceregent* of the *Supreme Infinite*, in the *material* World) is the *Medium* , through which *material* Things are seen and perceiv'd in our *System*, so the *essential Light* of the *Supreme infinite* himself, is the sole *Medium*, by and through which, his Nature and infinite Perfections are to be understood, and comprehended. And therefore as certainly, as the *Sun* sends forth his Light on the whole *material* World . . . so certainly, the *Sun of Righteousness*, the *Pattern* and *Archetype* of our *material Sun*, sends forth his enlightening and enlivening Beams on all the *System* of created intelligent Beings, and is, *that light which enlightens every Man that cometh into the World.*[7]

For Cheyne, then, a correspondence existed between the physical light and the spiritual light, and, like many other writers, he conceived light – sunlight – not solely in materialistic terms but also as performing a cosmological, even a spiritual, function.

5. THE OPTICAL REVOLUTION

In 1802 Thomas Young (1773–1829), again drawing on the analogy between sound and light, added a theory of interference to Euler's wave theory of light. He applied the principle of superposition to ascertain the net effect on an ether particle subjected simultaneously to two vibrations of the same frequency. An early formulation reads:

> When two Undulations, from different Origins, coincide either perfectly or very nearly in Direction, their joint effect is a combination of the Motions belonging to each.[8]

However, Young failed to grasp Huygens' principle and in practice he employed a two-ray theory of interference which accounted for a bright band if the path difference was a whole number of 'wavelengths' and a dark band if the path difference was $\frac{1}{2}$, $1\frac{1}{2}$, $2\frac{1}{2}$ . . . 'wavelengths'. Young boldly applied this law to explain a number of phenomena, including diffraction fringes (although he experienced some difficulty in deciding the ray paths) and 'Newton's rings' (assuming that the ray reflected at the rarer medium is retarded by one half-wavelength). Although he discussed these and other phenomena in wave-theoretic terms, he insisted that he had discovered a simple and general law of nature which was independent of all optical theories.

Largely independent of Young, Augustin Fresnel (1788–1827) developed a version of the wave theory that was both more solidly based in mathematics and made effective use of Huygens' principle. In his 1819 analysis of diffraction, he accounted for the intensity of the light at any point on the image by the vector sum contributed by all the elements of the wavefront touching the diffracting edge(s). Thus, Fresnel obtained light intensity curves for the diffraction fringes produced by an infinitely-extended straight edge, a single slit and a narrow opaque body. In 1819, the Paris Académie des Sciences awarded Fresnel a prize for his mathematically-precise explanation of diffraction. It has sometimes been claimed that both the judges and other scientists were swayed by the sub-sequently confirmed 'novel prediction' that if a small, opaque disc is placed in a suitable beam of light, a bright spot would appear at the centre of the shadow. However, John Worrall has shown that this phenomenon was of no exceptional importance compared with the other long-standing diffraction problems that Fresnel solved, and that Fresnel's memoir did not abruptly convert scientists to the wave theory.[9]

Of equal, if not greater significance than Fresnel's work on diffraction were his memoirs on polarisation and double refraction. In a series of experiments commenced with Arago, he investigated the problem of whether polarised light produces interference patterns identical to those formed by unpolarised light. Although the initial results did not point to any significant differences, Fresnel later found a major disagreement: in, say, a two-slit experiment, the familiar interference fringes were found to occur when the two beams were polarised in the same plane, but no such effect was observed with the beams polarised per-pendicularly to one another. This was a perplexing result since it suggested that light was not a longitudinal but a transverse vibration, with the untenable physi-cal implication that the luminiferous ether would have to be a solid. Only in 1821, four years after Young had suggested transverse vibrations, did Fresnel follow suit. In other experimental investigations, Fresnel discovered what became known as circular polarisation and also extended the theory of trans-verse vibrations in media to explain many instances of double refraction. Yet Fresnel's significance in the history of optics lies not only in his specific dis-coveries nor in his defence of the wave theory of light but also in his programme to reconstruct optics on a simple, coherent basis using a comprehensive mecha-nistic theory expounded in mathematical terms.

Principally in the 1830s, optics was at the centre of the scientific stage. The wave theory which became dominant by the end of that decade owed far more to Fresnel's theories than it did to Young's. Scientists of the period were impressed with this theory because 'it admits of mathematical expression' and because this mathematised theory enabled '[v]aried and comprehensive classes of phenomena to be embraced by it deductions'. By contrast the rival, corpus-cular theory lacked firm mathematical foundations. Moreover, while this latter theory spawned *ad hoc* hypotheses to accommodate diverse classes of pheno-mena, the wave theory manifested an internal simplicity and coherence.[10] The wave theory proved a potent research tool and it enabled rapid progress to be made on a number of problems, both traditional and new. For example, hav-ing derived an expression linking the length of an undulation with its velocity for a given medium, Augustin-Louis Cauchy offered a greatly-improved solution to the long-standing problem of refractive dispersion. Another example is William Rowan Hamilton's prediction of conical refraction in biaxial crystals – a prediction that was confirmed by Humphrey Lloyd. Finally we can cite George Airy's investigations into the effects of a metallic reflector on New-ton's rings produced by polarised light. Research in these and many other areas was greatly stimulated by the wave theory.

The historical importance of this revolution lies not only in a new, powerful theory for solving optical problems, but also in a new conception of physics. This conception is reflected in student texts and lecture courses which usually opened with a section on mechanics, followed by a section on optics in which the edifice of the wave theory was constructed on mechanical principles. Thus William Whewell labelled physical optics a 'secondary mechanical science'.[11] Moreover, from about 1830 the highly-successful, mathematically-based wave theory was generally taken as a model for physical theory. For realists and instrumentalists alike, the wave theory was high on the agenda in discussions of the philosophy of science. However, despite its successes, the wave theory did not command complete support and such respected optical writers as Biot in France and Brewster in Scotland went to their graves in the 1860s declaring that it was not the true theory of light.

6. AFTER THE OPTICAL REVOLUTION

The optical revolution of the early nineteenth century was the one occasion when optical theorising was at the centre of the scientific stage. After that period, as before it, theories of light have been less central although they have been closely interrelated to contemporary developments in other branches of science. This article concludes with two examples that illustrate this theme; examples which also show how innovations in other areas affected theorising about the nature of light.

In the third part of his paper 'On physical lines of force' (1862) James Clerk Maxwell laid the foundations of the electromagnetic theory of light. His dis-covery that the ratio of electric to magnetic units is equal to the velocity of light provided him with the crucial link between light and electromagnetism. The same paper also contains his bold assertion that 'we can scarcely avoid the inference that *light consists in the transverse undulations of the same medium which is the cause of electric and magnetic phenomena*'.[12] Maxwell based this claim on the correlation between both electromagnetic and optical equations and the formu-lae governing his mechanical models of the ether. Subsequently, the role of ether models became less explicit and he concentrated on showing how his electromagnectic equations specified the propagation of light in a medium; for example, in a crystal of known electrical and magnetic properties. For Maxwell and his followers, light became a species of electromagnetic radiation. (See art. 22, sect. 2.)

The second example connects optics with the major theories of early twen-tieth-century physics. In relativity theory the velocity of light enters as a fundamental constant (see art. 28), but the development of quantum theory bears a much more important and also a symbiotic relation to optical theorising. Concepts drawn from optics and also optical phenomena (such as line spectra and the photo-electric effect) were historically important in framing quantum theory, while that theory, in turn, provided new insights into the nature of light. In 1902 Philipp Lenard made the problematic discovery that, contrary to the wave theory, there was not a direct relation between the intensity of light falling on a photo-electric cell and the energy of displaced electrons, but that the energy depended solely on the wavelength. This anomaly was explained by Albert Einstein (1879–1955) in 1905 on the assumption, derived from Max Planck, that radiation is quantised, a quantum possessing the energy hv, h being Planck's constant, and v the frequency. Einstein also later attributed to the light quantum a momentum of hv/c, and he conceived a light quantum as a singular point surrounded by a vector field which decays with distance. Crucial insight into the nature of radiation was provided in 1923 by Arthur Holly Compton who discovered that in the scattering of X-ray from free electrons, the wavelength of the scattered radiation was greater than the incident radiation. This phenomenon indicated that the radiation, including light, is quantised. While this conclusion impressively supported Einstein's conception of the photon, Niels Bohr pressed in 1927 for a dualistic account according to which light sometimes behaves like a wave, sometimes like a particle. (See art. 29, sect. 2.) If most physicists in the 1830s believed that the nature of light could be known, their descendants of the 1930s could only offer an account of how light behaves under specified experimental conditions. For Bohr and his followers the question 'what is light?' can no longer be asked.

If the metaphysical connotations of light have become less prominent among optical writers since the early nineteenth century, they have certainly not disappeared. Maxwell, for example, could still speak of white light as 'the emblem of purity' and Einstein raised the velocity of light to the status of an absolute, while resisting all attempts to dissolve the reality of light.[13] For Maxwell and Einstein, as for many other scientists, the significance of light – and thus the scope of this topic – extends beyond physics.

NOTES

1. For physicists, optics is taken to include both physical and geometrical optics. In this article I have confined myself almost totally to physical optics.
2. D. C. Lindberg, *Theories of light from Al-kindi to Kepler* (Chicago, 1976); 'Laying the foundations of geometrical optics: Maurolico, Kepler, and the medieval tradition', in D. C. Lindberg and G. N. Cantor, *The discourse of light from the Middle Ages to the Enlightenment* (Los Angeles, 1985), pp. 1–65; S. M. Straker, 'The eye made "other": Durer, Kepler, and the mechanisation of light and vision', in *Science, technology, and culture in historical perspective*, eds. L. A. Knafla, M. S. Staum and T. H. E. Travers (Calgary, 1976), pp. 7–25; 'Kepler, Tycho, and the "optical part of astronomy": the genesis of Kepler's theory of pinhole images', *Archive for history of exact sciences*, 24 (1981), 267–93; 'What is the history of theories of perception the history of?', in

Religion, science and worldview. Essays in honor of Richard S. Westfall, eds. M. J. Osler and P. L. Farber (Cambridge, 1985), pp. 246–73.

3. I. Newton, 'A letter of Mr. Issac Newton . . . containing his new theory about light and colors . . . ', *Philosophical transactions of the Royal Society of London*, No. 80 (1671/72), 3075–87, quotation on p. 3081. Reprinted in *Isaac Newton's papers and letters on natural philosophy* ed. I. B. Cohen (Cambridge, Mass., 1958), pp. 47–59, quotation on p.53.

4. However, earlier in his career Newton had incorporated elements from the wave theory and, principally in the 1717 edition of the *Opticks*, he made use of an ubiquitous ether to explain optical phenomena, even imposing vibrations on that ether to account for 'Newton's rings'.

5. W. Whewell, *History of the inductive sciences, from the earliest to the present time* (3 vols., London, 1837), vol. II, pp. 390–462. Quotation on p. 394.

6. C. Huygens, *Treatise on light* (New York, 1962), p. 17.

7. G. Cheyne, *Philosophical principles of religion: natural and reveal'd* (London, 1715), pt. 2, 112.

8. T. Young, 'On the theory of light and colours', *Philosophical transactions of the Royal Society of London*, 92 (1802), 12–48, quotation on p. 34.

9. J. Worrall, 'Fresnel, Poisson and the white spot: the role of successful predictions in the acceptance of scientific theories', *The uses of experiment*, eds. D. Gooding, T. Pinch and S. Schaffer (Cambridge, 1989), pp. 135–57.

10. H. Lloyd, 'Report on the progress and present state of physical optics', *Annual report of the British Association*, 4 (1834), 295–413, quotation on p. 295.

11. W. Whewell, *History*, vol. II, pp. viii–x.

12. J. C. Maxwell, 'On physical lines of force', in *The scientific papers of James Clerk Maxwell* (2 vols., New York, n.d.), vol. I, pp. 451–513, quotation on p. 500.

13. —— 'On colour vision', in *The scientific papers of James Clerk Maxwell*, vol. II, pp. 267–79, quotation on p. 268.

FURTHER READING

J. Z. Buchwald, *From Maxwell to microphysics. Aspects of electromagnetic theory in the last quarter of the nineteenth century* (Chicago, 1985).

—— *The rise of the wave theory of light* (Chicago, 1989).

G. N. Cantor, *Optics after Newton. Theories of light in Britain and Ireland, 1704–1840* (Manchester, 1983).

D. C. Lindberg, *Theories of light from Al-Kindi to Kepler* (Chicago, 1976).

—— and G. N. Cantor, *The discourse of light from the Middle Ages to the Enlightenment* (Los Angeles, 1985).

V. Ronchi, *The nature of light: and historical survey* (London, 1970).

A. I. Sabra, *Theories of light from Descartes to Newton* (London, 1967).

A. E. Shapiro, 'Kinematic optics: a study of the wave theory of light in the 17th century', *Archive for history of exact sciences*, 11 (1973), 134–266.

41

COSMOLOGY: NEWTON
TO EINSTEIN

PIERRE KERSZBERG

1. NEWTON AND EINSTEIN ON COSMOLOGY

In December 1916, Albert Einstein (1879–1955) wrote to Michele Besso about a question of 'great scientific significance'.[1] The problem was how to interpret the fact that the universe is in equilibrium. Einstein wanted to reply to a suggestion that, for reasons of symmetry, it would be perfectly possible to conceive of matter uniformly filling all space to infinity; such a distribution would produce no field at all. Einstein's argument against this was as follows. Take a sphere of matter K centred at P. According to Gauss's principle, 'a gravitational flux through the surface K must exist, being created by the matter contained in K'. As a result, and quite independently of whether the space outside K was or was not filled with matter, 'the matter must fall towards P with an acceleration increasing as the distance from P decreases'. In these conditions, is it possible for the universe to endure at all? Einstein considers the possibility that the universe might be capable of reproducing the structure of the solar system, that is, the possibility of centrifugal forces hindering the fall of matter, but he suggests that such a motion cannot exist for any length of time because 'infinitely great differences of potential would give rise to very high stellar velocities, and these must have long since disappeared'.[2] Einstein intends his argument to be a proof that the symmetry of a homogeneous, infinite distribution of matter is an insufficient condition for eliminating the cumbersome assumption that the field at infinity is infinite. Imagine that the problem is due to the static distribution: if you allow high velocities to exist, these cannot continue for a long time – the shortness of their existence is, as Einstein surmises, proportional to their magnitude. And the only way of avoiding infinite potentials is to set at zero the mean density of matter at infinity, in which case we would be left with the equally 'distasteful conception'[3] of a natural centre to the universe.

In his argument, Einstein deploys the concept of field which marked the nineteenth century's great advance over Sir Isaac Newton's original formulation of the law of gravitational force. (See art. 22, sect. 2.) However, numerous problems and even outright contradictions were already apparent within the framework of Newton's original formulation. Strikingly enough, Newton (1642–1727) had encountered exactly the same hypothesis for explaining the equilibrium of the universe, and found it equally implausible. The suggestion came from Richard Bentley, who argued that if the universe were a uniform, infinite distribution of matter in Euclidean space, then the infinite attraction exerted by all masses on one side of some central particle would be compensated for by an infinite attraction on the other side. Newton replied 'that two equal infinites by the addition of a force to either of them, become unequal in our ways of reckoning'.[4] Those ways of reckoning, according to Newton, are the basis of mathematical reasoning, while the addition of a force is due to the slightest motion in the universe. If the infinites are equal, in accordance with Bentley's physical conception, then no motion at all is possible in the universe, even though equilibrium would be realised everywhere by virtue of nature's own forces. But if the infinites are unequal, in accordance with mathematics, then there is motion but no equilibrium. In either event, we face the very same impossibility: the occurrence of any particular kind of finite force in the universe may be understood irrespective of its inclusion in the whole universe. This formed the basis of Newton's discussion of the role of the supra-natural in the mechanical equilibrium of the universe.

In the solar system we find a variety of planets, comets and stars; a common pattern of orbits for the planets around the sun, as opposed to the erratic motions of the comets; one luminous centre for a multiplicity of opaque bodies. All this, according to Newton, bore witness to God's handiwork. This kind of non-uniformity had been accounted for successfully by the application of the law of gravitation; by contrast, Newton could not find a satisfactory response to the mathematical difficulties of the infinite. If the whole starry universe were finite, the result should be a central mass, blurred and undifferentiated. Newton went on to refuse the extension to the entire universe of the kind of equilibrium found in the solar system: a system in which centrifugal forces would deflect the fall of stars from their straight paths cannot be real, because the particular diversity exhibited in the solar system simply could not occur in this sphere. It is certain that Newton had this special problem in mind when he reverted to a famous solution adumbrated in the 'General Scholium' that ends the *Philosophiae Naturalis Principia Mathematica* (*Mathematical principles of natural philosophy*, 1687): 'if the fixed stars are the centres of other like systems, these must be all subject to the dominion of One . . . and lest the systems of fixed stars should, by their gravity, fall on each other, he (God) hath placed those systems at immense distances from one another'.[5]

Parallels (and contrasts) between Newton's and Einstein's discussion of the equilibrium of the whole universe indicate the main lines of cosmological thought from the later seventeenth century until the early twentieth century. It was certainly Einstein's intention that his epoch-making 'Cosmological Considerations' of 1917 should overcome the drawn-out and unsuccessful attempts to provide a satisfactory theoretical account of the equilibrium of the universe.[6] In fact, the great scientific significance attached to this problem is largely Einstein's own work, for the universal validity of Newton's laws of motion does not seem to have been severely undermined, throughout the eighteenth or nineteenth centuries, by the apparent impossibility of setting up a definite, concrete model of the universe. Rather, until the advent of general relativity, cosmological arguments tended to be either mixed up with their metaphysical implications or limited to purely astronomical research. The formal universality of Newton's laws supplanted cosmic order: physical bodies need not belong to a determined cosmic structure, so long as they all obey the same laws. Einstein's originality was to include cosmology within the scope of universal law, so that it became an integral part of physical science.

2. OBSERVATION, THEORY AND PRESUPPOSITION

In general terms, there are three major aspects of the cosmological problem from Newton to Einstein. From the observational point of view, the unquestioned acceptance of a Euclidean infinite space raised the problem of whether the stellar system was finite or infinite; in particular, it was not clear until the 1920s whether the stars were dispersed erratically throughout the sky or aggregated into one or more galaxies. But over and above this uncertainty, it seemed that by the end of the nineteenth century, astronomy had reached the zenith of its achievement. The historian of astronomy Agnes M. Clerke wrote in 1893 that where the Ancients merely described, Newtonian physics led to causal understanding, but only 'the third and last division of celestial distance may properly be termed "physical and descriptive astronomy"'. It seeks to know what the heavenly bodies are in themselves, leaving the *How?* and the *Wherefore?* of their movements to be otherwise answered'.[7] The one great advance after the invention of the telescope in the early part of the seventeenth century was when observational cosmology moved from a descriptive to a physical stage as the spectrometer and the camera were finally applied to astronomy in the second half of the nineteenth century. The theory of gravitation had very little to disclose in this area for, as Clerke went on to argue, 'it was virtually brought to a close when Pierre-Simon Laplace (1749–1827) explained to the French Académie des Sciences on November 19, 1787, the cause of the moon's accelerated motion. As a mere machine, the solar system, so far as it was known, was found to be complete and intelligible in all its parts'. As to the world beyond the solar system, 'the problems which demand a practical solution are all but infinite in number and extent' but their existence did not invalidate the type of theoretical approach already adopted in celestial mechanics.[8] From this point of view, the situation of nineteenth-century observational cosmology appears paradoxical because it offered a vision of the universe which was both well-founded and incomplete.

Development in cosmological theory arose from critical examination of the foundations of Newtonian science, especially the nature of its axioms. Cosmological significance was attached to the epistemologically distinct status of the laws of gravitation and motion. In his article in the *Encyclopédie*, Jean d'Alembert defined cosmology as a general physics which leaves room for metaphysics. The formulation of Newton's laws as differential equations by Laplace, William Rowan Hamilton and Siméon-Denis Poisson also widened the gap between physics and metaphysics; these equations describe local and instantaneous elementary processes, and while the finite processes can be obtained by integration, a complete knowledge of them involves the determination of initial conditions that remain independent of the theory. The differential equations thus seemed to imply a pre-existing order.

Underlying both observation and theory, a latent and implicit conception of totality held sway. Newton's mechanics was based on the rejection of almost all of the presuppositions embodied in a largely non-mathematical, Aristotelian view of the world. But one aspect of the non-Copernican world in particular was left quite untouched by Newtonian mechanics: the generally static conception of the universe as a whole. This conception of the ancient cosmos was only overthrown two and a half centuries after Newton's *Principia*. In their discussion of the large-scale implications of Newton's mechanics, both Newton and Einstein acknowledged the impossibility of combining any number of centres of forces with universal motion about these centres. But while Newton simply abandoned cosmology in the precarious position of appearing to explain nothing at all, Einstein derived some positive stimulus from it without changing the static condition. It was not until 1934 that Edward Milne and William McCrea could formulate a consistent Newtonian cosmology by dropping the assumption that the world is necessarily static, but this in turn was a response to the challenge of relativity.[9] (See art. 28.)

3. THE THEORETICAL SPECULATIONS

As Newton explained to Bentley, the new mechanics did not account for all the peculiarities of the solar system. Their supposed supernatural cause was also equated by Newton with the overall stability of the system. Several attempts were made in the first half of the eighteenth century to reconcile Newtonian and Cartesian physics (and hence Descartes' cosmogony as well). The fusion was not successful because Descartes did not allow for an interplanetary void

– and it was precisely this void that, in the Newtonian system, allowed inter-penetrating but seemingly independent orbits such as those of the planets and the comets. These attempts culminated in Daniel Bernouilli's model of the 1730s, in which the emergence of planets and comets was accounted for in terms of an extended solar atmosphere; this atmosphere was so tenuous that it really bore little resemblance to Descartes' original model. It was not until the end of the eighteenth century that Laplace was able to show, working solely within the Newtonian framework, that if the planets are subjected to a new, external influence they will spontaneously revert to a stable orbit. In fact, the peculiarities of the solar system then appear as the physical conditions of its stability.

Problems associated with the occurrence of centres of forces also took on a new dimension. Thomas Wright conjectured in 1750 that not just the earth, but the sun itself should lose its privileged centrality by proposing a Milky-Way-like model for the system of all stars. Wright was followed by Immanuel Kant (1724–1804) and by Johann Lambert who thought the Milky Way itself was only one member in a chain of similarly-structured systems of stars. Lambert's model is the first hierarchical model of the universe, with stars forming galaxies, galaxies forming clusters, clusters becoming superclusters and so on. In the nineteenth century, it was sometimes argued that this kind of specific spacing between the stars or the galaxies could annihilate Olbers's paradox, according to which, stars distributed uniformly throughout an infinite universe should result in a sky ablaze with light. (The paradox was first investigated by Edmond Halley in 1721 and Jean de Chéseaux in 1744. Olbers thought that the paradox could be overcome by postulating the existence of some light-absorbing inter-stellar matter.) The hierarchical hypothesis was revived by Carl Charlier in 1908 in the context of the gravitational problem: it was shown that a suitable arrangement of dimensions may also enable us to construct a universe with zero average density, thereby overcoming the problem of infinite gravity at infinity when the average density is finite. But the original form of Lambert's model was both finite and static. By contrast, Kant's early speculations in his *Theory of the Heavens* (1755) were highly distinctive although he later dismissed the absolute validity of any rational cosmology. Kant had a very original answer to the problem of how to make the existence of an indefinite number of centres of forces compatible with universal motion as predicted by the law of gravitation. His model was a dynamic one, derived from the concept of the simplest possible conditions prevailing at the moment of creation. The very first moment offered a way of combining centre and infinity, for the act of creation was endowed by Kant with a sort of transgeometric function on to a centre in an otherwise infinite universe. Kant thought he could derive the existence of an attractive force from an infinite diversity of specific densities among the primitive particles, and thus explain the production of organised material entities from the instability of the primeval chaos. In this universe, a sphere of ever more highly organised material entities is continually expanding from the point of highest specific density. By identifying creation and organisation in this way, Kant wanted to prove that the material powers of the world can only exhibit a divine, pre-established harmony.

But the price Kant paid for this bold extension of the limits of mechanical philosophy was enormous, because he was compelled to reject mathematical infallibility for his model. This tended to undermine the validity of the construction, for it appeared to violate the law of the conservation of angular momentum. (It must be borne in mind however, that it was not until Leonhard Euler in 1775 that the relationship between force and acceleration as we know it today was fully spelt out, and it is from this formulation that the law of the conservation of the angular momentum followed.) Independently of Kant, Laplace based his nebular hypothesis explaining the formation of the solar system, on the fact that the solar system could not generate its own angular momentum from nothing. Laplace started with a proto-sun already in a state of slow rotation; this vaporous mass proceeded to cool, contract and speed up so that successive rings were formed around the equator; each one of which could either condense into a planet, disintegrate into the group of asteroids (discovered between Mars and Jupiter early in the nineteenth century) or even form the rings circling Saturn. Contrary to Kant, Laplace's nebula was limited to the solar system and simply provided an explanatory and causal model for any conceivable system in the universe. Its impact was such that Auguste Comte, the positivist, found in it the ideal response to the theological discourse on the origin of the universe.

4. THE OBSERVATIONAL BASIS

While no historian of astronomy would deny today that such highly speculative schemes as those of Thomas Wright and Kant must be taken seriously in our evaluation of the development of cosmological ideas from Newton to Einstein, there is divergence of opinion over how pure speculation interacted with the growing body of observational evidence. Thus, historians such as Jacques Merleau-Ponty and John North are keen to draw a sharp distinction between the progress in observation, on the one hand, and physical theory versus philosophical issues on the other hand; Stanley Jaki goes as far as dismissing the cogency of those schemes that we describe today as speculative (see Further Reading). But Simon Schaffer has undertaken to raise the question of how metaphysics seems to have interacted with the astronomical work of William Herschel (1738–1822). Thus, in addition to the first systematic typology of nebulae, Herschel speculated on what he called 'the great laboratories of nature', that is, those seats of physico-chemical transformations in which entire cosmic processes of condensation and fragmentation could be generated or modified. In so doing, Herschel was probably echoing the eighteenth-century notion of an active principle, an idea that was proposed in order to overcome the Cartesian dualism between spirit and matter.[10]

While Kant based his conjectures on some reports of faint nebulous patches observed by a few astronomers (e.g. Pierre Maupertuis, in 1744) and on the first suspicion of proper motions among the stars (James Bradley in the early 1750s), the whole tradition of observational cosmology was actually inaugurated in the latter part of the eighteenth century, when William Herschel systematically directed his telescope to every part of the sky. His main achievement was the resolution of an increasing number of nebulosities into an aggregation of stars. He was equally convinced, however, that not every nebulosity could be resolved by increased telescopic power; following Laplace's scheme, some nebulae could serve as points of attraction for the formation of stars and planetary systems. Herschel also provided the first comprehensive description of the Milky Way, the definition of the solar apex, and the brilliant demonstration that the orbits of some binary stars can be accounted for in terms of the Newtonian force of attraction. In fact, the achievements of Laplace and Herschel are quite typical of the turn of the nineteenth century. Cosmological theory and observation began to be systematic; they no longer rested on *a priori* arguments or on narrowly selected facts. The two new guiding themes were the self-sufficiency of Newtonian gravitation and the use of probabilities in accounting for the emergence of certain physical structures. While Laplace's theories were explanatory, local and analytic, Herschel applied descriptive, global and synthetic methods in the service of an approach which became fully feasible only at the beginning of the twentieth century.

The distribution, as well as the constitution, of the nebulae was keenly debated until the early 1900s. It was not really until the 1920s that some consensus was finally reached, thanks to the classifications of Edwin Hubble (1889–1953) (which followed Curtis's demonstration of the extra-galactic character of the Andromeda Nebula in 1918). In 1847, the Earl of Rosse installed a massive telescope (a 72-inch reflector) at Birr in Ireland, which remained the largest available until it was finally surpassed by that of Mount Wilson (Hubble's telescope) in the 1920s. This enabled astronomers to resolve an increasing number of nebulae into stars, but it was precisely this increased telescopic power that was to precipitate a fundamental problem of interpretation. The problem was: how far is it possible to match the results bearing on the constitution of these nebulae with conjectures about their distribution? Michael Hoskins has commented: 'to equate all nebulae with star clusters would be to lend strength to the conviction that other island universes or galaxies exist beyond and outside our own', for those milky patches that are too distant to be resolved and yet occupy a substantial portion of the sky must certainly be located at enormous distances from the earth.[11] The problem posed a radical alternative: either all nebulae are star systems, or all those that cannot be resolved consist of gaseous, diffuse matter. In the latter part of the nineteenth century, the use of spectroscopy and photography convinced most of the astronomers that the assumptions underlying the island universe theory were incorrect. In particular, the discovery of the fine structure of Andromeda was conducive to the belief that Laplace's nebular hypothesis was somehow 'made visible', as Isaac Roberts had argued in 1888. By 1900, Simon Newcomb expressed the widespread view that 'it is a great encouragement to the astronomer that . . . he is gathering faint indications that it [the universe] has a boundary'.[12] But at the same time, the methods of astrophysics gave a new turn to the question concerning measurements of distance.

In the latter part of the seventeenth century, both Huygens and Newton computed the distances to some stars by assuming that all stars have the same intrinsic brightness as the sun. But when, in 1838, Friedrich Bessel measured stellar parallaxes for the first time (and proved in the process the validity of the Copernican theory by the use of an argument no longer confined in its application to the solar system) he took the proper motions of the stars, instead of their brightnesses, as his standard in measuring distance. His assumption was that the closer the object, the larger its proper motion would appear. Bessel drew from this the very important conclusion that stars vary a great deal in their intrinsic brightness. It was only in the early years of this century that indirect methods began to be used for the evaluation of greater distances. At distances where the spectra become far too tenuous to be measured, Henrietta Leavitt was able to establish an accurate relationship between the instrinsic brightness and the period of a particular type of variable star, the Cepheids (1912). When this method was applied to the smallest of the Magellanic Clouds in 1913, it was clear that this nebula was far more distant than any known star. This paved the way for Hubble to settle the question of distances, when he detected a Cepheid variable in Andromeda (1923).

The revival of the island universe theory was mainly due to the special attention paid by astronomers to one particular class of nebulae, the spiral nebulae. In 1898 Julius Scheiner showed that their spectra are comparable to the sun's spectrum. This seemed to confirm their affinity with star systems while also landing a serious blow to the Laplacian nebular hypothesis (an alternative hypothesis was suggested in 1904 by Thomas Chamberlin and Forest Moulton in which the formation of planetary systems was accounted for in terms of tidal effects between two neighbouring stars). In 1912 Vesto Slipher began to investigate the radial velocities of the spirals, and then in 1917 announced his conversion to the island universe theory. However, until the late 1920s, the real issues were blurred by Harlow Shapley's independent theory which was based on the identification of yet another class of nebulae as island universes – the globular clusters. Because these clusters systematically avoid the galactic plane, Shapley assumed that they are satellites of the Milky Way. This prompted him to develop a model of the Milky Way which was big enough to comprehend the spirals (cf. the Shapley-Curtis dispute of 1921, the so-called 'Great Debate'). In 1929 Hubble established the famous velocity–distance linear relationship which brought together the investigations of distances and the velocities of the spirals. Throughout the second decade of the twentieth century, three conjectures had managed to incorporate the radial velocities of nebulae in some systematic way: that of Campbell, which postulated a link between the velocities and the age of the nebulae (this hypothesis rapidly fell out of favour); that of Slipher, who suggested that the velocities were an effect of the proper motion of our galaxy; and finally that of Willem de Sitter (1872–1934), which proved to be the best because it relied on theoretical considerations borrowed from the theory of general relativity.

5. GENERAL RELATIVITY AND COSMOLOGY

In order to appreciate the cosmological import of general relativity, its antecedents must be traced in two very different areas of nineteenth-century science, thermodynamics and pure mathematics. In his treatise on *Opticks* (1st Latin edition, 1706), Newton had already argued that the quantity of motion in the universe would continually decrease, were it not for the miracle of God's handiwork in maintaining it; when decay and change affront the eternity of God, God seems to be willing to maintain the *status quo* rather than to oppose new forms of change. In Newton's conception, the comets were God's agents which replenished the sun with momentum. Similarly, the physicists of the nineteenth century seem to have based their fundamental cosmological ideas on the attempt to ward off the universe running down. Jean Fourier in 1824 was probably the first to point out that thermic and mechanical processes cannot be reduced to one another, yet heat, like gravity, is everywhere present. Fourier made a series of conjectures on the energetic properties of a cosmic substratum associated with space, but it was not until the second half of the nineteenth century, when the global implications of the heat engine formulated by Carnot in 1824 were first perceived, that the issue of decay of energy became explicit. (See art. 21, sect. 2.) William Thomson proposed a series of loosely cosmo-theological speculations about the irreversible energetic decay of the universe, while William Rankine suggested that out in space, vast concave ether walls collected and refocused the energy lost by stars. Uncertainty over the true relationship between heat and light prevented anyone from settling the question, but in the early twentieth century, it was by no means uncommon among scientists to invoke the name of Herbert Spencer, the philosopher who had endorsed the concept of endless cycles of 'evolution and dissolution'. When formulating his cosmological model in the gravitational context, Einstein argued that the behaviour of the gravitational potentials at infinity would no longer 'run the risk of wasting away'.[13] As to the nineteenth-century development of non-Euclidean geometries (see art. 42, sect. 2), there was a shift in the conception of mathematics, from describing our unique universe to describing various possible universes by way of commonly-satisfied axioms. In the 1870s, William Clifford speculated that the geometry of space might not be Euclidean, all physical laws being reducible to the variation of the curvature of space. Following the pioneering investigations of Gauss and Schweikart, Karl Schwarzschild developed the technique of parallax measurement in 1900 in order to test the reality of Euclidean geometry at the astronomical level. These attempts, however, clashed with Henri Poincaré's conventionalist approach to geometry, which tended to neutralise the interpretation of the results expected from such measurements.

Shortly after the publication of the first summarising memoir on general relativity in 1916 Einstein turned to cosmology. (See art. 28, sect. 2.) In that year he discussed with de Sitter the nature of the relativity of rotation and the degree of comparability between Newtonian and relativistic theories regarding boundary conditions. Einstein recognised that in general relativity, no boundary conditions could be generally covariant if they had simultaneously to satisfy Mach's principle: the requirement that there is no inertia relative to space but only an inertia of masses relative to one another. Accordingly, he dropped the concept of the infinite and built the so-called cylindrical universe, where space satisfies the Riemannian hyper-surface of a three-dimensional sphere and time remains linear. The fact that the flow of time was unaffected by the curvature of space allowed it to be cosmic time. In Einstein's opinion, a time that is identical for all observers accounted for the weakness of the relative stellar velocities. Another feature of the model was the introduction of the cosmological constant λ in the original field equations; strikingly enough, by the end of the nineteenth century, Seeliger and Neumann had already shown that a similar modification of Poisson's equation made possible a static universe which was Newtonian, infinite and homogeneous. Given this similarity, it seemed natural to identify λ with a repulsive force that would compensate for the cumulative effect of attraction at large distances. Just a few weeks after the publication of Einstein's paper, de Sitter offered a very strange and unexpected solution of the modified field equations, according to which an empty universe need not have the metric of Minkowski's pseudo-Euclidean space-time. The result was derived from a two-fold critique of Einstein's model: (1) any relativistic theory of the universe should include a curvature of both space and time, in accordance with Minkowski's conception of the continuum; and (2) the Machian requirement for the relativity of inertia is by no means a consequence of the formalism of the new theory of gravitation. At first, de Sitter did not believe his model was entirely empty, but that it simply showed how the causal relation postulated between the existence of matter and the curvature of space was untenable in large portions of space–time and that cosmic time also appeared to be implicated in this relation.

Until the early 1930s, the two models were generally regarded as antithetical. Thus, de Sitter was quick to show that no test body could remain at rest in his model of space-time, and that the curvature of time had the puzzling property of creating a singularity at the greatest spatial distance from any observer. For a long time there was confusion over the correct interpretation of this singularity. Einstein and Hermann Weyl (1885–1955) first thought this was a singularity of the field – as though all the matter of the original cylindrical model had been swept away into unobservable corners. In his *Space, Time and Gravitation* (1920), Arthur Eddington (1882–1944) was the first to realise that the effect was produced merely by the choice of co-ordinates. He developed this conception in his *Mathematical Theory of Relativity* (1923), in which he tried to combine the properties of motion with those of time in the de Sitter model. He took the λ term as the cause of a universal tendency for all test bodies to scatter; the mass-horizon itself was subject to the receding motion, so that he could describe it as an illusion of the observer at the origin. Eddington suggested that a complete picture of the de Sitter universe could be drawn by a continuous process from point to point. The curvature of time was responsible for a red shift of the spectral lines emitted by galaxies that increased with distance, and Eddington argued that this red shift was numerically equal to the effect created kinematically by a scattering motion (Doppler effect). In the same year, Weyl went on to show that the postulation of a common time for all particles at infinity in the past was a sufficient condition for the abolition of all horizons and the restoration of a unique picture. This new interpretation of Einstein's early conception of cosmic time implied a discrepancy between the two red shifts, i.e. a distance effect.

Quite independently, Aleksandr Fridmann (1922 and 1924), Georges Lemaître (1925 and 1927) and H. P. Robertson (1928) all found that the Einstein and the de Sitter models were not antithetical if an alternative interpretation of the occurrence of motion was elaborated. Instead of the classical conception of motion in space, they showed that an expanding space with co-mobile co-ordinates was the natural expression of what Lemaître called a 'fair compromise' between the two limiting cases. Weyl's distance effect was reinterpreted as an effect of the expansion of space, which accounted for the observed red shifts, so that what was soon known as Weyl's principle became the basis for all possible homogeneous, isotropic and non-static models of the universe. A positive response to these early suggestions of an expanding universe came very late, for it was not until 1930 that they were rediscovered, with Eddington exploring the instability of Einstein's model. In the class of non-static models with various geometries and rates of expansion, the term λ loses its original similarity to a repulsive force of a Newtonian kind and plays the role of an additional variable; some models are compatible with a zero value for this variable. That is why the justification of λ subsequently met with divergent interpretatîons. Some, like Eddington and Lemaître, thought it would crown Einstein's original theory of relativity, quite independently of the cosmological models, and provide a basis for the complete unification of all the fundamental forces of nature; others, like Einstein himself, preferred to dismiss it because its only basis was the erroneous belief that the universe was essentially static.

NOTES

1. A. Einstein–M. Besso, *Correspondance 1903–1955*, ed. P. Speziali (Paris 1972), p. 99.
2. Ibid., pp. 99–100.
3. A. Einstein, *Relativity. The special and the general theory. A popular exposition*, trans. R. W. Lawson (London, 1921), p. 107.
4. I. B. Cohen (ed.), *Newton's papers and letters on natural philosophy* (Cambridge, Mass, 1958), pp. 295–6.
5. I. Newton, *Mathematical principles of natural philosophy*, trans. A. Motte (1729) rev. F. Cajori (Berkeley, 1934), p. 550.
6. A. Einstein, 'Cosmological considerations on the theory of general relativity', in Einstein, *The principle of relativity* (New York, 1952), pp. 177–88.
7. A. M. Clerke, *A popular history of astronomy during the nineteenth century* (3rd ed., London, 1893), pp. 2–3.
8. Ibid., p. 528.
9. E. A. Milne and W. H. McCrea, 'Newtonian universes and the curvature of space', *Quarterly journal of mathematics*, 5 (1934), 73–80.
10. See S. Schaffer, 'The great laboratories of the universe: William Herschel on matter theory and planetary life', *Journal for the history of astronomy*, 11 (1980), 81–111.
11. M. A. Hoskin, 'Apparatus and ideas in mid-nineteenth century cosmology', *Vistas in astronomy*, 9 (1967), 79–85.
12. S. Newcomb, 'The unsolved problems of astronomy', in *Side-lights on astronomy. Essays and addresses* (New York, 1906), p. 6.
13. Einstein, 'Cosmological considerations', p. 181.

FURTHER READING

E. J. Aiton, *The vortex theory of planetary motions* (London, 1972).

R. Berendzen, R. Hart and D. Seeley, *Man discovers the galaxies* (New York, 1976).

M. A. Hoskin, *William Herschel and the construction of the heavens* (New York, 1964).

—— *Stellar astronomy: historical studies* (Chalfont St Giles, 1982).

S. Jaki, *The Milky Way: an elusive road for science* (New York, 1972).

J. Merleau-Ponty and B. Morando, *The rebirth of cosmology* (New York, 1976).

J. Merleau-Ponty, *La science de l'univers à l'âge du positivisme. Etude sur les origines de la cosmologie contemporaine* (Paris, 1983).

J. North, *The measure of the universe. A history of modern cosmology* (Oxford, 1965).

W. de Sitter, *Kosmos* (Cambridge, Mass., 1932).

R. W. Smith, *The expanding universe. Astronomy's 'great debate' 1900–1931* (Cambridge, 1982).

42

GEOMETRY AND SPACE

J. J. GRAY

Euclid's *Elements*, written *c.* 300 BC, is a rich and complicated work, which can be read in various ways. Its surprisingly logical structure, with its opening assumptions, basic definitions and elaborate network of deductions of many theorems, invites one to treat it as a purely mathematical or logical work. The assumptions and definitions themselves mostly codify what one tends to believe about simple, geometrical figures in physical space. Taken together, these two aspects ensure that the work presents many theorems in a way which suggests they are true statements about the world we inhabit. Indeed, it can seem that the veracity of these statements is a matter of logic, and not at all the result of an early exercise in mathematical modelling. Nonetheless, it was clear to at least some Greek mathematicians and philosophers that their study of geometry was based on some explicit hypotheses about space. For example, Aristotle presciently remarked in his *Physica* (II 9 200ᵃ 16–19) that:

> If the line is what we recognise it to be from our visual intuition, then the angle sum of a triangle is two right angles.

Because of the difficulties inherent in any study of a topic of this complexity, it will be helpful to follow the ensuing developments with three points in mind: (1) That the *Elements* have a logical deductive structure; (2) That the *Elements* are based on assumptions, often in the form of deductions, which reflect beliefs about physical space; (3) That various assumptions can be made about figures in physical space, the plausibility of Euclid's assumptions notwithstanding.

Not only have mathematicians read the *Elements* at various times in ways which stressed one of these aspects more than others, but historians have also chosen to prefer some readings, as they have attempted to recount the lengthy history of this part of geometry. Most importantly, some have emphasised the logical side of the investigations, others the empirical side.

1. EARLY INVESTIGATIONS

Of all the assumptions made in the *Elements*, the one which seems to have caused most concern was the fifth postulate, the 'parallel' postulate, which asserts:

> That, if a straight line falling on two straight lines makes the interior angles on the same side less than two right angles, the straight lines, if produced indefinitely, meet on that side on which are the angles less than two right angles [see Figure 42.1].[1]

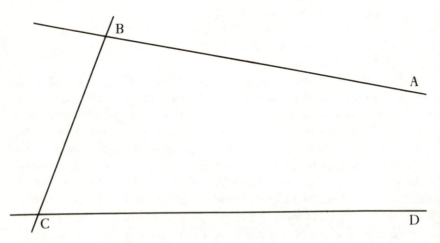

Figure 42.1: If angles *ABC* and *BCD* add up to less than two right angles, then the lines *BA* and *CD* meet in the direction of *A* and *D*.

The main reason this postulate attracted so much criticism was probably that it makes an assertion about the behaviour of lines BA and CD which meet at an arbitrary distance. For example, it is easy to see that if the interior angles are each chosen suitably close to a right angle, then the intersection of the lines can be millions of miles away. Plainly, this is not an assumption one is ever going to be able to verify, whereas the other postulates appear much more plausible.

The problem for Greek mathematicians was that, without the parallel postulate, very little in geometry could be proved at all. Although it is not needed to show that, given any line, 1, and a point P, not on 1, there is a line through P not meeting 1 (which is a consequence of *Elements*, I, 17); it is needed to show that the line so obtained is unique. It is the uniqueness of this line that makes parallel lines so useful in Euclidean geometry. It is required, for example, to show that the angle sum of any triangle is two right angles, to prove Pythagoras' Theorem and to construct scale copies of figures. Consequently, various attempts were made to obviate the parallel postulate.

Proclus, for example, thought that it 'ought to be struck from the postulates altogether, because it is a theorem'. And he even gave a (fallacious) proof, which purported to derive the postulate solely from the other assumptions and definitions of the *Elements*.[2] Had he succeeded, it would have been a particularly elegant solution, but his proof contained the assumption, not made by Euclid but equivalent to the parallel postulate, that the distance between parallel lines never exceeds a fixed amount, i.e. it is bounded.[3] Proclus's attempt, like many subsequent ones, ended by establishing only that some other assumption about lines is just as useful in geometry. Sometimes, as here, the new assumption was made tacitly, sometimes overtly; in neither case was the difficulty removed. For example, many writers defined a *parallel* to a given line as that curve which is everywhere equidistant from the line (like a railway line). But this is to assume that the curve so defined is straight, an assumption no more plausible than the one in contention.

It is clear that the best of these investigators, while they respected the logical structure of the *Elements*, also sought the 'right' characterisation of the straight line. Some argued that it should be redefined while others accepted Euclid's obscure definition ('a breadthless length which lies evenly with the points on itself') but appealed to certain alleged properties of lines in order to make their case. Attempts by Moslem mathematicians, for example, were of this kind, although they were generally more thorough-going than the earlier, Greek, accounts.[4] So too, in due course, were the earliest studies by Western mathematicians, of which perhaps the most substantial was the one by John Wallis (1616–1703) in 1663. Wallis, inspired by the work of the Persian mathematician Nasr-Eddin, showed that the parallel postulate was equivalent to the assumption that a scale copy of any figure can be made of any size. He argued, plausibly, that this assumption was in keeping with the rest of the *Elements*, but admitted that it was, strictly speaking, an extra assumption.

A significant advance was made in 1733 by Girolamo Saccheri (1667–1733), a Jesuit priest with an interest in mathematics and logic. In his *Euclides ab omni naevo vindicatus* (*Euclid freed from every flaw*), he considered replacing the parallel postulate by one of three hypotheses: (1) the angle sum of every triangle is greater than two right angles; (2) the angle sum of every triangle is equal to two right angles; (3) the angle sum of every triangle is less than two right angles. The second hypothesis is, of course, equivalent to Euclid's parallel postulate. He then aimed to show that each of the other two hypotheses was separately self-contradictory, thereby establishing the truth of Euclidean geometry on logical grounds, although, interestingly, he ascribed the ultimate source of the validity of his claims to the 'nature of the straight line'. He succeeded in proving that the first hypothesis did indeed 'destroy itself' (his phrase), but although he published what he thought was a proof that the third hypothesis likewise perished, his argument was fallacious. However, it did contain some interesting results which were later to be seen as valid theorems in a new geometry.

Saccheri was followed by Johann Heinrich Lambert (1728–77) who followed Saccheri's tripartite division, but was careful not to rush to judgement. Lambert also discovered new theorems in the geometry generated by Saccheri's third hypothesis; for example, given a triangle, the difference between two right angles and the angle sum of the triangle is proportional to the area of the triangle. He hoped that by finding more and more seemingly paradoxical results, he would eventually find a self-contradiction in the new geometry. However, he also knew that he had not succeeded. He seems to have believed in the end that a new geometry might be possible as the geometry of a surface, but not as the geometry of space. Perhaps he was dissatisfied with his work, because he knew that he had not seen through the question as clearly as usual, and he did not publish it. It was only published posthumously, in 1786.

2. FORMAL INVESTIGATIONS AND THE DISCOVERY OF NON-EUCLIDEAN GEOMETRY

Lambert's work did not end attempts to establish the truth of the *Elements*, but a new and more radical approach emerged at the start of the nineteenth century. While Adrien-Marie Legendre (1752–1833) defended the postulate in his influential *Eléments de Géométrie* (1794), which ran to several editions, a group of mathematicians loosely connected with Carl Friedrich Gauss (1777–1855) began to publish accounts of a new geometry that seemed to them to be physically plausible. This was founded on Saccheri's third hypothesis, probably suggested to them by reading Lambert's work (Saccheri's being by then forgotten). Gauss, together with Ferdinand Schweikart and his nephew Franz Taurinus, F. L. Wachter (a student of Gauss) and Friedrich Bessel, the astronomer, were reluctantly prepared to doubt the truth of the *Elements*. Taurinus gave a lengthy account of a geometry analogous to the geometry on the surface of a sphere, but then claimed, on singularly feeble grounds, that it could not be a geometry of space. And Gauss, who might have been expected to see most profoundly into the matter, could only conclude that the nature of space seemed to be an empirical question that could not be resolved *a priori*. The repeated failure of attempts to find a self-contradiction in a geometry based on the third hypothesis led them to think instead that it might be true, but this raised the question of the nature of geometry, which they were unable to broach successfully.

There are, in fact, two ways of approaching that question. One is to find a way of dealing more subtly with geometrical concepts, so as to examine the possibilities more closely. The other is to provide a fresh definition of the fundamental entities of geometry. As often in science, the two went together, with the philosophically obscurantist first approach in the lead. The chief protagonists were Nicolai Ivanovich Lobachevsky (1792–1856) in Russia and János Bolyai (1802–60) in Hungary, who each independently announced the existence of a new geometry that was a candidate for being the geometry of space. Lobachevsky published first, in Russian, in 1829. Bolyai's work appeared as an appendix to his father's two-volume treatise on geometry in 1831. Lobachevskii tried again, in French, in Crelle's new *Journal für Mathematik* in 1837, in a booklet in German in 1840, and in a French book written in 1855. Sadly, except for more or less private remarks, their discoveries appear not to have been accepted. To see why this was, it is necessary to look in a little detail at what they proposed.

Both men studied a three-dimensional space, and defined parallelism in a way consistent with the third hypothesis of Saccheri and Lambert. They then obtained three surfaces in this space; spherical geometry being valid for one, Euclidean geometry for another and Saccheri's third hypothesis being valid for the third. By transforming triangles from the first of these surfaces to the third, they showed how to derive trigonometrical formulae for triangles on the third surface from the familiar formulae of spherical trigonometry (which are valid independently of the parallel postulate). In this way they were able to prove all the basic results needed to give a complete, trigonometrical description of a new geometry of space. The overall impression of their work is very convincing. If a new geometry exists, then surely it is described by their formulae (which are identical to those written down by Taurinus, but derived in a much more meaningful way). But there remained the possibility that their initial definition of parallel lines was still logically inconsistent with the other assumptions of geometry, and for that reason their work could not command assent. Had a contradiction turned up, they would merely have established some results about the new functions that appeared in their trigonometric formulae, but those formulae would have turned out, after all, to be devoid of geometric meaning.

3. NEW IDEAS ABOUT GEOMETRY

However, if the ontological status of their formulae was in doubt, so too was the epistemology underlying the traditional position. The naïve conception of line and plane, not to mention that of physical space, had shown itself incapable either of defending the *Elements* or of creating a new geometry. The way forward was to give new foundations to the whole geometrical enterprise. In this development, the first crucial idea was due to Gauss who in 1827 published a theorem which showed that the curvature of a surface in space could be determined intrinsically; that is, it depended only on quantities which could be measured on the surface itself. Thus, measurements taken on a sphere could determine how curved it is, and it would not be necessary to step off the surface and look. In this approach, a plane emerges as one of the surfaces of zero curvature (the cylinder is another). Since, as he showed, two surfaces have the same intrinsic geometry if and only if their curvatures are the same at corresponding points, Gauss in this way characterised every possible two-dimensional geometry.

Gauss seems to have regarded this theorem as a deep fact about surfaces embedded in space, but in 1854 a brilliant student of his took the next crucial step of basing all of geometry on a generalisation of Gauss's idea. This was Bernhard Riemann (1826–66), who in 1854 put forward the view that any geometry was of this kind: it took place on a space (some kind of surface or three dimensional or even higher dimensional thing) upon which it was possible to speak of the distance between any two points.

Riemann showed how to generalise Gauss's idea of curvature so that an intrinsic description of any geometry was possible. The significance of this work was immense. For example, in a two-dimensional geometry, Gauss's result could be used to determine the curvature of the surface everywhere, because curvature does not depend on how the surface is embedded in Euclidean three-space; indeed, the surface need not be embedded at all. In this way the geometry of surfaces was shorn of any essential connection with the geometry of Euclidean space. All surfaces were on a par, and so, most importantly, were all three-dimensional geometries. The nature of physical space could now be investigated by proposing different mathematical models of it, but it could only be resolved empirically.

In this approach, plane geometry takes place on a two-dimensional surface of zero curvature.[5] A straight line is defined as the curve of shortest distance on the surface between any two of its points. For the first time it was possible to define a line without any appeal to intuition, and so to address Aristotle's original question.

It was also possible to give a geometrical meaning to the trigonometrical formulae of Bolyai and Lobachevsky. This was done by Eugenio Beltrami (1835–1900) who, in 1868, showed how to interpret them as describing the intrinsic geometry on a surface of constant negative curvature.[6] Beltrami drew a map of a non-Euclidean space, in exactly the sense in which the earth is described by maps in an atlas, when he depicted the new geometry on a disc. On his map, objects appear to contract as they move outwards, but this is a distortion of the map projection analogous to that of any terrestrial map. For the first time there was a securely-established alternative to Euclid's geometry. The new geometry, since it differs from Euclid's only in its definition of parallelism, is called 'non-Euclidean geometry'. Beltrami seems to have arrived at his ideas about two-dimensional geometries directly from reading Gauss, and independently of Riemann.

Thus far, the investigations were always conducted with some concern for their physical implications. But the successful promulgation of non-Euclidean geometry by Riemann and Beltrami inevitably destroyed mathematicians' ability to identify the space of the *Elements* with physical space. This raised the need both to give a new, formal account of space and to give a logical, deductive analysis of geometry which would not turn out in due course also to have begged essential questions. These needs were met, firstly by a series of axiomatisations of geometry that culminated in the work of David Hilbert (1862–1943), and secondly by an increasing use of the axiomatic method in all branches of pure mathematics. By the 1920s it was possible to base all mathematics on a theory of sets, and to view mathematical objects as sets of undefined elements carrying various sorts of extra structure. In this way even the most familiar objects, numbers and shapes, were given an entirely formal treatment.

For as long as this was a central aspect of contemporary mathematics, it was natural that historians of geometry, all of whom were themselves active mathematicians, would also see the history of non-Euclidean geometry as a struggle to discover an alternative axiomatisation. For that reason, the principal studies written around 1900, by Bonola and by Engel and Sträckel, emphasised the logical aspects of the story, and many later writers, relying on these works for their wealth of factual detail, have tended to take over their formulation of the matter. But now that the battle for axiom systems has long since been won, it is easier to appreciate that much early work was conducted with the aim of making mathematical sense of physical space.

The easiest way to see that the early investigations into the parallel postulate were not exercises in analysing axiomatic structures is to take an example of a geometry which is not Euclid's: the geometry on the surface of a sphere. Here the role of straight lines is played by arcs of great circles – the circles that are cut out on the sphere by planes through the centre of the sphere. See Figure 42.2: these curves are geodesics, marking out the shortest distance between any two points.

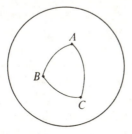

Figure 42.2: A sphere with a triangle on it composed of three great circular arcs, *AC*, *CB* and *BA*. Figure from Patrick J. Ryan, *Euclidean and non-Euclidean geometry* (Cambridge, 1986), p. 108.

Spherical geometry is in some ways familiar, in some ways unfamiliar. For example, any two great circles intersect (so there are no parallels), and triangles formed by three great circular arcs have angle sums greater than two right angles. This is not the geometry that Saccheri's first hypothesis might seem to correspond to, because it flouts another assumption of Euclid's, namely that lines are indefinitely extendable. Nonetheless, it is a geometry different from Euclid's, and some writers, like Lambert and Taurinus, mentioned it. Like Euclid, they ruled it out because in it, two lines can enclose an area, which they felt made it not a possible geometry for space. They did not say that it was a geometry different from Euclid's, which makes it plain that they were not looking for such a thing, but instead were only considering geometries that could be candidates for descriptions of physical space. Indeed, when Lobachevsky and Bolyai published their work, they explicitly recognised that the nature of space now had to be determined empirically and Lobachevsky went so far as to conduct an inconclusive set of astronomical observations.

4. THE IMPLICATIONS OF NON-EUCLIDEAN GEOMETRY

What have been the implications of the discovery of non-Euclidean geometry for mathematics? The theory of functions of a complex variable was shown to be intimately connected with non-Euclidean geometry, most influentially by Poincaré and Felix Klein in the 1880s.[7] Thurston's generalisation of their work dealing with three-dimensional spaces is widely regarded as one of the most important achievements of present-day mathematics. The study of various kinds of space of various dimensions, which derives from the work of Gauss and Riemann, was given a major boost by the discovery of such an important new geometry, and through the connection with the groups of transformations of a geometry there was a corresponding impact on the important theories of Sophus Lie and Elie Cartan.[8]

By contrast, the question of the nature of physical space was widely accepted as an empirical question, although curious limitations remained for quite a while. For example, it was believed until the start of the twentieth century that space had to have constant curvature, and only with the promulgation of Einstein's general theory of relativity was the curvature of space presumed to vary. There was no direct connection between Einstein's work and the discovery of non-Euclidean geometry, but there were a number of indirect ones. (See art. 28, sect. 2.) The formalism of general relativity is highly technical, and derives from studies of differential geometry made by Gregorio Ricci, Tullio Levi-Civita and others. They had attempted to work out the implications of Riemann's ideas for many mathematical processes that are unproblematic in Euclidean geometry, but which in non-Euclidean geometry become unexpectedly subtle, such as comparing the directions of vectors based at different points. What does it mean, for example, to say that two vectors on the sphere point in the same direction? And is it true that a vector can be taken round a closed curve without changing its direction? Their work, taught to Einstein by his friend

Michele Besso, enters naturally into general relativity when one observer's measurements are converted into another's by interpreting the problem as being about how to compare things, such as vectors, based at different points.

According to general relativity, space expands under a strong gravitational pull. This has implications for the path of light near a star, say, and the question becomes the investigation of the geometry near the star. Since we cannot step outside of space and look, this is a question of intrinsic geometry, and the simplest theoretical resolution of it is that the resulting geometry is one of negative curvature, the curvature becoming more and more negative as the star is approached. This is one way in which the question of the nature of space continues to be informed by the discovery of non-Euclidean geometry.

Mathematics, physics and the history of mathematics and science have all benefited from the discovery of non-Euclidean geometry. Philosophical battles have also been fought over it, and these too have been considered by historians. Joan Richards has looked at the reception of non-Euclidean ideas by English mathematicians, and finds that Euclidean geometry became interestingly entangled with a defence of *a priori* knowledge.[9] Imre Toth has studied Gottlob Frege's surprising rejection of non-Euclidean geometry.[10] He suggests that it derived from Frege's hostility to the new axiomatic methodology and his wish to guard against the creation of new mathematical objects and a plurality of axiomatic systems. It was suggested by Roberto Bonola, in his admirable history written in 1906, that the discovery itself was for a long time impeded by the widespread acceptance of Kantianism. This view is hard to appreciate without a clearer history of Kantianism than he presented, but it remains provocative. Also in this connection there have been studies of the philosophical views of, for example, Lambert and Riemann.[11] Lastly, Poincaré's conventionalist interpretation of geometry has its origins in debates about non-Euclidean geometry, and has recently been reconsidered.[12] It is likely that the discovery of non-Euclidean geometry, affecting as it does our ideas about mathematics, physical space and the practice of mathematics and science, will continue to be one of the most thought-provoking achievements of the nineteenth century.

NOTES

1. T. L. Heath, *The thirteen books of Euclid's elements* (Cambridge, 1956), vol. 1, p. 155.
2. G. R. Morrow, *Proclus: a commentary on the first book of Euclid's elements* (Princeton, 1970), pp. 58–61.
3. For details of this and subsequent attempts mentioned in this article, see the books by Bonola and Gray cited in the bibliography. The most thorough recent analysis of Greek investigations of the parallel postulate is I. Toth, 'Das Parallelenproblem im Corpus Aristotelicum', *Archive for history of exact sciences*, 3 (1967), 249–422.
4. A. P. Youschkevitch, *Les mathématiques Arabes* (Paris, 1976).
5. The cylinder, for example, has locally the same geometry as the plane, which is why printing is possible, and topology is needed to distinguish the two.

6. Negative curvature is exemplified by saddle-shaped surfaces.
7. See, for example, E. Scholz, *Geschichte des Mannigfaltigkeitsbegriffs von Riemann bis Poincaré* (Basle, 1980) and J. J. Gray, *Linear differential equations and group theory from Riemann to Poincaré* (Basle, 1986).
8. See a series of papers by T. Hawkins, including his 'Wilhelm Killing and the structure of Lie algebras', *Archive for history of exact sciences*, 26 (1982), 127–92.
9. J. Richards, 'The reception of a mathematical theory: non-Euclidean geometry in England, 1868-1883', in B. Barnes and S. Shapin (eds.) *Natural order: historical studies of scientific culture* (Beverly Hills, 1979).
10. I. Toth, 'Three errors in the *Grundlagen* of 1884: Frege and non-Euclidean geometry', proceedings of the International Frege Conference, Schwerin (GDR), 1984 (Berlin, 1984).
11. E. Scholz, 'Herbart's influence on Bernhard Riemann', *Historia mathematica*, 9 (1982), 413–40.
12. For a historically-based attempt to revive debate on the philosophy of geometry, see R.Torretti, *Philosphy of geometry from Riemann to Poincaré*, Episteme, vol. 7 (Dordrecht, 1978).

FURTHER READING

R. Bonola, *Non-Euclidean geometry*, tr. H. S. Carslaw, with a supplement containing *The science absolute of space*, by J. Bolyai and *The theory of parallels*, by N. I. Lobachevsky, tr. G. B. Halsted (New York, 1955).

F. Engel and P. Stäckel, *Die Theorie der Parallellinien von Euklid bis auf Gauss* (Leipzig, 1895).

J. J. Gray, *Ideas of space: Euclidean, non-Euclidean, and relativistic* (Oxford, 1979).

43

PARTICLE SCIENCE

HELGE KRAGH

The term *particle science* has not got an established meaning in the scientific vocabulary. I shall take it here to cover research aiming at accounting for the properties of matter by a few elementary particles of matter or perhaps even just one. In this sense, particle science expresses the age-old dream of a fundamental unity of matter, although this dream may also be given other interpretations (in terms of fields, for example).

Particle science has only reached maturity in this century with the emergence of elementary particle physics, but its history can be traced in earlier centuries. Although the history of particle science began with the atomists of ancient Greece, I shall concentrate initially on particle science in the nineteenth century, at which time it was cultivated primarily by chemists. I shall end with the current situation, *c.* 1980, by which time the subject had become primarily the concern of physicists. The interdisciplinary nature of early particle science is worth stressing: until well into this century it involved chemists as much as physicists. For example, it would be wrong to assume that the question of fundamental particles in the period 1890 to 1930 was dealt with only by physicists. Chemists' ideas of particle science and their relation to the ideas of physicists have as yet not received the attention they deserve.

Particle science, as defined in the present essay, concentrates on the discovery of new elementary particles and, as such, it supplies valuable material for a more general understanding of the concept of discovery. Yet the evidence suggests that there have been significant differences between these discoveries. Evidently not all particle discoveries belong to the same category. Some particles, such as the electron, exist in ordinary matter and were identified by low-energy experiments; other particles, such as the anti-proton, were manufactured in high-energy experiments under highly artificial conditions. Again, the discovery of some particles, such as quarks, involved theoretical constructions rather than direct experimental detection. Indeed, it may even be argued that (some) elementary particles were not discovered, but invented. In any case, particle discoveries are never instantaneous events since they involve both a theoretical and a social dimension. In order to count as a true discovery, the putative discovery claim has to gain social acceptance, which is often a protracted process. Whether or not a claim is accepted today is irrelevant from the point of view of history of science. Any socially-accepted discovery claim is, in principle, of equal historical interest and should be treated in the same manner. Furthermore, not only do the hundreds of particle discoveries need to be differentiated and classified but they also need to be compared with discoveries of other material objects such as planets or chemical elements. Such a work is likely to lead to interesting insights relating not only to the history of the physical sciences but also to their philosophy and sociology.

1. THE COMPOSITE ATOM IN THE NINETEENTH CENTURY

By the end of the eighteenth century, Newtonian corpuscularianism was generally accepted and further developed by Pierre-Simon Laplace (1749–1827) and his school of mathematical physics. (See art. 18.) According to the Laplacian programme the properties of matter should be explained in terms of imponderable fluids (such as heat and electricity) and ponderable atomic particles interacting through central forces. The nature of the forces, supposed to be analogous to Newtonian gravitation, was ignored by Laplace and his school but a few scientists offered corpuscular explanations for the forces. Thus George-Louis Lesage proposed in 1784 to account for gravitation by conceiving the ether as composed of minute particles.

During most of the nineteenth century, the majority of physicists and chemists (not always distinguishable professions) adhered to some version of the atomic doctrine. Matter was generally considered to consist of individual elementary atoms, as John Dalton (1766–1844) had postulated at the beginning of the century. According to Dalton each chemical element was identified with a specific kind of atom which was usually believed to be endowed with attractive and/or repulsive forces such as gravitational forces or, in earlier theories, atmospheres of caloric (the fluid of heat). Daltonian chemistry was a science of atomic (or molecular) particles but was not a particle science in the stricter sense adopted in the present article. It operated with a relatively large number of different atoms which differed in weight and size and had no common structure in terms of more fundamental entities.

The 'chemical atom' adopted by most chemists constituted a minimum atomism in which an 'atom' merely denoted the smallest unit of a certain element appearing in a chemical reaction. Chemists tended to conceive the atom operationally and not as the building-block of a theory of matter. According to this cautious, empirical view, questions about theory of matter were not included within the province of chemistry. Even among chemists who considered themselves atomists it was widely felt that chemistry should not deal with issues concerning 'the physical atom' or with questions about the ultimate nature of matter. Daltonian atomism was criticised on two fronts. Some people argued that atomism should be rejected because atoms were merely metaphysical concepts. Others rejected Daltonian atomism because of its lack of simplicity and disagreement with the idea of the unity of matter. The historical importance of these objections to atomism is a matter of dispute among historians of chemistry.

Throughout the century, there existed a counter-current which questioned the notion of indivisible Daltonian atoms by assuming that atoms are composite bodies made up of one or more fundamental particles. Thus, according to William Prout (1785–1850), a London physician, all chemical elements consist of multiples of hydrogen atoms. Prout's hypothesis, first ventured in 1815, won the support of Thomas Thomson (1773–1852) who became its most influential spokesman in the first half of the century. The idea was considered an interesting possibility by several continental chemists, including Jean-Baptiste-André Dumas in France and Jean Charles Galissard de Marignac in Switzerland. However, it was sharply criticised by Jöns Jacob Berzelius, Justus von Liebig and Jean-Servais Stas who argued convincingly that the atomic weights of the elements are not multiples of the atomic weight of hydrogen as one would expect from Prout's hypothesis. Hence, they concluded, the hypothesis is false.

Although this conclusion was generally accepted, the Proutian dream of the unity of matter continued to be explored in a variety of ways throughout the century. Speculative and often ingenious arguments were put forward in order to make the empirically-determined atomic weights fit with some modification of Prout's assumptions. One possibility was to reduce the magnitude of the hypothetical prime unit of matter, i.e. to consider all atoms, including hydrogen, to consist of 'sub-atomic' particles. This idea, first proposed by Prout in 1833, was supported by Marignac and Dumas and later developed by other scientists.

The general idea of composite atoms, including speculations of the possibility of transformation of elements, received strong impetus with the emergence of spectral analysis in the mid-century and with the establishment of the periodic system of the elements. Dmitry Ivanovich Mendeelev (1834–1907), who first developed the periodic system, rejected Prout's hypothesis and denied that the periodicity of the elements lends support to the idea of atomic structure. But other chemists thought differently. Julius Lothar Meyer, Julius Thomsen, Victor Meyer, Gustavus Hinrichs and Thomas Carnelley, among others, regarded the periodic system as evidence for the claim that atoms are composed of a common prime unit of matter. This theory was also supported by Norman Lockyer and William Crookes who mainly based their arguments on the study of spectra and electric discharges. At one stage, Crookes identified the rarefied 'fourth state of matter', cathode rays, as the prime matter.[1] Although neo-Proutians did not generally specify the nature of the hypothetical sub-atomic particles, some attributed specific qualities to them. For example, in 1867 Hinrichs introduced 'pan-atoms' (or 'pantogen') of atomic weight 0.5 or 0.25 and, twenty years later, Crookes speculated that helium, supposed to be of atomic weight 0.5, might be the prime matter. Still other scientists were willing to consider much smaller particles. To mention just one example, the German botanist Carl Wilhelm von Nägeli proposed in 1884 that all atoms should be considered as congregates of billions of ether particles which he termed 'Ameren'. The status of Proutian and neo-Proutian conceptions in the nineteenth century constitutes a rather confused picture. There were many ingenious ideas, often proposed by prominent scientists, but the trend remained outside mainstream science and did not lead to sound insights into the nature of matter. It was a programme, or a dream, rather than a research tradition. The idea of composite atoms was speculative in the sense that it seemed to be beyond experimental testing. Moreover, there were many contradictory theories of atomic constitution and none of them offered chemists any obvious advantages.

Although atomic theory was indisputably the foundation of most chemistry in the nineteenth century, many chemists questioned whether the theory should be interpreted realistically. They disliked speculations about the nature of the elements and wanted to use atomic theory merely as a useful instrument but not to claim that it represented reality. An extreme example of this instrumentalist approach was advanced in the late 1860s by the British chemist Benjamin Brodie (1816–80) who completely rejected the atomic theory. Brodie and his few allies wanted to base chemistry on a more general 'calculus of chemical operations' which was independent of all particulate theories of matter.[2] The attempt to free chemistry from atomic theory led to a lively debate in England but interest in Brodie's ideas was shortlived. However, later in the century anti-atomism reappeared more strongly.

While most nineteenth-century speculations about atomic structure arose among chemists, a similar programme was also followed by a few physicists who continued the Laplacian tradition. In order to account for various electrical, magnetic and optical phenomena, physicists developed tentative atomic models based on one or two hypothetical fundamental particles. In the mid-century the Italian physicist Ottaviano Mossotti proposed that the world is composed of a mixture of matter-atoms and ether-atoms interacting through inverse square forces. The German physicist Wilhelm Weber (1804–91) suggested in the 1850s that matter has an atomic constitution and that atoms are composed of imponderable positively and negatively-charged point particles. Partly in unpublished notes he developed this idea into an elaborate atomic model.

Weber claimed that this model would throw light not only on the physical properties of matter but also on such chemical problems as the periodic system and the nature of chemical affinity. This corpuscular theory of matter and electricity was in opposition to the electromagnetic field theories of Faraday and Maxwell. (See art. 22, sect. 2.) While his atomic theory attracted little attention, Weber's idea of tiny atoms of electricity won general support and was later further developed in Hendrik Antoon Lorentz's influential synthesis of Maxwellian electrodynamics and the electrical unit of matter. At the end of the nineteenth century, many physicists believed that material atoms were composed of positive and negative 'electrons', a term introduced by George Johnstone Stoney in 1891 but only generally used in its present sense a decade later. Another electrical particle, the ion, also entered physics and chemistry in the mid-century. It was introduced in 1833 by Michael Faraday (1791–1867) who, however, did not consider it as a real particle of electricity. Only with the experiments on electrolytic dissociation carried out in the 1850s by Johann Wilhelm Hittorf and later by Svante August Arrhenius did ions emerge as particles.

Atoms or hypothetical sub-atomic entities were often conceived as tiny 'billiard ball' particles satisfying the laws of Newtonian mechanics. However, more subtle notions of fundamental particles were also adopted. One such notion was Rudjer Josip Boscovich's theory of immaterial point atoms, pure centres of forces, which in England served as inspiration for Davy, Faraday, William Thomson (later Lord Kelvin; 1824–1907) and others. Another example of considerable interest is the vortex atomic model proposed by Thomson in 1867. According to this model, all atoms are ultimately vortices in the universal ether. Thomson and some other physicists, including J. J. Thomson, developed the vortex atomic theory to explain many electrical, chemical and gravitational phenomena but, at the end of the century, the theory was gradually abandoned. The vortex atomic theory was, like Boscovich's theory, a truly fundamental and unified theory of matter but not, perhaps, a typical particle theory. The vortex theorists saw particles like atoms and molecules as only apparent discontinuities in an otherwise continuous distribution of the universal ether.

In the last decade of the nineteenth century the atomic theory was generally accepted both by chemists and by physicists. However, not all scientists believed in a particulate view of matter. Under the influence of positivistic notions, the atomic theory met with considerable opposition, especially in Germany and France. This opposition was, to some extent, a continuation of an older romantic opposition which stressed the dynamic aspects of matter and rejected mechanistic corpuscularianism. In the 1890s anti-atomism was advocated by such prominent scientists as Wilhelm Ostwald, Ernst Mach, Pierre Duhem and Marcellin Berthelot who wanted to found the physical sciences on a new 'energetic' paradigm in which there was no room for atoms or other hypothetical particles. However, at the turn of the century, the opposition to particle science had lost much of its momentum and within a few years anti-atomism declined in importance. The reasons for its decline will become apparent in the next section.

2. ELECTRONS AND ATOMIC STRUCTURE

The electron, conceived as a fundamental sub-atomic particle, was introduced by J. J. Thomson (1856–1940) in 1897. Thomson's celebrated discovery has traditionally been seen as the result of a protracted controversy over the nature of cathode rays: together with other British physicists he argued that cathode rays were a stream of particles, while German physicists generally considered the rays to be pulse-like disturbances in the ether. However, recent scholarship has questioned this interpretation and argued that until 1896 cathode rays were not a topic of particular interest to British physicists.[3] Whatever caused Thomson to pursue his investigations, he produced experimental evidence in 1897 that cathode rays consist of sub-atomic 'corpuscles' and suggested that these particles are the ultimate constituents of all matter. Thomson's corpuscle was only gradually accepted as a proper elementary particle in the following years when it was further studied by Thomson and other physicists. At the beginning of the twentieth century, Thomson's particle was identified with the 'electron' which had been articulated in the theories of Lorentz, Poincaré and Larmor and with the modern electron which became an established elementary particle, the first of its kind.

Already in his work of 1897 Thomson suggested an atomic model based on electrons moving in circular orbits in a hypothetical positively-charged fluid. This model, the first version of the Thomson atom, was much elaborated during the following decade when it was widely accepted as a promising candidate for a realistic picture of the atom. At first, Thomson believed that atoms consist only of electrons which were thus regarded as true Proutian particles, each atom being composed of thousands of electrons. Thomson hoped to be able to explain even the positively-charged sphere as a manifestation of electrons and thus avoid a dualistic theory of separate kinds of electricity. However, in about 1908, it became increasingly clear that positive electricity had to exist in the atom in its own right. Thomson's electron-atom was adopted by several other physicists who in the period 1900 to 1910 proposed a number of alternative models. Jean Perrin in France (1901) and Hantaro Nagaoka in Japan (1903) suggested 'Saturnian' models in which the electrons revolve around a positive centre. Philipp Lenard in Germany (1903) pictured the atom in terms of 'dynamids', tiny electrical dipoles. Other models, suggested by Oliver Lodge and James Jeans in England and by Walter Nernst in Germany, operated with negative as well as positive electrons instead of Thomson's positively-charged fluid. In Lodge's model the atom consisted of alternating layers of positive and negative electrons. There were even models with 'neutrons', considered to be pairs of oppositely-charged electrons. Many of these short-lived models were deployed in chemistry, in particular in the explanation of the covalent chemical bond.

By 1910 the negative electron was recognised as an elementary constituent of all atoms but opinion was divided over the number of electrons and the nature of the positive charge. Some physicists regarded the electron as point-like and hence lacking internal structure, while others proposed elaborate models of the structure of the electron. In 1897 Thomson initially believed that the electron was a new element. However, although he soon abandoned this idea, it was later taken up by some other chemists. William Ramsay in 1908 and Johannes Rydberg in 1906 both argued that the electron should be treated like an element and have its place in the periodic system. The oil drop experiments of Robert Millikan in the years 1910–1916 did much to prove that the electron is really an elementary quantum of electricity. Millikan's conclusion was, however, questioned by the Austrian physicist Felix Ehrenhaft who claimed to have discovered sub-electronic charges, but the claim was ignored by the majority of physicists.

After 1913, Thomson's atomic model ceased to appeal to physicists and the Bohr-Rutherford nuclear atom became the new paradigm for particle physics. The electron kept its fundamental role but the positive charge was now seen as residing in the atomic nucleus as first suggested by Ernest Rutherford (1871–1937) in 1911. During the early years of the Bohr-Rutherford model the hydrogen nucleus gradually emerged as an elementary particle comparable with the electron. As mentioned above, there had been earlier speculations about positive atomic constituents but these were considered to be counterparts of the electron and were not identified with the hydrogen nucleus. The name 'proton' for the hydrogen nucleus was coined by Rutherford in about 1920. The proton is an example of a particle which was never 'discovered' in any direct sense but rather emerged slowly as a result of the success of the Bohr-Rutherford theory.

3. NUCLEAR CONSTITUENTS

In the 1920s, the consensus among physicists was that electrons play a double role in the atom: in a neutral atom of charge Z and mass number A there are Z electrons revolving around the nucleus which consists of A protons and A-Z electrons. In many schemes the α particle, considered to be a tightly bound system of 4 protons and 2 electrons, figured as an additional component in the nucleus. This picture of the atomic nucleus did not change with the advent of quantum mechanics in the mid-1920s. Initially quantum mechanics was a theory concerning the electron system and was not applied to the nucleus. The most popular model of the nucleus included protons, electrons and α particles but occasionally other nuclear particles were proposed. For example, Rutherford believed for some time that he had discovered a new particle, which he named X^{3++}, combining three protons and one electron. Other sub-units which were tentatively proposed were the $\alpha a'e$ particle (four protons and four electrons) and the μ particle (two protons and two electrons). A further particle which turned up in Rutherford's imaginative mind was the 'neutron' which appeared in the physics literature after about 1920. Rutherford believed this neutron to be a combination of a proton and an electron but attempts to detect the hypothetical particle proved unsuccessful. The term 'neutron' was first introduced by William Sutherland in 1899 who used it for a combination of a positive and negative electron into an ether particle. It was used in the same sense by Nernst in 1907. However, it would be misleading to see the Sutherland-Nernst neutron as a precursor of either Rutherford's neutron or Chadwick's neutron. These particles have only their name in common. Although several new nuclear particles were proposed in the 1920s, atomic theory was essentially a two-particle theory based on protons and electrons. Other particles, like the neutron or α particle, were systems of electrons and protons and not thought of as truly elementary constituents of matter. The climate of opinion in regard to new elementary particles was conservative, in the sense that such possibilities were totally excluded.

The two-particle consensus holds good even if the photon is included as an elementary particle. Corpuscular theories of light continued to receive some support even after the dominance of the wave theory in about 1830. However, the light quantum was only introduced in 1905 by Albert Einstein (1879–1955) who argued that light (and other forms of electromagnetic radiation) consists of discrete parcels of energy. (See art. 29, sect. 1.) Einstein's light quanta were not well received and it was only in the early 1920s that physicists accepted light particles or, as they had been called since 1926, photons. As a particle, the photon is very different from the electron (for example, the mass of the photon is zero) and it has its own complex history. Like the proton, the photon was never 'discovered' experimentally but grew out of a long series of experimental and theoretical arguments during the period 1905 to 1923.

By 1930, physicists began experimental research on the atomic nucleus with the result that the harmonious two-particle consensus was soon destroyed. The 1930s saw a number of new particles and the beginning of a new speciality in physics, elementary particle physics. Together with research on the nucleus, cosmic radiation was the prime source of information about the new particles. Although cosmic radiation had been studied since the First World War, it became a major research area of physics in the 1930s.

In order to explain various anomalies in nuclear physics, in particular the continuous β-spectrum, Wolfgang Pauli (1900–58) suggested late in 1929 that the nucleus might contain a number of very small neutral particles. Pauli called these hypothetical particles 'neutrons', a term which should not be confused with the neutrons of either Rutherford or Chadwick. At first Pauli believed that the mass of his 'neutron' was of the same order of magnitude as that of the electron. In the early 1930s, Pauli's particle was regarded with much scepticism but gradually it became more legitimate and most physicists accepted it as a real, although undetected particle. The main reason for this change of status was Enrico Fermi's influential theory of β-decay which from 1934 extended Pauli's idea. Fermi proposed to call Pauli's particle the 'neutrino', a name which was at once accepted. In the mid-1930s it became clear that the neutrino, if it existed, was weightless and not a nuclear constituent as Pauli had first suggested. Physicists generally believed that the neutrino, because of its extremely weak interaction with matter, was beyond experimental detection. Only in 1956 did Frederick Reines and Clyde Cowan manage to 'discover' the elusive neutrino by means of beams from a fission reactor. However, at that time the neutrino had been accepted as a real particle for at least twenty years.

In a celebrated experiment by James Chadwick (1891–1974) at the Cavendish Laboratory in 1932, *the* neutron was discovered. Chadwick at first believed that what he had discovered was Rutherford's neutron, that is, a proton-electron composite. More than a year after this experiment most physicists shared this view and hesitated to include the neutron among the true elementary particles: indeed, the atomic nucleus was usually considered to consist of protons, neutrons *and* electrons. The claim that the neutron was a new elementary particle, a third fundamental constituent of ordinary matter, was first made by the Russian physicist Dmitri Ivanenko in 1932 and was soon adopted by Werner Heisenberg in his theory of the atomic nucleus. The convergence of theory and experiment led in 1934 to the general acceptance of the neutron as an elementary particle; thus the electron was finally expelled from the nucleus after twenty years. In the mid-1930s it was realised that the proton and the neutron can be regarded as states of the same kind of particle for which the name 'nucleon' was coined.

In a series of papers, in about 1930, Paul Dirac (1902–84) pursued the old Proutian dream of a truly unitary theory of matter. On the basis of his relativistic theory of the electron, he suggested that the proton should be interpreted as a 'hole' in a hypothetical 'sea' of negative-energy electrons. By identifying the proton with an anti-electron (a name only later used) Dirac had reduced all matter to manifestations of just one fundamental particle. The electron in Dirac's theory thus corresponded to the hydrogen atom in Prout's old theory. However, Dirac's unitary theory of matter was short-lived since it was found to be inconsistent with both theory and experiment. As an alternative Dirac postulated in 1931 the existence of a new particle, the anti-electron or the positive electron, a 'mirror particle' of the ordinary negative electron. Although positive electrons figured quite frequently in physics and chemistry in the decades before Dirac, his positive electron, justified by the equations of quantum mechanics, has only a superficial similarity with, and no generic relation to, the positive electrons of Weber, Jeans and Larmor.

Dirac's theory of the positive electron was part of a more general theory in which there was also room for other 'anti-particles'. In 1933 Dirac introduced the negative proton as the anti-particle of the usual proton and later anti-neutrinos and anti-neutrons were also postulated. The anti-proton was occasionally discussed as a possible nuclear constituent, first by George Gamow in 1934, but it remained at the periphery of physics for the next twenty years.

Dirac's theory of anti-particles was at first regarded with scepticism. The anti-electron was only generally accepted by the physics community after 1932 when Carl Anderson (b. 1905) reported the discovery of positive electrons in cloud chamber photographs exposed to cosmic radiation. Anderson proposed calling these particles 'positrons'. It is significant that Anderson did not initially identify his positron with Dirac's anti-electron which played no role at all in the experimental discovery. It was only a year or so after Anderson's discovery that the position was recognised as vindicating Dirac's hypothetical particle. To say that Dirac predicted the positron, and Anderson discovered it, is thus only partially true; with the advantage of hindsight we can see that Anderson's particle is the same as that proposed by Dirac. At any rate, by 1933 the positron was an accepted, although exotic, member of the family of elementary particles.

Not only did Dirac predict the positive electron, he also conjectured the existence of another elementary particle, the magnetic monopole. Dirac proved in 1931 that such a particle, behaving like a single magnetic pole, is allowed according to the principles of quantum mechanics. In contrast to the positron, the monopole was ignored for more than thirty years. Only in the 1960s did the hypothetical monopole become an interesting particle and only then did the experimentalists begin to search for it. In spite of many attempts to detect the monopole, and even some claims to have succeeded, it has remained unconfirmed and hence hypothetical. The 'tachyon' is another hypothetical particle which has been sought in vain. Although tachyons may move faster than light they do not conflict with the theory of relativity. This was first suggested in the 1920s but these particles only attracted the interest of physicists forty years later. However, while monopoles are regarded as highly interesting entities which probably exist somewhere in the universe, tachyons have remained on the fringe of mainstream physics.

The 1930s saw the discovery of further new particles. At the end of 1931, Harold Urey and his co-workers discovered a heavy hydrogen isotope (deuterium), the nucleus of which was called a 'deuteron'. The deuteron consists of one proton and one neutron although at first, before the acceptance of the proton-neutron model, it was believed to consist of two protons and one electron.

Although not a true elementary particle the deuteron proved to be as important a particle for nuclear physics in the 1930s and 1940s as the α particle had been in the Rutherford era.

4. MESONS AND OTHER NEW PARTICLES

Cosmic radiation was the most fertile study field for early particle physics. It supplied physicists with the positron and some years later the meson, an entirely new kind of particle. In the mid-1930s, the absorption properties of cosmic rays presented a paradox to theoretical physicists who questioned whether relativistic quantum mechanics would still apply to the high energies present in cosmic radiation. The theorists were puzzled and in need of more data. In this context Carl Anderson and Seth Neddermeyer at the California Institute of Technology proposed in 1937 that cosmic radiation contains charged particles (mesons) with a mass intermediary between that of an electron and that of a proton. While Anderson's earlier discovery of the positron had been unexpected and unconnected to theory, this was not the case with the discovery of the meson; it resulted from a series of systematic experiments made in response to puzzles which faced the theorists. However, Anderson's discovery was not guided in any way by theoretical predictions of new particles. Such a prediction had in fact been made by the Japanese physicist Hideki Yukawa (1907–81) who, in 1935, proposed on theoretical grounds a 'U-particle' supposed to be a nuclear field quantum. However, Yukawa's theory, published in a Japanese journal, was unknown to Anderson and Neddermeyer in 1937. In the same year Yukawa's theory reached the West and his 'U-particle' was soon identified with the Anderson-Neddermeyer meson. The meson was quickly adopted by theorists in the late 1930s and it contributed significantly to the experimental knowledge of cosmic radiation. By 1940 most physicists accepted the following elementary particles: proton, neutron, electron, positron, neutrino, meson and photon. The Yukawa-Anderson-Neddermeyer particle, however, resulted in inconsistencies, gradually leading to the idea of two separate kinds of mesons.

Theoretical considerations as well as cosmic ray experiments seemed to demand that the Yukawa meson had properties not consistent with the Anderson-Neddermeyer particle. During the Second World War Japanese physicists tried to resolve the dilemma by proposing a two-meson hypothesis and French experimentalists claimed the existence of new mesons with masses intermediate between the Yukawa meson and the proton. However, it was only after the war that the two-meson theory became accepted and, in 1947, received experimental confirmation by Cecil Powell and his group in Bristol. At that time Powell did not know about the Japanese prediction. After 1947 it became accepted that mesons are of at least two kinds: the strongly interacting π meson (or pion) and the weakly interacting μ meson (or muon). Of these the first was recognised as the Yukawa meson while the μ meson is identical to the Anderson-Neddermeyer particle. Physicists rapidly accepted the duplication of mesons and were soon able to produce them artificially in accelerator experiments. While the pions discovered in the late 1940s were electrically charged (π^+ and π^-), in 1950 experimentalists succeeded in producing neutral pions which proved to have slightly smaller masses than the charged pions. Neutral mesons had also occasionally been considered by theorists since the late 1940s.

Shortly after the discovery of the pion, evidence was reported for the existence of new, unexpected particles. In 1947 George Rochester and Clifford Butler from Manchester produced cloud chamber photographs of what were then called 'V-particles', recognised in the following years as heavy mesons. In 1951 some 15 elementary particles were identified, including new mesons known as the τ meson, the Λ meson and the θ meson. With the diversity of new particles the scene of particle physics seemed at the same time confusing and challenging. And yet the explosion of elementary particles had hardly begun.

In the early 1950s particle physics was established as a new and exciting research field. New post-war technologies, especially high-energy accelerators and sensitive detectors, helped to transform the field into an American-dominated big science. Whereas in the period 1930 to 1950 the most important source of new particles had been cosmic radiation, in the 1950s accelerators took over. The neutral pion was the first particle among many to be discovered in an accelerator experiment. Likewise experimental detectors changed: in the early period cloud chambers and Geiger-Müller devices were the favoured detectors, later followed by the photographic emulsion which proved particularly useful in cosmic ray studies. In 1953 Donald Glaser (b. 1926) invented the bubble chamber which was developed into a powerful new detector; since the late 1950s it has been an integral part of high energy physics together with ever bigger accelerators.

During the 1950s and 1960s elementary particles continued to proliferate; soon there were more 'elementary' particles than the number of chemical elements. Apart from the particles already mentioned, the period saw new particles such as (in old symbols) Σ, Ξ, θ, K, and χ which all turned out to be unstable with lifetimes around 10^{-8} seconds. While these particles left directly-observable tracks in detectors, other particles, known as resonances, could only be identified indirectly. The first resonance particle, named Δ, was discovered in 1952, and in the early 1960s it was followed by many other meson resonances. Resonance particles are extremely short-lived (their lifetime is around 10^{-23} seconds) which is why they do not leave measurable tracks in detectors. Of the resonance particles reported in the 1960s many turned out to be spurious and soon disappeared from the catalogues of elementary particles. While all the new particles hitherto mentioned are 'hadrons' or strongly interacting particles, the list of weakly interacting 'leptons' (which includes electrons, neutrinos and muons) grew at a more modest rate. The only additions to this list came in 1962 when two distinct kinds of neutrinos (each with its own anti-particle), the electron-neutrino and the muon-neutrino, were experimentally confirmed.

5. FROM QUARKS TO GRAND UNIFIED THEORY

During this period there was no adequate theory to account for the proliferation of experimentally-detected particles. Lacking a proper theory of elementary particles, theorists introduced various phenomenological strategies in order to classify and better understand the plethora of particles. The most successful of these was the 'Eightfold Way' scheme proposed independently in 1961 by Murray Gell-Mann (b. 1929) from United States and Yuval Ne'eman (b. 1925) from Israel. The scheme succeeded in reducing all the hadrons to a few 'multiplets' each of which consists of a group of related particles. The Eightfold Way proved its instrumental power by Gell-Mann's prediction in 1962 of a hitherto unknown hadron, the Ω-particle. Two years later this particle was discovered in Brookhaven, USA, impressively confirming Gell-Mann's ideas.

The fertility of the Eightfold Way was further proved when it was developed into the so-called quark model, proposed independently by Gell-Mann and George Zweig in 1964. According to this model all hadrons 'consist' of sub-entities with fractional charges (2/3 and 1/3 of the electron's charge), called quarks. The word 'quark' was proposed by Gell-Mann while Zweig's proposal, 'ace', did not win support. Initially the quark model achieved only slender support in theory but it showed great phenomenological strength and promised a better, unified understanding of most high-energy experiments. Just as Mendeleev's periodic system and Bohr's atomic model had brought order and unity to the chaos of the chemical elements so, it was felt, the Eightfold Way and the quark model had reinstated order in the crowded world of elementary particles. The proton, the neutron, the mesons and all the other hadrons could now be considered manifestations of, if not composites of, just a few fundamental quarks.

The quark model won acceptance almost immediately but in its first years it faced opposition from a rival model for hadrons. The rival was the 'bootstrap' theory proposed by Geoffrey Chew (b. 1924) in 1961, a radical alternative to the quark theory. While the quark theory expressed the traditional Proutian or 'fundamentalist' aim of explaining the properties and existence of particles on the basis of more fundamental particles (quarks), Chew and other bootstrap theorists built up a non-reductionist, 'democratic' theory in which each hadron was seen as a composite of all others. In such a theory no particle is more fundamental than any other and hence the very notion of truly elementary particles disappears. The bootstrap theory was much discussed throughout the

1960s and was developed by Chew into a broader philosophical concept. However, particle physicists did not adopt it as a serious alternative.

In the decade following Gell-Mann's and Zweig's introduction of quarks, many experimenters sought evidence for free quarks. Despite such attempts and at least one claim to discovery (made in 1977 by physicists at Stanford University) the search was in vain. Isolated quarks were accepted as non-existent and the consensus emerged that quarks only exist 'confined' inside hadrons. Some physicists took this to mean that quarks are merely mathematical artefacts but, by about 1970, experiments with high-energy electron-nucleon collisions supplied evidence that the neutron and the proton are composed of confined clusters of three quarks. Other experiments in the late 1970s confirmed the existence of 'gluons', neutral particles which act as carriers of quark forces.

The original quark scheme included three separate quarks but, by the 1960s, some theorists argued for the possibility of a fourth, 'charmed' quark. This idea received dramatic confirmation in 1974 when two groups of American physicists independently succeeded in detecting a particle built up of charmed quarks, the J/ψ meson. This new meson was more than three times as heavy as the proton and it was soon succeeded by other heavy particles which confirmed the notion of 'charm'. The 1974 discovery of the J/ψ meson caused a minor revolution in particle physics, heralding what has been called 'the new physics'.

While quark physics deals with hadrons only, 'the new physics' was no less concerned with leptons. Theoretical attempts to unify weak and electromagnetic interactions resulted in a so-called electroweak theory, first proposed by Steven Weinberg and Abdus Salam in 1967. They predicted a new class of massive bosonic particles (known as W and Z particles) which transfer weak interactions. Such particles were suggested by the Swedish physicist Oskar Klein as early as 1938 but were ignored for more than twenty years. The W and Z particles of the successful Weinberg–Salam theory were widely accepted and were almost sure to receive experimental confirmation in sufficiently high energy accelerator experiments. Such experiments were performed in 1983 at CERN's super proton synchrotron. To nobody's surprise, although hailed in the press as a revolution in physics, conclusive proof of the new bosons was established. Another important discovery in accelerator experiments was made in 1975 when Martin Perl and his team at Stanford University found the first evidence for a 'third generation' of leptons, the τ lepton and its associated neutrino.

Since the 1970s, aspects of particle physics have been ever more integrated with problems of astrophysics and cosmology, in particular with the state of the very early universe. For example, it was realised that in order to make the standard Big Bang theory consistent with observations, there had to exist a third (and possibly a fourth) variety of neutrino. The discovery of the τ neutrino thus offered further support to the Big Bang theory. Grand Unified theory, an ambitious attempt to integrate electroweak and strong interactions in a single theoretical framework, predicted the existence of a class of new, fractionally-charged particles known as X and Y particles. These particles are believed to have been produced in great numbers in the earliest stages of the universe and to be responsible for quarks changing into leptons. The theory also predicts that the proton, hitherto supposed to be stable, is really unstable with a very long half-life. Experiments in the 1980s have failed to confirm either the assumed instability of the proton or the existence of X and Y particles.

Modern particle physics literature includes many other particles, most of which are probably either beyond experimental detection or are merely mathematical artefacts. This seems to be the case with the 'axion' and the 'Higgs boson'. The latter was argued theoretically in 1964 by Peter Higgs in England and is believed to be the carrier of a new force, the Higgs force. The Higgs boson, whether it exists as a detectable particle or not, plays an important role in recent attempts to understand the generation of particles in the Big Bang. Lastly, gravitation theory and its possible generalisation in a unified supergravity theory have given rise to yet more hypothetical particles. Quantised gravitational waves are called 'gravitons', being neutral and massless particles like the photons. Although never detected directly, they are generally believed to exist. Supergravity theories operate with other gravitational particles such as the 'gravitino', a hypothetical massive particle which is conjectured to act at very small distances.

Since the most recent period of particle physics is, like any living science, in a state of flux it may be difficult to subject it to traditional historical analysis. For example, analysing current particle physics within a broader historiographical framework, like those proposed by Kuhn or Lakatos, is inherently problematical; notions like 'crisis', 'revolution' or 'degeneration' seem to be inappropriate for the appraisal of the most recent developments in particle physics. (See art. 1, sects. 4 and 10.) However, this does not imply that these developments are outside the scope of history; in practice the historian will have to employ sociological tools and insights. Neither does it imply that general theories of scientific development are irrelevant to the history of particle physics. On the contrary, the field offers many illustrations of, for example, paradigm shifts, theory-laden observations and the tension between conservative and revolutionary approaches.

The history of particle science exemplifies the interplay of speculation, experiment and theory which is characteristic of modern physical science. Particle science, dealing with entities which are not directly observable, has always included a necessary element of speculation but theory only entered at the turn of the century when experimentalists supplied the theoreticians with new data. Since then, experiments have played a crucial role in particle science, to some extent even determining the theories of fundamental particles. Histories of particle physics, often written by physicists rather than historians, have tended to focus on theories and have neglected the role of technology. However, it may be argued that, in general, technological advances rather than purely scientific innovations have been the main source of progress in particle physics in this century.

NOTES

1. W. Crookes, 'On the illumination of lines of molecular pressure and the trajectory of molecules', *Philosophical transactions of the Royal Society*, 170 (1879), 87–134.
2. B. C. Brodie, 'The calculus of chemical operations', *Philosophical transactions of the Royal Society*, 156 (1866), 781–859.
3. J. L. Heilbron, 'Thomson, Joseph John', in *Dictionary of scientific biography*, ed. C. C. Gillespie, vol. 13 (New York, 1970–80) pp. 362–72. I. Falconer, 'Corpuscles, electrons and cathode rays: J. J. Thomson and the discovery of the electron', *British journal for the history of science*, 20 (1987), 241–76.

FURTHER READING

W. H. Brock, *From protyle to proton* (Bristol, 1985).

M. Brown and L. Hoddeson (eds.), *The birth of particle physics* (Cambridge, 1983).

D. J. Kevles, *The physicists* (New York, 1978).

D. M. Knight, *Atoms and elements* (London, 1967).

M. J. Nye, *Molecular reality* (New York, 1972).

A. Pais, *Inward bound* (Oxford, 1986).

A. Pickering, *Constructing quarks* (Edinburgh, 1984).

A. J. Rocke, *Chemical atomism in the nineteenth century* (Columbus, Ohio, 1984).

C. Schönbeck (ed.), *Atomvorstellungen im 19. Jahrhundert* (Paderborn, 1982).

44

THE FOUNDATIONS OF MATHEMATICS

PHILIP KITCHER

1. THREE TYPES OF FOUNDATIONAL ENTERPRISE

Many of the greatest mathematicians and philosophers have set themselves the task of finding a 'proper foundation,' either for mathematics or for some special branch of mathematics. They have declared the need to give clear definitions of mathematical concepts, to formulate rigorous proofs and to trace mathematical theorems to genuine first principles. But this consensus hides not only considerable divergence about how clear definitions, full rigour, and genuine foundations are to be achieved, but also differences in motivation. There are several quite distinct reasons why the enterprise of exposing the 'proper foundations' of mathematics has seemed important to mathematicians and philosophers, and we cannot hope to understand the activity or its history without appreciating these reasons.

The most obvious incentives for attending to definitions, proofs and first principles come from identifiable difficulties in the practice of some branches of mathematics. If mathematicians are employing problem-solving techniques that are recognisably powerful in some cases but that yield palpable errors or, worse, paradoxes in others, they will want to clarify the concepts they are using or scrutinise their methods of reasoning. History shows that mathematicians have frequently investigated the foundations of their subject precisely because they find it impossible to carry forward their technical research without clarifying concepts or modes of reasoning.

However, foundational activity also arises from other motivations. Sometimes mathematicians hope to enhance their understanding of the results in a particular mathematical field by making the interconnections as explicit as possible; they try to systematise the field and to make clear exactly what depends on what. If successful, the attempt may bring improved understanding even if there was no prior paradox or error. In setting a discipline in order, mathematicians are effectively behaving like natural scientists who seek explanations by trying to develop a unifying theory that will systematise a disconnected collection of empirical findings.

Finally, there may be purely philosophical motives for attending to the foundations of mathematics. For many thinkers, mathematicians and scientists as well as philosophers, mathematics has served as the paradigm for human knowledge because of the apparent certainty of its conclusions. The prior conviction that mathematical knowledge is absolutely unshakeable may inspire efforts to show exactly how this certainty is obtained. Alternatively, there may be concern about some particular area of mathematics which is seen as falling short of the indubitability that mathematical knowledge ought to possess, such that researchers try to remedy the defect by pursuing the subject's foundations. In either instance, the goal will be identical – first principles will be identified that are immediately certain and independent of sensory experience, and chains of reasoning will be developed that depend only on these principles as premises and proceed by inferential steps that preserve certainty.

It is important to distinguish these three main forms that the search for the foundations of mathematics may take if we are to see why some enterprises have succeeded and others failed. Mathematicians can achieve *problem-solving foundations* (foundations of my first type), which enable them to carry forward their technical research, without having either *explanation-yielding foundations* (my second type) or *certainty-conferring* foundations (my third type). Similarly, an endeavour to uncover explanation-yielding foundations may succeed even though the first principles that it identifies are not known immediately and for certain. Unfortunately, through rhetoric and lack of philosophical precision many earlier writers blurred the above distinctions. Moreover, while mathematicians sometimes write prefaces as if they were concerned to establish foundations of all three types, their practice usually belies the advertisement.

2. EARLY SEARCHES FOR FOUNDATIONS

Although mathematics has ancient roots in the civilisations of Mesopotamia, the first deductive organisation of the subject known to us is the *Elements* of Euclid (*c.* 300 BC). Euclid's presentation starts with some definitions, postulates and 'common notions', and on this basis, Euclid derives the main results of the geometry of plane linear figures and circles. Euclid does not, however, inform the reader what this presentation of the *Elements* was intended to achieve. Commentators on his work are more forthcoming, but they use ambiguous language and fail to distinguish between the various kinds of enterprise outlined above. Hence Euclid's work was able to serve as the paradigm for different types of foundational programme: he could be read as tracing the theorems of geometry to immediately certain first principles about the structure of space, or as showing how it is possible to provide an explanatory organisation of known mathematical results, without any commitment to the certainty of the first principles he adduced.

Despite Euclid's profound influence both on Greek geometers and on the mathematicians of the Renaissance and after, there was a flourishing mathematical tradition that did not receive the foundational treatment exemplified by the *Elements*. Babylonian mathematicians had discovered methods for solving practical problems that we would formulate using linear and quadratic equations, and the sciences of arithmetic and elementary algebra were carried forward during the medieval period by Arab and Indian mathematicians. The tradition continued to thrive in renaissance Italy, where the practice of challenging the skills of others stimulated several mathematicians to investigate questions that are, in our terms, tantamount to solving cubic equations. In 1545, Gerolamo Cardano (1501–76) published his *Ars magna*, in which he describes methods for solving various types of cubic equation, and also briefly mentions a foundational question.

Even before the explicit formulation of algebraic notation, workers in the theory of equations recognised that some problems afforded a smaller number of solutions than was normal. The defect could be remedied by allowing strange entities to count as solutions, such as 'negative numbers' or 'numbers whose square is less than zero', but there was considerable suspicion of the propriety of doing so. The Italian algebraists saw (in effect) that they could obtain exactly n roots for an equation of nth degree, but this seemed a slight benefit compared with the cost of dabbling in mysteries. In Cardano's phrase, such 'numbers' are 'subtile and useless'.

However, the seventeenth and eighteenth centuries were to witness a transformation of algebra and the flowering of algebraic analysis. Pierre de Fermat (1601–65) and René Descartes (1596–1650) independently showed how the algebraic notation of François Viète (1540–1603) could be applied to the solution of geometrical problems. Their new analytic geometry was able to generalise and extend the results of ancient Greek geometers (paradigmatically, Apollonius on conic sections). Building on the work of Descartes, Fermat and other mathematicians, Isaac Newton (1642–1727) and Gottfried Leibniz (1646–1716) independently formulated the principles of the differential and integral calculus. Using the new calculus, Newton and Leibniz computed the values of the areas under many curves, found the lengths of arcs, identified radii of curvature, constructed tangents and normals and solved problems about the motions of ideal particles. The Marquis Guillaume de l'Hôpital (1661–1701), author of the first textbook on the Leibnizian calculus, claimed that the new methods enabled mathematicians to solve problems which 'nobody previously had dared to attempt'.

Unfortunately, the new successes were purchased at a cost. In differentiation and integration, the fundamental operations of the new calculus, both Leibniz and Newton were compelled to use language that appeared to refer to ill-understood infinitesimal entities. The procedure for differentiation makes the trouble clear. If $y = f(x)$, we compute the quantity dy/dx by forming the difference $f(x + o) - f(x)$ and dividing by o. We write the result as $A + B[o]$, where the latter term contains all and only those expressions that are powers in o. Finally, we neglect terms in o by simply dropping $B[o]$ and declaring that $dy/dx = A$.

It is easy to appreciate why this (and kindred manipulations) should cause qualms. For if o is not zero, then by what right do we omit those terms that are powers in o? On the other hand, if $o = 0$ then the initial difference $f(x+o)-f(x)$ is also 0, and, perhaps more alarming, the procedure involves a division by zero. Hence there seems to be no way of justifying the algebra or of understanding the operations that are supposed to be performed. Early critics of the calculus, most notably George Berkeley (1685–1753), made the objection with considerable force. Nonetheless, the new methods were enormously fruitful, for, in the hands of Jakob Bernoulli (1654–1705), John Bernoulli (1667–1748) and Leonhard Euler (1707–83), they yielded conclusions that were both recognisably correct and significant in finding answers to traditional mathematical questions.

The successes of the calculus were not initially hampered by these difficulties and mathematicians had no motive to seek problem-solving foundations for the new algebraic analysis. However, in the works of Newton, Leibniz and their successors, there are remarks that can be interpreted as indicating either a desire for explanation-yielding foundations or for certainty-conferring foundations. Newton and Leibniz both pondered the question of whether the calculus could be reconstructed after the manner of 'the Ancient Geometers' (most prominently Euclid). Newton's preferred method of formulating the central concepts of the calculus embodied a kinematic conception of geometry (on which curves are viewed as generated by the motion of a point), and he articulated a justification of his conclusions about differentiation that we can identify, with hindsight, as a cryptic version of an appeal to the notion of a limit. Leibniz's published writings on the calculus appear pragmatic by contrast, for he seems willing to allow that the algebraic work is autonomous and that it does not need an interpretation in geometric or kinematic terms. The contrast is heightened in the works of eighteenth-century Leibnizians and Newtonians, for while Newton's successors continued to devote considerable energy to showing how the Newtonian calculus could be rendered according to the ideas of traditional geometry, the followers of Leibniz were more concerned to extend the scope of the new discipline.

During the eighteenth century, the issues surrounding the foundations of algebraic analysis became more complicated. In their attempts to differentiate and integrate recalcitrant functions, both Newton and Leibniz had introduced infinite series expansions and had used term-by-term integration and differentiation. Leibniz's method sometimes generated peculiar results, showing that the techniques had to be used cautiously. Nonetheless, in the hands of Euler, algebraic manipulations of infinite series expressions led to surprising discoveries. Euler recognised the distinction between convergent and divergent series, and he handled the latter with enormous artistry. Moreover, following the lead of Leibniz, Euler used complex numbers in the evaluation of indefinite integrals and he extended the work of Roger Cotes and Abraham de Moivre by giving a systematic treatment of the relations between exponential and trigonometric functions. Complex numbers could no longer be dismissed as 'subtile and useless' for they had a firm place within algebraic analysis.

Yet scholars with foundational worries could still protest that, for all its successes, algebraic analysis failed to live up to the standards of genuine mathematics. Infinitesimalist reasonings seemed only to work by luck, infinite series manipulations had to be performed with care (or with 'intuition'), and the reference to negative and complex numbers remained mysterious. Periodically during the eighteenth century mathematicians returned briefly to the foundational issues; but in retrospect, we can see these as mere unco-ordinated gropings towards the major ideas of the nineteenth century. In my judgement, the exciting achievements of algebraic analysis made a search for problem-solving foundations idle, and, while explanation-yielding foundations would have been a bonus, the prize was too small to divert creative mathematicians from extending the scope of analysis. So the recurrent lament that mathematics no longer accorded with the standards of Euclid did not translate into persistent foundational activity.

3. THE NINETEENTH CENTURY

Geometers, however, were attending to the substance of Euclid's *Elements*. Many mathematicians had found that the fifth postulate was less evident than the other four, and, in the centuries since Euclid, there had been periodic attempts to prove the fifth postulate, attempts which typically made use of equivalent principles. (See art. 42, sect. 1.) Following earlier, less careful discussions, Carl Friedrich Gauss (1777–1855), Janos Bolyai (1802–60) and Nicolai Lobachevsky (1792–1856) all recognised that the assumption of many parallels cannot be convicted of inconsistency simply on the grounds of its generating strange results. Their work gave rise to the first non-Euclidean geometry. Later in the nineteenth century, Bernard Riemann (1826–66) saw how to modify the Euclidean postulates so as to allow for a consistent geometry based on the assumption of no parallels, and he provided a general approach to geometry in terms of the theory of manifolds. Riemann's abstract treatment did much to allay the suspicions of those who worried that contradictions might appear in the later development of non-Euclidean geometry, and such concerns were finally put to rest through the construction of relative consistency proofs by Eugenio Beltrami and Felix Klein. Throughout this process there was a subtle shift in the status of geometry. For almost two millennia after Euclid, geometry had seemed to be a science based on immediate and indubitable insights into the structure of space. After Gauss, Bolyai, Lobatschevsky and Riemann, Euclidean geometry appeared as one among many possible geometrical systems. The mathematical task seemed to be that of investigating the systems, while it would be left to the physicist to decide which of them correctly characterises space. (See art. 42, sect. 2.)

A similar assessment resulted from the late-eighteenth-century assimilation of the complex numbers. Jean Argand, Caspar Wessel and Gauss independently demonstrated that the algebra of complex numbers can be represented geometrically by identifying numbers with points on the two-dimensional plane. William Rowan Hamilton (1805–65) subsequently provided an algebraic interpretation in which complex numbers were taken to be ordered pairs of reals. Seeking three-dimensional analogues of complex numbers, Hamilton formulated the algebra of quaternions, in which multiplication is noncommutative. His work in algebra, together with the nineteenth-century emergence of the concept of an abstract group from the theory of equations, fostered the belief in alternative algebraic structures, and suggested that mathematics consists in investigating these structures through axioms that uniquely characterise them.

The story of the foundations of analysis is more complex. Early in the nineteenth century, mathematicians working on problems generated by theoretical physics discovered that the lack of adequately-formulated central concepts of analysis handicapped their research. In his *Cours d'Analyse* of 1821, Augustin-Louis Cauchy (1789–1857) attempted to remedy the situation by providing definitions of the concepts of continuity, derivative and convergence in terms of the algebraic notion of limit. While Cauchy's treatment enabled him to give more comprehensible derivations of some of the main results of differential and integral calculus, it was not flawless. In particular, Cauchy endeavoured to resolve a controversy generated by the work of Joseph Fourier (1768–1830), who had claimed that arbitrary functions can be represented by trigonometric series. Opposing Fourier, Cauchy maintained that the sum of a convergent series of continuous functions is continuous (so that no convergent series of continuous functions can sum to a discontinuous function). As early as 1826, Niels Abel discovered that Cauchy's claim was false by finding a counterexample, but it took another three decades for mathematicians to explain in detail exactly how Cauchy had erred.

From this explanation mathematicians developed the theory of multiple limits and used it to distinguish between uniform and non-uniform continuity.

Building on earlier work of Peter Lejeune Dirichlet and Philip Seidel, Karl Weierstrass (1815–97) provided the systematic treatment in the lectures that he gave in Berlin after his inauguration in 1856. Weierstrass's inaugural address made it apparent that he had been led to consider the foundations of analysis by a desire to pursue technical work in analysis (specifically to complete the theory of elliptic functions). This desire could only be satisfied after he had attained a clearer view of the central concepts of analysis; yet many years passed before he could devote himself to that project.

However, not all those who pursued the foundations of analysis did so as a prerequisite for solving a technical problem. Cauchy's contemporary, the Czech philosopher and mathematician Bernard Bolzano (1781–1848), explicitly sought the reform of analysis so as to uncover the proper explanation for the main results of the discipline. Although, like Cauchy, Bolzano failed to establish limit-existence theorems, his work prefigured subsequent studies of the structure of the continuum. Thirty years later, Richard Dedekind (1831–1916) was similarly moved by the need to make the principles of analysis comprehensible in attempting to define the continuity of the real line. He proposed that real numbers 'correspond to' Dedekind sections of the rationals which made explicit, for the first time, the connection between the theorems of analysis and claims about infinite sets that Bolzano had already sensed. By the 1870s it had become obvious that Weierstrassian analysis was dependent on an explicit characterisation of the real numbers, and the available proposals – due to Dedekind, Charles Méray, Edward Heine and Georg Cantor (1845–1918) – all involved reference to infinite sets.

Some mathematicians suspected the concept of an arbitrary infinite set. Leopold Kronecker (1823–91) campaigned against the set-theoretic definitions of the real numbers used by his colleague Weierstrass, the set-theoretic constructions of Dedekind and, most of all, against Cantor's efforts to articulate the principles of transfinite set theory. Despite his objections, mathematicians faced with the choice between the strict arithmetisation of analysis favoured by Kronecker and the Weierstrassian reconstruction, recognised that arithmetisation could yield only fragments and they therefore opted for Weierstrass. Gradually, too, the power of Cantor's ideas became apparent. So the focus of foundational studies shifted from the justification of the principles of the calculus to the elaboration of set theory.

Meanwhile, significant changes occurred both in other parts of mathematics and in neighbouring areas of philosophy. After a placid history of over two hundred years, logic obtained new life in the nineteenth century, initially through the work of Bolzano and later through the researches of George Boole and Charles Sanders Peirce. But the major transformation was effected by Gottlob Frege (1848–1925). Originally trained as a mathematician, Frege came to believe that the search for rigour that had culminated in Weierstrassian analysis led to the investigation of the concepts of the arithmetic of the natural numbers. Influenced by Leibniz's claim that mathematics is a branch of logic, Frege set out to show that the concepts of arithmetic could be defined in terms of logical notions, and that the first principles of arithmetic derived from the laws of logic. To pursue his logicist programme, Frege needed a formal system of logic. Part of this was given in his *Begriffsschrift* (*Concept-script*) of 1879, and later extended in the two-volume *Grundgesetze der Arithmetik* (*Foundations of arithmetic*, 1893, 1903). In these works Frege developed a substantial part of modern formal logic.

Neither Frege's logical system nor his defence of logicism was positively received. Although *Begriffsschrift* was reviewed by several eminent logicians, few of Frege's contemporaries perceived that the daunting notation concealed a revolution in logic. Moreover, Frege had overestimated the kinship between the logicist programme and the enterprise of exposing the foundations of analysis. Mathematicians had chiefly been seeking problem-solving foundations; occasionally – as with Dedekind and Bolzano – for explanation-yielding foundations. What Frege promised to deliver seemed less relevant: a more philosophical inquiry into the grounds of our certainty in elementary arithmetic. If there were residual foundational disputes, then the mathematicians took them to lie in the discussions about infinite sets; discussions to which Frege's investigations did not seem pertinent.

However, some of Frege's contemporaries were also concerned to explore both logic and the foundations of elementary mathematics. In a little-appreciated monograph, *Was Sind und was Sollen die Zahlen?*, published in 1888, Dedekind also attempted a reconstruction of natural-number arithmetic and formulated the laws that characterise the natural numbers (the so-called Peano postulates). His motivations seem different from Frege's, in that Dedekind appears to have wanted explanation-yielding foundations and to have been indifferent to the philosophical tradition of searching for certainty-conferring foundations; a tradition linking Leibniz, Kant and Frege. Perhaps this explains why Dedekind was not concerned to specify the principles of his system with the precision and detail that Frege demanded, and why, in consequence, Frege failed to appreciate what he had accomplished.

Towards the close of the nineteenth century, Frege's efforts began to intertwine with those of other scholars. Building on earlier work by Moritz Pasch, who had perceived that Euclid's systematisation of geometry actually employs more premisses than are made explicit, David Hilbert (1862–1943) provided an axiomatisation of Euclidean geometry in which the deficiencies were repaired. He was also able to demonstrate that his system was consistent, relative to arithmetic. This success, together with the growing emphasis on mathematics as the study of axiomatic systems and the relative consistency proofs for non-Euclidean geometries, led Hilbert to formulate the problem of the foundations of mathematics in a way that accorded with the new image of mathematics. If mathematics is seen as the study of axiomatic systems, then the task of the foundationalist is to show that the systems are absolutely consistent.

That task became more urgent and Frege's logical investigations appeared more pertinent after Frege received a letter from Bertrand Russell (1872–1970) in 1902, which pointed out that his proposed system of logic was inconsistent. The problem affected not only Frege's logic but also Cantor's system of transfinite set theory, and it is most easily understood by reference to the latter. Cantor's system allowed that there should be a set of exactly those things that satisfy any arbitrarily chosen predicate (Frege's system contains an analogue of this principle). Russell pointed out that it follows that there is a set consisting of exactly those things that are not members of themselves. Call this set R. If R is not a member of itself then it is one of those things that are not members of themselves, and thus is a member of R. Conversely, if R is a member of itself then R belongs to the set whose members are just those things that are not members of themselves, so that R is not a member of itself after all. Since it must be the case that R belongs to itself or R does not belong to itself, we have a genuine contradiction.

Russell's paradox struck at the heart of Frege's system because without a principle permitting the transition from arbitrary predicates to sets, (or more exactly, to what he called 'extensions of concepts') Frege saw no way to establish the existence of infinitely many objects and thereby to generate the usual theorems about the sequence of natural numbers. However, logicism was not the only victim. Mathematicians quickly recognised that the theorems of Weierstrassian analysis depended on the assumed existence of infinite sets, and the most natural way of guaranteeing existence was to adopt Cantor's principle. Evidently this had to be restricted in some way to save classical analysis. Russell's paradox – and other related paradoxes of set theory – thus provoked several different types of foundational studies. Foundational work was required to solve pressing problems, to explain why classical mathematics seemed to work so well, and, for those steeped in the philosophical tradition, to confer on mathematics the certainty that had been called into question.

4. FOUNDATIONS OF MATHEMATICS: PHILOSOPHY OR MATHEMATICS?

The search for indubitable foundations prompted three main philosophical programmes. Logicists struggled to find principles that could plausibly be taken for principles of logic, that would avoid the contradictions of Frege's system and that would suffice for the derivation of theorems of arithmetic and analysis. The most prominent achievement of logicism was the three volume *Principia*

Mathematica (1910–13), jointly written by Russell and Alfred North Whitehead. Hilbert's profound essays on the foundations of mathematics outlined a different approach. Attuned to the new image of mathematics as the study of axiomatic systems, Hilbert suggested that certainty could again be assured by using an indubitable part of mathematics (roughly, primitive recursive arithmetic) to establish the consistency of the systems that are employed. With great ingenuity, Hilbert showed how formal systems could themselves be studied as mathematical objects, and how the statement of the consistency of these systems could be formulated as a mathematical assertion. His formalist programme was pursued with partial success into the 1930s.

A more radical foundational position was the intuitionism of Luitzen Brouwer (1881–1967). Taking up the complaints of Kronecker, Brouwer argued that the message of the paradoxes is that assertions of classical mathematics lack clear meaning. To talk of the existence of mathematical entities independent of the human power to construct such entities is to lapse into nonsense. The appropriate corrective is to require that any assertion of the existence of a mathematical entity should be based on a procedure for constructing it. This demand implies that the law of the excluded middle can no longer have unrestricted validity. Brouwer and his successors have laboured with considerable ingenuity to show that intuitionist analogues of classical theorems can be obtained. However, intuitionist analysis has proved considerably less powerful than its classical counterpart.

Few mathematicians and philosophers have been convinced by the complaint that the extra content of classical mathematics is rococo excess, and critics have objected that the restrictions imposed by intuitionists are arbitrary and unmotivated. Hilbert's formalist programme came to grief in a more dramatic way. In 1930, Kurt Gödel (1906–78) proved a pair of theorems which effectively deny the possibility of finding the kind of consistency proof that Hilbert sought. In a slightly strengthened version, due to Barkley Rosser, Gödel's first incompleteness theorem states that, in any consistent formal system adequate for arithmetic, there will be a statement A such that neither A nor its negation is provable in the system. The second therorem asserts the unprovability of a statement expressing the consistency of the system (provided that the system is consistent). Although the consistency of formal systems adequate for elementary additive and multiplicative arithmetic can be proved by employing stronger methods than those that Hilbert allowed (as demonstrated by Jacques Herbrand and Gerhard Gentzen) the employment of these methods does not accord with the standards of indubitability and consistency that gave epistemological point to Hilbert's programme.

The fate of logicism was more complex. In their reconstruction of arithmetic and analysis, Russell and Whitehead were forced to introduce axioms whose credentials as logical principles were suspect. By the 1920s there was wide-spread agreement that the axioms of choice, infinity and replacement cannot be defended as laws of logic, and the champions of logicism began consequently to transform their position. They drew inspiration from some of the ideas of Hilbert, Rudolf Carnap (1891–1970) and other logical positivists (see art. 54, sect. 2) who proposed in the 1930s that the axioms of a branch of mathematics are implicit definitions of the expressions occurring in them. In this way, mathematical knowledge starts with laws of logic and implicit definitions (which are indubitable in that our grasp of the meanings of the pertinent expressions suffices for our knowledge of the truth of the statements) and proceeds by deduction. This metamorphosis of logicism was severely criticised in a series of essays by Willard Van Orman Quine who advanced penetrating objections to the conception of truth-by-virtue-of-meaning on which the new logicism depended. By 1960, logicism, like the other two programmes that strove for certainty-conferring foundations, had been virtually abandoned.

But Russell's paradox did not only inspire the three philosophical enterprises whose history we have been tracing. The mathematical task of restricting the principle of Cantorian set theory that generated the troubles was undertaken by Ernst Zermelo (1871–1956), who formulated the iterative conception of set. Zermelo's set theory, extended by Abraham Fraenkel, sufficed not only for classical analysis but also for the description of those algebraic structures which have been vigorously studied by twentieth-century mathematicians. For the practising mathematician, the 'crisis' in the foundations of mathematics caused by the paradoxes of set theory has long been dissipated. The prevailing attitude, expressed eloquently by the group of mathematicians who write under the pseudonym Nicolas Bourbaki, is that the set theories of Zermelo and others provide a language in which to characterise and investigate the structures that are the proper object of mathematical research. This pragmatic attitude accords with that of Zermelo himself, who claimed explicitly that the credibility of his axioms depends not on their immediate indubitability, but on their ability to systematise and explain the results of classical mathematics.

From the point of view of mathematics, the 'foundational' subjects of logic and set theory have become parts of technical mathematics in their own right. In the early decades of this century, the formal logic of Frege and Russell was liberated from the assumption that logical statements have a fixed domain of discourse. Partly under the influence of the work of Peirce and Ernst Schröder, and partly through the investigations of Hilbert, the modern conception of an interpretation and a model was developed. Building on the work of Leopold Löwenheim, Thoralf Skolem established the important limitative theorem that any countable set of first-order sentences with an infinite model has a denumerable model. Gödel's incompleteness theorems paved the way for related results by Alfred Tarski on the concept of truth, and by Alonzo Church on the undecidability of first-order logic. Gödel's work was also seminal in the development of proof theory and recursive function theory. Since the Second World War, the theory of models has been further pursued and has established important connections with parts of algebra. One of its most celebrated accomplishments has been Abraham Robinson's development of non-standard analysis, and his revival of the long-derided notion of the infinitesimal. Finally, mathematicians have further articulated transfinite set theory; the investigations of Gödel and Paul Cohen have established the independence of Cantor's continuum hypothesis from the axioms of set theory and the independence of the axiom of choice from the remaining axioms.

These accomplishments are probably best seen as the fruitful articulations of those parts of mathematics which at one time earned the title 'foundational'. While contemporary philosophers continue to seek certainty-conferring foundations, their investigations now seem quite divorced from the technical mathematical work that interests professional mathematicians. Some philosophers have taken inspiration from remarks by Gödel, and have suggested that mathematics describes a universe of abstract objects – sets – and that the first principles describing this universe 'force themselves on us' as true. Others have offered ingenious attempts to revive logicism, to reformulate intuitionism, or to find a viable descendant of Hilbert's programme. But it is far from clear that any of these endeavours can answer to the original epistemological purpose of setting mathematics upon indubitable and immediate first principles.

Indeed, in the wake of Quine's influential critique of positivism, several philosophers, most notably Hilary Putnam and Imre Lakatos, have argued that the search for certainty-conferring foundations rests on a mistake. In Putnam's phrase, 'mathematics neither has nor needs foundations'. The present essay endorses this perspective, and while many philosophers have tried to read the history of the foundations of mathematics as exhibiting attempts by mathematicians to discover certainty-conferring foundations, my account portrays that history in terms of successes in obtaining problem-solving and explanation-yielding foundations. If mathematicians today evince any concern for foundations, they will concentrate on explanations and solutions to problems. Where there is no need for explanation and no urgent problem that requires conceptual clarification they will view philosophical inquiries as irrelevant and pointless. According to my version of the history of the foundations of mathematics, their attitude should come as no surprise. *Plus ça change, plus c'est la même chose.*

FURTHER READING

William Aspray and Philip Kitcher (eds.), *Essays on the history and philosophy of modern mathematics* (Minnesota Studies in the Philosophy of Science, Volume XI: Minneapolis, 1987).

Paul Benacerraf and Hilary Putnam (eds.), *Philosophy of mathematics: selected readings* (Second ed.: Cambridge, 1983).

H. J. M. Bos, 'Differentials, higher-order differentials and the derivative in the Leibnizian calculus', *Archive for history of the exact sciences*, 14 (1974), 1–90.

Joseph Dauben, *Georg Cantor* (Cambridge, Mass., 1979).

Michael Dummett, *Elements of intuitionism* (Oxford, 1978).

Gottlob Frege, *The foundations of arithmetic*, translation by J. L. Austin of *Die Grundlagen der Arithmetik* (Oxford, 1950).

Warren Goldfarb, 'Logic in the twenties: the nature of the quantifier', *Journal of symbolic logic*, 44 (1979), 351–68.

Judith Grabiner, *The origins of Cauchy's rigorous calculus* (Cambridge, Mass., 1981).

Ivor Grattan-Guinness, *The development of the foundations of anlaysis from Euler to Riemann* (Cambridge, Mass., 1970).

David Hilbert, *The foundations of geometry*, translation by E. J. Townsend of *Die Grundlagen der Geometrie* (Chicago, 1902).

Philip Kitcher, *The nature of mathematical knowledge* (Oxford, 1983).

Morris Kline, *Mathematical thought from ancient to modern times* (New York, 1972).

Imre Lakatos, *Proofs and refutations* (Cambridge, 1976).

Ernest Nagel, 'Impossible numbers' in *Teleology revisited and other essays* (New York, 1979).

Michael Resnik, *Frege and the philosophy of mathematics* (Ithaca, NY., 1980).

Jean van Heijenoort, *From Frege to Gödel: a source book in mathematical logic* (Cambridge Mass., 1967).

45

PROBABILITY AND DETERMINISM, 1650–1900

IAN HACKING

There have long been histories of the mathematical theory of probability. They reach back to the beginning of the nineteenth century, and Isaac Todhunter (1865) presents, in a way that is awesome in its thoroughness but which now seems lacking in insight, all the results known until 1820. With the exception of Karl Pearson's (1978) lectures of 1921–33, probability has seldom been placed in a larger framework of intellectual history. This situation is rapidly changing, and a spate of new work has just appeared or is in press. As for the various kinds of determinism, their evolution has been recounted ever since people began writing histories of philosophy. But there are still very few studies, so far, of probability *and* determinism and those that do exist are very recent. Hence this article is more a report on some current opinion than a presentation of a well-worked-out topic in the history of science.

1. DETERMINISM

Determinism is the name now generally given to any doctrine implying that for every event, there existed prior or timeless conditions that made the event inevitable. There are a great variety of such notions, not one of which is particularly clear, but each of which has, in its time, perplexed the most serious thinkers.

There is theological determinism, according to which the world inexorably unravels according to divine will or plan. There have been types of logical determinism, holding that all events occur with logical necessity. There is psychological determinism, a restricted form, according to which every choice made by a person is predetermined by earlier mental states including beliefs and motivation. This was the first sense given to the word 'determinism' (or rather *Determinismus*) and then only in the 1780s. Ideas of determinism may be old, but the word itself is quite a new one. Then there is physical-law determinism, according to which there are laws of nature that when applied to the state of the universe at a given time, determine the future course of the universe down to the finest detail. The word came to be used in this sense only in the 1860s. Before then, a not uncommon name for this idea was 'the doctrine of necessity' or some cognate phrase. Every type of determinism has seemed, in its day, incompatible with, or problematic for, free will, human choice and responsibility.

This article is chiefly concerned with physical-law determinism, which will usually be simply called determinism for short. Probability, with its connotation of chance and randomness, may seem contrary to determinism of this sort. Indeed when it became increasingly clear that twentieth-century microphysics demanded that the fundamental laws of nature must be of a probabilistic sort, the result was called indeterminism. It was, rather briefly, thought to make some space for freedom of the human will. Yet determinism and probability have almost always gone hand in hand.

Physical-law determinism became seriously entertained only with the advent of seventeenth-century natural science. That was precisely the era in which our modern conceptions of probability began clearly to emerge. It is perhaps no accident that Pierre-Simon de Laplace, arguably the greatest figure in the history of mathematical probability, is equally renowned for his work in celestial mechanics. It was he who gave us the most eloquent statement of the deterministic creed. 'All events, even those that, because of their minuteness, do not seem to obey the great laws of nature, follow from them as necessarily as the revolutions of the sun.' That is the opening sentence of his *Philosophical Essay on Probabilities*, which began as a semi-popular lecture in 1795, and it goes on to speak of the behaviour of the least atom.

2. PROBABILITY

Historians are widely agreed on two facts. First, the application of mathematics to probability begins in the middle of the seventeenth century. Secondly, it is natural to speak of a classical theory or classical period of probability going up to and including the lifetime of Laplace (1749–1827). After that, although old problems are continued, new ones appear, most notably those in which probability is slowly incorporated into the newly-forming social and life sciences. Although all such periodisations are suspect, for us they are convenient. Questions about probability and determinism in the classical period are substantially different from those that arise in mid-nineteenth century.

3. THE BEGINNINGS OF PROBABILITY AND ITS INTERPRETATIONS

The most famous early applications of mathematics to probability concern games of chance, and involve Blaise Pascal (1623–62), Pierre de Fermat

(1601–65) and Christiaan Huygens (1629–95). It is hardly surprising that mathematical probability should arise in this period. Games of chance involve numbers, including stakes, prizes and the central question of the fair price of a game. This was a time when anything numerical invited mathematical analysis. In the beginning the basic concept was not probability directly, but the expectation of a game. This may be thought of as the fair price for entering the game, or the long-run average pay-off in playing the game many times. Most modern treatments define expectation in terms of probability, but Huygens and his successors took the opposite route with equivalent consequences.

Hacking (1975) has argued that prior to this period not only was there no serious conception of mathematical probability, but also nothing much like our modern conception of probability at all. He holds that the present concept resulted from a radical mutation in various Renaissance concepts, including that of evidence. He also holds that physical-law determinism and probability are coeval. Garber and Zabell (1979) forcefully contest the second opinion, and more cautious writers such as Lorraine Daston (1988) certainly hold that it is, at the least, over-stated. However Daston does, as we shall see, provide important new arguments for a version of the first thesis, connecting the development of mathematical probability and determinism.

It has long been common to distinguish two fundamentally different sorts of probability ideas. In the one, probability denotes a stable relative frequency in repeated trials. In the other it has to do with the extent to which it is reasonable to believe a given proposition. S. D. Poisson (1781–1840) and in 1837 A. A. Cournot (1801–77) in 1843 marked the distinction by proposing two words, *chance* and *probabilité*. Laplace, who officially said that all probabilities are degrees of belief, regularly used the word *facilité* for something like the frequency conception. There has been some debate as to whether this duality goes back to the very first days of mathematical probability, or whether in the beginning only one or the other was uniquely intended. Each of these three possible positions has its defenders.

It may seem crucial to settle the question of interpretation before discussing the relationship between probability and determinism in those early days. For the idea of relative frequency, stable in the long run, may seem to imply some fundamental randomness and indeterminacy. This is not the case. Each item in a series of events could be fully determined, and yet the series itself exhibits nothing more to our eyes than stable frequencies. This is precisely the position even today of those who believe that the outcome of each toss of a die is fully determined by antecedent conditions and the laws of mechanics, while at the same time a sequence of tosses is subject to a calculus of relative frequencies. More to the point, there are also important theorems showing how frequency distributions can arise from fully deterministic processes.

4. DETERMINISM AND PROBABILITY IN THE EARLY DAYS

Historians agree that all the major contributors to the classical theory of probability were thorough-going determinists, at least in the realm of physical events. The first great mathematical theorist, Jakob Bernouilli (1654–1705) is as explicit in his *Ars Conjectandi* (posthumous, 1713) as the better-known statement of Laplace. So is Abraham De Moivre (1667–1754), whose *Doctrine of Chances* went through three editions, 1718, 1738 and 1756.

In this context it is not so easy to separate physical-law determinism from theological determinism. Pascal was a passionate convert to Jansenism; De Moivre and Bernoulli were of Huguenot backgrounds. One of the most bitter targets of the theologians preaching predestination was the vulgar belief in luck, fortune or chance. Renaissance thinkers were at home in a world of luck, which was exorcised by the new Protestant and counter-reformation theologies. Moreover, theology and providence were explicitly invoked to explain stable frequencies, both in the case of games of chance and in the new demographic data. Pearson (1978) has drawn particular attention to this aspect of De Moivre's thought, arguing that it is a feature of a 'Newtonian' world-view.

Many subsequent writers on the period have agreed. In 1710 John Arbuthnot (1667–1735) published 'An Argument for Divine Providence' based on his observation that in the city of London, for the previous 83 years, more boys had been born than girls. He argued that this shows that 'Art, not Chance' governs in the matter of the sex ratio. This is because he thought that chance meant a probability of 0.5 for a birth of either sex. We now say that it shows that the probability of a male birth exceeds 0.5. But it was certainly his opinion that this stable ratio was divinely, not causally, determined. De Moivre indicated that he shared this opinion. Stable birth rates with more boys than girls were regularly used in an argument from design for the existence of God – because there could be no other explanation. This idea was part of the motivation for the first great work of demography, J. P. Süssmilch's *Die göttliche Ordnung* of 1741. Thus, far from stable frequencies being thought incompatible with a form of determinism, they were taken as evidence for theological determinism and divine providence.

Returning to mathematical probability, Daston (forthcoming) presents the more striking thesis that determinism was not only an accompaniment to the classical theory of probability, but also a precondition for it. Her argument hinges on two distinct features. First, late Renaissance popular thought was intensely interested not only in fortune but in flukes and variability, in monsters, showers of fishes, hermaphrodites and the like. In a period of fifty years this fascination was replaced, at least in high culture, with an enthusiasm for natural, indeed mechanical, laws and the parallel drive towards physical-law determinism.

Secondly, it was generally held that mathematics could be applied only in the domain of what was absolutely fixed, determinate and necessary. This was part of a standard, almost universal, theory on the nature of mathematical knowledge. Thus there arose a problem of 'mixed mathematics', a concept analogous to what we now call applied mathematics. The science of the necessary was applied to the phenomena of nature. In celestial mechanics no one doubted that the laws of nature and the movements of the planets were fully necessary. But every application of mathematics had to meet the same standard, and hence, Daston argues, the early mathematicians of probability were not determinists simply as part of the common culture of their time. It was essential that they be determinists about aleatory events in order for them coherently to apply mathematics in that domain.

Daston is even able to offer a 'crucial experiment' in support of her analysis. It concerns the mathematician, alchemist and physician Geronimo Cardano (1501–76). Cardano did write a remarkable book on games of chance, and certainly had the mathematical ability used in the early works of probability a century after his death. But he was firmly convinced that games of chance operate by fortune or by luck and that their outcomes are in no way deterministic. Since he held that mathematics can only be applied to subject-matter whose events occur with necessity, he failed, Daston argues, to invent the mathematical theory of probability.

The seventeenth- and eighteenth-century workers who did invent probability mathematics did all avow a strict determinism in games of chance. It was, however, left to Laplace explicitly to deduce that determinism entails that all statements of probability are 'relative in part to our knowledge, in part to our ignorance'. This is commonly taken to mean that he understood probability statements as expressions of degree of belief relative to evidence. But as remarked above he also regularly used the word *facilité* to mean, apparently, the propensity of a physical arrangement to yield various events with a stable distribution of relative frequency.

5. DETERMINISM AND STATISTICS

Westergaard (1932) is an informative survey of the development of statistical practices, but does not consider related events in intellectual or political history. The first monograph-length study to do so is Porter (1986). One of the chief points is that social events are deemed to be governed by statistical laws. They are as deterministic as the laws of celestial mechanics.

Westergaard speaks of an 'era of enthusiasm' for statistics, from 1820–48. Although statistical data had been collected from time immemorial, for purposes of taxation and military recruitment, they had typically been regarded as secret state property. Only following the Napoleonic wars were statistical bureaucracies established to cover a far wider range of social experience. Moreover, in all the nations of Europe, digests of this information were published, at regular intervals. In France numerous bureaux directed their attention to social problems of disease, insanity and various types of deviancy such as suicide, crime and prostitution. These exerted a curious fascination on the public, for it appeared that the rates of suicide, of various kinds of crime and of conviction by jury, were constant from year to year. Even the ratios of modes of suicide were constant for different nations (carbon monoxide and drowning being preferred in France, while hanging and shooting were more common in England). This perceived stability suggested that these social phenomena are subject to deterministic law.

Porter describes the powerful effect this widespread conception had on Adolphe Quetelet (1796–1874). This Belgian astronomer became the premier nineteenth-century propagandist for statistics. During the 1830s he wrote extensively on the stability of frequencies of suicide, crime and the like, convinced that they were the expressions of deterministic law. However his most significant contribution was a combination of his astronomical and statistical knowledge.

C. F. Gauss (1777–1855) had brought his theory of errors to completion in the early years of the nineteenth century. Its immediate application was curve fitting of astronomical data. His work led to the law of errors, often called the Gaussian distribution and in 1893 named the normal distribution by Karl Pearson. Its frequency distribution is the familiar bell-shaped curve. By the 1840s Quetelet became convinced that the error curve had an entirely different application. Starting with the distribution of chest diameters from a table of Scottish soldiers, he became convinced that most biological and many social distributions conformed to the Gaussian distribution. Stigler (1986) recounts how, from a mathematical point of view, almost all of Quetelet's mathematical analysis was defective. He takes this to show the immense conceptual difficulty in transferring probability mathematics to social data. On the other hand, even if Quetelet was wrong, his conviction of law in the social domain had substantial consequences.

6. STATISTICAL FATALISM

One such consequence was a problem about free will. Suppose, for example, that about 15 people commit suicide in a given administrative unit every year. Let this be taken as a deterministic law of that region. Then, although it may not be determined that those particular individuals kill themselves, it is determined that so many will. Were they free not to? The problem was pressing, for this is the only sin for which it is logically impossible to make confession. Porter describes the confused reactions to this idea, including Henry Buckle's *History of Civilization* of 1857 which held, on Queteletian grounds, that the whole of history is subject to statistical determinism. This work was sensational in its day. It, together with Quetelet's work, provoked intense debate in Britain, France, Germany and Russia. In the end, statistical fatalism was rejected.

It is remarkable that when physics was made statistical with the advent of quantum mechanics, this was thought to make a space for free will. But 75 years earlier, when society was held in thrall to the first statistical laws, they were held to preclude free will. This indicates a substantial shift in the relations between conceptions of statistical law and determinism.

7. LAWS OF LARGE NUMBERS

Today the name, 'law of large numbers', is often taken to mean any of several formulations of the Central Limit Theorem in mathematical probability. Stigler provides an invaluable account of its evolution. Historically, however, the name was introduced by Poisson in 1835, in contrast to the theorem of Bernoulli published in 1713. The latter establishes that if the probability of an event is p, then in a long sequence of identical trials, the relative frequency with which the event occurs approaches p. Bernoulli gave excellent estimates of the rate of convergence. Poisson was, however, concerned with a situation in which the probability of the event varies according to some law from case to case. He showed that here too there is convergence. Indeed it is more rapid than in the Bernoulli case.

This directs one to a more general problem. Bernoulli studied homogeneous trials. In nature and especially in social affairs few chance set-ups are homogeneous. But one obtains stable frequencies from a variety of conditions with non-homogeneous trials. Why? How? An account of some of these researches is provided by Heyde and Seneta (1977). The relevance to determinism is as follows. One obtained stable frequency distributions from what appeared to be circumstances of 'chance'. Mathematicians tried to derive results proving that if the latter were law-like, then the law-likeness of the former was inevitable. Similar attempts were made to understand the application of the Gaussian law to social phenomena in terms of little underlying independent causes. Although in general the results were defective, they were believed to be in the right direction, and to explain how determinism could coexist with probability and statistical law.

8. DETERMINISM AND STATISTICAL LAW

Francis Galton (1822–1911), in many ways the founder of the modern theory of statistical inference, called the Gaussian law of error, applied to biological and social phenomena, 'the supreme law of unreason'. He was prepared to treat such laws as autonomous, not needing to be reducible to underlying causes in the manner of the preceding section. He was nonetheless a firm determinist. But the situation had changed. De Moivre had asserted that not only was the notion of chance impious, but also it was a mere word, signifying nothing. Chance and unreason were dangerous. By the time of Galton they had been tamed. Far from 'laws of chance' displacing determinism, they helped keep it in place in a world whose science was increasingly investigating random variability.

This is apparent in many different domains. The first, according to Michael Heidelberger (1987), may be 'psychophysics', the earliest quantitative empirical psychology. G. T. Fechner (1801–67) adapted the astronomers' law of error of observations to the study of our ability to distinguish different sensations; for example, to tell which of two slightly different weights is the heavier. Although he favoured indeterminism for a variety of reasons, one was the way in which it made sense of chance variations in judgement. Emile Durkheim (1858–1917), one of the founders of modern sociology, based his most famous study, *Suicide* (1897), on a century of French suicide statistics, and used them to determine the normalcy or pathology of a society. He urged that suicide rates indicate not facts about individuals, but laws acting upon a social ensemble as a whole. But where many today might think of this as indicating that the behaviour of individuals is a matter of chance, adding up to regularity in the large, Durkheim held to no such view. His laws acting upon social units were conceived of as deterministic, and the actions of individual agents, although free, were not thought of as violating physical-law determinism. An account of how Durkheim took over many of the concepts of medical statistics, and turned personal pathology into what he called social pathology, is to be found in Hacking (forthcoming).

9. PROCESSING THE DATA

During the nineteenth century every nation established statistical bureaucracies. Sometimes all statistical work was centralised in one dominant bureau, as in Prussia. In France data were typically collected by the several ministries, Justice, Education, etc. In Britain commercial data were administered by the Board of Trade, while vital statistics were collected by the Registrar General's Office (for England and Wales, with a comparable Scottish office). In the United States leadership was primarily furnished by individual states, the most notable of which was Massachusetts. The first article of the U.S. Constitution mandates that a census shall be held every ten years, in order to determine the representative districts. There was, however, no stable bureaucracy until 1860. As the ninth year of each decade rolled by, Congress would frantically pass bills authorising expenditures for the next census, and the census-takers themselves were almost entirely temporary patronage appointments. Only in 1880 and 1890 was the Bureau of the Census firmly in control on a full-time basis.

The collection of enormous quantities of data necessitated whole new techniques of compilation and calculation. William Farr, who administered the Registrar General's Office in London, pirated a large and excellent calculating machine designed by a Swedish inventor, W. Scheutz, and used it for the calculating and printing out of actuarial and annuity tables for 1860. In the United States, the census of 1890 yielded an almost unmanageable quantity of data, but a member of the bureau, W. Holerith, invented a calculator using punch cards, copying an idea from the automatic loom of Jacquard. His company is one of the three parent companies of today's giant, International Business Machines.

10. INFORMATION AND CONTROL

Throughout the century, and particularly in the decades before 1848, statistics were of great importance to social reformers, particularly of the utilitarian school. One of the most brilliant, although by no means the most bitter, attacks on the utilitarian statisticians is to be read in Dickens's novel *Hard Times* (1854). Schoolmaster Gradgrind forces his charges to learn endless statistical facts, when they cannot yet even pronounce the word 'statistics'. At the end, his son Tom goes bad and embezzles. He thrusts the spectre of statistical determinism at his father: 'So many people are employed in situations of trust; so many people, out of so many, will be dishonest. I have heard you talk, a hundred times, of its being a law. How can I help laws?' Dostoyevsky's *Notes from Underground* (1864) contains similar criticisms of the statistical determinism thesis which had just been made popular by the arrival of Buckle's *History* in Moscow and St. Petersburg.

One reason that the fashion for statistical law was the butt of such novelists was a genuine fear that the amassing of data and the accompanying inferred social laws would severely interfere with individual liberties. The philanthropists and utilitarians had a different view, holding that only by knowing the laws would it be possible to ameliorate the life and morality of the lower orders, and in particular of *les misérables* (a category frequently employed in French statistical analyses). This philanthropic-utilitarian drive was on the one hand the result of genuine revulsion at the terrible crowding and suffering of the new industrial cities. But it was also strongly motivated by a desire to bring control and order to the labouring classes.

It is possible to see these events as part of a larger movement to introduce new techniques of power in an industrial society. It is a case of what Michel Foucault, in *The History of Sexuality*, Vol. I, has referred to as 'biopower'. He conceived of this as acting on two axes. One is at the level of individual interventions in the family and its reproduction, heavily focusing, therefore, on sexual mores. The other is at the level of sweeping statistical analyses of the entire population, and attempts to govern or alter the population as a whole. One notorious example is the eugenics movement, founded by Francis Galton and continued by Karl Pearson, and which, when exported from Britain to the United States had substantial effects on immigration policy, forced sterilisation of prisoners, and the like. One convenient account of these developments is Daniel J. Kevles's *In the Name of Eugenics*. MacKenzie (1981) provides a broader account of the interaction between statistics and social interests.

No matter to what extent one may be inclined to follow or to reject Foucault's suggestions, one element of this history is plain to see. At first it may appear that regarding social phenomena as merely statistical phenomena may open the door to all kinds of indeterminism. Exactly the opposite was intended, and indeed all of us are now the subject of endless statistical surveys which take advantage of the new techniques of polling that require sampling only a small part of the population. One may venture the paradoxical-sounding statement that the more the indeterminism, the more the control.

11. A UNIVERSE OF CHANCE

Although statistical laws were increasingly regarded as autonomous, and not in need of reduction to underlying deterministic causes, it was not until the end of the century that there was an entirely forthright profession of anti-determinism. C. S. Peirce, the American pragmatist philosopher (1839–1914), openly avowed that we live in a 'universe of chance'. The events leading up to his paper entitled 'The Doctrine of Necessity Examined' (1892) have not yet been given adequate historical study, but some sketch of them is provided in Hacking (1983). There is an important interaction between the pragmatists Peirce and William James (1842–1910). James, who had had a serious crisis of will during his student years, insisted upon distinguishing 'soft' from 'hard' determinists. The former claim that physical-law determinism is consistent with free will, while the latter deny it. James thought that only hard determinism was coherent, and since he urged freedom of the will, he rejected determinism, although on no grounds except that it had undesirable consequences. In this respect he was importantly influenced by a body of French philosophers.

Peirce, however, rejected physical-law determination on the grounds that we had no reason to believe in it. All our evidence for uniformly necessary physical laws must be based on experience. Our experience shows merely approximate laws, subject to variations of error. All these laws are deducible, by laws of large numbers and the like, from the supposition that we live in a world of pure indeterministic chance. He was much influenced by his own experience in geodesy. He was personally acquainted with the vagaries of measurement. He invented many techniques, both mathematical and experimental, to overcome these sources of error but knew they could never be entirely eradicated. He was also deeply impressed by the statistical mechanics of James Clerk Maxwell (1831–79). Maxwell had derived the classical deterministic laws of gases from the postulation of purely random behaviour of molecules. Peirce conjectured that something similar would prove to be the case with all the most firm deterministic laws of physics. Incidentally, as Porter reports, Maxwell had been led to his model and his analysis after reading an account of Quetelet's research into social phenomena. In a sense he modelled his random distribution of molecular motion on social interactions. Maxwell himself may have held, at least at times, that his models were more than models, and that the underlying phenomena of gases are based on chance. He is very cautious in this respect. It was left to Peirce to make the first explicit and unguarded assertion that we live in a universe of chance.

12. CONCLUSION

Far from probability and physical-law determinism being incompatible, they are not only coeval but also mutually self-supporting until the end of the nineteenth century. However the developments of the nineteenth century gave rise to the notion of free-standing statistical laws, and hence to the possibility that one did not need to suppose an underlying determinism in order to obtain the universal regularities of the physics of the day. It was left to quantum mechanics to establish that this is more than a possibility. (See art. 29.)

At present only a few authors have addressed the historical connections between probability and determinism. There is much more to be done, and doubtless the above account will be revised. There is also a great need for work in the period from 1900 to 1936, from the beginning of the 'old' quantum mechanics to John von Neumann's 'No hidden variables' theorem of 1936. This theorem proves that no underlying causal and deterministic structure is consistent with the 'new' quantum mechanics developed between 1926 and 1927. Although there are many important histories of the quantum mechanics of this period, none adequately address the relation between probability and conceptions of determinism, both scientific and popular.

FURTHER READING

Daston (1988), Porter (1986) and Stigler (1986) are beautifully complementary. The first two authors are historians of science working in the tradition of history of ideas. Daston goes up to the early part of the nineteenth century, and Porter continues to the end. Stigler is a mathematical statistician who provides an account of the mathematical developments throughout the entire period discussed by Porter and Daston.
Lorraine Daston, *The reasonable calculus: classical probability theory, 1650–1840* (Prince-

ton, 1988). Writing in the tradition of the history of ideas, Daston connects the mathematical development with events in the insurance business and other practical affairs.

Daniel Garber, and Sandy Zabell, 'On the emergence of probability', *Archive for history of exact sciences*, 21 (1979), 33–53. An instructive antidote to Hacking (1975), it presents a substantial 'prehistory' of probability.

Ian Hacking, *The Emergence of Probability* (Cambridge, 1975). A philosophical account of the concept of probability from its beginnings until 1739.

—— 'Nineteenth-century cracks in the concept of determinism', *Journal for the history of ideas* 44 (1983), 455–75. An account of numerous tensions concerning determinism, in the context of philosophy, probability, and the physical sciences.

Michael Heidelberger, 'Fechner's indeterminism: from freedom to laws of chance', in Krüger *et al.* (1987) I, pp. 117–56.

C. C. Heyde and E. Seneta, *I. J. Bienaymé: statistical theory anticipated* (New York, 1977). Although the book is written around one mid nineteenth-century French mathematician, it provides a useful account of all nineteenth-century attempts to derive statistical homogeneities from underlying varying causes.

Lorenz Krüger *et al.* (eds.), *The probabilistic revolution*, Vol. I, *Ideas in history*; Vol. II, *Ideas in the sciences* (Cambridge, Mass., 1987).

—— 'The slow progress of probabilism: philosophical arguments in the nineteenth century', in Krüger *et al.* (1987) I, pp. 69–90. Connects difficulties in the development of probability with conceptual perplexity over determinism. These volumes represent the collective work of about 30 scholars, who deal with probability and most of the natural and social sciences in the period 1800–1930.

Donald A. MacKenzie, *Statistics in Britain, 1865–1930: the social reconstruction of scientific knowledge* (Edinburgh, 1981). An important work from the standpoint of sociology of knowledge, whose subtitle is self-explanatory.

Karl Pearson, *The history of statistics in the 17th and 18th centuries, against the changing background of intellectual scientific and religious thought*, lectures from 1921–1933, ed. E. S. Pearson (London, 1978). Just what its title implies; a lively and personal account by one of the founders of modern statistical inference.

Theodore M. Porter, *The rise of statistical thinking 1820–1900* (Princeton, 1986). Describes new practices of descriptive and analytical statistics, together with their impact on the larger current of ideas.

Stephen M. Stigler, *The history of statistics: the measurement of uncertainty before 1900* (Cambridge, Mass., 1986). This will long be the standard overview of mathematical statistics up to 1900. Although primarily a history of the mathematics, it is rich in personal anecdotes and curiosities.

Isaac Todhunter, *A history of the mathematical theory of probability from the time of Pascal to that of Laplace* (London, 1865; reprint 1949, 1965). An exhaustive recounting of technical results.

Harald Westergaard, *Contributions to the history of statistics* (London, 1932, reprint 1969). A thorough survey of descriptive and actuarial statistics from earliest times.

46

THE MIND–BODY PROBLEM

ROBERT M. YOUNG

There have been, throughout recorded history, representations of a separation between the corporeal and the spiritual – in religion, philosophy, folklore and myth. On the whole, the incorporeal realm has been seen as more enduring, efficacious and valued than the corporeal, which is often described as transient, of little value and even illusory.

However, this is not to say that the 'mind–body problem' of modern Western thought has a history stretching back through the mists of time. Indeed, for more than a thousand years prior to the seventeenth century, the reigning mode of explanation sorted out reality and causality along quite different lines or, rather, without the sort of lines associated with a short dichotomy between the mental and the physical. Nor were there sharp distinctions between ideas of causality, of what is ultimately real (ontology) and of how we can know with certainty (epistemology). All lay within an integrated Aristotelian (we should now say organismic) framework of causes or 'comings to be': the material cause (that out of which, or roughly, our concept of matter); the efficient cause (the source of energy: that which produces or imparts motion or shapes); the formal cause (that which gives form or plan in the sense of an architect's or craftsman's plan) and the final cause (the purpose or goal or that for which). All 'comings to be' – things, events, processes – were seen as constituted by all four causes, which could only be separately considered analytically. Debates about philosophy in the Renaissance were putting this framework under strain, so that the material and efficient causes were drifting towards one pole and the formal and final ones towards another. However, it would be anachronistic to treat these imputed poles as recognised extremes in a mind–body dichotomy. Other notions, such as that of 'substantial form' or ones invoking pre-Aristotelian, i.e. Platonic, concepts also put the form/matter dichotomy under strain.

If we cease to look at the pre-modern formulations and ask when the mind–

body problem became conceptualised in the ways which we can recognise as more or less our own, the answer lies in the philosophical writings of René Descartes (1596–1650) and in his place in the so-called 'Scientific Revolution' of the sixteenth centuries. I say so-called, because it would be a huge historical oversimplification to trace a single thread from his *Discourse on Method* (1637) or *Meditations* (1641) to the present. History is always messy, and intellectual history is no exception to this rule. In the case of the mind–body problem, this means that Aristotelian thinking never died and was perpetuated, for example, in the study of living phenomena ('biology' is a nineteenth-century term). Similarly, Platonic ideas of the universality of ideal forms linked to geometrical and numerical properties continued, as did mystical and alchemical notions which were intermixed with the persistence of Aristotelian and Platonic notions. These admixtures persisted in the work of the leading figures of the Scientific Revolution, for example, Copernicus, Kepler, Galileo and Newton. Moreover, materialist and atomist philosophies were being advocated, some of them drawn from classical sources, in the writings of Hobbes and Gassendi. (See art. 15.)

Even so, it is in the writings of Descartes that we find the full-blown paradox of the mind–body dichotomy. His method of radical doubt led to a single certainty: 'I think, therefore I am' – a theory of knowledge based on subjectivity linked to a theory of ultimate reality based on 'thinking substances' as one class of existence. Mind was being put forward as a self-contained sphere of enquiry.[1]

This pole of the dualism was linked to an equally strongly-held belief that causality in the material world is based on matter in motion, 'extended substances', obeying their own material laws. Introspection became the basis of certainty, while scientific knowledge of the external world depended on the laws of matter and motion.

These two bases for knowing opened up two closely-linked chasms in modern thought: the ontological (between mind and body) and the epistemological (between subject and object). Matter came to be defined in ways that made it amenable to treatment in mathematical terms and to the experimental method, leading to the notion that scientific explanation must be in terms of bodies: extension and shape, treated mathematically. Although misunderstanding Harvey's theory of the circulation of the blood, Descartes utilised it as the key to the comprehension of all of the rest of nature. This was merely the motion of material substances without a vital spirit or special causes but simply heat and the motions of the parts. The question of how much this left unexplained within the study of living nature will be discussed further on.

However, even on its own terms, the formulation of a reality consisting of extended substances and non-extended substances was fraught with difficulty. The non-extended substances were defined negatively as partaking of all the attributes that do not apply to body (i.e. which cannot be treated mathematically and experimentally). The essence of this was, of course, free will. We see in the philosophy of Descartes a grand historic compromise in which the claims of scientific explanation produced a definition of matter, while the claims of the church and moral responsibility produced a definition of mind. Yet those two were imcompatible.

How do body and mind interrelate in life and in knowing? This puzzle led to the classical 'problem of interaction', a perennial philosophical conundrum which still gets dismissed generation after generation until one thinks eventually of unanswerable questions such as how thoughts can cause actions or how unconscious fantasies can cause psychosomatic illnesses such as ulcers, asthma and colitis.

How do thoughts impact on particles of matter and how do material impacts cause thoughts, including the thoughts which lead from sensation to knowing? We are left wondering not only how we know anything for certain but how we have any experience at all, especially the experience of other minds. How can two sorts of basic substances which are *defined* so that they have nothing in common then have causal relationships in the 'having' of experience and the 'will-ing' of action?

If the scandalised tone of these questions seems eccentric, here are the opinions of two eminent philosophers, Whitehead and Burtt, reflecting on the mind–body problem and the closely-linked problem of knowledge.

> The seventeenth century had finally produced a scheme of scientific thought framed by mathematicians, for the use of mathematicians. The great characteris-tic of the mathematical mind is its capacity for dealing with abstractions; and for eliciting from them clear-cut demonstrative trains of reasoning, entirely satisfac-tory so long as it is those abstractions which you want to think about. The enor-mous success of the scientific abstractions, yielding on the one hand *matter* with its *simple location* in space and time, on the other hand *mind*, perceiving, suffering, reasoning, but not interfering, has foisted onto philosophy the task of accepting them as the most concrete rendering of fact.
>
> Thereby, modern philosophy has been ruined. It has oscillated in a complex manner between three extremes. There are the dualists, who accept matter and mind as on equal basis, and the two varieties of monists, those who put mind inside matter, and those who put matter inside mind. But this juggling with abstractions can never overcome the inherent confusion introduced by the ascrip-tion of *misplaced concreteness* to the scientific scheme of the seventeenth century.[2]

E. A. Burtt spells out the consequences of the doctrine for human self-knowledge.

> . . . it does seem like strange perversity in these Newtonian scientists to further their own conquests of external nature by loading on mind everything refractory to exact mathematical handling and thus rendering the latter still more difficult to

study scientifically than it had been before. Did it never cross their minds that sooner or later people would appear who craved verifiable knowledge about mind in the same way they craved it about physical events, and who might reasonably curse their elder scientific brethren for buying easier success in their own enterprise by throwing extra handicaps in the way of their successors in social science? Apparently not; mind was to them a convenient receptacle for the refuse, the chips and whittlings of science, rather than a possible object of scientific knowledge.[3]

Deep within the grand mind–body dichotomy lay the problem of parcelling out the qualities to assign to the separate realms. When one embarks on this task, new puzzles abound. The qualities which can be treated mathematically and which are thought not to vary according to subjective bias are called primary. It is a short list, and items keep falling off it. Extension and shape are the only enduring ones. Even hardness has a difficult time keeping its place, and physical theories based on forces and fields compete successfully with those based on atomic particles. But the realm of colour, odour and taste – the texture of experience – gets relegated to the domain of secondary qualities. These are seen as less real and are the effects of the vicissitudes of matter in motion. Aspects of this concept of 'primary and secondary qualities' were developed in the writings of Descartes, Galileo, Newton and Locke.

Whitehead is eloquent in his critique of the features and the consequences of the doctrine of primary and secondary qualities, a doctrine which lies at the basis of modern thought just as securely as the parent mind–body dichotomy.

Locke, writing with a knowledge of Newtonian dynamics, places mass among the primary qualities of bodies. In short, he elaborates a theory of primary and secondary qualities in accordance with the state of physical science at the close of the seventeenth century. The primary qualities are the essential qualities of substances whose spatio-temporal relationships constitute nature. The orderliness of these relationships constitutes the order of nature. The occurrences of nature are in some way apprehended by minds, which are associated with living bodies. Primarily, the mental apprehension is aroused by the occurrences in certain parts of the correlated body, the occurrences in the brain, for instance. But the mind in apprehending also experiences sensations which, properly speaking, are qualities of the mind alone. These sensations are projected by the mind so as to clothe appropriate bodies in external nature. Thus the bodies are perceived as with qualities which in reality do not belong to them, qualities which in fact are purely the offspring of the mind. Thus nature gets credit which should in truth be reserved for ourselves: the rose for its scent; the nightingale for his song; and the sun for his radiance. The poets are entirely mistaken. They should address their lyrics to themselves, and should turn them into odes of self-congratulation on the excellency of the human mind. Nature is a dull affair, soundless, scentless, colourless; merely the hurrying of material, endlessly, meaninglessly.

However you disguise it, this is the practical outcome of the characteristic scientific philosophy which closed the seventeenth century.

In the first place, we must note its astounding efficiency as a system of concepts for the organisation of scientific research. In this respect, it is fully worthy of the genius of the century which produced it. It has held its own as the guiding principle of scientific studies ever since. It is still reigning. Every university in the world organises itself in accordance with it. No alternative system of organising the pursuit of scientific truth has been suggested. It is not only reigning, but it is without rival.

And yet – it is quite unbelievable. This conception of the universe is surely framed in terms of high abstractions, and the paradox only arises because we have mistaken our abstraction for concrete realities.[4]

What a mess! Yet is well and truly still our mess. If we look at the goals of Newtonian explanation, we find him claiming that the whole business of natural philosophy is that from the phenomena of matter and motion we are to explain all the other phenomena. If we look at a modern textbook, we find roughly the same terms of reference. In the Royal Society document on *Qualities, Units and Symbols* (1975), we find the following on page 6:

> The value of a *physical quantity* is equal to the product of a *numerical value* and a *unit*. Neither any physical quantity nor the symbol used to denote it should imply a particular choice of unit, operations on equations involving physical quantities, units and numerical values, should follow the ordinary rules of algebra.

On page 8 it says,

> Each physical quantity is given a name and a symbol which is an abbreviation for that name. By international convention *seven* physical quantities are chosen for use as dimensionally independent base quantities: length (1), mass (m), time (t), electric current (i), thermodynamic temperature (T), amount of substance (n) and luminous intensity (Iv). *All* other physical quantities are regarded as being *derived* from the base quantities.

This is the bedrock of all explanation, and on it we must, in principle, erect *all* knowledge, all explanation.

Every attempt to transcend the mind–body dichotomy and the problem of interaction can be said to fall foul of some deep problem. As Whitehead said, there are basically three positions: dualists, materialists and idealists. In fact, the classification is somewhat more elaborate.

Classical Cartesian dualism invokes God at the point of interaction. For Descartes, the physical point of interaction where the miracle occurs countless times each day was the pineal gland or *conarium*. Modern *interactionists* take it as given that interaction between physical and mental events occurs, though they can in no sense explain it in causal terms.

One way of avoiding this scandal is to say that mental and physical events occur in parallel, without calling for interaction or a doctrine of mind–body causality. This approach was adopted by Malebranche (1638–1715), who invoked God to keep the mental and the physical events in step. Secular versions of *psychophysical parallelism* or the doctrine of concomitance have been widespread in the nineteenth and twentieth centuries. For example, they were held by the philosopher, psychologist and evolutionary thinker, Herbert Spencer, by John Hughlings Jackson, the father of modern neurology, who adopted it from Spencer, and by Freud, who applied Jackson's ideas in his first book, *On Aphasia* (1981) and continued to hold this view until his last writing, *An Outline of Psychoanalysis* (1940).

A recent exponent of psychophysical parallelism in neurology and philosophy is Hertwig Kuhlenbeck. The strength of the theory lies in its candour: psychophysical parallelists simply shrug their shoulders at the problem of interaction while making full use of the rich languages of mind and body. It can be argued that much of modern philosophy is parallelist in that elaborate theories of mental causation – the association of ideas – have been spelled out in the psychological writings of Locke, Hume, Hartley, James Mill, John Stuart Mill, G. H. Lewes, Spencer and Alexander Bain, among others, without, however, any denial of concomitant physiological mechanisms or commitment to causal explanations. The mental elements have been persistently described in ways which are closely analogous to concepts involving atoms and their interactions in physics. For example, in David Hartley's *Observations on Man* (1749), ideas and their associations paralleled postulated vibrations and 'vibratiuncles' in the brain. Similarly, William James commented on the close parallelism between the concept of the association of ideas and the neurone theory of the nervous system.

From this it is, of course, but one step to say – consistent with the doctrine of primary and secondary qualities – that the mental realm has no autonomy or causal efficacy, and that mind is merely an effect or epiphenomenon of physical and physiological processes. This is materialist monism or *materialism*, a doctrine which has had its advocates since antiquity and was assiduously advocated by Hobbes in the seventeenth century and by numerous philosophers in the nineteenth and twentieth centuries. Examples of this are the Helmholtz School of Physiology in nineteenth-century France and Germany and behaviourism in twentieth-century American psychology and British philosophy. There was a group of experimental physiologists in the mid-nineteenth century including Helmholtz, Brücke and Dubois-Reymond who held that there are no forces other than the ordinary physico-chemical ones operating in the organism, although they left room for the positing of, and research on, other natural and measurable forces.

The doctrine of behaviourism was developed in America in the early decades of the twentieth century. Its leading advocate was John B. Watson, who moved on from saying that psychology should adopt experimental methods for the study of organisms to saying that there are no minds, only observable behaviour. Thought became a sort of implicit speech. Behaviourism was closely linked to objective and operationist movements in physics and to astringent doctrines in philosophy which attempted to model philosophical thinking on the natural sciences. This point of view was most eloquently put in the analytical philosophy of Gilbert Ryle, whose *The Concept of Mind* (1949) was influential in the 1950s until the vein of psychological and philosophical behaviourism was played out, and researchers in both disciplines began to look again at meaning and subjectively in less restricted, though no less disciplined, terms.

A persistent problem with materialist monism from its ancient form to its modern-day advocates in physics, physiology and molecular biology is that the concept of matter bequeathed to us by the seventeenth century is simply too impoverished – too stripped of the qualities of lived experience – for it to be credible that *that* matter can produce life and mind. There is something unutterably bleak at the heart of the doctrine that there is only matter; foolish, too, as the above passage from Whitehead shows.

The classification I have given here is not exhaustive. For example, a variant of materialism is *identity theory*, whereby the logically separate domains of mental and physical are said to be based on an empirical identity: brain states. This leaves the subject's observations of his or her mental events in an ontological limbo. Other attempts to transcend the patent difficulties in the existing dualistic and monistic theories have postulated a *neutral monism* or have interpreted mind and body as two *aspects* of a single underlying reality. Those who advocate identity theory, neutral monism or aspect theory would, of course, argue that they have overcome the absurdities of traditional 'solutions' to the mind–body problem.

And yet the final choice – that there is only mind – is equally or possibly even more incredible. There has perhaps never been a consistent mentalist monist. Indeed, in *Individuals* (1959) P. F. Strawson went to some lengths to show that connection to some body in the past or present is essential to the identification of persons, things and other particulars. Perhaps Berkeley and some mystics were genuine idealist monists.

All of this leads one back to the drawing board. If interactionism, parallelism, materialism and idealism won't do, a way has to be found to grant matter its due, yet to give us back a recognisable world at the end of the day. In fact, real and sensible philosophers and scientists have rarely held pure versions of the above doctrine. In particular, they have persistently endowed matter with properties that go beyond the extremely short list of the seventeenth-century purists. For example, as the debate continued about what aspects of life, including human nature, could be described by the mechanical philosophy, J. O. de la Mettrie (1709–51) argued that *Man is a Machine* (1747), while enriching the concept of 'machine' enough to take the sting of despair out of his title for those who read his treatise carefully. Similarly, Albrecht von Haller (1708–77) argued that as long as we could do experiments, we could postulate whatever *biological* properties we need, e.g. sensibility or contractility. If one looks at a modern biological or physiological text, all sorts of properties are invoked without anyone (or practically anyone) intending to invoke special, vital or purely unmaterialistic forces. Thus 'inherent rhythmicity', 'pacemakers', 'organisers', 'homeostasis' and 'positive and negative feedback' are all concepts which span the realms of mechanism and purpose which were so starkly split in Cartesian dualism. Therefore, biological properties in the study of purposive mechanisms have broken through the strictest version of Cartesian dualism with its impoverished concept of matter.

Some have wished to elevate this transcendence of Cartesian dualism into a new philosophy and to argue for a doctrine of *emergence*. When hydrogen and oxygen combine to produce water, the property of wetness (absent in hydrogen and oxygen separately) is called an 'emergent'. Similar claims are made for the emergent properties of life and mind and, by some, spirit. This is an odd view. It is one thing to note what matter can do and thereby enrich our concept of it. It is quite another to hypostatise properties and give them a new ontological status and causal efficacy under the title of 'emergents'. It recalls Molière's Tartuffe, who explains that opium works because it has a 'soporific virtue'.

Another path by which the mind–body problem has been transcended is much trodden by the emergentists. It is the theory of evolution. The key point of evolution is its gradualism. At what point does mind appear? Animals evidently feel (though this was hotly debated in the wake of Cartesianism). Do they then think? Do they have a true language? Are they responsible? What, if any, are their rights? Do plants have the same rights as slugs, and do cats, dolphins and whales have the same rights as humans? Are less clever animals as responsible as bright ones? It could be argued that it depends on how much 'mind' a given creature has. Alternatively, it could be argued – and has been argued – that the linkage of mind, responsibility and will misses the whole point of relations among creatures and their world. Evolutionism undermines sharp dichotomies and makes a mess of scales of moral worth.

The attempt to retain a simple dichotomy between mind and body is also hard to maintain in the face of recent studies of psychosomatic symptoms. The title of a collection of clinical and philosophical studies makes the point nicely: it is *The Mysterious Leap from the Mind to the Body*.[5] Yet the messages of the psychosomatic symptom, when unravelled in psychoanalytic therapy, are perfectly legible in the languages of metaphor, pun and symbol. The crude concept of 'somatic [corporeal] compliance' seems a poor way of hiding our ignorance of how feelings get manifested physically as a symptom, a way of avoiding thinking about, and consciously knowing, human distress.

In this brief treatment, many aspects of the mind–body problem have been eschewed for the sake of clarity. If one cast one's net more broadly, one would have to agree with Feigl: 'It is truly a cluster of intricate puzzles – some scientific, some epistemological, some syntactical, some semantical, and some pragmatic. Closely related to these are the equally sensitive and controversial issues regarding teleology, purpose, intentionality, and free will'.[6]

Rather than remaining split by the mind–body problem, it would surely be better to find a way of knowing that (to paraphrase Gilbert and Sullivan) the meaning isn't matter and never idle patter of a transcendental kind. Nature is a meaningful unity, of which our philosophies must be seen as a part. Those, like Rorty, who would dissolve the history of the great questions of ontology and epistemology – of mind/body and subject/object – into a moving army of metaphors, seem to me to be appropriately gentle:

> These so-called ontological categories are simply the ways of packaging rather heterogeneous notions, from rather diverse historical sources, which were convenient for Descartes' own purposes. But his purposes are not ours. Philosophers should not think of this artificial conglomerate as if it were a discovery of something pre-existent – a discovery which because 'intuitive' or 'conceptual' or 'categorical' sets permanent parameters for science and philosophy.[7]

That is to say that what we mean by reality, including minds, bodies, persons and other dimensions of nature, is inside history and open to historical revision and reconceptualisation. It is to be hoped that the concepts will be friendly rather than tyrannical.

NOTES

1. R. Rorty, *Philosophy and the mirror of nature* (Princeton, 1980), p. 120.
2. A. N. Whitehead, *Science and the modern world* (London, 1985), p. 70.
3. E. A. Burtt, *The metaphysical foundations of modern physical science*, 2nd ed. (London, 1932), pp. 318–19.
4. Whitehead, (1985), pp. 68–9.
5. F. Deutsch, (ed.), *On the mysterious leap from the mind to the body* (New York, 1959).
6. H. Feigl, 'The 'mental' and the 'physical' ', in H. Feigl *et al.*, (eds.), *Minnesota studies in the philosophy of science* (Minneapolis, 1958), Vol. 2, pp. 370–497, at p. 373.
7. Rorty, (1980), p. 125.

FURTHER READING

R. G. Collingwood, *The idea of nature* (Oxford, 1945).

R. Descartes, *Discourse on method and the meditations* (trans. E. A. Sutcliffe, Harmondsworth, 1968).

P. K. Feyerabend and G. Maxwell, (eds.), *Mind, matter and method: essays in philosophy and science in honor of Herbert Feigl* (Minneapolis, 1966).

A. von Haller, 'A dissertation on the sensible and irritable parts of animals', with an introduction by O. Temkin, *Bulletin of the history of medicine*, 4 (1936), 651–99.

H. Kuhlenbeck, 'The meaning of 'postulational psychophysical parallelism' ', *Brain*, 81 (1958), 588–603.

G. Ryle, *The concept of mind* (London, 1949).

P. F. Strawson, *Individuals: an essay in descriptive metaphysics* (London, 1959).

A. Vartanian, *La Mettrie's L'homme machine: a study in the origins of an idea* (Princeton, 1980).

R. M. Young, 'Animal soul', in P. Edwards, (ed.), *The encyclopedia of philosophy* (London, 1967), vol. 1, pp. 122–7.

R. M. Young, 'Freud: scientist and/or humanist', *Free Associations*, 7 (1968), 7–35.

47

PARADIGMATIC TRADITIONS IN THE HISTORY OF ANTHROPOLOGY

GEORGE W. STOCKING

1. DEFINING THE DOMAIN OF ANTHROPOLOGY

In 1904 Franz Boas defined the domain of anthropological knowledge as 'the biological history of mankind in all its varieties; linguistics applied to people without written languages; the ethnology of people without historic records; and prehistoric archeology'. More than any other 'anthropologist', Boas (1858–1942) may be said to exemplify the putative unity of this domain, since (virtually alone among his confrères) he made significant contributions to each of these four inquiries in the course of his long career. But despite the fact that he was perhaps the most important single figure in the institutionalisation of an academic discipline called 'anthropology' in university departments in the United States, Boas already felt in 1904 that there were 'indications of its breaking up'. The 'biological, linguistic and ethnologic-archeological methods are so distinct', he believed, that the time was 'rapidly drawing near' when the two former branches of anthropology would be taken over by specialists in those disciplines, and 'anthropology pure and simple will deal with the customs and beliefs of the less civilized peoples only . . . .'[1]

Given the weight of institutional inertia and of residual commitment to the norm of disciplinary unity, it remains arguable today whether Boas' prediction is yet likely to be achieved. Nevertheless, the fact that its leading practical exemplar regarded the unity of anthropology as historically contingent rather than epistemologically determined suggests that no general historical account of that 'science' may take its unity for granted. In spite of the all-embracing etymological singularity of the term anthropology (Greek *anthropos*: man; *logos*: discourse), the diverse discourses that may be historically subsumed by it have only in certain moments and places been fused into anything approximating a unified science of humankind. In continental Europe in Boas' time, 'anthropology' referred (and often does today) to what in the Anglo-American tradition has been called 'physical anthropology'. As such, it was distinguishable from and historically opposed to 'ethnology' – a discourse that, etymologically, was somewhat more diversitarian (Greek *ethnos*: nation).

In this context, the historical development of anthropology may be contrasted to two ideal typical views of disciplinary development. The first is a Comtean hierarchical model in which the impulse of positive knowledge is successively extended into more complex domains of natural phenomena. The second is a genealogical model in which, within each domain, disciplines may be visualised as growing from a single undifferentiated 'ur' discourse (with the biological sciences developing out of natural history, the humanities out of philology and the social sciences out of moral philosophy). As against these two fission models, 'anthropology' in its inclusive Anglo-American sense is better viewed as an imperfect fusion of modes of inquiry that were quite distinct in origin and in character – deriving in fact from all three of these undifferentiated 'ur'-discourses.

In so far as a common denominator may be extracted from Boas' contingent descriptive definition of anthropology, it would seem to imply an opposition between Europeans, who have written languages and historical records, and 'others', who have not. Indeed, it may be argued that the greatest retrospective unity of the discourses subsumed within the rubric 'anthropology' is to be found in this substantive concern with the peoples who were long stigmatised as 'savages', and who, in the nineteenth century, tended to be excluded from other human scientific disciplines by the very process of their substantive-cum-methodological definition (the economist's concern with the money economy; the historian's concern with written documents, etc.). From this point of view, to study the history of anthropology is to study the attempt to describe and to interpret or explain the 'otherness' of populations encountered in the course of European overseas expansion. Although thus fundamentally (and oppositionally) diversitarian in impulse, such study has usually implied a reflexivity which re-encompassed European self and alien 'other' within a unitary humankind. This history of anthropology may thus be viewed as a continuing (and complex) dialectic between the universalism of 'anthropos' and the diversitarianism of 'ethnos' or, from the perspective of particular historical moments, between the Enlightenment and the Romantic impulse. Anthropology's 'recurrent dilemma' has been how to square both generic human rationality and the biological unity of mankind with 'the great natural variation of cultural forms'.[2]

2. THE BIBLICAL, DEVELOPMENTAL AND POLYGENETIC TRADITIONS

A second unifying tendency within Boas' definition is historical, or more generally, diachronic, since history in the narrow sense seemed precluded by the lack

of documents. For Boas, the 'otherness' which is the subject-matter of anthropology was to be explained as the product of change of time. Although Boas in
fact wrote on the verge of a revolutionary shift towards a more synchronic
anthropology, the history of anthropology up until his time may be schematised
in terms of the interplay of two major diachronic traditions that were, in a broad
sense, paradigmatic, both of them counterpointed by a more synchronic tradition which, because of its heterodoxy, only very briefly achieved paradigmatic
status. In the discussion that follows, these traditions will be designated as the
'biblical' (or 'ethnological'), the 'developmental' (or 'evolutionist'), and the
'polygenetic' (or 'physical anthropological').

The ultimate roots of anthropological thought are more often traced to the
Greek than to the biblical tradition. However, it may be argued that during the
period of European expansion the underlying paradigmatic framework for
the explanation of 'otherness' derived from the first ten chapters of Genesis.
Many intellectual currents contributed to anthropological speculation, among
them environmentalist and humoralist assumptions from the Hippocratic and
Galenic traditions, hierarchical notions from the 'Great Chain of Being',
mediaeval conceptions of the monstrous, etc. But the dominant paradigmatic
tradition (paradigmatic in the sense of providing a more or less coherent *a priori*
framework of assumption defining both relevant problems and the data and
methods for their solution) was that iconically embodied in the second of John
Speed's 'Genealogies of Holy Scriptures' in the King James Bible. There,
growing from the roof of the Ark resting on the top of Mt. Ararat in Armenia,
was a genealogical tree with three major branches: the descendants of Japhet in
Europe, of Sem in Asia and of Ham in Africa, traced on out to their various
representatives in the ancient world ('Phrigians', 'Bactrians', 'Babylonians',
etc.).[3] In this context, the fundamental anthropological problem was to establish
putative historical links between every present human group and one of the
branches of a biblical ethnic tree that linked all of humankind to a single descendant of Adam and Eve. Since what had diversified humankind in the first
instance was the confusion of tongues at Babel, the privileged data for re-
establishing connections were similarities of language, augmented by such
similarities of culture as survived the degenerative processes which were a concomitant of migration towards the earth's imagined corners. Since all humans
were offspring of a single family, and ultimately of a single pair, the physical differences among them were secondary phenomena, characteristically attributable to the influence of the environments through which they had migrated
during the six millennia allowed by the biblical chronology, if not to the direct
intervention of God (as in 'the curse of Ham').

The biblical anthropological tradition, which saw the (characteristically
degenerative) differentiation of humankind in terms of movement through space
within a limited and event-specific historical time, may be contrasted with a

Graeco-Roman paradigmatic tradition deriving from the speculations of Ionian materialists. Perhaps most influentially embodied in Lucretius's *De Rerum Natura*, this tradition saw time as an enabling rather than a limiting factor, and conceived diachronic change in progressive processual rather than degenerative historical terms. Rather than losing divinely given knowledge as they moved through space in time, human groups acquired knowledge gradually, responding to organic needs and environmental stimuli in an adaptive utilitarian manner, as they groped their way forwards step by step from a state near the brutes to that of the most advanced civil society. Although human differentiation was construed in terms of status on a generalised developmental scale rather as the product of a specific sequence of historical events, the Graeco-Roman paradigm was still in a broad sense diachronic.

While the biblical and the developmental traditions represent the dominant paradigmatic alternatives in Western anthropological thought before 1900, it is useful to distinguish a third major paradigmatic tradition: the polygenetic. Foreshadowed in tribal and classical notions of autochthonous origin, it became a matter of more serious speculation in the aftermath of the discovery of the New World, the peopling of which posed a major problem for the orthodox monogenetic tradition. A few writers, most notoriously Isaac de la Peyrère in 1655, went so far as to suggest that the peoples of the New World did not descend from Adam. However, it was nearly a century before Linnaeus (1707–78) included mankind (American/choleric; European/sanguine; Asiatic/melancholic; African/phlegmatic) in the *System of Nature* (1735), and still a generation later before systematic comparative human anatomical data began to be collected. Even then, most of the early physical anthropologists remained, like Johann Blumenbach (1752–1840), staunchly monogenist. But given the growth of comparative data within the framework of a static pre-evolutionary view of biological species, a 'polygenetic' approach to human differentiation became in the nineteenth century an alternative to be considered seriously. From this point of view, human 'races' (often distinguished by the forms of their crania) were, like animal species, aboriginally distinct. Unaffected by the forces of environment, they had remained constant throughout the relatively short span of human historical time – as the images on the 4,000 year-old monuments discovered by Napoleon's expedition to Egypt confirmed.

3. THE DARWINIAN REVOLUTION AND THE DIFFERENTIATION OF NATIONAL ANTHROPOLOGICAL TRADITIONS

Although Rousseau (1712–78) had envisioned in 1755 a unified science of man carried on by philosopher-voyagers who, shaking off 'the yoke of national prejudices', would 'learn to know men by their likenesses and their differences',[4] it was more than a century before his dream began to be realised. For most of that time, the vast bulk of anthropological data was collected incidentally by travellers, missionaries, colonisers and naturalists. In so far as the activity was tied to a knowledge-tradition, it was much more likely to be that of natural history than social theory. Furthermore, the forms of 'anthropology' institutionalised in the major European nations differed strikingly in their relation to the three paradigmatic traditions just described.

During the pre-Darwinian nineteenth century, the focal anthropological issue was posed by the explosion of the data of human diversity that was produced by European expansion, in the context of advances in the regnant sciences in the human and biological domains – comparative linguistics and comparative anatomy. From a classificatory and/or genetic point of view, the central question was 'is mankind one or many?'. Until mid-century, comparative Indo-European (i.e. Japhetic) linguistics provided a model of inquiry which promised to provide a classification of humankind in terms of its most distinctive feature, but which would also link all human groups to a single source. Exemplified in the works of the staunchly monogenist James Cowles Prichard (1786–1848), this goal was institutionalised in several of the 'ethnological' societies founded around 1840.

By the 1850s, however, a distinctly physical anthropological current, modelling itself on comparative anatomy and often polygenist in tendency, had begun to separate itself from the ethnological (formerly biblical) paradigm. Foreshadowed in the works of certain French investigators, and in the 'American School' of Samuel G. Morton (1799–1851), this trend was realised institutionally in the 'anthropological' societies founded by Paul Broca (1824–80) in Paris in 1859 and by James Hunt (1833–69) in London in 1863. Although the term 'anthropological' had in fact been previously employed as a theological/philosophical category, it was now used to affirm the need for a naturalistic study of humankind as one or more physical species in the animal world.

This newly asserted physical anthropological tendency in fact proved resistant to Darwinism, which seemed to the polygenetically-inclined simply a new and speculative form of monogenism. However, the Darwinian revolution was to have a major impact on speculation in the older ethnological tradition. On the one hand, the greatly extended 'antiquity of man', confirmed by the discoveries at Brixham Cave in 1858, made the gradual formation of contemporary races by modification of a single ape-like progenitor seem more plausible. On the other, the revolution in time made extremely unlikely the ethnological task of establishing plausible historical connections over the whole span of human existence. Furthermore, Darwinism posed a problem for which the new 'prehistoric' archeology offered extremely inadequate evidence: providing a convincing evolutionary account of the cultural development that might link modern man with an ape-like ancestor. In this context, the developmental paradigm came again to the forefront of anthropological attention in the last third of the nineteenth century, especially in the Anglo-American tradition.

During this period, socio-cultural evolutionists attempted to synthesise the data of contemporary 'savagery' collected by travellers and naturalists (including that now obtained by correspondence or in response to more formal questionnaires such as the *Notes and Queries in Anthropology* prepared by a committee of the British Association for the Advancement of Science in 1874). By arranging such present synchronic data on a diachronic scale, it was possible for 'armchair' anthropologists to construct generalised stage-sequences of development in each area of human culture. In Britain, E. B. Tylor (1832–1917) traced the evolution of religion from primitive 'animism' through polytheism to monotheism, while John McLennan (1827–81) followed the evolution of marriage from primitive promiscuity through polyandry to monogamy. In the United States, Lewis Henry Morgan (1818–81) traced a more general development from 'lower savagery' through three phases of 'barbarism' up to 'civilisation'.

These sequences depended on a generalised assumption of human 'psychic unity', which enabled anthropologists to reason backwards from an irrational 'survival' in a higher stage to the rational utilitarian practice underlying it. However, the sequences thus reconstructed by the 'comparative method' in fact assumed a polar opposition between 'primitive' and 'civilised' mentality. And in the mixed Darwinian/Lamarckian context of late nineteenth-century biological thought these cultural evolutionary sequences took on a racialist character. The human brain was seen as having been gradually enlarged by the accumulative experience of the civilising process, and the races of the world were ranked on a double scale of colour and culture (as when Tylor suggested that the Australian, Tahitian, Aztec, Chinese and Italian 'races' formed a single ascending cultural sequence). While much of day-to-day anthropological inquiry reflected a continuing interest in the ethnological affinities of different groups, what is sometimes called 'classical evolutionism' was both the theoretical cynosure and the dominant ideological influence in anthropology in the later nineteenth century.

In general, anthropological thought in the late nineteenth century attempted to subsume the study of human phenomena within positivistic natural science. However, 'anthropology' itself was by no means a trans-national scientific category. In England, the post-Darwinian intellectual synthesis of ethnological and polygenist tendencies in 'classical evolutionism' was reflected institutionally in 1871 by the unification of the Ethnological and Anthropological Societies in the Anthropological Institute. In the United States, a similarly inclusive viewpoint was evident in J. W. Powell's governmental Bureau of Ethnology (1879), which, despite its title, had as its avowed mission the organisation of 'anthropologic' research among American Indians. In principle if not always in practice, 'anthropology' in the Anglo-American tradition attempted to unify the four fields later specified by Franz Boas. By contrast, on the continent where

Darwinism did not exert such a strongly unifying influence, 'anthropology' continued to refer primarily to physical anthropology. Although Broca's École d'Anthropologie included chairs in sociology and ethnology, those studies had for the most part a quite separate development, largely under the aegis of Emile Durkheim (1858–1917) and his students. And although by 1900 the fossil gap between existing primate forms and the anomalously large-brained Neanderthals had been narrowed by the discovery of 'Java Man', physical anthropology continued to be heavily influenced by a static, typological approach to the classification of human 'races', primarily on the basis of measurements of the human cranium, using the 'cephalic index' developed by Anders Retzius (1796–1860) in the 1840s.

4. THE CRITIQUE OF EVOLUTIONISM IN AMERICAN CULTURAL ANTHROPOLOGY

In this context, the critique of evolutionary assumption elaborated by Franz Boas between 1890 and 1910 contributed to a revolutionary re-orientation in the history of anthropology. Born of a liberal and assimilated German-Jewish family, and trained in both physics and geography, Boas began his career from a position of cultural marginality and scientific intermediacy, somewhere between the dominant positivistic naturalism on the one hand, and the romantic and *Geisteswissenschaft* traditions, on the other (an opposition classically delineated in his 1885 essay on 'The Study of Geography').

After a year of ethnogeographic fieldwork among the Baffin Island Eskimo, Boas settled in the United States, carrying on general anthropological fieldwork among the Indians of the Pacific northwest, where he worked under the auspices both of Powell's Bureau of Ethnology and a committee of the British Association for the Advancement of Science chaired by Tylor. By 1896, Boas had developed a neo-ethnological critique of 'the comparative method' of classical evolutionism. Arguing on the basis of a study of the borrowing and diffusion of cultural elements among Northwest Coast Indians, he insisted that the detailed historical investigations of specific culture histories must precede the attempt to derive laws of cultural development. Parallel to this, Boas criticised the evolutionary idea of 'primitive mentality', arguing that human thought generally was conditioned by culturally varying bodies of traditional assumption – a viewpoint sustained also by his analyses of American-Indian grammatical categories. Similarly, his physical anthropological researches – including a study of the modification of headform in the children of European immigrants – called into question racialist arguments based on cranial typology.

Boas' anthropology was characteristically critical rather than constructive. Nevertheless, his work laid the basis for the modern anthropological conception of culture as pluralistic, relativistic and largely freed from biological determinism. His student, A. L. Kroeber (1876–1960), a major articulator of the cultural viewpoint, initially invoked the autonomy of the cultural in 1917, simply as a heuristic device, and since then, there has been a recurrent anthropological interest in the culture/biology interface. But the general thrust of Boasian anthropology was to mark off a domain from which biological determinism was excluded. Initially, that delimitation depended on an insistence on the essentially historical character of cultural phenomena, as exemplified in Edward Sapir's *Time Perspective in Aboriginal American Culture: A Study of Method* (1916). But if the first generation Boasians occasionally spoke of themselves as the 'American historical school', the major thrust of Boasian anthropology after 1920 was in fact away from historical reconstruction. On the one hand, the emergence of a more time-specific archeology (with the development of stratigraphic approaches after 1910, augmented after the Second World War by carbon 14 dating) tended to devalue historical reconstructions based on the distribution of 'culture elements' over 'cultural areas'. On the other , the Boasian interest in the cultural basis of human psychological differences led towards a synchronic study of the integration of cultures and of the relation of 'culture and personality' – tendencies archetypified in Ruth Benedict's widely-influential *Patterns of Culture* (1934).

Although the 'culture and personality' movement and the study of 'acculturation' were being superseded by the 1950s by more sociologically oriented approaches, 'culture' remained the predominant focus of anthropological inquiry in the United States. As graduate training began its explosive spread beyond the four centres founded before the First World War (Harvard, Columbia, Berkeley and Pennsylvania) and the half dozen additions of the inter-war period, it usually continued to include at least introductory training in each of the 'four fields'. Most practitioners, however, had long since specialised in no more than one of them; and physical anthropologists, linguists and archeologists had, during the inter-war period, founded their own professional organisations. While the American Anthropological Association (founded in 1902) continued to include specialists in all four fields, it was dominated by those who specialised in what Boas and the first generation of his students still called 'ethnology' – which by the 1930s was in the process of being rechristened 'cultural anthropology'.

5. FIELDWORK, FUNCTIONALISM AND BRITISH SOCIAL ANTHROPOLOGY

In Great Britain, the early twentieth-century 'revolution in anthropology' took a somewhat different course. As in the United States, where the Boasians carried on and elaborated the 'fieldwork' tradition pioneered by the Bureau of Ethnology, a key factor was the development of a corps of academically-trained ethnographic fieldworkers. However, what was to become the archetypical field situation for British anthropologists differed considerably from that of their early Boasian counterparts. In the United States, where transcontinental railways facilitated relatively short visits to Indian reservations, ethnographers studied the 'memory culture' of elder informants, often by collecting 'texts' (which Boas thought might provide for a non-literate culture the equivalent of the documentary heritage that was the basis of humanistic study in the Western tradition). By contrast, British ethnographers, travelling weeks by sea to the darker reaches of the world's largest empire, became the archetypical practitioners of extended 'participant observation' of the current behaviour of still-functioning social groups. Foreshadowed in the work of Baldwin Spencer (1860–1929) and Frank Gillen (1855–1912) among the Australian Arunta in 1896, implemented among the graduates of A. C. Haddon's Torres Straits Expedition (1898) and by younger members of the 'Cambridge School' in the first decade of the century, the 'lone-ethnographer' model of inquiry was in fact formalised by W. H. R. Rivers (1864–1922) in his description of the 'concrete method' for the 1912 revision of *Notes and Queries*. The person most closely associated with this development, however, was Bronislaw Malinowski (1883–1942), who came from Poland in 1910 to study under Edward Westermarck (1862–1939) and Charles Seligman (1873–1940) at the London School of Economics. During the First World War, Malinowski spent almost two years among the Trobriand Islanders off the Northeast Coast of New Guinea, and in 1922 he gave the new methodology its mythic charter in the opening chapter of *Argonauts of the Western Pacific*.

During the 1920s, Malinowski moved briefly toward Freudian psychoanalysis by offering the matrifocal Trobriand family to suggest a modification of the universal Oedipus Complex. However, there was no British analogue to the American culture and personality movement. The latter may be regarded as offering an explanatory alternative to nineteenth-century evolutionary assertions of racial mental differences. In Britain, however, the critique of evolutionism focused not on its biological implications, but rather on its tendency, archetypified in the *Golden Bough* of James G. Frazer (1854–1941), to explain human behaviour in intellectualist utilitarian terms. By 1900, attacks had already begun on Tylor's doctrine of animism, which had explained human religious belief as a premature and failed science (with the experience of dreams and death suggesting the hypothesis of a soul distinct from the human body). Echoing William James, R. R. Marett (1866–1943) suggested a 'pre-animistic' basis of religious belief in the much more effect-laden Melanesian concept of *mana* (an awe-inspiring supernatural power manifesting itself in the natural world). During the following decade, theoretical discussion centred on the mixed socio-religious phenomenon of totemism, which McLennan had defined in 1869 in terms of the linkage of animistic belief and exogamous matrilineal social organisation. To this, William Robertson Smith (1846–1894) had added the idea of the occasional communal consumption of the totem animal – an armchair conception which to Frazer seemed confirmed ethnographically by Spencer and Gillen's research among the Arunta. In the decade before the First World War, social anthropological debate swirled about the problem of totemism, with special reference to the Arunta and other Australian data, which were assumed by evolutionists to provide evidence of the most primitive human state.

It was in this context that British anthropology, which in its Tylorian and Frazerian phase gave priority to the problem of religious belief, shifted towards the study of religious ritual, and more generally, toward the study of kinship and social organisation, which had been a special concern of the American evolutionist Lewis Henry Morgan during his pre-evolutionary 'ethnological' phase. Building on his own pioneering ethnographic study of the Iroquois in the 1840s, Morgan had attempted to solve the problem of the peopling of America by using an ethnographic questionnaire to collect world-wide data on *Systems of Consanguinity and Affinity* (1869). Recast in developmental terms, his distinction between the 'classificatory' and 'descriptive' systems of kinship provided a conceptual framework for the ethnographic work of his Australian correspondents Lorimer Fison (1832–1907) and A. W. Howitt (1830–1908). Augmented by the 'genealogical method' developed by Rivers in the Torres Straits in 1898, Morgan's approach was eventually to provide the conceptual groundwork for modern British social anthropology, although not, however, until it had been detached from its diachronic evolutionary framework.

That process took place in two phases in the work of Rivers and his student A. R. Radcliffe-Brown (1881–1955). Rivers himself underwent a 'conversion' from evolutionism to a diffusionary 'ethnological analysis of culture' in 1911. However, his attempt to reconstruct *The History of Melanesian Society* (1916) was still heavily dependent on the evolutionary concept of 'survival' which assumed that certain existing social customs or kinship terms need not be explained in terms of their present function, but rather in terms of their correspondence with prior social organisational forms. In contrast, Radcliffe-Brown moved away from evolutionism via the more functionalist sociology of Emile Durkheim. His break with Rivers focused specifically on the utility of 'survivals' in sociological analysis, and involved a general rejection of any 'conjectural' approach to diachronic problems in 'social anthropology', which in 1923 he took some pains to differentiate from 'ethnology'.

At that time British anthropology was excited by the confrontation between the 'heliolithic' diffusionism of Rivers's disciples Grafton Elliot Smith (1871–1937) and William Perry (1889–1940) at University College London and the psycho-biological functionalism of Malinowski at the London School of Economics. Sustained by grants from the Rockefeller Foundation, Malinowskian functionalism had, by 1930, become the dominant British current. But during the next few years some of Malinowski's more important students shifted their theoretical allegiance to Radcliffe-Brown, who after two decades of academic wanderings (from Cape Town to Sydney to Chicago), finally succeeded in 1937 to the chair at Oxford. Although the Association of Social Anthropologists formed at Oxford in 1946 included representatives of several different viewpoints, it was Radcliffe-Brown's synchronic natural scientific study of 'social systems' – overlaid upon the Malinowskian fieldwork tradition – that gave British social anthropology its distinctive character.

6. THE SYNCHRONIC REVOLUTION, THE 'CLASSICAL PERIOD' AND THE EMERGENCE OF INTERNATIONAL ANTHROPOLOGY

Despite these differences of phase and focus, there were many common features in the development of British social and American cultural anthropology in the first half of the twentieth century. In both countries, anthropology in the pre-academic museum period had been oriented largely towards the collection of material objects (whether artefacts or bones) carried into the present from the past; in both cases there was a dramatic turn towards the observational study of behaviour in the present. Although an interest in evolutionary or historical questions never disappeared entirely from either national tradition, anthropological inquiry was no longer primarily conceived in diachronic terms. And while Radcliffe-Brown insisted, during his Chicago period, on the differences between his viewpoint and the more dilute 'functionalism' of some American cultural anthropologists, there is a looser sense in which one may speak of synchronic functionalism as a paradigm in the Anglo-American tradition. This was even more the case after the Second World War, when American anthropologists went overseas in large numbers for fieldwork, and began at home to feel the influence of functionalist theory in American sociology.

In both countries, one may speak of anthropology as having become 'ethnographicised'. Although the goal of cross-cultural comparison and scientific generalisation continued to be acknowledged, the most distinctive common feature of Anglo-American anthropology in what may be called its 'classical' period (c. 1925–c. 1965) was the central role of ethnographic fieldwork. Rather than providing items of information for armchair anthropological theorists, fieldwork became the certifying criterion of membership in the anthropological community and the underpinning of its central methodological values; i.e. participant observation in small-scale communities, conceived holistically and relativistically, and given a privileged role in the constitution of theory. In both countries, this ethnographically-oriented study of social and cultural behaviour tended to separate from and to dominate the other anthropological subdisciplines, although in the more pluralistic structure of American academic life, the ideal of a 'general anthropology' uniting the traditional 'four fields' continued to have a certain potency.

Elsewhere, however, the course of sub-disciplinary development was rather different. On the European continent, where the inclusive 'four field' tradition had never taken root, physical anthropology continued to have a largely separate development on into the twentieth century, and to be relatively unaffected by the Boasian critique – especially in Germany, where during the Nazi period, the discipline was redefined as *'Rassenkunde'*. In Germany and in central Europe, the ethnological tradition continued to be strongly diffusionist and historical up until the mid-twentieth century, although some ethnographic fieldwork was carried on. In France a modern ethnographic tradition did not develop until after the founding in the 1920s of the Institut d'Ethnologie, in which Durkheim's nephew Marcel Mauss played a leading role. It was not until 1982 that the French equivalents of cultural anthropologists were to take the lead in founding the Société d'Anthropologie française after the American model. This development reflected not only the intellectual interchange that had occurred between the French and the Anglo-American traditions after 1960 under the influence of the 'structuralism' of Claude Lévi-Strauss (b. 1909) but also the influence of a tendency that can be called 'international anthropology', or the internationalisation of the Anglo-American tradition.

Although international congresses of 'anthropologists' or 'prehistorians' or 'Americanists' had been held periodically since the 1860s, it is only since the Second World War that International Congresses of Anthropological and Ethnological Sciences have been held on a regular basis over a long period (in Philadelphia, Moscow, Tokyo, Chicago, Vancouver, Delhi and Zagreb). Reinforced after 1960 by the international journal *Current Anthropology*, edited by Sol Tax (b. 1907), these congresses have been at the same time forums for diversity and media for the diffusion of a certain homogenising tendency, in which socio-cultural anthropology in the emergent Anglo-Franco-American mode has predominated, but the other major sub-disciplines have continued to be represented. However, the embracive 'four field' conception associated with the American tradition has still had a certain inertial influence, reinforced by the overwhelming numerical predominance of American anthropologists within the world anthropological community.

7. THE 'CRISIS' AND 'REINVENTION' OF ANTHROPOLOGY

In the very period in which an 'international anthropology' began to be realised, however, there were dramatic changes in the world historical relationship of the peoples who had traditionally provided the scholars and the subject-matter of anthropological inquiry. For more than a century, the anticipated disappearance of 'savage' (or 'primitive' or 'tribal' or 'pre-literate') peoples under the impact of European expansion had been a major impetus to ethnographic research, which was carried on under an umbrella of colonial power. By the 1930s, these categories had already become problematic, and field research was beginning to be undertaken in 'complex' societies. But despite the postwar interest in peasant communities and the processes of 'modernisation', anthropology retained its archetypically asymmetrical character, as a study of dark-skinned 'others' by light-skinned Euro-Americans. With the end of colonial empires, however, the peoples anthropologists had traditionally studied were now part of 'new nations' oriented towards rapid socio-cultural change and their leaders were often unreceptive to an inquiry which, even after the critique of evolutionary racial assumption, continued to be premised on socio-cultural asymmetry. Indeed, many Third World intellectuals now began to regard as ideologically retrograde (and even as racist) the characteristic modern anthropological attitude of relativistic tolerance of cultural differences. What had served in the 1930s to defend 'others' against racialism seemed now to justify the perpetuation of a backwardness founded on exploitation. In the politically-charged context of major episodes of post-colonial warfare, there had developed by the late 1960s what some were inclined to call the 'crisis of anthropology'.

The sense of malaise – which was widespread in the human sciences – manifested itself in a number of ways: substantively, ideologically, methodologically, epistemologically, theoretically, demographically and institutionally. In the face of rapid social change and restrictions on access to field sites, it was no longer realistic, even normatively, to regard the recovery of pure, uncontaminated non-European 'otherness' as the privileged substantive focus of anthropological inquiry. Nor was it possible to regard such inquiry as ethically neutral, or innocent of political consequences. A new consciousness of the inherently problematic reflexivity of participant observation called into question both the methodological and epistemological assumptions of traditional ethnographic fieldwork. In the context of a general questioning of positivist assumption in the human sciences, there were signs of a shift from homeostatic theoretical orientations to more dynamic ones. And even the very growth of the field was now a problem, as the government funding of the 1950s and 1960s began to be restricted, and PhDs began to overflow their accustomed academic niches, beyond which anthropology had yet to establish a viable claim to significant domestic social utility. In the face of predictions of the 'end of anthropology', there were, by the early 1970s, radical calls for its 'reinvention'.

The majority of anthropologists, however – reflecting either a residue of prelapsarian confidence or a sense of the weight of institutional inertia – seem to have taken for granted that the discipline would carry on indefinitely. And indeed, it seemed clear that by the mid-1980s, the crisis had been domesticated.

A decade after the call for the discipline's 'reinvention', the major academic anthropology departments continued to carry on a kind of 'business as usual', despite the difficulties of funding research and the still-constricted job market for the students they were training. Nevertheless, it seems clear that the 'classical' period of modern anthropology had come to an end sometime after 1960, and the usual business of post-classical anthropology differed in significant respects from what had gone before.

8. REFLEXIVITY, FISSION AND THE DUALISM OF THE ANTHROPOLOGICAL TRADITION

At the demographic centre of the discipline in the United States, the centrifugal forces observed by Boas in 1904 had multiplied. It was no longer a question simply of the coherence of the four major subdisciplines, but of a multiplication of 'adjectival anthropologies' (applied, cognitive, dental, economic, educational, feminist, historical, humanistic, medical, nutritional, philosophical, political, psychological, symbolic, urban, etc.) – many of them organised into their own national societies. And while it was possible to interpret this proliferation as a sign of the continued adaptive vigour (or the successful reinvention) of the disciplinary impulse, there was inevitably concern about how, in the last decade of the twentieth century, that impulse might be defined.

Once the reflexivity implied in the original anthropological impulse had been raised permanently to disciplinary consciousness, and the forces of sociocultural change had removed many of the more obvious distinctions on which an asymmetrical anthropology had been premised, it was clear that 'anthropology pure and simple' would *not* 'deal with the customs and beliefs of the less civilised peoples only'. But it was less clear how a more anthropologically-embracive study would be carried on. In many situations, both in the developing countries and the traditional centres of the discipline, the line between anthropology and applied sociology was no longer clear. At the same time, the traditional concern with exotic 'otherness' persisted, although now once again historically and textually oriented, in the context of rapid cultural change and the reaction against positivistic natural scientific models. Not only were particular cultural groups beginning to be studied in more historical terms, but the distinctive features of 'otherness' itself – including now the notion of the 'tribe' – were beginning to be seen as contingent products of the historical interaction of European and non-European peoples in the context of world historical processes. As the manifestly observable differences between peoples diminished, culture was pursued into the crevices of encroaching homogeneity. In this context, there was an increasing sense of the problematic character of the central concept in terms of which 'otherness' had long been interpreted by anthropologists.

For more than a century, the idea of culture had been the single most powerful cohesive force in anthropological inquiry. Although that concept was relativised and given an autonomous determinism by the Boasian critique of evolutionary racial assumption, biological and evolutionary concerns were not eliminated from anthropology. And while a systematic evolutionary viewpoint was slow to inform physical anthropology and archeology, the period after the Second World War saw important developments in the field of 'paleo-anthropology', as well as the resurgence of a submerged neo-evolutionary tendency within American cultural anthropology. During the same years, in the context of a closer association with Parsonian sociology, cultural anthropologists began to think more seriously about just what 'culture' was. By the end of the 1960s, a conceptual polarisation was beginning to be evident. On the one hand, there was a tendency – most strikingly evident in what came to be called symbolic anthropology – to treat cultures in humanistic idealist terms as 'systems of symbols and meanings', with relatively little concern for the adaptive, utilitarian aspect of cultural behaviour. On the other hand, there was a materialist countercurrent which insisted that culture must be understood scientifically in adaptive evolutionary terms, whether in the form of 'techno-environmental determinism', or in the even more controversial form of 'socio-biology', which seemed to many to threaten a resurgence of racialist thought in the human sciences.

Although the vast majority of American anthropologists came to the defence of Margaret Mead (1901–76) when a critique of her Samoan fieldwork was generalised as an attack on the notion of cultural determinism, it is by no means clear that the ambiguities of the culture concept have been resolved. Indeed, it might be argued that beneath the recent polarisation lies the paradigmatic opposition that characterised thinking about human differences prior to the early twentieth-century 'revolution in anthropology'. In the case of Graeco-Roman developmentalism, the continuity with neo-evolutionism is manifest; in the case of the biblical/ethnological paradigm, it is less clear cut. But the fact that the emergence of symbolic and 'interpretive' anthropology is spoken of as the 'hermeneutic' turn, and also the fact of preoccupation with linguistic phenomena, suggest a level at which it may exist. Be that as it may, the historically constituted epistemic dualism underlying modern anthropology is real enough, and seems likely to endure. From this point of view, Boas – who in other writings insisted on the independent legitimacy of both the *natur-* and the *geisteswissenschaftliche* approaches to the study of human phenomena – may perhaps serve as a guide to the future as well as to the past of the discipline.

NOTES

1. F. Boas, 'The history of anthropology', as reprinted in G. Stocking, (ed.), *The shaping of American anthropology, 1883–1911: a Franz Boas reader* (New York, 1974), p. 35.
2. C. Geertz, *The interpretation of cultures* (New York, 1973), p. 22.

3. J. Speed, 'The genealogies of holy scriptures', in *The Holy Bible: a facsimile in a reduced size of the authorised version published in the year 1611* (Oxford, 1911), no. 2.

4. J. Rousseau, *Discourse on the origin and foundations of inequality*, in R. D. Masters, (ed.), *The first and second discourses* (New York, 1964), p. 211.

FURTHER READING

P. J. Bowler, *Theories of human evolution. A century of debate, 1844–1944* (Baltimore, 1986; Oxford, 1987).

C. Hinsley, *Savages and scientists: the Smithsonian Institution and the development of American anthropology, 1846–1910* (Washington, DC, 1981).

M. Hodgen, *Early anthropology in the sixteenth and seventeenth centuries* (Philadelphia, 1964).

R. Kemper and J. Phinney, (eds.), *The history of anthropology: a research bibliography* (New York, 1977).

B. Rupp-Eisenreich, (ed.), *Histoires de l'anthropologie (xvi⁻–xix⁻ siècles)* (Paris, 1984).

J. S. Slotkin, (ed.), *Readings in early anthropology* (Chicago, 1965).

W. Stanton, *The leopard's spots: scientific attitudes toward race in America, 1815–1859* (Chicago, 1960).

G. Stocking, Jr., *Race, culture and evolution: essays in the history of anthropology* (New York, 1968).

—— (ed.), *The shaping of American anthropology, 1883–1911: a Franz Boas Reader* (New York, 1974).

—— (ed.), *Observers observed: essays on ethnographic fieldwork [History of Anthropology, vol. 1]* (Madison, Wis., 1983).

—— (ed.), *Functionalism historicized: essays on British social anthropology [History of Anthropology, vol. 2]* (Madison, Wis., 1984).

—— (ed.), *Objects and others: essays on museums and material culture [History of Anthropology, vol. 3]* (Madison, Wis., 1985).

—— (ed.), *Malinowski, Rivers, Benedict and others: essays on culture and personality [History of Anthropology, vol. 4]* (Madison, Wis., 1986).

—— *Victorian anthropology* (New York, 1987).

—— (ed.), *Bones, bodies, behavior: essays on biological anthropology [History of Anthropology vol. 5]* (Madison, Wis., 1988).

48

PHYSIOLOGY AND EXPERIMENTAL MEDICINE

JOHN V. PICKSTONE

In common with all scientific disciplines, physiology can be characterised at two levels: as a set of claims about an aspect of nature, or as a set of people and institutions which produce and reproduce such claims. Since the content and the scope of the claims has varied over time, together with the social collectives concerned, definitions are bound to be elusive. But for about the last century, 'physiology' has usually meant a set of propositions about the *functioning* of human and animal bodies, established by means of experiment. 'Physiologists' have been laboratory-based investigators, usually in medical schools. The workings of *plants* are not normally included; the term *general physiology* usually directs attention to the cellular level and to properties which animals and plants have in common, but even here the emphasis tends to remain on animal, especially higher animal, cells.

In the sense just given, 'physiology' is largely synonymous with 'experimental physiology'. It is a meaning developed in the middle of the last century, largely by German academics who, distancing themselves from anatomy and zoology, regarded their work as a basis for medicine, and saw chemistry and histology as ancillary methods in the experimental establishment of body functions. Physiology, so understood, was a paradigm for the investigation of complex systems; it stood, with the new experimental physics, as part of the frontier of science in the late nineteenth century.

By 1900, experimental physiology was firmly institutionalised in the medical schools of Europe and the United States. Since then, its identity has become less clear, mainly through the differentiation of disciplines which were, at least in part, its offspring. Differentiation could be by method and cognate physical disciplines (for example, biochemistry or biophysics), or by division according to 'systems' (for example, nutrition, endocrinology or neuro-sciences), in which aspects of physiology have been variously combined with adjacent aspects of other pre-clinical and clinical sciences.

However, even when the identity of 'experimental physiology' was clear as a medical school discipline, the word 'physiology' on its own had a much wider currency that historians neglect at their peril. Popular works on physiology taught lay men and women how their bodies functioned and how such functions were best maintained. Such books were influenced by scientific novelties and by the standing of medical science, but they were also part of a long tradition of advice manuals – guides to the 'nature' of men and women.

1. MEDICAL THEORY

The etymological root of 'physiology' is 'study of nature'; it meant 'natural philosophy'. But within the medical tradition of classical Greece it could refer more specifically to that part of nature which was relevant to medicine – the nature of man. In renaissance Europe this meaning of physiology became stabilised: physiology was the theoretical part of medicine, dealing with the normal and abnormal workings of the body. Thus the great masters of eighteenth-century medicine, Boerhaave in Leiden and Haller in Göttingen, taught physiology in this sense; such was also the case at Montpellier or Edinburgh. In the latter, William Cullen was professor of the 'Institutes of Medicine'. It was in these contexts that new models of the body were explored. Boerhaave preferred mechanism; Haller and the Montpellier school were vitalists; Cullen developed a species of vitalism based on the operations of the nervous system as mediating between environment and organism, body and mind. Such synthetic systems were designed to give order to the observations of medical men and to relate them to the structures uncovered by anatomists. The general mode of medical theorising remained within the classical scheme of *balance*; balance within the organism and between the organism and its environment. The preferred model could shift from mechanical tubes and chemistry (as preferred in the scientific revolution), to tension or slackness of fibres, or to degrees of irritability or to the heightened or depressed activity of the nerves, but the doctrines were generally holistic, environmentalist and tending to a linear scale of excess or deficit.

It would, however, be wrong to see these systems as wholly arbitrary or lacking in new empirical content. The work of Harvey (see art. 36) and his followers in the seventeenth century had radically altered man's understanding of the functions of the heart and the lungs. Whatever means one chose to try to explain the contractions of the heart, it was agreed that the blood circulated out through the arteries and back through the veins; the arteries carried nutriment and vital spirits to the various organs and the veins carried away blood altered by these organs. This involved a substantial shift from the Greek position. So, too, did the discoveries of lacteal and lymphatic vessels during the seventeenth and eighteenth centuries. Here were new systems which served, respectively, in the absorption of food from the gut, and for the absorption of fluids from skin or other organs.

The new knowledge was derived from anatomy and also from microscopy, chemistry and mechanics. Some of it involved experiments on living organisms, notably Harvey's demonstrations of the circulation. Harvey had shown these experiments to surgeons; they could also be demonstrated to students. And, of course, several of the medical teachers themselves sought new knowledge through experimentation. William Hunter and his colleagues in London not only explored the lymphatics anatomically, they also experimented to show their role in absorption. Haller's most famous treatise reported whole series of experiments designed to show that muscle was irritable (i.e., it responded to stimulation by contraction), but that only the nervous system was sensitive (i.e., it gave rise to sensation). By and large, the body of such experiments can properly be referred to as 'animated anatomy'. The investigators tried to show organs in action, believing that each anatomical system was responsible for a particular body function.

The medical theorists of the eighteenth century have provided a popular subject for historians of a philosophical persuasion and Lester King's work provides an excellent introduction. There is relatively little, however, published on the *social* history of the major medical schools. Here, perhaps, Edinburgh leads the way, for there is now an extensive literature on the Scottish Enlightenment which combines intellectual, social and political perspectives. For studies of medicine, Chris Lawrence's work is outstanding. A recent collection on William Hunter helps extend this analysis to London and gives entry to other contemporary schools (e.g. Halle).[1]

2. PHYSIOLOGY BETWEEN 1789 AND 1830

Before we explore this break with 'medical theory', we should perhaps emphasise the strong continuities between eighteenth-century physiology and much of the teaching in medical schools during the nineteenth century.

In Germany, with the renewal of the university system after the battle of Jena, medicine came to share in a strong intellectualist tradition which gave social status rather than practical knowledge. Some medical theorists became *Naturphilosophen*; transcendental anatomy developed, seeking symmetries, recurrent patterns and underlying models; so too did the science of subjective sensation. Morphology and psychology remained strongly German sciences, but they also had followers in France and Britain, and one should be wary of separating German medicine too deeply from that of the rest of Europe. It used to be fashionable to depict German medicine as lost in speculation until at least the 1830s, but this habit is yielding before new investigations, particularly the recent work of Lenoir, who has stressed the strong continuity of empirical yet teleological 'biology' extending from late eighteenth-century Göttingen to the Berlin of Johannes Müller around 1840.[2]

Lenoir concentrated on the German attempts at a science of development; one which would encompass the *series* of adult animals (from simple to complex), as well as the developmental stages of higher animals. It would cover function as well as form, variety (and taxonomy) as well as individual anatomy. But Lenoir's study is largely at the level of ideas, and it does not explore the linkages of medicine to this general programme for life sciences; we still need more detailed and more social historical studies of the major German schools. But in as much as many of Lenoir's subjects were professors of anatomy (or anatomy and physiology), their orientation. one presumes, helped provide a theoretical context for early nineteenth-century German medicine.

It was not until about 1840 that the laboratories of these anatomists/physiologists/zoologists produced young investigators who wished to specialise in a newly-defined, narrower, physiology. For them, functions were not to be understood within a systemic view of animal life, but as physical and chemical products of the structures concerned.

In Britain, there were scarcely any *separate* institutions for 'physiology' until after about 1840, and no substantial positions in medical schools until the 1870s. Until then, 'physiology' was a subject taught by young clinicians to medical students. The subject remained largely anatomical in its orientation, though with a substantial contribution from medical chemistry. (See art. 31, sect. 1.) This was because the new schools which grew up in London and the English provinces were based on anatomy schools, and because alternative approaches, especially vivisection, were more problematical in Britain than in France.

Initially the anatomical base was that worked out by the Hunterian surgeon/anatomists, including comparative anatomy. From about 1830, the 'advanced' London institutions, notably the new *university* medical schools, began teaching French 'general anatomy' – the tissue doctrines we shall shortly describe. At about the same time, microscopy began to increase in popularity, as better instruments became available. Here was a novel, scientific, relatively uncontentious way to study form and deduce function. Some of the teachers concerned were able to add new knowledge, and some medical practitioners carried out physiological experiments as a hobby, but most of the information was coming from Europe, from the broad life-science of Germany, where microscopy was rapidly taken up, and from the more specifically medical physiology produced in France by Marie-François-Xavier Bichat (1771–1802) and, especially, François Magendie (1783–1855). The historiography of physiology in England was, until recently, illumined by only two or three (good) papers; Stephen Jacyna is now advancing our knowledge considerably.[3] The historiography of French physiology has long been seen as crucial, and is correspondingly contentious.

There are several reasons for this concentration on France. When history of physiology was mostly written by physiologists, they usually presented François Magendie as the pioneer of their discipline. His pupil, Claude Bernard, was the more sophisticated French exponent, but it was Magendie who had set himself up as a prophet of experimental physiology. He had started a journal for physiology and he had cut himself off from the 'vitalism' and 'systems' of Bichat, in which he was raised. German physiologists might see Ludwig as the major influence on by far the largest school, but British physiologists tended to hark back to William Harvey as the founder of experimentalism. However, Magendie could clearly not be neglected. He was, in fact, explored by one of the founders of modern historiography of medicine, Owsei Temkin, who, together with Erwin Ackerknecht and Erwin Rosen, laid the basis for our understanding of the transformations of physiology (and of medicine) around 1800. Their initial emphasis, though always broad, was philosophical. What were the intellectual roots of Magendie's attitudes to physiological experiment and explanation? How should we distinguish and classify the 'vitalisms' and 'materialism' seen in the French and German traditions?

But these historians were also concerned with the context of this new French physiology – the post-Revolutionary Paris School of Medicine. Such doctors as Laennec and Corvisart had pioneered a view of disease as localised organic lesion, and thousands of medical students had regarded a trip to the Paris schools as a necessary part of their training. How were historians to explain these events, and how might they be related to Magendie's advocacy of experimental physiology?[4]

The issues have been further heightened over the last two decades by the writing of Michel Foucault. He achieved his greatest fame for studies of power and knowledge manifest in attitudes to prisons and sexuality. His early 'historical' work included a study of transformations in natural history and in zoology, plus a book on 'The Birth of the Clinic'. Foucault's claims were anti-historical; he looked for structures of understanding and for medicine, he reported major shifts around 1800. Indeed, he saw the contemporary shift in natural history/zoology as part of a general re-orientation of epistemological structures also evidenced in the study of language and economics.[5]

Foucault did not attend to details, nor to the concordance or otherwise of his different books. British and American historians have shown a wide range of reactions. Some dismiss Foucault and his followers as continental obscurantists, careless of real history, while others maintain that he produced insights of major significance and ways of understanding shifts in deep logic which shallower continuities may hide. The issue is open as yet; there are only a few studies which have shown how structuralist insights can animate historiography which nevertheless meets the evidential standards of more empirical schools.

It was Temkin who showed that the new view of internal disease was essentially an internalisation of the view taken previously by surgeons of *external* lesions. Now physicians would also seek for lesions *within* the body. These could be found by post-mortem examination, or they could be 'sounded-for', in life, using stethoscopes or other techniques of clinical examination. Temkin's suggestion about experimental physiology, recently elaborated by Lesch, was that it too should be seen as a product of surgery – vivisection was surgical technique turned to investigation rather than remedy.

Lesch develops this suggestion by emphasising Magendie's debt to the experiments on death which Bichat described in the latter half of his book *Recherches Physiologiques sur la vie et la Mort* (1800) a work which also contains Bichat's views on vital properties. Lesch thus depicts a double Bichat, who wrote vitalism for physicians, but who could also devise a new kind of experimental physiology which appealed to surgeons. This interpretation stands opposed to the more traditional view, which has stressed the unity of Bichat's work and the distance between it and Magendie's experimentalism. Both Albury and Pickstone have recently underlined that view in seeking to understand the epistemological and social gaps between Bichat and Magendie. The points at issue here are of general interest, deserving more exploration both for Paris and for other medical capitals. They involve the place of physiology at the level of disciplines and institutions, but also in relation to changing models of society.[6]

In early nineteenth-century France, physiology sat uncomfortably between medicine, natural science and popular culture. Magendie had support from the zoologist Cuvier and the physicist Laplace, but there was no separate section for physiology in the Academy of Sciences. The term 'physiology' became widespread – e.g. in Brillat-Savarin's *Physiologie du Gout* or in Balzac's *Physiologie du Mariage* and it served as talisman for naturalistic approaches to man. It was also the title for various synthetic activities in life sciences, for which the term 'biology' would later be used, but the role of experimental physiology in medicine remained peripheral. Magendie regarded his experiments as the only sure way to a scientific medicine; he worked extensively in experimental pharmacology, which was of more direct service to medical practitioners. His results were taken up by medical teachers, but his attempts to institutionalise the discipline were only a partial success.

The procedures of physiology were regularised in Germany and it was there that independent institutes of physiology became widespread in universities, thus setting a pattern for Britain, America and, indeed, France. Unfortunately we know relatively little about the social history of this movement, or even about the details of its intellectual history. Students will still depend largely on Rothschuh, supplemented by the articles of Cranefield and others on 'reductionism' around 1848. For fuller knowledge we shall have to await the extension to Germany of the rounded historical investigations now available for British physiology and some aspects of the history of physiology in France.[7]

The key institution appears to have been the Berlin laboratory of Johannes Müller (1801–58) where, in the 1830s and 1840s, a whole series of anatomists, physiologists and zoologists were trained. It was here that the German 'biological' tradition began to fragment, along with the synthetic teleological programme which had served to unify it.

It is usual to cite here the 'group of four' – Helmholtz, Brücke, Du Bois-Reymond and Ludwig – whose fraternity in physiology dated from about 1848, when they were also involved in political liberalism. The first three were students of Müller; all went on, via positions which combined physiology with anatomy or pathology, to head institutes devoted to physiology alone. Helmhotz, of course, then moved on to physics; Du Bois-Reymond became distinguished and relatively unproductive; Brücke, in Vienna, worked on a wide range of topics, anatomical as well as physiological; Ludwig, especially at Leipzig, educated over two hundred collaborators, including a large proportion of the next generation of physiologists. Institutes of chemistry became widespread around the mid-century; while separate physiological institutes became common from the 1860s.

These developments in physiology have provided one of the classic case-studies in historical sociology of science: the arguments by Joseph Ben-David and his collaborators that disciplinary growth took place chiefly because of competition between the universities. Germany, in contrast to France, was pictured as having a highly pluralist, emulative system where the prestige of research was established; universities sought out bright young physiologists to head new institutes. Thus, for a few decades, the products of older laboratories (e.g. Müller's at Berlin), found rewarding posts with relative ease, and physiology was established as a separate discipline throughout the whole of the system. Once this system was 'full', matters became more difficult. Typically, young men trained in physiology then moved into related fields, taking with them the methods and presumptions of the parent discipline. In some cases the effect would be the renovation of existing subjects, e.g. the growth of experimentalism in embryology. More promising were new subjects, such as hygiene, for which there was official demand. The growth of clinical science, which we will discuss later, owes something to this 'out-migration' from classical physiology.[8]

This general model has been very useful. But historians have begun to question its assumptions and to ask deeper questions about control of university appointments. Steven Turner, for early nineteenth-century Prussia, has emphasised the power of the Ministry of Culture to over-ride the wishes of university staff. Research reputation was indeed translated into appointments but not, in this case at least, by free competition between universities. One enters a world of real politics.[9]

Turner's work is not particularly concerned with physiology or medicine; very little (English) writing is. A notable and promising exception is the recent study by Arleen Tuchmann on Heidelberg University, exploring the replacement in 1843 of Friedrich Tiedemann by Jacob Henle and Karl Pfeufer. University medical faculties, at least in Baden, were under pressure to provide a more 'practical' education; there was competition from surgical schools; students wanted more modern courses and so did the (industrial-bourgeois) state authorities. 'Practical' and 'modern' here meant clinical methods (French school), plus microscopy (at which Henle was accomplished). Tuchmann then goes on to discuss the perceived pros and cons of a distinctively 'experimental' physiology.[10]

3. CLAUDE BERNARD

Claude Bernard (1813–78) has been a favourite subject for historians, philosophers and for physiologists. All three groups have analysed, repeatedly, the *Introduction to the Study of Experimental Medicine*, where Bernard made the case for physiology as an experimental subject, transcending the observations of clinical medicine, anatomy or natural history. The book presents a hypothetico-deductive account of science which has attracted philosophers. It is also the basic text for the notion of experimental 'control'. This can mean the careful regulation of experimental procedure by which a phenomenon can be *controlled* at will. More specifically, Bernard described the control experiment, i.e., that in which the animal suffers all but the single interference in question, so allowing the experimenter to separate the specific effect from others which the whole procedure may involve. Bernard argued for the *determinism* of physiological phenomena, in the sense that experimentalists could produce and reproduce them in specified ways.

These two linked notions were of enormous importance, way beyond the single discipline of physiology. So, too, on a different level, was the idea of *homeostasis* (Walter Cannon's term) which Bernard introduced in his famous statement that the fixity of the internal 'milieu' was the condition of the free life. This meant, roughly, that the constancy of body fluids in higher animals was the precondition of their sophisticated functions and their relative independence of external factors such as temperature.

The interest of Bernard's book also derives from his use of his own experiments to illustrate his themes. Historians have amused themselves comparing these accounts with the original published papers or, better, the laboratory notebooks; Bernard, like many investigators, tailored the examples when preaching. Holmes has gone beyond this level, to provide a meticulous reconstruction of Bernard's work in animal chemistry, and he continues to devote himself to this fine detail of historical analysis. Others are now concentrating on a broader, institutional analysis, so situating more precisely Bernard's advocacy of French science, particularly physiology.

Bernard, like his master, worked at the margins of medicine. The Collège de France was his main base, the Société de Biologie, a group of science-minded doctors, being his immediate reference group during his formative years as an investigator. His physiology was carefully placed with respect to existing disciplines and power-bases. It was experimental and so transcended natural history, though Bernard also lectured on general physiology (which for him meant the physiology of tissues). His chemical studies were not organic chemistry (and so went beyond Dumas and his school), because there was no guarantee that chemical processes in living bodies followed the patterns seen *in vitro*. He looked down on *clinical* medicine, for that had relied on collections of observations which, even in statistical form, gave no basis for certitude. Hypotheses and experimental tests were the royal road to an understanding of the body which would allow control of physiological and pathological processes.[11]

The immediate context was France in the 1860s, worried about German supremacy, her scientific and medical institutions little changed from the Revolutionary period. Through the work of Weisz and Coleman we are beginning to understand more thoroughly the objects of the rhetoric and the reasons for its lack of effect.[12]

4. THE INSTITUTIONALISATION OF PHYSIOLOGY IN BRITAIN AND THE UNITED STATES

It is, perhaps, for Britain that some of the best historiography of physiology has been produced. In part, this is because the main historical work has been carried out later and so has benefited both from the strong traditions of British social history and from the growth of the 'Darwin industry'. More recently it has begun to benefit from increased attention to medical education and to government support for science.

The key studies are by Richard French and Gerald Geison. The former began by exploring the comparative physiology of Romanes, but went on to produce a full social history of the anti-vivisection movement, which heavily conditioned the growth of animal experimentation in Britain. Geison provided a monograph on the Cambridge school of physiology, established by Michael Foster in the 1870s and of continuing importance within this peculiarly 'clubby' discipline. It is through Geison's work that we can see the characteristic dynamics of the discipline during its formative decades in Britain.[13]

At this time, the British university system was changing rapidly. Cambridge, and to some extent Oxford, was developing natural sciences, pulled one way by internal reformers and pushed in another by external criticisms displayed in governmental reports. In the provinces, university colleges were developing, initially under the auspices of the University of London. From about 1880, these became separate (or federal) institutions which tended to incorporate the local, private, medical schools. The regulation of medical qualifications under the Act of 1858, allowed medical educators to raise standards of entry to medicine, increasing the amount of science expected of medical students.

Thus Oxford and Cambridge, provincial medical faculties and the London medical schools came to provide the main characteristic English locations for the development of physiology. We should not forget, though, the Scottish universities, or the importance of largely non-medical institutions, such as state colleges at South Kensington, the Fullerian chair at the (charitable) Royal Institution and the prestigious Royal Society.[14]

Physiology, as a separate discipline, fared best in Cambridge, which, together with Oxford and University College London, came to dominate the Physiological Society. To a much greater extent than say chemistry, physiology was a metropolitan discipline; only Edinburgh and Liverpool were significant exceptions to that pattern. The reasons are fairly clear. In Cambridge, and especially at Trinity College, there was financial support for bio-medical sciences; good students were available because they intended to go on to medicine. There were a few prestigious clinicians to lend support but there was no medical faculty and hence no overwhelming concern with practice. Physiology therefore developed in parallel with physics; it claimed support through links with Darwinian biology and at Cambridge, much of the work involved experiments on lower animals, thought to show more clearly (in principle, or merely as a matter of fact) the fundamental nature of phenomena such as the heartbeat. Thus was established a tradition of research on nerve and muscle which helped give British physiology world standing by the beginning of the twentieth century.

In Manchester, by contrast, as Stella Butler has shown, the full-time physiologist tended to become a teacher and administrator. Neither his students nor his clinical colleagues had much time for laboratory science.[15]

By the end of the century the position had changed a little. Physiology in Oxford was established; there were also laboratories in most of the London medical schools. In Liverpool, C. S. Sherrington was investigating reflexes, part of a massive programme of research which he continued later at Oxford. At Liverpool he was part of a development in medical sciences that included public health, bacteriology, biochemistry and tropical medicine. By the 1890s, partly because of the new bacteriology, medical science was acquiring the power to draw large investment from industrialists (especially as legacies). At University College London, Ernest Starling acquired a new laboratory institute and was able to develop the department's teaching and research considerably. We shall return below to the question of physiology's direct utility.

The work on the heart, in Cambridge and London, as well as the work of Starling (and William Bayliss) on hormones, was clearly opening up new means of exploring and explaining medical phenomena. Physiologists were then presenting patterns of integrated activity which matched the turn of century emphasis on co-ordination and efficiency in economic and political life.[16]

In the United States the pattern was not dissimilar. The models were mostly German, though with some specifically British components. Our historical knowledge of the art comes as yet, largely from institutional studies and biographies; the recent volume edited by Gerald Geison is particularly useful.

Again, physiology as a discipline was closely tied to the development of new forms of medical education. To the extent that the scientification of medical schools took place before 1900, physiology was a major beneficiary. In the schools which were 'renovated' in the twentieth century, biochemistry, as the subject of the day, was the more usual bridge between scientific and clinical concerns. Robert Kohler's work on biochemistry, in Europe as well as in the United States, is exemplary in its attention to the institutional dynamics of discipline formation.

The Johns Hopkins University in Baltimore was the model institution for new medical science and medical teaching in the United States. Its funds came from an industrialist while its spirit came from educators and doctors who had studied in Germany. When a new medical school was attached, its major figures were a pathologist/bacteriologist (Welch), a scientific surgeon (Halsted), an anatomist (Mall) and an encyclopaedic physician (Osler). Experimental physiology was taught, from 1876, by Henry Newell-Martin, an Irishman who had been a protégé of Huxley and of Foster. Martin was appointed to a chair of 'biology'; but his successor, W. H. Howell, was clearly identified with 'physiology', having studied with Ludwig as well as with Martin.

At Harvard, another Ludwig student, H. P. Bowditch, was appointed in 1871, becoming a full professor of physiology in 1876. He trained many of the experimentalists who took the newly-created chairs in the 1890s. The American Physiological Society was founded in 1887, and by the First World War, American physiology was well established. World-famous figures included two more products of Harvard: W. B. Cannon, disciple and successor of Bowditch, investigator of homeostasis and stress; and Harvey Cushing, neurophysiologist and major founder of modern neurosurgery.[17]

5. PHYSIOLOGY AND EXPERIMENTAL MEDICINE

As the attention of historians has shifted to twentieth-century history, to state involvement and to theory–practice relationships, we have come to know more about the growth of 'clinical research' or 'scientific medicine'. As critics of present medicine complain about medical curricula which say 'everything about molecules and nothing about people', so we have a further reason for exploring the nature and effects of the projects over the last century which aimed to 'make medicine a science'. Physiology, as a body of knowledge and as a social institution, was centrally involved in these projects.

The outlines are now emerging. The pioneers of clinical research have left records of their models and their successes; historians have begun to uncover the clashes of interest and the political manoeuvring which the pioneers preferred to leave in obscurity.

We know for example from American practitioner-historians, that German models were paramount, but we lack direct studies of these German exemplars, and so are in danger of idealising them. German experimental medicine appears as an offshoot of physiological institutes. If the workings of the body, in health and disease, could be understood in physiological terms; if, as became common in the late nineteenth century, disease could be understood as loss of *function*, then could not the hospital ward serve as a laboratory, where physical and chemical measurements could be made, and from which fluid (or tissue) samples could be sent for histological or chemical analysis? Was not this the royal road to a medicine as rigorous as the 'pre-clinical' sciences? Clinical medicine could be a real university subject, not an apprenticeship to the techniques of good practice.

There were one or two individual doctors who could bring the new physiology into ordinary practice. The most striking, perhaps, was James McKenzie, a general practitioner in the mill town of Burnley, Lancashire, who recorded venous and arterial pulses in an attempt to improve prognoses for heart disease. There were other practitioners who were ready to use the instruments of physiological medicine, especially the thermometer. But the heartland of the new movement lay in universities. Research needed time and status; it required, in effect, that professors of medicine be full-time researchers and teachers, not part-time teachers also heavily engaged in high-income private practice.

Here was an antithesis crucial to the development of recent medicine, not least in Britain and the United States. In Germany, the long association of medicine and universities, plus the relatively high status of professors, may have made plausible and more practicable the idea of clinical science. In the United States, the medical schools had been independent or loosely attached to weak colleges, while hospitals had been civic charities where teaching (let alone research) was ancillary. However, such was the power of the professional ideal in post-bellum America, so rich in potential did medical science seem and so ready were the corporate-rationalisers to invest the funds of Rockefeller and Carnegie, that full-time clinical chairs and clinical research were the established pattern in the better medical schools before the First World War.[18]

In Britain, by that time, most provincial city infirmaries had come largely under the control of medical schools, but clinical teaching often remained an adjunct to practice rather than to research. The Medical Research Council (founded in 1913) and the reformers of London University tried to establish clinical research, but with limited success. Thomas Lewis, a physician trained in physiology at University College London, and influenced by McKenzie, built up a research group, first working on cardio-vascular problems, then diversifying into studies of metabolism.[19] Several full-time chairs of medicine were established, often with American money, but with mixed results. A few biochemists, pathologists and pharmacologists might venture into clinical problems, but few clinicians understood research – at least so the physiologists claimed.

Yet it was between the wars that clinical physiology could first claim impressive practical successes. During the First World War, the British state had found physiologists useful in studies of fatigue and other 'functional' disorders. The 1920s brought insulin and cures for pernicious anaemia; whatever the role of clinical intuition or individual obstinacy in these breakthroughs, physiology had provided the background and the means of development. Physiologists no longer needed to rely on claims about the educational or fundamental nature of their subject; like the microbiologists and pharmaceutical chemists, they had cures to their credit. Thus, pre-clinical scientists were coming to the cutting-edge of medicine. Surgeons and physicians sometimes resented it.

6. PHYSIOLOGY AFTER THE SECOND WORLD WAR

Even in Britain, clinical research became securely established under the National Health Service from 1948. In the London Postgraduate Medical School and elsewhere, British clinical researchers gained international standing. Physiologists with clinical training now tend to work in clinical rather than in pre-clinical departments. The latter have become the preserve of medical scientists without clinical qualifications.

Physiology continues as a discipline, indeed, it grew rapidly in the 1960s and 1970s. Biochemistry has separated but 'biophysics' is usually under the parental roof; studies of membrane transport and nerve and muscle action form a crucial part of the modern discipline. Studies of particular *organs* may well be conducted in departments of cardiology or endocrinology, depending partly on how 'clinically relevant' they seem. At the level of whole systems, physiology draws on chemical engineering and control systems to construct models of feed-back and equilibrium. Integrative studies of the nervous system show a tendency to link with psychology, computer science etc. as part of the neuro-sciences.

As a result of these various processes of discipline formation, the identity of physiology is less clear than it was a century ago. It would now be possible to design a new medical school without a physiology *department*, though not without studies of organ and tissue function. A century ago, the discipline of physiology signified the search for causal explanations of body processes; by now that attitude is widely diffused through a range of disciplines which, in whole or part, might be regarded as physiology's progeny.

NOTES

1. L. S. King, *The medical world of the eighteenth century* (New York, 1971); C. Lawrence, 'The nervous system and society in the Scottish enlightenment', in B. Barnes and S. Shapin (eds.), *Natural order: historical studies of scientific culture* (Beverly Hills, 1979); W. F. Bynum and R. Porter, (eds.), *William Hunter and the eighteenth-century medical world* (London, 1985).

2. T. Lenoir, *The strategy of life: teleology and mechanics in nineteenth-century German biology* (Dordrecht, 1982); W. Pagel. 'The speculative basis of modern pathology. Jahn, Virchow and the philosophy of pathology', *Bulletin of the history of medicine*, 18 (1945), 1–43.

3. See, for example, Edwin Clarke and L. S. Jacyna, *Nineteenth-century origins of neuroscientific concepts* (Berkeley, 1987).

4. J. E. Lesch, *Science and medicine in France. The emergence of experimental physiology, 1790–1855* (Cambridge, Mass., 1984); O. Temkin, *The double face of Janus and other essays in the history of medicine* (Baltimore, 1977); E. Ackerknecht, *Medicine at the Paris Hosopital 1794–1848* (Baltimore, 1967); T. Gelfand, *Professionalising modern medicine. Paris surgeons and medical institutions in the eighteenth century* (Westport, Conn., 1980).

5. M. Foucault, *The birth of the clinic* (London, 1973), *The order of things* (London, 1970). Foucault's translator has produced an excellent guide: A. Sheridan, *Michel Foucault: The will to truth* (London, 1980).

6. Lesch, (1984); J. M. D. Olmsted, *François Magendie, pioneer in experimental physiology and scientific medicine in nineteenth-century France* (New York, 1944); W. R. Albury, 'Experiment and explanation in the physiology of Bichat and Magendie', *Studies in the history of biology*, 1 (1977), 47–131; J. V. Pickstone, 'Bureaucracy, liberalism and the body in post-Revolutionary France: Bichat's physiology and the Paris School of Medicine', *History of Science*, 19 (1981), 115–42.

7. K. Rothschuh, *History of physiology* (Huntingdon, New York, 1973); P. F. Cranefield, 'The organic physics of 1847 and the biophysics of today', *Journal of the history of medicine*, 12 (1957), 407–23, also 21 (1966), 1–7.

8. J. Ben-David, 'Scientific productivity and academic organisation in nineteenth-century medicine', *American sociological review*, 25 (1960), 828–43 and A. Zloczower, *Career opportunities and the growth of scientific discovery in nineteenth-century Germany, with special reference to physiology* (Hebrew University thesis), (New York, 1981).

9. R. S. Turner, 'The growth of professional research in Prussia, 1818 to 1848 – causes and context', *Historical studies in the physical sciences*, 3 (1971), 137–82.

10. A. Tuchmann, 'Science, medicine and the state: scientific medicine at the University of Heidelberg, 1830–1870' (Ph.D thesis, University of Wisconsin, Madison, 1985), to be published.

11. J. M. D and E. H. Olmsted, *Claude Bernard and the experimental method in medicine* (New York, 1952); F. L. Holmes, *Claude Bernard and animal chemistry* (Cambridge, 1974).

12. W. Coleman, 'The cognitive basis of the discipline. Claude Bernard on physiology', *Isis*, 76 (1985), 49–70; R. Fox and G. Weisz, (eds.), *Organisation of science and technology in France* (London, Paris, 1980).

13. R. D. French, *Antivivisection and medical science in Victorian society* (Princeton 1975), and G. L. Geison, *Michael Foster and the Cambridge school of physiology* (Princeton, 1978).

14. On British medicine see M. J. Peterson, *The medical profession in mid-Victorian London* (Berkeley, 1978).

15. S. V. F. Butler, 'A transformation in training: the formation of university medical faculties in Manchester, Leeds and Liverpool, 1870–84', *Medical history*, 30 (1986), 115–32.

16. See S. V. F. Butler 'Science and the education of doctors in the nineteenth century: a study of British medical schools with particular reference to the uses and development of physiology', (PhD. thesis, UMIST, Manchester, 1982).

17. Gerald L. Geison (ed.), *Physiology in the American context, 1850–1940* (Bethesda, Md., 1987); R. E. Kohler, *From medical chemistry to biochemistry. The making of a biomedical discipline* (Cambridge, 1982); J. H. Warner, 'Science in medicine', in S. G. Kohlstedt and M. W. Rossiter,

Historical writing on American science. Perspectives and prospects (Baltimore, 1986); K. M. Ludmerer, *Learning to heal: the development of American medical education* (New York, 1985).

18. A. M. Harvey, *Science at the bedside. Clinical research in American medicine, 1905–1945* (Baltimore, 1981) and see A. Flexner, *Medical education, a comparative study* (New York, 1925).

19. On McKenzie, Lewis and 'clinical research' see C. Lawrence, 'Moderns and ancients: the "new cardiology" in Britain 1880–1930', *Medical history*, Supplement No 5, 1985, 1–33.

FURTHER READING

Edwin Clarke and L. S. Jacyna, *Nineteenth century origins of neuroscientific concepts* (Berkeley, 1987).

R. D. French, *Antivivisection and medical science in Victorian society* (Princeton 1975).

G. L. Geison, *Michael Foster and the Cambridge school of physiology* (Princeton, 1978).

A. M. Harvey, *Science at the bedside. Clinical research in American medicine, 1905–1945* (Baltimore, 1981).

F. L. Holmes, *Claude Bernard and animal chemistry* (Cambridge, 1974).

R. E. Kohler, *From medical chemistry to biochemistry. The making of a biomedical discipline* (Cambridge, 1982).

T. Lenoir, *The strategy of life: teleology and mechanics in nineteenth-century German biology* (Dordrecht, 1982).

J. E. Lesch, *Science and medicine in France. The emergence of experimental physiology, 1790–1855* (Cambridge, Mass., 1984).

J. M. D. Olmsted, *François Magendie, pioneer in experimental physiology and scientific medicine in nineteenth century France* (New York, 1944).

J. M. D. and E.H. Olmsted, *Claude Bernard and the experimental method in medicine* (New York, 1952).

K. Rothschuh, *History of physiology* (Huntingdon, New York, 1973).

J. Schiller, 'Physiology's struggle for independence in the first half of the nineteenth century', *History of Science*, 7 (1968), 64–89.

J. Schiller, *Physiology and classification. Historical relations* (Paris, 1980).

O. Temkin, *The double face of Janus and other essays in the history of medicine* (Baltimore, 1977).

49

GEOGRAPHY

DAVID N. LIVINGSTONE

Since the institutionalisation of geography as a university discipline in Britain in the decades around 1900, the history of the subject has been a part of the staple student diet of the aspiring geographical professional. When the geography diploma was first introduced in Cambridge, for example, the General Board of Studies recommended in 1904 that 'the history of geographical discovery' should constitute one of the six papers comprising the Part I examinations, and that in Part II 'the history of geography' should likewise be represented.[1] Doubtless reflecting this emphasis, numerous works dealing with geography's history have been issued over the years to initiate the subject's apprentices into the mysteries of their chosen craft. Some of these have made real contributions to the history of science. Among them, special mention might be made of John K. Wright's *The Geographical Lore at the Time of the Crusades*, along with his numerous essays on geography's history; Eva G. R. Taylor's work on the history of navigation (the so-called 'mathematical practitioners' in England during the Tudor, Stuart and Hanoverian periods) and on sixteenth- and seventeenth-century English geography; Clarence J. Glacken's monumental survey of western attitudes to nature from classical times to the end of the eighteenth century, entitled *Traces on the Rhodian Shore*; and Gordon Davies's *The Earth in Decay* – a history of British geomorphology to 1878.

Despite the enduring qualities of works like these, and the long-standing interest in the evolution of the geographical tradition, however, much writing on the history of geography has been conducted with a 'prehistorical' historiography that is internalist (paying scant attention to broader social and intellectual contexts), presentist (perceiving history as the inevitable movement from an ill-informed past to an enlightened present) and hagiographic (focusing on the great names). Because most of these efforts are what have been christened 'textbook chronicles' – in-house treatments of disciplinary development for consumption within the geographical community – their stance has invariably been characterised by the concern to contemplate the past solely in terms of the present. In most cases, the underlying motivation is to furnish students with historical spectacles through which they can better see the current state of geography's affairs. In too many instances, therefore, the history of the subject is presented with a view to justifying partisan definitions of the field. In his classic monograph *The Nature of Geography* (1939), Richard Hartshorne, for instance, was not too embarrassed to include a whole section under the rubric 'Deviations from the course of historical development.' This spirit has continued to characterise much published work on the history of geography as practitioners have legitimated, or criticised, such diverse visions as 'geography as exploration', 'geography as map-making', 'geography as the study of land forms', 'geography as regional description', 'geography as society–nature relations' or 'geography as spatial science' from the heroes of the past. Accordingly, many histories amount to little more than a chronological tableau of great names, dates and theories with little regard for either the social or intellectual contexts within which geographical knowledge was produced and communicated.

In recent years, however, there have been several attempts by historians of geography to seek some rapprochement with history of science. Thus there have been those who have looked to the Kuhnian model to decipher the history of geography, others who have focused on the institutional links between its internal domain and external relations, and still others who have emphasised the importance of informal socio-scientific circles or colleges. The interest in metaphor common among philosophers of science has also found favour with historians of geography. Concurrently, the biographical milieux of the discipline's leading practitioners has continued to exert a perennial fascination and is complemented by a newer emphasis on the ways in which geographical praxis crystallised the ideological commitments of its practitioners. Still, significant though these developments have been, they represent in no sense a coherent statement of geography's historiography. They are better seen as symptomatic of a growing dissatisfaction with the available surveys and a concern for a contextual reading of the discipline's history.

The inappropriateness of an internalist reading of geography's history, however, stems not just from its historiographical naïvety, but more especially from the very nature of the discipline itself. For geography has always been practised in close association with other academic pursuits and has often been used to subserve policy ends whether in terms of imperial enterprises or planning programmes. Indeed, the very diverse visions of what constitutes the geographical tradition may well reflect the changing relationships that the discipline has sustained with a range of other intellectual pursuits. It is precisely because geography has variously drawn conceptual sustenance from primary geographical exploration, from the earth sciences, from practical arts such as navigation and map-making and from the nascent social sciences – anthropology, sociology, economics and politics – that it has remained an essentially contested tradition. In geography's case, then, the systemic relationships between science and society are only too plainly displayed.

Geography's story can be – and often has been – traced back through the chronicles of medieval Christian adventurers and Muslim scholars – travellers like Ibn-Batuta and Ibn-Khaldun – to the classical writings of figures like Thales, Anaximander, Erastosthenes, Strabo and Ptolemy. Their records, together with the voyages of the Scandinavian Vikings and the mathematics and explorations of the Chinese, did much to increase knowledge of the terrestrial globe and to advance the art of cartography. Nonetheless, geography, as it developed in the West, owes its scientific status less to these contributions than to two more recent developments in western culture, namely, the so-called 'age of discovery' and the post-Reformation rise of modern experimental science.

Indeed these two movements were related in not unimportant ways. First, what distinguished the fifteenth-century European explorers from medieval forebears such as Marco Polo was precisely their self-perception as engaging in a process of something called 'discovery'. Secondly, many of them shared an awareness that, as explorers, they were behaving as scientists; that is, that they were, as O'Sullivan puts it, 'engaged in an effort to convert cosmographical theory into practice. The voyages of discovery were, in a way, large-scale experiments, proving or disproving the Renaissance concepts inherited from the ancient world'.[2] Naturally, the relationship between theory and discovery was often fuzzy in the minds of those early voyagers lustful for adventure and fame, and zealous of finding fortune in the new trading empires. And it is true that while the names of Portuguese explorers like Diego Cão, Bartholemew Dias and Vasco da Gama, Englishmen like Sir Francis Drake and John and Sebastian Cabot, and discoverers sent out from Spain like Christopher Columbus, Ferdinand Magellan and Hernando Cortés, are now well known, their discoveries made rather less impression on the educated public of their day than might have been expected. Still, the re-publication of Ptolemy's *Geography* in 1406, and the new translation of Strabo's work later in the century did much to arouse new interest in the world and its exploration. The result was that in the century and a half from 1400 to 1550, most of the world's coastlines were for the first time reduced to map form. Alongside this achievement, the navigating needs of maritime nations during the later fifteenth century began to be met by a marriage of academic science and practical skills in the form of instruments to enable the calculation of latitude and other 'haven-finding arts'. Besides, the encounter with strange varieties of humanity raised anthropological and theological questions that had to be grappled with for the first time; indeed, the study of racial differences and their implications has continued to fascinate students of human geography.

If knowledge of the earth's surface and its inhabitants was thus expanded through the voyages of discovery – richly chronicled by men like Richard Hakluyt, Walter Ralegh, Thomas Harriot and Samual Purchas and splendidly mapped by Belgian and Dutch cartographers such as De Jode, Mercator, Jodocus Hondius and Petrus Plancius – the intellectual impact of the Reformation and the 'scientific revolution' also soon began to be registered by geography's practitioners. In Lutheran Germany, for example, a new understanding of the doctrine of divine Providence was exploited by Bartholomew Keckermann (c. 1571–1609) who urged the emancipation of geography's methods and aims from theology. In his *Systema Geographicum* of 1611, he explained that geography was the science which dealt with the measurement of the earth and proceeded to delineate the content of geography's subject-matter in its 'general' and 'special' aspects. This duality – already hinted at in the geographical writings of John Dee (1527–1608), an Elizabethan map-maker, alchemist and occult practitioner whose work, incidentally, like that of William Cuningham and Thomas Blundeville, links geography to the hermetic and cabalistic traditions – was later to be taken up by Bernhardus Varenius (1622–50) who pushed on to a more critical evaluation of the Geography of the Ancients. Varenius's *Geographia Generalis* of 1650 soon became the standard authority on the subject, its status being further increased by the fact that two Latin editions (of 1672 and 1681) were issued by Sir Isaac Newton. For Varenius, *geographia generalis* (or universal geography) is a thoroughly deductive science, mathematically grounded and derived from the system of Copernican astronomy; *geographia specialis* (or particular geography), by contrast, 'describes the constitution and situation of each single Country by itself' and is therefore empirical and inductive.[3]

In seventeenth-century Britain, similar currents of thought found expression in the writings of the Puritan geographer Nathanael Carpenter (1589– c. 1628). In *Geography Delineated Forth in Two Bookes* (1625), Carpenter, while hesitating between the Ptolemaic and Copernican systems, also distinguished a general and a special geography, this time using the terms 'Sphaericall' and 'Topicall'. But in contrast to Keckermann who offered a series of regional vignettes of various countries under his 'special geography', Carpenter outlined a methodology for the study of regions itemising measurement, mapping, location and modes of description. Yet for Carpenter, no less than for Keckermann, theological convictions underlay his geographical philosophising. In his *Philosophia Libera* of 1622, he had already defended the theological propriety of a 'free science' – a science liberated from the authority of the Ancients and the cult of Aristotle, and bound only by the Scriptures as the touchstone of truth.

In this marriage of geography and theology, Carpenter, of course, was by no means unique, although other writers were perhaps more concerned to keep geography subservient to divinity. This was so in the case of Peter Heylyn (1599–1622) author of *Microcosmus: or A Little Description of the Great World* who was later better known as a theologian, and in the writings of the sometime clergyman Samuel Clarke (1599–1683). In point of fact, throughout the seventeenth and eighteenth centuries, and for that matter well into the nineteenth century, geography was almost invariably practised in a context derived from natural theology. The great physico-theologists Thomas Burnet (c. 1635–1715) and John Ray (1627–1705) did much to bequeath to history a vision of nature as teleologically determined and providentially controlled. To them, as later to William Paley (1734–1805), the world of nature was nothing less than a functioning revelation of divine purpose, and to explore it was to delve into the very mind of the Creator. As Johann Gottfried von Herder (1744–1803) insisted, geography and history were, respectively, the theatre and book for God's ordering of the world. Geography was the theatre, history the book.

If the teleological argument thus energised the study of geography for some, it was precisely the concern to disengage theology from geography that motivated others. In the case of Georges Louis Buffon (1707–88), director of the Jardin du Roi in Paris, the questioning of natural theology was implicit, but the impact of his *Histoire Naturelle* was both profound and lasting, not least on the thinking of Herder and Kant. Perhaps more than anyone else in the eighteenth century, Buffon laid the foundations for biogeography, challenging the Linnaean taxonomy by downplaying morphology and employing the notion of hybrid sterility, and urging that fauna are the products of their regional environments and adapted to their climatic zones. It was this aspect of his thinking that was to have such a lasting influence on Humboldt and other contemporary biogeographers. (See arts. 19 and 24.)

The anti-teleological bias was also crucial for Immanuel Kant (1724–1804) who presented lectures on physical geography at the University of Königsberg from 1756 to 1796. He further pursued Keckermann's strategy by subjecting the design argument to philosophical scrutiny and concluded that geography could not be studied through physico-theological spectacles. Since God was now banished to the outer fringes of the shadowy noumena, it was futile to search for him along the course of river beds, behind the laws of mountain-building or in the ebb and flow of tides. For Kant, then, geography was theologically neutral and encompassed both the study of the physical world and the behaviour of its human inhabitants including their commercial, political, religious and cultural activities. Besides, it had the added privilege of occupying a strategic role in the endeavour to unify human learning – a function akin to Bacon's universal science.

If Kant's geography was born, as it were, in the armchair, the same can hardly be said of Alexander von Humboldt (1769–1859), the putative founder of modern geography. His was an out-of-doors geography although it perpetuated the Kantian spirit by detaching science from Christianity and seeking in geography a universal and unifying science. First and foremost, Humboldt saw himself not as a dilettantish wanderer or adventurous explorer, but as a scientific traveller. In 1790 he travelled in Western Europe with J. G. Forster and in 1799 sailed for Venezuela where he spent some four years journeying over the *llanos*, from Caracas to the Orinoco, across the Andes and along the high valleys to Bogotá and Quito, and finally through the coastal plains of Mexico. Equipped with the latest instruments for measurement and with a passion for accuracy in observation, he revealed himself an inveterate collector and chronicler and spent his days fixing astronomical observations, mapping, accumulating geological and botanical specimens and recording the habits and appearance of the peoples he encountered. Plant geography, climatology, cartography and geophysics (particularly terrestrial magnetism and meteorology) were thus central to Humboldt's science. And yet Humboldtian science, as Cannon has designated it, was anything but the sterile accumulation of facts; rather it was concerned with the 'accurate, measured study of widespread but interconnected real phenomena in order to find a definite law and a dynamical cause'.[4] Indeed, this idea of the interconnectedness of things was to be the theme that ran like a high voltage current through Humboldt's incomplete *magnum opus*, the five volume *Kosmos: a Sketch of a Physical Description of the Universe* (1845–1862). Throughout, in his depiction of the harmonious unity of the universe, in his analysis of the relations between the world of nature and human beings and in his epistemological reflections on the nature of scientific and historical knowledge, the same motif of unity in diversity reasserts itself.

By now, geography as a science had acquired some of the basic concepts and trade skills that would in large measure characterise its future practitioners. Cartographic techniques were plainly central to the whole procedure of fieldwork and landscape observation, as was the ability to use various instruments designed for surveying, recording and standardising measurements. Then the recognition of the immensity of time, as James Hutton (1726–97) broke through Ussher's 4004 BC time barrier, heralded a reassessment of theories about the history of the earth and, soon, the antiquity of the human species.

Still, despite the detailed philosophical critique of the teleological argument by writers such as Kant, Hume and Spinoza, and despite several efforts to exorcise geography of the ghost of the physico-theologists, natural theology in one form or another continued to furnish the common context within which science in general and geography in particular was transacted. This is not to say that it provided a unified or coherent framework for research: natural theology took many forms and performed many different functions, some intellectual, some social. But that the design argument was generally assumed was rightly underscored by H. R. Mill when, in 1901, he observed:

748

Teleology or the argument from design had become a favourite form of reasoning among Christian theologians and, as worked out by Paley in his *Natural Theology*, it served the useful purpose of emphasizing the fitness which exists between all the inhabitants of the earth and their physical environment. It was held that the earth had been created so as to fit the wants of man in every particular. This argument was tacitly accepted or explicitly avowed by almost every writer on the theory of geography, and Carl Ritter distinctly recognized and adopted it as the unifying principle of his system.[5]

While Mill was perhaps too willing to locate the roots of natural theology in the writings of Paley – other less utilitarian versions were available – the basic thrust of his diagnosis was quite sound. In Britain, for example, Mary Somerville, already author of a volume entitled *On the Connexion of the Physical Sciences* produced her pioneering *Physical Geography* in 1848. Here she assured her readers that 'the great cosmical phenomena . . . are the ministers of the manifold designs of Providence' and that the pattern of human centres of civilisation demonstrated the 'arrangement of Divine Wisdom'. In the United States, Matthew Fontaine Maury, celebrated author of the *Physical Geography of the Sea* (1855), took an even more stringent teleological line. The thoroughly empirical tenor of the work impressed its reviewers at the time, but this did not prevent Maury from urging that, for example, the land–water proportions of the globe and the energy transfers between earth, sea and air (described in mechanistic vocabulary), were expressive of a natural law guided by Providence.[6]

Teleological reasoning in geography, however, was not restricted to mechanistic construals of natural theology. Organic analogies with a more idealist emphasis also found favour. This was especially so in the case of Arnold Guyot, Princeton's Professor of Physical Geography and Geology from 1854 to 1880. Perpetuating many of the assumptions of the *Naturphilosophie* of his native Switzerland, Guyot presented his *Earth and Man* (1849) as a geographical testimony to the grand harmonies of nature that universally bore witness to the control of Providence. His volume was a frontal attack on traditional geographies with the physiographic inventories and commercial catalogues; instead it advocated an interpretative geography grounded on ecological principles and stressing the interrelationships in nature. 'All is order, all is harmony in the universe', he insisted, 'because the whole universe is a thought of God'.[7]

Throughout, Guyot's geography perpetuated the spirit of his mentor Carl Ritter (1779–1859), a contemporary of Humboldt and likewise resident in Berlin. Educated in the innovative methods of Pestalozzi and personally encouraged by him, Ritter occupied a position as history professor at Frankfurt before turning more exclusively to geography and moving to Berlin in 1820. His great work was *Erdkunde*, an encyclopedic project in which he intended to chart 'Earth Science in Relation to Nature and the History of Man'. The work was never completed and by the time of his death only Africa and Asisa had been surveyed. Nevertheless his objectives and methods were clearly displayed: his intention was to establish 'the unity of law among the diversity of phenomena' and to illustrate the predestinarian history of the human race on the face of the earth. Not surprisingly his human geography, like Guyot's, tended to lapse into a form of environmental determinism that surrendered human culture to the dominating control of physical environment.

Numerous other writers on geography displayed a similar sympathy for the procedures of natural theology: among these mention might be made of Alexander Winchell, Nathaniel Shaler, David Thomas Ansted, Daniel Coit Gilman, Archibald Geikie and Thomas C. Chamberlin, to name but a few. Undoubtedly, natural theology provided the common intellectual context for geography as much as for biology. But just as significant were the ideological services that it could provide. In his analyses of Victorian natural science, in essays now drawn together as *Darwin's metaphor: nature's place in Victorian culture* (1985), Robert M. Young has spoken of the transfer from one theodicy based on natural theology to another grounded in the new scientific laws of nature. As he sees it, this shift in intellectual authority merely legitimated the social order preferred by particular interest groups. Nature, in other words, replaced God as the basis for the value system of the intellectual establishment. One does not have to espouse Young's entire philosophical programme to see the relevance of his proposals for the history of geography in the modern period. A single instance will suffice.

Throughout the nineteenth century, geographers were fascinated with questions about the origin and distribution of the different human races. The geographical interest in race, it should be noted in passing, also highlights the developing links geography cultivated both with the social science tradition and with medicine. In the early days of the Royal Geographical Society, for example, James Cowles Prichard regularly presented reports on ethnogeographical themes, and these ties were further cemented through the later writings of figures such as Charles E. Pickering, William Z. Ripley and Franz Boas, all of whom took geographical distribution and physical environment seriously into account. On the medical front, geographers became more and more interested in questions about human acclimatisation, particularly the acclimatisation of the white race to the tropics, and several medical practitioners were resorted to for the latest medical opinions on the subject. Such interest, of course, could easily be given an ideological twist. In Guyot's case it was the Creator who had placed certain human types in the tropical zones where they would never achieve any degree of civilisation because the physical environment was not conducive to social advancement. In the case of Alexander Winchell it was 'Nature' that had herded them 'in regions where they would never mingle in the stir of social and national struggles'.[8] A clearer shift from theology to nature as justification for the white race's place in society can scarcely be imagined. These are not isolated instances. Similar conceptual manoeuvres are discernible in the writings of Robert DeCourcy Ward, Francis A. Walker, Nathaniel S. Shaler, Daniel Coit Gilman, James Bryce, William Z. Ripley and later Ellsworth Huntington. Moreover, these sentiments were from time to time pushed beyond academic analysis to political prescription as when geographers lent their support to various nativist movements, eugenics crusades or immigration restriction policies.

The shift from natural theology to natural law as the acceptable mode of scientific explanation was not always so ideologically focused. The development of biogeography is illustrative. In the pre-Darwinian period, and in some cases long afterwards, utilitarian and idealist versions of the design argument permeated studies of the geographical distribution of plant and animal life, and patterns of migration. The writings of William Kirby, William Swainson, Andrew Murray, John Cowles Prichard and Louis Agassiz reveal this in different ways, on topics ranging from entomological to anthropological distribution. But with the advent of Darwinism, natural evolution soon became the appropriate explanatory vehicle as in, for example, Henry Walter Bates's naturalistic account of the phenomenon of mimicry in butterflies. The introduction of evolutionary principles thus began the tradition of ecological biogeography which subsequently numbered among its practitioners figures like Marion Newbigin, H. C. Cowles, F. C. Clements and later Arthur Tansley.[9] Of course there were hidden ideological implications in the epistemological shift and these surfaced dramatically when biogeography touched on questions about the origin and migrations of mankind; the feuds between monogenists and polygenists – to take a single instance – clearly illustrate this.

If geography was not immune to ideological forces, neither was it practised in an institutional vacuum. A variety of geographical societies helped give structure to the practice of the discipline and, in some cases, to shape the content of geographical knowledge. Space only permits some observations on one of these, although organisations such as the Royal Scottish Geographical Society, the United States Geological Survey and the LePlay Society within the English-speaking world, never mind elsewhere, would equally deserve scrutiny. The Royal Geographical Society, founded in 1830, was only one of many learned societies established in the period to organise and delineate specific forms of knowledge. It rested the case for its *raison d'être* on the fact that geography's 'advantages are of the first importance to mankind in general, and paramount to the welfare of a maritime nation like Great Britain, with its numerous and extensive foreign possessions'. These aims were reflected in the journal's articles and in the society's membership. The vast majority of communications were either records of journeys and explorations, or were concerned with specifying the precise location of sites, often with cartographical accompaniment, while the original 460 members were either 'men of high social standing' or drawn from the ranks of the military.[10] The RGS thus had a social clientele rather different from that of more technical societies such as the Geological and

751

the Astronomical and this tended to foster an amateurish and dilettantish image. Still, there were numerous distinguished scholars associated with the Society, notably Bentham, Hooker, Murchison, Sedgwick, Darwin, Galton, Huxley and Wallace, not to mention Bates, its assistant secretary for nearly thirty years. Indeed, there were occasions when the interests of the imperial and scientific factions fused. European imperial expansion in the tropics and sub-tropics, for example, provided the context for the increased scientific and medical attention that was devoted to the question of acclimatisation, while on the political front the expertise of geographers was often called upon in disputes about the precise location of international boundaries. (See art. 60.)

The RGS also played a crucial role in the institutional advancement of geography elsewhere in British society, particularly in the educational sphere. Through its efforts, geography became a recognised university subject at Oxford and Cambridge. In fact the RGS provided financial resources for sharing the stipend of these early geography lectureships. The establishment of university chairs in the subject had to wait until the early years of the twentieth century. Thus began the growth of university geography in Britain. In 1903 the one chair of geography was at University College London and was occupied by L. W. Lyde; by 1920 there were four geography chairs, and by 1950 the number had risen to sixteen. Since then growth has been exponential, with some sixty chairs of geography being occupied in 1980.

Throughout the period of its early modern growth, one of geography's dominant theoretical principles was the doctrine of environmental determinism. That this dogma could perform ideological functions is already clear from the racial geographies that were issued at the time and which made environment the cause of ethnic superiority or inferiority. Its roots, plainly, were earthed in the teleological tradition that had been kept alive by the natural theologians. But further reinforcement could be gleaned from certain versions of evolutionary theory.

The impact of evolutionary thinking on geography was certainly substantial. Organicism, change through time, ecological models and adaptation were just some of the Darwiniana to sweep through the subject. But these were not of exclusively Darwinian preserve. They were shared by other versions of the evolutionary story. Besides, the major thrust of Darwinism – random variation and natural selection – ran counter both to natural theology (at least in its Paleyan mould) and to a deterministic environmentalism. Indeed, the flourishing of environmental determinism in nineteenth- and early twentieth-century geography would seem anachronistic in the light of these currents of thought were it not for the emergence of an alternative evolution model more to the liking of those with a necessitarian bias, namely, neo-Lamarckism. For one thing, with its metaphysics almost as explicit as its science, neo-Lamarckism facilitated the survival of a teleological interpretation of nature. And then, because it emphasised the direct impress of environment on organisms and the heritability of the characteristics thus acquired, it became attractive to many geographers, given their now-typical fascination with the interrelationships between organism, environment and society. Not that they were self-consciously neo-Lamarckian in outlook; rather, when they filtered out of the evolutionary literature those themes least appropriate for their purposes, they were invariably left with a Lamarckian residue.

In the United States, geography's initiation into Lamarckian evolution began with Nathaniel Shaler (1841–1906) who, like other leaders in this new School of American Biology – notably Cope, Hyatt and Le Conte – had come under the spell of Louis Agassiz. For Shaler, there was an immediate causal link between specific social groups and their physical environments; geographical conditions, he insisted, 'strongly impressed themselves on the character of a race' with the result that contemporary local cultures were the cumulative expression of ancestral experience transmitted from generation to generation.[11] Shaler's influence, of course, was widespread, and no more so than in the case of William Morris Davis (1850–1934) whom he taught at Harvard and who was to emerge as the 'great man' of American geomorphology. Davis indeed is conventionally regarded as codifying the Darwinian influence on physical geography through his cyclical interpretation of landform development – the cycle of erosion. But his evolution was decidedly more Lamarckian in emphasis. Not only did he advance a causal account of the relationship between 'physiographic control and organic response', but he displayed a persistent recapitulationist tendency to be 'more impressed with the mystery of growth from egg or seed to adult [a life cycle] than . . . with the cumulated effect of small scale changes over many generations'.[12] Both were thoroughly neo-Lamarckian instincts.

Shaler and Davis were far from unique in the evolutionary path they followed. John Wesley Powell (1834–1902) took the Lamarckian route in physiography and ethnology. Frederick Jackson Turner (1861–1932) assumed the same version when he accounted for the unique qualities of the American nation as socio-political responses to its physiographical features, as did Albert Perry Brigham (1855–1932) who published *Geographic Influences in American History* in 1903, and Ellen Churchill Semple (1863–1932) author of *Influences of Geographic Environment* (1911). Brigham's chief intellectual source, doubtless, was his teacher Shaler, but Semple drew inspiration from the work of the German naturalist-traveller Friedrich Ratzel (1844–1904). Certainly hers was a vulgarisation of Ratzelian *Anthropogeographie*. But Ratzel *had* found the work of Moritz Wagner particularly congenial and it was from his Lamarckian biology that Ratzel gleaned the migration theory.

Ratzel, of course, has an independent significance in geography's history, not least for his single-handed attempt to create a science of society that would bridge the natural and human sciences. Central to his project was the concept of *Lebensraum*, a notion he developed in his *Politische Geographie* of 1897. Viewing the state as an organism, he urged that the character and destiny of a People or *Volk* were umbilically tied to an area or definite space (*Raum*). Later, conventional wisdom has it, this theme was to gain notoriety with its absorption into the politics of German National Socialism. But recent revisionist accounts make clear that the environmental determinism of the Ratzelian perspective – perpetuated in the geopolitical writings of Karl Haushofer and Richard Hennig – never fitted comfortably with the genetic racism of mainstream Nazism.[13] Indeed until the post-Second World War period, when the naturalism of Ratzel's anthropo-geography was superseded by an emphasis on culture (although Ratzel did reveal a sensitivity to the moulding power of Kultur in *Die Vereinigten Staaten von Nord-Amerika*), the German geographical tradition continued to build on the foundations laid by Ferdinand Von Richtofen (1833–1905) who emphasised the physical basis of the subject, and Alfred Hettner (1851–1941), founder of the influential *Geographische Zeitschrift* in 1898.

The same environmentalist conception of geography, with its attendant evolutionary Lamarckism, was also widespread in British geography. Perhaps chief among its advocates was Sir Halford J. Mackinder (1861–1947) who was no less concerned to find in geography a means of holding together the natural and social sciences under one explanatory umbrella. But there was never any doubt in his mind which had priority; to use his own words, 'no *rational* political geography can exist which is not built upon and subsequent to physical geography'. Mackinder's zoological training and his enthusiasm for Bagehot's *Physics and Politics* made his determinist vision of what he termed 'geographical causation in universal history' all too predictable. Not that the agency of human beings was entirely obliterated. Mackinder always believed that a nation could wrest the initiative from nature and change the course of history by taking hold of the world's key environments, 'the natural seats of political power'. 'Who rules East Europe commands the Heartland' he wrote; 'Who rules the Heartland commands the World Island; Who commands the World Island commands the World'.[14] Herein lay the attraction of Mackinder's geography for Haushofer and the German geopoliticians.

For all that, the causal factor in Mackinder's writings was attractive to many. Sir James Bryce, geographer-historian and distinguished British transatlantic ambassador, 'heartily agreed' with him, because as he saw it 'geography was not a science of description, but of causality, and its function was to exhibit the way in which a variety of physical causes played, firstly upon one another, and secondly upon man'.[15] It was a heady vision – reducing history to geography, politics to pedology, culture to nature; and it attracted many geographers, some newly professionalised and anxious to find a scientific basis for their endeavours. In Britain, Holdich's study of world political geography, Lyde's work on race, and Howarth's writings on climate and civilisation betray the same outlook. Meanwhile, James Fairgrieve was interpreting the 'ascent of man', the shifting locus of high civilisation and the pattern of world political power as the outcome of geographical control. In Australia, Griffith Taylor (1880–1963) advanced what he called 'stop-and-go determinism', while in America, the apex of environmental determinism, still with direct links to biological Lamarckism, was reached in the highly influential writings of Ellsworth Huntington (1876–1947) on race, civilisation and climate.

The tradition of environmental determinism, however, was never uncontested, nor indeed was the conservative political stance it often presupposed. On the latter front radicals such as Elisée Reclus and Peter Kropotkin used geography to challenge the *status quo* rather than to support it. Reclus (1830–1905), author of the monumental nineteen-volume *Nouvelle Géographie Universelle: la Terre et les Hommes* – a work as much aesthetic as scientific – possessed a deep-seated humanitarianism that gave him a love for the human race and a concern for social justice. The anarchistic humanism of Kropotkin (1842–1921) sprang from a profound dissatisfaction with the nastier social implications of Darwinism. So in *Mutual Aid* he put forward the case for co-operation as a crucial evolutionary factor and, having seen the selective advantage conferred by acquired sociability, came to the conclusion that Lamarck had been unjustifiably neglected. The social implications of his geography were therefore supportive of collectivism rather than *laissez-faire* individualism.[16]

So far as environmental determinism was concerned, dissenters came from a variety of intellectual contexts. Paradoxically, the very Lamarckian doctrine that had given such a 'scientific' boost to environmentalism, revealed that it had resources to challenge it as well. Because Lamarckians believed that organisms could consciously adapt themselves to their environments and pass on the benefits by use-inheritance, their version of evolution reserved an important place for mind, will and consciousness. Geographers suspicious of a monistic environmental determinism could therefore find scientific consolation here. Patrick Geddes (1854–1932), for example, emphasised from time to time the significance of social heritage – the accumulated enregistration of learned experience – and used it to support urban planning and educational initiatives rather than consigning society to the power of environment. Herbert John Fleure (1877–1969), a Fellow of the Royal Society, had been critical of Weismann's neo-Darwinism ever since his student days in zoology, and his geographical work confirmed his Lamarckian inclinations as he accounted for the patterns of cultural behaviour in terms of the acquired 'experience of millennia'. Fleure's geography therefore sprang from the idealist strain in Geddes's outlook and undergirded his anxiety lest geography should fail to appreciate 'the importance of the human will and of man's power to modify his surroundings'.[17] Andrew J. Herbertson, another of the Geddesian circle and enthusiast for Le Play's trilogy 'lieu-famille-travail' as crucial for human geography, displayed similar sympathies neatly revealed in his posthumously published, but tellingly entitled paper, 'Regional environment, heredity and consciousness'. For Herbertson, the 'regionalising ritual' – specifying and elucidating the character of the world's great natural regions – was fundamental to geography, and in this he reflected the critique of environmental determinism emanating from a different conceptual source, Vidal de la Blache (1845–1918) and the vibrant tradition of French cultural geography.[18]

Vidal's influence on French geography was indeed profound, so much so that the so-called *tradition vidalienne*, articulated through the journal he founded, *Annales de Géographie*, was perpetuated long after his death. His concern was to liberate geography from what he saw as the snare of environmental determinism by urging that environment merely provides a range of possibilities which human cultures can manipulate according to their needs and capacities. Humanity, therefore, creates its own habitat, rather than languishing as the fatalistic victim of a heartless nature. Hence the term 'possibilism', often used to characterise this tradition. As to the sources for this critique, Vidal drew on the historical work of Lucien Febvre and on the modish neo-Kantiansim then dominating the philosophical horizon. The outcome was an emphasis on the region because it was in specific physical milieux that distinctive *genres de vie* – modes of life – found expression. Vidal himself illustrated this complex, yet balanced, interweaving of human society and environmental settings in his celebrated *Tableau de la Géographie de la France* (1903). And the tradition he established was perpetuated by Albert Demangeon, Jean Brunhes and Camille Vallaux.

A third strand of determinist critique can be located in the cultural geography of Carl Sauer (1889–1975) and the Berkeley school. There is a sense, of course, in which the roots of this critique go back to the cultural anthropology of Franz Boas who began his scholarly career as a physical geographer. His work among the Inuit led him to question his environmental determinist assumptions and to look to other factors in the moulding of human cultures. The liberal humanism and cultural relativism to which this brought him was mediated to Sauer via Boas's students Alfred Kroeber and Robert Lowie, also at Berkeley. From them, Sauer got his notion of culture history as the basis of social science and he focused on material culture – artefacts and so on – as indicative of the cultural diversity that gave character to particular places over the face of the earth. Still, while Sauer's inspiration derived less from biology and philosophy than from anthropology, the naturalism of Chamberlin in geology and of Cowles in ecology were influential, as was neo-Kantianism in the form of American pragmatism. In Sauer's geography, then, 'man' and 'culture' were superorganic entities irreducible to individuals and possessing an inherent logic of their own. And his concern was therefore to break with the environmentalism of geography's recent past because of its mono-causal implications, to work with a more flexible view of the relations between humanity and land-scape and to reinvigorate the classical German tradition of chorology – the regional paradigm.[19]

Many geographers found this brand of regional geography particularly attractive. Some produced regional monographs of lasting significance, and E. Estyn Evans's luminous writings on the personality of Ireland must rank among the best. Still, the focus on geography as regional description found its chief philosophical apologist in Richard Hartshorne whose immensely influential monograph *The Nature of Geography* – so influential perhaps because of the lack of any coherent alternative – argued the regional case from a partisan review of historical sources. To him, geography was an idiographic science that centred on the particularity of places and the behaviour, whether social, economic or political, of their inhabitants. This scenario was subsequently challenged by Fred Schaefer in a paper entitled 'Exceptionalism in Geography' published in the *Annals of the Association of American Geographers* during 1953. Schaefer's critique was designed to transform geography into a true science by urging that it become a law-seeking, explanatory discipline articulating theories that were universally applicable, not regionally specific, and therefore not 'exceptional'.[20] The debate opened the door to the admission of logical positivism into geography, and its curriculum was defended in William Bunge's *Theoretical Geography* first published in 1962 and in David Harvey's *Explanation in Geography* in 1969. Meanwhile W. L. Garrison in the United States and Peter Haggett in Britain were introducing location theory – a set of theorems seeking to explain the location of economic activities – to geography. Through their efforts and the writings of Walter Isard, an economist, the earlier economic theorising of such German figures as Von Thünen, Alfred Weber, Walter Christaller and August Lösch brought a new theoretical awareness to Anglo-American economic geography. Subsequently these re-evaluations led to an interest in the space economy, especially among those geographers working within the tradition of Marxian political economy, to a systems analytic approach to environment and society, or to a mathematised behavioural geography that looked to psychology to explain decision-making processes. In general terms, then, positivism for geographers meant quantification and so, during the 1960s and afterwards, the subject was exposed to its fair share of statistical methods. The degree to which these new craft competences represented professional vested interest in creating a 'spatial science' may well leave this episode open to the critiques of the 'strong programme' of the sociology of knowledge.

Since the early 1970s, the number of academic geographers has mushroomed; the vast majority of geographers who have ever lived are undoubtedly alive today. This alone makes any evaluation of recent trends a particularly difficult task. Besides, the subject has witnessed the emergence of numerous competing theoretical perspectives. Some advocate a more strenuous engagement with issues of social relevance. Indeed, there have always been geographers sympathetic to that cause whether their concern has been for the conservation of natural resources, welfare or the third world. Others have espoused one or other of the traditions of modern Marxism and spawned radical sub-movements and journals mirroring the precise hue of their own political colours. Again this outlook has a distinguished lineage stretching back to figures such as Reclus and Karl Wittfogel. Still others have urged a return to what they see as a revivification of the spirit of Vidalian geography (though often ignoring his natural science aspirations for *géographie humaine*), calling for a humanistic reinstatement of men and women as feeling, thinking, knowing subjects and building on the earlier contributions of Kirk, Lowenthal and Wright. And some have pushed on beyond the reductionism of a fundamentalist Marxism and the subjectivism of the new humanists to a structurationist geography that endeavours to take seriously the complex transformations of social, economic and political structures through the agency of human subjects.

It is still much too early to attempt any rigorous, contextual analysis of these newest debates. If a revised edition of this *Companion* were to be undertaken say fifty years from now, the time might then be ripe to begin such an assessment. In the meantime, it is clear that the evolution of modern geography over the past four centuries or so has been the history of a diversified tradition – often reactive, frequently contested and periodically refocused. And it is precisely because geography has drawn theoretical inspiration from both the natural *and* the social sciences, because it has been implicated both in imperial enterprises *and* in political radicalism, and because it has made robust contributions to wider scientific theory as with, say, the opening up of the world by geographical exploration or the insights of ecological biogeography, that the absence of genuinely contextual histories of the subject is to be so lamented. Certainly there have been attempts to chart geography's efforts to articulate its own conceptual identity; but since these 'internal' concerns have been so informed by professional, social and theoretical 'externals', the failure to take them seriously into account has too often resulted in chronologies that only serve as precursors to fully-fledged history. If geographical thought and practice is in any sense the story of humanity's attempts to comprehend or control or change its natural and social environment, then the history of this enterprise is as much a history of the societies that produced geographical knowledge as a history of the geographical knowledge societies have produced.

ACKNOWLEDGEMENT

I am grateful to Fred Boal, Gordon Herries Davies, Derek Gregory and Jon Hodge for valuable comments on this essay.

NOTES

1. See D. R. Stoddart, *On geography and its history* (Oxford, 1986), p. 108.
2. D. O'Sullivan, *The age of discovery 1400–1550* (London and New York, 1984), p. 3.
3. Quoted in J. A. May, 'The geographical interpretation of Ptolemy in the Renaissance', *Tijdschrift voor Economische en Sociale Geographie*, 73 (1982), 359. On geography in Lutheran Germany, see M. Büttner, 'The significance of the Reformation for the reorientation of geography in Lutheran Germany', *History of science*, 177 (1979), 139–69.
4. Susan Faye Cannon, *Science in culture: the early Victorian period* (New York, 1978), p. 105.
5. H. R. Mill, 'Geography', *Encyclopaedia Britannica* (14th ed., London, 1929), p. 147. See also Y-F. Tuan, *The hydrologic cycle and the wisdom of God: A theme in geoteleology* (Toronto, 1968).
6. M. Somerville, *Physical geography* (4th ed., London, 1858), pp. 339, 486, 493; M. F. Maury, *The physical geography of the sea* (New York, 1855), pp. 68, 92–4.
7. A. Guyot, *The earth and man: lectures on comparative physical geography in its relation to the history of mankind* (New York, 1897, first published 1849), p. 82.
8. Guyot, *Earth and man*, p. 251; A. Winchell, *Preadamites: or a demonstration of the existence of men before Adam; together with a study of their condition, antiquity, racial affinities, and progressive dispersion over the earth* (Chicago, 1880), p. 157.
9. See M. P. Kinch, 'Geographical distribution and the origin of life: the development of early nineteenth century British explanations', *Journal of the history of biology*, 13 (1980), 91–119; P. Scott, 'History of biogeography', in J. A. Taylor (ed.), *Themes in biogeography* (London and Sydney, 1984), pp. 1–24. The shift in explanatory context is discussed more generally in D. N. Livingstone, 'Natural theology and neo-Lamarckism: the changing context of nineteenth century geography in the United States and Great Britain', *Annals of the Association of American Geographers*, 74 (1984), 9–28.
10. Chairman's address, *The journal of the Royal Geographical Society of London*, 1 (1832), p. vii (The rather different setting in Scotland is discussed in E. N. Lochhead, 'The Royal Scottish Geographical Society: The setting and sources of its success', *Scottish geographical magazine*, 100 (1984), 69–80). D. R. Stoddart, 'The RGS and the "new geography": Changing aims and changing roles in nineteenth century science', *Geographical journal*, cxlvi (1980), 190–202.
11. N. S. Shaler, *The story of our continent* (Boston, 1892), p. 166. For a full discussion of Shaler see D. N. Livingstone, *Nathaniel Southgate Shaler and the culture of American science* (University, Alabama, 1987).
12. W. M. Davis, 'The faith of reverent science', *Scientific monthly*, 38 (1934), 395–421.
13. M. Bassin, 'Race *contra* space: the conflict between German *Geopolitik* and national socialism', *Political geography quarterly*, forthcoming. For a general outline of Ratzel's life see H. Wanklyn, *Friedrich Ratzel. A biographical memoir and bibliography* (Cambridge, 1961).
14. H. J. Mackinder, 'On the scope and methods of geography', *Proceedings of the Royal Geographical Society*, 9 (1887), 143; idem, 'The geographical pivot of history', *Geographical journal*, 23 (1904), 421; idem, *Democratic ideals and reality: a study in the politics of reconstruction* (Harmondsworth, 1944, first published 1919), p. 113.
15. J. Bryce, 'The relations of history and geography', *Contemporary review*, 49 (1886), 426–33; idem, 'Discussion following H. J. Mackinder "On the scope and methods of geography" '. *Proceedings of the Royal Geographical Society*, 9 (1887), 170–2.
16. The best introduction to Reclus is G. S. Dunbar, *Elisée Reclus. Historian of nature* (Hamden, CT., 1978); on Kropotkin see M. A. Miller, *Kropotkin* (Chicago, 1976).
17. See J. A. Campbell, *Some sources of the humanism of H J. Fleure* (University of Oxford School of Geography Research Paper No. 2, 1972).
18. A. J. Herbertson, 'Regional environment, heredity and consciousness', *Geographical teacher*, 8 (1915), 147–53.
19. See R. T. Trindell, 'Franz Boas and American geography', *Professional geographer*, 21 (1969), 328–32; J. N. Entrikin, 'Carl O. Sauer, philosopher in spite of himself', *Geographical review*, 74 (1984), 387–408; M. Williams, ' "The apple of my eye": Carl Sauer and historical geography', *Journal of historical geography*, 9 (1983), 1–28.
20. R. Hartshorne, *The nature of geography: a critical survey of current thought in the light of the past* (Lancaster, Penn., 1939); F. K. Schaefer, 'Exceptionalism in geography: a methodological examination', *Annals of the Association of American Geographers*, 43 (1953), 226–49. A general

survey of these and subsequent developments is available in R. J. Johnston, *Geography and geographers. Anglo-American human geography since 1945* (London, 1979).

FURTHER READING

B. Blouet (ed.), *The origins of academic geography in the United States* (Hamden, CT., 1981).

M. Bowen, *Empiricism and geographical thought: from Francis Bacon to Alexander von Humboldt* (Cambridge, 1981).

J. Browne, *The secular ark. Studies in the history of biogeography* (New Haven and London, 1983).

A. Buttimer, *Society and milieu in the French geographic tradition* (Chicago, 1971).

R. J. Chorley, A. J. Dunn and R. P. Beckinsale, *The history of the study of landforms or the development of geomorphology. Volume one. Geomorphology before Davis* (London, 1964).

R. J. Chorley, R. P. Beckinsale and A. J. Dunn, *The history of the study of landforms or the development of geormorphology. Volume two. The life and work of William Morris Davis* (London, 1973).

P. Claval, *Essai sur l'évolution de la géographie humaine* (Paris, new edition, 1976).

G. L. Davies, *The earth in decay. A history of British geomorphology 1578 to 1878* (London, 1969).

G. Dunbar, *The history of modern geography: An annotated bibliography of selected works* (New York and London, 1985).

C. J. Glacken, *Traces on the Rhodian shore. Nature and culture in Western thought from ancient times to the end of the eighteenth century* (Berkeley, 1967).

D. Gregory, *Ideology, science and human geography* (London, 1978).

D. N. Livingstone, 'The history of science and the history of geography: interactions and implications', *History of Science*, 22 (1984), 271–302.

J. H. Parry, *The age of reconnaissance. Discovery, exploration and settlement 1450–1650* (London, 1963).

D. R. Stoddart (ed.), *Geography, ideology and social concern* (Oxford, 1981).

—— *On geography and its history* (Oxford, 1986).

E. G. R. Taylor, *Late Tudor and early Stuart geography* (London, 1934).

Y-F. Tuan, *The hydrologic cycle and the wisdom of God: A theme in geoteleology* (Toronto, 1968).

J. K. Wright, *The geographical lore of the time of the Crusades* (New York, 1925).

SECTION IIC: THEMES

50

SCIENCE AND RELIGION

JOHN HEDLEY BROOKE

1. INTRODUCTION

In his *Science and the Modern World* (1925), the philosopher A. N. Whitehead deemed it a matter of urgency that the proper relations between science and religion should be clarified. The models through which the natural world had been analysed and manipulated, and the symbols through which humanity had customarily found meaning and purpose in life were both so powerful that it was essential to determine their relationship.

To achieve a consensus on such an issue has proved highly problematic, for the task presupposes the existence of criteria by which the legitimate domain of the sciences may be differentiated from that of religion. Claims to have established such criteria have generally been controversial, the boundaries have shifted with time and as great a diversity of opinion probably exists today as when Whitehead issued his plea. In certain forms of existentialist theology, for example, scientific and religious discourse are completely isolated, the former referring to I – it relations, the latter to I – thou situations. For as influential a Protestant theologian as Rudolph Bultmann, the Christian doctrine of Creation did not refer to the origins of the physical world, but rather to the creation within the believer of an authentic stance towards his earthly predicament.

By contrast, twentieth-century process theologians such as Charles Hartshorne, taking their inspiration from Whitehead himself, have made scientific knowledge, notably concepts of organic evolution, germane to a religious vision in which God both participates in, and is affected by, events in the material world. By contrast again, there are vociferous minorities who affirm that creationism can be 'scientific' and that neo-Darwinian hypotheses fail to conform to some preconceived standards of verifiable (or falsifiable) science. In contemporary quarrels between creationists and evolutionists, competing concepts both of legitimate science and legitimate religion are brandished in the context of a conflict having educational and political dimensions.

2. THE COMPLEXITY OF THE RELATIONS BETWEEN SCIENCE AND RELIGION

Since these three broad patterns – of isolation, integration and conflict – have repeatedly occurred in the past, any history of the relations between scientific and religious movements is bound to be complex. Indeed, different models of their 'proper' relationship have served different social, political and religious ends according to time and circumstance. Thus an emphasis on the integration of scientific and religious beliefs often appears in those societies where an emerging scientific community has to make conciliatory gestures towards powerful religious authorities. This may also happen when religious apologists themselves seize a particular scientific innovation as a resource for defending the rationality of their faith, or for legitimating their own religious tradition against others.

An emphasis on the isolation of science and religion has often occurred as a reaction against facile syntheses which have disintegrated as science, or religious sensibilities, have changed. A complete separation has also been attractive as a protective strategy and one which, during the nineteenth century, also reflected the diverging demands of a professional career in both science and academic theology. An emphasis on conflict has appeared either when religious authorities have sensed a challenge to their spiritual values and world-view, or when the scientific community, as in late nineteenth-century Britain, sought to consolidate what it saw as a new set of professional standards and pre-rogatives which deliberately excluded the clerical amateur. As F. M. Turner has argued, the Victorian conflict between science and religion was, in one sense, a by-product of a profound social shift in which power, authority and prestige were passing from one part of the intellectual nation to another. At the same time, the disintegration of a long tradition of relative harmony was reflect-ing the growth of scientific specialisms in which a clerical presence all but dis-appeared. The number of Anglican clergymen presiding over sections of the British Association for the Advancement of Science fell from 41, for the period 1831 to 1865, to three for the period 1866 to 1900.

The rhetoric of T. H. Huxley, to the effect that extinguished theologians lay around the cradle of every new science like snakes around the body of Her-cules, was the aggressive manifestation of that shift in the social context and ideology of science. Amid the controversies surrounding Darwin's *Origin of Species* (1859), such rhetoric could appear amply justified. It resulted, however, in historical analyses which reified both science and religion, projected the con-flict backwards and even located it in pre-Christian societies. In his *History of the Warfare of Science with Theology* (1896), A. D. White made much of the fact that the Stoic, Cleanthes, had denounced the heliostatic astronomy of Aristar-chus as impious, without pausing to consider whether such an occurrence might not have been recorded precisely *because* of its exceptional character. In popular literature on the history of science, the 'conflict' thesis, as enunciated by J. W. Draper, has often been taken as axiomatic: the history of science is 'a narrative of the conflict of two contending powers, the expansive force of the human intellect on one side, and the compression arising from [traditional] faith and human interests on the other'.[1]

This view has been seductive because it chimes with common knowledge about the fate of such innovators as Bruno and Galileo, and with what is known of the religious fury which greeted eighteenth- and nineteenth-century texts in which man was made a product of nature, and in some cases an accidental one. It also chimes with historical models of secularisation which give a prominent place to the manner in which the sciences have transformed our understanding of the natural world, whether by shrinking the domain of the miraculous, or by shrinking the significance of man himself in a universe shown to be overwhelmingly vaster and older than was formerly imagined. It ties in, too, with models of secularisation which stress the role of applied science and technology in transforming societies from a condition in which there is a perceived dependence on Providence to one in which there is greater dependence on the works of man.

Without disputing that scientific and religious interests have not infrequently been locked in confrontation, particularly in the context of educational priorities, scholars have increasingly found the 'warfare' axiom inadequate to cope with the rich tapestry of interaction that has occurred in the past. In the long process of disaggregation, whereby newly-emerging sciences differentiated themselves from what had once been the queen of the sciences, complex patterns of subordination and insubordination arose. In fourteenth-century Paris, for example, Nicole Oresme developed a powerful critique of physical arguments habitually used against the Earth's axial rotation, but his enterprise was subordinate to the theological goal of showing that human reason was impotent to settle the issue. Even at the end of the seventeenth century, it was still possible for Newton to say that part of the business of natural philosophy was to consider the question of God's relation to the physical world. Indeed, one of the defects of the conflict model is that it posits two competing mentalities, disregarding eminent scientific figures who were either clerics or who had a strong religious commitment. Newton himself provides one of the most spectacular examples of the integration of scientific and religious interests in one and the same mind. Not only was he attracted to alchemical texts, with their rich religious symbolism, but he was as much concerned to find the correct rules for interpreting biblical prophecy as for interpreting the planetary orbits.[2]

This is not to imply any correlation between religious orthodoxies and science. With his anti-Trinitarian theology, Newton would be a representative of the many men of science who have deviated from the religious norms of their culture. However, it does acknowledge that scientific and religious interpretations of the natural world have frequently been seen as complementary rather than as mutually exclusive. The many schemes of theistic evolution which flourished in the late nineteenth century would illustrate one form of complementarity. Even Darwin's bulldog, T. H. Huxley, conceded that Darwinism had no more damaged theism (however grave its implications for Christianity) than had the first book of Euclid. The rigid categories of 'science versus religion' have proved inadequate even in those contexts in which they seem most applicable. Immediate responses to Darwin's theory of natural selection included scepticism from notable physicists, but a guarded welcome from certain clergy who, like the Anglicans Frederick Temple and Charles Kingsley, valued the opportunity to divest their Christianity of the demeaning image of God as conjuror.

3. REVISIONIST HISTORIOGRAPHY

Reacting against the insensitivity of rationalist polemics, historians of science are now more likely to stress that what may look like conflicts between science and religion often turn out to be instances of internecine scientific controversy (in which religious interests may have intruded on either side), or internecine religious controversy (into which concepts of scientific authority are imported). One of the more engaging theses to emerge from such revision states that certain traditions within Christian theology were conclusive to, rather than obstructive of, intellectual changes and the re-evaluation of practice, which allowed a critical, empirical science to displace the natural philosophy of Aristotle.[3]

Rolf Gruner has pointed out that the case has undoubtedly been overstated by religious apologists, tempted to tie the rationality of modern science to a unique metaphysical system, but Marxists and other secular historians have come to recognise that religious beliefs could provide presuppositions, sanctions and even motives for new styles of scientific enquiry.[4] As crucial a conception as that of physical *laws* was regarded by the Marxist, E. Zilsel, as having its origins in the theological conception of a divine legislator who had imposed his will, like an absolute monarch, on the physical world.[5] This interpretation is at least consistent with the pronouncements of such seventeenth-century celebrities as Kepler, Descartes, Boyle and Newton, who variously claimed to be searching out the laws which God had impressed upon His creation.

In the works of Francis Bacon one can perhaps see most clearly how religious beliefs could function as a sanction for science. It was Bacon's contention that scientific activity which promised practical benefits was to be valued because it would help to restore man's dominion over nature, sacrificed when Adam fell from grace. Bacon's advocacy of experimental methods was also justified in theological terms in that a spirit of humility was presented as a prerequisite both of a Christian piety and of a submissive posture before the facts of nature, which only human arrogance would try to determine from *a priori* considerations. Since God had been free to make any world He chose, which world He *had* made could only be discovered by reading the book of His works for oneself, without deference to the pretended authority of earlier commentators. Such a correlation between a voluntarist theology and the justification of empiricism was not uncommon during the seventeenth century and it was not confined to Protestant thinkers. In France, the Minim friar Marin Mersenne (1588–1648) attacked the Aristotelian conception of a central, *natural* place for the Earth by suggesting that there were no natural places in the universe: created objects were where God had freely chosen to put them. Mersenne even attacked Kepler, on similar grounds, for having presumed to space the planetary orbits according to preconceived geometrical criteria.

That religious commitment could provide motivation for scientific activity has been a more controversial claim – not least because motives are notoriously elusive. Where scientific conclusions have assisted the differentiation of one religious position from another, they have, however, often been valued for that reason. According to the controversial thesis of R. K. Merton, the rapid expansion of scientific activity in seventeenth-century England had much to do with the dissemination of Puritan values.[6] Puritan reformers allegedly saw scientific study as an acceptable calling because the injunction to glorify God could be met in at least two ways: by producing knowledge that would alleviate suffering and knowledge which revealed God's power and wisdom. Inquiry into the secondary causes by which natural phenomena were produced was a permissible use of that gift of reason which distinguished man from beast and which, when properly exercised, diverted him from sensuality. Whilst Merton has been justly criticised for an indiscriminate application of the term 'puritan', and for failing to appreciate that the soteriological concerns of puritan divines could result in a low priority being accorded to scientific endeavour, other scholars, notably Charles Webster in *The Great Instauration* (1975) have located a religious motivation for science. This is in the millenarian ideals of those puritan reformers who saw in the restoration of man's dominion over nature a necessary precondition of Christ's earthly rule.

Opinions remain divided, however, as to whether radical puritanism or moderate Anglicanism provided the more auspicious milieu for the advance of scientific understanding (C. Webster (ed.), *The Intellectual Revolution of the Seventeenth Century* (1974).) The question arises because the kind of science advocated by puritan radicals, such as Oliver Cromwell's army chaplain, John Webster, often bore a closer resemblance to the magical philosophies of the Renaissance, with their emphasis on spiritual illumination, than to an emerging mechanical philosophy. The latter, in England, gained ground among those, like Robert Boyle, who had clearly reacted against the extremism of puritan sects, complaining that Christianity was being jeopardised by their proliferation. Presenting himself as a priest in the temple of nature, Boyle, among others, developed a natural theology which capitalised on mechanical images of nature, providing a Christian theism with a rational foundation via the argument from design.

Theses affirming congruence between puritanism and applied science, or between moderate Anglicanism and a more cerebral science, are extremely difficult to test; there is the ulterior problem that even if the correlations were established, they need not imply a direct input from the religion to the science. It is always possible that religious and scientific predilections could independently reflect an underlying social and economic change. Tendentious references to the Anglican *origins* of modern science must also appear parochial when the emerging scientific movement is brought within a wider European focus, and appear positively chauvinistic towards non-Christian civilisations in which, as with Islam in the eleventh and twelfth centuries, analytical tools were forged and significant strides made in such areas as algebraic geometry and physical optics.[7]

Merton's thesis, and the many variants of it, nevertheless continue to attract attention because they constitute a special case for a broader generalisation – that, in the Christian West, Protestantism was more conducive to scientific growth than Roman Catholicism. The grounds for such an assertion usually include the absence among the Protestant churches of a strong and centralised system of censorship, the likelihood that a reforming mentality in the religious sphere would create a predisposition towards the reform of natural philosophy (or vice-versa), and that the Roman Church had more vested interests in the philosophy of Aristotle. The trial of Galileo before the Holy Office in 1633 continues to symbolise the contrasts.[8] A generation later, England's foremost Copernican populariser, John Wilkins, ended his days not under house-arrest but as a bishop in the Anglican church and Lent Preacher to the King. Catholic critics of the new cosmology, with one eye on the Netherlands, would even refer to the Calvinist-Copernican theory, suggesting a degree of convergence between the two spheres of reform.

4. THE CHALLENGE OF COPERNICANISM

The diffusion of Copernican astronomy (see art. 14, sect. 3) does indeed throw some light on religious attitudes towards scientific innovation during the first half of the seventeenth century, but closer examination shows the issues to have been extremely complex. First there was the philosophical question of whether a mathematical hypothesis, designed principally to predict the angular position of the planets, need be admitted as a representation of physical reality. Initially, only those scholars such as Rheticus, Kepler, Galileo and Copernicus himself, who took mathematical elegance to be a touchstone of truth, were inclined to give a realist interpretation to the heliostatic model. Second, the theological implications of shifting humanity from the centre of the cosmos were not as clear-cut as is often supposed. There was a profound disorientation, to be sure, but it was still possible for Kepler to argue that mankind retained a privileged position, since the Earth occupied the central orbit around what Kepler believed, in defiance of Bruno, to be the most resplendent sun in the universe. Even within the rubric of Aristotelian cosmoslogy, there was a sense in which man was promoted rather than degraded: he had the exhilaration of whirling in the superlunary region of perfection, transported from that central pit which Galileo dubbed the sink of all refuse in the universe. Indeed, Wilkins reported that a common objection against the Copernican system was that it elevated man above his true station.

A third complication concerns the challenge of Copernicanism to biblical authority. Such difficulties as were posed by Joshua 10 v. 12 and Psalm 93 v. 1 were in principle removable by adopting a principle of biblical accommodation. As formulated by Calvin, the argument was that the Holy Spirit had made due allowance for the frailty of the human intellect when guiding the authors of Scripture, thereby ensuring that spiritual meanings would be clear to all. Accordingly, it was suggested that they had utilised the language of common-sense observation rather than technical astronomy, since the latter would baffle the uninitiated and give them an excuse for disregarding the more urgent matter of their salvation. It was a line of argument which a friendly cardinal, Carlo Conti, mooted to Galileo.

A fourth complication is that Galileo's fate may not be an accurate symbol of the attitude of Roman Catholic authorities towards new learning in general because there were peculiar political dimensions to the case. Not only had Galileo alienated Jesuit philosophers, notably Christopher Scheiner, with whom he had a priority dispute concerning the discovery of sunspots, and Horatio Grassi, with whom he differed on the nature of comets; but he also managed to offend his former ally, now Pope Urban VIII. This he did by including in his *Dialogue Concerning the Two Chief World Systems* (1632) an argument for the Earth's diurnal and orbital motions based on the tides, which violated Urban's injunction to avoid such physical considerations.

Galileo's case was not helped by the fact that most of the evidence he adduced in support of a moving Earth was equally compatible with the alternative cosmology of Tycho Brahe which allowed all the planets, with the exception of the Earth, to revolve around the sun, the latter orbiting the Earth and carrying the planets with it. Furthermore, Galileo's tragedy was not so much the result of inherent animosity between the Catholic Church and scientific enquiry, as a reflection of the political and doctrinal consequences of the ongoing battle *between* Catholicism and Protestantism. Galileo did adopt the principle of biblical accommodation but, by suggesting that the miracle of the long day of Joshua was actually more comprehensible in a Copernican universe, he heightened the suspicion that, like his friend Paolo Sarpi who had led a Venetian revolt against the papacy, he was a crypto-Protestant.

In response to the threat of Protestant expansion, the Council of Trent had earlier decreed that where the Church Fathers had achieved a consensus on the interpretation of a particular biblical text, that consensus was to be respected. As Galileo himself pointed out, this placed him in a bind because the Church Fathers could not be expected to have interpreted Scripture *his* way, given that Copernican astronomy could not have been known to them. Undoubtedly there are layers of political intrigue still to be uncovered. One recent suggestion is that the real issue behind Galileo's trial was not so much the Copernican system as an atomic theory of matter Galileo had developed which, through its break with Aristotelian conceptions of primary and secondary qualities, posed a direct challenge to the Catholic interpretation of the Eucharist.[9] With Galileo's view of the relationship between matter and form, as with that of Descartes later, it was difficult to see how the bread and wine could change into the body and blood of Christ without visible changes.

5. THE MECHANICAL PHILOSOPHY AND CHRISTIAN THEOLOGY

The revival of interest in atomic and particulate theories of matter during the early seventeenth century (see art. 15, sect. 3.2) certainly did create difficulties for Christian apologists – and not merely in the context of the Eucharist. As presented in Lucretius's *De Rerum Natura*, the atomic philosophy of antiquity made the world a chance product of atomic collisions, the processes occurring within it needing no deity for their explanation. It was, however, possible to harmonise atomism with a doctrine of Providence by arguing that God was not only responsible for the original organisation and motion of the atoms, but also for sustaining their motion.

By stressing the passivity of the ultimate particles of matter (I know of no man, Boyle was later to say, who has satisfactorily made out how matter can move itself), it was possible to construct a mechanical philosophy of nature which actually had theological advantages. In France, for example, Mersenne was attracted to the mechanical science of Galileo, in part because a mechanical philosophy could be useful in rebutting the allegation of Protestants that the Catholic Church constantly turned marvels into miracles in order to impress the laity. Wounded by such allegations, Mersenne looked for criteria that would help his Church to discriminate between natural marvels and genuine miracles. A mechanical philosophy could then become attractive because it helped to define the boundaries of a natural order. Another advantage of a mechanical philosophy appealed to Protestants perhaps more than to Catholics: in so far as God was made directly responsible for moving matter, one had the means of emphasising His sovereignty over His creation, whilst at the same time performing the service for the physical sciences of ridding the universe of angels, spirits and demons. These were all intermediate spiritual agencies which, however much they might appeal to platonists, could be seen to detract from God's absolute transcendence and absolute control.

For both Boyle and Newton, there was a fundamental analogy between our ability to move our limbs (showing the power of mind to move matter) and God's activity in the world. Though the mechanical philosophy, as developed by Descartes and Hobbes, was often seen as a danger to Christian belief, it was always possible to argue that, properly understood, it reinforced the rational grounds of belief. A universe that resembled the great clock of Strasbourg rather than a living organism, simply had to have an intelligent Designer.

That there were theological gains as well as losses in a mechanised universe draws attention to one of many ironies in the history of the relations between science and religion in the West. A philosophy of nature which, in the seventeenth century, was often justified in terms of a voluntarist theology, later became the very resource which deists and free-thinkers would use in their attacks on the Christian religion. If there is a sense in which a mechanistic science, grounded in the concept of physical law, was the offspring of a Christian culture, it was an offspring which could easily turn rebellious. The clockwork universe, which for Robert Boyle, pointed to God's continual involvement in the world, was soon to be exploited by the deists of the Enlightenment to transform Him into a benevolent, but absentee, clockmaker.

6. NEWTON'S SCIENCE

In that historical process, the science of Newton occupied a pivotal place (see art. 16.) On the one hand, his laws of motion and gravitation were a gift to deists such as Voltaire who could exploit a mathematically-defined natural order against what they saw as the superstition of Catholic theology and the political repression with which it was allied. On the other hand, there were aspects of Newton's philosophy of nature, formulated in reaction against the mechanical philosophy of Descartes, which enriched rather than depleted the evidence for an active Providence. The gravitational force was invisible, its action inexplicable in mechanistic terms. Leibniz denounced it as unintelligible for that very reason. Moreover, Newton grounded the universality of his law of gravitation in the doctrine that God not only constituted space, but was omnipresent in a universe, the laws of which He had freely chosen. Newton's science also gave fresh impetus to the argument from design in that the planets would not have gone into closed orbits in the first place, had not the deity calculated the correct transverse component of their velocity with which to impel them. Newton's God was a mathematician no less brilliant than Newton himself. But He was also the God of the Bible who had been active in human history. As if to underwrite the doctrine of an active Providence, Newton insisted that the solar system would run down if it were not for the occasional reformation in which God had a hand. The ambivalence in Newton's position is revealed, however, by an ambiguity concerning whether God intervened directly to ensure the stability of the system, or whether He used secondary causes, vested in comets, to achieve the required effect.[10]

Consequently, how Newton's science was interpreted depended on the presuppositions of its interpreters. There were Anglican divines such as Richard Bentley, Samuel Clarke and William Derham who, as popularisers, made the most of its theistic possibilities. By contrast, the free-thinker and political radical, John Toland, found himself obliged to reinterpret Newton's philosophy of matter, insisting that forces which Newton had deemed not to be inherent in matter were precisely that.[11] From William Whiston, in England, who believed Newton's science would reinforce a literal reading of Scripture, to free-thinkers in France, for whom Newton's science was a paradigm of what human reason could achieve, there were almost as many interpretations of the theological significance of Newton's work as there were theological commentators. Opposition to Newton's natural philosophy could also be justified on theological grounds. Thus Leibniz, who may have associated a voluntarist theology with the menace of an absolutist monarchy, resisted Newton's scheme on the grounds, among others, that only a second-rate clockmaker would need to repair His creation.[12]

7. SCIENCE AND RELIGION IN THE ENLIGHTENMENT

Other aspects of the relation between science and religion in the Enlightenment conform to this general point. It was not that a sequence of incontrovertible scientific discoveries drove God out of His world, or even that a unique scientific method had come into being, by the standards of which the claims of established religion could be judged defective. It was rather that the disclosures of the sciences were adopted both by religious protagonists and antagonists according to the exigencies of the moment. More often than not, attacks on the authority of Scripture were based on arguments which emphasised cultural relativism (every religion seemed to have its miracles) or which impugned the rationality and even the morality of traditional Christian doctrines. It is true, however, that powerful images of scientific and technical progress were often invoked, as in the *Encyclopédie* of Diderot and D'Alembert, to enrich an ideology of social reform. And there is no doubt that scientific enquiry, and pre-eminently a science of man, was encouraged by the philosophes, as by Joseph

Priestley in England, because it was thought to inculcate modes of thinking which would be destructive of popular superstition and, eventually, of arbitrary political power. Detailed studies nevertheless suggest that even within otherwise coherent groups seeking intellectual liberation and greater religious tolerance, there were often fundamental disagreements, as there were between Diderot and D'Alembert, over what constituted archetypal and authoritative forms of scientific reasoning: the immediate authority of an empirical fact, as in an observational science such as experimental physiology, or the highly formalised deductive authority of a geometrised mechanics.

The ambivalence of 'factual' discoveries, with respect to the significance which could be attached to them, can perhaps best be illustrated by three innovations in the life-sciences which were seized by mid-18th-century French materialists to bolster their position. Reports of the spontaneous generation of micro-organisms, ostensibly achieved by John Needham, were invoked to support the idea that life could emerge from non-life without the aid of gods. The discovery of the property of 'irritability' by Albrecht von Haller, (whereby a muscle fibre would automatically contract when stimulated) could be construed as evidence that matter had the intrinsic power to move itself. And the astonishing discovery of Abraham Trembley that, when a hydra was chopped to pieces, each piece would regenerate into a complete organism, could easily be exploited by those who, in a literally soul-destroying exercise, argued that matter had inherent powers of self-organisation. And yet each of these discoveries could be interpreted quite differently by the non-materialist. Needham himself was a Catholic priest who was accused by Voltaire of having faked a miracle. Haller interpreted his force of irritability as analogous to Newton's force of gravitation, ultimately a manifestation of God's causal agency in the world. And whether the hydra had a soul or not actually had very little bearing on the status of the human soul.

A similarly equivocal pattern obtained in the physical sciences late in the eighteenth century, when Laplace and Lagrange showed that Newton's solar system was self-stabilising and did not require the reformations that Newton had proposed. On one interpretation, God had been further edged out of His world. That may have been the interpretation which Laplace aspired to, for in the 'nebular hypothesis' by which he accounted for the origin of the solar system, teleological considerations were rigorously excluded. However, for natural theologians in Britain and America, a self-stabilising system was evidence of even greater ingenuity on the part of the Creator than one which required a service contract.[13] As the Cambridge mathematician and philosopher William Whewell observed in the 1830s, a savage inspecting a steam-engine would be no less likely to attribute the machinery to intelligence on being shown the self-regulatory part of the mechanism.

8. THE PLACE OF NATURAL THEOLOGY

If materialist philosophies were more common in France than in England during the eighteenth century, and if natural theology, with its celebration of the design argument, was more prominent in England, this undoubtedly had much to do with the fact that there were fewer political incentives in England, where a degree of religious toleration had already been achieved, to pit science against religion. In France, and other Roman Catholic countries, there was generally a sharper divide between religious orthodoxy and heterodoxy than in England, where the existence of a spectrum of tolerated opinions had the effect of pointing up the importance of a natural theology which, for the most part, they had in common. As Roy Porter has observed in *The Enlightenment in National Context* (Cambridge, 1981), since there was no Pope, no Jesuits, no comparable grip of the clergy on the family through confession, an integration of science and religion could be sustained in England as part of a wider cultural phenomenon of comprehensiveness which historians have contrasted with the polarities of Enlightenment rhetoric in France.

Despite the well-known critiques of physico-theology advanced by David Hume in Scotland and Immanuel Kant in Germany, the argument from design continued to flourish as part of popular scientific culture in the English-speaking world until well into the nineteenth century. Since references to design in nature were useful in disarming clerical opposition to scientific innovations, they actually fulfilled a more urgent need in Britain in the decades following the French Revolution than before. The conservative backlash, from which Priestley suffered, coupled with a burgeoning evangelical revival, focused attention on scientific concepts which might prove dangerous in the hands of political radicals. The evolutionary speculations of Erasmus Darwin, for example, had been tolerated until the 1790s but, by the first decade of the nineteenth century, they were being treated with abuse. The durability of natural theology in Britain also owed something to the fact that proponents of the design argument were not always so unsophisticated as to expose themselves to the force of Hume's critique. It was sometimes acknowledged, as by Whewell, that claims for design were more a means of corroborating an already existing faith than a pretended *proof* of God's existence or attributes.[14]

Since the literature of natural theology marks the most sustained tradition in which science and religious belief were integrated, it is important to consider what relevance the theologising might have had to scientific practice, and vice versa. Even among those historians who have kept the relevance of the theology to a minimum, there has been an acknowledgement that commitment to a conventional natural theology tended to dispose naturalists towards creationist rather than evolutionary interpretations of the history of living systems (N. C. Gillespie, *Charles Darwin and the Problem of Creation* (1979)). This should not be surprising given that both Hume and Kant showed how the design argument logically presupposed a Creator. From a post-Darwinian perspective, it is therefore easy to regard the preoccupation with design as an obstruction to liberal scientific thinking. The role of teleological considerations in the life-sciences was not, however, a purely negative one. Not only did the study of biological adaptation prosper as evidence was sought for divine contrivance, but in reconstructing past creatures from fossil fragments, the exercise was often regulated by the belief that the organism had been an integrated whole in which each part was functionally correlated with others. It is another of the ironies that, whilst Darwin's theory of natural selection displaced the teleological argument of William Paley, it nevertheless drew on an extensive range of data which had been accumulated under a natural theology paradigm.

On the relevance of science to natural theology, the key question is whether the design argument could survive a series of difficulties which arose in the wake of the historical sciences. That the appearance of design in the organic world was an illusion had been argued from antiquity by sceptics who had observed that living things would never have survived at all had they not been well adapted. The implication was that many non-viable creatures might have come into existence, only to perish as victims of an uncoordinated combination of limbs and organs. During the late eighteenth century evidence for extinct species came to light. Buffon, for example, was deeply impressed by the remains of mammoths in the colder parts of the globe. Since large mammals tended to be found in equatorial regions, Buffon could support his contention that the Earth had cooled from an incandescent state, having had its origins in material ejected when a comet collided with the sun. During the long process of cooling, conditions had so changed on the Earth's surface that many species could well have become extinct. It was Georges Cuvier, however, who did most to establish the fact of extinction by reconstructing fossil species from fragmentary remains in the Paris basin. Whereas his contemporary, Lamarck, by-passed the uncomfortable fact of extinction by suggesting that one form had gradually changed into another, Cuvier insisted that there were fossil forms which had no living analogues. They had been extinguished by local catastrophes, when the inundation of land, for example, might destroy many species simultaneously.

The fact of extinction was a blow to the kind of natural theology that had been erected on a principle of plenitude: that God had created, and cared for, every creature it was possible to create. For many observers, such as the poet Tennyson, the indifference of nature as revealed by the geologists could be emotionally disturbing. Nevertheless, in seeking to quell such disturbance, the defenders of natural theology had little difficulty in making the fossil record an ally rather than a foe. If each species, during the span of its existence, had been well adapted to its environment, one could still argue for design from the manner in which the history of organic forms and the Earth's physical history had

775

been synchronised. Indeed, the Cambridge geologist, Adam Sedgwick, used the fossil record in the 1830s to attack both atheists and deists. Since there was a time when every species in the fossil record had not existed, the atheist was denied the comfort of eternal living forms. The deist, too, had his come-uppance because the progressive creation revealed by the fossil record indicated a Creator involved in, rather than absent from, His Creation.

Under pressure from the historical sciences, natural theology was forced to diversify but it was not immediately destroyed. In the scientific literature of the 1830s, 1840s and 1850s, it is possible to discern at least three quite different versions of the design argument. Some naturalists still stuck to variants of the teleological argument as personified by Paley: each part of an organism had a function for which it was perfectly adapted, or at least as perfectly adapted as correlation with other parts would allow. A more sophisticated argument had, however, taken shape in response to the concept of a unity of structure among vertebrates which Geoffroy Saint-Hilaire had developed in opposition to teleo-logical reasoning. The comparative anatomist, Richard Owen, suggested that all vertebrates were indeed modelled on a skeletal archetype which should, however, be construed as an idea in the mind of the Creator. It was the adap-tation of the archetype to the specific needs of each species which, according to Owen, constituted the best argument for design – one which could accommo-date features of an organism which did not have an immediate purpose – male nipples for example. But a third version was also taking shape, in the mind of Charles Darwin among others.[15] This was the view, expounded most forcibly by the Oxford mathematician and philosopher, Baden Powell (1796–1860), that the most cogent evidence of design was to be found in the laws of nature, not in the domain of the inexplicable. That so many diverse laws conspired together to produce a viable world had also impressed Whewell, whose statement to the effect that divine wisdom was as discernible in the laws of nature as in pre-sumed instances of intervention was conveniently borrowed by Darwin to legit-imate his naturalistic account of speciation.

9. DARWINIAN EVOLUTION

In early drafts of his theory, Darwin had construed the evolutionary process as nature's way of ensuring that species remained in perfect adaptation to their environment. He was also prepared to embrace a broader teleology in that the evolutionary process could be presented as the means to another, foreseeable, end: the production of organisms of increasing complexity. In mature versions of Darwin's theory, however, the concept of perfect adaptation was replaced with concepts of relative and differential adaptation, allowing natural selection to be in constant operation and thereby attenuating the force of references to design. The fact that the process of natural selection could counterfeit design meant that his theory constituted the single most powerful objection that could be levelled at the design argument in its traditional guise. Nevertheless, several Christian commentators, notably Asa Gray in the United States, positively welcomed Darwin's theory for the light it might throw on the classic paradox: why should a beneficent and omnipotent God permit so much suffering in the world? That problem was one of the many sources of Darwin's own agnosticism, but Gray's point was that one could now go some way towards rationalising it if pain and suffering were inevitable concomitants of a struggle for existence which was itself a *sine qua non* of the process of creation. Gray, who did so much to popularise Darwin's theory in the United States, suggested that the problem of suffering was far greater for Paley's creationist theology than for a Darwinian theist who could see its purpose in the creative economy of nature. Darwin's own tentative formula, that the laws of the evolutionary process might have been designed with the details left to chance, also had attractions for rationalist theologians who could exonerate the deity for the more devilish by-products.

The volatility of the public reaction to Darwin's *Origin of Species* was not unrelated to the larger crisis in Christendom provoked by historical criticism of the Bible. In his *Life of Jesus*, made available to the English-speaking world through George Eliot's translation of 1846, D. F. Strauss had insisted that a truly historical approach to the gospels required the recognition that the evangelists had interpreted Christ's life and death through a series of beliefs and expectations peculiar to their own generation and no longer admissible in the modern world. The miracles they ascribed to Christ, in portraying him as the Messiah, had been naturally but retrospectively transferred to him in line with expectations drawn from earlier Messianic prophecy. Scientific and historical criticism were now converging, since both geology and evolutionary biology underlined the mythological elements in the Genesis creation narrative, and since Darwin had effectively removed one of the last great miracles: the origin of species.

Not surprisingly, Darwin's theory continues to be seen as a watershed in the historical relations between science and religion (see art. 24, sect. 4.) Recent scholarship, however, has favoured the view that in the ensuing debates concerning human evolution, many issues were brought to the fore which had already been discussed in earlier contexts. These issues were whether mankind was a product of nature or a late addition; whether the process of evolution was, in any sense, goal-directed; whether the workings of the human mind could be construed in exclusively naturalistic terms; whether a naturalistic account could be offered for the emergence of the human conscience and finally, whether religious beliefs were themselves by-products of evolution, socially inculcated and culture-specific. In his *Descent of Man* (1871), Darwin gives a brief sketch of the emergence of religious beliefs, stressing the ease with which belief in one or more gods could arise from a primitive animism. Religious beliefs had even played a role in human evolution by reinforcing particular ethical codes which, in turn, might have been of survival value to the communities which espoused them. Darwin did not intend to undermine the foundations of morals. Quite the reverse: he argued that the golden rule ('as ye would that men should do to you, do ye to them likewise') was the highest but *natural* outcome of the development of social instincts. For many of his contemporaries, however, who were clinging to moral absolutes as the lifeline of a faith that had already been badly shaken, the effect of Darwin's analysis could be desolating. His own wife could not stomach the proposition that all morality had grown up by evolution and excised from his *Autobiography* a passage which compared a child's belief in God with a monkey's fear of a snake.

Both before Darwin and after, the dialogue between transformist and anti-transformist positions was charged with political meanings. In second-Empire France, the transformist Geoffroy Saint-Hilaire perceived himself to be fighting a scientific establishment, dominated by the presuppositions of Cuvier. In Britain, as Adrian Desmond has emphasised, the transformism of Lamarck proved attractive to a counter-culture of materialists and radicals but was generally suppressed by such dignitaries as Charles Lyell and Richard Owen, the latter trampling on the Lamarckian Robert Grant at a critical juncture in his career.[16] The social and political connotations of transformism were such that Darwin was troubled by the thought that to admit the mutability of species was like confessing to a murder. His own theory, however, stood in a somewhat paradoxical relation to the political climate of his time. By adding scientific authority to Herbert Spencer's concept of the survival of the fittest, he seemed to reinforce the values of a *laissez-faire* capitalism, but at the same time undermined the religious foundations on which those values had often been sustained. The rapid dissemination of his theory also had much to do with the fact that it could be invoked to support colonialist and imperialist ideologies in which the racial superiority of white anglo-saxons was commonly taken for granted.

The continuity between humans and animals, which for Darwin was corroborated by a comparable range of emotional expression in both, was also politically attractive to secular thinkers who wished to undermine the credibility of institutional religion. In England, T. H. Huxley showed particular hostility to the Roman Catholic, St George Jackson Mivart, who tried to integrate biological evolution with the teachings of his Church. In so doing, Mivart attacked Darwin's concept of natural selection, epitomising for Huxley the unacceptable intrusion of religious values into scientific debate. The most aggressive statement of the new naturalism was made by the physicist John Tyndall in his Belfast address to the British Association for the Advancement of Science in 1874: 'We claim and we shall wrest from theology the entire domain of cosmological theory'.[17] But it was in Germany where the programme was most relentlessly pursued, by materialists such as Ludwig Buchner and Carl Vogt, and by the monist Ernst Haeckel who saw in evolution the basis of a new religion. The fact that Darwinian phylogenies were associated with secularist and materialist propaganda helps to explain why, in France for example, it was not until the 1890s that Catholic commentators began to look at all sympathetically at Darwin's original theory, having at last recognised that it might be disentangled from the rhetoric with which it had been invested. It has been argued by James Moore in his study of *The Post-Darwinian Controversies* (1979) that among Protestants in Europe and America it was actually religious conservatives who had the best resources with which to come to terms with Darwin, in that they were able to resist facile liberal syntheses in which central Darwinian concepts such as natural selection and evolutionary divergence were frequently caricatured. One of the grounds on which Moore affirms his paradoxical thesis is an alleged structural parallel between the reconciliation of natural selection with Providence and the reconciliation, with which Calvinists in particular were only too familiar, between human freedom and divine sovereignty. It is difficult to deny, however, that Darwinian evolution gave the greatest impetus to religious radicalism. Thus David Strauss welcomed Darwin's account of human evolution precisely because it showed that man had risen not fallen. The former view gave hope to the human race, whereas the traditional doctrine of original sin was cause only for despair.

Too sharp a polarity between Darwinian secularism and religious commitment can, nevertheless, conceal many intermediate positions which, during the late nineteenth and early twentieth century, capitalised to a greater or lesser degree on the fact that Darwin's mechanism of natural selection, far from being scientifically sacrosanct, remained highly problematic.[18] Rechristianising the evolutionary philosophy of Herbert Spencer, the Scotsman and liberal evangelical, Henry Drummond, went so far as to claim that Christianity and Evolution were one and the same: each had as its object the making of more perfect living beings. So complete a fusion was only possible, however, if altruism had a higher profile in the evolutionary process than Darwin had indicated. Many other schemes of theistic evolution, notably that of Teilhard de Chardin in the twentieth century, have gained their theological plausibility only in so far as they have departed from neo-Darwinian orthodoxy by importing *a priori* concepts of perfection towards which the evolutionary process is said to be converging. In Teilhard's system, which has been much criticised for its poetic licence in the use of scientific metaphor and for its ascription of incipient forms of life and consciousness to matter itself, the perfection of Christ both symbolises and presages a focal point to which the cosmic process, through the emergence and heightening of human consciousness, is said to be converging.

In the late nineteenth century, many thinkers were just as disenchanted with the ambitious claims of the scientific naturalists as they were with the claims of traditional Christianity (F. M. Turner, *Between Science and Religion* (1974)). The idea that scientific knowledge should be the basis of a new culture, that scientists would be the new arbiters of moral worth, smacked of turning science into a substitute religion which for some, like Darwin's cousin Francis Galton, it almost certainly was – with eugenics as the new creed of human perfectibility. In opposition to such scientism stood some of the leading scientific figures of the nineteenth century: the physicists Clerk Maxwell, William Thomas (Lord Kelvin) and George Stokes, the geologist Charles Lyell (who, whilst a convert to Darwinian evolution, never renounced the view that there were distinct features of the mind which eluded reduction to natural selection) and Alfred Russel Wallace who, as co-founder with Darwin of the theory of natural selection, was nevertheless drawn into spiritualism to account for human creativity and aesthetic appreciation in such spheres as mathematics and music. As he reflected on the religious experience of mankind, the American psychologist William James observed that science would never defeat religion, or entirely usurp its role, because it could not answer the most fundamental human needs which were bound up with the inner world of the psyche. Developing a pragmatic conception of religious truth, he argued that if a religious belief enriched the life of the person who held it, it could be considered true for that person.

10. SCIENCE AND RELIGION IN THE TWENTIETH CENTURY

The twentieth century has witnessed many 'scientific' critiques of religion. Those deriving from Darwin, Marx and Freud have become almost commonplace. Moreover there has been a powerful philosophical tradition, taking its inspiration from the logical positivism of the Vienna school (see art. 54, sect. 2), which has persisted in affirming a dichotomy between scientific propositions which are in principle falsifiable (even if they are not verifiable) and religious claims which are to be rejected because, as with propositions about the love of God, they conform to neither of those criteria. On the other hand, certain developments within the sciences themselves have created extra space for dialogue between scientists and theologians. Thus the development of quantum mechanics not only created difficulties for a crude scientific determinism, but by drawing attention to the limitations of scientific models, also contributed to a climate in which both scientists and theologians became more prepared to regard their formulations as partial models rather than all-encompassing dogmas. The argument has sometimes been taken to an extreme in which neither scientific theories nor religious doctrines are presumed to represent an external reality, but are assumed to fulfil a purely instrumental role in the two totally different contexts in which they are used. Indeed, a conspicuous feature of twentieth-century literature on the subject has been the prevalence of attempts to insulate theology from any implications which might be drawn from the natural sciences.

One variant of this insularity thesis was mentioned in the introduction: Bultmann's existentialist analysis of the doctrine of Creation. Instrumentalist accounts of both scientific and religious models constitute the grounds of another. A third variant occurs in the work of linguistic philosophers who, claiming a pedigree from Wittgenstein, insist that scientific and religious vocabularies belong to two distinct language games, the one characterised by object detachment, the other by personal commitment. Yet other variants attempt to establish the proposition that scientific and religious language relate to different 'aspects' or 'dimensions' of human experience. Such attempts to protect theology from the relevance of science can, however, seem unduly defensive and, as W. H. Austin has argued in *The Relevance of Natural Science to Theology* (1976), few stand up to vigorous analysis.

In creating space for dialogue, the most significant development has probably been the loss of that faith which, in the Enlightenment, had been placed in science as the key to solving all human problems. Even before the First World War shattered so many illusions, doubts had been expressed about the negative consequences of a technological society, in which unemployment might be increased and the environment rendered more dangerous. It is not merely that atomic bombs and industrial pollution have turned Utopian fantasies into nightmares but, contrary to the triumphalist images of the nineteenth century, science has actually generated problems which it is itself powerless to solve. Many of these are familiar enough in the sphere of medical ethics. Indirectly, as with new penumbras of ignorance created by nuclear technology, they affect us all. The interface between science and moral accountability is one along which religious values can still have relevance as is argued in *The Touch of Midas*, edited by Sardar (1984). There are, however, no neat religious solutions to what are unprecedented moral dilemmas. Many scientists understandably remain suspicious of any attempt to import what can appear simplistic or alien values into policy decisions, especially if they are perceived as harbingers of fanaticism. Nor is there likely to be any consensus achieved on such matters within closed religious communities. There is, for example, considerable disagreement among contemporary Muslim writers as to what a distinctively 'Islamic science' would look like and how a secularised western science can be purged of its materialistic connotations. One conclusion which the history of science has, however, established is that under different value-systems, different priorities are accorded to different subjects of scientific research, and different directions delineated for its practical application. As long as the world's religions continue to stake a claim in the elaboration of those values, the two domains of science and religion are unlikely to be completely severed.

NOTES

1. J. W. Draper, *History of the conflict between religion and science* (London, 1875), Preface.
2. F. Manuel, *The religion of Isaac Newton* (Oxford, 1974).
3. R. Hookyaas, *Religion and the rise of modern science* (Edinburgh, 1972).
4. Rolf Gruner, 'Science, nature and christianity', *Journal of theological studies*, 26 (1975) 55–81.
5. E. Zilsel, 'The genesis of the concept of the physical law', *Philosophical review*, 51 (1942), 245–79.
6. R. K. Merton, *Science, technology and society in seventeenth-century England* (New York, 1970).
7. J. and M. Jacob, 'The Anglican origins of modern science', *Isis*, 71 (1980), 251–67.
8. G. De Santillana, *The crime of Galileo* (Chicago, 1955).
9. P. Redondi, *Galileo eretico* (Turin, 1983). English translation: *Galileo heretic*, transl. by Raymond Rosenthal, (Allen Lane, 1988).
10. D. Kubrin, 'Newton and the cyclical cosmos: providence and the mechanical philosophy', *Journal of the history of ideas*, 28 (1967), 325–46; also available in C. A. Russel (ed.), *Science and religious belief* (Open University Press, 1973), pp. 147–69.
11. M. C. Jacob, *The Newtonians and the English revolution* (Hassocks, 1976).
12. S. Shapin, 'Of gods and kings: natural philosophy and politics in the Leibniz–Clarke disputes', *Isis* 72 (1981), 187–215.
13. R. L. Numbers, *Creation by natural law: Laplace's nebular hypothesis in American thought* (Seattle, 1977).
14. J. H. Brooke, 'Indications of a creator: Whewell as apologist and priest', in M. Fisch and S. Schaffer (eds.), *William Whewell* (Oxford, forthcoming.)
15. J. H. Brooke, 'The relations between Darwin's science and his religion', in J. R. Durant (ed.) *Darwinism and divinity* (Oxford, 1985), chap. 2.
16. A. Desmond, *Archetypes and ancestors* (London, 1982).
—— *The politics of evolution* (forthcoming).
17. J. Tyndall, Presidential Address to the 1874 meeting of the British Association for the Advancement of Science, reproduced in G. Basalla, W. Coleman and R. Kargon (eds.), *Victorian science* (New York, 1970), pp. 441–78, pp. 474–5.
18. P. J. Bowler, *The eclipse of Darwinism* (Baltimore, 1983).

FURTHER READING

I. G. Barbour, *Issues in science and religion* (London, 1966).
J. Dillenberger, *Protestant thought and natural science* (London, 1961).
C. C. Gillispie, *Genesis and geology* (New York, 1959).
N. C. Gillespie, *Charles Darwin and the problem of creation* (Chicago, 1979).
T. Glick (ed.), *The comparative reception of Darwinism* (Austin, 1974).
D. C. Lindberg and R. L. Numbers (eds.), *God and nature: historical essays on the encounter between Christianity and science* (Berkeley, 1986).
D. Ospovat, *The development of Darwin's theory* (Cambridge, 1981).
A. Peacocke (ed.), *The sciences and theology in the twentieth century*.
Z. Sardar (ed.), *The touch of Midas: science, values and environment in Islam and the West* (Manchester, 1984).
S. Schaffer, 'Godly men and mechanical philosophers: souls and spirits in restoration natural philosophy', *Science in context*, 1 (1987), 55–85.
K. Thomas, *Religion and the decline of magic* (Harmondsworth, 1973).
F. M. Turner, 'The Victorian conflict between science and religion: a professional dimension', *Isis* 69 (1978), 356–76.
—— *Between science and religion* (New Haven, 1974).
C. Webster (ed.), *The intellectual revolution of the seventeenth century* (London, 1974).
R. S. Westfall, *Science and religion in seventeenth-century England* (New Haven, 1958).

51

SCIENCE AND LITERATURE

GILLIAN BEER

1. BOUNDARIES OF EXPLANATION

Science and literature have always been related. Scientists share language with other writers and learn the stories of their culture. Literature is produced within the conditions of expectation marked out by current scientific understanding of the physical world and by the technological advances which result from scientific theory. However, though such relations may seem self-evident, their study – and the study of further historically-varying connections between science and literature – have been a fairly recent academic interest. The polarisation of science and literature itself is also of comparatively recent date.

We may be far from the position of the alchemical writer Michael Maier who saw his work *Atalanta Fugiens* (1617) as reaching its full scientific effectiveness only when it was read both silently and aloud, its emblems pored over and copied, its instructions carried out and related to everyday life, and sections of it sung polyphonically. Such *gesamtkunstwerk* is no longer part of the scientific enterprise nor indeed, of the literary. Nevertheless, the overlapping of science and literature has not been obliterated. Well into the nineteenth century scientists were citing literary material as part of their evidence (as the geologist Charles Lyell cites Ovid in *Principles of Geology* (1830–33). Despite intermittently voiced suspicions of the stultifying effects of scientific analysis on the imagination (a suspicion first strong in the Romantic period), creative writers have continued to draw on scientific theories and discoveries. They have also sought to invoke scientific authority for their work – if only to demonstrate how much more thorough-going is the artist's understanding of events. An example of suspicion of science is that of William Hazlitt in his influential essay *Poetry in General* (1818) which profoundly affected the second generation of Romantic poets in England. He declares that 'there can never be another Jacob's dream. Since that time, the heavens have gone farther off, and grown astronomical.

They have become averse to the imagination, nor will they return to us on the squares of the distances.'[1] An example of the half-ironic invocation of the explanatory authority of science can be seen in the opening sentence of Joseph Conrad's novel *Victory* (1915): 'There is, as every schoolboy knows in this scientific age, a very close chemical relation between coal and diamonds.' Conrad then plays on the discourses common to science and to finance:

> The world of finance is a mysterious world in which, incredible as the fact may appear, evaporation precedes liquidation. First the capital evaporates, and then the company goes into liquidation. These are very unnatural physics, but they account for the persistent inertia of Heyst, at which we 'out there' used to laugh among ourselves. An inert body can do no harm to any one.[2]

Conrad disturbs the autonomy of scientific language, and by implication science, by showing how its terms overlap with those of capital. He invites the reader to share an intellectual knowledge of 'inert bodies' which seems comically out of scale with the implied laziness of Heyst. The 'unnatural physics' of finance already augurs the instability of all law, natural, economic or social. The 'out there' is both the isolation of the colonist and of the 'objective' observer.

Writers, scientific and literary, have often made it their business to disturb creatively the boundaries of the terms within which they work. John Tyndall, for example, opens his essay on *The Scientific Use of the Imagination* by provocatively expanding the term 'poetry':

> To spur up the emotions, on which so much depends, as well as to nourish indirectly the intellect and the will, I took with me two volumes of poetry, Goethe's 'Farbenlehre', and the work on 'Logic' recently published by Mr. Alexander Bain.[3]

Tyndall here cross-faces the habitual expectations of what kind of text will stir the emotions (works on optics and logic are not usually assumed to do so) and asserts the poetry of the intellect. His project in the essay is to insist that empiricism and speculation are not opposed activities, and that scientific activity is imaginative activity.

At very much the same period that Tyndall was seeking to close the gap between science and other imaginative enterprises, Sir Leslie Stephen, one of the first major literary analysts, was claiming 'a scientific basis' for literary criticism. It is important at the outset to recognise that there has been a recurrent yearning for the scientific model in the literary theory of the past hundred years, even in periods when many creative writers, such as D. H. Lawrence and George Bernard Shaw, were repudiating the scientific enterprise. Stephen offers a description based on one major activity of Victorian science – taxonomy – and makes a claim to objectivity, or to the role of observer, which has been a classic characterisation of the scientific. (That heuristic description is itself now the subject of much controversy, as may be seen in Stephen Toulmin, *The Return to Cosmology, Postmodern Science and the Theology of Nature* (1982) and

Evelyn Fox Keller, *Reflections on Gender and Science* (1985).) Stephen, writing very much at the beginning of a separate practice of 'literary criticism' and before its acceptance into the university curriculum, seeks to distinguish criticism from oratory or persuasion and to assert the 'testability' of literary value.

> Though criticism cannot boast of being a science, it ought to aim at something like a scientific basis, or at least to proceed in a scientific spirit. The critic, therefore, before abandoning himself to the oratorical impulse, should endeavour to classify the phenomena with which he is dealing as calmly as if he were ticketing a fossil in a museum . . . When we are seeking to justify our emotions, we must endeavour to get for the time into the position of an independent spectator, applying with rigid impartiality such methods as are best calculated to free us from the influence of personal bias.[4]

Whereas Tyndall emphasises emotion and imagination in the scientific enterprise, Stephen emphasises classification and impartiality in that of the literary critic. Each creatively transgresses the stereotype by adopting terms considered appropriate to a contrary field. Stephen goes further, to point out a paradox in the activity of scientific and literary analyst alike: 'To be an adequate critic is almost to be a contradiction in terms; to be susceptible to a force, and yet free from its influence; to be moving with the stream, and yet to be standing on the bank'. That sentence, Toulmin suggests, already pinpoints a predicament later intensified in modern scientific theorising; the loss of the detached spectator 'out there' has been a characteristic movement in recent scientific thinking.

What needs to be done, and is now beginning to be done, in studying 'Science and Literature', is a careful analysis of the diverse relationships concealed within the 'and', as well as the differing priorities in the ordering: 'Science and Literature' and 'Literature and Science'. Built into these pairs are assumptions not only about connection but also about which enterprise comes first or even which matters more. This essay will present examples of differing levels of allusion to science within specific literary texts. It will track some of the patterns ascribed historically to relations between science and literature, and it will examine the argument that scientists inevitably work within the constraints of current cultural assumptions which have, at least in the past, been most influentially expressed in literature. The extreme consequence of this argument is sometimes taken to be that science is simply a form of writing like any other and, like most writing, will be vitiated by the loss of its cultural context. First let us consider the terms 'science' and 'literature' and the questions of belief implied in their designation.

2. TERMS AND BELIEF

When the literary theorist I. A. Richards set out to describe and to distinguish between scientific and poetic language, he called his essay, at first, *Science and*

Poetry (1926). In the next edition the title ran, less readily, *Poetries and Sciences*. This manoeuvre brings out a central difficulty: can either science or literature be a unitary system? Much modern literary theory would deny that literature is an autonomous domain of writing, thus Stanley Fish writes in *Is there a Text in This Class?* (1980): 'What will, at any time, be recognised as literature is a function of a communal decision as to what will count as literature'. Rather than literature exhibiting 'certain formal properties that compel a certain kind of attention . . . paying a certain kind of attention . . . results in the emergence into noticeability of the properties we know in advance to be literary'.[5] Fish is here reacting against the assumption of a 'canon' of literary works and, alongside writers like Pierre Macherey in *A Theory of Literary Production* (1978), against the emphasis on the individual author; the production of a text, he argues, is an act of reading within a specific historical culture. Macherey substitutes the term 'production' for 'creation', thereby claiming a materialist, even a technological, analogy and repudiating the theistic and individualistic. While literary theory in its post-structuralist phase has been emphasising textuality (reading process, variety of discourse, illimitability of interpretation), writers in the history of science, such as Martin Rudwick in *The Great Devonian Controversy: The Shaping of Scientific Knowledge among Gentlemanly Specialists* (1985), have demonstrated that scientific knowledge is the product of people in social interaction and have brought to the foreground the cultural and political constituents of such knowledge-formation (e.g. Robert M. Young, *Darwin's Metaphor* (1985)). The position of the 'author' has been differently treated in the history of science and of literary theory but the emphasis on the role of cultural interaction has had a similar importance in both. The past hundred years of increasingly institution-based science have seen a movement into a multitude of specialisations with little manifest interconnection and very diverse vocabularies. Most scientists, however, seem to remain content with the professional description of themselves as scientists and of the activity in which they are involved as science. 'Science' is an old term often used to cover both the particular methods of empirical enquiry and also the products of that enquiry alike (we shall find it many times in Francis Bacon's initiating work in the late sixteenth and early seventeenth century); 'scientist' is comparatively recent, becoming much used only in the earlier nineteenth century to separate, and privilege, the professional pursuit of knowledge of the material world. At about the same time the word 'literature' acquired a new designation, coming to mean particularly both 'the body of writings produced in a particular country or period, or in the world in general' *and* by the 1860s, the more restricted sense of 'writing which has claim to consideration on the ground of beauty of form or emotional effect'. 'This sense' remarks the Oxford English Dictionary, from which these definitions are quoted 'is of very recent emergence both in English and French'. The separation and intensification of terms almost certainly accompanies a newly-marked separation of activity, the outcome of which was to be the topic of the controversy surrounding C. P. Snow's, *The Two Cultures* in the 1950s.

Since the time of Snow's essay, however, the powerful influence of, predominantly, French theorists, such as Foucault and Serres, has emphasised the contiguity of the various projects which we summarise within the terms 'science' and 'literature'. Their work has emphasised the power strategies which underpin discourse and in the case of Serres, the endless simultaneity of science and myth. Serres has harkened back to the idea of archaic laws of the imagination which condition all discovery, in a surprising refurbishment of the myth of origins: 'The sacred mythic and religious words are' [in Western culture since the *Odyssey*] 'spoken at the same time and in the same breath as those of science and of journeys'. He suggests that 'the realms of the subjective and the objective are no longer at odds ... they are both order *and* disorder'.[6] Serres is here implicitly alluding to his own earlier work on Zola's response to, and implication in, thermodynamic theories (*Feux et signaux de brume: Zola*, 1975). The amalgamation of discourses and the unsteadying of contracts of belief between reader and text is typical of Serres's work. It is a process which had begun already in Zola's appropriation of Claude Bernard's innovatory work on methodology as in *Introduction à l'étude de la médicine expérimentale* (1865). Zola adapted Bernard's observations concerning controlled experiments and the making of prognoses in *Le roman expérimental* in order to justify his own novelistic methods and themes. He explored the cultural and genetic determinisms of a family and a society in the Rougon-Macquart series and claimed for the novelist some of the same verifiability and prognostic power which experiment was introducing into rule-bound medicine. As so often, scientific ideas and methods are at their most powerful in literary works when it is possible to loosen the terminology and punningly transgress the terms provided. If we are to analyse accurately some of the typical generative movements of science *into* literature, we should not look for tight equivalence but rather for fugitive allusion, a changing of contractual terms of belief and paradoxical appropriations of ideas in an incompletely argued form. It is worth noting both how recent is the drawing of linguistic lines of demarcation around 'literature' and the 'scientist' and also the urgency with which literature has raided scientific ideas in the past hundred years, while scientists have, on the face of it during that time, made allusion less and less to literature.

What does this imbalance signify? The specialisation of the terms literature and science in the nineteenth century records a process which has led to an emphasis on contrary visions. Contradictory views of what science itself signified are to be found within the European Romantic movements of the late eighteenth and early nineteenth centuries. *Naturphilosophie* suggested that scientific discovery might unfold an organic whole realised in manifold forms, while the simultaneously increasing emphasis on experiment led forward into discrete specialisations. Sometimes poets like William Blake asserted that science serves the insights of myth:

> The Atoms of Democritus
> And Newton's particles of light
> Are sands upon the Red Sea shore
> Where Israel's tents do shine so bright.[7]

More sardonically, Emily Dickinson in mid-century observed:

> 'Faith' is a fine invention
> When Gentlemen can *see*–
> But *Microscopes* are prudent
> In an Emergency.[8]

The equivocation upon poetic belief and philosophical (that is to say, natural scientific) belief is the unsteadying topic of Keats's 1820 poem *Lamia*, which takes up the Hazlitt essay quoted earlier. The ambiguously-natured Lamia, alternately woman and serpent, creates a palace of erotic delights for the wooing of her lover, Lycius. Their loving security is short-lived. The aged 'philosopher' Apollonius literally sees through Lamia so that her illusionary world and self withers, bringing with it the death of Lycius. The analytical enquiry here jeopardises the fleeting truths of poetry and the ephemeral delights of sensory life; once Lamia is *known* by the philosopher her ambiguity becomes fraudulence, her visioned palace simply delusion. The analytical powers of science and the univocality of scientific discourse become the object of dread. It is as if, even magically, any system of explanation which separates out and names parts would make it impossible to put them back together again. (Keats was a medical student before anaesthesia or disinfectants so that the suppressed image of the surgeon's knife or of an experiment which necessitates the death of the subject has a historical and personal bearing.)

Also implied in the poem is an argument about how to value the univocal discourse of science, with its authentication from a substantial referent in the physical world, as against multivocal poetic discourse with its simultaneity of referents, no one of which is given authenticating primacy. Propositions can be invalidated by new evidence. Is this true of poetry? Can poetry? The problem of substantiation has continued to be claimed as a primary distinction between the literary and the scientific. Poetry is free of time because it does not claim to represent knowledge up to this point in time, argues Maurice Blanchot in *L'Espace littéraire* (1955). It has no origin in the real world.

I. A. Richards attempted a less metaphysical answer to the same linguistic problem of what styles of belief are demanded by literary and scientific texts from the reader. He contrasts, without preference, the 'statements' of science and the 'pseudo-statements' of literature. Despite the derogatory connotations of 'pseudo', Richards is attempting a dry and clear distinction which will preserve the fullness of poetry. Statement (which we might now call propositional discourse) demands belief; pseudo-statement does not; indeed, Richards argues that, in watching a tragedy, it is crucial that we 'cut our pseudo-statements free from belief and yet retain them, in this released state, as the main instrument by which we order our attitudes to each other and the world'. Richards denies that there can be any conflict between pseudo-statements and 'statements proper such as science provides'. However, the admirably autocratic division (as so often in other such discussions) immediately begins to blur over the word 'belief'. Richards appears to confuse 'believing in' and 'believing that': 'We need no beliefs, and indeed we must have none, if we are to read *King Lear*'.[9] Watching the play we need not believe in the historical examples but we set out with an implied prior, communal belief that children should not be cruel to their parents.

Derrida's strategy of 'ungrounding' is an attempt to take this question of belief towards a different solution. Instead of privileging either science or literature as a discursive form, he seeks to do away with traditional oppositions, to erase ideas of origin and to emphasise the problematical nature of meaning in all texts: 'Deconstruction cannot be restricted or immediately pass to a neutralization: it must, through a double gesture, a double science, a double writing – put into practice a *reversal* of the classical opposition *and* a general *displacement* of the system'.[10] Derrida's immensely influential thought has unsettled assumed relations between scientific and literary meaning and their recomposition alongside other writings. It has probably contributed to a move (which also pre-dates him) away from seeing 'science' as source and 'literature' as embellishment.

3. ORIGINS AND INTERCHANGE: TWO MODELS

Questions of priority have bedevilled discussion of the relations between science and literature, particularly in literary theory and criticism. Is a work of literature explained by exposition of the scientific theories or discoveries to which it alludes? How full an explanation does such a procedure offer? The work of some pioneers such as Marjorie Hope Nicolson in *The Breaking of the Circle: Studies in the Effect of the 'New Science' upon Seventeenth Century Poetry* (1950) and *Newton Demands the Muse: Newton's Opticks and the Eighteenth Century Poets* (1946) tended, with great erudition, to settle the work of literature upon what was seen as its scientific base. It refers the work back to prior conditions of its intellectual production. The scientific referent may blur or excise other simultaneous significations. The result may be to over-stabilise reading even though the critic may be praising (as Nicolson was) innovation and disturbance.

The opposing view is that literature provides fresh ideas, which are then later systematically demonstrated by scientists. This view may make scientists appear as over-zealous demonstrators of what has already been thought, as in George Bernard Shaw's evident misunderstanding of the need for diversity and thoroughness in marshalling scientific explanation. Shaw, in the preface to *Back to Methuselah*, contemptuously argues that 'If very few of us have read *The Origin of Species* from end to end, it is not because it overtaxes our mind, but because we take in the whole case and are prepared to accept it long before we have come to the end of the innumerable instances and illustrations of which the book mainly consists'.[11] Elizabeth Sewell's *The Orphic Voice: Poetry and Natural History* (1961) asserts that 'Biology has mistaken its mythology. It needs poetry rather than mathematics or language-as-science to think with.' Sewell was herself much influenced by Michael Polanyi's work *Personal Knowledge* (1958) which argued that both scientific hypotheses and poetry surpass the writers' powers of exposition. The break-up of systematisation implied in such work is carried out in a more thorough-going way in Paul Feyerabend's *Against Method* (1975). Both philosophers of science and literary theorists and practitioners have thus challenged the autonomous nature of scientific language, the absolute objectivity of scientific method and its priority of language.

The disadvantages of posing either science or literature as source or origin for the other has given rise to another current model: that of interchange, or even simultaneity. Within this account, particular discoveries or particular literary works may initiate fresh perceptions for the other field but the emphasis is on interaction. The activity of metaphor is particularly important in this mode of analysis.

One development of recent years has been the readiness to use literary critical techniques to analyse works written originally as scientific texts (and thereby in some periods implicitly claiming exemption from cultural analysis). Earlier instances of this approach were Stanley Hyman, *The Tangled Bank: Darwin, Marx, Frazer and Freud as imaginative writers* (1962) and Jacques Barzun's *Darwin, Marx and Wagner* (1958). Morse Peckham has demonstrated in works like *Man's Rage for Chaos* (1965) the extent to which 'scientific' texts yield information about cultural and imaginative processes, as well as codifying discovery in language. The present writer's *Darwin's Plots* (1983) offers a detailed analysis of the language with which Darwin had to work and shows how the discourse he shared with other writers of the time privileged concepts such as design and creation. He had to write against the grain of the inherited language in order to precipitate his own thesis. The cultural constituents of a shared tongue make for enriching difficulty: Darwin's theories very rapidly moved out into the common culture with multiple and often contradictory readings of their social and imaginative implications.

One of the most rewarding fields in which literary analysis has been applied to texts written with a theoretic and therapeutic intent is in the recent work on Freud's case-histories. A considerable number of feminist critics such as Toril Moi have worked on the Dora case-history (e.g. C. Bernheimer (ed.), *In Dora's Case: Freud–hysteria–feminism* (1985).) Peter Brooks in *Reading for the Plot* (1984) has demonstrated how the story plotted by Freud employs the narrative expectations of early twentieth-century readers and the narrative assumptions of a writer steeped in Victorian fiction, as Freud was. (See also Sebastiano Timpanaro, *The Freudian Slip: psychoanalysis and textual criticism* (1976).) Such criticism takes away from scientific writing its privileged address and subjects it to the analytical procedures considered appropriate for other texts. The method does not challenge the efficacy of the scientific text nor does it under-mine the claims of the scientist to demonstrate empirically his propositions. It does examine the processes of encoding by which assumptions shared *beyond* science are built into scientific statement. Conclusions are reached within science which harbour the procedures of language and which are to some extent controlled by them. Evelyn Fox Keller discusses the underlying meta-phors of Plato and Bacon and the gendered epistemologies of scientific language in her *Reflections on Gender and Science* (1985). Few would deny scien-tific writing its propositional status, with the implicit expectation of testing, correction and moving on to a further stage of argument. What is now denied is that scientific writing, or science, occupies a domain exempt from language and from cultural determinations, though many of the accretive discoveries of science will break loose from the cultural tongue in which they were first described.

A study which well demonstrates the gains and difficulties of the 'inter-change' model is that of Stephen Kern, *The Culture of Time and Space 1880–1918* (1983). Kern excellently demonstrates the multiple interactions of ideas and events in the sciences, visual arts, politics, literature, film, techno-logy, architecture and international war and peace. The work, like its subject-matter, presents itself as a shifting series of relations and momentary group-ings. Kern notes how technological changes redefine culture; both literature and science were transformed by the advent of the telephone and the aero-plane. Kern carefully does not separate off scientific and literary material from other constituents of a culture or study solely their interactions. Instead, he encourages the reader to take account of a variety of material changes and spe-culations. He thus dispels any suggestion that one form of experience has supremacy. Kern, like other recent historians and literary theorists, has learnt to pay attention to Arthur Lovejoy's warning that we should not seek to make the thought of an individual or an age all hang together.[12] As it happens, this warning allows Kern paradoxically and perhaps over-insistently to suggest that irreconcilability is particularly pronounced in the age he studies: thus it becomes itself a cohesive principle. This aesthetic yearning towards 'imitative form' is marked in much literary cultural history (and indeed is one of the modes of naturalisation sometimes favoured by scientific theorists).

Although we cannot do without a model of dialectics it needs to be one which is more sinuous than four square (emphasising the emergence of an unforeseen third term and the generation of further potential contraries, rather than simply the locked opposition of two terms). Thus in examining the relations of science and literature, we need to get beyond definitions which pose them as isolated contraries or a privileged pair and instead to re-immerse them in the multiplicity of forces that generate the specific text, the particular discovery and which fire the individual imagination. We need, that is, both to sustain an awareness of what is peculiar to a work and can be analysed in that work, and to observe the diverse forces in its production and its contribution to those forces. Its reproduction as later reading within the conditions of future historical culture will be different again, and will result in further interchanges.

4. THE BODY AND DESIGN

Although the interchange model appears somewhat novel at present, it has some curious and ancient precedents. One axis on which the connection of science and literature turns is that of philosophy, another is the human body. These diverse (or apparently diverse) domains of language have together provided the microcosm/macrocosm analogy. This analogy was objectively believed from Paracelsus through to the time of Newton. Even more recently, in the softer form of anthropomorphism, it continues to haunt our patterning of the world about us. As Marjorie Hope Nicolson observes, Paracelsian homologies inform the writing of Kepler, even while his contention that the planets moved about the sun in ellipses, not circles, undermined the earlier belief in the perfect circle as the pattern of all existence. Kepler writes: 'As the body produces hair on the skin, so the earth produces plants and trees, and as in the former lice are generated, so in the latter caterpillars, crickets, and many other insects and sea-monsters'.[13] Such close analogies did not die out with the seventeenth century. We can observe even a writer like Darwin, intent on destabilising the centrality of humankind, having difficulty with the double meaning of a phrase like 'the face of nature' in which the sense of 'surface' is less prominent than that of 'human visage'.[14] The implicit presence of the human body in writing and language has made it hard to expunge from the terminology of science, as a glance at any number of *Nature* will demonstrate. This is true even where the context of use subdues the human referent almost to invisibility. During the Renaissance, human activities were commonly used to represent the order of the universe and we find examples of this in John Davies's *Orchestra* where atoms and stars alike perform a dance:

Since when they still are carried in a round,
And changing come one in anothers place,
Yet doe they neyther mingle nor confound,
But every one doth keep the bounded space
Wherein the daunce doth bid it turn or trace.[15]

Such a poem is an attempt at serious play upon concepts poised easily and equally within the myth and science of the time. It depends ultimately upon the idea of design, in which a benign intent displays and patterns all the possibilities of the universe.

As long as scientists and writers could both figure their activity as theistic, manifesting the workings of God in the material world, or in the human person, or in the organisation of fiction or poem, no alienation of one activity from the other was implied, though the scale of commitment might differ. Henry Fielding saw the novelist's task essentially as the magnanimous ordering of the world so as to represent God's governance truthfully. Even a century later than Fielding, the great physicist James Clerk Maxwell used, in his 1870 lecture on molecules, a reflexive argument from design to insist on the benign ordering of molecular structures. The asserted equivalence between the properties of intelligence and of the world it greets were used to enforce inherent order. This is so in Henry Fielding's eighteenth-century writing where the reader's attentiveness is gratified by the complex and perfect working-out of the plot of his novel *Tom Jones*: the meeting of these two aspects can unostentatiously represent the order of God who, in Pope's words, fills, bounds, connects and equals all. This feature of epistemology, in which the mind gratefully finds the likeness of its procedures in the material world, and takes for granted the stories told in the culture, is one of the most persistent of all tropes. It is a meeting point for science and literature in which the two practices tend to reinforce each other unless the most alert and scrupulous scepticism is sustained.

Analogy as something more than a rhetorical trope for calling attention to shared characteristics persists into the nineteenth century in science. One of Clerk Maxwell's first papers, for example, is entitled 'Are there real analogies in Nature?' and Darwin, despite his proper methodological scepticism concerning the force of analogy as evidence, found himself driven to observe and value analogy between his widely separated domains of study and to argue for 'true affinities' within morphology. In literature, analogy has continued to be used without compunction as an ordering principle, although much post-modern literature is encyclopedic rather than classificatory in its procedures. William Golding's novel, *Pincher Martin* (1956) offers a malign version of the microcosm/macrocosm theme, in which a narcissistic Everyman is shipwrecked on an island which proves to be his own tooth. The collapse inward of perceived exteriority is one of Golding's cruellest comments on modern man's place in nature. No space is left for the observer; he is entirely implicated.

The analogy between the practice of doctor and writer, as well as the figure of the doctor, is one of the main points of connection between science and literature. The double role of the doctor – pastoral in his relations and empirical in his enquiries – was an intriguing one for novelists in the nineteenth century, allowing them to explore contradictions (Lydgate in George Eliot's *Middlemarch*) as well as to provide resolutions (the last volume of Zola's Rougon-Macquart series, *Docteur Pascal*.) In novels, doctors can figure as altruistic heroes who can bring the book romantically and ethically to a satisfactory conclusion (Dr. Woodcourt in Dickens's *Bleak House*). The inadequacies of medical training may, more sardonically, become the material of painful description, as in Charles Bovary's maladroit operation on a club-foot in Flaubert's *Madame Bovary*. But the importance of doctors for the novelist was probably more in their social functions than their scientific: doctors could circulate professionally within a very wide social range; they knew more than most about their patients; they were observers of the community and sometimes at odds with its values (Fitzpiers in Hardy's *The Woodlanders*). Doctors – and quasi-medical men – were and are the most familar face of scientific discovery in society. It is in the doctor's surgery that people most directly acknowledge science. In *Tristram Shandy*, Dr Slop also provides a bridge (of a slippery kind) across to the subject of nature. His familiarity, as an obstetrician, with female anatomy becomes a focus for jests about enquiry and 'knowing' which depend upon the long-established association of women and nature. The lewdness of the scientist probing nature is suggested in this figuration of active male and passive female. Nature is the object of enquiry, never the enquirer. The doctor, ideally, controls and heals, diagnoses and offers prognoses. The novelist may adopt this as a model for his own procedure, as Zola does. But the doctor also bungles and mismanages, mistakes diseases and offers false remedies. Sterne adopts the doctor as an example of this sort in his own novelistic proceedings: *Tristram Shandy*'s pleasures rely on the manifest attempts and failures of both writers and obstetricians to control the recalcitrant energies of living and dying.

5. SCIENTISTS IN LITERATURE

We shall not find in literature widespread reference to the ordinary doings of scientists. We shall look in vain for novels and plays set in the laboratory, unless it is a laboratory at the moment of war. (Nigel Dennis's *Cards of Identity* (1960) deals with the sinister practices of experiment, as did H. G. Wells's *The Island of Dr Moreau*; recently there have been one or two studies of Einstein.) But reference to science in fiction or drama outside science fiction is nearly always to the scientist as a magical, isolated individual whose experiments breach taboos of knowledge (as in Mary Shelley's *Frankenstein* (1819)) or to the scientist as the type of human power (Mann's *Dr. Faustus*) or as the human implicated in the machinations of the state, oppressed and surviving by stratagem (as in Brecht's *Galileo*). The scientist can stand as intellectual martyr or represent the extreme individualism of knowledge-seeking which breaches the bounds of society and of religion (as in the *Faust* legend and its literary forms). In Marlowe's version of the story, Dr. Faustus is presented essentially as libido, exacting from the natural and social world all possible pleasures and ignoring the aftermath of retribution. The scientist can become the form of excess, even of rapaciousness, and certainly of obdurate self-seeking (in both senses) as in Goethe's *Faust* and Thomas Mann's *Dr. Faustus*. It is not surprising that Freud should have used a passage from Goethe's *Faust* to complete his analytical description of the paranoid dilemma, in which the self, having destroyed the world for its own gratification and in its own terror at the withdrawal of love, must then build that world anew in its own image, using only the materials of the psyche. So when we look for the 'scientist in literature' we shall not find him or her so much at the level of social description as at that of myth.

There is a striking contrast between the level at which scientific theory is present in the ordering of novels and of poems. The condensation and linguistic innovation of lyric poems has meant that scientific ideas have offered puzzles to the poet from Sir Philip Sidney through to Adrienne Rich. These puzzles bear within them the recurrent and absorbing questions of teleology, design, autonomy, power and love. Very recently, Adrienne Rich and Diane Ackerman have responded to scientific and technical domains of experience in their poetry. Making sense of experience (even when it is a non-sense) is a goal shared by literature and science, and a consequent difficulty in their claim to truth-telling. Description takes for granted a teleology or discoverable pattern. This pattern will frequently be discovered to conform to pre-existing expectations, as Empson brilliantly records in his poem 'Doctrinal Point'.[16] The mind retrieves from the universe the patterns that the mind has traced upon it. This circularity, or uneasy dance, is a more recent version of the design argument, which we may have supposed reached its formation and conclusion in eighteenth-century work such as Pope's *Essay on Man*.

The industrial revolution and technology have shaped the experience of western culture since the nineteenth century and the classic realist texts of the period record that shaping. More recently, however, science fiction has used scientific theories and technological advances to imagine futures and track alternatives. Science fiction explores possibilities and refuses to discriminate between the possible and the impossible. It relies upon the reader's incredulity for its pleasures as much as on the writing's power of convincing us while we read even of that which is impossible. Of current science fiction writers Stanislaw Lem offers the most astounding virtuoso capacity to embroil us in experiences outside our sensory register and simultaneously to use such experiences to satirise current society. Since it is a fiction of ideas and types, of possibilities rather than realist representation, science fiction often cannot be distinguished from Utopian writing. In Isaac Asimov, Doris Lessing and Stanislaw Lem an assertive humanism unsettles our assumptions and makes strange the everyday. The idea of plurality of worlds and journeys to the moon had already entered fiction in the seventeenth century: H. G. Wells and Jules Verne developed both that idea and the concept of penetrating the reaches of our environment which we never ordinarily enter. Novelists such as Ursula le Guin and Margaret Atwood have used the future as a setting in order to force a recognition of the current repression of women. The imagined future can present a brutally exaggerated enactment of covert current assumptions. It can, equally, challenge our current practice by taking for granted what seem to us extraordinary freedoms. The amount of 'science' in science fiction varies greatly: in Asimov and particularly in Lem technical description is crucial, whereas some writers like Ursula le Guin seem to work far more within a William Morris Utopian tradition. Doris Lessing appropriates genetic ideas for her exploration of human destructiveness and the potential renewal of life. These themes haunt many works of science fiction but Lessing works them out with rare imaginative stamina and ethnographic thoroughness. The endemic danger of good science fiction is sentimentality, though repetitive violence is the style of the pulp-fiction which shares the title. Stanislaw Lem's sardonic eye on our assumptions keeps the easy solution at bay, so that in *Tales of Pirx the Pilot*, he can mingle satire and a kind of technological theology in which Pirx is Everyman, the irreducible human figure who can yet outgo the machinery to which he is bound.

Finally, by no means all the recent works which release characters and readers from the constraints of ordinary physical possibility could be classified as 'science fiction'. In Gabriel García Márquez's *One Hundred Years of Solitude*, people fly, levitate, live way past a hundred years and attract clouds of butterflies. The book opens by showing how a technology advanced beyond the expectations of a particular society will appear to be magic, for example, 'the false teeth of eternal youth'. Yet the work nonetheless shows its people confined by the chilling obduracies of human experience, particularly violence, forgetfulness and political oppression. So, recent developments in 'magical realism' have drawn on ideas of uncertainty and probability gleaned from scientific theory of this century, but not stringently in line with scientific arguments or practice.

Vigorous interchange of ideas and concerns between scientists and literary writers should not lead us to expect thorough-going and sustained congruity. We may be misled if we value, or seek, a systematic representation of scientific ideas in works of literature. We are far more likely to find a fugitive insight or generalised acceptance. Ideas do not remain static when they change context: science and literature transform rather than simply transfer. The dearth of literary citation and quotation in modern scientific papers should not mislead us into assuming that science is immured within its own domain. The stories privileged in a culture tend to be privileged also in its scientific work. If simplicity, hierarchy or synchrony are values, they will also be readily discovered.

Students in the field of 'science and literature' need to resist one-to-one systematisation. To recognise fugitive appropriation, slack application or covert story, without seeking to convert them into stable explanation, does not at all mean that the critic's observations are without stringency. Quite the contrary. Such a position demands considerable knowledge and restraint. Instead of seeking a single origin, the observer must scan a whole constellation of associated and unsettled material. That material will need to be drawn from the domains of science and literature and also from other cultural formations.

NOTES

1. W. Hazlitt, *Lectures on the English poets* (London, 1910) p. 9.
2. J. Conrad, *Victory* (London, 1948), p. 3.
3. J. Tyndall, *Essays on the use and limit of the imagination in science* (London, 1870) p. 15.
4. 'Charlotte Bronte', *Cornhill magazine*, 36 (1877), 723–4.
5. S. Fish, *Is there a text in this class?* (Cambridge, Mass., 1980), p. 10.
6. M. Serres, *Hermes: literature, science, philosophy* (Baltimore, 1982), pp. xxi, 82.
7. W. Blake, *Complete writings*, ed. G. Keynes (London, 1966), p. 418.
8. E. Dickinson, *Complete poems* (London, 1970), p. 185.
9. I. A. Richards, *Science and poetry* (London, 1926), p. 24.
10. J. Derrida, *Margins of philosophy* (Brighton, 1982).
11. G. B. Shaw, *Back to Methuselah*, Bodley Head Bernard Shaw (London, 1970–4) vol. 5, pp. 298–9.
12. A. Lovejoy, *Essays in the history of ideas* (1948; rptd. New York, 1970) pp. xiv–xv.
13. Quoted Nicolson from *Harmonice Mundi* in *The breaking of the circle* (Evanston, Illinois, 1950), p. 13.
14. L. Jordanova (ed.), *Languages of nature* (London, 1986), pp. 223–8.
15. Sir John Davies, *'Orchestra' in the poems of Sir John Davies* ed. R. Krueger (Oxford, 1975) p. 94.
16. W. Empson, *Collected poems* (London, 1955), p. 39.

FURTHER READING

Gillian Beer, *Darwin's plots: evolutionary narrative in Darwin, George Eliot, and nineteenth century fiction* (London, 1983).

S. F. Cannon, *Science in culture: the early Victorian period* (New York, 1978).

I. F. Clarke, *The pattern of expectation 1644–2001* (London, 1979).

Alen Friedman and Carol Donley, *Einstein as myth and muse* (Cambridge, 1985).

Stephen Jay Gould, *Ontogeny and phylogeny* (Cambridge, Mass, 1977).

Ludmilla Jordanova (ed.), *Languages of nature* (London, 1986).

Evelyn Fox Keller, *Reflections on gender and science* (New Haven, 1985).

Stephen Kern, *The culture of time and space 1880–1918* (London, 1983).

Edith Kurzweil and William Phillips, (eds.), *Literature and psychoanalysis* (New York, 1983).

Trevor Levere, *Poetry realised in nature: Samuel Taylor Coleridge and early nineteenth century science* (Cambridge, 1981).

George Levine, (ed.), *One culture* (Madison, 1987).

Arthur O. Lovejoy, *The great chain of being: a study in the history of an idea* (Cambridge, Mass., 1936).

Andrew Martin, *The knowledge of ignorance: from Genesis to Jules Verne* (Cambridge, 1985).

Ronald Martin, *American literature and the universe of force* (Durham, NC, 1981).

George Rousseau (ed.), *Organic form: the life of an idea* (London, 1972).

Michel Serres, *Hermes: literature, science, philosophy*, ed. J. Harari and D. Bell (Baltimore, 1982).

Sally Shuttleworth, *George Eliot and nineteenth-century science* (Cambridge, 1984).

52

SCIENCE AND PHILOSOPHY

GEORGE MACDONALD ROSS

1. ETYMOLOGY

Since its beginnings in Greece, many of the central issues of Western philosophy have arisen out of scientific problems: the nature of matter, space, time and causality; the roles of reason and of experience in scientific explanation; problems of infinity, continuity, change and motion; the extent to which human behaviour is explicable in materialist and determinist terms; whether there are fixed kinds or species of things in nature; and so on.

Yet in modern usage, the terms 'science' and 'philosophy' and cognates such as 'scientific' and 'philosophical' are so sharply distinguished that they are often treated as polar opposites. 'Science' suggests a body of objective, concrete facts which have been established by empirical investigation and mathematical techniques, and are expressed quantitatively. 'Philosophy', on the other hand, conjures up abstract speculation, loaded with subjective value-judgements. Indicative of the contrast is the fact that there is clearly something amiss if the scientists of different cultures come up with conflicting results; yet no one is surprised, or even particularly shocked, by the radical differences between philosophy as it is carried out in English-speaking countries, the continent of Europe, the socialist world or the East.

Although different people articulate the contrast between science and philosophy in different ways, the very fact that they are contrasted can easily lead to the conclusion that they differ in *essence*, and therefore that they cannot overlap or merge into one another. This conclusion deepens on the assumption that, when a word is used meaningfully, it must connote a unique essence which is its meaning. Largely because of the influence of Wittgenstein, this assumption is no longer generally accepted by philosophers. In examining the range of theories as to the relation between science and philosophy, I shall first consider those which assume that there is an essential difference, and which attempt to specify a sharp line of demarcation between the two activities. I shall then consider those which postulate a grey area which is as much the province of the philosopher as of the scientist.

There is, however, a further, related assumption which dominates many people's thinking on the issue. This is the assumption that the essential meaning of terms such as 'science' and 'philosophy' must be broadly stable through time and space: that when thinkers in different historical periods or in different cultures use these terms (or their equivalents in other languages), they must be striving to articulate the same distinction as us. Now it is at least plausible to suppose that late twentieth-century speakers of English are in rough agreement about the everyday meanings of the terms, and that they disagree only over their tighter definition for theoretical purposes. But there is absolutely no basis for any assumption that their meanings, whether in their ordinary language or in their theoretical use, should not have changed dramatically over time, or have evolved differently in different cultures. This is in fact the case with 'science' and 'philosophy'. But before tracing their evolution during the modern period, it is important to establish how they were understood previously.

Even here there is a problem of contamination between the traditional meanings of the terms, and subsequent attempts to redefine them in accordance with new theories as to their interrelations. All early modern writers were brought up on classical Latin, and (to a lesser extent) on ancient Greek. They normally wrote, and presumably also thought, in Latin; and, unlike most medievals, they aspired to a correct classical style. It is therefore difficult to establish how far they were using key terms in a classical or in a modern sense. When theorising about their use of language they often appealed to classical definitions, even if these diverged from their own actual practice. On other occasions they offered new coinages, but in practice lapsed into the traditional meanings of the terms. Again, in the context both of what we now know as science, and of what we now know as philosophy, it was the Greeks who made the running; and many Latin words were recognised as being no more than translationese for the Greek. Even quite basic philosophical terms, such as *substantia realis*, or *qualitas*, were deliberately coined by Cicero, Boethius and other translators as equivalents of Greek words.

In the case of 'science', or *scientia* in Latin, there is relatively little difficulty. It simply meant 'knowledge' or 'understanding', as opposed to mere belief or practical skill. It was used to translate the Platonic *episteme*, or highest grade of knowledge combined with understanding; but beyond that it had none of the connotations of the modern term 'science'. Indeed, in a Platonic context it would be the philosopher rather than the empirical investigator of nature who was possessed of *episteme* or *scientia*.

'Philosophy', or *philosophia* is more problematic. In Greek it meant 'love of *sophia*', and it was often equated with *sophia* itself. The Romans adopted the term as equivalent to *studium sapientiae*, or the pursuit of *sapientia*, and they also often equated it with *sapientia* itself. But how did *sophia/sapientia* differ from *episteme/scientia*? Conventionally, the distinction is that between wisdom and knowledge. And for us there is indeed a considerable difference between the two concepts: a person can be wise without being a polymath, or knowledgeable but foolish. However, this distinction used not to be so sharply drawn. At least until the seventeenth century it was generally assumed that worldly wisdom (or *sophia* or *sapientia*) went hand in hand with superior knowledge.

As an example of how these terms have changed their meanings, consider the following passage from Hobbes's *Leviathan*, chapter 5:

> As, much experience, is *Prudence*; so, is much Science, *Sapience*. For though wee usually have one name of Wisedome for them both; yet the Latines did always distinguish between *Prudentia* and *Sapientia*; ascribing the former to Experience, the latter to Science.[1]

Hobbes equates *scientia* and *sapientia*, and distinguishes them both from *prudentia*. His 'prudence', as the capacity to predict the future on the basis of experience, is roughly what we would call 'science'; and yet we might now be inclined to say that prudence is precisely what distinguishes wisdom from mere knowledge, or philosophy from science.

No doubt the concept of a *philosopher* generally had all sorts of overtones: at his best he was the learned sage possessed of supreme rationality, esoteric insight and practical wisdom. But there was no such person as a *scientist* with whom he could be contrasted – any seeker after knowledge could be called a philosopher. Indeed, it was not until well into the nineteenth century that the word 'scientist' was first coined. The old equation of the two terms still survives in the use of the term 'natural philosophy' for physics in Scottish universities, in the title Ph.D. (as distinct from the DD, MD and LL D of the old 'higher' faculties) and until recently in the name 'moral sciences' for philosophy at Cambridge.

So far the discussion has turned on the etymology of the terms 'science' and 'philosophy'. But the fact that these particular terms fail to mark our modern distinction does not prove that the distinction was not made. If we look more closely at the sub-divisions made within the all-embracing science/philosophy, we will find something closer to, but by no means identical with, the modern distinction. The crucial concept here is that of nature (*physis*, *natura*). But again we have to beware of importing modern concepts. Aristotle wrote about *physica*, and Newton wrote about *philosophia naturalis*; the scope of their respective studies was broadly similar in intention, but neither corresponded either to 'physics' or to 'philosophy of nature' in their modern senses. 'Physics' has been narrowed, so as to exclude chemistry, geology, etc.; and the term 'philosophy of nature' has been hi-jacked (via the German *Naturphilosophie*) to mean metaphysical speculation about the nature of the physical world, as contrasted with science, or *Naturwissenschaft*. In practice, *physica* or *philosophia naturalis* came somewhere between the two: it was broader than physics, in that it covered the whole of terrestrial inanimate nature; but it certainly did not exclude what we would now call metaphysics or ontology.

Discounting the metaphysical element, *philosophia naturalis* would correspond roughly to the modern 'natural science' – though there would still be differences as to whether it included astronomy (as supra-terrestrial), or botany, zoology and the 'human sciences'. Thus, for example, we now quite happily distinguish ethics from the scientific study of human behaviour; but it is far from obvious which would be meant by the expression 'moral philosophy' in the seventeenth century. It may be that the commonly felt disquiet at classing human studies as sciences derives from the way in which the modern English word 'science' evolved from the older distinction between the natural and the human. In German, by contrast, the term *Wissenschaft* corresponds more closely to the epistemological concept of *scientia* or *philosophia*, denoting a methodology rather than an area of study.

In short, the fact that we still use the terms 'science' and 'philosophy', but in senses which are very remote from earlier usages, is a hindrance rather than a help in trying to understand how the world of the intellect was mapped during the early modern period. Instead, we need to look at the actual division of labour within the academic curriculum.

2. UNIVERSITIES AND SCIENTIFIC SOCIETIES

Until the reforms of the eighteenth and nineteenth centuries, the universities broadly retained their medieval structure. They normally consisted of the lower faculty of Arts or Philosophy (these names were interchangeable), and the higher faculties of Theology, Medicine and Law. All students had to graduate in Arts before proceeding to one of the higher faculties, and there were no facilities for advanced study in Arts subjects. The age at which students normally followed the Arts course was roughly equivalent to modern secondary-school age. Consequently Arts subjects tended to be held in relatively low esteem.

The Arts curriculum varied in balance and content during different periods and at different universities, but the general pattern preserved the ancient division into the seven Liberal Arts. These were grouped into three foundation subjects (the *trivium*, or 'three ways'): Grammar, Dialectic and Rhetoric; and into four more advanced subjects (the *quadrivium*, or 'four ways'): Arithmetic, Geometry, Music and Astronomy.

Grammar originally meant the study of Latin language and literature (including historical and other texts), but during the Renaissance it was often widened to include Greek and even Hebrew or Arabic. Dialectic and Rhetoric covered formal and informal reasoning, and were greatly expanded to include Aristotle's major works in philosophy and physics. The quadrivium was largely mathematical, given that Music was concerned with harmonic ratios in abstract, and Astronomy with the calculation of the positions of heavenly bodies. On the other hand, Geometry often amounted to geography, and Astronomy to astrology.

If we now ask where science and philosophy were to be found, the answer is that, with the exception of medicine and the more philosophical aspects of theology and law, they were both scattered through the curriculum of the Faculty of Arts/Philosophy, and neither had any clearly marked identity. Certain individuals might have a proclivity towards metaphysics, logic, language, literature, mathematics, astronomy, physics or biology, but there was no hint of the modern idea of specialists being qualified only in their own sphere, still less of the modern Arts/Science divide. There was no such person as a professional philosopher any more than there was a professional scientist. Indeed, despite the fact that we tend to think of the medieval universities as obsessed with philosophy, philosophy as a specialism took longer to emerge than science. In both cases, however, the modern concepts evolved mainly outside the university system.

With very few exceptions, the proponents of the new science and of modern philosophy had either a non-academic profession, or none at all. They therefore had no need to concern themselves with academic distinctions between one subject and another. Apart from a general reluctance to become embroiled in dangerous theological controversy, they were happy to enter any field of inquiry to which their interests and aptitudes led them, and they were not especially concerned with the question of precisely when they were crossing disciplinary borderlines. (See art. 63.)

However, the seeds of demarcation were already being sown. The seventeenth century saw the foundation of a number of societies and journals, a few of which were, from the start, effectively 'scientific' in the modern sense – in particular the Paris Academy of Sciences, and the Royal Society of London for Improving Natural Knowledge, and its associated journal. But the majority of academies, whether actualised or merely planned, embraced the whole of human knowledge. Similarly the newly-established learned journals, such as the *Journal des Scavants*, the *Acta Eruditorum*, and the *Nouvelles de la République des Lettres*, were, as their names imply, by no means limited to the results of scientific research, but covered the whole world of learning.

The distinction between the new institutions and the old was not primarily a difference in the subjects studied, but a difference of approach. Initially the difference is describable in terms of a humanist reaction against the universities.

Whereas the universities prided themselves on having developed a new form of Latin relevant to their needs, the humanists castigated their language as 'barbarous', and promoted a return to classical forms and vocabulary in Latin, also encouraging the use of the vernacular for serious writing. Again, the university syllabus was centred on the Aristotelian corpus, whereas the humanists paid much more equal respect to all Classical thinkers. Plato in particular tended to be adopted as a counterweight to Aristotle – hence the popularity of the title 'Academy' among the new institutions.

The Platonic element was important for fostering one idea which was to contribute towards the ultimate separation of 'science' from other disciplines, namely its emphasis on mathematics. By the end of the seventeenth century, no-one could hope to participate in physical science without a knowledge of mathematics far beyond the scope of the normal university graduate. Another complementary idea, also developed in reaction to university practice, was a growing belief in the value of experience as contrasted with mere book-learning. As we shall see in the next section, this approach was dominant from the start in institutions such as the Royal Society.

The universities were not wholly insulated from these new developments; but when they took up the new ideas they incorporated them within their existing structures. This had the effect of delaying the institutionalisation of the emergent distinction between science, philosophy and other disciplines. Thus, the new Cartesian science was taught in a number of French and Dutch universities – but within the Arts curriculum, and only as part of the total Cartesian 'philosophy'. Similarly, at Cambridge the new mathematics and science came to dominate the curriculum – but they were still only part of the general Arts curriculum. Again, the Scottish universities came to be at the forefront of mathematical and scientific development, but without ever divorcing science from the philosophical principles in which it was seen as rooted.

A striking example of the context in which experimental science was introduced into the seventeenth-century university system is provided by a letter of 3rd June 1699 from Johann Bernoulli to Leibniz. At the time, Bernoulli was teaching in the Arts Faculty of the University of Groningen in the Netherlands, and he was one of the first Northern Europeans to give a course on experimental physics. His letter provides a graphic instance of the way in which experimental science was perceived as an integral part of humanist philosophy, and as antagonistic mainly to traditional theology:

> Since I know that you are completely at home in every branch of science, it comes as no surprise to me that you are also a poet.

He then recounts a quarrel with some theologians in the university, and continues:

If you only knew what I have had to put up with here at the hands of these idiots and ignorant philistines, I am sure I would have your sympathy. It is enough to say that, in order to deem me worthy of their odium, they have branded me as avant-garde, and as the introducer of 'theatrical wisdom' (that is what they insist on calling Experimental Philosophy, which I am the first to teach here). Such is the revulsion of these pathetic little men against the humanities.[2]

In fact, the modern distinction between science and other disciplines, as also the modern conception of philosophy as a distinct academic subject, became generally institutionalised only during the nineteenth century. However, this is not to say that no-one ever conceived of the separability of science from the humanities in general, and from philosophy in particular. In the next section we shall consider some of the more important attempts at a sharp demarcation.

3. SOME ATTEMPTS AT DEMARCATION

The most influential early attempt at a demarcation was that of Francis Bacon, who championed the experimental method against the more or less unquestioning Aristotelianism of the universities. But despite his reputation as the 'father of experimental philosophy', he failed to free his own view of nature from Aristotelian assumptions. Moreover, his notion of an experiment had little to do with the modern notion. Although we might be tempted to translate *experimentum* as 'experiment', and *experientia* as 'experience', there was as yet no terminological distinction between a controlled experiment and any experiential datum. For Bacon, the experimental method meant no more than assembling a large mass of one's own or reported experiences, and then classifying them for the purpose of extracting empirical generalisations. (See art. 53.)

Bacon was indeed an empiricist, but only in the traditional sense still retained in the word 'empiric'. The ancient 'empirical' school of medicine (and the sceptical school of philosophy which derived from it) held that all theories were unsound, and that the physician should rely solely on remedies that had been found to work, without worrying about their theoretical justification. It is understandable that 'empiric' should have become a pejorative term, implying reliance on hearsay and tradition rather than on scientific knowledge. Even as late as 1755, Samuel Johnson in his *Dictionary* could define EMPIRICISM as 'Dependence on experience without knowledge or art; quackery.' During the modern period, many philosophers saw empiricism in the same light; and even the most ardent admirer of Baconian method would have to concede that works such as his *Sylva Sylvarum* were in practice little more than a farrago of old wives' tales, not significantly different from the *Magia naturalis* of his contemporary della Porta (though della Porta, too has been hailed as a forerunner of modern experimentalism).

However, Bacon's theoretic stance sparked the imagination of subsequent thinkers. In particular, the ideology of the Royal Society was grounded in the ideal of the 'plain historical method', where 'historical' simply meant 'empirical', but without the latter term's contemporary overtones of charlatanry. Now it is certainly true that much of the Society's activities consisted in the detailed observation of natural phenomena. It is also consistent with this approach that Newton should have claimed not to fabricate hypotheses – hypotheses were the stock-in-trade of the scholastics and the natural magicians, whereas the moderns had to do with actual phenomena. Yet Newton's principal achievement was the discovery of the *mathematical* principles of natural philosophy, to which he contributed no new empirical evidence. Apart from his optics, his experimental work was mainly in the sphere of chemistry, and carried out in a way which hardly distinguishes him from the medieval alchemists.

Again, although the Royal Society was opposed to the philosopher Aristotle, it was not necessarily opposed to philosophy as such. There was a general recognition that the new scientific methodology required a philosophical formulation, such as Locke attempted to provide. Yet in attempting to provide this formulation, Locke defined a crucial shift in the balance of power between philosophy and science, at least within the Anglo-Saxon tradition. In place of the traditional idea that the study of nature was subservient to a general philosophy, he made the philosopher the 'underlabourer' for the scientist. But even here we must be careful to avoid anachronism. What Locke saw himself as the underlabourer for included both the empirical study of nature and theoretical hypotheses of the sort officially spurned by Newton, such as corpuscularian explanations of the cause of vision or of the chemical properties of matter. On the other hand, he often supported his own theses with empirical arguments, and much of what he did might now be classed as psychology or linguistics. Although his *Essay* is currently treated as a canonical *philosophical* text, much of its contents are glossed over as 'not really philosophy'. It is far from clear that he would have been more insulted at having part of his work dismissed as non-philosophical, than at having the rest classified as philosophical in the modern sense.

Hume has shared a similar fate, but he left no room for doubt as to his position. He set out to do for the mind what Newton had done for matter. However much we might wish to make Hume an archetypal philosopher as contrasted with a scientist such as Newton, Hume himself accepted no such contrast:

> If we take in our hand any volume; of divinity or school metaphysics, for instance; let us ask, *Does it contain any abstract reasoning concerning quantity or number?* No. *Does it contain any experimental reasoning, concerning matter of fact and existence?* No. Commit it then to the flames: for it can contain nothing but sophistry and illusion.[3]

It is clear that Hume saw no half-way house between the sophistical metaphysics of university philosophy and the new empiricism of which he believed his own work was a part. Where we would draw a line between philosophy and science, he perceived only a single enterprise. Yet it is obvious to any modern critic that only a small proportion of Hume's own reasoning can properly be described as 'experimental'. Despite his ideology, Hume was in fact doing what we would now describe as philosophy.

With the gradual emergence of the modern distinction between science and philosophy in the nineteenth century, it became all the more necessary to define a legitimate role for philosophy as distinct from science on the one hand, and from questionable metaphysics on the other. One tendency was to sharpen the contrast between science and metaphysics by absorbing legitimate philosophy into the ambience of science, and rejecting anything else as mere superstition. This approach used generally to be known as 'positivism', and, more recently, as 'scientism'.

The term 'positivism' was coined by Auguste Comte, in his *Cours de philosophie positive* of 1830–42. In this work, he implicitly treated philosophy as a meta-discipline, concerned with the organisation and validation of the positive sciences. However, he had little to say about the status of philosophy as such, and his idea of positivism as a secular religion distances him very much from later positivists. (See art. 53.)

J. S. Mill, who acknowledged his general debt to Comte, took the significant step of characterising his philosophical work as a branch of logic. In his *System of Logic* of 1843, he was primarily concerned with what we would now call philosophy of science: in particular the problem of defining the conditions under which a scientific theory is to be counted as true. In the context of Mill's extreme empiricism (so extreme that he regarded even the truths of mathematics as empirical generalisations), his appeal to logic was incapable of supporting his substantive philosophical claims about the nature of science; yet the idea of philosophy as essentially a *logical* discipline was to become extremely influential.

The seeds of a revolution in thinking about the nature of philosophy were sown by Gottlob Frege's *Begriffschrift* of 1879. This work laid the foundations not only of a fully mathematicised logic, but also of a formal theory of language and meaning. Frege himself was a Platonist, preserving an absolute distinction between *a priori* mathematical/logical knowledge, and *a posteriori* scientific knowledge. However, his subsumption of traditional areas of philosophy under mathematical techniques laid the way for his followers to sharpen the distinction between legitimate philosophy and illegitimate metaphysics, by associating the former more closely with science.

Thus Bertrand Russell further emphasised the fundamental unity of logic and mathematics by placing the foundations of mathematics in logic, in his *Principia Mathematica* of 1910–13 (written in conjunction with A. N. Whitehead). Moreover, his extensive writings on the theory of knowledge betray a marked hostility towards traditional metaphysics. He saw the task of philosophy, at least in its theoretical aspect, as that of establishing the foundations of empirical science, and of doing so by means of a methodology which was itself broadly scientific. Russell's own emphasis was on logic, and to a lesser extent on language. It is indicative of his emphasis on logic and of his scientism at this phase of his career that he described his own philosophical system as 'logical atomism'.

The identification of genuine philosophy with the systematic and scientific study of logic and language was even more marked in Ludwig Wittgenstein's *Tractatus Logico-Philosophicus* of 1921. However, the theory of meaning advanced in this work was so strictly scientistic that it left no scope for the meaningfulness of theorising about meaning. As Wittgenstein himself said of the philosophy of the *Tractatus*:

> My propositions serve as elucidations in the following way: anyone who under-stands me eventually recognises them as nonsensical, when he has used them – as steps – to climb up beyond them. (He must, so to speak, throw away the ladder after he has climbed up it.)[4]

The Vienna School of logical positivists continued the project of developing a purely scientific philosophy. One of the most influential proponents of logical positivism in the English-speaking world has been A. J. Ayer. In his *Language, Truth and Logic* of 1936, his main thesis was that there are only two types of meaningful utterance: those that are empirically verifiable, and those that are tautologies, or true by definition. This division cuts across the Arts/Science divide, since it classes history, linguistics and empirical social studies along with the physical sciences; and logic and the little that survives of philosophy with mathematics as tautological. Metaphysics, theology and much else are con-demned as meaningless.

Logical positivism was subject to two main criticisms in particular. First, as with Wittgenstein's *Tractatus*, it could give no account of its own status as con-sisting neither of empirical generalisations, nor of vacuous tautologies. Second, since scientific generalisations and theories were infinite in scope, they could never be empirically verified, and should therefore strictly be rejected as 'meta-physical'.

Karl Popper, in his *Die Logik der Forschung* of 1934, attempted to get round the latter problem by means of the concept of falsifiability rather than that of verifiability. He maintained that genuine science was demarcated from pseudo-science in that only scientific claims were subject to possible empirical falsifica-tion, and that claims should be conjectured to be true, and always provisionally so, even after they have survived concentrated attempts to falsify them. Popper's approach copes with the problem that a universal generalisation, such as 'All crows are black', cannot be verified by any finite number of observations of black crows, since it can indeed be falsified by a single observation of a white one. However, scientific theories, as opposed to mere generalisations, are more problematic, since they are rarely overturned as the result of the falsification of a single experimental prediction. The more one is forced to accept the reasonableness of *ad hoc* explanations which save a theory from apparent falsification, the less are scientific theories distinguishable from metaphysical ones, which are themselves in any case not wholly immune from empirical considerations. Moreover, although Popper supplies an account of the rational processes involved in testing scientific theories, the process of moving from the current state of a science to the production of a new theory is left as intuitive, and not obviously different from the conceptual leap involved in developing a new metaphysical theory. (See art. 54.)

A very different, though minority, approach to demarcation arose from Wittgenstein's later work. In the *Philosophical Investigations* of 1953, the primary locus of meaning was shifted from the experience of the individual observer of physical phenomena to communities of language-users sharing a common 'form of life'. This tended to make all theoretical pronouncements problematic, whether metaphysical, theological or scientific. At one end of the spectrum, some of Wittgenstein's followers turned to an extreme form of reductionism, according to which theoretical statements have meaning only in so far as they are translatable into ordinary language – a position not significantly different from the reductionism of positivists such as Ernst Mach. At the other end, scientific, religious and (less commonly) philosophical discourse have been accepted as autonomous 'language-games', each valid within a particular 'form of life', but not mutually translatable. This relativistic view may be an accurate reflection of the *de facto* state of virtual non-communication between scientists and philosophers in the latter part of the twentieth century; but it entirely begs the question of whether or not there is in fact an overlap in their domains of activity.

It might be expected that the scientism of much twentieth-century philosophy, especially in the English-speaking world, would have led to a close cohabitation between scientists and philosophers. This was indeed the case during the earlier part of the century; but, paradoxically, the long-term effect has been an increasing isolation of philosophy from other disciplines. The prevailing orthodoxy within the university departments of philosophy has been that philosophy is essentially concerned with the study of logic and language; but such studies have largely been pursued in their own right, without any reference to science. This phenomenon can be explained both externally and internally.

Externally, the tendency towards isolation has coincided with the growth of large university departments, jealous of their disciplinary autonomy; and the accident of history that philosophy has been designated an Arts subject has raised institutional barriers to its co-operation with science. More specifically, the emergence of the philosophy of science as a distinct discipline has resulted not only in a further distancing of philosophy as such from science, but in new problems as to the relationship between philosophy and the philosophy of science, and between the philosophy of science and science.

Internally, philosophers have generally emphasised the *a priori* nature of their activity. Their stance has always posed problems about how philosophy connects with science, especially when science is viewed as essentially empirical. It is therefore perhaps hardly surprising that the two enterprises should have drifted apart. On the other hand, the very distinction between the *a priori* and the *a posteriori* has come under attack from philosophers brought up within the positivist tradition. In particular, W. V. O. Quine, in his seminal paper 'Two Dogmas of Empiricism' of 1951, rejected the analytic/synthetic distinction on which logical positivism had been based. One of the consequences he drew was that scientific theories were 'underdetermined' by the evidence – that is to say, conflicts between competing scientific theories could not be decided by empirical criteria alone, but required considerations which were broadly philosophical. Thus, although positivism started out with the project of absorbing part of philosophy into science and rejecting the rest, at least one branch of the tradition has ended up by recognising a continuity between the two disciplines.

4. THEORIES OF CONTINUITY

Despite the crudity of the traditional contrast between 'rationalism' and 'empiricism', it is useful for marking two sharply distinct approaches to the relation between science and philosophy. Whatever their ambiguities and disagreements as to the scope and role of *a priori* reasoning, so-called 'empiricists' have agreed on the primacy of experiential knowledge in a major area of human intellectual activity, whether or not it is appropriate to describe this area as 'science'; and they have tended to reduce philosophy to at best a service role. The 'rationalists', on the other hand, have always emphasised the importance of *a priori* reasoning, both mathematical and logical, in the construction of natural science, and have seen empirical enquiry as in some sense subordinate to more general and abstract concepts and principles.

Modern rationalism drew much of its inspiration from Plato. For Plato, true knowledge had to do only with the eternal, underlying Forms, which were the objects of pure intellect, or *nous*. Sense experience yielded only belief, and was concerned with the semi-real, material world of change. As such, sense experience was at best a stimulator to enquiry and a hindrance rather than a help in the search for genuine knowledge.

Descartes' position was broadly in the same tradition: the intrinsic properties of matter are size, shape and motion; physical science must therefore be reducible to a sort of a temporalised geometry, which will be the proper object of reason rather than of experience. Any non-geometrical properties of things in the world as we experience it are mere affectations of the mind, and belong to the dream-like world of experience rather than to reality itself. On the other hand, the world of experience does derive from reality itself, and provided that we can subsume experimental data under the correct concepts, it provides valuable, if incomplete, information about it. In practice, Descartes was no less reliant on empirical research than, say, Einstein in our own century. But the priority of philosophy is clear; and in his *Principles of Philosophy* (1644), intended as a university text-book, Descartes starts out from epistemology and metaphysics, as the essential preconditions of a conceptually-correct description of nature. To start from experience would mean confining oneself to the description of human experiences, rather than of the real world.

Despite the continuity between philosophy and science in Descartes' approach, he at least implicitly recognised a distinction between 'first philosophy', or *meta*physics (the topic of the *Meditations on First Philosophy*), and 'philosophy', or mostly *physics* (the topic of the *Principles of Philosophy*). Leibniz, while sharing Descartes' belief in continuity, was more conscious of the difference between the two levels of activity. His major contributions to scientific theory (e.g. his development of the infinitesimal calculus, his critique of Newton's concepts of space and of gravitation, his development of the concept of energy, his rejection of atomism and his concept of organism) depended heavily on his metaphysical ideas; yet, presumably because of an increasingly anti-metaphysical climate of opinion, he often deliberately divorced his arguments from their metaphysical backing. It is a pity that his diplomatic cast of mind prevented him from forcing a more explicit dialogue with empiricist contemporaries on the relation between philosophy and science.

But again there is the problem of the very concepts of 'philosophy' and 'science'. Even a century later, it is difficult to apply modern distinctions to a philosopher such as Kant. In one sense, Kant was the demarcator *par excellence*; and the subsequent history of the division of the sciences in Germany, and then in the rest of the world, cannot be fully understood without reference to his work. He did as much as anyone to lay the foundation for the idea of philosophy as a distinct discipline in its own right – but mainly through his example in writing the *Critique of Pure Reason* (1781), rather than as a result of his theoretical pronouncements. He himself saw his own work as lying outside the future division of the sciences, and preparatory both to a 'scientifically' worked-out metaphysics (concerned with God, immortality and freedom), and a securely based natural science. What we would regard as the archetypally philosophical part of his work could eventually be discarded, like Wittgenstein's ladder.

As far as natural science was concerned, he made frequent genuflexions to empiricism (for example, his famous dictum that 'All knowledge begins with experience', and his repeated insistence that we can have no knowledge of anything which transcends experience); yet his approach to scientific knowledge was dominated by epistemological considerations, and he made Newtonian science subservient to general principles of reason. However, there is an important ambiguity about the way in which he saw science as subservient to reason. On one interpretation, he was simply reinforcing the rationalist assumption that the material provided by scientific research must be understood in terms of forms or concepts derived from reason itself. On another interpretation, he was subordinating science to a conceptual framework which he happened to believe was unique to all rational beings, but which might in fact be different for different cultures, eras, or even individuals. (See art. 53.)

Despite the central role played by science in Kant's own system, the consequence of its success was to give philosophy, especially on the Continent, a new confidence in its independence from, and indeed superiority over, physical science. For much of the nineteenth century, philosophy hardly existed as an academic subject in England; whereas in most of the rest of Europe (including Scotland) it was an autonomous discipline enjoying high prestige.

The Scottish Enlightenment of the mid-eighteenth to the mid-nineteenth centuries provides a striking instance of how a continuity between science and philosophy can be preserved at the level both of practice and of education. A number of illustrious Scottish philosophy professors, such as Thomas Reid, Adam Ferguson and Dugald Stewart, started their careers as teachers of science or mathematics; and the main thrust of their work was to develop a methodology and framework of concepts common to science and philosophy. Reid, for example, sought to refute scepticism by means of a number of *a priori* principles basic equally to science and to philosophy, while at the same time recognising that the empirical methods normally characteristic of natural science could equally be applied to traditional problems of mental philosophy. Their general emphasis was on epistemological issues which arise from science, such as those relating to causality and to the nature of scientific method; and some scholars have seen this as having had a crucial influence on the development of British physics as a whole during the relevant period.[5] The debate between Sir William Hamilton and William Whewell in the 1830s highlights the Scottish resistance to the Cambridge ethos of drawing a sharp line of demarcation between the emergent natural sciences and traditional arts subjects; and the eventual erosion of the Scottish ideal of continuity is one of the sadder episodes in the history of education.[6]

By contrast, few of the major figures in Continental philosophy, such as Hegel, Kierkegaard or Nietzsche showed more than a passing interest in science. This is true even of Marx, despite his characterisation of his own philosophy as 'scientific' – though later Marxists have developed a Marxist philosophy of science, which analyses the creation and acceptance of scientific theories in broadly socio-economic terms. (See art. 6.)

During the present century, all the main movements arising from within the Continental philosophical tradition have often, although not invariably, remained aloof from science. Phenomenology, Existentialism, Structuralism and Post-Structuralism have focused on topics such as the nature of individual consciousness, society, culture and language; and discussion of the traditional philosophical issues arising from science has largely been left to philosophically-inclined scientists, such as Mach, Poincaré and Duhem, and to the members of the Vienna Circle, as well as physicists involved in the development of Relativity Theory and Quantum Mechanics.

Kant himself can hardly be blamed for the failure of his followers to maintain his vision of the essential continuity of philosophy and science. As it happens, one of his central themes, namely the idea of science as operating within a framework of concepts which are not themselves empirical in origin, has been taken up in the present century. For example, Thomas Kuhn, in *The Structure of Scientific Revolutions* of 1962, distinguishes between 'normal' and 'revolutionary' science. In the normal stage, scientific activity consists in working out the details of an already-entrenched general theory. As long as progress seems relatively smooth, there is little motivation for examining the bases of current theory, and such examination is often positively discouraged. Only when there is a crisis do scientists go back to basics; and when a new theory emerges, it is 'incommensurable' with the previous orthodoxy, in that the conceptual frameworks are mutually incompatible: what is true in one framework is not so much false as inexpressible in the context of the other. (See art. 54.)

It may be that, in the manner of all revolutionaries, Kuhn overestimates the extent both to which scientific activity can be neatly compartmentalised into normal and revolutionary phases, and to which concepts are mutually untranslatable. However, he does express sharply the idea that scientific theory involves conceptual considerations, and that the major difference between one theory and another is as much conceptual as empirical.

This combines neatly with a shift in the consensus as to the nature of philosophy. The gradual separating off, first of the natural and then of the human sciences from philosophy, left it looking for a role – and one that would still be distinct from that of theology. In retrospect we can see that the canonical 'philosophers' of the modern period were, at least in part, doing something distinct, even if none of them was capable of articulating what it was. In the past, philosophers constructed 'systems', which were not clearly distinguishable from ambitious scientific theories. In recent times, especially in the English-speaking world, philosophers have taken on the role of conceptual analysts. It is not their task to say what is or is not the case about reality, or even about moral or aesthetic issues, but to help clarify the concepts through which others settle such questions on an empirical or personal basis.

So, if we combine the two approaches, it emerges that science in its revolutionary aspect essentially involves philosophical issues, since it centres round conceptual change. This analysis is amply confirmed by historical fact. There is no need to rest the case on the early modern period, when there was no meaningful distinction between the person of the philosopher and that of the scientist. Even during the scientific revolution of the early twentieth century, by which time the two roles had become institutionally distinct, most scientists at the forefront of scientific advance were well educated in philosophical ideas, and were deeply conscious of how their work fitted into continuing philosophical debate.

It may seem obvious to class, say, Einstein and Heisenberg as scientists; yet much of their work was contiguous with that of Russell and Whitehead, for example. Again, an amateur such as General Smuts, who coined the term 'holism',[7] was still capable of keeping up the tradition of integrating philosophy and physics in a way which has since been maintained by philosophically-minded scientists such as D. Bohm[8] and K. G. Denbigh.[9]

It is implicit in Kuhn's thesis that, at times of ferment in basic science, there should be considerable cross-fertilisation of ideas between science and philosophy. Both sides gain from such interaction: not only is science helped by philosophical work on logic and evidence, and on the concepts of space, time and matter; but philosophy is revitalised by having to take account of current scientific theories. In periods of 'normal science', however, there is a marked tendency for disciplines to retreat within artificial boundaries.

5. CONCLUSION

Despite the antiquity of the terms 'science' and 'philosophy', they acquired their present meanings only during the nineteenth century. With the benefit of hindsight, we can find much activity which we would call 'scientific' or 'philosophical' in earlier periods; but the respective practitioners did not see themselves as divided into distinct camps, or at least not in a way we would recognise today. Generally, much of what we now call philosophy was tacitly accepted as a proper part of science (or 'philosophy' as it was then called), but contrasted with the useless 'school metaphysics' of the universities. It was only when philosophy more or less as we now know it became a university specialism in the nineteenth century that it became possible for scientists to leave the more philosophical aspects of science to specialist philosophers.

Many scientists and philosophers consider the twentieth-century trend towards greater specialisation to have been a good thing, and regard philosophy no less than physics as a technical discipline which can be practised properly only by experts. Others on both sides regret the institutional divorce, and would welcome a *rapprochement* between science and philosophy. This would, in effect, involve a breaking down of Kuhn's distinction between normal and revolutionary science, so that even during 'normal' periods, scientists maintained more of an interest in fundamental concepts and methodology, and philosophers were more willing to apply their theories and techniques outside philosophy itself.

NOTES

1. T. Hobbes, *Leviathan*, ed. C. B. Macpherson (Harmondsworth, 1968), p. 117.
2. G. W. Leibniz, *Mathematische Schriften*, ed. C. I. Gerhardt, (7 vols., Halle, 1855–63), vol. 3, p. 590.
3. D. Hume, *An enquiry concerning human understanding*, ed. L. A. Selby-Bigge (3rd ed., Oxford, 1976), Sect. XII, Part III, p. 165.
4. L. Wittgenstein, *Tractatus logico-philosophicus*. Tr. D. F. Pears and B. F. McGuinness (London, 1961), proposition 6.54, p. 74.
5. e.g. R. Olson, *Scottish philosophy and British physics, 1750–1880* (Princeton, NJ, 1975).
6. cf. G. Davie, *The democratic intellect* (Edinburgh, 1961).
7. J. C. Smuts, *Holism and evolution* (Cambridge, 1926).
8. D. Bohm, *Wholeness and the implicate order* (London, 1980).
9. K. Denbigh, *An inventive universe* (London, 1980).

53

THE DEVELOPMENT OF PHILOSOPHY OF SCIENCE 1600–1900

ERNAN McMULLIN

In 1600, the terms 'philosophy' and 'science' did not mean quite what they would later mean in 1800, say, or in 1850. And in 1600 the label 'philosophy of science' would have made no sense at all. So the enterprise of tracing the development of philosophy of science from 1600 to 1850 involves a more-than-ordinary degree of extrapolation. Our story divides rather readily into three periods. First is the century of the 'Scientific Revolution'; it can be argued that the imposition of the strong term 'revolution' can most easily be justified by pointing to the shift that occurred at this time in people's perceptions of how a properly 'scientific' knowledge of nature is to be attained. After this comes an intermission, when the procedures of the 'new science' were questioned, extended and clarified. Finally there is the period of new initiatives in philosophy, when reflection on the implications of the new approaches for the nature of knowledge generally led to far-reaching reformulations of philosophy itself.

1. IN POSSESSION

In 1600, the received view in philosophy of science would assuredly have been that of Aristotle. The account of what constitutes the ideal of knowledge (*scientia*) would have been substantially that given in the *Posterior Analytics* two thousand years before. Science is a matter of *demonstration*, a special kind of 'showing' (*apodeixis*), where the relations of property to essence and property to property are laid out in deductive fashion. Its starting-point is a set of propositions (principles, axioms) which are recognised as true in their own right; the danger of a regress is thus avoided. The ability to recognise the link between predicate and subject in these propositions requires a high degree of familiarity, and hence prior experience, with the subject-matter. The entire edifice of demonstration depends on the faculty of intuition (*epagoge*) that enables the knower to grasp the truth and even the necessity of the basic propositions.

The affinity between this model of science and the axiomatic geometry that so captivated the Greek mind is obvious. Aristotle proposes it as an ideal for knowing generally, while recognising that in practice it may be unattainable in many domains where one may have to be content with premises (and hence conclusions) that are only 'true for the most part'. Still, 'eternal and necessary knowledge' is the goal where possible; its preconditions are two: an ontology of natures or essences and an anthropology that discovers in man the powers of intuition requisite to grasping directly the causal relations within essence. Science has thus two functions, one probative and one explanatory. To demonstrate is not just to prove something to be true; one must show *why* it is true, that is, one has to trace the causal relationship that makes the claim hold by necessity.

This account of science was not drawn from a survey of Aristotle's own extensive work in biology, say, or in physics. Indeed, the discrepancy here between theory and practice has been a source of puzzlement to scholars of a later time.[1] Generations of Aristotelian commentators later explored the hints given in the Organon as to how intuition might be supplemented in the gaining of *episteme* (science). It seemed as though a hypothesis would first have to be tested in terms of its ability to explain in a causal way the property being demonstrated; it would then have to be shown to be the *only* explanation if the demonstration were to function as it should. This topic of *regressus*, as it came to be called, the movement from experienced effect back to cause (*demonstratio quia*), and from this cause deductively forward to effect (*demonstratio propter quid*), was widely discussed by Renaissance theorists of method; it would have been a standard topic in expositions of the 'received view' in 1600.

There was, of course, another view by then, and it had been in contention for several centuries. It was in part his account of science that had led the nominalists of the fourteenth century to reject Aristotle's philosophy. The pretensions to demonstration on the part of that philosophy had provoked strong criticism already in the middle of the thirteenth century as Aristotle's 'natural' works became known in the Latin West; theologians like Bonaventure argued that such a science implicitly abridged God's freedom since it suggested that the main features of the world can be no other than they are. The condemnation by the Archbishop of Paris in 1277 of a set of theses drawn somewhat loosely from the works of Aristotelian natural philosophers (including Thomas Aquinas) was prompted in part by this suspicion. Gradually other arguments drawn from logic and metaphysics were formulated, and a distinctively different account of science emerged. (See art. 35.)

Accordingly to the nominalists, words function simply as conventional signs for singulars; there are no universal natures or essences. Instead of beginning

817

from general propositions holding true by necessity, the natural philosopher must start from the other end with sensible singulars and rely on analogies sufficient to sustain generalisations. The necessity of causal connection that underlay the entire structure of Aristotelian science is rejected; the empirical co-occurrence set in its place can at best support only probable assertion.

This is, of course, a much weaker conception of science than the Greek one. It was attractive to the Reform theologians of the sixteenth century who saw in the authority that had been granted to Aristotle a challenge to the integrity of the Christian message. The notion of demonstration licensed an autonomous source of 'necessary' knowledge; it seemed to many that this could not be permitted, since it established a potential rival to the revealed Word of God. Nevertheless, it would be fair to say that in the universities of Italy, France and England, the dominant philosophy of science in 1600 was that of Aristotle, modified in a multitude of ways by the labours of countless commentators but still substantially the intuitive–deductive account of the ideal of knowing sketched in the *Posterior Analytics*.

By 1700, this account had been, if not entirely swept away, at least supplanted to a very large degree. There were still traces of the older view, as we shall see, in some of the new accounts given; and Aristotle's account of science still had some defenders, particularly in the Italian universities. However, there was not a single major philosopher whose philosophy of science would still have been regarded as Aristotelian. There was much else that changed in this century of change. But if these changes add up to a 'revolution' in the domain of natural knowledge, it would be the shift in what counts as knowledge and how it is to be gained that would merit this label first and foremost.

2. REVOLUTION

The seventeenth century was not long under way before the conviction spread that an entirely new conception of science was needed, involving a new method for the attainment of knowledge. Bacon and Descartes had little in common in the way of intellectual background. But they were united in the conviction that a new start had to be made, not just in natural science but, at the second level, in the theory of science itself. They were committed to a revolution (though, they would not, of course, have used that term); one that would centre first and foremost on method. Though Bacon belonged to the generation before Descartes (he died in 1626, two years before Descartes composed his first work, the *Rules for the Direction of the Mind*), he is much the more radical of the two in his rejection of the 'infinite error' of the received view. It seems best, then, to treat Descartes first; there is more of Aristotle in him than he appears willing to admit.

The affinity between the *Rules* and the *Posterior Analytics* is, indeed, quite striking. Science, we are told, is 'true and evident cognition' (Rule II). Merely probable knowledge must be rejected; for a claim to count as science, it must lie beyond all doubting. Where Aristotle seeks a necessity rooted in the nature of things, Descartes requires a certainty based on the quality of ideas. To achieve such certainty, only two mental operations are admissible, intuition and deduction. Intuition is 'the undoubting conception of an unclouded and attentive mind, and springs from the light of reason alone' (Rule III).[1] Since 'truth and falsity can be a matter of the understanding alone', what we must seek are those 'truths for the knowledge of which the human reason suffices' (Rule VIII). They are arrived at by an intuitive apprehension of simple natures, 'which either our experiences or some sort of light innate in us enable us to behold as primary and existing *per se*' (Rule VI). Science rests securely on these self-evident principles, from which other propositions may then be derived by deduction.

Achieving science through a combination of intuition and deduction is clearly Aristotelian in inspiration. But the differences are also plain. Descartes's intuition is an inspection of ideas in the mind; the ideas acquire authority as a testimony to simple natures, not because of their relationship to experience but because of their intrinsic intelligibility. This is rationalism in close to its purest form; though earlier empirically-minded thinkers had sometimes accused Aristotelians of a similar distance from experience, it is important to notice that Aristotle himself never lost hold of his grip on the experiential. *Epagoge* for him was an intuition schooled by a learning through the senses; it was directed to the world known through the senses.

Descartes draws the model of science much more explicitly from mathematics than Aristotle did; nothing is to be allowed as science unless it attains the certitude of arithmetic and geometry. Among the sciences, only they 'are free from the taint of falsity and uncertainty' (Rule II). The simple natures from whose interrelation science begins must, then, be mathematical or quasi-mathematical in character, and the style of deduction they license will be that of geometry, not of the syllogism. The distance that Aristotle had set between physics and mathematics is here abolished.

It is important to remember, however, that Descartes left the *Rules* in unfinished draft. Modern reconstructions of the rationalism/empiricism debate generally take the rationalism of the *Rules* as one of the poles. Yet it is not at all clear that this is fair to Descartes. After all, he did withhold the *Rules* from publication. And in the *Discourse on Method* (1637), his most influential statement on the nature of scientific knowing, he modified the rationalism of the *Rules* in important ways. In the intervening decade, his work in optics and physiology had evidently brought home to him the difficulty of carrying through the optimistic reductionism of the *Rules*. Though he was still persuaded that intuition could serve to provide the principles of mechanics, he had also come to realise that it would not suffice to enable him to penetrate the diversity and complexity of the perceived world and discover the hidden causes of this immense variety. From the principles of mechanics he could derive the most general features of the terrestrial realm. 'But I must also confess that the power of nature is so ample and so vast and these principles are so simple and general, that I observed hardly any particular effect such that I could not at once recognise that it might be deduced from the principles in many different ways' (Part VI). In other words, though it was not difficult to find *sufficient* causes of the refraction of light or the formation of crystals or the action of magnets, it was much more difficult to show that these were the *actual* causes. To show that, he concedes, the only course he can think of is to find 'experiences' that will serve to decide which of the possible causes is the true one.

This sounds impressively empirical. Some historians have, indeed, been led to regard Descartes as the founder of the hypothetico-deductive method. But two important reservations must immediately be expressed. There is very little sign that Descartes ever *did* make use of experimental test as a means of discriminating between different explanatory hypotheses. His *Principles of Philosophy* (1644) is full of ingenious explanations of a whole range of physical phenomena, most of them highly speculative, their plausibility deriving only from their general consistency with the principles of his mechanics. He makes no attempt to devise experiments that would serve to discriminate between the explanations he gives and other equally plausible ones. Furthermore, his confidence never wavers in the certainty and self-evidence of the principles of his mechanics; there is never any question of testing *them* empirically. Indeed, when his critics pointed out that they appear to be clearly at odds with experience in regard to the phenomena of collision, his answer was to say that unperceived disturbing influences must be at work, thus blunting any possible experimental test of the principles themselves.

Descartes is, in effect, distinguishing between two different sorts of 'science'. The more basic, in practice restricted to mechanics, rests on self-evident principles, reached through the exercise of reason on ideas possessed by all. The other infers to underlying causal structure; though he admits the hypothetical character of the inference, he tends in practice to minimise this feature as far as possible. This second type of science relies heavily on metaphor and hence on imagination; Descartes concedes that though imagination is not properly a part of understanding, it is an indispensable aid to it.

If Descartes was not a true rationalist, neither was Bacon a true empiricist. Indeed, it might be argued that the *New Organon* (1623), the final statement of his lifelong plan for the 'great instauration' of science, was the most telling critique of empiricism of his century. 'By far the greatest hindrance and aberration of the human understanding proceeds from the dullness, incompetency and deceptions of the senses. . . . The sense by itself is a thing infirm and erring,' he warns (I, aph. 50).[2] The senses are incompetent for the purposes of science mainly because the 'things invisible' that explain the properties of even the most familiar things lie beyond the reach of the senses: 'Every natural action depends on things infinitely small, or at least too small to strike the sense' (II, aph. 6). Until these are comprehended, there is no true science. The senses can lead us, at best, only into the 'outer courts' (II, aph. 7). And their deliverances are further weakened by the fact that the words we use are 'framed according to the capacity of the vulgar' and impose partially arbitrary 'lines of division' on the world (I, aph. 59). Any attempt to alter those lines 'to suit the true divisions of nature' will thus be resisted.

Bacon is critical of the 'empirical school of philosophy' (he mentions only Gilbert by name) because it finds its foundations in the 'narrowness and darkness' of too few experiments (I, aph. 54, 64). In consequence, its exponents 'fly to universals' too quickly. Instead, induction must rise from the evidence of the senses 'by a gradual and unbroken ascent', arriving at 'the most general axioms last of all' (I, aph. 19). Is this a matter of generalisation, of finding broader and broader empirical regularities? Bacon has often been interpreted as an inductivist in this sense, and his language (in particular what he says about 'forms') sometimes lends itself to this reading. But he makes it clear that empirical generalisation is *not* enough. One must 'penetrate into the inner and further recesses of nature' (I, aph. 18), and for this mere generalisation the fact-gathering of the 'ant' (I, aph. 95) is not enough. What is needed is a transformation of sense-experience by the understanding, enabling a proper 'interpretation' of nature to be made. From such a 'league between the two faculties, the experimental and the rational, such as has never yet been made, much may be hoped' (I, aph. 95).

The 'rational' shows itself in the devising of the 'just and orderly process' by which hypotheses are to be tested. 'Let trial be made . . . ': one is constantly reminded that Bacon's life had been spent as a lawyer, not as a philosopher. What he calls 'induction' is not just a matter of generalisation from observed similarities. Indeed, he warns against this process; the most deep-rooted error of intellect, he says, is to be 'more moved by affirmatives than by negatives'. Thus, one must analyse nature by 'rejections and exclusions', bearing in mind that 'the negative instance is the more forcible of the two' (I, aphs. 46, 105).

Much of Book II of the *New Organon* is occupied by an elaborate taxonomy of the different types of 'instance' or test to which hypothesis is to be subjected. These are not yet experiments in the full sense; even the famous 'crucial experiment' discriminates between different causal hypotheses merely by searching for appropriate contexts in nature where these may be tested. Bacon often writes as though the 'indissoluble union of natures' he seeks were simply a matter of co-occurrence. But the examples he chooses (the cause of the tides, the nature of heat), make it clear that the cause is to be tested by its *consequences* and not directly observing it to co-occur with its supposed effect. He assumes that in practice an exhaustive list of possible causes can be generated and all of these then eliminated save one. Though science is no longer of the necessary, it is not yet of the probable.

One further typically Baconian theme ought be noted. When he says that knowledge and power 'meet in one' (I, aph. 4), he means not only that a real science of nature will bring in its train 'troops' of practical outcomes of benefit to mankind but that such outcomes are a 'sign', a 'testimony', of science itself (I, aphs. 73, 74). Since the new method seeks the testimony of science not in self-evidence but in empirically-testable consequences, the close bond between 'light' and 'fruit' is assured; Bacon warns, however, against the premature concern for fruits that he sees as characteristic of the 'empirical school'.

Between them, Descartes and Bacon set philosophy of science on a new course. But the directions had been sketched only in the most general way. Galileo and Boyle went on to make the notion of experiment much more definite. Instruments were needed both to extend the range of the senses and to provide accurate measurement. And the causal tangle of the natural order had to be artificially simplified by devising 'experiments', that is, controlled laboratory situations, where correlations and causal hypotheses could be reliably tested. Neither Galileo nor Boyle wrote a manual on the methods of science as Bacon and Descartes had done. Though each has much to say about the procedures required to achieve genuine science, their remarks are elicited by the scientific problems at hand rather than by a concern for larger philosophical issues. In our terms, they write as scientists, not as philosophers. It is with them, perhaps, that the now-familiar separation between 'philosophy' and 'science' might be said to begin.

There is an obvious tension within Galileo's conception of science. On the one hand, he speaks in Aristotelian terms of the 'natural sciences whose conclusions are true and necessary'.[3] And in his mechanics, he often cites simplicity or naturalness as warrant for the principles he proposes. On the other hand, he also appeals to experiment, or more broadly, to empirically testable consequences, effectively treating his claims as hypotheses whose warrant derives not from any intrinsic evidence or necessity but from the continued verification of observational inferences drawn from them. This hypothetico-deductive approach is especially characteristic of his work in areas of physics other than mechanics; in his discussions of sunspots or the vacuum, for example.

The tendency to place mechanics in a special knowledge category and to view its principles as self-evident or intuitively warranted, recurs again and again in the history of the philosophy of science. Galileo had a particular reason to be tempted in this regard. His law of fall did not require any reference to a cause of motion; it was purely descriptive and attractively simple. It could thus be accounted for by postulating that 'Nature habitually employs the first, simplest, and easiest means'.[4] But Galileo was not satisfied with this mode of proof alone. He realised he had also to invoke 'the very powerful reason that the essentials successively demonstrated by us correspond to . . . that which physical experiments show forth to the senses'. The 'essentials successively demonstrated' are not inductively arrived at; they are mathematically simple and antecedently plausible hypotheses.

Where Galileo disagreed most strongly with Aristotle, perhaps, was in his belief that 'the Book of Nature is written in the language of mathematics'. His affinities here are plainly with Plato and Archimedes, but his mathematicism is more radical than Plato's, since Plato believed the sensible world to copy the unchanging realm of mathematical Form only in an imperfect way. Galileo deals with the messiness of the sensible world by developing a complex (and not always consistent) notion of 'impediment'. The aim is to 'remove somewhat from the sensible world to show . . . the architecture with which it must have been built'.[5] The consequent idealisation is what makes Galilean science possible, and is Galileo's most enduring legacy to philosophy of science. It takes two main forms, depending on whether one is simplifying the material context within which experiment is carried on, or constructing a schematic theoretical model.

Boyle was sceptical of the 'geometric way' of approach to science through axioms and deductions. He did not trust reason in this role any more than Bacon had. Yet he was also critical of the 'mere empiric' who performs experiments simply to gather data, without having a specific question in mind that needs answering. Science progresses by formulating hypotheses and then testing them by means of experiments contrived especially for that purpose: 'Experience is but an assistant to reason, since it doth indeed supply informatives to the understanding; but the understanding remains still the judge, and has the power or right to examine and make use of the testimonies that are presented to it. . . . Sense does but perceive objects, not judge them.'[6]

Besides judging the validity of experimental results, reason will also be engaged in the evaluation of hypothesis. Boyle lists six criteria for a 'good' hypothesis and four additional requirements for an 'excellent' one. An excellent hypothesis ought not be forced; it ought to predict novel and testable consequences, and ought to be the only (or at least the best) explanation available. This is a far more sophisticated use of reason than the deduction and induction of the earlier tradition. And, as Boyle admits, it can certify a hypothesis only as probable, that is, worthy of approval (*probabilis*). But since the observable properties of bodies are to be explained ultimately by recourse to the invisible 'corpuscles' of which they are composed, a hypothesis that can give access, however tentative, to these is to be prized. It is Boyle's 'corpuscular philosophy' above all, that leads him to make experiment the primary tool of his science.

Not everyone was as persuaded of the epistemic role of experiment as Boyle was. There were still those who defended the older axiomatic notion of science. Hobbes and Spinoza both attacked the new-fangled reliance on 'engines difficult to be made'. Hobbes argued that experimental techniques imposed artifice on nature; the answers received were prompted by the questions put. Besides, sense-experience can never be a sufficient warrant for the necessary truths of which true science consists. These principles are definitional in character, as he takes the axioms of geometry to be. Geometry, in consequence, may be the only true science yet available to man. The necessity of the definitions is internal to them; it rests on the arbitrary convention by which men agree to relate in a certain way the names the definitions contain. Truth thus consists in the 'right ordering of names'. Since disputes about the imposition of names may easily occur, the King has the right to decide in such cases which conventions should be adopted; the maintenance of civil order takes precedence over other values, even in the determination of truth. A stronger contrast with Bacon, the stern critic of ideology, could hardly be imagined. How linguistic conventions are to afford truths about the world Hobbes never discusses.

Indeed, he retreats from this extreme conventionalism elsewhere in his work. Sometimes he suggests that principles may be seen to be true in the light of their self-evidence or again, in the light of clear and distinct ideas caused in us by motions of bodies. More surprisingly, he concedes in *De corpore* that in physics we have to make do with hypotheses, since the objects we deal with there are not within our power and the principles of their operation are placed within them by God, not by human convention. Working back from effect to cause can at best, then, yield only probability. But he never really took seriously the role of experience in the testing of hypothesis; it was sufficient, he thought, to assess its conceivability in rational terms and to ensure that the phenomena already known were deducible from it. This was, of course, just the sort of licence to speculation that Bacon and Boyle had been concerned to curb.

It seems fitting to end this review of a century of profound change with John Locke's *Essay Concerning Human Understanding* (1690), where the separation between the new and weaker sort of 'science' of nature, yielding at best only probability, and the older demonstrative ideal of knowledge is most effectively underlined. Locke reaffirms the traditional doctrine of two types of knowledge, intuition and demonstration, but he gives it a rationalist twist by construing knowledge in this strict sense as the perception of agreement or disagreement between ideas. Not surprisingly, he finds that we have no such knowledge of bodies, nor can there be any prospect of attaining it at some later time. For the secondary qualities of bodies could be explained only with reference to the 'minute and insensible parts' of which bodies are composed. Yet the configuration of such parts responsible for a particular secondary quality cannot be observed, and even if it could be, no necessary connection of ideas could be shown between the shapes and motions of the corpuscles responsible for the secondary qualities and the sensations corresponding to them. The language of 'ideas' leads Locke into some confusion here, but he sees quite clearly that the new style of arguing from effects back to unobserved and even unobservable causes cannot, in principle, yield 'science' in the traditional sense of that term.

But he does not, for that reason, dismiss the quest. Instead, he elaborates upon a faculty of 'judgement' that yields probability, 'likeliness to be true', instead of certainty. Though it is a 'twilight state' by comparison with knowledge in the strict sense, it is sufficient for the conduct of life and must not, therefore, be dismissed by the philosopher. He distinguishes between two uses of judgement, one relatively reliable that allows us to formulate such generalisations as 'fire melts lead' on the basis of our constant experience, the other much more speculative that enables us to propose hypotheses about the underlying causes of these same regularities. These hypotheses are guided by analogy, but they will remain mere conjecture unless they are controlled by experimental discrimination between alternatives on the basis of testable predictions. Locke does not elaborate on the methodology of test, but by 1690, he did not need to do so.

3. INTERMISSION

The crucial transition in philosophy of science in this century was from a broadly rationalist notion of science, relying on necessary connections between ideas, to a 'consequentialist' one, according to which a hypothesis is evaluated not just for its coherence with principle but more revealingly by its empirically testable consequences. The scaling-down of the traditional expectations of science, the certainty, self-evidence and demonstrative character that had set it apart from changeable 'opinion', was not easy to accept and, indeed, was not accepted by all. The implications of the new and apparently successful experimental approach to nature took time to sink in.

Newton, for one, did not favour so radical a change. His success in discovering 'mathematical principles' in optics and mechanics led him to defend a conception of 'experimental philosophy' that utilised only deduction and induction: 'propositions are deduced from the phenomena and afterwards made general by induction'.[7] Retroduction (to use a convenient modern term for hypothetical argument from observed effect to unobserved cause) is not required for science proper; only induction, understood as generalisation, qualifies the certainty of the deductive mathematics employed. Though not yielding strict demonstration, 'yet it is the best way of arguing which the nature of things admits of'. The wider the induction, the stronger it is; if exceptions should be discovered through experiment, the original conclusion 'may then begin to be pronounced with such exceptions as occur'. Newton does not say that the exceptions *refute* the original 'conclusion', only that they qualify it as approximate.[8]

This inductivist account of science is a compromise. It does not recognise the causal hypotheses of the 'corpuscular philosophy'; not only are the empirically untestable explanations of the Cartesians excluded but the inferences to unobserved causes that had by then become standard in the experimental tradition of Bacon and Boyle are also called into question. Newton does not banish these latter entirely, but he gives them the status of 'query' only. The axiomatic geometric treatment of light in the *Opticks* is sharply separated from a long series of ingenious speculative proposals regarding vibrating media and the 'small particles of bodies' that he takes to be responsible for a 'great part of the phenomena of nature'.[9] One might suppose that these 'queries' are so labelled because they are still tentative, and that Newton anticipates they may later progress to the status of science proper. But no amount of further evidence can make these inferences to unobservable entities conform to the schema of deduction followed by induction to which Newton wanted to limit the 'experimental philosophy'.

The plausibility of this scheme derives in part from the ambiguity in the explanatory constructs, *force* and *attraction*, around which the *Principia* is built. Newton assumes that the forces governing a motion can be inferred from a description of the motion itself. They are to be taken, he says, 'mathematically, not physically' and the reader is enjoined 'not to imagine that by those words I anywhere take upon me to define the kind or the matter of any action, the causes or the physical reasons thereof'.[10] This convenient separation of the 'mathematical' and the 'physical' enables him to bracket all questions about how forces function as *causes*, while retaining enough of a causal overtone to suggest he has somehow explained *why* the motion occurs. The inductivist model of science works here because force is being construed merely as a propensity. Newton was left with the problem of how to deal with force as 'active principle', and how to relate such discussion with the inductivist science from which it seems in principle to be excluded. In the years that followed the writing of the *Principia*, he returned to this problem again and again. But he never succeeded in resolving it.

Berkeley saw more clearly than most the tensions within the Newtonian account of science. The inductivist side he could accept; the business of physics is to establish descriptions of motion ('laws') that are as general as possible, and that serve the practical purpose of prediction. The attack on hypothesis he would carry much further than Newton had: 'To throw light on nature, it is idle to deduce things which are neither evident to the senses nor intelligible to reason'.[11] He was critical, in consequence, of Newton's use of terms like 'attraction' which purport to *explain* motion but in reality do nothing more than describe it. It is not the business of physics to seek efficient causes, he argues; they lie in principle beyond its reach in the realm of metaphysics. Physics must accept its limitation to what can be perceived; its goal must then be to describe and hence to predict, nothing more. One can see why some have found in Berkeley's philosophy of science the first full-blown version of the position later to be called instrumentalism.

Though his starting point was a phenomenalism not unlike Berkeley's, Hume adopted a far more radical position; indeed, he may be said to have called into question even the possibility of a philosophy of science, understood as an account of how science is possible. He divides the objects of inquiry into relations of ideas (as in mathematics) and matters of fact. Demonstration is impossible in the case of the latter, since their contraries never actually imply a contradiction. Only causal reasoning might carry one beyond the immediate testimony of sense and memory. But how is it to do this? To say that C is the 'cause' of E is no more than to say that in the past, C and E have been constantly conjoined in our experience. Since C and E both have to be perceptible, causal inference to the 'secret structure of parts' on which the perceived qualities of bodies have been claimed to depend is impossible.

What is worse, inference from past conjunction to a similar relationship in the future has nothing by way of argument to support it; demonstration is excluded and recourse to the assumption that the future must resemble the past leads to regress. The best that can be done is to explain why we *believe* that a particular observed correlation serves as a guide to the future. Hume thinks we can account for this by invoking a process of habituation, an association of ideas, brought about by the repetition of similar conjunctions of events. But he is emphatic that the belief cannot be justified by any form of argument. It is a product of 'natural instinct', a 'necessary result of placing the mind in such circumstances',[12] not something of which a logical account can be given.

The Newtonian context of Hume's analysis is unmistakable. When Newton's inductivism and his proscription of hypothesis are carried through by a mind more philosophically critical than his own, this kind of sceptical outcome is not surprising. Hume takes for granted that induction is the only possible source of justification for ampliative claims about matters of fact. He ignores, and indeed may have been unaware of, the role that structural theory had come to play in sciences other than mechanics. Where is the medium, the 'interposing idea', he asks, that would allow one to infer from effect to unobserved cause or from cause to an as yet unobserved effect? The answer Boyle would have given was testable hypothesis and he would have gone on to note that the criteria for such a hypothesis involved much more than constant conjunction. But the sophistication of the earlier tradition had been momentarily eclipsed, and the ambiguity of Newton's primary constructs, *force* and *attraction*, gave phenomenalism a purchase it could never otherwise have claimed.

One philosopher, in particular, made himself responsible for the spread of Newton's 'rules of philosophising'. Thomas Reid was convinced that Newton's contributions to methodology were as important as his work in mechanics.

Drawing together Newton's scattered remarks on method, he constructed a full-blown inductivist philosophy of science, construing induction as generalisation. 'Our senses testify particular facts only: from these we collect by induction, general facts which we call laws of nature. . . . Thus, ascending from what is less to what is more general, we discover as far as we are able natural causes or laws of nature.'[13] The scientist must shun hypothesis, since it can never lead to real knowledge. Though Reid is not altogether clear on this, it seems that inferences to causes, themselves not directly observed, are to be excluded from science. Newton is politely chided for his own use of such hypotheses in optics. Reid criticises the screen of ideas that Berkeley and Hume had placed between mind and world, and argues that Hume's dissolution of the world into discrete events with no relations other than external ones of co-occurrence makes science of any sort impossible. Yet he agrees with Hume that our belief in the uniformity of Nature cannot be justified on the grounds of logic or experience; the 'inductive principle' on which science depends has to be seen as an effect of the constitution of the human mind. The step from Reid to Kant is not a long one. But Reid's major legacy to later philosophers of science is a distrust of theory, together with an emphasis on fact and also on law as a properly regulated collection of facts.

All of the writers discussed so far took mechanics, or more broadly physics, as paradigm. But there was one other who did not. In his *New Science* (1725), Giambattista Vico (1688–1744) argued that if one seeks the universal and eternal principles that are proper to a science, one must look to the products of human making, notably to the history of human institutions. Physics deals with natures that are opaque to us, and hence we can achieve only 'the semblance of probability' there. But our intuitive ability to understand the desires and needs that bind the human race together across the ages permits us to formulate 'axioms' (he lists no fewer than 114!) that enable a reconstruction to be made of the patterns of development and decay through which nations must pass. And the fact that this reconstruction accounts so well for the known details of human history confirms (he says) the principles of his inquiry as effects do postulated causes. Though these principles are, in the first instance, 'discovered within the modifications of our own human mind', they are not *a priori*, since the modifications are the product of a common human experience. Here, then, are three very different thinkers, Hume, Reid and Vico who turn to mind to discover the source of the universality (or at least the generality) characteristic of science. The next effort to do this will be on a far larger and grander scale.

4. NEW INITIATIVES

Kant's philosophy of science is without doubt the most ambitious we have yet encountered. The *Critique of Pure Reason* (1781) marks a new sort of initiative:

for the first time, the existence of a successful natural science prompts a far-reaching reconsideration of the entire range of philosophical topics, from metaphysics to ethics and philosophy of religion. It is impossible to do justice here to Kant's convoluted system, gradually developed over many years. Almost every detail of its interpretation is strenuously debated. A few general remarks must suffice.

His early work in the natural sciences and his exposure to the empiricism of Hume led him in time to distrust the rationalist metaphysics of his teachers. He was persuaded by Hume that experienced repetition cannot of itself be a sufficient ground for the universality and necessity of natural science, let alone of metaphysics. But there was a fixed point: 'It is fortunately the case that although we cannot assume that metaphysics as a science is real, we can confidently say that certain pure synthetic knowledge *a priori* is real and given, namely mathematics and pure natural science. . . . We have therefore some, at least, uncontested synthetic knowledge *a priori*, and do not have to ask whether such knowledge is possible (for it is real), but only how it is possible'.[14] The problem of the first *Critique* (1781) is not to validate Newtonian physics but to find a framework within which its validity as science is explained; this framework will then prove sufficiently comprehensive (Kant hopes) to ground the broader science of metaphysics. There is only one possible solution and that is to turn to the constitution of the human mind itself. Only on that basis might one explain how some judgements can be prior to experience without reducing to merely nominal definitions: 'The understanding is itself the source of the laws of nature'.[15]

Kant searches within sensory experience for traces of an *a priori*, and finds them in the ideas of space and time. These, he argues, are the *form* of our experience; they structure it to be of the kind it is without themselves being experienced as objects. The unity of human consciousness requires further that appearances must be synthesised by concepts of a special kind which impose a 'law' or 'rule' upon them, thus constituting objects for the intuition. This proof of the necessity of our possessing such concepts, the categories of the understanding, is what Kant calls a 'transcendental deduction', that is, an argument directed to the real possibility of experience. These categories then enable one to formulate the synthetic *a priori* principles required to make a proper natural science possible.

Does this mean that the natural science Kant took as paradigm, Newtonian physics, is itself synthetic *a priori*? This apparently simple question has deeply divided Kant scholars. Part of the problem is that Kant is not altogether consistent in specifying the precise logical relationship between Newtonian physics and the synthetic *a priori* principles that are the hallmark of the critical philosophy. There is an ambiguity in his notion of a 'pure natural science'. Is it presupposed (and if so, in what sense) by Newton's physics, or could it be identical with it or some part of it? Or is the success of Newton's physics a premiss in the construction of pure natural science? How far does the establishment of possibility make contact with the content of the actual laws of empirical science? Kant does say that 'natural science contains *a priori* synthetic judgements as principles', and gives as one example: 'In all communication of motion, action and reaction must always be equal'.[16] This certainly *sounds* like Newton's Third Law of Motion. In the *Metaphysical Foundations of Natural Science*, he argues that the possibility of matter (the objectivity of the concept of matter, in his terms) requires the attribution to matter of 'fundamental' or constitutive forces of attraction and repulsion. And in direct contradiction to Newton: 'The attraction essential to all matter is an immediate action through empty space of one matter upon another'.[17]

Newton's three Laws, and the eight Definitions that precede them, define the fundamental notions of mass, inertia, momentum, force, action and reaction that constitute what one might call a 'general' mechanics, that is, a framework sufficient for the understanding of motion in general. The notions are interlocked in such a way that each part involves all the others. When Kant makes the use he does of them in the first *Critique* and in the *Metaphysical Foundations*, he seems to be attributing *a priori* status to the general mechanics of the *Principia*. More specifically, he criticises Newton's absolutes of space and time and shows how an inertial frame can be defined without them; his proof commits him to claiming that the three Laws have to be presupposed in order to define a true (or actual) motion, and hence the notion of a spatio-temporal framework itself. This further requires a means of comparing the masses of bodies; Kant argues that this must implicitly involve the Law of Universal Gravitation as a presupposition. Newton's refusal to allow gravitational attraction at a distance as an essential property of bodies left him, Kant argues, with no way of justifying (other than in a weak inductive fashion) the proportionality of attraction and mass that he requires to hold universally. An inductive argument will not do here, since there is a question of giving objective meaning to the Newtonian space-time framework before inductive argument can begin. This is an illustration of what Kant means by claiming that only *his* form of transcendental idealism can 'ground' an adequate empirical realism.

Kant was, then, the last and perhaps the greatest exponent of the 'classical' notion of science going back to Aristotle. In the *Preface* to the *Metaphysical Foundations*, he summarises his views: 'Only that whose certainty is apodeictic can be called science proper'. When, as in chemistry, the laws proposed are based merely on experience, 'they carry with themselves no consciousness of their necessity'. Furthermore, 'a doctrine of nature will contain only so much science proper as there is applied mathematics in it'. For both of these reasons, a purported science like chemistry proposing laws of force between parts of matter that cannot be constructed *a priori* along transcendental lines is no more than a 'systematic art'; it is 'merely empirical' and thus can never become 'science proper'. Kant does not interdict the use of hypothesis or unobservable entities like ether or magnetic matter. And his construal of matter in terms of forces eliminates the puzzle that Locke had found so dismaying of how to infer to the sizes and shapes of the 'minute parts'. But it is clear that for him hypothesis must lie on the side of 'systematic art', useful but not really *science*. The principles of a true science must be constructible independently of actual observation; in the end, the only natural science that can lay claim to possess such principles is Newtonian mechanics.

Hegel disagrees with Kant's high assessment of Newton, and he also rejects postulated entities out of hand, adopting as tight a phenomenalist limitation on theorising as Berkeley did: 'What is not subject to observation does not exist in this sphere; for to exist is precisely to be for another, to make oneself perceptible'.[18] But he praises Kant's transcendental approach to the foundations of natural science, while claiming for himself a philosophy which does not make nature as given in sense perception the basis of science, but which goes to the absolute Notion for its determination. His order of procedure differs from Kant's: 'The philosophy of nature takes up the material which physics has prepared for it empirically at the point to which physics has brought it, and reconstitutes it so that experience is not its final warrant and base. . . . [Philosophy must] translate into the Notion the abstract universal transmitted to it, by showing how this universal, as an intrinsically necessary whole, proceeds from the Notion'.[19] His 'absolute mechanics' is thus dependent on experience in the sense that empirical discovery must come first. But it transcends experience in the sense that its laws are revealed as the necessary working out of the Notion. The stages in this 'working out' are discovered not by a transcendental deduction but by an imaginative dialectical linking of the empirical starting point to the Notion. How this process yields necessity is not made clear. But Hegel insists that it does, as do the later exponents of *Naturphilosophie*.

Despite the historicism he displays elsewhere, Hegel appears to hold that the philosophy of nature is moving towards the status of necessary truth, and that in some respects this has already been attained. In so far as there are barriers to its further attainment, they derive not so much from the contradictions that history still has in store, as from what he calls the 'impotence of Nature'; the fact that it preserves the determination of the Notion only abstractly. This sets limits to philosophy; the Notion cannot comprehend the infinite variety of forms that are the contingent products of Nature. A proper science of such products is thus not just difficult or slow in the making; it is impossible. Here again is the distinction between a 'pure' natural science of necessary principles, whose paradigm for Hegel is optics, and an empirical quasi-science of contingent forces and structures like chemistry.

Up to this point, philosophy of science has been derivative from, or sometimes at the centre of, a general theory of knowledge or of mind. Vico and Hegel point to the history of human institutions as a means of discovering how reason operates. But it is only in the early nineteenth century that philosophers of science turn to the history of science as a major (for Comte and Whewell, *the* major) source of insight as to the nature of scientific activity itself. Comte claims that each science goes through three stages, the theological, the metaphysical and finally the 'positive' where the vain search for an absolute knowledge is abandoned, and energies are turned to the only achievable scientific goal which is the discovery of empirical laws, 'relations of succession and resemblance'. What characterises the 'positive spirit' is the search for such laws in every domain of nature; though the methods of the different natural sciences are irreducibly different and there are complicated patterns of interdependence between them, they have in common a stress on exact prediction, which is both the test and the practical outcome of the discovery of law. This is true in the social domain just as much as in the natural, though the laws are much harder to establish there.

Comte may have been the first to assert that prediction and explanation are symmetrical: a law-like connection serves equally well to predict as to explain. Hypothesis is important – he is critical of the Newtonian legacy of distrust in regard to hypothesis – since law-like connections cannot be discovered without the aid of provisional formulations that are gradually improved, or if necessary rejected. The laws of nature are, indeed, 'hypotheses confirmed by observation'. He is also critical of the traditional empiricist assumptions in regard to fact and observation: 'In order to make an observation, our mind requires some theory. If, in contemplating the phenomena, we did not immediately connect them to some principles, it would not only be impossible to combine these isolated observations . . . for the most part, we could not even perceive them.'[20] By 'theory' here, Comte means a hypothetically-proposed law. He rejects retroductive inference to unobserved cause. 'Science must study only the laws of phenomena and not the mode of production.' Theories that make use of constructs such as 'atom' or 'ether' are permissible, as long as it is realised that these latter are no more than 'logical artifices', heuristically useful perhaps, but providing no evidence of objective existence. Comte's opposition to what would later be called 'scientific realism' was to become a hallmark of the positivism inspired by his work.

This was the time when the label 'philosophy of science' was first used, and when 'scientists' now began for the first time to devote serious attention to the history of science. Whewell's *Philosophy of the Inductive Sciences, Founded upon their History*, (1840) develops the theme that only a detailed study of the history and practice of the sciences can furnish the basis for an adequate theoretical account of what science is. This study leads him to a detailed and highly suggestive account of 'induction', understood both as discovery and as verification. Induction is not a matter of generalising from particulars in a straightforward logical way, as logicians supposed. It is, first and foremost, an untidy inventing of hypotheses meant to 'colligate', or bind together, the known facts and to reveal new ones. The first step here is the crucial one of finding the appropriate 'conceptions' that will enable the facts to fall together in an intelligible unity. This is the distinctive contribution of mind, a contribution overlooked by empiricists. But induction also involves verification. A good hypothesis should explain the phenomena already observed, as well as predicting new kinds of phenomena. Prediction alone gives some measure of truth. But when a 'consilience of inductions' occurs, when hitherto unrelated areas of inquiry fall together under a single hypothesis, this can give us a conviction of the certainty of the hypothesis. Consilience involves both scope and simplicity. More important, as a criterion it requires the scientist to track the hypothesis over time, to assess the resources it has shown from bringing an increasing coherence to an ever wider domain, or conversely, the ways in which its development has been *ad hoc*. Whewell's nuanced discussion of consilience was a major contribution to the discussion of the criteria of theory-assessment.

There was, however, a disturbing tension in his work between the sophisticated historically-based analysis of topics like consilience and the rationalist Kantian principles never far in the background. He claims to find in the natural sciences a number of axioms or necessary truths whose character can be explained only by the presence in our minds of certain 'fundamental ideas', akin to Kant's Categories (though much more numerous). These truths are backed, not by a static transcendental deduction, but by a gradual process of discovery, a 'progressive intuition', on the part not of everyone but only of highly trained people who gradually are led to a clearer apprehension of the Ideas involved. There are in the end more echoes here of Plato than of Kant, and the theological justification Whewell presents for the ultimacy of the Ideas is less persuasive than Kant's transcendental route to a similar goal.

Another scientist, perhaps the best known English scientist of his generation, John Herschel (1792–1871), carried out an almost equally thorough review of the procedures and presuppositions implicit in scientific practice. The philosophy of science he formulated bears, however, no trace of rationalist necessity. Science is a search for lawlikeness in nature; the goal of induction is to discover the causal relations, or invariable correlations, between phenomena. Herschel proceeds to formulate, rather as Bacon had done but with a great deal more precision, a series of rules of experimental practice which enable the scientist to discover these correlations. But there is a second concept of cause in his work also when he speaks of unobservable agents that are known to us only by their effects. These are to be discovered by formulating explanatory hypotheses and ultimately constructing coherent theories of as broad a scope as possible. Because the examples of unobservable causes he adduces are Newtonian forces or the new 'fields' of Faraday, he is led to assume that the 'laws of action' of these causes can be arrived at by means of a 'direct induction'. This is the same ambiguity which we already saw in Newton's own work. Herschel does not appear to realise that his 'induction' takes two very different forms depending on whether it is simply a discovery of invariable correlations between phenomena or a postulation and indirect testing of non-phenomenal entities. The hazy causal status of forces tends all too easily to obscure this all-important distinction.

The most widely-read philosopher of science of the mid-century was assuredly John Stuart Mill (1806–73). Yet his work in philosophy of science showed very little originality or depth. The famous 'Methods' of Agreement, Difference and Concomitant Variation, were taken over directly from Herschel; his own contribution was little more than to find convenient names for them. Mill was a philosopher, not a scientist. (The distinction was now becoming a fairly sharp one in vocational terms). His empiricism had none of the qualifications that familiarity with actual scientific practice had led Herschel and Whewell to recognise. In his *System of Logic* (1843), he presents induction as a straightforward logical operation, a 'generalisation' from experience. 'It consists in inferring from some individual instances in which a phenomenon is observed to occur, that it occurs in all instances of a certain class; namely in all which resemble the former in what are regarded as material circumstances.'[21] It requires a single general resupposition, the principle of the uniformity of nature. His attempt to justify his principle in advance on the grounds of a broader induction is fallacious; the implications of a radical empiricism had been understood far more clearly by Hume.

Mill distinguishes between 'empirical laws', regularities which hold only under limited circumstances, and 'basic laws of nature', absolutely invariable sequences. The aim of science is to determine the basic laws and to deduce the empirical laws from them, showing why these take the form they do under the limitations specified. But this distinction seems to require something more than the mere fact of past co-occurrence, which is all that the methods of agreement and difference can show. One further testimony to the distance between doctrinal empiricism and working science: since the cause of a phenomenon must itself be a phenomenon, Mill excludes the possibility of causal inference to unobservable entities and thus reduces theory to law. The affinities between his approach and that of the logical positivists in our own century are unmistakable; these affinities were amply recognised by the positivists themselves.

But there was another philosopher of science to whom later positivism owed a much greater debt. Ernst Mach (1838–1916) was one of the outstanding scientists of the latter half of the nineteenth century, contributing to fields as diverse as mechanics, physiology and psychology. His interest in history of science was lifelong; like Whewell and Herschel, he held that an adequate philosophy of science must be based on analysis of the history and practice of the sciences themselves. Like Whewell, however, he brought to that analysis a prior theory of knowledge, in his case the phenomenalism of Berkeley and Hume rather than the rationalism of Kant. According to him, science rests on a secure starting-point in the 'sensations' of which we are irrefutably aware; science must itself be construed, therefore, as being about sensations (recalling the 'ideas' of the earlier empiricist tradition). The aim of science is to formulate 'laws', that is, economical descriptions of sensations, enabling more effective prediction and communication. (This emphasis on sensations led to his being violently attacked as an 'idealist' by Lenin). When tested, scientific laws appear to refer to elements that cannot be directly certified in sensation, there must be a way to reformulate the laws in acceptably phenomenalist terms. He goes to great lengths to reconstruct Newtonian mechanics so as to make 'force' no more than a description of accelerated motion; the law of inertia (since it refers to an unobservable motion under no forces) becomes an implicit definition of force, and the absolutes of space and time are replaced by references to comprehensive sets of observable motions.

Mach's celebrated rejection of atomic theory was prompted by a strongly anti-metaphysical approach to theory generally. Theories do not (he maintains) provide the deeper understanding that scientists often suppose they do. They are merely temporary substitutes for proper description in terms of sensations alone. The analogies on which they are based may have some heuristic value, but unless a theory also serves the practical ends of economy (and in the case of atomic theory, Mach became convinced that it did not), it has no distinctive contribution to make to scientific understanding. Understanding or explanation must be rigorously limited to the level of description of what can be observed. Though the wave theory in optics is a successful instrument of prediction, this does not imply that it provides any deeper understanding of the underlying nature of light than our sensations alone can give. Mach repudiated, more emphatically than anyone had done before him, the goal of theoretical explanation, explanation of observed regularity in terms of underlying structure, bequeathed by the 'corpuscular philosophers' of the seventeenth century and seemingly central to the achievements of nineteenth-century science. The distinction between two forms of empiricism was now clear; one a broader view subscribed to by most philosophers of science which held that all evidence in science must ultimately come from the senses, the other a more radical form, which would imply that any entity proposed as explanatory must *itself* be capable of being sensed.

As the century drew to an end, the lines were thus relatively clearly drawn between two opposing camps. There were the followers of Mach, who distrusted any ampliative claim made for science, beyond that of a larger and more economic generalisation. And then there were the critics of positivism and phenomenalism who argued that scientific theory could, in fact, penetrate into what Newton called 'the invisible realm'. The hope that this explanation could rely on 'primary' qualities as its tool, on sensible qualities that could be extended indefinitely downwards and outwards from familiar mid-level experience, had, it is true, been almost abandoned; the role of imagination in creating a language appropriate to the invisible realm was becoming apparent. And this, of course, offered a fresh weapon to radical empiricism.

Another issue separating philosophers of science bore on rationality rather than realism. What kind of logic, if any, ought/do scientists follow? The followers of Kant still favoured an axiomatic–deductive format for at least some parts of natural science, notably mechanics. Empiricists in the tradition of Mill supported an inductive logic that could enlarge probability to virtual certainty by the progressive application of well-defined rules. Others, for whom Duhem would become a spokesman, insisted that the assessment of theory was not a matter of simple logical rule and that rationality had to be construed in broader terms than either deductive or inductive logic offered.

Philosophers of science of all stripes called on the history of science in support of their claims, but the morals they drew from history always seemed to be conditioned by their own prior commitments. Philosophy of science did, however, appear to be more 'decidable' than other more traditional parts of philosophy, since its assertions are (or at least in some sense *ought* to be) immediately conditioned by what actually goes on in science. Scientists could, therefore, claim a priority of expertise in certain respects over the professional philosopher. The major figures in philosophy of science as the century ended were nearly all, in fact, distinguished scientists in their own right.

With Poincaré and Peirce we are already on the brink of a decidedly new period. Einstein's two theories of relativity would shortly challenge Kantians and phenomenalists alike. But the themes for this new period had for the most part already been announced. The philosophers we have just been discussing would not find the arguments of Carnap or Popper, of Kuhn or van Fraassen, entirely unfamiliar.

NOTES

1. The translation is that of E. S. Haldane and G. R. T. Ross, *The philosophical works of Descartes* (New York: Dover, 1955).
2. The translation is that of James Spedding *et al.*, *Works of Francis Bacon* (Boston: Taggard and Thompson, 1863) vol. 8.
3. *Dialogue concerning two chief world systems*, transl. S. Drake (Berkeley, 1953), p. 53.
4. *Two new sciences*, transl. S. Drake (Madison, 1974), p. 153.
5. *Dialogue*, p. 15.
6. *The christian virtuoso, the works of Robert Boyle* (London, 1772), ed. T. Birch, vol. 5, p. 539.
7. Letter to Cotes, *Correspondence of Sir Isaac Newton and Professor Cotes*, ed. J. Edleston (London, 1850), p. 156.
8. *Opticks* (New York, 1952), Query 31, p. 404.

9. Ibid., p. 376.
10. *Principia*, transl. A. Motte and F. Cajori (New York, 1962) Book I, Definition VIII, pp. 5–6.
11. *De motu* (1721), *The works of George Berkeley*, ex. A. A. Luce and T. E. Jessup (London, 1948), vol. 4, p. 40.
12. *An enquiry concerning human understanding* (1751), Section V, Part I.
13. *Works of Thomas Reid*, ed. W. Hamilton (Edinburgh, 1846), vol. 1, p. 57.
14. *Prolegomena to any future metaphysics*, transl. P. Lucas (Manchester, 1953), par. 4.
15. *The critique of pure reason*, transl. N. K. Smith (London, 1933), A127.
16. *Critique of pure reason*, B17.
17. *Metaphysical foundations of natural science* (1786), transl. J. Ellington (Indianapolis, 1970), chap. 2, Proposition 7, p. 61.
18. *Philosophy of nature* (1830), transl. A. V. Miller (London, 1970), p. 118.
19. Ibid. p. 10.
20. *Cours de philosophie positive* (Paris, 1830), vol. 1, p. 9; translated in L. Laudan, 'Towards a reassessment of Comte's "méthode positive" ' in *Science and hypothesis*, chap. 7, p. 146.
21. *A system of logic* (New York, 8th edition, 1874), p. 223.

FURTHER READING

Ralph M. Blake, Curt J. Ducasse and Edward H. Madden, *Theories of scientific method: the renaissance through the nineteenth century* (Seattle, 1966).
Maria Righini Bonelli and William Shea (eds.), *Reason, experiment and mysticism in the scientific revolution* (New York, 1973).
Gordon Brittan, *Kant's theory of science* (Princeton, NJ, 1978).
Gerd Buchdahl, *Metaphysics and the philosophy of science* (Oxford, 1969).
Robert Butts and John Davis (eds.), *The methodological heritage of Newton* (Toronto, 1970).
Robert Butts and Joseph Pitt (eds.), *New perspectives on Galileo* (Dordrecht, 1978).
Robert Butts (ed.), *Kant's philosophy of physical science* (Dordrecht, 1986).
Desmond Clarke, *Descartes' philosophy of science* (Manchester, 1982).
I. Bernard Cohen, *Revolutions in science* (Cambridge, Mass., 1985).
Robert S. Cohen and Raymond J. Seeger, *Ernst Mach, physicist and philosopher* (Dordrecht, 1970).
Ronald N. Giere and Richard S. Westfall (eds.), *Foundations of scientific method: the nineteenth century* (Bloomington, 1973).
Nicholas Jardine, *The birth of history and philosophy of science* (Cambridge, 1984).
Larry Laudan, 'Theories of scientific method from Plato to Mach: a bibliographical review', *History of science* 7 (1968), 1–63.
—— *Science and hypothesis* (Dordrecht, 1981).
Kathleen Okruhlik and James R. Brown (eds.), *The natural philosophy of Leinbiz* (Dordrecht, 1985).
David Oldroyd, *The arch of knowledge. An introductory study of the history of the philosophy and methodology of science* (London, 1986).
Steven Shapin and Simon Shaffer, *Leviathan and the air pump* (Cambridge, 1985).

54

THE DEVELOPMENT OF PHILOSOPHY OF SCIENCE SINCE 1900

M. J. S. HODGE AND G. N. CANTOR

1. BEFORE LOGICAL POSITIVISM

For anyone writing in the English-speaking world in the present decade, a synoptic account of philosophy of science in this century will inevitably make one development the dominant theme: the rise and fall of logical positivism. Originally, logical positivism was the philosophy of the Vienna Circle, so called, led by Moritz Schlick (1882–1936) in the Austrian capital in the 1920s, and spreading from there to Britain and the United States as many of its adherents left Hitler's Europe. It was called logical positivism or logical empiricism (we shall take the two labels to be equivalent) because it held that, in any theory in physical science, logical structure can be distinguished from empirical content; whereas, by contrast, in mathematics which is more or less reducible to logic, there is no empirical content. The name logical positivism was apt, then, because this philosophy combined the new logicism (mathematics grounded in logic) of Gottlob Frege (1848–1925) and the older positivist tradition of Auguste Comte (1798–1857) that contrasted natural sciences as positive, empirical knowledge with metaphysics as speculative and vacuous (see art. 53; sect. 4).

We shall let the rise and fall of logical positivism dominate our account of twentieth-century philosophy of science. But we begin by insisting that the philosophical study of science did not stand idle for two decades after the century's opening, waiting for the Great War to end and for Schlick to gather his circle. So, to indicate the state of discussion at that time, we will glance at three writers already active before the War. Other choices might have been made, but Pierre Duhem (1861–1916), Ernst Cassirer (1874–1945) and Bertrand Russell (1872–1970) are especially instructive, in illustrating the paramount significance of two nineteenth-century legacies – from Immanuel Kant and from Comte – and in showing the different comparisons and contrasts then being drawn between mathematics, natural science and metaphysics.

The definitive version of Duhem's account of science is in his book of 1906 (second edition, 1914): *La Théorie Physique: Son Objet, Sa Structure*. Although Duhem was not ultimately a positivist, his view of physical theory is explicitly so. For he is as insistent as Ernst Mach and others had been that a physical theory is entirely independent of metaphysics; for it is not an explanation but a system of mathematical propositions that represents empirical laws and observable phenomena without pretending to disclose their underlying causes (see art. 53; sect. 4). Where Duhem broke new ground was in the further conclusions he drew from this positivist view. Galileo and the Church need never have clashed, Duhem held, if both had agreed to regard Galileo's theories, correctly, as representations of the celestial motions rather than as docrines about the real nature of astronomical phenomena. Again, a law of physics is not, for Duhem, true or false, but only approximate. Futhermore, physical laws are not tested one at a time, in isolation, but in groups. So when an experiment disagrees with prediction, the physicist learns that one of the hypotheses in the group is faulty, but the experiment does not indicate which one. Indeed, there can be no crucial experiments that decide between two theories by indicating the falsity of one of them.

Physical theories classify phenomena, Duhem holds, and with the progress of science we do come to believe that the classifications are natural ones corresponding to real distinctions in nature; but this belief, although often reasonable, is never justifiable by any reasoning from the facts themselves. As for physical and metaphysical theory, the only relationship Duhem finds between them is analogy. Duhem, both a master of thermodynamics and a loyal Roman Catholic, suggested that the equilibrium principles fundamental to thermodynamical theory were analogous to the principles of natural motion presupposed by Aristotle's (and so also Thomas Aquinas's) metaphysical cosmology. However, for Duhem, no physical theory ever confirms or contradicts any cosmological thesis. The positivism in his view of science serves, therefore, not to discredit metaphysics but to sever it from physics.[1]

The Marburg Kantian tradition, in which Cassirer was raised, had always understood the relationship between natural science and metaphysics very differently. For Cassirer, Kant had repudiated the possibility of metaphysics, in the sense of an *a priori* science of reality as it is independently of our knowledge of it, and had inaugurated instead a transcendental philosophical inquiry into science itself, into the fact that science exists as knowledge (see art. 53; sect. 4). This inquiry is not a psychological but a logical inquiry into the problem of knowledge as it arises for science, an inquiry into experience as the object of science, the object that makes science possible as knowledge.

Cassirer pursued this inquiry on the critical idealist assumption that this experience is actively constructed by scientific theorising. It has not then been constructed once and for all when some privileged structure of theory has been achieved. Even before the new physics of relativity theory and quantum mechanics had discredited anything like Kant's own explication of space and causation as presupposed by Newtonian physics, Cassirer had broken with Kant's privileging of that physics; and he duly embraced first relativity and then quantum mechanics within his neo-Kantian transcendental philosophical programme. Kant was right in holding that geometry contributes to our synthesising of phenomena into a definite concept of the world of experience as a single totality; but, Cassirer says, relativity shows that axioms other than the Euclidean can do this for us. Again, the uncertainty relations of quantum theory are irreconcilable with Kant's deterministic foundation for all physics, but the principles of conservation of energy and momentum, that can connect quantum with classical physics, show that some causal presuppositions are still required even if Kant's own need correction. There is, then, here too a neo-Kantian philosophical task, which is to ask what this correction includes and what its epistemological significance may be.[2]

Characteristic as they are of Cassirer's philosophy of science, such tasks are intrinsically historical, in that the principal preoccupation is with the epistemological innovations – in the Kantian sense of the logic of knowledge, the explication of the presuppositions of scientific concepts – that are implicit in developments in scientific theorising. That many of Cassirer's writings are constructed as historical analyses derives from his view of his relationship to Kant, a view that was paramount in determining how he saw his own programme in philosophy.

Russell's leading pre-First World War publication was *Principia Mathematica* (1910–13), the treatise in three volumes written with Alfred North Whitehead. The authors' greatest debt was to Frege's efforts to refute and replace Kant's view that the truths of arithmetic are synthetic and *a priori*. For Kant a judgement is synthetic if the predicate is not definitionally included in the subject term. The predicate is not so included when it is said (the example is Kant's own) that all bodies are heavy, but is included when it is said, in an analytic statement, that all bodies are extended. Although he took them to be synthetic, Kant thought that the truths of arithmetic could be known *a priori*, that is, independently of finding them instantiated in our experience of the world; whereas our knowledge of the truths of chemistry – that water, say, is a compound not an element – does depend on experience.

In his writings of the 1880s, Frege's programme for exhibiting arithmetic as a body of analytic truths and *a priori* knowledge required defining arithmetical concepts in logical terms – number in terms of class membership for instance – and deriving arithmetical truths by deducing them from logical truths, such truths as that a proposition is either true or false but not both. *Principia Mathematica* was offered as an extension and consummation of this quest for foundations for mathematics in logic (see art. 44).

Russell himself moved beyond this quest to an even more general philosophical programme that has been dubbed his logical constructionism. The guiding principle for this logical constructionism was, wherever possible, to substitute constructions out of known entities for inferences to unknown entities. This principle, Russell argued, often allows one to dispense with abstraction. For example, instead of making a risky inference that relations of equality arise from some abstract common quality, all the formal purposes of this common quality can be served by the membership of the group of terms having this relation of equality to a given term. Going beyond cases of relational properties, such as equality, to theoretical or hypothetical entities such as electromagnetic fields or electron particles, Russell was to argue that for these too, similar constructions can be provided. However, here the constructions have to include as elements sense data, the sensory givens of colour, shape, sound and so on. For Russell, logical constructionism has to be complemented by comprehensive conjectures, attempts at a philosophical synthesis of all the fundamental pre-suppositions made by the different sciences concerning the constitution of the universe – the events of the relativity physicist and the sensations of the physiological psychologist, for example. Such conjectures, Russell insists, are appropriate to scientific philosophy, and in acknowledging their continuity with older metaphysical theorising, he appears unwilling to separate science from metaphysics. Far from rejecting such philosophical enquiries as mere metaphysics, Russell would bring them into science through logical constructions.[3]

The spirit and letter of Russell's logical constructionism set decisive precedents for a short book by his young friend Ludwig Wittgenstein (1889–1951), the *Tractatus Logico-Philosophicus* (1921) a main aim of which was to clarify the relationship between language and the world. A principal thesis of the book is that clarification is to be found in a relation of picturing between elementary propositions and the elementary facts that they depict. This proposal suggested that the theories of empirical science are to be contrasted with those of logic and mathematics; in empirical science facts are pictured, while the purely formal truths of logic and mathematics do no depicting. (See art. 52.)

2. LOGICAL POSITIVISM

Our sampling of pre-First World War philosophies has now prepared us to appreciate what was novel in the logical positivism of Schlick and the Vienna Circle. For they combined, as no one had before, logicist opposition to the Kantian synthetic *a priori* in explicating mathematics, with a positivist elimination of metaphysics and legitimation of physical science through an empiricist criterion of factual meaning. For, consider the logical positivists' various criteria of cognitive meaning in general and of factual meaning in particular: for instance, 'a sentence makes a cognitively meaningful assertion, and thus can be said to be true or false, only if it is either (1) analytic or self-contradictory or (2) capable, at least in principle, of experiential test'.[4] All such criteria were deliberately designed to eliminate metaphysics altogether as meaningless and so linguistically impossible. The novelty of logical positivism resided, therefore, not in either of the two strands indicated by the name of the movement, but in their conjunction.

Logical positivism was not just a philosophy of science, but a comprehensive philosophical teaching including distinctive analyses of mind and morals. It had, moreover, a distinctive Enlightenment ideological character, explicitly harking back to the eighteenth century as the first age of Enlightenment, and repudiating the Counter-Enlightenment thrust of the Romantic age that had opened the nineteenth century. The immediate rationale for their new Enlightenment commitment was the struggle, as the Viennese philosophers saw it, that had to be fought against not only conservative political positions but also the associated threatening hegemony of obscurantist Hegelian metaphysics and reactionary Catholic theology prominent in many Austrian and some German universities. In a later phase, especially in the United States in the years after the Second World War, logical positivism often served further ideological and institutional roles. It was a dominant school of thought when philosophy of science was emerging as an autonomous discipline within the wider academic profession of philosophy. The American protegés of such emigrés as Carnap, Feigl, Hempel and Reichenbach were among the first people whose professional academic identity was primarily constituted by overt pursuit of a career in philosophy of science as such. At the same time, the commitment to Enlightenment ideals of reason and freedom could motivate ideological opposition to the authoritarian and totalitarian tendencies perceived to be entrenched in the political regimes of the Socialist bloc countries.

Of all the philosophy of science texts written by logical positivists since the Second World War, one – Rudolf Carnap's *Philosophical Foundations of Physics* (1966), since retitled *An Introduction to Philosophy of Science* (1974) – is especially instructive; for it consistently relates its analyses of particular theories and concepts to the most general resources and preoccupations of Vienna Circle philosophy. Throughout Carnap's entire presentation of the philosophy of science, one task dominates; and that is to distinguish on the one hand the logical, the formal, the analytic, the *a priori*, the purely mathematical, or the definitional and, on the other, the empirical, the factual, the *a posteriori*, the applied and the physical. Indeed, one can say that this task constitutes his philosophy of science by providing both its agenda and its strategies for pursuing that agenda. Philosophy of science is a logical, analytic exercise conducted upon science with the aim of distinguishing what is, and, conversely, what is not, logical and analytic in science.

The character of this enterprise is manifest both in treatments of particular theories and concepts and in the accounts given of wider topics such as laws of nature, causality and theories in general. The particular theory that receives most attention is, naturally enough, Einstein's theory of relativity considered as a theory of the physical structure of space. Here, tellingly, Carnap recalls that this was the subject of his doctoral thesis and so provided his own entrée into philosophy of science. No less tellingly, the subject as he now examines it leads, as it did so often in Vienna in the 1920s, to a critique and rejection of Kant's synthetic *a priori*; with an endorsement of Schlick's aphorism that empiricism itself can even be defined by this rejection.

The account of space, with its anti-Kantian conclusion, depends throughout on the contrast between mathematical geometry and physical geometry. These two are 'excellent paradigms of two fundamentally different ways of gaining knowledge: the aprioristic and the empirical', a distinction that can provide 'valuable insights into important methodological problems in the theory of knowledge'.[5] The non-Euclidean, Riemannian geometry adopted by Einstein is, as mathematics, a purely formal, logical system with no empirical content. It yields an account of the physical structure of space in Einstein's theory of gravitation, because it is there conjoined with additional definitional decisions about measurement conventions. For, Carnap argues, if suitable decisions are made, then it becomes an empirical question as to which geometry yields the simplest physics for gravitating bodies. To that extent, it becomes an empirical problem to determine what is the physical structure of space.

Carnap's philosophical, which is to say logical, analysis is practised on Einstein's theory as a product, an achievement that is given, with its structure and content complete, and needing, from the philosopher, only explication. Likewise, with those items, such as laws and theories, that are the characteristic structures of science in general; Carnap takes these to be given. Indeed they are given in that they are definitively characteristic of all natural science, in that any process or programme of empirical, explanatory inquiry would only count as science if it were producing structures that comprise confirmable empirical laws and testable theoretical laws and therefore structures that constitute physical theories. Philosophical questions about processes and programmes resolve themselves, consequently, into logical questions about those structures.

Carnap analyses explanation – in conformity with a long empiricist tradition refined by other logical positivists such as Hempel – as argument, so that the structure of explanation is the structure of an argument form. The form includes at least one premise that is a law statement, for explanation of a fact involves subsuming the explained fact under a law of nature, a covering law in the phrase since become standard. Laws of nature and laws of logic are to be contrasted as, once again, falling on either side of the great divide that separates the empirical from the analytic. Likewise, too, with probability: statistical probability is empirical and owes its meaning to its verifiability in observed frequency trends; logical or inductive probability is a relation between the conclusion of an argument and the premises. Inductive logic is, therefore, like deductive logic in being concerned with logical relations between statements, not with the facts of nature; and an inductive logic, once constructed, would allow an assignment of numerical values to the logical probabilities – the partial implications – holding between the evidence for a hypothesis and the hypothesis itself. However, while it is 'possible to apply an inductive logic to the language of science' it is not possible 'to formulate a set of rules, fixed once and for all, that will lead automatically, in any field, from facts to theories'.[6] In devising a new system of theoretical concepts, Carnap emphasises, creative ingenuity is needed.

Although recognised as indispensable, such creative ingenuity lies outside the scope of Carnap's account of theories. For, to a logical positivist or empiricist, the principal challenges presented by theories – and, by the non-observable terms, such as electron, that they include – are the challenges of meaning and confirmation. Meaning requires verifiability or at least confirmability, potential confirmation; whereas confirmation requires that this potential be realised. Theories are problematic, both as to their meaning and their status as knowledge, unless they can be related appropriately to observations that are not problematic. As Carnap saw it, the distinction, between theories and facts as given by observation, is essential to the very formulation of the issues central to a logical positivist's philosophy of scientific theory.

Central therefore, too, are 'correspondence rules', the statements that link theoretical concepts and statements to observation and so make possible this meaning and this knowledge. First, as to knowledge; a statement, that the temperature of a gas is proportional to the mean kinetic energy of the molecules, connects a non-observable in molecular theory, the kinetic energy, with an observable, the temperature of the gas. Such a rule allows, therefore, for empirical laws to be derived from theoretical laws. Such rules allow also meaning or interpretation. A term in a mathematical axiom system, such as 'number', can be provided with an interpretation through a definition in logic, as Frege and Russell have shown. But the axiomatic terms in a postulate system in physics – 'electron' and the like – can and must be given an interpretation, albeit a partial one, by correspondence rules that connect those terms with observable phenomena. This interpretation being incomplete, new rules of correspondence can always be added. Progress in physical science often consists in establishing more and more correspondence rules that allow wider and wider arrays of laws and facts to be subsumed within a single theory. Maxwell's unifying subsumption of electrical, magnetic and optical laws within a single theory depended on establishing appropriate correspondence rules, connecting theoretical terms and statements in a single theory with empirical laws in these three domains. It is here that Carnap endorses, implicitly, the standard logical positivist view of scientific change and progress: namely, that such change is progressive especially when it achieves unification through successive subsumptive reductions. For what is achieved in Maxwell's theoretical optics is a reduction of optics to electromagnetic theory; in that the optical laws – under specified conditions and through the correspondence rules – can be deduced as corollaries of the laws of that electromagnetic theory.

It is, then, not true that logical positivism had nothing to say about scientific change. In progress by unification through reduction, it had an ideal of progressive change, an ideal that was thought to have been often instantiated in the natural sciences since the Renaissance. However, what is true is that for logical positivism the articulation of this ideal was directly derivative from prior considerations concerning the conditions for meaning and confirmation in theories. It was, then, derivative from the analysis of theories as partially interpretable logical calculi. The agenda of logical positivist philosophy of science included no concern with the history of science, except where that history could serve as a source of illustrative cases exemplifying philosophical conclusions derived from logical analysis as applied to the structures, the logical forms, taken to be typical of the products of science: scientific theories themselves.

From the early 1930s onwards, logical positivist philosophy of science had a persistent and respected critic in Karl Popper (b. 1902), who was in Vienna in the 1920s, although never a member of Schlick's Circle. Popper's philosophy had its origin in a single proposal: falsification, as a resolution of two fundamental issues: first, the demarcation of science from any non-scientific theorising including metaphysics, and, second, induction. To be scientific a theory must be capable of falsification, Popper decided. This demarcation does not make falsifiability a criterion of meaning. Not meaning but learning was Popper's concern. If we can learn that a theory is false by establishing that it has made false predictions, then that theory can contribute to the growth of knowledge that is characteristic of any scientific enterprise. Learning, and so the progressive growth of knowledge, does not involve, therefore, any inductive inferences. On one traditional characterisation of induction, it consists in inferring that a statement of law is true or probable from finding instances of the law within experience. But, argued Popper, in his *Logik der Forschung* (1934) or *Logic of Scientific Discovery* in English translation (1959), induction is neither valid nor needed. All that is needed to learn from experience is to infer, in accordance with the deductive validity of *modus tollens*, from falsity in the deductive consequences of a theory to the falsity of the theory itself.

Science, as conjectures and refutations, needs no inductivist justification.

Rather it is to be legitimated through appropriate methodological conventions that are taken to constitute a normative definition of science as an activity having certain aims. If the aim of science is agreed to be a progressive succession of theories that are more and more informative (and so more and more falsifiable and, indeed, logically improbable) then success in the pursuit of that aim will require whatever methodological conventions will ensure the continued formulating and testing of theories. The logic of *modus tollens* (which implies that what has a false consequence is itself false) is necessary but not sufficient for this; for, logically, a theory can be protected from falsification in the face of any given facts, by reformulating it appropriately or conjoining it with suitable supplementary assumptions. The logical analysis of theory testing shows, therefore, Popper insists, that deductions must be complemented by decisions that exclude saving theories by such evasive and protective measures. Logical deductions and methodological decisions together can constitute the critical rationality of science without recourse to inductive or probability logics. Moreover, the aims of science and success in their pursuit can be explicated without reference to anyone's beliefs or feelings of certainty or uncertainty. The theoretical products and critical operations on them, that comprise the communal and individual learning that is science, are to be analysed into statements and entailments that have the objectivity of logical entities and relations rather than the subjectivity of psychological processes.

In its anti-psychologism, Popper's philosophy is indebted to the logicism of the Fregean tradition; but it does not develop that tradition by concentrating on meanings, definitions and the elucidation of theoretical structures through their reformulation in logical calculi serving as artificial languages. Rather the emphasis is on what logic can and can not do for the theory of method, rationality and progress. When that is appreciated, Popper concludes, the positivist quest – to find the justification for a superstructure of theory in a solid base of fact uncontaminated with theory and its attendant uncertainty – is discredited. Science as learning does not require either foundational justification or certainty, only guessing and testing. There are no observational statements that have no theoretical ingredient anyway. Any statements that can be used in testing any theory include theorising in their own formulation and deployment. The positivist teaching is mistaken, misled by its anti-Kantianism, Popper holds, in its very understanding of theory and observation; and in so far as that understanding is definitive of what it is to be a positivist, he is adamant that he is no positivist. Nor does he accept the positivist elimination of metaphysics. Realism about scientific theories, the untestable, unfalsifiable conjecture that theoretical scientific terms refer to real entities and processes in the world, is upheld by Popper as a metaphysical programme, complementary to science although demarcated from it.

3. AFTER LOGICAL POSITIVISM

Despite Popperian assertions to the contrary, Popper's teachings did not play a major part in the downfall of logical positivism. That downfall has yet to be given a critical history, but there would be little disagreement that at least three factors would have to be considered. The first is that the assumptions about language and logic that had been so central both to logicism and to logical positivism, were taken to have received, from the early 1950s onwards, a variety of telling criticisms. Two very different critics, both knowledgeable of the positivists' teachings, were W.V.O. Quine (b. 1908) and Ludwig Wittgenstein. Quine attacked not only the distinction between analytic and synthetic truths, but also the whole contrast between logical and empirical enquiries. Wittgenstein, in his *Philosophical Investigations* (1953), dissociating himself from many of the views he had shared with Russell earlier in his life, argued that the uses, and so meanings, of a natural language will always be misunderstood in attempts to elucidate them by representations of formal structures.

A second challenge to logical positivism came from the history of science. In the 1950s historians of science, most notably A. Koyré who was acknowledged by many as the doyen, were far from innocent of philosophical predilections (see art. 1). Moreover, although many historians were unaware of it, whenever Koyréan interpretations of history were sought, the new historiography of science was drawing, through Koyré, on philosophical debts to Hegel rather than to Hume and to opponents of positivism such as Meyerson rather than to positivists such as Mach. History of science and logical positivist philosophy of science were now so divergent philosophically that the history of science had the resources for a philosophical critique of logical positivism. And that, in the late 1950s and early 1960s, is exactly what began to take place.

Thirdly, the broad cultural innovations of the 1960s included reassertion of Counter-Enlightenment attitudes that often conflicted with the ideological character of logical positivism (see art. 58). Philosophical students of science were challenged, by these newer attitudes, to show that they were not uncritical in their own attitude to science and not presuming in advance that a philosophy of science must always reveal the legitimacy rather than the limitations of scientific rationality.

Probably the first philosopher of science to exploit Wittgenstein's *Philosophical Investigations* in challenging the presuppositions of empiricism was Norwood Russell Hanson in his *Patterns of Discovery* (1958). As his title suggests Hanson was concerned with innovative thinking in science, particularly in modern physics. Traditional empiricist and positivist teachings, with their emphasis on justification and verification rather than on discovery and transformation seemed to throw little light on the creative aspects of science or on periods of rapid change. Moreover, they seemed especially unenlightening when confronting the practice of particle physicists who talk confidently about such unobservable entities as electrons, positrons and mesons. Hanson's response was to concentrate on the role of perception and the Wittgensteinian dictum that 'seeing is not only the having of a visual experience; it is also the way in which the visual experience is had'.[7] Since there is no one correct way of having visual experience, two scientists can experience the same event in two entirely different ways, each interpreting the event through his or her own complex of beliefs and expectations. So, to take what was to become a standard example, both Ptolemy and Copernicus might watch the setting of the sun; but while both would, presumably, have exactly similar retinal images, the first would 'see' the moving sun travelling beyond the horizon, while the second would 'see' the sun in an apparent motion due to the diurnal rotation of the earth. Each would give different accounts of the sunset, accounts grounded in their respective cosmological theories. Generally, then, Hanson insisted that observations are not theory-neutral but are 'theory-laden'.

This Wittgenstein–Hanson line of argument explicitly repudiated any distinction between facts and theories such as positivism upheld. It is a repudiation that has raised a host of problems besetting philosophy of science ever since. If facts and theories are not distinct but theories infuse facts and the choice of facts, while facts are only significant in respect to theories, then scientific theorising is without a purely empirical base. In the extreme this leads to a complete relativism, with Ptolemy and Copernicus looking at the world in different ways. Neither way is better and neither is true, since each theory interprets the sunset in its own terms. Moreover, the notion of progress – which was for Enlightenment thinkers the very touchstone of science – also disappears. What is at issue in all these cases is, first, the claim that because Ptolemy and Copernicus 'see' the world in different ways they must describe it in different languages, or, in Wittgensteinian terminology, play different 'language games'. And second, since the meaning of terms is defined by other terms in the same language there is no way of translating between the two languages: for Ptolemy and Copernicus the meanings of 'sunset' are totally different. The languages are therefore 'incommensurable'.

These concerns arising from the Wittgenstein–Hanson tradition found their most celebrated exposition in Thomas S. Kuhn's *The Structure of Scientific Revolutions* (1962). Kuhn, trained in physics, decided that the history of mechanics could not be comprehended within a simple accumulationist view of scientific knowledge, since such a thesis implies that earlier writers are to be judged anachronistically, in terms of later developments. Rather, he concluded, the history of a scientific descipline is marked by discontinuities. The first stage in such a history is characterised by the existence of a number of contending schools of thought each pursuing its own goals, methods and problems. At some point this diversity is replaced by consensus among practitioners; they all follow the same 'paradigm' – the word is taken from Wittgenstein. Perhaps the most serviceable of Kuhn's definitions of paradigms is: 'These I take to be universally recognized scientific achievements that for a time provide model problems and solutions to a community of practitioners'.[8] Thus, for example, Newton's *Principia* (1687) provided scientists with a way of defining and solving physical problems in terms of particles of matter and attendant forces; moreover it set acceptable standards for scientific work, specified the kind of apparatus to be employed in research, and served other such functions. In all, the paradigm is a way of looking at the world and a way of talking about it.

In those, often extended, periods when a particular paradigm holds sway, scientists pursue 'normal' science, a game in which they solve the puzzles set by the paradigm. For example, scientists working within the paradigm of Newton's *Principia* sought the precise force laws governing electrostatic action and the interaction between light particles and material bodies. While this characterisation applied to much of science, there were occasions when anomalies accumulated to such an extent that the discipline would be thrown into a state of crisis. One resolution of the crisis would be the appearance of another paradigm which would rapidly gain the community's allegiance. Here we have a 'scientific revolution', with the new paradigm representing a break from the old. Kuhn expresses the relationship between the two paradigms in a striking simile: 'Like the choice between competing political institutions, that between competing paradigms proves to be a choice between *incompatible modes of community life*'. Again, a paradigm change causes 'scientists to *see the world* of their research-engagement differently;' it is 'a relatively sudden and unstructured event *like the gestalt switch;*' the protagonists '*necessarily talked through each other*'.[9] All of these similes and metaphors bear on themes prominent in the Wittgenstein–Hanson tradition.

In analysing scientific revolutions, Kuhn claims that the preceding and succeeding paradigms are incommensurable with no intertranslation possible. Thus the word 'mass' which appears in both Newtonian and Einsteinian languages has different meanings in each; mass being independent of velocity in the first but velocity dependent in the second. However, Kuhn was clearly uncomfortable with this radical thesis and argued that there were nevertheless a number of inter-paradigm standards – such as simplicity and consistency – which saved science from indiscriminate relativism and reinstated such traditional values as progress and rationality. Kuhn's prevarication on such issues also alerts us to the diversity and inconsistencies in his philosophical heritage. While Wittgensteinian themes doubtless provide many of the key philosophical features of his theory, these are freely intermixed with elements drawn from Piaget's theory of child development, Whorfian comparative linguistics, Continental idealism, Quine's philosophy of logic and language and even from old-fashioned positivism.

Yet Kuhn needs to be located in at least two other ways. One is as a historian of science who has written extensively on the histories of thermodynamics, Copernicanism and quantum theory. Although it would be naïve to assume that *The Structure of Scientific Revolutions* is the generalisation of his experience as a historian, it is certainly true that his historical knowledge helped in his selection of philosophical ideas and that he makes extensive use of historical examples. The other discipline Kuhn needs to be related to is sociology, especially the sociology of science. In *Structure*, Kuhn insists that the paradigm is located in a scientific community, in a group that has been socialised to see the world in a particular way, a scientific community that is a Wittgensteinian language community. Kuhn accordingly rejects the view that science is to be understood solely in terms of scientific ideas, and instead places great emphasis on the institutions of science, especially those which train scientists and maintain consensus, such as textbooks. Not surprisingly, *Structure* has provided a major stimulus for sociologists of science such as Michael Mulkay, Barry Barnes, David Bloor and Trevor Pinch, some of whom have also tapped the more sociological themes to be found in Wittgenstein (see arts. 5 and 8). However, it should be pointed out that Kuhn's sociology, like other aspects of his work, is conservative in that he hardly ever allows ideas or events outside science to influence its development. He conceives the scientific community to be, normally, both isolated from society at large and self-regulating.

In contrast to Kuhn's rather faltering deployment of the Wittgenstein–Hanson tradition, Paul Feyerabend has used it vigorously to attack both empiricism and rationalism. He uses the claim that all observations are theory-laden to dispose of the view that the aim of theories is to represent or explain a fixed, external world. Instead, for Feyerabend, scientific theories are acts of the imagination which create the world we perceive. Accordingly, he argues for an uncompromising version of the incommensurability thesis. Like Kuhn, he rejects, too, successive subsumptive reductions as a mode of progress for science, for the deductions needed for the reductions require meaning invariance for their validity.

Further, theories of rationality have no part in our understanding of science since they not only threaten to limit our creativity but also, according to Feyerabend, fail to appreciate how new theories have introduced new standards of evaluation: rationality and, likewise, scientific method are not fixed and ahistorical. How, then, are we to understand not only the knowledge claims of science but also public statements on scientific rationality and scientific method? For Feyerabend, utterances on these subjects constitute the political and propaganda aspects of science. Taken together with the incommensurability thesis, this implies that the science we now accept, or that any previous generation accepted, is not the result of a dispassionate, empirically-constrained search for truth, but the result of political pressures that have eliminated alternatives from the public domain. What Feyerabend sees as most needed for both science and philosophy of science is the stripping away of the dogma and authority by which they are currently fettered; indeed the individual's scientific beliefs should be as free from public and state interference as his religious beliefs. Only then would science be both free and humane, he insists.

4. BEYOND POST-POSITIVIST PHILOSOPHY OF SCIENCE

It is in Feyerabend's writings that one finds the most vivid echoes of the neo-Romanticism so characteristic of 1960s counter-culture. It would be tempting, therefore, to suspect that the generational wheel has since turned on yet again to bring us, once more, a revival of Enlightenment sentiments in philosophy of science. But no such suspicion is born out by any survey of present trends. One reason for this is that science has become an object now of many kinds of characterisation. Twenty years ago the logical and the historical approaches seemed to constitute the main choices. Today, anthropological theories of society, semiotic theories of man, deconstructionist theories of discourse and a host of other resources are drawn upon, so that it is difficult to say where philosophy of science begins and ends and where other disciplinary ventures take over (see arts. 4, 5 and 10). Such a state of the art makes generalisations unwise; but two impressions may be worth recording because they will serve to make connections with other contributions to this *Companion*.

The first is that, for philosophers who have stayed with the traditional issues raised by scientific theorising, two topics have seemed especially pressing: rationality and realism. Rationality has been given urgency as a topic, especially by the use made of post-positivist philosophy of science by sociologists of scientific knowledge; for these sociologists have often repudiated all principles of rationality in favour of an explicit relativism (see art. 12). Realism, on the other hand, has been given a new lease of life by developments in the theory of meaning, reference, truth and interpretation associated with philosophers such as Sellars, Davidson, Kripke and Putnam (see art. 13).

The second impression is that one concern which remains dominant among philosophers in general, namely language, is providing a bridge between the English-speaking world and the world of Continental European philosophy; and that this bridge is already of consequence for current attempts to advance philosophical understanding of science. Books such as Richard Rorty's *Philosophy and the Mirror of Nature* (1979) have argued for links joining current mainstream English-speaking preoccupations – with meaning, reference, truth and interpretation – to the post-structuralist, often neo-Nietzschean developments associated with Michel Foucault, Jacques Derrida and others in France. Such links may open up possibilities for the philosophy of science, but it is too early to say yet what they may include (see art. 10). Especially, it is not clear whether they will lead to rapprochements between what the French used to call Anglo-Saxon philosphy of science and yet other philosophical traditions such as Marxism.

Quite inconclusive as these closing reflections may be, they will have served their purpose if they have reinforced the earlier impression that, for better or worse, philosophy of science has moved a long way from where it was when logical positivism was in the ascendant. They will have served their purpose, too, if they have helped to highlight one generalisation that must emerge from any survey of the philosophy of science over the long run of several generations: namely, that philosophy of science is a very inconstant enterprise, and is so for a good reason. For it is likely at any time to be redirected, both in its agenda and its resources, by innovations in the sciences, by developments in philosophy and by wider cultural transformations as well. Indeed, in its most fruitful phases it has been responding to all of these things.

NOTES

1. P. Duhem, trans. P. Wiener, *The aim and structure of physical theory* (New York, 1977). Appendix: 'Physics of a believer', pp. 273–311.
2. P. A. Schilpp (ed.) *The philosophy of Ernst Cassirer* (Evanston, Illinois, 1949); E. Cassirer, trans. W. C. Swabey and M. C. Swabey, *Substance and function, and Einstein's theory of relativity* (New York, 1953); E. Cassirer, trans. O. T. Benfey, *Determinism and indeterminism in modern physics* (Newhaven, 1956).
3. B. Russell, 'Logical atomism', in A. J. Ayer (ed.), *Logical positivism* (New York, 1959), pp. 31–50.
4. C. G. Hempel, 'The empiricist criterion of meaning', in A. J. Ayer (ed.), *Logical positivism*, p. 108.
5. R. Carnap, ed. M. Gardner, *An introduction to the philosophy of science* (New York, 1974), p. 125.
6. Carnap, *Introduction*, p. 33.
7. N. R. Hanson, *Patterns of discovery* (Cambridge, 1958), p. 15.
8. T. S. Kuhn, *The structure of scientific revolutions* (Chicago and London, 1962), p. x.
9. Kuhn, *Structure*, pp. 94, 111, 122 and 132. Emphases added.

FURTHER READING

P. D. Asquith and H. E. Kyburg (eds.), *Current research in philosophy of science* (East Lansing, Michigan, 1979).

Harold I. Brown, *Perception, theory and commitment: the new philosophy of science* (Chicago, 1979).

A. F. Chalmers, *What is this thing called science?* (Milton Keynes, Second edition, 1979).

Ian Hacking, *Representing and intervening. Introductory topics in the philosophy of science* (Cambridge, 1983).

—— (ed.) *Scientific revolutions* (Oxford, 1981).

W. Newton-Smith, *The rationality of science* (London, 1979).

David Oldroyd, *The arch of knowledge. An introductory study of the history of the philosophy and methodology of science* (London, 1986).

F. Suppe, *The structure of scientific theories* (Urbana, Illinois, Second edition, 1977).

55

THE CLASSIFICATION OF THE SCIENCES

NICHOLAS FISHER

1. 'THE TRUE ORDER OF KNOWLEDGE'

Apart from librarians, few people today give much consideration to the classification of knowledge. And yet if there were not someone to take it seriously, the seeker after that knowledge would very soon get lost in the library, and knowledge itself would become radically inaccessible, especially with today's geometrical escalation of information. In the nineteenth century, on the other hand, the period of ever-increasing specialisation that saw the establishment of the chief scientific disciplines, the classification of the branches of knowledge was a preoccupation by no means confined to bibliographers. From practising scientists, philosophers and encyclopaedists, to polymathic figures such as Auguste Comte and Herbert Spencer who took almost all knowledge to be their province; all felt it necessary to discuss 'the true order of knowledge' as some sort of prolegomenon – to a full understanding of science in general or of a particular science, or to proper education in science, or to a workable library classification. At the end of the century these many systems were surveyed by Ernest Cushing Richardson, the Princeton Librarian, and by Robert Flint DD, Emeritus Professor of Divinity at Edinburgh, in exhaustive works which, because the topic is no longer academically fashionable, may never be superseded.

The main impression that emerges from the nineteenth-century literature is of virtually unbridgeable dissent. That, after all, is why so many scholars felt it incumbent upon them to produce schemes of their own, invariably accompanied by criticism (sometimes very academic) of the shortcomings of their predecessors.

2. HISTORICAL DEVELOPMENTS IN THE CLASSIFICATION OF THE SCIENCES

One area, however, in which the organisation of knowledge was no academic question, and was becoming ever more essential at the beginning of this century, was the library. Despite the apparent dissent, Henry Evelyn Bliss was able in 1929 to detect a 'scientific and educational consensus' as to the organisation of knowledge. This embraced library practice as well as the usual school and college curriculum. What he thought was needed in that era of postwar reconstruction was co-operative research informed by social need, with real efficiency achieved by division of labour according to scientific disciplines – an echo of Francis Bacon. In this new real world philosophical classification of the sciences was firmly made subordinate to the utilitarian demand for rapid, complete and accurate retrieval of scientific information.[1]

In the twentieth century, working scientists would tend to acknowledge Bliss's consensus: at least at the core, the main disciplines (including some new ones) are well characterised by their subject-matter, as well as by their professional identity. If, for the sociologist of science, 'science is what scientists do', this is also very much the case for the specialist disciplines. With occasional exceptions, scientists and natural philosophers have for the last 300 years had little care for the niceties of philosophical classification and have defined their discipline in terms of their activity and their interests. Thus for the chemist Charles Everitt writing in the eleventh edition of the *Encyclopaedia Britannica* in 1910,

> CHEMISTRY . . . the natural science which has for its province the study of the composition of substances. In common with physics it includes the determination of properties or characters which serve to distinguish one substance from another, but while the physicist is concerned with properties possessed by all substances and with processes in which the molecules remain intact, the chemist is restricted to those processes in which the molecules undergo some change . . .

Two general points occasioned by this quotation should be made before embarking on the main historical developments in the classification of the sciences. One is to note the pervasiveness of the territorial metaphor, in which the system of the sciences is seen as a map of knowledge, with chemistry having a 'province'. We can express the strength of the twentieth-century consensus by saying that the boundary outlines have changed very little in the last 80 years. There may have been border disputes, and new exploratory techniques may have yielded levels of detailed knowledge in certain areas which our grandfathers could not have dreamed of. There is also greater cooperation across boundaries now – something of a Common Market – a welcome change after the nationalisms of the nineteenth century. Some territories have risen in importance while others have declined; the province of chemistry, for instance, seems to be becoming depopulated, at least relative to its one-time colony, molecular biology. And within each territory, cities and regions have waxed and waned. But the boundaries have been remarkably stable. One great danger for the historian of science is that these taken-for-granted borders seem so natural to the late twentieth-century mind that there is a tendency to assume that they have always been there. As a result people look for 'biology' and 'physics' before the nineteenth century, and if they come across early references to 'chemistry', they think of it as coextensive with the present territory. Similarly it would be incorrect to see the sciences of the past as divided from the rest of knowledge into 'two cultures' (continents?). Until about a hundred years ago, knowledge was seen as an integrated whole. Since then there has been drift apart.

The other point, raised by the *Britannica*'s mention of distinguishing one substance from another, is the extent to which classification of the sciences may be compared to classification of the objects of science. Logically, the procedures are of course the same, and the zeniths of the two traditions were roughly coincident in time, early in the nineteenth century. Nevertheless, the two classificatory traditions have remained largely distinct, with little cross-membership, since the one is concerned with objects and other with activities. One point in common, though, between the two traditions, is that for both, classification is far more than pigeon-holing division. A good classification of animals will attempt to express the totality of relationships in the animal kingdom; a good classification of knowledge will try to integrate the whole 'circle of the sciences'.

3. THE ARISTOTELIAN TRADITION

One other feature common to the two traditions is that both have their origins in Aristotle. Not only did he invent the logic of classification, but he remains one of the very few taxonomists of the natural world who were also seriously involved in the systematisation of knowledge.

For Aristotle, unlike some of his mediaeval followers, classification was never an end in itself. Nor, perhaps surprisingly, were the classifications of this philosopher supposed truly to correspond to the real order of nature; they were not 'natural' in the eighteenth- or nineteenth-century sense. For these reasons he left no fixed systems: despite the efforts of some historians of science to reconstruct *the* Aristotelian classification of animals, Aristotle stressed that these might be arranged according to different criteria, depending on the aim of the classification. The closest he came to a definitive classification was a scale of perfection, later to be transformed into the *Scala Naturae*, or Great Chain of Being. (See arts. 35, 52 and 53.)

As for his organisation of knowledge, Flint tells how Aristotle adopted a threefold division of science, into Theoretical, Productive and Practical, criticising him severely for classifying according to the aims of the sciences, rather than their inherent natures.[2] Apart from this brief passage in the *Metaphysics*, though, of which Flint makes so much, Aristotle in the *Nicomachean Ethics* defines five kinds of intellectual virtues, art (*techne*), scientific knowledge (*episteme*), rational intuition (*nous*), practical intelligence (*phronesis*) and wisdom (*sophia*). This would yield a second classification of philosophy or knowledge according to mental qualities. It is not reconcilable with the first, nor with a third (and the most important) of Aristotle's divisions of learning, which is the content-based classification enshrined in the titles of his treatises.

From these a hierarchical 'system' can be constructed in which metaphysics stands at the apex as the 'First Philosophy', the most abstract and therefore the most widely applicable of the sciences. Mathematics is less general and less abstract, and is followed by physics, the science embracing what can be known by perception and experience. This is not of course the same as the 'physics' of today, and includes much if not most of what we would now call 'science', being concerned with matter and change in all their manifestations. For instance it includes 'psychology': *psyche*, soul, is the agent of change in the living world, and its study includes the manifestation in plants of vegetative or nutritive soul. But it also of course covers the activity of the rational soul, the faculty that distinguishes man from the rest of nature. Man's social nature is dealt with as ethics and politics, increasingly concrete and specialist, and his creative activity under poetics and rhetoric. In looking at man, at the base of the pyramid, we return to the classification of knowledge according to ends.

Outside the hierarchy stands logic, both a necessary preliminary to philosophy, and a tool (*organon*, instrument) common to all scientific argumentation. Aristotle's logical works contain the formidable apparatus with which mediaeval logicians assigned all propositions to their proper categories – the very basis of the philosophy of classification. Also in Aristotle's logic there is a hint of yet another classification of knowledge, according to the nature of the propositions in question: propositions may be ethical, physical or logical. This tripartite division was later to be the basis of Stoic classification of the sciences.

Aristotle's major categorisation by subject-matter, as in his treatises, was not just an academic division of knowledge. It was also an agenda for scientific investigation. Geoffrey Lloyd has described Aristotle as 'the founder of systematic research'. At the Lyceum, his school in Athens, he assigned these areas for investigation to his friends and pupils. For instance, Aristotle's own zoological work was complemented by that of his pupil Theophrastus in botany and mineralogy. All this work was governed by Aristotle's empirical method. The research programme was never of course completed, and much of the work, particularly that done after Aristotle's death, has been lost. The inspiration and the programme were lost too.

In the Latin Middle Ages the educational curriculum was dominated by the Trivium and Quadrivium, pre-Aristotelian in origin, which together made up the seven 'liberal arts'. Grammar, dialectic and rhetoric, on the one hand, and arithmetic, geometry, astronomy and music on the other, represented the undergraduate preparation for the higher or professional studies of medicine, law and theology. In the late Middle Ages, additionally, virtually the full Aristotelian corpus became available. Given the level of bare literacy that was presumed at university, it was just not possible to integrate two systems of knowledge of such very different levels of sophistication – and of scope and arrangement. The latter difficulties are graphically illustrated by Bliss's modern diagram which combines the two.[3] The triangular 'province' of the Trivium and the parallelogram of the Quadrivium occupy a very small area of the medieval circle of knowledge – which was itself rather restricted, as was soon to be recognised.

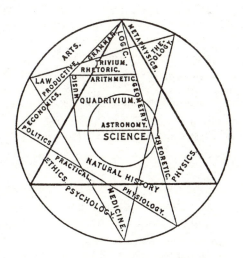

4. CLASSIFICATION IN THE RENAISSANCE: THE BACONIAN TRADITION

Several of the 'new men' of the Renaissance who realised the importance of craft knowledge, which had been too little considered during the Middle Ages, and, inspired as they also were by the symbolic importance of Columbus's discovery of the New World, set out to draw the map of an expanded world of learning anew. The most thorough-going and innovative of these new map-makers was Francis Bacon, who has also, to this day, been the most influential.

Enough has been written elsewhere about Bacon's rejection of scholasticism and of authority (particularly that of Aristotle), about his new inductive method, or his wish to incorporate the knowledge, the organisation and the aims of mechanics. What is of concern here is his new classification of knowledge and its part in his dreams of the new science. (See art. 53.)

Like Aristotle, Bacon was a born organiser (although faced with the prolixity of his works, and their numerous digressions, the reader would be forgiven for doubting this). Collectively, his writings on philosophy have the character of an (uncompleted) encyclopaedia, which ranges from Acceleration, through Grammar, Manures and Sleep, to Zoroaster. His language throughout is classificatory, locating the information within his framework of knowledge: there are instances and kinds and classes, lists and tables, definitions and exemplars.

Although he never came near to finishing his classification of the sciences (indeed on his own admission, he could scarcely be said to have begun), it played a crucial part in his 'Great Instauration' – the establishment of the true new philosophy. Faced with the falsity of the old, and the attachment of men to settled ways of thinking,

> There was but one course left, therefore, – to try the whole thing anew upon a better plan, and to commence a total reconstruction of sciences, arts, and all human knowledge, raised upon the proper foundations.[4]

Bacon well recognised that this ambitious project could not be achieved by one man, or even in one generation. What was needed was to get the framework, the agenda right, so that the fulfilment could be left to others.

The work is in six Parts:–

1. The Divisions of the Sciences.
2. The New Organon, or Directions concerning the Interpretation of Nature.
3. The Phenomena of the Universe; or a Natural and Experimental History for the foundation of Philosophy.
4. The Ladder of the Intellect.
5. The Forerunners; or Anticipations of the New Philosophy.
6. The New Philosophy; or Active Science.[5]

Only the second part, Bacon's new inductive method, was left in anything like a definitive state. The third is to be found as his brief *Parasceve*, 'Preparative towards a natural and experimental history', with its 'Catalogue of particular histories by titles' (130 in number), as well as in some more developed illustrative examples. The last three parts were not even attempted; the last indeed was for some distant future generation. But the vital division of the sciences was the prelude to the whole enterprise, providing the new agenda, the map for the explorers:

> In laying out the divisions of the sciences however, I take into account not only things already invented and known, but likewise things omitted which ought to be there. For there are found in the intellectual as in the terrestrial globe waste regions as well as cultivated ones.[6]

So again, inevitably, there is nothing definitive. (It is a feature of classifications of the sciences that they are almost never completed.) The most developed sketch explicitly presented as an agenda for future research, is in *The Advancement of Learning* of 1605, amplified in its Latin translation *De augmentis scientiarum* eighteen years later.

Bacon's fundamental division was according to the three faculties of the rational soul – memory, imagination and reason – from which flow history, poesy and philosophy. This was an exhaustive classification, in the sense that it comprises all possible forms of learning. Bacon would appear to be the first to have used the metaphor of the tree of knowledge: these three branches meet in a stem of *Philosophia prima*, which should support them. If this first philosophy has not done so hitherto, it is because it has been particularly neglected, 'which cannot but cease and stop all progression'. For successful pursuit of the new science, then, knowledge must be seen as a whole unified in this stem.

Bacon has been criticised by philosophers from Hobbes to Quinton for the indeterminacy of his division according to the faculties of the mind: there are few mental operations which can be said to employ one faculty to the exclusion of the others. But since all subsequent subdivision by Bacon and his successors has followed other criteria, the original basis of the division into history, poesy and philosophy (or science) matters little: they have proved useful in practice since they have been made to represent genuinely discrete activities.

Of the four sub-divisions of history, natural, civil, ecclesiastical and literary (that is, of learning), the first and last are of interest to the historian of science, particularly natural history, which is further divided into history of nature in course (regularities), of nature erring (aberrations) and of nature wrought (mechanical arts). This last is 'of all others the most radical and fundamental towards natural philosophy; . . . it will give a more true and real illumination concerning causes and axioms than is hitherto attained'. So the branches of learning very much intermingle. This complication is underlined by Bacon's alternative division of natural history not according to object, but according to use, into narrative and inductive. The latter becomes the foundation of philosophy, the third part of the Great Instauration. Given this feedback loop, it is not surprising that no one has yet successfully set out Bacon's division of knowledge in tabular form.

In some ways the sub-division of philosophy is more straightforward than that of history – at least, once revealed religion has been separated from philosophy proper as a special category of *scientia*, knowledge. The first division is according to object: philosophy (natural theology), natural philosophy and human philosophy (individual and civil, the former including medicine as well as logic and ethics).

Natural philosophy is then divided by aim 'into the Inquisition of Causes, and the Production of Effects; Speculative and Operative, the one searching into the bowels of Nature, and other shaping Nature as on an anvil'.[7] The former divides into 'physic special', concerned with efficient, and to a lesser extent material, causes (what the twentieth century would consider science proper), and metaphysic, concerned with formal causes (in Bacon's view the main object of natural philosophy) and to a very much lesser extent with final causes. The residual Aristotelianism of Bacon's framework is clear. Of the divisions of operative science, mechanics is the result of the application of physic, and magic of metaphysic. It is to magic that Bacon looked for radical technological change, as the 'science which applies the knowledge of hidden forms to the production of wonderful operations'. Today we may see the results of this 'magic' in the productions of modern technology.

Bacon made mathematics, both pure and applied, a 'great Appendix of Natural Philosophy'. This has been taken as a symptom of his failure properly to value the role of mathematics in natural science – perhaps justly. But it is also clear that given the criteria Bacon used, there was otherwise no place for mathematics; it had to stand outside as a tool for all the sciences, as logic had been for Aristotle.

To return to the overall aim of Bacon's 'Divisions of the Sciences', the reason why this had to be the first step in the Great Instauration was partly to point to gaps in current knowledge which had to be made good before science could efficiently progress. *Terra incognita* is a recurrent theme in *The Advancement of Learning*: 'Thus have I made as it were a small Globe of the Intellectual World, as truly and faithfully as I could discover; with a note and description of those parts which seem to me not constantly occupate, or not well converted by the labour of man'.[8] Just as important, if not more so, was the division of that labour. Baconian science, with its exhaustive natural histories and its painstaking inductive method, was a long hard slog, only to be achieved by planned teamwork. We have a glimpse of what Bacon envisaged in the hierarchical organisation of the workers in Salomon's House in his fable *The New Atlantis* (1626), from Interpreters of Nature, through Compilers and Merchants of Light, down to novices and apprentices. The organisation of knowledge and the organisation of labour made practicable what might otherwise have seemed an impossibly ambitious dream:

> . . . touching impossibility, I take it that all those things are to be held possible and performable, which may be done by some persons, though not by every one; and which may be done by many together, though not by one alone; and which may be done in the succession of ages, though not in one man's life; and lastly, which may be done by public designation and expense, though not by private means and endeavour.[9]

Bacon's influence, on scientists in particular, is a complex and controversial story. It can be traced in the foundation of the Royal Society of London, though that body did not divide its membership into classes according to their sciences as the French Académie did. It is prominent in the educational writings of John Amos Comenius, but is harder to find in any developments of the curriculum in the classroom. What is undeniable is his continuing influence on the tradition of the organisation of knowledge, as practised by the encyclopaedists of the eighteenth and nineteenth centuries, and the librarians of the nineteenth and twentieth.

5. THE DEVELOPMENTS OF THE EIGHTEENTH CENTURY

It was not the lack of knowledge or the gaps that worried Ephraim Chambers as he compiled his *Cyclopaedia* in 1728, or his successor Diderot two decades later. It was the sheer quantity of information that threatened to swamp the learned world. Both used modifications of Bacon's tree (or was it a map of the intellectual globe?) to help them reduce the chaos to order. For Chambers,

> a reduction of the body of learning is growing every day more necessary . . . For want of this, the sciences remain in great measure at a stand, or can advance only imperceptibly; since the whole life of those who should make discoveries, is spent in learning what is already found out.[10]

Diderot agreed: the *Encyclopédie* was just in time; the next generation would have found it impossible to cut through the jungle of knowledge, and he adopted as a motto for the 'Prospectus' the above quotation from Bacon about the impossible being possible with enough cooperation. Further, he confirmed Bacon's status as a patron saint of the *Encyclopédie* by saying that if this were to be a success, then

> the chief credit will be due to Chancellor Bacon, who set out the plan for a universal dictionary of the sciences and of the arts at a time when, so to speak, neither sciences nor arts existed. When it was impossible to write the history of what men knew, this extraordinary genius set out the history of what they had to learn.[11]

There were changes in detail between Bacon's plan or tree and those of his successors. Indeed, although Chambers stayed within Bacon's overall framework, there was radical rearrangement of the parts. Diderot and d'Alembert went further back to the original. But the really significant change lay in their altered perceptions of the categories: instead of Bacon's natural divisions based on the fixed and universal character of the human mind, they introduced the notion of conventional, negotiated divisions. For Chambers,

> In the wide field of intelligibles, appear some parts which have been more cultivated than the rest . . . These spots, regularly laid out, and conveniently circumscribed, and fenced round, make what we call the *Arts and Sciences* . . .
> They were divided, by their first discoverers, into a number of subordinate provinces, under distinct names; and have thus remained for time immemorial, with

little alteration. And yet this distribution of the land of science, like that of the face of the earth and heavens, is wholly arbitrary; and might be altered, perhaps, not without advantage, Had not Alexander, Caesar, and Gengiskan lived, the division of the terraqueous globe had, doubtless, been very different from what we now find it: and the case would have been the same with the world of learning, had no such person been born as Aristotle . . . [12]

D'Alembert in the *Discours préliminaire* to the *Encyclopédie* of 1751 got his metaphors thoroughly mixed, but expressed much the same sentiment:

> But, as in general Maps of the World, Objects are placed nearer or more remote, and appear differently, according to the Point wherein the Eye is supposed to be placed; so the Form of our Systematical Tree will vary, according to the Point from which we view the World of Science. We may therefore figure to ourselves as many different Systems of Knowledge, as there are general Maps of different Projections: and each System may have some Advantage over the rest.[13]

This new view of the tree or map of knowledge was a result of introducing a historical view: the present make-up, with all its contingencies, was the result of progress in human knowledge (a well-known Enlightenment preoccupation), and this progress had of course been uneven. According to D'Alembert, the 'metaphysical' account of the systematic division of knowledge was supposed to fix the tree, the historical account to show the order in which material should be laid before the reader (so that ontogeny might recapitulate phylogeny).

Very little of this shows up in the *Encyclopédie* proper – one of the clearest examples of the division between theory and practice in the classification of the sciences. The order there is alphabetical, of course, but categorisation and connections were supposed to be shown by assignment to a discipline at the beginning of each article, as well as by cross-references, particularly at the end. In fact, categories such as '*mythologie*', '*machine*' and '*histoire moderne*' are used, which are perfectly self-explanatory, and perfectly properly applied, but which do not occur in the encyclopaedic tree. Only very occasionally do we find an entry such as

> ART, s.m. (*Ordre encyclop.*, *Entendement*, *Mémoire*, *Histoire de la nature*, *Histoire*, *de la nature employée*, *Art*). Terme abstraite et métaphysique . . .

which provides a full reference to the classificatory table. It is clear that the main purpose of this table was to be an editors' agenda: like Bacon's classification, it told them what needed to be covered. But it had little relevance to or relation to the reader.

One final point about the scheme of the *Encyclopédie*: in recognising the part played by historical contingency in the growth of knowledge, d'Alembert abandoned any claim that the classification might be 'natural'. If the artificial scheme of Diderot and d'Alembert could be said to have any guiding principle beyond Baconian mental faculties, it is the accidental proximity to man of Buffon's contemporaneous *Histoire naturelle* (which, Buffon claimed, was in fact the most 'natural' of all).

6. NINETEENTH-CENTURY TRENDS

Several developments in the century or so following the publication of the *Encyclopédie* contribute to an impression of increased activity in the classification of the sciences. The *Encyclopédie méthodique*, intended to follow up the success of the *Encyclopédie*, was actually divided into separate sciences – as was an English counterpart, the *Encyclopaedia Metropolitana*. But despite an interesting methodological preface by Samuel Taylor Coleridge, this work had little influence. Indeed, encyclopaedists generally had a decreasing influence on the organisation of knowledge during the nineteenth century, as the growth of sophisticated specialist knowledge far outran their ambition to bring the frontiers of research to a general readership, and they settled for dilution for a mass audience. Other early nineteenth-century movements had implications for the classification of the sciences: the rise of specialist journals and specialist societies, the sectionalisation of general scientific societies such as the British Association for the Advancement of Science, the foundation of specialist chairs in universities and the revisions of school curricula. Those who wish to follow the very great number of authors who wrote on the classification of the sciences in the nineteenth century, in what I have already described as a tradition of rather sterile and academic dissent, can do so in Flint (riding with him his two hobby-horses as he damns those who exclude theology and blasts those who do not consider psychology a science). (See art. 64.)

For all the activity, however, there were few significant developments in the classification of the sciences during the nineteenth century. Most writers continued to use as differential criteria the operations of the mind and the properties of nature in all possible permutations, following the Baconian tradition. Some did attempt innovation. For instance, William Whewell sought to introduce a Kantian Guiding Idea which informed each science; no one followed him. In retrospect the most significant new dimension was that of time. After 1859 those classifications that paid attention to the chronological development of science were able to take advantage of the power of the evolutionary metaphor.

Studies in the conjectural history of the progress of human society from savage origins to the polite present had been widespread in the Enlightenment, particularly in Scotland and in France. These celebrations of progress would identify a number of stages (four was the normal number) as rungs on the upward ladder which all societies had to climb. This was the background to Auguste Comte's *Cours de philosophie positive* of 1830, in which he introduced his 'great fundamental law of the development of human thought', namely that all ideas and all branches of knowledge must necessarily pass through three stages (*états*). In the theological stage (itself marked by progression from fetishism through polytheism to monotheism) any explanation is supernatural, fictitious; in the metaphysical it is abstract; in the highest, scientific, stage it is positive – that is, laws such as Newton's suffice for complete explanation.

Comte identified six fundamental sciences – mathematics, astronomy, physics, chemistry, physiology (also called biology) and social physics (or sociology). These go through the stages in a staggered sequence, reaching the final positive stage in the above order, which is the order of increasing concreteness. Social physics had not reached it yet. A central feature of this series is that each of the earlier sciences is a prerequisite for a proper understanding of, and progress in, subsequent sciences (hence the staggering), which has obvious educational implications. Moreover, Comte's organisation is not as one-dimensional as reported so far: each of these fundamental sciences has dependent on it not only subsequent sciences, but also its 'own' applied sciences. A full table would have an elaborate branching structure. And the classification is firmly and fundamentally hierarchical, since it is based on these relations of dependence.

One of Comte's main purposes was to write theology and metaphysics out of the canon of valid modern knowledge. He was therefore concerned to discredit Bacon and d'Alembert, and everyone else who had incorporated these anathemas, and who had based their divisions on 'various diverse faculties of the human mind' – themselves radically pernicious, because metaphysical. His own classification, he claimed, represented the arrangement taken for granted by working scientists, as well as corresponding to historical reality. It is difficult to test Comte's claim. Certainly in its simplicity his series could be said to approximate to the disciplines practised by contemporary scientists (with the exception of sociology, which in a real sense Comte was the first to put on the map). And certainly scientists had little truck with faculties of the mind.

One scientist who did publish at much the same time was Ampère, in 1834, whose elaborate dichotomous division of learning into 128 parts (2^7), with its extravagant Greek neologisms, may be said to be the most ambitious attempt of the century to classify the sciences by content. The major disciplines do indeed occur in the same order as Comte's, but one can hardly compare 128 with 6! Later in the century, scientists such as Wundt, Ostwald and Karl Pearson produced schemes where again the disciplines are in Comte's order. Perhaps we can see the beginnings of Bliss's 'scientific and educational consensus'. But we may also note that the scale from abstract to concrete goes back to Aristotle.

A philosopher who devoted a lot of paper to proving Comte wrong, but whose own scheme is very comparable, was Herbert Spencer. Given the strength of Spencer's influence in the United States, and the importance of the American tradition in the curriculum and in library classification in cementing the consensus, we must look briefly at his scheme. Spencer devoted his long essay 'The genesis of science' of 1854 to demonstrating both that the sciences could not be arranged in a linear series and that Comte's series did not represent the order of historical evolution (the first use of the word in this context). Ten years later in 'The classification of the sciences' he put forward his own alternative, distinguishing Abstract science, treating of forms (logic, mathematics), Abstract–concrete, dealing with elements of phenomena (mechanics, physics, chemistry, etc.), and Concrete, concerned with phenomena as wholes (astronomy, geology, biology, psychology, sociology, etc.). Apart from the fact that these three groups are distinct, the only substantial change from Comte's order is the repositioning of astronomy as more concrete than physics. Moreover, there was a historical filiation, at least among the last group:

> is it not manifest that in the group of sciences – Astronomy, Geology, Biology, Psychology, Sociology, we have a natural group that admits neither of disruption nor change of order? Here there is both a genetic dependence, and a dependence of interpretations. The phenomena have arisen in this succession in cosmical time; and complete scientific interpretation of each group depends on scientific interpretation of the preceding groups.[14]

This order of cosmic evolution (from monad through organism to society) had originated in the *Naturphilosophie* tradition in Germany, as exemplified in the classifications of Schelling, Oken and Hegel. Spencer had devoted a part of his earlier essay to discrediting the latter two of these. It is typical of the literature of the classification of the sciences that having denied the possibility of recapitulating creation and of serial arrangement, Spencer should have adopted both of these.

7. THE DEWEY DECIMAL CLASSIFICATION AND BEYOND

It was with great good sense that the 25-year old Melvil Dewey introduced his Decimal Classification in 1876 with the barest of prefaces, and no philosophical justification whatever. It was thus left to sink or swim on its practical merits. Because of these it has prospered, with rather minor modifications over the years, to become the most widely-used system in the English-speaking world. Its advantage over the many alternative systems (some of which have greater claims to correspond with the 'natural' order of knowledge) would appear to be its simplicity and flexibility.

From the start, purist librarians found Dewey's artificial separations, such as language from literature, objectionable. E. C. Richardson, for instance, thought that a good book classification 'should follow as nearly as possible the order of things. A properly classified library is perhaps the nearest thing that there is to a microcosm'. He himself identified 'the order of things' with the 'world history or evolution' that we have already encountered in Schelling and Spencer. For Richardson, 'the closer a classification can get to the true order of the sciences and the closer it can keep to it, the better the system will be and the longer it will last'.[15]

As a principle of survival in the struggle for existence among library classifications, this is simply wishful thinking. What is required is some compliance with the practice of scientists and other scholars – whether or not this corresponds to the 'true order of knowledge' – and adaptability to changing academic environments. As Ampère would have found, neither the organisation of knowledge nor everyday language can be changed overnight, however compelling the reasons. In the library, as in the proverb, possession is nine-tenths of the law. Those systems that were in place when consensus was hardening in the early years of this century have only got stronger, and are now virtually set in concrete. And with the establishment of the 'scientific and educational consensus', the tradition of the innovative classification of knowledge has withered away.

Outside Eastern Europe, where the classification of the sciences still survives in a tradition established by Engels in his *Dialectics of nature*, essentially the only historian of science to have discussed the topic since the war is R. G. A. Dolby in a recent paper on the nineteenth-century tradition. His discussion of the decline of the tradition in this century gives reasons other than the establishment of consensus: his focus is the philosophical tradition, and that was never consensual. He sees the main reasons for the decline in the internal exhaustion of the tradition and the artificiality of its products, where I would see a loss of the market for those ever-different products as consensus took hold. These explanations are entirely complementary. In what follows I will not further distinguish Dolby's explanations from my own.

If researchers in Aristotle's or Bacon's time could benefit from being told by a classification of the sciences where the main gaps in knowledge were, this was by no means the case by the twentieth century. By 1900, the map of the sciences had as few *terrae incognitae* as that of the terraqueous globe; new research was now generated within each science, perhaps by a new technique or through the articulation of new theories. (Recently, it is true, hybrids have developed through cooperation across disciplinary boundaries, but not because anyone has identified a yawning gap between them.) Moreover, most European and North American universities – certainly those with any aspiration to first rank – would have had a good spread of disciplines by 1900. If new chairs were founded subsequently, it would have been unusual for the arguments to have been premised on classificatory gaps. Utility was a far more usual selling point.

Philosophy of science has changed too. To the extent that there was an identifiable speciality of that name before the end of the last century, classification of the sciences, with the stress on unification quite as much as differentiation, was a very strong component. In the twentieth century, differentiation is more of interest to funding bodies than to philosophers, and any discussion of unification has tended to be in the reductionist terms associated with Neurath and Carnap and the proposed *International Encyclopedia of Unified Science* with its basis in logical empiricism. Reductionism (whether Comtian or more recent) has not proved attractive to biologists, and recently there has been a resurgence of holism, in parallel to the wider social reaction against the 'technological fix'.

After 200 years of progressive abandonment by encyclopaedists of the ordering of knowledge, the editors of the *Encyclopaedia Britannica* have adopted an ordered arrangement for the latest edition (1978), essentially following Spencer's evolutionary model from matter and energy, building up through various manifestations of human society to finish with a philosophical overview. Though this was met initially with mixed reactions, it has now been generally accepted, not least because its order reflects the consensus exemplified in most university and general libraries.

To return to our starting point, it is librarians who are most concerned with the classification of the sciences today. They have to make everyday professional decisions so that readers may read; these decisions are only really noticed when they are wrong. The organisation of knowledge is a thankless task. No one has ever got it right, of course, in any absolute sense, but if there is a decent classification system and sensible decisions are made within it, they will be taken for granted. As far as the user is concerned, perhaps that is as it should be.

NOTES

1. H. E. Bliss, *The organization of knowledge and the system of the sciences* (New York, 1929), part I.
2. R. Flint, *Philosophy as scientia scientiarum and a history of classifications of the sciences* (Edinburgh and London, 1904).
3. H. E. Bliss (1929), p. 402.
4. J. M. Robertson (ed.), *The philosophical works of Francis Bacon* (London and New York, 1905), p. 241.
5. Ibid., p. 248.
6. Ibid.
7. Ibid., p. 458.
8. Ibid., p. 175.
9. Ibid., p. 425.
10. E. Chambers, *Cyclopaedia* (2nd ed., 2 vols., London, 1741), vol. 1, p. xxiv.
11. D. Diderot, *Oeuvres complètes* (ed. by J. Proust *et al.*, Paris, 1975–), vol. 5, p. 91; see also ibid., p. 85, and vol. 7, pp. 234–5.
12. J. M. Robertson (1905) p. ix.
13. J. le R. d'Alembert, *The plan of the French Encyclopaedia* (London 1752), p. 48.
14. H. Spencer, 'Classification of the sciences', in *Essays: scientific, political, and speculative* (2nd ed., 3 vols., London, 1875), vol. 3, p. 48.
15. E. C. Richardson, *Classification, theoretical and practical* (New York, 1901), p. 87. See also 3rd ed. (New York, 1930).

FURTHER READING

H. E. Bliss, *The organization of knowledge and the system of the sciences* (New York, 1929).

A. Broadfield, *The philosophy of classification* (London, 1946).

R. Darnton, 'Philosophers trim the tree of knowledge: the epistemological strategy of the *Encyclopédie*', in his *The great cat massacre and other episodes in French cultural history* (New York and London, 1984), Chap. V.

R. G. A. Dolby, 'Classification of the sciences: the nineteenth-century tradition', in R. F. Ellen and D. Reason (eds.), *Classifications in their social context* (London, New York and San Francisco, 1979), pp. 167–93.

R. Flint, *Philosophy as* scientia scientiarum *and a history of classifications of the sciences* (Edinburgh and London, 1904).

M. Foucault, *The archaeology of knowledge* (London, 1972).

G. E. R. Lloyd, *Aristotle: the growth and structure of his thought* (Cambridge, 1968), Chap. V: 'The founder of systematic research'.

F. Machlup, *Knowledge: its creation, distribution, and economic significance*, vol. 2: *The branches of learning* (Princeton, 1982).

J. Needham, 'Integrative levels; a revaluation of the idea of progress', in his *Time: the refreshing river* (London, 1943), pp. 233–72.

C. F. A. Pantin, *The relations between the sciences* (Cambridge, 1968).

E. C. Richardson, *Classification, theoretical and practical* (New York, 1901).

A. Quinton, *Francis Bacon* (Oxford, 1980).

P. Speziali, 'Classification of the sciences', in P. P. Wiener (ed.), *Dictionary of the history of ideas* (4 vols., New York, 1973), vol. 1, pp. 462–7; see also W. Tatarkiewicz, 'Classification of the arts', ibid., pp. 456–62.

56

MARGINAL SCIENCE

SEYMOUR H. MAUSKOPF

This article is in two parts. The first part is devoted to a survey of the literature on the definition of marginal science (or 'pseudo-science', a term which will be used interchangeably with marginal science in this article) and its demarcation from science. The second part treats the history and historiography of selected examples of marginal sciences.

1. DEFINITIONAL PROBLEM

The philosopher Marx Wartofsky offered this definition – or pair of definitions – of marginal science, which he termed 'pseudo-science':

> . . . it is what appears as science, or represents itself as science. Or else it is what science proper – the scientific establishment, or the scientific inquisition – marks off as heretical.[1]

The disjunction implicit in these two options is at the basis of the so-called 'demarcation problem'. In what I shall term the 'cognitive' approach to this problem, the attempt is made to devise a set of criteria (concerning theory and/or methodology) by which activities ostensibly pursued in order to generate natural knowledge can be evaluated as truly scientific or not.

In what may be termed the 'social' approach, the demarcation between science and pseudo-science is seen as being more dependent upon socio-cultural and even socio-political factors than on cognitive ones. Activities called 'marginal' or 'pseudo-scientific' (or whatever the epithet of the time) are so labelled because the convention-setters of that time – 'the scientific establishment, or the scientific inquisition' in Wartofsky's words, dislike or fear these activities and consequently mark them off as 'heretical'.

The cognitive approach is the older historiographical one. Although, in a sense, going back to Aristotle, its modern form stemmed from the progressivist tradition of the nineteenth century, by which science was characterised as making cumulative advance; it did so by deploying an increasingly refined scientific method.[2] In its historical corollary, activities which might have been associated with science in an earlier stage of its theoretical and methodological development, were sloughed off later because the natural knowledge they claimed to examine and substantiate appeared to be more and more incredible in the light of more advanced theory and because the methods employed in the investigation appeared to be flawed in the light of refined experimental and quantitative techniques of true science. Thus, George Sarton characterised the advance of modern science:

> The growth of science entails the gradual purification of its methods and even of its spirit. Men of science have made abundant mistakes of every kind; their knowledge has improved only because of their gradual abandonment of ancient errors, poor approximations, and premature conclusions. It is thus necessary to speak not only of temporary errors but also of superstitions, which are nothing but persistent errors, foolish beliefs, and irrational fears.[3]

Twentieth-century logical positivists have tried to devise a comprehensive criterion for distinguishing science from other activities purporting to assert factual knowledge (not just pseudo-science, but, e.g. religion) in the empirical verifiability of its statements. Intended as a corrective to this programme, and directed more specifically to discriminating between science and pseudo-science was Karl Popper's criterion of falsifiability. His thesis was that scientific propositions could never be established with certitude through a process of verification, but they did have the defining characteristic of being falsifiable through the discovery and deployment of counter-evidence obtained through observation and experiment. It was, indeed, through falsification that scientific propositions are winnowed and refined and hence, science advances. In pseudo-science, by contrast, propositions were invulnerable to falsification.

In recent times, the progressivist historical view of scientific advance has come under scrutiny; this was brought to a focus in Thomas S. Kuhn's *The Structure of Scientific Revolutions* (1962). By the 1960s it had become far less axiomatic to historians of science that one could speak of scientific progress in terms of cumulative theoretical and methodological advance. Moreover, to those more philosophically than historically orientated, similar scrutiny was being directed at the positivist and Popperian definitions of scientific propositions; it became apparent that every system of science contained propositions which were virtually immune to any kind of empirical 'testing' (verification or falsification) and which might only be called into empirical question when that scientific system was itself being undermined (an example would be the principle of inertia or Newton's Second Law of Motion). Hence, neither the positivist nor the Popperian criteria could be used comprehensively to demarcate scientific from pseudo-scientific propositions and theories.

Meanwhile, a number of sociologists and historians of the late 1960s and 1970s took a radically opposed view of science (and hence the demarcation issue) to the cognitive approach espoused by the positivists and progressivists. A covert assumption of the cognitive approach is that natural knowledge is culturally transcendent and the methods employed in its discovery (at least, the 'proper' methods) are culturally invariant, even if these methods only came gradually to be refined. There was, of course, a venerable historical tradition which in principle opposed the assumptions of cultural transcendence and invariance: the Marxist. The structure of natural knowledge at any given time and place was, to the Marxists, epiphenomenal, a product and reflection of economic and social structures. But the traditional Marxist historians of science, as represented by J. D. Bernal, for example, were still also progressivists. Science had 'advanced' in the quality of its world-view, its theories and its methods.

The above-mentioned sociologists and historians have built on Marxist epiphenominalism but have carried it far towards a relativistic picture of science, no doubt influenced both by developments in the historiography of science challenging the positivistic and progressivistic points of view and by the more general turn towards interest in the social history of science. In what I have called the 'social' approach, science (both as natural knowledge and as investigatory methods), far from being socially and culturally transcendent, is socially, culturally and even politically determined. Needless to say, the demarcation issue is analysed very differently by the espousers of the social approach from the way used by the positivists and progressivists. For example, in an essay titled 'The Social Construction of Scientific Knowledge', the historian of science Everett Mendelsohn treats the sundering of science from pseudo-science and magic in the seventeenth century in a fashion that would have been virtually unrecognisable to George Sarton:

> What drove Hermeticism, alchemy and magic from the system of knowing nature? It is not clear that intellectual strength by itself was creating the bifurcation. My claim is that the consolidators among the second generation [of the Scientific Revolution] responded to the political realities of their day and consciously banished from consideration, in their new foundations, those areas which would transcend the authority of those whom they did not wish to offend.[4]

And Roger Cooter extends this mode of analysis to post-seventeenth century science generally and couches his analysis in more overtly Marxist terms:

> As Everett Mendelsohn among others has tried to make clear, the process of identifying certain bodies of knowledge as 'incorrect' (because of their having unquantitative human, social, or metaphysical dimensions) in order to establish the impression of other bodies of knowledge as transcendent touchstones of truth was 'socially imposed and self-consciously accepted' during the emergence of the capitalist order in the seventeenth century.[5]

As of this writing, neither the cognitive nor the social approach to the demarcation issue has achieved commanding ascendancy over the other. The goal of the cognitive approach – to provide a comprehensive set of demarcation criteria – has certainly not been met and there are some who doubt that it is in principle reachable. At the same time, the relativism of the social approach (implicit or explicit) leaves open many issues of theory and method concerning which critical analysts can and still do raise disturbing questions. At most, it can be said that philosophers (and debunkers) tend to pursue the cognitive programme whereas sociologists and social historians of science, the social. The more general historians who have undertaken historical study of marginal or psuedo-science tend to ignore explicit confrontation with the demarcation issue.

2. HISTORICAL OVERVIEW: FROM 1700 ONWARDS

Much of the most provocative scholarship dealing with the Scientific Revolution (1500–1700) has been devoted to examining the so-called occult or pseudo-scientific traditions. Attention has centred on the hermetic, Paracelsian, natural magical and alchemical traditions. Although the evaluation of the role of these traditions in the development of early modern science – and even of how they were evaluated in their own time – remains controversial, there is reasonable consensus that they remained important components in the thought and work of most of the scientists of this period. The alchemy of Newton is perhaps the most striking (and one of the latest) cases.

The year 1700 appears to mark a rather sharp divide in scientific sensibilities concerning these traditions. Unfortunately, little concrete historical study has been given to the passage from seventeenth century to the eighteenth in regard to the occult and pseudo-scientific traditions. One book which does explicitly treat this topic – in the peripheral American colonies – is Herbert Leventhal's *In the Shadow of the Enlightenment: Occultism and Renaissance Science in Eighteenth Century America* (1976). Leventhal consideres a wide range of pre-eighteenth-century beliefs about the world, some of which would be best defined as 'going-out-of-date science' (geocentricity, the theory of four elements) and others of which belong more clearly to the occult and pseudo-scientific (astrology, witchcraft). What Leventhal shows was that there was a supersedure of older scientific views by new ones by about 1730 but a continuation of the more occult and pseudo-scientific beliefs and practices, especially in popular culture. The historian of Paracelsianism, Allen Debus, has recently studied the perseverance of Paracelsian and hermetic beliefs in eighteenth-century France; he has found ample evidence that Paracelsian medicine and alchemy survived not just in out-of-the-way places and popular culture but among the social and, to a degree, the scientific elite as well. Clearly, this subject has only begun to be carefully investigated; much more work needs to be done to ascertain which occult and pseudo-scientific traditions survived into the eighteenth century, among what social and professional strata of society, and when and how they came to be sharply disjoined from 'true' science.

This evaluation also holds true for the historiography of marginal sciences of later times, although there is certainly no dearth of claimants for scrutiny by historians of science. However, there are some cases which have received extended historical treatment. I shall briefly discuss three from the period 1775 to 1875: mesmerism, *Naturphilosophie* and phrenology. Then I shall conclude with more detailed discussion of the historiography of a modern marginal science, parapsychology.

Mesmerism, associated with the theory ('animal magnetism') and therapy of Franz Anton Mesmer (1734–1815), represents perhaps the first fully fledged struggle between a marginal science seeking legitimacy and an official scientific establishment (the Paris Academy of Science, the Faculty of Medicine and the Society of Medicine). The conflict arose after Mesmer's move to Paris in 1778 and resulted in the official debunking of mesmerists' claims by committees of these official bodies. Mesmerism has attracted the attention of social historians and historians of the behavioural science as well as historians of eighteenth-century French science.

The evaluation of Mesmer and mesmerism remains as controversial today as in Mesmer's time. Some view Mesmer as little more than a charlatan. Others, perceiving the significance of mesmerism for abnormal psychology and psychiatry a century later, evaluate Mesmer's activities much more positively.[6] Two recent studies have considered the scientific status of mesmerism: one, by Robert Weyant, has judged it to have been pseudo-scientific on cognitive grounds; the other, by Geoffrey Sutton, attempting to analyse the scientific status of mesmerism in its own time, adopts what I have termed the social approach to the demarcation problem and concludes that social and professional factors were more important than cognitive ones in determining mesmerism's poor reception by the eighteenth-century French scientific establishment.

Consideration of the other two examples, *Naturphilosophie* and phrenology, have had an important place in the historiography of science in recent decades. Moreover, much of the research has had a rehabilitative goal: to show their importance for advances in mainstream science. In the case of *Naturphilosophie* (the organismic and dynamical world view associated with German Romanticism and embodied particularly in the writings of F. W. J. Schelling (1775–1854)), the object of much of the historical research has been to demonstrate the influence on major advances in electrodynamics, thermodynamics and chemistry. No attention has been focused directly on the demarcation issue but, ironically, the marginal status of *Naturphilosophie* has been emphasised in its very rehabilitation. For in the process of tracing connections between *Naturphilosophie* and mainstream scientific developments, historians have often contrasted the former unfavourably – as fancifully speculative – with the latter. The discussion of the influence of the *Naturphilosoph*, Lorens Oken, on Humphry Davy by the historian of science, David Knight, provides a succinct example:

> This all seems utterly lunatic, and yet it is not so very far from the speculation of Davy, but Davy succeeded in using such ideas to generate experimentally testable consequences.[7]

The rise in interest in *Naturphilosophie* occurred in the 1950s and 1960s; the 1970s and 1980s have witnessed a comparable interest in phrenology. This was the system of psychology developed by Franz Joseph Gall (1758–1828) and his disciple Johann Gaspar Spurzheim (1776–1832) in which fundamental mental functions and behavioural traits were defined and related to the structure of the brain and the skull. Phrenology enjoyed considerable scientific and popular success during the first third of the nineteenth century. However, from the first, it was also embroiled in controversy and, after mid-century, came to be rejected as pseudo-scientific.

Although judicious analyses and evaluations of phrenology had been written earlier by historians of medicine, recent exploration of phrenology's scientific and cultural significance began with the publication in 1970 of Robert M. Young's *Mind, Brain and Adaptation in the Nineteenth Century*. Young focused on phrenology's scientific import: its patrimony in the development of localisation of brain function and in the systematic study of human and animal behaviour. His approach was close to that of the historians of *Naturphilosophie*: rehabilitative in demonstrating phrenology's scientific significance yet critical of its methodology and its theory.

Led in part by Young himself, a veritable research industry devoted to phrenology had emerged by the mid-1970s. Interest shifted from the scientific to the socio-cultural context: phrenology as popular science and social movement, especially in Britain during the Industrial Revolution. Regarding the evaluation of phrenology *vis-à-vis* the demarcation issue, some of the literature is overtly and even aggressively 'social'. In so far as its authors subscribe to the view that scientific knowledge is socially and culturally determined, they view the conflict between phrenology and its critics relativistically, with phrenology receiving a sympathetic evaluation and the scientific objectivity of the critics being dismissed as illusory.

The historiography of phrenology has exhibited what is perhaps the clearest and most coherent development of any literature on marginal science, moving over time from a rehabilitative effort initially couched in terms of the contribution of phrenology to neuro-anatomical development to a much more social and relativistic orientation. In its development, this literature has reflected the more general shifts of interest and orientation in history of science over the past forty years.

Compared to nineteenth-century science, the scientific enterprise has, in this century, become much vaster, more sharply drawn professionally and commands a much greater proportion of the societal resources. At the same time, it has become more complex and heterogenous, due both to fragmentation into increasing numbers of disciplines and specialties and extensions into new domains of knowledge. The boundaries between science and other activities (including those purporting to be scientific) are thus, paradoxically, both sharper and more difficult to draw unambiguously. For example, are the social sciences and psycho-analysis truly 'scientific'?

Of the many candidates for marginal scientific status in the twentieth century, only a few have received serious detailed historical study.[8] In the remainder of this article, I shall examine in detail one particular example of twentieth-century marginal science: psychical research and parapsychology. I choose it for three reasons: it comes as close as any example to being paradigmatic for modern marginal science; it has received detailed treatment from historians and sociologists of science; and I myself have contributed to the historical study of this field.

3. PSYCHICAL RESEARCH

Psychical research was formally organised in 1882 with the founding in London of the Society for Psychical Research (hereafter denominated as 'SPR') by a group of English scientists and intellectuals. The SPR's objective was to examine anomalous phenomena associated with spiritualism which had been attracting considerable attention for the previous three decades. These were mainly manifested in spiritualist seances and involved purported communication by discarnate spirits of the dead through the agency of a psychic 'medium'. The SPR also concerned itself with the investigation of a variety of purported psychic abilities of the living, such as telepathy (mind-to-mind communication without sensory intermediary), clairvoyance (object-to-mind communication without sensory intermediary), and telekinesis (or psychokinesis: mind-matter interaction).

English-organised psychical research, soon imitated in the United States and eventually in most Western countries, espoused a programme of utilising the methods of science (experimental and quantitative where possible) to study their anomalous phenomena and this has remained the programme of psychical researchers and parapsychologists ever since, although the field also embraces activities which are not, strictly speaking, experimental.[9] The term 'parapsychology' was applied by J. B. Rhine in 1934 to the experimental research he and his students at Duke University were carrying out on psychical abilities; it has come to supplant 'psychical research' to a considerable degree in the United States as the generic term for the field.

Parapsychology is paradigmatic of marginal science in that it has always claimed the mantle of scientific method and objectivity and attracted outstanding intellectuals and scientists to its support, particulary in the late nineteenth century. The original SPR numbered among its membership before the First World War many of the leaders of late Victorian culture including the philosopher Henry Sidgwick, and scientists such as William Crookes, A. R. Wallace and the majority of the important British physicists. To some degree, advocacy and patronage of parapsychology has been maintained by eminent scientists in this century in Britain and other countries. Yet the very credibility of the phenomena parapsychologists study is questioned by many in the scientific community. Consequently, parapsychology has always had its detractors who view parapsychologists and their supporters as gullible and/or deceitful.

The condemnations of the evidence for psychical phenomena and abilities have usually centred around the issues of fraud and replication. The critics assert that there exists no good evidence; all claimed as such is flawed either in the experimental design itself or through the chicanery of the subjects and/or experimenters.[10] It should be said that there has been little consensus historically even within the parapsychological community as to what constitutes the valid data base. Behind the scepticism of the critics lies the consideration of the improbability of psychical phenomena, at least in the light of the post-seventeenth century scientific world-view, an improbability fully recognised by the founders of organised psychical research themselves.

The scientific status of parapsychology remains unsettled and controversial today. It is perhaps best captured by the field's relationship with the American Association for the Advancement of Science. In 1969, parapsychology was granted membership in that national forum; yet parapsychologists have been unsuccessful in publishing their work in the Association's journal, *Science*, even though that journal has published critical articles on parapsychology. In its still-unresolved scientific status, parapsychology differs from *Naturphilosophie* and phrenology. It differs from them in another major respect which, I believe, has influenced the nature of the historical literature on this field: parapsychology has not produced any obvious 'pay-off' for mainstream scientific advance. Therefore, it has not attracted the kind of rehabilitative research efforts from historians of science that have characterised the historiography of *Naturphilosophie* and phrenology.[11] It has an extensive and sophisticated historical literature, but it is not so central to the historiography of science as is that on *Naturphilosophie* and phrenology. However, parapsychology has undoubtedly received more attention from philosophers and sociologists of science than have the other examples I have examined. Before turning to the historical literature, I shall give some attention to the philosophical and sociological studies of parapsychology.

As reference to Henry Sidgwick suggests, philosophers have long been interested in parapsychology. Philosophers of positivistic orientation have tended to view parapsychology critically. However, there are also philosophers in the analytical tradition currently attempting to provide both conceptual context and support for parapsychology.[12]

More pertinent to this article is the recent work of sociologists of science on parapsychology, notably that of Harry Collins, Trevor Pinch and James McClenon. Collins and Pinch have been leaders among the recent sociologists and historians of science who have adopted the view that natural knowledge is socially and culturally conditioned, and consequently espouse what I have termed the social approach to the demarcation issue. In a number of articles and in the book, *Frames of Meaning*, (1982), they analyse and evaluate debates over paranormal phenomena – particularly parapsychological ones – between their investigators (and supporters) and the sceptics in mainstream science, focusing on the issue of experimental evidence and its replication. They have stressed their belief that the social and epistemological components are inseparable and therefore:

> It would seem that evidence is so bound up with society or social group which gives rise to it that theories held by members of radically different scientifico-social groups cannot be adequately tested against each other by experiment. It matters not whether the evidence is intended to corroborate, 'prove' or refute the theories in question.[13]

Their perspective makes them sympathetic towards the claims of parapsychology. A similar perspective and sympathy is manifested by the American sociologist of science, James McClenon, in his delineation of parapsychology's status in the American scientific community as 'deviant science'. By this he means any purportedly scientific activity which counters 'scientism', his term for the dominant post-seventeenth century physicalist ideology of science. Because of its heretical stance towards 'scientism', parapsychology has been rejected as illegitimate by the scientific elite; it has managed to survive, in McClenon's analysis, because it has been able to draw upon lay support and (like deviant activities outside of science, such as organised crime) to imitate the organisational structure of its oppressor. For McClenon, methodological and theoretical issues *per se* concerning parapsychology are subordinate to the social and political relationship between parapsychology and its mainstream scientific adversaries.

A more impassive analysis of parapsychology's situation in the United States was given somewhat earlier by another American sociologist, Paul D. Allison. Allison, like McClenon, grants that parapsychologists have made decisive moves towards professional organisation and that the methodological issue of 'replication' does not seem to be the crucial one in comprehending why parapsychology has been so frustrated in attaining scientific legitimacy. But, whereas McClenon appears to place the onus on the scientific power structure, Allison sees it as stemming as much from inherent features of parapsychology: 'its threat to basic scientific assumptions and its origins in and continued association with the occult.' Finally, Allison sees the continued connection to and financial reliance upon lay persons by parapsychologists as a major liability to their goal of scientific legitimation.

As was mentioned earlier, the historical literature itself has not shared the rehabilitative goal that characterises much of the studies on *Naturphilosophie* and phrenology; nor has the sympathetic 'social' orientation of some of the sociologists of science been emphasised. Most of the historical literature has concentrated on the rise of spiritualism in the nineteenth century and its partial transformation into psychical research; it has been written by social and cultural historians who are primarily concerned with embedding these developments in their contemporary society and culture. No doubt the reason for the focus on the nineteenth century is because of the sudden and dramatic rise of spiritualism in mid-century and the widespread interest in psychical research among the intellectual and social elites in the last quarter of the century.

The pioneer work, and point of departure for later studies, was written not by a professional historian but by an English psychologist associated with the SPR, Alan Gauld. In *The Founders of Psychical Research* Gauld both details the research carried out by the active leadership of the SPR in its early decades and situates the rise of English psychical research in the cultural matrix of Victorian England, associating it in particular with the 'reluctant doubt' of traditional religious belief that pervaded late Victorian intellectual life (see art. 50, sect. 9). Gauld is sympathetic towards the enterprise of psychical research and defends the credibility of the evidence amassed by these early psychical researchers.

The religious theme delineated by Gauld is explored in a wider cultural context by the historian Frank M. Turner in the biographical studies which comprise his book *Between Science and Religion: The Reaction to Scientific Naturalism in Late Victorian England* (1974). As indicated by the title, the principal theme of this book is the crisis which confronted many Victorian intellectuals who could no longer accept traditional Christianity but who also found no place in the ascendant materialistic world-view for the issues which really mattered to them – human values, ethics and destiny. Of the six biographies, only two are of prominent psychical researchers (Henry Sidgwick and F. W. H. Myers; three if one includes A. R. Wallace). But of concern to Turner (as to Gauld) is the motivation for the taking up of psychical research by Victorian intellectuals. He finds as motivation the search for a means of moving beyond Victorian naturalism to a more comprehensive and human-centred world-view without abandoning the advantages of scientific rationality and method. Turner's is one of the first studies of nineteenth-century intellectual history to grant a serious place to psychical research. Turner himself is unconcerned with the issue of the veracity of the research itself.

The scientific and intellectual elites that are the focus of both Gauld's and Turner's books are also featured in another study of the rise of English psychical research but are dealt with from a very different viewpoint. Brian Wynne sees the rise of psychical research (and indeed, the 'ethereal' cast of much late-nineteenth-century English psychics) in Marxist terms as a response on the part of these elites to the threat posed to their social milieu by industrialisation. To him, Turner's 'scientific naturalism' is 'the cosmological backcloth of industrialisation' associated with an 'aggressively-ascendant industrial middle class'. Of particular relevance to the rise of psychical research was the invasion of the traditionalist academic sanctuary of Oxbridge by middle class utilitarian 'professionnalisers'. The early English psychical researchers included a large number of prominent physicists (the 'Cambridge School') both among the active leaders and supporters. Wynne sees them as constituting, along with other academic leaders of the field such as Henry Sidgwick, the upper class, conservative resistance to the new industrial society. One way they manifested their resistance was through the search for a supra-material, spiritualist cosmology both in physics and in psychical research.

Although Wynne obviously subscribes to the view that natural knowledge is socially constructed, he does not relate this viewpoint explicitly to the demarcation issue regarding psychical research. One might infer that, in so far as ethereal physics and psychical research were both expressions of the reactions of conservative elites in his view, neither was necessarily more or less scientific than the other. But Wynne does not, in fact, address the issue.

Two major books by intellectual and cultural historians dealing with psychical research have adopted a somewhat different focus from that of Gauld and Turner; spiritualism figures at least as prominently as psychical research in each and attention is directed to the middle and lower classes as well as to the elites. The first of these books, *In Search of White Crows: Spiritualism, Parapsychology and American Culture* (1977) by Lawrence Moore also departs from the earlier historical literature on psychical research by focusing on the United States rather than on England. The second, *The Other World: Spiritualism and Psychical Research in England, 1850–1914* (1985) by Janet Oppenheim parallels Moore's book in many ways.

The most important parallel between these two books is the relationship each draws between the ascendancy of mid-nineteenth-century spiritualism and social reform movements. Moore relates spiritualism in the United States to the abolitionist and feminist movements; Oppenheim to Owenite working-class movements. Both see spiritualism as a surrogate – and indeed, a competitor – to traditional religion. In each book, the analysis of spiritualism to society and culture is complex and subtle. This analysis can be seen as complementary to the studies of phrenology by historians like Roger Cooter.

The treatment of psychical research (parapsychology to Moore) is in marked contrast, particularly in Moore's book. Moore sees spiritualism as running its course as a focus of social meliorism by about 1880: the subsequent parapsychological activity is much less socially interesting to Moore and he treats it with brevity and disdain. Oppenheim is more subtle and generous to English psychical research but the long and detailed portion of her book devoted to exploring the relationship between psychical research and the contemporary sciences is titled, significantly, 'A Pseudoscience'. Her characterisation of psychical research is in line with this denomination. In neither book is parapsychological research taken seriously as being scientific.

The assumption behind the focus of historical investigation of psychical research in the nineteenth century would appear to be that, by the early twentieth century, spiritualism and organised psychical research had receded from social and cultural importance. This assumption seems to be manifest in the time period comprehended by Oppenheim in the very title of her book: 1850–1914; moreover, she evaluates the more recent period as one in which 'few influential or renowned scholars endorse the claims of parapsychology'. But Oppenheim makes no attempt to account for the shift from socio-cultural importance to marginality of English psychical research.

However, this issue has been addressed in *The Secularization of the Soul* (1982) by John J. Cerullo, which deals with the intellectual and cultural milieu of English psychical research through the first decades of the twentieth century. Cerullo's argument is complex and not altogether convincing to me but it does bring him to confront explicitly the issue of the change in socio-cultural status of English psychical research early in this century. He agrees with his fellow historians that both spiritualism and psychical research were responses to – and surrogates for – traditional religion. Both spiritualists and psychical researchers were attempting to recapture an ineffable noumenal core for man – a soul – which Cerullo sees as having been lost in the rational world of Protestantism and science. But he differs with the other historians of these subjects in that he perceives a deep difference between spiritualism and psychical research: the spiritualists were most concerned with the question of the survival after death of this ineffable entity whereas the psychical researchers were interested in identifying such an entity in living man, even though many of them had been led to psychical research from spiritualism. By the turn of the century, Cerullo asserts that one formulation of this core of being in terms of an unconscious 'secular soul', the 'subliminal self' of F. W. H. Myers, had come to dominate psychical research.

Cerullo argues that for a time (roughly the first two decades of this century), Myers's conception of the subliminal self appealed to many among the educated middle and upper classes who had left traditional religion but found the routinised industrial and bureaucratic society empty of meaning and value. Myers's concept was itself supplanted by another formulation of the unconscious inner man deemed by Cerullo to be of greater utility in coping with modern life: that of Sigmund Freud. It was, thus, the advent of Freudianism that made psychical research culturally marginal.

Cerullo does not address the evidential aspects of psychical research at all; hence the issue of the scientific status and success of psychical research is not taken up. In the unpublished dissertation by Molly Noonan, 'Science and the Psychical Research Movement', the one other work of which I am familiar which treats the question of the marginalisation of psychical research, the questions of scientific status and – more interestingly – relation to other developing sciences are taken up. Noonan's study focuses on the original American Society for Psychical Research (ASPR, 1884–89). This group, composed largely of a scientific elite, attempted to parallel and replicate the work of the SPR without success. Noonan sees the lack of productivity in the experimental research programme of the ASPR as important in driving into hostility the experimental psychologists, notably G. Stanley Hall and his student Joseph Jastrow. Moreover, experimental psychology itself was just becoming established as an autonomous and legitimate scientific discipline and its leaders in the United States were particularly sensitive to association with questionable and experimentally sterile enterprises. In contrast, medical scientists, particularly neurologists and psychotherapists, were somewhat more receptive to psychical research because many of the topics of the field were to direct interest to investigators of abnormal mental traits. Although Noonan would characterise modern parapsychology as a pseudo-science (because of its contemporary valuation), she recognises that it has not always had this status. Cerullo's and Noonan's approaches to comprehending the change undergone by psychical research around the turn of the century suggest promising complementary directions for further historical research.

The history of parapsychology for countries other than England and the United States has received scant attention. This is also true of the history of the field in these two countries for the period after 1920. The major exception is the work of Seymour H. Mauskopf and Michael R. McVaugh synthesised in their book, *The Elusive Science: Origins of Experimental Psychical Research* (1980). This book deals with parapsychology in the period 1915 to 1940. During this time, parapsychology was reinvigorated in its bid for scientific legitimacy by the work of J. B. Rhine at Duke University. In 1934, Rhine published the first fruits of the experiments he and his students had been carrying out since the start of the decade in the book, *Extra-Sensory Perception*.[14] Rhine claimed to have achieved the long-awaited desideratum for scientific acceptance: success in studying psychical abilities (clairvoyance and telepathy) in controlled experimental situations, and it is the experimental tradition prior to and including Rhine's work on which the book concentrates. Equal attention is given to other themes: the nature of the community of parapsychologists and its organisation (both in the United States and abroad) and the reception of Rhine's work by this community and mainstream scientists.

The authors are non-judgemental *vis-à-vis* the demarcation issue; they attempt to examine parapsychology in so far as possible in the same way that historians of science study other scientific communities and research, paying close attention to the details and complexities of the history. This approach enables them to move beyond the dichotomy of dismissing parapsychology as a pseudo-science or defending it in terms of the relativistic sociological view-point. For example, they perceive that there are important cognitive differences between parapsychology and more orthodox sciences, the primary one being the great difficulty in securing experimental control over psychical phenomena and abilities. Moreover, they conclude that this and other differences were significant in the difficulties that the field encountered in achieving scientific status. But at the same time they endeavour to treat parapsychological research with the same seriousness and sympathy which they would bring to the study of any other area of scientific research. Thus, they structure their history of parapsychological research around the model of general scientific development proposed by Thomas S. Kuhn. Rhine's book *Extra-Sensory Perception* is seen as constituting the first successful 'paradigm' for the field – and one which might well have led to its dramatic expansion had Rhine's experimental claims been more readily matched than in fact proved to be the case.

The approach of Mauskopf and McVaugh also leads them to see the relation between parapsychology and other sciences (particularly psychology) as being more complex than do the debunkers or supporters of the field, none of whom have carried out historical research to the degree of detail of Mauskopf and McVaugh for the time period which they cover. Most interesting in this regard is their account of the reception of J. B. Rhine's work by psychologists in the 1930s, where they have discovered a wide range of reactions among them (sometimes indeed within an individual psychologist) extending from suspicion and hostility to genuine scientific puzzlement and interest in the reported results. Given the uniquely unsettled scientific status of parapsychology, the approach of Mauskopf and McVaugh is perhaps the most reasonable one for handling the history of this controversial field.

NOTES

1. 'Introductory remarks', in M. P. Hanon, M. Osler, R. G. Weyant (eds.), *Science, pseudo-science and society* (Waterloo, Ont., 1980), p. 4.
2. L. Laudan, 'The demise of the demarcation problem', R. Laudan (ed.), *The demarcation*

between science and pseudo-science (Blacksburg, VA, 1983), pp. 7–35. See also R. Wallis, 'Science and pseudo-science', *Social science information, 24* (1985), 585–601.

3. G. Sarton, *A history of science: Hellenistic science and culture in the last three centuries* BC (New York, 1965), pp. vii–viii.

4. In E. Mendelsohn, P. Weingart, R. Whitley (eds.), *The social production of scientific knowledge* (Dordrecht, 1977), pp. 17–18.

5. R. J. Cooter, *The cultural meaning of popular science: phrenology and the organisation of consent in nineteenth-century Britain* (Cambridge, 1984), p. 18.

6. C. C. Gillispie, *Science and polity in France at the end of the old regime* (Princeton, 1980), chap. 4 ('Scientists and charlatans'); H. F. Ellenberger, *The discovery of the unconscious* (New York, 1970), chap. 2 ('The emergence of dynamic psychiatry').

7. D. M. Knight, 'Steps towards a dynamical chemistry', *Ambix, 14* (1967), 187–8.

8. Psychoanalysis has received, of course, very extensive historical treatment and also consideration *vis-à-vis* the demarcation issue from its critics. See, for example, A. Grünbaum, *The foundations of psychoanalysis: a philosophical critique* (Berkeley, 1984).

9. The investigation of hauntings, dowsing, faith-healing and the monitoring of mediums and psychics are some of them.

10. C. E. M. Hansel, *ESP: a scientific evaluation* (New York, 1966); A. Flew, 'Parapsychology: science or pseudo-science?', in M. P. Hanon, M. Osler, R. G. Weyant (eds.), *Science, pseudo-science and society*, pp. 55–75.

11. There does exist a historical literature written by those within the field, often polemical but nevertheless carried out with care, e.g. T. H. Hall, *The strange case of Edmund Gurney* (London, 1964). There are also some important collections of published papers such as *William James on psychical research*, ed. G. Murphy and R. O. Ballou (New York, 1960).

12. C. D. Broad, *Lectures on psychical research* (London, 1962); B. Brier, *Precognition and the philosophy of science* (New York, 1974); S. E. Braude, *ESP and psychokinesis: a philosophical examination* (Philadelphia, 1979).

13. H. M. Collins and T. J. Pinch, *Frames of meaning: the social construction of extraordinary science* (London, 1982), p. 184.

14. (Boston: Boston Society for Psychic Research, 1934). It was in this work that Rhine introduced the term 'parapsychology'.

FURTHER READING

There are a number of collections containing essays devoted to the issue of marginal science; they are listed in order of date of publication:

B. Barnes and S. Shapin (eds.), *Natural order: historical studies of scientific culture* (Beverly Hills, 1979).

M. P. Hanon, M. Osler, R. G. Weyant (eds.), *Science, pseudo-science and society* (Waterloo, Ont., 1980).

R. Laudan (ed.), *The demarcation between science and pseudo-science* (Blacksburg, VA, 1983).

S. H. Mauskopf (ed.), *The reception of unconventional science* (Boulder, CO, 1979).

R. Wallis (ed.), *On the margins of science: the social construction of rejected knowledge* (Keele, 1979 [Sociological Review Monograph 27]).

The journal, *The zetetic scholar*, edited by the sociologist of science, Marcello Truzzi, is a forum for debate about marginal science.

Marginal science after 1700

B. Capp, *English almanacs, 1500–1800* (Ithaca, 1979).

A. G. Debus, 'The Paracelsians in eighteenth century France: a renaissance tradition in the age of enlightenment', E. Mendelsohn (ed.), *Transformations and traditions in the sciences: essays in honor of I. Bernard Cohen* (Cambridge, 1984), pp. 193–214.

H. Leventhal, *In the shadow of the enlightenment: occultism and renaissance science in eighteenth century America* (New York, 1976).

Mesmerism

R. Darton, *Mesmerism and the end of the enlightenment* (Cambridge, 1968).

G. Sutton, 'Electric medicine and mesmerism', *Isis*, 72 (1981), 375–92.

R. G. Weyant, 'Protoscience, pseudo-science, metaphors and animal magnetism', Hanon, Osler, Weyant, (eds.), *Science, pseudo-science and society*, pp. 77–114.

Naturphilosophie

B. Gower, 'Speculation in physics: the history and practice of *Naturphilosophie*', *Studies in history and philosophy of science*, 3 (1973), 301–56.

D. M. Knight, 'The scientist as sage', *Studies in romanticism*, 6 (1967), 65–88.

T. S. Kuhn, 'Energy conservation as example of simultaneous discovery', M. Clagett (ed.), *Critical problems in the history of science* (Madison, 1959), pp. 321–56.

H. A. M. Snelders, 'Romanticism and naturphilosophie in inorganic natural sciences, 1797–1840: an introductory survey', *Studies in romanticism*, 9 (1970), pp. 193–215.

R. C. Stauffer, 'Speculation and experiment in the background of Oersted's discovery of electromagnetism', *Isis*, 48 (1957), 33–50.

Phrenology

E. Ackerknecht and H. V. Vallois, *Franz Joseph Gall, inventor of phrenology and his collection*, trans. Clair St. Leon (Madison, WI, 1956).

R. J. Cooter, 'Phrenology: the provocation of progress', *History of science*, 14 (1976), 214–34.

—— *The cultural meaning of popular science: phrenology and the organisation of consent in nineteenth century Britain* (Cambridge, 1984).

S. Shapin, 'The politics of observation: cerebral anatomy and social interests in the Edinburgh phrenology disputes', Wallis (ed.), *On the margins of science*, pp. 139–78.

O. Temkin, 'Gall and the phrenological movement', *Bulletin of the history of medicine*, 21 (1947), 251–321.

R. M. Young, *Mind, brain and adaptation in the nineteenth century* (Oxford, 1970).

Parapsychology

P. D. Allison, 'Experimental parapsychology as a rejected science', Wallis (ed.), *On the margins of science*, pp. 271–91.

H. M. Collins and R. J. Pinch, *Frames of meaning: the social construction of extraordinary science* (London, 1982).

J. J. Cerullo, *The secularization of the soul* (Philadelphia, 1982).

A. Gauld, *The founders of psychical research* (London, 1968).

J. McClenon, *Deviant science: the case of parapsychology* (Philadelphia, 1984).

S. H. Mauskopf and M. R. McVaugh, *The elusive science: origins of experimental psychical research* (Baltimore, 1980).

L. Moore, *In search of white crows: spiritualism, parapsychology and American culture* (New York, 1977).

M. Noonan, 'Science and the psychical research movement' (Philadephia, 1977 [Ph.D. dissertation, Department of the History and Sociology of Science, University of Pennsylvania]).

J. Oppenheim, *The other world: spiritualism and psychical research in England, 1850–1914* (Cambridge, 1985).

F. M. Turner, *Between science and religion: the reaction to scientific naturalism in late Victorian England* (New Haven, 1974).

B. Wynne, 'Physics and psychics: science, symbolic action, and social control in late Victorian England', Shapin (ed.), *Natural Order* pp. 167–86.

57

SCIENCE, ALIENATION AND OPPRESSION

ROBERT M. YOUNG

Neither 'alienation' nor 'oppression' is in any sense unique to the modern era or to the Industrial Revolution and its aftermath. Yet most would say that the resonances of both concepts are primarily Marxist and derive from the critique of the capitalist mode of production developed by Karl Marx, Frederick Engels and various Marxist writers from the mid-nineteenth century to the present. These resonances are quite appropriate, and in a short essay it would be folly not to concentrate on Marxism. But at least three gestures must be made before pursuing this restricted brief. Firstly, practically every religion, culture and philosophical tradition has its own story of how humans came to be estranged or alienated from the gods or a god, from a bountiful nature and from one another. By the same token the subsidiary concept of oppression – the power that some people have over others – is ubiquitous and may be seen in emperors and subjects, masters and slaves, chiefs and indians, lords and serfs, capitalists and workers, conquerors and the conquered, men and women, parents and children, straights and gays and whites and blacks. Thus some sense of alienation and of oppression has been in need of explanation wherever there has been disharmony among people.

The Judaeo–Christian tradition locates the origins of these phenomena in the temptation of Eve by Satan. It was in the wake of partaking of the fruit of the tree of knowledge of good and evil that humans experienced self-estrangement, poverty, shame, the pain of childbirth, thorns, human labour, human – including sexual – conflict and death. It was thus that Adam and Eve came to be driven out of harmony with themselves, with each other and with nature – and out of the Garden of Eden. It was their son Cain who slew his brother Abel and was made the first fugitive and vagabond. He was driven from the presence of the Lord and 'dwelt in the Land of Nod, on the East of Eden'.[1] The Christian path to de-alienation (overcoming original sin) is said to have been brought about by the Incarnation and Crucifixion through Christ's redemptive suffering. Similarly, in the Western philosophical tradition people offended the gods – Greek and Roman – and could never adequately propitiate them. As a result, human knowledge came to be acquired in mediated ways, glimpsed as shadows in a cave, rather than directly and intuitively.

However, there is no need to look even this broadly or to still other cultures in the Middle East, Far East, the Americas or Australasia. Marx's early writings take us to his own immediate predecessors, Ludwig Feuerbach and G. W. F. Hegel, and to conceptions of the alienation of the human spirit from knowledge of essences, from plenty, from the deity and from social and sexual harmony. Alienation was estrangement, separation and objectification. All of these find their modern classical expression in Hegel's *Phenomenology of Mind*. But even if we take this beginning, it quickly proliferates figures and traditions. Most conceptions of alienation have several dimensions of distressing separation and estrangement – from self, from one's fellow humans, from nature, from one's labour, one's product, one's humanity and from the deity or gods. A wider history of the post-Hegelian concept would embrace the writings of at least the following figures, most of whom interacted in important ways with Marxism: Kierkegaard, Heidegger, Nietzsche, Schopenhauer, Weber, Simmel, Durkheim, Tillich, Fromm, Fanon, Illich, Whyte (*The Organisational Man*), Arendt, Marcuse and writers on liberation theology.

If one were to pursue these positions in anything approaching a systematic way it would lead to careful discussion of phenomenology, existentialism, the sociology of work, the histories of colonialism, racism, imperialism, patriarchy and feminism. Each of these in one way or another intersects with the scientific world-view, especially the alienation from nature in a sharp dichotomy in philosophy and in the philosophy of science between the knowing subject and the known object. The entire Hegelian tradition (including humanistic Marxism) juxtaposes to these a more interactive or dialectical concept of I/thou to I/it. It could be argued that in each and every case of alienation and oppression, the requisite distancing could not occur without a psychological and philosophical split which projected away from the self an alien Other, be it nature, other persons, or any cut-off object.

The movement from Hegel to Marx can be summarised as follows: 'Feuerbach criticised Hegel's view that nature is a self-alienated form of Absolute Mind and that man is Absolute Mind in the process of de-alienation. For Feuerbach, man is not a self-alienated God, but God is self-alienated man – he is merely man's essence abstracted, absolutised and estranged from man. Thus, man is alienated from himself when he creates, and puts above himself, an imagined alien higher being and bows before him as a slave. The de-alienation of man consists in the abolition of that estranged picture of man which is God . . . Marx agreed with Feuerbach's criticism of religious alienation, but he stressed that religious alienation is only one among the many forms of human self-alienation'.[2]

Some of Marx's earliest writings were reflections on Feuerbach. He roots his analysis in practical activity and focuses on the human labour of production within capitalism, in which the capitalist owns the means of production and the labourer sells his or her labour power. Here is the classical source of Marx's concept of alienation: 'Labour produces not only commodities: it produces itself and the worker as a *commodity* and does so in the proportion in which it produces commodities generally.

'This fact expresses merely that the object which labour produces – labour's product – confronts it as *something alien*, as a *power independent* of the producer. The product of labour is labour which has been congealed in an object which has become material; it is the *objectification* of labour. Labour's realisation is its objectification. In the conditions dealt with by political economy this realisation of labour appears as a *loss of reality* for the workers; objectification as *loss of the object* and *object-bondage*; appropriation as *estrangement*, as *alienation*'.[3] Marx concludes that 'the worker is related to the *product of his labour* as to an *alien* object'.[4] 'The worker therefore only feels himself outside his work, and in his work feels outside himself. He is at home when he is not working, and when he is working he is not at home'.[5]

The worker is alienated from (1) his own act of production within the labour process, (2) the product of his labour, (3) his fellow worker and (4) his own human nature or 'species-being'. Labour, the product, other humans and one's own sense of humanity become alien – over against the self as something strange and threatening. Behind all this, for Marx, lies the concept of private property: 'Alienated labour has resolved itself for us into two elements which mutually condition one another, or which are but different expressions of one and the same relationship. *Appropriation* appears as *estrangement*, as *alienation*; and *alienation* appears as *appropriation*, *estrangement* as true *enfranchisement*.

'We have considered the one side – *alienated* labour – in relation to the *worker* himself, i.e. the *relation of alienated labour to itself*. The *property-relation of the non-worker to the worker and to labour* we have found as the product, the necessary outcome of this relation of alienated labour. *Private property*, as the material summary expression of alienated labour, embraces both relations – the *relation of the worker to work, to the product of his labour and to the non-worker*, and the relation of the *non-worker to the worker and to the product of his labour*'.[6]

Some objectivist Marxists have criticised the use of the concept of alienation, because they wish to purge Marxism of concepts they see as humanistic. They wish instead to use concepts such as exploitation, division of labour and private property (which, as we have just seen, Marx equated with alienation). I have no sympathy with this view and merely report it.

The important next step in the understanding of 'science, alienation and oppression' is that for Marxists alienation is the predominant form of objectification in the modern era. This occurs by means of the property relations of the capitalist mode of production. A crucial link for understanding science in terms of alienation is to see the process at a deeper level – one in which objectification occurs in the philosophies of nature and of science in the capitalist mode of production as a world-view, just as it does in the capitalist mode of production as a way of making things for sale. There are at least four ways that the link between science and the scientific world-view, on the one hand, and alienation and oppression, on the other, can be made. The first is through the historical relations between scientific revolution, the rise of capitalism and the Protestant revolution. The second is through a conceptual analysis of the scientific world-view and the ways in which nature became alienated, objectified and reified. The third is by means of the role of science and technology and the fundamental change in the labour process which occurred in the Industrial Revolution from formal subordination in pre-industrial capitalism to real subordination in machinofacture, leading to ever-subtler forms of pacing, surveillance and control in automation, Taylorism and, most recently, micro-processor-controlled production. Fourthly, the history of oppression both draws on raw materials from colonial countries and sells manufactured goods to them, intensifying human suffering in the form of literal and wage slavery. After the rise of industrial capitalism the same countries, no longer under colonial rule, suffer economic oppression as the falling rate of profit in the metropolitan countries leads to more intensive exploitation. Native workers are used for gathering materials and for actual manufacturing processes, as multi-national corporations increasingly site their factories in Third World countries where labour is cheap and relatively unorganised.

Each of these approaches is, to put it mildly, a large topic. Before embarking on any of them, however, it is as well to point out that my brief is to describe the role of alienation and oppression. This means that I am focusing on one side of a profoundly dialectical phenomenon – the interpenetration of good and bad, enabling and controlling, enriching and impoverishing phenomena. In the Enlightenment, the nineteenth century and in our own time science has come to be identified and even equated with progress, reason and human benefit. It would be silly to argue that science is always and everywhere, i.e. inherently, alienating and oppressive. Yet it would be equally silly to say that it is only in the abuse of science that alienation and oppression occur. Science enlightens and brings about progress but *also* alienates and oppresses. My own view is that we need to be fully ambivalent about science and progress.

The close interrelations between the development of scientific instruments and theories in astronomy, navigation, ballistics and mining, as well as between medicine, agriculture and the study of living phenomena; the development of world trade, mercantile capitalism and urbanisation; and the development of a view of the relations between God, the individual and the redemptive value of work are all so intertwined and mutually constitutive that the scientific, capitalist and Protestant revolutions of the sixteenth and seventeenth centuries are a single reconstitution of the world, the world-view and the structure of relations among people and peoples. They have in common a splitting-off of moral value, mind and responsibility – concerning purpose or final causes – from the labour process itself. This occurs in science, in manufacturing and in moral relations. A mechanical world-view comes to replace an organismic one. Fact and value, thing and purpose and body and mind become sharply dichotomised, just as labour power gets separated off from the worker.

In this way, abstraction from science and from nature becomes the rule, so that what matters is not the sensuous particularity of persons, processes and things but the value of labour power and of commodities. The same alienation occurs in the scientific world-view. What matters to science is that which is amenable to mathematical handling – matter and motion. These preoccupy the thinkers who are developing the modern world-view (see art. 46). The commodity exchange abstraction, like the abstractions of science, treats objects as shorn of their secondary qualities and the social relations embedded in them and in which they have their being. Both are forms of misplaced concreteness.

Marx says in the *Grundrisse*: 'Considered as values, all commodities are qualitatively equal and differ only quantitatively, hence can be measured against each other and substituted for one another (are mutually exchangeable, mutually convertible) in certain quantitative relations. Value is their social relation, their economic quality. A book which possesses a certain value and a loaf of bread possessing the same value are exchanged for one another, are the same value but in a different material. As a value, a commodity is an equivalent for all other commodities in a given relation. As a value, the commodity is an equivalent; as an equivalent all its natural properties are extinguished; it no longer takes up a special qualitative relationship towards the other commodities; but is rather the general measure as well as the general representative, the general medium of exchange of all other commodities . . . as a value, every commodity is equally divisible; in its natural existence this is not the case'.[7]

When Marx writes about the fetishism of commodities in *Capital*, he is describing an objectification and estrangement which is exactly parallel to that which has happened in the filtering out of the sensuous qualities of nature in the scientific world-view. He writes, 'A commodity appears at first sight an extremely obvious, trivial thing. But its analysis brings out that it is a very strange thing, abounding in metaphysical subtleties and theological niceties'.[8] He goes on to describe how we can relate to a table for years and continues: ' . . . but as soon as it emerges as a commodity, it changes into a thing which transcends sensuousness. It not only stands with its feet on the ground, but, in relation to all other commodities, it stands on its head, and evolves out of its wooden brain grotesque ideas, far more wonderful than if it were to begin dancing of its own free will . . . The mysterious character of the commodity-forms consists therefore simply in the fact that the commodity reflects the social characteristics of men's own labour as objective characteristics of the products of labour themselves, as the socio-natural properties of these things. Hence it also reflects the social relation of the producers to the sum total of labour as a social relation between objects . . . It is nothing but the definite social relations between men themselves which will assume, here, for them, the fantastic form of a relation between things'.[9]

Science, manufacturing and commerce become preoccupied with what can be treated objectively. The world, the worker and the product get treated as objects, not as subjects. All values other than those amenable to science or to exchange get filtered out. Social relations get reduced to things: they become reified. The features amenable to abstract treatment become the most interesting ones at the expense of their qualities as colours, odours, tastes or beautiful living organisms. Once again, this is what is meant by the misplaced concreteness of the modern world-view. In his classical essay on 'Reification and the Consciousness of the Proletariat' Lukács comments acidly on the outcome of this process. He says that 'the more intricate modern science becomes and the better it understands itself methodologically, the more resolutely it will turn its back on the ontological problems of its own sphere of influence and eliminate them from the realm where it has achieved some insight. The more highly developed it becomes and the more scientific the more it will become a formally closed system of partial laws. It will then find that the world lying beyond its confines, and in particular the material base which it is its task to understand, its own *concrete underlying reality* lies, methodologically and in principle, *beyond its grasp* . . . science is thereby debarred from comprehending the development and the demise, the social character of its own material base, no less than the range of possible attitudes towards it and the nature of its own formal system'.[10]

Lukács makes quite explicit the links I have been describing above: 'It is anything but a mere chance that at the very beginning of the development of modern philosophy the ideal of knowledge took the form of universal mathematics: it was an attempt to establish a rational system of relations which comprehends the totality of the formal possibilities, proportions and relations of a rationalised existence with the aid of which every phenomenon – independently of its real and material distinctiveness – could be subjected to an exact calculus.

'This is the modern ideal of knowledge at its most uncompromising and therefore at its most characteristic, and in it the contradiction alluded to above emerges clearly. For, on the one hand, the basis of this universal calculus can be nothing other than the certainty that only a reality cocooned by such concepts can truly be controlled by us. On the other hand it appears that even if we may suppose this universal mathematics to be entirely and consistently realised "control" of reality can be nothing more than the objectively correct contemplation of what is yielded – necessarily and without our intervention – by the abstract combination of these relations and propositions.[11]

'But here we can see that this results in the assimilation of all human relations to the level of natural laws so conceived. It has often been pointed out in these pages that nature is a social category. Of course, to modern man it must look as if the point of view which we have just outlined consisted simply in applying to society an intellectual framework derived from the natural sciences'.[12] He then points out that this way of thinking led, according to Marx, to thinking of nature and humanity in commodity terms: 'After Hegel had clearly recognised the bourgeois character of the "laws of nature"', Marx pointed out that 'Descartes with his definition of animals as mere machines saw with the eyes of the manufacturing period, while in the eyes of the Middle Ages, animals were man's assistants'; and he adds several suggestions towards explaining the intellectual history of such connections. Tönnies notes the same connection even more bluntly and categorically: 'A special case for abstract reason is *scientific* reason and its subject is the man who is objective and who recognises relations, i.e. thinks in concepts. In consequence, scientific concepts which by their ordinary origin and their real properties are judgements by means of which complexes of feelings are given names, behave within science like commodities in society. They gather together within the system like commodities on the market. The supreme scientific concept which is no longer the name of anything real is like money, e.g. the concept of an atom or of energy'. Lukács concludes: 'What is important is to recognise clearly that all human relations (viewed as the objects of social activity) assume increasingly the objective form of the abstract elements of the conceptual systems of natural science and of the abstract substrata of the laws of nature'.[13]

I have gone to some lengths to trace the connections between the scientific world-view, the fetishism of commodities and the concept of alienated labour, since there have been writers (both Marxist and non-Marxist) who have failed to see the warrant in Marxist writings for these connections.[14]

The scientific world-view was increasingly linked to people's daily lives by the union of science and technological rationality to the process of manufacturing as the history of capitalism moved from manufacture to machinofacture – from the system where outworkers made things with their own instruments to where the means of production were owned by the capitalists and were concentrated and brought near to sources of power. Formal subordination of workers through quotas and prices was progressively replaced by real subordination by control of the actual movements of the workers through pacing by machines. In one of the most important passages in the history of thought, Marx puts forward a conception of the history of technology as a moving resolution of forces with science at the heart of capital's control.

It would be possible to write a whole history of the inventions made since 1830 for the sole purpose of providing capital with weapons against working-class revolt. We would mention, above all, the self-acting mule, because it opened up a new epoch in the automatic system.

Nasmyth, the inventor of the steam-hammer, gave the following evidence before the Commission on Trades Unions, with regard to the improvements in machinery he himself introduced as a result of the wide-spread and long-lasting strikes of the engineers in 1851. 'The characteristic feature of our modern mechanical improvements, is the introduction of self-acting tool machinery. What every mechanical workman has now to do, and what every boy can do, is not to work himself but to superintend the beautiful labour of the machine. The whole class of workmen that depend exclusively on their skill, is now done away with. Formerly, I employed four boys to every mechanic. Thanks to these new mechanical combinations, I have reduced the number of grown-up men from 1,500 to 750. The result was a considerable increase in my profits.' (10th Report of Commissioners on Organisation and Rules of Trades Unions, 1868)

Ure says this of the colouring machines used in calico printing: 'At length capitalists sought deliverance from this intolerable bondage' (namely the terms of their contracts with the workers, which they saw as burdensome) 'in the resources of science, and were speedily re-instated in their legitimate rule, that of the head over the inferior members.' Then, speaking of an invention for dressing warps, whose immediate occasion was a strike, he says: 'The combined malcontents, who fancied themselves impregnably intrenched behind the old lines of division of labour, found their flanks turned and their defences rendered useless by the new mechanical tactics, and were obliged to surrender at discretion.' Of the invention of the self-acting mule, he says: 'A creation destined to restore order among the industrious classes . . . This invention confirms the great doctrine already propounded, that when capital enlists science into her service, the refractory hand of labour will always be taught docility.'[15]

This is oppression.

The subsequent phases of this process can be seen in the history of machinofacture as new inventions occurred in the factory system, for example, in mass production and in the moving assembly line (derived from meat packing). The next phase in direct control of workers was the development of 'scientific management' at the hands of Frederick W. Taylor. His aim was to apply the methods and assumptions of science to the most detailed movements of workers – all of this in the name of efficiency. His research was the fountainhead of all forms of work-study and direct control over the labour process. His aims were quite explicit: 'To prove that the best management is a true science, resting upon clearly defined laws, rules and principles, as a foundation. And further to show that the fundamental principles of scientific management are applicable to all kinds of human activities, from our simplest individual acts to

the work of our great corporations, which call for the most elaborate co-operation . . . It is hoped, however, that it will be clear to other readers that the
same principles can be applied with equal force to all social activities: to the
management of our homes; the management of our farms; the management of
the business of our tradesmen large and small; of our churches, our philanthropic institutions, our universities and our governmental departments'.[16]

The full implementation of this vision depended on subtle and ubiquitous
means for surveillance, pacing and control. These are only becoming fully
available in the wake of the development of micro-processor-controlled manufacturing. Therefore, the goals set by Ure and by Taylor are only in sight of fulfilment as the twentieth century draws to a close. The theorectical elaboration
of this vision, in conceptions based on the management sciences, systems theory
and what has been called by James Martin *The Wired Society*, is in prospect
unless a fundamentally different approach is taken to the union of the scientific
world-view with the capitalist mode of production.

In what follows I shall only be able to give an example of the other dimensions of the relations between science, alienation and oppression. In what I have
said above I have attempted to lay out the most general features of these
relations. The tracing of the connections between those and the particular
examples listed below would far exceed the space available.

The essential link between the scientific world-view and human alienation
and oppression occurs through the labour process in both theory and practice.
The theory is that of technological rationality and the practice is a technology-
driven form of work. The most eloquent critique of this has been made by
Herbert Marcuse in *One Dimensional Man* (to which the reader is most sincerely
referred). Marcuse says, 'The scientific concept of a universally controllable
nature projected nature as endless matter-in-function, the mere stuff of theory
and practice. In this form, the object-world entered the construction of a technological universe – a universe of mental and physical instrumentalities, means
in themselves . . . Only in the medium of technology, man and nature become
fungible objects of organisations. The universal effectiveness and productivity
of the apparatus under which they are subsumed veil the particular interests
that organise the apparatus. In other words, technology has become the great
vehicle of *reification* – reification in its most mature and effective form. The
social position of the individual and his relation to others appear not only to be
determined by objective qualities and laws, but these qualities and laws seem to
lose their mysterious and uncontrollable character; they appear as calculable
manifestations of (scientific) rationality. The world tends to become the stuff of
total administration, which absorbs even the administrators. The web of domination has become the web of Reason itself, and this society is fatally entangled
in it. And the transcending modes of thought seem to transcend Reason
itself.'[17]

Which example should one choose? Here are some candidates: the role of military research through 'research and development' from nuclear physics to higher mathematics, optics, chemical and biological warfare, containerisation and high resolution photography; the management-based research and development policies pioneered by the Rockefeller Foundation including the international organisation of hygiene and tropical medicine, the Green Revolution, primatology, the social sciences and molecular biology; behavioural control in drugs (an industry providing a topic in its own right), conditioning, cerebral implants and psychosurgery; management sciences and operational research; the new technologies and property relations of genetic engineering, fertilisation and childbearing; and, finally, Social Darwinism in international relations, in business and in social theory. I trust that the large domain of the concepts of alienation and oppression *vis-à-vis* science will begin to become apparent.

The example I shall sketch is the global assembly-line in micro-processor production. The history of information transmission from telegraphy to wireless telegraphy to the thermionic valve and then to transistors and micro-processors is itself almost wholly constituted by patronage from the military and the financial community. But what is so striking about the current manufacturing of these 'computers on a chip' are the conditions which, in their way, recall the worst excesses of the Industrial Revolution of the eighteenth and nineteenth centuries. Because of the falling rate of profit in the United States, American corporations set up factories in the Far East, sinking the shallowest roots in the community so that they can up the stakes whenever the labour force becomes uppity. Young women are recruited from villages and given very close work. Their eyes do not last long and they get called 'granny' in their early twenties. The companies develop programmes to develop metropolitan tastes in clothes, perfumes, jewellery and gadgets, thus binding the young women closer to long hours and lower wages. Health conditions in the 'clean rooms' are bad and various toxic substances are abroad, even with special clothes and ventilation. When the women are too ill or their sight goes, they lose their jobs and many find their way into the only other lucrative trade that is available in the urban setting: prostitution. These are the conditions and the human costs by which the micro-processors at the heart of so many gadgets get made, for example, watches, hi-fi systems, home computers and computer-programmed washing machines. These working conditions and labour relations also exist in free-trade zones in the First World, e.g. on the California/Mexican border and in Eire, but there are, in those places, some regulations which partially ameliorate what I have described as quite normal in South-East Asia.[18]

In order to oppress other people, they must be seen as alien. The scientific world-view separates matter from mind and fact from value, while the capitalist mode of production separates the worker from the finished product and the work from the worker via the wage. Both senses of value – the moral and the economic – get separated off from the human. Much human benefit has been derived from science and from capitalism, but these are rather like a saving clause in a bad treaty.

NOTES

1. Genesis, Chapters 3 and 4 to verse 16.
2. G. Petrovic, 'Alienation', in T. Bottomore *et al.*, (eds.), *A dictionary of Marxist thought* (Oxford, 1983), pp. 9–15, at p. 15.
3. K. Marx, *Economic and philosophic manuscripts of 1844* (Moscow, 1961), p. 69.
4. Ibid., p. 70.
5. Ibid., p. 72.
6. Ibid., pp. 82–3.
7. K. Marx, *Grundrisse: foundations of the critique of political economy (rough draft)* (1857–8) (London, 1973), p. 141.
8. K. Marx, *Capital: a critique of political economy*, 3 vols. (London, 1976), vol. 1, (1867), p. 163.
9. Ibid., pp. 163–5.
10. Georg Lukács, *History and class consciousness: studies in Marxist dialectics* (1923), (London, 1971), pp. 104–5.
11. Ibid., p. 129.
12. Ibid., p. 130.
13. Ibid., p. 131.
14. See R. Young, 'Science *is* social relations', *Radical Science Journal*, 5 (1977), 65–129.
15. K. Marx, *Capital*, (1867, 1976), pp. 563–4.
16. F. W. Taylor, *The principles of scientific management* (1911) (New York, 1967), pp. 7–8.
17. H. Marcuse, *One dimensional man: the ideology of industrial society* (1964), (London, 1968), pp. 136–7.
18. Pacific Research Center, 'The changing role of South East Asian women: the global assembly line and the social manipulation of women', Special Joint Issue of *Pacific research* and *S. E. Asia chronicle* (Mountain View, Calif., 1978–9).

FURTHER READING

H. Braverman, *Labour and monopoly capital: the degradation of work in the twentieth century* (London, 1974).

S. Chorover, *From Genesis to genocide: the meaning of human nature and the power of behavioural control* (London, 1979).

J. Israel, *Alienation from Marx to modern sociology: macrosociological analysis* (Boston, 1971).

C. V. Jones, *Most secret war: British scientific intelligence 1939–1945* (London, 1978).

E. and M. Josephson (eds.), *Man alone: alienation in modern society* (New York, 1962).

W. Leiss, *The domination of nature* (New York, 1972).

L. Levidow and R. M. Young (eds.), *Science, technology and the labour process* 2 vols. (London, 1981, 1985).

S. Milgram, *Obedience to authority: an experimental view* (London, 1974).

D. Noble, *The forces of production: a social history of industrial automation* (New York, 1984).

B. Ollman, *Alienation: Marx's conception of man in capitalist society* (Cambridge, 1971).

Theodore Roszak, *The making of a counter-culture: reflections on the technocratic society and its youthful opposition* (London, 1970).

R. Schacht, *Alienation* (London, 1971).
A. Sohn–Rethel, 'Science as alienated consciousness', *Radical science journal* 2/3 (1975), 65–101.
A. N. Whitehead, *Science and the modern world* (London, 1985).

58

ORTHODOXIES, CRITIQUES AND ALTERNATIVES

J. R. RAVETZ

1. INTRODUCTION

The concept of 'alternative science' has been current for a very brief period, about two decades at most; hence a historical survey of the movement lacks the normal preconditions in reflective source-materials: prior scholarly productions and separation in time. But, however recent, it is of great importance for any projection of the shape of science in the future; and the period in which the idea was born, the 1960s, is definitely in the past. Also, a genuine history, rather than a mere chronicle, is made possible by the essential feature of this movement; its roots lie in the establishment of our sort of science in the seventeenth century. Its ideology was then given a very clear expression, partly in programmatic terms and partly in contrast to other conceptions of natural knowledge then prevalent. The contradictions within that ideology, some latent and others then capable of resolution, could subsequently, with the advance of science, be suppressed or ignored. With the recent full maturing of science in its organisation, effectiveness and power, these contradictions have become manifest. This explains the apparent paradox that in a period of the greatest triumphs of science, its opponents became most strident and effective. Out of the movement of criticism on all issues, new foci of practice and reflection have come to exist and to find stable niches in society. These are what we call 'alternatives'.

2. EARLY CONTRADICTIONS AND THEIR RESOLUTION

The early vision of modern science was explicitly millenarian in Bacon, and implicitly so (within the limits of their respective styles) in Galileo and Descartes. From their writings, we may distil the prophetic message: that through the study of an abstract aspect of nature, through a style of enquiry that was alienated from its object but open to all, error would be banished, ignorance abolished and truths easily achieved that would be powerful, beneficial and safe. Thus a straight and narrow path of enquiry into Nature was to be the gateway to the material and moral redemption of mankind.

For analysing the contradictions in that programme, we may rephrase it in terms of certain themes. That is, this style of science promised the *security* of gaining truth (and avoiding error) through *discovery* within a particular *reality*; its social practice was one of *openness* (to all participants and also in its results); to its external patrons it promised ideological *innocence* in its teachings and the practical *beneficence* of its powers in application. All this is an ideology; and it was an essential part of the endeavour, in the Scientific Revolution and for some three centuries to follow.

The aspect of the ideology of science that was later to become its greatest strength, *security*, was the weakest point in the early programme. Galileo's attempt at a scientific proof of the Copernican system failed disastrously; Descartes's general physics was obviously speculative; and Bacon induced very little indeed successfully. Nor did the initial protestations of *innocence* carry sufficient weight, particularly with those Roman Catholic authorities who had cause for concern. The claims of *openness* were more successful, although (perhaps because of) being restricted to the more polite orders of society.

The problems of *reality* also solved themselves; although some of the great earlier discoveries of modern science (such as those of Kepler, Gilbert and Harvey) were made within the framework of 'animated' world-views, the accelerating secular change in common-sense consciousness was soon making such 'alternative' world-pictures implausible and obsolete. The progress of *discovery* within the new paradigm, in the seventeenth century and beyond, seemed to guarantee beyond doubt that this is the one and only secure way to the True.

Although the practical *beneficence* of the new science took a long time to materialise, it seems that its public were generally prepared to take that on trust. Jonathan Swift's portrait of addled natural philosophers and corrupt 'projectors' of Laputa (in *Gulliver's Travels*) was only part of his general denunciation of secularised eighteenth-century high society. The powers of the new science also had a quality of *innocence*: with the decline of the magical arts, there were no longer secrets too powerful to be revealed. All effects were proportionable to their natural causes, and so the idea of science producing real evil was nearly a logical impossibility until our own times.

3. EARLY CHALLENGES, RESOLVED AND UNRESOLVED

Thus did the ideology of modern science gain its form, and increase steadily in strength during the eighteenth and nineteenth centuries. One of the greatest strengths of that ideology was that it saw science as simple and absolute, the antithesis to mere belief or to 'ideology' itself.

The earliest conflicts involving science were easy victories. The perennial struggle about *openness* surfaced in the French Revolution, with vain complaints that Lavoisier's chemical nomenclature made a barrier against all those artisans who lacked the erudition to master his classicisms. The issue of *reality* erupted with *Naturphilosophie*; and with its downfall, the hardest of world-views generally ruled supreme. The triumph of Darwinism was due only in part to the overwhelming weight of its separately inconclusive arguments; equally it was the conviction of its audience that no other sort of explanation could be 'scientific'.

By the sort of double-think that is possible only within a well-established ideology, science's propagandists could continue to proclaim its *innocence* (as the vehicle of simple truth) while vigorously attacking what for the unlettered majority of people was the foundation of their personal morality: religion revealed through sacred texts. The *beneficence* of science was equally secure; while the propagandists of industrialisation lauded science as their own, those who spoke for the suffering masses were equally determined to enlist it; thus Marx called his the 'scientific' Socialism, which would replace the futile 'Utopian' varieties.

The *security* of scientific knowledge grew to the point of becoming a new dogma. Those who debated such questions as the nature of 'force' in the eighteenth century, or of infinity in projective geometry, or atomism in chemistry in the nineteenth century, never doubted that there was a unique true solution. Outsiders who criticised the foundations of a science, as did Bishop Berkeley on the calculus, were dismissed as not possibly being really serious. Even the great 'critical' philosopher Kant took Newton's mechanics, along with Euclid's geometry, as the necessary framework for our experience of the world.

By the later nineteenth century some independent spirits were beginning to uncover obscurities and contradictions at its base. Their intent was not at all destructive; they wished only to strengthen science against certain weaknesses that had developed through its years of easy triumphs. But directly and indirectly they prepared the groundwork for the revolutions, philosophical and scientific, of the next century. Ernst Mach's critical history of mechanics showed that Newton's idea of 'force' was confused and anthropomorphic, his 'mass' was incomprehensible and 'absolute space' non-scientific.[1] Thus, for nearly two hundred years scientists had been living in an illusion of security; their paradigm science could then be seen to be resting on very shaky conceptual foundations. Similar developments afflicted mathematics. Non-Euclidean geometries created a schism between 'intuition' and mathematical truth; while a series of interrelated developments in theories of sets, of infinite numbers and aggregates and of logic, led to a full blown 'foundations-crisis' at the end of the century. (See arts. 42 and 44.)

Within the space of a very few years, Albert Einstein made discoveries which would soon revolutionise the foundations of the world-picture of physics and also of scientific truth; hence this greatest triumph of *discovery* would fatally weaken the traditional *security* of science. The combination of his theoretical work with that of the revolutionary 'atomic physics' eventually led to the atomic bomb, which shattered the *beneficence* of science as well.

The first philosopher to appreciate the full significance of Einstein was Popper; with his 'falsification' he jettisoned the True of science to save the Good, as realised through the intellectual integrity of the (legendary) Einstein who dared the world to prove him wrong (1963). Popper was far ahead of his time; through three decades of his career he witnessed the dominance of the last 'triumphalist' philosophy of science.[2] This was logical-positivism, born in anti-clerical struggles in Vienna, and transplanted by refugees in ideologically neutralised form to the English-speaking world. By the time Popper came into prominence, his message for science was anachronistic. The revolution within philosophy of physics of the earlier twentieth century had given way to a revolution of consciousness and experience, in which the old ideology of science was a principal object of rejection and contempt. (See art. 54.)

4. THE RADICAL CRITIQUE OF THE 1960s

Although the millenarian aspirations of the 1960s, in politics and in experience, are now reduced to an object of historical study, the permanent changes achieved then should not be underestimated. The concept 'alternative', including science, is a mark of these. The conditions for that revolution in consciousness were multiple. First, there was a new class, of 'affluent' youth, enjoying incomes to spend and markets organised around their desires. They were also free of the bondages of parental control, of fear of poverty and of ambition for advancement. They could cultivate new experiences ranging over idealistic politics, communal lifestyles, intense aesthetic experience and altered states of consciousness.

In relation to science, this 'counter-culture' was full of contradictions. Its devotees would cheerfully utilise all its benefits, including the standard equipment of post-war domestic technology, high-technology music and synthetic mind-expanding drugs. Yet on the ideological plane, science was a prime focus of attack. All the contradictions in the ideology of science that had been latent, through the centuries of triumph, now became manifest.

Continuing with the philosophical theme, we have Kuhn's epochal *The Structure of Scientific Revolutions* (1962), influential perhaps because of its confusions, ambiguities and ironies. Its effective message was of a science whose content is strongly 'arbitrary', where 'progress' consists of an alternation between anti-critical puzzle-solving within paradigms and anti-rational combats between paradigms.[3] In vain did Popper protest that Kuhn's 'normal science' is a menace to civilisation; equally vainly did Lakatos try to blend Popperian idealism with Kuhnian realism in his 'methodology of scientific research programmes' (1971).[4] The *security* of science was irretrievably lost for some generations to come. (See arts. 12 and 54.)

The executioner of scientism was Paul Feyerabend, who showed in *Against Method* (1975) that for every principle of method or even of intellectual integrity, there was a violation committed by some great scientist, usually Galileo. Although his professed message was 'playful anarchism' he formed the link between epistemology and radical activism. He had been in Berkeley in the late 1960s, experienced police tear-gas in the classrooms and also 'alternative medicine'. Thenceforth for him science was a white male middle-class racket, protecting itself by a dogmatic orthodoxy as intolerant as any other in history.[5]

Although Feyerabend was in a small minority among philosophers of science, his message of denial of the beneficence of science had already been expounded on many fronts. Ecological consciousness among the reading public was created suddenly with Rachel Carson's *Silent Spring* (1963); and, within a remarkably few years, the American government had environmental legislation drafted and enacted. More radical ecological messages came from Paul Ehrlich, with his *Population Bomb* (1966), and from Barry Commoner, with *Science and Survival* (1966) which blamed post-war high-technology consumerism rather than just people. Most radical of all was the communalist-Christian Ivan Illich, in his broadside attacks on all the institutions of Western science-based intellectual culture; these included *De-Schooling Society* (1971), *Energy and Equity* (1974) and *Medical Nemesis* (1975). In a more practical vein, E. F. Schumacher showed that 'aid' to the poor nations was counter-productive, materially as well as ethically. His vision was of 'intermediate' (later 'appropriate') technology, described as *Small is Beautiful* (1973) but founded on his 'Buddhist economics' conception of the meaning of work and ultimately on his own private religious experience.

With the beneficence of science falling into disrepute, its innocence could not be far behind. It was in the public record that with the A-bomb, science had tasted sin, and that with the H-bomb it had found it sweet. The evil and insanity of nuclear 'deterrence' were appreciated by only an eccentric few until the Cuba crisis of 1962; thenceforth this greatest production of the scholars brought back visions of the sorcerer's apprentice, and worse. The complicity of American science in some of the most reprehensible dirty tricks of the dirty Vietnam war was signalled by dissident students and researchers, culminating in a research-strike at MIT itself. And even within the world of 'pure science', the image of the slightly eccentric other-worldly searcher of old-fashioned academic science gave way, in the age of industrialised science, to 'Professor Grant Swinger' (immortalised by Dan Greenberg in *Science* magazine in 1969),[6] and to the real-life swashbuckling opportunist Jim Watson, who, some fifteen years after the great event, cheerfully revealed the squalid side of his Nobel-prize-winning achievement (1968).[7] Further, problems of quality control, with the implication that many scientists will not or cannot do work of adequate quality, have intruded into the governing of science in an age of restricted support; and there has been no shortage of cases of flagrant, even flamboyant, fraud and plagiarism in prestigious fields and institutions.[8]

This loss of innocence also affected scholarly reflection on science as a human activity. Up to the 1960s, historians of science, as led by such as Sarton, and sociologists of science, as led by such as Merton, were at one with the great popularisers and propagandists in presenting a picture of science, and also of scientists, in which anything but the Good and the True in consequences and in behaviour, was nearly inconceivable. But, after the messages of Kuhn and Feyerabend had been assimilated, historians eagerly lifted the lid off questionable scientific practices among the great, so that the situation was eventually summed up in a classic paper, 'Should the History of Science be rated X?' by Steven Brush (1974).[9] (I attempted to comprehend the positive and negative aspects of science as a social activity, combining a Polanyi-ite theory of craft knowledge of research with a Marxist conception of 'industrialised science', and concluding with a call for 'critical science' (1971).) A new generation of epistemologically-radical social scientists soon found their target in the old faith that science proceeds by *discovery* of something objective out there. Scientific knowledge was shown to be the product of social construction, of negotiation among interests, or merely 'relative' to a professional consensus and capable of being illuminated by the approach of cultural anthropology; the seminal work in 'the scientist as aboriginal' being *Laboratory Life* by Latour and Woolgar (1979).[10] The collapse of the old positivistic faith among philosophers of science was complete by the end of the 1970s: though of course there would always be those in the mathematical-behavioural sciences who had not heard of Kuhn any more than they had of Heisenberg. (See arts. 5 and 7.)

The inherited ideas on *discovery* in science were further eroded by the movements of environmental activism that got underway in the later 1960s. Hitherto, no one had seriously considered the prospect of the impotence of science as worthy of serious reflection. To be sure, in previous generations the limits of our knowledge, as of disease, had been painfully obvious; but there was the sense that the progress of knowledge would eventually eliminate all such ignorance. However, with the environmental crises of modern times, a new category appeared, which we can call science-based ignorance. The new technologies, particularly nuclear power, created problems of risks and pollution, for which no available body of scientific knowledge was adequate. The great statesman of nuclear engineering in America, Alvin Weinberg, exposed the problem with his idea of 'trans-science' (1972). For this his paradigm case was the determination of the number of mice necessary for the assurance of the safety of environmental radiation at Federal standards: some eight billion (8.10^9) would be required. Other problems, such as those called 'zero-infinity risks', and (again from Weinberg) 'Faustian bargains' in which future generations are to cope with our pollutants, have emphasised the radical insufficiency of scientific inputs to urgent policy issues. The contradictions are both cognitive and social. On risks questions, the official task of scientific reassurance is either to prove the impossibility of the undesired event, which is logically impossible; or to prove its 'acceptability' to a suspicious public, which is practically impossible. Worse, the awareness of technologies that are 'unforgiving' or 'brittle' spread more quickly among protestors and critical scientists than among designers and expert-apologists. Finally, the prevalence of very ordinary weaknesses of morale and discipline among managers and operatives in extraordinary sensitive and dangerous installations deprived such enterprises of all credibility among their critically concerned publics.

Environmental politics also punctured another element of the old faith of science, that of its *openness*. For, in such struggles, only a part of the relevant information is 'public knowledge', produced by academic scientists whose rewards are derived through the conventions of citation. Crucial information will be 'corporate know-how': data on processes or pollutions which are the private property of institutions, private or State. In this sort of science, the art is to provide non-information, disinformation, misinformation, anything but the real thing, to those standing in the way of this particular manifestation of progress. Even within the traditional university research sector, the 'open society' of science is in retreat, as more funding for research comes in contracts rather than in grants, and (as in fields like biotechnology) scientists become inventors and entrepreneurs as well as discoverers. Other aspects of the traditional openness of science have also failed the test of critical scrutiny. Entry or advancement has been no more immune to the effects of prejudices based on class, race or sex than in other fields of human endeavour. Even if such regrettable practices are now less tolerated than in the past, their becoming known represents a change in the public image, the self-image and the ideology of science. These are themselves as real, and as important for the activity, as the social practices that they reflect.

Reality itself came up for effective questioning in the 1960s, for the first time in several centuries. This was not then in the form of a competing research programme, or paradigm, for mainstream science itself. Rather, altered states of consciousness, made possible on a mass scale by the achievements of modern chemical science, were invoked in a challenge to the billiard-ball universe that constitutes the metaphysical orthodoxy of science. This formed the basis for a wide-ranging critique of the supposed inhumanity and corruption of the modern scientific enterprise, in the name of the 'Counter-culture'. In such an environment, venerable pseudo-sciences moved in from the margins of respectability, to capture the interest and commitment of even the best-educated young people.

Thus in the 1960s many aspects of science that were previously unquestionable were subjected to critical scrutiny, on a large scale, in public, and to some extent from within the community that supplies science with its recruits and with its principal audience and social support. One decade of convulsions in the realm of ideas is far from sufficient to effect a rapid radical change in the large-scale social enterprise to which they relate. But in spite of the subsiding of the ferment of the 1960s, many of the ideas that achieved plausibility and power then have survived, maintaining a stable existence on the margins, some remote but some quite close, to the mainstream of the contemporary scientific-technical enterprise.

5. SOME EFFECTIVE 'ALTERNATIVE' APPROACHES

Even during the 1960s, there was a variety of positive, practical initiatives devoted to resolving particular problems revealed in the general critique. These took permanent shape during the following decade, along with critical movements that appeared quite suddenly at the end of the decade of ferment (as radical feminism); and now there is a goodly spread of stable, partly-institutionalised activities that in one way or another can be called 'alternative'.

The least impact on science has been made by the more traditional Socialist, or Marxist, critique. To see how the 'development of the means of production' can be systematically evil (as in warfare and pollution) requires a perspective not to be found in the Marxist canon; and the continued failure of the established Socialist societies to provide an example of success in science could not but weaken the force of the Marxist critique of capitalist science. The quaintly-named 'British Society for Social Responsibility in Science', which quite rapidly transformed itself from a club of left-of-centre academics to a ginger-group of young radicals, settled down to providing a valuable service in the field of occupational hazards, and also in providing a base for young professionals protesting the incompetence and corruption in their established state-welfare institutions. But there never appeared a mass base, or even an effective organised constituency, in any of the groups to which such a movement necessarily appeals. The contradiction of a movement *for* the workers, which was not *by* the workers, was never resolved. The movement for 'alternative technology' did not fare much better in terms of recruits and successful designs. Windmills and methane digestors could not fit in with modern industrial systems; and industrial processes that were small-scale, non-polluting, human *and* profitable have been elusive in practice.

By contrast, the issue of 'the environment' has found a broad and stable constituency, though not as yet a single mass institutional base. The issue is well expressed by American acronyms: NIMBY (Not In My Back Yard) groups opposing LULUs (Locally Unwanted Land Uses). These have all the strengths, and weaknesses, of special-interest activist movements. For them, the beneficence and openness of science are in discredit, as well as the innocence and integrity of the corporate 'experts', where their local interests are affected. They derive much of their strength from ideologically-committed national pressure groups, such as Friends of the Earth, or (in the USA) such as the 'Citizens' Clearing-house on Hazardous Wastes'. An essential element in their struggles is a new sort of 'scientific discovery': that of investigative journalism, usually on television, which exposes the callous inhumanity of selected corporate offenders and the impotence or complicity of State regulatory agencies.

Local 'environmental' campaigns are symbiotic with a militant 'ecological' movement, which interprets high-technology catastrophes (as Bhopal, Challenger, Chernobyl and the Rhine-poisoning) as symptoms of a deep sickness in the style and values of modern science-based civilisation. Through magazines (such as the *Ecologist*) and activist groups (such as *Greenpeace*) they drive home the message of the corruption of established science, be it on the whales, civil nuclear power or the tropical rain forests. Their positive programme calls for a transformation of lifestyles and values, along the lines of such mystical-communitarian prophets as Gandhi and Schumacher. As yet they have an effective political base only in West Germany; but unless the problems they address are either resolved or are overwhelmed by ones which are far worse, they will not go away.

In response to the ecologists' political challenge, a cynical analysis is that there are no votes in sewage. But there are votes in the home, where children, growing or as yet unborn, are exposed to insidious hazards. Through such issues, women's movements escape the contradictions inherent in their standard complaints about science: is it bad because it discriminates against women, or is it the sort of sexist, soulless grind that no sensitive person would want to go into anyway? For 'housewives' epidemiology' uses disciplined methods, sometimes quite inventive, to supplement and expose official statistics that show 'no evidence of harm' from suspected pollutants. Although on a relatively small scale as yet (after the first flush of enthusiasm in the 1970s), women's 'self-health' groups constitute a radical alternative to prevailing medical ideas about what is significant and what is 'normal' in the functions and problems of women's bodies. In that sense, they are unavoidably political; and to the extent that they make the subjective feeling of being a woman into a self-aware and shared experience, they lay the seeds for a demystification of male-dominated knowledge and ways of knowing, of which modern science is the paradigm case.

The success of 'alternative' approaches is perhaps best seen in medicine. Largely through the triumphs of bacteriological medicine (perhaps owing more than is generally admitted to soap, sewers and window-screens), the classic infectious diseases have been brought under control. Now, health hazards are known to relate as much to life-style as to germs. The legendary ancient Chinese principle of paying a doctor to keep one healthy is reflected in the American Health Maintenance Organisations. Psychogenic disease, forgotten for some centuries, has become respectable again. Different approaches to healing, until very recently dismissed and denounced as the province of charlatans and quacks, are now given grudging respect for their accomplishments, if not for their theories; examples are homeopathy, herbalism, chiropractic and acupuncture. This last, involving the manipulation of 'Qi' energy, may be a meeting point for orthodox and alternatives, as for 'East' and 'West'. Practitioners and researchers, in China and elsewhere, apply a scientific approach to the study of Qi, and let the two styles complement each other in a single course of therapy.

All such developments are still on the margins of regular medical practice; and as marginal activities they are conducted in a very different social style. They are more 'open', not only in the sense of presenting fewer barriers in the form of lengthy training, but also exhibiting none of the exclusiveness that the 'medical sects' of earlier times employed to maintain their shreds of prestige. The openness extends to varieties of the healing art that are 'alternative' in the extreme; indeed some which in England had been classed as witchcraft until the 1950s. Healing by laying on of hands, with or without contact, with or without theories of orthodox religion or of unorthodox spirituality, is now regularly administered by some thousands of persons. It is of course possible that their achievements will follow on those of Qi-energy in being explained within a slightly enriched scientific world-picture. But in the meantime, such a practice constitutes a challenge to the reality defined by the prophets of the scientific revolution, and accepted unquestioningly in the world of science ever since. It is all the more effective for being quiet, non-antagonistic and outwardly consistent with any lifestyle or medical treatment. Its practitioners and clients need not think of themselves as metaphysical revolutionaries; individually, they believe themselves simply to be giving and receiving help. It is thereby less vulnerable to being outlawed on the one hand, or to being commercialised or co-opted on the other.

With this last activity we have come a long way from what is currently accepted as 'science' in any sense of the term. But the challenge of the 'alternative' approaches is that this is itself a product of history, whose original contradictions, latent through some centuries of triumph, have now matured and manifested. What sort of interaction will develop between orthodox science and its critics and its alternative approaches is for future historians to study. But we can be sure that the orthodoxy will never be the same as in its three triumphalist centuries before the middle of our own.

NOTES

1. On Mach's philosophy, see art. 53.
2. K. R. Popper, *Conjectures and refutations* (London, 1963).
3. T. S. Kuhn, *The structure of scientific revolutions* (Chicago, 1962).
4. I. Lakatos and A. Musgrave (eds.), *Criticism and the growth of knowledge* (Cambridge, 1971).
5. P. Feyerabend, *Against method* (London, 1975).
6. D. S. Greenberg, *The politics of American science* (Harmondsworth, 1969).
7. J. D. Watson, *Double helix* (New York, 1968).
8. J. R. Ravetz, *Scientific knowledge and its social problems* (Oxford, 1971).
9. S. G. Brush, 'Should the history of science be rated X?', *Science*, 183, (1974), 1164–72.
10. B. Latour and S. Woolgar, *Laboratory life: the social construction of scientific facts* (London, 1979).

FURTHER READING

R. Carson, *Silent spring* (London, 1963).

B. Commoner, *Science and survival* (London, 1966).

P. R. Ehrlich, *Population bomb* (London, 1968).

P. F. Feyerabend, *Against method* (London, 1975).

——, *Science in a free society* (London, 1978).

I. D. Illich, *De-schooling society* (London, 1971).

H. Nowotny and H. Rose (eds.), *Countermovements in the sciences: the sociology of the alternatives to big science* (Dordrecht and London, 1979).

J. R. Ravetz, *Scientific knowledge and its social problems* (Oxford, 1971).

E. F. Schumacher, *Small is beautiful* (London, 1973).

59

NATIONALISM AND INTERNATIONALISM

BRIGITTE SCHROEDER-GUDEHUS

Scientific theory and practice are by nature international. This is so at least in the natural sciences, where knowledge is generated and communicated regardless of national boundaries, where it is cumulative regardless of national origin, and where new insights and discoveries have to be recognised universally before they can be added to the common achievement of science. 'Universalism' and 'communality' have been established as norms of scientific activity.[1] Their actual observance translates into the time-honoured practice of discussion and publication, of international exchange and collaboration. 'Scientific internationalism' is viewed as a matter of discourse and as a matter of practice. It resides in the conviction that international agreement on theory and method and international communication and collaboration among scientists are inherent to scientific work and scientific progress.[2] Scientists are therefore not only used to interacting with their counterparts from foreign countries but also depend on this interaction, since it guarantees them access to both the research front and professional recognition.

In retrospect, the history of science unfolds as a co-operative enterprise with a distinctly trans-national character. The scholars' day to day experience of common purpose, common standards and liberal communication with their peers abroad evolved for a long time quite unperturbed, it seems, by the spasms of international politics. Whether in times of peace or war, scholars corresponded with one another all over Europe. They moved easily from one country to another, spending years away from their homelands. Leibniz, for example, lived in Paris, Descartes in Holland while Euler lived firstly in St Petersburg, later in Berlin and then again in St Petersburg. The story of Sir Humphry Davy has often been told to prove that science was never at war; he went to Paris in 1813 in the middle of Anglo-French military conflict, to accept the prize that the Academy of Sciences had bestowed on him. Even plans to unite all academies of sciences in a European federation were advanced time and again by great savants, from Bacon to Leibniz and Comte. Although these ideas never materialised, the academies were bound together by a network of inter-institutional and personal relations. These ties were strengthened by bestowing membership on foreign scientists, although, as a form of international co-operation, these appointments soon lost practical significance and developed into mere gestures of reciprocal courtesy.

This does not mean, however, that within this cosmopolitan republic of letters scientific achievement, as an intellectual exploit, had not been a matter of collective pride and envy and, therefore, a possible source of tension between co-operation and competition. Scientific discoveries were not only a matter of personal fame; the glory they brought to the scientist also accrued to his native country or, where national consciousness was still in its infancy, to his prince. Scientific communities started staking their claims in terms of collective world rank and leadership. After the prominence of English and Scottish science in the seventeenth and eighteenth centuries, France took over at the turn of the nineteenth century, until Germany set out to repatriate the science of chemistry and to belie the dictum that 'la chimie est une science française'. However, difficult conflicts of loyalty between the principles of scientific internationalism and the fatherland's claim to undivided commitment, which were so common later on, hardly occurred before the nation state had gradually evolved into its modern form after the French Revolution and taken ideological hold of its citizenry and before scientific research had become a factor of industrial and then military strength in the late nineteenth century.

Yet scientific internationalism experienced what seemed to be its most spectacular manifestation in the nineteenth century. It was a period of intense scientific growth: with the expansion of knowledge came disciplinary differentiation, increasing theorisation and data collecting. Doing science became a profession; the abstracting journal had to be invented to deal with the flood of scientific publications. The diffusion of knowledge, and scientific intercourse in general, greatly benefited not only from improved printing and publishing techniques but also increasingly from the development of more and cheaper means of transportation. Great scholars and renowned institutions attracted foreign students and assistants and their discoveries and work became the dominant avenues through which schools of scientific thought and practice spread from one country to another.[3] These intellectual influences were not confined to theories and research problems but extended to institutional models and concepts of academic life and teaching methods, such as the École Polytechnique, Liebig's seminar or, later, the German university and research system in general. However, foreign theories, concepts and techniques from abroad were not always received without difficulties, especially when they ran counter to the views prevailing within powerful national groups. This was illustrated by successive failures to elect Darwin to the French Académie des Sciences where Lamarck-ians were dominant. Intellectual resistance would occasionally take on the accent of patriotic warnings against the surrender to foreign influence, or point to the imprint of foreign mentality, as happened later, during the First World War, when Pierre Duhem rejected relativity as a product of German *esprit géométrique*. Duhem had been interested in the study of national styles in the pursuit of science, especially physics, since the 1890s.[4]

One of the most spectacular reflections of scientific internationalism in the nineteenth century was the development of international congresses and associations. From one or two congresses held annually in the 1850s, their number grew steadily to an average of thirty at the turn of the century. International scientific and scholarly associations proliferated at the same rate during that period, rising to more than 500 on the eve of the First World War. Much of this co-operation was generated in response to problems arising from scientific and technical progress and on the initiative of public administrations. The greater part, however, reflected the needs of national research communities, constantly expanding with the growth and increasing differentiation of scientific disciplines. At the end of the century, the academies felt compelled finally to form a federation, the International Association of Academies, in the hope of providing the authoritative co-ordination which, they felt, was necessary to forestall the ill effects of unbridled initiatives in international co-operation. The eagerness to establish contacts and collaboration with foreign counterparts was not, however, particular to scientists. It pervaded practically all sectors of human activity and thought, from practitioners of law to philatelists and from apple-growers to the advocates of international arbitration. The number of international meetings and organisations did not increase at a higher rate in science than it did in other fields. Nevertheless, with its unquestioned claim to universality and its prestigious tradition of foreign relations, science enjoyed specific status. Scientific internationalism was in the public eye. Those involved in projects and speculations on peaceful solutions to international disputes and on a new world order liked to point to the international scientific community as a potential model.[5] Scientists themselves were generally not insensible to the parallel. However, actual commitments on their behalf to the prevention of international conflict scarcely extended beyond lofty references to bridge-building and the supra-national fraternity of science, uttered by distinguished scientists delivering cere-monial speeches or writing obituaries.

Indeed, the impressive expansion of international scientific activities and the enthusiastic endorsement of international co-operation in the late nineteenth century occurred during a period of increasing political tension and great power rivalries. Public opinion was deeply involved in these rivalries which, in some instances, had become important elements of collective self-awareness and national sense of purpose. Although one cannot presume, of course, that all men of science were necessarily unanimous on specific matters of their country's foreign policy, it is fairly obvious that few, if any, would have taken exception to the principle that the nation's power and prestige should be given highest priority over any other consideration. It was a matter of both personal patriotism and corporate interest that motivated the scientific communities to endeavour to see their contribution to their country's strength and glory properly recognised by both government and the public. As the so-called science-based industries began to prove their importance in the struggle for world markets, the argument that scientific pre-eminence was crucial to great power status became all the more convincing. Although a close link between research on the one hand, and industrial or military implementation on the other, existed in only a few scientific disciplines, the state found itself enjoined to finance research for the sake of the national interest. Inevitably, such declarations assumed nationalistic overtones – one of the favourite arguments being that, without adequate backing for research, the country was in danger of being overtaken by the scientific advances of other nations.

It seems difficult to imagine how this attachment of science to national interest could be reconciled with the commitment to scientific internationalism and the enthusiasm for international collaboration witnessed by the growing number of meetings, associations and projects. There can be no doubt, indeed, that during this politically troubled period the norms of science had an international constituency. If any proof were needed, it is certainly provided by the institution of the Nobel prizes at the turn of the century: the very possibility of creating the award depended entirely on the world-wide recognition and acceptance of the criteria which the awarding body would bring to bear on its decisions. The apparent contradiction between scientific internationalism and patriotic fervour became the object of much scrutiny and soul-searching when the international scientific community split wide open in 1914 and remained entrenched in opposite camps for years after the war was over. Some questioned the authenticity of pre-war internationalism; others blamed its loss on the insanity of war. Gradually, it became popular to view the nineteenth century as the golden age of international science, lost forever after the 'perversion' of science in the war effort, particularly in the development of toxic gas. This view is simplistic in that it tends to interpret the scientists' tendency to overlook national boundaries and political disagreements as correlative to more or less identical tendencies in their outlook on world politics. Harping on the dilemma scientist-citizens were facing in 1914, many later observers seem to suppose that the majority of those living at the time viewed the problems of international scientific collaboration exclusively or primarily in terms of adherence to either nationalism or internationalism. The case is otherwise. The international dimension of the collaborative structures was far from being the principal issue at stake when scientists in the generations before the First World War met to form their organisations or to elaborate their joint projects: it was really no more than an accessory feature. The question most widely and most seriously discussed in this context by both organisers and bystanders had more to do with the changes in the social conditions of research and in the production of knowledge than with reflections on internationalism and world order. Scientists were striving to come to terms with the transformations that scientific activity as such had undergone in the span of a generation.

Scientific knowledge had, by the end of the nineteenth century, ramified into a great number of disciplines and specialties, and scientific activity required more and more people with competence in clearly restricted fields. Whether or not one deplored this fragmentation, research had ceased to be an essentially individual occupation and was, in many fields, in the process of becoming an organised activity. More than ever, agreement had to be reached over nomenclature and units of measurement; large-scale observations and compilations required the introduction of division of labour as did the objective of reducing expenditure through large shared projects. The various forms of international scientific collaboration come out, indeed, primarily as prolongations of organisational requirements that had initially appeared at national level. Disciplinary differentiation versus the unity of science and the transformation of research into a collective, organised activity versus the creative effort of the individual were the topics of discussion among men of science and, indeed, of all scholarly disciplines at the turn of the century. The proponents of the division of labour claimed that scientific activity should be opened to consideration of efficiency and rational organisation; they occasionally went so far as to point to industrial productivity and the factory, or to the laws of evolution and functional adaptation, to demonstrate the advantages of international scientific cooperation. 'What is wanted in science is organisation!'[6] The International Association of Academies was in fact the first attempt to centralise the coordination of international scientific activities, that is, to organise those activities internationally in keeping with the 'great international scientific enterprise'.[7]

Scientific internationalism – the 'ideology' that was supposed to enable men of science to benefit from the advantages of international collaboration and recognition, yet to remain irreproachable patriots – advanced all the more easily in that the two poles of potential conflict were separated by a seemingly neutral no man's land: common enthusiasm for the rational organisation of scientific work.[8] Scientific internationalism was then neither conceived nor regarded as a force to offer opposition to constraints that might one day bear upon the individual at the political level. Except in the writings of outspoken pacifists, there are scarcely any statements to be found about the bridges of science holding up in the event of conflicts involving the nation's vital interests. 'Par la science, pour la patrie' was the catchword of the French Association for the

Advancement of Science, but stands very well for the dominant attitude in all national scientific communities. (See art. 61.)

In the months following the outbreak of the First World War, scientists in all the countries involved set out enthusiastically to participate in the war effort; those who could not expect their competence to be of immediate military or economic use threw themselves at the front of the psychological war. There were a few exceptions, of whom Albert Einstein was without doubt the most prominent. Einstein's overwhelming importance and renown (as well as the tendency to ascribe political bearing to scientific internationalism) has made it popular to consider pacifism as being a standard component of a 'true' scientist's mental set-up. Yet Einstein was extremely isolated in Germany and he had no equivalent among scientists in other countries at war. Among those men of learning who refrained from joining the battlefield of threats and insults and who openly deplored the collapse of collaboration and civilised relations, the proportion of scientists was by no means preponderant.

After the war, the international scientific community remained deeply divided. Neither the principles of scientific internationalism nor the well-proven effectiveness of international co-operation were able to overcome the obstacles of acrimony and vindictiveness that had built up during the military conflict, when many of the pre-war links were ostentatiously severed. Medals and honorary degrees had been returned, membership of academies and learned societies publicly revoked or renounced and many international scientific organisations disbanded. However, within the boundaries of military alliances, international scientific and technical co-operation continued. Before the war ended, a group of Western academies – of the United Kingdom, France, Italy, Belgium and the United States – decided to replace the old International Association of Academies with a new organisation that would exclude representatives from the Central Powers and their allies. The International Research Council was officially founded in 1919 by the academies or equivalent organisations of countries that had been at war with Germany; academies of former neutral nations were invited to join and did so in 1920. The Council set out immediately to create international scientific unions which were to replace the pre-war associations and congresses in all major disciplines, and serve to unite international scientific activities under its umbrella.

The 'boycott' of German science was officially justified with the moral necessity to put an end to the German drive for hegemony – a tendency which the founders of the Council had observed as much in German science as in the Kaiser's foreign policy. The unfortunate 'appeal to the civilised world', signed by 93 German intellectuals in October 1914, was cited as the expression *par excellence* of the German professors' arrogance, their endorsement of crime and their compromise with power. This document was deemed to provide sufficient grounds to have them rejected from the circle of civilised nations. Regarding the norms of scientific internationalism, the most militant proponents of the boycott conceded that these limitations imposed on international collaboration might well temporarily impair the progress of knowledge, but, given the moral imperatives, they were ready to accept these disadvantages. Fairly effective during the early post-war years, the boycott gradually lost its hold as the international climate improved in the wake of French-German *rapprochement*, thereby depriving the hard-liners of a psychologically supportive environment. However, it took pressure from the governments – who were anxious that public opinion should not work against their policies of reconciliation – to get scientific institutions moving in the same direction and to obtain an invitation to the German academies to join the International Research Council. Political pressure on leading academics prevailed in England, France and Belgium. It failed in Germany. German scientists had reacted with extreme bitterness to their exclusion from international scientific affairs and it had not taken them long to launch a no less militant 'counter-boycott'. They claimed, moreover, that scientific performance and scientific prestige had to make up for the other elements of great power status which Germany had lost through its defeat and that the imperatives of national survival had to take precedence over scientific internationalism. The German academies handled the official invitation dilatorily, and did not join the Council (or its successor, the International Council of Scientific Unions, formed in 1931) until after the Second World War.

While the differences between organised international scientific co-operation before and after the First World War are striking, it is more difficult to assess the commitment to scientific internationalism on the individual level. Personal contacts among scholars of former enemy countries and joint projects between them had been discreetly restored soon after the war had ended, and efforts had been made – especially on the part of the neutral academies – to lessen the effects of the boycott and to hasten its revocation. Emerging fields such as nuclear physics generated a certain amount of international collaboration without much attention being paid to the policies of official organisations. Political rifts within the international scientific community continued, however, to have repercussions in matters involving competition and recognition, such as candidacies for the Nobel prize, invitations to academic functions or publication practices of scientific journals.[9] In the late 1920s, international scientific relations were proceeding with less and less interference from the official 'umbrella' organisation. The scientists who had been most instrumental in bringing about this 'normalisation' did not consider scientific internationalism a matter of political commitment. Some had, on the contrary, a record of staunch patriotism, such as Fritz Haber, who had not hesitated during the war to transform his chemistry into a deadly weapon. These scientists simply considered international communication and collaboration an indispensable factor of scientific progress.

The new upswing of international collaboration went to pieces in the early 1930s, when Hitler came to power in Germany. 'Internationalism' of any kind was anathema to national-socialist ideology; science – just as any other product of the human mind – was proclaimed to be racially determined, and Jewish scientists were dismissed and driven out of the country in their hundreds. Many others, such as Albert Einstein, who happened to be abroad, decided not to return. It should be mentioned, though, that while the postulate of 'Aryan science' was the most blatant repudiation of scientific universalism, it was not the only one.[10] The extreme form of Lamarckism known as 'Lysenkoism' became the official doctrine of the Soviet Communist Party only in 1948, but Trofim Lysenko had professed his interpretation of evolution since the 1930s and had succeeded in dismissing Mendelian genetics (it was only in the 1960s that 'Lysenkoism' was definitely discredited).[11]

The number of refugees increased when, during the Second World War, German armies occupied one European country after another. Niels Bohr who fled from Denmark in 1943 was one of the most prestigious exiles. Many of them found refuge in Britain and in the United States, and a few contributed to that dramatic demonstration of international scientific collaboration, the atomic bomb.[12]

Some of these nuclear scientists – among whom Niels Bohr was prominent – were convinced that the availability of nuclear explosives required changes in the concept and conduct of international relations and foreign policy commensurate with the unprecedented power of the new weaponry. They hoped that the threat of nuclear destruction would force diplomats and politicians to seek the only alternative to a deadly arms race, that is, international co-operation in all fields related to nuclear energy. They were eager to point out that the leaders of world politics would only have to follow the long established practice of the international scientific community, the practice of openness and mutual trust. These hopes did not materialise,[13] but physicists remained at the forefront in the struggle for *détente*. They did have their moments of glory, for example in the early years of the Pugwash movement, when American and Soviet physicists met in defiance of the Cold War.[14] They were instrumental in opening and maintaining lines of communication between East and West and became associated as closely as ever with the diplomats involved in the discussions surrounding nuclear disarmament and arms control, such as in the 1958 Conference of Experts and in the nuclear test ban negotiations of the early 1960s.[15]

Invariably, scientific internationalism has had to contend with new obstacles. New loyalties have emerged in conflicts over social justice and economic order. While the claims of patriotism may have softened over the generations, the traditions of international science are challenged in the post-war world by difficulties of another order of magnitude. Considerations of national security and the diminishing distance between basic research and technical application have restricted the free movement of scientists and scientific ideas more than ever before. As important assets to national strength, scientists enjoy considerable attention from their governments on whom, in turn, they depend for their livelihood and the material conditions of their work. While international collaboration has reached unprecedented volume, scope and institutionalisation, the relationship between science and the state has dramatically tightened.[16]

CONCLUSION

The political attitudes of scientists as citizens have been increasingly studied since the 1960s with due attention to periods of international conflict, such as the First World War and its aftermath, which was obviously less fraught with transnational ideological concerns than the Second World War. Since scientists in all countries at war aligned themselves very much in the same way as the educated population in general, their attitudes attracted the historians' interest mainly in so far as these attitudes were unexpected or deviant, that is, in contrast to what were supposed to be the principles of scientific internationalism. It is in this perspective, then, that most of the work has been undertaken.[17] Only a few studies have so far addressed themselves directly to the concept of 'scientific internationalism' and its meaning and significance in connection with political attitudes.[18]

As with all investigations into attitudes and behaviour, research into scientific internationalism and scientists' actual adherence to internationalist values has had to face methodological problems regarding reliable indicators. As public pronouncements of prominent scholars are clearly insufficient, the above-mentioned studies have largely drawn on unpublished archives, which not only contain the private utterances of a wide range of scientists, but also document their gestures and actions. The statistical analysis of nominations for the Nobel prize, that is, of nominators' preferences in terms of nationality of the nominees, has tapped a source of valuable precision.[19]

The extracting of historical evidence to support the contention that scientific internationalism is not a political concept and that, especially, it does not make a man of science immune against nationalist agitation, has prompted criticism from disapproving scientists who, often on the basis of personal recollections or the life stories of particular scholars, have tried to correct what they consider to be unjustified charges.[20] The rhetoric of scientific internationalism as a virtuous pursuit ultimately to the benefit of world peace tends also to be perpetuated at least tangentially in official institutional histories and treatises.

Those who are determined to hold onto their view that scientists derive some intrinsic feeling of internationalism in political matters from the universality of science have still further disappointments in store. Recent developments in the sociology of science may well, indeed, lead to a critical reappraisal of one of the basic constituents of scientific internationalism, that is, the universal nature of scientific knowledge itself. So far, reflections on the existence of specific national traits have been restricted to characteristics of research activities, such as scientific styles, theoretical versus empirical dispositions and research directions, as well as to mental aberrations such as the proclamation of 'Aryan' science. Now the 'constructivist' view of science endeavours to demonstrate that cultural and social factors, operating both within the research community and in interaction with the surrounding society, affect the content of science as well as its direction.[21] To the extent that the view of a culturally and socially determined content of scientific knowledge gains acceptance, the postulate of universality will be directly challenged.

The difficulty of reaching a consensus on nationalism and internationalism in science that would also include the practitioners of the scientific *métier* does not come from differences of *problématique* and approach alone. The difficulty is also rooted in the fact that the notions of 'nationalism' and 'internationalism' suffer from a high degree of imprecision; they are not, after all, ahistorical concepts.

NOTES

1. D. Crane, 'Transnational networks in basic science', *International organisation*, 25, 3 (1971), 585–601; see also *Sociology of the scientific community* (Section II/8).
2. P. Forman, 'Scientific internationalism and the Weimar physicists: the ideology and its manipulation in Germany after World War I', *Isis*, 64 (1973), 155; J. J. Salomon, 'The internationale of science', *Science studies*, I (1971), 23–42.
3. L. Graham, 'The formation of Soviet research institutes: a combination of revolutionary innovation and international borrowing', *Social studies of science*, 5 (1975), 303–29; H. Hawkins, 'Transatlantic discipleship: two American biologists and their German mentor', *Isis*, 71 (1980), 197–210.
4. See on Duhem's observations on national characteristics of science H. W. Paul, *The sorcerer's apprentice. The French scientists' image of German science, 1840–1919* (Gainesville, 1972), pp. 54–76.
5. L. S. Woolf, *International government*. Two reports prepared for the Fabian Society Research Department (London, 1916), p. 317; G. Sarton, 'L'histoire des sciences et l'organisation internationale', *Isis*, 29 (1938), 311–25.
6. M. Foster, 'The international medical congress', *Nature*, 49 (1894), 563.
7. Koenigliche Akademie der Wissenschaften, Mathematisch-physikalische Klasse, *Sitzungsberichte*. Munich, 16 November 1901, vol. 31, p. 420.
8. P. Forman, *Isis*, 64 (1973), 153–6.
9. E. Crawford, J. L. Heilbron, 'The Kaiser-Wilhelm-Institute in Basic Science and the Nobel Institution', in *Wissenschaft im Spannungsfeld von Politik und Gesellschaft*. Festschrift zum 75 jährigen Bestehen der Max-Planck-gesellschaft zur Förderung der Wissenschaften (Munich, 1989).
10. A. D. Beyerchen, *Scientists under Hitler. Politics and the physics community in the Third Reich* (New Haven, 1977).
11. D. Joravsky, *The Lysenko affair* (Chicago, 1985).
12. M. Gowing, *Britain and atomic energy, 1939–1945* (London, 1964); R. G. Hewlett and O. E. Anderson, *History of the US AEC*. Vol 1: *The new world, 1939–1946* (Philadelphia, 1962);

S. R. Weart and G. Weiss-Szilard, *Leo Szilard: his version of the facts* (Cambridge, Mass., 1978); S. R. Weart, *Scientists in power* (Cambridge, Mass., 1979).

13. M. J.Sherwin, *A world destroyed. The atomic bomb and the grand alliance* (New York, 1975).

14. J. Rotblat, *Scientists in quest for peace. A history of the Pugwash Conferences* (Cambridge, Mass., 1972); M. J. Pentz and G. Slovo, 'The political significance of Pugwash' in W. W. Evan, (ed.), *Knowledge and power in a global society* (London and Beverly Hills, 1981), pp. 175–203.

15. R. Gilpin, *American scientists and national policy making* (Princeton, 1962); H. K. Jacobson and E. Stein, *Diplomats, scientists and politicians. The United States and the nuclear test ban negotiations* (Ann Arbor, 1966). J. F. Pilat, R. E. Pendley and C. K. Ebinger (eds.), *Atoms for peace: an analysis after thrity years* (Boulder, 1985).

16. D. Dickson, *The new politics of science* (New York, 1984); P. Forman, 'Behind quantum electronics: national security as basis for physical research in the United States, 1940–1960', *Historical studies in the physical sciences*, *181*, (1987), 149–229.

17. See, e.g. C. S. Gruber, *Mars and Minerva. World War I and the uses of higher learning in America* (Baton Rouge, 1975); H. W. Paul, *The sorcerer's apprentice. The French scientists' image of German science, 1840–1919* (Gainesville, 1972); D. J. Kevles, 'Into hostile political camps . . .', *Isis*, 62 (1970), 47–60; L. Badash, 'British and American views of the German menace in World War I', *Notes & records of the Royal Society London*, 34 (1979), 91–121; J. Dauben, 'Mathematicians and World War I: the international diplomacy of G. H. Hardy and Gosta Mittag-Leffler', *Historia mathematica*, 7 (1980), 261–88.

18. P. Forman, *Isis*, 64 (1973), *Les scientifiques et la paix. La communauté scientifique internationale au cours des années 20* (Montreal, 1978); —— 'Division of labour and the common good: the International Association of Academies, 1899–1914' in C. G. Bernhard, E. Crawford and P. Soerbom (eds.), *Science, technology and society in the time of Alfred Nobel* (New York, 1982), pp. 3–20; P. Alter, 'The Royal Society and the International Association of Academies', *Notes & records of the Royal Society London*, 34 (1980), 241–64; A. H. Teich, 'Politics and international laboratories: a study of scientists' attitudes', in A. H. Teich (ed.), *Scientists and public affairs* (Cambridge, Mass. 1974), pp. 173–235. See also D. C. Watt's review of M. J. Sherwin, *A world destroyed*, in *Science*, 194 (8 Oct. 1976), 174–5.

19. E. Crawford, John L. Heilbron (1989); E. Crawford, 'Internationalism in science as a casualty of the First World War: relations between German and Allied scientists as reflected in nominations for the Nobel prizes in physics and chemistry', *Social science information*, 27 (1988), 2, 163–201.

20. E.g. A. G. Cock, 'Chauvinism and internationalism in science: the International Research Council, 1919–1926', *Notes & records of the Royal Society London*, 37 (1983), 249–88.

21. See *Sociological theories of scientific knowledge* (Section II/9).

FURTHER READING

E. Crawford, J. L. Heilbron, 'The Kaiser-Wilhelm-Institute in basic science and the Nobel Institution', in *Wissenschaft im Spannungsfeld von Politik und Gesellschaft. Festschrift zum 75 jährigen Bestehen der Max-Planck-gesellschaft zur Förderung der Wissenschaften* (Munich, 1989).

P. Forman, 'Scientific internationalism and the Weimar physicists: the ideology and its manipulation in Germany after World War I', *Isis*, 64 (1973), 151–80.

H. W. Paul, *The sorcerer's apprentice. The French scientists' image of German science, 1840–1919* (Gainesville, 1972).

B. Schroeder-Gudehus, 'Division of labour and the common good: the International Association of Academies, 1899–1914', in C. G. Bernhard, E. Crawford, P. Sorbom (eds.), *Science, technology and society in the time of Alfred Nobel* (Oxford, New York, 1982), pp. 3–20.

60

SCIENCE AND IMPERIALISM

LEWIS PYENSON

In his Massey Lectures for 1974, sponsored by the Canadian Broadcasting Company, George Steiner recalled Claude Lévi-Strauss's discussion, a generation earlier, of what happened when men and women from the North Atlantic world discovered peoples existing in innocence and unity with nature:

> Coming upon these shadows of the remnants of Eden, Western man set out to destroy them. He slaughtered countless guiltless peoples. He clawed down the forests, he charred the savannah. Then his fury of waste turned on the animal species. One after another of these was hounded into extinction or into the factitious survival of the zoo. This devastation was often deliberate: it resulted directly from military conquest, from economic exploitation, from the imposition of uniform technologies on native life-styles. Millions perished or lost their ethnic heritage and identity.

It made little difference whether the invaders were mercenary or spiritual, if they sought to rob or to instruct:

> The gifts which the white man had brought – medical gifts, material, institutional – proved fatal to their recipients. Whether he came to conquer or to proselytize, to exploit or to medicate, Western man brought devastation. Possessed, as it were, by some archetypal rage at his own exclusion from the Garden of Paradise, by some torturing remembrance of that disgrace, we have scoured the earth for vestiges of Eden and laid them waste wherever we have found them.[1]

These were, in Steiner's view, among the principal discontents of the civilising mission.

However one views the mission – as an impetus or as a justification for expansion – it will be evident that the final product has generally been a world away from the intended result. Despite nearly a century of resident French law professors and magistrates, Napoleonic Code lies shredded in present-day Iran and Vietnam. The tradition of political diversity and freedom of expression, so central to the Netherlands, is conspicuously absent in modern Indonesia. Universal suffrage, a central tenet of twentieth-century Britain, is nowhere to be found in present-day South Africa.

1. THE SPREAD OF WESTERN TRADITIONS

The reflection of European canons is frequently distorted in former colonies and satrapies, though this is not so when dealing with force and those who control it. Generalissimos and field marshals the world over wear the jackets and caps of British junior officers during the First World War, albeit weighted down with a bit more wampum. Roughnecks, game wardens and nurses also wear similar uniforms. Instruments of record are standard issue: in place of clay tablets, scrolls, and tree-bark one finds books and the standard-issue side-arm of educated women and men – the ball-point pen. The engines of power – machine guns, automobiles, hydro-electrical power stations, nuclear reactors – all look basically alike. Here small variations on common themes reveal much about cultural values and a civilisation's heritage. The presence or absence of a Western cravat in a military uniform, of an abacus in a market town or of a crucifix in a hospital ward give voice to the varieties of cultural adaptation.

While costume, architecture, modes of conveyance, means of destruction and even the design of machinery easily admit of some variation, the same may not be said about the mathematical laws ascribed to the physical world. One finds $F = ma$ and $PV = nRT$, not $F = ma^2$ or $PV = nRe^T$, whether taught in Rabat or Bandung, Tananarive or Quito. In contrast with the qualitative sciences, which provide evidence of astonishing cross-cultural mutations, on the periphery of the Western world physical laws are often conveyed unsceptically to a fault, as if local Immanuel Velikovskys, Herbert Dingles, David Bohms and Joseph Webers have been reluctant to publicise unfashionable scientific points of view.[2] It would be a mistake to ascribe such uniformity to practical concerns: Newton's laws are no more required for building reliable bridges than Copernicus's system was an indispensable element of sure navigation. Manipulating the mathematical laws of nature is seen as an unambiguous sign of having become civilised, in much the way that nineteenth-century European capitalists patronised science in order to appear before the world as cultured men. This observation is central to any discussion of science and imperialism.

2. STUDY AND MUSEUMS IN COLONIAL LOCATIONS

Our present understanding suggests that historians who seek to understand the relationship between imperialism and Western technology, agriculture, medicine, geology or anthropology will have to be prepared to face the daunting prospect of disentangling the ideological and practical uses of these disciplines from the rather more abstract claims of disciplinary discourse.[3] A tropical botanical garden or hospital obviously served the practical interests of imperialist overlords while catering to the rather more abstract, intellectual pursuits of European-trained researchers. Anthropological expeditions, while seeking knowledge about essential human proclivities, served to catalogue indigenous social structures in a way useful to the military authorities. The point here is less to discourage scholars from studying such questions than to suggest the difficulty of dealing with pure science in these fields as it relates to the imperialist condition.

One approach for analysing the descriptive sciences and the forces of imperialism has been taken by Susan Sheets-Pyenson in her continuing study of natural history museums in colonial and neo-colonial locations. There are many advantages of this focus with regard to a comparative study. Most obviously, the museums represent major commitments of material and human resources in the service of science at places peripheral to imperial, metropolitan centres. The architecture housing museum activity, no less than its social organisation, directly reflects imperial dreams and designs. Museums are intended both to instruct local peoples and to advance scientific knowledge. Museum curators deal extensively with metropolitan and local colleagues, as well as with a broad spectrum of people of all sorts representing local potentates and distant princes. What facilitates a connection here with pure learning is the extraordinarily feeble link between colonial museums and the immediate practical needs of colonial exploiters: museums are instruments of a metropolitan civilising mission. That the focus of the present essay is directed to the exact sciences must not obscure significant research now undertaken by students of the descriptive sciences.[4]

3. HOW RESEARCH WAS ESTABLISHED

Beyond the North Atlantic world, research and teaching in the exact sciences have for the past 150 years closely followed the pattern set in the principal industrial nations of Europe and North America – with Western objects of veneration being variously forced on and invited into non-Western settings. Studying the diffusion of these sciences bears especially upon our understanding of cultural imperialism. Metropolitan strategies for spreading science in a 'national' mould and peripheral responses to imperialist incursion come into clear focus when restricted to the activity of physicists and astronomers as vectors of new ideas. Practical considerations, such as finding cures for tropical diseases or deposits of gold and oil, recede in favour of examining how largely impractical scientific discourse served the ends of empire. Ultimately, such an inquiry extends the promise of deciding the extent to which 'pure' scientific discourse has, in the recent past, been insulated from socio-economic reality.[5]

The topic of cultural imperialism and exact sciences is most clearly engaged by considering imperialist strategies for creating institutions abroad. Among the many facets to building institutions on the periphery, the most transparent is that dealing with the movements of scientists acting as vectors of scientific diffusion. In pursuing this line of investigation, no identity need be hypothesised between individual career aims and national policies or goals. Western scientists on the periphery will be seen to have worked in patterns reflecting their metropolitan training. In seeking to explicate the laws governing their new physical surroundings, they found inspiration from the work of their teachers. At the same time, just like a physicist or astronomer situated in a provincial European setting, they generally adapted their styles of research to local conditions. They were, at all events, caught in a system about which they were poorly informed. Referring to the ferocious exploitation of Latin America by the North Atlantic world, Eduardo Galeano has observed:

> For its foreign masters and for our commission-agent bourgeoisie, who have sold their souls to the devil at a price that would have shamed Faust, the system is perfectly rational; but for no one else, since the more it develops, the greater its disequilibrium, its tensions, and its contradictions.[6]

Given their self-image as representatives of higher learning, the physicists and astronomers in 'heathen' regions kept at arm's length from forced-labour gangs and plantation squalor. They also fulfilled a role as agents of imperial design, but not without experiencing something of the uncertainties faced by Galeano's wretched victims. In their stories one reads the dialectic of master and servant, and the counterpoint of tradition and innovation.

4. THE BLOCHIAN TRADITION

As will have been evident from the preceding discussion, comparative history serves to cast strategies of cultural imperialism in bold relief. The technique of comparison, wielded incisively and convincingly by Marc Bloch and his followers, requires most centrally that one phenomenon be considered in several settings. Blochian comparatists would reject, for example, an attempted comparison between German professors of paleontology and German professors of physics at the national university of La Plata, Argentina; nor would they admit to the comparative corpus a study of French, Italian, American and German astronomers at that university. To deal with the overseas diffusion of the exact sciences, the most fruitful approach seems to involve two levels of comparison: for a given kind of scientific endeavour, interest is focused on comparable settings that received institutions inspired by different imperialist nations.[7]

5. PROBLEMS AND CRITICISMS

Having identified the central relevance of comparative history of science, it is well to address, if only to deflect, the criticisms that may be levelled against the present undertaking. A traditional-minded colleague may protest that there is not, as yet, a body of specialised texts which permit a fruitful comparison to be made. The range of linguistic tools required for such a comparison is dauntingly complex. The archives, if they exist, are scattered around the world in various states of preservation and decay. The scientific significance of research in these undeveloped countries is far from clear. Finally, until we understand the dimensions of science in the North Atlantic world, it is premature to study its diffusion to non-Western settings.

The response to these criticisms may be summarised in the following way. The reputed lack of secondary sources reflects nothing more than bibliographical insouciance. Science in imperial settings has been the object of intense and detailed analysis, not a little of it appearing from presses in such places as Buitenzorg, Manila, Shanghai, Beirut, Tananarive and Montreal. The history of scientific institutions beyond the North Atlantic world is probably documented in print at least as extensively as that of institutions situated in metropolitan centres.[8] The shelf list of the New York Public Library reveals that much of this published literature is readily available to researchers in the North Atlantic world.

It seems strange that historians, of all people, would throw up their hands when faced by a large and relevant literature in a new language. Young men and women have, after all, the enthusiasm to learn what is required, while senior scholars tenured in academical bowers have the leisure to acquire new tools of the trade. Confessions of linguistic insufficiency are, in any event, largely an English speaking affliction. As the twentieth century draws to an end, and as the dominance of English as a language of learning and trade erodes, many scholars will find themselves acquiring the elements of Indonesian, Japanese and Arabic, among other non-Western tongues.

As far as archives go, they are where you find them. Many thousands of linear feet of unpublished material await the historian of science in such locations as Jakarta, Mexico City and Buenos Aires, and well mapped-out holdings may be found in metropolitan centres of empire. Historians of the Dutch, French and British empires have, in fact, mined metropolitan archives for generations. It should be emphasised that paper in the tropics, suffering no extreme fluctuations in temperature and humidity, survives rather better than in temperate climates, even taking account of damage sustained by insects and fungus.

Historians of science have certainly devoted much of their attention to chronicling great discoveries and innovations, and for this reason it is not irrelevant to indicate that Nobel prizes, up to 1970, were awarded to a dozen researchers who spent a substantial portion of their life in colonies or in settings beyond the North Atlantic world.[9] It can hardly be justifiable, however, to assign the study of the history of science according to the incidence of medals and prizes. Historians of science are mistaken if they think to define their role as the *chiens de basse-cour* of the scientific academies.

6. THE RELATIONSHIP BETWEEN SCIENCE AND WESTERN EXPANSION

To focus history of science exclusively on Western Europe because that is where, during the period before 1900, modern science flowered, would be like submerging the histories of Western European democracies in that of Great Britain simply because Westminster is the mother of parliaments. One need not embrace Immanuel Wallerstein's notion of the modern world system to affirm that much of Western European culture (in its broadest sense) is of extra-European origin. Examples of this are cocoa, coffee, tea, tobacco, sugar, opium and hashish, which gave rise to what David Landes has called 'the big fix'; foodstuffs such as potatoes, tomatoes and spices, whose diffusion fills a large literature in social history; shrubs, flowers and domestic pets; fabrics and manufactures; strategic materials, jewels and precious metals; heraldic symbols and figures of popular speech. Both the discourse and the institutional organisation of modern science owe debts to researchers in Africa, Asia, the Americas and Oceania, and one of the clearest ways to understand that indebtedness is to study the relationship between science and Western expansion.

The obverse of the Western debt to the non-Western world is the process of modernising traditional societies along Western lines. Especially in explications and analyses of technology-transfer, the spectre of 'cultural imperialism' has loomed large. The diffuse literature on development and modernisation often takes as a fundamental tenet that, over the recent past, scientific discourse or technological expertise acted as if it were a spring or branch grafted on to one or another host stalk.[10] It is more apt, however, to consider the transferred discourse as a graft on *metropolitan* culture. The situation is much as Karel Čapek described it in another context. Čapek, who provided us with cautionary tales of robots and the unpredictability of evolution, observed:

> When all is ready the gardener tries the blade of the knife on the tip of his thumb; if the grafting-knife is sufficiently sharp it gashes his thumb and leaves an open and bleeding wound. This is wrapped in several yards of lint, from which a bud, rather full and big, develops on the finger.[11]

Scientific institutions in imperialist settings are roses on the bloodied thumb of the outstretched imperial hand. Whether and how such institutions relate to the question of autonomous development depends on texture and instance, but it may well be that their impact in this regard is less significant than generally assumed. Writing about Western education in modernising Indonesia, Slamet Iman Santoso has emphasised:

> A cultural change is a process of life, and a process in history, and probably more governed by irrational than rational or scientific forces. Science can to a certain extent only illuminate the process and make the best of it.[12]

A problem more tractable than the one Santoso proposes, though perhaps one not extending the promise of responding to a 'national need', would be to focus on the role of Dutch engineers in transforming and controlling the colonial regime of the Dutch East Indies.[13]

7. WHO THE SCIENTISTS WERE

If, then, one chooses to study scientific institutions, properly speaking, as mechanisms of scientific diffusion and as instruments of geopolitical or economic aims, individual scientists will, more often than not, form the centre of discussion. Individuals are, after all, the authors of scientific texts conceived on, and issued from, the periphery of empire. The texts may not often mark turning-points in the history of science, although even on this point the historian should be prepared for surprises. We may interpret the meanings of cultural imperialism in many ways; in the human ambitions and failings of men and women engaged in research at places considered by their colleagues to be the ends of the earth, in the cynical or unsophisticated manipulation of their lives by metropolitan functionaries and local governors and in their astonishment at being at the centre of an extraordinarily rich and confusing mixture of Western and non-Western cultures. These relatively unknown actors, outliers in every sense of the word, are the key to understanding science and imperialism.[14]

It is natural to ask whether the outliers carrying out research on the periphery constitute an identifiable set or class, or whether they are just men and women with unusual careers. Certainly the major colonial powers recruited scientists to support colonial or imperialist ambitions, both formally and informally. One need only recall La Condamine's expedition to Ecuador, Captain Bligh's voyage to Tahiti, Darwin's passage on the 'Beagle', Bragg's professorship in Adelaide, Rutherford's in Montreal, Clay's in Bandung and Einstein's travels to Argentina and the Far East. Religious societies placed hundreds of scientist missionaries overseas. The French, German, British, Dutch and American empires had greater or lesser corps of colonial scientists. And though hundreds of scientists emigrated overseas in a private capacity, many of these men and women, even when they became nationals of their place of residence, actively sought to further the interests of their native land.

926

8. SCIENCE IN THE COLONIES

A sense of the whole may be obtained from the writings of Edouard de Martonne, commandant in the colonial infantry of French West Africa and head of that colony's geographical service. He was a skilled physical scientist marooned in a place largely bereft of high French culture. The research in astronomy and geophysics carried out by his colony was far less impressive than that carried out by French institutions in Madagascar, Lebanon and China, and by analogous institutions in German, Dutch and British possessions.[15] About 1930, de Martonne agreed to produce a treatise defining the profession of *savant colonial* for Georges Hardy, an eminent apologist of French colonial policy who rose to become rector of the University of Lille. De Martonne's book (for which analogous treatments may be found in English, German and Dutch) is a stirring defence of the tasks of scientists who stand on the thin red line protecting metropolitan civilisation. Forming more of an emotional plea for attention than a record of the actual decisions taken by metropolitan policy makers, it provides a clear record of aspirations and ideologies.

Science in the colonies, in de Martonne's view, had a purpose no different from that of science in the metropolis. In both cases, scientists worked for the greater glory of the imperialist power and this dedication was, as a matter of course, to enrich all mankind:

> 'For you, that is to say, for France, for humanity!' These are words that do not appear explicitly in the contract signed in the [colonial] offices of the rue Oudinot, but they are understood implicitly in the moral pact undertaken [by the scientist] with science and with the country.

It was certainly true, for de Martonne, that scientists in the colonies encountered many more obstacles than among their colleagues in the metropolis, 'where spiritual gestation is easier, creation is clearer, where the intellectual worker benefits from a thousand intangible factors that aid his task'. For this reason, the colonial scientist had to exercise great moral fortitude and self-discipline. His role was central to the imperialist civilising mission. 'Science, inserted into our colonial conquest, will counterbalance, up to a certain point, the mercantilism that is everywhere rampant.' The colonial scientist, no doubt just like the colonial administrator, would help colonised people to transcend, 'bit by bit, the eternal childhood' where they simply copied European activity, and in this way he would help them replace 'the automatic repetition of gestures by the progressive exercise of reason'. In carrying out scientific research, the scientist gave substance to European claims of superiority. 'The mastery of nature by the man of science inspires singular respect in primitive peoples, who fear all aspects of nature.' The colonial scientist would, by his abstract activity, repress independentist feelings among subject races:

At a time when, in almost all colonies, claims are being advanced by native elites intoxicated by their recent knowledge as by a new wine, it is wise to temper this overly hurried presumption by demonstrating our scientific superiority, which alone is able perhaps to curb minds without repressing them [*d'enchaîner les esprits sans les comprimer*]: These pupils of civilisation must be persuaded that the degree of emancipation increases naturally with the degree of culture, and that nothing can replace the maturity brought by science and the awareness of these values.[16]

The colonial scientist had to respond to practical issues, but de Martonne saw his calling as an ideologically-motivated activity in pure learning. He spoke for the many hundreds of scientists who, by 1930, were employed in one or another colonial corps, as well as for numerous others who carried out scientific research overseas as altruists or as mercenaries.

9. IMPERIALIST STRATEGY

Preliminary evidence allows for the positing of a model to indicate how science has been used to further the overseas political goals of imperialist nations in their colonies and spheres of influence. The evidence is based on studies of the exact sciences as probes into the means and ends of what might loosely be called cultural imperialism.[17] An open-ended use of the term 'cultural imperialism' is deliberate. Given the present state of our knowledge, it seems best to refrain from confining the term to an overly-restrictive definition. Attitudes towards cultural imperialism exhibit variation with regard to metropolitan powers and latitude in colonial dependencies, but there is a consistent belief that the example of carrying out scientific research *overseas* constituted a cultural beachhead in the entrenchment of metropolitan domination. As de Martonne put it in his visionary programme of 1930, *savants* in the colonies were 'agents' for the propagation of metropolitan (in his case, French) 'culture', just as 'colonists and functionaries are agents of social and economic expansion'.[18]

The comparative nature of the preceding discussion permits extraction of preliminary generalisations in the form of a descriptive model. The model focuses on three, orthogonal axes of imperialist strategies: the *functionary* axis, the *research* axis and the *mercantilist* axis. These axes may be thought of as being much like the x-y-z coordinates of analytical geometry. They are suggested as a way of picturing in concrete terms the rather abstract strategies that are under discussion. It lies far from the intent here, however, to enlist the model in the service of 'quantifying' cultural imperialism.[19]

A strategy in the direction of the functionary axis would emulate French practice: a tight union of academic, military and religious interests where the desire to follow original research was depressed, if not extinguished, and where a

scientist in foreign parts remained entirely subordinate to metropolitan direct-
ives. In the French experience, a physicist or astronomer overseas was first and
foremost a functionary. He could be recalled if he incurred the displeasure of
colonial or metropolitan overlords – be these administrators in a governor
general's office, junior ministers in Paris or Jesuit superiors in France. The
guiding lines of late nineteenth- and twentieth-century French policy may be
seen succinctly in an address of 1936 by Alfred Lacroix, perpetual secretary of
the Academy of Sciences, on scientific research in French overseas territories.
In Lacroix's view, there was 'no room in our colonies for new, major agencies of
purely scientific research'. Rather, it was 'necessary to locate in the metropolis
the centre of action for scientific research carried out in *la France d'Outre-Mer*'.
The metropolitan *savants* would assign younger scientists clearly defined and
limited tasks to be carried out overseas. When their tasks were accomplished,
'the study of the material [acquired] and the discussion of the collected observations would be done in France'.[20]

The research axis suggests the drive behind German practice: a loose union
of academic, business and military interests, where the research ethic remained
paramount. A German scientist overseas was, above all, a seeker of new knowledge. He was for the most part on his own, and he pursued science by wits and
wiles. The ideology may be seen in a proposal to the Prussian Kultusministerium of 1908 written by six distinguished Göttingen scientists who argued in
favour of constructing an astrophysical branch of their university's observatory
at Windhoek, in German South West Africa:

> Scientific activity in the colonies is certainly the most noble claim that, in this
> sense, can be advanced. A colonization like that of an observatory already provides
> a seat of civilization. If it is known that an astrophysical observatory is located at
> Windhoek, the impression of wasteland and inefficiency, which seems to exist in
> wider circles about life in the Southwest, may be diminished.[21]

The scientists expressed the view that the practice of pure learning would, as a
matter of course, be relevant to the imperial designs of the state. Their proposal, in this case, bore no fruit.

Finally, a strategy in the direction of the mercantilist axis would have scientists serving business interests; research would be subordinated to solving one
or another problem in technology. Highly skilled scientists travelled overseas to
pioneer Belgian mines in Katanga and set up Canadian nuclear facilities in
Argentina, for example, but Belgian and Canadian *savants* did not initially set
up institutions of higher learning overseas. Belgium and Canada have traditionally favoured mercantilist strategies of cultural imperialism.[22]

10. VECTORS OF THE CIVILISING MISSION

Where do the Netherlands fit into this picture? Dutch practice involved a union
of academic and commercial interests, one where scientists acted as official

representatives of their state. The state, in fact, generally acted to finance higher learning only when the path had been cleared by private interests and when academic researchers had already committed themselves to the enterprise. A striking expression of the ideology behind this union may be found in a speech given in 1920 by K. A. R. Bosscha, one of Java's richest plantation owners, during the opening ceremonies of the physics laboratory at the Bandung Institute of Technology. Bosscha, who had endowed the building, left the laboratory's research programme entirely up to the new professor of physics. The governor general, in his speech, expected technicians to be produced at the institution but did not point to any direction for work at the laboratory. The professor of physics, Jacob Clay, left no doubt that he would be engaging in pure learning.[23] The Dutch experience, then, would be represented by a vector with positive components projected along all three axes.

In the absence of detailed studies, one may attempt to place the strategies of other imperialist nations in relation to these three axes. American strategy would rank high in the research ethic and high in responsiveness to metropolitan direction (there were observatories in Chile, Peru and Argentina which were controlled by metropolitan astronomers, Rockefeller Foundation investments in China and religious missionaries in Lebanon) but it does not seem centrally concerned with extracting natural resources or selling American goods. United Fruit and Standard Oil, having the United States Marines at their command, did not seem to have required the services of scientists as cultural imperialists. British strategy (for the moment leaving aside the educational vortex of the metropolis), while ranking high on the research axis, involved few controls exerted by metropolitan authorities: Canadian, Australian, South African and Indian physicists followed their lights in carrying out research. For the British, however, unlike the Americans, the trade interest was paramount: observatories were erected at coaling stations around the world in order to provide mariners with accurate time signals and weather reports. One may guess that Japanese strategy manifested strong mercantilist and functionalist characteristics while being rather weak along the research axis; at least such seems to have been the pattern in Japanese management of the Tsingtau observatory, captured from the Germans in 1914. Finally, there are imperialist countries exhibiting weak or non-existent magnitudes in the direction of any of the three axes: those on the Iberian peninsula come immediately to mind.

The institutions of higher learning that figure in such an analysis are situated in uncharted territory from the point of view of the academic historians of science who have, over the past generation, concentrated on documenting the momentous rise of knowledge in Europe and the United States. As our century draws to a close, however, the forgotten universities and observatories will loom large, in much the way that historians have come to focus attention on peoples and civilisations bypassed by an army of writers afflicted with unwavering,

Eurocentric vision. Understanding science that until now has remained largely without a history will be essential for arriving at a fuller appreciation of modern research as an inter-cultural activity.

ACKNOWLEDGEMENT

A portion of my research has been supported by the Herbert C. Pollock Award of the Dudley Observatory.

NOTES

1. George Steiner, *Nostalgia for the absolute: Massey Lectures, fourteenth series* (Toronto, 1974), p. 32.
2. I do not have a sense for the geographical distribution of heretical science, but no culture has a franchise on unfounded speculation or implausible deduction. Three cases from the southern hemisphere are instructive in this regard: Argentina's Ronald Richter, as portrayed by Mario Mariscotti in *El Secreto Atómico de Huemul: Crónica del origen de la energía atómica en la Argentina* (Buenos Aires, 1985); Brazil's César Lattes, as interviewed by José Hamilton Ribeiro, 'César Lattes, o Quixote da ciência', *Século 21*, no. 3 (1980), 48–55; and New Zealand's A. W. Bickerton, as considered by R. M. Burdon, *Scholar-errant: a biography of Professor A. W. Bickerton* (Christchurch, 1956).
3. On British technology in Africa and Asia: Daniel R. Headrick, *Tools of Empire: technology and European imperialism in the nineteenth century* (New York, 1981). On British agriculture: Lucile H. Brockway, *Science and colonial expansion: the role of the British Royal Botanic Gardens* (New York, 1979). On tropical medicine: Ann Beck, *Medicine and society in Tanganyika, 1890–1930: a historical inquiry* (Philadelphia, 1977) [American Philosophical Society, *Transactions*, 67, pt. 3], and Helmut J. Jusatz, 'Wandlungen der Tropenmedizin am Ende des 19. Jahrhunderts', in Gunter Mann and Rolf Winau, (eds.), *Medizin, naturwissenschaft, Technik und das Zweite Kaiserreich: Vorträge eines Kongresses vom 6. bis 11. September 1973 in Bad Nauheim* (Göttingen, 1977), 227–38. The special case of the French Institut Pasteur awaits detailed study, but see: C. Mathis, 'L'Oeuvre colonial de l'Institut Pasteur', *Actes et comptes-rendus de l'association colonies-sciences*, 7 (1931), 202–20. On geology in the French colonies, Raymond Furon, *Histoire de la géologie de la France d' Outre-Mer* (Paris, 1955) [*Mémoires du Muséum national d'histoire naturelle*, series C, 5]; on geology in the British colonies, Robert A. Stafford, 'Geological surveys, mineral discoveries, and British expansion, 1835–71', *Journal of Imperial and Commonwealth history*, 12 (1984), 5–32. The full spectrum of descriptive sciences in the Netherlands East Indies is surveyed in: Jakarta, Koninklijke Natuurkundige Vereeniging, *Een eeuw natuurwetenschap in Indonesië 1850–1950* (Jakarta, 1950).
4. Susan Sheets-Pyenson, 'Henry Augustus Ward and museum development in the hinterland, 1860–1890', *University of Rochester Library bulletin*, 38 (1985), 38–59; 'How to "Grow" a natural history museum: collections in colonial locations, 1850–1900', *Archives of natural history*, 15 (1988), 127–47; 'Cathedrals of science: the development of colonial natural history museums during the late nineteenth century', *History of science*, 25 (1987) 279–300; 'Civilizing by nature's example: the development of colonial natural history museums, 1850–1900', in Nathan Reingold and Marc Rothenberg (eds.), *Scientific colonialism, a cross-cultural comparison* (Washington, 1987), pp. 351–27; and especially Sheets-Pyenson's synthetic work, *Cathedrals of science: the development of colonial natural history museums during the late nineteenth century* (Montreal, 1988).
5. These points have been elaborated in Lewis Pyenson, *Cultural imperialism and exact sciences: German expansion overseas, 1900–1930* (New York and Berne, 1985); *Empire of reason: exact sciences in Indonesia, 1840–1940* (Leiden, 1989).
6. Eduardo Galeano, tr. Cedric Belfrage, *Open veins of Latin America: five centuries of the pillage of a continent* (New York, 1973), p. 14.
7. The issue of comparative history is considered in Lewis Pyenson, *Cultural imperialism* (1985),

pp. 295–9, and in Lewis Pyenson and Susan Sheets-Pyenson, 'Comparative history of science in an American perspective', *History of science in America: news and views*, 3, no. 3 (1985), 3–7. Current debate on the status of comparative history may be found in the pages of the *American historical review*, 85 (1980), 753–857, 1055–1166; 87 (1982), 123–43; and also in *Comparative studies in society and history*, 22 (1980), 143–221. A summary dismissal of comparative history is found in G. R. Elton's *Practice of history* (London, 1984), pp. 42–3.

8. Substantial histories have been published about the Jesuit scientific institutions in Beirut, Shanghai, Manila, Quito and Guatemala; all varieties of scientific institution in Canada, Australia and New Zealand; all kinds of secular institution of higher learning in Argentina and Brazil. To chronicle and justify their civilizing missions, the major imperialist nations provided extensive surveys of scientific works in the colonies.

9. Ronald Ross (1902), Ernest Rutherford (1908), William H. Bragg and William L. Bragg (1915), Charles Nicolle (1928), Christiaan Eijkman (1929), Chandrasekhara V. Raman (1930), Bernardo A. Houssay (1947), Hideki Yukawa (1949), Frank MacFarlane Burnet (1960), John C. Eccles (1963), Schinichiro Tomonaga (1963), Luis F. Leloir (1970).

10. A sense of the bewildering profusion of literature, as well as the widespread acceptance of the notion that Western technology is a 'package good', may be found in Jorge A. Sábato, *Transferencia de tecnología: Una selección bibliográfica* (Mexico City, 1978).

11. Karel Čapek, *The gardener's year*, tr. M. and R. Weatherall (1931; Madison, 1984), p. 88.

12. Slamet Iman Santoso, *Pembinaan watak tugas utama pendidikan* (Jakarta, 1981), p. 313.

13. Jacques van Doorn, *The engineers and the colonial system: technocratic tendencies in the Dutch East Indies* (Rotterdam, 1982) [Erasmus University Rotterdam, Comparative Asian Studies Programme, 6].

14. Gordon Wright, *Insiders and outliers: the individual in history* (San Francisco, 1981), pp. 4–5.

15. Edouard de Martonne, *Rapport sur les travaux astronomiques et géodésiques exécutés en Afrique Occidentale française avant la guerre 1903–1914* (Paris, 1923) [reprinted from *Afrique française*, 33 (1923), no. 4]; de Martonne, 'Magnétisme', in Comité d'études historiques et scientifiques de l'Afrique Occidentale française, *Etat actuel de nos connaissances sur l'Afrique Occidentale française*, 2 (Paris, 1926?), 353–92. Compare Georges Perrier, 'Les Travaux actuels de la Section de géodésie du Service géographique de l'Armée française', in Perrier, *Conférences faites en décembre 1925 à l'Université et à l'Ecole polytechnique de Prague* (Prague, 1929) [Masarykova Akademie Prace, Section of Natural History and Medicine, Publication no. 47], pp. 35–46.

16. Edouard de Martonne, *Le savant colonial* (Paris, 1930), quotations in sequence on pp. 151, 78, 21, 21–2, 76, 164.

17. Evidence for the model is elaborated in Lewis Pyenson, 'Pure learning and political economy: science and European expansion in the age of imperialism', in Robert Visser, *et al.*, (eds.), *New trends in the history of science* (Utrecht, in press).

18. De Martonne, *Le savant colonial* (note 16), p. 32.

19. Comparative history need not end in typologies. Aristotelian kinds seem difficult to extract from certain cases, such as that of the history of colonial cities. G. A. de Bruijne, 'The colonial city and the post-colonial world', in Robert Ross and Gerard J. Telkamp (eds.), *Colonial cities: essays on urbanism in a colonial context* (Dordrecht, 1985), pp. 231–43, on p. 236.

20. Alfred Lacroix, 'Pour une organisation des recherches scientifiques dans nos territoires d'outre-mer', *Actes et comptes-rendus de l'Association Colonies-sciences*, 13 (1937), 21–5, quotations on pp. 23–4. Lacroix's vision, unlike de Martonne's, reflected political realities.

21. Felix Klein, Eduard Riecke, Karl Schwarzschild, Woldemar Voigt, Emil Wiechert and Hermann Wagner to Kultusministerium, 14 July 1908, cited in Pyenson, *Cultural imperialism and exact sciences* (1985), p. 303.

22. This observation is by no means to deny the use of metropolitan and international scientific organisations, on the part of Canada and Belgium, to further colonial or imperialist ambitions. A striking case of the latter is how King Leopold II created and patronised the International Association for the Exploration and Civilisation of Africa in 1876 as a means of carving out a place in the sun for Belgium. In 1884–5 the International Association received widespread recognition as the Congo Free State, a *de jure* sovereign power but a *de facto* satrapy of the Belgian monarchy. The charade ended in 1907 when the Belgian parliament assumed control of the Congo Free State as Belgium's first colony. Science was absent from the International Association's agenda, unless the adventures of H. M. Stanley, its hired agent, are considered to belong to the annals of geography.

23. All the speeches are printed in Technische Hoogeschool te Bandoeng, *Opening van het Natuur-kundig Laboratorium door Zijne Excellentie den Gouverneur-Generaal van Nederlandsch-Indië, 18 maart 1922* (Bandung, [1922]). See Pyenson, *Empire of reason* (1989) pp. 143–5.

FURTHER READING

L. Pyenson, *Cultural imperialism and exact sciences: German expansion overseas, 1900–1930* (New York and Berne, 1985).

—— *Empire of reason: exact sciences in Indonesia, 1840–1940* (Leiden, 1989).

N. Reingold and Marc Rothenberg (eds.), *Scientific colonialism: a cross-cultural comparison* (Washington, 1987).

S. Sheets-Pyenson, *Cathedrals of science: the development of colonial natural history museums during the late nineteenth century* (Montreal, 1988).

61

SCIENCE AND WAR

D. E. H. EDGERTON

The relationship between science and war is much discussed but little studied. Neither historians of science nor military historians have paid the subject much attention, though both acknowledge its importance. This makes a historiographical review difficult; it becomes a plea for further research as much as a survey of what has been done.

In the absence of detailed inquiry, discussion has tended to myth. Typically the myths are those of Pandora and her Box, Prometheus (and indeed, 'The Modern Prometheus', Frankenstein), and, perhaps most famously of all, Vishnu the preserver, like 'a thousand suns', becoming 'Death, the destroyer of worlds'. By some accounts, science knew sin for the first time: innocent, truth-seeking and international, science was corrupted by worldliness or a fatal Faustian desire to know too much. Scientists become tragic gods creating 'wonder weapons' born of innocence, and therefore especially powerful: the First World War becomes the 'chemists' war', the Second the 'physicists' war'.

But all good myths have counter-myths. The ultimately peace-creating effects of weapons so terrible that only the mad or evil would force their use is, of course, the cliché of the 'nuclear age' and, indeed, of the early 'air age'. The argument goes back at least to the last century; Alfred Nobel used it with respect to his new explosives and propellants. Indeed the history of the mythology surrounding science and war would constitute an interesting study in itself, especially since the *Book of Revelations* has a place in the strategic thought of former United States President Reagan and his Secretary of Defense.

Ideological considerations explain at least some of the reasons for the lack of a significant historiography of the relations between science and war, especially in the Anglo-Saxon world. Since the nineteenth century, liberals have argued that war is destructive whereas science is seen as both the cause and the effect of progress. War is an aristocratic, feudal hangover; science, the promise of a peaceful future.[1] This antithesis, which suggests that any connections are contingent and unfortunate, has led to a serious mis-specification of questions about the relationship. Why were some scientists attracted to work on military projects? What psychological defect did they suffer from? Were the temptations of the technically sweet devil just too great? In other words, the question becomes one of the 'social responsibility of the scientist'. When war is justified, however, this same social responsibility requires the scientist to act as a modernising agent, not just by providing new weapons, but by replacing obscurantist and reactionary military thought with a rational scientific ethos.

Other political traditions have been less reticent in acknowledging the links between science and war. Nationalistic, militaristic and statist traditions of thought make no bones about the link between science and war. Culture, including scientific culture, does not exist independently of the State, and since states are inevitably in conflict, science too is inextricably involved. This tradition is, of course, notable in Wilhelmine and Nazi Germany, but also expressed itself in Edwardian Britain in the form of such anti-liberal, pro-science lobbies as the British Science Guild (see below). A modern echo of this view may be found quite explicitly in the works of Correlli Barnett, who argues that the British ruling class was so committed to an idealistic liberal ideology that it failed to build up the military, scientific and industrial power of Britain in the twentieth century.

Another important anti-liberal tradition is the Marxist one, which holds that capitalism is a cause of war, and that under capitalism, therefore, science and war are necessarily closely linked. Only under socialism could war be overcome and only then would science be able to undertake its liberating mission. To these traditional perspectives may be added a modern feminist approach, seen for example in the work of Brian Easlea, which sees both science and war arising not from aristocratic hangovers corrupting science, or from capitalism, or from the natural rivalry of nation-states, but from the dominance of men in society. Other modern critical viewpoints have been slow in taking up the theme. An exception is Bruno Vitale, who argues that there are significant affinities between the armed forces and science, especially in that both seek order.

Special mention needs to be made of E. P. Thompson who, in an influential manifesto for the modern peace movement, has argued that the continued development of nuclear weapons has transcended traditional arguments relating propensity to wage war to social structure. We no longer have a logic of imperialism, or of rivalry between nation-states, but a 'logic of exterminism', that has grown out of the contingencies of post-war history and which now controls economy and society on both sides of the Iron Curtain.

The historiographical importance of differing approaches to the understanding of war in modern society can best be illustrated by considering the still limited, but growing, historiography of the relationship between war and economic and technical development. The anti-liberal and anti-Marxist German historian, Werner Sombart, argued before the First World War that war was creative of progress and, more specifically, that war had a hand in the creation of industrialism. In the inter-war years, despite the damage that the war had done to liberalism as a political movement, the view that war was essentially destructive gained new force. Sombart's thesis came to be associated closely with German militarism and Nazism, which prompted Anglo-Saxon liberals, notably J. U. Nef, to reaffirm the liberal view.[2] This historiographical debate, dormant for many years, is now re-emerging. Merritt Roe Smith has argued that the American System of Manufactures owed more to military requirements for interchangeable parts than it did to 'Yankee ingenuity', free enterprise and a liberal economy. David Noble, also concerning himself primarily with manufacturing technology, has argued that the military have played a very important role in developing such technology so that it de-skills workers, making them part of a strictly delineated hierarchical system. The dynamics of modern capitalism and modern militarism are no longer seen as the opposing ideal types of Herbert Spencer's 'industrial' and 'militant' societies.

An important exception to this trend may be found in the work of Mary Kaldor, who has developed the traditional liberal argument in a new and unexpected way. She argues that military technology, particularly in peacetime, suffers from 'baroque' accretions, with the consequence that the military effectiveness of a nation advances less quickly than its technological sophistication. At the same time, the technology of production remains stagnant, acting as a drag on the economy as a whole. She attributes these effects to the special combination of dynamic capitalist industry and conservative (peacetime) armed forces.

While the historiography of technology and war has thus advanced beyond the banal argument that the main contribution of the military to technology has been money, the broader discussion of science and war has not. Since an excellent survey of the American literature has already been prepared by Alex Roland, in what follows I shall try to tease out various aspects of the relationship in the twentieth century, using evidence principally from British history, but developing arguments of more general relevance. I shall discuss (1) what scientists themselves have made of the question; (2) relations between scientists and the military; (3) the militarisation of science; and (4) the impact of science on the conduct of war.

1. 'PUBLIC SCIENCE' AND WAR

The attitude of British scientists towards war and preparation for war has changed over time in ways which reflect wider changes in their social and political thought. Just as it is misleading to see a constant tradition of scientific reformers from the early nineteenth century onwards, advocating public support of science but frustrated by political conservatism and an anti-industrial and anti-scientific culture, it is wrong to see scientists holding on to the progressive nostrums of nineteenth-century liberal thought as they related to war. Attitudes to state funding of science and to war both changed, but this has not been adequately examined in the literature.

The story is often told of the utter unpreparedness of Britain in 1914 to fight a scientifically and technologically sophisticated Germany. The voices that complained about this before the war, notably the British Science Guild, are seen as prescient advocates of the need for state support for science, just as Lyon Playfair had been in an earlier period. What is not usually pointed out is that the British Science Guild was not simply a lobby for science, but rather, in Frank Turner's words 'a conservative, social imperialist pressure group seeking to combine the intellectual prestige of science with the political attraction of efficiency and empire'.[3] Turner argues further that before 1914, these scientists 'were defining the character of modern warfare and the manner of its preparation so as to enhance their own possible contribution to it and subsequent recognition through it'.[4]

A second theme in discussion of the First World War is the lament that it broke up the international community of science. Although it is often implied that scientists only reluctantly accepted this, the recent evidence suggests that scientists were prominent in arguing for it. Indeed, German scientists were kept out of international scientific organisations for many years, branded as war criminals (see art. 59). Certainly science was more national after the war than before, but this was in part the consequence of scientists' arguments that science be organised for national purposes. It is disingenuous and unhistorical to argue that it was a disgrace that the international scientific community was disrupted, but 'a good thing' that the state greatly increased its support for science. In arguing for the latter, scientists in part denied the former. The Germans had not been simply intellectual teachers, but political teachers too.

'Public science' changed after 1918. The prussianisation of the British state and its relationship to science, brought about by the war, changed the parameters of the argument. The war had provided much evidence of the potential of science when linked to the state and to industry. Britain became self-sufficient in many industries where Germany had dominated before the war. But it was, perhaps, poison gas that had the most lasting effect on thinking about the relationship between science and war. Despite the efforts of some inter-war scientists (including J. B. S. Haldane) to present gas as just another legitimate weapon of war, it continued, and indeed continues, to be regarded as particularly dastardly. It had not been particularly efficacious as a weapon, but it came to symbolise the power and the misuse of science.

In the 1930s, the social relations of science movement was acutely aware of the arguments which linked science and the private armament firms (dubbed the 'Merchants of Death', the 'Secret International' etc.) as causes of war. For the Marxists this posed no difficulties, but for the others it did. Even in 1940 the influential Penguin Special, *Science and War*, while advocating a much greater use of science by British state and industry, omitted to mention the most obvious use of scientists in war: the design and development of new offensive weapons. Attention was fixed firmly on the protection of the civil population, the rational organisation of the armed forces, economy and society and, almost in passing, on defensive weapons. Moreover, as the publisher put it in his introduction:

> It should be appreciated that until now, the world of science has had little to say about the use to which scientific advances have been put. Had it been otherwise, and had scientific methods played their part in home and international affairs, war might have been avoided.

This public re-affirmation of the liberal view was not evidence of any reluctance among scientists to create new weapons. If there was no lobby like the British Science Guild arguing openly for science on militaristic grounds, it was partly because that battle had been won in the 1914–18 war, and partly because of fears that associating science with weapons of war would undermine long term public support for science in peacetime.

Though it may have seemed so in the Britain of the 1930s, *scientific* modernisation was never the sole prerogative of social and political progressives. Certainly in Britain the celebratory identification of science, technology and war, was nothing like as strong as it was in Germany, as shown in the works of Ernst Jünger,[5] or in Italy, where the Futurist Marinetti could declare in the 1930s:

> War is beautiful because it establishes man's dominion over the subjugated machinery by means of gas masks, terrifying megaphones, flamethrowers, and small tanks. War is beautiful because it initiates the dreamt-of metallisation of the human body. War is beautiful because it enriches a flowery meadow with the fiery orchids of machine guns. War is beautiful because it combines the gunfire, the cannonades, the scents, and the stench of putrefaction into a symphony. War is beautiful because it creates new architecture, like that of the big tanks, the geometrical formation flights, the smoke spirals from burning villages, . . .[6]

However, it did exist on a very limited scale in, for example, aviation circles. Britain's leading fascist, Sir Oswald Mosley, was a notable supporter of science, but, with the exception of biological ideas, the relationship between the interwar British right and science has not been adequately explored.

In the Second World War British science had a 'good war'. Scientists were defending both their countries and science itself. Whereas Wilhelmine

Germany could not be portrayed as an enemy of science (although some had tried), Nazi Germany obviously was. The association of science and democracy was used to powerful ideological effect, both against totalitarianism and for and against the democratic control of science. This became the very stuff of the 'freedom versus planning' debate of the 1940s, which was much stimulated by the war. The Cold War added an ironic twist. The proponents of planning then argued against the use of science for military purposes, while the proponents of scientific freedom chose to ignore the extent to which even the purest of sciences were being directed to military ends, by defining military science as 'technology'.

One is thus tempted to conclude that, since 1918 at least, the rhetoric of British public science has portrayed the realities of the relationship between science and the military ever less accurately. One might argue that as the relationship between science and war got closer, the more ingenious became the argument that they had nothing in common.

2. SCIENCE-MILITARY RELATIONS

The liberal stereotype of progressive science and backward armed forces has been influential in discussions of the place of science and scientists in the conduct of war. Science is regarded as essentially civilian and free, answerable only to nature; the military are regarded as creatures of tradition, subject to superior officers, preparing to 'fight the last war'. In this scheme, science-military relations are necessarily difficult, with science ultimately having the upper hand. As Bertrand Russell put it, 'One nuclear physicist is worth more than many divisions of infantry . . . It is to steel and oil and uranium, not to martial ardour, that modern nations must look for victory in war'.[7]

Armed forces are often presented as being peculiarly resistant not only to free thought but also to new weapons. This is sometimes applauded as a reminder of a golden age of chivalrous warfare, and at other times condemned as dangerous and irresponsible backwardness. However, while there is certainly much truth in the picture of socially and politically conservative armed forces, technical conservatism must be treated more cautiously. There are important differences between armed services and between different historical periods. In general, we might expect the Royal Navy to be more interested in science than the Army, the Royal Engineers more than the Grenadier Guards and the Royal Air Force more than all the others. As a particular example, we might take the case of Sir Alfred Ewing, famous for naval and diplomatic code-breaking in the First World War. From 1890 he was Professor of Mechanism and Applied Mechanics at the University of Cambridge. In 1902 he was appointed Director of Naval Education, as part of the wide-ranging technical modernisation of the Royal Navy which predated the war. A second example is that of the Royal Air

Force which was created in 1918 as an independent service around a particular technology, with a particular strategic mission: the long-range bombing of civilian and industrial centres.

As well as being wary of over-generalising across armed services, historians of the relation of science to the military need to make their picture historically specific and to be aware of the wider tensions which operated in the conduct of war. At the beginning of the First World War middle-class Europeans rushed to enlist to escape the humdrum materialism of everyday life. One such was Henry Gwyn Jeffreys Moseley, whose death at Gallipoli was used both at the time and since as evidence that the British military were reluctant to use scientists for scientific purposes. In fact Moseley was offered scientific work but chose to volunteer.

As is well known, the Great War turned quickly from being a contest in patriotic enthusiasm to a quagmire of grimly calculated carnage fed by the laboratories and factories of the belligerents. Such a dramatic difference between expectation and outcome led to important conflicts between civilians and professional soldiers, from the highest levels in the direction of the war down to the shopfloor of the munitions industry. Civilian scientists and other experts certainly met resistance from the professionals, as we know from studies of the largely civilian Munitions Invention Department of the Ministry of Munitions and the Board of Invention and Research of the Admiralty. However, such difficulties probably tell us less about the alleged anti-scientific bias of the armed forces than about bureaucratic infighting in general, including rivalries between civilian newcomers and the established scientific and technical branches of the fighting services. In any case, such considerations should not obscure the obvious integration of science, industry and war that took place in a few short years.

The relationship established during the war broke down considerably after the war, but never reverted to what it had been. Even the Department of Scientific and Industrial Research, though primarily a civil body, worked in an atmosphere in which civil technology was more readily accepted as essential to the fighting capacity of a nation. The DSIR's Fuel Research Board was, for example, closely involved with the oil-from-coal programme. The BBC was strongly encouraged to develop television, partly to create industrial capacity to produce cathode ray tubes. On the eve of the Second World War, Britain was much readier than it had been in 1914 to fight a 'scientific' war. Indeed, it was hoped that war would not be based on sheer numbers in uniform; the whole stance of the rearmament programme was towards air warfare rather than a commitment to infantry. That classic example of military science in Britain, the development of radar, took place from the 1930s, and resulted from the close collaboration of service and civilian scientists together with serving officers.

During the Second World War, scientists found themselves not only designing new weapons but also having important advisory roles on the conduct of operations, using the newly developed techniques of operational research (OR). As machines came into conflict with each other, statistical methods had to be used to assess outcomes and their most efficient use. Furthermore, operational research was used to calculate economic costs and benefits of particular weapon systems in terms of the costs of producing a weapon, against the economic cost to the enemy of the destruction caused by that weapon. Operational research was *par excellence* the science of total war.

Of course these developments did not take place without friction. There was resistance to 'long-haired professor types', and scientists did have to argue publicly and forcefully for a greater status for science in the government machine. But, by the end of the war, the importance of scientists in the waging of war was firmly established as never before. The availability of 'scientific manpower', the proper organisation of the Scientific Civil Service and civilian scientific advice to government, became important points of discussion in peace as well as war.

3. THE MILITARISATION OF SCIENCE

The link between science and war changed science. This is not simply a question of the importance of military funding for science, important as this has been. It is also a question of the way military-funded science has been practised, and what kind of science has been performed. Clearly it has been developed in a variety of sites, from within the armed services, in state civil organisations, in private firms and in universities. We have, as yet, little systematic knowledge of the changing patterns of funding and direction of military research. However, we can usefully contrast the lack of importance of university-based military science in Britain as compared with the United States after the Second World War.

Clearly, the requirements of secrecy have affected the character of military research to some extent. This is not simply a question of secrecy between scientists in different countries, but also among scientists in a particular country, even between scientists working on the same project. The process of compartmentalisation, of information on a 'need to know' basis, would seem to imply a certain kind of research as well as hierarchy and scientific administration. Our detailed knowledge of how important military projects were administered is very limited. Notable exceptions are Gowing's study of the nuclear weapons programme, Hackmann's study of sonar and Haber's comparative study of the poison gas programmes of the First World War. It is surely remarkable, given the importance of military funding for science and the increasing concern of historians of science with scientific institutions, what little work has been done in this field. There is an obvious need for comparative studies across countries and across different kinds of laboratories doing military work, as well as a clearer picture of the importance of military-funded science as a fraction of total scientific activity, especially for the period before 1939.

4. THE IMPACT OF SCIENCE ON THE CONDUCT OF WAR

Throughout the twentieth century there has been a tendency to exaggerate the impact of science and technology on the character and outcome of warfare. References to the 'Chemists War' and the 'Physicists War' are all too common and all too misleading. Just as it is not easy to measure the importance of particular technologies in promoting economic growth, it is difficult to assess the importance of particular technologies to the outcome of war. How can we, for example, compare radar with penicillin, or DDT or anti-malarials; the demagnetisation of ships with proximity fuses or condoms with plastic explosives? In the case of war, the problem is much complicated by special contingencies. For example, the destruction of a particular aircraft on its way to bomb a particular target may be militarily more important than the general capacity to destroy aircraft. Furthermore, in warfare what is of interest is not absolute increases in military capacity brought about by science and technology, but relative differences, taking into account countermeasures. It is a profound irony that the cost-benefit analysis of weapons has greatly developed in the nuclear age, and has indeed become the very stuff of nuclear politics, when such weapons have the capacity to obliterate the world and the analysts with it.

In general terms, however, the argument can be made that in total war the scientific and technical capacity of nations has affected their capacity to wage total war. In the First World War, Germany was able to draw on its highly-developed science-based industries for a whole range of goods, including synthetic ammonia and nitrates, both for offensive operations and for the maintenance of the home front. Britain had to build up its science-based industry to meet the German military challenge in a way that had not been necessary to meet the German commercial challenge before the war, and broadly speaking, the science, technology and industry of the British and German Empires were evenly matched along the Western Front. Neither gas nor tanks were able to change the course of the war, though submarines nearly did.

It is important to note, however, that specific sciences and technologies were seen by some as a means of avoiding the mobilisation of a nation's entire scientific, technical, industrial and human resources. In the inter-war years, military theorists looked above all to two mechanical inventions, the aeroplane and the tank, which, it was hoped, would lead to short decisive encounters involving relatively small forces. The tank would make trench warfare obsolete; the aircraft would destroy industrial capacity and civilian morale. Such hopes need to be seen as being both modern and anti-modern; modern in that it was technology that was vital to armed force, and anti-modern in that what was sought was a return to older forms of heroic and professional warfare. But the Second World War, like the First, became a total war. The extent to which the outcome was decided by differences in scientific and technical resources, and the utilisation of those resources, is a difficult question to decide. After all, the major battles of the war took place on the Eastern Front and not on the more technically-intensive Western Front. In the Far East, the technical factors were different again. But from a purely British perspective, science was seen as critical to Britain's successes as a fighting nation. Radar, IFF, H2S, Oboe, Asdic, bouncing bombs, penicillin, PLUTO, jet aircraft and midget submarines all quickly became part of the legends of war. The more recent revelations about the 'battle of the beams', and, especially, the breaking of the German 'enigma' and 'fish' codes have added the very special fascination of secrecy and also strengthened the picture of sleepy British 'boffins' rising to the challenges of war in a particularly creative way. The implied claim that British science was more successful than German science, has not, however, been examined in any detail.

Of course, the most famous example of the relations between science and war, the atomic bomb, came too late to have anything except a minor impact on the outcome of the Second World War. Thereafter however, the possession, if not the use, of nuclear weapons has been at the very centre of discussion about strategic and tactical doctrine, and the number, power and accuracy of nuclear weapons and delivery systems have become issues of the utmost importance. The effects of possession of nuclear weapons on the wars that have been fought, and the possible effects of such weapons in preventing war, has also been subject to intense debate.

4. CONCLUSIONS

The relationship between science and war raises many issues other than the social responsibility of the scientist. The liberal perspective ignores the reality of very close links between science and the military, and cannot adequately account for the patterns of the relationship; indeed, its assumptions obscure much that is critical to our understanding. The interrelationships between science and war have had major consequences for both war and science which have hardly been addressed in the literature.

NOTES

1. Recent sociological and historical work has explored the question of ideological and social-theoretical approaches to war in some detail. See in particular: M. Shaw (ed.), *War, state and society* (London, 1984); A. Giddens, *The nation state and violence* (Cambridge, 1985); C. Creighton and M. Shaw (eds.), *The sociology of war and peace* (London, 1987); B. Semmel, *Liberalism and naval strategy: ideology, interest, and sea power during the pax britannica.* (London, 1986).

2. See J. M. Winter's excellent survey, 'The economic and social history of war' in J. M. Winter (ed.), *War and economic development: essays in memory of David Joslin* (Cambridge, 1975).
3. Frank M. Turner, 'Public science in Britain, 1880–1919', *Isis*, 71 (1980), p. 602.
4. Ibid., p. 603.
5. See Herf, *Reactionary modernism: technology, culture and politics in Weimar and the Third Reich* (Cambridge, 1985).
6. Quoted by Walter Benjamin in 'The work of art in the age of mechanical reproduction', in Walter Benjamin, *Illuminations* (Fontana, London, 1973), pp. 243–4.
7. B. Russell *The impact of science on society* (London, 1952), p. 85.

FURTHER READING

Correlli Barnett, *The audit of war: the illusions and realities of Britain as a great nation* (London, 1985).

A. G. Cock, 'Chauvinism and internationalism in science: the International Research Council, 1919–1926', *Notes and records of the Royal Society of London*, 37, no. 2 (1983), 249–88.

B. Easlea, *Fathering the unthinkable* (London, 1985).

D. E. H. Edgerton and P. J. Gummett, 'Science, technology and economics in the twentieth century', in G. Jordan (ed.), *British military history: a supplement to Higham's guide to the sources of British military history* (New York, 1988), pp. 477–99.

M. M. Gowing, *Britain and atomic energy, 1939–1945* (London, 1964).

M. M. Gowing, *Independence and deterrence: Britain and atomic energy, 1945–1952*, vol. I, *policy making*; vol. II, *policy execution* (London, 1974).

L. F. Haber, *The poisonous cloud: chemical warfare in the first world war* (Oxford, 1985).

B. C. Hacker and S. L. Hacker, 'Military institutions and the labour process: non-economic sources of technological change, women's subordination, and the organisation of work', *Technology and culture* vol. 28, no. 4 (1987), 743–75.

W. D. Hackmann, *Seek and strike: sonar anti-submarine warfare and the Royal Navy, 1914–1954* (London, 1984).

J. Herf, *Reactionary modernism: technology, culture and politics in Weimar and the Third Reich* (Cambridge, 1985).

A. Hodges, *Alan Turing: the enigma of intelligence* (London, 1983).

M. Kaldor, *The baroque arsenal* (London, 1982).

R. M. Macleod and E. K. Andrews, 'Scientific advice in the war at sea, 1915–1917: the board of invention and research', *Journal of contemporary history*, 6 (1971), 3–40.

W. H. McNeill, *The pursuit of power: technology, armed force and society since AD 1000* (Oxford, 1983).

M. Pattison, 'Scientists, inventors and the military in Britain. 1915–19: the munitions invention department', *Social studies of science*, 13 (1983), 521–68.

M. Pearton, *The knowledgeable state: diplomacy, war and technology since 1830* (London, 1983).

A. Roland, 'Science and war' in S. G. Kohlstedf and M. W. Rossiter (eds.), *Historical writing on American science: perspectives and prospects* (Baltimore, 1985).

Merritt Roe Smith, (ed.) *Military enterprise and technological change: perspectives on the American experience* (Cambridge, Mass., 1985).

E. P. Thompson *et al.*, *Exterminism and cold war* (London, 1982).

B. Vitale, 'Scientists as military hustlers' *Issues in radical science*, edited by the Radical Science Collective, *Radical science*, 17 (1985), 73–87.

P. G. Werskey, *The visible college* (London, 1978).

J. M. Winter (ed.) *War and economic development* (Cambridge, 1975).

Also see papers in: 'Cooperative research in government and industry', symposium at the 17th international congress of the history of science, Berkeley, Cal., *Historical studies in the physical and biological sciences*, 18 (1987), part 1.

62

SCIENCE EDUCATION

W. H. BROCK

1. HISTORIOGRAPHY

Like the history of science, history of education is part of the wider story of the history of society. In the words of Asa Briggs, it is 'social history broadly interpreted with the politics, the economics and . . . the religion put in'.[1] Such a definition explains why historians of education are interested in the history of science, and vice versa. Science and technology have played major roles in shaping modern society, and although the historian may choose to emphasise either the intellectual or the social processes which stimulated or hindered the development of western society, the growth of modern science and medicine and their technical exploitation cannot be fully understood without considering how their curricula are learned and acquired by one generation after another. The study of scientific and technical institutions, or of the educational systems and facilities of different countries, or of the financial support given to scientific teaching and research, helps the historian of science to understand the dynamics of scientific development. Accordingly, historians of science share some territory with historians of education. Like the latter they can approach territorial problems through local studies, comparative national history, quantitative (cliometric) analysis, administrative history, working-class social history ('history from below') and intellectual history.

To avoid an exhaustive but dreary catalogue approach, or the production of a series of vignettes, historians of science education continually need to raise fundamental questions about society's ideas of, and attitudes towards, education at different periods. Why teach science? How is science teaching linked with innovation in mathematics, technology or medicine? To what extent does a society's interest in science teaching (or lack of it) depend on religious, economic or political factors? What is the status of the scientist, or science teacher, and what careers are open to them? Was science taught formally, or by example, or heuristically, and at what cost? Should the curriculum be specialised or general?

What particular sciences are the most popular for instruction purposes and why? How does one country's system affect another's? To what extent is there agreement over methods of instruction and examination? Which are the influential textbooks? What do they indicate concerning contemporary attitudes? Can the influence of past science teaching be seen in the contemporary organisation and development of the subject? By composing its history around such questions the historian of science education will ensure that the specialism becomes an integral part of history like the history of science itself.

A potent example of the way in which a contemporary British debate is both informed and misinformed by knowledge of the history of education is 'declinism'. Ever since Jacob Bronowski's and C. P. Snow's analyses of Britain's relative decline as a world scientific power in terms of two opposed artistic and scientific cultures, it has been fashionable to use 'education' as a unique explanation for national decline. Barnett, Roderick and Stephens, and, most notably, Wiener, have all argued that the failure of Britain's governing and industrial classes to develop a more practical, applied and technical system of education in the 1880s is the direct cause of Britain's present position in the world. Hobsbawm's explanation that Britain's present-day position is an inevitable consequence of colonial imperialism and of being the first European country to industrialise, is rejected as unsatisfactory.[2]

Such 'declinism' is historically and historiographically too simplistic. It has yet to be proved convincingly that there is a direct correlation between 'technical' education and improved economic performance, fashionable though this equation may be. It also has to be remembered that the fundamental role of any educational system – up to the secondary level at least – is conservative: the transmission of a culture's heritage. Indeed, before 1914 all European nations had developed remarkably similar educational systems for their elites. The declinist thesis also lays too much stress upon 'aristocratic', 'pre-industrial' and 'countrymen's' cultural values while failing to consider the possibility that scientists, engineers and industrialists may not themselves have deliberately distanced their activities from manual and craft images of science and industry in order successfully to enhance their status as professional men and women. Finally, there has been a failure by economists and historians of education to recognise the perennial rhetorical nature of declinist arguments.

It is mainly because of class attitudes, *laissez-faire* and narrow views of liberal education as 'superior' to technical training, which had worked satisfactorily in the first phase of industrialisation, that educational and economic historians have tended to view scientific and technical education in Great Britain as somehow 'held back'. Support for such a view is, of course, readily found in nineteenth-century scientific rhetoric of 'decline', beginning with Charles Babbage's peevish *Reflections on the Decline of Science in England* (1830). Babbage held up France as the model for Britain to follow while ignoring Scotland and the richness of English provincial science. Later men of science, particularly those like Lyon Playfair and Edward Frankland, who had studied in Germany with Liebig or Bunsen in the 1840s, praised the German states for the way they had created (following Prussia's example at the beginning of the nineteenth century) a highly organised, technically-trained society through a state system of education. In fact, as historians of French and German science education have pointed out, the 'decline' argument was relative and rhetorical: both French and German scientists often complained that their respective scientific and technical educational systems were dangerously inferior to a 'foreign' system and even commented enviously on the mixed state and voluntary/philanthropic systems which generally prevailed in Great Britain until after the First World War.[3] No doubt there have been significant differences in the responses to, and the impact of, the argument in different decades and in different countries, and the history of education would be greatly enriched by a detailed comparative study of the argument's continuity and historiography.

Whatever the contemporary justification for the rhetoric of 'decline', it (along with social Darwinism) was undoubtedly effective in making European nations competitive during the second phase of the Industrial Revolution when electricity began to complement steam power and gas as an energy source and the chemical industry became dependent upon engineering. A detailed understanding emerged of synthetic pathways and thermodynamics rather than the empirical, analytical, 'boilerman' approach of most chemical technology before 1860. The German infra-structure of pharmaceutical education had a tradition of practical workbench experience in privately-run Chemical Institutes long before Justus von Liebig exploited it for the production of chemists who might apply their analytical knowledge to the relief of man's estate by improving agriculture, fighting disease, maintaining health and exploiting chemical laws for commercial gain. This gave the German states some competitive advantage over other nations. However, given the large numbers of British chemists whom Liebig taught, his tremendous popularity in Britain and the way the Giessen method of training was copied and exploited by A. W. Hofmann in the privately-financed Royal College of Chemistry (founded in 1845), it is doubtful whether Britain really 'lagged' behind in chemical education.[4] Nor, given the fact that most German *Gymnasium*-educated men who entered university had received a purely classical education, was the British schools' anti-scientific bias all that unusual. Where Germany differed was in her manufacturers' willingness to absorb graduates and to spend time transforming them into industrialists.

Historians of science and education have done a good deal of work on French, German and American science and education, but apart from some partial studies of Japanese and Russian science teaching, little has been done on other countries. No one has yet attempted a global synthesis of the history of science education, or even a comparative analysis of European development, and apart from a major study of the emergence of the female scientific community in America, surprisingly little has been published on the history of the educational development of women scientists in Europe.[5]

2. SCIENCE EDUCATION IN GERMANY

After its defeat by Napoleon in 1806, Prussia, followed by the other German states, mobilised itself for European spiritual and intellectual leadership. It did this by formally developing government-controlled segmented systems of primary, secondary and tertiary education which would ensure that the state had an elite and an efficient class of officials and learned professions. To this end, the *Gymnasium*, or grammar school, rather than the *Volkschule*, or primary school, became the focus of attention. For it was the ancient-languages-based curriculum of these *Gymnasien* that formed the basis of the school-leaving examination (*Abitur*) which allowed middle-class pupils to matriculate to universities or obtain direct entry into various state examinations for the civil service. Other types of secondary school, which failed the severe accreditation test for the *Abitur*, became known as *Realschulen* (modern schools). Although the latter developed science teaching, their pupils were unable to matriculate at universities until legal battles had been fought in the 1860s and tended instead to take their higher education in the *Technische Hochschulen* (technical schools or polytechnics), whose examination was considered inferior to that of universities. As in Great Britain, therefore, until 1900, when all secondary school pupils were admitted to the *Abitur*, most German scientists of the top rank had had severely classical educations and first experienced science at university.

The whole purpose of education in Germany's many universities was to achieve success in state examinations which allowed entry into government service, including the professions of pharmacy, medicine and academic teaching. However, with the expansion of faculties of philosophy, which became imbued with the ideology of *Wissenschaft*, or the search for knowledge, an increasing number of students throughout the nineteenth century, particularly foreign students, stayed on at university to take a doctoral degree. This, like the higher degree of *Venia Legendi* or *Habilitation*, called for independent research and the composition of a thesis. It was in this atmosphere that teaching and research laboratories emerged, beginning with Liebig's internationally renowned chemical laboratory at the University of Giessen in 1824. The development of experimental research was greatly aided by the competition for prestigious professorial staff that occurred between the various German state governments prior to unification in 1870.

The first subject to be put in this laboratory mould was chemistry, principally because pharmacy and the growth of agricultural and industrial chemistry, after

1848, created new career opportunities for trained chemists. A second avenue of expansion was provided by physiology, which became regarded as a necessary part of medical knowledge from the 1840s onwards. At first teaching was carried out by professors of anatomy; however, between 1855 and 1874 some 26 German scientists were appointed to new chairs in physiology. By the mid-1870s, however, this period of expansion was over; consequently physiological research began to lose momentum and the brightest *Privatdozenten* (qualified university teachers without chairs who were allowed to give extra-curricular lectures) began to move into other specialisms, such as pathology, biochemistry and psychology.

Germany remained a continuing seat of productivity in laboratory-based sciences up until the First World War. By then, Germany's *Hochschulen* had become accredited 'technical universities', able since 1899 to award the doctorate to students for research in applied science. The Berlin *Hochschule* at Charlottenburg, which was established in its final form only in 1875, played a decisive role in the rationalisation of the several scientific and technical institutions of South Kensington in London into the Imperial College of Science and Technology in 1907. In using the 'decline' argument, British scientists and commentators repeatedly looked to Germany; however, Germany's output of science graduates, impressive and important though it was, must always be kept in proportion. Science graduates were always heavily outnumbered by those graduating in law, medicine, the humanities and (before 1911) in theology.

3. SCIENCE EDUCATION IN FRANCE

The revolution of 1789 destroyed the old universities and church-based schools and replaced them with an integrated, centralised education system which was, and remains, unique in Europe. Until the 1850s, the curriculum of French state schools (*lycées*) was severely classical and, like the German *Gymnasien*, it culminated in an intensely difficult examination, the *baccalaureate*. In 1852, under the influence of industrial demands for a more technically competent work-force, bifurcation was permitted whereby some students could choose to take a science-based *baccalaureate*. The same pressure led to the regional development of faculties of applied science in former university towns. Although these developments were extremely important for France's industrial development, Paris, and the specialised *grandes écoles* like the Ecole Polytechnique, which had replaced the universities as training academies for government servants, continued to be powerful magnets drawing off provincial scientific talent, as the careers of J.–B. Dumas, Claude Bernard and Louis Pasteur illustrate. Like Britain, French education throughout the nineteenth century was also complicated by intense religious debates over the content and purpose of education, debates which scientific modernists and secularists had decidedly won by 1914.

4. SCIENCE EDUCATION IN THE UNITED STATES

Unlike in Europe, a state examination system controlling entry into the professions and government service was never developed in the United States; consequently, higher education never came to confer status upon individuals in the way it always demarcated elite groups in Europe. Private fee-paying local academies, based upon English Anglican and nonconformist models, were the principal sources of education in eighteenth-century America; like their English counterparts, they provided an all-round curriculum which included mathematics and science for a commercial vocation.

Although academies continued to provide a secondary education in the nineteenth century (some of them developing into degree-conferring institutions), they were generally superseded by free public high schools which were maintained by boards of local ratepayers. This system, which originated in Massachusetts in the 1820s, acted as a stimulus to the establishment of the school board system of secular schools established in Britain in 1870 and their successors, the local authority schools, after 1902. As in English schools, American school science before the 1870s was predominantly 'catechistic' and didactic, and only the wealthier academies and school boards possessed demonstration apparatus. The introduction of laboratory instruction into schools, colleges and universities was promoted by a number of factors. These were: the great influence of Herbert Spencer's essays on education (which portrayed science as *the* crucial subject in the educational curriculum of an industrialised society); the effects of the Morrill Land Act of 1862 (whereby Congress donated federal land for the establishment of vocational training colleges of agricultural, mechanical and industrial arts); the publicity given to the curricula of German *Realschulen* and of Swedish and Russian industrial schools which exhibited at the Philadelphia World Fair in 1874 and the growing numbers of American scientists who, by 1880, had received a German university education. After 1890, as in Great Britain, few American public schools were built without chemistry and physics laboratories. The so-called 'Harvard' lists of pre-matriculation experiments in physics and chemistry which were recommended for use in American schools in 1886 closely resembled those issued by Edward Frankland and Frederick Guthrie for Department of Science and Art classes in Britain some years earlier.

5. SCIENCE EDUCATION IN ENGLAND AND WALES

For centuries, education in England and Wales was the responsibility of the Church of England, and it was not until the end of the Victorian period that the clerical monopoly of schools and universities ended and secular education was accepted as a legitimate alternative to 'godliness and good learning'.[6] It is for this reason that so much of English scientific activity took place within an essentially religious context. Until the early nineteenth century, university students were of what we should now regard as school age, and before the seventeenth century there is little point in distinguishing between school and university. Scientific instruction, as far as it went, consisted in the main of Aristotelianism imbedded in the curriculum of 'the seven liberal arts'.

Britain's pre-eminence in the first phase of industrialisation was founded upon a combination of capital, good natural mineral resources, the development of transport systems for both internal and external export trades and a native inventiveness which produced innovations which gave Britain an overwhelming lead over European nations. This industrial success had little to do with the gentry's traditional educational institutions, though its effectiveness undoubtedly owed much to many informal educational agencies such as the networks of eighteenth-century itinerant lecturers who spread intelligence, and to the 'modern' and commercially-minded curriculum of the noncomformist academies and the many proprietory schools which were established to provide education and training for the children of dissenters who were unwelcome at Oxford and Cambridge or at the Anglican endowed schools.

Both Oxford and Cambridge came in for a good deal of criticism in the early part of the nineteenth century for their religious exclusiveness, their privileges and the narrowness of their curricula. It was not until the 1870s, however, prompted both by internal reformers such as William Whewell and Charles Daubeny and by government interference, that college-teaching Fellows at these universities ceased to be clergymen before anything else and became, instead, dons in the modern sense, concerned with advancing as well as preserving knowledge. It is noticeable that in Europe and the United States, and to some extent in Scotland, the absence of a clerical monopoly led to an earlier emergence of a secular academic profession.

Nevertheless, mid-century reforms at Oxford and Cambridge did have important ramifications for science: in 1850 Oxford created Honours examinations schools in mathematics and science which ended the monopoly of classics, while in 1851, Cambridge complemented its already important mathematics degree course with one in the natural sciences. These new science degrees, despite their origins in 'liberal education' ideology, laid a solid foundation for the more laboratory-based and research-oriented science degrees of the 1880s.

Meanwhile, religious tests and the narrowness of the Oxbridge syllabus had led to the foundation of the secular University of London in 1826. Its eclectic degree included an astonishing array of sciences; moreover, its charter of 1836 recreated the University as an examining body which, in the next 50 years, allowed the affiliation of dozens of London, provincial and overseas institutions. One of the first to affiliate, and to offer London degrees, was Owens College, Manchester, which, once its science classes had begun to attract the interest of its industrial community, became, in turn, the model for other civic university colleges. The federal structure of the University of London also became a model for universities in Ireland, Canada, India, Australia and New Zealand, all of which followed its 1859 precedent of establishing separate bachelor degrees in arts and sciences.

The British national system of education was established barely a century ago, in 1870. Before then, well over a million working-class children between the ages of six and ten years received no education whatsoever, and it is estimated that a further half-million aged between ten and thirteen also never attended school. The 1870 Education Act was a belated recognition by the state that the voluntary elementary schools established by the Anglican National Society for Promoting the Education of the Poor in the Principles of the Established Church (founded in 1811) and the mainly nonconformist British and Foreign School Society (founded in 1808), whose sectarianism bedevilled nineteenth-century elementary education, were quite unable to cope. Nevertheless, it must be borne in mind that elementary education was not made compulsory until 1876 and then only up to the age of ten. Providing a child aged between ten and thirteen had passed the fourth standard (*i.e.* that expected of a ten year-old) in the '3R's, he or she was allowed to enter the labour market. Although the minimum age for school exemption was raised to twelve years in 1899 (with crucial exemptions in agricultural districts) it is clear that the chances of an English or Welsh working-class child adopting a scientific career in the nineteenth century were extremely low. This is not to deny the fact that a few British scientists emerged from the voluntary schools before 1870 and, more positively, from the non-sectarian Board schools after that date. Indeed, the principles of self-help and informal education ran deep in Victorian society. For the determined child and ill-educated adult, educational chances were offered by apprenticeship, Mechanics' Institutes and mutual improvement societies. In addition, the ideologies offered by phrenology, socialism and even spiritualism, the cheap books and periodicals made possible by the steam press and the repeal of 'taxes on knowledge' after 1855, and, above all, the teaching and examination system offered by the government's Department of Science and Art after 1853, undoubtedly offered routes into scientific careers. This is shown by the famous case of Oliver Lodge, and also by John Perry and Richard Wormell, who made valuable contributions to the cause of science teaching. Nevertheless, the point remains that, for most of the nineteenth century, there was no royal highway to a scientific career for working-class children, but only a few ladders. Indeed, it should be remembered that the vast majority of British children left school at the age of fourteen until 1947 and until then (and even since) have had to rely on 'night school' and 'day release' systems for any further educational advancement.

Great Britain was scarcely exceptional in this respect. Although both France

953

and Germany had established elaborate state systems of education at the beginning of the nineteenth century (Italy not until 1878), in practice, recruitment into secondary and higher education and hence into significant scientific careers, was restricted, as in Britain, to the middle- and upper-classes. For these classes, entirely different systems of education operated, ranging from home education to the *lycées* of France, the *Gymnasien* of the German states and the endowed, grammar and proprietory schools of Britain, which commonly educated children up to the ages of sixteen or nineteen.

Not until 1902 did the British government provide, through local authority taxation, a system of secondary education for all, thus giving a university route for ordinary working-class children via a 'free place' system based upon scholarly prowess. The independent academically-orientated private schools became the models for these local authority schools by providing a ready-made tradition of standards of scholarship, internal organisation and an ideal of corporate ('team') spirit, as well as aspirations for university entrance and for the learned professions. Unfortunately, although this model made science teaching obligatory, the new state schools, by adopting it, discouraged the technical and vocational training which had begun to emerge in the higher classes of state elementary schools before 1900. In the absence of a sufficient number of state secondary schools, 'free places' were bought by local authorities in endowed grammar schools – a system which led later in the twentieth century to the controversial '11-plus' examination system. Fees were finally abolished by the 1944 Education Act which mandated local authorities to provide and maintain elementary and secondary education for all children aged between five and fifteen. (Compare the situation in the United States, where the last state to abolish fees was New Jersey in 1871.) Authorities were then encouraged to divide secondary pupils by attainment and vocational aptitude between grammar schools, which were academically orientated and well-equipped with science laboratories; technical schools for those less academically gifted whose craft skills were high; and secondary modern schools for the residuum. Another option of large, multilateral or comprehensive schools which catered for varieties of academic ability, was taken up by very few local authorities before the 1960s, but is now the nearly-universal state system in England and Wales, as in the United States.

6. SCIENCE EDUCATION IN SCOTLAND

For the historical reason that the Church of England was never established in Scotland, the education system there developed differently, and this may well have affected the production of scientific manpower from this part of the United Kingdom. Many historians of science have been interested in the study of styles of science in different countries, or in particular local studies of science and have analysed the ways in which scientific culture is related to the educational facilities and structures of the national and local community. Attention has focused particularly on Scottish science, its birth during the Enlightenment, and its maintenance, expansion and decline within specific institutions, especially the universities. The Scots, despite their union with the English kingdom in 1707, retained a very considerable educational independence. During the eighteenth century their five universities (and particularly those at Edinburgh and Glasgow) challenged and overtook Oxford and Cambridge in science and medicine. Because they allowed matriculation without imposing a religious test, the Scottish universities proved particularly attractive to English dissenters, most of whom had been educated in the nonconformist academies until the foundation of the University of London (by Scots-educated reformers) in 1826. The magnetism of the University of Edinburgh, in particular, was systematically strengthened by the Town Council which successfully established an influential medical school. This, together with the ancillary sciences like chemistry which it encouraged, was significant for the production of men of science from the 1720s onwards. These developments owed much to Edinburgh's decision, in 1708, to abolish 'regenting' (the system whereby arts students were tutored in all subjects by one academic), thus allowing the appointment of specialist professors. This decision, taken initially to raise the intellectual attainment of Scottish clergy, gave students the opportunity to specialise and, more significantly, stimulated dedicated teaching from professors whose incomes depended upon the sizes of classes they were able to attract. Like English university education, whose purpose was to 'enlarge' the mind through the study of classics and logic at Oxford, or mathematics and classics at Cambridge, Scottish universities also emphasised the mental, rather than the vocational, value of study. However, they enacted it through what has been described as 'democratic individualism', for these universities were open to privileged and under-privileged students alike; they taught a wide range of subjects at elementary level and knitted the miscellany together with doses of philosophy. (See art. 53) Consequently, scientists like William Thomson (later Lord Kelvin) and James Clerk Maxwell, who attended Scottish universities, as well as the University of Cambridge, went through a good general education in Scotland, including natural philosophy, which could be capped by specialised mathematical studies in England.

7. TECHNICAL EDUCATION

As we have seen, class attitudes have prevailed in British education; each form, or system, of education was felt to be appropriate to a particular class. Grammar schools had been endowed for the middle classes, some of whom might also enjoy a university education which was otherwise reserved for the wealthy. Technical education was a lower form of education appropriate only for artisans, not for gentlemen. Engineering was a craft; its pioneers were self-taught, and to their practical knowledge they had coupled a 'self-help' determination. Industry was essentially a collection of craft-based firms. This empirical approach had worked and from it had grown the strong tradition that engineering was something to be learned on the job.

The state itself was disinclined to intervene in educational matters and most educational philosophy (e.g. that of Herbert Spencer) began with the assumption that state intervention – as in France after the Revolution – led to state control. This *laissez-faire* attitude was complemented by that of most British manufacturers (though exceptions, like Bernhard Samuelson, can be cited) who had little use for, and no understanding of, the value of research or of scientific education. For them, a scientifically-trained workman seemed an unwise investment since the artisan would therefore understand the principle of the process and would possibly move to a competitor or even raise capital to begin a rival business.

The situation on the continent was different; there the image of the engineer as a highly-educated professional man had originated in the mining academies and military schools of France, Germany and Hungary in the eighteenth century and had been transposed to the Ecole Polytechnique in 1796. This, in turn, had set the pattern for later technological institutions (*Technische Hochschulen* or 'Polytechnics') founded in Germany and Switzerland.

The doctoral degree, which is now the *sine qua non* of scientific professionalism, has only been awarded for post-graduate research in British universities since 1918. Before then the higher, examined degree of D.Sc. was available to graduates of a particular university but rarely taken. Post-graduates from other universities (as at Cambridge University's Cavendish laboratory after 1895) had to make do with a demeaning 'research' B.A. or B.Sc. Therefore, British students in search of research experience tended to attend German universities, as did Americans, where their efforts were rewarded by the Ph.D. It should be noted, however, that before the 1870s the German doctorate awarded to foreigners was often of an honorary nature and frequently worthless as a measure of competence. Nevertheless, research degrees on the German model were strongly advocated by members of the British and American scientific communities who gave evidence to educational inquiries and who obtained positions of influence after the 1870s. In the event, it was the economic and political necessity of colonial cohesion made necessary by the First World War, the Foreign Office's concern to wean American students away from German contamination, and the availability of post-graduate research grants by the Department of Scientific and Industrial Research which prompted universities to introduce the doctoral degree.

Although the British government had patronised the sciences in many ways before 1914 – notably through the administration of an annual grant to several universities and colleges from 1889 – the creation of the DSIR was a landmark in the relationship between science and government in Britain and a model for the Commonwealth. Until its demise in 1964, the DSIR encouraged and financed research in universities and colleges, awarded stipends to post-graduates and established and maintained a host of useful research institutions. Until the second half of the nineteenth century it had never been considered a duty of European universities to produce trained men for industry. However, the expanding industries at the end of the nineteenth century – industries based on metallurgy, chemicals and convenience foods – were precisely those in which science graduates were needed, if only for quality control of raw materials and products, let alone for research and development. The fact that the social and economic processes, which compensated for the diminishing imperial advantage which Great Britain had enjoyed, were the very sorts of changes which 'declinists' and the emerging professional scientists vociferously demanded, has made the connection between economic success and investment in science education appear more casual than it really was.

The 'civic universities', technical colleges and polytechnics of Manchester, Sheffield, Leeds and Birmingham, were largely founded by industrialists who were alarmed and disturbed by the position of Britain's industries in the face of German and American competition. (There are comparisons to be made here with the regional Science Faculties of France and the German and Swiss *Hochschulen*.) That these science colleges were founded in provincial cities, rather than as extensions of Oxbridge, was due to the physical growth of Victorian cities, their concomitant civic pride and their coexistence with industry. They also represented a reaction against the Oxbridge commitment to non-vocational 'liberal' education, though in so far as the provincial colleges were forced to take London external degrees, even the most vocational of them, like Mason's College, Birmingham, admitted the Arts into their curricula. As it was, the coming of competitive examinations for the professions after 1860 meant that by 1900 even Oxford and Cambridge had come to accept financial aid from industry, and were cultivating industrial careers for their graduates through their newly-established Appointments Boards.

That business and industry were able and willing to recruit more graduates than ever before during the Edwardian era was due to the increasing scale of industrial enterprise, the shortage of managerial staff and the gradual introduction of research methods and laboratories in industries that were under competition from large-scale German and American firms. Even so, the number of graduates involved remained small compared with Germany, the majority being forced to choose schoolteaching as a career. However, the coming of the Ph.D. and the consequent gain in research experience, coupled with the appearance of many new science-based technologies thrown up or catalysed by the First World War (such as radio, aircraft and fibres, all of which needed technical expertise to maintain and develop them), led to the firm establishment of research and development laboratories in a number of industries. These became increasingly willing to employ Ph.D. or B.Sc. students from the universities.

In the 1920s and 1930s, consequently, industries were increasingly well disposed and philanthropic towards the universities and (in the 1950s) towards private schools. Thus, industrial money poured into Cambridge where (despite some difficulties over which piper, academic or industrial, should call the tune) research in physics, chemistry and biochemistry remained basic and unapplied in excellent laboratory facilities endowed by industry.

Inevitably, there were some voices raised against the increasingly closer symbiosis of university and industry. For example, despite his American experience, Abraham Flexner, in his *Universities, American, English and German* (1931), deplored the way specific technologies, like brewing and glass-making, had come to dominate civic universities such as Birmingham and Sheffield. Although both these departments made fundamental contributions to biochemistry and the physics of materials, for Flexner they were neither 'liberal nor university quality'. Socialist critics, like J. D. Bernal and Julian Huxley were similarly critical; albeit for the different reasons that industry's support was, in their eyes, leading to the neglect of the more socially-relevant biological sciences. But whether existing departments were admired or criticised, one point, already fairly clear, was put beyond doubt by the developments of the Second World War. Universities could specialise in their teaching of science, as they did in research, and still produce graduates who would be as acceptable to industry as they were to the civil service and the academic world.

NOTES

1. A. Briggs, 'The study of the history of education', *History of education*, 1 (1972), p. 5.
2. J. Bronowski, *Science and human values* (London, 1961); C. P. Snow, *The two cultures and the scientific revolution* (Cambridge, 1959), reissued as *The two cultures: a second look* (Cambridge, 1964, 1978); C. Barnett *The collapse of Britain's Power* (London, 1972) and 'Technology, education and industrial and economic success', *Journal of the Royal Society of Arts* (No. 527, 1979), 117–30; G. Roderick and M. Stephens, *Education and industry in the 19th century: the English disease* (London and New York, 1978); Idem. (eds.) *Where did we go wrong? Industrial performance, education and the economy in Victorian Britain* (Lewes and Philadelphia, 1981); M. J. Weiner, *English culture and the decline of the industrial spirit 1850–1980* (Cambridge, 1981). (Weiner's original title, 'English culture and the *containment* of industrialism', was sensationalised by his American publisher; see *New society*, 17 (1983), 274–5.)
3. H. W. Paul, 'The issue of decline in 19th century French science', *French historical studies*, 7 (1972), 416–40; P. Lundgreen, 'Education for the science-based industrial state? The case for nineteenth-century Germany', *History of education*, 13 (1984), 59–67.
4. See, however, R. F. Bud and G. K. Roberts, *Science versus practice. Chemistry in Victorian Britain* (Manchester, 1984). For Liebig's method, see J. B. Morrell, 'The chemist breeders: the research schools of Liebig and Thomas Thomson', *Ambix*, 19 (1972), 1–46.
5. M. W. Rossiter, *Women scientists in American: struggles and strategies to 1940* (Baltimore and

London, 1982); R. MacLeod and R. Moseley, 'Fathers and daughters: reflections on women, science and Victorian Cambridge', *History of education*, 8 (1979), 321–33.

6. C. M. Heward, 'Industry, cleanliness and godliness: sources for and problems in the history of scientific and technical education and the working classes, 1850–1910', *Studies in science education*, 7 (1980), 87–128.

7. G. E. Davie, *The democratic intellect: Scotland and her universities in the nineteenth century* (2nd edition, Edinburgh. 1964).

FURTHER READING

W. H. Brock, (ed.), *H. E. Armstrong and the teaching of science, 1880–1930* (Cambridge, 1973).

——'From Liebig to Nuffield. A bibliography of the history of science education, 1839–1974', *Studies in science education*, 2 (1975), 67–99.

D. S. L. Cardwell, *The organisation of science in England* (London, 1957; revised ed. London, 1972).

C. M. Heward, 'Industry, cleanliness and godliness: sources for and problems in the history of scientific and technical education and the working classes, 1850–1910', *Studies in science education*, 7 (1980), 87–128.

E. W. Jenkins, *From Armstrong to Nuffield. Studies in twentieth-century science education in England and Wales* (London, 1979).

E. W. Jenkins, 'Some sources for the history of science education in the twentieth century, with particular reference to secondary schools', *Studies in science education*, 7 (1980), 27–86.

D. Layton, *Interpreters of science. A history of the Association for Science Education* (London, 1984).

C. E. McClelland, *State, society and university in Germany, 1700–1914* (Cambridge, 1980).

H. W. Paul, *From knowledge to power. The rise of the science empire in France, 1860–1939* (Cambridge, 1986).

63

THE ORGANISATION OF SCIENCE AND ITS PURSUIT IN EARLY MODERN EUROPE

ROGER L. EMERSON

The organisation and pursuit of science has always been regulated by two broad determinants: by the concepts believed to describe the natural world as it exists and by the institutions which support, guide and define the roles played by those who study nature. The first of these made the pursuit of science in the seventeenth and eighteenth centuries integral parts of natural history and natural philosophy, themselves portions of more comprehensive philosophic systems.[1] The second relates the pursuit of science to the increasing social complexity of modern societies and to their reliance upon specialised knowledge in every field of inquiry. This essay in a summary way will try to discuss these determinants of scientific activity.

Prior to the mid-nineteenth century, there was no generally recognised domain of science. Indeed, the word *science* as referring primarily to ' "Natural and Physical Science" and thus restricted to those branches of study that relate to the phenomena of the material universe and their laws' did not come into common use until the 1850s.[2] The concerns of present-day scientists were scattered over a variety of fields and were investigated by intellectuals who seldom specialised in any one. They did, however, generally recognise the same basic ordering of what men claimed to know. It is to that we should first turn because it did much to determine the kinds of people who engaged in science, the directions their science took and the uses which were found for it.

I. THE BIBLE AND EARLY EUROPEAN THOUGHT

Early modern European thinkers found the basic divisions in what they believed to lie in the manner in which their beliefs were justified. Religious beliefs almost always depended upon authorities and rested ultimately upon revelations conveyed to men in supernatural ways. Christianity possessed mysteries not to be rationally comprehended. These beliefs or truths belonged exclusively to the realm of grace, not nature, and pertained to the salvation of men. The Bible, however, contained historical information and comments on the natural world which were also regarded as authoritative and privileged. The accounts of the Creation, the fall of man and the history of the early ages of the world contained in Genesis applied to the natural world and could not be learned from analyses of the data of experience or through reasoning, although these activities might confirm the biblical history. Because revealed truths were usually seen as more certain and better warranted than other propositions derived from mere sense and reason, revelation and biblical history constituted a limit for natural knowledge and pushed its pursuit in areas likely to confirm religious belief just as they tended to foreclose other avenues of development.[3] One could explain the Noachian flood, confirm its existence, date it or plot its effects but one could not safely deny its occurrence.

Conceptions of an uncreated, eternal, merely material universe were outlawed by a higher truth, as were merely naturalistic accounts of human development over a time span which exceeded a rought limit of 6,000 years. For most of those who pursued scientific inquiries, these limitations did not create problems since they remained convinced Christians. Such men tended to believe that revealed and natural knowledge gained through sense and reason were compatible, complementary, God-given and not in conflict. Natural knowledge buttressed religious belief which in turn completed and limited cosmological speculations. Natural knowledge could show or make probable the design in nature which allowed men to infer the existence of a Creator. The fullness of the created world, revealed to the taxonomists and naturalists who recorded a seemingly endless and rapidly growing list of new minerals, plants and animals, humbled men's pride, as did the novel and beautiful regularities increasingly discovered by investigators of every sort. Those could and did lead to the pious outlook of men as diverse as Sir Thomas Browne, M.D. (1605–82), the Honourable Robert Boyle (1627–91), Colin MacLaurin (1698–1746) or Thomas Reid (1710–96), to cite only British examples.

The pursuit of natural knowledge had religious import throughout this period, a fact which was equally clear to such French men of letters and science as Fr Marin Mersenne (1588–1648), Fr Nicholas de Malebranche (1638–1715), Voltaire [François–Marie Arouet] (1694–1778) or some of the scientific writers who contributed to the *Encyclopédie* edited by Jean LeRond d'Alembert (1717–83), and Denis Diderot (1713–84). Protestants may have stressed these religious elements more than Catholics but the most widely read work of physico-theology produced in the eighteenth century was the *Spectacle de la nature* (1732–50) written by Abbé Noel-Antoine Pluche (1688–1761). The association of science with religion was also encouraged by censorship which operated throughout Europe until *c.* 1700 and thereafter was absent as an oppressive reality only in Holland, Britain and a few other small territories.[4] Without remembering the connection between religion and science it would be difficult to account for the large number of scientists recruited from the ranks of the clerics or the even greater number of men who justified and popularised science, not for its utility but because it supported religious beliefs and helped to make men moral by humbling their pride and leading them to the moral tenets of a natural religion.

2. NATURAL KNOWLEDGE

If knowledge was divisible into revealed and natural, the latter could also be divided and had been since classical times into three great disciplines: logic and metaphysics, moral philosophy and natural philosophy.[5] To the first belonged an abstract consideration of all existing things (ontology) such as space, time, substances and the forms of valid arguments about these. To the second principally belonged the study of spirits and minds (pneumatics) – God, angels, men – and of their active powers. Natural philosophy dealt with bodies and the reasons or causes for their changes and modifications. All three divisions of philosophy were seen as systematically related but the division of natural knowledge in this fashion meant that science was pursued by men whose principal concerns might not be scientific. The philosophic unity of natural knowledge was preserved until the end of the eighteenth century but it underwent important changes which affected the organisation and pursuit of science.[6] As it did so, all portions of what was conceived as a single conceptual structure changed when any important element of it was altered. One could not generally alter one's metaphysics without also perceiving a need to change one's physics or moral philosophy, just as one could not adopt new methods in one part of the system without having them affect other portions of it.

3. THE SCHOLASTIC TRADITION IN BRITAIN

In Britain, the scholastic philosophy prevailing in the sixteenth century was transformed after the time of Francis Bacon (1561–1626) by empiricist ideas which he had been the first to state with force, if not always with clarity. If all natural knowledge derived from experience, as he tended to argue, then philosophers needed to show that this was so. Empiricism entailed an epistemological revolution and a programme. It meant that the concepts of the metaphysician had to be shown to be derivable from experiences and reflection on these. Philosophers such as John Locke (1632–1704) and David Hume (1711–76) undertook this task and were emulated by Frenchmen such as

Etienne Bonnot, Abbé de Condillac (1715–80). Doing this required thinkers to give a new status to concepts such as *space*, *time* and *substance* which now tended to become ideas produced by human minds rather than objective things in a universe directly known *a priori*. The categories which defined nature were becoming dependent upon experience and thought and could, would, change over time, a point explicitly made in Adam Smith's (1723–90) posthumously published *History of Astronomy* (1795)[7] (see art. 1, sect. 4). Empiricism could explain the progress of knowledge and its relativity to men and their minds. At the same time it required a thorough-going investigation of every area of thought.[8] Men like Francis Hutcheson (1694–1746), after 1730 the Glasgow University Professor of Moral Philosophy, dedicated their scholarly careers to showing that moral philosophy too could be restructured on an empirical base.[9] This meant a more detailed and critical attempt to understand the human mind; it meant, in short, a much better psychology. Since moral philosophy also dealt with ethics, natural law, jurisprudence and economics, Hutcheson's work put these too on empirical foundations which were broadened by his successors in Scotland such as David Hume (1711–76), Henry Home, Lord Kames (1696–1782), Smith and Dugald Stewart (1753–1826). As they pursued these branches of natural knowledge they helped to found the modern sciences of anthropology, psychology, political economy and sociology.

4. EMPIRICISM

Empiricist philosophy made epistemology the primary philosophic study. In doing so it profoundly changed the position and function of logic.[10] The old forms of deductive argument were supplemented by a logic of discovery, found in induction, operating upon the data of casual observations or those produced and controlled by critical investigations and experimental methods. To expand knowledge by observations systematically and critically made became the objective of many *virtuosi* throughout Europe during the seventeenth century. This promoted natural history but it had equally important effects upon antiquarian and historical studies.[11] These reflected humanist concerns with a classical past, the discoveries of explorers and the chorographies often produced by men such as Robert Plot (1640–96) whose surveys of regions of Europe looked toward practical improvements and technical developments. Increasingly the critical methods of the natural philosophers and the natural historians shaped the work of antiquaries and improving surveyors. These developments also fed into the materials which would give rise to new social sciences not only in Scotland but in the France of Anne–Robert–Jacques–Turgot, Baron de l'Aune (1727–81) and Marie J.T.A. N. de Caritat, Marquis de Condorcet (1743–94) (see art. 67, sect. 1). What was true of these studies was even more evident in those which concerned bodies. Here experimental methods were clearly formulated, not only in Britain where Robert Boyle, Robert Hooke (1635–1703) and Sir Isaac Newton (1642–1727) gave expression to them but also in Italy where Galileo Galilei (1564–1642) and his followers stated them, as did Pierre Gassendi (1592–1655) and various members of the Parisian *Académie des sciences*. The results were thus quickly apparent in hydrostatics, chemistry, in new sciences of motion, dynamics and rational mechanics, in the optics of Newton and the microscopy of many Dutch, French and British observers.

Empiricism as a programme which relied upon an analytical and critical evaluation of experience and upon an experimental method (which in thought experiments could even be employed in moral philosophy) increasingly displaced rationalist philosophy of an *a priori* sort. Not only Aristotelianism but Cartesianism and, outside Germany, Leibnizianism were discredited by c.1800. Indeed, the European Enlightenment is largely the story of the triumph of empiricism and scientific methods defined in the seventeenth century and extended to every field of inquiry during the eighteenth. The unity of philosophical systems which had been based upon the unfolding or deductive elaboration of the meaning of their substantial concepts known *a priori* was slowly replaced by a methodological unity imposed by concepts and truths held to be probable, contingent and likely to change in the future as knowledge expanded. It was also constituted by the acceptance of methods of analysis and synthesis seen as applicable to every field.

By 1800 the systematic unity of natural knowledge had considerably lessened as philosophers came to see various disciplines as the probable constructs of the men who studied them and not necessarily reflective of what truly existed. The idea of a completed philosophic system remained but for a thinker like Immanuel Kant (1724–1804) its purpose was regulative of human effort: it represented an ideal of reason which men could state but to which they could not attain. Moreover, empirical methodologies applied to discrete sets of data allowed for the organisation of disciplines which could be treated as autonomous. The chemistry of Antoine Lavoisier (1743–94) or the economics of Jeremy Bentham (1748–1832) bore little systematic relationship to the study of *body* as it was formerly conceived or to moral philosophy as it had once been pursued. In the long run, empiricism and its attendant methods favoured the emergence of independent sciences pursued by specialists not very mindful of the religious, moral or other implications of what they did. With those changes came others related to ideas about natural knowledge which had long been held in the West.

5. NATURAL PHILOSOPHY

Natural philosophy worked at in a systematic context had usually been pursued for ends extrinsic to itself. It had also generally been conceived as a search for causes. These led to metaphysics and that, at last to God. In its ancient and scholastic forms, it had prized that knowledge most which was abstract, spiritual and contemplative. Preference had been clearly given to what was theoretical (and usually speculative) in character and not to what was concrete and mired in the mundane things of experience. Philosophy had remained aloof from the arts which it could 'explain' even though their practitioners were usually seen as unable to understand the principles which governed what they did. Natural philosophy was not alien to educated physicians, surgeons, astrologers, alchemists, architects or even artists, engineers and gunners, but it seldom involved many artisans until after the first third of the eighteenth century. Deplored by the humanists of the sixteenth century, by Christian pansophists and Baconians and finally by the philosophes, these attitudes about knowledge died hard. As they did the pursuit of science by men informed by artisans or by the artisans themselves became more common. Popular expositions of science, lectures, toys and instruments designed to reach amateurs and artisans began in the eighteenth century to bridge the gulf between the theorists and the doers. Also contributing to this end were many technical 'how to' books which ranged from cheap broadsides to the expensive and elegant encyclopedias, of which Diderot's and d'Alembert's is surely the most impressive.[12]

While philosophy had kept aloof from practice it had insisted both in the ancient world and in that of the modern scholastics that every theoretical discipline had its practical employment. From this it followed that improvements in theory should lead to improvements in practice and thus to the amelioration of conditions in this world. So long as theoretical changes had no important and noticeable impact upon practice or conditions it was not urgent that theories be changed or that scarce resources be spent upon the pursuit and development of sciences. Support for cartographers, fort builders, navigators, astrologers, physicians and architects might be found but state support for specialised institutions to promote natural knowledge came generally after *c.* 1650 and even then was most concerned with practical inquiries. Only after the 'new science' had been seen to have some important practical consequences was it promoted for these reasons. Even then the expectation that it would be useful was greater than its ability to change much for the better. Despite that, scientific pursuits found new favour among seventeenth-century Europeans. Bacon and Tommaso Campanella (1568–1639) had at the beginning of the century set out visions of societies which supported, and benefited from, the pursuit of useful natural knowledge. The *New Atlantis* (1626) and *the City of the Sun* (1623) were dreams which moved pansophists and other men seeking a regenerated world endowed with a proper philosophy.[13] Theirs and other similar schemes inspired men who knew that some progress had been made and that more was possible. 'Scientists' who had hitherto been found isolated in a great variety of places increasingly began to collect in clubs and societies dedicated to the pursuit of new philosophies which for many were meant to lead to certainties, a regenerated religion and a world improved, if not restored to its pristine state. It is now time to consider the places in which men had pursued science and those novel ones whose creation was for the first time dedicated to the professional furtherance of natural knowledge.

6. SCIENTISTS AND THE CHURCH

Many of the places which supported the work of early modern scientists are to be found in the various churches of the period. Most ecclesiastical establishments had some posts which offered the necessary leisure, income and independence for the pursuit of some activity. Even in the eighteenth century a surprising number of European Catholic scientists held church livings. Among them were such men as the French astronomer Nicolas-Louis de Lacaille (1713–62), the Austrian mathematical physicist Rudjer Josip Bošković (1711–87) and the Irish biologist Abbé John Turberville Needham (1713–81). Protestant countries had fewer such places but they did not wholly disappear, particularly in England and in those parts of Lutheran Germany in which episcopalian systems survived. Indeed, some of the brighter scientific reputations in eighteenth-century England belonged to the Reverends John Theophilus Desaguliers (1638–1744), Stephen Hales (1677–1761) and Joseph Priestley (1733–1804). Dutch and Scottish Calvinists had their share of natural philosophers but they tended more often to be men who had trained as clerics but had been called to more secular professions, as was the case with Professors Herman Boerhaave, MD (1668–1738), Colin MacLaurin (1698–1746) and John Playfair (1748–1819).[14]

Throughout Europe the churches generally controlled, staffed or supervised the universities, colleges and higher schools as well as their teachers. This meant that until well after 1800 most of those who introduced students to science, philosophy and mathematics were either already in orders or were under the jurisdiction of men who were, or were themselves contemplating a clerical career. This surely worked to preserve the connections between science and religion. Indeed, it probably channelled researchers into areas such as natural history and botany which were seen as useful for apologetic purposes and which were also not too demanding. Educational institutions also decided to some extent what was studied and what flourished by the places assigned to various subjects and by the men who taught them. Mathematics, philosophy and astronomy were all arts subjects often taught by younger men who looked forward to the securing of better chairs in faculties of medicine or divinity. Since the arts chairs were generally older and by 1700 often less well endowed, they were not always desirable or conscientiously filled. Moreover, the science-related teaching positions in the sixteenth century universities never amounted to more than 10 per cent of all chairs if medical posts are excluded. Until the eighteenth century the prestige of science in the colleges and schools was not great and it is not surprising that science struggled to find a supportive audience for its endeavours even in seventeenth century England.[15] Science fared better in eighteenth-century universities. Yet even at Edinburgh University in the 1760s only five of eleven arts chairs were science-related and these included neither the most prestigious – Moral Philosophy – nor the most lucrative – Greek.[16] Grammar and other schools sometimes sheltered scientists by avocation but few of these taught even much mathematics until after *c.*1730.

7. SCIENTISTS AND THE COURT

Civil establishments in the early modern period found increasing numbers of places for intellectuals, including some scientists. The most prominent among these were courts. Every court and many noble households had resident physicians, surgeons, astrologers and astronomers, engineers/architects/surveyors and other intellectual odd-job men whose skills involved numeracy and some practical ability. Leonardo da Vinci (1452–1519), Johannes Kepler (1571–1630), Sir Chistopher Wren (1632–1723) and Georges-Louis Leclerc, Comte de Buffon (1707–88) are among the many men of science who held court offices. For these functionaries there were incentives to innovate. The better they performed their jobs, the more glory they gave to their patron and the more likely they were to reap in rewards.

In the sixteenth, seventeenth and eighteenth centuries governments became increasingly separated from royal households. As they did so they were bureaucratised into departments which even then tended to multiply as they became more specialised. As this process worked itself out more places were created in which scientists could find support and useful employment. Armies needed the skills of men like Niccolò Tartaglia (*c.* 1499–1577), an Italian mathematician and military engineer who served the Duke of Urbino; and they continued to employ them in ever-increasing numbers throughout this period. In Scotland by 1760 there were probably four men teaching gunnery and fortification outside the five universities within whose walls the five professors of mathematics almost certainly included these subjects in one of their courses. The Scots whom they taught provided a disproportionate percentage of the officers in the technical services of the British army. Elsewhere special schools, often with distinguished teachers, arose to fill this need. Pierre–Simon Laplace (1749–1827) taught at the Ecole Militaire, Gaspard Monge (1746–1818) at the Ecole Royale du Génie de Mezières and John Robison (1739–1805) was for some time a Professor of Mathematics to the Imperial Corps of Sea Cadets in St Petersburg. After the Napoleonic Wars such schools were to proliferate across Europe as nations imitated those established in the Old Regime and perpetuated under state auspices in post-revolutionary France.[17] Navies were no less productive of places for scientists. Galileo's new sciences were related to his work at the Venetian Arsenal, as was much of the science done by Henri-Louis Duhamel de Monceau (1700–82)[18] who in a variety of places was involved with French marine affairs. Conquests and the prospects of conquests also made work for the learned. The reputation of Sir William Petty (1623–87) as a surveyor, like Sir Hans Sloane's (1660–1753) as a botanist, came from work done in recently conquered Ireland and Jamaica. The crews of Captain James Cook (1728–79) and Louis de Bougainville (1729–1811) contained similar sorts of men. Less often this was true of colonial officials but all the eighteenth century empires could point to some savants such as Cadwallader Colden (1688–1776) or those who joined colonial scientific societies.[19] By the late seventeenth century most major states had numerous other departments with one or more figures whose activities furthered the advance of science or served as a reward for such work. What was true of government departments was becoming increasingly true of large private concerns and commercial companies.

8. SCIENTISTS AND INDUSTRY

The great trading companies of the seventeenth century sometimes hired experts to work on complex technical problems concerned with navigation and their trades. Other corporations, such as those which drained the English Fenlands or built the great London water pumps, also employed men who occasionally became notable mathematicians, engineers and surveyors as well as contributors to science. It is worth recalling in this context that Sir Jonas Moore (1617–79), the promoter of the Royal Observatory at Greenwich, had worked as a surveyor in the Fens, as a tutor and for the government in a variety of offices. The great canal which linked the Garonne with the Rhône river system or the fountain pumps at Chantilly and Versailles did as much for France and perhaps even more for hydraulics, as the work of Edme Mariotte (1620–84) and Henri Pitot (1695–1771) suggests.

Wherever there was large-scale commercial and industrial expansion during the seventeenth and eighteenth centuries, wherever great capitals were applied in a way requiring technological change, places were created for men who might and often did contribute to science, or at the very least functioned as members of its audience and as its consumes.[20] By c. 1720 a greater speculator such as James Brydges, the first Duke of Chandos (1673–1744), might constantly retain technical advisors to assess the feasibility of mining, insurance or other ventures or to find ways of making them more profitable. Chandos was well served by the Reverends John Harris (?1667–1719) and John Theophilus Desaguliers and later by James Stirling (1692–1770), men whose scientific activities were also supported by clerical posts and a teaching position.[21] There was perhaps less of this on the continent but there state advisors often filled these roles. In both environments there was an increasing need not only for engineers but for chemists. In Britain by the mid-eighteenth century, entrepreneurs like James Watt (1736–1819), Josiah Wedgwood (1730–95), or Drs John Roebuck (1718–94) and James Hutton (1726–97) had become chemists themselves. Others like them paid such men as Joseph Black (1728–99), Joseph Priestley (1733–1804) or the French chemists Pierre-Joseph Macquer (1718–84) and Claude Louis Berthollet (1748–1822) to act as consultants. What was true of chemistry was by the end of this period also the case in agriculture, mining, insurance and engineering. Men such as Lavoisier, Dr Andrew Coventry (1764–1832), the first Professor of Agriculture at Edinburgh University, James Hutton, the Rev. Richard Price (1723–91) or John Robison could all have made comfortable livings as freelance technical experts. At the end of the 1790s John (later Professor Sir John) Leslie (1766–1832) was doing so and working on his *Experimental Inquiry into the Nature and Properties of Heat* (1804).

9. THE DEVELOPMENT OF SCIENCE IN EUROPE

As social, economic and technological complexity grew in Europe, the pursuit of science tended to be seen in altered ways. Its relation to religion and morality weakened and justifications for scientific activities were cast more in utilitarian terms. Scientific progress could make men happy by making life richer, easier and productive of more pleasure to increasing numbers. Most of the eighteenth century philosophes tended to see it in this way. If it was methodologically independent and not bound to a particular place in the economy of knowledge, then science was an autonomous activity which could be pursued for its own sake and within institutions appropriate to it. Haltingly, Europeans began to create these in the form of academies and societies dedicated to the furtherance of natural knowledge.

Fourteenth-, fifteenth- and sixteenth-century Italian humanists found that their literary and critical interests were not welcomed in the universities or by scholastics. Because of that, they tended to seek and find places outside the schools, in the chanceries of city states, at courts and in the entourages of despots and merchant princes such as the Medici. Throughout the 1400s such men had organised clubs, most of which were unspecialised in nature and few of which paid much attention to science or even mathematics.[22] They did help to popularise the idea that learning could and ought to be revived and they interested some of the social elite in this goal which was generally associated with the belief that the material social and political conditions of life could also be changed for the better. These humanists also often placed a higher value upon the practical knowledge possessed by craftsmen. That side of humanism aided the development of science by publishing the works of Roman engineers and architects such as Vitruvius (1st century B.C.) or by collecting and editing whatever antiquity had known about medicine and many other fields. Georgius Agricola's [Georg Bauer (1494–1555)] *De re metallica* (1556) is exemplative of this side of humanist interests although its provenance is German, not Italian. Most Italian and French Renaissance academies were literary in orientation but their platonism and enthusiasm for ancient learning gave them some interests in mathematics, science and technology.

By 1600 these small beginnings of the academic organisation and support of science were being undercut by the repressive influences of the Counter-Reformation. This continued in seventeenth-century Italy and was to some extent responsible for the demise of two important academies: the *Accademia dei Lincei* (1603–29) and the *Accademia del Cimento* (1657–67). Both of these were technically private ventures sponsored by noblemen although the latter, despite its lack of a formal constitution, was closely related to and supported by the Grand Dukes of Tuscany. Both bodies had evolved from even less formally organised clubs of *virtuosi* as did most of the important academic bodies elsewhere.[23] Both helped in different ways to define what scientific academies should be or become. The Lincei, partly because Galileo was a member, established experiments as an important, usual and privileged means of advancing science, and the academy as a body both sanctioning this method and authenticating the results. It functioned, as did later societies, as a reference group for other scientists, as a clearing house for information and as a focus for interests made more general by its work. These in turn were legitimated and given social significance by aristocratic patronage and by the gentility and usefulness of its members. All of this was clear in Rome before Bacon's similar views were widely known, or known in Italy. What the Lincei stood for became known in Europe as the difficulties or 'persecution' of its most prominent member, Galileo, began to be of interest to European intellectuals, particularly those in Protestant Holland and Britain. That the *Accademia del Cimento* should have provided another institutionalised instance of the outlook and methods of Galileo and his associates shows that these had rooted but that they could flourish only if nourished with resources provided by very generous patrons willing to protect scientists from those who feared their conclusions. Most of the important friends and correspondents which the academicians of Tuscany had found by 1667 were, unfortunately, outside Italy. Many were by then already associated with similar bodies.

French and English *virtuosi* can be found meeting informally to discuss a variety of concerns from the late 1500s on, but the patterns of their organisation were to vary with the politics of the two countries. In France the organising proclivities of absolutist regimes led to a greater control of culture and to its guidance by the state. The still remaining Renaissance academies tended to receive charters from the crown and in Paris the Académie Française (1635) provided an early model for the institutionalised pursuit of science. Private discussion groups appear in the Paris of the 1620s and more elsewhere are referred to by the intellectuals of that time. None seem to have been exclusively scientific in outlook. In Paris the most successful academic venture, Théophraste de Renaudot's (1586–1653) Bureau d'Adresse (1633–42) enjoyed the sponsorship of Cardinal Richelieu (1585–1642) and the protection of the state it sought to serve by promoting the acquisition and use of natural knowledge.[24] Renaudot's Bureau had successors but their private patrons lacked the resources and commitment to support the programme desired by scientists and seen as useful by royal advisors such as Jean–Baptiste Colbert (1619–83) who was interested in science and appreciated its promise as a prop to industry and the activities of the state. Colbert was also not unaware that the successful promotion of learning would bring honour and *gloire* to Louis XIV who desperately craved both. In 1666 a French *Académie des Sciences*[25] was founded in Paris when Louis decided to emulate his English cousin, Charles II, who in 1662 had chartered the Royal Society of London.[26]

10. SCIENCE AND PHILOSOPHY IN BRITAIN

The British experience with academies had been less extensive than that of Italians and Frenchmen but up to the 1640s it was essentially the same. A few clubs and societies had existed but so had worried statesmen who wished to control intellectuals. James I had refused to allow antiquaries to meet in London and had refused to charter a society for them. Control of cultural activities had been an aim of Archbishop William Laud (1573–1645) as well as of Cardinal Richelieu. In England the groups of intellectuals meeting to discuss science and philosophy were probably fewer and smaller than the French clubs but by the 1640s they emerge with some clarity in the freer world created by the Puritan Revolution. That also made places at Oxford and Cambridge for more proponents of the new learning and experimental philosophy. The Restoration of Stuart rule in 1660 did not greatly upset the institutional gains which had been made but did bring to the circles of the *virtuosi* returning exiles excited by the science of continental thinkers which they wished to promote in England. Robert Boyle, Sir William Petty or Bishop John Wilkins (1614–72) might have been Puritan in sympathy but William, Viscount Brouncker (c. 1620–88), Sir Robert Moray (1608–73) and Sir Kenelm Digby (1603–65) were enthusiasts for the same activities from within the Royalist camp. Any English society promoted after 1660 would have to reconcile or agree to ignore many of the interests brought to it by both sets of men. The pansophist, improving, religious elements of the first group were modified and balanced by the politically conservative and statist outlook of the other. Both groups had to recognise that attitudes about individual liberty, the limits of royal authority and the purposes of government had changed greatly in England between *c.* 1640 and 1660. They also worked in a limited state with little extra cash for such marginal activities as the pursuit of science.

The Royal Society of London founded in 1662 was a voluntary society which controlled its own affairs, agenda, officers and membership and which lacked the propaganda and ideological functions assigned to the French Royal Academy which had many more ostentatious, public ceremonial functions supportive of both the monarchy and church. Unlike the French Royal Academy, it received little financial aid from the Crown and paid only a few men to devote all of their time to the pursuit of natural knowledge. It was less able to sustain long-term projects and relied far more on the work of *virtuosi* who were less able to further and develop research traditions than were the paid *pensionnaires* of the *Académie des Sciences*.

These two great societies became the model for many later academies which divided institutionally into statist and voluntary bodies.[27] And they both encouraged the formation of unchartered societies. In the English-speaking world the 1680s and 1690s saw either the founding or attempts to found *virtuoso* societies in Oxford, Dublin, Boston and three of the Scottish university towns (Aberdeen, St. Andrews and Edinburgh).[28] These were to be satellites of the Royal Society of London which would review, publish and in some measure direct their work. The societies later founded at Peterborough, Spalding, Norwich, Edinburgh, Philadelphia and Charlestown (Charleston, SC) fulfilled that dream to some extent.[29] Outside the British world such societies were later in developing and generally less important, although they tended to recruit members from the same social strata and to pursue similar programmes. The French *Académie des Sciences* found imitators within that realm in various provincial capitals and large cities. Although few of these bodies employed many professional scientists, those academies looked to Paris for their standards and for guidance. Absolutist regimes elsewhere in Europe after 1700 also promoted many more bodies to do for their countries what Louis XIV and Colbert expected the Parisian Academy to do for France.

II. THE EUROPEAN ENLIGHTENMENT

All of these new institutions had a profound effect upon the pursuit of science. They gave it prestige, social legitimation, recognition and an important place outside the schools and church but within the state among the complex of institutions promoting secular novelties. Defining new roles, they created for the first time scientific careers and a new if small class of professional scientists who served as their permanent and full time functionaries. Because they were recognised, approved and increasingly successful and useful, they promoted the pursuit of science among the classes for whom approval, success and utility were most important – professional men, gentlemen who had to make their way in the world and those who sought to be regarded as polite and useful members of society. The academies and societies were all committed to the use of experimental methods which they saw as not only providing men with new knowledge but all as eliminating old errors, superstitions and ignorance. They were also promoters of mathematics which some men increasingly saw as the real language of natural philosophy. The academies' attitudes toward knowledge supported and helped to drive the European Enlightenment which they did much to define. Societies everywhere became exemplars of good science not only for their respective kingdom but for the European Republic of Letters. Indeed, this Republic and the cosmopolitan ideals it expressed reflected the institutionalisation of science in these new bodies. Their transactions, memoires, journals and other published works created a new medium for the exchange of information and speeded the dissemination and criticism of new ideas. Even though many of these institutions were also committed to chauvinistic ends, their publications, research programmes, prize competitions and work as state agencies gave a direction to national and international scientific activities which had formerly been lacking in Europe. This can be seen not only in the common European pursuit of problems which engaged the attention of men in London, Paris and later Berlin, Uppsala or St Petersburg but also in co-operative undertakings such as the observations of the Transit of Venus in 1761 and 1769.[30]

As the academies pursued their projects, they also tended to make science more clearly a distinctive activity requiring rigorous training and specialised expertise. Their own standards and the work of their professional members had encouraged specialisation and had raised the expected levels of performance so that by 1800 few amateurs and *virtuosi* were to be found among those making significant contributions to natural knowledge. As servants of their respective states the academies increasingly showed how useful specialised bodies possessing scientific knowledge could be to the governments which chartered or supported them.

12. THE GROWTH OF SCIENTIFIC INSTITUTIONS

The success of the great academies can be measured in numerous ways by the end of the eighteenth century. Everywhere private and government-supported scientific institutions were more numerous and visible. Even post-revolutionary France preserved its national academy (albeit under a new name, the Institut de France) and set up more specialised bureaux. After 1750 great numbers of new societies and academies are to be found in Europe and the European colonies.[31] Most were located in provincial centres where urban growth, improved education, specialised industries and the existence of state institutions or universities allowed for the recruitment of enough intellectuals to form a general purpose club. Most of these groups found some place for the discussion if not the active pursuit of science. In these contexts science cannot and should not be too sharply separated from improving interests in agriculture, technology, industry or the desirable social and political changes related to these. Many provincial intellectuals found in these milieux encouragement, an audience and some help in sharpening minds and methods which they would employ in science done elsewhere. Among these bodies were institutions like the numerous Economic Societies formed after *c.* 1760 which brought to bear upon social questions the outlook of the empirical natural philosophers. Between 1750 and 1770 from Spain to Russia governments themselves did much to promote such bodies.[32] Medical, agricultural, improving and other often ephemeral groups appeared in response to plagues, subsistence crises, changes in regimes and a general increase in knowledge and desires to change societies in ways generally set out with varying degrees of radicalism by the French philosophes.

Another set of institutions are to be found in English cities such as Birmingham, Derby, Leeds, Manchester, Newcastle and Sheffield. There, literary and philosophical societies grew up sponsored by businessmen who oriented their scientific activities to the industrial concerns which they had as entrepreneurs and manufacturers.[33] The older bodies had been generally aristocratic and professional in outlook; these were industrial. The older societies had tended to be agricultural and statist in orientation; these were not, just as they were not as elitist and conservative in their politics or Anglican in their religion. All of these late eighteenth-century developments pushed the use of science in new areas, among new classes and found for it a new audience.[34] They also showed the degree to which science had penetrated social strata which in 1700 were just being appealed to by books, lecturers, instrument makers and divines. A new audience had indeed been created for science (see art. 65), one which in the nineteenth century would demand more and better teaching of science subjects but which would also support pseudo-sciences such as Mesmerism and phrenology. The pursuit of science would hereafter seldom be confined to the principal cities or so exclusively within such elitist institutions as the academies had been.

13. THE EFFECTS OF THE FRENCH REVOLUTION

The French Revolution dramatically changed the organised pursuit of science in France and foreshadowed later developments both there and elsewhere. The First Republic insisted upon its totalitarian right to order all activities and to harness all talents for the public good. Science no less than other concerns was brought under the direction of the state. As the Republican regimes ceased to lurch from crisis to crisis, scientific pursuits in France were organised in new educational institutions, government departments and research establishments, all of which were better funded than had previously been the case. As this happened science's old ties to religion and to the cosmopolitan pursuit of philosophy tended to be broken by what was later to be called positivism and by the nationalist patriotism which scientists were expected to feel. Those attitudes, rather than the more pacific cosmopolitanism of the Enlightenment, began to mark the new scientists. The use of scientific methods to analyse society and governments was discouraged and would later surface as part of the programme of radical socialists. The French government remained a supporter of research but it was channelled toward military uses and civilian employments seen as having benefits for those with power. France spread through Europe many of these attitudes and some of the new-made institutions. In the English-speaking world this period was more notable for private initiatives which led not to government-funded and controlled institutes but to more societies now beginning to take on a distinctly modern look. At the top were those which now increasingly tended to honour achievement, such as the Royal Societies of London or Edinburgh. On the second rung specialised and at least partly professionalised bodies tended to direct inquiries in areas such as botany or geology while at a third level one finds provincial societies with relatively unspecialised interests of a practical sort. In addition to these, many more institutions catering to the needs of special groups were to be found, ranging from new laboratories and classrooms in the universities to working men's scientific societies, often looked at with suspicion by their betters.[35] In this freer world, science has long been incorporated into other institutions which contributed to its organised pursuit.

NOTES

1. Schematic representations of the relations of the arts, sciences and realms of knowledge and faith can be found in many places, including some editions of the works of Bacon, Hobbes, Locke and Hegel as well as in encyclopedias such as those edited by Ephriam Chambers (c. 1680–1740) and Denis Diderot (1713–84).

2. *The compact edition of the Oxford English Dictionary*, (2 vols., Oxford, 1971), vol. 2, pp. 2668:222.

3. R. S. Westfall, *Science and religion in seventeenth-century England* (New Haven, 1958); G. Reedy, SJ, *The Bible and reason: Anglicans and Scripture in late seventeenth-century England* (Philadelphia, 1985); D. C. Allen, *The legend of Noah: renaissance rationalism in art, science and letters* (Urbana, 1963; originally published in *Illinois studies in language and literature*, 33 (1949, Nos. 3–4).

4. An extensive list of European physico-theological works is given by W. Philipp, 'Physicotheology in the age of Enlightenment: appearance and history', *Studies on Voltaire and the eighteenth century*, LVII (1967), 1233–67.

5. Barbara J. Shapiro, *Probability and certainty in seventeenth-century England: a study of the relationships between natural science, religion, history, law, and literature* (Princeton, 1983).

6. R. W. Meyer, *Leibnitz and the seventeenth-century revolution* (trans. J. P. Stern, Cambridge, 1952), pp. 38–65. R. Harré, 'Knowledge,' in *The ferment of knowledge: studies in the historiography of eighteenth-century science* (eds.) G. S. Rousseau and R. Porter (Cambridge, 1980), pp. 11–54.

7. The best edition of this essay is contained in *The Glasgow edition of the works and correspondence of Adam Smith* (6 vols. Oxford, 1976–1981) III (1980), ed. by I. S. Ross, D. D. Raphael and A. S. Skinner, pp. 31–105. Smith's views on the progress of science resemble those offered by T. S. Kuhn in *The structure of scientific revolutions* (2nd ed., Chicago, 1970).

8. E. Cassirer's, *The philosophy of the Enlightenment* (trans. F. C. A. Koelln and J. P. Pettegrove, Princeton, 1951) works out that programme in detail.

9. T. L. Hankins, *Science and the Enlightenment* (Cambridge, 1985), pp. 158–90.

10. W. S. Howell, *Eighteenth-century British logic and rhetoric* (Princeton, 1971); V. M. Bevilacqua, 'Adam Smith and some philosophical origins of eighteenth-century rhetorical theory', *Modern language review*, 63 (1968), 559–68. The changes which came to literature have been discussed by W. P. Jones, *The rhetoric of science: a study of scientific ideas and imagery in eighteenth-century English poetry* (London, 1966); H. Brown, *Science and the human comedy* (Toronto and Buffalo, 1976); M. H. Nicolson, *Newton demands the muse* (Princeton, 1946); *Voyages to the moon* (New York, 1948).

11. J. M. Levine, *Dr. Woodward's Shield: history, science and satire in Augustan England* (Berkeley, Los Angeles, London, 1977); *Humanism and history: origins of modern English historiography* (Ithaca, London, 1987), pp. 14–15.

12. A. E. Musson and E. Robinson, *Science and technology in the industrial revolution* (Manchester, 1969), pp. 10–200, *passim*; D. Diderot, J. LeR. d'Alembert, *Encyclopédie ou dictionnaire raisonné des sciences, des arts et des métiers* (Paris, 1751–80).

13. F. E. and F. P. Manuel, *Utopian thought in the western world* (Cambridge Mass., 1979), Part III, pp. 205–410; C. Webster, *The great instauration* (London, 1975).

14. Some of these men are noticed by E. G. Ruestow, *Physics at seventeenth and eighteenth-century Leiden: philosophy and the new science in the university* (The Hague, 1973); others appear in *Martinus Van Marum: life and work* ed. E. LeFebvre and J. G. de Bruijn; IV, G. L'E. Turner and T. H. Levere (Leyden, 1973), pp. 3–102.

15. J. Ben-David, *The scientist's role in society: a comparative study* (Englewood Cliffs, 1971), pp. 50–5.

16. J. B. Morell, 'The University of Edinburgh in the late eighteenth century: its scientific eminence and academic structure', *Isis*, 62 (1971), 158–71.

17. The careers of these and many other similar men are recounted in two splendid accounts of the institutionalisation of science in eighteenth-century and early-nineteenth-century France: C. C. Gillispie, *Science and polity in France at the end of the Old Regime* (Princeton, 1980), M. Crosland, *The society of Arcueil: a view of French science at the time of Napoleon I* (Cambridge, Mass., 1967).

18. 'Duhamel de Monceau', Jon Eklund in *Dictionary of scientific biography* (16 vols., ed. C. C. Gillispie, New York, 1970–80), Vol. iv, pp. 223–5.

19. Those in the American British colonies are noticed in R. P. Stearns, *Science in the British colonies of America* (Urbana, 1970); B. Hindle, *The pursuit of science in revolutionary America 1735–1789* (Chapel Hill, 1956); many of the colonial societies are noticed in J. E. McClellan, *Science reorganized: scientific societies in the eighteenth century* (New York, 1985); typical of the scientific interests and pursuits of many enlightened bureaucrats were those of Jean-Marie Roland de la Platière discussed by C. A. LeGuin in 'Roland de la Platière: a public servant of the eighteenth century', *Transactions of the American Philosophical Society* (N. S. 56: Part 6 (1966)).

20. This has been documented for Scotland by A. and N. L. Clow, *The chemical revolution* (London, 1952); a sceptical discussion of the ties held to exist between science and industry can be found in Peter Mathias, *The first industrial nation: an economic history of Britain 1700–1914* (2nd ed., London and New York, 1983), pp. 110–165. This includes a helpful bibliography.

21. L. Stewart, 'The selling of Newton: science and technology in early eighteenth-century England', *Journal of British studies*, 25 (1986), 178–92.

22. References to the literature on these early bodies can be found in E. W. Cochrane, *Tradition and enlightenment in the Tuscan academies 1690–1800* (Chicago, 1961), pp. 1–33; W. E. K. Middleton, *The experimenters: a study of the Accademia del Cimento* (Baltimore and London, 1971), pp. 1–15; Ben-David, (1971), pp. 55–70.

23. M. Ornstein, *The role of scientific societies in the seventeenth century* (3rd ed., New York, 1938); H. Brown, *Scientific organizations in seventeenth century France* (New York, 1967); McClellan, (1985), pp. 41–66.

24. H. M. Solomon, *Public welfare, science, and propaganda in seventeenth century France: the innovations of Théophraste Renaudot* (Princeton, 1972).
25. R. Hahn, *The anatomy of a scientific institution: the Paris Academy of Sciences, 1666–1803* (Berkeley, Los Angeles, London, 1971).
26. M. Hunter, *The Royal Society and its Fellows 1660–1700: the morphology of an early scientific institution* (British Society for the History of Science, Mongraph 4, 2nd ed. 1985), Dorothy Stimson, *Scientists and amateurs, a history of the Royal Society* (New York, 1948); Margery Purver, *The Royal Society: concept and creation* (London, 1967).
27. See Appendix II.
28. T. K. Hoppen, *The common scientist in the seventeenth century: a study of the Dublin philosophical society 1683–1708* (London, 1970), pp. 210–11; McClellan, (1985), p. 57; R. L. Emerson, 'Science and the origins and concerns of the Scottish Enlightenment', *History of science*, 26 (1988), 333–66.
29. Musson and Robinson, (1969), pp. 138–42; R. L. Emerson, 'The Philosophical Society of Edinburgh 1737–1783', *The British journal for the history of science*, 12 (1979), pp. 154–91, 14 (1981), 133–76, 18 (1985), 255–303; R. S. Bates, *Scientific societies in the United States* (New York, 1945).
30. H. Woolf, *The transit of Venus: a study of eighteenth-century science* (Princeton, 1959).
31. The French societies are brilliantly described by D. Roche in *Le siècle des lumières en province: académies et académiciens provinciaux 1680–1789* (2 vols., Paris and the Hague, 1978). Others are noticed in McClellan (1985) and Bates (1945).
32. There is no general work on the economic societies but see R. J. Shafer, *The economic societies in the Spanish world 1763–1821* (Syracuse, 1958); Franco Venturi, *Italy and the Enlightenment* (trans. Susan Corsi, ed. Stuart Woolf, London, 1972), pp. 265–291; Roche, (1978); Roger Hahn: 'The Application of science to society: the societies of arts', *Studies on Voltaire*, 25 (1963), 829–36.
33. These are all noticed in McClellan (1985) or Musson and Robinson, (1969); see also R. E. Schofield, *The Lunar Society of Birmingham: a social history of provincial science and industry in eighteenth century England* (Oxford, 1963).
34. There is now a considerable literature dealing with the shaping of scientific activities by the local contexts and interest of scientists. Many of those studies are noted in *The ferment of knowledge* (Rousseau and Porter, 1980).
35. Douglas McKie, 'Scientific societies to the end of the eighteenth century' in *Natural philosophy through the 18th century*, (ed.) Allan Ferguson (London and Totowa, 1972; first printed London, 1948), pp. 141–2.

APPENDIX

Selected Scientific Academies and Societies *c.* 1560–1800.

'*' denotes an incorporated society; the absence of a '*' denotes a private one. Place-names are shown in italics where the society published materials. Dates ending with '—' mean that the date of dissolution is unknown or that the society still continues. Information on these and other bodies is given in the works whose titles appear in the notes.

Dates	Name	Place
c. 1560s	Accademia Secretorum Naturae	Naples
c. 1600–57	Accademia dei Lincei	Rome
1622–24	Societas Ereunetica	Rostock
1633–42	Bureau d'adresse	Paris
1651–90	Oxford Philosophical Society	Oxford
1652–72–95	Collegium Naturae Curiosum/Academia Caesarae-Leopoldina naturae curiosorum*	*Schweinfurt*

Dates	Name	Place
c. 1662–	Royal Society of London*	*London*
1666–1793	Académie royale des sciences*	*Paris*
1666–75	Académie de physique*	*Caen*
1672–95	Collegium curiosum sive experimentale	*Altdorf*
1677–98	Accademia di Fisico-mathematica	Rome
1680–1714	Accademia Geografico-storia-fisica	Venice
1683–1708 (intermittent)	Dublin Philosophical Society	*Dublin*
1683–88	Boston Philosophical Society	Boston
1697–1712?	'Virtuoso Meeting' (intermittent)	Edinburgh
1700–44–	Societas Regia Scientiarum/Académie royale des sciences et belles lettres de Prusse*	*Berlin*
1706–93	Société royale des sciences*	*Montpellier*
1710–*c.*1760; 1810–	Gentlemen's Society	*Spalding*
1712–93	Académie royale des sciences et belles lettres*	*Bordeaux*
1714–1804	Accademia delle Scienze dell'Instituto*	*Bologna*
1717–1846	Spitalfields Mathematical Society	London
1723–46	The Honourable the Improvers in the Knowledge of Agriculture of Scotland	*Edinburgh*
1724–93	Académie royale des sciences, belles lettres, et arts*	*Lyons*
1725–1917	Academia Scientiarum Imperialis Petropolitanae*	*St Petersburg*
1725–40–93	Académie des sciences, arts et belles lettres*	*Dijon*
1728–	Societas Regiae Scientiarum*	*Uppsala*
1731–	Dublin Society For the Improvement of Husbandry, Agriculture and Arts	*Dublin*
1731–93	Académie royale de chirurgie*	*Paris*
1731–37	Medical Society	*Edinburgh*
1734–78–	(Royal) Medical Society*	Edinburgh
1737–83	Philosophical Society of Edinburgh	*Edinburgh*
1737–41	Collegium Curiosorum/Kungliga Svenska Vetenskaps Akademie*	*Stockholm*
1743–	Det Kongelige Danske Videnskabernes Selskab*	*Copenhagen*
1743–47	American Philosophical Society	Philadelphia
1746–60–	Natural History Society/Norwich Botanical Society	*Norwich*
1746–	Naturforschende Gesellschaft	*Danzig*
1746–	Naturforschende Gesellschaft	*Zurich*
1752–93	Académie royale de la marine*	*Brest*
1752–	Königliche Societät der Wissenschaften*	*Gottingen*
1752–1804	Hollandsche Maatschappij der Wetenschappen*	*Haarlem*
1754–	Royal Society of Arts*	*London*
1754–	Akademie gemeinütziger Wissenschaften*	*Erfurt*
1755–64	Edinburgh Society for Arts, Manufactures and Commerce	*Edinburgh*
c. 1757–	Société d'agriculture, de commerce, et des arts*	Rennes

Dates	Name	Place
1758–68	American Society for Promoting and Propagating Useful Knowledge	Philadelphia
1759–	Churbayerische Akademie der Wissenschaften*	*Munich*
1759–	Ökonomische Gesellschaft*	*Berne*
1759–83–93	Société royale des sciences/Académie royale des sciences*	*Turin*
1760–67–	Det Trondhjemske Selskab/Det kongelige Norske Videnskabers Selskab*	*Trondheim*
1761–93	Société d'agriculture*	*Paris*
1763–95	Academia Electoralis Scientiarum et Elegantiorum Literatum Theodoro-Platina*	*Mannheim*
1764–70–	Real Conferencia Fisica/Real Academia de Ciencias Naturales y Artes*	Barcelona
1766–91	Lunar Society	Birmingham
1768–	American Philosophical Society*	*Philadelphia*
1768–	Fürstlich Jablonowskische Gesellschaft*	*Leipzig*
1768–92	Zeeuwsch genootschap der Wetenschappen*	*Middleburg*
1769–91–	Privatgesellschaft in Böhmen Wissenschaften/ Böhmische Gesselschaft	*Prague*
1769–	Bataafdersch Genootschap der Proefonder-windelijke Wijsbegeerte*	*Rotterdam*
1773–	Medical Society of London	*London*
1777–93	Collège de pharmacie*	*Paris*
1777–93	Société Royale de Médecine*	*Paris*
1777–	Bath Agricultural Society	*Bath*
1778–	Teylers Tweede Genootschap*	*Haarlem*
1779–	Gesellschaft de Naturforschenden Freunde*	*Halle*
1780–	American Academy of Arts and Sciences*	*Boston*
1780–95	Societas Meteorologicae Palatinae*	*Mannheim*
1781–	Literary and Philosophical Society	*Manchester*
1782–	Accademia dei Naturalisti	Bergamo
1783–	Accademia real das ciências*	*Lisbon*
1783–	Literary and Philosophical Society	Derby
1783–	Royal Society of Edinburgh*	*Edinburgh*
1783–179?	Société des Sciences Physiques	*Lausanne*
1784–	(Royal) Highland Society of Scotland	*Edinburgh*
1785–	Royal Irish Academy*	*Dublin*
1786–99–	Connecticut Society of Arts and Sciences*	*Hartford & New Haven*
1788	Linnean Society	*London*
1793	Literary and Philosophical Society	Newcastle-Upon-Tyne
1799–1807–	British Mineralogical Society/Geological Society	*London*

64

PROFESSIONALISATION

J. B. MORRELL

1. THE DEVELOPMENT OF PROFESSIONALISATION

For Dr Johnson, the word 'profession' provided no problems: it simply meant a calling, a vocation, or known employment. By early Victorian times, a concern with status and respectability had ensured that a profession was deemed to be different from a trade or a handicraft: professional people dealt with people *qua* people, while tradesmen and artisans provided things for their physical wants. For early Victorians the classic professions were the three learned ones of divinity, law and medicine, plus the armed forces; hence a profession was a vocation in which a professed knowledge of some aspect of science or learning was applied to human affairs or in the practice of an art founded upon such knowledge. This notion was sufficiently elastic to permit more and more people, such as engineers, architects and teachers, to be embraced by it. At the end of the nineteenth century, some pundits such as Herbert Spencer considered the growth of professions to be the essential feature of civilised society; they were concerned, not with the defence, maintenance or regulation of life, but with its augmentation. This wide definition could, therefore, include dancers as well as scientists. By the mid-twentieth century the sociological interest in elites, bureaucracies and industrialisation had revealed that professionalisation was a major feature of industrial societies. It has even been asserted that an industrialising society is essentially a professionalising one, and that in industrial societies everyone will soon be professionalised. This very brief survey shows that the notion of a profession has never been static. On the contrary, it has changed drastically over time; it has been a social semantic construct, the changing meanings of which have reflected the way in which more and more occupations have acquired the status and power of a profession.

Even so, there is a vast sociological literature on professionalisation in which many attempts have been made to define the distinguishing characteristics of the process by which an occupation is transformed into a profession. The most popular approach has emphasised traits, in that it has sought to give an exhaustive list of the crucial characteristics of professionalisation with medicine and law prominent as the paradigmatic, prestigious learned professions. The consensus generated by the 'trait' approach seems to be that a profession was and remains a full-time vocation defined by the following characteristics: the possession of skill based on systematic, theoretical and esoteric knowledge; the provision of exacting and specialised training; procedures for testing and certifying the competence of members; organisations, often self-regulating and state-sanctioned, to enforce standards, maintain a strong sense of corporate identity and exert a degree of monopoly and adherence to the norm of altruistic, though remunerated, service to clients and to society at large. Such findings stress that professions existed in part to deal with the vital practical affairs of the general public and of individual lay clients, via the application of esoteric knowledge. In the world of pure science, however, there has often been a distinct lack of clients and only potentially was there specific application. Clientless non-applied science has concerned functionalist sociologists of science, who have been concerned to defend the probity of science as a profession by invoking a static set of distinguishing attributes.

2. THE CARR–SAUNDERS/WILSON APPROACH

For historians of professions and of professionalisation, the sociological approach is too 'essentialist' and sometimes simply naïve, but they have long had an alternative model, and a classic one at that. Over fifty years ago A. M. Carr–Saunders and P. A. Wilson described in general terms the process by which various occupations gained the characteristics of a profession, citing many case histories.[1] They saw professionalisation as an aspect of occupational development and strategy, in which the desire for higher status, autonomous control of conditions of work and control of the market in the interest of higher rewards (financial and honorary), were all prominent. Such an approach is not incompatible with a sequence of 'stages', roughly corresponding to the list of attributes of the sociologists, but without prejudice to whether any particular occupation attained every stage. The Carr–Saunders/Wilson approach does not postulate that every professionalising occupation went through the same stages in the same order. Instead, it acknowledges the full force of the basic fact that today's professions are those occupations which have succeeded over time in establishing their claim to the advantages long enjoyed by the three learned professions; some occupations have been more successful than others in the game of occupational aggrandisement.

This occupational strategy model of professionalisation has several advantages. It is not deterministic in that it does not envisage professionalisation as a necessary consequence of industrialisation via the division of labour and the growth of bureaucracy; it avoids the anachronism of imputing professionalising aims and needs to people who were often simply trying to upgrade their occupation; it encourages us to see professionalisation as a process involving the pursuit of various forms of power, including success in persuading the public to pay well for services rendered; and it admits the possibility that any professional association could not only seek to impose a code of practice on its members but could also try to establish a specific identity and increase corporate rewards by acting, on occasion, like a pressure group or trade union. With respect to science, the Carr–Saunders/Wilson approach discourages as futile any attempt to say precisely when science became a profession in a particular country. The several 'stages' of professionalisation did not suddenly and simultaneously all come into being; the process was gradual and its various 'stages' appeared at different times. Moreover, although Carr–Saunders and Wilson were well aware of the importance of science and technology as promoters of professionalisation, they found it impossible to discuss science as a homogeneous activity analogous to law and medicine, but profitable to focus on different disciplinary practitioners such as engineers, chemists and physicists. Significantly their index carried no entry for science or scientists.

3. SCIENCE AS A VOCATIONAL PURSUIT

During the nineteenth century, science in Europe and the United States was incompletely and very slowly transformed from the pastime of leisured individuals into a regular vocational pursuit. In that process, at least six features became prominent, features which we can retrospectively recognise as 'stages' of professionalisation.

(1) There was an increase in the number of full-time paid positions, directly or indirectly linked to the possession of scientific knowledge. In France the typical scientific career became that of teacher, examiner or official in a state-supported bureaucracy which was centralised in Paris; French savants were state functionaries. In the German states before unification, the dominant scientific career became that of professor in a state university. After unification, university posts were supplemented by careers with corporate firms and in research institutes supported by the imperial government. In Britain, where individualism and localism were more prevalent, the period 1820–50 saw a doubling of scientific chairs in the universities. Everywhere the link between posts and money was important. It was this question of remuneration which in 1852 provoked Thomas Huxley to lament that 'science in England does everything – but *pay*. You may earn praise but not pudding'.[2] By the end of the century 'pudding' was more widely available.

(2) Specialist qualifications, which functioned as public certification of scientific competence, were established. Such qualifications, which tended to displace both private patronage and market forces, stressed achievement as measured by examinations. An obvious example was the German university Ph.D. which ambitious young chemists, fresh from the pleasures of research in a German university laboratory, began to sport in the early 1840s. (See art. 62, sect. 2.) Less well-known was the introduction of bachelor's degrees in science in the early 1850s at the two old English universities, Oxford and Cambridge.

(3) Training procedures were developed especially through the university laboratory, which was transformed from its previous use as a preparation room for a professor into a central teaching device as important as the lecture room, a training ground where apprentices learnt the tacit and practical skills of their subject, and the home of research schools. By the 1850s the university laboratory, in the hands of first Justus von Liebig and then R. W. von Bunsen, provided for science an equivalent of the Renaissance artist's studio, in that it offered induction into the scientific guild through pupillage under a master practitioner.

(4) In published research there was a rapid growth of specialisation, shown in the development of esoteric technical languages, in the greater application of analytical mathematics and in the deployment of arcane experimental techniques. A mere glance through the famous nineteenth-century review journals, such as the *Edinburgh* and the *Quarterly*, reveals that specialist sciences were detaching themselves from general culture and were becoming inaccessible to Dr Johnson's willing common reader. In other words, various sciences were being demarcated as specific areas of skill, knowledge and expertise.

(5) There was growing group solidarity and self-consciousness among the students of natural knowledge, especially as expressed linguistically and institutionally. Witness the coining of the word 'scientist' in 1833 by William Whewell at the third meeting of the British Association for the Advancement of Science. The assembled cultivators of science yearned for a term which would collectively designate the students of knowledge of the material world, as opposed to the literary, religious, moral and philosophical worlds. Institutionally-shared interests were most manifest in the various national associations which were formed to promote science, e.g. in Switzerland in 1815, in Germany in 1822, in Britain in 1831, in Italy in 1839 and in the United States in 1848. (See art. 63, sects. 9–13.)

(6) In lieu of the approval of a satisfied client, various reward systems, geared to recognise the best practice, were developed. Thus, venerable national scientific societies and academies often became less functionally effective in promoting

science but more concerned with conferring honours. For instance, in the early nineteenth century, medical men found the fellowship of the Royal Society to be financially useful: for them FRS meant 'fees raised since'! By the end of the nineteenth century, the acquisition of the coveted letters FRS had become the ultimate form of national recognition available to British scientists. In 1901, with the inauguration of the Nobel Prizes, the reward system of science became internationalised and reached its apogee.

4. HISTORY OF SCIENCE IN THE UNITED STATES

There is no doubt that the Carr–Saunders/Wilson approach yields dividends when applied sensitively. Nowhere is this more apparent than in the history of American science. Twenty years ago two prejudices about science in the United States were rampant. One was that it was essentially a twentieth-century development, a view which demoted Benjamin Franklin and Josiah Willard Gibbs to the rank of freaks. The second, derived from Alexis de Tocqueville's *Democracy in America* (1835-9), was that in the nineteenth century the United States was indifferent to basic research because of the irresistible opportunities for gadgeteers and inventors associated with industrialisation, shortage of labour and westward expansion. These two prejudices have been shown to be myths largely by applying the professionalisation model to the career of American science. The sixty years from *c.* 1820 to *c.* 1880 are now viewed as a transition period between that of colonial dependency on Europe and that of independent professional maturity, achieved by adapting European models to a republican country and then, with the invention of research foundations, transcending them.[3]

Several of the stages of professionalisation stand out. The growing self-consciousness of American scientists, widely scattered over many states, was shown in the founding of the American Association for the Advancement of Science in 1848. Although dismissed by a disillusioned member as the Amazing Asses Adverse to Science, the Association as the first national body for science was quite different from existing local societies such as the American Philosophical Society which met in Philadelphia. With respect to full-time paid jobs, the federal government discarded the suspicion of federal aid to scientific projects, which had characterised presidents from Jefferson to Jackson. For instance, after 1879 when existing state geological surveys were combined into the US Geological Survey, its director John Wesley Powell rapidly made it into a well-funded organisation providing employment for many geologists. Specialist qualifications began to appear in mid-century. Led by Louis Agassiz, the Lawrence Scientific School at Harvard produced ten B.Sc. degrees a year between 1851 and 1871, while at Yale the private philanthropy of Joseph

Sheffield enabled it to become in the 1860s the first American university to put graduate training in science on a formal basis; Yale granted fourteen Ph.D. degrees in science that decade, the first star pupil being Josiah Willard Gibbs. With respect to research schools based in laboratories, the establishment from the 1870s of new blue-print research-orientated universities was crucial, perhaps the most important being Johns Hopkins at Baltimore (founded in 1876) and Harper's Bazaar, as it was called, at Chicago (founded in 1892). The new emphasis on the laboratory research school was nicely revealed in the career of Ira Remsen, a New Yorker who studied in Germany under Friedrich Wöhler and Rudolph Fittig. As the dominant figure in American university chemistry before the First World War, Remsen created on the banks of the Patapsco a powerful American version of Fittig's school at Tübingen. All these examples show that the professionalisation model gave useful purchase on American science by revealing how professionals eventually supplemented or supplanted devotees as scientific leaders and researchers. Perhaps because of the American obsession with the functions of elites in a democracy, the professionalisation model is still in vogue as an approach to the history of science in the United States. In 1985 Arnold Thackray and his collaborators produced the first book-length empirical study of the history of American chemistry from 1876 when the national Chemistry Society was founded. It assembles impressive statistics, showing long-term trends, as a necessary preliminary to the full history of the American chemical profession.[4]

5. PROFESSIONALISATION IN FRANCE

The case of France provides a most interesting example of the application of the professionalisation model: after some heady euphoria about its virtues, doubt has now set in. In the period of the *ancien régime*, the crucially important work is that of Roger Hahn on the Parisian *Académie des Sciences*.[5] From the absolute monarchy of Louis XIV to the imperial dictatorship of Napoleon I, the *Académie* was one of Europe's most prestigious institutions. In his book on the *Académie*, Hahn took his cue from Colbert, who designed it as an arm of the state and financed it as such, by choosing as his main theme the changing and interdependent loyalties of the *Académie* to both science and state. Throughout his analysis of the pre-revolutionary situation, Hahn assumed that state-sponsored institutions like the *Académie* publicly sanctioned science and offered the prospect of scientific careers in regular well-paid positions. Thus he saw institutionalisation and professionalisation as propelling scientific advance before 1789. Subsequently, Hahn produced the provisional results of a 'prosopographical' study of more than 300 working members of the *Académie* prior to 1789. According to Lawrence Stone the barbarous term 'prosopography' has a mundane meaning: the investigation of the common characteristics of a group of actors in history by means of collective study of their lives. Clearly, Hahn expected his survey of academicians as a group to confirm his previous assumption that they were incipient professional scientists. His results showed otherwise. The collective life of the academicians did not encourage cohesiveness, and they did not form a well-paid occupational group. Financially they fared better under the Sun King than under his successors, and in any case their financial rewards were more like old-age pensions than salaries. Only the old and distinguished were able to live off the proceeds of being an academician. The others depended on government posts, often holding more than one at a time, for their income. It appears that the much vaunted and lauded financial sponsorship of the *Académie* by the government before 1789 did not offer a professional career to academicians, some of whom failed to get adequate remuneration or were forced into jobs which were inimical to their research.

The Napoleonic period has been seen by Maurice Crosland as central to the professionalisation of science. He claims that it was in France in about 1800 that science emerged for the first time in modern history as a profession.[6] Although Napoleon's patronage of the Société d'Arcueil, a brilliant informal research group led by Laplace and Berthollet, was indirect, the general drift of Crosland's account of the Society is that Napoleon contributed to the valuable French tradition of government patronage of science. In a similar way, he argues that Gay-Lussac, one of Arcueil's star products, was one of a first generation of professional scientists, appropriately educated via specialised training. Certainly, Gay-Lussac made a lucrative career in Paris, not least through the *cumul* system of holding several posts simultaneously, then a common practice.

In contrast to Crosland's view that in the Napoleonic period men of science were less sensitive to politics than other scholars, Dorinda Outram has stressed that the formation of a scientific career at that time was inextricably connected with politics. Using the case of Georges Cuvier, who was castigated by contemporaries as a politician and place-monger, Outram has attempted to move away from a concern with institutions and with issues such as professionalisation towards a closer examination of patronage, especially that of an informal kind. She reveals how Cuvier was a masterly political negotiator who survived several very different forms of government. For her the central questions concern power, politics, vocation and authority, and not institutions or professionalisation: in fact she sees the longer period 1793–1830 in France as one in which there were no professional and meritocratic careers smoothly and easily open to talent. Instead, she argues that careers were not taken up but were made by individuals playing the patronage game in a rapidly changing society, and that such private politicking co-existed uneasily with the ideology of the nonpolitical nature of science which those individuals publicly espoused.[7]

In a wide-ranging survey of science in nineteenth-century France, Robert Fox has questioned the utility of the professionalisation model. He stresses that accomplishment in science should not always be equated with professionalisation. Indeed, he reveals the incompatibility between the intellectual and bureaucratic concepts of the savant, and emphasises that by the early 1900s advancing professionalisation had yielded a blighted harvest for French scientists. Fox takes the occupational strategy approach so that, instead of focusing on the creation of the profession of science, he examines the fitful changes in the work of academic scientists in response to changing government policies and, later in the nineteenth century, to industrial opportunities.[8]

6. PROFESSIONALISATION IN BRITAIN

The distinction between unpaid gentlemen and paid players has often been applied to the history of English science. Given that the virtuoso figure of the natural philosopher was different from the modern specialised scientist, it is easy to assume that this shift was the same as the transformation of science pursued by devotees into that done by professionals. This view, which may well apply to Victorian Ireland, has been subjected to criticism apropos England. For example, Roy Porter acknowledges that geology first became professionalised through the Geological Survey, founded in 1835; but he stresses that such professionalisation reinforced rather that subverted gentlemanly geology in that professionals were paid to do what they wanted to do anyway as amateurs. In his enthusiasm to avoid being lured by the professionalisation model, Porter underestimates the differences between the Survey's professionals and the gentlemanly devotees with regard to the procedures employed in field-work.[9]

Pressure groups in the scientific world seem prima facie to be well suited to historical analysis in terms of professionalisation. The very name of the British Association for the Advancement of Science seems to indicate that the professionalisation model might give fruitful purchase; so, too, do its avowed aims of obtaining greater public attention to science and of removing public obstacles to its progress. It is true that the Association rapidly became a very successful pressure group. Yet, according to Morrell and Thackray, its most important lobbies of government were not attempts at professionalisation: they were undertaken to nourish the career interests and research programmes of the voluntarist and gentlemanly coterie which controlled the Association. It is significant that the early Association deliberately ignored several matters concerned with professionalisation, such as the creation of full-time paid posts by government, the provision of government honours and pensions and action of certification and pupillage. The prime aim of the gentlemen who managed the Association was not to prepare the ground for professionals who might eventually challenge their cherished dominance. Thus the professionalisation model gives little purchase on the Association's function as a pressure group. The notions of career interests, research programmes, intellectual property and collective exploitation are more illuminating.[10]

The emphasis on gentlemanliness in Victorian English science shows no sign of waning. It is a central assumption of Martin Rudwick's amazingly detailed study of an important geological controversy of the 1830s that gentlemen were more concerned than professionals with competitive career-making and matters of priority. For the former, science was a lifetime's vocation; for the latter, a livelihood.[11] Again, if the last thirty years of the nineteenth century were of general importance for professionalisation as a national phenomenon, that did not mean that in those years the devotee or amateur was snuffed out. On the contrary, amateurisation also thrived, in field sciences and physical sciences alike, via associations which were not professional qualifying bodies concerned with the apparatus of certification but were less exclusive alternatives to the established disciplinary societies. It is true that the founding of the Institute of Chemistry in 1877 was important as the first institution for a group of professional scientists; it is also true that amateurs exerted themselves institutionally through, for example, the Geologists' and the Astronomical Associations (founded in 1858 and in 1890). In natural history too, amateurisation had prospered through natural history field clubs, of which the parent was the Berwickshire Naturalists' Club (founded in 1831). These clubs were so popular that by the 1870s regional amalgamations began to occur, the first such federated group being the Yorkshire Naturalists' Union founded in 1877.

Though professionalisation tends to be used by the unwary as an imprecise Protean term which explains nothing, it is still fruitful when sensitively employed in its Carr-Saunders/Wilson mode. Recent work by M. J. Peterson and A. J. Engel on English medicine and education shows that the notions of professions and professionalisation still beckon alluringly and profitably. They do have heuristic power in research, they provide continuity of theme and approach and they bring into focus a good deal of scattered information, thereby converting it into evidence. Even so, the occupational strategy approach to professionalisation in the social history of science is now seen as being useful, subject to certain caveats. (See art. 1, sect. 13; art. 3, sects. 2–4.) We must not impose unqualified modern notions of professionalisation on the institutions and individuals of the past. If we do so, we offer nothing more than goal-directed history. Again we must avoid ascribing professionalising needs and aims willy-nilly to institutions; that is vulgar functionalism and institutional animism. Instead we must be alert to the possibility that past institutions were vehicles, not just for professionalisation but for the making of careers, the exercise of patronage and the promulgation of ideologies by controlling coteries. Above all, we must acknowledge that past cultivators of science could pursue many interests, which could include or not a concern with the occupational upgrading of science in general or of one of it constituent disciplines.

NOTES

1. A. M. Carr–Saunders and P. A. Wilson, *The professionals* (Oxford, 1933).
2. L. Huxley (ed.), *Life and letters of Thomas Henry Huxley* (2 vols., London, 1900) vol. 1, p. 100.
3. N. Reingold, 'Definitions and speculations: the professionalisation of science in America in the nineteenth century', in A. Oleson and S. C. Brown (eds.), *The pursuit of knowledge in the early American Republic: American scientific and learned societies from colonial times to the Civil War* (Baltimore and London, 1976), pp. 33–69.
4. A. Thrackray, J. L. Sturchio, P. T. Carroll and R. Bud, *Chemistry in America 1876–1976: historical indicators* (Dordrecht, 1985).
5. R. Hahn, *The anatomy of a scientific institution: the Paris Academy of Sciences, 1666–1803* (Berkeley, 1971); idem, 'Scientific careers in eighteenth-century France' in M. P. Crosland (ed.), *The emergence of science in Western Europe* (London, 1975), pp. 127–38.
6. M. P. Crosland, *The society of Arcueil: a view of French science at the time of Napoleon I* (London, 1967); idem, 'The development of a professional career in science in France' in Crosland, *The emergence of science*, pp. 139–159; idem, *Gay-Lussac: scientist and bourgeois* (Cambridge, 1978).
7. D. Outram, 'Politics and vocation: French science, 1793–1830', *British journal for history of science*, 13 (1980), 27–43; idem, *Georges Cuvier: vocation, science and authority in post-revolutionary France* (Manchester, 1984).
8. R. Fox, 'Science, the university, and the state in nineteenth-century France' in G. L. Geison (ed.), *Professions and the French State, 1700–1900* (Chapel Hill, 1984), pp. 66–145.
9. R. Porter, 'Gentlemen and geology: the emergence of a scientific career, 1660–1920', *The historical journal*, 21 (1978), 809–36.
10. J. B. Morrell and A. W. Thackray, *Gentlemen of science: early years of the British Association for the Advancement of Science* (Oxford, 1981).
11. M. J. S. Rudwick, *The great Devonian controversy: the shaping of scientific knowledge among gentlemanly specialists* (Chicago and London, 1985).

FURTHER READING

A. J. Engel, *From clergymen to don: the rise of the academic profession in nineteenth-century Oxford* (Oxford, 1983).

T. J. Johnson, *Professions and power* (London, 1972).

M. J. Peterson, *The medical profession in mid-Victorian London* (Berkeley, 1978).

C. A. Russell, N. G. Coley and G. K. Roberts, *Chemists by profession: the origins and rise of the Royal Institute of Chemistry* (Milton Keynes, 1977).

65

SCIENCE AND THE PUBLIC

STEVEN SHAPIN

1. INTRODUCTION AND SURVEY

A remarkable feature of present-day science is that we know, or think we know, with self-evident certainty who is a scientist and who is a layperson, where science ends and where other forms of culture begin. And it is no less remarkable that the judgements of scientists and the laity on these matters display such a measure of agreement. In few instances are we even aware of engaging in decision. It is as if the notions of 'science' and 'the public' could simply be read from their exemplars by inspection. Even historians and sociologists of science, on the occasions when they do consider the categories of science and the public, tend to focus upon the relations between two known entities, rather than analysing how the entities are themselves constituted.

The task here is to describe and explain aspects of the historical construction of these categories. On what bases, and for what purposes, have boundaries been drawn between scientific and other forms of culture, between the social role of the practitioner of natural knowledge and other social roles? In the course of addressing these questions we will move from the self-evident to the problematic. At the end of the exercise we will, in a sense, know less about the entities 'science' and 'the public' than we did at the outset. But we also know that much of what we previously took to be self-evident knowledge was inadequately founded. Our recompense for knowing less will be a potential programme for empirical and theoretical research.

We start by describing the elements of 'the canonical account' – our contemporary common wisdom about the historical relations between science and the public. We then consider certain dimensions along which practitioners of science and other forms of culture have historically been discriminated, paying particular attention to the social and cultural correlates of the notion of intellectual 'competence'. Certain forms of scientific practice involved the acquisition and deployment of intellectual skills which were not prevalent in lay culture or in the culture of the generally literate. Such a cultural gulf was not, however, a 'natural' or inevitable feature of the place of science in the overall map of culture. We describe several systematic attacks upon the propriety and legitimacy of a scientific culture thus divorced from the common-sense and ordinary competences of the wider public. And we examine the significance of mid- to late-nineteenth-century Scientific Naturalism as a vehicle for establishing and validating important modern social and cultural boundaries between science and the public. The production and justification of specific items of scientific knowledge is often dependent upon decisions about who is a competent practitioner and who is a member of the laity. Episodes are described in which public testimony about natural phenomena was evaluated according to its social source, and we point to the endemic roles of trust and authority in scientific communication. Some aspects of communication between members of the scientific community and the public are examined, in terms of what practitioners want from the public and how, in specific circumstances, it was judged proper and politic to secure those desiderata. Special attention is paid to the function of 'natural theology' as a bridge between scientific and lay culture, and to the vehicles by which scientific knowledge was channelled to the public. Finally, we discuss what the public and the state have wanted from men of science. The roles of patronage and of utilitarian concerns are assessed, and the social and cultural consequences of professionalisation for relations between science and the public are examined.

2. THE CANONICAL ACCOUNT OF HISTORICAL RELATIONS BETWEEN SCIENCE AND THE PUBLIC

The self-evidence of our knowledge of the categories of 'science' and 'the public' is supported by a canonical account of their historical relations. In the past the relations between science and the public were intimate, pervasive and consequential. What belonged to science was poorly demarcated from what did not, just as the role of the man of science was scarcely discriminated from other social roles. The public and other social and cultural structures were powerful compared with science. Public concerns could influence not only the direction of scientific work but also, at times, the content of scientific knowledge. As we come closer to present times, those relations have radically changed. Indeed, it might be said (in the canonical version) that science has progressively shed its public and circumscribed the role of the public, as well as that of non-scientific intellectuals, in scientific affairs. This shedding and disciplining of the public have been the conditions for the production of properly scientific knowledge, for wherever science has been substantively influenced by public concerns, there reliable and objective knowledge has been compromised. As the categories of the public and of science have become disentangled, so the roles of each have been codified. The public's role now consists solely in acceding to scientific judgements and in rendering support for activities that scientists have deemed desirable or essential. If the public takes a more active role, it runs the risk of eroding the scientific character of the knowledge in question. It could be said that the past three centuries have witnessed an inversion of the power relations between science and the public. Where science – to the extent that it can be recognised as a discrete activity – was once influenced or interfered with by the public and other institutions, the scientific community now controls its own proceedings, stipulates the nature of proper relations between itself and the public, and even extends its influence importantly into the arena of public affairs.

There is much to recommend the canonical account. The relations between science and the wider public *have* altered dramatically since the seventeenth century. These changes *have* involved the winning by the scientific community of far greater autonomy in ordering its own affairs; they *have* involved a substantial shift in political power to scientific practitioners and away from interested non-practitioners and public institutions. The canonical account presents us with matters which need careful description and explanation. The weakness of that account is the attendant, and largely unacknowledged, tendency to equate description with explanation, and to make out of a series of historical events a process which is its own explanation. That tendency, commonly manifested in studies of scientific 'professionalisation', locates in the historical process an immanent force by which the modern relations of science and public have been progressively unveiled.[1]

Modern historical practice, like modern science, tends to suspect the legitimacy of teleological explanations. In this area, the most effective antidote to teleological temptations is the display of the enormous labour expended by individuals in the past in constructing the very categories of 'science' and 'the public' and in stipulating the proper nature of transactions between them. There was nothing 'natural', 'inevitable' or 'immanent' in these developments; they were massive historical achievements. The work that allows us to apportion items to 'science' and to 'the public' was done in specific historical settings, for specific purposes. Moreover, these classifications were widely contested. Different groups of interested persons upheld divergent views of what science was or ought to be and how the boundaries between it, other forms of knowledge and public concerns should be drawn. We start, therefore, with a sketch of how the categories of science and the public have been defined, defended and, on occasion, subverted. Following that, the discussion can shift to the relations that have subsisted between these categories: the concerns of the scientific community *vis-à-vis* the public; the concerns of the public and public institutions *vis-à-vis* scientific culture and the scientific community and the consequences that have flowed from these engagements.

How, then, have the entities 'science' and 'the public' been delineated in history? In what do these categories consist, and on what grounds are they set in opposition? We can analyse the social and cultural dimensions along which 'science' and the 'public' have historically been arrayed, and we can examine a number of revealing historical moments at which the boundary between the two categories has been constructed and subverted, drawn, redrawn and defended.

3. CULTURAL COMPETENCE AND THE GULF BETWEEN SCIENCE AND THE PUBLIC

One of the most obvious means by which we, and people in the past, discriminate between 'science' and 'the public' involves the notion of cultural competence. Accredited members of the scientific community are those deemed to have acquired relevant cognitive and manipulative skills that members of the public do not possess. As a result of this differential acquisition of skills, there is a discrepancy between what the public know how to do, or what they understand, compared to what qualified scientific practitioners can do or what they know. This discontinuity of competences is, of course, a historical phenomenon: it is something that has developed over time to its present situation. However, it did not proceed at the same rate in all sciences, nor has it been linear or uncontested in its development. As Thomas Kuhn has shown, the first scientific area to develop a gap of comprehensibility between its qualified practitioners and the generally-educated public was that of the mathematical sciences, including astronomy, optics and statics, as well as mathematics proper.[2] Even in antiquity, practitioners of these sciences did not expect that members of the generally-educated public would read their productions, or, if they did read them, would understand them. In the sixteenth century, Copernicus said that he wrote for other mathematicians and not for the literate public in general. The mathematical physics of the seventeenth-century Scientific Revolution, similarly, was not comprehensible as such by non-mathematically-qualified intellectuals, nor did those who produced it think that it ought to be. To evaluate Newton's mathematical works one had to be a mathematician; it is traditionally doubted whether more than a handful of contemporaries did in fact read and understand *The Mathematical Principles of Natural Philosophy*. If indeed, as Galileo and others said, the Book of Nature was written in the language of mathematics, then scientific texts ought to reflect that reality. Ability to speak and to read esoteric mathematical and technical, rather than everyday, languages was therefore an effective discriminator of who could be a competent scientific practitioner and who could not.

Needless to say, the same general situation obtains today, although, as we have seen, it is far older than the social institution of professionalised science.

993

Yet it is well to remind ourselves that the professionalised state of modern science means that there is wide agreement in our society as to who is an expert bearer of reliable natural knowledge; it does not mean that natural knowledge is solely located in the minds and texts of accredited scientists, nor is it necessarily accurate to assume that 'what the public think' about natural processes and objects is merely a simplification or dilution of scientists' expert knowledge. Compared to the abundance of academic material we now possess about the beliefs of tribal societies concerning the natural world, it is remarkable how little we know, and have sought to know, about the 'ethnoscience' of our own, modern western societies. Peter Burke's programme dedicated to the study of popular culture and its relations with 'high' culture has not yet made a significant impact on the history of science proper. Thus, with the exception of a small, but admirable, body of work in medical history and sociology, we have scarcely any understanding of the range of beliefs entertained by lay members of our society, how these beliefs may relate to those maintained by scientists and what purposes may be fulfilled by lay thinking about nature. Research by such medical sociologists as Cecil Helman strongly suggests that the public of modern western societies possesses a fairly elaborate set of beliefs about disease, its causes and indicated treatments. These beliefs are found to be not only qualitatively distinct from the beliefs of physicians but are actively deployed by patients to secure from their doctors the therapies that patients deem appropriate.[3] We are a very long way from understanding 'public science' in this sense, but we can at least recognise the historical submergence of lay beliefs about nature as a problem and as a legitimate topic of historical inquiry.

4. THE CULTURAL GULF ATTACKED

The cultural gap surrounding the mathematical physics of the Scientific Revolution was neither a pervasive feature of all sciences, nor was it universally considered to be either an inevitable feature of scientific progress or an acceptable and desirable state of affairs. Indeed, some commentators regarded a gulf of incomprehensibility between the common sense of the public and the culture of scientific intellectuals to be a sign that something was amiss with the latter. Paracelsus in the sixteenth century, and his numerous followers in the seventeenth century, argued that the sequestration of official intellectuals from everyday empirical experience and their socialisation into esoteric ways of knowing and speaking guaranteed that what they claimed to know was defective. Genuine natural knowledge for Paracelsians was founded upon sympathetic engagement with ordinary sensory experience. This was why miners, practical chemists and husbandmen were said to know more and know better than university professors and university-trained physicians. Proper knowledge was properly public knowledge, generated by using the knowledge-acquiring techniques of ordinary members of society.

This structuring of the nature and legitimacy of the cultural relations between science and the public is recurrent. For example, Charles Gillispie has shown how the radical Jacobins of Enlightenment France contested the morality and validity of the official Newtonian science of the Paris *Académie des Sciences* by pointing to its divorce from the world of ordinary experience. Popular herbalist medical men criticised the knowledge and efficacy of 'allopathic' physicians in nineteenth-century America along similar lines. In nineteenth-century Britain the phrenological followers of Gall and Spurzheim (see art. 56, sect. 2.) questioned the scientific standing of academic psychology: a genuinely scientific study of the mind ought, they said, to be grounded in the observational competences available to the ordinary public, rather than depending upon the trained 'introspection' of university elites. And in the early twentieth century the phenomenologist Edmund Husserl identified a 'crisis' in the state of science. The 'Galilean' idealisations of modern mathematical science did not in fact pertain to or explain the world of lived experience. One could cite instances of this sort indefinitely. But the point should be evident: one of the most basic dimensions along which the knowledge of the scientific community and the knowledge of the public is arrayed has historically been a field of contest. There appears to be nothing inevitable about the existence of a cultural gulf dividing the knowledge or the ways of knowing of scientists and the public.

The strand of mathematical science represented a distinctively 'private' (or, at least, esoteric) form of culture, divorced from the experiences, competences and comprehension of the ordinary public or even from members of the ordinary educated elite. However, there was another strand of science, particularly important during the Scientific Revolution of the seventeenth century, and this stipulated the public character of science. The tradition of observational and experimental sciences which derived partly from the philosophical programme of Francis Bacon, implemented and publicised by Robert Boyle and his colleagues in the early Royal Society of London, was one that vigorously insisted upon the necessity of a public presence in proper scientific practice. Indeed, in its strong form this Baconian and Boylean programme identified the lack of that public presence and public participation as an adequate sign that the practice in question was not scientific. Alchemy, for example, was castigated for the privacy of its practice and the secrecy of its practitioners. Scholasticism was condemned for its esoteric language and for the refusal of its proponents to submit their claims to the test of ordinary (and artificial) experience; and some of those who endeavoured to model empirical science upon mathematical and demonstrative methods were labelled 'modern dogmatists', who wished to make ordinary experience submit to the transcendent domain of logical and geometrical inference. Was experience to be the test of knowledge, or was the evidence of the senses to be subjugated to special, non-experiential procedures that dictated what nature 'must' be like, or was like 'in essence' or 'ideally'?[4]

The Baconian goal of 'the levelling of men's wits' had both epistemological and social dimensions. Having such a goal implied that the methods employed in empirical science and those that characterised everyday reliable observation and validation would overlap substantially; it also meant that the social boundaries between members of the scientific community and the public would be such as might easily be crossed. The style of writing and discoursing appropriate to the new experimental programme should, it was said, be such as facilitated public comprehension. Jargon, florid prose and esoteric language in general were to be rejected, precisely because such linguistic traits erected a boundary between the new enterprise and the wider public whose participation was being solicited. Yet, for all the rhetoric of seventeenth-century publicists which stressed the open and public character of their preferred science, the reality was far more complex and problematic. The 'public' that actually participated in the new experimental programme was a carefully selected and disciplined public. There is no accurate sense in which one could say that this was a form of practice open to all members of society. Even the much-advertised 'popularity' of the new science must, as Michael Hunter's research on Restoration science shows, be treated with caution. Moreover, from the latter part of the seventeenth century, the experimental enterprise co-existed with a revitalised and culturally aggressive mathematical programme. Mathematical practices in general, and the celebrated Newtonian mathematical philosophy of nature in particular, were definitely not public practices; nor, as has already been noted, were public comprehensibility or public participation said to be necessary for their truth and power to be granted. Seventeenth-century practitioners therefore lived with the tensions intrinsic and extrinsic to at least two forms of relationship between science and the public. Only occasionally did these tensions manifest themselves.

5. SCIENTIFIC NATURALISM AND THE COMMON CULTURAL CONTEXT

By the nineteenth century, certain of the divergences between public conceptions of nature and those said to be proper to legitimate science were being systematically addressed. The Scientific Naturalist movement of the mid-to-late Victorian period was characterised by efforts to eject from what counted as scientific thinking those elements that had previously linked public and scientific culture. Anthropomorphic, anthropocentric and teleological views of nature were identified by writers such as Huxley and Tyndall as fallacies of the public (or clerical) mind: wherever they intruded themselves, there an objective conception of nature was at risk. A human-scaled and human-shaped nature

– congenial to public common sense – was to be replaced with one in which human beings and human experience were themselves naturalised and had to find their place along with other natural processes, other animate and inanimate bodies. In the early modern period, the idea that man was the measure of all things formed a heavily-trafficked bridge between science and other forms of culture and between science and public discourse. That bridge was dismantled by the triumph of Darwin and other Naturalist scientists.

The consequences of the Naturalist victory, and of the secularisation of codified natural knowledge, for the relations between science and the public have not yet been systematically studied. R. M. Young has argued that one result was a 'fragmentation' of a previously 'common cultural context' linking scientists, clerics and laypersons. One could speculate that it was in this setting that lay perceptions of nature and natural processes were submerged and, ultimately, became invisible. The triumph of secular science consisted in the achievement by its qualified practitioners of hegemony and of professional legitimacy. Orientations to nature not accredited by the sanctioned scientific community did not have to be eliminated; it was sufficient, as F. M. Turner's work has shown, that they have no public forum and no political purchase.[5]

Aspects of this submergence have been discussed in Gillian Beer's work on the language of evolutionary science. She points to an apparent paradox, viz. that some of the key nineteenth-century texts that spelled out the divorce between properly scientific conceptions and public fallacies were, in fact, written for 'any educated reader' and worked with a language and a set of cultural assumptions shared between natural scientists and the educated public. Moreover, as the nineteenth- and twentieth-century public reception of Darwinian thought makes clear, a teleological account of evolutionary processes remains pervasively popular despite the agreement of the relevant scientists that it is grossly inappropriate.[6] It may be that our public language contains the ineradicable residues of the teleological, anthropocentric and anthropomorphic cosmology in which it was shaped. To the extent that scientific statements are couched in, or even appear to be couched in, ordinary public language, problems may be endemic. On the one hand, scientists may decide that certain scientific conceptions simply cannot be expressed in the public language. On the other hand, scientists' endeavours to use that public language may involve metaphors and analogies whose resonances they cannot expect to hold in place and control. In either case, the differentiation of scientific and public culture has precipitated serious problems of translation whose nature is largely undefined and whose remedies are unclear. Can the public comprehend science without learning the specialised languages and linguistic meanings of the scientific community? Are all attempts to 'popularise' science doomed to failure or fraud? Are modern science and its public divided by the illusion that they possess a common language?

6. SCIENTIFIC TESTIMONY AND THE PROBLEM OF PUBLIC TRUST

The problematic nature of the relations between the scientific community and the public goes back at least to the origins of systematical empirical science. Indeed, those relations are to be found at the very core of empirical knowledge; they are implicated in decisions about what is to count as knowledge. Within the rhetoric and the practice of seventeenth-century empirical science a fundamental problem of social relations was recognised and addressed. If, as was insisted, eye-witnessing was to be the hall-mark of proper scientific procedure, and if, as practical exigencies dictated, most of one's knowledge was to be founded upon testimony and trust, how did one go about evaluating testimony about empirical phenomena and processes? Who was to be believed and trusted in such matters? Although various candidate solutions to the practical problems posed by testimony were offered during the seventeenth century, the matter was dealt with for the most part by deploying criteria of creditworthiness that were routinely used by sectors of the public. For example, one might trust the word of a gentleman – in science as in social life in general. By the eighteenth century, and especially in France, the scientific enterprise was beginning to be much more clearly differentiated. The visible institutionalisation of science in the Paris *Académie* was both a means and a sign of the distinction that now existed between the man of science and the public. Within such a setting the question of what reports would count as knowledge, and therefore of how natural reality would be construed, were assessed according to whether such reports stemmed from the scientific community proper or from members of the public. Westrum has written of an especially telling episode in mid-to-late eighteenth-century France in which reports from the public retailing the fall of 'meteorites' were systematically discredited by members of the *Académie*, whose current thinking was that these phenomena did not exist, on the grounds that such lay persons were credulous and undisciplined observers. It is a state of affairs that still exists. Public claims about the natural world, where they conflict with what scientists reckon as true or plausible, are not in general seriously engaged with by the scientific community.[7] The costs of doing otherwise would, of course, be enormous. Sheer practicality necessitates the use of some sort of filter selecting which claims scientists can effectively consider. Nevertheless, the effect of such distinctions is to define out of the domain of science novel claims to knowledge that stem from the public – for the reason that this is their derivation. Further examples of the cognitive consequences of distinctions between the public and the scientific community could be cited *ad libitum*. Yet the general point is evident: membership and non-membership in the scientific community is continually being negotiated. The scientific community (and various sectors of it) and the public (and its special institutions and interest groups) are ceaselessly at work in defining themselves, and the nature of the distinctions that divide them. In the course of so doing they also define what is to count as knowledge and the proper means of securing it.

7. WHAT SCIENTISTS WANT FROM THE PUBLIC AND HOW THEY TRY TO GET IT: THE PROBLEM OF LEGITIMACY

When members of the scientific community explicitly address themselves to the public at large, what is it that they want, and how do they go about achieving it? In historical settings where science is neither well institutionalised nor recognised as a valuable enterprise in its own right, members of the scientific community commonly desire public acknowledgment of their legitimacy. They want it recognised that the systematic pursuit of natural knowledge is an acceptable and, ideally, a laudable activity; that its products are innocuous or even valuable. Such recognition is seen as a pre-condition for acquitting the day-to-day goals of men of science, e.g. the disinterested pursuit of knowledge and the free deployment of cognitive and manipulative skills. But in a pre-institutionalised setting this value and legitimacy had to be argued for and won. R. K. Merton's 1938 thesis about the connection between seventeenth-century English science and Puritanism centrally concerns this aspect of the relations between science and the public.[8] Merton showed that English virtuosi and natural philosophers publicly argued for the legitimacy of the new science by displaying its compatibility with dominant modes of culture and their sentiments, in this case with Puritan strands of religion. The systematic pursuit of natural knowledge, it was argued by spokesmen of science, was in no way inimical to or incompatible with religion. Indeed, religious purposes were to be as effectively (or even more effectively) realised by the study of God's Book of Nature as by more traditional religious practices. (See art. 50, sect. 3.)

From the seventeenth century up to and including much of the nineteenth century, members of the scientific community continued to assert the public legitimacy of their enterprise via 'natural theology', an exercise predicated upon the argument that legitimate religious functions could be well served through the scientific study of nature and the public deployment of scientific findings. If religious authorities, and the public that accepted religious canons, could be convinced that science was useful in these ways, then the much-wanted recognition of the legitimacy of science might be secured. From the Boyle Lectures (starting in 1692) to the Bridgewater Treatises of the 1830s, the culture of natural theology was one of the main vehicles by which scientists addressed the public and advertised the cultural and moral goods that scientific activity might deliver. A consequence of these transactions between science and the public was the entrenchment in scientific culture of those orientations (such as teleology) that were deemed to be essential to the public religion. Only with the vigorous campaign of the Scientific Naturalist movement of the 1860s, 1870s and 1880s was the culture of natural theology broken down. Another sort of argument addressed from the scientific community to the public became current, designed to secure another desideratum. As we have seen, a secularised nature that no longer sustained religious verities was presented to the public. Strictly speaking, the public and practitioners of other forms of culture were told that they were to have no moral interest in this secularised nature. Scientists (now properly so called) were the only experts with a legitimate interest in, and with legitimate rights to pronounce upon, the domain of secularised nature. The public were told to expect substantial utilitarian benefits from the activities of authentic scientists (indeed, they were told that they had already enjoyed such benefits); but they were at the same time instructed that the only proper role that could be served by the public was to encourage and support the programmes of work and conceptions decided upon by autonomous scientists. If the public were substantially to interfere with the autonomy of the scientific community, it would not in fact receive the benefits that might accrue from science: they would kill the goose that lays the golden egg. The objectivity of knowledge would be corrupted, and the useful outcomes that could only arise from objective knowledge would not be realised. A more docile public emerged together with the role of the professional scientist and the secularised nature in which he operated.

8. CHANNELS OF COMMUNICATION BETWEEN SCIENCE AND THE PUBLIC

Until the nineteenth century the channels linking the public to scientific pronouncements were, in general, diffuse. We know that certain natural theological exercises were preached to specific congregations, and we now have some knowledge of the audience for science in a range of relatively inclusive scientific societies and academies from the seventeenth to the nineteenth centuries. But we still have little knowledge of the readership for texts that represented the findings of sciences to a wider audience or that appropriated scientific findings for public purposes. Karl Hufbauer has made one of the few systematic attempts to ascertain the readership of given scientific (and quasi-scientific) works, in this instance via subscription lists for a range of eighteenth-century German chemistry texts.[9] However, there has not yet been a concerted response by historians of science to the programme of research on the culture of publishing and reading associated with the work of Robert Darnton on the *Encyclopédie* and Elizabeth Eisenstein on print culture and Copernicanism. We need more studies of the vehicles used to communicate between science and the public, not least because the conventions and distribution of these vehicles may have had an important bearing upon public perceptions of scientific claims and therefore upon their careers.

In the seventeenth century, periodicals like the *Philosophical Transactions* of the Royal Society of London and the *Journal des savants* distributed scientific information and opinion among a broad community of the philosophically interested, though much scientific interchange continued to be conducted by letter and without the intervention of print. Nor should one forget the extent of face-to-face interaction in the seventeenth and eighteenth centuries between men of science and laypersons in public venues such as coffee-houses, taverns and exchanges. During the eighteenth century, itinerant lecturers in Britain staged scientific spectacles for public consumption, and Schaffer has shown how public demonstrations of phenomena created by the Leyden jar functioned as theologically important dramatic manifestations of God's power latent in nature.[10] By the eighteenth and early nineteenth centuries, printed channels for conveying scientific knowledge to the laity had vastly expanded: in Britain *The Ladies' Diary* (founded in 1704) and *The Gentleman's Diary* (founded in 1741) were important vehicles for mathematical communication; the *Gentleman's Magazine* (founded in 1731) contained significant quantities of medical information and the *Edinburgh Review* (founded in 1802) was the first of a large number of nineteenth-century British periodicals that defined the place of science in the wider culture and whose conflicting political and religious orientations offered readers divergent interpretations of the meaning of scientific claims. R. M. Young has shown how the fragmentation of the common cultural context may be traced in the changing place of science in the nineteenth-century general periodical literature.

The differentiation and specialisation of science meant that scientific knowledge no longer enjoyed a matter-of-course place in general culture. Yet that same differentiation created an opportunity for the explicit 'popularisation' of science, and, thus, for literary forms designed to convey otherwise inaccessible or impenetrable scientific knowledge to sectors of the public. From the late eighteenth century there developed, especially in Britain and America, a thriving industry devoted to the production and distribution of a vast number of 'popular' scientific texts, pamphlets and periodicals, ranging from moralistic tracts for the children of the lower orders to straightforwardly technical manuals for craft and industrial workers. The purposes of these various enterprises of popularisation and the portrayals of nature and of natural knowledge that they proffered have only begun to be assessed.[11] In our own century the roles of newspapers and magazines and of non-print media, notably photography, radio, television, film and museum exhibitions, in shaping (and representing) public perceptions of science, technology and medicine also remain largely unexplored, while serious studies of the role of 'science fiction' in the relations between the scientific community and the public are similarly scarce.

Scientific knowledge, in various forms, had been an element in the curricula of universities since their founding in the Middle Ages. However, the public reached by universities, even by the more open and accessible of these institutions, was small. The development in the nineteenth century of a 'schooled' society, and the integration of scientific knowledge into the curricula of schools, marked a fundamental change in the relations between science and the public. In Britain voluntary adult schools for skilled workers (the Mechanics' Institutes) offered almost exclusively scientific instruction from the 1820s, but it was not until much later in the nineteenth century, and into this century, that all children in Britain and elsewhere in Europe and America were receiving a compulsory education that contained significant elements of the natural sciences and mathematics. The nature and effect of this exposure has yet fully to be explored. However, it merits serious attention from historians of science, as school is certainly the major source of the modern public's knowledge of science and of how scientists go about securing their knowledge. The embedding of science into structures of authority like the classroom may have far-reaching consequences for shaping the public's sense of the certainty to be expected of science and of the manner in which scientific knowledge is made. Whether these sensibilities accurately correspond to the realities of science is debatable.

9. WHAT THE PUBLIC WANTS FROM SCIENCE AND HOW IT TRIES TO GET IT: THE PATRON AND THE STATE

If what the scientific community largely wanted from the wider public was recognition, legitimacy and support, what did the public want from men of science and the knowledge they were producing? And what consequences have there been for science of this public interest? As has already been suggested, a public persuaded that science was potentially useful knowledge might express their desire for the promised outcomes. (In this sense, public wants are not independent of the scientific community's historical work in identifying and cultivating those wants.) The public might want to see men of science actively at work addressing and satisfying technological and economic needs. Again, aspects of Merton's thesis deal with these relations between science and public interests and with their effects on scientific work. Merton documented certain 'foci of interest' that characterised the scientific proceedings of the seventeenth-century Royal Society. Scientific interest was not, he found, randomly distributed across the whole range of disciplines and problem areas; it was in fact concentrated in certain theoretical areas that, he argued, were those bearing the most evident relationship to pressing technical and economic problems. Sectors of the seventeenth-century English public came to believe that science might possess answers to economic and military problems they desired to solve. As a consequence, men of science found it advisable, expedient, or simply interesting to work preferentially in these areas.

From the Renaissance up to and including the eighteenth century, one of the most consequential social links connecting science and public concerns was patronage. In the relative absence of secure institutionalised positions and career structures for men of science, the role of the individual patron in the direction of scientific work was crucial. The patron offered support, subvention and encouragement, protected the man of science from enemies, and suggested topics of inquiry and trajectories of research. The study of patronage in science still lags somewhat behind the assessment of its role in the fine arts and literature. We need to know more about the structure and effects of the relationships between individual men of science and their patrons, for example, between Galileo and the Medici, Robert Hooke and Sir John Cutler, Thomas Hobbes and the Cavendish family, Cassini and Colbert, Leibniz and the Guelphs, William Herschel and George III, Priestley and Shelburne and Cuvier and Tessier.[12] It was in the nature of the patronage relationship that it was largely *ad hoc* and not standardised. The terms of contract might be explicit or informal, the patron's interests might affect the recipient's work strongly or not at all (it might, indeed, be the receiver of patronage who effectively controlled the relationship); or public concerns might correspond to those of the patron in a wide variety of ways. Newton, evidently, kept his disciples' noses firmly to his philosophical grindstone, and his influence with government and universities ensured that his patronage was intellectually compelling. In the early eighteenth century James Brydges, first Duke of Chandos, manipulated a vast empire of public works and influenced the shape of applied science practised by Desagulier, John Keill, Richard Bradley and many others. Darwin's presence on the *Beagle* was the immediate result of patronage and the indirect product of public interest in empire, while the scientific outcome of that appointment bore little connection with the public concerns that brought it about.

In eighteenth-century Scotland, the patronage relationship merged with a more diffuse nexus in which the cultural leadership of certain sectors of society was acknowledged by men of science, with effects upon the direction and nature of scientific work. In that setting, a powerful audience of improving Lowland landowners, persuaded that the pursuit of sciences relating to the terraqueous globe might aid them in their search for greater yields, profits and rents, influenced Scottish men of science to cluster their researches in geology, mineralogy and meteorology. C. J. Lawrence has argued that public concerns with explaining the state of Scottish society and legitimating certain versions of proper social order influenced eighteenth-century Lowland physicians and physiologists to produce a specific view of bodily organisation and its nervous integration.[13]

Since the eighteenth century, the patronage system has been progressively replaced by professionalised (frequently bureaucratic) career structures and formal relations between science and the public. Now it is the state that speaks for (or claims the right legitimately to speak for) the public and to voice public interest in the conduct of science. This state of affairs developed at varying rates and for different reasons in different national settings. The persistence of patronage and of pluralistic and diffuse connections between science and the state is evident throughout much of the nineteenth century in Britain. In France the old regime effectively forged a set of institutional structures and ties between science and the state that the Napoleonic reforms largely translated into a new idiom. The government of Prussia invented key aspects of the scientist's role virtually as a by-product of bureaucratic concerns with the reform of the universities.

But it was in the United States that one of the most intractable problems afflicting modern relations between science and the public was most directly confronted. The scientific community up to and including the nineteenth century had argued for public support largely on utilitarian grounds. Pure science, it was repeatedly said, would ultimately yield applied science and economic benefits. In a democratic society, the state was justified in spending public money on these grounds and on no others. The recipients of public monies had to be publicly accountable. (In the middle and later part of the nineteenth century there were considerable *constitutional* objections to Federal support for an enterprise that could not guarantee contributions to the national welfare, and there continue to be enormous problems securing resources for scientific studies whose useful outcomes are not acknowledged by the public or its representatives.) These terms of public support carried with them substantial troubles. The demand for accountability appeared radically incompatible with the autonomy that, scientists said, was the condition for the health of science, its capacity to yield objective knowledge, and, thus, to produce the knowledge upon which technological innovation could be based. The relations between science and the public in modern democratic societies would seem to be entangled in deep contradictions, partly deriving from the rhetorical structures historically used by the scientific community to justify itself to the public, partly the effect of engagements between a particular institution (science) and the enveloping public institutions whose interests may materially diverge.[14]

Throughout the nineteenth and twentieth centuries, and especially after the Second World War, the scale of state support for science vastly expanded, and in no areas more spectacularly than in those of direct or indirect military interest. It is now difficult to imagine what the social institution of science would look like divorced from its military ties. The effect of these links on the scientific community, including scientists' professed norm of openness, has scarcely been examined, still less their consequences for public perceptions of the nature of science, its autonomy and its value. If the golden egg explodes and strews radioactive isotopes over the countryside, one may perhaps understand the public's willingness to consider doing violence to the goose who has historically claimed the egg as her own.

10. PUBLIC ORDER AS SCIENTIFIC TOPIC: CONCLUSION

Historically, the public have wanted much more from natural knowledge than technical and economic utility. Nature has traditionally been a theatre in which moral dramas are enacted and a classroom in which moral lessons can be learned. A socially (as well as technically) usable nature has been demanded of those entrusted with the task of producing representations of it. However, here it is not merely incautious but grossly inaccurate to speak loosely of 'the public's' interest. As with economic goods, the conception of moral goods inevitably divides the public into groups with differing interests. In the late seventeenth and early eighteenth centuries, Low Church Anglican apologists demanded a morally usable conception of nature in which God could be seen actively to intervene, while their deist opponents required a visibly self-sufficient nature. Such moral use of science divided the public into those who approved and disapproved of Newtonian natural philosophy, in whole or in part.[15] In the nineteenth century distinct geologies, with conflicting attitudes towards what counted as stratigraphical and palaeontological facts, catered for sectors of the public with different investments in the natural world and its uses in religious and moral argumentation. Perhaps the most celebrated public appropriation of codified scientific work is Social Darwinism. There were sectors of the public that rejected Darwin's naturalistic findings on moral and religious grounds; others held the text stable while contesting its implications for man and the moral order.

The triumph of Darwinism, and of the Naturalistic movement of which it was part, signalled the end of an era of public interest in the constitution of scientific knowledge. With the secularisation of nature, the relations between science and the public were, as the canonical account rightly suggests, fundamentally altered. A culture that represents nature as morally vacuous lays down the conditions for a radical distinction between those professionally concerned with the explication of secular nature and the general public with their moral concerns. The modern public were to have no business with the framing of scientific representations and with the conceptual content of scientists' work. The converse did not, of course, apply. In the late nineteenth century the eugenics movement offered a naturalistic account of the social order, an enterprise carried on in the late twentieth century by sociobiologists. Nor are naturalistic theories of public order confined to the specifically biological: much, if not the whole, of modern social science is founded upon agreement that social order and the formation of public interests ought to be naturalistically analysed. There can be no more striking evidence of the changing relations between science and the public since the seventeenth century. Where once the public were powerful in relation to the making of scientific knowledge, there is now widespread assent to the proposition that public life is a legitimate topic for naturalistic scientific inquiry.

NOTES

1. The 'canonical account' described here is obviously a pastiche of approaches employed by many writers. An author whose view comes closest to the canonical account is Joseph Ben-David, see esp. his *The scientist's role in society: a comparative study* (new ed., Chicago, 1984; orig. publ. 1971), and 'Organization, social control, and cognitive change in science', in Ben-David and Terry Nichols Clark (eds.), *Culture and its creators: essays in honor of Edward Shils* (Chicago, 1977), pp. 244–65.
2. Thomas S. Kuhn, 'Mathematical versus experimental traditions in the development of modern science', in Kuhn, *The essential tension: selected studies in scientific tradition and change* (Chicago, 1977), pp. 311–65.
3. Cecil G. Helman, ' "Feed a cold, starve a fever" – folk models of infection in an English suburban community, and their relation to medical treatment', *Culture, medicine and psychiatry*, 2 (1978), 107–37; Charles E. Rosenberg, 'The therapeutic revolution: medicine, meaning and social change in nineteenth-century America', *Perspectives in biology and medicine*, 20 (1977), 485–506.
4. Steven Shapin and Simon Schaffer, *Leviathan and the air-pump: Hobbes, Boyle, and the experimental life* (Princeton, 1985); Shapin, 'Robert Boyle and mathematics: reality, representation, and experimental practice', *Science in context*, 2 (1988), 25–61.
5. Robert M. Young, *Darwin's metaphor: nature's place in Victorian culture* (Cambridge, 1985), chaps. 2 and 5; Frank M. Turner, 'The Victorian conflict between science and religion: a professional dimension', *Isis*, 69 (1978), 356–76; Morris Berman, ' "Hegemony" and the amateur tradition in British science', *Journal of social history*, 8 (1975), 30–50.
6. Gillian Beer, *Darwin's plots: evolutionary narrative in Darwin, George Eliot and nineteenth-century fiction* (London, 1983); also R. M. Young, (1985) ch. 4.
7. Ron Westrum, 'Science and social intelligence about anomalies: the case of meteorites', *Social studies of science*, 8 (1978), 461–93; idem, 'Science and social intelligence about anomalies: the case of UFOs', *Social studies of science*, 7 (1977), 271–302.
8. Robert K. Merton, *Science, technology and society in seventeenth-century England* (new ed., New York, 1970), esp. chs. 4–6.
9. Karl Hufbauer, *The formation of the German chemical community (1720–1795)* (Berkeley, 1982); idem, 'Chemistry's enlightened audience', *Studies on Voltaire and the eighteenth century*, 153 (1976), 1069–85.
10. Simon Schaffer, 'Natural philosophy and public spectacle in the eighteenth century', *History of science*, 21 (1983), 1–43.
11. See, for example, James A. Secord, 'Newton in the nursery: Tom Telescope and the philosophy of tops and balls, 1761–1838', *History of science*, 23 (1985), 127–51; Greg Myers, 'Nineteenth-century popularizers of thermodynamics and the rhetoric of social prophecy', *Victorian studies*, 29 (1985–86), 35–66.
12. For selected examples, see Dorinda Outram, *Georges Cuvier: vocation, science and authority in post-revolutionary France* (Manchester, 1984), esp. chap. 5; Richard S. Westfall, 'Science and patronage: Galileo and the telescope', *Isis*, 76 (1985), 11–30; John Gascoigne, 'Politics, patronage and Newtonianism: the case of Cambridge', *The historical journal*, 27 (1984), 1–24.
13. Steven Shapin, 'The audience for science in eighteenth-century Edinburgh', *History of science*, 12 (1974), 95–121; Christopher Lawrence, 'The nervous system and society in the Scottish Enlightenment', in Barry Barnes and Steven Shapin (eds.), *Natural order: historical studies of scientific culture* (Beverly Hills, 1979), pp. 19–40.

14. George H. Daniels, 'The pure-science ideal and democratic culture', *Science*, 156 (1967), 1699–1705.
15. Margaret C. Jacob, *The Newtonians and the English revolution, 1689–1720* (Ithaca, N.Y., 1976); idem, *The radical enlightenment: pantheists, freemasons and republicans* (London, 1981).

FURTHER READING

Roger Cooter, *The cultural meaning of popular science: phrenology and the organization of consent in nineteenth-century Britain* (Cambridge, 1984).

Charles C. Gillispie, 'The *Encyclopédie* and the Jacobin philosophy of science: a study in ideas and consequences', in Marshall Clagett, (ed.), *Critical problems in the history of science* (Madison, Wisconsin, 1959), pp. 255–89.

Gerald Holton and William Blanpied, (eds.), *Science and its public: the changing relationship*, Boston studies in the philosophy of science, vol. 33 (Dordrecht, 1976).

David Layton, *Science for the people: the origins of the school science curriculum* (London, 1973).

Roy S. Porter, 'Science, provincial culture and public opinion in enlightenment England', *British journal for eighteenth-century studies*, 3 (1980), 20–46.

Steven Shapin and Barry Barnes, 'Science, nature and control: interpreting mechanics institutes', *Social studies of science*, 7 (1977), 31–74.

Susan Sheets-Pyenson, 'Popular science periodicals in Paris and London: the emergence of a low scientific culture, 1820–1875', *Annals of science*, 42 (1985), 549–72.

Terry Shinn and Richard Whitley (eds.), *Expository science: forms and functions of popularisation*, Sociology of the sciences, volume IX, 1985 (Dordrecht, 1985).

Larry Stewart, 'Public lectures and private patronage in Newtonian England', *Isis*, 77 (1986), 47–58.

Frank M. Turner, 'Public science in Britain, 1880–1919', *Isis*, 71 (1980), 589–608.

66

SCIENCE AND POLITICAL IDEOLOGY, 1790–1848

DORINDA OUTRAM

1. INTRODUCTION AND HISTORIOGRAPHY

Few topics have aroused such sustained debate, and posed such acute methodological problems in the history of science, as the relations between science and political ideology. The problem is especially acute for the period 1790–1848 because this was a period of great change and flux both in the content and institutionalisation of science, and in the whole field of political ideology. In particular, in France, the Revolution which began in 1789 and ended in 1799, had produced radical and enduring questioning of previously held political ideas; a questioning which had affected most other European countries to a greater or lesser degree. At the same time, during the period 1790–1848, Britain experienced the first thoroughgoing industrialisation. This brought with it social strains, economic changes and a search for new ideas on many sides, to challenge or to justify the new social and political order which industrialisation brought with it.

In these circumstances, it is not surprising that the history of science has failed to reach any historiographical consensus, or even a coherent tradition of approach to this question. Science and politics were generally, until quite recently, held rigidly separate by the practitioners both of science and of the history of science. History of science uncritically accepted the claims of nineteenth-century science that it was a value-free, apolitical activity, and it thus made little or no sense to integrate scientific and political ideas. In spite of obvious counter-examples in the real world such as Social Darwinism, or eugenics, this denial, within the history of science, of the links between science and politics held sway at least until the late 1950s.

After that time, history of science itself gradually began to loosen its links with science, and to reforge its links with general history. A growing perception of the history of science as a historical discipline in its own right, rather than as an ancillary discipline to the sciences, allowed the gradual entry into the field of the problem of the relations between science and political ideology. At the same time, the increasing polarisation between right and left, which was a hallmark of political life in the 1960s in France, the United States and to a lesser extent Great Britain, also refocused attention on the pre-history of many radical ideologies which had pre-figured Marxism and socialism. All these changes ushered in more explicit recognition of connections between science and political ideology.

However, such considerations remained limited in scope. Attention was focused almost exclusively on the relationship between the life sciences and the social sciences which was allegedly forged by their debt to an evolutionary theory commonly ascribed to Lamarck. Political ideology was also given in many cases a restricted definition applying only to minority creeds such as Owenism, or Saint-Simonism. History of science did not reflect the wider tendency in history as a whole, especially due to the impact of the *Annales* historians in France, to cease to focus on closely-defined ideologies, and to turn attention more to general political outlooks or assumptions prevalent in society at large: the so-called *mentalités*.

From the mid-1970s, historiography entered a new phase, characterised by a much sharper awareness of the critical functions inherent in historical enquiry, and in the history of science in particular. Attention turned from minority movements to the much wider enquiry into the relationship between the popular diffusion of science (through the printing press, Mechanics' Institutes and informal debating societies) and high-profile, though mainly middle-class organisations such as the British Association for the Advancement of Science. It should be noted, however, that such an approach is very much confined to the history of science in Britain and the United States. Little has been done to produce any synthetic examination of this topic in relation to France or to other parts of Europe, in spite of considerable evidence that, especially after 1815, science in these regions did become a popular cultural commodity, and in spite of the fact that proto-Socialist or Utopian creeds such as Saint-Simonism were of considerable importance in organising a new form of class-consciousness among the French working-class in particular.

The new emphasis on the interaction in lower social groups between science and political ideology has also been very much influenced by a consistently left-wing political orientation. With the exception of the vigorous and rigorous empiricism of Thackray and Morrell's account of the early years of the British Association for the Advancement of Science, much of this orientation has adopted ideas of the relationship between ideology and power in society which draws heavily on contemporary Marxism. However, many proponents of recent approaches to the topic are not themselves committed in other respects to this ideology. (See art. 6.)

This does not mean to say that the Marxist approach has produced ideas which are consistent with each other, nor does it provide a single view of science's functions in the construction of political ideology, or political ideology's role in shaping the reception and functions of scientific ideas. Let us examine some recent approaches to the problem which will bear out this point. On one account, the diffusion of science has been identified with the 'social control' required in the expanding industrial sector of the aspiring industrial work-force by the entrepreneurs in particular, and the middle-classes in general. It is argued that the diffusion of positive scientific technical knowledge as well as disciplined work attitudes through such institutions as Mechanics' Institutes created a fusion of interest and outlook between workers and owners, while at the same time blocking off enquiry into other areas of science whose political implications might have been far more debatable. Science, it is argued, e.g. by Cooter (1985), was an essential element in the creation of a cultural hegemony which tried fundamentally to delegitimate the opinions of those workers whose ideas were directly opposed to those of the manufacturers or which stemmed from a pre-industrial artisan outlook. But this view, plausible though it seems, has also been subjected to criticism. Inkster has pointed out that there was no single dominant class in the England of the early 1800s. Social friction did not simply oppose masters to men; it also opposed land-owners to industrialists, new urban areas to old and province to metropolis. Each such fragment certainly attempted to use science, amongst other aspects of culture, to create cultural control or to challenge opposing groups. According to this view, as Inkster writes:

> Science was not a counter-culture, nor was it integral to the ruling cultural stock. Rather, science was a malleable thing, allowing much creativity, individuality and competition, representing a means of social mobility to some, of social expression to others, a measure or tool of socio-intellectual control (through sanctions and rewards) to yet others.[1]

This approach to science as a functional object mediating social and political conflict has been most consistently worked out in the works of Steven Shapin and Barry Barnes. Different reactions to and definitions of such pseudo-sciences as phrenology have formed one of the main case-studies for this thesis. Social interests, it has been argued, turn science and its definition into an expression of their social *mentalité*, and use them in their conflicts with other interest groups. Using inputs from anthropology, Shapin argues, with Mary Douglas, that a belief is sustained by its persuasiveness in negotiating social relations and not simply by its technical possibilities of 'explaining' what happens in the natural world itself.

There has, however, been much criticism of the Barnes-Shapin-Cooter approach. If scientific theories and cosmologies are developed as socially useful instruments of persuasion, why do theories fail? The answer here should be that social forces have changed, and need new theories to lock in and form new ideologies. But this argument also depends on a successful identification of social and political change, always a notoriously controversial judgement to make. There are also other problems. Their anthropological perspective does have the merit of rescuing science from the pedestal on which it was placed by a traditional, apolitical historiography. However, the arguments common in the Barnes-Shapin school, against the possibility of retrieving the intentions of individual scientific practitioners seem unconvincing, especially for a period where science, still far from fully institutionalised, continued to be largely carried out by individuals. Above all, the major premiss of the Barnes-Shapin-Cooter historiography, that is, that the major conflicts over science are really about the authority to interpret reality socially, is suggestive, but not proven, even though argued from many interesting coincidences of assumptions, imagery and interest. Also, if scientific theorising is so malleable that it can be readily appropriated for the making of social and political ideologies and justifications, we need to know what distinguishes science from any other body of knowledge or belief with equally accessible resources. This is a special problem, owing to Shapin's denials of causal links between the actual content of science, and the political beliefs arising from it. In the case of phrenology, for example Shapin concedes that:

> A successful demonstration that British phrenology was *involved with* a plethora of social-reformist movements does not justify asserting that phrenology *caused* people to favour social reform or that the phrenological system of ideas *entailed* certain social policies.[2]

To answer this point, Shapin has emphasised the technical interests and procedures which become codified and identified as specifically scientific.

2. FROM THE FRENCH REVOLUTION TO THE BEGINNINGS OF INDUSTRIALISATION (1789–1830)

It should be clear by now that no historiographical consensus exists on the topic of the relations between science and ideology in this period. Nor is this a surprising state of affairs. As Inkster points out, we cannot ascribe one single definition to science in this period, let alone a single set of political implications. But we can say that all the debate which accompanied the definition of approaches to our topic has left certain very basic questions still completely untouched. It will be impossible here to do more than list these omissions; but they can be used as indications for some future developments in this area of the history of science. The first point to be made is that science, although considered in most of the historiography as an object *fed into* or *applied to* areas of ideological formation such as social and political conflict, did indeed, through its vocational ideology, also make claims about the nature of authority in the world; claims which were, in many ways, identical to those current in political attitudes in society at large at the end of the eighteenth century. Few investigations have been made of these claims, apart from that contained in Outram, *Georges Cuvier: vocation, science and authority in post-revolutionary France* (1984). The operation of these ideological claims in the political world, and their interaction with other political creeds of the time, is a major theme of this book. A second area of omission in the historiography lies in its failure to identify the very broad shifts in political *mentalités* in this period. Equally, little or no sustained attention has been paid to the consequences of the Revolution in France. While general historians debate as a matter of course the way the Revolution changed not only formal structures of power, but also created a whole new cultural field for the emergence of political ideologies of new types, there is little of this discussion in the field of history of science. In their task, of course, historians of science are not helped by historians of politics and ideas who, conversely, display generally little awareness of the input of science into this crucial political and cultural shift. A fourth unanswered question is much simpler and equally important: why was it that science *should* have had any input into political ideology? Why was it that men were so ready to combine descriptions of the natural world with their political ideologies?

Clearly, these questions raise issues which are far too large to be discussed here. What will be attempted instead should be treated as more in the nature of guidelines for possible approaches to these questions, rather than answers to them. Before we can even begin this task, some semantic points have to be considered. Neither 'science' nor 'ideology' was used in its modern meaning in this period. Science was a word primarily used in French to denote a vague idea of knowledge or knowing, and did not come to its modern meaning until the early twentieth century. In English, natural philosophy was the equivalent term until the late nineteenth century. It is worth remembering that even the word 'scientist' itself is a late formulation, first being used by William Whewell in 1833. '*Idéologie*' also existed in French in the late eighteenth and early nineteenth centuries, but was mainly used in a restricted philosophical sense: the *idéologues* were contemporary philosophers concerned with the problem of the formation of ideas from sense-impressions. *Idéologie* is sometimes found in this period in both English and French in the sense of 'systems of political ideas explicitly articulated'; but although this usage exists, it is uncommon. For its full development the term 'ideology' had to await the work of Marx and the later development of Marxist and socialist theory in this century.

So, in attempting to approach our four questions, we have to make the point at the outset that we must avoid being misled by anachronistc terminology. It is also important to draw another consequence from our semantic enquiry: that it is impossible to see science on the one hand and political ideology on the other as two discrete objects which interact in predictable ways. At this point we should also recognise the reservations of historians of political ideas, such as Sheldon Wolin, who have discussed at length the inability of the men of this period to locate and define the political sphere as a clear autonomous area of human life. Such autonomy, again, is very much a twentieth-century viewpoint. All this means that historians must be guilty of anachronism if they think in terms of science and political ideology being two clearly demarcated, unambiguous areas reacting on each other but unaffected by that reaction. We need to think much more in terms of descriptions of nature, and of the practitioners of science, operating in a *common context* with descriptions of and hopes for the political world.

Now let us return to our major questions. After the qualifications introduced above, it would not be found surprising that the vocational ideology of science itself made explicit claims about the authority of its practitioners, claims which the more astute of them, such as Cuvier, found it easy to translate into real political authority. The ideal scientist, it was claimed, was so in virtue of a character of austere probity, which would have nothing to do with the machinations and intrigues of courts and patrons. Such a character's absolute rectitude and solitary self-sufficiency guaranteed his very capacity to see and interpret the natural world correctly. This ideal also had a great deal in common with that of republican rectitude which qualified men for public life and legitimated their authority both in France in the revolutionary period, and in the immediately post-colonial United States. It made the claim to scientific vocation a valuable political resource at a time when actual political ideologies were confused, hostile and fragmented, and when political life itself, especially in France, was chaotic. The claim to control neutral ground was also, in these circumstances, the claim to control a rare and valuable public resource. On this were based many of the claims of nineteenth-century science to mediate between different social classes and even between different nations through the even-handed, apolitical, value-free distribution of its discoveries to mankind. It is thus impossible to regard science as an unpolitical input into political ideology: science itself contained claims about the nature of authority.

This naturally brings us to consider how science interacted with the broader political *mentalités* of this period, a theme which most historians have ignored in favour of assessing the input of science into clearly defined, explicit systematic exposés of political ideologies. But broader, inexplicit, often unexamined assumptions in society at large about the relations between natural orders and political systems have to be taken into account before we can understand much of the rationale behind the making of links between science and more clearly defined explicit ideologies. In the much broader assumptions of the age, we can say that science and political ideology were linked through the medium of widely-held religious beliefs, beliefs which in their broad outline were common to both Protestant and Catholic traditions. Over-simplifying enormously, we can say that the two traditions held that both the natural and the social order had been created and were held in place by Divine Will. Often, religious authorities in both traditions interpreted the natural order as an allegory for the social hierarchy, and also insisted that both bore clear marks of the benevolent intentions of the Creator to his Creation. Both religious traditions, though to a far greater extent in the case of France, also saw the figure of the monarch as the meeting point of the natural and the social order under God. The king combined in his own person both the natural body of a man, able to live the biological, natural life of a man and ultimately die, and also, at the same time, the image of the 'body politic', the undying, representative body (the king is dead, long live the king), who existed on earth by God's will. He was therefore an image both of divine authority over the created and social worlds, and of the relationships of hierarchy within the social order itself (the members all being subordinate to the head). It was very long-standing political and religious attitudes such as these which made it 'natural' for images of the natural world to be requisitioned when men were discussing political ideas. As we have seen above, the vocational ideology of science itself also validated claims to have apolitical authority in the public world. These two levels worked together and reinforced each other, and go some way towards explaining one of the basic questions raised by our theme; after all, why *should* men have used accounts of, or assumptions about the natural world to inform their political ideology? This reinforcement of ideas also shows the extent to which, by the 1790s, science and political ideology did at some basic cultural level ultimately form a common context, rather than two sharply demarcated automonous spheres.

The period from 1790 to 1830, however, also saw great challenge and modification in such pre-existing *mentalités*, and these were changes which could not fail to affect the common context which we have just discussed. The impact of the revolutionary era is also a difficult one to assess in any global or general way. Different countries, and even different social classes within the same country, were very different in their reactions to the ideological shifts and challenges of the revolution. Nor was it the case, even in France itself, that the old basis of the common context abruptly disappeared even after the physical death and political annihilation of the monarch and the monarchy between 1792 and 1793. After 1815, when monarchy was restored in France, strenuous efforts were made by both church and state to reimpose as absolute all the dogma, including that of the King's two bodies, on which the old regime had rested. The period 1790-1830 can be considered then as a period of transition, when many apparently incompatible ideological viewpoints existed; it was also, of course, a period when science itself went through many developments of its own, which will be considered later.

Bearing these qualifications in mind, we can begin to examine in more detail the actual impact of the French Revolution, which broke out in 1789, on the relations of science and ideology. The first point to make is that the period of the Revolution between 1789 and September 1792 not only changed France from a historic monarchy to a new republic, changed every structure of local and central administration and dispersed or killed a very large portion of France's previous ruling class, but also changed the entire nature of politics, and in so doing also changed the nature of political ideology as well. It changed politics from being primarily a court politics, where transactions of power usually took the form of face-to-face negotiation between the members of the numerically restricted political elite, to a politics where power lay in the control and creation of mass movements and organised factions, and where a broader public opinion became a political force for the first time. In this situation, the nature of political ideology was also bound to change. The old regime in France had, of course, seen much coherent criticism of the monarchy; but it had not been a society where such thoughts about, or theories of, politics (e.g. to cite the most influential texts, Jean-Jacques Rousseau's *Contrat Social* or Montesquieu's *Discours sur l'esprit des Loix*) had become the blue-prints of coherent political groups. This was so for two reasons. First, as we have seen, pre-revolutionary politics in France were not carried on through the medium of modern-style political parties or pressure groups. Second, political philosophy itself before the Revolution in France was of a quite different kind from that which succeeded it after 1789. After 1789 historians now argue that ideology became an integral part of politics for the first time. And as politics for the first time became an affair involving everyone, rather than a small elite, then ideologies were bound to splinter and to reflect the different needs and purposes of the many different social and interest groups that had recently entered the new political arena. In the place of a basic consensus in society about the place of political authority, Divine Will, social hierarchy and the natural order, a consensus typified by the common habit of picturing society and the political order through the metaphor of the body politic, the revolutionary period saw the emergence of tightly defined non-consensual political ideologies. These were often aimed at a radical restructuring, not only of politics but also of the entire social order, including the relations between the sexes. Such ideologies, which would include Owenism in the United Kingdom, or Fourierism and Saint-Simonism in France, later gained many adherents both in Britain and the United States.

The more extreme phase of the French Revolution also made another substantial innovation in the field of ideology, with its outright attack on the beliefs and practices of Christianity itself. This 'dechristianisation campaign', as historians such as Michel Vovelle have termed it, lasted from the end of 1792 to the beginning of 1794. It was never successful all over France, and was not even unanimously accepted even by the leading politicians and groups of the Revolution. But it did make very visible a new determination to destroy the Church not only as an organisation, but also as a set of beliefs. Religious worship, for example, was forbidden, and the production of religious images and works of piety was banned. From the Revolution onwards, the input of Christian thinking into ideology became debatable ground. Such beliefs had previously legitimated certain attitudes towards the natural order and its relationship with the social and political order, as both being hierarchies held in place by a benevolent Deity. Once that legitimation was challenged, science, especially in France, began to stand forward as an autonomous source of legitimation, divorced from its theological under-pinnings. This is another reason why the new political ideologies, especially in France, incorporated, and appealed to, the findings of science in their thinking about society. Science could now be a source of legitimation because it was possible to view it as a body of knowledge and practice detached from the politically implicated belief-system of Christianity.

But the fact that science performed this function, especially in France, did not necessarily mean that all the political ideologies it supported were of one kind. It cannot be too strongly emphasised that this period following the Revolution saw the production of conservative, liberal and even Utopian ideologies, while at the same time the older *mentalités*, though strongly challenged, were still of importance for large segments of the population.

It is also true that if 'political ideology' does not represent a monolithic object, neither does the term 'science'. The early nineteenth-century was not a period when scientific specialisms had yet appeared in a strongly defined way. Much science was still produced by amateurs, and only a fortunate few were able to find fully-paid posts. Nor were the boundaries clear between science and non-science. Many individuals were able practitioners in both areas. Within science itself, many different outlooks and traditions jostled for predominance. A positive, analytical approach to the interrogation of nature, which stressed the asking of 'answerable' questions to closely defined areas of enquiry, looked askance at the rival tradition which attempted to view nature as an organically-related whole, without insisting on the boundaries between different scientific disciplines. Science itself was no more a monolithic intellectual entity than 'political ideology'.

These two trends had their own political images. The organic tradition had within it a strong tendency towards what we might call epistemological democracy: because the world was to be understood as a unified whole, it followed that individuals did not necessarily need an esoteric specialist training to be able to make valid observations about the nature of the natural world. The analytical tradition, on the other hand, stressed a much greater degree of specialised training, and went hand in hand with contemporary moves towards increasing specialisation within, and professionalisation of, science in the mid-century.

During the French Revolution, the organic tradition briefly triumphed in the successful artisan movement to close the Paris Academy of Sciences and other corporate bastions of formal, analytical science, a movement described in the closing sections of Roger Hahn's *The Anatomy of a Scientific Institution: the Paris Academy of Sciences 1666–1803* (1971). These events had given this trend in science, and in French science in particular, a reputation for association with social and political radicalism. These associations were fed for Britain in particular by the life and work of the chemist Joseph Priestley, who emigrated to America in 1792. 'Any man', he wrote, 'has as good a power of distinguishing truth from falsity as his neighbours'.[3] For Priestley, science was inherently anti-authoritarian: 'This rapid progress of knowledge will, I doubt not, be the means under God of extirpating all error and prejudice, and of putting an end to all undue and usurped authority in the business of religion as well as of science.'[4] Attitudes such as Priestley's, combined with the connections of 'democratic science' and the French Revolution, in some quarters soon gave French science a seditious image in other countries. Conservatives, such as the Edinburgh professor John Robison, denounced the French Revolution as a *philosophe* conspiracy, and included noted scientific free-thinkers like Priestley amongst their targets. Such attitudes led to a strong movement in Britain to capture science for conservative purposes. A concrete manifestation of this attitude was the Seditious Societies Act of 1799 which required licensing of all public meetings dealing with controversial subjects. Although it now seems clear that these acts were really only for short periods, and used selectively to deal with proven radicals, there is also evidence that popular 'democratic' science, in the form of working men's meetings, was adversely affected. Above all, the Act contributed to efforts by the conservative Royal Society of London to control other scientific societies by acting as referee on their suitability to obtain licensing. All this shows that any given moment could produce both conservative and radical functions for science. In Britain, in particular, this period saw only a partially successful attempt to link science, theology and political conservatism. William Paley's classic *Natural Theology: or Evidences of the existence and attributes of the Deity, collected from the appearances of nature* (1802), a textbook used continuously in university education until late in the nineteenth century, argued that natural orders and political orders were analogous to one another, and that although the inferior ranks in each seemed to endure disproportionate suffering, this was cancelled out in the long run by the disposition of other benefits. The message was clear; apparent injustices in the social hierarchy must be endured rather than challenged. But strong though this conservative version of science was in Britain, the conservative ideology itself was in constant flux. By 1830, the Scots divine Thomas Chalmers was arguing for a natural theology which could recognise that the physical, and hence the social worlds were not immutable, but changing systems.[5]

This discussion should have helped to make it clearer why the new radical ideologies of the early nineteenth century existed, why they should be in any way related to science, and what the claim to be 'scientific' could imply. This is an important topic to clarify because nearly all the new ideologies of the early nineteenth century, (including Marxism itself, a little beyond the close of our period) do make claims to be 'scientific', do denigrate other ideologies in terms of their alleged 'non-scientific' nature and do claim authority from the fact of that 'scientificness'. Marx and Engels, for example, rejected Owenism, the English socialist movement of Robert Owen, as 'not scientific' but 'Utopian'. The Owenites themselves claimed a wholly scientific foundation to their projected re-structuring of society, a foundation which would substitute 'system and science' for 'chance and error'. William Thompson, a prominent Owenite, wrote of the 'New Science of Society, or Social Science, the science which determines . . . happiness or misery . . . by circumstances over which each individual has hitherto had little control'.[6] In other words, science here means the application of determinate social and ideological conditions to human thought and behaviour. Owenites hoped to use such tools to promote the principle of individual interests perpetuated by religion, marriage and private property. These were the principles on which to oppose the universal fragmentation and alienation engendered by modern commercial society.

An even more interesting case-study in the relations between science and the new ideologies is provided by Saint-Simonism. This sect, founded by Claude-Henri de Saint-Simon (1760–1825), produced a scheme for industrial Utopia based on a rigid hierarchy of labour. Although always strongest amongst the French middle-class, this movement had made contact with Owenism in Britain by the 1830s. From the beginning, Saint-Simon made it clear that science was an integral part of his social philosophy. In his *Lettres d'un habitant de Genève à ses contemporains* (1802), he noted that it was in considering our social relations as physiological phenomena that he thought of this project (of a new social science). Specifically, it seems clear that Saint-Simon was strongly influenced by the physiological research of Xavier Bichat. Bichat produced experimentally based 'positive' facts, different from the philosophical theorising of contemporary life-scientists in the 'organic' tradition such as Lamarck. He also defined life as a dynamic function of the interplay of external environment and internal milieu. Bichat's famous definition of life itself as 'an ensemble of functions which struggle against death', indicated a view of organised bodies not as stable entities, but as continuously struggling for, and sometimes approaching, a state of equilibrium. It was this image which enabled Saint-Simon to abandon the steady-state abstraction which dominated the enlightenment thinkers' views of society, and to substitute for it an idea of human society as being, like a natural organism, full of crisis and change whilst retaining its basic structure. These were ideas which prefigure the arrival in France of the stresses and tensions of industrialisation. Saint-Simon saw that medical and physiological research demonstrated that men are not born equal, and that their rationality was dependent on their biological organisation. Thus, the eighteenth-century ambition to construct one universally viable social system to accommodate legions of identical men of reason was an aberration. In this respect, Saint-Simon differs radically even from such contemporary thinkers as Condorcet and Cabanis. Above all, Saint-Simon was one of the first ideologists to see society in terms of the production of work. His understanding of science helped him in this. Bichat and others who followed his definitions, such as Cuvier, defined organic phenomena as those which constituted a system whose separate components were arranged in relations of mutual dependence, and were only understandable as such. But the arrangement was by implication functional; the system existed to do work, and this was precisely Saint-Simon's idea of society: a fluid, transformational, productive economy of forces. Saint-Simon was also reinforced by Bichat's idea of metabolism, the function which transforms simple inputs into complex levels of organisation which time and the onslaught of external forces break down. Thus metabolism again provided a powerful analogy for social integration and dissolution, and analogy enabled Saint-Simon to integrate the biological with the social. Such metaphors were critical in shaping Saint-Simon's view of social structures. They also allowed him to reach a model of community in which individual uniqueness was a condition of wholeness, not its enemy, because organic solidarity is a product of shifting relationships. Just as much as the Owenites, though in a far more defined way, science enabled Saint-Simon to produce a social ideology which opposed any idea of an automatic opposition between individual and society.

To sum up: this period saw an immense pressure for change in both science and ideology. Science was used to sanction both conservative and Utopian ideologies and was itself the bearer of messages about public authority. Politics and culture changed in such a way in this period throughout the western world, and particularly in Western Europe, as to allow the emergence of new, tightly-defined non-consensual ideologies, which co-existed alongside many other attitudes towards the relations of nature and politics. In all cases, however, science was invoked to a greater or lesser degree to validate political beliefs and outlooks, whether new or old.

3. INDUSTRIAL EUROPE AND THE COMING OF REVOLUTION (1830–48)

The period from 1830 to 1848 saw the decisive phase of industrialisation for much of Western Europe and the United States. For Britain, France, Belgium, Holland, central and northern Germany and the northern United States, mass production of goods in large factories had become commonplace, and was no longer confined to iron, steel and chemicals, but had extended to consumer goods such as clothes and textiles. To distribute this increased volume of industrial products, transport systems dependent on the rapid and reliable steam engine came into being, and started to create the conditions for the emergence of genuinely national and international markets for the first time. National governments became heavily involved both in the planning and in the financing of the new transport networks, and, in the countries concerned, the middle classes became more numerous and visibly better-off than they had been before. They benefited by having the capital to invest in the new financial structures which were inseparable from industrial advance and which were in many cases secured by state investment.

For the working class, the consequences of industrialisation tended to be less happy. Industrialisation enforced a change from production in small artisan workshops to large anonymous factories. Instead of being entrusted with the making of a whole object, workers typically found themselves entrusted only with specific fragmentary and repetitive tasks. This division of labour caused many artisans to feel threatened by the progressive de-skilling and hence social and economic degradation which would accompany their entry into factory labour. It is not surprising that many of the new ideologies which grew out of the experience of industrialisation came not from industrial workers, but from threatened artisans.

It seems clear that industrialisation brought with it a steady increase in tensions between the social classes. Governments, while often investing heavily in the infrastructure of industrialisation, such as railways, usually saw it as no part of their function to intervene in the social or economic consequences of the new organisation of production. Employers were thus able to depress wages (to raise profits) without hindrance from any central authority, and also without challenge from labour movements which in any case existed only in embryo form in this period. Miserable working and living conditions were the result for the majority of industrial workers. The new large factories also required the rapid expansion of towns to accommodate the increased labour force, and the result was the creation of squalid working-class districts in the greatest possible contrast to the comfortable living conditions of the middle class. Such developments made startlingly visible the contrasts between the lives of the workers, and those of the middle-class entrepreneurs and consumers who profited by their labours.

Under the pressure of all these new and complex circumstances, political ideology and science also came to alter their relations. Industrialisation, dependent as it was on the massive application of technology, was altering the social, economic and geographical map. The struggle to claim 'scientificness' as a validation for political ideologies in some quarters was matched in others by attempts to repudiate it altogether. These reactions cannot simply be broken down along class lines. Many artisans, for example, particularly in Britain, repudiated science and technology altogether, seeing it as a force which gave other social classes exploitative power over them. In France, however, the situation was different. Utopian socialism, preached by such leaders as Etienne Cabet, found much support amongst threatened artisans for the demand for a direct democracy based on civic education, censorship and modern technology. His movement rejected violence, and claimed that socialism would arrive through the conversion of the bourgeoisie by peaceful propaganda. Change in the social control of the means of production would mean that technology could be harnessed for the good of all. At its best, Cabet's paper the *Populaire* had 4,500 subscribers and when read aloud in homes, cafés and outdoor meetings, may have reached an audience of 200,000, mainly from the older craft towns and among the threatened trades such as tailors, shoemakers, cabinet-makers and hand-loom weavers. By 1846, however, Cabet's movement was in crisis. The bourgeoisie remained impervious to socialist persuasion, and the economic depression of the late 1840s heightened class tensions and shattered dreams of class collaboration and the neutral use of science and technology as distributors of benefits among all classes of society. In the revolutionary situation of 1848, Cabet offered no solution except flight, urging his followers to emigrate to model communities in America.

Nor were the middle classes any more united in their reactions to the problems posed by industrialisation. Liberalism has often been presented as the middle-class creed *par excellence*, a creed which was to form the basis of the revolutions all over Europe in 1848, when the middle class attempted to seize political power from old governing elites. Broadly speaking, liberals believed that the state should not intervene in social and economic problems, but simply 'hold the ring' between the competing interest groups whose interaction constituted the fabric of civil society. This was not a creed of much interest to social groups at the receiving end of exploitation. Liberals also campaigned for various political rights such as liberty of the press, free assembly, freedom from arbitrary arrest and imprisonment and for a degree of representative government, limited, however, by property, age and gender restrictions. Given orderly principles of government along these lines, and the free play of market forces in the economy, liberals expected that societies would develop with ordered progress. It is not our purpose to point out here how shortsighted the liberal demand was for an orderly re-distribution of political power in favour of the upper sections of the male middle-class, unbacked by a redistribution of social and economic power. This was to be the cause of the collapse of the liberal revolutions of 1848 in the face of radical demands from the working class. But we should note here that liberalism did accompany commitment to, or attraction for, certain kinds of scientific theory; for example, Charles Lyell's idea of geological change, influential from 1832 onwards, which highlighted the steady operation of constant causes, rather than the cataclysmic upheavals which had featured in much of the geology of the eighteenth century. Liberalism also favoured a certain beneficent view of science as a whole, as operating to smooth over social division by such neutral gifts as gas street-lighting or cheap transport through steam power.

It should, however, not be forgotten that the middle class, especially in France, also housed political ideologies of a quite different kind. Middle-class intellectuals tried hard in the years after 1830 to convert the working classes to developed versions of Saint-Simonism. They contrasted the rule of parasites, such as clergy and landowners, with the technocratic elite committed to industrial expansion, where each would contribute according to his capacity in a society held together by a religion of humanity. A clearly class-conscious ideology, let alone an unambiguously class-conscious attitude to science, was slow to emerge in this period, and led to many ambiguities in the attitudes of those who sought, from both sides, to bridge the gap between the needs and experiences of threatened artisans and exploited industrial workers, and the more socially reformist elements of the middle class.

The period before 1848 also saw the continuation of a strong tradition of European conservatism, in the works of such thinkers as Joseph de Maistre. They hoped for the return of the social consensus between ruler and governed, which they saw as the hallmark of the world before the French Revolution. Unlike the followers of liberalism, they remained openly hostile to science, which they saw not as an even-handed conferrer of blessings and reconciler of social tensions, but as a disruptive force, socially unrooted, and proceeding by a critical rationality which called into question the historical and customary basis of society. Science was also disliked by such thinkers because of the strong opposition which it appeared to mount to religious revelation and hence to the teachings of, especially, the Catholic Church. Such attitudes were to culminate in Papal condemnation of modern science in any encyclical of 1849.

To sum up: science and political ideology, due to the stresses of industrialisation, lived in even greater tension than they had before. Attitudes to science did not, however, break down strictly along class lines, although, unsurprisingly, hostility to science did tend to come from opponents of industrialisation, whether threatened artisans, aristocrats or middle-class conservatives. Industrialisation made the appropriation of science even more of a prize than before, because it made the potential impact of science and technology upon the social and economic world so much more visible.

NOTES

1. Ian Inkster, 'Seditious science: a reply to Paul Weindling', *British journal for the history of science*, 14 (1981), 181–7; 182.

2. S. Shapin, review of David de Guistino, *Conquest of mind: phrenology and Victorian social thought*, *British journal for the history of science*, 10 (1977), 177–9; 178.
3. J. Priestley, *An examination of Dr Reid's enquiry into the human mind on the principles of common sense* (London, 1774), p. 74.
4. J. Priestley, *Experiments and observations on different kinds of air* (3 vols., London, 1774–77), I, xiv.
5. Crosbie Smith, 'From design to dissolution: Thomas Chalmer's debt to John Robison', *British journal for the history of science*, 12 (1979), 59–70.
6. *The economist*, 3 February 1821; cited in Barbara Taylor, *Eve and the new Jerusalem: socialism and feminism in the nineteenth century* (London, 1983), p. 19.

FURTHER READING

Roger Cooter, *The cultural meaning of popular science: phrenology and the organisation of consent in nineteenth-century Britain* (Cambridge, 1985).

C. C. Gillispie, *Genesis and geology: a study in the relations of scientific thought, natural theology and social opinion in Great Britain, 1790–1850* (New York, 1959).

B. Haines, 'The inter-relations between social, biological and medical thought, 1750–1850: Saint-Simon and Comte', *British journal for the history of science*, 11 (1978), 19–35.

Ian Inkster, 'London Science and the Seditious Meetings Act of 1817', *British journal for the history of science*, 12 (1979), 192–6.

Ian Inkster, 'Seditious science: a reply to Paul Weindling', *British journal for the history of science*, 14 (1981), 181–7.

Isaac Kramnick, 'Eighteenth-century science and radical social theory: the case of Joseph Priestley's scientific liberalism' *Journal of British studies*, 25 (1986), 338–53.

D. Mackenzie, 'The political implications of scientific theories: a comment on Bowler', *Annals of science*, 42 (1985), 417–26.

Frank Manuel, *The prophets of Paris* (Princeton, 1978).

D. Outram, 'Politics and vocation: French science 1793–1830', *British journal for the history of science*, 13 (1980), 27–43.

D. Outram, *Vocation, science and authority in post-Revolutionary France: Georges Cuvier* (Manchester, London, and Dover, New Hampshire, 1984).

S. Shapin, 'Phrenological knowledge and the social structure of nineteenth-century Edinburgh', *Annals of science*, 32 (1975), 219–43.

S. Shapin and S. B. Barnes, 'Science, nature and control: interpreting Mechanics' Institutes', *Social studies of science*, 7 (1977), 31–74.

Crosbie Smith, 'From design to dissolution: Thomas Chalmers' debt to John Robison', *British journal for the history of science*, 12 (1979), 59–70.

A. Thackray and J. B. Morrell, *Gentlemen of science: early years of the British Association for the Advancement of Science* (Oxford, 1981).

P. Weindling, 'Science and sedition', *British journal for the history of science*, 13 (1980), 139–53.

67

NATURAL SCIENCE AND SOCIAL THEORY

THEODORE M. PORTER

The term 'social science' first emerged in the milieu of Condorcet during the French Revolution, but the aspiration it embodies dates at least to the seventeenth-century Scientific Revolution, and in a loose way, to classical antiquity. Since the time of Galileo and Bacon, and especially since Newton, natural philosophy has stood for the possibility of attaining reliable, objective knowledge. As a model for social thought, it offered a possibility of escape from the tyranny of faction and partisan politics. Scientists, it appeared, are somehow able to achieve consensus about the fundamentals of the issues they study. For more than three centuries, natural science has served as a prototype for the authority of reason, which seemed an agreeable contrast to the regime of status, wealth and prejudice.

The urge to elevate politics above *mere* politics by achieving a consensus of experts has decidedly technocratic implications. But it is far from clear that the scientific model has, on balance, worked against openness and participation in politics. Social science has been allied, though ambivalently, to the Western liberal tradition, often taking some understanding of the dignity of individuals as its premise. Moreover, the social sciences have not been able to force a consensus, particularly when practical applications are at issue. In part this is because conflicting political or social visions are often only masked by the ostensibly neutral language of science. In the present context, however, it is especially significant that the natural sciences present neither a unified nor any single readily-appliable model for social science. Science envy, far from elevating political and social thought above politics, has provided instead a pervasive idiom of debate.

1. IMAGES OF THE NATURAL: MECHANICAL AND MATHEMATICAL

The creation of human sciences in modern Europe depended on that process of intellectual secularisation by which nature and natural philosophy gradually assumed the authority of Christianity to interpret and define the meaning of events in the world. In this context, natural images and analogies have gained moral force, and they have been integral to the conceptual development of social thought. Probably the most influential model for knowledge in modern history, and certainly the pre-eminent one in the eighteenth century, was mechanics. It can hardly be said that the Enlightenment philosophes undertook systematically to build a sound science on precepts and analogies drawn from Newton. They were, in fact, scarcely able to distinguish the methods followed by Newton from those set forth by Bacon or Locke, and they tended to attribute the mathematical simplicity and elegance of the new planetary astronomy to a spirit of patient empiricism – coupled, to be sure, with genius. Hence it was possible to claim the authority of Newton for efforts that in hindsight appear more nearly journalistic than scientific. Still, Newtonian analogies were an indispensable part of the Enlightenment language of social criticism and advice, the first sustained attempt to place the 'social art' on a scientific footing.

Critics of the Enlightenment would later claim that this fondness for mechanical analogies only proved that the philosophes were lacking a proper conception of the social. But it was certainly not a mere misconception. Perhaps the absence of a coherent organicist alternative inhibited Montesquieu, whose scientific aspirations accorded poorly with his adherence to an intricately differentiated society of estates and orders. However, what caused confusion in Montesquieu conformed splendidly to the aims of Voltaire, Turgot and Condorcet. The Newtonian world was a well-ordered machine. His astronomy showed how natural philosophy could be used to cut through the appearance of complexity and reveal the simple reality underneath. It was a model both for understanding society and for reforming it.

Thomas Hobbes (1588–1679) had already demonstrated impressively the power of the mechanical idiom in his *Leviathan* (1651). A mechanical world permitted no essences, but only individuals, stripped by analysis of all claims to hereditary rights or prerogatives. Hobbes's mechanism led to nominalism, flattening the verbal landscape as it had flattened the social. Meaning in language arises from definitions, which may be chosen at will so long as they are adhered to consistently. By choosing intelligently he could apply deductive reason, as in geometry, which he took as his model. Similarly, structure in society – laws, contracts, political authority – derives from the social contract, though here, as in geometry, consistency of definition leads inexorably to a certain set of arrangements. Hobbes deduced a system of compelling simplicity, a contract among equal, atomic individuals to create a sovereign in whom all power was invested. There was neither need for nor possibility of subdividing the power.

This, of course, was not the only possible reading of the mechanical analogy, as the subsequent American discussion of checks and balance clearly indicates.[1] Most philosophes, of course, agreed with Locke that the social contract should be binding on the sovereign as well as the subjects so that power would not be absolute. But a comparison between Newtonian physics and politics almost always supported a faith that political institutions could be simple and rational. This was most clearly in evidence in the French Enlightenment. Keith Baker shows how French philosophes such as Turgot (1727–81) and Condorcet (1743–94) allied themselves to king and bureaucracy against the centrifugal forces of aristocracy, church and municipal autonomy. The Newtonian apotheosis of natural harmony resulting from the operation of a few elementary laws was admired by social philosophers precisely because it helped to discredit the traditional corporate order. The old regime, presupposing that sin and disorder were the natural condition of man, depended on guilds to regulate labour, intricate customs to maintain favourable trade and the authority of the church to uphold morals. The encyclopedists and physiocrats would leave these things to nature where possible, trusting in the spontaneous order that emerges from the interactions at least of enlightened individuals. Where administration is necessary, it should be simple and centralised. As Turgot explained to Louis XVI, it is best to 'govern like God by general laws,' not by 'particular acts of will.'[2]

The political viewpoint underlying this dedication to mechanical analogies also made possible the first serious application of numerical reasoning to the body politic. Models of society were never sufficiently concrete during the seventeenth and eighteenth centuries to permit the deduction of mathematical relationships governing them. But the possibilities of statistics were increasingly appreciated during the eighteenth century, and the application of number to society was greatly facilitated by the availability of a viewpoint that could see human individuals where most eyes saw only nobles, clergymen, officeholders, tradesmen, labourers and peasants.

Political arithmetic, ancestor of statistics, was the first of the quantitative sciences of society. From the time of its founders, John Graunt and William Petty, it was modelled on the new natural philosophy. Condorcet, Laplace and Quetelet later argued that the progress of the physical sciences provides an indispensable example for the social and political ones, and that what they demonstrate concretely is the importance of mathematics. This was and is a controversial claim, but it is certainly the viewpoint whose influence among social thinkers seeking to emulate the natural sciences has been most enduring. By the mid-nineteenth century the quantitative ideal had become largely independent of the general Enlightenment mechanical metaphor, although particular analogies continued to prove useful for mathematisation.

But the ideal of mathematical social science was able to become so widely influential largely because the mechanical viewpoint had, in a sense, gained its victory by the early nineteenth century. The simplicity of mechanics – a society of individuals born equal under the law – came to be taken for granted in most of Western Europe. The ideal of an organic, corporate society like the old regime did not vanish, of course. It was, if anything, more clearly articulated and more eloquently defended after the combined effects of the French and Industrial Revolutions had gone a long way towards destroying it. But in the nineteenth century it was almost always put forward as an alternative to the existing mechanical or bourgeois order, based on atomic individuals in competition with one another. The most popular and influential of the new human sciences in the early nineteenth century were individualistic ones: phrenology (a mechanised view of the brain), political economy and statistics. These became especially important after about 1830, which, as Eric Hobsbawm argues in *The Age of Revolution* (1962), marked a crucial transition in the history of class alignments in the West.

Statistics was perhaps the new science most characteristic of attitudes in the nineteenth century. From about 1830 to 1880 it was the most promising candidate to become the general science of society. Statistics was pursued as an agent of reform by citizens – rarely professional scientists – concerned by the growth of cities and the accompanying unrest. The 'statists' of the 1830s and 1840s sought to bring order to the new urban slums, in the form of education and sanitation. They tended to be sceptical of classical political economy, usually because they distrusted both its *laissez-faire* politics and its deductive approach. But they lived in the same intellectual world as J. B. Say and David Ricardo, one composed of individuals born free and equal, though not always brought up in the most propitious circumstances. Blending in various measures a faith in competitive individualism and rational bureaucracy, they embodied the twin ideals of the Enlightenment mechanical viewpoint.

In Voltaire's France, where the society of estates was still dominant, bureaucracy and individualism were allies. In Britain they were not, for there centralisation was widely seen as a threat to freedom – and not just to that of the most privileged orders. The tensions inherent in an individualist social science, however, were most directly confronted by Condorcet. He believed, more devoutly than most philosopes, that government should rest on the consent of the governed. But he had scarcely more faith than Voltaire in the rationality of the untutored masses, and his own career was dedicated to the promotion of a comprehensive, thoroughly elitist organisation of science within which an effective science of society could be established. The latter was to be thoroughly mathematical, and was unlikely to be comprehensible to the average citizen.

Condorcet's conception of the relation between scientific truth and social values, moreover, was strongly at variance with democratic government. He was in this respect much like Rousseau. Although the 'general will' was to be determined by a vote, the citizens in Rousseau's ideal state did not cast ballots according to their private interest. Rather, they endeavoured to vote in accordance with the true public interest, which existed independently of what the various individuals in the state thought or wanted. Similarly, Condorcet supposed that there was a correct course of state action in any given circumstances that was accessible to science, and that could not be reduced to the hopes and aims of the various citizens. Even if the voters perceive accurately their own private interests, an election may not lead to the proper decision for a society. Condorcets's theory of elections predicts a correct result only when the voters have a high probability of knowing what is best for society. He clearly thought it more likely that scientific experts would reach correct decisions than that the mass of citizens would.

During most of his career, Condorcet championed the claims of a monarchy he hoped to make enlightened. Like Turgot, he believed that a concentration of power offered the best prospect of rational administration if men of enlightenment could control it. He argued that under such men the people will not really have lost their rights, since political order would rest not on mere power, but on reason and nature. But Condorcet took natural rights seriously, and the French Revolution gave him the incentive to reconcile popular government with the demands of social science. He did not argue that the citizens were disqualified from governing themselves by their lack of scientific expertise. Most of his own work on the 'social art' had been devoted to the theory of elections and judicial decisions, and during the Revolution he emphasised the study of election arrangements that would be most likely to represent the true will of the electorate. His Society of 1789 worked for scientific education, which he thought would enhance the prospects of effective self-government. What he expected, however, was not so much a society of competent authorities as one whose members would be able to recognise the superior judgement of their scientific betters. That is, popular sovereignty is not destroyed, but enhanced, if the people choose to set up committees of experts to reach solutions to difficult problems.

The tensions within the self-styled Newtonian approach to society are also exemplified in the work of Lambert-Adolphe-Jacques Quetelet (1796–1874), whose aims and methods were in many respects similar to Condorcet's. Quetelet, however, followed his mechanical prototype more closely; indeed, an obsession with physical analogies is the distinctive feature of his approach to social science. Quetelet was of a different generation, and had, to a much greater extent than Condorcet, made the transition from a moral science of precepts to a social science of laws. But Quetelet would make laws of society the basis of reform activity. This was a role for which mechanical laws were ill-suited, and Quetelet's German followers tended for this reason to see him as a social determinist, and hence an opponent of attempts at reform. That he certainly was not. Rather, he was inconsistent.

Mechanical analogies came naturally to Quetelet, since the mathematical roots of statistics were in astronomy. As an ambitious young astronomer in 1823 he had received authorisation from the government of the United Netherlands to venture to Paris, where he was to learn how to set up and operate an observatory. There he contracted an infatuation for mathematical probability, by then used routinely in the reduction of astronomical observations, and also applied to demographic problems by Laplace, Joseph Fourier and Poisson. Here was powerful evidence for Laplace's dictum that the methods of the natural sciences constituted the proper basis for the social ones.[3] From the observatory he set up upon his return to Brussels he studied not just the stars, but also statistics.

Quetelet's idea was to found social mechanics on the concept of the average man, which was like the centre of gravity in celestial physics. To do this implied that humans were fundamentally alike – that, like the force of gravitation in a sphere, the deviant effects of peripheral members of the 'social body' must cancel one another out. This he was prepared to accept, even applaud, since it accorded with his Aristotelian sense that virtue is a just mean between vicious extremes. Quetelet conceived himself, after all, as a moderate bourgeois reformer threatened by intransigent aristocrats on one side, the dangerous *peuple* on the other. He was equally pleased with the idea of statistical social laws, which he interpreted as fully comparable to the mechanical laws of the heavens. This, too, was a token of order in a world that seemed always to be on the verge of revolution. He recognised only one difference between his laws on the 'trajectory' of the 'social body' and those of mechanics: social laws, being statistical did not determine the behaviour of individuals with complete determinism. In this way Quetelet could salvage free will, and perhaps disarm criticism, without (he thought) in the least undermining the certainty of the collective laws regulating the whole society. That was the virtue of statistics, which permits social laws to be uncovered even where the individual actions are too complex or too numerous to be understood in detail.

Quetelet thus thought the analogy between mechanical and social laws complete. The historical path of society could be calculated from statistical data in the same way as a planet's. The social system was subject to conservation of living force, so that all attempts to block progress must in the end fail. Only abrupt forces, or revolution, can delay progress, and these are consequently to be avoided at all cost. The idea for which Quetelet is best known, that natural variation generally conforms to the normal distribution, derived also from physical analogies. That curve was known in his time as a law of the distribution of measurement errors, particularly in astronomy. Human variation thus became for him a kind of measurement error, a set of accidental fluctuations from the golden mean that he idealised as somehow embodying the purpose of nature. This doctrine of the exemplary average, incidentally, provided for an almost automatic harmony between social science expertise and a government *for* the people, if not *by* the people. Every person was in effect, represented by the average man.

Quetelet, however, seems not to have been much troubled by issues of sovereignty.

Mechanical social models could lead almost to fatalism. Henry Thomas Buckle (1821–62) would later take Quetelet's social mechanics to what might be seen as its logical conclusion, and argue that since society was rigidly lawlike, legislation could only be the effect, never the cause, of social change. Purged of its deterministic implications, however, the mechanical viewpoint connoted simplicity, and was an ally of the rationalist reformer. Quetelet was obliged to place the legislator outside the system of social laws, but having done so, these laws became proof that society was predictable, and that reforms could be undertaken with confidence that the desired result would be attained. The same was true of James Mill and Jeremy Bentham, who treated politics and jurisprudence as problems in geometry. Edmund Burke provides an illuminating contrast. He objected to mechanical thinking because he opposed rationalistic reform, identifying it with the shallow optimism and ignorance of history that had led to cataclysm in the form of the French Revolution. During the 1830s and 1840s, John Stuart Mill pondered over the differences between his father and Macaulay and between Bentham and Coleridge. This was, indeed, the central issue in his *Logic* (1843). As ever, he tried to find the synthetic position that would incorporate what was best in both doctrines. But here there was no compromise. He finally decided that society is basically mechanical, and not chemical, since it consists of autonomous human individuals, each acting according to associationist principles.[4] Hence the joint effect of two actions, or reforms, will be their sum, and not something entirely different, as when oxygen and hydrogen combine to make water. Mill deemed this conclusion a decisive refutation of conservative romantics, who see in society something ineffable and hold that massive reform is always dangerous because its effects can never be predicted. Mechanics for Mill was practically synonymous with rationality. For him, as for most of its advocates, it was an indispensable ally of liberalism and reform.

2. SCIENCE AND AUTHORITY

If the mechanical and statistical conceptions of society tended to be liberal ones in the late eighteenth and early nineteenth centuries, their implications were by no means necessarily democratic. As was clear with Condorcet, a science of society was unlikely to be understood by the masses, and the persistent fear of revolution in much of Europe for more than a century after 1789 gave the prospect of moving politics from the streets to the study of a strong appeal. Approaches like the statistical one may have tended to treat society as a sum of individuals, but Quetelet's willingness to dissolve diversity in averages is hardly indicative of an excessive appreciation of individuality.

If truly authoritarian uses of science tended to be associated with organicism, there is also some ambiguity here. Organicism in social thought arose in opposition to what was seen as rationalistic excess, and many adhered to it as an alternative not merely to physics, but to science. Burke's thoughts are again revealing, though he was a moderate by the standards of the Lake Poets who followed him. The state, like a sick father, should be tended solicitously, not hacked to pieces and reassembled at whim. Sentiment, not reason, is the proper faculty for man in society; reason leads to analysis and criticism, when reverent caution is needed. One of the great virtues of the old organic order, according to Joseph De Maistre and later Claude-Henri de Saint-Simon, was that it did not call for an excess of critical thought. People were born in their place, where they would remain throughout their lives, and were told what to believe by the church. Even Auguste Comte (1798–1857) who in some respects belongs in the organicist tradition, but who, like Saint-Simon, worshipped science, thought that with himself science had reached its proper end. Thus, faith in the unlimited possibilities of human progress, which since Turgot had been closely associated with belief in the progressiveness of science, was transformed by Saint-Simon and Comte into a historical progression whose proper end was found in their own work. Anticipating, as he did, the fruition of history in the organic stability of positivism, Comte had very little enthusiasm for future research. If the frequently-noted connection between liberalism and the rise of science has any reality more enduring than the circumstance that natural philosophy was available in the Enlightenment as an alternative to the intellectual hegemony of the church, it is that science is dynamic, open-ended and dependent on the free expression of opinion. Apart from the social sciences, this freedom is restricted largely to matters of, at most, indirect political import, and often confined to the scientific community. But even that was more than Comte was prepared to allow; he would freeze science, leaving it as a body of doctrine rather than an uncontrollable activity.

Comte saw his work as the culmination of all of science, not merely of biology. His background was in the Ecole Polytechnique, the great French engineering school, and although he was expelled before finishing, he later earned an income examining candidates there in mathematics. Comte was one of many polytechnicians who became associated with the social visionary Saint-Simon, and Friedrich Hayek has argued powerfully that Saint-Simonian scientism represents the hubris of the engineer. Certainly Comte and the Saint-Simonians treated society as a thing to be engineered. But Comte did not systematically apply the methods or concepts of the physical sciences to sociology. He was an enthusiastic admirer of *idéologue* physiologists like Cabanis and Bichat, who denied that physiology could be reduced to mechanics, though he rejected their vitalism. Although he called the science of society 'social physics' until 1835, when Quetelet placed that term in the title of his most important book, Comte used 'physics' in its traditional sense, as merely an experimental or observational science. He denounced all attempts to apply mathematics to sociology, and he thought probability misguided and puerile. He did argue that mathematics, astronomy, physics and chemistry had to become positive sciences before sociology could, in part because certain doctrines from these sciences were needed by sociology. But this was part of an explanation for the historical order of development of the sciences, not a plea to base sociology on physics or chemistry.

Neither, to be sure, would Comte reduce sociology to physiology, the fifth science in his famous hierarchy. His admiration for the Paris physiologists was qualified by regret that they had failed to perceive the autonomy of social science. Sociology had to await the development of physiology, chemistry and physics not mainly because of specific doctrines but because sociology was so complicated that it required a maturity of mind available only through the pursuit of these other sciences. Sociology for Comte was a properly constructed history. It was based on the three stages, theological, metaphysical and positive, through which social science must pass. Since the character of a society is determined by its prevailing ideas, the history of sociology is very nearly identical with the history of society itself. But popular ideas lag behind science, so that in transitional periods all three phases will be represented in the population at once. That, incidentally, was one reason Comte so distrusted statistics, and especially the use of broad averages, which must conflate what historical analysis permits the sociologist to keep distinct. Mechanical analogies were meaningless here. So also was objectivity, the independence of the researcher from his subject-matter. Unlike Quetelet's social physics, where the reforming social scientist stood outside the system of laws he studied, Comte's scheme looped back on itself. For him, as for Hegel, true history was a history of mind, and his very discovery of positive sociology implied that the world would soon be re-created in its image. Science itself, not the human body or physical matter, was the principal subject of Comte's sociology, and it could not be studied by the methods of physiology or chemistry.

Still, the purpose of Comte's system was to define the new form of social organisation that was to emerge as a corollary of his historical schema, and his thoughts on social planning were distinctly organicist in character. Saint-Simon seems to have been the pioneer here, although Comte, as his personal secretary from 1817 to 1824, was probably responsible for such intellectual rigour as is to be found in his mentor's writings during this fruitful period. Saint-Simon's earliest scheme for a new comprehensive science of society was, at least in intention, based on Newtonian physics; like Charles Fourier, he was impressed by universal gravitations as a model for a law of passionate attraction that would bind together the social world as gravity did the physical. This, however, was the most superficial analogy. The relation of physiology to social science was more fundamental. Saint-Simon based his social organisation on the division of humanity into three biological types, thinkers, artists and workers. The individual, accordingly, is not autonomous or self-subsistent, but inherently a part of society. Society, in turn, has its own physiology, just like the human body.

Comte held to this schema, charging the scientists to define belief and the artists to preside over the ceremonial and emotional aspects of the positivistic 'religion of humanity'. He rejoiced in the anti-individualistic aspects of this scheme, which were in fact built in to his hierarchy of the sciences. There was no place in it for psychology, which he deemed metaphysical since it was based on introspection rather than on proper observations and experiments. Also, the search for timeless laws of mind must be futile when the main divisions of history are so closely bound to changing patterns of thinking and explanation. Comte would allow psychology only as phrenology, a branch of physiology. Similarly, he disdained political economy as an impermissible abstraction of one class of phenomena from the comprehensive science of society, and one that was full of misperceptions because of its narrowness. For Comte, as Hayek observes, even individuality was an abstraction; only society was real. Like Dostoevsky's Grand Inquisitor, Comte and Saint-Simon viewed freedom negatively – an unwanted burden for the individual, and for society a source of frightful disorders like the recent revolution.

Whereas the philosophes made science an ally of pluralism by opposing it to the church, Comte bound science to a prospective religion and developed its full potential as an enemy of liberalism. Like Saint-Simon, he admired the 'organic' order which, in his view, had prevailed under the aegis of medieval Catholicism. The only problem with the Roman church was that it had failed, because it had come into conflict with science. This was the source of the terrible disorder that began with Protestantism and culminated in the French Revolution. Saint-Simon called this a critical period; Comte identified it as society's metaphysical stage. It was a lamentable development, but the clock could not be turned back. Fortunately, the dialectic of history promised a restoration of organic order, as society entered its positive phase, the last stage of history. Positive social science would end the chaos and establish the authority of a new dogma, one that could endure, since it was true. Now that the truth had been found, freedom of conscience no longer had any point. Social decisions would henceforth be made by a scientific elite, in the same way as other scientific truths were discovered and accepted. Comte devoted his late career to the scientific religion of humanity, one full of positivistic saints and festivals aptly labelled by T. H. Huxley as Catholicism minus Christianity.

The works of Saint-Simon and his followers, particularly the remarkable *Doctrine of Saint-Simon* (1829) prepared after his death, practically defined the modern socialist tradition, and were highly appreciated by Marx and Engels. The relation between 'science' and socialism, however, has been inconsistent. When Marx contrasted his own 'scientific' approach with his 'Utopian' predecessors, he meant that their infatuation with ideas precluded a proper appreciation of history. Marx subscribed to what he called materialism, holding that economic change and the accompanying dialectic of social classes guaranteed the triumph of communism in its due time. The idealists, he held, thought that the triumph of socialism only required that someone think of it. This was unfair to the Saint-Simonians, who believed in a dialectic of ideas – one connected with social history – so that the idea of socialism would only occur when the time was ripe. Science to Marx and Engels seem to have meant materialism, or rather dialectical materialism, for they insisted also on the universality of history, even in the natural world.[5] Kant's cosmic evolution and Darwin's biological evolution thus exemplified for them the materialistic dialectic, as did the Heraclitean fire. Although Marx and Engels also identified science with certainty, and used the claim that they alone had comprehended society scientifically to discredit rivals, there is nothing in their thought like the all-embracing scientific religion with which Comte would render freedom archaic.

The Comtean plan for using science to restore social integration, and to supplant a democratic chaos in politics, has perhaps been more influential in sociology, though its authoritarian features have, in most cases, been much attenuated. Sociology has often been allied to organicism, since it requires a level of reality above the individual. Emile Durkheim, an admirer of Comte, dissolved individuality in a sea of social forces. He also used the organic metaphor to justify a scientific politics, making the sociologist into a social physician who learns to distinguish between the normal and the pathological.[6] But even sociology has largely been won over to the advisory posture of the methodological individualists in economics, defined by J. M. Keynes: it is the task of politics to determine the ends; science can only establish the means.[7] Moreover, organicism has by no means been uniquely or consistently allied with opposition to individual freedom. Organic structure and diversity have often been valued as ways of protecting liberty against the encroachments of the centralised state. Mill and de Tocqueville feared that the disappearance of social differentiation might lead to a debasement of culture under the oppressive weight of democratic opinion. Both Hobbes's imagined dictatorship and the real totalitarianism of our own time rest on a levelling of distinctions and destruction of organisations outside the state.

3. SOCIETY AND EVOLUTION

Both the physiological and mechanical models of society have been very loose ones. Both are based almost entirely on analogy, which can be useful only to the extent that the analogy of subject-matter suggests some analogy of concepts or methods. But these can be variously interpreted. A mechanical conception might imply the possibility of analysis to homogeneous individuals, or the use of mathematics or some other form of deduction, or merely serve as a model of order through simplicity. A social physiologist might also analyse, expecting, however, to find diversity rather than homogeneity in the constituents. Organicism has also led to the appreciation of history, by analogy with biological development. In short, not only do physics and biology present very different models, with divergent political implications for social science, but there is still a wide range of possible lessons to be learned after the model has been agreed upon. Even the most dedicated imitators, like Quetelet, found themselves with a serious problem of adaptation, and were forced to be original in spite of themselves.

The biological theory of evolution presented a model for social science of a different character, since it offered the prospect of reducing the social sciences to the biological. Reduction, of course, was no new ambition, and reductions to physics had been attempted by various crackpot materialists, but the extension of evolutionary theory to include the development of society was plausible enough to be taken seriously by the best thinkers of the late nineteenth and early twentieth centuries. This included the first two generations of professional social scientists in the vast American university system, and many in Germany and Great Britain as well. In retrospect, it appears that much social theory was no more than analogous to evolution, but in the absence of a theory of genetics the distinction was unclear.

This was even less a case of an active donor and passive recipient than most instances of interdisciplinary influence. The historical approach to social science, having flourished briefly during the Scottish Enlightenment, was making a comeback in Britain during the 1850s with the works of Herbert Spencer and Henry Thomas Buckle, both influenced to some extent by Comte. Historicism was prevalent in late nineteenth-century Germany, and Ernst Haeckel's approach to evolution, with its heavy reliance on the evidence of embryology, had, as he himself pointed out, much in common with the philological reconstruction of lost texts. Darwin, of course, had received a vital stimulus from Malthus's theory of population, and probably also from the classical economic theory of the free market. The 'common context' of biological and social theory that Robert M. Young has observed in early nineteenth-century Britain was in many ways continuous with the evolutionary approach to society at the end of the century. Darwin's contribution to the triumph of evolutionary social theories was considerable, but not decisive, and in many ways he stood in the shadow of Herbert Spencer. Although the powerful case he made for evolution in *The Origin of Species* (1859) was largely responsible for its acceptance, the mechanism of natural selection was not widely adopted. Around 1900 it was thoroughly out of favour, even among biologists.[8]

The best-known influence of evolutionary theory on social thought is also the most misunderstood: Social Darwinism. Natural selection, it is still often supposed, served to justify a brutal *laissez-faire* economics and to legitimate the depredations of the robber barons. The Yale economist William Graham Sumner is routinely invoked here: progress in society as in nature requires that the able receive the rewards of their achievements, and that the unfit be eliminated. Similar sentiments were expressed by Andrew Carnegie and John D. Rockefeller. Social Darwinism has been held responsible for late nineteenth-century racism and imperialism, and for eugenic initiatives culminating in the Nazi atrocities.

But this sort of argument reflects an almost complete indifference to the actual affiliations of ideas. Even Carnegie's Social Darwinism dissolved into a social gospel, as he gave unprecedented sums to foundations and charities. What has been called Social Darwinism in Austria, the sociological ideas of Ludwig Gumplowicz, was really a theory about the origins of class differences in racial conquest, and involved no vindication of force by biological progress. The most important and influential of the 'Social Darwinists', Herbert Spencer, was a Darwinian only in the loosest sense. He had become convinced of biological evolution before the publication of the *Origin*, and remained an advocate of the Lamarckian mechanism of use inheritance throughout his life. In social, as in biological evolution, Spencer thought the actual elimination of the unfit a relatively insignificant cause of progress. He opposed state-sponsored welfare not because he thought the poor should die, but because he felt some spur to activity was essential if they were not to lapse into an idleness that would become hereditary, and lead to the growth of useless, dependent classes. Spencer's theory was biological, to be sure, but natural selection had only a slight role. His reasoning was closer to that of classical political economy, which is where his intellectual roots were. Until the enormous consolidation of business enterprise late in the nineteenth century, at least, free enterprise was valued primarily as an incentive to efficiency for all market participants, and not as a way of eliminating the weakest. Protection and collusion would allow inefficiency, which would indeed be passed on from generation to generation. Spencer biologised social theory in part by treating biology as economics.

The main inspiration for Spencer's architectonic system had indeed come from biology, but not from Darwinian or even Lamarckian evolution. His was much grander than that, a theory of cosmic evolution modelled on the embryological theory of Karl Ernst von Baer. Von Baer saw individual development as a process of progressive differentiation, which Spencer would call the transition from the homogeneous to the heterogenous. Spencer made the universe an organism, one that became steadily more organised. The progress of society from savagery to barbarism to civilisation as political and economic structures became more elaborate was a corollary of this universal principle. Because differentiation took place spontaneously, without the need for central direction, it was compatible with *laissez-faire*. Centralism, in fact, could only disrupt it; this was the abstract basis for his opposition to the growth of the state. This same opposition left him cool to imperialism. There is no question that Spencer thought European peoples more advanced, both biologically and socially, than other races. So also did Darwin. Spencer was partly responsible for ranking the peoples of the earth from lowest to highest on a chain that could be identified with the historical progress of an advanced people like the English. He was, however, no advocate of racial purity or colonial expansion, either paternalistic or exploitative.

The 'scientific' racial doctrines that were so fashionable from about 1870 to the 1920s, and in some quarters up to the Second World War, had their origins mainly in anthropometry, and perhaps ultimately in phrenology. Quetelet, characteristically, was one of the early enthusiasts of skull measurement, but he decided in favour of monogenism on the basis of a rather tenuous demonstration that the distribution of skull measurements in the world conformed to the error law. More portentous was the conclusion of Armand de Quatrefages after the Franco-Prussian War that the Prussians were not Europeans at all, but some low race of East Asian origin. His anthropometric reasonings were refuted by Rudolf Virchow. By this time anthropometry under Paul Broca (1824–80) had become widely-accepted as an explanation of culture; Broca's ideas were further developed by Paul Topinard and, more tendentiously, by Otto Ammon and Georges Vacher de Lapouge. By the 1880s, skull measurement had not only proved (once again) to the satisfaction of Europeans their own superiority, but had led to a division of Europeans themselves into three invidious categories: Nordic, Alpine and Mediterranean. The proper hierarchy of races – and of the sexes – was evidently known *a priori*, because it proved necessary to try out a variety of physical criteria of superiority to get the correct results. The most influential of these was the cephalic index, a measure of long-headedness, whose determination supported manufacturers of calipers for generations.

The evolutionary interpretation of this hierarchy was most often Lamarckian, or, to be more precise, Haeckelian. It presupposed that evolutionary change is mainly the result of new behaviours by adults, and that these lead to the modification of organs, which will be passed on to offspring. Because the striving of the organism plays so large a role, change is almost by definition improvement, and this was confirmed by Haeckel's biogenetic law ('ontogeny recapitulates phylogeny'), which held that an individual of a higher type passes through all lower organic types in the process of becoming an adult. This provided an ostensibly simple, and in actuality a suitably flexible criterion for determining the highest races. For mankind the head was obviously of special importance, so this approach could be made to support the anthropometric one. The inevitable conclusion was that northern European men were most advanced; the inferiority of all others could be seen from the circumstance that their development did not take them quite so far beyond the ape stage, as revealed by slope of forehead and cephalic index, among other things.

The biogenetic law, and the hierarchy it justified, inspired or were incorporated into a remarkable variety of researches. Among them were studies of childhood, where the supposed phylogenetic parallels to the stages of individual development were interpreted by G. Stanley Hall, among others, as dictating a certain educational programme. Lombroso's criminal anthropology stipulated that capacity for morality was a late evolutionary development, and that perhaps forty per cent of criminals were sufficiently backward biologically that reform was not really possible. Frank Sulloway has demonstrated how much of Freudian psychoanalysis was rooted in his Lamarckian version of evolutionary biology, particularly in Haeckel's biogenetic law.[9] Freud correlated infant sexuality with the phylogenetic sequence through which the child was passing – hence the oral and anal stages had an evolutionary basis. The maturing individual did not so much pass through these stages as accumulate them, so that adults retained, often unconsciously, the impulses of lower organisms. Fixation in a pre-adult stage caused neurosis.

Freud was not the only thinker inspired by evolution to place greater emphasis on man's animal nature. William McDougall founded a school of social psychologists early in the twentieth century which emphasised the role of instinct in human behaviour. The presumption of irrationality that informed the new political science of Graham Wallas used McDougall to support this pessimistic understanding of mass politics.[10]

Probably the most influential evolution-based movement of social ideas – and, to a degree, political action – was the effort to improve the human biological character through state action. This drew on the anthropometric theories of race, and for a time on Haeckel's biogenetic law, though it was more closely associated with the Darwinian mechanism of natural selection and with Mendel's laws than with Lamarckian inheritance; its main influence dates from 1900 or 1905, when Lamarck and Haeckel were already falling into disrepute among biologists. At its heart was eugenics, which is often treated as a form of social Darwinism. But this is to confuse two very different programmes simply because they reflect a similar disdain for the lower classes. Social Darwinism means *laissez-faire*. Eugenics required vigorous state action. It would be more accurate to label it 'Socialist Darwinism', for it had much in common with the socialism of the Fabians, though opponents of socialism were often willing to support this form of state intervention, since it would intrude mainly into the lives of the poor. It was almost always justified in terms of the preservation of society or fitness of the race rather than as a way of leading to happier, healthier, more creative persons.

Walter Bagehot argued in *Physics and Politics* (1867) that the struggle for existence in modern civilisation occurred mainly between nations, not between individuals. Modern political organisation conferred an enormous advantage, but progress also required the activity and dynamism of free individuals. To be oppressed by the 'cake of custom', the dead weight of tradition, virtually guaranteed defeat. Bagehot's social competition, then, did not demand centralised planning and public ownership in advanced societies, but discouraged it. The era of so-called social Darwinism, however, was one in which both the role of the state and the bureaucratic ambitions of many intellectuals grew enormously. None were more impressed by the possibilities of expertise than Karl Pearson, who saw the competition between nations as a compelling argument for systematic organisation. In a time of heightened international competition, of Darwinian struggle between nations, the British could no longer afford the waste and inefficiency of a competitive economy and decentralised institutions. To ensure survival, he insisted, required socialism, which he defined simply as the primacy of the social.

Pearson's arguments, and Pearson's career, provide some of the best reasons for denying any inherent affinity between science and liberalism. He maintained in *The Grammar of Science* (1892) that scientific method was uniquely suited to his anti-individualistic socialism because it produced consensual knowledge. The efficient state must eschew all judgements based on individual peculiarities or personal whimsy, and that rules out democracy as well as the dictatorship of an individual. Politics and administration must become the business of science and, since science is no affair of the average man, the social struggle requires elevation of an intellectual elite. Pearson viewed the statistical methods he worked out as invaluable tools for this new administrative science.

Within this grand evolutionary vision, Pearson also emphasised the importance of biology at another level. Maximum social fitness required the best possible individuals. Reproductive patterns in modern society did not lead to this. He argued that scientists and professionals are most valuable socially, but often childless, while those he identified as the dregs of society were enormously prolific. In short, eugenic measures appeared to be necessary not merely for progress, but even to halt the decline. Francis Galton, Pearson's mentor in both statistics and eugenics, had, beginning in 1865, advanced what may be seen as a liberal programme of eugenics, relying on public opinion rather than state coercion to raise the birth rate of the upper classes and reduce that of the lower. He got no support. By 1900 eugenics had begun to gain public interest, but now Galton as well as Pearson hoped to make reproduction the business of the state. Public education would not suffice for social progress; Galton and Pearson believed they had shown that nature far outweighed nurture in the production of able, intelligent and socially useful children.

Eugenics had considerable intellectual support in Britain, and, to a somewhat lesser extent, throughout Europe. It provided one component, though not the main one, of the Nazi racial programme. In the United States, as Daniel Kevles shows, it became a mass movement, and several thousand eugenic sterilisations were actually carried out. More to the point of the present essay, the arguments of eugenists were mainly responsible, along with racial theories of anthropometric origin, for the widespread hereditarianism among social scientists, especially in the United States, during the first two decades of the twentieth century.

The biological approach to the human sciences was pursued most avidly by psychology, a field whose professional identity derived from the quest for the dignity of a proper science. Until about 1900, scientific psychology meant psychophysical experimental measurements, as championed by Gustav Fechner and Wilhelm Wundt, whose laboratory trained the first generation of psychologists in Europe and America. Then the psychophysicists were joined by comparative psychologists, whose field can be traced to the efforts of the devout Darwinian George Romanes to narrow the mental gap between man and the apes. For several decades after John B. Watson, the emblem of American psychology was the rat running a maze. The behaviourists assumed that psychology must be confined to external phenomena, and never resort to introspection, and that there is no fundamental difference between man and animals. In particular, they held that the mind (if so metaphysical a term may be permitted) is passive: it receives stimuli and produces responses in a simple, associationist fashion. Perhaps the branch of psychology with the greatest influence on society was intelligence testing, which in Britain and especially the United States became a standard tool of state schools. As championed by Charles Spearman, Cyril Burt, Lewis Terman and L. L. Thurstone, intelligence testing reflected the conviction that quantification is the essence of science, and that what can be measured must exist. On just what *was* being measured, these men differed, but the intelligence testers showed a strong tendency from the beginning to view their results as reflecting hereditary endowment, and not just culture. No convincing explanation has been given for this propensity of psychologists. In many cases, their hereditarianism derived from elitist cultural exclusiveness. But its prevalence probably also reflected the desire of psychologists to give their results some solidity by grounding them in biology – a phenomenon by no means restricted to intelligence testing.

One of the most celebrated early findings of the intelligence testers was the thoroughly bogus discovery, as a result of the testing of American recruits in the First World War, that northern Europeans were more intelligent by far than Italians, Slavs, Jews and blacks. This fitted in well with the racialist orientation of American sociologists, who until the 1920s had at most a dim sense of their distinctiveness from psychologists. But during the inter-war period the enormous American academic community began to draw a sharp line between social and natural science – with most psychologists continuing to prefer to see themselves on the natural science side. That division had been a commonplace since the 1870s in Germany, where nature and history were generally seen as opposites. In France, Emile Durkheim's *Rules of Sociological Method* (1895) followed Comte in insisting that social science was quite distinct even from psychology – indeed, that behaviour was so much determined by social forces that sociological explanation is the only sort possible.

In the United States, the rebellion against biology was led by cultural anthropology, and in particular by the German Jewish immigrant Franz Boas. Boas, remarkably, had come to anthropology from physics by way of geography. It was in part as a psychophysicist that he became convinced of the importance of the culture concept, for he found that Eskimos and Northwest Indians differed from him even in the colours they saw and the sounds they heard. The anthropologists objected to racial hierarchies, and found in culture something thoroughly unbiological by which to place human societies outside the domain of nature. As sociologists began to push for institutional autonomy, they became increasingly appreciative of such reasons for intellectual autonomy as well. Since 1945 the rigid separation between social and natural phenomena has been almost *de rigueur* among intellectuals in Europe and America, and even more so elsewhere. The consensus has been only slightly disturbed by such movements as socio-biology, which, ironically, has had its greatest impact on anthropology.

The acceptance of a nature-culture distinction does not imply that social thinkers have lost interest in the ideal of natural science. This essay has dealt entirely with relations between the *theories* of natural and social science. The attempt by social thinkers to put into effect somehow the *method* of natural science did not always reflect a belief that social theories should be grounded in biology or physics, and in the last fifty years it almost never has. But the 'scientific method' has been notoriously elusive, and the history of attempts to capture it for the study of society is mainly a history of a search for prestige, for the authority and certainty of 'scientific law' in the slippery domain of human studies. The scientific method has been so variously interpreted by social thinkers, and often with so little evidence of serious thought about what natural scientists actually do, that its invocation is usually more justly interpreted as a convenient apologetic than a serious intellectual statement. The one important exception (and quantification) to this is mathematics, whose centrality to certain areas of natural science is such that it has been often taken as the distinctive feature of proper science. That misperception has doubtless intensified the interest of social scientists in mathematics, leading to much abuse but also opening some fruitful lines of research.

It may be noted in conclusion that interdisciplinary influences have not always proceeded from above to below in the Comtean hierarchy. Darwin's debt to Malthus is well known; those of the physicist James Clark Maxwell and of Francis Galton to Quetelet's social statistics are scarcely less impressive. In this century, too, evolutionary biologists and ecologists have often benefited from mathematical analogies or statistical techniques developed by economists and sociologists.[11] And this should not be surprising, for it is altogether characteristic of the relations among the sciences. Successful reduction has been relatively rare in the natural sciences, and rarer still in the social. If the grand mechanical analogies of the Enlightenment, and the evolutionary schemes of 1900, were too sweeping, a more nuanced perception of analogies has often provided new ways to confront problems. Rather less has been accomplished by pursuing a unitary scientific method.

NOTES

1. See Otto Mayr, *Authority, liberty, and automatic machinery in early modern Europe* (Baltimore, 1986); also Gideon Freudenthal, *Atom and individual in the age of Newton: On the genesis of the mechanistic world view*, Peter McLaughlin, trans. (Dordrecht, 1986).
2. Keith Baker, *Condorcet: from natural philosophy to social mathematics*, (Chicago, 1975), p. 207. See also William Sewell, *Work and revolution in France: the language of labor from the Old Regime to 1848* (Cambridge, 1980).
3. See Laplace, *Essai philosophique sur les probabilités* (1825; Paris, 1986), p. 117.
4. See John Stuart Mill, *Autobiography* (1873; Boston, 1969), pp. 95-7.
5. See Friedrich Engels, *Socialism: utopian and scientific* (1875; New York, 1982).
6. Emile Durkheim, *The rules of sociological method* (1895), Stephen Lukes, ed., W. D. Halls, trans. (New York, 1982), chap. 3.
7. J. N. Keynes, *The scope and method of political economy* (Cambridge, Eng., 1891).
8. See Robert M. Young, *Darwin's metaphor: nature's place in Victorian culture* (Cambridge, 1985), chap. 2; Peter Bowler, *Evolution: the history of an idea* (Berkeley, 1984).
9. Frank Sulloway, *Freud, biologist of the mind: beyond the psychoanalytic legend* (New York, 1979).
10. Reba Soffer discusses McDougall and Wallas in *Ethics and society in England: the revolution of the social sciences, 1870–1914* (Berkeley, 1978).
11. There are several nice examples in Sharon Kingsland, *Modelling nature* (Baltimore, 1985).

FURTHER READING

Keith Baker, *Condorcet: from natural philosophy to social mathematics* (Chicago, 1975).
Robert Bannister, *Social Darwinism: science and myth in Anglo-American social thought* (Philadelphia, 1979).
John W. Burrow, *Evolution and society* (Cambridge, 1966).
Hamilton Cravens, *The triumph of evolution: American scientists and the heredity-environment controversy, 1900–1941* (Philadelphia, 1978).
Peter Gay, *The Enlightenment: an interpretation*, vol. 2 (New York, 1969).
Stephen Jay Gould, *The mismeasure of man* (New York, 1981).
—— *Ontogeny and phylogeny* (Cambridge, Mass., 1977).
Friedrich Hayek, *The counterrevolution of science* (Glencoe, Ill., 1952).
Daniel J. Kevles, *In the name of eugenics: genetics and the uses of human heredity* (New York, 1985).
Gertrud Lenzer (ed.), *Auguste Comte and positivism* (New York, 1975).
Donald MacKenzie, *Statistics in Britain, 1865–1930: the social construction of scientific knowledge* (Edinburgh, 1981).
Frank Manuel, *The new world of Henri Saint-Simon* (Cambridge, Mass., 1956).

Frank and Fritzie Manuel, *Utopian thought in the western world* (Cambridge, Mass., 1979).

J. D. Y. Peel, *Herbert Spencer: the evolution of a sociologist* (New York, 1971).

Theodore M. Porter, *The rise of statistical thinking, 1820–1900* (Princeton, 1986).

Robert J. Richards, *Darwin and the emergence of evolutionary theories of mind and behaviour* (Chicago, 1987).

George Stocking, *Race, culture, and evolution: essays in the history of anthropology* (New York, 1968).

THE CONTRIBUTORS

Barry Barnes, Science Studies Unit, University of Edinburgh, UK.

Gillian Beer, Girton College, Cambridge, UK.

Larry Briskman, Department of Philosophy, University of Edinburgh, UK.

W. H. Brock, Victorian Studies Centre, University of Leicester, UK.

John Hedley Brooke, Department of History, University of Lancaster, UK.

G. N. Cantor, Department of Philosophy, University of Leeds, UK.

J. R. R. Christie, Department of Philosophy, University of Leeds, UK.

K. Danziger, Department of Psychology, University of York, Ontario, Canada.

D. E. H. Edgerton, Centre for the History of Science, Technology and Medicine, University of Manchester, UK.

Roger Emerson, Department of History, University of Western Ontario, Canada.

Raymond E. Fancher, Department of Psychology, University of York, Ontario, Canada.

Nicholas Fisher, Department of History and Philosophy of Science, University of Aberdeen, UK.

Robert Fox, Linacre College, Oxford, UK.

Alan Gabbey, (formerly) Department of History and Philosophy of Science, University of Belfast, UK.

Bill Gerrard, Department of Economics and Related Studies, University of York, UK.

J. V. Golinski, Churchill College, Cambridge, UK.

J. J. Gray, Faculty of Mathematics, Open University, Milton Keynes, UK.

Gary Gutting, Department of Philosophy, University of Notre Dame, Indiana, USA.

Ian Hacking, Institute for the History and Philosophy of Science, University of Toronto, Ontario, Canada.

John Henry, Science Studies Unit, University of Edinburgh, UK.

M. J. S. Hodge, Department of Philosophy, University of Leeds, UK.

Pierre Kerszberg, Department of General Philosophy, University of Sydney, Australia.

Philip Kitcher, Department of Philosophy, University of California, San Diego, USA.

Helge Kragh, Department of History, Cornell University, USA.

Larry Laudan, Department of Philosophy, University of Hawaii, USA.

Rachel Laudan, Department of History, University of Hawaii, USA.

David N. Livingstone, Department of Geography, Queen's University, Belfast, UK.

Michael S. Mahoney, Program in History of Science, Princeton University, USA.

Jane Maienschein, Department of Philosophy, Arizona State University, USA.

Seymour H. Mauskopf, Department of History, Duke University, Durham, North Carolina, USA.

Ernan McMullin, Department of Philosophy, University of Notre Dame, USA.

A. George Molland, Department of History and Philosophy of Science, University of Aberdeen, UK.

Neil Morgan, 6 Seymour Avenue, Bristol, UK.

J. B. Morrell, Department of European Studies, University of Bradford, UK.

W. H. Newton-Smith, Balliol College, Oxford, UK.

Thomas Nickles, Department of Philosophy, University of Nevada, Reno, USA.

R. C. Olby, Department of Philosophy, University of Leeds, UK.

Dorinda Outram, Department of Modern History, University College, Cork, Ireland.

Carleton E. Perrin, deceased, (formerly) Division of Natural Science, York University, Ontario, Canada.

John V. Pickstone, The Centre for the History of Science, Technology and Medicine, University of Manchester, UK.

Trevor Pinch, Department of Sociology, University of York, UK.

Roy Porter, Wellcome Institute for the History of Medicine, London, UK.

Theodore M. Porter, Department of History, University of Virginia, Charlotte, USA.

Lewis Pyenson, Département d'Histoire, Université de Montréal, Canada.

J. R. Ravetz, (formerly) Department of Philosophy, University of Leeds, UK.

Michael Redhead, Department of History and Philosophy of Science, University of Cambridge, UK.

George MacDonald Ross, Department of Philosophy, University of Leeds, UK.

Simon Schaffer, Department of History and Philosophy of Science, University of Cambridge, UK.

Brigitte Schroeder-Gudehus, Institut d'Histoire et de Sociopolitique des Sciences, Université de Montréal, Canada.

John A. Schuster, Program in History, Philosophy and Politics of Science, University of Wollongong, Australia.

Steven Shapin, Department of Sociology, University of California, San Diego, USA.

Phillip R. Sloan, Program of Liberal Studies, University of Notre Dame, Indiana, USA.

Crosbie Smith, Unit for History, Philosophy and Social Relations of Science, University of Kent, UK.

Roger Smith, Department of History, University of Lancaster, UK.

John Stachel, The Collected Papers of Albert Einstein, Boston University, USA.

George W. Stocking, Department of Anthropology, University of Chicago, USA.

Martin Tamny, Department of Philosophy, University of New York, USA.

John R. G. Turner, Department of Genetics, University of Leeds, UK.

Andrew Wear, Wellcome Institute for the History of Medicine, London, UK.

M. Norton Wise, Department of History, University of California, Los Angeles, USA.

Robert M. Young, Free Association Books, London, UK.

INDEX OF NAMES

INDEX OF SUBJECTS